THE FACTS ON FILE
COMPANION TO THE

BRITISH SHORT STORY

ANDREW MAUNDER

Facts On File

An imprint of Infobase Publishing

The Facts On File Companion to the British Short Story

Copyright © 2007 by Andrew Maunder

Facts On File, Inc.
An imprint of Infobase Publishing
132 West 31st Street
New York, NY 10001

ISBN-10: 0-8160-5990-X
ISBN-13: 978-0-8160-5990-4

Library of Congress Cataloging-in-Publication Data

The Facts On File companion to the British short story / [edited by] Andrew Maunder.
    p. cm.
  Includes bibliographical references and index.
  ISBN 0-8160-5990-X (acid-free paper)
1. Short stories, English—History and criticism—Encyclopedias. I. Title: Companion to the British short story.
II. Maunder, Andrew. III. Facts on File, Inc.
  PR829.F33 2006
  823 .0109—dc22   2006006897

Text design adapted by James Scotto-Lavino
Cover design by Cathy Rincon

Printed in the United States of America

VB Hermitage 10 9 8 7 6 5 4 3 2 1

This book is printed on acid-free paper.

CONTENTS

INTRODUCTION

The acknowledgment of the short story's place in Britain's literary history is one of the most striking developments of recent years. The British short story—from Walter Scott's tales of rural Scottish laborers to Arthur Conan Doyle's adventures of the metropolitan master of disguise Sherlock Holmes to Virginia Woolf's experiments in depicting human consciousness—has come to be read and studied in high schools, colleges, and universities across the world and recognized as an "adventurous, inventive, very various and, above all, a discovering form," to quote Malcolm Bradbury (8). The aim of this new book—intended as a companion to Abby Werlock's *Facts On File Companion to the American Short Story*—is to provide insight into the wealth and variety of the British version of this favorite American form. The book maps out some of the main strands that have shaped the British short story and novella since the early 19th century. It provides up-to-date discussions of key stories and story collections as well as discussions of the careers of all the most widely studied exponents of the genre—for example, James Joyce, Joseph Conrad, Katherine Mansfield, D. H. Lawrence, Thomas Hardy, Henry James, Oscar Wilde, Rudyard Kipling, Elizabeth Bowen, and William Trevor. In selecting the stories and writers to cover in this volume, the editor has combed through popular anthologies and literature textbooks, in both the United States and Great Britain. This volume also includes essays on other "lost" or neglected authors who have more recently started to find their way into the classroom,

such as George Egerton, Bram Stoker, Mary Butts, and Margaret Oliphant. Furthermore, this book also aims to help students and readers whose interests are taking them beyond the classroom and who want to find out more about the British short story as it is being written today. Therefore, it also contains discussions of younger writers whose bold experiments with the short story have started to make an impact on the literary scene: Will Self, Toby Litt, Nicola Barker, and Janice Galloway, among many others. The book analyzes, as well, some of the historical and cultural conditions under which the short story has developed in Britain and considers the recurrence of key themes, such as class, women's roles and ambitions, Englishness, the British Empire, and crime and detection.

One of the things this book has not tried to do is to reinforce old-fashioned and stereotyped ideas about "merrie England," with the short story "marooned among buffers and buffoons, bucolics, butties and Blimps," as the writer A. S. Byatt has put it (15). Instead—and appropriately for the 21st century—the book recognizes the deeper political and cultural dimensions of the terms *English, Irish, Welsh,* and *Scottish* and what it means to be British, distinctions that are usefully illuminated by the contributors here. Additionally, the book includes discussions of works by important and widely studied writers from the former British colonies—such as Henry James (United States), Olive Schreiner (South Africa), Katherine Mansfield (New Zealand), Salman Rushdie and Anita

Desai (India), and V. S. Naipaul (Trinidad/India). To include these writers is to use the term *British* in a fairly expansive, rather than proprietorial, way. It is done on the basis that these are writers who, for some years, lived and made a considerable part of their careers on the British mainland and whose work can partly be read as coming out of, or throwing light on, various elements of the British short story, its development, and its scope. The British Empire was a fruitful source for writers at the beginning of the 20th century—Kipling and Maugham in particular—who can never be disregarded. Now British literature has a postcolonial dimension, made up of an assortment of different global voices and progenies that make up a multicultural body of literature. These authors look back to the early 20th century and also forward, bringing a non-European cultural awareness to the confines of British fiction.

One of the reasons that this volume has been published now is that the time is right for a fresh look at the British short story. In the United Kingdom, the form is enjoying a revival in its fortunes. Prompted partly by the rise of university and college creative writing courses in which the short story has been adopted as one of the most obvious teaching tools, claims for the genre's importance have started to reappear in a multitude of settings. In 2004 Small Wonder, Britain's first annual literary festival devoted exclusively to the short story, was launched. The launch, in that same year, of the £10,000 International Orange Award for New Writing (a spin-off from the £30,000 Orange prize for fiction), together with the National Short Story Prize in 2005, the Frank O'Connor award (also 2005), and the long-standing Bridport prize, is part of an increasing awareness that the short story deserves critical (and financial) recognition and should be taken seriously, as it is in the United States. It is, moreover, a form in which many of the leading British fiction writers of the past 20 years have revealed particular talents. To pick up Giles Gordon's and David Hughes's anthology *The Best British Short Stories 1986–1995,* replete with stories by A. S. Byatt, Martin Amis, Julian Barnes, J. G. Ballard, Adam Mars Jones, Fay Weldon, and Rose Tremain, is to be reminded, as the editors point out, of the short story's "vigour and met-

tle, its social awareness and literary acumen" (Gordon and Hughes, 7). Moreover, to log on to the British Arts Council's Web campaign, "Save Our Short Story" (theshortstory.org.uk), with its stock of new works by Ian Rankin, Ali Smith, Michael Faber, and others, is likewise to be reminded of the form's diversity and depth and to realize that it is not the exclusive property of the literati, encompassing the detective story, the thriller, the science fiction story, the horror story, "Chick Lit," "Lad Lit," travel writing, erotica, and more.

The discussions that occupy these and other short story sites, plus a browse among bookstore shelves and the Web pages of Amazon.com, reveal that those interested in the British short story have plenty to read. In addition to the influential anthologies that appear in the classroom—from Malcolm Bradbury's *Penguin Book of Modern British Short Stories* (1987) and A. S. Byatt's *Oxford Book of English Short Stories* (1998), through Susan Hill's *Penguin Book of Modern Women's Short Stories* (1996; 1998), to David Marcus's *Best New Irish Stories* (2005), not to mention larger literature anthologies, such as the Norton—there are multiple collections by such landmark practitioners of the genre as Rudyard Kipling, Thomas Hardy, Katherine Mansfield, Virginia Woolf, and Agatha Christie. Then there are the recent collections of stories by authors whose work has started to become the subject of reevaluation and rediscovery, such as Viking's *Complete Short Stores of Muriel Spark* (2001) and *The Music at Long Verney* (2001), a collection of Sylvia Townsend Warner stories originally published in the *New Yorker.* In 2005 new collections appeared of work by two colorful but overlooked exponents of the 1930s and 1940s short story: Julian Maclaren-Ross and Michael McLaverty. Readers can also debate the short stories broadcast daily on BBC Radio Four, where stories by Oscar Wilde and Elizabeth Taylor (not the actress) are read alongside new work by Stevie Davies, Mick Jackson, and Jackie Kay. A new magazine, *Prospect,* gives a proportion of its space to short story writers, and in August 2005 in a move toward on-line publishing, Amazon.com announced that it would do the same. Unlike literary prizes, which at worst can be read as cynical exercises in marketing and at best as contentious, this willingness of publishers and agents to back the short story seems concrete testimony to the genre's renaissance.

I use the term *renaissance* because one of the issues I want to consider in this introduction is the historiography of the British short story and its critical fortunes. What does the short story mean to us? What role has it played in Britain's literary heritage? Answers to this question fluctuate wildly. There is the short story as exquisite miniature, "art in highly concentrated form," as William Boyd has described it, whose effects are akin to those of the multivitamin pill "a compressed blast of discerning, intellectual pleasure." There is another British short story—the British short story that is narrow, insipid, inward-looking, and commercial, whose publishers insist upon gimmicky themes in order to attract readers, "Thirty-one Irish tales of drink" or "Fifteen humorous stories about sports" being typical tag lines (Marvor, 5). Another section of the current literary establishment has tended to present the British short story as a "bastard" genre and as an "endangered species" (Ezard, 8). William Trevor, long acclaimed as the undisputed master of the form, recently noted that for much of the 1980s and 1990s the short story was an incredibly "unpopular" genre with British publishers, who got it into their heads that the reading public did not like—or couldn't cope with—the genre. There was some truth in this, as Trevor acknowledges. Contrary to what one might think, the short story, Trevor explained, does not sit easily in a market that demands easily digestible fare. "You play a different game with the short story. You demand far more of the reader than you do with a novel, or television" (quoted in Lane). Helen Simpson has likewise suggested that in the sound-bite culture of the 21st century, one in which we demand spoon-feeding and instant gratification, the short story—a form by nature "nervous . . . adrenalised, very quick, not restful" that works by "giving you the raw ingredients and telling you to make the meal yourself"—had lost much of its appeal (Lane, 23). Then there is the viewpoint that sees the British short story as provincial and twee, a pale imitation of its vital U.S. counterpart, "culturally redundant and economically unviable" as the editor of *Prospect,* Alexander Linklater, recently observed when explaining the vision behind the

National Short Story Prize. This version of the short story has encouraged the long-held view that the story is done better in America, and that it is only in America, thanks to publications like the *New Yorker,* that the short story is properly appreciated (Levy, 27). So familiar is this argument that the richness and variety of the British short story tends to get pushed to one side, despite the prevalence of British short fiction in today's classrooms, in both the United States and Great Britain. Whatever one's take on the genre, these different views of the short story have set the terms for a critical debate that has been played out for many years and has now taken off once more.

What, then, is the "British short story"? From what did it originate? How do we classify and define it? One response is that despite a great deal of discussion, its history remains fairly indeterminate, so much so that it is usual to preface accounts of its genesis and development with mention of its multifariousness. Writing about the short story as it exists in the 21st century, Philip Hensher suggests that "it's impossible to diagnose the state of the short story, make any suggestion where it might be going, since it's impossible to say where it has come." The British short story also seems to be a genre difficult to pin down. "On the whole," argues Hensher, "the classic short story runs from 5,000–10,000 words, and prefers the single situation to plot and subplot entrelacement." John Mullan suggests a similar length but writes of the short story's ending as making us feel that "we are stopping short of resolution or conclusion." The hackneyed notion that the short story is merely "practice space for fiction" has also come in for a good deal of scrutiny (McCarthy, 27). Many argue that short stories are harder to write than long fiction. Bill Naughton wrote that "[i]n a novel there is scope to spell things out and in effect to tie up all loose ends, but in a quality short story little must be said yet everything implied" (quoted in Ezard, 8). Susan Hill argues that "every word must tell—there is . . . no room for in-filling" since the short story is "an unforgiving form" (9). There is thus a sense that the form requires a special kind of skilled—or possibly brutal—craftsmanship. This involves "cutting it really quite savagely so it becomes bare, removing every ounce of skin and flesh so you're just left with the bones," as William Trevor recently put it (Lane, 23). To use the short story as a way of carrying out a panoramic critique of society is not something that many recommend. Instead the consensus has always been that the short story is what Trevor calls "the art of the glimpse" (Coldstream, 9). It does not present whole lives but fleeting moments in a life through a dramatic or poignant incident or a turning point. This may be an incident that triggers conflict between characters or marks a change in the mind-set of another and that is followed through to a kind of resolution. The short story's very shortness and ability to be read at one sitting can be an advantage, helping create the kind of "unified effect" recommended by its "patron saint," Edgar Allan Poe, and still advocated today (Levy, 27).

The contradictions that critics identify have been formulated in many ways, but as well as disagreements about form, about word-length, about the use of labels—the difference, for example, between the tale and story—there is the confusion arising out of the fact that, as Philip Hensher suggests, the British short story is a Frankenstein's monster of a genre, one "which makes its way in life as best it can, without anything much in the way of respectable forebears." As has been noted, it is difficult to ascribe an essential "Britishness" to the form, in contrast, for example, to the way that critics of the American short story tend to recognize an "essential Americaness" (Lee, 11). So while there are plenty of antecedents for the short story, the consensus has generally been that in Britain it was not until late in the 19th century that the short story, at least as a "concentrated form of writing" (Bradbury, 11), was born. In 1905, Hilaire Belloc, writing in the *Manchester Guardian,* pronounced the short story "a very modern thing." "What brought it into being," he added, "has not been discovered, though the subject has been discussed at great length" ("Short and Sweet"). More recently, Roger Luckhurst noted that the term "short story" was not used until 1884 (17).

Explanations for the late emergence of the short story in Britain have taken several forms. In a notable article, "The Tardy Evolution of the British Short Story," Dean Baldwin describes the genre as "one of the more curious anomalies of literary history." He goes on:

By the 1840s the genre was already established in America, and within two decades it had taken root in Germany, Russia, and France. I am speaking here, of course, of the modern short story, defined loosely as Poe's story of "single effect," not simply of fiction shorter than the typical novel. This modern story did not achieve prominence in Britain until the 1880s, even though Britain would appear especially likely to develop the genre, since during the period of the story's "invention," if we may call it that, Britain was a world leader in the writing and dissemination of fiction. (1)

According to this version of events, the late emergence of the British short story is a result of the dominance for most of the 19th century of the full-length novel as the chief fictional form. It was not until the creation of a new mass of readers, following the education acts introduced between 1870 and 1890, that the short story came into its own. This legislation led to compulsory elementary education for all but had the side effect of prompting a flood of new cheap magazines and papers, many of which gave a central place to short fiction. Magazines such as *Titbits* and *The Strand*—the latter featuring the first appearances of the famous detective Sherlock Holmes—gained mass readerships and places "at the centre of respectable popular British culture" (MacDonald, 154). Moreover, while the novel did not die out, many authors appreciated the fact that the short story involved much less complicated business arrangements. The *Atlantic Monthly,* in explaining "the present popularity of the short story with authors and public alike," suggested that "here is a form of literature easy to read and write. The author is often paid as much for a story as he earns from the copyrights of a novel, and it costs him one tenth the labor. The multitude of magazines and other periodicals creates a constant market, with steadily rising prices. . . . The public pays its money and takes its choice" (Perry, 250). In this way, the genre saturated the culture and commerce of an era that saw massive shifts in the way literature was acquired, produced, and consumed. "Short stories broke out everywhere," recalled H. G. Wells of the 1890s (Richardson, 45).

Moreover, there were so many magazines that, as Wells noted, even stories "of the slightest distinction" tended to find an outlet.

Merely labeling or bestowing a birth date to something does not, of course, mean that it did not exist before. So while it has been convenient to suggest that the short story did not bulk very large before the burst of activity in the 1880s, it is still possible to find examples in the earlier part of the 19th century. As the present volume reveals, there are plenty of texts that have some kind of relationship to the modern short story, even if the formal shapes used and labels given them—"tale," "sketch," "fable," "short tale"—are different. In moving the scope of our survey backward chronologically, the aim has also been to provide a more inclusive, if not totally comprehensive, overview of the 19th-century short story, one that recognizes the strong legacy of development left by previous generations of writers and editors, including Maria Edgeworth, Walter Scott, Mary Shelley, Mary Russell Mitford, and Charles Dickens. Their influence still often goes unrecognized. For example, despite Percy Fitzgerald's claim that "Dickens always seemed to hanker after the short story" (quoted in Thomas, 2), Dickens's seemingly relaxed approach—his loose definition of the short story as "anything told orally by a narrator within the story or as anything shorter than four serial instalments"—has helped ensure that this element of his writing has tended to be viewed very much as secondary to his novels (Thomas, 3). This viewpoint, however, ignores such influential texts as *Sketches By Boz* (1834–36), *A Christmas Carol* (1843), and the much-anthologized ghost story "The Signalman" (1866), among others. Moreover, Dickens's involvement in the magazine market of his day through *Bentley's Miscellany* (1837–39), *Household Words* (1850–59), and *All the Year Round* (1859–70) ensured that he was a powerful catalyst in the short story's emergence. The magazines Dickens edited showcased works by his protégés and rivals, notably Wilkie Collins, Elizabeth Gaskell, and Anthony Trollope, writers who began to turn the concise sketch or anecdote into a story with a definite, often suspenseful, plot. Theirs are often realist stories, meaning that they use recognizable characters and carefully described settings and they focus on the demands of society upon the individual.

However, a parallel development in the 1850s was the growing interest in "sensational" stories of crime and deviance, often taking place within the supposedly safe confines of the family home. When taken together, mid-century stories by Collins, George Eliot, Thomas Hardy, Joseph Sheridan le Fanu, Ellen (Mrs. Henry) Wood, Mary Braddon, Lucy Clifford, and Rhoda Broughton cover a remarkably wide range of subjects: murder, adultery, degeneration, love, adventure, betrayal, and weird or "uncanny" events—hauntings, the return of the dead, second sight. These stories are a long way from the cozy, rose-tinted image of the mid-Victorians as a staid, earnest, and rather dull bunch. As short stories they are also more various than the standard criticism often makes out, focusing in uncomfortable ways on sexual passion, marriage, and homes in which violence, or the possibility of violence, is always lurking.

One of the things the present volume also tries to do is to point out types of short story that are proving of particular interest to critics in 2006, including works by writers who have tended to languish outside the literary canon. For example, among the anthologies of 19th-century British short stories recently reissued, several have focused on the 1890s, or the fin de siècle as it tends to be known. This has prompted suggestions from feminist critics that "the best work of the decade was in the short story rather than the novel" and that much of it came from women writers (Showalter 1995, 12). Elaine Showalter writes:

> The novel was a problematic genre for *fin de siècle* women writers, as many of them realised. Too often it tended to the didactic, episodic and stiff, whereas the short story was supple, impressionistic and intense. Women writers in the 1890s found in the short story a suitable form for the new feminist theories of the decade: the exploration of female sexuality and fantasy; the development of a woman's language, and the critique of male aestheticism. (1995, 12)

Recent critics of the short story have followed Showalter in thinking about the feminine dimension to many short stories of the late 19th century. This includes the ways in which many texts can be seen to deal at least in part with the so-called Woman Question, presenting questions and viewpoints about female emancipation, about a woman's rights to education and professional training and to earning and keeping her own income and property.

The fin de siècle has traditionally been seen as notable for stories by writers associated with the short-lived decadent and aesthetic movements, notably Ernest Dowson and Oscar Wilde, whose texts were often associated in the public mind with "outrageous" expressions of perversity and sensuality, full of ideas of ennui or moral exhaustion. However, it was the small-scale short stories by such New Woman writers as George Egerton, Ella D'Arcy, Vernon Lee, and Ella Hepworth Dixon (among others) that seeped into the literary market and helped create widespread feeling that modern woman was trying to rebel against domestic life. Readers of the late-Victorian and Edwardian short story—by men as well as women—can easily see these texts as symbols of early feminist rebellion. Many writers of the time were preoccupied with the issue of woman—the independent woman, the unfulfilled woman, monstrous woman, the "erotomaniac," the emancipated woman who committed the cardinal sin of unsexing herself by personally rejecting marriage and sacred motherhood altogether—and the short story was "a particularly appropriate vehicle for the expression of ex-centric, alienated vision," as Claire Hanson suggests (3). Overall, the increasing emphasis given to the women's short story by recent feminist critics can be seen as a rebuke to the tendency on the part of certain 20th-century critics to claim the short story as male preserve, even, as has been suggested, using phallic language to do so. Notable here is H. G. Wells's pronouncement that "in order to produce its 'one single vivid effect,' the short story must 'seize the attention at the outset, and never relaxing, gather it together more and more until the climax is reached.'. . . [It must] 'explode and finish before interruption occurs or fatigue sets in'" (quoted in Brown, xviii). Wells's account, which seems intended to privilege men's literary work, is unusual in its explicitness, but it does square with attempts by the literary intelligentsia of the 1890s to "reclaim the kingdom of the English novel for male writers, male readers and men's stories," as Showalter puts it (1992, 142). This mission helped ensure that many fine short stories by women were brushed aside and ignored by those responsible for putting anthologies together and for teaching the short story—at least until recently (Showalter, 142).

Because authorship itself was undergoing significant change and becoming more obviously professional, it is no surprise that some writers used the short story to talk about what it was to be an author or artist—as did Henry James in "Greville Fane" (1892) and "The Real Thing" (1892) and Vernon Lee in "Lady Tal" (1892). For others, the very shortness of the short story was the obvious form for the new breakneck speed of the modern age with its trains, steamships, motorcars, omnibuses, telegrams, and telephones. Bliss Perry believed the short story to be "a kind of writing perfectly adapted to our over-driven generation, which rushes from one task of engagement to another and between times, or on the way, snatches up a story" (251). This idea that the short story thrives in a disordered, fast-paced, fragmented society has remained a popular one, as has the idea that it is a form particularly suited to conveying a peculiarly "modern" sense of dislocation and uncertainty. The strength of the British short story has often been what Wendell Harris has described as its ability "to isolate, to portray the individual person, or moment, or scenes in isolation detached from the great continuum." In this way the short story is often held up as "the natural vehicle for the presentation of the outsider" and also "for the moment whose intensity makes it seem outside the ordinary stream of time . . . or outside our ordinary range of experience" (11).

One of the realizations that will emerge from a reading of the present volume is that trying to disentangle the moral, social, and aesthetic dimensions of the short story at the beginning of the 20th century is a complex undertaking. There is no exact starting point, no single Poe-like figure who stands out, although the French realist writer Guy de Maupassant and the more impressionistic Russian Anton Chekov are often cited as influential figures (Fedderson, 22). The years leading up to the outbreak of World War I in 1914 saw the culture of the short story expanding: detective fiction including G. K. Chesterton's Father Brown stories;

colonial stories by Kipling and Maugham, with their examination of the so-called white man's burden in the far-flung reaches of the British Empire; suffragette fiction, sympathetic to women seeking the vote; children's fiction, including Beatrix Potter; and the sharp, satiric observations of the Edwardian social scene by E. M. Forster and the author known as Saki (Hector Hugh Munro). Clearly, at any moment in the history of fiction a range of styles is likely to be in evidence as older writers continue to publish alongside members of a younger generation. This seems to have been particularly true in the first two decades of the 20th century, which saw the gradual emergence of the loose literary movement known as modernism, involving a dismissal of many of the previous generation of Victorian writers by a new literary intelligentsia. This was coupled with bold experimentations with narrative techniques, with point of view, with time and space, with new visions made up of the scattered impressions of individual consciousnesses and selves. Henry James, Oscar Wilde, Thomas Hardy, and Joseph Conrad are often seen as the precursors to the high modernist short story—important hinges between the Victorian outlook on the one hand and the modern 20th-century viewpoint on the other—before it was injected with new vigor by James Joyce and D. H. Lawrence, among others. The works of both these writers are notable for their focus on the drab, but often tragic, lives of working- and lower-middle-class characters, for their striking use of symbolism, and for their challenges to the barriers of what could and could not be said.

Modernism, however, is equally associated with members of the so-called Bloomsbury Group, named after a salubrious area in central London near the British Museum where many of them lived and met. The group comprised a wealthier but loose coterie of artists and writers including Virginia Woolf and Katherine Mansfield. Like Lawrence and Joyce, the work of these two women writers has also been seen to represent something strikingly new and different but also unsettling. Somerset Maugham, another influential short story writer who argued that the best stories are "well made" and "strongly plotted," accused Mansfield of writing plotless stories "using atmosphere to 'decorate a story so thin' that it could not exist without its trimmings" (Shaw, 16). Nonetheless, the best-known modernist short stories—including Mansfield's "The Garden Party," Woolf's "Kew Gardens," and Joyce's "The Dead"—have been viewed as sublime pieces of craftsmanship in which their authors, far from being restricted by word length, use the formal limitations of the short story as a tool for innovation and experimentation in the depiction of human psychology and the representation of individual subjectivities and impressions. Although it is often suggested that the modernists were heavily influenced by the impressionism of Chekhov (May, 51), the modernists' own important—some would say self-important—sense of their mission was spelled out by Virginia Woolf in 1918 when she discussed the writer's task: "If we are not mistaken, it is his purpose to catch and enclose certain moments which break off from the mass, in which without bidding things come together in a combination of inexplicable significance, to arrest those thoughts which suddenly, to the thinker at least, are almost menacing with meaning" (Burgan, 269).

Although the modernists have often been charged with self-aggrandizement and snobbery, collections such as Mansfield's *Bliss* (1920), Woolf's *Monday or Tuesday* (1921), and Lawrence's *England, My England* (1922) suggested to observers of the 1920s and 1930s that the short story could still be an exciting literary form. Elizabeth Bowen, looking back from the perspective of 1945, believed these works "captured, as truly as anything in our literature, the psychological atmosphere of that time," that is, the early 1920s (13). As the essays in the present volume discuss, Woolf and Mansfield saw the overriding aim of the modernist story as an attempt "to represent slight incidents of implication within the structures of an intensively managed fictional form," something in evidence in the titles of such much-anthologized works as Woolf's "The Moment" and Mansfield's "Prelude" (Burgan, 268).

The success of the modernists' attempts to "make a 'sudden arrest' of the moment" was a theme taken up in 1924 when Alfred C. Ward recorded the shift that had taken place in short story writing. He argued that the new techniques were symptomatic of the "contemporary mind," which was no longer to regard human life as fixed within plainly defined and immutable boundaries. Life is now depicted as an affair of jagged and blurred edges, of hazy and indefinable outlines, where dim half-lights afford little opportunity for clear discernment. The conscious and the subconscious intermingle; death and life are uncertainly poised; the subconscious impinges upon the unconscious. (16)

Ward had mixed feelings about this kind of writing. He disapproved of it when it resembled "a fashionable Freudian 'pathological' pamphlet" but he appreciated, as later critics have done, the creative ambition behind such attempts—"a genuine wish to explore new fields of thought opened up by advances in psychological study." Ward had no patience with those who privileged plot and who claimed, as Maugham had done, that "nothing happens" in these stories. Ward explained that what was being conveyed was very significant: "the emotional processes which transpire within two beings who are passing through probably the most tremendous experiences possible" (18–19).

Some of these experiences were, of course, those that involved coming to terms with the bloodbath of World War I (1914–18). Whether they supported or opposed the war, both male and female writers, including Rudyard Kipling, Arthur Machen, Mary Butts, and Radclyffe Hall, tried to find new ways of writing about trauma and the kinds of demands placed on the individual at home and at the front. So powerful are many of these stories that, as Trudi Tate has noted in her anthology *Men, Women, and the Great War,* "[o]ur own knowledge of the events of the Great War often comes through literary works," and the short story becomes "one of the key ways in which war was written as history" (4). Later, the widespread sense after the war of a chance for "a fresh start" "helped accelerate" the new modernist generation's search for different ways of diagnosing and representing human experience (Goldie, 29–30). The modernist sense of fragmentation, of fleeting glimpses, of loss, of exclusion and estrangement, of disintegration and instability, is evident in many of the stories written in response to the conflict.

Predictably perhaps, something of this instability is apparent in the subsequent history of the 20th-century short story. Periodicizing is still a difficult task, and as Malcolm Bradbury argues, it is "harder to suppose that there is a single or clear cut tradition" (14). Not all writers of the 1920s or 1930s were modernists. This was the so-called golden age of the detective story, when Agatha Christie and Dorothy L. Sayers reached their peak. The 1930s were also good decades for A. E. Coppard and H. E. Bates, whose lyrical tales of the countryside helped encourage a sense of Englishness that was still rural, as well as for the elegant stylists Elizabeth Bowen and Elizabeth Taylor.

The 1920s left a legacy of experimentalism, but some commentators observed a lack of social or political commitment. This was a charge levied by Edward O'Brien, writing in the introduction to *The Best Short Stories* (1934), in which he claimed that English writers were "so preoccupied with economy of effect" that their work appeared "sterile and inbred." "I believe deeply," he wrote, "that the English short story is in danger of being abandoned to delicate . . . young men who write beautifully about nothing." He finished on a familiar note by asking, "Is not the American short story much more the more memorable, much the more vital?" (10). Certainly one of the things that seemed to emerge in the 1930s was a sense that that the short story was not fulfilling its potential for recording the human condition. This was particularly evident after the outbreak of World War II in 1939. Writing "The Short Story in England" for *Britain To-Day* as the end of the war seemed to be in sight, Elizabeth Bowen predicted that the short story would emerge as "the ideal prose medium for war-time creative writing," that "war-time London, blitzed, cosmopolitan, electric with anticipation now teems, I feel, with untold but tellable stories, glitters with such scenes that cry aloud for the pen. So must our other cities, our ports and sea-coast, our factory settlements, our mobilized countryside." "I forsee," she added, "a record crop of short stories immediately after the war" (15–16).

These predictions did not quite come to fruition, however. During the war the short story was certainly encouraged in magazines such as *Horizon* (1940–50), which published works by Graham Greene, Frank

O'Connor, Evelyn Waugh, Elizabeth Bowen, and H. E Bates. Also influential was *Penguin New Writing* (1940–50), which published Rosamund Lehmann and Elizabeth Bowen alongside American writers like Saul Bellow, Eudora Welty, and Tennessee Williams. Other magazines included *Orion, Daylight,* and the *Windmill,* as well as the more middle-brow *Penguin Parade* (1937–48) and *English Story,* whose editor, Woodrow Wyatt, also championed the short story as "the poem of the modern world," amenable to being written by those who were employed in the armed services in between sentry duty or on leave (6). By 1945, however, there seemed to be much less inclination on the part of many writers to write about this war than there had been to write about World War I, and there seemed much more resistance to retrospection generally. Partly this was due to practicalities. In 1940 Woodrow Wyatt reported that "the short story in this country has fallen on lean days" and ascribed the decline to paper shortages (5–6), together with editors' unwillingness to take risks and the closure of several magazines. P. G. Wodehouse—admittedly an unlikely writer of wartime stories—wrote to a friend in the aftermath of the war lamenting the collapse of the once buoyant *Strand Magazine,* asking "Where can [a writer] sell his stories?" and recalling 17 magazines from his childhood "and probably a dozen more that I've forgotten." Wodehouse's apparent inability to sell stories may well have had something to do with his status as persona non grata following his own undistinguished—and, some claimed, traitorous—war, in which he foolishly made pro-German broadcasts before moving to the United States, but his own view was that magazines died of "slanting" (the demand that all stories be written to a pattern) and "names" (printing anything by anyone famous even if it was substandard) (Dutton, 8). Other writers made similar complaints.

Most critics who have written on the post-World War II short story make the point that after 1945, the decline of magazines meant that there was no longer a ready outlet for short fiction. According to this version of events, the novel and poem began to prove more amenable templates for creative work that wanted to capture the strange mood of dullness and renewal in the postwar years. Dennis Vanetta describes the post-

war short story as "for the most part middle-aged and graying around the temples," its main practitioners having been born before World War I (35). Malcolm Bradbury also gives a similar message in his classic anthology *The Penguin Book of Modern British Short Stories.* Bradbury, however, sees the "New Look" postwar tradition of the short story as more complex than might be supposed—one of "realistic or reportorial narrative," which captures something of the post-1945 world of rationing and bureaucratization, versus "the notion of it as an art of language, of experimental form and symbol," this new tradition in turn sometimes "led in the direction of the strange, the fantastic, the grotesque, the surreal and the mythic." He also suggests that the short story that emerged in the drab postwar years could be divided into traditions, "one pre-eminently social and one pre-eminently experimental, but a sequence of constant attempts at reconciliation" (13). As if to prove his point, Bradbury's now-classic collection begins with stories by Malcolm Lowry, Elizabeth Bowen, and Samuel Beckett—the last about as experimental as writers got in the 1950s—and moves through V. S. Pritchett, Jean Rhys, and Muriel Spark to the more abrasive stance of two of the so-called angry young men representative of the social revolution taking place in Britain in the 1950s: Kingsley Amis and Alan Sillitoe (Vanetta, 34).

Bradbury's collection attempts to give the reader a snapshot of the social concerns of 1950s short fiction, together with the sense that fiction was being written outside the narrow confines of London. Moreover, this was not simply provincial fiction or working-class fiction. The presence of Bowen and Beckett is a reminder that throughout the history of the British short story, fundamental to its development has been the work of writers originating from outside England in her old colonies. In Ireland writers as different as George Moore, Bram Stoker, Oscar Wilde, and W. B. Yeats emerged at the end of the 19th century, followed by Frank O'Connor, Bowen, and Beckett in the 20th. All helped redraw the map of what Irish short stories might look like. The significance of the short story in Irish literary culture has been much commented on, but recently C. L. Dallat, reviewing Faber's *Book of New Irish Short Stories 2004–5* writes that the genre has long recognised-roots in the demands of societies in flux: where long-stable cultures in England and France led inexorably to the long-gestation novel, the new-founded 19th century U.S., seismic 20th-century central Europe and post-independence Ireland all opted for brevity, the latter context producing a particular flourishing in the hands of [Sean] O'Faolain, [Liam] O'Flaherty and [Frank] O'Connor, all more or less involved in the early-20th century struggle. (10)

Frank O'Connor called the short story the genre of "submerged population groups" who find themselves in "frontier" or "outsider" situations (20), perhaps making use of "local colour" situations. This is also a theme taken up in accounts of Welsh writing. In a recent article on the English-language short story in Wales, Tony Brown quotes Claire Hanson's explanation why the short story seems to appeal to sections of the writing population. According to Hanson, "The formal properties of the short story—disjunction, inconclusiveness, obliquity—connect with its ideological marginality, and with the fact that the form may be used to express something suppressed/repressed" (2). In Wales, both Welsh and Anglo-Welsh writers—the latter doubly marginalized in that they are neither Welsh nor English—including Margiad Evans, Dylan Thomas, Rhy Davies, and Caradoc Evans, wrote through the Great Depression and the two world wars to take in the industrial and the pastoral, social struggle and nationalist idealism, conscious that theirs were "ex-centric" voices, cut off from the center of power and influence, London.

A similar picture has been found in Scotland, the home of a long-developed tradition of published storytelling from Walter Scott at the beginning of the 19th century to the "weird tales" of Margaret Oliphant and Robert Louis Stevenson at the end. Since then the Scottish tradition has encompassed Muriel Spark, Alistair Gray, and, more recently, Irvine Welsh, Bernard McLaverty, James Kelman, A. L. Kennedy, Janice Galloway, and Margaret Elphistone. Writing in the 1980s—a time when the economic north/south divide (and literary divide) that existed in Britain was becoming more acute—some like Kelman and Welsh, began to use the language of the streets to give voice

to the marginalized or unemployed working classes. Others, Liam McIlvanney claims, invoke political as well as literary alienation from the rest of Britain, their stories all giving voice with considerable linguistic adventurousness to "people whom literature habitually ignores" (McIlvanney, 184). They have been lauded for refusing to "trim their Scottish sails to suit the prejudices of editors and marketing managers of London publishers" (Glen, 30) and for refusing to perpetuate the picture of Britain as cozy, southern, metropolitan, comfortable, and cricket-playing and as synonymous with England. A series of notable anthologies in the late 1980 and 1990s, among them Polygon's *Original Prints: New Writing from Scottish Women* (1985–89), James Robertson's *A Tongue in Yer Heid* (1994), and Harper Collins's *Three Kinds of Kissing* (1993), the first of an annual series of collections of new writing, allowed Scottish writers—both names and unknowns—to make their voices heard south of the border.

Like the list of authors included in Malcolm Bradbury's anthology, the choice of contemporary (post-1980) authors and stories given space in the present volume is partial in both senses of the word and can only serve as a reminder of the dimensions of the short story and the complex questions the form continues to provoke. As has been suggested, a sense that there remains a difficulty in coming to grips with the British short story is currently much in evidence in the British press. However, one thing most critics do agree on is that the form has been shaken up since the early 1980s. Twenty-five years ago Chris Bigsby echoed the thoughts of many in the literary world when he suggested that British fiction had become "a cosily provincial, deeply conservative, anti-experimental enterprise, resistant to innovation," reflecting what many saw as the ethos of Margaret Thatcher's hard-line Conservative government (to 1990) with its strong tendency toward nationalism (Morrison, 4). This was partly overturned with the emergence of a generation of young writers born after World War II, voices that signaled a shift from realism as the preferred mode to writing that came to be termed postmodern. Although publishers and agents had by this time begun to push young authors toward the novel form, in the mid-

1980s supporters of the British short story could point to Ian McEwan's macabre explorations of depraved and socially unacceptable behaviour, Martin Amis's vicious satires on the greed and materialism of the decade, and Graham Swift's fictional cocktails of torment, alienation, and fragmentation as a body of work that suggested "revitalization" plus "new voices and new styles," as Elaine Showalter has noted (2002, 67). By this time, readers had slowly begun to be aware also of the revisionist work of a new generation of women short story writers, notably Angela Carter and Michèle Roberts, who combined formal experimentation and feminist themes. Carter's magic realist vision is epitomized in *The Bloody Chamber* (1979), her second collection of short stories, which takes on traditional (misogynistic) fairy tales, already endlessly rewritten, and re-presents them with gothic, feminist, and overtly sexual elements; *Black Venus* (1985), similarly intertextual, continues her appropriation of other texts, her retelling (demythologizing) of myths, and the growing recognition that "the narrative constructions of history must always be partial and problematic" (Morrison, 24). Recent work by A. S. Byatt and Kate Atkinson has continued this tradition of taking up the histories of different characters across different time periods; Byatt, like Carter, returns to folktales and fairy tales, and Atkinson, similarly historically aware, merges social and political events and anxieties into the context and textures of her women's lives. Atkinson came to prominence in the 1990s, by which time the literary world was also seeing the first stories from a new generation of writers born in the 1960s: Will Self, Toby Litt, Philip Hensher, Nicola Barker, and Nicola Simpson, writers whose work has sometimes proved controversial and shocking in its postmodernist take on a post-Thatcher Britain of shoplifters, celebrities, sleaze, and rent boys, plus the obligatory sex, drugs, and rock and roll. More recently, collections such as *All Hail the New Puritans* (2000), *Speaking with the Angel* (2000), and *England Calling* (2002) have helped redefine the possibilities of the short story genre, adding to the immense complexity and scale of the form as it has been and still is produced by British writers.

At the beginning of this introduction I suggested that these are exciting times for the British short story, with its diverse and not very ordered history. The selections of essays that make up the present book are intended to reflect this. The intention has been to provide insight into the wealth and variety of the British short story, to offer new readings and new perspectives on some of the most popular stories and novellas of this period, and to give a sense of what A. S. Byatt has described as the "threads of connection and contrast" that run through them (14). Above all, the inclusion of essays about contemporary writers and texts is intended to signal that the British short story is very much alive and worthy of further study.

BIBLIOGRAPHY

Baldwin, Dean. "The Tardy Evolution of the British Short Story," *Studies in Short Fiction* 30, no. 1 (1993): 1–10.

Basham, Diana. *The Trial of Woman: Feminism and the Occult Sciences in Victorian Literature and Society.* London: Macmillan, 1992.

Belloc, Hilaire. "Short and Sweet." *Guardian* (October 30, 2004). Available online. URL: http://books.guardian.co.uk/fromthearchives/story/0,,1339120.html. Accessed July 10, 2006.

Bowen, Elizabeth. "The Short Story in England." *Britain To-Day,* May 1949, pp. 12–16.

Boyd, William. "Brief Encounters." *Guardian* (October 2, 2004). Available online. URL: http://books.guardian.co.uk/departments/generalfiction/story/0,,1317931,00.html. Accessed July 10, 2006.

Bradbury, Malcolm. *Penguin Book of Modern British Short Stories.* London: Penguin, 1988.

Brown, Tony. "The Ex-centric Voice: The English Language Short Story in Wales," *North American Journal of Welsh Studies* 1, no. 1 (2001). Available online. URL: http://spruce.flint.umich.edu/-ellisis/VolOne.html.

Burgan, Mary. "The 'Feminine' Short Story in America." In *American Women Short Story Writers,* edited by Julie Brown, 267–280. New York: Garland, 1995.

Byatt, A. S. *Oxford Book of English Short Stories.* Oxford: Oxford University Press, 1998.

Coldstream, John. Introduction. In *The Daily Telegraph Book of Contemporary Short Stories.* London: Headline, 1995.

Dallat, C. L. "New Voices Abroad," *Guardian* (May 28, 2005). Available online. URL: http://books.guardian.co.uk/reviews/0,,1492925,20.html. Accessed July 10, 2006.

Duguid, Lindsay. "Before It Becomes Literature: How Reviewers Have Dealt with the English Novel." In *On Modern British Fiction,* edited by Zachary Leader, 294. Oxford: Oxford University Press, 2002.

Dutton, J. A. P. "Why Magazines Die." *Guardian,* 25 June 2005, p. 8.

Ezard, John. "Orange Prize for First Time Writers Boosts Short Stories." *Guardian,* 25 April 2005, p. 8.

Feddersen, R. C. "A Glance at the History of the Short Story in English." In *A Reader's Companion to the Short Story in English,* edited by Erin Fallon et al., xxii. London: Fitzroy Dearborn, 2001.

Fitzgerald, Percy. *Memories of Charles Dickens with an Account of* Household Words *and* All the Year Round. London: Simpkin, Marshall, Hamilton, Kent, 1913.

Glen, Duncan. *The Bright Writer's Guides to Scottish Culture 2.* Edinburgh: Arkos, 1995.

Goldie, David. *A Critical Difference: T. S. Eliot and John Middleton Murray in English Literary Criticism 1919–28.* Oxford: Clarendon, 1998.

Gordon, Giles, and David Hughes. *The Best of Best Short Stories 1986–1995.* London: Minerva, 1995.

Hanson, Clare. *Re-reading the Short Story.* London: Macmillan, 1989.

Harris, Wendell. "Vision and Form: The English Novel and the Emergence of the Short Story," *Victorian Newsletter* 47 (1975), 11–16.

Hensher, Philip. "Fables and Foibles." *Observer* (April 9, 2000). Available online. URL: http://books.guardian.co.uk/reviews/generalfiction/0,,157234,00.html. Accessed July 10, 2006.

Hill, Susan. *Contemporary Women's Short Stories. An Anthology.* London: Penguin, 1995.

Lane, Harriet. "Just Stick to the Brief," *Observer,* 5 September 2004, pp. 20–23.

Lee, A. Robert. *The 19th Century American Short Story.* Totowa: Barnes and Noble, 1985.

Litz, A. Walton. *Major American Short Stories.* New York: Oxford University Press, 1908.

Levy, Andrew. *The Culture and Commerce of the American Short Story.* Cambridge: Cambridge University Press.

Linklater, Alexander. "Reclaiming the Story," *Prospect Magazine* 114 (September 2005). Available online. URL: http://www.prospect-magazine.co.uk/article_details.php?id=7025. Accessed July 10, 2006.

Luckhurst, Roger. *Science Fiction.* Cambridge: Polity, 2005.

MacDonald, Peter D. *British Culture and Publishing Practice 1880–1914.* Cambridge: Cambridge University Press, 1997.

Marvor, Alex. "Why We Need More Soho Dandies." *Observer* (December 5, 2004). Available online. URL: http://books.

guardian.co.uk/reviews/classics/0,, 1360523,00.html. Accessed July 10, 2006.

May, Charles. *The Short Story.* New York: Twayne, 1995.

McCarthy, Thomas. "The Art of the Short Story." *Guardian,* 27 August 2005, p. 27.

McIlvanney, Liam. "The Politics of Narrative in the Post-war Scottish Novel." In *On Modern British Fiction,* edited by Zachary Leader, 181–208. Oxford: Oxford University Press, 2002.

Morrison, Jago. *Contemporary Fiction.* London: Routledge, 2003.

Mullan, John. "Brief Lives." *Guardian* (June 26, 2004). Available online. URL: http://books.guardian.co.uk/elements/story/0,,1447617,00.html. Accessed July 10, 2006.

O'Brien, Edward. *The Best Short Stories.* London: Jonathan Cape, 1934.

O'Connor, Frank. *The Lonely Voice: A Study of the Short Story.* New York: World, 1963.

Perry, Bliss. "The Short Story." *Atlantic Monthly* 90 (1902), pp. 245–55.

Pykett, Lyn. *The Sensation Novel.* Plymouth, England: Northcote, 1994.

Rennison, Nick. *Fifty Contemporary British Novelists.* London: Routledge, 2002.

Richardson, Angelique, ed. *Women Who Did: Stories by Men and Women 1890–1914.* London: Penguin, 2002.

Shaw, Valerie. *The Short Story: A Critical Introduction.* London: Longman, 1983.

Showalter, Elaine. "Ladlit." In *On Modern British Fiction,* edited by Zachary Leader, 60–76. Oxford: Oxford University Press, 2002.

———. *Sexual Anarchy.* London: Bloomsbury 1992.

———. "Smoking Room." *Times Literary Supplement,* 16 June 1995, p. 12.

Tate, Trudi. *Women, Men and the Great War. An Anthology of Stories.* Manchester: Manchester University Press, 1995.

Thomas, Deborah A. *Dickens and the Short Story.* Philadelphia: University of Pennsylvania Press, 1982.

Vanetta, Dennis, ed. *The English Short Story 1880–1945.* New York: Twayne, 1985.

Ward, Alfred C. *Aspects of the Modern Short Story: English and American.* London: University of London Press, 1924.

Wyatt, Woodrow. Foreword. *English Story,* fourth series, edited by Woodrow Wyatt and Susan Wyatt, 6. London: Collins, 1943.

A

ACID HOUSE, THE IRVINE WELSH **(1994)**
Irvine Welsh's *The Acid House* (1994) is a collection of
21 short stories and a novella. Many of these stories
bear the hallmark of Welsh's novels in that they often
take place in Scotland and have drugs, sex, and random violence as themes. Many of his characters also
speak with a strong Scottish dialect, forcing the reader
to engage with a culture and style that differs from
Standard English. Robert A. Morace, in *Irvine Welsh's
Trainspotting* (2001), suggests correctly that Welsh's
use of language in *Trainspotting* (1993), and by extension in later works, is more specific and challenging
than is immediately apparent: "Welsh's linguistic
assertion of Scottish identity is in fact an assertion
more particularly of a Scottish sub-cultural identity,"
specifically, working-class youth culture, whose language is not that of "cultured Edinburgh" (27–28).
The cultural identities of the characters and the language they use are intertwined. The dark humor that
infiltrates Welsh's novels can also be found in this
collection.

The title story, "The Acid House," focuses on Coco
Bryce, a self-proclaimed football hooligan. The acid of
the title refers to the LSD that Coco takes before a life-
changing experience. With a flash of lightning he
inhabits the body of a newborn baby, and the souls of
Coco and the baby are swapped. This use of fantasy
and science fiction is ironic: Coco, in the baby's body,
continues to swear foully, and the body of the once-
powerful Coco has now been taken over by the baby;

consequently, Welsh undermines these subgenres
through his central antihero.

Experimentation with form in this collection is most
evident in a section of "The Acid House" when Welsh
escapes from realism by deftly combining Coco's past
and present lives. His past is signified with boxes of
dialogue spoken by his teachers and father, and these
are fitted in across the page interspersed with the
repeated word "light." This playing with form and use
of postmodern techniques reflects the effects of LSD on
Coco and adds pathos to his characterization. It
emerges that the violence he has meted out he learned
as a child from the adults around him.

Welsh's writing returns to the excesses of masculinity in all of his work and manages to value and parody
masculinity simultaneously. On the whole, specific
masculine, working-class values are repeatedly ridiculed here, yet these values are also portrayed with a
certain amount of sympathy. The scorn Coco feels for
his new middle-class parents is shared by the reader as
Welsh attacks the subterfuge of what it is to be a new
man in the 1990s.

The stories in *The Acid House* are often dependent on
Scotland and the stereotype of a Scotsman as a reference point for the various narratives, but this is not left
unquestioned. In a sequence that is evocative of
Trainspotting, Euan, the narrator of "Eurotrash," says,
"The Scots oppress themselves by their obsession with
the English which breeds the negatives of hatred, fear,
servility, contempt and dependency" (17). This story is

set in Amsterdam, implying that this distance gives the narrator the chance to reflect objectively on the politics of his victim status. The role played by the Scots in their own colonization is a theme that recurs elsewhere in Welsh's work, notably in *Trainspotting*.

Welsh also moves away from Scotland in stories such as "The Last Resort on the Adriatic," in which the narrator Jim commits suicide in a memorial to his dead wife. In "Where the Debris Meets the Sea" Santa Monica is the setting, but there is a return of sorts to Scotland as Welsh satirizes celebrity culture and gives Kim Basinger and Madonna improbably strong Scottish accents. Their manufactured importance is ridiculed as they sit lusting after unknown noncelebrities who live on schemes (housing projects) in the working-class district of Leith, and finally they realize they can only dream of going there for a holiday.

This collection is also exuberant in its focus on the so-called underclasses. In "Granny's Old Junk," for example, both the grandson and Granny are heroin addicts. Drug use is a recurring area of interest in Welsh's work, and his refusal to moralize about the dangers for the chemical generation means that he avoids preaching. This may be read as irresponsibility or, conversely, as a refusal to simplify a problem endemic in contemporary British life. Welsh is an adult writer, and he allows the reader to judge his characters from a rarely seen perspective. These stories offer a glimpse of another culture, and they challenge the metropolitan English middle-class sensibility. The fiction of a romantic Scotland (as a satellite of England) is reversed.

Paul McGuigan directed a film in 1998 titled *The Acid House,* based on three of these short stories: "The Granton Star Cause," "The Soft Touch," and "The Acid House."

BIBLIOGRAPHY

Morace, Robert A. *Irvine Welsh's Trainspotting.* New York: Continuum, 2001.
Irvine Welsh: The Unofficial Site. Available online. URL: http://www.irvinewelsh.com. Accessed January 24, 2006.
The Official Irvine Welsh Site. Formerly available online. URL: http://www.irvinewelsh.net. Accessed July 1, 2004.
Welsh, Irvine. *The Acid House.* London: Cape, 1994.

Julie Ellam

"ADVENTURE OF CHARLES AUGUSTUS MILVERTON, THE" ARTHUR CONAN DOYLE (1904) This story first appeared in the STRAND MAGAZINE in the set of stories called *The Return of Sherlock Holmes*. It is one of Sir ARTHUR CONAN DOYLE's Sherlock Holmes stories and focuses on the power of the master blackmailer Charles Augustus Milverton. Since Milverton's victims are afraid of the public revelations police involvement will bring, they turn to Holmes instead. Milverton threatens to publish compromising letters from Lady Eva Blackwell to a man in whom she was once interested. Holmes agrees to help her by trying to purchase the letters from Milverton, but Milverton's price is too high. To find a way to steal the letters from Milverton's home, Holmes goes undercover as a plumber. Watson accompanies him, but the two of them are surprised when Milverton returns. A woman then arrives and accuses Milverton of having caused her husband's death by sending him letters of hers. She then shoots the blackmailer dead and leaves the house. Holmes takes the opportunity to burn all the incriminating documents. He and Watson agree that they will not do anything to help the authorities find Milverton's killer, even though they know her identity.

This is a classic example of Holmes intervening to assist a woman in trouble because a corrupt man threatens her. Holmes's obvious disgust at Milverton—he calls him "the worst man in London" (791)—fuels his desire to thwart the master blackmailer. On the one hand, Holmes is helping a potential victim of a criminal; on the other hand, he assists a woman in keeping a secret from her fiancé. Holmes thwarts the potential power of public opinion and social scandal as he takes the side of Lady Eva and her secret. Her letters are described as merely imprudent, which highlights the injustice Victorian society would visit on a woman and her reputation for even a small infraction. The story, with its tension between private errors and vices and public exposure, is also typical of the way Holmes often works. He plays the role of judge and jury, and he is willing to break the law to bring a morally just conclusion to a case. In other stories he impersonates a clergyman ("A SCANDAL IN BOHEMIA"), causes a person's death ("The ADVENTURE OF THE SPECKLED BAND"), and decides to let a thief go without punishment ("The Adventure of the Blue Carbuncle").

BIBLIOGRAPHY

Conan Doyle, Arthur. *Sherlock Holmes: The Complete Novels and Stories.* Vol. 1. New York: Bantam Books, 1986.

Linsenmeyer, John. "Why Charles Augustus Milverton Should Be Canonized and Not Cannon-Balled," *Baker Street Journal: An Irregular Quarterly of Sherlockiana* 50, no. 1 (Spring 2000): 36–40.

Susan Bernardo

"ADVENTURE OF THE SPECKLED BAND, THE" ARTHUR CONAN DOYLE (1892)

This locked-room mystery was published in February 1892 in the STRAND MAGAZINE, a popular illustrated periodical aimed at a middle-class family audience. By the time contemporaries encountered "The Speckled Band," Sherlock Holmes and his friend Dr. Watson were familiar from two short novels and a handful of stories. Although audiences have been captivated by the Holmes stories, Sir ARTHUR CONAN DOYLE, a physician and historical novelist who wrote popular fiction to make money, felt that the mysteries' quality fell short of his other, less popular novels. Conan Doyle did, however, appreciate "The Speckled Band" enough to rewrite it for the stage in 1910.

"The Speckled Band" is of interest for a number of reasons, including its gothic elements, potentially sexual imagery, colonial connections, and incidental discussion of class and profession. The gothic reveals itself through exaggeratedly virtuous and demonic character types and through a decayed, half-empty house. These elements emphasize the supernatural appearance of the story's events, making Holmes's rational solution to the crime more surprising in comparison. The gothic elements also introduce the potential of submerged incestuous desire between the powerful but insane stepfather and his innocent, victimized stepdaughters. This conclusion, based on the gothic elements, is supported by the phallic image of the snake that crawls nightly into the victims' room through a small air shaft. "The Speckled Band" creates tension by portraying potentially inappropriate sexuality, but it places the emphasis of Dr. Roylott's relationship with his stepdaughters on financial rather than physical victimiza-

tion. This emphasis has inspired interpretations that concentrate on the story's imperial allusions and challenge the reading of the snake as a symbol of "destructive male sexuality" (Jann 121). Such interpretations provide roots for different readings of the snake and the other Indian elements that find a more positive or powerful view of both colonized cultures and the feminine in the story.

An impoverished aristocrat who survives first by taking up a profession (medicine) in the colonies and then by marrying a woman with an independent income, Dr. Roylott complicates discussions of class in the story. He is problematic enough to be killed, an unusual conclusion for a Holmes mystery. A gentleman and a professional, an Englishman and a former resident of India, a strong energetic man and a leisured landowner, Roylott crosses boundaries that make his character dangerous for individuals and for society. Pushed to crime to preserve his social and economic status, he uses professional and imperial knowledge to carry out his task. Holmes concludes, "When a doctor does go wrong, he is the first of criminals. He has nerve and he has knowledge." The interpretation of Roylott and the viper becomes central to supporting any argument about the story.

BIBLIOGRAPHY

Conan Doyle, Arthur. *The New Annotated Sherlock Holmes.* Edited by Leslie S. Klinger. New York: W. W. Norton & Company, 2004.

Jann, Rosemary. *The Adventures of Sherlock Holmes: Detecting Social Order.* New York: Twayne Publishers, 1995.

Wynne, Catherine. *The Colonial Conan Doyle: British Imperialism, Irish Nationalism, and the Gothic.* Westport, Conn.: Greenwood Press, 2002.

Andrea Cabus

ADVENTURES IN CAPITALISM TOBY LITT (1996)

Adventures in Capitalism was TOBY LITT's debut collection and, according to Malcolm Bradbury, foretold a novelist whose "fresh contemporary style . . . will sing in the ears of a generation" (3). The collection is divided into two sections, "Early Capitalism" and "Late Capitalism," and each story is set in the present. Litt wages brutal assaults on the MTV generation and explores the surreal, postmodern existences lurking beneath the veneer of perfection in consumer lifestyles.

"It Could Have Been Me and It Was," first in the volume, is the story of Brian, a man who wins the lottery and then decides to believe the messages in every advertisement but refuses to believe any humans. This story introduces a prominent theme in Litt's work, that of the body. At one point Brian claims that "the whole world competed for my body and cash" (6), emphasizing the cannibalistic and global nature of consumerism.

Elsewhere in the collection, "The Sunflower" is a wonderful pastiche of the Kafkaesque tale of paranoia, featuring a magazine reader who turns into a sunflower. After spending the majority of his life as a recluse, he is unmasked and becomes the subject of exhaustive media attention in a tale reminiscent of that of the Elephant Man or a circus freak. The final story in the collection, "When I Met Michel Foucault," is a haunting, vicious coup de grace in which the narrator avoids any deification of the 20th-century icon when he encounters him in an S&M club, marking, labeling, and scarring Foucault's body with a heated poker. This meeting reinforces the relationships Litt has previously identified between the body and consumerism, pornography and power, fantasy and identity.

Among all of these pithy epithets and dark comparisons, Litt still maintains a degree of critical awareness by cleverly mixing absurd humour with biting satire. He demonstrates an awareness of the conventions of narrative by breaking them and creates a perceptive celebration of material vacuity in contemporary culture, showing its potential interest as a subject for literature.

BIBLIOGRAPHY

Bradbury, Malcolm. "Real Life," *Independent*, 26 May 1996, p. 3.
Litt, Toby. *Adventures in Capitalism*. London: Secker and Warburg, 1996.

Martin Colebrook

ADVENTURES OF SHERLOCK HOLMES, THE ARTHUR CONAN DOYLE (1891–1892)

These 12 detective stories were first published as a series in the *STRAND MAGAZINE*, 1891–92, and then as a collection by George Newnes in 1892. After the novellas *A STUDY IN SCARLET* (1887) and *The Sign of Four* (1890), Sir ARTHUR CANON DOYLE employed the shorter form for subsequent stories featuring Sherlock Holmes, not returning to the novel until *The Hound of the Baskervilles* (1902). *The Adventures of Sherlock Holmes* comprised the first 12 stories to be included in the *Strand Magazine*: "A SCANDAL IN BOHEMIA," "A Case of Identity," "The Red-Headed League," "The Boscombe Valley Mystery," "The Five Orange Pips," "The MAN WITH THE TWISTED LIP," "The Blue Carbuncle," "The SPECKLED BAND," "The Engineer's Thumb," "The Noble Bachelor," "The Beryl Coronet," and "The Copper Beeches." The stories mark a departure from the embedded narration form of the longer stories and show modifications in the character of Holmes, from the decadent figure of the novellas to a more ascetic character (for example, as Ian Ousby points out, Holmes's use of cocaine is greatly reduced). The short stories are, perhaps deliberately considering the intended family readership of the *Strand Magazine*, less sensational than the first novellas, which featured corpses in bloodied rooms and macabre deaths by exotic poisons. By contrast, the *Adventures* are mostly based in romantic and political intrigues, financial conspiracies, and ingeniously planned robberies; only three of the stories ("The Boscombe Valley Mystery," "The Five Orange Pips," and "The Speckled Band") involve a murder investigation.

The stories make use of tropes used extensively in late Victorian detective fiction and developed in the 20th century, most significantly the threat of the criminal foreigner and the return of a colonial past with criminal consequences ("The Engineer's Thumb," "The Boscombe Valley Mystery," "The Five Orange Pips") and the instability of identity ("A Case of Identity," "The Man with the Twisted Lip"). In other stories, the mystery lies in explaining an unusual set of circumstances, usually connected to a criminal plot; for instance, in "The Red-Headed League," Holmes must find out why only a red-headed man should be employed by a mysterious organization to copy out pages from an encyclopedia. The short story form allowed Doyle to establish a structural technique that would become familiar to readers: Many of the stories open with Watson's musings in Baker Street, followed by a display of Holmes's powers of detection, then the entrance of a client who relays a mysterious narrative leading to the central investigation, before Holmes solves the mystery and explains his reasoning at the conclusion. The repetition of this form may have contributed to Holmes's popularity with readers of the *Strand;* it also allowed formalist critics to propose a structural "grammar" for the 56 Holmes short stories written by Doyle.

Each story was accompanied in the *Strand* by as many as 10 illustrations by Sidney Paget, and the tendency of later editions to omit these presents certain methodological difficulties for those studying the stories, not only because it provides a different textual experience from that of the *Strand,* but also because of the close relationship between Doyle's text and Paget's visual representations. The images were largely responsible for the establishing the visual iconography associated with Holmes (the other major influence was the American actor William Gillette's stage portrayal in the early 20th century), to such an extent that Doyle's later descriptions of Holmes were consciously altered to better fit Paget's depiction, which was itself modeled on Paget's brother William.

BIBLIOGRAPHY

Doyle, Arthur Conan. *The Adventures of Sherlock Holmes.* London: Newnes, 1892.

Ousby, Ian. *Bloodhounds of Heaven: The Detective in English Fiction from Godwin to Day 6.* Cambridge, Mass.: Harvard University Press, 1976.

Stashower, Daniel. *Teller of Tales: The Life of Arthur Conan Doyle.* London: Allen Lane, 2000.

Christopher Pittard

AESTHETICISM   Aestheticism was a 19th-century literary, artistic, and cultural movement influenced by the aesthetic philosophies of the German romantic school, by the art criticism of John Ruskin, and by French writers such as Théophile Gautier and Charles Baudelaire. Aspects of aestheticism can be found in the poetry and painting of the British Pre-Raphaelites (see PRE-RAPHAELITISM) from the 1850s on and in the work of Edgar Allan Poe in America. As a cultural movement, however, aestheticism reached its height in the 1870s and 1880s, before developing into the decadent aestheticism of the 1890s. Artists and writers associated with aestheticism include James McNeill Whistler, Walter Pater, and OSCAR WILDE.

Aestheticism advocates the principles of art for art's sake: Art is an end in itself; art need not serve moral, didactic, or political ends; art should not be judged by nonaesthetic criteria. Stylistically, aestheticism is characterized by preciosity, archaisms, and sometimes obscurity. Aesthetes insisted that any subject matter could be made beautiful in art, and therefore some aesthetes treated the perverse, the abnormal, and the morbid in their work. Ideologically, aestheticism represented a revolt against the materialism of Victorian middle-class culture and the effects of industrialization and mass production. Aesthetes retreated into the world of art in an attempt to transcend what they regarded as the ugliness of middle-class Victorian life. At the same time, however, aesthetes sought to beautify their own surroundings, to experience life in the spirit of art. As such, aestheticism's influence extended beyond literature and art into the realms of fashion, furniture design, the decorative arts, and architecture.

Though aestheticism is most often discussed in relation to painting, poetry, and the decorative arts, its influence is also notable in the short fiction of the late Victorian period. On the one hand, aestheticism characterized a genre of short story with a sumptuous, almost poetic style. Often the plot is slight, the emphasis being on mood and character, the embodiment of intellectual insights in an imaginative form, and the representation of the artist figure or sensitive individual struggling to realize an ideal in an inhospitable environment. Notable examples of such stories appear in Walter Pater's *Imaginary Portraits* (1887), Oscar Wilde's *The HAPPY PRINCE and Other Tales* (1888) and *A House of Pomegranates* (1891), Arthur Symons's *Spiritual Adventures* (1905), and ERNEST DOWSON's *Dilemmas* (1895). On the other hand, aestheticism and the aesthete figured as important subject matter in much late 19th-century short fiction, often treated negatively. Some of HENRY JAMES's short stories of the 1880s and 1890s, for example, including "The Author of Beltraffio" (1884), "The Lesson of the Master" (1888), and "The Middle Years" (1893), explore the personal costs of the aesthete's extreme devotion to art.

Aestheticism has traditionally been associated with male artists and writers. Recent scholarship, however, has drawn attention to women's participation in the movement and the ways in which they embraced, rejected, or sought to reconfigure aestheticism (see Schaffer and Psomiades). Women writers also drew attention to the problematic aspects of aestheticism in their short fiction, notably the male aesthete's objectification of women, emotional distance, and narcissism. Examples of this treatment of aestheticism can be found in VERNON LEE's "LADY TAL" (1892), Sarah Grand's "The Undefinable: A Fantasia" (1894), ELLA D'ARCY's "The PLEASURE PILGRIM" (1895), and Ada Leverson's "A Suggestion" (1895).

BIBLIOGRAPHY

Harris, Wendell V. *British Short Fiction in the Nineteenth Century: A Literary and Bibliographic Guide,* 72–81. Detroit: Wayne State University Press, 1979.

Reed, John. "From Aestheticism to Decadence: Evidence from the Short Story," *Victorians Institute Journal* 11 (1982–83): 1–12.

Schaffer, Talia, and Kathy Alexis Psomiades, eds. *Women and British Aestheticism.* Charlottesville and London: University Press of Virginia, 1999.

Kirsten MacLeod

AFTER DARK WILKIE COLLINS (1856) A number of WILKIE COLLINS's contributions to CHARLES DICKENS's *Household Words* were reprinted in a short story collection titled *After Dark* (1856) published in two volumes by Smith Elder. The stories included "The Traveller's Story of a TERRIBLY STRANGE BED," "The Lawyer's Story of a STOLEN LETTER," "The French Governess's Story of Sister Rose," "The Nun's Story of Gabriel's Marriage," and "The Professor's Story of the Yellow Mask." "The Lady of Glenwith Grange" was the only story that not been published previously.

The stories are contained within a frame narrative titled "Leaves from Leah's Diary." Leah Kerby serves as amanuensis for her husband, an itinerant artist whose temporary blindness forces him to take a break from his painting. During William Kerby's convalescence, Leah transcribes several mystery tales that her husband entertains her with "after dark." These are not William's own stories, however; they have been recounted to

him "by accident" by his various clients as they sit for their portraits. Leah plans to publish these stories in a collection titled *After Dark* and hopes that the sales of the book will make up for the lost income caused by her husband's unemployment.

Set during the 1789 French Revolution, "The French Governess's Story of Sister Rose" is a tale about a young woman named Rose and her devoted brother Louis Trudaine. Rose marries the treacherous aristocrat Charles Danville, who betrays his brother-in-law when he reports Trudaine's suspicious behavior to the revolutionary authorities. What Danville does not realize, however, is that the clandestine activities of Trudaine and Rose are part of an effort to help Danville's royalist mother seek asylum outside of France. Though brother and sister are condemned to the guillotine, their lives are saved by a former servant who has since become a police agent. Three years after the Reign of Terror ends, Rose and Trudaine expose Danville before he can commit bigamy. His mother disowns him, and he is killed in a duel by the father of the woman he had intended to marry.

"The Angler's Story of The Lady of Glenwith Grange" is told by a gentleman farmer named Mr. Gathwaite who has employed Kerby to paint one of his bulls. One morning, when the bull refuses to be a cooperative "sitter," Garthwaite and Kerby decide to go fishing. During the day's angling, Garthwaite recounts the extraordinary story of the reclusive Miss Ida Welwyn, also known as the Lady of Glenwith Grange. Years earlier, Ida Welwyn had promised her dying mother that she would always take care of her infant sister, Rosamond. Through her sister's devotion and attention, Rosamond matures to be an accomplished and beautiful lady who is highly regarded throughout society. After rejecting two marriage proposals, Rosamond falls in love with the dashing Baron Franval, whom she meets in Paris. Ida though she secretly dislikes and distrusts the Baron, allows him to marry her beloved sister on the condition that she and Rosamond are never to live apart. Ida's "vague sense of terror" is finally confirmed with the appearance of a French police agent who exposes the Baron as an imposter. The man Rosamond has married is, in fact, an escaped convict who bears an uncanny likeness to the real Baron Franval. The criminal is killed while attempting to escape, and Rosamond dies of shock. Ida Welwyn returns to Glenwith Grange to spend her remaining years caring for Rosamond's child and the neighboring "peasant population."

"The Professor's Story of the Yellow Mask" is recounted to Kerby by an eccentric Italian political exile, Professor Tizzi, who has spent his life researching "the principle of life." As he sits for his portrait, Professor Tizzi tells Kerby the story behind a strange decorative object that he keeps in his study: a stuffed poodle named Scaramuccia that once belonged to a young woman named Nanina. The story begins with Father Rocco, the brother of the master-sculptor Luca Lomi, who devises a plan for Luca's daughter, Maddalena, to marry Count Fabio d'Asocoli, who is studying under Luca. Father Rocco believes that the Count's inheritance, which supposedly originates from stolen Church money, can be rightfully restored if Maddalena marries Fabio. The only obstacle to this plan, however, is Nanina, a poor young model and the true love of Fabio, whom Father Rocco persuades to leave Pisa. Though Fabio subsequently marries Maddalena, she tragically dies in childbirth the following year. To prevent Fabio from remarrying, Father Rocco employs a woman, who also once had designs on Fabio's wealth, to impersonate Maddalena at a masked ball. Wearing a yellow mask over a cast of Maddalena's face, the woman reveals herself to Fabio as his dead wife and almost shocks him to death. Nanina, who has returned to Pisa, nurses Fabio back to health while also proving over time that he was tricked by Father Rocco.

After Dark represents one of Collins's earliest experiments with a multiple narrators, a polyphony of voices that leaves the reader to discern whether narrative control is ultimately exercised by a particular voice (the male artist, the female amanuensis, the lawyer, the governess, the farmer, the nun, the political exile) and, if so, what the implications of that dominant voice are. While the framing narrative provides a formal link for the stories, there are certain recurring motifs and thematic impulses that can be traced throughout the collection, such as disguise and mistaken identity, secrets and lies, crime and detection, dreams and the super-

natural, and death and resurrection (also referred to as "the dead alive").

BIBLIOGRAPHY
Collins, Wilkie. *Complete Short Fiction*. London: Constable, 1998.

Maria Bachman

ALL HAIL THE NEW PURITANS NICHOLAS BLINCOE AND MATT THORNE (EDITORS) (2000) According to their introduction, the editors of this collection of 15 short stories sought to bring together a group of "like-minded writers and set them a challenge." These contributors are Matthew Branton, Candida Clark, Anna Davis, Geoff Dyer, Bo Fowler, Alex Garland, Daren King, Simon Lewis, TOBY LITT, Rebecca Ray, Ben Richards, Scarlett Thomas, Tony White, and the two editors. The challenge comes in the form of a 10-point "pledge" or manifesto, devised by the editors and outlined in their introduction. The contributors—entirely made up of published, British writers, nearly all of them, at the time, in their late 20s or 30s and living in the southeast of England—were chosen by the editors beforehand, and each story was written specifically for the anthology. They were all completed between November 1999 and April 2000, thereby creating a focused cross section of a generational movement at a specific time. The only criterion for inclusion was that the candidate "would be responsive to the New Puritan challenge" and follow the manifesto; in the editors' view this form of "pre-editing" was sufficient, and the resulting stories, predictably, are somewhat uneven and resemble each other only in sharing a rather dark tone (with two exceptions) and having been written under the same restrictions.

According to Blincoe and Thorne, the 10-point pledge was created both as a challenge to the contributors and as a reflection of what was already "so original and challenging" about recent fiction (ii). To a certain extent, the pledge was meant to advance a "new wave" in fiction—stressing simplicity, purity, clarity, and integrity—and simultaneously aiming "to blow the dinosaurs out of the water"(vii)—a reference presumably to the previous generation of British writers not considered to adhere to these qualities. They specifically mention the work of Martin Amis and Salman Rushdie.

"The New Puritan Manifesto" comprises the following 10 rules:

1. Primarily storytellers, we are dedicated to the narrative form.

2. We are prose writers and recognise that prose is the dominant form of expression. For this reason we shun poetry and poetic licence in all its forms.

3. While acknowledging the value of genre fiction, whether classical or modern, we will always move towards new openings, rupturing existing genre expectations.

4. We believe in textual simplicity and vow to avoid all devices of voice: rhetoric, authorial asides.

5. In the name of clarity, we recognise the importance of temporal linearity and eschew flashbacks, dual temporal narratives and foreshadowing.

6. We believe in grammatical purity and avoid any elaborate punctuation.

7. We recognise that published works are also historical documents. As fragments of our time, all our texts are dated and set in the present day.

8. As faithful representations of the present, our texts will avoid all improbable or unknowable speculation about the past or the future.

9. We are moralists, so all texts feature a recognisable ethical reality.

10. Nevertheless, our aim is integrity of expression, above and beyond any commitment to form. (vii)

While the title of the collection is taken from a song by the British rock group The Fall, the concept itself probably owes more to film than it does to music. The Dogme 95 movement, for instance, is an obvious inspiration for the New Puritans, in that the filmmakers' manifesto bans the use of light or sound sources not naturally appearing in the scene and essentially intends to proclaim a new and purer alternative to Hollywood studio productions. Having drawn the connection, though, it must be noted that the New Puritans were faced with no true equivalent to the highly powerful Hollywood system to define themselves against, and the manifesto struggles to come up with a full 10 com-

mands. Some of the rules, the editors later admitted, were included simply to challenge their contributors (e.g., point 5) and not as part of the New Puritan aesthetic. Such restrictions, perhaps more than anything else, led some of the early reviewers to label the collection a mere publicity stunt.

This assessment is not entirely fair. It is still very early to gauge accurately the influence of the anthology, but it has been a success in terms of publicity and sales. Croatian, German, and French editions all appeared within the first few years, and groups allying themselves to the New Puritans include the Crack group in Mexico and the FAK in Croatia. There is something refreshing in the New Puritan desire to find middle ground between simple genre fiction on the one hand and playful postmodernist stylization or pure artiness on the other hand. The stories share a rewarding context of contemporary moral questioning within a focused sense of faithfully rendered time and place, and they seem to define successfully the New Puritan aesthetic as well as any manifesto, whether the anthology is considered a mere stunt, a needless attempt at revolution, or a breakthrough in early 21st-century literature.

BIBLIOGRAPHY
Blincoe, Nicholas, and Matt Thorne, eds. *All Hail the New Puritans*. London: Fourth Estate, 2000.

Rod Rosenquist

AMIS, KINGSLEY (1922–1995)   Born in London, Amis served in the British Army, Royal Signal Corps, from 1942 to 1946; attended Oxford University; and from 1949 to 1961 was a lecturer in English at the University College of Swansea in Wales. With novels such as *Lucky Jim* (1954), a satire of university life; *That Uncertain Feeling* (1955), about the professional and sexual conundrums faced by a Welsh librarian; *I Like It Here* (1958), about the adventures abroad of a xenophobic philistine; and *Take a Girl like You* (1960), about the cultural strains on the relationship between a young woman from the industrial north and a more cosmopolitan young man from London, he gained himself a reputation as one of the so-called angry young men of the immediate postwar period.

Known primarily for his novels, Amis also wrote short stories throughout his career, but he generally regarded them as either warm-ups or false starts to novels. *My Enemy's Enemy* (1962) includes three stories about class tensions among British soldiers during the last months of World War II: "Court of inquiry," "I Spy Strangers," and the title story. The collection also includes two stories concerning the English inability to understand the Welsh: "Interesting Things" and "Moral Fibre." *Collected Short Stories* (1980) includes all of these stories except the last, as well as previously uncollected stories that exploit the conventions of the espionage, mystery/detective, and science-fiction genres. Two of the best previously unpublished stories are "Dear Illusion," concerning a poet who knows that his acclaimed work is inferior but continues to be praised even for a new collection that he has purposely made second-rate, and "Who or What Was It?" in which Amis provides an exercise in postmodern literary schizophrenia that literally climaxes with his watching his fictive alter ego make love to his wife.

BIBLIOGRAPHY

Amis, Kingsley. *My Enemy's Enemy*. London: Gollancz, 1962. New York: Harcourt, 1963.

————. *Collected Short Stories*. London: Hutchinson, 1980.

Bell, Robert H., ed. *Critical Essays on Kingsley Amis*. New York: G. K. Hall, 1998.

Gardner, Philip. *Kingsley Amis*. Twayne's English Authors Series, no. 319. Boston: Twayne, 1981.

Salwak, Dale, ed. *Kingsley Amis in Life and Letters*. New York: St. Martin's, 1991.

Martin Kich

AMIS, MARTIN (1949–)

Born in Oxford on August 25, 1949, Martin Amis is the son of KINGSLEY AMIS. Unlike his father, who wrote safely within the aesthetic conventions of realism, Martin uses a playful voice that calls attention to the narrative as a work of fiction. Emerging from his father's shadow, Martin earned a reputation as the enfant terrible of the London literary scene and was even called "the rock star of English literature" by the BBC. As Amis would be the first to say, he is now too old to remain the literary scene's bad boy. Amis grew up in England, America, and Spain before graduating from Oxford University in

1971. Afterward, he worked as a book reviewer for the *Observer,* as an editorial assistant for the *Times Literary Supplement,* and again as a book reviewer for the *New Statesman.* Amis has been a prolific essayist throughout his career. The collections *The Moronic Inferno and Other Visits to America* (1986) and *Visiting Mrs. Nabokov and Other Excursions* (1993) include essays on the two writers most admired by Amis: Vladimir Nabokov for his verbal games and Saul Bellow for colloquial speech taken from the streets of America.

In 1973, Amis published his first novel, *The Rachel Papers,* about 19-year-old Charles Highway's seduction of a young woman. What might be called black romantic comedy, the novel is ultimately more interested in wordplay than in foreplay. *Money: A Suicide Note* (1984) describes the addiction to the 1980s-style instant gratification experienced by narrator John Self, who moves between London and New York trying to arrange a film deal. A much-talked-about scene takes place when Martin Amis appears in his own novel as a character hired to work on Self's screenplay. A favorite of rock bands Blur and Elastica, *London Fields* (1989) describes Keith Talent's dart matches in a west London pub while femme fatale Nicola Six plots her own murder amid much millennial angst. Amis moves beyond adolescent humor in *Time's Arrow* (1991), a novel written in reverse sequence about the Holocaust. The narrative moves backward chronologically from a typical American suburb as seen by Tod Friendly (aka Odilo Unverdorben) toward the concentration camp Auschwitz.

The themed short story collection *Einstein's Monsters* (1987) warns of nuclear catastrophe. Framed by "Thinkability," the introductory essay on nuclear weapons, many of the stories link personal tragedy to 20th-century events. "Bujak and the Strong Force, or, God's Dice" presents characters deeply affected by World War II—namely the bombing of Nagasaki, the Polish occupation, and Auschwitz—in describing Bujak's response to a violent attack on his family. "Insight at Flame Lake" is told through two sets of diary entries, one by a schizophrenic and the other by a nuclear scientist. Characters avoid all excitement only to achieve banal lives in the satiric "The Time Disease." The fable "The Little Puppy That Could" describes a postapocalyptic landscape in which nuclear holocaust survivors struggle to appease a mutated animal. "The IMMORTALS" views an atomic attack from the perspective of an undying being who has walked the Earth since its creation. Critics expressed dissatisfaction with the simplistic politics at odds with the sophisticated writing in the collection.

The British tabloids printed stories about Amis with great frequency during the mid-1990s. First, rumors that Amis had broken with longtime literary agent Pat Kavanagh, wife of Amis's friend JULIAN BARNES, in favor of the American agent Andrew Wylie increased scrutiny into the large advance Amis had demanded for his next novel. Stories soon followed about the separation from his wife, an illegitimate daughter, a cousin's murder, and, farcically, his expensive dental work. As Amis pointed out, his novel *The Information* (1995) focuses on the main character's midlife crisis. The events that had transformed Amis from literary to media celebrity came to an end with the death of his father in October 1995. Many of these events are eloquently described in *Experience: A Memoir,* published in 2000.

Heavy Water and Other Stories (1999) brought together pieces published between 1976 and 1997, many of them in the *New Yorker* magazine. Several stories prolong a single joke, as does "Career Move," which reverses the fortunes of a poet and a screenplay writer, and "STRAIGHT FICTION," which imagines a world in which heterosexuals are the minority. "What Happened to Me on My Holiday" is told in the dialect of an American adolescent whose resistance ("resizdanze") to clear speech reflects a struggle to understand death. "The Coincidence of the Arts" examines the effects of race and class through the silent, and indirectly violent, affair between a British painter in New York and an African-American woman who unexpectedly reveals her cockney accent at the story's end. "State of England," one of the best stories of the collection, embodies changes to the nation through the figure of Big Mal, a bouncer attending his son's Sports Day after having left the family for another woman. The story is framed around the father-son race, which Mal has been running metaphorically for years as he struggles to find a stable place for the white working-class male within multicultural, supposedly classless England. Another well-known story from the collection is "LET ME COUNT THE TIMES." While the early stories may feel like writing exercises, the later stories express Amis's characteristic themes of sexual intrigue, racial anxiety, and grotesque bodily attention. Reviewers have pointed out that Amis is the most American of the British authors writing today.

Amis is admired primarily for his vivid style, which combines amusing observation and scathing satire. He is at his best when writing about the grotesque, or physical shortcomings that embody moral shortcomings, and much of his humor arises from the nastiness for which he earned his reputation as an iconoclast. Amis has a morbid fascination with the embarrassments of the body; for example, few writers have mined sexual impotence with such fertility. This attention to bodily decay corresponds with larger themes of impending apocalypse—nuclear, planetary, or even personal. He returns repeatedly, some would say excessively, to the intertwined subjects of pornography, perversion, violence, drugs, and money. While these themes reflect his weaknesses for tedious plots, caricature, and puerility (yet another story about masturbation?), what redeems Amis's fiction is an ever-vibrant prose encompassing street slang as well as crafted metaphors. We find ourselves mesmerized by his grotesque characters even— or especially—at their most repugnant.

BIBLIOGRAPHY

Amis, Martin. *Dead Babies.* London: Jonathan Cape, 1975.
———. *Einstein's Monsters.* London: Jonathan Cape, 1987.
———. *Heavy Water and Other Stories:* Jonathan Cape, 1998.
———. *Visiting Mrs. Nabokov and Other Excursions.* London: Jonathan Cape, 1993.
Chaundy, Beb. "The Martin Amis Experience." Available online. URL: http://news.bbc.ro.uk/i/hiluk/744791.htm. Accessed July 2, 2006.
Dern, John A. *Martians, Monsters, and Madonna: Fiction and Form in the World of Martin Amis.* New York: Peter Lang, 1999.
Diedrick, James. *Understanding Martin Amis.* Columbia: University of South Carolina Press, 1995.
Morrison, Susan. "The Wit and the Fury of Martin Amis," *Rolling Stone,* 17 May 1990, pp. 95–102.
Wilson, Jonathan. "A Very English Story," *New Yorker,* 6 March 1995, pp. 96–106.

Matt Rubery

"AMOUR DURE" Vernon Lee (1887) A supernatural tale first published in *Murray's Magazine* and then included in Vernon Lee's collection *Hauntings* in 1890. It is one of the best-known examples of the Victorian ghost story and has been reprinted in many anthologies.

The story spans the period of August to December 1885 and is written as a series of diary entries by Spiridion Trepka, a young Polish scholar employed by a German university, who has recently arrived in the fictional Italian town of Urbania to write a work of history. While working in the town archives, he becomes fascinated by the story of a mysterious 16th-century woman named Medea di Carpi, whose many suitors met with violent ends and who was murdered on the orders of her brother-in-law, Duke Robert. Spiridion becomes increasingly obsessed with Medea and neglects his scholarly work to seek out traces of her life. Spiridion is particularly fascinated by a portrait miniature he uncovers, in which Medea wears a necklace inscribed with the motto "Amour Dure—Dure Amour" (love endures—hard love).

After several months, Spiridion receives a letter in Medea's handwriting asking him to meet her at a local church. He suspects a hoax, but he goes anyway and sees a woman in black who resembles Medea. Convinced he has finally come into the presence of the past, Spiridion returns to the church the next day only to find it shuttered and full of cobwebs. Spiridion then receives another letter from Medea, asking him to destroy a silver effigy that Duke Robert had placed inside a statue in order to prevent his soul from encountering Medea's in the afterlife. Now maniacally devoted to Medea, Spiridion destroys the statue and the effigy on Christmas Eve. While writing his final diary entry, he hears a step on the staircase. The last words he writes are "AMOUR DURE—DURE AMOUR!" (122). The story concludes with an anonymous note stating that a local newspaper had reported the mutilation of the statue and the discovery of Spiridion Trepka dead of a stab wound.

"Amour Dure" draws upon a wide range of literary and artistic sources. Medea is named after a woman from Greek mythology who killed her own children to punish her unfaithful husband. Lee's tale is most directly influenced by romantic writers such as E. T. A. Hoffmann and Théophile Gautier, whose supernatural stories often concerned uncanny hauntings from the past. Lee also draws upon the fascination of many Victorian writers, such as Robert Browning and Walter Pater, with Renaissance Italy. Lee's description of Medea's portraits, finally, alludes to a 16th-century portrait of a woman named Lucrezia Panciatichi by the Italian painter Agnelo Bronzino.

Although it takes the form of a ghost story, "Amour Dure" is also about history. By writing in the voice of an obsessed male scholar, Lee underscores the problematic desires that motivate our relationship to the past. Spiridion begins as a scholarly student of history but ends up unable to distinguish between objective facts and subjective desires. Lee in this way suggests that the Victorian fascination with the past is often a disguised indulgence in personal fantasy. Lee also comments on the role of women in history. Medea seems to be a femme fatale (fatal woman), but over the course of the story Lee suggests that she is ruthless as a result of circumstances, not nature. Passed from one man to another, Medea can gain freedom only by using her beauty to control those in power. Medea's ghostly seduction of Spiridion is one more attempt to turn the tables on the men who seek to define and control her.

BIBLIOGRAPHY

Colby, Vineta. *Vernon Lee: A Literary Biography.* Charlottesville and London: University of Virginia Press, 2003.

Lee, Vernon. "Amour Dure." Available online. URL: http://www.litgothic.com/Authors/titleindex.html. Accessed July 15, 2005.

Stableford, Brian. "Haunted by the Pagan Past: An Introduction to Vernon Lee." *Infinity Plus Non-fiction.* Available online. URL: http://www.iplus.zetnet.co.uk/introduces/lee.htm. Accessed May 5, 2006.

Zorn, Christina. *Vernon Lee: Aesthetics, History, and the Victorian Female Intellectual.* Athens: Ohio University Press, 2003.

Matthew Potolsky

"AMY FOSTER" Joseph Conrad (1901) First published in the *Illustrated London News* in 1901, "Amy Foster" was republished in *Typhoon, and Other Tales* in 1903. According to biographer Frederic Karl,

JOSEPH CONRAD'S idea for the subject of the story came from his friend and sometime collaborator Ford Madox Ford, who mentioned it in his *Cinque Ports* (514). The story of a misunderstood Polish castaway powerfully captures English xenophobic fears at the turn of the century.

"Amy Foster" uses a frame narrative like the one Conrad famously used in HEART OF DARKNESS; an unnamed narrator retells the story he heard from his friend Dr. Kennedy, a country doctor with a "penetrating" mind who takes an interest in the personalities of the villagers who are his patients. Kennedy tells of Amy Foster, a stoic and reserved young woman whose "heart was of the kindest" and who takes pity on a wandering tramp whose ravings terrify the other people he encounters. As it turns out, Yanko is not a tramp but a Polish castaway who survived the wreck of a ship that was taking him from his home in Austria to America, where he hopes to find work and start a new life. The frightened and bewildered Yanko is pelted with stones by children and locked in a barn by a farmer who fears him. Taken in by a neighbor, Yanko gradually proves himself by his hard work and heroism and learns English. A handsome man, he courts and marries Amy Foster, who has fallen in love with him. Once she has his child, however, she comes to fear Yanko's alien ways, especially the prayers and songs he croons in Polish, longing for his son to share his language and assuage his loneliness. Her passion for him becomes "fear resembling the unaccountable terror of a brute." He dies in a fever, abandoned by his terrified wife. In a last bit of irony, the reader is told that their boy is called Johnny, meaning Little John, the translation of Yanko's name.

Conrad's story, told in a realist style, is deeply infused with irony and symbolism. The bay looms behind the quiet life of the village in the first lines of the story, representing the presence of the rest of the world that the townspeople cannot quite keep out. Conrad, heavily influenced by the adventure tale, uses the expected outlines of the story of a castaway washed up in a new land to tell a much darker, ironic story. Yanko's kindness and intelligence cannot overcome the prejudices of the townspeople against his foreignness; he comes to represent essential human loneliness, the loss of idealism, and turn-of-the-century fears of solipsism, all common themes in Conrad's works. Echoing the central question of Conrad's *The Nigger of the "Narcissus"* (1897), Amy fears that Yanko is "shamming" illness, highlighting the story's themes of miscommunication and fears of an inauthentic self. The description of the now "passive" and "inert" Amy, who becomes brutishly terrified of her kind husband, also references contemporary discourse on atavism and degeneracy, which Conrad further explores in his 1906 novel *The Secret Agent*. One of the story's deepest ironies is that it is the English who are cruel and un-Christian, not the foreign man they fear. Conrad's own history as a Polish immigrant to this area of England clearly influenced "Amy Foster," which highlights failures of communication between people of different ethnicities and between men and women, as well as concerns about the author's ability to communicate with his audience.

BIBLIOGRAPHY

Conrad, Joseph. *Typhoon and Other Tales*. Oxford: Oxford University Press, 2002.

Karl, Frederick R. *Joseph Conrad: The Three Lives*. New York: Farrar, Straus & Giroux, 1979.

Knowles, Owen, and Gene M. Moore. *Oxford Reader's Companion to Conrad*. Oxford: Oxford University Press, 2000.

Ellen Burton Harrington

ANGELS AND INSECTS A. S. BYATT (1992)

Published in 1992, *Angels and Insects* continues A. S. BYATT's interest in the Victorian era, which was established with her Booker Prize–winning novel *Possession: A Romance* (1990). The two novellas published as *Angels and Insects* are "MORPHO EUGENIA" and "The Conjugal Angel," the latter concerned with angels and the former with insects. Set in the mid-19th century, "Morpho Eugenia" recounts the experiences of the naturalist William Adamson during his time at Bredely Hall, where he is staying with his aristocratic patron, the Reverend Harald Alabaster. Adamson marries one of Alabaster's daughters, Eugenia, but after discovering her incestuous relationship with her brother Edgar he leaves for the Amazon once again. He is joined on this expedition by Matty Crompton, with whom he had been compiling a natural history book for children while at Bredely Hall. In this novella, Byatt addresses the mid-19th-century conflict between science and religion that arose in response to Darwin's theory of natural selection. "The Conjugal Angel" similarly treats the complex relationship between science and religion by considering the position of spiritualism in the 1870s. The protagonists of this novella, Lilias Papagay and Sophy Sheekhy, are amateur mediums who hold séances for their social circle. This circle includes the historical figures Captain and Emily Jesse; the sister of Alfred Tennyson, Emily was engaged to Arthur Hallam but married Captain Jesse after Hallam's death. All present at the séances, including Captain Jesse, presume that Emily attends in the hope of receiving a message from her former fiancé. When Arthur sends a message that he and Emily will be joined in the hereafter, Emily surprises everyone by refusing to have anything to do with the arrangement. For Emily, as for several other members of the group, communing with the dead prompts a fuller appreciation of the living.

Although these novellas are located at different points in the Victorian era and concern different characters, they are subtly linked. The title of the collection refers to both novellas, and they are concerned with the challenges posed to religion in the 19th century from both science and spiritualism. Moreover, the ending of "Morpho Eugenia" provides a subtle intertextual link to the plot of "The Conjugal Angel"; the ship that Matty and Adamson set sail on, *The Calypso,* is captained by Arturo Papagay, Lilias Papagay's husband. The ending of "Morpho Eugenia" is ambiguous, leaving its protagonists "on the crest of a wave" (160) hovering between the ordered English world they are escaping and the Amazon to which they are headed. Although Arturo returns at the end of "The Conjugal Angel," there is no such resurrection for Matty and Adamson, so the ambiguous ending of "Morpho Eugenia" is never resolved. In adopting such an elusive technique for closure, Byatt recalls Charlotte Brontë's *Villette* (1853), which refuses to resolve the question whether the protagonist returns safely or drowns at sea.

The novellas belong to the genre of neo-Victorian fiction, a mode of contemporary fiction that engages with the Victorian past through an adoption of Victorian characters, locations, or themes. Byatt's most famous work in that genre, *Possession,* adopts a dual plot to explore the interrelations between the 19th and 20th centuries. In contrast, the novellas in *Angels and Insects* are located entirely in the 19th century and adopt a narrative voice that appears consistent with 19th-century fiction. Yet Byatt remains aware of the 20th-century perspective of her readers and manages to incorporate it neatly into her stories without diminishing or patronizing the 19th-century context. Thus, while an opposition between 19th-century belief and 20th-century skepticism might be expected in "The Conjugal Angel," Byatt complicates the issue by revealing the coexistence of an array of positions regarding spiritualism in the 19th century. She most expertly achieves this through the incorporation of various stanzas from Tennyson's 19th-century poem, *In Memoriam* (1850); an elegy to Arthur Hallam, it articulated many of the Victorian anxieties and questions concerning religion and its place in the modern world.

BIBLIOGRAPHY

Byatt, A. S. *Angels and Insects.* London: Chatto & Windus, 1992.

Schor, Hilary M. "Sorting, Morphing and Mourning: A. S. Byatt Ghostwrites Victorian Fiction." In *Victorian Afterlife: Postmodern Culture Rewrites the Nineteenth Century,* edited by John Kucich and Dianne F. Sadoff, 234–251. Minneapolis and London: University of Minnesota Press, 2000.

Louisa Hadley

ANNUALS AND GIFT BOOKS

Assemblages of short stories, poetry, and engravings, appearing for the most part from the 1820s to the 1850s. The British annual industry originated with the publication in 1822 of Rudolph Ackerman's *Forget-Me-Not.* Ackerman received his main inspiration from similar collections that were popular at the time in France and Germany, but the roots of the genre can also be traced to the personal albums and pocket books of the early 19th century in England. In these books, people, usually women, would transcribe their favorite poems and other literary pieces into a decorative volume to give as a remembrance to a friend or loved one. An early commercial example of such a book is Robert Southey's *Annual,* published in

1799 and 1800, which collected poems from various poets for publication but did not include the illustrations that would become such a prominent fixture of the later gift books.

In the couple of years following the publication of Ackerman's *Forget-Me-Not,* a small number of rivals appeared, notably *Friendship's Offering, or the Annual Rembrancer* in 1823 and *The Literary Souvenir, or Cabinet of Poetry and Romance,* edited by Alaric Watts, in 1824. These annuals were generally published in early November so as to be available for purchase as gifts for the Christmas and New Year holidays. Consequently, the books are generally associated with the year following publication, such as *The Literary Souvenir* for 1825, which would have been published late in 1824. The number of annuals steadily increased each year until, by 1831, more than 60 productions were in circulation. The most successful of them was *The Keepsake,* founded by Charles Heath, a prominent engraver. *The Keepsake* was produced annually for the years 1828 to 1857, outlasting Ackerman's *Forget-Me-Not,* the last volume of which was for the year 1847. The only other annual to exceed 20 volumes was *Friendship's Offering,* which was available from 1824 until 1844.

Such a high number of contending volumes necessarily led to considerable competition among editors to secure suitable talent to fill their pages. In this regard, the standard was set by Charles Heath, who hired a new editor, Frederic Mansel Reynolds, for *The Keepsake* in 1828, and the two gentlemen traveled the country that year to secure contributors among the literary world's elite. They offered large sums of money to Sir WALTER SCOTT, William Wordsworth, and Samuel Taylor Coleridge, for example, all of whom contributed to *The Keepsake* (in addition to other annuals) despite the qualms they and many other established writers had about damaging their literary reputations by associating with what they perceived to be a less dignified industry. Another popular poet of the time, Thomas Moore, was greatly perturbed to discover the unauthorized inclusion of some of his lines despite his repeated rejection of Heath's offers. Nevertheless, *The Keepsake* for 1829 offered works by an unprecedented collection of writers, including Scott, Wordsworth, Coleridge, Moore, Laetitia Elizabeth Landon, Felicia

Hemans, Robert Southey, MARY SHELLEY, and Percy Shelley. Editors quickly decided, however, that securing such a large number of famous writers was not necessary for financial success, and, although later contributors to the annuals included CHARLES DICKENS, Lord Tennyson, John Ruskin, and Robert and Elizabeth Barrett Browning, subsequent editions of *The Keepsake* and other annuals typically included much fewer big names.

The particular significance given to the name recognition of contributors, especially in the earlier editions of the annuals, resulted in somewhat relaxed standards for the literary merit of the actual compositions included in the volume. Writers such as Scott or Wordsworth, who considered the gift book beneath their standards, often submitted work that had previously been rejected by other publishers or of which they were not particularly proud. Other writers, working under the strict guidelines imposed by the editors, would compose pieces especially for the annuals. Often, however, these writers would be commissioned to compose a short story or poem to complement an engraving that had already been secured. As a consequence, the selections would occasionally appear stilted or unnatural, and their relationship to the accompanying embellishment would seem forced. Mary Shelley is just one writer who acknowledged the pressure of these conditions, and a number of the 19 stories she contributed to *The Keepsake* involved some literary concessions on her part. Thereafter, although many famous authors contributed to the annuals, most of the works found in them do not qualify among the best-known or most appreciated of their careers.

In many ways, however, the identity of the contributors to the annuals, as well as the quality of their offerings, was of less significance than the general appearance of the book itself. Designed to appeal to the middle-class consumer intent upon appearing fashionable, the gift books boasted gilt edges; delicate bindings of leather or silk, often vibrantly red or purple; and, most important, elegant engravings using the most recent steel-plate technology. Steel plates were more durable than the copper plates they replaced and allowed for crisper images. To take advantage of this new development, editors persuaded some of the most prominent artists of the time to contribute their work. For example, J. M. W. Turner, from whom Heath commissioned 120 pictures during this period for his different publishing ventures, contributed 17 illustrations for *The Keepsake* from 1828 to 1837. Other artists included Robert Smirke, C. R. Leslie, and Richard Westall. Ironically, such details were employed to emulate the hand-crafted books often found in gentlemen's libraries, but they were created in modern factories using the latest equipment to produce thousands of identical volumes for the marketplace.

The bourgeois tone of the gift books was further encouraged by their subject matter. Selections overwhelmingly depicted sentimental domestic scenes, replete with weeping lovers, mothers, and children. These stories have also been seen to perpetuate conventions and standards for morals and behavior. Sacrifice, devotion, and filial piety were celebrated virtues. Some publishers considered it their responsibility to protect their readers from impropriety; their works were designed to offer a sanctuary from the worries of the outside world. At the same time, however, the increased focus on the experiences of women and the preponderance of female contributors—and, increasingly, editors—for the annuals has more recently begun to be recognized as a more subversive phenomenon, occurring as it did at a time when women had little access to public careers. Further, the recurring use of exotic locales and story lines offered temporary escape from the increasingly restrictive social conditions of the middle class.

Although the quality of the contributions to the annuals has frequently been disparaged, their importance, especially for writers of fiction, should not be overlooked. The early 19th-century literary world was largely focused on poetry, while publishers of fiction generally sought out the three-volume novel. Popular magazines (*see* MAGAZINES, VICTORIAN) had offered some other venues for shorter fiction, though their editors often preferred novels, which would appear in serialized form. With the gift books arose a venue wherein writers of short stories could find an increased audience, one that perhaps required the flashy trappings of the exquisitely presented books to develop an interest in the literature included inside, and the proliferation of these annuals allowed for greater numbers of writers, whether beginners or veterans, to explore the possibilities offered by the genre.

BIBLIOGRAPHY
Booth, Bradford Allen, ed. *A Cabinet of Gems.* Berkeley: University of California Press, 1938.
Boyle, Andrew. *An Index to the Annuals: The Authors 1820–1850.* Worcester, England: A. Boyle, 1967.
Faxon, Frederick. *Literary Annuals and Gift Books: A Bibliography 1823–1903. Reprinted with Supplementary Essays by Eleanore Jamieson and Iain Bain.* Middlesex, England: Private Libraries Association, 1973.
Ledbetter, Kathryn. "Lucrative Requests: British Authors and Gift Book Editors," *Papers of the Bibliographical Society of America* 2 (1994): 207–216.
———. "'White Vellum and Gilt Edges': Imaging *The Keepsake*," *Studies in the Literary Imagination* 30, no. 2 (1997): 35–49.

Adam Mekler

"ANTHEAP, THE" DORIS LESSING (1953)

Originally published in DORIS LESSING's second collection of short fiction, *Five* (1953), "The Antheap" relates the growth from childhood to young adulthood of Tommy, the son of white settlers in southern Africa. As elsewhere in her short fiction (e.g., "The OLD CHIEF MSHLANGA"), Lessing uses a child's viewpoint to explore the processes of both enculturation into racist ideology and resistance to such acculturation.

The antheap of the title refers to the place where Tommy meets secretly with Dirk, the son of the white mine owner Mr. Macintosh and a black woman who lives in the African compound on the mine. That Dirk is Macintosh's son is known by all on the mine but can be acknowledged by no one, as young Tommy discovers when he asks his mother why Dirk is a different color from the other African children: "'why do you ask?' said Mrs. Clarke, with anger. Why, she was saying, do you infringe the rule of silence?" (311). The allegedly childless Mr. Macintosh takes an increasingly paternal interest in Tommy, paying for the education that will provide him with a promising future, but Tommy cannot forget that he is a changeling who has usurped the place of the real son, who is abandoned to a life of poverty and dangerous toil on the mine. An intense relationship develops between the boys, and Tommy becomes the means through which some of the father's riches are channeled to their rightful recipient, passing on to Dirk the education that he is receiving in a city school.

The story explores themes of friendship, justice, and freedom, aiming never to underestimate the difficulties involved in a relationship that transgresses social codes. As a child, Tommy is taught to understand that his becoming a man involves operating the racial exclusions that his society is based upon: "'You're too big now to play with a lot of dirty kaffirs,'" his mother tells him (307). And young Tommy himself thrills to the self-importance he feels when Dirk tries to sell him a duiker: "'Damned cheek, too much'" (309). Despite the older Tommy's recognition of the injustice of Dirk's situation, the boys are nonetheless frequently set in conflict over the privilege that Tommy cannot seem to help but believe he has a right to: "Slowly [Tommy] understood that his emotion was that belief in his right to freedom which Dirk always felt immediately" (346). Tommy's belief in his own freedom, as well as the possibility of his accepting as natural Dirk's lack of freedom, becomes an issue in one of the sculptures of Dirk that the promising artist Tommy produces: "'Why haven't I any hands or feet? . . . Surely it needn't be wood. You could do the same thing if you put handcuffs on my wrists'" (346–347), demands Dirk, responding to the disempowerment that he perceives in Tommy's representation of him. In what is perhaps a moment of deliberate self-reflexivity, Lessing's text here touches on the politics of representation, on the way that producing a representation of someone—in either visual art or fiction—involves the exercise of a certain power.

Finally however, the boys both understand themselves to be bound together in a relationship that is deeper than liking, or being alike, and "closer than brothers" (320). At the close of the story the boys have won an agreement from Macintosh to send them both to university: "The victory was entirely theirs, but now they had to begin again, in the long and difficult struggle to understand what they had won and how they would use it" (349). Joining Tommy and Dirk together in the plural "they," this ending is merely a beginning

for the boys. Their job is rather like that of the reader, to interpret what has taken place and what it will mean for the future.

BIBLIOGRAPHY
Lessing, Doris, *This Was the Old Chief's Country: Collected African Stories*. Vol. 1. 1953. London: Michael Joseph, 1973.

Victoria Margree

APPLE FROM A TREE AND OTHER STORIES, AN Margaret Elphinstone (1991)

Magic subversion and ecological agenda coexist in Margaret Elphinstone's collection of short stories. Quirky creatures populate the stories, which retain a strong humanity, even when cast in the fantastic genre. Human characters often hallucinate to grasp the unintelligible, and their visions subversively enlighten their view of the world, questioning their own beliefs and defying rational understanding. Epistemological and social issues coexist strongly in the majority of the stories, as the supernatural challenges rational thinking and critically investigates modern society.

The first story of the collection, "The Green Man," bears evident links to the Scottish ballad tradition. Evocative of fairyland, the Green Man's name, Lin, also establishes a specific connection with Tam Lin, the legendary hero of the Scottish ballad. The casual encounter with the Green Man accelerates a critical process of doubting already planted in the heroine, Sara's, mind. As reality gradually loses its apparent order, a dramatic urge of artistic inspiration runs through Sara's creative work. Eventually, the sacrificial death of the Green Man, whose elusive interpretation associates him with notions of fertility as well as otherness, allows life and rebirth for the planet.

The modern world's doomed state is the background to two related stories, "Conditions of Employment" and "The Cold Well." In the first story, fortune-telling priestess Miranda's fantastic encounters with characters from a remote past are juxtaposed against her more realistic visits into the ordinary present world. Both stories stress the importance of magical vision and the ability to foresee, imagine, and view things in an alternative way. "The Cold Well," inspired by the author's visit to Sellafield nuclear station, reinforces the sense of danger incumbent on the natural world. In stark contrast to the cool and pristine waterfalls described at the beginning of the story, earth, water, fire, and air, separated from their natural harmonious symbiosis, are turned against each other in the dangerously artificial world of the nuclear station visited at the end of the story.

The contrast between two clashing worlds is the focus of "An Apple from a Tree." An apple bite initiates Alison's friendship with a strange creature seemingly landed from another dimension in the middle of Edinburgh's Botanic Gardens: Nosila is, literally, Alison's inverse double. Deceptively attractive and naive, Nosila is in fact a destabilizing force in her new context. Brought to this world through a gesture evocative of original sin, the creature represents the unknown other world, embodies a moral code, and impersonates a social behavior radically different from Alison's own. Failed attempts of communication with human beings compensated by strong emotional bonds with houseplants and vegetables suggest that Nosila springs from a world closer to nature than Alison's Edinburgh. A second bite into the magic apple throws the two out of the Botanic Gardens and onto the thick grass of Nosila's world, where the sky is blue and the forest untouched. As the story develops, the awareness dawns that the possibility of them inhabiting the same world is unlikely.

Like Sara and Miranda, Alison is alienated from her own world. All human characters from the collection undergo a process of self-growth catalyzed by their extraordinary experiences. The supernatural encounters in the stories from *An Apple from a Tree* push the boundaries of realism open to accept the irrational within the rational and, rather than invite a suspension of disbelief, ultimately question the existence of rigid boundaries between real and supernatural worlds.

BIBLIOGRAPHY

Elphinstone, Margaret. *An Apple from a Tree and Other Visions.* London: The Women's Press, 1991.

Monica Germana

"ARABY" JAMES JOYCE (1914) One of JAMES JOYCE's most frequently anthologized works, "Araby" is the third in the trilogy of stories in his 1914 collection, DUBLINERS, which Joyce described in a letter to the publisher Grant Richards as "stories of my childhood." Like its predecessors, "The Sisters" and "An Encounter," "Araby" tells the story of an unfortunate fall from innocence, as a young boy comes to recognize the sorry state of the world in which he lives. On the whole, Joyce's home city is not kindly portrayed in these stories; he set out in *Dubliners* to produce what he called "a moral history of my country," with a particular focus on the supposed "centre of paralysis," Dublin itself. "Araby" and the other stories of Dublin's youth are tales of initiation into this gray world.

As is the case with most of the stories in *Dubliners,* "Araby" takes its inspiration from remembered fragments of the author's own childhood, including the Joyce family's sometime residence on Dublin's North Richmond Street, the Christian Brothers' School that Joyce and some of his siblings briefly attended, and the "Araby" bazaar that passed through the city in May, 1894, when Joyce would have been 12 years old. Yet although Joyce's life is deeply woven into his art, neither "Araby" nor any of his other works are merely autobiographical. These remembered elements come together in a story of a young boy in the intense grip of his first love, who imagines himself dispatched on a romantic quest by his beloved, only to realize in the end that his romantic notions were the naive fantasies of a child.

The dismal state of Joyce's Dublin is suggested in part by the gloomy atmosphere of the story. We are twice reminded in the opening moments that North Richmond Street is "blind." At its dead end is an empty house, and along one side is a school whose description likens it to a prison. The "brown imperturbable faces" of the other houses suggest a neighborhood of pious moralists keeping each other under constant surveillance. The young boy's own home is redolent of a past that persists in a stale and unpleasant form: The "air, musty from having been long enclosed, hung in all the rooms." The house's former tenant, a priest who passed away there, has left numerous uninspiring reminders of himself, from the rusty bicycle pump in the garden to the "old useless papers" scattered about the place. The narrator hints that the old man was at home among the street's "brown imperturbable faces" when he tells us that the supposedly charitable old man left all of his money to unspecified "institutions" and only the furniture of his house to his sister.

"Araby" is set in the short days of winter, whose cold and dark further underscore its gloomy atmosphere. Throughout, light contends weakly with an encroaching darkness. The boys' evening play takes place among houses "grown sombre" and beneath a violet sky toward which "the lamps of the street lifted their feeble lanterns." As the boy arrives at the nearly empty bazaar in the story's closing moments, the lights are turned off in the gallery of the hall, leaving him "gazing up into the darkness." Amid the persistent gloom, however, stands the radiant object of the boy's devotion, Mangan's sister, "her figure defined by the light."

The young boy's ability to see dazzling light in the midst of overwhelming darkness is a function of the romantic idealism that is gradually stripped from him by his decidedly unromantic world. Even the scattered leavings of the dead priest, which include Sir WALTER SCOTT's historical romance *The Abbot,* together with the memoirs of the adventurous criminal-turned-detective, Eugène François Vidocq, afford him fuel for his romantic imagination. Until the story reaches its sad conclusion, the boy is able to keep the darkness at bay, running happily through the darkened street with his young friends and transforming the clamor of the market on a Saturday evening into the backdrop for his imagined knight's quest. There he imagines "that I bore my chalice safely through a throng of foes"; however, the boy's adventure-story version of his world is challenged by the songs of the street singers, with their allusions to O'Donovan Rossa and other reminders of "troubles in our native land." The boy imagines his adventurous life despite the political troubles whose effects are felt and sung all around him. For a while, he imagines himself able to transcend such concerns and inhabit a thrilling realm of heroism and perfect love.

However, in the end his world will not sustain these happy illusions. The name of the Araby bazaar promises an Eastern exoticism entirely absent from the tawdry affair he finally experiences. Having imagined himself a questing knight, the boy encounters in Araby his Chapel Perilous, a defiled temple where "two men were counting money on a salver," and his heroic self-image crumbles during his encounter with the young woman at the stall he visits, who clearly regards him as a young nuisance. He witnesses in the flirtatious but shallow exchange between the young woman and the two gentleman a version of love considerably less operatic than the devotion that brought him to Araby, and he comes to see himself as a much smaller being than the gallant hero who undertook a sacred quest for his beloved, regarding himself in the final moment "as a creature driven and derided by vanity."

In recounting the boy's journey from passionate innocence to jaded cynicism, Joyce employs a narrative technique that is subtle but effective. The story is told from a first-person retrospective point of view that enables us to perceive two distinct but intimately related voices in the narration: that of the devoted young boy able to imagine himself a knight-errant "in places the most hostile to romance" and that of the subdued older man, recalling his younger self with an ironic detachment born of disappointment. The narration brings us inside the mind of the youthful lover, perplexed and overwhelmed by emotions that he can interpret only in the languages he knows: that of religious devotion and the stories of adventure and romance. Throughout, though, we are reminded that the young boy's "confused adoration" is being recalled by his older and sadly unconfused self. The gloomy opening description of North Richmond Street, with its houses "conscious of decent lives within them," gazing at each other "with brown imperturbable faces," clearly reflects the perspective of the older man rather than that of the boy who careened through the same street in play. And the explicit judgment in the narrator's recollection that "her name was like a summons to all *my foolish blood*" (emphasis mine) reflects an ironic self-perception that the young boy does not at that moment have. These two voices eventually converge in "Araby"'s closing paragraph, when the narrator declares, "I saw myself as a creature driven and derided by vanity," revealing the origin of that ironic perspective in the moment of his sad fall from romance to cynicism.

BIBLIOGRAPHY

Ellmann, Richard. *James Joyce.* 1959. Revised edition, Oxford: Oxford University Press, 1982.

Gifford, Don. *Joyce Annotated: Notes for Dubliners and A Portrait of the Artist as a Young Man.* Berkeley: University of California Press, 1982.

Joyce, James. *Dubliners: Text, Criticism, and Notes.* Edited by Robert Scholes and A. Walton Litz. New York: Penguin USA, 1996.

Brian Patton

"ARTHUR SNATCHFOLD" E. M. FORSTER (1928/1972)

Although E. M. FORSTER produced sufficient material in his writing career for three collections of short stories, he published only two collections in his lifetime: *The Celestial Omnibus* (1911) and *The Eternal Moment* (1928). *The Life to Come and Other Stories* was collected after Forster's death in 1970 and was published in 1972. This was not the only instance of this happening. In 1971, *Maurice,* a novel that Forster had first drafted as early as 1913 and returned to many times throughout his life, also received its first publication posthumously. Its frontispiece reads "Dedicated to a Happier Year." The reason for the delay in publishing these two texts was that Forster believed that their homosexual content would damage his and others' reputations. Forster died only three years after homosexuality was first legalized in Britain, so even though he had enjoyed a successful literary career, he believed that no publisher would go near these works.

The Life to Come and Other Stories features a variety of settings—from the more traditional, dramatic, and realist settings of "Arthur Snatchfold" and "Ansell" (both similar to that of *Maurice*) to the fantastical "The Life to Come" and the comic "The Obelisk." The story "Arthur Snatchfold" is similar in structure to the latter half of *Maurice.* It tells the story of the bisexual Sir Richard Conway, who, while staying at his friend Donaldson's country mansion, meets and becomes involved with Arthur Snatchfold, the estate's milkman. The morning after they meet they have sex in the woods. Later, Donaldson tells Conway that Snatchfold was caught and convicted of "gross indecency" on "evidence of a medical character." Snatchfold goes to prison without revealing the identity of his lover. The story concludes with Conway guiltily relieved but also changed by the experience. He acknowledges this to himself by writing down Arthur's name "in order that he might not forget it. He had only heard the name once, and he would never hear it again."

There is a variety of Forsterian themes at play in this story, the most obvious of which is that of the working class emancipating the upper class through a single act of coitus. This model of Uranian democracy is derived from the thought and writings of Edward Carpenter, a friend of Forster's. And the working-class man was typically a man of the forest—an autochthonous man of the earth. Forster's use of this symbol is out of step with 20th-century modernity. Instead, it suggests a pastoral nostalgia for a more equal world. Carpenter holds the notion that men can become equals through sex, the ultimate democratizer. Forster's notion of queer desire in "Arthur Snatchfold" presents a radical vision of same-sex desire, not because the desire was against the law but because it suggests that society's codes of behavior are artificial and unnatural and therefore can be broken.

BIBLIOGRAPHY

Bristow, Joseph, ed. *Sexual Sameness: Textual Differences in Lesbian and Gay Writing.* London: Routledge, 1992.

Forster, E. M. *The Life to Come and Other Stories.* London: Penguin, 1972.

Martin, Robert K., and George Piggford, eds. *Queer Forster.* Chicago: University of Chicago Press, 1997.

Vybarr Cregan-Reid

ASHENDEN W. SOMERSET MAUGHAM (1928)

Ashenden, a collection of 16 interconnected stories, is based on W. SOMERSET MAUGHAM's own experiences as a British secret agent in Switzerland and Russia during World War I. When first published, the stories seemed so authentic that Winston Churchill accused Maugham of breaching the British Official Secrets Act. As a consequence, the author burned 14 unpublished Ashenden texts. The collection is extremely important in the development of British espionage fiction, and both John le Carré and Len Deighton give *Ashenden* as a source of inspiration for their novels. What makes the stories innovative is that, in contrast to the lurid adventures depicted in the spy fiction of E. Phillips Oppenheimer and William le Queux, the action in the *Ashenden* stories is often unglamorous, inconclusive, and even anticlimactic.

The stories are narrated in the third person but almost exclusively give the point of view of the protagonist, Ashenden, "a writer by profession," who is recruited to work for British intelligence during World War I. Ashenden's experiences as an agent are recounted in a predominantly unemotional language, appropriate to the rather reserved and intellectual protagonist. However, he is not without feeling and often sympathizes with the predicaments and sufferings of the other principal characters (sometimes his enemies). Plots sometimes extend over two or more stories (for example, "The Hairless Mexican" and "The Greek"), but the collection as a whole is deliberately fragmentary. Endings are often ambiguous ("Miss King" and "The Flip of a Coin") or inconclusive ("Gustav" and "A Chance Acquaintance"). Ashenden's activities are usually dishonorable—they involve blackmail, lying, and aiding a murderer. Settings are frequently drab—small Swiss and French towns, shabby streets, and second-rate hotels—although the last six stories have the aura of great political events in the background and glamorous settings, such as a luxuriously furnished British Embassy. A notable feature of the collection is that several stories contain further stories within them, for example "The Hairless Mexican," "His Excellency," and "Love and Russian Literature."

"R" tells briefly of Ashenden's almost casual recruitment by his spymaster, the enigmatic and unscrupulous Colonel R. Two linked stories, "A Domiciliary Visit" and "Miss King," show Ashenden at work in Geneva. In the first tale, two Swiss policemen question him in his hotel room; in the second he plays cards with a beautiful Austrian agent and two anti-British Egyptians, after which he is called to the deathbed of a elderly English lady, who, although she has always professed a dislike for Britain, dies with the word "England" on her lips. Ashenden, however, has no idea what this dying word means for Miss King. "The Hairless Mexican" and "The Greek" depict an encounter with a sinister Mexican assassin who, with Ashenden's help, murders an innocent man by mistake. In "A Trip

to Paris" and "Giulia Lazzari" Ashenden and R blackmail a prostitute in order to entrap an Indian nationalist. "Gustav" presents espionage as a cynical way of making money, and in "The Traitor" Ashenden again tricks a British traitor to his death. The remaining six stories show Ashenden's work in an unnamed country and in Russia just before the Revolution of 1917. The stories center on a British ambassador who, despite his glittering success, thinks his life a failure; a determined Polish nationalist; a beautiful Russian woman who is Ashenden's former lover; and the talkative and prim American businessman Mr. Harrington, whose death, because of his refusal to abandon his dirty washing, is representative of the sordid and ironic events that these cynical, but not unfeeling, stories depict.

BIBLIOGRAPHY

Bloom, Clive, ed. *Spy Thrillers: From Buchan to Le Carré.* Basingstoke, England: Macmillan, 1990.

Maugham, W. Somerset. *Ashenden.* 1918. London: Mandarin, 1991.

David Malcolm

ASPERN PAPERS, THE Henry James (1888)

One of the most enduringly popular of Henry James's shorter fictions, *The Aspern Papers* was first published in serial form in the American journal *Atlantic* from March to May 1888. Its central theme concerns the attempt by the story's anonymous narrator—an American literary historian—to procure documents relating to the life of an imaginary expatriate American romantic-era poet named Jeffery Aspern. These documents (chiefly love letters), he believes, are in the possession of Aspern's former mistress Juliana Bordereau, who, now elderly and very infirm, lives alone with her middle-aged niece in a crumbling palazzo in Venice. Taking advantage of the two women's financial straits, the narrator installs himself as a boarder in their home, hoping to find a means of obtaining the papers, if necessary after Juliana's death. But the stress of waiting proves to be too much for the narrator, who eventually succumbs to the temptations of proximity and attempts to steal the letters. He is caught in the act by Juliana herself, who denounces him as a "publishing scoundrel." The only alternative offered to him is the suggestion by the younger Miss Bordereau that he join the family, by marrying her and thereby gain legitimate access to the papers. Although he has trifled with her affections, the narrator refuses to marry a "ridiculous, pathetic, provincial old woman" to gain his ends. Instead, he flees Venice, and the precious papers are painstakingly burnt one by one.

The story, with its mixture of comic, gothic, and realist elements, has intrigued critics since the time of its publication. First, the identities of James's characters and the broad outline of his story parallel certain facts surrounding the history of Claire Clairmont, former mistress of the infamous romantic poet Lord Byron (1788–1824). In old age, Clairmont accepted an American lodger named Captain Silsbee, who was himself in pursuit of papers pertaining to Byron and his fellow poet Percy Shelley. James included these details in his notebook, but his alterations to the original story he had heard are important and give some indication of the tale's wider significance. For example, James relocates the story from Florence to Venice, using Venice's blend of cosmopolitanism, historical continuities, and unique landscape as a metaphor for his questioning of the priorities of literary criticism and the importance of privacy even among public figures. Venice's palaces, outwardly austere and inward-looking, mask the private gardens inside which, like the secret lives of the inhabitants, provide the literal and figurative means by which the narrator gains admittance to the Bordereaus. Likewise, the narrator's anonymity (and pseudonymity) contrasts with the scrutiny he intends to give the lives of his hostess and her dead lover. Last, James's model for Aspern himself has caused much speculation, though the truth is probably that James created him as a kind of hybrid figure, representative of many literary figures whose works have fostered ruthless investigations into their authors' private lives.

BIBLIOGRAPHY
Klujeff, Marie Lund. "The Shades of Tone: The Narrator's Tone of Voice in Henry James's 'The Aspern Papers.'" In *Reinventions of the Novel: Histories and Aesthetics of a Protean Genre,* edited by Karen-Margrethe Simonsen, Marianne Ping Huang, and Mads Rosendahl Thomson, 191–202. Amsterdam: Rodopi, 2004.
James, Henry. *The Aspern Papers and Other Stories.* Oxford: Oxford University Press, 2001.
Reeve, N. H., ed. Henry James: *The Shorter Fiction: Reassessments.* Basingstoke, England. Macmillan, 1997.

John Ballam

ATKINSON, KATE (1951–)
Kate Atkinson was born in York in 1951 and studied English literature in the University of Dundee. She cites American short story writers, particularly Robert Coover and Donald Barthelme, as important influences. She won the *Woman's Own* short story prize in 1988 and the Ian St James Award for "Karmic Mothers = Fact or Fiction?" in 1993. Atkinson came to public attention, however, with her Whitbread-winning debut novel *Behind the Scenes at the Museum* (1995), a cross-generational, tragicomic account of one British family with a *Tristram Shandy*–like narrative. *Human Croquet* (1997) and *Emotionally Weird* (2000) also deal with time, memory, family, and consciousness but make greater use of her trademark techniques of narrative fragmentation, intertextuality, and ambiguous elements of fantasy.

Her short stories over the same period, such as "This Dog's Life" (1997), "Inner Balance" (1998), and "A Partner for Life" (2000), proved well suited to radio adaptation, showing an interest in dramatic narrative also reflected in her writing of two plays. Atkinson's first volume of stories, NOT THE END OF THE WORLD (2002), also places acute observation of everyday domestic experience in surreal quasi–magic realist contexts. But in keeping with her insistence on the importance of the short story, she makes wide use of its possibilities. Departing from the earlier novels' first-person voices, *Not the End of the World* contains 12 distinct yet interlinked third-person narratives that take up the stories of different characters across different times. Each story develops another aspect of the previous ones to produce an amorphous whole. References to classical mythology are interwoven throughout, and the opening and closing sections frame the volume with their account of two women making lists and spinning tales amid what might—or might not—be the end of the world. Atkinson's *Case Histories* (2004) returns to the novel form, but its multilayered tracing of three central stories shows the ongoing influence of the short story mode on her work.

BIBLIOGRAPHY

Atkinson, Kate. *Behind the Scenes at the Museum.* London: Doubleday, 1995.

———. *Human Croquet.* London: Doubleday, 1997.

———. *Not the End of the World.* London: Doubleday, 2002.

Muireann O'Cinneide

"AT THE END OF THE PASSAGE" RUD-YARD KIPLING (1890)

"At the End of the Passage," one of RUDYARD KIPLING's Indian tales, was first serialized in 1890 and appeared in the 1891 collection *Life's Handicap.* It deals with themes familiar to Kipling's Indian fiction: the grueling day-to-day work involved in the running of British India and the incursion, or apparent incursion, of the supernatural.

The story opens with four friends, Hummil, Spurstow, Mortram, and Lowndes, spending an evening at Hummil's bungalow. The pressures of work and the ravaging heat combine to make them, especially Hummil, lackluster and weary. Later Hummil confides to Spurstow, a doctor, the full extent of the nightmares that afflict him. Spurstow administers morphine and advises him to take time off, but Hummil declines. Alone, he is confronted with an apparition of himself but endeavours to rationalize the experience. However, a week later he is discovered dead, having apparently died of pure fright. He is hastily buried, and life amid the excruciating Indian summer goes on.

The story employs standard gothic motifs: delirium, nightmares, doubles. Also, like much gothic fiction, it is ambivalent: It is impossible to determine if the events depicted have a genuinely supernatural cause or result from psychological disturbance. Certainly the strain of the work to which Hummil is subjected appears conducive to hallucination. At the same time, the suggestion of some external agency at work is not easily discarded, especially in view of native superstitions as expressed by Hummil's servant Chuma, and the sheer extent of the horror in Hummil's dead eyes.

Kipling's emphasis in this story is also the appalling work conditions that cause Hummil to break down—the kind of hardships Kipling felt were generally suppressed or misrepresented in official accounts of Anglo-Indian life. The discrepancy between such reports and the grim reality is made painfully clear in this story as the four friends, worn out in rendering service to the empire, read a newspaper report of a politician accusing Anglo-Indians of living in luxury while oppressing the natives. And much of the narrative is given over to describing the overpowering heat, loneliness, and boredom that they suffer. Furthermore, there is the burden of overwork: Hummil has had to take on extra duties after the death of a colleague apparently driven to suicide. Moreover, it is implied that he might have been saved if his friends had not been too busy to keep an eye on him.

However, Kipling wishes to draw attention not only to the strains of Anglo-Indian working life but also to its unsung heroism. Hummil's refusal to take some leave arises out of a noble desire to spare Burkett, the man who would have to take over, as Burkett has family commitments. Spurstow is impressed, declaring that he thought such acts of selflessness belonged in the past. Beyond this, Hummil's sacrifice goes virtually unrecognized. But for Kipling, it is all the more remarkable on that account—one example among many in his Indian fiction of the kind of valor upon which the great Indian empire rests, and for which it grants scant reward.

BIBLIOGRAPHY

Kipling, Rudyard. *Life's Handicap.* Edited by A. O. J. Cockshut. Oxford: Oxford University Press, 1987.

Gurdip Kaur Panesar

AWARDS AND PRIZES

Reviewers and critics agree that literary prizes are significant for the promotion and exposure of writers and their work. Unlike in the United States, where the Pulitzer Prize for Fiction considers short story collections as well as novels, Britain's leading literary awards such as the Booker, Whitbread, and Orange prizes are open only to novels. The wide publicity and commercial success enjoyed by the winners of these prizes consolidate authors in the literary canon and extend the scope of the contemporary novel to a wider and more international readership. By comparison, the prizes for which short story collections are eligible are relatively unknown outside the book trade and attract little media attention. Also, compared with the Booker's £50,000 and the Orange's £30,000, the prize money offered by short story awards is comparatively low.

Until recently, the Macmillan Silver PEN was the only award specifically given for short story collections. However the launch in 2004 of the £10,000 International Orange Award for New Writing (a spin-off from the £30,000 Orange prize for fiction), the National Short Story Prize in 2005, and the Frank O'Connor Award also in 2005 suggests a growing recognition of the importance of the form. In addition, the genre benefits from other, smaller prizes that nominate an unpublished short story such as the International PEN David T. K. Wong Prize for Short Fiction, the V. S. PRICHETT Memorial, and the Bridport prizes. The most important literary prizes awarded for short story collections are the Somerset Maugham Award, the WHSmith Award, the Guardian First Book Award, the Geoffrey Faber Memorial Prize, the James Tait Black Memorial Prize, the Commonwealth Writers Prize, and the Macmillan Silver PEN Award.

Created and endowed in 1947 by SOMERSET MAUGHAM to enable British authors under the age of 35 to enrich their writing by spending time abroad, the Somerset Maugham Awards are granted to writers on the strength of a published work of fiction (novel or short story collection), biography, history, philosophy, travel, or poetry. Authors must be British subjects by birth. The awards are administered annually by the Society of Authors, and each winner receives £3,500. The first to win the Somerset Maugham Award for a short story collection was Nigel Kneale in 1950 for *Tomato Cain and Other Stories.* More recent recipients include IAN MCEWAN in 1976 for *First Love Last Rites,* Clive Sinclair in 1981 for *Hearts of Gold,* ADAM MARS-JONES in 1982 for *Lantern Lecture,* and Helen Simpson in 1991 for *Four Bare Legs in a Bed.*

The Guardian First Book Awards were launched in 1999 to replace the Guardian Fiction Prize, which was awarded annually since 1965 to a work of fiction. Addressed to first-time authors, the current Guardian Awards are open to fiction, poetry, biography, memoir, history, politics, science, and current affairs. The annual award is worth £10,000 to the winner, and the selection is made by a panel of critics and writers, chaired by the literary editor of the newspaper. In its 38 years of operation, only once has a short story collection been awarded the prize, Pauline Melville's *Shape-Shifter* (1990).

Founded in 1959, the WHSmith literary Award is judged by an independent panel of three judges who call in books from publishers. Writers from the United Kingdom, the Commonwealth, or the Irish Republic are eligible. The prize is awarded annually to all genres of literature, and its current value is £10,000. The WHSmith has been awarded to short story collections three times since its inception. Winners include NADINE GORDIMER in 1961 for *Friday's Footprint,* V. S. PRITCHETT in 1990 for *A Careless Window and Other Stories,* and ALICE MUNRO in 1995 for *Open Secrets.*

The Geoffrey Faber Memorial Prize was established in 1963 as a memorial to the founder and first chairman of the publishing firm Faber & Faber. The value of the prize is £1,000, and it is awarded in alternate years to a work of poetry and a work of prose fiction. The author must be under the age of 40 at the time of publication. Three reviewers, nominated by literary editors of newspapers and magazines that regularly review fiction and poetry, choose the winner. WILL SELF's *The Quantity Theory of Insanity* is the only short story collection to win the prize (1993).

Established in 1919, the James Tait Black Memorial Prizes are awarded annually to fiction and biography written in English and originating with a British publisher. They are two of the most prestigious awards in Britain. Each of the two prizes is worth £3,000 to the winner. In 1943 Mary Lavin's *Tales from Bectine Bridge* became the first short story collection to win the prize. It was followed by *Allegro Positions* by Jonathan Keates in 1983. No short story collection has been awarded the prize since.

The Commonwealth Foundation established the Commonwealth Writers Prize in 1987 to encourage the upsurge of new Commonwealth fiction. The prize is awarded annually to a work of prose fiction (novel or short story collection). It is divided into two categories: Best Book Award and Best First Published Book Award of £10,000 and £3,000, respectively. The work must be written originally in English by a citizen of the Commonwealth. There is no restriction on setting, theme, or mode. There is no requirement that the work should discuss the Commonwealth. The prize has been awarded to short story collections three times since its inception. Winners include Olive Senior in 1987 for *Summer Lighting,* John Cranna in 1990 for *Visitors,* and Pauline Melville in 1991 for *Shape-Shifter.*

The Macmillan Silver PEN Award is sponsored by Macmillan publishers, ST Dupont, and English PEN and is awarded annually to a collection of short stories. The winner is chosen from nominations made by the vice presidents and members of the PEN executive committee only; entries are not required. Winners receive £500 plus a silver Dupont pen. The most recent recipients include WILLIAM TREVOR in 2001 for *The HILL BACHELORS* and Bill Broady in 2002 for *In this Block There Lives a Slag.* In 2000, English PEN founded the International PEN David T. K. Wong Prize for Short Fiction. The prize is awarded every other year to previously unpublished short stories of between 2,500 and 6,000 words from writers worldwide. The first prize is £7,500.

The V. S. Pritchett and Bridport prizes are also awarded for unpublished short stories. The Royal Society of Literature founded the former in 1999 to commemorate the centenary of the eponymous short story writer. Residents and citizens of Great Britain and Ireland are eligible to enter. The value of the prize is £1,000. The Bridport Prize is endowed by the Bridport Arts Centre and invites entries for original poems and stories. The total value of the award is £4,500 divided among the winners of the first (£3,000), second (£1,000), and third (£500) prize. In 2001 the top 26 stories and poems were published in the Bridport Prize 2001 anthology.

In 2005, the National Endowment for Science, Technology and the Arts (NESTA), supported by BBC Radio 4 and *Prospect* magazine, launched the largest award for a single short story in the United Kingdom. The National Short Story Prize awards £15,000 annually for the winning story, £3,000 for the runner-up, and £500 for three other short-listed stories. Additionally, BBC Radio 4 will broadcast the short-listed stories, and *Prospect* will publish the winning entry. Finally, the single largest prize in the world for a collection of short stories, the Frank O'Connor International Short Story Award sponsored by O'Flynn Construction, was introduced in 2005. The Chinese author Yiyun Li received €50,000 for her debut collection of short stories, *A Thousand Years of Good Prayers.* It is hoped that the award will be held biannually.

The short story has been neglected by the mainstream prize industry even for the less important prizes for which single-author collections are eligible, which favor novels in their winning lists. The Somerset Maugham Award has chosen short story collections over novels only five times since its inception. The WHSmith Award was running for nearly 31 years before it nominated a story collection for the first time in 1990, followed by one more in 1995, while the Guardian First Book Award has included only one collection of short fiction in its lists of winners. Thanks to the recent launch of a number of high-profile prizes for short story collections, things may be about to change. It remains to be seen whether the successful promotion of a major prize will help offset the trade's constant privileging of novels and secure for the short story a permanent place on the literary calendar.

Vana Avgerinou

B

BAINBRIDGE, BERYL (1934–) Born in the north of England, in Lancashire, on November 21, 1934, Beryl Bainbridge grew up and began her career as an actress in Liverpool. Her first novel, *A Weekend with Claud,* was published in 1967. Bainbridge is regarded primarily as a novelist, and her popularity has led to her being created a Dame of the British Empire (equivalent to a knighthood) and being shortlisted for the Booker Prize five times. Bainbridge has published more than 15 novels as well as nonfiction pieces and two editions of short stories. Some of her novels have been been adapted into films, including *An Awfully Big Adventure* in 1995 starring Hugh Grant and Alan Rickman. Bainbridge's novels are an eclectic mix of historical analyses, such as *Every Man for Himself*'s focus on the *Titanic*'s maiden voyage, and realist novels set in England that explore the tumultuous relationship between the sexes in the domestic sphere.

Michiko Kakutani, writing for the *New York Times,* provides a starting point for an analysis of Bainbridge's stories, in his remark, "Reading these stories, it's clear that Ms. Bainbridge has a dry, dark-humored wit as well as a sharp eye for incongruous details." This sharpness undoubtedly comes from Bainbridge's "tight plotting" (*Guardian*), which subverts seemingly normal and mundane issues into gripping "snapshot" stories. Bainbridge draws on her career on the stage to explore performance within the domestic sphere, and the stories suggest that life is the most dramatic performance of all.

In "Mum and Mr. Armitage" the pair's long-awaited arrival at the hotel and the liveliness they bring backfires when Miss Emmet, an old spinster, endures an event with Mum and Mr. Armitage that forces her to stand up to these two characters, causing them, Mum especially, to become the figures of fun and gossip. "People for Lunch" is a humorous and dark story pivoting on two couples being made to have lunch in the garden by the teenage son who will not move from the sofa. The lunch party becomes a spectacle: A private act is taken into the public domain for all to see (including drunken passersby returning from the pub), highlighting the farcicality of the lunch party. "Perhaps You Should Talk to Someone," narrated by an adolescent called Katie, similarly focuses on the performative element of life and the social expectation that one should be adept in manipulating the truth. The lack of boundary between life and the stage is cleverly conveyed in "CLAP HANDS, HERE COMES CHARLIE," which concentrates on the estrangement between family members attending a production of *Peter Pan.* The story ends with the husband's death and Tinkerbell's resurrection, suggesting that art overtakes life.

Bainbridge's stories leave the reader thinking: Her narratives lack conclusions, yet they all seem to have a moral attached that the reader is meant to incorporate into his or her own life. Furthermore, houses are not homes: Conciliation and comfort are absent in the domestic sphere. This is poignantly represented in the story "Helpful O'Malley," in which an overseer,

O'Malley, lets a room to Edith, a girl who wants to escape from her dying mother but ends up committing suicide in the cold and lonely room after a chat with O'Malley. The domestic sphere is threatening, not comforting—a space where harm can occur.

This concern with domesticity and its ambivalence aligns Bainbridge with other 20th-century women writers of short stories, such as KATHERINE MANSFIELD and ELIZABETH BOWEN. The fluctuating narrative positions in Bainbridge's stories are similar to those of Margaret Atwood: The reader is more knowing than the character and is placed in a godlike position to pass judgment on the characters' actions and decisions.

BIBLIOGRAPHY

Bainbridge, Beryl. *Collected Stories.* London: Penguin, 1994.
———. *Watson's Apology and Mum & Mr. Armitage and Other Stories.* New York: McGraw-Hill, 1988.
———. *A Weekened with Claud.* London: Hutchinson, 1967. Republished as *A Weekend with Claude,* London: Duckworth, 1981.
Guardian. "Beryl Bainbridge (1934–   )." Guardian Unlimited. Available online. URL: http://books.guardian.co.uk/authors/author/o,,-14,00.html. Accessed March 31, 2006.
Kakutani, Michiko. Review of *Mum and Mr. Armitage, New York Times,* 11 July 1987.
Smith, Jules. "Beryl Bainbridge". Contemporary Writers. Available Online. URL: http://www.contemporarywriters.com/authors/?p=auth10. Downloaded on March 31, 2006.

Lucy Le Guilcher

BALLARD, J. G. (1930–   )

Best known for his novels *Crash* (1973) and *Empire of the Sun* (1984), James Graham Ballard is also a prolific short story writer. He slid into writing SCIENCE FICTION in the mid-1950s because its generic content approximated Ballard's own concerns (time, technology, the unconscious) in a way that more mainstream fiction did not. Ballard has also benefited, as a professional writer, from the genre's dependence on short fiction.

Ballard was born into a colonial family in Shanghai, a city marked by crime, poverty, and commerce. When Shanghai fell to the Japanese in 1941, Ballard and his parents were incarcerated in a prisoner-of-war camp, a key moment when (as he has often remarked) Ballard realized that reality was little more than a stage set that could be disassembled. Following the war, Ballard was sent to the Leys School in Cambridge to complete his education. He began to study medicine at Cambridge University in 1950 but dropped out after his second year. Ballard pursued a number of jobs during the 1950s, including advertising agent and test pilot, and also married his wife, Mary (who died in 1964), and raised a family. When his stories "Prima Belladonna" and "Escapement" were published, respectively, in *Science Fantasy* and *Terra Novae* in 1956, Ballard became a full-time writer.

Ballard received encouragement from Ted Carnell, the editor of *Terra Novae.* Carnell, who had launched the journal in 1947, was keen to promote younger writers even when (as in Ballard's case) they drew criticism from more traditional readers of science fiction. In 1964 Carnell appointed the young MICHAEL MOORCOCK to be his successor. Moorcock immediately retitled the journal *New Worlds* and began to replace the writers of Carnell's generation with his own contemporaries as well as slightly older writers such as Brian Aldiss. Most of all, Moorcock was inspired by Ballard's exploration of new styles and content.

Ballard's early short stories, marked by a variety of influences from avant-garde literature, surrealism, and psychoanalysis, established the characteristic themes of his fiction. "The Voices of Time" (1960), for example, offers a series of striking images and metaphors to describe the passage of time and the effects of entropy. "The Terminal Beach" (1964) is the first of what Ballard called his "condensed novels." Plot and story are virtually nonexistent, and the text is divided into titled subsections, further disrupting narrative development and foregrounding its own artifice. The text is primarily concerned with the outer landscape, in particular with images derived from nuclear radiation and with the recesses of the mind (which Ballard termed "inner space").

Although Ballard has received considerable recognition as a novelist, he is particularly well suited to writing the short story because of the form's emphases on character over plot, single effects over lengthy description, and ambiguity over narrative resolution. The strategies he deploys, however, allied to his subject matter of urban landscapes, media technologies, and mass consumerism, are quite unlike those of the traditional short story and have instead been identified with postmodernism. These elements are, perhaps, most effectively combined in Ballard's cycle of condensed novels, *The Atrocity Exhibition* (1970), a surrealistic and fractured attempt in which to understand the political and social upheavals of the 1960s through an unstable, anonymous protagonist.

Despite the disorienting look of texts such as *The Atrocity Exhibition,* as well as later collections such as *Myths of the Near Future* (1982) and *War Fever* (1990), Ballard's concentration on lone characters is an extreme proof for FRANK O'CONNOR's claim that the short story is innately drawn to outsiders. For other writers concerned with the alienation of contemporary society, such as MARTIN AMIS, IAN MCEWAN, and WILL SELF, Ballard has proved to be an important influence. (See also "DREAM CARGOES.")

BIBLIOGRAPHY
Ballard, J. G. *The Complete Short Stories*. London: Flamingo, 2001.
Luckhurst, Roger. *The Angle between Two Walls: The Fiction of J. G. Ballard.* Liverpool: Liverpool University Press, 1997.
Stephenson, Gregory. *Out of the Dream and into the Night: A Thematic Study of the Work of J. G. Ballard.* New York: Greenwood Press, 1991.

Paul March Russell

BARKER, NICOLA (1966–)

Born in Ely, Cambridgeshire, Nicola Barker spent much of her childhood in South Africa before returning to the United Kingdom to take a place at King's College, Cambridge. After graduating she worked in a variety of jobs before her first collection, the prize-winning *Love Your Enemies,* was published to great acclaim in 1993. This was followed by *Heading Inland* (1996) and more recently by *The Three Button Trick* (2004), which incorporates the best from both earlier collections. Her most recent novel is *Clear,* inspired by the U.S. magician David Blain's suspension in a Perspex box in London in 2003. Barker's stories are often about people willing to go to physical or mental extremes, or they involve people caught up in fantastical situations. In "Inside Information," Martha, a shoplifter, becomes pregnant

and thinks she can turn this to her advantage. Suddenly she finds herself harried by her fetus, which can talk and has a mind of its own. The story "Layla's Nose Job," about a 16-year old London girl with an extraordinarily long nose who finds that plastic surgery uncovers (rather than hides) her dark side, is typical of Barker's interest with those who are outsiders or are alienated from society. Barker's work is sometimes criticized for its excessive use of images, but for many critics she represents a breath of fresh air. In Ali Smith's words, Barker is "an energiser for the more moribund forms of Englishness and English fiction" (14).

BIBLIOGRAPHY
Barker, Nicola. *Behindlings*. London: Flamingo, 2002.
———. *Clear.* London: Flamingo, 2004.
———. *Heading Inland.* London: Faber, 1996.
———. *Love Your Enemies.* London: Faber, 1993.
———. *The Three Button Trick.* London: Flamingo, 2003.
Smith, Al. "The Tapeworm and the Tumor," *Guardian* 5 (5 July 2003), 14.

Peter Matthias

BARNES, JULIAN (1946–)

Julian Barnes was born in Leicester, England, on January 19, 1946. The child of two French teachers, Barnes was educated at the City of London School and Magdalen College, Oxford, where he studied modern languages. After graduating with honors in 1968, he worked as a lexicographer for the *Oxford English Dictionary* supplement. Barnes studied to become a barrister but soon decided on a writing career, preferring to write book reviews for the *Oxford Mail* and the *Times Educational Supplement* than practice law: "I came to realise that there was more pleasure in [writing reviews] than any prospect of a trespass case and £100" (Hawtree, 19).

His talent for fiction became evident in 1975, when his first published short story, "A Self-Possessed Woman," appeared in *The Times Anthology of Ghost Stories.* The story centers on Philip, the editor of an academic journal, and his interactions with Mrs. Beesley, a medium capable of contacting the spirit world and transcribing the thoughts and unfinished works of deceased authors, including James Joyce and William Makepeace Thackeray. Although Barnes's first attempt at short fiction, the story reveals his superb sense of irony, his interest in authors and authorship, and the interplay between truth and fiction—themes he would revisit in later works of fiction.

Barnes's first collection of short stories proper, CROSS CHANNEL (1996), centers on the complex relationship between England and France. The stories in *Cross Channel* explore issues familiar from Barnes's longer works of fiction (adult relationships, love, history, and truth), but each also attempts to illuminate the similarities and differences between the two cultures. Known for his exacting attention to detail and a heavy use of factual information, Barnes, in the best stories in the collection, uses the factual nuances of daily life to illustrate these larger themes. The opening story, "Interference," concerns Leonard Verity, an English composer on the verge of death who is living in a small French village with his mistress Adeline. Verity has recently finished what he considers his final masterpiece and desires to hear it performed before his death, but Adeline fails to ask the villagers not to run their electrical equipment. The resulting interference with his radio signal occurs just as he dies and symbolizes the disjunction between the English and French. Similar conflicts can be found throughout the collection, whether in a cricket match between English and French clubs, an Englishwoman's yearly pilgrimage to visit French World War I memorials, or a train journey through the Channel Tunnel.

In his second and most recent collection, *The Lemon Table* (2004), Barnes takes aging and death as his overall theme. The lemon is the Chinese symbol for death, and the book takes it title from a restaurant in Helsinki where, at the beginning of the 20th century, artists like the composer Sibelius used to sit at a "lemon table" to talk about death. In much the same way, each story in the collection addresses the topic, but Barnes does not portray late life as a genteel quieting of the spirit. Instead, the characters in *The Lemon Table* are extensions of their former selves, full of love, hatred, jealousy, anger, sympathy, and humor.

Unlike Barnes's stories published in the early 1980s, the pieces in *Cross Channel* and *The Lemon Table* are more highly refined in structure, with deeper layers of meaning and more carefully crafted language and tone. The characters are also more developed and the rela-tionships more complex. Because the stories are unified by a central theme, critics have often drawn comparisons with Barnes's earlier works, such as *A History of the World in 10½ Chapters*. In fact, after reading *The Lemon Table,* critic André Alexis commented, "I felt a little as if I'd read a novel." Whether writing a novel or collection of stories, Barnes is highly skilled at weaving together weighty themes with a deep understanding of humanity and a willingness to uncover the humor and ironies of life.

BIBLIOGRAPHY

Alexis, André. "Not a Lemon in the Bunch," *The Globe and Mail,* 17 July 2004, p. D7.

Barnes, Julian. *Cross Channel.* London: Jonathan Cape, 1996; New York: Knopf, 1996.

———. (as Dan Kavanagh). "The 50p Santa," *Time Out* (London), December 1985, pp. 12–13.

———. "Hamlet in the Wild West," *Columbia: A Magazine of Poetry and Prose* 24/25 (1995): 59–62.

———. *The Lemon Table.* London: Jonathan Cape, 2004; New York: Knopf, 2004.

———. "One of a Kind," *London Review of Books,* 18 February–3 March 1982, pp. 23–24.

———. "On the Terrace," *Punch,* 28 October 1981, pp. 746–748.

———. "A Self-Possessed Woman." In *The Times Anthology of Ghost Stories,* 132–149. London: Jonathan Cape, 1975.

———. "Trespass," *New Yorker,* 24 November 2003, pp. 86–93.

———. "The Writer Who Liked Hollywood," *New Statesman,* 2 July 1982, pp. 18–20.

Birkerts, Sven. "Julian Barnes." In *British Writers,* edited by George Stade and Carol Howard. Supplement IV, 65–76. New York: Scribner, 1997.

Guignery, Vanessa. "Julian Barnes in Conversation," *Cercles* 4 (2002): 255–269. Available online. URL: http://www.cercles.com/n4/barnes.pdf. Accessed May 5, 2006.

Hawtree, Christopher. "Novel Escapes," *Times Saturday Magazine* (London), 13 January 1996, pp. 18–19, 21–22.

Oates, Joyce Carol. "But Noah Was Not a Nice Man," *New York Times Book Review,* 1 October 1989, pp. 12–13.

Pateman, Matthew. *Julian Barnes.* Writers and Their Work. Tavistock, Devon, England: Northcote House in association with the British Council, 2002.

Roberts, Ryan. *Julian Barnes Website.* Available online. URL: www.julianbarnes.com. Accessed May 5, 2006.

Ryan Roberts

BARSTOW, STAN (1928–   )

A former engineering draftsman, Stan Barstow began to write stories and novels in the 1950s partly as an alternative to the daily grind of office life. His background is a northern English working-class one, and he is often associated, perhaps misleadingly, with other realist regional writers of his generation, notably John Braine, KINGSLEY AMIS, ALAN SILLITOE, and David Storey—so-called angry young men whose work focuses on the aspirations of working-class and lower-middle-class young men trying to come to terms with the pressures of family and environment.

Barstow became famous with his novel *A Kind of Loving* (1960). This story, about an intelligent, respectable young man (Victor Brown) who gets his girlfriend Ingrid pregnant and has to adjust to living with the consequences because "life is no fairy tale," is set, like most of Barstow's fictional works, in the mythical industrial town of Cressley, located somewhere in West Yorkshire. It is notable for its evocation of time and place, for its first-person narrative, and for its frank treatment of sexual relationships. Victor and Ingrid's story is continued in two sequels, *The Watchers on the Shore* (1966) and *The Right True End* (1966), works in which the characters struggle to come to terms with what Ingrid von Rosenberg describes as "feelings of disorientation, insecurity, loneliness" (147). These are recurring themes in Barstow's work, notably in the title story of his first short story collection, *The Desperadoes* (1961), about a gang of male teenagers. Barstow's second collection, *A Season with Eros* (1971), gives more prominence to working-class and lower-middle-class women characters. (Some critics have suggested that Barstow's early representation of women is misogynistic, but his later work seems less so.) Disparaged by some critics for unadventurous technique, these later stories are rich in religious symbolism. Such symbolism is also apparent in the stories that make up *The Glad Eye* (1984), in which the focus is often on vulnerable, middle-aged women worn down by circumstances (or by their husbands) who are driven to act in a way that is entirely out of keeping with what those around them expect. Like all Barstow's work, these stories are striking for his refusal to romanticize male-female relationships, highlighting instead how economics and class can often override the best of intentions. Barstow's work is highly regarded, thanks largely to the skill and compassion with which he depicts the lives and aspirations of the northern working classes.

BIBLIOGRAPHY
Barstow, Stan. *The Desperadoes and Other Stories.* London: Joseph, 1961.
———. *The Glad Eye and Other Stories.* London: Joseph, 1984.
———. *A Season with Eros.* London: Joseph, 1971.
Haywood, Ian. *Working-Class Fiction.* Plymouth, England: Northcote House, 1997.
Rosenberg, Ingrid von. "Militancy, Anger and Resignation: Alternative Moods in the Working Class Novel of the 1950s and Early 1960s." In *The Socialist Novel in Britain,* edited by H. G. Klaus, 145–165. New York: St. Martin's, 1982.

Andrew Maunder

BATES, H. E. (1905–1974)

A former reporter and clerk, Herbert Bates wrote novels, poetry, and short stories from 1926 until his death in 1974. He was a protégé of Edward Garnett and GRAHAM GREENE, both of whom were instrumental in getting his early work published. Bates's first collection of short stories, *Day's End,* was published in 1928. Their mostly rural settings were inspired by the Midlands county of Northamptonshire, where Bates grew up, and his interest in how the countryside was affected by the spread of industrialization. Bates's interest in rural life is a recurrent feature in his work and is most famously apparent in *My Uncle Silas* (1939), a series of anecdotal tales centering around the lovable and often drunken Uncle Silas, said to be based on Bates's uncle, Joseph Betts. Versions of these stories were filmed in 2003 with Albert Finney in the title role. The anarchic atmosphere of the character is taken up again in *The Darling Buds of May* (1958), the first in a wildly successful series of stories featuring the larger-than-life Pop and Ma Larkin and their children. The Larkins refusal to marry, their avoidance of income tax, and their relaxed attitude to life clearly appealed to readers who wanted escape from the stifling conformity of 1950s Britain. Sequels followed: *A Breath of Fresh Air* was published in 1959 and *When the Green Woods Laugh* in 1960. The stories were televised in the 1980s and 1990s and gained another popular following. Often overlooked in histories of the short story, partly because his work often seems devoid of any political or social edge, Bates was like A. E. COPPARD in his interest in the form (he published an important critique, *The Modern Short Story,* in 1941) and his wish to record the changing face of the English countryside and its customs.

BIBLIOGRAPHY

Baldwin, Dean R. "Atmosphere in the Stories of H. E. Bates," *Studies in Short Fiction* 21 (1984): 15–22.
———. *H. E. Bates: A Literary Life.* Selinsgrove, Pa.: Susquehanna University Press, 1987.
Bates, H. E. *The Darling Buds of May.* London: Michael Joseph, 1958.
———. *Day's End and Other Stories.* London: Cape, 1928.
———. *Fair Stood the Wind for France.* London: Michael Joseph, 1944.
———. *My Uncle Silas.* London: Cape, 1939.
———. *Seven by Five: Stories 1926–1961.* London: Michael Joseph, 1963.
———. *The Two Sisters.* London: Cape, 1926.
Flora, Joseph, ed. *The English Short Story 1945–1980.* Boston: Twayne, 1985.

Andrew Maunder

"BEACH OF FALESÁ, THE" ROBERT LOUIS STEVENSON (1892)

"The Beach of Falesá" is a story of colonialism in the South Seas that shocked many of ROBERT LEWIS STEVENSON's admirers when it was first published in the *Illustrated London News* (1892). It is related in the first person by British trader John Wiltshire, who is sent to the mission station of Falesá. Upon landing, he is introduced to other Britishers on the island: the drunken Captain Randall and Case, the principal trader on the island, who initially appears affable. Case suggests that Wiltshire take a native "wife" and picks out a likely girl, Uma. Wiltshire acquiesces and goes through the requisite sham marriage ceremony as practiced by whites in the region. He feels ashamed of such a travesty but is genuinely taken with Uma, as she is with him. Thereafter he settles down to business but is perturbed to find the islanders avoiding him, and he finally enlists Case's help in finding out what they have against him. Case informs him that, while he is not exactly tabooed, the natives harbor some kind of superstition about him. Case refuses to help him any further, and Wiltshire realizes that Case is quite happy with the situation, as it means he has a monopoly on trade on the island. Wiltshire finally extracts the whole truth from Uma: He is being shunned because Case has helped spread some unsavory rumors about her. Wiltshire thus realizes the trick Case has played on him, setting him up with a girl of whom the islanders are wary. At this point the missionary Tarleton arrives. Wiltshire meets with him to arrange a proper marriage ceremony for himself and Uma. Tarleton then proceeds to reveal how unscrupulous Case really is and how, by devious means, he has established great influence among the islanders and eliminated rivals in the past. Subsequently Wiltshire also learns that Case has instituted a kind of devil worship to keep the islanders in perpetual awe. He goes to see for himself and uncovers the paraphernalia with which Case beguiles the natives: an Aeolian harp, a luminous painted idol, and such items. Later he is agreeably surprised to find that Maea, one of the tribal chiefs, has come over to his side, having fallen out with Case over a girl. Heartened by this unexpected support, Wiltshire determines to expose Case as a fraud. This leads to a final conflict with Case in which Wiltshire, although wounded, stabs Case to death. Wiltshire is eventually moved to another station but remains in the South Seas, unable to return to England to fulfill his modest dream of running his own public house; although he evidently remains loyal to Uma and has children by her, he frets over their future as half-castes.

In some ways, "The Beach of Falesá" reads like a typical colonial adventure tale, with a resourceful hero and wily villain, treachery, dark deeds by night, and a spectacular (and extremely violent) climax; all of this is set against a backdrop of tropical sunshine and beaches and dimly visible natives who, with the notable exception of Uma, do not really emerge as characters in their own right. But in many other ways this text is starkly different from the usual run of glamorous, exotic adventure stories much in vogue among the British reading public at that time. The most notorious aspect is its frankness about sex and miscegenation, and the paragraph concerning the illegal marriage of Wiltshire and Uma was removed altogether when the story was first serialized (an act of censorship that infuriated Stevenson). The Europeans in the story are unflatteringly portrayed: the scheming Case, the ineffectual Tarleton, and the wholly degenerate Randall, who is described as being like some sort of hairy grey animal. All of this is filtered through the medium of Wiltshire, who, although he declares himself to be plainspoken, is of course being disingenuous to a degree: He is still keen to win the local struggle for mastery with Case, and in his account of the final confrontation he dehumanizes Case by referring to him more than once as a "brute" while appearing no less brutish himself in stabbing his adversary many more times than is necessary. Despite this ending, we also get a sense of Wiltshire's basic decency. Although he evinces a familiar colonialist tendency to look down on the natives, the Kanakas, he genuinely cares for Uma and later for their children. She is not merely a beautiful woman, an exotic alien object but, as he fully acknowledges, a true friend, and his only friend in the place in the absence of any solidarity among the whites. At the same time it would be wrong to assume that, just because he is able and willing to expose the shady dealings of whites in the area, he has any unusual sympathy for the natives. He has limited horizons; his chief concern is simply to detail the business rivalries in the region and his own part in them. Unlike the tragic realism of JOSEPH CONRAD, or even of Stevenson's own later story "THE EBB-TIDE," there is no tragic awareness here, no percipient analysis of the human condition, nor even any of the systematic exploration of evil that characterizes some of Stevenson's other works.

BIBLIOGRAPHY

Linehan, Katherine Bailey. "Taking Up with Kanakas: Stevenson's Complex Social Criticism in, 'The Beach of Falesá,'" *English Literature in Translation 1880–1920* 33 (1990): 407–422.

Menikoff, Barry. *Robert Louis Stevenson and "The Beach of Falesá": A Study in Victorian Publishing.* Palo Alto, Calif.: Stanford University Press, 1984.

Stevenson, Robert Louis. "The Beach of Falesá." In *South Seas Tales.* Edited by Rosslyn Jolly. Oxford: Oxford University Press, 1999.

Gurdip Panesar

"BEAST IN THE JUNGLE, THE" HENRY JAMES (1902)   First published in HENRY JAMES's 1902 collection, *The Better Sort,* "The Beast in the Jungle" is among the most anthologized of his short stories. Often read as a fable about failure, the tale of John Marcher is also seen as an internalized ghost story since the protagonist's own fears haunt him. Ten years before the narrative begins, Marcher has met May Bartram near Pompeii on the day of a significant discovery, and he has told her he feels destined for something terrible. She inquires whether he has met the beast. When the story opens, the narrator has forgotten the specifics of this earlier encounter, but the sense that his life is going to be marked by a terrible event has remained with him. This secret creates a bond between the two, and May accepts his offer to watch with him for the manifestation of the beast.

Circumstances bring them together in London: She has inherited money and can live independently. They fall into a habit of going out to the theater and dinner together and of talking with the verbal intimacy of spouses. He is at times aware that the arrangement benefits him more than it does her, but he convinces himself that he is not selfish in seeming to rob her of the ordinary womanly rewards, such as marriage and children, in life. May seems to know him and to understand his secret, as if she were the perfect angel in the house without being of his household.

When May becomes ill and is obviously dying, Marcher finds that the irregularity of their attachment does not allow him to attend to—or even to visit—her, on whom he has come to depend. He spends the year after her death abroad, and on his return to London, he visits her grave. In the cemetery, he sees a man mourning for his dead wife, and here he encounters the beast. The grief Marcher sees brings the realization that he has failed: He, whose name suggests a military perseverance, had been a noncombatant in life. In trying to escape his fate, he had met it.

Biographical critics read the story as a reworking of James's mysterious friendship with the American novelist Constance Fenimore Woolson, whose letters James destroyed when she died in Venice, possibly a suicide. (He also destroyed his letters to her when he helped clear out her rooms.) Some biographical critics see in the tale James's fear of what he might have been, had he not acted on his belief in doing, in pursuing actively the challenges of living. Marcher is often classed with James's artist-failures, unable to handle his medium, life. Other interpreters see the story as a covert expression of male homosexual panic. Marcher knows he is different, and the life he lives in public differs from the one he lives in private. When he realizes he should have desired May, he may be recognizing that he ought to have preferred women, as Eve Sedgwick argues. One might, however, argue that Marcher ought simply to have preferred something and found, rather than lost, his life.

BIBLIOGRAPHY

Goodheart, Eugene. "What May Knew in 'The Beast in the Jungle,'" *Sewanee Review* 61 (2003): 116–27.

James, Henry. *Complete Stories*. New York: Library of America, 1996.

Johnson, Courtney. "John Marcher and the Paradox of the 'Unfortunate' Fall," *Studies in Short Fiction* 6 (1969): 121–35.

Sedwick, Eve Kosofsky. *Epistemology of the Closet*. Berkeley and Los Angeles: University of California Press, 1990.

Karen Keck

BECKETT, SAMUEL (1906–1989)

Samuel Barclay Beckett was born near Dublin, the second son of an upper-middle-class Protestant family. He was an outstanding student at Trinity College, where he specialized in romance literatures. During extended spells in Paris in the 1920s and 1930s, Beckett became acquainted with JAMES JOYCE, whose influence is noticeable in Beckett's early works, especially the collection of short stories *More Pricks Than Kicks* (1934). Beckett published his first novel, *Murphy,* in 1938, and he went on to redefine the possibilities of drama with such plays as *Endgame* (which many regard as his finest dramatic work), *Krapp's Last Tape, Happy Days,* and *Not I.* He also created works specifically for radio, television, and film. Although more famous for his dramatic work, Beckett continued to produce challenging and experimental prose, for example, the short story "PING" (1966) and the "late trilogy" *Company, Ill Seen Ill Said,* and *Worstward Ho* (1980–83). Beckett won the Nobel Prize in 1969 for "his writing, which—in new forms for the novel and drama—in the destitution of modern man acquires its elevation." He wrote and worked in the theater almost until his death in Paris in December 1989.

Beckett has received possibly more critical attention than any other 20th-century writer due to his art's enigmatic, difficult nature. Beckett's work can seem pessimistic, as the figures in his texts are often physically decrepit and lost within a godless world that they cannot explain yet cannot leave; they must go on, creating fictions, playing games, bantering pointlessly, or just waiting. A humanistic perspective sees Beckett's main concern as the expression of the human condition within an absurd universe, as many of his characters struggle to express their essential identity but are thwarted by the language they are condemned to use. Poststructuralist views of Beckett see a deconstruction of all forms of expression, revealing not an essential identity but a play of linguistic and textual forms revolving around an illusory core that gives rise to expression, but that (as nonexistent) can never be reached. That Beckett's work can create such radically different interpretations is tribute to the questions it raises. Despite images and situations of despair, a rich vein of black humor evocatively blurs the distinction between tragedy and comedy. Beckett's work in all genres and forms is one of ceaseless experimentation inspired by the beliefs that "form is content, content form" and that there is "nothing to express" yet the "obligation to express." From the turn to first-person narration in "FIRST LOVE" (1946) to the cold, mathematically objective style of "The Lost Ones" (1970), it was in the short story that Beckett made some of his most radical formal attempts at the impossibility of expression.

BIBLIOGRAPHY

Knowlson, James. *Damned to Fame: The Life of Samuel Beckett.* London: Bloomsbury, 1996.

Knowlson, James, and John Pilling, eds. *Frescoes of the Skull: The Later Prose and Drama of Samuel Beckett.* New York: Grove Press, 1979.

Ricks, Christopher. *Beckett's Dying Words.* Oxford: Clarendon Press, 1993.

Trezise, Thomas. *Into the Breach: Samuel Beckett and the Ends of Literature.* Princeton, N.J.: Princeton University Press, 1990.

Paul Stewart

"BELEAGUERED CITY, A" MARGARET OLI-
PHANT (1880)   The first of MARGARET OLIPHANT's popular series *Stories of the Seen and Unseen,* "A Beleaguered City" belongs to the subgenre of Victorian-era supernatural tales, such as CHARLES DICKENS's *A CHRISTMAS CAROL.*

In "A Beleaguered City" Oliphant uses different narrators to give evidence about how the worldly and materialistic conduct of the inhabitants of the French town of Semur causes "the dead to rise from their graves" and take possession of the town. After darkness settles over the city, a mysterious force ushers the townspeople out of their homes and locks them outside the town walls. The reason for this evacuation is demonstrated early in the story: The people of Semur have made a god of money and neglected their religious responsibilities. But far from being a sentimental sermon, this novella thoughtfully explores contemporary debates between religion and science, spiritualism and materialism. The story's most obvious spokesman for materialism is the vulgar Jacques Richard, who proclaims, "There is no bon Dieu but money." But more interesting is Martin Dupin, the mayor of Semur and the story's primary narrator, who does "not pretend, in these days of progress, to have retained" his religious faith. He too is a materialist, but he idolizes rationality and science.

Reason proves an inadequate savior in this story, for the scientists cannot explain the spectral message that appears on the cathedral doors, and more important, the spirits do not reveal themselves to the avowedly rational characters. Thus, the mayor's devout wife Agnes has a vision of their deceased daughter, Marie, but the secular Dupin is unable to communicate with the child himself. Likewise, the priest is humiliated to find that the spiritual world does not reveal itself to him but rather to the village "dreamer," Lecamus. Yet the narrative does not fully endorse extreme spiritualism either and shows a distrust of fanatical religious feeling. Madame Veuve Dupin's account of events leads the reader to regard Sister Mariette's smile of calm resignation as a deficiency rather than a virtue—after all, the aged nun can disregard the material world only because she has no son or husband among the watchers. And even as the ghostly invasion of Semur seems

designed to challenge Dupin's secularism and pull him toward religious faith, Dupin's serving of the mass and triumphal Te Deum do not ultimately signal his full conversion.

This novella can also be read as an allegory of interpretation. The supernatural event is inexplicable, so the entire community works to interpret it. Indeed, the text exists as Dupin's official history of the city's possession, and to that purpose he asks several other characters to add their accounts "to ensure a complete testimony." Readers should note that rather than fill in the holes, the multiple narrators often give conflicting accounts that highlight the complex nature of interpretation. Dupin's interpretive authority is initially undermined because he cannot explain or control these strange happenings, but his credibility is further damaged when the townspeople begin to suspect that the siege is a divine punishment for his refusal to allow the Sisters of St. Jean to say mass in the local hospital. Ultimately, the reader cannot accept Dupin's rational account because even his own mother contradicts him by sympathizing with the sisters of St. Jean.

BIBLIOGRAPHY

Oliphant, Margaret. *A Beleagured City and Other Tales of the Seen and Unseen.* Edinburgh: Canongate, 2000.

Katherine Malon

"BISHOP'S LUNCH, THE" MICHÈLE ROBERTS (1993)   "The Bishop's Lunch" appears in *During Mother's Absence,* a collection of MICHÈLE ROBERTS's short stories that was first published in 1993. The collection may be considered an unofficial sequel to Roberts's novel *Daughters of the House* (1992), which was short-listed for the Booker Prize and was awarded the W. H. Smith Literary Award. Like the novel, each story in *During Mother's Absence* foregrounds maternal absence in a young woman's life. The emphasis is placed not on the loss itself but on the way in which physical absence cannot sever the bond between mother and daughter.

Michèle Roberts's religious background is rooted firmly in Catholicism although as an adult she has rejected its formal structure, which was imposed upon her as a child. She often, however, invokes God and religious themes within her work. These themes are contextualized within a feminist agenda and are used to expose the patriarchal values underpinning the foundations of Catholicism.

"The Bishop's Lunch" is the story of Sister Josephine of the Holy Face, a novice who is responsible for the kitchen duties at the convent. This includes preparing a banquet for the Bishop during his traditional visit on Easter Sunday. She knows the Bishop will expect a sumptuous feast much different from the nuns' normal fare. Sister Josephine is no great cook and fears she will not be able to prepare the feast; her fears are alleviated when she opens her black notebook and finds that her mother has copied her family recipes into it. To obtain the necessary ingredients for the recipes, she must borrow the gardener's shotgun as well as secretly raid the henhouse for eggs before they are sold. The nuns never connect these mysterious disappearances with the Bishop's lunch, and Sister Josephine's feast is considered a miracle.

In this story, Roberts combines two of her most prevalent themes, food and God, while subtly demonstrating the lasting power of maternal influence. Initially, Sister Josephine is portrayed as having rejected her mother in favor of the Church. In fact, she is unhappy with her kitchen responsibilities because they remind her of her mother's life. Josephine never learned to cook from her mother because she "hungered for transcendence, for the ecstasy of mystical union" (85) and was not interested in learning domestic chores. Yet these are the duties she is asked to perform at the convent. She appeals to God for assistance with her culinary dilemma, something she would not normally do as "God, being male, [is] above such trivia" (86), but it is her mother who answers her prayer. With her mother's assistance, Sister Josephine performs an Easter miracle.

BIBLIOGRAPHY

Plummer, Patricia. "Re-writing the House of Fiction: Michèle Roberts's *Daughters of the House*." In *Engendering Realism and Postmodernism: Contemporary Women Writers in Britain,* edited by Beate Neumeier, 63–85. Amsterdam: Rodopi, 2001.

Roberts, Michèle. *During Mother's Absence.* London: Virago, 1993.

Wandor, Michelene, ed. *On Gender and Writing.* London: Pandora Press, 1983.

Sherah Wells

BIT ON THE SIDE, A William Trevor (2004)

This recent collection by WILLIAM TREVOR appeared when he was 76 years old, and it has been suggested that the tone of the stories betrays Trevor's age. A distaste for modern, superficial culture is apparent when characters complain (through free indirect speech) about the intrusion of modern music into the public sphere. In "Justina's Priest," Father Clohessy laments the playing of Bob Dylan's "The Times They Are A-Changin'" (perhaps the song's message disturbs the representative of a declining church more than the loud music itself); the omniscient narrator of "Graillis's Legacy" condemns the inanity of "a brash disc-jockey" who "pumped out his chatter before a cacophony began"; in "On the Streets," a character feels that music in a bar sounds "more like a noise than anything else"; and Trevor's contempt for the vapid "Musak that was playing, jazzy and sentimental" in the background of the title story is made clear through the choice of derogatory nouns and adjectives.

Inevitably, the lives of many of Trevor's contemporaries are coming to an end: Trevor's enhanced awareness of mortality seems to manifest itself in the collection's higher-than-usual quota of stories involving death. In the quietly gothic story "Sitting with the Dead," two ghoulish old sisters spend much of their time visiting, without invitation, bereaved families accompanying corpses and their often lugubrious surviving spouses. Jackdaws (small crows) are deliberately slaughtered by a frustrated and slyly malevolent boarding school maid in "Traditions." A more serious killing occurs in "On the Streets," which tells of an impoverished breakfast waiter who outdoes a career of petty theft by stalking and then murdering a supercilious customer. In "Solitude," a bourgeois family flees Britain and pays former domestic assistants to remain quiet about the inconvenient death of the mother's illicit lover. And in the sarcastically titled "Big Bucks," a young couple's desire for a new life in America is motivated in part by the fact that some of the man's relatives have died when carrying out the only available work—fishing in the treacherous waters offshore. A sense of closure, then, dominates many of the stories.

Closure comes to many of the adulterous relationships that, as ever, characterize companionate relationships in "Trevorland." Trevor's stories have often elicited sympathy for characters who pursue sexual affection outside of marriage. In "Graillis's Legacy," an adulterous affair has ended because the male character's older lover has died; although aware that the woman has written him into her will to celebrate the limited time that they enjoyed together, he seeks to exclude himself legally from her will (through embarrassment or guilt?). An apparently interracial affair between Mrs. Bouvrie and Mr. Azam in "Rose Wept" ends because the woman's aging husband will no longer work overtime to distract himself from his wife's infidelity. In the collection's concluding story—the title story—a different sort of life change causes the separation of two middle-aged lovers. The woman gets divorced, changing the whole tenor of the affair. The reader, inspired by the deceptively dismissive title, may cynically feel that the relationship has lost its illicit excitement for the male. But we are left in no doubt that there was an "intensity" to the affair, and both characters walk away proudly at the story's end: Their affair was a secret and short-lived triumph, but a triumph nonetheless. While most of the stories involve narratives of closure and ending, the lasting impression from this title story and the collection as a whole is one of reasoned satisfaction: At least these characters were able to enjoy some amorous diversion, however ephemeral and retrospective these joys now seem.

BIBLIOGRAPHY
Adair, Tom. "Return to Trevor-Trevor-Land," review of *A Bit on the Side. The Scotsman,* 16 May 2004. Available online. URL: http://news.scotsman.com/features.cfm?id=555572004. Accessed May 8, 2006.
Fitzgerald-Holt, Mary. *William Trevor: Re-imagining Ireland.* Dublin: The Liffey Press, 2003, 173–189.
Lee, Hermione. "Old Ireland, Far Hence," review of *A Bit on the Side. The Guardian,* 12 June 2004. Available online. URL: http://books.guardian.co.uk/review/story/0,,1236079,00.html. Accessed May 8, 2006.
Ormsby-Lennon, Hugh. *Fools of Fiction: Reading the Fiction of William Trevor.* Dublin: Maunsel and Co., 2004.
Trevor, William. *A Bit on the Side.* London: Viking, 2004.

Kevin De Ornellas

"BLACK VENUS" ANGELA CARTER (1980)

This story was originally published in 1980 in the series Next Editions and was reprinted in 1984 in ANGELA CARTER's collection *Black Venus.* The common concern of the stories gathered in this volume is the demystification of famous historical and/or literary figures who have become crystallized and canonized in the Western collective imagination (see also "The KISS"). "Black Venus" retells the story of Jeanne Duvall, Charles Baudelaire's Creole mistress. Carter tries to rewrite history by shifting the focus from the iconic French author to a marginal figure, usually relegated to the footnotes of poetry books and of biographical studies on Baudelaire.

Through her revisionist approach to the authorized version of history, Carter is obviously interested in exploring the relationship between fact and fiction and the reasons that Jeanne's story has been easily silenced. The strong political agenda of "Black Venus" combines feminist and postcolonial concerns: Jeanne is doubly other and marginalized, because of both her gender and her ethnicity. However, in her attempt to give Jeanne a voice, Carter is careful to avoid speaking for her and turning her into a mere literary object or anecdotal curiosity. Carter's solution to this quandary is the adoption of a self-conscious narrator, who explicitly mistrusts his or her, or indeed anybody's, ability to tell Jeanne's true story. This attitude is in striking discord with Baudelaire's relationship with Jeanne, who was not only his mistress but also a source of inspiration and the subject of his cycle of poems titled "Black Venus."

Carter points out how Jeanne's role as a muse to the great poet further confines her to silence and misrepresentation, since she is typecast as the exotic mistress who paradoxically combines both the innocence of her Edenic faraway land and the corruption of an unrestricted sensuality. While Jeanne complains that Baudelaire will not pay for hot water for her bath, the poet is prey to the romantic fallacy that the woman's sweat smells like cinnamon. Jeanne's straightforward pragmatism is provocatively juxtaposed to Baudelaire's self-absorbed idealism. Carter traces back the premises of this opposition to the conservative identification of man with culture and woman with nature, a model that is mentioned in the short story with ironic distance.

The common Western image of the Caribbean as an unspoiled and desirable paradise is also challenged. Baudelaire's clichéd perception of Jeanne's homeland is rendered by Carter in the tones of a shallow and unsophisticated pop song. Baudelaire's lofty, iconic status as the groundbreaking figure of French symbolism is further desecrated by the allusion to his squalid sugar daddy role. Jeanne, on her part, remains untouched by the poet's rhetoric and his literary efforts (which are branded as "scribbling"), while recoiling in horror at the mere recollection of the widespread poverty of the colonies. Mockingly, the poet's ennui, the existential boredom typical of the modern human condition that Baudelaire captured so suggestively in his writing, is translated rather prosaically into Jeanne's mundane boredom. An even more demythologizing comment on the poet's work is offered when Jeanne uses Baudelaire's discarded manuscript to collect the ashes of her cheroot.

At a first glance, the relationship between Baudelaire and Jeanne appears mutually exploitative, if grounded on a common feeling of alienation. However, Carter makes sure to emphasize that it is only Jeanne who is literally dispossessed and exiled, as well as economically dependent on her paramour. Jeanne's subordination to Baudelaire is repeatedly foregrounded, perhaps nowhere more overtly than halfway through the story, when Carter grafts her creative reconstruction of the Creole mistress, about whom very little is known, onto a thin layer of factual information: Significantly, while Jeanne's date of birth remains obscure, there is a clear, reliable record of when she first met the French poet. Yet the conclusion of the story departs from any historical accuracy. Although it is known that Jeanne died before Baudelaire, Carter, with typical black humor, represents her surviving her lover to return to the Caribbean, where she is able to open a brothel with the profits from the sale of the poet's manuscripts. The closing paragraph of the story is an ironic reference to the only legacy from Baudelaire that Jeanne is truly able to disseminate around the world: Short of circulating the poet's writing, Jeanne "will continue to dispense, to the most privileged of the colonial administration, at a not excessive price, the veritable, the authentic, and the true Baudelairian syphilis."

BIBLIOGRAPHY

Carter, Angela. Black Venus. London: Chatto and Windus, 1985.

Gamble, Sarah. Angela Carter: Writing from the Front Line. Edinburgh: Edinburgh University Press, 1997.

Matus, Jill, "Blonde, Black and Hottentot Venus: Context and Critique in Angela Carter's 'Black Venus'" In Angela Carter, edited by Alison Easton, 161–172. London: Macmillan, 2000.

Schmid, Susanne. "'Black Venus'—Jeanne Duval and Charles Baudelaire Revisited by Angela Carter." Erfurt Electronic Studies in English (February 1997). Available online. URL: http://webdoc.sub.gwdg.de/edoc/ia/eese/artic97/schmid/2_97.html, Accessed May 8, 2006.

Stephania Ciocia

BLISS AND OTHER STORIES KATHERINE MANSFIELD (1920)

The first important collection of KATHERINE MANSFIELD's work and a touchstone for the MODERNIST short story. Bliss brought together stories composed from 1916 to 1919; at this time, Mansfield was living through the last years of the WORLD WAR I and traveling to France and Italy in the hope of curing the tuberculosis that would eventually kill her. Despite the upheaval in her life, this was a period of great productivity for her. The stories in Bliss share a number of common themes, exploring the nature of human personality and sexuality, alienation, loneliness, and malaise. The collection is characterized by a bitter sense of irony; a hard, clean style; and a Chekhovian psychological realism. It is also notable for Mansfield's experimentation with narration.

The stories in Bliss include "Prelude," "JE NE PARLE PAS FRANÇAIS," "Bliss," "The Wind Blows," "Psychology," "PICTURES," "The Man without a Temperament," "Mr. Reginald Peacock's Day," "Sun and Moon," "Feuille d'Album," "A Dill Pickle," "The Little Governess," "Revelations," and "The Escape." "Prelude" was first published in 1917 by Leonard and VIRGINIA WOOLF's Hogarth Press and went generally unnoticed, although it is now considered one of Mansfield's finest stories. "Je ne parle pas français" was published privately by John Middleton Murry, Mansfield's husband, in 1918. In 1919 "Bliss" was published in *The English Review* and "Pictures" and "The Man without a Temperament" in *Art and Letters.* In 1919 Grant Richards expressed interest in publishing a collection of Mansfield's stories, but Murry interceded and contacted Michael Sadleir of the publishing firm Constable, who would pay more for the collection. Mansfield read proofs for the publication while in a sanatorium in Italy, and the book was released in 1920. She believed *Bliss* for the most part to be trivial, but it was well reviewed in the *Times Literary Supplement,* the *Athenaeum,* and the *Observer* and sold quite well (4,000 copies in 1920–21). Sadleir submitted the collection for the Femina-Vie Heureuse prize, for which it placed third. According to the jacket blurb, "In theme, in mordant humor, and in keen realistic outlook, she [Mansfield] is the nearest thing to the modern Russian story writers and to de Maupassant that England has produced. . . . The stories have a wry chic, and tell, with a cruel and detached irony, of sorrows and of sudden brutal joys." In their depiction of "moments of being," the stories represent the height of the genre in modernism and reveal, as many reviewers noted, the influence of Anton Chekhov and OSCAR WILDE and a representation of psychology indebted to Sigmund Freud.

Mansfield's interest in psychology is evident in stories like "The Man without a Temperament." Critics have seen a biographical origin in this text coming from her relationship with Murry during her illness; he was quite pained by the character of Robert, a husband traveling with an invalid wife and seeking to fulfill her needs while sublimating his resentment at being taken from his own life in England. The story flashes back to moments in their marriage when she was well and vibrant, and it juxtaposes scenes of their static existence abroad to show how illness has trapped them both. Robert's position is ambiguous, as the reader is never certain of the extent of his resentment. The narration never allows us inside the man's head, and we are left to draw conclusions from the moments Mans-

field presents: a tired woman insisting her husband go for a walk without her while other guests sneer at his passivity, a final scene where she asks him if he truly minds being away with her, only to hear him say, "Rot." The story is notable for its sense of stasis, of entrapment, and of the alienation between two people in a stifling intimacy.

Other stories similarly explore psychology with more of Mansfield's characteristic satire. "Bliss" shows a series of revelations on the part of Bertha Young, who first realizes her own attraction to her husband only to discover his adulterous affair. "Psychology" intertwines a satire of intellectuals who delight in conversations about philosophy and literature while failing to understand and communicate their own feelings for each other. In this story, the narration is focalized through the alternating point of view of a man and a woman who meet regularly for conversation. The plot consists of a series of moments when they realize their feelings for one another, but their own desires and needs are so frightening that each retreats into empty discussion of "psychological literature." The irony of the story lies in their professing to understand psychology while failing to understand their own psychology and that of their companions.

Mansfield's satire comes to the fore in "Mr. Reginald Peacock's Day." In this story, a singing teacher imagines himself as an artist who is irresistible to his female pupils. The reality of his existence is revealed through his relationship to his wife, who, in his mind, fails to treat him as the artist he really is. The banality of his marriage and everyday life is juxtaposed with a vision of himself that is shown to be ludicrous. Here Mansfield seems to be making a particular comment on the nature of the artist and the impossible tension between the way one views oneself and the truth of one's own life. A similar irony is present in "Pictures," the story of an aging singer who believes herself still capable of performing. She travels from agency to agency, fantasizing about being discovered, only to wind up in a café going home with a middle-aged man; we are left to assume that she will have sex with him for money, the only recourse left to her.

This portrayal of the isolated, alienated woman and the possibility of deviance in human sexuality is also very much a part of "The Little Governess." Here, a young girl is traveling to Germany for her first job as a governess. She is exhorted by her agency to be wary of strangers, and her position as a young woman alone is shown to be a dangerous one. An old man takes an interest in her that she believes to be benevolent, and he offers to protect her and show her around the city where she is to meet her future employer. The old man's purpose, however, is to engage her sexually, and she flees back to her hotel, only to discover that her employer has already been there looking for her. She is left alone in a strange land, and the reader must suppose that further victimization is imminent. "The Little Governess" has much in common with "Je ne parle pas français," in which another young woman is abandoned and faced with sexual predation. These stories, like "Bliss," are notable for their frank depiction of sexuality, in terms of both desire and depravity.

"Prelude," a story that has garnered much critical attention for its depiction of sexuality, for its postcolonial aspects, and for its symbolism, is possibly the most significant text in the collection. One of Mansfield's New Zealand stories, it forms, with other texts like "At the Bay" and "The Doll's House" that draw on her childhood, a bildungsroman, portraying a child's coming to awareness of sex and mortality. The story is focalized varyingly through the child Kezia, based on Mansfield herself, and through her parents, Linda and Stanley Burnell. The plot is the family's move to a larger and better house, indicating their upward class mobility. At the same time, Linda is revealed to be pregnant, an outward manifestation of her husband's physicality and what she perceives as his overwhelming desire. Her dislike of sex and her children, indeed of her own body, is symbolized by an aloe that grows in the yard of the house and the violent animal imagery that permeates the story. Kezia is only dimly aware of these feelings, but they are revealed to be part of her growing consciousness as the story progresses.

The theme of alienation, the awareness of psychology, and the exploration of sexuality that made *Bliss* so worthy of attention upon its publication in 1920 has also made it a key text of modernism, and critics continue to find Mansfield's considerations of gender, exile, and the unconscious seminal to discussions of that era.

BIBLIOGRAPHY

Alpers, Antony. *The Life of Katherine Mansfield*. New York: Viking, 1980.

Kaplan, Sydney Janet. *Katherine Mansfield and the Origins of Modernist Fiction*. Ithaca: Cornell University Press, 1991.

Kobler, J. F. *Katherine Mansfield: A Study of the Short Fiction*. Boston: Twayne, 1990.

Mansfield, Katherine. *Bliss and Other Stories*. London: Bloomsbury, 1994.

Nathan, Rhoda, ed. *Critical Essays on Katherine Mansfield*. New York: G. K. Hall, 1993.

Robinson, Roger, ed. *Katherine Mansfield: In from the Margin*. Baton Rouge: Louisiana State University Press, 1997.

Scott, Bonnie Kime. *Refiguring Modernism*. 2 vols. Bloomington: Indiana University Press, 1995.

Janine Utell

BLOOD JANICE GALLOWAY **(1991)** The first collection of stories by JANICE GALLOWAY comprises 25 stories, apparently self-contained but all interlinked by a manifest coherence of style and imagery and the anecdotal surface of their plots: The various episodes and situations are told through a visceral style, vivid imagery, and a surreal cinematic perspective that inevitably distorts everyday situations into exquisitely grotesque scenarios. The collection received significant critical attention and acclaim: Short-listed for the *Guardian* Fiction Prize, People's Prize, and Saltire Award, the volume was also a *New York Times* Book of the Year.

Mundane rituals—such as the routine visit of an anonymous "Health Visitor" to an equally nameless "Old Woman" in "Scenes from the Life No. 26: The Community and the Senior Citizen" or the dentist's appointment in "Blood"—are the raw material Galloway starts from to carve extraordinary stories that palpitate with the emotionally charged characters' experiences. An apparently ordinary situation typically hides sinister elements of veiled danger, permanent damage, or worse, death. The victims are often harmless recipients of the inexplicable reactions of family members, partners, and close relations, as in "Scenes from the Life No. 23: Paternal Advice" and the last, and longest, story of the collection, "A Week with Uncle Felix." In the first of the two stories, written in the concise style of a script, a father deliberately allows his baby to fall on the floor from a fireplace to teach his son a lesson: Trust no one. The paternal bond accentuated by the names given to the characters—Sammy and Wee Sammy—is violently distorted. More subtly, in the second story, a disturbing relationship develops between the apparently emotionless 11-year-old Senga and her paternal uncle Felix.

The uncanny episodes at the core of the stories from the collection all reveal Galloway's intent to unmask the illusion of tranquillity given by familiar, homely, and domestic settings, in order to reveal the dark undercurrents running through characters' everyday lives and their dysfunctional relationships. In "Love in a Changing Environment," the negative evolution of the relationship between the two unnamed characters is cleverly observed through the near magical realist setting of the story. A surreal atmosphere created by the scented warmth of the bakery above which the couple live reflects the happy stage of their emotional and sexual liaison; both rapidly fade when a change of ownership transforms the bakery into a butcher's shop: The acrid smell of organic decay accelerates the friction and, ultimately, the envisaged end of their relationship.

Human relationships are the object of Galloway's acute investigation; taboos and prejudice are equally laid bare. Behind the typically unsatisfying bonds is the inability to communicate between man and woman, mother and daughter, teacher and pupil. "David," a short story about a teacher's quick one-night stand with a pupil, explores the uncontrollable power of boundless passions, challenging moral etiquette and gender stereotypes in an accurate portrait of female eroticism. Elsewhere, strong, traumatic emotions transpose ordinary experience into a horrifying nightmare. The imagery employed in the opening section of "Blood" escalates a tooth extraction to a much more traumatic violation of the woman's body, a sinister motif reinforced by the recurring blood imagery and the gory ending.

Physical and emotional scars, complemented by traumatic visions and, at times, surreal hallucinations, all contribute to the unsettling mood shared by all the stories in the collection. Exploring life beyond the precarious facade of social conventions, moral codes, and,

generally, clichés of a modern Scottish society, the stories often suggest unexpected nuances even in the fragmented sketches of "Scenes from Life No. 29: Dianne," "It Was," "The Meat," and "Nightdriving."

BIBLIOGRAPHY
Galloway, Janice. *Blood*. London: Cape, 1991.

Monica Germana

BLOODY CHAMBER, THE ANGELA CARTER (1979)

The Bloody Chamber collects 10 of ANGELA CARTER's short stories, linked by their common source material, familiar tales from the folk tradition including "Bluebeard," "Snow White," "Beauty and the Beast," "PUSS IN BOOTS," and "Little Red Riding Hood." As the volume's title suggests, in Carter's hands these tales often bear little resemblance to the generally tamer versions best known to contemporary readers and moviegoers. The combination of sex and violence implied by *The Bloody Chamber* gestures back to the often gruesome nature of the ancient oral tales that began to enter the literary realm only when they were gathered and recorded by such early folklorists as Charles Perrault and Jacob and Wilhelm Grimm. The title also highlights some of the other kinds of narratives informing Carter's tales: the gothic fictions of writers such as Poe, Hoffman, and LEFANU and, most controversially, the pornographic writings of the Marquis de Sade.

Carter's interest in fairy tales was an abiding one, evident throughout her body of fictional writing for both adults and children, and even more so in her work as an editor and translator, which yielded *The Fairy Tales of Charles Perrault* (1977), *Sleeping Beauty and Other Favourite Fairy Tales* (1982), *The VIRAGO BOOK OF FAIRY TALES* (1990), and *The Second Virago Book of Fairy Tales* (1992). As she wrote in the preface to her edition of Perrault, these old tales represent "the great mass of infinitely various narrative that was, once upon a time and still is, sometimes, passed on and disseminated through the world by word of mouth—stories without known originators that can be remade again and again by every person who tells them." However, Carter had little interest in fairy tales as vehicles for mere fantasy and escapism. In an interview with John

Haffenden published in 1985, Carter abruptly and comically dispatched Hans Christian Anderson and J. R. R. Tolkien with his "horns of elfland faintly blowing," arguing that "too much imaginative richness makes Jack a dull boy; and no good at killing giants" Carter's tales are not about escape but about confrontation and critique. In her afterword to *Fireworks* (1974), she praised the tale for its unsettling, antimimetic qualities, which—unlike the more realistic tendencies of the short story—prevent readers from discovering in it "a false knowledge of everyday experience" (122).

The Bloody Chamber appeared in the same year as Carter's controversial polemic *The Sadeian Woman and the Ideology of Pornography,* which was her contribution to a deeply divisive debate among feminist thinkers at the time on the subject of pornography. In a phrase that became notorious, she envisioned a "moral pornographer" who "might use pornography as a critique of current relations between the sexes" (20–21). Carter regarded Sade as a "terrorist of the imagination" whose shocking representations of sexual cruelty made glaringly apparent the power imbalance underlying both the sexual and the broader social relations between men and women in his society.

Fairy tales, too, reflect the unequal relations of power brought to light by Sade and so afforded Carter the opportunity to engage in some imaginative terrorism of her own. Marriages of young maidens to handsome princes are to be found in her collection, but Carter's tales leave little of the more accustomed romantic idealism intact. Marital relationships in *The Bloody Chamber* tend to involve negotiations between unequal partners. The title story, for instance, is Carter's version of "Bluebeard," but her revised title shifts attention from the monstrous groom to both his chamber of horrors and the marital chamber into which he brings his bride, an innocent who married not for love but to "banish the spectre of poverty from its habitual place at our meagre table." Her husband, the Marquis, receives in turn her eroticized virginity in an exchange whose imbalance of power is signified by his wedding gift, "a choker of rubies, two inches wide, like an extraordinarily precious slit throat."

This theme of patriarchal marriage as an economic exchange involving unequal partners is picked up again in the collection's two versions of "Beauty and the Beast," "The COURTSHIP OF MR. LYON" and "The Tiger's Bride." Carter described these tales as a partial response to Bruno Bettelheim, author of the landmark study *The Uses of Enchantment: The Meaning and Importance of Fairy Tales* (1976), who viewed "Beauty and the Beast" in a positive light, as an account of a young woman transferring her emotional attachment from father to lover. In her tales, Carter is keen to highlight the economic underpinnings of this transfer, as Beauty becomes a commodity exchanged between a debtor father and a creditor Beast. However, such limiting patriarchal constructions of the feminine are not shown here to be inescapable. Although "The Courtship of Mr. Lyon" ends with Beauty having been manipulated into accepting the role of the bourgeois Mrs. Lyon, "The Tiger's Bride" ends very differently, with the unnamed Beauty figure embracing her own bestial nature, refusing the status of victim and engaging with the Beast as a lustful equal—a pattern that recurs in "The COMPANY OF WOLVES," Carter's version of "Little Red Riding Hood."

For many of Carter's readers, *The Bloody Chamber* marks a pivotal point in her career, standing between the incisive feminist and postmodern critiques of her earlier work and the yoking of that critical approach to the new narrative exuberance and playfulness so obviously present in her final novels, *Nights at the Circus* (1984) and *Wise Children* (1991). Certainly, the volume that led one commentator to nominate Carter the "high priestess of post-graduate porn" (Bristow and Broughton, 1) cemented her reputation as a bold explorer of our common cultural inheritance who takes the familiar and renders it strange and startling.

BIBLIOGRAPHY

Bacchilega, Cristina. *Postmodern Fairy Tales: Gender and Narrative Strategies.* Philadelphia: University of Pennsylvania Press, 1997.

Bristow, Joseph, and Trev Lynn Broughton, eds. *The Informal Desires of Angela Carter.* London: Longman, 1997.

Carter, Angela. *The Bloody Chamber and Other Stories.* London: Gollancz, 1979.

———. *Fireworks: Nine Profane Pieces.* London: Quaitet, 1977.

———. *The Sadeian Woman and the Ideology of Pornography.* London: Virago, 1979.

Hafferden, John. *Novelists in Interview.* London: Methuen, 1985.

Roemer, Danielle M., and Cristina Bacchilega, eds. *Angela Carter and the Fairy Tale.* Detroit: Wayne State University Press, 1998.

Brian Patton

"BLUE CROSS, THE" G. K. CHESTERTON (1910)

"The Blue Cross" appeared in *The Storyteller* magazine in September 1910 and heralded the first appearance of G. K. CHESTERTON's most famous and enduring creation, Father Brown. The story, and the five further stories that followed at monthly intervals, were combined with six more Father Brown stories that appeared in *Casell's Magazine* to create *The Innocence of Father Brown* in July 1911. Because of the popularity of the stories, the publication of *The Innocence of Father Brown* was widely anticipated, and it received gracious reviews. Negative criticism focused on the inability of the character of Father Brown to support an anthology of stories. Many critics have identified a lack of consistency in the character across a number of stories, and others have criticized the stories for their perceived lack of substance. However, the popularity of the first collection ensured that Father Brown continued for a further 37 stories, providing Chesterton with an enduring and profitable character. Father Brown never received the literary or creative recognition afforded to Edgar Allan Poe's or Arthur Conan Doyle's detectives, but during the early 1900s he was considered second only to Sherlock Holmes. The adaptation of "The Blue Cross" into the 1954 film with Sir Alec Guinness as Father Brown and the mid-1970s TV series ensured that the character's influence was felt by modern detectives such as Columbo and Father Dowling. If detectives are "identified by their methodologies or approaches" (Kayman, 44), as Martin A. Kayman claims, Father Brown's unique and unusual style of detection makes him a very distinctive detective. There are two principles that simply but effectively distinguish Father Brown from other detectives: Father Brown is an invisible and innocuous figure, and he has an innocent knowledge afforded by his role as a priest.

A reader could be forgiven for thinking that "The Blue Cross" introduces a cynical and flawed French detective rather than Chesterton's innocuous priest detective. The narrative follows Valentin, the chief of Paris Police and "the most famous investigator of the world," as he tracks Flambeau, the bold and daring "colossus of crime." At the crucial moment of capture, after Valentin has followed Flambeau by a number of unusual clues, it is revealed that another detective figure, Father Brown, has outsleuthed Valentin and, without prior knowledge of Flambeau's criminal behavior, has anticipated and thwarted the villain's crime. Unlike Holmes or Poirot, Father Brown is not a pretentious or ostentatious great detective. Instead, he is a scruffy, overlooked, and underestimated priest. He is introduced at the beginning of the story as a subject for pity. Valentin describes him as having "a face as round and dull as a Norfolk dumpling" and "eyes as empty as the North Sea" (2001, 5). Yet his appearance and vocation causes Flambeau to underestimate him, allowing Father Brown to leave outrageous clues for Valentin to follow and to ascertain the true nature of Flambeau's criminal intentions by testing his tolerance. Father Brown reasons that an innocent man would express annoyance if he found salt in his coffee and express outrage when overcharged, while a man with something to hide would not. When Flambeau drinks his salty coffee and pays an exorbitant bill, Father Brown knows something is wrong, manages to identify Flambeau's technique for theft, and uses it against him. Because Father Brown has remained so inconspicuous, when he reveals his denouement Flambeau is left "stunned with the utmost curiosity" (2001, 25).

Flambeau's astonishment turns to disbelief when Father Brown reveals what Joseph Pearce has termed his "innocent wisdom" (2001, 92). While Father Brown initially knows nothing of Flambeau's criminal plot, he displays an intuition for criminal behavior. Father Brown explains, "Has it never struck you that a man who does next to nothing but hear men's real sins is not likely to be wholly unaware of human evil?" (2001, 25–26). In his autobiography, Chesterton provides an explanation for the origin of "The Blue Cross," the Father Brown character, and in particular, the concept of innocent wisdom. Chesterton describes his surprise that his friend, Father O'Connor, should have a more detailed knowledge of criminal behavior than he, because the generally accepted opinion of priests was that they knew nothing of real-world transgressions. In Chesterton's own words, "That the Catholic Church knew more about good than I did was easy to believe. That she knew more about evil than I did seemed incredible" (1937, 328). When enlightened on a point of vice and crime by Father O'Connor, Chesterton describes a "curious experience to find that this quiet and pleasant celibate had plumbed those abysses far deeper than I" (1937, 326). What ultimately distinguishes Father Brown from other detectives is not his religion but the benefits his religion affords him. Through the practice of reason that he considers essential to theology and the personal experience of confession that provides intimate knowledge at a distance, Father Brown is able successfully to reconcile intuition and reason. Consequently, Father Brown predicts and manipulates both the criminal and the detective but does so unobtrusively.

Similarly, the stories themselves are distinctive by not being unusual. There are no razor-wielding orangutans or pigmy assassins. Crimes, when they do take place in a Father Brown story, have the most commonplace explanation but often the least-expected outcome. In "The Blue Cross" Chesterton introduces an ingenious and plausible detective in a tale that is no less amazing because it is so easily comprehendible.

See also "The SECRET GARDEN" and "The HAMMER OF GOD."

BIBLIOGRAPHY

Chesterton, G. K. *Autobiography*. London: Burns, Oates and Washbourne, 1937.

———. *The Best of Father Brown*. London: Dent, 1987.

———. *Father Brown*. London: Penguin, 2001.

Coren, Michael. *Gilbert: The Man Who Was G. K. Chesterton*. London: Cape, 1989.

Father Brown (1954). Directed by Robert Hamer. Written by Thelma Schnee and Robert Hamer. Columbia Pictures, 1954.

Pearce, Joseph. *Wisdom and Innocence: A Life of G. K. Chesterton*. London: Hodder and Stoughton, 1996.

Sullivan, John, ed. *G. K. Chesterton: A Contemporary Appraisal*. London: Paul Elek, 1974.

Tony Garland

"BLUSH, THE" ELIZABETH TAYLOR (1958)

First published in the *New Yorker* and collected in *The Blush and Other Stories*, this is perhaps ELIZABETH TAYLOR's most anthologized short story. A. S. BYATT included it in the *Oxford Book of English Short Stories* (1998), and it was also selected by Patricia Craig for *The Oxford Book of Modern Women's Stories* (1994). "The Blush" centers on Mrs. Allen, a childless upper-middle-class woman in a village outside London. The lonely, betrayed protagonist is soul sister to many other isolated characters in Taylor's work. Her final revelation of her own ignorance and the capacity in others to deceive is one of the most powerfully realized moments in Taylor's fiction.

"The Blush" is also a feminist exploration of women's roles in 1950s England, a portrayal that is informed by social class as well. In "The Blush," Taylor subtly negotiates the boundaries between gender and class from the first sentence: "They were the same age—Mrs. Allen and the woman who came every day to do the housework." The two women are thus overtly compared from the outset, and Mrs. Allen continues throughout the story to see her life in relation to that of Mrs. Lacey, her charwoman. The first issue between the women is introduced in this initial sentence: work. Mrs. Allen is a wealthy woman of leisure, and Mrs. Lacey is the woman she hires to perform her traditionally female work. However, the issue of labor is not quite so simple, it turns out: Mrs. Allen "listened—as they worked together in the kitchen—to Mrs. Lacey's troubles with her family." The two women in fact often work side by side in Mr. Allen's home, female laborers maintaining its order and beauty. They are, in a sense, close, having worked together in the Allen home for many years. Although Mrs. Allen is critical of Mrs. Lacey's rebellious children, the childless woman also defends her housecleaner from the gardener's snide criticisms: "'She works hard, and deserves a little pleasure—she has her anxieties,' said Mrs. Allen, who, alas, had none."

That Mrs. Allen has no anxiety—that she has, in particular, no children—is the crux of the story. In this sense, the tale is about another kind of labor, both giving birth itself and the work of raising children, about pain and joy missed. The second sentence of the story introduces this element: "'I shall never have children now,' Mrs. Allen had begun to tell herself. Something had not come true; the essential part of her life." While Mrs. Allen imagines "her children in fleeting scenes and intimations," she listens, over the years, to Mrs. Lacey's catalog of her difficulties with her children, "grumblings about her grown-up son who would not get up till dinner-time on Sundays . . . the adolescent girl who moped and glowered and answered back." Mrs. Lacey is rumored in the village to have done "all too little" for her children when they were young: "The children, one night after another, for years and years, had had to run out for parcels of fish and chips while their mother sat in The Horse & Jockey drinking brown ale." Mrs. Allen herself is usually alone, but when she goes out, she sips sherry at the Chequers, where "no one ever sat down, but stood and sipped and chatted as at a cocktail-party, and luncheons and dinners were served, which made it so much more respectable: no children hung about outside, because they were all at home with their Nannies." While Taylor depicts the poignancy of the blowsy Mrs. Lacey's children waiting outside the Horse & Jockey, where they "pressed their foreheads to the window and looked in at the dark little bar," Taylor also implicitly comments on the ease of the middle-class mothers' lives, with their children "at home with their Nannies."

The pain of Mrs. Allen's life lies in her gradual awareness that she is wasting her time waiting for life to begin—in the larger sense, for children who will not be born, but more insistently for her husband to return from the many evenings when he "was kept late in London": "She knew that it was a wasteful way of spending her years—and looking back, she was unable to tell one of them from another—but she could not think what else she might do. Humphrey kept on earning more and more money and there was no stopping him now." Mrs. Allen's Christian name is, significantly, Ruth. She is the dutiful wife who has been, like her biblical forerunner, the dutiful daughter: "Whither soever thou goest, I also shall go." In Taylor's quietly dark story, the ideal of female patience and loyalty is called into question, exposed as the male-constructed social ideal that it is.

Ruth Allen is certain she knows her successful husband's tastes, however, and she is willing to garden and clean and walk the dog—and wait for him to come home. She is especially glad that the respectable, class-conscious Humphrey Allen has not met the "slackly corseted" Mrs. Lacey, with "her orange hair and bright lips and the floral patterns that she always wore." She is worried about what he might think: "Her relationship with Mrs. Lacey and the intimacy of their conversations in the kitchen he would not have approved, and the sight of those calloused feet with their chipped nail-varnish and yellowing heels would have sickened him."

Mrs. Allen's world is rudely shaken, however, by two events. First, Mrs. Lacey tells her that she is pregnant again: "Mrs. Allen felt stunned and antagonistic. 'Surely not at your age,' she said crossly." Then the much older Mr. Lacey, "quite ageless, a crooked, bow-legged little man who might have been a jockey once," confronts Mrs. Allen at her home demanding that she stop asking Mrs. Lacey to babysit every night so that she and her husband can attend cocktail parties. Mrs. Allen is mystified. She feels "at sea" and "perilously near a barbarous, unknown shore and was afraid to make any movement towards it." Mr. Lacey continues his tirade: "'I'm boiling over some nights. Once I nearly rushed out when I heard the car stop down the road. I wanted to tell your husband what I thought of you both.'" Mrs. Allen knows that she has not asked Mrs. Lacey to babysit and makes the connection between her husband's absences and Mrs. Lacey's lies.

The story ends with Mrs. Allen promising the deluded Mr. Lacey that she will not ask his wife to babysit for her again at night. It is not clear whether she is simply stunned, or whether she is protecting herself, her husband, Mr. Lacey, or even Mrs. Lacey. After Mr. Lacey bicycles away from the house, Ruth Allen's body registers the shameful realization of her own husband's betrayal: "Then she felt herself beginning to blush. She was glad that she was alone, for she could feel her face, her throat, even the tops of her arms burning, and she went over to a looking-glass and studied with great interest this strange phenomenon." The blush expresses on the body her deep embarrassment at her ignorance of her husband's sordid liaison with her own housecleaner.

This union now promises to give the prolific Mrs. Lacey yet another child—this time, a child of Humphrey Allen's, the child Ruth Allen has been denied. Indeed, although Mrs. Lacey is rumoured to be promiscuous, it is even possible that all of Mrs. Lacey's children have been fathered by Mr. Allen while he denies children to his yearning wife. It is difficult to tell how deep the betrayal and the sense of evil are in this situation, and for Mrs. Lacey, it is inflected by class bitterness as well: "She was an envious woman: she envied Mrs. Allen her pretty house and her clothes." Since all the years of Ruth Allen's waiting have become blurred—"looking back, she was unable to tell one of them from another"—we cannot discern the temporal boundaries of her betrayal.

Oddly, however, Mrs. Allen's blush also seems empowering. While blushes throughout English literature signal female modesty, Ruth Allen's blush seems to be a marker of a more complex reaction. Although the blush manifests her shame, it also seems to be a liberating release, perhaps the sign of sexual desires long repressed. Ruth wants to see this roseate glow in the mirror and almost scientifically "studied with great interest this strange phenomenon." She seems to have recognized that she is part of the animal kingdom, and her observation of the blush is empirical. Mrs. Allen's rosy display issues from her revelation of sexual knowledge; the "burning" that spreads across her face, throat, and even arms seems sexual, even orgasmic. She has fallen from innocence, and her fallenness is marked by the scarlet ruddiness of her body. Even in the midst of her shame, she seems fascinated with her body's power, reflected back to her in the looking glass, and this final mirror image may suggest a new identity for Ruth Allen. Her promise to Mr. Lacey that his wife will not be going out at night on her employers' behalf suggests an imminent confrontation with Mr. Allen that might well end his trysts. Perhaps Mrs. Allen's blush is the harbinger of a new life in which the demands of her own body will be recognized—a life in which she will no longer wait for her prince to come.

BIBLIOGRAPHY
Taylor, Elizabeth. *The Blush*. London: Peter Davies, 1958.

Deborah Deneholz Morse

BOWEN, ELIZABETH (1899–1973)   Born in Dublin, the daughter of a long-established Anglo-Irish family, Elizabeth Bowen spent her time shuttling between the family's ancestral home, Bowen's Court in Kildorrey, County Cork, and London, where she worked during WORLD WAR II. Bowen described herself as "a writer for whom places loom large," a quality inspired perhaps by the early deaths of her parents and the peripatetic existence she led as a child and young adult. The careful evocation of place is most apparent in the early novel *The Hotel* (1927); in *The Last September* (1929), which features a portrait of the Bowen home; and in her most famous novel, *The Heat of the Day* (1949), set in the London blitz. London in wartime is also the setting of her most anthologized short stories, "MYSTERIOUS KOR," "The DEMON LOVER," and "In the Square."

Alongside its emphasis on loneliness and family breakup, Bowen's work is characterized by a focus on the upper and middle classes, people whose seemingly secure lives, based on restraint and good manners, are suddenly put under threat. Bowen was interested in what she termed "the cracks in the surface of life," something that is apparent in her short stories, notably "Summer Night" and "A Love Story." These deal with characters whose ordered lives are disrupted by the unexpected emergence of passion, which they struggle to suppress. Others have supernatural elements; notably, "Foothold" (1929), "The Cat Jumps" (1929), and "The Apple Tree" (1931) combine uncanny or ghostly elements with a modern setting. One of Bowen's final collections, *A Day in the Dark and Other Stories* (1965), contains a short essay in which Bowen reviews the use of supernatural tropes in her own work.

This essay is one of a number of pieces which Bowen wrote about the short story as a genre. The most extensive of these is her introduction to the *Faber Book of Modern Stories* (1937), in which she called for "poetic tautness and clarity" and suggested its affinities with the cinema: "neither sponsored by a tradition. . . . [B]oth, still, are self-conscious, show a self-imposed discipline and regard for form." (7). (See also "The NEEDLECASE.")

BIBLIOGRAPHY
Bowen, Elizabeth. *Ann Lee's and Other Stories*. London: Sidgwick and Jackson, 1926.

———. *Collected Stories.* London: Cape, 1980.

———. *The Demon Lover and Other Stories.* London: Jonathan Cape, 1945. Published as *Ivy Gripped the Steps.*

———, ed. *The Faber Book of Modern Short Stories.* London: Faber, 1937.

———. *Joining Charles and Other Stories.* London; Constable, 1929.

Glendinning, Victoria. *Elizabeth Bowen.* London: Weidenfeld, 1977.

Hoogland, Renée. *Elizabeth Bowen.* New York: New York University Press, 1994.

Lee, Hermione. *Elizabeth Bowen.* London: Vintage, 1995.

Andrew Maunder

"BOWMEN, THE" ARTHUR MACHEN (1914)

"The Bowmen" first appeared in the *Evening News* (London) on September 29, 1914. Set in WORLD WAR I, this supernatural tale recounts a fictional battle between British and German soldiers. The British forces are on the verge of suffering a crushing defeat. Their numbers have been reduced by half. In a desperate moment, a British soldier appeals to St. George, using a motto he recalls from the plates of a vegetarian restaurant he once frequented: "Adsit Anglis Sanctus Georgius" ("St. George help the English"). The plea conjures up a ghostly army of bowmen from the Battle of Agincourt—King Henry V's famous English victory over the French, immortalized in Shakespeare's play *Henry V* (1599)—and, in a short time, with the help of this heavenly host, the British soldiers defeat a 10,000-strong German army. Because the dead German soldiers have no wounds, the Germans conclude that the British used poisonous gas during the battle. Though inspired by the accounts of the real-life Battle of Mons of August 1914, the supernatural aspects of the story, ARTHUR MACHEN insisted, were entirely fictional. The story was a "composite," he said in the introduction to the tale, of the legendary notion of spiritual intervention in wartime, of RUDYARD KIPLING's story of a ghostly regiment ("The Lost Legion"), and of Machen's interests in medievalism (296). Still, the reportorial style of the narrative convinced many that the story was true. In the year following its publication it attracted wide interest and controversy. Numerous "real-life" accounts corroba-

rating the story began to circulate, including those of military officers, soldiers, and battlefield nurses. Theosophists wrote books and preachers preached sermons on the subject and, within a short time, the story was popularized as the legend of "the Angels of Mons," a title under which the tale sometimes appears. In August 1915 "The Bowmen" was issued in book form along with similar tales by Machen in order to capitalize on the interest generated by the legend. Spurred by the ongoing controversy, the book sold 3,000 copies in the first day, 50,000 in three months, and 100,000 in a year and was translated into six languages. Though it was Machen's most successful work, he reaped no financial benefits from it as the rights to it were owned by the *Evening News*. The story is slight in itself. Machen said of it that he "had failed in the art of letters" but "succeeded, unwittingly, in the art of deceit" (297). Its importance lies not in its artistic merits but in what it reveals about the mindset of the British nation during World War I. The tale provided consolation and hope to a public terrified at the unexpected toll the war was exacting on its nation. Despite the materialist and industrialist character of the age, the British people were not immune to a belief in the miraculous. Indeed, as Adrian Eckersley has argued, "The Bowmen" reveals "the tensions under which the credulous and incredulous confronted one another in this era of materialism, when scientists were often appalled at the sheer inhuman mechanism of the cosmos they envisioned and religion became a counterweight and comfort against the inhumanity of their vision" (222).

BIBLIOGRAPHY

Clarke, David. "Rumours of Angels: A Legend of the First World War," *Folklore* (October 2002). Available online. URL: http://www.findarticles.com/p/articles/mi_m2386/is_2_113/ai_95107633. Accessed May 8, 2006.

Eckersley, Adrian. "Arthur Machen." In *Dictionary of Literary Biography.* Vol. 156, *British Short-Fiction Writers, 1880–1914: The Romantic Tradition,* edited by William F. Naufftus, 216–224. New York: Gale, 1996.

Machen, Arthur. "The Bowmen." In *The Collected Arthur Machen,* edited by Christopher Palmer, 295–302. London: Duckworth, 1988.

Kristen MacLeod

BOYD, WILLIAM (1952–)

William Boyd was born in Accra, Ghana, in 1952 to English parents, who were then dispatched in Africa. According to the author himself in his book *Protobiography* (2005), his childhood and early adolescence were marked by airports and flights to Scotland, where he spent his holidays with family relatives. This travel, he points out, brought about a fascination with airplanes that is recurrently reflected in stories such as "On the Yankee Station" or "Extracts from the Diary of Flying Officer J," both published in *On the Yankee Station* (1982). When he was nine, his parents sent him to Scotland to proceed with his schooling, and this period proved to be a turning point in both personal and literary terms. Tired of an educational system that he considered stifling, Boyd abandoned the suffocating atmosphere of British prep schools to become acquainted with other cultures and languages. This interest took him to Nice University, where he attended several courses on French language and literature that he nostalgically remembers in "Alpes Maritimes" and "Gifts," two other stories in *On the Yankee Station*.

After his time in France, Boyd returned to England to start a degree at Oxford University, where he consolidated his literary tastes and, more important, wrote his first fictional accounts. Once he completed his degree, the novelist-to-be began to lecture in literary theory at St Hilda's College while working on a Ph.D. dissertation he never finished. He soon felt that teaching was not rewarding enough and left Oxford to become a full-time writer. By this time Boyd had managed to write two novels that remain unpublished and a number of short stories that appeared in several newspapers and journals that would later be compiled in *On the Yankee Station*.

In 1981 his first novel, *A Good Man in Africa,* came out. He was awarded several literary prizes and started to be acknowledged as the successor of KINGSLEY AMIS and Evelyn Waugh. Boyd was recognized as a master of humor, irony, and farce, which he exhibits more conspicuously in his second and third novels, respectively. *An Ice-Cream War* (1982) and *Stars and Bars* (1983) confirmed Boyd's extraordinary versatility and ample literary scope, ranging from antiwar satire to farcical portraits of both American and British societies.

Although Boyd is best known for his novels, the role played by the short story is, according to the author, crucial to understand some of the issues he tackles in his longer works: "My own case is perhaps typical: I have written eight novels but I cannot stop writing short stories—something about the short form . . . lures me back again and again" (2004, 24). Furthermore, Boyd's relationship with the short story has been productive on several levels. It allows him to experiment with forms, characters, and themes and to become initiated in the complex and sometimes hostile editorial world. *On the Yankee Station* was his first collection, and it already shows traits that characterize most of his stories. In his illuminating "Brief Encounters," written for the *Guardian* in 2004, Boyd argues that reduction and concision are the elements that differentiate the short story from the novel and also the traits that endow his stories with a very singular dimension. *On the Yankee Station* is full of autobiographical details, perfectly discernible in "Killing Lizards," in which he depicts the tranquil existence of a boy living in Africa with his parents; in "Alpes Maritimes;" and in "Gifts." Boyd's stories in this collection gravitate around motifs that he deals with more extensively in his novels: The figure of the expatriate, the African scenarios, and the use of satire become distinguishable features of narratives that analyze the unpredictability of ordinary situations. *On the Yankee Station* is also full of literary allusions and influences, for instance, the very noticeable Dickensian touches in "Bat Girl," in which Boyd draws on the same facts versus imagination dichotomy that CHARLES DICKENS explores in *Hard Times* (1854), and the Swiftean approaches to the odors and shortcomings of the human body in "Historie Vache," reminiscent of the episode in which the eponymous hero of Jonathan Swift's *Gulliver's Travels* observes and smells at close range the bodies of the enormous Brobdingnagian women.

In stylistic and formal terms, short stories have been an essential groundwork for Boyd, who has attempted to depart from the more realistic framework of his novels to survey more postmodern and challenging literary forms. *The Destiny of Nathalie "X"* (1992) epitomizes this technical evolution, especially in the title story, in which Boyd uses a layout that echoes the structure of a film script to satirize the vices and follies of Hollywood's show business. In "Adult Video," the story that opens his last collection, *Fascination* (2005), Boyd recuperates the starring character of both "Alpes Maritimes" and "Gifts" and places him in an Oxford context. There, the author analyzes the intricacies that underlie academic and cultural life through the tense relationship of a doctoral candidate and incipient novelist with his thesis supervisor. But above all, "Long Story Short," the closing story of *On the Yankee Station,* emerges as one of the most brilliant and playful narratives Boyd has ever written, in which his direct way of addressing the reader, his way of re-creating himself as a fictional character, and the manipulative nature of the story turn it into a noteworthy piece of literary geniality. It is also important to mention that, besides being a basic means for formal experimentation, the short story has allowed Boyd to delineate some of his most memorable characters. Such is the case of Morgan Leafy, the protagonist of *A Good Man in Africa,* who appears for the first time in "Next Boat to Douala" and again in "The Coup" in *On The Yankee Station* evidencing the same foolishness and vices as in Boyd's first novel. Also, Logan Mountstuart is the central character of "Hotel de Vouyageurs" (in *The Destiny of Nathalie "X"*), in which Boyd provides some general hints about this protagonist of *Any Human Heart.*

BIBLIOGRAPHY

———. "Brief Encounters," *Guardian,* 2 October 2004.
———. *The Destiny of Nathalie "X."* London: Penguin, 1995.
———. *Fascination.* London: Penguin, 2005.
———. *The New Confessions.* London: Penguin, 1987.
Boyd, William. *On the Yankee Station.* London: Penguin, 1982.
———. *Protobiography.* London: Penguin, 2005.

Juan F. Elices

BRADDON, MARY ELIZABETH (1835–1915)

In her 55-year career, the almost preternaturally prolific Mary Elizabeth Braddon produced more than 80 novels, dozens of short stories, and a substantial number of plays and articles—as well as six children, a maelstrom of critical controversy, and a loyal, eager readership that continues to this day. Shrewdly aware of the public interest in scandal and sensation,

Braddon invariably wrote to sell. Her steamy page-turners upended conventional Victorian morality by featuring seemingly respectable protagonists, often women, who were guilty of sordid crimes and self-interested calculation. Like her friend and sometime-mentor Edward Bulwer-Lytton and her popular contemporary WILKIE COLLINS, she supplied absorbing accounts of, as she put it in a letter to Bulwer, "crime, treachery, murder, slow poisoning, and general infamy" to an insatiable reading public (Wolff, 12). Yet despite the stream of often formulaic fiction written, sometimes pseudonymously, for the penny press, Braddon took the art and craft of writing seriously. Like Jane Austen, she closely observed social class and customs and exposed the corruption lurking beneath the veneer of civil propriety. Melding the convoluted plotting and extremes of gothic romance with the everyday realism of the domestic drama, Braddon followed Collins's lead and helped forge a new genre—a kind of DETECTIVE FICTION in which the gothic heart of darkness is found not in some misty otherworld but in the uncomfortably close and familiar. Her most enduring work reveals her preoccupation with duplicitous societal strictures and women's precarious lot.

In an 1865 review of *Aurora Floyd,* the second in what Braddon termed her "pair of Bigamy novels" (the first being the spectacularly successful *Lady Audley's Secret*), an admiring HENRY JAMES noted Braddon's "turn for colour," her artistry, "audacity," and "pluck." "Uncommonly clever," Braddon "created the sensation novel" and turned her own "wide experience" to fictional account: "She knows much that ladies are not accustomed to know but they are apparently very glad to learn. The names of drinks . . . the talk natural to a crowd of fast men at supper, when there are no ladies present but Miss Braddon" (594). It was Braddon's wide experience that so shocked and titillated more restrained Victorian sensibilities. Though born to a middle-class family, Braddon knew early privation and loss and was forced to reckon with the grimmer shades of grey in ambiguous, duplicitous adult relations. Her father, Henry, was charming and feckless, a failed solicitor who was unfaithful to his wife, Fanny White Braddon. The couple separated when Braddon was five, and finances were always a worry. By the time

Lady Audley appeared in 1862, Braddon had already flouted time-honored codes for ladylike discretion by taking to the stage to support herself, her mother, and her elder sister and then becoming involved with a married man. Her acting career was relatively short-lived, lasting from 1852 until about 1860, when the writing trade beckoned and proved to be more lucrative. Her liaison with publisher John Maxwell was a lifelong affair, from its inception in 1861 until the death of her cherished, stalwart, if sometimes irascible "Max" in 1895. Maxwell's first wife was mentally ill, like the fictional Bertha Rochester, and was being cared for by relatives. Braddon became the amiable, estimable stepmother to Maxwell's five children and gave birth to six children of her own (one son died in infancy). In 1874, after Maxwell's first wife died, he and Braddon were able to "legitimize" the relationship that had stirred such social antipathy and critical scorn.

In an unpublished memoir, Braddon wrote, "The history of my life is for the most part the history of the books I have written and the books I have read" (quoted in Wolff "Devoted Disciple," 35). The sheer magnitude of her accomplishments makes the words "ambition" and "discipline" seem paltry. Her work was shaped by market demands—a market she herself helped create—yet works such as *The Doctor's Wife* (1864), *Birds of Prey* (1867), *Charlotte's Inheritance* (1868), *The Cloven Foot* (1879), and *Ishmael* (1884) show the clear influence of French realists Gustave Flaubert and Honoré de Balzac and of her later attraction to Zola's naturalism. During the proliferation of the magazine trade in the 1860s, John Maxwell published periodicals for all classes of readers, and Braddon wrote stories for and serialized novels in most of them, from hack-work thrillers for the *Halfpenny Journal* to more earnest efforts directed at the middle- and upper-class readers of *Temple Bar* and *Belgravia*. She edited *Belgravia* from 1866 to 1876, also writing much of its content. *Belgravia*'s popular Christmas annual of stories and poems reemerged as *The Mistletoe Bough* in 1878. Braddon edited and contributed to it for most of its 15-year run.

It is safe to assume that all of Braddon's stories originally appeared in periodicals before being collected in the eight editions that appeared in her lifetime, though a few sources remain untraced. (Her novel *All Along the River* was originally issued in two volumes, and the third in the typical three-volume format was composed of eight short stories; some sources list two additional collections: *Figure in the Corner,* 1879, and *Great Journey,* 1882. American and other foreign editions were sometimes retitled.) As does her longer fiction, her stories demonstrate her versatility and fluctuate in style, theme, and literary intent. She was a virtuoso of the ghost story, a hugely popular but still critically undervalued genre that held sway in the Victorian imagination and furnished chills around many a fireside. "At Chrighton Abbey," first published in *Belgravia* in 1871 and then collected in *Milly Darrell and Other Tales* (1873), typifies the traditional ghost story with its slow buildup of tension and accumulation of believable supernatural portents. "The Cold Embrace," from her first story collection, *Ralph the Bailiff and Other Tales* (1862) (first printed in Maxwell's *Welcome Guest,* 1860), is notable for its eerie narrative wryness and the inevitability of the faithless, narcissistic artist's demise at the spectral hands of his carelessly rejected betrothed. As in countless folktales of beyond-the-grave visitations, Braddon's hauntings are often personal rather than historical, born of unresolved emotional need. As in her less uncanny sensation fiction, plots hinge on suicide and suffering, crime, guilt, and revenge. Commonplace cruelties and everyday ambiguities are thematic mainstays. "The Shadow in the Corner," from *Flower and Weed and Other Tales* (1883; first published in Charles Dickens's *All the Year Round,* 1879), is a wrenching exposé of social class and female vulnerability. Other ghost tales include "Eveline's Visitant" and "How I Heard My Own Will Read" from *Ralph the Bailiff and Other Tales,* "Her Last Appearance" and "John Granger" from *Weavers and Weft and Other Tales* (1877), "Dr Carrick" from *Flower and Weed,* and "My Wife's Promise" from *Under The Red Flag and Other Tales* (1886). "Good Lady Ducayne," published in the *Strand Magazine* (1896), is a vampire tale that may well have influenced the 1897 *Dracula,* written by Braddon's friend Bram Stoker.

Many of the tales make use of Braddon's theatrical background and offer portraits of colorful types as well as intriguing glimpses into her own early experience. In "Too Bright to Last," from *Weavers and Weft* (1877;

originally published in the *Belgravia Christmas Annual* in 1871), a young woman is stranded by her scapegrace father and survives by taking to the stage. "Across the Footlights" (first printed in the *Mistletoe Bough* in 1884 and then in *Under the Red Flag* the same year) evokes the world of the Theatre Royal in Brighton, where a young Mary Seyton (Braddon's stage name) and the fictional Rosalie Morton appear. In "Thou Art the Man," from *Flower and Weed,* a suspicious theatergoer turns amateur sleuth and proves that his first love was murdered by the star of a Drury Lane play in which the actor/killer mimics, all too closely, the real crime. Though her ghostly tales and detective fiction are best remembered and most often anthologized today, Braddon's subversion of Victorian codes and depiction of women's social and economic place in other works are of particular interest to feminist scholars.

BIBLIOGRAPHY

Braddon, Mary Elizabeth. *The Cold Embrace and Other Ghost Stories.* Edited by Richard Dalby. Ashcroft, British Columbia: Ash-Tree Press, 2000.

———. *The Fatal Marriage and Other Stories.* Edited by Chris Willis. Hastings, England: The Sensation Press, 2000.

———. *Milly Darrell and Other Tales.* 1873. Boston: Elibron Classics, 2002.

———. *One Fatal Moment and Other Stories.* Edited by Jennifer Carnell. Hastings, England: The Sensation Press, 2001.

———. *Under the Red Flag and Other Tales.* 1884. Boston: Elibron Classics, 2002.

———. *Weavers and Weft.* 1877. Boston: Elibron Classics, 2002.

Carnell, Jennifer. *The Literary Lives of Mary Elizabeth Braddon.* Hastings, England: The Sensation Press, 2000.

James, Henry. "Miss Braddon," *Nation,* 9 November 1865, pp. 593–594.

Willis, Chris. "Mary Elizabeth Braddon and the Literary Marketplace." Available online. URL: http://www.chriswillis.freeserve.co.uk/meb2.html. Accessed April 26, 2006.

Wolff, Robert Lee. "Devoted Disciple: The Letters of Mary Elizabeth Braddon to Sir Edward Bulwer Lytton, 1862–1873." *Harvard Library Bulletin* 12 (1974): 5–35, 129–161.

———. *Sensational Victorian: The Life and Fiction of Mary Elizabeth Braddon.* New York: Garland Publishing, 1979.

Kate Falvey

"BREAKING SUGAR" A. L. KENNEDY (1997)

This story is from A. L. KENNEDY's *ORIGINAL BLISS.* In a number of very favorable reviews of this collection, critics noted Kennedy's predilection for characters who can be moved only by extreme circumstances, as if their responses have been dulled by more quotidian offenses, together with the puzzles in her work that challenge a reader's comfortable responses to realistic fiction. This second characteristic is apparent in "Breaking Sugar," which focuses on the relationship between the unnamed female narrator, a married former academic, and her boarder, Mr. Haskard, a systems analyst. While her husband, Nick, is at work, the narrator follows Haskard's direction to take the furniture out into the lawn so she can see how "dead and insubstantial our achievements and defenses are" (114). Haskard's strangeness is also marked by his hobby: He travels to places where people have been wronged—the site of "a supremely avoidable mining disaster" or "the pool where Witchfinder General Matthew Hopkins was thrown, bound hand and foot" (119)—to say he is sorry. Haskard apologizes for what the reader imagines is his complicity as a member of the offending human race. Typically Kennedy makes it hard for us to know what to make of this: Certainly there are things for which we should feel guilty, but just as certainly it seems wrong to think that we can ever adequately apologize for them. Our desire to express solidarity with Haskard's efforts is undercut when we discover that the photos he takes of these sorry landscapes "had a certain emptiness, as if he had arrived too late to catch the heart of it" (119). If this is the sum of our response, Kennedy suggests, it is not enough.

The narrator and Haskard consummate their unusual relationship by smashing sugar cubes with a hammer against a breadboard, unleashing flashes of violet light. This aesthetic experience is written as if it had epiphanic undertones for the narrator. Maybe something significant is being released by this act, but again, Kennedy through her narrator, deflates the scene when she explains that the explosions are a natural process, part of the breaking of the sugar's crystal form. The narrator keeps this nocturnal activity secret from her husband, even when he tastes the sugar on his bread. It would be easy to see the act of breaking the sugar cubes aligned with Haskard's apology, as if by apologizing he too was releasing light or energy heretofore trapped in the landscape. But then, where does the light come from in these scenes of culturally sanctioned tragedy, and is it right to make equivalent, for example, "torture and execution of Welsh resisters" (119) and the narrator's personal, aesthetic-epiphanic moment in the kitchen? And what does it mean that the residue of such experiences adds a barely perceptible sweetness to the food we eat?

Kennedy's stories often probe the gulf between what makes her characters do and what her readers are willing to bear, and "Breaking Sugar" is no exception. In mostly flat and realistic prose, Kennedy presents a strange woman's relationship in terms that are only subtly upsetting, but then offers little direction about how to interpret her story.

BIBLIOGRAPHY

Kennedy, A. L. *Original Bliss*. London: Jonathan Cape, 1997.

Matthew Dube

"BRIGADIER GERARD" ARTHUR CONAN DOYLE (1894)

During a long and prolific writing career, Sir ARTHUR CONAN DOYLE created three of the most memorable characters in series fiction: the quintessential detective Sherlock Holmes, the indomitable man of science Professor Challenger, and the swashbuckling French soldier Etienne Gerard. Popular literature in the early 1890s witnessed a resurgence of interest in the Napoleonic era of the early 1800s. The victory over Napoleon at Waterloo continued to play a special role in British national memory, especially in contrast to the dirty little wars of imperial adventurism that since 1815 had occupied British attention. The Napoleonic wars with their romantic aura offered a rich field for adventure writers, who capitalized on the period's hold on the popular imagination with stories crafted from the enemy's viewpoint (Tracy, 173).

The character of Brigadier Gerard was modeled on the life and military career of Baron Jean Baptiste de Marbot (1782–1854), a French cavalry officer and personal favorite of the Emperor's, whose memoirs were first published in 1844. An English translation appeared in 1892 and became an immediate best seller (Tracy 173–174). After reading Marbot's memoirs, which had been recommended to him by George Meredith, Conan Doyle saw the opportunity for crafting a new hero to replace Sherlock Holmes. Doyle would later comment that his three years of painstaking research on the Napoleonic era resulted in only "one little book of soldier stories" (Carr, 91).

The first story featuring Brigadier Gerard appeared in December 1894 and was published in the STRAND MAGAZINE, which had featured the Sherlock Holmes tales. The Brigadier Gerard adventures came out over a 15-year period leading up to Professor Challenger's debut in 1912. Conan Doyle's accounts of Gerard's exploits are distinguished for their careful attention to historical detail. The stories cover every major campaign and battle of the Napoleonic wars, from the French victories at Zurich in 1799 to the defeat of Napoleon at Waterloo in 1815, and correspond closely to their model Marbot's career in Napoleon's service (Tracy, 175).

BIBLIOGRAPHY

Carr, John Dickson. *The Life of Sir Arthur Conan Doyle*. New York: Carroll & Graff, 1949.
Doyle, Arthur Conan. *The Complete Brigadier Gerard*. Edinburgh: Canongate, 1996.
Tracy, Jack. "How the Brigadier Came to Be Written." In *Brigadier Gerard*, edited by Jack Tracy, 173–182. New York: Jove, 1982.

Tony Rafalowski

BRITISH EMPIRE

Although the British Empire had its beginnings long before the 19th century, it was not until the second half of that century that it made its greatest impact on British literature. This was the age of high imperialism, more aggressively expansionist in character than formerly, and the culmination of a period stretching back to the last decades of the 18th century, when Britain lost its American colonies to revolution but rapidly began to acquire global possessions elsewhere. The annexation of Bengal consolidated the British hold upon India; the Victorian age saw further gains from New Zealand to Canada and participation in the European-wide "scramble for Africa." (The whole of Ireland, too, remained under

British sway until 1916, but in view of its proximity and similarity of language and custom, it is generally regarded as a special case.)

In the first half of the Victorian era, literary awareness of empire remained largely confined to travel writing and essays by writers including CHARLES DICKENS and ANTHONY TROLLOPE; there were also the juvenile seafaring adventure tales of Captain Marryat and R. M. Ballantyne, and the colonial influence is discernible in some adult novels, such as *Vanity Fair* (1847) by William Makepeace Thackeray, who was born in India. But later in the century the empire came to figure more extensively in mainstream fiction. Engaging with empire liberated writers from domestic concerns and allowed them to deal in the exotic mode while foregrounding Western ideals and values. Indeed, the bulk of this writing operated on a fundamental (often racist) assumption of difference, maintaining a certain distance between colonizer and colonized and thus allowing colonized places to function as the site of difference or otherness, of the unknown, leading to wonder, excitement, and adventure. On the simplest level, this meant tales of youthful escapades of the kind exemplified in the work of G. A. Henty and the stories that saturated juvenile magazines like *Boy's Own*, tales of young colonial heroes going abroad, fighting battles, mastering natives, and making their fortunes; this fiction was also seen to inculcate sound imperial values in the young. The columns of the new adult magazines, too, were replete with stories, whether short stories or serialized novels (like some of Rider Haggard's African romances), in which exotic places featured as a convenient backdrop for tales of magic, mysticism, and the supernatural. However, around the beginning of the 20th century there appeared a body of fictional writing, now regarded as seminal, that took a more complex approach and in which the Empire provided a sharp focus for all manner of fears and insecurities.

RUDYARD KIPLING made his name with his early short stories about India, but while *The JUNGLE BOOKS* gave an exhilarating picture of life in the Indian wilds, stories from his other collections such as *PLAIN TALES FROM THE HILLS* (1888) were rather different. These stories exhibited a new literary sophistication in employing irony and economy of method to build up a picture of Anglo-

Indian life largely shorn of exotic glamour. For example, in "The MAN WHO WOULD BE KING" the two vagabonds who go to create a empire for themselves in Kafiristan are scarcely empire heroes in the traditional mold, and their story is told at a wry distance by a cynical narrator working in a stifling press office. Kipling thus suggests that the dreariness and drudgery of life in this office, and not grand exotic adventure, represent the true reality of the Raj. Throughout his Anglo-Indian fiction Kipling deals with ordinary folk, from soldiers to administrators, emphasizing the hardships they face and the problematic relationships, isolation, and overwork, often leading to physical and mental breakdown. This is what happens, for example, to the protagonists of "The PHANTOM RICKSHAW" and "AT THE END OF THE PASSAGE," stories in which Kipling employs the gothic mode not just for its own sake but in order to highlight the psychological strains and stresses of Anglo-Indian life.

Derangement is also a theme of JOSEPH CONRAD's writing about Africa, most famously in *HEART OF DARKNESS* (1899). This novella deals with the Belgian rather than British Empire but expresses concerns seen to be common to all modern colonialism. The sardonically-titled "An Outpost of Progress," which appeared in *TALES OF UNREST* (1898), similarly features European violence, madness, and degeneracy in the primordial heart of Africa. Other tales in this collection deal with the Far East (as many of Conrad's later celebrated stories and novels were to do), and although more in the traditional romance-adventure mode they carry the same sense of the sheer immensity and incomprehensibility of tropical regions. In such stories the other threatens to, and sometimes actually does, overwhelm.

Another distinct geographic locale that features in empire writing of the era is the South Seas. ROBERT LOUIS STEVENSON's "The BEACH OF FALESÁ" (1892) is groundbreaking in its squalidly realistic account of white corruption in the region and ends with its narrator caught in the classic colonial dilemma of wavering between two worlds, committing himself to his native wife and children while still longing to return to England. "The Ebb Tide" (1894) anticipates Conrad in its tragic realism and highly wrought symbolism, exploring not only the perversion of colonialist ideals but raising pertinent questions about the human condition.

Such writing reveals the anxieties that beset Empire even at its seeming height, and with the dawn of the 20th century, particularly with the protracted, inglorious spectacle of Britain's controversial entry into the Boer War in South Africa (1899–1900), a waning of confidence in the imperial project became more pronounced. Doubts about the legitimacy of imperialism, fears of contamination through "primitive" contact, and worries over Britain being gradually overhauled by increasingly powerful competitors on the world stage all accumulated in the rush to the cataclysm of world war. Thereafter writers like SOMERSET MAUGHAM and E. M. FORSTER continued to engage with the related themes of empire and the exotic in their short stories and novels. Also, the empire began to "write back," initiating a new phase of postcolonialism as authors from the colonies and later from the independent nations found their own voice and began to tell their own stories while casting a critical eye over the slow dwindling and final extinction of the British Empire, on which, it was once fondly believed, the Sun would never set.

BIBLIOGRAPHY

Brantlinger, Patrick. *Rule of Darkness: British Literature and Imperialism 1830–1914.* New York and London: Cornell University Press, 1988.

Boehmer, Elleke, ed. *Empire Writing: An Anthology of Colonial Literature 1870–1918.* Oxford: Oxford University Press, 1998.

Gish, Robert. "The Exotic Short Story: Kipling and Others." In *The English Short Story 1880–1945: A Critical History,* edited by Joseph M. Flora, 1–38. Boston: Twayne, 1985.

Gurdip Panesar

BRONTË, CHARLOTTE (1816–1855)   Born in Thornton, Yorkshire, Charlotte Brontë was the third daughter of six children of Patrick Brontë, an Evangelical minister, and his wife, Maria. Her two older sisters, Maria and Elizabeth, died in 1825 at the ages of 11 and 10 of tuberculosis contracted at Cowan Bridge Clergy Daughters' School in Lancashire. Brontë and her younger sister, Emily, who also were at the school then, were brought home immediately; Cowan Bridge later was depicted in her first published novel, *Jane Eyre* (1847), as the appalling girls' school, Lowood. Brontë also wrote three other novels under the pseudonym

Currer Bell: *Shirley* (1849), *Villette* (1853), and the posthumously published *The Professor* (1856). Her heroines are complexly written and portrayed, chronicling the often frustrating economic and social situations in which single, middle-class women frequently found themselves.

Brontë began writing at a young age, her imagination fueled by reading the likes of Sir Walter Scott's romances, Richard Burton's *Arabian Nights,* and, especially, Lord Byron's poetry. She and her brother Branwell first collaborated on a collection of stories and plays centered around the fictional Glass Town (1826–30); he focused on the political intrigues while she created passionate tales about her romantic hero, the Duke of Wellington, and his son, Arthur Wellesley. From 1830 to 1833, Brontë wrote on her own, often incorporating characters from Glass Town. Stories such as "Albion and Marina" (1830), "The Bridal" (1832), and "The Foundling" (1833) feature themes that dominate her novels: tragic love, moral fortitude, self-esteem, and repressed emotion.

Beginning in 1834, while Emily and Anne cowrote stories about the imaginary land of Gondal, Charlotte and Branwell joined together again to invent Angria (1834–39). Her manuscripts about the Duke of Zamorna and other characters continued developing the issues important to Brontë, and at least two of them, "High Life in Verdopolis" (1834) and "Henry Hastings" (1839), feature prototypes of Jane Eyre: plain young women whose intellect and passion are anathema to societal conformity.

By 1838, when she was 22 years old, Brontë's writing was becoming more mature and realistic; "Stancliffe's Hotel" (1838) includes a character addicted to opium, mirroring her brother's growing obsession with the drug that would eventually contribute to his death in 1848. Her final Angrian-related work, a novelette titled "Caroline Vernon" (1839) about a young woman seduced by Zamorna, anticipates the psychological range and depth of her novels.

Noted for powerful descriptions of their heroines' emotional and mental states, Brontë's stories argue for women's self-esteem and independence in a society that deems them insignificant. *The Professor* (written in 1846) was produced following Brontë's return from

Belgium after falling in love with the married headmaster of the Pensionnat Heger. In *Shirley,* set during the Luddite riots of 1811–12, Brontë invented a determined and independent estate owner, Shirley Keeldar, and in *Villette,* she created perhaps her most complicated heroine, Lucy Snowe. Lucy's struggle to construct an identity while constrained by external class and economic strictures is complicated by an internal battle about her own sense of worth. (See also "NAPOLEON AND THE SPECTRE.")

BIBLIOGRAPHY

Alexander, Christine. *The Early Writings of Charlotte Brontë.* Oxford: Basil Blackwell, 1983.

———. *An Edition of the Early Writings of Charlotte Brontë.* 2 vols. Oxford: Basil Blackwell, Shakespeare Head Press, 1987–91.

Barker, Juliet. *The Brontës.* New York: St. Martin's, 1995.

Fraser, Rebecca. *The Brontës: Charlotte Brontë and Her Family.* New York: Ballantine, 1988.

SueAnn Schatz

"BROOKSMITH" HENRY JAMES (1891)

At just over 7,000 words, "Brooksmith" is one of HENRY JAMES's most compact tales. An unnamed narrator recounts the decline and presumed death of Brooksmith, butler and "most intimate friend" to Oliver Offord, a retired diplomat who dies leaving Brooksmith £80 and the culture that unfits him for his station. As a frequent guest at Offord's exclusive parties, the narrator claims that Brooksmith has tremendous social gifts: He is no less than "the occult artist" behind the stimulating conversation. However, the narrator often reveals his own snobbery, and his frequent, unfounded inferences make him unreliable. Brooksmith himself says little, suggesting that he may be less interested in salon talk than the narrator insists. And while Brooksmith descends into casual work and poverty in full view of the narrator, neither the narrator nor any of his social circle do anything to help. Rather, they lament the disappearance of the parties and justify their inaction by dismissing as beneath an artist such prosaic expedients as setting Brooksmith up in a shop or public house. Citing Brooksmith's inability to rise beyond his class—even in death Brooksmith is imagined changing the plates of the gods—critics have remarked on the tale's subtle social criticism. More recent commentary has enlarged on the narrator's unreliability.

James's remarks on the tale's genesis (in his notebooks and the preface to his New York edition) reveal that the "germ" for "Brooksmith" concerned a maid condemned to return to her people after becoming accustomed to her recently departed mistress's brilliant talk. In light of these origins, the tale's treatment of gender is intriguing. The narrator's hostility toward women spans the social spectrum: The ladies of England are incapable of cultivating a salon, while Brooksmith lives among "vague, prying, beery females." Moreover, Brooksmith's relationship to his master and the narrator's keen pursuit of Brooksmith suggest a homoerotic subtext. "Brooksmith" first appeared May 2, 1891, in *Black and White* and *Harper's Weekly,* in Britain and the United States, respectively. The tale was first collected in *The Lesson of the Master* (1892).

BIBLIOGRAPHY

Anesko, Michael. *"Friction with the Market": Henry James and the Profession of Authorship.* New York: Oxford University Press, 1986.

Drummond, Rory. "The Spoils of Service: 'Brooksmith.'" In *The Finer Thread, the Tighter Weave: Essays on the Short Fiction of Henry James.* edited by Joseph Dewey and Brooke Hovath, 69–81. West Lafayette, Ind.: Purdue University Press, 2001.

James, Henry. *The Complete Notebooks of Henry James.* Edited by Leon Edel and Lyall H. Powers. New York: Oxford University Press, 1987.

———. *Complete Stories.* New York: Library of America, 1996.

Winnie Chan

"BROTHER JACOB" GEORGE ELIOT (1864)

GEORGE ELIOT described her short story "Brother Jacob" (written in 1860, published in the *Cornhill* 1864) as a "slight tale." "Brother Jacob," a story about deception, imperial venture, and self-interest, was the first piece written after her true identity had been disclosed to the public and one of only two independent short stories by the famous novelist.

The story is a fable, written with a satiric tone. Eliot portrays the unashamed, brazen David Faux as he plots to steal his small inheritance from his mother's room and travel to the West Indies. His plan is foiled by his "idiot" brother Jacob, who catches him in the act. After failing to distract and pacify Jacob with candy from the confectioner's shop at which he was an apprentice, David allows Jacob to follow him, only to leave him asleep on a stagecoach. David fails to make a fortune in the Indies, and the tale is picked up years later in the market town of Grimworth, where David (now Edward Freely) has set up a pastry and confection shop. The women at Grimworth, while at first snubbing the shop on the principle that no respectable (or self-respecting) woman would purchase cakes when she could make her own, succumb to the attractive products and become enamored with both Freely and his goods. Freely/Faux is eventually uncovered by the return of Jacob, who recognizes his "brother Davy," and the townspeople reaffirm the threat to domestic harmony and social rank David presented.

Sugar and its consumption contribute much of the rich symbolic material in the story. As Susan de Sola Rodstein notes, "sugar—in the middle decades of the 19th century in England, was the locus of intense moral and economic debate over slavery, emancipation, free trade, and social definition" (295). David, at first a confectioners' apprentice, later represents the imperial adventurer who seeks a fortune first in the West Indies and then in a quiet market town, all through the slave-produced commodity sugar. Indeed, David at some level enslaves his brother Jacob, the women of Grimsworth, and even his potential wife "Penny Palfrey" through the sweets he produces and the "sweet" self-image he projects; Eliot describes this as "gradual corruption." Eliot's tale explicitly links sugar with the imperialist mind-set, so that we come to see that Freely's goods are not the airy, harmless substances we might believe we are consuming.

Eliot's fable—a perfectly dramatized exaggeration of human greed and its influence—also emphasizes the way Edward Freely's capitalist venture destroys communal and familial bonds. As Richard Mallen explains, the fable is about "the triumph of small-town virtue over a corrupting capitalism and democratic leveling. It is also a tale about the triumph of an explicit, authoritarian trust over an implicit, free-market trust" (50). Jacob, in his insatiable appetite for David's sugar prod-ucts, demonstrates the "idiocy" of a Victorian public that enables such capitalists to dupe the consumer. However, Eliot does award Jacob the ability to "uncover" the secret of Freely's enterprise and identity, symbolically uncovering the British national's participation in the slave trade of sugar and the public's eager support.

Social class in Grimworth is resolutely upheld, causing the suspicion leveled at the stranger Freely upon his arrival. As his "place in the scale of rank had not been distinctly ascertained," he challenges the aristocratic code of class and profession with his unknown origin and his trade. The fable refutes this challenge, yet not with an unblemished return to order. Readers now see the greed and imperialist ties that lie within Britain, as Jacob, David, and the Grimworth residents each enjoy the sugar (and the other commodities it represents) even though such sweets might lead relationships and integrity to rot and decay.

BIBLIOGRAPHY
de Sola Rodstein, Susan. "Sweetness and Dark: George Eliot's "Brother Jacob," Modern Language Quarterly 52 (1991): 295–317.
Eliot, George. The Lifted Veil and Brother Jacob. London: Penguin, 2001.
Mallen, Richard D. "George Eliot and the Precious Mettle of Trust," Victorian Studies 44, no. 1 (2001): 41–75.

Erin V. Obermueller

BROUGHTON, RHODA (1840–1920)

Rhoda Broughton was born near Denbigh, North Wales, the third of four children of a clergyman. The family moved to the ancestral family home at Broughton, Staffordshire, when Broughton was young. Broughton Hall, originally built in the early 14th century, would later serve as the setting for Broughton's first published novel, Cometh Up as a Flower (1867). Her first foray as an author came by way of SHERIDAN LEFANU, Broughton's uncle by marriage, who arranged to have her first manuscript, Not Wisely but Too Well, published in the Dublin University Magazine; he also submitted it to his publisher, Bentley and Son. Although George Bentley rejected Not Wisely but Too Well on the basis of reader Geraldine Jewsbury's poor review, he did agree to publish Broughton's second manuscript, Cometh Up as a

Flower, in its place as a two-volume novel. Eventually Broughton revised *Not Wisely* and went on to write 24 more novels.

These novels made Broughton one of the most popular novelists of the late Victorian era. The plots were basic, centering around the foibles and idiosyncrasies of the English country gentry, but it was her sharp, satiric barbs aimed at upper-middle-class pretentiousness that won over readers. While best known as a novelist, Broughton worked steadily as a writer of short stories, and magazine editors were eager to take her work. In 1873 she published a collection of short stories, *Tales for Christmas Eve,* later retitled *Twilight Stories* for a new 1879 edition. (While she occasionally published individual short stories, *Twilight Stories* is her only known compilation.) Although her short stories are not scrutinized as much as her novels, several literary scholars believe that these storytelling endeavors helped Broughton develop the crisp style and biting dialogue that mark her later novels.

Twilight Stories contains five ghost stories, and the state of being unconscious (literally and figuratively) is a recurring theme. Broughton specifically targets those who scoff at dreams and premonitions as well as those who do not follow their instincts. For example, in both "The Man with the Nose" and "Behold It Was a Dream," the main character's dreams that something evil will happen are ridiculed as the product of an overactive imagination; at the end of each story, however, the protagonist's fears have been realized. The main characters in "The Truth, the Whole Truth and Nothing but the Truth" and "Under the Cloak" also fear something unknown, yet they do little to evade the danger. A ghost appears in a dream in "Poor Pretty Bobby," the most conventional of the stories and the least interesting.

BIBLIOGRAPHY

Broughton, Rhoda. *Cometh Up as a Flower.* London: Bentley, 1867.
———. *Twilight Stories.* London: Home and Van Thal, 1979.
Sadleir, Michael. *Things Past.* London: Constable, 1944.
Wood, Marilyn. *Rhoda Broughton: Profile of a Novelist.* Stamford, England: Paul Watkins, 1993.

SueAnn Schatz

BUCHAN, JOHN (1875–1940)

John Buchan was born in Perth, Scotland, the eldest son of a minister in the Free Kirk of Scotland. He began his prolific literary career when he was still a student, first at Glasgow University and then at Oxford. He was part of a flourishing Scottish literary scene led by Hugh MacDiarmid and was also part of the English establishment, pursuing a successful career as a barrister and member of Parliament—his political career culminating with the post of governor-general of Canada, from 1935 to 1940.

Despite his political success, Buchan never abandoned his literary career, writing fiction as well as nonfiction works, including a biography of WALTER SCOTT (1932). During the interwar period, he focused mainly on the thriller genre, his novels being a means of propaganda for Britain's imperial and anti-German policy. These works, including the famous *The Thirty-Nine Steps* (1915), were extremely popular, but they gave him the reputation of an old-fashioned, misogynistic writer whose rather shallow plots were centered on English country houses and London Clubs. In fact, although he chose to move south to England for his career, he set many fictional and nonfictional works in his native Scotland, especially during the last years before his death. His own favorite novel, *Witch Wood* (1927), tells the story of a moderate Presbyterian minister, David Sempill, who is confronted with devil worship in his Scottish community and whose compassion is at odds with the religious extremism of his days. Often compared to the works of James Hogg and ROBERT LOUIS STEVENSON, it is one of the novels that have led to a renewal of interest in Buchan in the past few years as well as a critical reassessment of his works, whose real depth and sophistication are now acknowledged.

Although he is mainly famous as a novelist, Buchan also wrote essays and poetry as well some 60 short stories, the majority of which were published in four collections: *Grey Weather* (1899), *The Watcher by the Threshold* (1902), *The Moon Endureth* (1912), and *The Runagates Club* (1928); other short stories were published in *Scholar Gipsies* (1896) or in magazines. "On Cademuir Hill," his first short story, appeared in the *Glasgow University Magazine* in 1894 and deals with a gamekeeper who, being caught in a poacher's trap, thinks back on his life and analyzes the influence that drink and religion have had on him. Buchan's early short stories were inspired by his holidays in the Borders in Scotland; his protagonists usually were young Oxford scholars who found mystery in unknown lands, first in Scotland and then in Africa, which Buchan discovered when he went to South Africa (1901–3) with the High Commission, working on reconstruction after the Boer War.

Whether the contrast is between England and Scotland or between Britain and Africa, the same notion of a precarious balance between civilization and primitivism is to be found in Buchan's novels and short stories. It is generally assumed that this preoccupation was mainly due to his experience of the WORLD WAR I, but it is already present in the novella *The Power House* (1913), in which the conspirator Lumley utters what is perhaps Buchan's most famous line: "You think that a wall as solid as the earth separates civilisation from barbarism. I tell you the division is a thread, a sheet of glass. A touch here, a push there, and you bring back the reign of Satan." Although Buchan wrote some realistic stories, usually set in Scotland, his strong mystical sense also led him to write a number of supernatural short stories. One of the most famous is "The Watcher by the Threshold," whose narrator is summoned to the Highlands by his cousin after her husband has become possessed by the devil. Buchan was to deal with this theme of the survival of pagan rites in his later novels *The Dancing Floor* (1926) and *Witchwood* (1927).

BIBLIOGRAPHY

Buchan, John. *Complete Short Stories.* London: Thistle, 1997.
———. *Supernatural Tales.* Edinburgh: B&W Publishing, 1997.
———. *The Watcher by the Threshold.* Edinburgh: Canongate, 1997.
Lownie, Andrew. *John Buchan: The Presbyterian Cavalier.* London: Constable, 1995.
Webb, Paul. *A Buchan Companion: A Guide to the Novels and Short Stories.* Stroud, England: Alan Sutton, 1994.

Benjamine Toussaint-Thiriet

"BURNING BABY, THE" DYLAN THOMAS (1936) Entered in the "red notebook" (a notebook containing drafts of 9 stories) and dated September 1934, "The Burning Baby" was published in *Contemporary Poetry and Prose* in May 1936. The story is characteristic of Thomas's early prose work with its surreal and poetic imagery, its obsession with the sexual and the pagan, and its inclusion of elements of Welsh folklore such as Druids and changelings. Thomas got the idea for his story while on a visit to Aberystwyth in 1934 to meet the Anglo-Welsh writer Caradoc Evans. Another writer Glyn Jones, told him the story of the Welsh doctor William Price of Llantrisant (1800–1893), an intellectual and druidic figure who sang pagan addresses to the Moon and named his much-loved illegitimate son Iesu Grist (Jesus Christ), because he believed him destined to recover the lost secrets of the druids. When the son died at the age of five years, Price burned the body on a hill in Caerlan fields, chanting wild laments. Price's successful defense of himself at a subsequent trial made cremation legal in Britain.

This plotline underwent considerable changes in Thomas's treatment of his material. Clearly influenced by Caradoc Evans, the story mocks religious hypocrisy in its grotesque portraiture of a lecherous and incestuous minister, called Rhys Rhys, who impregnates his own ugly daughter—"her hair smelt of mice, her teeth came over her lip, and the lids of her eyes were red and wet" (23)—and burns the fruit of their incest, a newborn baby, alive. The story begins with echoes of Old Testament language: "They said that Rhys was burning his baby when a gorse bush broke into fire on the summit of the hill. The bush, burning merrily, assumed to them the sad white features and the rickety limbs of the vicar's burning baby" (22). Rhys Rhys, who falls in love with his daughter "on a fine Sabbath morning in the middle of summer" (22), is morbidly obsessed with the sinfulness of the flesh. On the same day he has touched his own daughter's body for the first time, he preaches in church: "That night he preached of the sins of the flesh. O God in the image of our flesh, he prayed. His daughter sat in the front pew, and stroked her arm" (23). Thomas effectively satirizes and attacks here the guilt-ridden perversity ascribed to the Nonconformist clergy. The highly dramatic and apocalyptic scene of the immolation of the child again shows the vicar's horror at the corruption of (his own) flesh: "Burn, child, poor flesh, mean flesh, flesh, flesh, sick sorry flesh, flesh of the foul womb, burn back to dust, he prayed" (27f).

The gothic character of the story is further enhanced by the vicar's eldest son, a changeling and idiot with green hair and tuberculosis who has had strange sexual adventures, for his sister "was to him as ugly as the sowfaced woman Llareggub who had taught him the terrors of the flesh. He remembered the advances of that unlovely woman" (25). This is the first appearance of the name Llareggub ("Bugger all" spelled backwards), which was to reappear in Thomas's play *Under Milk Wood*. This boy carries a dead, bleeding rabbit throughout the story, which serves to release feelings of cruelty and perverse emotion; he howls with the wind and in a "sanatorium he coughed his lungs into a basin, stirring his fingers delightedly into the blood." Morbid horror, disease, sexual obsession, and disgust create a horror tale that combines cruelty, madness, and incest into a surreal, nightmarish story.

Written shortly before Thomas's 20th birthday, "The Burning Baby" shows a solipsistic adolescent preoccupation with the ugly underside of sexuality, with insanity, violence, evil, sin, and redemption, as well as with the sinister connection among religion, sexuality, and death. Symbolist, surrealist, and gothic elements of Welsh folklore are intermingled in a kind of lyrical prose that presents reality as a phantasmagoria of images and perceptions, giving Thomas's language intense sensual power, though perhaps less subtlety. This style is typical of Thomas's early stories, which "explored the relation between immediate reality and archetypal symbols" (Vernon Watkins, quoted in Ackerman, 93). In 1938, after a three-year pause in the composition of prose, Thomas suddenly began writing in a totally different vein with "The Peaches," drawing a clear line between his poetry and his prose.

BIBLIOGRAPHY

Ackerman, John. *Dylan Thomas*. London: Macmillan, 1996.
Thomas, Dylan. *Early Prose Writings*. Edited and with an introduction by Walford Davies. London: Dent, 1971.
Peach, Linden, *The Prose Writing of Dylan Thomas*. Basingstoke: Macmillan, 1988.

Heike Grundmann

BUTTS, MARY (1890–1937)   "There is no head or tail to this story, except that it happened. On the other hand, how does one know that anything happened? How does one know?" These opening lines of Mary Butts's short story "Brightness Falls" exemplify the mystical and extraordinary quality of her short fiction. Her stories have been compared to those of HENRY JAMES, Marcel Proust, D. H. LAWRENCE, and KATHERINE MANSFIELD both in her lifetime and in the present, yet her writing has an individual, elliptical, and supernatural quality that makes her difficult to classify. Bryher (Annie Winifred Ellerman), in her memorial to Mary Butts shortly after the writer's death, claimed that her stories have a spoken and visual quality that classifies them as poems, and in fact Bryher's assessment reflects the same nebulous, inquisitive, and inspirational quality suggested by the quotation above. The stories are both poetic and magical and explore Butts's contemporary world with an eye clearly prefiguring that of the 21st century.

Born December 13, 1890, at Salterns, her family home in Dorset, England, the first child of Captain Frederick John Butts and Mary Jane Briggs (30 years his junior), Butts grew up in an affluent and educated family. As the great-granddaughter of Thomas Butts, a patron and friend of the romantic poet William Blake, Butts's home was filled with original Blake paintings. Such a collection affected her imagination and, along with her education in Greek, Latin, and their mythologies, served as an early inspiration for her writing. The Blake paintings offered Butts a way to look beyond the realities of the seen world into what she called the "unseen world," a concept that permeates most of her fiction.

After the death of her father when she was 14, her mother remarried 15 months later and sent Mary to boarding school in Scotland, where she received one of the best educations available for girls at the time but where she also experienced loneliness and emotional hardship. She eventually became estranged from her mother and her beloved younger brother Anthony, mainly over issues of money; studied briefly at Westfield College in London from 1909 to 1912; attended the London School of Economics from 1912 to 1914; and worked with London County Council, the Children's

Care Committee, and the National Council Against Conscription during the early years of the war. During this time, she had an affair with Eleanor Rogers and began her 21 years of journal writing in 1916. She also met the poet and publisher John Rodker, married him in 1918, and had one child, Camilla, in 1920. Shortly after Camilla's birth, Butts left her with a friend in London and went away to Paris with Cecil Maitland, a Scottish artist and Joyce critic whom she had met while married to Rodker. She had already been involved with drugs, but Maitland deepened that involvement (cocaine, opium, hashish, heroin) and introduced her to Aleister Crowley ("The Great Beast") and his occult group in Cefalu, Italy. She soon became disenchanted with Crowley, and Maitland eventually left her damaged and hurt. He had been, she claimed, the love of her life.

Butts then pursued a wildly bohemian life in London, Paris, and Villefrance, France. She moved easily among artists, writers, lesbians, and homosexuals in the avant-garde world of the 1920s, all the while writing and working on her art in spite of her addiction to opium and involvement with other drugs. Her wild lifestyle stunned even the other bohemians of the period, and records of her behavior appear in numerous memoirs of the times. Although she knew and interacted with her fellow modernists (including Gertrude Stein, VIRGINIA WOOLF, T. S. Eliot, Ezra Pound, JAMES JOYCE, W. B. Yeats, and Ford Madox Ford), she remained an independent woman and never belonged to any group. By 1930 drugs and poverty led to a breakdown from which her mother rescued her. In the same year, Butts married Gabriel Aitken, a young English artist. Aitken, however, was an alcoholic and a homosexual, and in 1934 he left her at their home in Sennen Cove, near Land's End in Cornwall. She spent the remainder of her life in the natural world that she had loved as a child, became an Anglo-Catholic, and continued writing. She never relinquished her addiction to opium and died in 1937 after being rushed to a hospital in Penzance, where she died after an operation for a gastric ulcer.

Mary Butts published five novels; an autobiography of childhood; dozens of poems, essays, and reviews; and three collections of short stories: *Speed the Plough and Other Stories* (1923), *Several Occasions* (1932), and *Last Stories* (1938). Most of her stories deal with her contemporary society, both urban and rural, and with the mystical aspect of both worlds. In these worlds Butts explores sexuality, especially homosexuality, with an openness and honesty rare for her time. Her examination of a physically and psychically injured World War I soldier in "Speed the Plough" illustrates such interest. Lying in a London hospital bed imagining all sorts of expensive fabric in the clothes displayed in the English fashion magazine *The Sketch,* which often included the "Kirchner album" of beautiful young women, this soldier's interest is not in the women but in the fabrics and clothing. Sent to the country to recuperate, he creates in his mind a London dress shop as he milks cows and finds himself sickened by the connection to female sexual reproduction. Clothing and fabric become something of a veil between the masculine and feminine worlds—an aesthetic metaphor for the young, homosexual soldier. It ends with the soldier back in London, once again a dressmaker, serving a young society girl in a fitting room, on his knees, "vertical in black cloth, and grey trousers, and exquisite bow tie," pinning up a hem, in a submissive position but in control. The young girl looks down frowning, but he finds himself lost in "A roll of Lyons brocade, silver, and peach, [that] was pliant between his fingers as the teats of a cow." This story is complex and intriguing in its representation of male desire and female external trappings, which offer insights to Butts's sympathetic yet complicated understanding of and interest in homosexual men, a theme she returns to again and again in much of her fiction.

Butts is perhaps at her best when she imbues her stories with contemporary life and female manifestations of power drawn from a primal goddess source. These stories transport the reader to the avant-garde world of the 1920s but also transcend time and place to a supernatural realm. Stories like "Brightness Falls," "Friendship's Garland," and "Widdershins" pit rural and urban values against each other while the characters quest for healing in a postwar world. Incorporating mystical and mythical images into stories whose characters have names like Daphne and Cynthia, Butts captures mythical references for her own purposes. In "Friendship's Garland," for example, Butts appropriates the Daphne/Apollo myth for modern interpretation. Daphne, in her attempt to escape the metaphorical rape of her artificial society, where "things are not natural, marble like cheese, red velvet, and plaster gilt," experiences a metamorphosis and epiphany as she conjures a vision of a sanctified (biblical and mythical) tree and finds that the tree "was also myself." When the vision clears, she discovers that, after stripping the makeup from her face, the face presented to city society, one look in the mirror reveals, "I looked like a child that has been dipped in dew." It is the sanctity of nature and myth that transforms her and transports her from the dis-ease of the wounded and misguided society, ironically a society that is also an essential aspect of these characters' lives. Other stories like "From Altar to Chimney-piece" (Butts's indictment of Gertrude Stein and her salon: "men and women who think art synonymous with vice") present a much darker view of the sacred and profane, blending biographical events with occult secrets. "Madonna of the Magnificat," another attempt at fusing the natural and supernatural worlds, modernizes Mary, the Virgin Mother. Butts's character suggests the free-spirited, profane side of Mary, perhaps the "Mary" Mary Butts herself might have been. The blendings of sacred and profane permeate, enliven, and enrich the stories as they and the female characters create their own kind of power.

At her death Mary Butts was in negotiation with T. S. Eliot at Faber and Faber for a collection of short stories; they were subsequently published posthumously by Bryher, who owned Brendin Publishing Company. Butts's short fiction, as well as her longer works, is infused with a mythical and mystical quality, a dazzling complexity of language, powerful female characters, and a true sense of magic.

BIBLIOGRAPHY
Blondel, Nathalie, ed. *The Journals of Mary Butts.* New Haven: Yale University Press, 2002.
———. *Mary Butts: Scenes from the Life.* Kingston, N.Y.: McPherson & Company, 1992.
Butts, Mary. *From Altar to Chimneypiece: Selected Stories.* New York: McPherson & Company, 1992.
———. *Last Stories.* London: Brendin Publishing Co., 1938.
———. *Several Occasions.* London: Wishart & Co., 1932.
———. *Speed the Plough and Other Stories.* London: Chapman & Hall, 1923.
———. *With and Without Buttons and Other Stories.* Manchester, England: Carcanet Press, Ltd., 1991.
Foy, Roslyn Reso. "Brightness Falls: Magic in the Short Stories of Mary Butts," *Studies in Short Fiction* 36, no. 4 (Fall 1999): 381–399.
———. *Ritual, Myth, and Mysticism in the Work of Mary Butts: Between Feminism and Mysticism.* Fayetteville: University of Arkansas Press, 2001.
Hamer, Mary. "Mary Butts, Mothers, and War." In *Women's Fiction and the Great War.* Edited by Suzanne Rait and Trudi Tate, 219–240. Oxford: Oxford University Press, 1997.

Roslyn Reso Foy

BYATT, A(NTONIA) S(USAN) (1936–   )
A. S. Byatt was born on August 24, 1936, in Sheffield, England. Her father was a judge and writer, and her mother was a secondary school teacher who later gave up her career to care for her children. In 1957, Byatt earned her B.A. at Cambridge University and later pursued graduate work at Bryn Mawr College, Pennsylvania, and Somerville College, Oxford University. During the period 1962–83, Byatt taught in the department of liberal studies at the Central School of Art and Design, London, and was, in the latter part of that period, a senior lecturer in English and American literature at University College, London. Beginning in 1978, she was periodically employed as a British Council lecturer. This position provided the opportunity to travel extensively to places like Spain, Germany, Australia, Hong Kong, China, Korea, and India; these experiences (as she herself recognizes) have greatly influenced Byatt's fictional writing. In 1983, she began writing full time and has since had a prolific and renowned career publishing numerous novels, short stories, and collections of literary criticism. Her accomplishments in the field were recognized in 1990 when she was awarded the prestigious CBE (Commander of the Order of the British Empire).

For the first half of her career, Byatt primarily published novels, beginning in 1964 with *Shadow of a Sun* (later reprinted as *The Shadow of the Sun*), a novel that examines the difficulties faced by women artists and intellectuals. This theme is taken up in much of her later work, including her best-known work, *Possession: A Romance* (1990). The novel received the Booker Prize and was later made into a major Hollywood film. *Possession* is the story of two modern Victorian scholars who uncover an illicit love affair between two of the 19th century's most prominent poets, Randolph Henry Ash (based on Robert Browning) and Christabel Lamotte (based on Elizabeth Barrett Browning and Christina Rossetti). The story engages one of Byatt's most prominent fictional themes: the relationship between the past and the present, or what she refers to as "the relationship between living and dead minds."

Much of Byatt's fiction is set in the 19th century, which has earned her a reputation as a "postmodern Victorian." In her fiction, she plays with the conventions of 19th-century realism and of postmodernism to create engaging narratives that simultaneously entertain the reader while they call into question the nature and function of storytelling. Byatt often tests the bounds of realism by incorporating elements of fantasy, fairy tale, and ghost story into narratives that otherwise adhere to the realist tradition. The relationship between language and lived experience is central to all of her work, and her readers are continually asked to consider the function of reading and writing and the impact of those acts on individuals and communities. These themes are taken up at considerable length in two of her works of literary criticism: *Passions of the Mind: Selected Writings* (1991) and *On Histories and Stories: Selected Essays* (2000). In these and other nonfiction writings, Byatt names her primary influences as George Eliot, Honoré de Balzac, and Iris Murdoch.

In 1987 Byatt published her first collection of short stories, titled *Sugar and Other Stories*. She has since published five other collections of short fiction: ANGELS AND INSECTS (1992), The MATISSE STORIES (1993), *The Djinn in the Nightingale's Eye* (1994), *Elementals: Stories of Fire and Ice* (1998), and *Little Black Book of Stories* (2004). The short stories contained within each collection are held together by theme and focus, while still able to stand alone as autonomous narratives. The 11 tales in *Sugar and Other Stories* are linked by themes like the struggle of the female intellectual and the legacy of generations in

"Racine and the Tablecloth" and "Rose-Coloured Teacups"; writerly ambition and the relationship between writing and mortality in "Loss of Face," "On the Day That E. M. Forster Died," and "Precipice-Encurled"; and human mortality and the notion of spiritual and physical decay in "The July Ghost," "The Next Room," "The Dried Witch," "The Changeling," and "In the Air." All of these themes culminate in the final story, "Sugar," a seemingly autobiographical story of a woman who tries to decipher the truth about her family's history after her father's death and, in so doing, comes to understand the ways in which storytelling helps shape experience and understanding.

Angels and Insects contains two novellas, "MORPHO EUGENIA" and "The Conjugial Angel," each of which is set in the 19th century and takes up two of the period's most pressing concerns: science and spiritualism. The tales in *The Matisse Stories* are each inspired by one of Henri Matisse's paintings. The shared central theme of "Medusa's Ankles," "Art Work," and "The Chinese Lobster" is the complex formation of a personal aesthetic, and as such, each tale contemplates the relationship among sight, thought, and feeling. *The Djinn in the Nightingale's Eye: Five Fairy Stories* is a delightfully entertaining and clever collection of adult fairy tales inspired by *The Arabian Nights* and Turkish poetry; it includes "The STORY OF THE ELDEST PRINCESS." The six narratives in *Elementals: Stories of Fire and Ice* blend characteristics of fairy tale and realism to create stories whose central theme is the nature of desire and longing. The most remarkable tale in this collection is "Cold," the story of an ice princess who risks her own life and liveliness to move to the desert kingdom of her lover, whom she desperately longs to be near. Byatt's next collection of short fiction, *Little Black Book of Stories*, contains five sophisticated tales that are part fairy tale, part ghost story. "A Stone Woman" is about a woman who, after the loss of the elderly mother, finds that she is turning into stone. "The Thing in the Forest" is a tale of two young girls who see something dreadful in a forest and return to the scene as middle-aged women. All the stories in the collection bring together the fantastic, the horrific, and the everyday in order to examine the tie between the natural and the supernatural.

BIBLIOGRAPHY

Alfer, Alexa, and Michael J. Noble. *Essays on the Fiction of A. S. Byatt.* Westport, Conn.: Greenwood, 2001.

Byatt, A. S. *Angels and Insects.* London: Chatto, 1992.

———. *The Djinn in the Nightingale's Eye: Five Fairy Stories.* London: Chatto, 1994.

———. *Elementals: Stories of Fire and Ice.* London: Chatto, 1998.

———. *Little Black Book of Stories.* London: Chatto, 2004.

———. *The Matisse Stories.* London: Chatto, 1993.

———. *Passions of the Mind: Selected Writings.* London: Chatto, 1991.

———. *Still Life.* London: Chatto, 1985.

———. *Sugar and Other Stories.* London: Chatto, 1987.

———. Introduction to *The Oxford Book of English Short Stories,* edited by A. S. Byatt, xv–xxx. Oxford: Oxford University Press, 1998.

Dusinberre, Juliet. "A. S. Byatt." In *Women Writers Talking,* edited by Janet Todd, 181–195. New York: Columbia University Press, 1980.

Franken, Christien. *A. S. Byatt: Art, Authorship, Creativity.* London: Palgrave, 2001.

Hope, Christopher. *Contemporary Writers: A. S. Byatt.* London: Book Trust/British Council, 1990.

Kelly, Kathleen Coyne. *A. S. Byatt.* Twayne's English Authors Series 529. New York: Twayne, 1996.

Lana Dalley

C

"CANTERVILLE GHOST, THE" Oscar
Wilde (1887) First published in the *Court and Society Review,* "The Canterville Ghost," subtitled "a Hylo-Idealistic Romance," concerns an American minister, Mr. Hiram B. Otis, who buys a haunted English mansion from Lord Canterville. When warned about the ghost by Canterville, Mr. Otis replies only that since Americans live in a modern country and have everything that money can buy, if there is a ghost they would just as soon have it in a museum. Canterville tells Otis that the ghost has been around since 1584 and makes an appearance before any family death. Otis refuses to believe that there is any ghost, and the purchase is completed.

The Otis family consists of Hiram; his wife, the New York belle Lucretia R. Tappan; their eldest son, Washington; their 15-year-old daughter, Virginia; and their twins, nicknamed the "Stars and Stripes." Upon entering their new home, Mrs. Otis notices a bloodstain which the housekeeper identifies as the blood of Lady Eleanore de Canterville, murdered by her husband Sir Simon in 1575. It is Sir Simon's ghost that haunts Canterville. He survived his wife for nine years before disappearing under strange circumstances, and his body was never discovered. Washington promptly removes the stain with Pinkerton's Champion Stain Remover and Paragon Detergent. The next morning, the bloodstain has returned, as it does each morning after Washington removes it. One night, Mr. Otis is awakened by the clanging of metal and the appearance of the Can-

terville ghost. With red eyes, long gray matted hair, ragged clothes, and chains hanging from his wrists and ankles, the ghost is furious when Otis calmly requests that he use Tammany Rising Sun Lubricator to silence the noise of the chains. When the ghost flees, groaning in an attempt to terrify the family, the twins throw pillows at him. In 300 years, the Canterville ghost has not been so insulted. He mentally runs through his list of brilliant performances, all of which resulted in the death or madness of those he frightened, and vows revenge.

The humiliation of the ghost continues, and he finally resorts to stealing Virginia's paints to restore the bloodstain that Washington removes daily. His groans cause Mrs. Otis to recommend Dr. Dobell's tincture for indigestion to the ghost, and the twins set up a mock ghost that terrifies him. The ghost resolves to himself that these are gross materialists incapable of appreciating him, and he determines to do only his minimal duty as a ghost. He even tries the Rising Sun Lubricator and finds that it does indeed oil his chains well. After a butter slide set up by the twins trips him, he vows to try his most terrible disguise, Reckless Rupert, or the Headless Earl. But the twins douse him with water and laugh at him. The Canterville ghost gives up his nocturnal wanderings, and the family generally assumes that the ghost is gone.

One day, Virginia notices the ghost sitting alone in the tapestry chamber. He admits to killing his wife and then says that her brothers starved him in retaliation.

The ghost tells Virginia that he cannot sleep and that he wishes to die, but that he cannot until the prophecy written on the library window is fulfilled. The prophecy requires a golden girl to pray and weep for the soul of the ghost. She agrees, and they disappear together. At midnight, Virginia reappears to her frantic family with a beautiful box of jewels and with the news that the ghost is dead. She takes her family into a chamber where a gaunt skeleton stretches out his hand for an out-of-reach water jug. The family holds a funeral for the ghost, and not long after, Virginia marries her sweetheart, a duke. The story closes when the duke asks her what happened when she was locked up with the ghost. Virginia refuses to answer, and only blushes when the Duke asks if she will tell their children.

In "The Canterville Ghost," OSCAR WILDE draws on fairy tales, the popular gothic conventions of the 19th century, and the portrait of the American abroad to shape his comic ghost story. Possible sources for the ghost of Sir Simon include Alfred Tennyson's poem "Maud" as well as Samuel Taylor Coleridge's "Christabel." Wilde also emphasizes Sir Simon's performance of a role, the importance of masks and appearance, and the discrepancy between the public and private self, all of which are repeated themes in Wilde's work. The clearly allegorical names of the children—Washington, Virginia, and the Stars and Stripes—suggests that they come from a country in which everything can be bought and commodified, in which the bloodstains from the past are easily removed with the newest brand of detergent. Henry Labouchere, who endorsed Wilde's lecture tour in America in 1882, hoped that Wilde's hyperaestheticism might offer a corrective for America's hypermaterialism, and it is this hypermaterialism that characterizes the Americans of Wilde's story. That England's ghosts and skeletons simply fail to haunt the American Otis family is a central point in "The Canterville Ghost." The ghost cannot haunt the American family, and it is only in the young girl Virginia that Wilde hints at a more vexed relationship to the past. She eventually marries a duke, making her father uneasy that she is united with a titled figure of the past. She is the character most aligned with the ghost, and she disappears with him for hours for which she will not account. At her husband's urging to tell

what occurred between her and the ghost, or at least to tell their children one day, Virginia only blushes, though it remains unclear whether she blushes at the allusion to sexuality within the marriage, at the mystery of her time with the ghost, or at some combination of the two.

BIBLIOGRAPHY
Wilde, Oscar. *The Canterville Ghost and Other Stories.* New York: Dover, 2001.

Julieann Ulin

"CAPTAIN OF THE *POLE-STAR*, THE"

ARTHUR CONAN DOYLE (1883)   While still a 23-year-old medical student, before creating the wildly popular character of Sherlock Holmes, ARTHUR CONAN DOYLE published "The Captain of the *Pole-Star*." Conan Doyle's tale is a ghost story set aboard an arctic expedition, narrated by John McAlister Ray, a young medical man. Conan Doyle's own experience as a ship's doctor aboard the whaling ship *Hope* in the Arctic Circle no doubt inspired this unsettling story of a captain haunted by memories the narrator can only imagine. The narrative also foreshadows Conan Doyle's later interest in spiritualism.

The story takes the form of a diary kept by John Ray aboard a Scottish whaler, chronicling increasingly disturbing events that take place as the ship approaches the far reaches of the north. Although sympathetic to the nervous disorders that can plague men on a long and lonely voyage, the skeptical Dr. Ray nevertheless finds rational explanations for occurrences that convince the crew that the ship is cursed and that they are being haunted. The ship's captain, Craigie, manifests strange behavior during the voyage, and at odd times this seemingly cultured and intellectual man becomes irrational, distraught, and even violent. The narrator is intrigued by him but does not believe that the captain's behavior is caused by anything other than emotional or psychological distress. As the events in the diary come to a climax, the captain appears to glimpse a figure on the ice and becomes deeply agitated, then elated. Captain Craigie leaps onto the ice, speaking fondly to what the narrator characterizes as "a wreath of mist, blown swiftly in a line with the ship," and disappears. When his frozen body is found a day and half later, it is in the attitude of an embrace and covered by a swirl of ice crystals that seem to be, to some of the crew, in the "shape of a woman." Dr. Ray ends his diary here, and Conan Doyle includes an afterword by the young man's father, noting that he, the father, has learned that the captain, as a young man, had loved a woman who died "under circumstances of peculiar horror" while Craigie was at sea.

"The Captain of the *Pole-Star*" is an interesting character study of both the captain and the narrator. The doctor begins the diary as a practical, skeptical man who is, as his father describes him in the afterword, "unimaginative." He scoffs at the crew members' superstitions and seeks to find rational explanations for their fears and his own uneasiness. The captain can also be read as a double of the narrator. Both are well-educated men, and the narrator is devoted to a young woman named Flora, whom he misses and regrets having left behind as the journey becomes progressively dangerous and bizarre. The captain's fate may be a cautionary one for the younger doctor, since the captain's beloved met her horrible death while he was away, and Captain Craigie has apparently never been able to forget, or perhaps to forgive himself. As the diary comes to a close, the narrator finds himself more open to the supernatural and remarks that from his experiences on the *Pole-Star,* he has "learned never to ridicule any man's opinion, however strange it may seem." The events described and the conclusions reached in the story are tantalizingly ambiguous and suggest a fin de siècle meditation on the inadequacy of rational explanations in the face of human emotion and supernatural phenomena.

BIBLIOGRAPHY

Conan Doyle, Arthur. "The Captain of the *Pole-Star*." In *Victorian Ghost Stories,* edited by Michael Cox and R. A. Gilbert, 283–303. Oxford: Oxford University Press, 1991.

Anita Rose

CAPTAINS COURAGEOUS Rudyard Kipling (1897)

This short novel is one of the products of Rudyard Kipling's residence in the United States from 1892 to 1896. What Kipling described as a "boy's

story" was first published in serial form in *McClure's Magazine* in the United States and in *Pearson's Magazine* in Britain, and in book form by Macmillan in 1897. The title comes from one of Kipling's favorite ballads, "Mary Ambree." *Captains Courageous* is a story of maturation and redemption, a pattern of action that recurs throughout Kipling's work. It is set mostly on the Atlantic Ocean over the Grand Banks, fishing grounds off the southeast coast of Newfoundland, although later parts of the text take place in the fishing port of Gloucester, Massachusetts, and on the West Coast of the United States. The time setting is approximately the 1890s. The protagonist is Harvey Cheyne, the spoiled and arrogant son of a multimillionaire American businessman and of a weak and indulgent mother. At age 15, on a trip to Europe with his mother, Harvey falls from the liner into the sea. He is rescued by a Portuguese fisherman, Manuel, who carries him in his small fishing boat, or dory, to the schooner *We're Here,* of which he is a crew member.

On board the *We're Here,* Harvey faces an incredulous reception from the fishermen. The captain and owner, Disko Troop, considers him mad when Harvey tells of his father's wealth and his own importance. Troop offers him work on board the schooner (for $10.50 a month), and when Harvey indignantly and offensively refuses, strikes him. Troop's son Dan, who is the same age as Harvey, does partly believe him, however, and during a conversation with the boy, Harvey begins to acknowledge that he has behaved badly, apologizes to Troop, and begins work aboard the *We're Here.* He soon meets the entire multiethnic crew of the schooner, who return in the dories from fishing. Of these the only one who gives any credence to Harvey's account of his background is the black cook, who is gifted with second sight and predicts that "one day he will be your master, Danny."

Immediately after his apology to Troop, Harvey begins working on the *We're Here.* This occurs early in chapter 2, barely one-seventh of the way into the text. The remaining seven chapters present Harvey's experiences of life aboard the fishing schooner as it searches for, catches, and processes fish over a summer on the Grand Banks. Harvey engages in heavy physical labor; eats food that is new to him; is educated in sailing by crew members; gets to know them, their pasts, and their eccentricities; observes the skill of Disko Troop in finding the best fishing grounds; lives through bad weather and the varying moods of the sea; experiences the music and the traditional lore of fishermen; encounters violent death, danger, and the supernatural; and meets with the wide range of vessels and people that work on and pass through the Grand Banks. "'Tis beautiful to see how he takes to ut," remarks one of the crew of the *We're Here*.

The last two chapters of *Captains Courageous* are set on shore. Harvey's father, also called Harvey Cheyne, learns of his son's survival and with his wife arranges a record-breaking train journey from the West Coast of the United States to Gloucester. There the parents are reunited with their son and observe the change that a few months have made in his character. Formerly spoiled and rude, Harvey has become mature. The fabulously wealthy Cheynes and the Troops learn to respect each other, the text provides more details of fishermen's and their families' lives, and the elder Cheyne confides in his son and offers to bring him into his business empire. The text ends with Harvey agreeing to go to college to prepare himself for his role as his father's heir.

Critics have often pointed out that Harvey's conversion from spoiled brat to hardworking sailor is very rapid. The focus of *Captains Courageous* is the experiences that make him mature, rather than any internal conflicts of the protagonist. Harvey is saved by hard physical work, an encounter with the sturdily independent lower classes, and integration into a community. He learns to respect the immense skill of the fishermen and also the power and danger of the natural world. He sees death close up. Kipling did much research to get the details of life aboard an 1890s fishing schooner accurate, and critics have noted and praised the text's realism. This includes the specifics of the Cheynes' cross-country railway journey in chapter 9. The descriptions of the sea have also been singled out as impressive elements in the short novel. All these are aspects of Kipling's writing as a whole, as is his use of a range of voices (different dialects, languages, and technical registers). Critics have also pointed out that *Captains Courageous* has a U.S. focus. Troop and

Cheyne senior embody an old/new, East/West, and labor/capital opposition that has been seen as Kipling's allegorical vision of Gilded Age America. The multiethnic and polyglot characters, too, suggest the ethnic and linguistic variety of the late 19th-century United States. In this regard, it should be noted that Troop and Cheyne are integrated at the end (although the Cheynes are masters and the Troops men), and the diversity of characters is firmly under the control of those of Anglo-Saxon origin.

A film version of *Captains Courageous,* with substantial changes to Kipling's original plot, was a box-office success in 1937.

BIBLIOGRAPHY

Carrington, Charles. *Rudyard Kipling: His Life and Work.* London: Macmillan, 1955.

Kipling, Rudyard. *Something of Myself and Other Autobiographical Writings.* Edited by Thomas Pinney. Cambridge: Cambridge University Press, 1990.

Ormond, Leonee. "*Captains Courageous*: Introduction." The Kipling Society: Readers' Guide. Posted October 27, 2003. Available online. URL: http://www.kipling.org.uk. Accessed May 9, 2006.

Stewart, J. I. M. *Rudyard Kipling.* London: Victor Gollancz, 1966.

David Malcolm

CARTER, ANGELA (1940–92)

Angela Carter's writing went largely unappreciated until the 1980s, although she wrote her first novel, *Shadow Dance,* in 1965. As Lorna Sage acknowledged in her obituary after Carter's premature death from cancer in 1992, "it wasn't until the eighties that readers caught up with her." Catching up, and keeping up, with Carter's vibrant and turbulent imagination is a task well worth undertaking. Now acknowledged as one of Britain's foremost late 20th-century writers, whose work regularly appears on university reading lists and is popular material for Ph.D. theses, Carter's writing still retains the ability to shock and surprise, to make us see the world differently and dramatically.

Born in Sussex in 1940, Carter spent her childhood in Yorkshire and London, graduating with a degree in English from Bristol University in 1965. She received some early recognition for her work when she won two prizes: the John Llewellyn Rhys Prize for *The Magic Toyshop* in 1967 and the Somerset Maugham Award for *Several Perceptions* in 1968. The latter of these funded her travels to Japan, where she spent several years. FIREWORKS: NINE PROFANE PIECES (1974), Carter's first collection of short stories, draws heavily on this period of her life, detailing the experience of being an outsider and an observer of life. These autobiographical elements are particularly apparent in three of the stories: "Flesh and the Mirror," "A SOUVENIR OF JAPAN," and "The Smile of Winter." Dealing with loneliness, isolation, and self-identity, these stories blur the boundary between appearance and reality, as appearance, or artifice, becomes the reality. This collection includes many elements that are exploited further in Carter's later fiction, introducing taboo topics such as incest, playing with gothic features, and questioning notions of gender and sex. As Carter acknowledged, her feminism also developed during this period. Nevertheless, Carter's fiction displays her ambivalent relationship with the feminist movement, as she insists on an antiessentialist stance, rooting her women in material and historical conditions. This difficult association with feminism found its epitome in Carter's reworking of the Marquis de Sade's writings in *The Sadeian Woman: An Exercise in Cultural History* (1979), a book that upset many readers and critics with its conscious use of pornography and defense of de Sade.

Despite her early success, Carter's writing remained relatively unknown during the 1970s, as she published the novels *The Infernal Desire Machines of Doctor Hoffman* (1972) and *The Passion of New Eve* (1977). Carter's work is deliberately revisionist, taking on and debunking myths and tales, and always challenging expectations. In the speculative dystopian world of *The Passion of New Eve,* Evelyn becomes Eve at the hands of a terrifying, many-breasted mother figure. Questioning notions of gender, mythology, and genre, Carter presents a fantastic, postmodern, and grotesque fiction. This impulse continues in *The BLOODY CHAMBER* (1979), her second collection of short stories, which takes on traditional fairy tales, already endlessly rewritten, and re-presents them with gothic, feminist, and overtly sexual elements (e.g., "PUSS-IN-BOOTS"). In "The COMPANY OF WOLVES," Red Riding Hood and the wolf become highly sexualized characters, developing aspects implicit in the original tales, and the girl becomes an active participant in her fate, though the ending of this story is controversial, as some critics see Red Riding Hood as complicit in her own rape. This story was later made into a film of the same name, directed by Neil Jordan. This collection began the resurgence of interest in Carter's work, a revival that continued into the 1980s and turned into a deluge after her death.

Carter's final two novels were her most popular in many ways. Cementing Carter's movement to a concentration on female subjects, these novels are fantastic, soaring flights of exuberant and comic imagination. *Nights at the Circus* (1984) sees Fevvers, a fin de siècle aerialist and possessor of real (or are they?) wings since puberty, move from a childhood in a whorehouse through a series of adventures that lead her to the Siberian woodland. It is the voice and sheer womanliness of Fevvers, an eel-pie-eating Winged Victory, that dominates this novel, and she is linked by critics such as Aidan Day with the figure of Jeanne Duval in the title story of *BLACK VENUS* (1985), a collection that brings together stories Carter published between 1977 and 1982 and continues Carter's revision of myth and history. So Jeanne Duval, Charles Baudelaire's mistress, is rescued from the objective position of muse, "my monkey, my pussy-cat, my pet," to be portrayed as a woman with her own bad-tempered voice. And Lizzie Borden, known for the murder of her parents and a nursery rhyme based on these events, steps from the children's rhyme to become an unmarried woman suffocated by eternal daughterhood in "The FALL RIVER AXE MURDERS." *Wise Children* (1991), Carter's last novel, moves from circus to theater to produce its own unforgettable voices in the shape of the Chance sisters and their long lives on the wrong side of the blanket: They are illegitimate daughters of the great Shakespearian actor Sir Melchior Hazard. The Lucky Chances present a tumbling, boundary-defying family history many see as the best narrative Carter produced.

Carter's work has always challenged expectations and categorization, from gender to genre. Trying to fit her novels and stories into boxes, critics have labeled it magic realism, dystopian fiction, science fiction, and even pornography. Her wide-ranging intellect and impressive imagination make her work an intertextual paradise, in which Shakespeare revels with the 20th-century French philosopher Jacques Derrida and Hollywood meets fairy tale. Consisting of nine novels, four collections of short stories (her last, *American Ghosts and Old World Wonders,* was published posthumously in 1993), three collections of nonfiction pieces, and a variety of essays, articles, and scripts, Carter's oeuvre is no less extensive than her imagination. (See also "The Lady of the House of Love.")

BIBLIOGRAPHY

Carter, Angela. *American Ghosts and Old World Wonders.* 1993. London: Vintage, 1994.

———. *Black Venus.* 1985. London: Vintage, 1996.

———. *The Bloody Chamber.* 1979. London: Vintage, 1995.

———. *Fireworks.* 1974. London: Virago, 1988.

———. *Shaking a Leg: Collected Journalism and Writings.* London: Chatto and Windus, 1997.

Day, Aidan. *Angela Carter: The Rational Glass.* Manchester: Manchester University Press, 1998.

Gamble, Sarah. *Angela Carter: Writing from the Front Line.* Edinburgh: Edinburgh University Press, 1997.

Gamble, Sarah, ed. *The Fiction of Angela Carter: A Reader's Guide to Essential Criticism.* Hampshire, England: Palgrave Macmillan, 2001.

Sage, Lorna. "The Soaring Imagination," *Guardian,* 17 February 1992, p. 37.

Sarah J. Falcus

CHESTERTON, GILBERT KEITH (1874–1936)

Born in Campden Hill, London, on May 29, 1874, Gilbert Keith Chesterton was the first son of Edward Chesterton, an estate agent, and Marie Louise Grosjean; his brother, Cecil, was born in 1879. Chesterton was a day pupil at St. Paul's preparatory school in Hammersmith from 1887 to 1892, where he participated in the junior debating club, an experience that would set the stage for a life of intellectual debate in many forms: short fiction, essays, and journalism. In 1893 Chesterton entered University College, London, taking classes in Latin, French, and English. His focus was the study of fine arts at the Slade School, and he intended to become a book illustrator. He left the university without a degree in 1895, and he declares in his

Autobiography that it was the most troubling period of his life. Chesterton pronounces the *L'art pour l'art* movement and French decadence as nihilistic and decries impressionism, then in vogue, as "obviously something highly subjective and sceptical. . . . It naturally lends itself to the metaphysical suggestion that things only exist as we perceive them, or that things do not exist at all. The philosophy of Impressionism is necessarily close to the philosophy of Illusion" (1937, 89). This profound rejection of a Nietzschean universe "beyond good and evil" resonates in all of Chesterton's writing, and the spiritual crisis of his years at the Slade mark the beginning of his conversion from conventional, middle-class Anglicanism to Roman Catholicism in 1922. One of his earliest short stories, "The Diabolist," describes this crisis of conscience at the Slade. The narrator encounters a red-haired gentleman who questions his orthodoxy, asking, like Oscar Wilde's Dorian Gray, "shall I not find in evil a life of its own?" The narrator rejects this philosophy, rushing past a fire in the streets: "I did not know whether it was hell or the furious love of God." "The Diabolist" first appeared in November 1907 in the *Daily News* and, along with a selection of other short fiction, was published in *Tremendous Trifles* in 1909.

After leaving the Slade, Chesterton found work in the publishing house Redway and then with T. Fisher Unwin, where he remained until 1902. He met Frances Blogg in 1896 and married her in 1901. Two volumes of his poetry appeared in 1900, *Greybeards at Play* and *The Wild Knight and Other Poems;* neither was a financial success, but the early years of the new century marked Chesterton's entry into the world of professional journalism, and he began to contribute essays and short stories to a variety of journals. In 1902 the *Daily News* gave Chesterton an opinion column; in 1905 he moved to a weekly column in the *Illustrated London News,* which he would write for the next 30 years. Chesterton's writing career was prolific and diverse, with 80 books, 4,000 essays, and more than 200 short stories to his credit. His love of argument, inculcated at St. Paul's, led to a series of public debates with many of the eminent wits of his age, most notably George Bernard Shaw and H. G. Wells, both of whom became lifelong friends despite their often extreme differences of opinion on spiritual, literary, and political matters. Chesterton's reputation as an apologist for Christian orthodoxy is perhaps his most enduring intellectual legacy, and many of his essays on spiritual life remain in print. *Orthodoxy*, subtitled "The Romance of Faith" and published in 1908, "is not an ecclesiastical treatise but a sort of slovenly autobiography," as Chesterton writes in the introduction. Dale Alquist, president of the American Chesterton Society, argues for *Orthodoxy*'s centrality to the Chesterton oeuvre. The essay/narrative of Chesterton's journey from the "insanity" of reason to the "paradox" of faith "is a mystery. It is a knot that cannot be untied. But while the modern intellectual may choke on the paradox, it is the daily bread of the common man. Because the common man has something that the modern intellectual is sadly lackin: common sense" (Alquist, 25). Chesterton converted to Roman Catholicism in 1922, at age 48, and was an eloquent defender of the faith for the rest of his life.

Chesterton is most famous for Father Brown, the unassuming hero of 49 short detective stories. Chesterton began writing about the Catholic priest who moonlights as an amateur sleuth in 1911, when he published the first of five collections, *The Innocence of Father Brown*. Father Brown follows in the footsteps of ARTHUR CONAN DOYLE's Sherlock Holmes, but he represents the common man, without the aesthetic excesses and scientific precision of Doyle's character. Father Brown solves crimes through his insights into the shared condition of humanity as a fallen people; all are sinful, and all are capable of redemption. In "The Secret of Father Brown" (1927), the small, shabbily dressed priest explains that he is able to solve crimes because he has committed them himself, not literally yet not figuratively, either: "I mean that I thought and thought about how a man might come to be like that, until I realized that I really was like that, in everything except actual final consent to action" (*Best of Father Brown*, 5). Through Christian empathy he is able to understand the motivations of the killers and thieves who populate the stories, and therefore Father Brown is granted insight into both the crimes and the follies of human existence that they represent.

Father Brown represents a sort of Everyman with a keen eye, and the stories are perfect puzzles of human motivation, in which every necessary clue to solving the puzzle is set before the reader. Father Brown's instincts are generally sharper than those of the average reader, yet the final revelation is always something that anyone mindful of the clues and insightful about human nature could have discovered for himself. This accessibility makes the Father Brown stories unusual in the genre of detective fiction, which often introduces plot elements in order to produce the final revelation. Chesterton considered these conventional last-minute plot twists insulting, insisting that readers enjoy being fooled but not tricked. As Alquist writes, Chesterton "loved being surprised to learn that the countess had killed the professor. But he hated to be introduced to the countess for the first time at the very tail end of the story" (163).

Large in body (6′4″ and weighing nearly 300 lbs.) and large in reputation during his lifetime, Chesterton today receives scant critical attention, and while much of his work remains in print, his stories are not often included in the major student anthologies. Two critical journals, the *Chesterton Review,* distributed by the Intercollegiate Studies Institute, and *Gilbert Magazine,* published by the American Chesterton Society, work to keep his philosophies and his literature in the public eye. While much of the critical literature devoted to Chesterton remains hagiographic in nature, recent studies such as Mark Knight's *Chesterton and Evil* (2004) and John Coates's *G. K. Chesterton as Controverialist, Essayist, Novelist and Critic* (2002) place Chesterton within the slippery cultural context of the first decades of the 20th century. Knight argues convincingly that Chesterton's work is undervalued in part because he cannot be located "within the framework of modernism" (2) and suggests that the Edwardian period is critically neglected as the space of transition from the fin de siècle culture of the decadents to the modernism of Bloomsbury and Joyce. Falling into a space between major cultural movements and belonging to neither, Chesterton is perceived as culturally conservative and distinctly middlebrow in his concerns. Alquist's *The Apostle of Common Sense* celebrates Chesterton for his wit and wisdom and for the timely relevance of his spiritual guidance in an increasingly secular world. (See also "The SECRET GARDEN," "The HAMMER OF GOD," and "The BLUE CROSS.")

BIBLIOGRAPHY

Alquist, Dale *G. K. Chesterton: The Apostle of Common Sense*. San Francisco: Ignatius Press, 2003.

Chesterton, G. K. *All Things Considered*. London: Methuen & Co., 1908.

———. *Autobiography*. London: Burns, Oates and Washbourne, 1937.

———. *The Best of Father Brown*. London: Dent, 1987.

———. *The Club of Queer Trades*. London: Penguin Books, 1984.

———. *The Incredulity of Father Brown*. Harmondsworth, England: Penguin Books, 1958.

———. *The Innocence of Father Brown*. Oxford: Oxford University Press, 1988.

———. *The Man Who Knew Too Much*. London: Darwen Finlayson, 1961.

———. *Orthodoxy*. London: Bodley Head, 1927.

———. *The Scandal of Father Brown*. London: Cassell, 1935.

———. *The Secret of Father Brown*. Harmondsworth, England: Penguin Books, 1974.

———. *Tales of the Long Bow*. London: Cassell, 1925.

———. *Tremendous Trifles*. New York: Dodd, Mead and Co., 1909.

———. *The Wisdom of Father Brown*. Harmondsworth, England: Penguin Books, 1974.

Coates, John. *Chesterton and the Edwardian Cultural Crisis*. Hull, England: Hull University Press, 1984.

———. *G. K. Chesterton as Controversialist, Essayist, Novelist and Critic*. Lampeter, Wales: Edwin Mellen Press, 2002.

Conlon, Denis J., ed. *G. K. Chesterton: A Half Century of Views*. Oxford: Oxford University Press, 1987.

Coren, Michael. *Gilbert: The Man Who Was G. K. Chesterton*. London: Jonathan Cape, 1989.

Ffinch, Michael. *G. K. Chesterton: A Biography*. London: Weidenfeld & Nicolson, 1986.

Knight, Mark. *Chesterton and Evil*. New York: Fordham University Press, 2004.

Pearce, Joseph. *Wisdom & Innocence: A Life of G. K. Chesterton*. San Francisco: Ignatius Press, 2001.

Lisa Weihman

CHRISTIE, AGATHA (AGATHA MARY CLARISSA MILLER CHRISTIE MALLOWAN) (1890–1976)

Agatha Christie is one of the most popular detective fiction writers of the 20th century. She wrote 76 novels, 158 short stories, and 15 plays. She also wrote and published several books of poetry.

Born in Torquay, England, on September 15, 1890, at the family home Ashfield to Clara "Clarissa" Miller (neé Boehmer) and Frederick Alvah Miller, Agatha was the third and last child in the family. She was educated at home until her mother decided that she should go to a finishing school in Paris in 1906 at age 16. In 1910, she left finishing school and returned to live with her mother at Ashfield; her father had died in 1901. As a young woman in her early 20s, Agatha had many proposals of marriage but finally accepted Archibald Christie, an officer in the Royal Flying Corps. They were married on December 24, 1914, and two days later Archibald left for the war. Agatha Christie was 24 and already working as a volunteer nurse at Torbay Hospital in Torquay. While working at the hospital Christie was offered a position working in the dispensary. It is clear from reading her autobiography, published posthumously in 1977, that working in the dispensary contributed to her knowledge and understanding of how to use and administer drugs of all kinds, especially poisons. While she worked in the dispensary she began writing her first detective novel, *The Mysterious Affair at Styles* (1920).

Encouraged by her husband, Agatha Christie submitted her first novel for publication to Methuen. Methuen rejected the manuscript, citing that it was not suitable material for the press; after trying another publisher, Christie finally settled on The Bodley Head. Published in 1920, this novel introduced one of literature's most famous detectives, second only to Sherlock Holmes, Hercule Poirot. Her first novel sold 2,000 copies, but Christie only received £25 for her efforts. Under her contract with The Bodley Head she had no royalty rights, nor did she have serial rights to her work; the serial rights were sold to the *Weekly Times* for £50. Thus were the pitiful beginnings of what would ultimately become an illustrious literary career.

Archibald and Agatha Christie divorced in April 1928. Agatha Christie married her second husband, Max Mallowan, on September 11, 1930. Christie met Mallowan while visiting the archeologist Leonard Woolley and his wife, Katharine, in Iraq. Mallowan was 14 years younger than Agatha, but their marriage was far happier than her first. Throughout their marriage Agatha helped Max with his archeological work. She learned how to photograph the pottery that was unearthed at the sites and to catalog her husband's findings. Christie kept her first married name because her publishers, William Collins Sons and Co., Ltd., with whom she had signed in 1922, felt that she had made her literary reputation with that name and therefore, the name was important in continuing to please her reading public. However, in her private life she was always known as Mrs. Agatha Mallowan.

Christie was comfortable writing in different genres, and by the time she published her first novel she had already written many poems; a collection called *The Road of Dreams* was published in 1924. She published six novels under the pseudonym Mary Westmacott: *Giant's Bread* (1930), *Unfinished Portrait* (1934), *Absent in the Spring* (1944), *The Rose and the Yew Tree* (1948), *A Daughter's a Daughter* (1952), and *The Burden* (1956). Christie is also credited with writing the longest-running play on the London stage: *The Mousetrap*, written in 1951, opened on October 6, 1952, at the Theatre Royal, Nottingham; and the play is still being performed daily at its permanent home in London at St. Martins Theatre.

Whatever genre Christie was working with when writing her detective stories, her gifts was creating interesting puzzles for her readers to solve. It was unnecessary for readers to see the details of gory crimes; the excitement of a Christie story was unraveling the clues. What made Christie's stories so ingenious was her ability to complicate her plots in the simplest of ways. She deliberately sent the reader on a false trail by initially focusing on the real criminal as a prime suspect in a case. However, she would then produce clues that drew the reader's attention to an innocent person, easily leading the reader down the incorrect path. Christie's ability to manipulate the reader served her well; her detective fiction remains as popular today as it was when it was first published.

Although known primarily as a novelist, Christie was also a prolific short story writer. To retain her own and her reader's interest in the short stories, Christie took the opportunity to reintroduce readers to certain detectives whom she had already developed in her novels. In her first novel, *The Mysterious Affair at Styles,* she introduced her now famous Belgian detective, Poirot. Consequently, when she was asked to put together a book of short stories, she once again turned to Poirot. *Poirot Investigates* was published in 1924, and *The Big Four* was published in 1927. Both sets of short stories were mostly culled from the magazine the *Sketch,* albeit with a few stories written quickly to round out the two volumes.

It seems, however, that although Poirot was very popular with readers, Christie herself was disappointed that she had made him so old. This was a regret that she also had with Miss Jane Marple, who begins life in *The Murder at the Vicarage* (1930) at about 65 or 70, but then never grows any older. Christie also chose to publish four volumes in which she writes six stories each about her two famous detectives. These volumes are *The Regatta Mystery* (1939), *Three Blind Mice* (1950), *The Adventure of the Christmas Pudding* (1960), and *Double Sin* (1961).

Although Christie produced more than 158 short stories, she seems to have felt that this was an inadequate genre for the detective story. She writes in *An Autobiography* that "[t]he short-story technique, I think, is not really suited to the detective story at all. A thriller, possibly—but a detective story, no" (349). She goes on to explain that "the right length for a detective story is fifty-thousand words . . . [sometimes] . . . sixty thousand or seventy thousand are more acceptable" and palatable to the reading public (348). In other words, Christie believed that the novel was a better vehicle for her detective stories.

However, there are several detectives whom Christie never introduced in a novel and whom she developed only for the short story. She especially liked Mr. Harley Quin and Mr. Satterthwaite in *The Mysterious Mr. Quin* (1930). She wrote about Mr. Quin only when the mood struck her; he was a special character to her from her childhood, and therefore she refused to write a series of Mr. Quin stories for any one magazine. Mr. Parker Pyne in *Parker Pyne Investigates* (1934) is not a detective but a retired civil servant who considers himself concerned with matters of the heart. Christie also wrote two volumes of short stories that did not have detectives in their plots. *The Hound of Death* (1933) was a volume of stories about the supernatural world, and *The Listerdale Mystery* (1934) focuses on stories about deception and romantic love.

Agatha Christie was recognized formally for her literary achievements in 1956 when she was named a Commander of the British Empire. In 1971, she was further recognized for her place in English literature and the arts by being declared Dame of the British Empire by Queen Elizabeth II. She died on January 12, 1976, at age 85. (See also DETECTIVE FICTION.)

BIBLIOGRAPHY

Bunson, Matthew. *The Complete Christie: An Agatha Christie Encyclopedia.* New York: Pocket Books, 2000.

Christie, Agatha. *The Adventure of the Christmas Pudding.* London: William Collins Sons and Co., 1960.

———. *An Autobiography.* New York: Dodd, Mead, and Co., 1977.

———. *The Big Four.* London: William Collins Sons and Co., 1927.

———. *Double Sin.* New York: Dodd, Mead and Co., 1961.

———. *The Hound of Death.* London: William Collins Sons and Co., 1933.

———. *The Labours of Hercules.* London: William Collins Sons and Co., 1947.

———. *The Mysterious Mr. Quin.* London: William Collins Sons and Co., 1930.

———. *Parker Pyne Investigates.* London: William Collins Sons and Co., 1934.

———. *Partners in Crime.* London: William Collins Sons and Co., 1929.

———. *Poirot Investigates.* London: William Collins Sons and Co., 1924.

———. *The Regatta Mystery.* New York: Dodd, Mead and Co., 1939.

———. *The Road of Dreams.* London: Geoffrey Bles Publishers, 1924.

———. *Star over Bethlehem.* London: William Collins Sons and Co., 1965.

———. *Three Blind Mice.* New York: Dodd, Mead and Co., 1950.

Gill, Gillian. *Agatha Christie: The Woman and Her Mysteries.* New York: The Free Press, 1990.

Rowland, Susan. *From Agatha Christie to Ruth Rendell: British Women Writers in Detective and Crime Fiction.* Houndmills, England: Palgrave, 2001.

Barbara Tilley

CHRISTMAS CAROL, A CHARLES DICKENS (1843)

The first of CHARLES DICKENS's *Christmas Books, A Christmas Carol in Prose; Being a Ghost Story of Christmas* is a fairy-tale-like ghost story that has contributed much to the formation of the Christmas story as a genre. Written in October and November 1843, it was specifically produced for the Christmas season, which began to be transformed into and was increasingly commercialized as a family celebration during the mid-Victorian era. *A Christmas Carol* was followed by *The Chimes* (1844), *The Cricket on the Hearth* (1845), *The Battle of Life* (1846), and *The HAUNTED MAN* (1848).

The story recounts the miserly Ebeneezer Scrooge's spiritual transformation through four ghostly visitations. "[A] squeezing, wrenching, grasping, scraping, clutching, covetous, old sinner . . . secret, and self-contained, and solitary as an oyster," he is "an excellent man of business on the very day of [his partner's] funeral," which he "solemnised . . . with an undoubted bargain" (7–8). As the opening thus assures the reader of Jacob Marley's death seven years earlier, it moreover emphasizes Scrooge's spiritual death-in-life. Scrooge then ridicules his nephew's seasonal greetings, begrudges his clerk his half-holiday, and repulses charitable organizations, which he regards as interference with the natural "decrease [of] the surplus population" (12). He has little patience with the trappings or the spirit of Christmas: "every idiot who goes about with 'Merry Christmas' on his lips should be boiled with his own pudding, and buried with a stake of holly through his heart. He should!" (10).

At home in his "gloomy suite of rooms" (14), he finds them haunted, as the knocker is transformed into Marley's face. Scrooge soon hears an ominous clinking of chains, and Marley's ghost appears through the door, dragging, like a tail, a chain made of "cash-boxes, keys, padlocks, ledgers, deeds, and heavy purses wrought in steel" (17). The ghost's gothic paraphernalia have been updated to suit the Victorian businessman. Marley has come to warn Scrooge that his dead partner's fate might become his own, yet he promises hope of escape. Scrooge is to be haunted by three spirits: the Ghost of Christmas Past, the Ghost of Christmas Present, and the Ghost of Christmas Yet to Come. The first ghost takes Scrooge on a journey back in time, which reflects the Victorians' growing fascination with time travel. Scrooge sees "his poor forgotten self as he used to be" (27) at school and then working at a warehouse, increasingly eaten up by "the master-passion, Gain" (34). Vicariously reliving the past, he weeps over his childhood self, remembers his nephew as he sees his now-dead sister, and compares the joyful family Christmas of his old love with his own loneliness.

His sympathy with humankind reawakened, he welcomes the Ghost of Christmas Present to teach him another "lesson" (40). He is led to see the festive joy in the suburban dwelling of his clerk, Bob Cratchit, overshadowed by Tiny Tim's declining health, and with horror, he notices two wretched children, Ignorance and Want, the outgrowths of human indifference, attached to the ghost. The Ghost of Christmas Yet to Come proceeds to show him his own death, his corpse "plundered and bereft, unwatched, unwept, uncared for" (64). As Scrooge wakes up on Christmas Day, he rejoices in a new "glorious" day (72). Feeling reborn, he goes forth to send a prize turkey to the Cratchits, donates money, and becomes "as good a friend, as good a master, and as good a man, as the good old city knew" (76).

As its full title, *A Christmas Carol in Prose; Being a Ghost Story of Christmas,* promises, the story experiments with different genres (Miller, passim). The preface announces it as a "Ghostly little book" aimed to "raise the Ghost of an Idea" to "haunt [the readers'] houses pleasantly." While Ebenezer Scrooge is clearly meant to be frightened into compliance with the spirit of Christmas, the description of his encounters with the ghosts remains intently humorous, at times verging on the comical. Thus, when alerted to the "ponderous chain" that will fetter him after his death, "Scrooge glanced about him on the floor, in the expectation of finding himself surrounded by some fifty or sixty fathoms of iron cable" (19). Haunted by the ghost of his former bunsiness partner Jacob Marley, he likewise attempts to exorcise the vision by blaming it on a "disorder of the stomach": "You may be an undigested bit of beef, a blot of mustard, a crumb of cheese, a fragment of an underdone potato. There's more of gravy than of grave about you, whatever you are!" (18). Yet his jokes, as his reliance on a commonsense rejection of the supernatural, quickly wear thin. If Scrooge dismissed the Christmas spirit with his famous exclamation, "Bah! [. . .] Humbug!" (9), in the opening chapter,

after the first visitation, he "tried to say 'Humbug!' but stopped at the first syllable" (22).

The story's popularity has rested as much in the brilliant simplicity of the tale as in its evocation of 19th-century London and Victorian Christmas festivities. Peter Ackroyd speaks of "the poor, the ignorant, the diseased, the wretched" beyond the hearth, who induce us to "enjoy the flames of the Christmas fire more because of the very shadows which it casts" (414). Yet its themes have also been seen as peculiarly modern and ultimately contemporary. The 1988 film *Scrooged,* starring Bill Murray, recast Dickens's tight-fisted businessman as a successful yuppie; a 2000 film version more directly turned him into a loan shark. The countless adaptations also include a Disney production in 1983, with Scrooge McDuck appropriately playing Scrooge; *The Muppet Christmas Carol* (1992); and *Blackadder's Christmas Carol* (1988), evincing the extent to which Scrooge's story (Davis, passim) has entered popular culture.

BIBLIOGRAPHY

Ackroyd, Peter. *Dickens.* London: Sinclair-Stevenson, 1990.
Collins, Philip. "The Reception and Status of the *Carol,*" *Dickensian* 89 (1993): 170–172.
Davis, Paul. *The Lives and Times of Ebenezer Scrooge.* New Haven: Yale University Press, 1990.
Dickens, Charles. *Christmas Books.* Edited by Eleanor Farjeon. 1954. Reprint, London: Oxford University Press, 1966.
Miller, J. Hillis. "The Genres of *A Christmas Carol,*" *Dickensian* 89 (1993): 193–206.

Tamara Wagner

"CLAP HANDS, HERE COMES CHARLIE" Beryl Bainbridge (1985)

The decline of British power and influence in the international sphere following World War II was paralleled by substantial changes in life in Britain. The cherished, if idealistic, version of England as a "green and pleasant land" was subject to the strains of postwar urban development, and the concept of a common culture that comforted even those who were essentially excluded from most of its benefits began to dissolve in the face of radical changes accelerated by the rise of a surly, disaffected generation seething with contempt for the traditional symbols of English life.

BERYL BAINBRIDGE's "Clap Hands, Here Comes Charlie" focuses on a working-class family riven by a generational divide that is intensified by their precarious economic status and compounded by a clash in cultural values. Charlie Henderson, the middle-aged "head" of the household, lives in a state of permanent vexation at his inability to provide either a sufficient income or any sense of direction for his family. His son Alec, still living at home and educated beyond his employment prospects, maintains a mordantly ironic perspective toward everything. Mrs. Henderson, a cleaning woman, tries to encourage a relatively civil level of discourse in their high-rise apartment but is nonplussed by Alec's apparent total disrespect for his father. For Charlie, the real problem is that they no longer live "in a proper house"; he regrets the absence of a garden plot, an accessible street, even windows that can be opened—small but significant symbols of the old ways. The benefits of efficient plumbing no longer seem sufficient compensation for living "as though inside the cabin of an aeroplane."

As the story opens, Mrs. Henderson has been given tickets to a performance of *Peter Pan* by an employer who feels that offering money as a Christmas bonus "is so degrading," although Mrs. Henderson, aware of the necessity for adequate compensation for labor, "had never, when accepting money, felt degraded." On the night of the performance, the Hendersons are joined by their daughter Moira and her uncontrollable son Wayne; this begins a continuing series of small crises involving Alec's wild driving and Charlie's futile attempts to gain some degree of control over Alec's antics. During the trip, Charlie begins to muse about how much the area has changed, recalling with nostalgic fondness "men playing football in the street" of a living village, to which Alec rejoins that the "whole area had never been anything but a slum," dismissing Charlie's recollections as "Never-never land."

The reference to J. M. Barrie's well-known play *Peter Pan* leads toward the second part of the story. Here, the narrative moves from an omniscient perspective to a detailed record of Charlie's responses as the play commences. Charlie finds the first act "old fashioned and cosy," and then dozes through the second and third acts, dreaming of fishing in an old canal where "a damn big crocodile crawled up the bank with a clock ticking inside it." During the intermission, Alec interprets the action as "obvious. Mr. Darling longs to murder his offspring," declaring, "Like fathers in real life. They're always out to destroy their children," to which Charlie hisses "He talks a load of codswallop. I'd like to throttle him."

As the play approaches its famous conclusion, Charlie suffers a heart attack, receding into unconsciousness as the audience is exhorted to "clap for Tinkerbell." While the entire audience is totally captivated by the imaginative power of the dramatic presentation, Charlie's gasps for help are dismissed as a distraction. "Shut up, Charlie," Mrs. Henderson cries, in thrall to the entreaties of Peter Pan to revive Tinkerbell while Charlie, a veritable "lost boy," slides away from a world in which he no longer has a place.

BIBLIOGRAPHY

Bainbridge, Beryl. *Collected Stories*. London: Penguin, 1994.

Leon Lewis

CLASS

Class is a key dimension of character and a principal motivator of conflict in British fiction. In sociology the term refers to socioeconomic distinctions causally related to differences in power and opportunity, applying to groups and individuals distinguished by their class positions: upper (aristocratic), middle (professional), and working (manual labor). The most prominent and controversial approach to the issue of class derives from Karl Marx and Friedrich Engels's mid-19th-century declaration in *The Communist Manifesto* that "the history of all hitherto existing societies is the history of class struggles." This claim sets the tone for Marxist literature and criticism and for an emphasis on class consciousness in the analysis of culture. Class analysis in this lineage has provided a model for dealing with other dimensions of social difference, including those relating to gender, ethnicity, language, and culture. While other prominent theories of class (for instance, those of Max Weber) have influenced literary criticism, Marxist materialism, emphasizing the primacy of "objective conditions," allows cultural processes and products to be judged in terms of the economic realities present to subjects inside and outside the text. Seen in this light, fiction and criticism draw attention either to or away from the existence of class difference, tension, or animosity.

While class distinctions may have diminished in importance in British society, especially through the 20th century, fiction in the British tradition may be regarded as typically class-conscious compared with writing from the United States. In the pre-Victorian period class difference and distinction were major themes in the works of Jane Austen, especially *Pride and Prejudice* (1813). Mary Shelley's *Frankenstein* (1818) may be read as a study of class creation (the birth of the proletariat) brought on by the Industrial Revolution. Later Emily Brontë's 1847 *Wuthering Heights* provides a poignant study of the ruinous interaction of romantic interests and class consciousness, while many of ANTHONY TROLLOPE's stories focus on the trials and tribulations of the new professional middle-classes—lawyers, clergymen, doctors, engineers—and their attempts to rise in the world. Elsewhere the most prominent fiction writers dealing with class relations are ELIZABETH GASKELL and CHARLES DICKENS. At the end of the century an interest in the aristocracy makes itself felt in OSCAR WILDE's writings of the 1890s; here the aristocracy, who live off the income from land, are objects of glamor, admiration, and deference but also satire. In contrast, ARTHUR CONAN DOYLE's Sherlock Holmes character, though himself a Bohemian, serves middle-class interests, protecting society threatened by such clever evil-doers as Dr. Moriarty. By this time, thanks in part to the interest in naturalism, writers like ARTHUR MORRISON and ISAAC ZANGWILL had begun to focus their attention on working-class characters and problems.

Although striking encounters between the classes occur in E. M. FORSTER's "ARTHUR SNATCHFOLD" and KATHERINE MANSFIELD's "The GARDEN-PARTY," it has been argued that D. H. LAWRENCE is the most class-conscious of 20th-century short story writers. In Lawrence's "The HORSE DEALER'S DAUGHTER," the money nexus in class mobility is clearly sketched in Mabel's situation: "[S]o long as there was money, the girl felt herself established, and brutally proud, reserved." Through the character of an ailing doctor, Jack Fergusson, the story also provides the reader with a view into working-class life, a view characteristic of Lawrence's works more generally: "Nothing but work, drudgery, constantly hastening from dwelling to dwelling among the colliers and iron-workers." However, the story also points out the dignity of labor: "It was a stimulant to him to be in the homes of the working people, moving as it were through the innermost body of their life. His nerves were excited and gratified. He could come so near, into the very lives of the rough, inarticulate, powerfully emotional men and women."

The clash between particular class interests is also a theme in SOMERSET MAUGHAM's 1926 story "The Outstation," in which the context of colonial Malaya allows issues of class and race to interact. The resident's life and duties as the highest authority in a remote area are ones in which class position and mobility, as they exist in England, have no relevance, yet class was and is always Mr. Warburton's principal motivation: "It was marvelous to watch the ingenuity he used to mention his distant relationship to the noble family he belonged to; but never a word did he say of the honest Liverpool manufacturer from whom, through his mother, a Miss Gubbins, he had come by his fortune. It was the terror of his fashionable life that at Cowes, maybe, or at Ascot, when he was with a duchess or even with a prince of the blood, one of these relatives would claim acquaintance with him." Through this protagonist we see class pretensions and the sheen of noble birth presented as all-encompassing and powerful. Warburton's antagonist is his assistant Cooper, a man born and bred in the colonies, who dresses in the native style but finds himself in constant and finally fatal conflict with the Malays because—according to Warburton—he cannot "draw the line." On meeting Warburton, Cooper expresses the view that "the war has done one good thing for us. . . . It's smashed up the power of the aristocracy." He expounds for his superior's benefit his vision of a snob-free, if not classless, future, "a business government by business men. I was born in a Crown Colony and I've lived practically all my life in the colonies. I don't give a row of pins for a lord. What's wrong with England is snobbishness. And if there's anything that gets my goat it's a snob." When Warburton's request to his superiors to have Cooper removed is refused, he is told that he attaches too much importance to a man's position and that times have changed.

Changing attitudes also make themselves felt, albeit more slyly, in P. G. WODEHOUSE's comic Jeeves stories of the 1920s and 1930s. Here the idle aristocracy on the wane has a duty to keep up impressions but may not be in the best position to know how this is done. Bertie Wooster's man Jeeves—"a brainy chap"—is not only is constantly lauded as more intelligent than his boss but has a better conception than his master of how a Wooster can fulfill the gentlemanly expectations his extended family and society have of him. The fun is in the contradictions implied by this class collaboration, the function of which is to keep the world in proper order. The Jeeves stories provide the middle-class reader with a fantasy of the idle life and the American reader with a fantasy of the old English world of immutable values. In either case an opportunity is afforded to read the world's uncomfortable bustle from above.

After World War II, the class map of Britain slowly changed, "removing many of the frameworks through which social roles and English identities had once been defined," as Randall Stevenson puts it in *The Last of England?*, his study of the period from 1960 to 2000. Yet it is still the case, as Stevenson argues, that "England did end the period as it began, with social stratifications still more clear-cut than almost anywhere else in the world" (3). Differences in accent still remain, as does the presence of what we might call, for want of a better word, an "under-class," people disenfranchised, unemployed, and living outside the system. In fictional terms, class, law, and multiple forms of transgression have provided themes for WILL SELF and for IRVINE WELSH's stories in *The Acid House* (1994). Welsh's working-class characters are presented as routinely beyond the law. In the story "The Shooter," class and dialect are conflated, so that the protagonist narrator slips seamlessly in and out of the story's framing dialogue. First-person narration distinguishes the protagonist from the dangerous Gal, in whose service he appears to be half-willingly enlisted. Gal is newly released from prison and is a character with scores to settle. Despite the first-person delivery, the protagonist appears to have quite different intellectual and class pretensions when in dialogue and when narrating.

—So what're ye saying, Gal?
—Either we forget it, or we make him take us seriously

I let his words play round inside my head, checking and double-checking their implication, an implication in reality I had instantly recognized.
—So what dae we dae?

Just as D. H. Lawrence's medical man in "The Horse Dealer's Daughter" offers the middle-class reader a glimpse of the grimier life, so in Welsh's story the vicarious excitement of danger among the under-class is easily conveyed through identification with a character capable of educated middle-class diction. Ability to intellectualize guarantees in the end, however, neither moral nor tactical advantage. The protagonist ends the story with a sawn-off shotgun pointed in his face, accompanied with the words, "I heard that you were seeing quite a bit of my missus when I was inside mate."

BIBLIOGRAPHY

Lawrence, D. H. *England, My England and Other Stories.* London: Penguin, 1995.

Marx, Karl, and Friedrich Engels. *The Communist Manifesto.* Edinburgh: Edinburgh University Press, 1998.

Maugham, W. Somerset. *The Collected Short Stories.* London: Penguin, 1977.

Stevenson, Randall. *The Last of England? Oxford English Literary History. 1960–2000.* Oxford: Oxford University Press, 2004.

Welsh, Irvine. *The Acid House.* London: Cape, 1994.

Wiener, Martin. *English Culture and the Decline of the Industrial Spirit 1850–1980.* Cambridge: Cambridge University Press, 1981.

Wolfreys, Julian, and William Baker, eds. *Literary Theories.* London: Macmillan, 1996.

Christoper Kelen

CLIFFORD, LUCY (1846–1929)
The widow of a celebrated mathematician, William K. Clifford (d. 1879), Lucy (Mrs. W. K.) Clifford wrote novels and plays to support herself and their two young daughters. She was close friends with HENRY JAMES and many other literary personalities of the day. She became

famous in her own right with her novel *Mrs. Keith's Crime* (1885), in which a terminally ill widow kills her dying daughter instead of leaving her to die alone. The novel was striking for its first-person narrative, which looks forward to the stream-of-consciousness technique adopted by the next generation of modernist writers. Many of Clifford's other novels concern vulnerable women who are brutalized by men or women but find the strength of character to act according to their consciences rather than societal expectations. Disparaged in later life by an envious VIRGINIA WOOLF as a hack, Clifford was nonetheless a skillful and innovative writer who achieved a good deal of popularity. Publishing short stories in a variety of popular magazines gave her a wide audience, even though her work was often considered depressing in its refusal to romanticize male-female relationships. Clifford's work fell out of favor after WORLD WAR I but recent reevaluations have begun to place her work in the tradition of NEW WOMAN writers, thanks to her portrayals of independent women struggling for survival in a world that does not value them. These include "The END OF HER JOURNEY" (1887) and the novella "A Woman Alone" (1898). Notable too are her stories for children, including "The Mother" and "Wooden Tony," the study of an autistic child.

BIBLIOGRAPHY

Chishol, Monty, and Marysa Demoor, eds. *"Bravest of Women and Finest of Friends": Henry James' Letters to Lucy Clifford.* Victoria, Canada: University of Victoria, 1999.

Clifford, Lucy. *Anyhow Stories, Moral and Otherwise.* London: Warne, 1882.

———. *The Last Touches and Other Stories.* London: Black, 1892.

———. *A Woman Alone.* London: Macmillan, 1898.

DeMoor, Marysa. "Self-Fashioning at the Turn of the Century," *Journal of Victorian Culture* 4 (1999): 276–291.

Silver, Anna K. "The Didactic Carnivalesque in Lucy Lane Clifford's The Mother," *Studies in English Literature* 40, no. 4 (2000): 727–737.

Andrew Maunder

COCK AND BULL WILL SELF (1992)

A literary sensation on the strength of his breakout collection of interwoven short stories—1991's *The Quantity The-ory of Insanity*—WILL SELF continued to impress with 1992's *Cock and Bull,* a pair of novellas that take conventional notions of gender and turn them inside out. Inspired by Kafka's *The Metamorphosis,* in which Gregor Samsa wakes up one day to find himself turned into a giant insect, Self offers the story of Carol, a woman whose clitoris lengthens into a penis, and John Bull, a man who grows a vagina behind his knee. In both cases Self examines the impact these physical metamorphoses have on the gender identity of his protagonists. Critics and reviewers did not quite know what to make of *Cock and Bull*'s absurdist premise. Some applaud its playful approach to gender (Harbord). Others accuse it of being too clever by half and of using dexterous wordplay to obscure what is a vulgar sort of determinism (Kakutani). The confusion is understandable because the author himself claims to be undecided, explaining that, when asked what the story is about:

> I'd give various answers: that it was about my rage with feminist arguments that all men are rapists by virtue of possessing the requisite weapon; that it was about the breakdown in gender distinctions which implied that all it was to be either one or the other was a mix and match of the requisite parts; that it was about my own nature, for, as Cocteau remarked, all true artists are hermaphrodites. (2006, 285)

Ultimately, Self suggests that the question can be boiled down to this: Is gender biologically or culturally determined? Taking Carol as our example, we can conclude that the answer is, quite simply, yes.

At first glance, Carol appears to be a blatant instance of biological determinism. Her growing penis provides a masculine sense of empowerment—"an acute awareness of a solid and mechanical species of causation in the world" (54)—while it also fuels her aggressive tendencies, culminating in rape. And yet Carol's metamorphosis has cultural rather than biological origins. Significantly, her penis emerges at the very moment she becomes aware of her hapless husband's shortcomings: Ruled by the bottle and his overbearing mother, Dan turns out to be not much of a man. His abdication

COLLECTIONS AND ANTHOLOGIES 77

of a strong male role leaves the relations between the sexes out of balance (at least, as traditionally conceived). Carol's penis thus emerges as a biological response to a cultural imperative, rushing in to fill the void left by Dan's deficient masculinity.

Cock is also about the nature of narrative itself, suggesting that the experience of gender needs to be understood as a story we tell about ourselves. Crucially, the story of Carol and hapless Dan comes to us at a remove. *Cock* is narrated to a nameless listener by a character described only as a fussy university don. His account of Carol's metamorphosis is increasingly interrupted by a variety of hateful rants, culminating in a vicious attack on his listener, who, as he is being raped, realizes that the don is none other than the newly empowered Carol. Her penis has prompted a masculinity that is toxic in its attitude toward otherness, which must be relentlessly feminized and dominated through both words and brute force.

If *Cock* concludes that the penis makes the man, *Bull* explores the impact of a wayward vagina on the lad. John Bull, British Everyman, wakes up one morning to find a vagina nestled behind his knee. Convincing himself that it is a burn or wound, Bull immediately consults his doctor. This is in sharp contrast to Carol, who, glorying in her "frond," has absolutely no intention of seeking treatment. Dr. Margoulies, Bull's sleazy general practitioner, calms his hysterical patient down, though he is less interested in his Bull's well-being than in the erotic potential of his new orifice, an obsession with tragicomic implications.

Beyond Bull and Carol's shocking transformation, their interactions with secondary characters provide occasion for Self to develop themes that he would continue to obsess over throughout the 1990s. Foremost among them is an abiding suspicion of the medical establishment's claims on what constitutes mental health. Starting with *The Quantity Theory of Insanity*, the target of Self's satire is the scientific obsession with measuring, classifying, quantifying—the indignities of attempting to reduce subjective experience to a function of objective knowledge. As such, two characters in particular come in for harsh treatment. Dave 2—Dan's Alcoholics Anonymous sponsor in *Cock*—is the perfect foil for Self's merciless send-up of the banal affirmations of therapy.

Meanwhile, Dr. Margoulies, who soothes Bull's anxiety over his "troublesome gash" while plotting his seduction, is a stand-in for the mendacity of modern medicine.

BIBLIOGRAPHY

Harbord, Janet. "Performing Parts: Gender and Sexuality in Recent Fiction and Theory," *Women: A Cultural Review* 7, no. 1 (Spring 1996), 39–47.
Kakutani, Michiko. "Comic Novellas on Metamorphoses," *New York Times,* 31 May 1993, p. 20.
Self, Will. *Cock and Bull.* London: Bloomsbury, 1992.
———. *Junk Mail.* New York: Black Cat, 2006.

Matt Kavanagh

COLLECTIONS AND ANTHOLOGIES

The rise of the periodical in the 19th and early 20th century fostered the development of the modern short story. It also spawned another literary genre, the short story collection. Because MAGAZINES refused to print stories already having appeared in collections, most writers of the period wrote stories expressly, if not exclusively, for magazine publication. Unlike the large advances publishers offered for novels, short story collections generated only minimal revenue for their authors through royalties based on a per-book basis. Nor did the genre offer much financial return for its publishers. Dean Baldwin's archival research has demonstrated that short story collections "seldom if ever became top sellers and frequently barely broke even" (37). Understandably then, short story collections accounted for less than 5 percent of new books published in Britain between 1919 and 1939 (40).

Still, a majority of prominent 19th- and early 20th-century writers published short story collections. The genre represented a stepping-stone to a successful career, particularly for young, unpublished writers looking to forge relationships in the literary marketplace. Forward-thinking publishers who recognized an as yet undiscovered talent would eagerly purchase an author's short stories at a relatively low price in exchange for first option on the author's first novel. One result of this process was, and continues to be, that most short story collections are editorially compiled miscellanies and do not constitute any coherent, aesthetic vision on the part of their authors. Such collections are often familiarly denoted by the titular convention "[name of first story in the collection] and Other Stories." For all of these reasons, scholars have traditionally disregarded the short story collection in discussions of modern literary genres, of which the novel is generally accepted as king.

But not all short story collections are compiled by editors, and when looked at from a certain perspective, the short story collection belongs to a generic lineage stretching back much farther than the continuous, linear narrative characteristic of the novel, which came into popular usage only in the 18th century. As a group of individual stories, the short story collection exhibits structural affinities with the tale-telling traditions of oral cultures. Works such as Homer's *Iliad* and *Odyssey* show that ancient storytellers, or singers, composed stories based around characters, events, or settings and performed them for groups. The epic sagas of ancient Ireland belong to groups known as story cycles. For example, stories related to the life of king Conchabar of Ulster belong to the Ulster cycle, and stories about the exploits of the warrior Finn MacCumaill belong to the Fenian Cycle. Religious texts such as the Bible, the Koran (Qur'an), and the Bhagavad Gita exhibit a similar structure to the short story cycle in that they are whole texts comprised of individual, often unconnected episodes.

An early British progenitor of the modern short story cycle was medieval cyclical drama. The York, Wakefield, Coventry, and Chester cycles make up the Corpus Christi plays. Each cycle dramatizes a different series of biblical events from Christ's birth to the Crucifixion and Resurrection. The cycles were performed on holidays, always in their entirety. More recent notable ancestors of the short story collection include lyric and epic cycles such as Chaucer's *Canturbury Tales* (1387–1400), Malory's *Le Morte d'Arthur* (1470), sonnet sequences of the Renaissance, and Alfred Lord Tennyson's *Idylls of the King* (1859). In the 19th century, the short story collection developed alongside another composite form, the Victorian poem sequence, of which Elizabeth Barrett Browning's *Sonnets from the Portuguese* (1850), George Merideth's *Modern Love* (1862), and Robert Browning's *The Ring and the Book* (1868–69) are examples.

In many cases, the periodical format itself encouraged authors to compose stories linked by character, setting, or theme. If one story achieved popularity, a magazine editor was likely to ask its author to submit another related story. This practice naturally led to the advent of the village sketch tradition, the nearest precursor to the modern short story collection. Britain's MARY RUSSELL MITFORD's *Our Village* (1824) represents an early village sketch collection. More prominent examples of the genre include ELIZABETH GASKELL's *CRANFORD* (1853), GEORGE ELIOT's *Scenes of Clerical Life* (1858), Jane Barlow's *Irish Idylls* (1893), and GEORGE MOORE's *The Untilled Field* (1903). Arnold Bennett notably carried on this tradition into the 20th century in *The Grim Smile of the Five Towns* (1905) and his subsequent Five Towns collections. Generally speaking, though, the village sketch achieved greater prominence in America, with writers such as Washington Irving, Nathaniel Hawthorne, and Herman Melville.

By the late 19th century, many authors began experimenting with different ways of composing and arranging their stories for volume publication without external pressure from the periodical marketplace. HENRY JAMES perhaps provides the best example. In *Terminations* (1895), *Embarrassments* (1895), and *The Better Sort* (1903), he experimented with a variety of unifying techniques that he brought together to integrate his most mature short story collection, *The Finer Grain* (1910). Many modernist authors followed James in constructing highly integrated short story collections of the highest aesthetic order. JAMES JOYCE's *DUBLINERS* (1914) is the most important, but D. H. LAWRENCE's *The PRUSSIAN OFFICER AND OTHER STORIES* (1914) and VIRGINIA WOOLF's *MONDAY OR TUESDAY* (1921) are worthy of note.

Britain's most prodigious 20th-century short story writers often composed stories in groups and published collections exhibiting varying degrees of unity. Prominent early 20th-century British short story collections include H. E. BATES's *The Black Boxer: Stories* (1932), A. E. COPPARD's *Silver Circus* (1928), ALDOUS HUXLEY's *Mortal Coils: Five Stories* (1922) and *Brief Candles* (1930), Liam O'Flaherty's *Spring Sewing* (1924), and V. S. PRITCHETT's *When My Girl Comes Home* (1961) and *ON THE EDGE OF THE CLIFF* (1980).

Authors of short story collections from around the world are indebted to the 19th-century Russian masters. Alexander Pushkin's *Tales of Belkin* (1831), Mikhail Lermontov's *A Hero of Our Time* (1840), and Ivan Turgenev's *Sportsman's Sketches* (1852) are among the most influential Russian examples of the genre.

In comparison with the continuous narrative of the novel form, scholars emphasize the short story collection's discontinuous, episodic nature and therefore its formal correspondence with modern life. James Nagel has argued that the genre is particularly well suited to expressing the disjuctive experiences of displaced ethnic minorities.

BIBLIOGRAPHY

Baldwin, Dean. "'Short Stories Don't Sell': British Short Story Collections, 1919–1939," *Short Story* 2, no. 1 (1991): 33–45.

Ingram, Forrest L. *Representative Short Story Cycles of the Twentieth Century: Studies in a Literary Genre.* The Hague: Mouton, 1971.

Nagel, James. *The Contemporary American Short-Story Cycle: The Ethnic Resonance of Genre.* Baton Rouge: Louisiana State University Press, 2001.

Aaron Zacks

COLLINS, WILLIAM WILKIE (1824– 1889)

Collins was born in London, the eldest son of the popular landscape painter, William Collins, R.A. At age 22, he was admitted as a law student to Lincoln's Inn; in 1851 he was called to the bar, though ultimately he never practiced law, deciding to pursue a literary career instead. In that same year, Collins met CHARLES DICKENS through a mutual friend, the artist Augustus Egg. Dickens invited Collins to perform in one of his amateur theatricals, a production of Bulwer-Lytton's play *Not So Bad as We Seem,* and for the next 16 years the two men were close personal friends, traveling companions, and valued colleagues. Collins frequently contributed to Dickens's journals, *Household Worlds* and *All the Year Round,* and between 1856 and 1861 he and Dickens also collaborated on a number of projects, including the dramatic version of *The Frozen Deep* (1856), "Perils of Certain English Prisoners" (1857), and the short story "No Thoroughfare" (1867). Despite this mutually rewarding relationship, for years

Collins was seen aesthetically as a kind of lesser Dickens, a protégé, critics claimed, whose work never quite matched the scope and finesse of his older mentor.

For someone who was master of the intricate plot, it is no surprise that Wilkie Collins himself lived a personal life that was more complicated than that of his fictional characters. Simultaneously maintaining two independent households, Collins lived with two women and chose to marry neither of them. In his later years, he circulated the polite fiction that one mistress, Caroline Graves, was his housekeeper, and when he visited his second mistress, Martha Rudd, with whom he had three children, he assumed the persona of William Dawson, Barrister. In addition to these sexual indiscretions, Collins was addicted to laudanum, regularly consuming doses reputedly strong enough to be fatal to those who were unaccustomed to the drug's effects. While those close to Collins knew the truth about his unconventional life, they managed to demonstrate true Victorian reserve by refusing to discuss his peccadilloes publicly.

For over a century, Wilkie Collins has been remembered primarily as the man who invented sensation fiction, and his literary reputation rested primarily on *The Woman in White* (1860), considered one of the best Victorian mystery novels, and *The Moonstone* (1872), generally acknowledged as the first English detective novel. However, during a literary career spanning four decades, Collins was quite prolific in a variety of genres: In addition to 25 novels, he wrote as many as 15 plays, over 50 short stories, and more than 100 articles.

Always something of a radical in his personal and professional life, Collins was more openly critical of Victorian social conventions and gender norms than most of his contemporaries. Many critics have made a compelling case for a transgressive Collins, noting the anarchic and asocial impulses that underscore so much of his fiction. In fact, Dickens, who serialized Collins's early work in his weekly journals, attempted to censor Collins's writing because of his tendency to be "unnecessarily offensive to the middle class" (quoted in Stang, 200). "Mad Monkton" for instance, a story that takes hereditary insanity as its subject, was rejected for publication in 1853 in *Household Words* because Dickens believed that it would offend the sensibilities of his readers. It was published a few years later in *Fraser's Magazine* and then subsequently included in Collins's second short story collection, *The Queen of Hearts* (1859).

Throughout his fiction, Collins explores the boundaries and margins of his culture's taboos, blurring the distinctions between dark and light, self and other, masculine and feminine, sanity and insanity, challenging and redefining the hierarchies and taxonomies that Victorian novelists so often reaffirm. Collins may very well be classified as the first modern Victorian, for much of his fiction centers on identity and alterity. Virtually every story Collins wrote contains doubles, doppelgangers, alter egos, and reflected selves. Moreover, his fictional world is one in which the inner mind is constantly manifesting itself in conscious and unconscious revelations; it is a world of dreams and somnambulism; it is a world marked by endless secrets—secret pasts, secret diaries and letters, secret selves; it is a world constantly under surveillance—spying, watching, eavesdropping. Though critics of his novel *Armadale* (1866) complained that Collins chose "vermin as his subjects" and reviewers of *No Name* (1862) found his sympathetic treatment of illegitimate, disinherited, and vengeful women "unwholesome," "perverse," and "polluting," Collins continued to explore the psyches of his "freaks" as fictional case studies of what it was like to be marginalized or cast as a misfit in Victorian England.

Collins repeatedly employs multiple narrators and multiple narrative techniques, and thus, as critics have noted, issues of inscription and textuality are also a key feature of his fiction. His texts, from the short story collection AFTER DARK (1856) through major works such as *The Woman in White* (1861), *The Moonstone* (1872), and *The Law and the Lady* (1875), are themselves textual montages—letters, affidavits, first-person accounts, diaries, wills, letters within diaries, letters within letters. His narrative technique is far more complicated, for instance, than the dual narrators Dickens employs in his great narrative experiment, *Bleak House* (1851), and was well in advance of the multivocal journal structure of BRAM STOKER's *Dracula* (1897).

While Collins's greatest literary successes were achieved in his novels, the many short stories he wrote, particularly those written early in his career, are significant contributions to the gothic tale of terror ("A TERRIBLY STRANGE BED") and the emerging form of the detective story ("The STOLEN LETTER"). While the formal constraints of the genre do not always allow for the labyrinthine plots or complex experiments in character development for which Collins was especially famous, his early tales, replete with deceit and duplicity ("The Lady of Glenwith Grange"), mystery and murder ("The DIARY OF ANNE RODWAY"), suspense and the supernatural ("The OSTLER"), and terror and tyranny ("Sister Rose"), clearly foreshadow many of the prevailing themes of his full-length fiction. And though these tales of terror and mystery may have been overshadowed by the popular success of his novels, they are nevertheless just as richly rewarding in their capacity to entertain and enthrall. To paraphrase the hard-to-please young woman who listens to the tales recounted in *The Queen of Hearts*, Collins's short stories seize hold of the reader's interest and keep her reading breathlessly until the very end.

Many of Collins's short stories were first published in various periodicals and then later collected in *After Dark* (1856) and *The Queen of Hearts* (1859), both of which feature an innovative framing narrative that links and attempts to unify the disparate stories. Two later collections, *Miss or Mrs? and Other Stories in Outline* (1873) and *Little Novels* (1887), also feature stories that had been publisher earlier in various American and English periodicals. (See also "WHO KILLED ZEBEDEE?")

BIBLIOGRAPHY

Clarke, William M. *The Secret Life of Wilkie Collins.* Chicago: Ivan R. Dee, 1988.

Collins, Wilkie. *Complete Short Fiction.* London: Constable, 1998.

———. *Mad Monkton and Other Stories.* Oxford University Press, 1998.

Nayder, Lillian. *Wilkie Collins.* New York: Twayne, 1997.

Peters, Catherine. *The King of Inventors: A Life of Wilkie Collins.* London: Secker and Warburg, 1991.

Pykett, Lynn. *Wilkie Collins (New Casebooks).* New York: St. Martin's, 1998.

Stang, Richard. *The Theory of the Novel in England.* New York: Columbia University Press, 1959.

Wilkie Collins Pages. Available online. URL: http://www.
    wilkiecollins.com. Accessed May 9, 2006.

Maria K. Bachman

"COMFORT, THE" James Kelman (1998)

"Contrary to what might be expected I have no time at
all for these macho-bastards, the kind that run about
chasing nooky—especially when they're 35 years old
and married for nearly ten years." Tommy, the cautiously upstanding narrator of James Kelman's "The
Comfort," contrasts his own maturity with the behavior of his philandering friend. Chic only visits when he
needs to avoid the wife he is cheating on; their alcohol-
fueled "male-bonding" is really just a way of evading
the responsibilities of adult relationships. As a middle-
aged divorcé, Tommy himself has no place in family
life, and because an unemployed single man is neither
husband nor father nor provider, he has no social or
economic function the authorities would recognize.

The two characters appear trapped in a situation
where all the avenues of traditional masculine authority
are blocked. They leave Tommy's flat for what seems
safer ground: the male preserve of the working-class
pub. But here they are immediately confronted with a
potent emblem for a useless, dependent masculinity: a
drunken man, skinny with white hair, dressed in "a pair
of joggers and one of these vests that show off yer biceps
but he was so fucking skinny the joggers needed braces."
The man's bared biceps, conventional signifiers of
strength and virility, become a mocking reminder of his
fragility and dissipation, just as his advanced age is made
ridiculous by his alcoholic degeneration to a childlike
incomprehension. Tommy sees a reckless immaturity in
the man, and his nagging warnings to Chic to "go careful in this place" cast him in the ideologically feminine
role of passive, hand-wringing observer. In a largely
unemployed working-class community that offers scant
for opportunity for "manly" proactiveness, certainty and
resolution, Kelman offers an uncomfortable picture of
male fragility and mutual dependence.

BIBLIOGRAPHY
Kelman, James. *The Good Times.* New York: Anchor Books,
    1999.

Scott Hames

"COMING OF ABEL BEHENNA, THE"
Bram Stoker (1914)   This story collected in the
posthumously published *Dracula's Guest* is about the
power of the past to haunt the present. Bram Stoker
also makes use of the plot device of the fatal return, a
popular narrative in many 19th-century texts. Most of
the action takes place in Pencastle, a small Edenic fishing port in Cornwall. The narrative is driven by the
demands made by the heroine, Sarah Trefusis, and her
greedy mother that, as a married woman, Sarah be provided with a comfortable lifestyle by one of her suitors,
Eric Sansom or Abel Behenna. Abel, having staked his
claim to Sarah by the lucky toss of a coin, dutifully
sails off to China and the East Indies to satisfy her hunger for money. Sarah while remembering her relationship with Abel, but having "woman's weaker nature,"
consoles herself with Eric. For his own selfish motives,
Eric persuades Sarah that Abel is dead. Having satisfied
herself that she can access the money freshly deposited
in Abel's bank account, Sarah agrees to replace Abel
with Eric. Two weeks before the wedding, there is a
violent storm and a ship is wrecked in the harbor.
Climbing aboard to help rescue the crew, Eric comes
face to face with one of them, Abel, and refuses to save
him. However, even when apparently out of the picture, Abel has the power to disrupt events, and he does
so on Eric and Sarah's wedding day, the day that was
supposed to be Abel and Sarah's wedding day. He
comes back from the most frightening destination of
all, death, to demand recognition of his rights—to
Sarah, to his money, and to the domesticity he has
been promised. The story ends when Abel's corpse is
discovered outside Eric's cottage, his hand outstretched
toward Sarah in a gesture of accusation.

There are several ways of interpreting the story.
Most obviously Abel's return from the dead and his
biting back, as it were, can be read as a bleak comment
on the failure of romantic love in a world full of competing individual appetites and ambitions. The story
can also be read as a narrative about exclusion.
Removed from Sarah, separated from her and from
Pencastle, Abel becomes a creature of margin as well as
burden. Once out of sight he is also out of mind, and
once Sarah has agreed to marry Eric, he can return
only as a troubling ghost. Reading out from the story

into the wider context of 1890s imperialism with which Stoker's readers would have been familiar, there are grounds for suggesting that this is also a cautionary story about imperial as well as domestic exploitation: Abel becomes part of the empire, spending his days in foreign lands and sending his hard-earned money back home. When he finally returns, an unexpected and unwelcome visitor glimpsed by terrified witnesses, he is represented in terms that emphasize his foreignness, or otherness: "a strange seaman whom no one knew," a "porpoise," a weird creature "like a pig with the entrails out" (117–18); he is no longer the handsome young man Sarah remembers but a less-than-human being who exists only to support the English home. Critics interested in issues of gender might also say that what makes this story especially interesting is the use it makes of the triangle configuration, so common to Victorian fiction, of one woman loved by two men; the woman marries the losing suitor after the first has disappeared. As a female character in a short story about male friendship written by a man, the function of Sarah seems fairly predictable: By captivating both men, this sadistic character allows Stoker once again to associate the figure of woman with death and destruction and moral emptiness. She is a life-denying rather than life-giving force. "[H]er one intention . . . was so to arrange matters that [she] . . . should get all that was possible out of both men." "'Both these men want ye,'" her mother tells her, "'and only one can have ye, but before ye choose it'll be so arranged that ye'll have all that both have got!'" (100). In this sense "The Coming of Abel Behenna" is a thoroughly misogynistic text in its analysis of male-female relations.

BIBLIOGRAPHY

Stoker, Bram. *Dracula's Guest and Other Weird Stories.* London: George Routledge, 1914.

Andrew Maunder

"COMPANY OF WOLVES, THE" ANGELA CARTER (1979) One of ANGELA CARTER's most famous short stories, "The Company of Wolves" was first published in the innovative and imaginative 1979 collection of fairy-tale themed stories, *The BLOODY CHAMBER.* "The Company of Wolves" skillfully inter-

weaves peasant superstitions, such as old wives' tales and folk remedies, with the Little Red Riding Hood theme, fully displaying Carter's penchant for myth, folklore, and fairy tales. Carter believed that folklore and literature represented "vast repositories of outmoded lies, where you can check out what lies used to be a la mode and find the old lies on which new lies are based" (quoted in Easton, 22). She also argued that throughout history, the process of storytelling has helped perpetuate a constructed, as well as a constricting, reality for each successive generation, which is especially evident in gender role mythology and its psychological implications. Therefore, with "The Company of Wolves," a provocative and sensual reimagining of "Little Red Riding Hood," Carter has crafted a tale that serves the dual function of both illustrating how expected cultural traditions are indoctrinated in future generations and challenging those expectations, which she accomplishes by altering the classic fairy tale.

"The Company of Wolves" begins by describing in poetic yet realistic prose the dangers of living in close proximity to the forest, especially in winter when the wolves are starving because "the wolf is carnivore incarnate and he's as cunning as he is ferocious" (212). Intermingled with the atmosphere of fear created by the wolf and the descriptions of the "grave-eyed children" who "always carry knives" (213) to protect themselves from these creatures, is werewolf lore, tales of humans who have been transformed into wolves. These tales, woven within the larger framework of the story, include the account of a witch who transforms the guests at a wedding banquet into wolves when the man she wishes to marry weds another. A second tale recounts the story of a woman whose husband went outside to urinate, only to disappear. When he returns several years later to learn that his wife has married another man and borne that man's children, he changes into a wolf once more. However, when this particular werewolf is chopped apart with a hatchet, his human form is visible beneath the wolf's skin. With these tales, Carter deftly illustrates the inherent metaphorical connection between man and beast. In myth, folklore, and fairy tales, the wolf has traditionally been representative of man's savage animal nature, and women have been considered merely their prey. However, that is not the case in Carter's fairy tale; in her rendering of Little Red Riding Hood, the wolf meets his match.

In "The Company of Wolves," although a little girl in a red cape journeys through the forest to her grandmother's house, she does not meet a wolf along the path but instead meets a handsome huntsman, who is really a wolf in the guise of a man. The two become acquainted as they walk through the forest and decide to have a race to see which one of them will arrive at Granny's cottage first. If the huntsman, who carries a compass, wins the race, he will be rewarded with a kiss. The huntsman arrives at Granny's house first and devours her, just like in the original fairy tale, but that is where the similarities end. Carter's version of "Little Red Riding Hood" features an erotic conclusion quite different from the more famous versions of the tale written by France's Charles Perrault and Germany's Grimm brothers. In Perrault's adaptation, Little Red Riding Hood and her grandmother are consumed by the wolf, never to be heard from again. In the Grimm brothers' version, the two are eaten by the wolf, only to be rescued—cut out of the wolf's belly—by a woodcutter. Instead, "The Company of Wolves" borrows its conclusion from the lesser-known oral version of the fairy tale, "The Story of the Grandmother," in which the character of Little Red Riding Hood performs a striptease for the wolf instead of becoming the wolf's victim. Reciting the memorable lines, including "what big teeth you have" (Carter, 219), Carter's Little Red Riding Hood ceremoniously removes her clothes and throws them into the fire as the wolves howl outside the cottage. In the end, rather than being devoured by the wolf, this Little Red Riding Hood, who "knew she was nobody's meat" (Carter, 219), climbs into bed with the wolf, allowing the reader to draw his or her own conclusions as to the outcome. Whether she joins the huntsman in his company of wolves is left undetermined, but at the very least, Carter's Little Red Riding Hood has acknowledged the beast within herself, a vital component of self-knowledge and a powerful statement for feminism, as it is a substantial representation of gender equality.

"The Company of Wolves" displays Carter's unique style, irreverent wit, and unrelenting ambiguity, but the story also exhibits Carter's astute observations about the effects of social and political ideologies on human existence, and on women in particular. For Carter, writing represented a way to contest or demythologize these ideologies that most people take for granted as truth. As Carter herself once said, "my life has been most significantly shaped by my gender. . . . I spent a good many years being told what I ought to think, and how I ought to behave, and how I ought to write, even, because I was a woman and men thought they had the right to tell me how to feel, but then I stopped listening and tried to figure it out for myself" (quoted in Easton, 2). And so she has: Although "The Company of Wolves" has the appearance of a rather archaic fairy tale, by revealing that the wolf is an innate beast that exists in both men and women, implying that an egalitarian society is the ultimate utopia, the ambiguous story ironically proves to be enlightening.

BIBLIOGRAPHY
Bristow, Joseph, and Trev Lynn Broughton, eds. *The Infernal Desires of Angela Carter: Fiction, Femininity, Feminism.* New York: Addison Wesley Longman Inc., 1997.
Carter, Angela. *Burning Your Boats: The Collected Short Stories.* New York: Penguin, 1995.
Easton, Alison, ed. *Angela Carter: New Casebooks.* New York: St. Martin's, 2000.
Gamble, Sarah. *Angela Carter: Writing from the Front Line.* Edinburgh: Edinburgh University Press, 1997.
Tucker, Lindsey, ed. *Critical Essays on Angela Carter.* New York: G. K. Hall & Co., 1998.

Trudi Van Dyke

CONRAD, JOSEPH (1857–1924) Joseph Conrad grew up with multiple senses of himself as Polish, French, English, Catholic, revolutionary, gentleman, seaman, and author. This cosmopolitan writer suffered from a perpetual sense of exile after spending much of his life wandering the globe—an anxiety seen in the concern of his characters as to who is "one of us." Józef Teodor Konrad Korzeniowski was born on December 3, 1857, in Berdyczew, a Ukrainian province of Poland under tsarist rule. Conrad's patriotic father, Apollo Korzeniowski, was arrested for involvement with a conspiratorial Polish group and was deported with his wife Ewa Bobrowska to the Russian town Vologda. Reading was a refuge for Conrad throughout these years in exile: "I don't know what would have become of me if I had not been a reading boy." After the early death of his parents from tuberculosis, Conrad remained in Poland with his uncle Tadeusz Bobrowski until age 17, when he announced a wish to become a sailor, formed in part from the seafaring romances of Frederick Marryat. In 1874 Conrad traveled to Marseille, where he sailed to the West Indies aboard French merchant ships and later worked as a carrier of illegal arms for Spanish Carlists. This phase of his life ended abruptly with a self-inflicted gunshot wound to the chest—what is thought to have been a suicide attempt, though Conrad explained the incident as the outcome of a duel.

Conrad knew no English until age 21. After arriving in Lowestoft, England, in 1878, he slowly acquired the language, passed the marine examinations, and became a British citizen in 1886. He wrote literature in English from then on: "You may take it from me that if I had not known English I wouldn't have written a line for print, in my life." He received encouragement from literary acquaintances Edward Garnett, Stephen Crane, H. G. WELLS, R. B. Cunninghame Graham, JOHN GALSWORTHY, and Ford Madox Ford, with whom he collaborated on two novels. During his 16 years with the British Merchant Service, he traveled the world's oceans to Europe, Asia, Australia, the Americas, and Africa. HENRY JAMES remarked of these travel experiences, "No one has known—for intellectual use—the things you know." A traumatic expedition as a steamboat captain for a trading company in the Belgian Congo (now Democratic Republic of the Congo) in 1890 seriously undermined his health and spirits. He went to sea just once more between 1890 and 1896, as chief mate of the *Torrens* carrying passengers to Australia, before returning to the manuscript he had been working on for the past five years. In 1896 he married Jessie George, with whom he had two sons, born in 1898 and 1906.

Conrad's literary career consists of three periods: the early phase of sea stories and Eastern settings (1895–1903), the middle phase of political themes and Western settings (1904–11), and the late phase of miscellaneous and retrospective writings (1912–24). His first novel, *Almayer's Folly: A Story of an Eastern River,* begun in 1888 and published in 1895, and *An Outcast of the Islands* (1896), vividly re-create Malaysian settings in which isolated Dutch traders suffer from ambition and failure, depicted through complex shifts in time and perspective. Reviewers compared these novels favorably to those of ROBERT LOUIS STEVENSON and RUDYARD KIPLING. Conrad's voyages aboard the *Vidar* throughout the Malay Archipelago also provided material for *Lord Jim* (1900), *Victory* (1915), *The Rescue* (1920), and numerous stories. A trip from Bombay to Britain in 1884 inspired *The Nigger of the "Narcissus": A Tale of the Sea* (1897), a novella rich in symbolism describing the black American sailor James Wait's morbid influence over a ship's crew. The novel's celebrated preface, published separately as *The Art of Fiction* in 1902, is a statement of Conrad's artistic intent to discover an essential reality behind appearances: "My task which I am trying to achieve is, by the power of the written word, to make you hear, to make you feel—it is, before all, to make you *see*."

Conrad's short fiction, which makes up 31 of 43 fictional works, is central to his literary reputation. The collection *TALES OF UNREST* (1898) consists of five stories serialized in magazines between 1896 and 1897. The African and Malaysian tales are the collection's best. "An Outpost of Progress" takes place in a remote trading post in central Africa, where two European traders unintentionally participate in the slave trade. The white narrator of the first Malay story, "THE LAGOON," reveals Arsat's guilty secret of family betrayal, and a former captain (who anticipates Conrad's narrator Marlow) narrates the second story, "KARAIN: A MEMORY," in which the respected chief Karain receives a coin from Queen Victoria's 1887 Jubilee as a charm to ward off the spirit of a murdered friend. The collection shares with the early novels its unifying themes of destructive obsessions and ethical lapses following failed romantic idealism within a colonial environment. Conrad conveys the psychological complexity of experience through an ornate descriptive style commonly referred to as literary impressionism.

Youth: A Narrative, and Two Other Stories (1902) portrays seamen in youth, maturity, and old age. Based on Conrad's experience aboard the *Palestine* from 1881 to 1883, "YOUTH: A NARRATIVE" is Marlow's nostalgic account of his first voyage at age 20 to the East, now seen with the ironic distance of an experienced seaman. The last story, "The End of the Tether," describes the moral decline of an aging steamboat captain who conceals his blindness from the ship's crew. It is the second story, HEART OF DARKNESS, written in February 1899, that is Conrad's most famous novella, upon which much of his reputation rests today. A fictional version of Conrad's experiences in Africa in 1890, the story is Marlow's vividly impressionistic account of a journey deep into Africa in pursuit of Kurtz, the legendary manager of the inner station whose moral ideas become a source of fascination to Marlow. Kurtz is the driving mystery of the narrative and has intrigued readers since the story appeared with his controversial behavior and enigmatic dying words. The story's ambivalent stance toward imperialism—Conrad has been both praised for criticizing European imperialism and accused of racism—has led to lively critical debates in recent decades.

The novella *Typhoon,* published in the *Pall Mall Magazine* in 1901 and in book form with "AMY FOSTER" in 1903, describes Captain McWhirr's efforts to guide the steamship *Nan-Shan* through a severe storm. "Falk: A Reminiscence" portrays a taciturn Scandinavian tugboat owner who confesses to cannibalism. An adaptation of the third story, "To-Morrow," was to become Conrad's first play, *One Day More* (1905). The later novels shift from Eastern maritime settings to Western political settings, as in *Nostromo: A Tale of the Seaboard* (1904), which describes a South American revolution, and *The Secret Agent: A Simple Tale* (1907), which describes a failed terrorist attack on the Greenwich Observatory. *A Set of Six* (1908) includes political stories set in disparate parts of the world, though their contrived plots are less admired than those of the early stories. "The SECRET SHARER: An Episode from the Coast" appeared in *Harper's* in 1910 before being republished with two other stories. One of Conrad's best, this story describes the meeting between an inexperienced young captain anchored in the Gulf of Siam and his alter ego Leggatt, an escaped prisoner from a nearby ship who persuades the captain to help him escape.

These were difficult years for Conrad, troubled as he was by depression and gout, his wife's knee injury, and

financial strains. Conrad suffered a nervous breakdown in 1910 after completing *Under Western Eyes* (1911) and moved to Capel House in Ashford, Kent. The collection *'Twixt Land and Sea: Tales* (1912) returned to sea stories about challenges faced by inexperienced captains. The storyteller Marlow returns in *Chance: A Tale in Two Parts* (1913), which became a best-seller in America. Similar themes of love and violence recur throughout the story collection *Within the Tides: Tales* (1915). While the last decade of his life brought professional success to a writer who had struggled financially throughout his career, the late fiction suffers from sentimentality, tendentiousness, and overplotting. The outbreak of war in 1914 forced the Conrads to cut short a visit to Poland and agonized a man with allegiances to multiple European countries. He afterward wrote *The Shadow-Line: A Confession* (1917), four more novels, and several stories published posthumously in 1925 as *Tales of Hearsay.* Conrad died of a heart attack on August 3, 1924, at age 66.

BIBLIOGRAPHY
Conrad, Joseph. *Complete Short Stories of Joseph Conrad.* Edited by Samuel Hynes. New York: Ecco, 1992.
———. *The Mirror of the Sea: Memories and Impressions.* London: Methuen, 1906. New York: Harper, 1990.
———. *A Personal Record.* New York: Harper, 1912.
Guerard, Albert J. *Conrad the Novelist.* Cambridge, Mass.: Harvard University Press, 1958.
Knowles, Owen, and Gene M. Moore, eds. *The Oxford Reader's Companion to Conrad.* Oxford and New York: Oxford University Press, 2000.
Leavis, F. R. *The Great Tradition: George Eliot, Henry James, Joseph Conrad.* London: Chatto and Windus, 1948.
Meyers, Jeffrey. *Joseph Conrad: A Biography.* New York: Scribner, 1991.
Stape, J. H., ed. *The Cambridge Companion to Joseph Conrad.* Cambridge and New York: Cambridge University Press, 1996.

Matthew Rubery

CONSTITUTIONAL HELEN SIMPSON (2005)
In the title story of HELEN SIMPSON's fourth collection, a science teacher takes her regular lunchtime stroll around Hampstead Heath. This is her "constitutional," a reassuringly old-fashioned concept, far removed from

power-walking, jogging, or similar goal-oriented forms of exercise: "The thing about a circular walk is that you end up where you started, except, of course, that you don't" (106). But the title also evokes corporeality. It encapsulates Simpson's concerns in the collection as a whole: mortality, the passing of time and the persistence of cycles and routines, both natural and man-made. While the settings are superficially domestic and mundane and the tone is lightly ironical, the effect is often unsettling and the humor darkly disturbing. In "Constitutional," as the lunch hour ticks away, the first-person narrator considers the perversities of her own biological clock. On the cusp of middle age, at the very moment when her faculties may be in decline, she has become pregnant for the first time.

Like the rest of the stories in the collection, "Constitutional" juxtaposes images of physical decay with humdrum reality. The black humor is at its most pronounced in "Every Third Thought," which chronicles a virtual epidemic of death and disease in deepest suburbia: "'They said his tumour's the size of an orange,' she said, blowing her nose. 'I'd just bought a net of oranges for juicing and they went straight in the bin. I do wish doctors would keep away from food when they're making their comparison'" (23).

In "Early One Morning," the school run maps out another circumscribed route, like the trek around the heath in "Constitutional." Taking the children to school and back again, stuck in the congestion, Simpson's protagonist seems to be moving in ever-decreasing circles. In Simpson's previous collection, *Hey Yeah Right Get a Life,* Simpson's typical heroine was an educated, youngish woman struggling to reconcile her sense of autonomy with the demands of motherhood. Now, on the wrong side of 40, she is even more conscious that time is slipping away beyond her control.

Simpson is especially good at capturing children's voices, suggesting in "Early One Morning," as so often in her work, an ultimate complicity between mother and child. In "The Year's Midnight," Marion soothes a child who is having a tantrum at the baths, going through the well-practiced rituals of maternal optimism: "the more she, Marion, insisted that they would have a happy Christmas, the more likely it became that they all really would" (19). "The Year's Midnight" is set in a swimming pool at the winter solstice, "and so she was also aware of swimming in the dark sea of Time with the old year wheeling wearily across the sky above her, the sun very low and weak, and somewhere beneath the horizon the unmarked infant new year waiting its turn" (11). Seasonal change, especially the coming of winter, interacts with the biological and social life cycles of Simpson's characters.

Often, the characters are stuck in obsessive or repetitious behavior. In "The Phlebotomist's Love Life" (a title that returns to circulation, this time of the blood, a recurring image in the collection), the outraged protagonist asks everyone she meets for his or her opinion on the Gulf War. "The Tree," the only story narrated by a man, charts the disasters set in motion by his senile mother's fixation on the dead tree in her garden. He is a surveyor, someone who "worries for a living" (55), looking out for the telltale signs of damage. As in houses, so in humans, decrepitude awaits. This is not exactly a consoling message, but it is redeemed by the wit and energy of Simpson's fast-paced prose.

BIBLIOGRAPHY

Simpson, Helen. *Constitutional.* London: Jonathan Cape, 2005.

———. *Hey yeah Right Get a Life.* London: Vintage, 2001.

Ailsa Cox

COPPARD, A. E. (1878–1957)

Born of working-class parents in Folkstone, Kent, Alfred Edgar Coppard left school at age nine, becoming variously an errand boy, a professional athlete, and a clerk. Sensitive about his lack of formal education, Coppard read voraciously before starting to publish poetry and short stories. The hardships of his early life are described in his autobiography, *It's Me, O Lord!* (1957), but they also feature in his fiction. The story "My Hundredth Tale" tells of a Coppard-like writer living in isolation in a primitive hut who has affairs with three women; he rejects the first two but is rejected by the third, for whom he is too uncouth. Literary recognition arrived at age 43 with the publication of the collection *Adam and Eve and Pinch Me* in 1921. Coppard quickly followed this with *Clorinda Walks in Heaven* (1922) and *The Black Dog and Other Stories* (1923).

Although Coppard believed that a short story was harder to write than a full-length novel, he quickly established himself as an innovative exponent of the form with a distinctive style. H. E. BATES wrote, "Mr. Coppard has long cherished the theory that short story and film are expressions of the same art, the art of telling a story by a series of subtly implied gestures, swift shots, moments of suggestion, an art in which elaboration and above all explanation are superfluous and tedious." Coppard makes considerable use of repeated motifs and symbols that are often taken from the natural world. Although he was acclaimed for his supernatural or "weird" fiction, he was most famous for his short stories set in rural England, in particular Oxfordshire and Berkshire. His moving accounts of countryfolk and misfits struggling to eke out a basic existence present the countryside not as an idyllic retreat but rather as a place where natural beauty exists alongside violence, cruelty, and betrayal. The climax of "The Silver Circus" comes when a pair of elderly laboring women realize that they been deceived by the same man and their mutually supportive friendship is irrevocably damaged. Coppard's much anthologized story "The Higgler," which first appeared in the collection *Fishmonger's Fiddle* in 1925, is a tragic tale of an itinerant salesman in poultry and eggs who is offended when a farmer's widow seems to want to sell him her quiet daughter along with her farm. Later, trapped in an unhappy marriage with a dour, humorless woman, he suddenly realizes that the daughter was in love with him but was too shy to let him know. The damage has, however, been done.

Coppard was a presence throughout the 1920s and 1930s but refused to ally himself with any particular school or movement. In his fiction he developed a deceptively simple form of short story populated by characters that were in marked contrast to those favored by MODERNIST writers, and he thus helped establish another route for the genre's development in British literature.

BIBLIOGRAPHY

Bates, H. E. *The Modern Short Story: A Critical Survey.* London: T. Nelson, 1941.

Coppard, A. E. *Adam and Eve and Pinch Me: Tales.* Berkshire, England: Golden Cockerel Press, 1921.

———. *Clorinda Walks in Heaven.* Berkshire, England: Golden Cockerel Press, 1922.

———. *Fishmonger's Fiddle: Tales.* London: Cape, 1925.

———. *The Man in the Caravan.* London: Phoenix, 2003.

Gindin, James. "A. E. Coppard and H. E. Bates." In *The English Short Story, 1880–1945: A Critical History,* edited by Joseph M. Flora, 113–141. Boston: Twayne, 1985.

Andrew Maunder

CORELLI, MARIE (1855–1924)

CORELLI, MARIE (1855–1924) Marie Corelli is the pseudonym of Mary Mills (later Mackay), born in Bayswater, London, as the illegitimate child of Scottish poet Charles Mackay and his servant, Mary Mills, who later became his second wife in 1859; she was sister to one half-brother, Eric Mackay. Called "Minnie" as a child, Corelli lived at Fern Dell at Box Hill, Surrey, with George Meredith as a neighbor. Precocious in intelligence and musical learning (she played the harp, mandolin, and piano), she was educated privately by governesses except during a brief period when she attended a convent school. Obsessively protective of her carefully cultivated and self-dramatizing persona, she adopted various names, beginning with "Signoria di Corelli" when she embarked on an early career as an improvisator on the piano and ending with "Marie Corelli" when she became an author; her musical efforts were short-lived because in 1886, at age 30, she published her first novel, *The Romance of Two Worlds,* with Richard Bentley. In 1876 her mother died; as a result, her childhood friend and ultimately lifelong companion, Bertha Vyver, joined the household and moved with the family to London in 1883. Most likely the best-selling author of all Victorian novelists after the publication of *Sorrows of Satan* (1895), Corelli was also prolific. She wrote 25 novels ranging from lurid romances to outlandish science fiction, several articles and opinion pieces, and more than 30 short stories, which were collected in *Cameos* (1896), *The Song of Miriam and Other Stories* (1898), *Delicia, and Other Stories* (1907), and *The Love of Long Ago and Other Stories* (1920). Exemplified in her short fiction are many of the themes and concerns of Corelli's longer works, such as mysticism ("The Distant Voice"), science ("Lead Kindly Light"), and women's roles ("The Stepping Star"); these are compounded by her lurid tales of exotic locales and occult proceedings, which often also include commentaries or thinly disguised essays on imperialism, journalistic corruption, and child poverty ("Tiny Tramps"). Despite her interest in strong career women, Corelli distanced herself from the NEW WOMAN writers of her day and was against the suffragette movement (see SUFFRAGETTE FICTION). Unlike most Victorian writers, Corelli did not first publish her stories in periodicals, but they were often published in more than one collection or were initially distributed to the public as novellas. A phenomenon of publishing and popular culture, Marie Corelli died at Stratford on Avon, where she lived from 1901 to her death.

BIBLIOGRAPHY

Corelli, Marie. *Cameos.* London: Hutchinson, 1896.
————. *Delicia and Other Stories.* London: Constable, 1907.
————. *The Love of Long Ago and Other Stories.* London: Methuen, 1920.
————. *The Song of Miriam and Other Stories.* London: Hutchinson, 1897.
Federico, Annette. *Idol of Suburbia.* Charlottesville: University Press of Virginia, 2000.

Sarah Maier

COSMOPOLITAN (1886–   )

First issued in 1886, *Cosmopolitan* was part of the late-Victorian "magazine revolution" of the 1890s (see MAGAZINES). This revolution saw the emergence of a number of cheap advertising-based (as opposed to subscription-based) magazines catering to a middle-class readership. Through the 1880s and 1890s, led by owner John Brisben Walker (1889–1905), *Cosmopolitan* was a general-interest illustrated magazine, though it contained notable fiction. H. G. WELLS's novella *War of the Worlds* was serialized in 1887, and other important contributors of this period included RUDYARD KIPLING, ARTHUR CONAN DOYLE, Mark Twain, W. W. Jacobs, THOMAS HARDY, Jack London, and HENRY JAMES. Under William Randolph Hearst's ownership (1905–51), *Cosmopolitan* entered a period of muckraking before becoming a fiction-dominated periodical in 1912, a trend that lasted until the 1940s. By 1925, the magazine carried, on average, four serials and 12 short stories alongside a few feature articles. This formula was popular, bringing the magazine's circulation to nearly 1 million between 1915 and 1925. *Cosmopolitan* paid well for its fiction, up to $5000 for a short story and $40,000 for a serial in the 1930s. As such, it attracted prominent popular fiction writers during this period, including William SOMERSET MAUGHAM, P. G. WODEHOUSE, Rafael Sabatini, Ring Lardner, and Louis Bromfield. After the war, as fiction declined in popularity, *Cosmopolitan* changed its format and focused its market on the middle-class housewife. In the 1960s, under Helen Gurley Brown, *Cosmopolitan* underwent a radical change, becoming a magazine devoted to "sex and the single girl," a focus it retains today. In terms of its role in the history of the short story, *Cosmopolitan* is significant as an indicator of the most popular writers and short story genres of the 1890s through the 1940s.

Kristen MacLeod

"COURTING OF DINAH SHADD, THE"

RUDYARD KIPLING (1890)   One of RUDYARD KIPLING's many stories of life among noncommissioned soldiers in India, "The Courting of Dinah Shadd" was first published in *Harper's Weekly* in the United States in 1890. It also gave its name to the volume of short stories published by Harper Brothers in September 1890, an edition that Kipling considered pirated. In 1891 Kipling published the story in a collection in the United States titled *Mine Own People,* with an introduction by HENRY JAMES. It was published in Britain in *Life's Handicap: Being Stories of Mine Own People,* also in 1891. Kipling wrote it in early 1890, after he had left India; it is a story that echoes earlier work but also points toward the sophisticated narratives and dark visions of his later writing.

The story is placed second in the standard Macmillan edition of *Life's Handicap,* between two other stories of a trio of soldiers who recur in several Kipling texts; Mulvaney, the Irishman; Ortheris, the London cockney; and Learoyd, the Yorkshireman. "The Incarnation of Krishna Mulvaney" recounts a drunken adventure involving a sedan chair, an Indian temple, and "the wives and daughters of most of the kings of India." "On Greenhow Hill" interweaves Learoyd's account of the death of a girl he has loved with Ortheris's preparations to shoot a deserter. "The Courting of Dinah Shadd" echoes these stories in its narrative complexity and pessimism.

The epigraph to the story is a poem that asserts—ironically, as it turns out—that all women "Are sisters under their skins" in their desire to get the man they want. The text deals with sexual rivalry (among men also), but it approaches its topic indirectly. Mulvaney's story of courting Miss Shadd is doubly framed in an account of army maneuvers in India and of an encounter with Mulvaney, Ortheris, and Learoyd. The unnamed narrator listens to Mulvaney talk as the soldiers involved in the maneuvers entertain themselves in camp. Mulvaney starts with a reminiscence of watching *Hamlet* in Dublin and then asks the narrator "Did you iver have onendin' devilmint an' nothin' to pay for it in your life, sorr?" He proceeds to tell of his falling in love with Dinah Shadd and his fighting another soldier to win her. He reveals that within half an hour of Dinah's agreeing to his courtship, he had flirted with another woman, the disreputable Judy Sheehy, and gave her to understand that he wanted to marry her. The next day, he and Dinah were confronted by Judy and her drunken mother. Mulvaney refused to marry Judy, whereupon Mrs. Sheehy laid a terrible curse on him. Dinah, after first rejecting him, stuck by Mulvaney and shared the curse. Mulvaney reveals that the curse—of professional failure, moral disappointment, and childlessness—has come true, but he and Dinah have remained married.

Mulvaney's narration is given in the phonological transcription of dialect that Kipling uses in many stories (and that George Orwell and SALMAN RUSHDIE have found annoying). However, this technique is an attempt to let Mulvaney's lower-class and provincial voice be heard clearly. This and the complex narrative give a freshness to Mulvaney's sordid tale. Kipling also gives the Mulvaneys' disappointed lives some dignity. His language and that of Mrs. Sheehy is often rhetorically powerful, his and Dinah's sufferings are poignant, and the double framing allows Kipling to place Mulvaney's failure in the context of general transience ("Today, of all those jovial thieves . . . not one remains") and of heroic figures like Hamlet and Prometheus. The story fits in with the other dark and disturbing tales that make up *Life's Handicap.*

BIBLIOGRAPHY

Kipling, Rudyard. *Collected Stories.* London: Everyman, 1994.

David Malcolm

"COURTSHIP OF MR. LYON, THE" AN-GELA CARTER (1979)   Originally published in British *Vogue,* "The Courtship of Mr. Lyon" is one of the nine pieces contained in *The BLOODY CHAMBER and Other Stories* (1979), Angela CARTER's feminist rewriting of traditional fairy tales. In particular, "The Courtship of Mr. Lyon" is based on Madame Leprince de Beaumont's "Beauty and the Beast," which Carter had already translated and edited for her volume *Sleeping Beauty and Other Favourite Fairy Tales* in 1982. Some critics have therefore seen *The Bloody Chamber* as Carter's commentary on her own previous work, and Carter herself has emphasized the metanarrative aspect of this collection by describing it as "a book of stories about fairy stories."

"The Courtship of Mr. Lyon" is one of two rewritings by Carter of "Beauty and the Beast" and, at a first glance, is the most faithful to the original: Beauty's father is a ruined gentleman who takes temporary shelter in a grand, and apparently empty, mansion, from whose garden he plucks a white rose to take to his daughter as a present. This gesture provokes the sudden appearance and indignation of the owner of the house, the Beast, who can be pacified only by the promise that the thieving trespasser will come back accompanied by his beautiful daughter. Later, in exchange for Beauty's company, the Beast offers to help restore her father's fortune; when Beauty finally makes her way back to her father, she forgets her promise to visit the Beast, who begins to languish. Beauty's providential return and proffer of love not only rescue the Beast from his deathbed but reinstate his human form and trigger the conventional happy ending in the couple's marriage. In contrast, Carter's other version of the story, "The Tiger's Bride," which immediately follows "The Courtship of Mr. Lyon" in *The Bloody Chamber,* ends with Beauty's metamorphosis into a tiger rather than the Beast's transformation into a prince.

The most superficial difference between "The Courtship of Mr. Lyon" and the original fairy tale is that Carter's version is set in the modern world, albeit one that is scantily sketched, rather than in the indeterminate past of the "once upon a time." The Beast is Mr. Lyon, a country gentleman rather than a spellbound prince, and once they have regained their fortune, Beauty and her Father start enjoying the glamour of city life in London. Even more defamiliarizing, within a fairy tale context, is the way Beauty's father first enters Mr. Lyon's mansion because of mechanical problems with his car. Similarly, the feeling of suspension of reality that pervades Mr. Lyon's mansion cannot be ascribed to the magic quality of the fairy-tale setting. Instead, Beauty's father puts it down to the eccentricity typical of the very rich, for whom the rules of everyday reality do not seem to apply. The materiality of these details emphasizes the patriarchal, capitalist economy of exchange within which Beauty is effectively imprisoned.

This strategy reflects Carter's rejection of Bruno Bettelheim's reading of the traditional "Beauty and the Beast" as the story of a girl's necessary maturation from daughter to bride. Rather, Carter points out how Beauty's fate is that of a commodity passed on from one master to the next within the patriarchal order. Women's servility and subjugation to men is further emphasized by the presence of the white (like Beauty) bejeweled spaniel, the only other female creature in the story, whose status seems to hover between that of lady of the house, governess, and prized possession. More overtly, not only does Mr. Lyon demand that Beauty be brought to dinner as compensation for the theft of the white rose (again, Beauty's own white complexion seems like a fair exchange for the stolen flower), but Beauty herself perceives the extension of her stay with the Beast as the rightful price for the reversal of her father's fortune. Beauty appears to be incapable of escaping this perverse logic when, at the end of the story, she is once again victim of an emotional blackmail, this time perpetrated by Mr. Lyon rather than her father.

Several critics, however, have pointed out how, even as Carter drops hints about the oppressiveness of patriarchal ideology, Beauty in fact undergoes as positive a metamorphosis as Mr. Lyon does, through the blossoming of their mutual love. Beauty's selfless commitment to the Beast represents the assumption of responsibility in place of the frivolity and shallowness of life as a spoiled socialite—in which guise she first appears, delighted by the prospect of a shopping expedition to buy, significantly, furs with her father's money. According to this reading, Beauty renounces the pleasures of the glittering metropolis for the much

less glamorous life in the country and the genuine love of what Margaret Atwood describes as a "somewhat tatty dying animal." Even so, the ending of the story is anticlimactic and ironic: Domesticity is finally represented as tranquillity verging on stasis, even decay, as the closing image of the fallen petals seems to suggest.

BIBLIOGRAPHY

Atwood, Margaret. "Running with the Tigers." In *Flesh and the Mirror: Essays on the Art of Angela Carter,* edited by Lorna Sage, London: Virago, 117–135. 1994.

Carter, Angela. *The Bloody Chamber.* 1979. London: Vintage, 1995.

Stephania Ciocia

COUSIN PHYLLIS Elizabeth Gaskell (1864)

Cousin Phyllis is one of Elizabeth Gaskell's later works and one in which she returns to the rural Cheshire of her youth. *Cousin Phyllis* was first published by George Smith in his *Cornhill Magazine* (see MAGAZINES) in four monthly parts from November 1863 to February 1864. Part two included an illustration by George du Maurier that has since become iconic. The entire novella is narrated by Paul Manning, who, as a mature man, is recollecting his days at Hope Farm and his acquaintance with Phyllis and Holdsworth. He describes a rural idyll in which the heroine, Phyllis Holman, discovers romantic love for the first time in her life. As an only child growing up in an isolated farming community she has been overprotected by her devoted parents, who fail to observe her developing sexuality. Railway construction in Cheshire brings two young railway workers into regular contact with Phyllis, her parents, and Hope Farm, where they live and work. Phyllis's father, Mr. Holman, is a Nonconformist minister (i.e., not a member of the Church of England or Roman Catholic Church), as well as a farmer. The young men are Mr. Holdsworth, an engineer, and Paul Manning, who is both Holdsworth's assistant and Phyllis's cousin. Although the railway itself does not affect the farm, the presence of the young men, especially Holdsworth, disturbs the Edenic quality of this rural environment. Phyllis, who is 17 when the story begins, experiences an emotional and sexual awakening that she tries to conceal from her parents.

This tale does not have a happy ending. Holdsworth, the young man who has captured Phyllis's heart, takes a position at very short notice in Canada. Because of the suddenness of his departure he is unable to declare his feelings to Phyllis, but he confides in Paul. Seeing Phyllis so sad after Holdsworth's departure, Paul tells his cousin that Holdsworth loves her and hopes to marry her on his return. As time passes, however, Holdsworth's letters to Paul include references to a new friend: a French-Canadian girl named Lucille Ventadour. Before returning to England Holdsworth sends news that he has married Lucille. Learning of Holdsworth's marriage so disturbs Phyllis that she becomes critically ill with brain fever. Her admission to her parents that she loved Holdsworth compels Mr. and Mrs. Holman to acknowledge their daughter's progress from childhood to young adulthood. Phyllis recovers from her physical illness, but the story ends on a note of uncertainty regarding her future life. Alternative endings were considered by the author but discarded.

The novella is regarded by many scholars as Gaskell's finest work and the culmination of her shorter fiction. It charts Phyllis's emotional journey, the exchange of innocence for experience, which proves to be painful for her and for those who truly care about her. The story is often praised for its accuracy of description, but details here do more than describe appearances: They signify a character's inner life. Major signifiers are Phyllis's pinafore, which she is wearing in Gerald du Maurier's illustration and which denotes her early innocence, and her recurring blushes, which indicate her subsequent emotional turmoil. This emphasis on human feeling, together with a fusion of religion and nature, is one of the reasons that *Cousin Phyllis* has attracted much critical attention.

BIBLIOGRAPHY
Elizabeth Gaskell. *Cranford and Cousin Phyllis*. London: Penguin, 1979.

Irene Wiltshire

CRANFORD ELIZABETH GASKELL (1851–1853)
An episodic novel of linked stories set in Cranford, a fictitious country town in northern England. First serialized in *Household Words,* a weekly magazine edited by CHARLES DICKENS, between December 1851 and May 1853, *Cranford* appeared in volume form in June 1853. An additional episode, "The Cage at Cranford," was published in Dickens's *All the Year Round* in November 1863.

Cranford is based on ELIZABETH GASKELL's childhood memories of the small town of Knutsford, Cheshire. As a fond record of an old-fashioned backwater, the story has primarily been praised for its charm, domestic detail, and vivid creation of a rural society dominated by a close-knit group of impoverished gentlewomen. Recent interest in the material conditions of domestic life in Victorian Britain has revealed that industrialization, imperialism, and the new consumer society are central to the story's treatment of class and gender issues.

Cranford has thus been read as an insightful point of entry into discussions of the 19th-century transport system and commercialism and of developments in the patterns of production, distribution, and consumption (Hall). This new interest in the story's socioeconomic background, however, has also accentuated the intriguing ambiguity of its representation of gender relations. In its exploration of sexual politics, it has been alternately interpreted as a satire on embittered spinsters and as a fond detailing of middle-class feminine gentility. The opening sentence propels the reader into the center of this ambiguity: "In the first place, Cranford is in possession of the Amazons; all the holders of houses, above a certain rent, are women." In Ancient Greek mythology, the Amazons are warrior women who live without men, and while the genteel ladies of Cranford form a community of women in which men of their class are practically nonexistent and not necessarily welcome unless they are first successfully domesticated, or feminized, the comparison of these women to a race of warrior women is replete with fond ridicule. As Nina Auerbach pointedly puts it, at first sight "the appellation 'Amazons' seems simply to chuck these sweet ladies under the chin; but the Amazons bob up repeatedly in Victorian writing, usually to be banished as soon as evoked." More recently, Eileen Gillooly has likewise endeavoured to account for the aggressive humour of this charming tale by showing how "in possession of the Amazons" can be read differently: While Cranford seems to be a town that belongs almost exclusively to women, Cranford also possesses the Amazons by locking them away from the world.

The narrative situation is significant for the story's many paradoxes. The first-person narrator, Mary Smith, is a much younger woman than the majority of Cranford ladies and is a visitor. She is intimately familiar with the ways and means of Cranford, but nonetheless she is an outsider or, at best, a partial participant. She can even be seen as an anthropologist who observes the cultural context of her anecdotes with an outsider's bemused, or amused, fascination (Schor). Residing with her widowed father in "the great neighbouring commercial town of Drumble," with which preindustrial Cranford is repeatedly contrasted, Mary undertakes extended visits to some of the central characters, notably to Deborah and Matty Jenkyns and Miss Pole. With a mildly aloof sense of detachment she recounts that every inhabitant of Cranford has "her own individuality, not to say eccentricity, pretty strongly developed." Mary's own personality, however, is treated with a similar irony. Her somewhat stiff conservatism, especially in terms of dress, provides a comical contrast to Matty Jenkyns's endearing youthfulness, if not childishness. This comes to the fore in the episode "Signor Brunoni," as Miss Matty expects Mary to import a fashionable sea-green turban into old-fashioned Cranford. Her desire exemplifies the strangely comical representation of attempts to domesticate the exotic, the alluringly but threateningly foreign male seemingly embodied by Brunoni, alias Samuel Brown. Instead, Mary purchases "a pretty, neat, middle-aged cap"—"anxious to prevent [Miss Matty] from disfiguring her small gentle mousey face with a great Saracen's-head turban." The later chapter "The Cage at Cranford" takes this even further as Mary proves as ignorant of new Paris fashions as the Cranford ladies. The promised French "cage"—a skirt-shaped construction worn under the dress when extensive skirts became fashionable—is misinterpreted as a new habitation for Miss Pole's Polly-Cockatoo. Such double irony pervades the stories.

Not initially intended as a novel, *Cranford* contains episodic anecdotes, and their most prevalent characteristic is indisputably their humor. Among the most memorable episodes is an Alderney cow dressed in flannel after its fall into a lime pit, which causes it to lose all its hair: "Do you ever see cows dressed in grey flannel in London?" Considering that the cow's owner is an old lady who "looked upon [the cow] as a daughter," Captain Brown's initial jokes about the necessary flannel waistcoat and drawers harbor the aggressive humor that ruptures the seemingly smooth idyll. One of the few men temporarily admitted into Cranford society, Captain Brown, like Brunoni, embodies a disruptive male element. Given the captain's literary debates about Dickens's *Pickwick Papers*—significantly the fictional chronicles of an all-male club—as opposed to the old-fashioned pomposity exemplified by Deborah Jenkyns's reading of the 18th-century essayist Samuel Johnson, his death becomes doubly symbolic: He is run over by a train shortly after reading the *Pickwick Papers* but also while saving a child, thereby atoning for his identification with industrialization and progress. Likewise, Peter Jenkyns's transvestism at once is extremely funny and has a sinister side to it as he impersonates his masculine sister Deborah in a pose of feminine weakness: nursing a mysterious infant with maternal effusion.

In contrast to this carnivalesque moment, Peter's later return from India to save his sister Matty from comparative poverty incongruously reasserts male dominance. Impoverished after the failure of a Joint-Stock Bank in which the Miss Jenkyns are shareholders, Matty has discreetly been selling tea, vacillating on the borderlines of gentility, of the "elegant economy" in which trade figures as vulgar: "'Elegant economy!' How naturally one falls back into the phraseology of Cranford! There, economy was always 'elegant,' and money-spending always 'vulgar and ostentatious.'" Peter's fortuitous return replenishes domestic gentility, yet this use of the colonies as an offstage source of fortune is more intriguingly counterpoised by Mrs. Brown's narrative of having carried her last surviving child "from station to station, from Indian village to village." This multilayered use of India, Indian muslin, the East India Company, and fashionable turbans has led Raphael Samuel to single out *Cranford,* in his analysis of the interplay of the imperial and the domestic, as a central counterexample to Edward Said's seminal discussion of appropriating European orientalism. Like its intriguing insights into the domestic effects of industrialization and the new consumer society, its self-conscious and self-ironic portrayals of Orientalism and

Orientalia prove that *Cranford* is much more than the comical idyll that has alternately been praised and condemned for its sentimental charm.

BIBLIOGRAPHY
Auerbach, Nina. *Communities of Women: An Idea in Fiction.* Cambridge, Mass.: Harvard University Press, 1978.
Gaskell, Elizabeth. *Cranford.* Edited by Elizabeth Porges Watson. Oxford: Oxford University Press, 1998.
Gillooly, Eileen. *Smile of Discontent.* Chicago: Chicago University Press, 1999.
Hall, Catherine. "The Butcher, The Baker, The Candlestick maker: The Shop and Family in the Industrial Revolution." In *The Victorian City,* edited by R. J. Moris and Richard Rodger, 307–321. London: Longman, 1993.
Schor, Hilary M. *Scheherezade in the Marketplace: Elizabeth Gaskell and the Victorian Novel.* Oxford: Oxford University Press, 1992.

Tamara Wagner

CROMPTON, RICHMAL (1890–1969) A

former schoolteacher who retired because of ill health at age 33, Richmal Crompton wrote novels and stories, initially as a sideline but increasingly to support herself and her widowed mother. She was extremely successful from the end of World War I until her death from a heart attack in 1969. She became famous for her "William" stories—filling almost 40 volumes—in which an unkempt, cheery, and irrepressible boy and his gang of friends known as "the Outlaws" get into scrapes and face the wrath of the authorities, represented by parents and teachers. The stories are striking for their celebration of William's anarchic antiauthoritarian stance and for their conservative evocation of a certain type of ordered middle-class village life in 1920s and 1930s England: a world of cooks, housemaids, tea parties, tennis tournaments, and cycling. Even when the novels move forward into wartime (William remains at age 11), life goes on much as it always has done, despite the arrival of evacuees and rationing. Many of the stories concern William's attempts to best pompous adults, including his family, who rarely share his view of the world; others involve his attempts to extricate himself from the clutches of his sole female admirer, the lisping Violet Elizabeth Bott, daughter of the nouveau riche Mr. and Mrs. Bott, whose money comes

from sauce. Disparaged in later life by Crompton, who claimed to be weary of having to give the public a new book every year and who was also perpetually disappointed that her novels for adults never sold half so well, the William stories are nonetheless the work of a skillful and witty writer, and the character is still a national institution in the United Kingdom. Unlike that of Enid Blyton, Crompton's work has never fallen out of favor, and recent reevaluations have begun to recognize her central place in the landscape of 20th-century popular culture and the historical currents of which she is a part.

BIBLIOGRAPHY
Cadogan, Mary. *Richmal Crompton: The Woman behind William.* London: Unwin, 1986.
Crompton, Richmal. *Just William.* London: Newnes, 1922.
———. *William the Fourth.* London: Newnes, 1924.
———. *William the Conqueror.* London: Newnes, 1926.
———. *William the Outlaw.* London: Newnes, 1927.
———. *William the Showman.* London: Newnes, 1937.

Andrew Maunder

CROSS CHANNEL JULIAN BARNES (1996)

Cross Channel was JULIAN BARNES's first book of short fiction. It collects 10 stories about the English experience of France over 350 years, from the 17th to the early 21st century. Five of these tales were first published in the *New Yorker* and *Granta.* Drawing on a broad array of storytelling techniques and styles—from Regency letters to first-person accounts in cycling slang—these stories articulate a number of Barnes's primary thematic concerns, such as truth and its verifiability and our relationship to the past. "Experiment," a fine example of Barnes's wit, examines questions of truth through the narrator's investigation of the past of his uncle, who claimed that he was once mistaken for a surrealist because of his poor pronunciation of French. In "EVERMORE," the best story of the collection, Barnes explores questions of memory and the inaccessibility of the past through the story of a British proofreader who pays her yearly visit to the grave of the brother she lost in World War I.

Although the stories are all set in France, they do not seek to depict the French way of life as perceived by English travelers. Barnes uses the French otherness rather as decor to address the notion of Englishness through issues as diverse as religion, food, language, love, sexuality, and art. As pointed out by a *Times Literary Supplement* reviewer, Barnes's characters remain, despite their encounter with French culture, thoroughly English. For example, in "Interference," a vain English composer, who has retired to a French village because "it [is] not permitted to be an artist in England," will listen only to BBC concerts and will not interact with the villagers, whom he sees as a nuisance: In "Hermitage," two Victorian spinsters buy a run-down vineyard in France and obstinately stick to their high (British) principles as they reestablish it.

Assembled in a nonchronological order, the stories switch at random from a somber evocation of the persecution of Huguenots in the 17th century ("Dragons") to a vernacular account of a Tour de France in the 1990s ("Brambilla"), or from a cricketer's view on the aftermath of the French Revolution ("Melon") to a poignant commemoration of World War I ("Evermore"). The haphazard order and the diversity of tone have led reviewers to point out a lack of coherence in *Cross Channel,* even if its final piece attempts to unite the whole collection: "Tunnel" abounds in allusions to the preceding tales and informs the reader that the stories in the collection have all been written by the protagonist, an elderly writer (a visionary self-portrait by Barnes) who rides on the Eurostar train in the year 2015 and sifts through his favorite traveling memories.

In addition to a lack of unity, negative critiques have identified an overwhelming profusion of historical facts. However, despite these less favorable reactions, *Cross Channel* has been well received on both sides of the Channel. Reviewers have praised Barnes's wit, erudition, and elegance of style, as well as his ability to re-create the language and atmosphere of each time period in this fragmented but inventive portrait of three centuries of cross-channel history.

BIBLIOGRAPHY

Barnes, Julian. *Cross Channel.* London: Jonathan Cape, 1996.
Furbank, P. N. "If the French Were Shorter in Flaubert's Day, Did They Need to Be Less Fat in Order to Be Called 'Fat'?" *London Review of Books,* 4 January 1996, p. 22.
Kempton, Adrian. "A Barnes'-Eye View of France," *Franco-British Studies* 22 (1996): 92–101.
Mangan, Gerald. *"Très british,"* Times Literary Supplement, 19 January 1996, p. 24.

Virginie Renard

"CROSS LINE, A" GEORGE EGERTON (1893)

This story by GEORGE EGERTON (Mary Chavelita Dunne Bright) first appeared in the influential collection KEY-NOTES. Published in 1893 by Elin Mathews and John Lane, it was the first book in a series of 33 volumes, 13 of which would be written by so-called NEW WOMAN writers. These works openly explored female sexuality, questioned women's options, attempted to render the psychological states of women, and experimented with narrative. In all of these, Egerton led the way, not only freeing others to write "like women" but most surely pioneering the way for D. H. LAWRENCE, whose 1921 novel *Women in Love* explores the sexual and psychological tensions between lovers in like manner to "A Cross Line."

Egerton's story begins with a man's voice described significantly as "profane," "indelicate," "vulgar," and unwelcome. The voice is heard by a woman sitting on a "felled tree" in the middle of a wilderness with "lopped" branches all around. Nearby "a little river rushes along in haste to join a greater sister that is fighting a troubled way to the sea." These images reflect the woman's troubled psychological state: Surrounded by vibrant nature, she, like many of the trees, has been tamed, but her spirit continues to rebel through flights of fantasy. The voice becomes a whistle, and then the man appears. He is a stranger, and she is to him at first only "the female animal," as if he has just chanced upon some interesting bug. The pair discuss fishing, but their dialogue slowly transforms into a courtship dance, in which each is sexually drawn to and repulsed by the other. There is no physical contact, however, because they recognize a line they should not cross because the woman is married. The woman then returns to her husband, who is by all accounts an attentive lover and satisfactory companion. They seem to be happily married, although Egerton realistically portrays their struggles to communicate as if there were a line between them, a line drawn by gender, one that they cannot cross.

As summer continues in the peaceful country existence for this couple, the monotony becomes oppressive, and the wife escapes into a fantasy world of adventure and sexual freedom. She also becomes introspective about who she is as a woman among women. In 1932 Egerton wrote, "There was only one small plot left for her to tell: the *terra incognita* of herself, as she knew herself to be, not as man liked to imagine her—in a word to give herself away, as man had given himself away in his writings" (58). Yet, the woman in this story identifies a line that must not be crossed: Women must give but never want. They are expected to tame the wild beast in men, but they are not, cannot be passionate themselves. But this woman declares, "I have been for myself and helped myself, and borne the burden of my own mistakes." Finally she affirms her identity in a community of women and mothers (her own mother, who is dead, and a maid whose child is also dead) and opts to accept motherhood over licentiousness, for she is pregnant and remains sexually faithful to her husband.

BIBLIOGRAPHY

Egerton, George. "A Cross Line." In *Nineteenth-Century Short Stories by Women: A Routledge Anthology,* edited by Harriet Devine Jump. New York: Routledge, 1998.

———. "A Keycycle to Keynotes." In *Ten Contemporaries: Notes towards their Definitive Bibliography.* Edited by John Gadsworth, London: Ernst Benn Ltd, 1932.

McCullogh, Kate. "Mapping the 'Terra Incognita' of Women: George Egerton's *Keynotes* (1893) and the New Woman Fiction." In *The New Nineteenth Century: Feminist Readings of Underread Victorian Fiction,* edited by Barbara Leah Harman and Susan Meyer, 205–223. New York: Garland, 1996.

Stetz, M. D. "George Egerton," *Turn of the Century Women* 1, no. 1 (1984): 2–8.

Brenda Ayres

DAHL, ROALD (1916–1990) The only son of Harald Dahl and Sofie Magdalene Hesselberg, Roald Dahl was born on September 13, 1916, in Llandoff, Wales. Although Roald was not yet four years old at the time of his father's death in 1920, he acquired his father's lifelong passions for fine furniture, painting, and gardening, themes that occur regularly in Dahl's fiction. It was Sofie, however, who exerted the most influence on her son's literary future by introducing the boy to the fantastic fairy tales and legends of her native Norway.

Dahl entered Llandaff Cathedral School when he was seven, a time he remembered mostly for his trips to the local candy shop. In 1925, Dahl became a pupil at St. Peter's Preparatory School in Weston-Super-Mare, where he first encountered the stern headmasters and corporal punishment he would later write about in his short stories. At age 13, Dahl began attending the famous Repton Public School in Derbyshire. Here he endured the same sort of brutal flogging at the hands of a sadistic prefect as William Perkins does under Foxley in Dahl's short story "Galloping Foxley."

At the outbreak of the World War II in 1939, Dahl enlisted as an aviator in the Royal Air Force, serving primarily in southern Europe and northern Africa. Eventually, after having suffered numerous injuries of varying severity, Dahl was declared an invalid and was transferred to Washington, D.C., as an air attaché in 1942. While in Washington, Dahl met C. S. Forester, who requested that the young aviator provide him with an account of his experiences during the war. Initially planning to write a feature for the *Saturday Evening Post* based on Dahl's narrative, Forester was so impressed with the young man's writing that he refused to change a word. With Forester's encouragement, a newly published essay, and a check for $900, Dahl set out to become a professional writer.

With the exception of *The Gremlins* (1943), a children's book Dahl adapted from a screenplay he had written for Disney, the majority of the author's early fiction was written for an adult audience. Over the next 15 years, Dahl published short stories in the *Saturday Evening Post,* the *New Yorker,* and *Harper's,* earning a reputation as a master of the short story form. In 1953, Alfred Knopf released *Someone Like You,* a collection containing some of Dahl's most famous tales. Stories such as "Taste," "Lamb to the Slaughter," "A Dip in the Pool," "Skin," and "The Sound Machine" display the unsettling tension that continues to draw readers to Dahl's prose. Adroitly blending humor, innocence, and elements of the macabre into short stories with surprising plot twists, Dahl quickly built a large audience in both the United States and his native England. A rare critical and popular success, Dahl was awarded the prestigious Edgar Award by the Mystery Writers of America on three occasions. With the simultaneous release of *Tales of the Unexpected,* an anthology of Dahl's adult short stories, and broadcast of the eponymous television series, the author solidified his place among the best postwar short story writers in English.

Despite the tremendous success of Dahl's adult-oriented short stories, much of the author's fame rests on the popularity of his children's books, many of which are regarded as classics. Shortly after Dahl's marriage to Patricia Neal in 1953, the author's experiences as a father telling bedtime stories to his daughters inspired him to try his hand at children's literature. The unparalleled popularity of *James and the Giant Peach* (U.S., 1961; U.K., 1967) and *Charlie and the Chocolate Factory* (U.S., 1964; U.K. 1967) introduced the author to a new audience and made Dahl a household name.

After divorcing Patricia Neal in 1983, Dahl married Felicity Crosland and continued writing children's literature until his death on November 23, 1990. Since his death, the U.K. editions of Dahl's books have sold more than 30 million copies, making the author one of the 20th century's most read writers.

BIBLIOGRAPHY

Dahl, Roald. *The Collected Short Stories of Roald Dahl.* London: Penguin, 1992.

———. *Tales of the Unexpected.* New York: Vintage, 1979.

———. *The Wonderful Story of Henry Sugar and Six More.* London: Jonathan Cape, 1977.

RoaldDahl.com. "Roald Dahl Biography." The Official Roald Dahl Website. Available online. URL: http://www.roalddahl.com. Accessed May 10, 2006.

Treglown, Jeremy. *Roald Dahl: A Biography.* New York: Farrar, Strauss & Giroux, 1994.

Warren, Alan. *Roald Dahl.* San Bernadino, Calif.: Borgo Press, 1988.

Erik Grayson

DAISY MILLER HENRY JAMES (1878) Originally subtitled "A Study," this novella was first published by Leslie Stephen, the father of VIRGINIA WOOLF, in the *Cornhill Magazine* (see MAGAZINES). The choice of a British press cost HENRY JAMES his American rights. The sheer amount of pirated versions, however, hints at the succès de scandale the book turned out to be in the literary marketplace on both sides of the Atlantic: Daisy-Millerites celebrated the textual subtleties of observation, while the (less numerous) anti-Daisy-Millerites disparaged it as a foreign and all-too-abrasive judgment on American citizens abroad.

The story of the young American naif sojourning in Europe was generally received as a theatrical comedy or tragicomedy of manners, even more so since James himself reworked his plot into a three-act comedy in 1883, characteristically failing at the dramatic medium. Critics have often commented on the text's uncomfortable blend of the comic and mythic and the overly melodramatic structure peppered with a substantial amount of symbolically significant names, like "Daisy," the spring flower suggesting freshness and innocence; a would-be lover whose name puns on winter-born; an inappropriately immobile Mrs. Walker; and the conflagration of old and new money imagery in the hotel's name, Trois Couronnes.

Yet taking into account that even a literary master may accommodate effects generally associated with sentimental domestic traditions, it seems more fruitful to approach the text as a cultural study by an artistic expatriate. *Daisy Miller* furnishes an early example of James's so-called international theme, which juxtaposes unsophisticated American travelers with an old Europe brimming uneasily with a profound, often strikingly carnal, knowledge of the world. As a structuring device, this theme traces the choreographies of curiously transitory identities, which circulate across boundaries of all sorts. Moreover, the characteristically Jamesian point of view can already be detected in the use of a third-person narrative voice as a central intelligence, embodied in the young American, Frederick Winterbourne. The novella thus focuses on the observer, and Daisy as the object of the gaze is accessible for the reader only through his jaundiced eyes. Winterbourne's voice, however, is still framed by that of a first-person narrator whose minute hesitations and slips of the tongue prevent readers from an unproblematic identification with the male protagonist, calling into question his reliability as a storyteller and his frequently clinical judgments.

The novella begins with Winterbourne, just come over from Geneva, seated in the garden of the fashionably cosmopolitan hotel Trois Couronnes in the Swiss resort of Vevey. A disconnected bachelor with voyeuristic leanings, he is fully absorbed by his gentlemanly existence whose dated moral parameters account for his difficulty in understanding a fresh young woman, Daisy Miller, who is literally crossing his path.

The girl, with her fragmentary social know-how, seems on conscious display, adorned with a fan as an image of both feminine grace and challenge. In a recourse to a trope of realist writing, the text presents her as an unprotected daughter and a victim of flawed nurturing. She is associated with an uncultivated and alarmingly dysfunctional family background: Her father remains a blank, being far off on business; her mother is a hypochondriac dressing in Daisy's discarded clothes; her younger brother is a xenophobic, provincial, and aggressively newly rich brat.

Fascinated with her good looks and confused by her candor, Winterbourne tests her to see to what violation of social codes she can be lured. Yet her behavior—when she upholds her suggestion of a boat trip à deux to Chillon, paying no heed to the warnings of the courier Eugenio, and even urges Winterbourne to come and see her in Rome—threatens to overwhelm the neat categories of her suitor's obsessively itemizing mind. In his desperate attempts to make her legible by finding epithets and attaching labels, he seeks the feedback of his ilk in the expatriate American community of which his aunt Mrs. Costello is a crucial part. Here, among people more European than the Europeans, Daisy is unremittingly judged for letting herself be talked about in picking up chance acquaintances.

The subsequent geographical shift notwithstanding, rumors about Daisy fill the air in Rome as well. Confronted with her Italian cavalier, the gentleman lawyer Giovanelli, Winterbourne suddenly finds himself a substitute Eugenio dedicated to safeguard her. When the young woman is caught walking with both men in the Pincian Gardens in a blatant trespass of codes of propriety and refuses to heed Mrs. Walker's urgent remonstrations, the American diaspora finally closes its ranks by ostracizing Daisy publicly as "damaged goods." The object of this moral outrage, however, defiantly and deliberately leaves Winterbourne still at sea with regard to her possible engagement with Giovanelli.

Moreover, she even ventures to pay a nocturnal visit to the Colosseum with the Italian, even though the sacrificial site is notorious for its miasmal atmosphere.

Winterbourne overhears their plans and seems to arrive finally at his sought-for ultimate reading of Daisy. He settles on the worthlessness of his former object of attention, and this pivotal scene is followed by the laconic report of her death by fever, which she contracted during her nightly excursion. Ambiguously, her loss of life in spring is either sentimentally readable as a willed suicide motivated by Winterbourne's rejection of her or as a mere outcome of her imprudence. Winterbourne himself admits that confusion as to the young woman's character still lingers in his mind, even more so since Daisy's mother fulfills her daughter's last wish in informing him that Daisy was never Giovanelli's fiancée.

With his return to Geneva, however, which seems motivated by some foreign lady who is sojourning there, the plot comes full circle: Any illusion of personal development is shattered, as Winterbourne continues in his determination to censor otherness in order to maintain the social entropy that is required for his survival as a gentleman gigolo.

In this novella about the male gaze, everybody is busy forging fictions about others to such an extent that none of the narratives can be authenticated. Always alive to alternative options, the text resists the very conventions of realistic characterization on which it relies. The central consciousness is forever failing to arrive at ultimate certainty; the excess of sobriquets attached to Daisy drains them of any defining function. The gossip that characterizes the settings of Rome and Geneva may well look back on long traditions of moral absolutism, be they Catholic or Calvinist, yet it never fully manages to blot out Daisy's plain formulation of relativity: "People have different ideas."

The novella furnishes an example of indeterminacy and the provisionality of identities that came to be registered as a distinctively Jamesian hallmark. Moreover, in setting its characters afloat on a sea of rumors while telling a tale of failed communication and epistemological insecurity, the text anticipates a central concern of modernist writing.

BIBLIOGRAPHY

Bell, Millicent. *Meaning in Henry James.* Cambridge, Mass.: Harvard University Press, 1991.

Fogel, Daniel Mark. *Daisy Miller: A Dark Comedy of Manners.* Boston: Twayne, 1990.

Graham, Kenneth. "Daisy Miller: Dynamics of an Enigma." In *New Essays on Daisy Miller and The Turn of the Screw,* edited by Vivian R. Pollak, 35–63. Cambridge: Cambridge University Press, 1993.

James, Henry. *Daisy Miller and Other Stories.* Oxford: Oxford University Press, 1998.

Weisbuch, Robert. "Henry James and the Idea of Evil." In *The Cambridge Companion to Henry James,* edited by Jonathan Freedman, 102–119. Cambridge: Cambridge University Press, 1998.

Sandra Gottfreund

D'ARCY, ELLA (1857–1937)

Thought to be one of the most promising young female writers of the 1890s, D'Arcy was by some accounts first published by Charles Dickens, Jr., in his magazine *All the Year Round;* the first available proof of publication is for her story "The Expiation of David Scott," a conventional melodrama of love, jealousy, and revenge, which appeared in *Temple Bar* in December 1890. Although her early effort was poorly reviewed by the *Athenaeum,* D'Arcy continued to publish sentimental stories such as "An April Folly," "A Modern Incident," and "The Smile" under the pseudonym Gilbert H. Page in the *Argosy* between 1891 and 1893. These early stories are not of the caliber of her later stories.

D'Arcy's career in short fiction really began with the publication of her master work, "The Elegie," in *Blackwood's* in November 1891. It was later published in her first collection, *Monochromes,* with John Lane for his Keynote Series in 1895. In this story, a young woman, Marie the daughter of an aristocrat, idolizes a young composer, Emil Schoenemann. They become engaged, but her father banishes him to Paris for seven years to test his faithfulness. Marie remains true to the decadent Schoenemann while his cynicism increases. He finally returns to her and finds her on her funeral bier: Marie has died rather than be forced to marry her cousin. Schoenemann composes a magnificent elegie from the sensation of her death, but it is clear that he is not overwhelmed with grief. This story foregrounds themes that are, from this point forward, extensively considered in D'Arcy's work. The concept of the demands of genius and its companion, solipsism; the

real versus idealized woman; and the battle of the sexes. Another example of her best work is "The PLEASURE-PILGRIM," also published in *Monochromes,* which contains masterly characterization of a neurotic British writer and his exploitation of a young American woman with advanced ideas whom he ultimately convinces to kill herself to prove her love. These stories, especially "The Elegie," established D'Arcy as a writer influenced by French naturalism; recently she has also been considered a NEW WOMAN writer and a possible female decadent (see DECADENCE).

This French influence, combined with psychological realism and a stark consideration of character as well as gender and sex, caused D'Arcy's work to be rejected by mainstream publications as full of depressing episodes and squalid realism, but William Blackwood remained a strong supporter even of her short novel *The Bishop's Dilemma* (1898). HENRY HARLAND, the editor of the new periodical *The YELLOW BOOK,* noted her originality and established her not only as a consistent contributor (her work appeared in 10 of 13 volumes) but as the informal subeditor of the quarterly. Her writing during this time continued to discuss, from a scathing perspective, both men and women's responsibilities within contemporary debates on the relations between the sexes, religion, sexuality, and marriage. Harland removed her from her position as subeditor when she continually questioned his judgment over editorial decisions; there is some speculation that she was removed after the decline of an intimate relationship between the two.

D'Arcy published a further collection, *Modern Instances* (1898) for John Lane, and her oeuvre is completed by four stories published from 1899 to 1910. Various sources posit D'Arcy as unmotivated despite her early success at the *Yellow Book,* where she and HENRY JAMES were the only two well-reviewed authors in the first volume. The depth of D'Arcy's stories has also been critically undervalued, perhaps because of her limited number of texts, but there is no lack of intense interrogation of social issues in her existing fiction; in addition, she had a striking ability to create the mental atmosphere of her characters.

D'Arcy never married but had affairs with several men and was the object of the unrequited affection of

CHARLOTTE MEW. She died in London at Saint Pancras Hospital on September 5, 1937.

BIBLIOGRAPHY

D'Arcy, Ella. *Modern Instances.* New York: Garland, 1984.
————. *Monochromes.* New York: Garland, 1977.
————. "The Pleasure Pilgrim." In *Nineteenth Century Short Stories by Women,* edited by Harriet Devine Jump, 283–306. London: Routledge, 1998.
Fisher, Benjamin. "Ella D'Arcy: A Commentary," *English Literature in Transition* 35, no. 2 (1992); 179–211.
Windholz, Anne. "The Woman Who Would Be Editor: Ella D'Arcy and *The Yellow Book,*" *Victorian Periodicals Review* 29, no. 2 (1996): 116–130.

Sarah Maier

DARK NIGHT'S WORK, A ELIZABETH GASKELL (1863)

Serialized in CHARLES DICKENS's magazine *All the Year Round* (January–February 1863), ELIZABETH GASKELL's *A Dark Night's Work* details the devastating effects of a tragic secret shared by Edward Wilkins, a widowed lawyer in the rural town of Hamley, his daughter Ellinor, and his coachman Dixon. One night, during a heated, drunken argument, Wilkins accidentally kills his law partner, Mr. Dunster. Dixon is summoned by his master for assistance, while Ellinor accidentally stumbles onto the scene. Fearful of what the authorities will do to Wilkins, the trio decides that the crime must be covered up. The two men then set out for a "dark night's work" of digging a grave for Dunster. They succeed at diverting suspicion from Wilkins. The local community assumes that Dunster has run off to America and taken his partner's fortune with him. The three cannot, however, escape the guilt they feel. Ellinor falls ill for an extended period of time, while Wilkins descends into alcoholism. Although by tacit agreement, the trio never discuss the matter, Ellinor never again feels close to her father and has little contact with her old friend Dixon. Wilkins eventually dies a pathetic man, having squandered his fortune and alienated his daughter. Ellinor retires to a cathedral in East Chester with her governess, Miss Monro. Dixon, the ever-dutiful servant, stays behind to keep watch over the garden where Dunster lies. Eventually, the remains are discovered when workmen building a railroad excavate the ground. Ellinor, who is touring Italy at the time, learns that Dixon has been charged with the murder, and by the time she can return to England, he has been convicted of the crime. Fortunately, Ellinor's former fiancé, Ralph Corbet, is the judge for the case. Once she reveals that her father was the killer, Corbet has Dixon released. Finally free from guilt, Ellinor marries Reverend Livingstone, an old suitor. In the story's final scene, Dixon is seen keeping watch over the couple's two children, and it is said that Miss Monro visits them often.

Consisting of 16 chapters, more than 160 pages, and an extensive narrative that features several interwoven plot lines, *A Dark Night's Work* is more properly called a novella than a short story. Indeed, some sources, such as the Gaskell Web Project, consider it a full-length novel. Disputes over length strained the long-standing professional relationship between Gaskell and Dickens. Ironically for the contemporary reader, *A Dark Night's Work* is of interest primarily for what it lacks. Its title and its focus on the haunting effects of a grisly crime of the kind favored by sensation writers WILKIE COLLINS and ELLEN WOOD suggest that this would be a gothic tale, but the story contains little that is shocking or scary. The only two disturbing events, Dunster's death and the burial of his body, are only spoken of, not narrated directly.

Gaskell's aim here is not to frighten but rather to instruct. The plot, which is built around a series of improbable coincidences, conveys the simple moral lesson that one cannot escape the past. For years after the murder, the humble life of devotion and charity work that Ellinor leads offers her no solace from the guilt she feels. But after confessing her part in the crime in order to clear Dixon's name, she finally achieves atonement. More important, she also earns the reward of marriage, the life's goal of Victorian women and the end to which 19th-century realist narratives overwhelmingly aspire. Although Ellinor's union with Reverend Livingstone seems inevitable from the moment he enters the text, it can occur only after she becomes worthy of marriage by laying bare the deceit on which her life has rested.

BIBLIOGRAPHY

Foster, Shirley. *Elizabeth Gaskell: A Literary Life.* Basingstoke, England: Palgrave Macmillan, 2002.

Gaskell, Elizabeth. *A Dark Night's Work and Other Stories.* Edited by Suzanne Lewis. Oxford: Oxford University Press, 1992.

Stephen Severn

"DAUGHTERS OF THE LATE COL-ONEL, THE" KATHERINE MANSFIELD (1922)

Published in *The GARDEN PARTY* and concerned, like the title story of the collection, with "the diversity of life and how we try to fit in everything, Death included" (Mansfield 1985, 259), this story was written one year before KATHERINE MANSFIELD's own death and was considered by many reviewers a "cruel" piece when it was published. Like most fictions by Katherine Mansfield it is difficult to recount, being plotless—Mansfield despised "nice 'plotty' stories" (Mansfield 1985, 239)—although the title of the story tells something of what it is about. Josephine and Constantia, the two middle-aged, unmarried and, childless protagonists of the story, have existed only in relation to their father, a symbol of Victorian patriarchy and imperialism. When the colonel is dead, the two women discover that although they are no longer obliged to obey his rule, their lifelong submission to his authority has stripped them of their potential for independence: They are unable to get away from the claustrophobic space of his house and exchange a world of escapist fantasies for the potential dangers of freedom and external reality.

As in "Prelude" and "At the Bay," one of the main achievements of "The Daughters of the Late Colonel" lies in its complex and modernist structure based on a significant tension between linear continuity and spatial contiguity—between the apparently logical succession of scenes and the illogical juxtaposition of images and unstated links. Section one begins in the sisters' bedroom, a week after their father's death, an event that will never be directly named until the last section of the story. From the start, Josephine and Constantia's reaction to their loss appears both comic and pathetic, a mixture of embarrassment, nervousness, and paralysis. In section two, we realize that the sisters' fearful attitude to Nurse Andrews and their servant Kate replicates their father's tyranny over them. Section three records the sisters' remembered horror at the gothic sight of their father opening "one eye only" just before dying in his bed. Section four centers on a decorous visit from the vicar, in the drawing room, the day of the Colonel's death. The conversation shows the sisters' guilt and anxiety when confronted with male authority. Section five takes us back at the cemetery, when Josephine imagined their father's resurrection and revenge for the fact that they buried him.

In section six, the two women try to face their fears and weaknesses for the first time as they enter their father's room, two mornings after his funeral. Constantia deliberately locks the Colonel's wardrobe and takes the key out, a symbolic gesture of punishment that reminds Josephine of the day when she pushed her brother Benny into the pond. But in the section seven, as they are back in the dining-room, inner tension increases again: The sisters wonder what memento of their father they should send Benny while unconsciously making a link between domestic tyranny and the empire (we infer here that the colonel served in the colonial service in Ceylon). Deciding on a watch, a male symbol of historical and chronological time, Josephine then wonders in section eight whether their adult nephew Cyril should not have it. Until the end of section nine, the dining room dissolves in a happy memory of one of Cyril's visits as a child. Sections ten and eleven take us back to the present and to the daughters' indecisiveness and unlived lives.

The final section of the story focuses on a series of metaphorical objects and images that embody the possibility for the sisters to escape from patriarchal order and develop their own female identities. The music from the barrel organ in the street defies the military order imposed on them by their father, the sparrows chirping on the window-sill echo Josephine's "queer little crying noise" inside her, and the moonlight and the sea suggest a reconciliation with female rhythms and limitless territories. But when Constantia turns to her sister to articulate what she has glimpsed of this new fantasized life, the expected moment of self-revelation evaporates into oblivion: "I can't say what I was going to say, Jug, because I've forgotten what it was . . . that I was going to say." As Mansfield wrote to a friend in June 1921, "All was meant, of course, to lead up to that last paragraph, when my two flowerless ones turned with that timid gesture, to the sun. 'Perhaps now . . .' And after that, it seemed to me, they died as surely as Father was dead" (Mansfield 1985, 224). The sisters' awakening is smothered by their upbringing and education.

The mixing of time and space in the 12 numbered sections of the story reminds us that for many modernist writers time is both subjective and objective; it is a complex flow of fragmented moments challenging the logical causality usually associated with time sequence. In this story, the illusion of chronological linearity created by the numbered sections is rapidly dismissed by the confusing function of the temporal ellipses and typographical gaps and by the sisters' successive movements in the different rooms of the house. The use of flashbacks within the sections or in between them underlines the retreat into the subjective memory of an "eternal" past that functions like a prison. As the story unfolds and time elapses, the structuring of the narration draws attention to the circularity of the short story: Suspended in time, the daughters are unable to experience the cyclical time of creative and maternal capacity, an inability that seems to be confirmed by the absence of the mother in the story. But the structure of Katherine Mansfield's story also has symbolical implications linked with its dramatic frame and main thematic impulses. "The Daughters of the Late Colonel" is a story concerned with Oedipal romance, with the neurotic fixity of gender roles, with authority and suppressed desire, alienation and freedom, life and death. If the story is indeed cruel, this cruelty is not primarily addressed to the sisters, whose unfulfilled lives are rendered poignant and humorous by Mansfield's technique of point of view and free indirect style. It is rather the result of a harsh yet indirect criticism on a Victorian patriarchal system that victimizes its women to the point of making them unaware of their own potential.

BIBLIOGRAPHY

Fullbrook, Kate. *Katherine Mansfield.* Bloomington: Indiana University Press, 1986.

Hanson, Clare, and Andrew Gurr. *Katherine Mansfield.* London: Macmillan, 1981.

Kleine, Don W. "Katherine Mansfield and the Orphans of Time," *Modern Fiction Studies* 24, no. 3 (Autumn 1978): 423–438.

Mansfield, Katherine. *The Garden Party and Other Stories.* London: Penguin, 1998.

———. *The Letters and Journals of Katherine Mansfield: A Selection.* 1977. Edited by C. K. Stead. 4th ed. Harmondsworth, England: Penguin Books, 1985.

Anne Besnault-Levita

DAUGHTERS OF THE VICAR D. H. LAWRENCE (1911)

This novella contrasts life-giving and life-denying attitudes, key themes in D. H. LAWRENCE's stories. Salient details of Midlands country life give this story its realism: A miner's widow plans brussels sprouts, meat, and apple pie for dinner; moleskin trousers smell of mining; snowflakes on a train window and the mining lift entrance viewers. Fabular elements appear, too: A proud, dark, and beautiful eldest daughter (Mary) trades her body for status, marrying for money; the stubborn, blond, and plain second daughter (Louisa) vows to marry for love. Written in 1911 as "Two Marriages," Lawrence revised the story in 1913 and 1914 before publication in *The Prussian Officer and Other Stories* to focus on emotional and erotic life.

Lack of money and admiration appear as barriers to happiness for the vicar and his wife, who move from Cambridge when an influx of miners swells the population of Aldecross. Despite a meager income, the couple instill their sense of superiority and their bourgeois values in their children. The vicar's ill health brings a young clergyman to town; he represents the amassing of learning, perhaps money, at the cost of vitality. Slight in build, Mr. Massy seems "an abortion," "infantile," and defective in masculinity. He physically repulses the older daughter, yet she admires his "abstract goodness" and morality. Because of her impoverishment and because her father considers it "not a bad match," Mary accepts Massy's proposal. She "paid with her body" and "bought her position," she thinks. A domineering husband, Massy becomes an obsessively anxious father, endangering his wife's health. Children force Mary to recognize that she cannot deny the body.

A mining family also exhibits warped sexuality. The Oedipal situation echoes Paul Morel's plight in the novel *Sons and Lovers,* itself autobiographical. Widowed Mrs. Durant binds her youngest son to her: Alfred feels ashamed, incompetent, and unmanly. Enlisting "makes a man of him," yet after returning, nearly 30 years old, he still cannot leave home. When cancer kills his mother, his grief is reminiscent of Morel's. As Keith Cushman shows, earlier versions of the story portray Louisa as a substitute mother. In the published version, Louisa breaks through class difference, social conventions, and self-consciousness to a transforming passionate connection with Alfred. Deferential, distant, and nearly mute, Alfred cannot respond to her initial overtures. Impassioned "beyond herself," she declares that she wants to stay with him. A transfiguring "agony" bares their "souls" and leads to lovemaking. The 13th of 15 sections ends with their laughter about the smudges on Louisa. Louisa's father calls their engagement "unseemly" and wants to avoid as much "loss of prestige as possible," so the couple plan to emigrate to Canada.

The crucial scene of washing a man's body appears in *Sons and Lovers, Aaron's Rod,* and *Lady Chatterley's Lover.* Written earlier, "ODOUR OF CHRYSANTHEMUMS" uses the washing of a corpse to show essential separateness and a failed marital connection. In *Daughters of the Vicar,* revelation of male beauty galvanizes Louisa's desire; washing and a mother's death unite a vicar's daughter and a mama's boy.

Like *Middlemarch* in its focus on two sisters, *Daughters* treats issues raised in *The Rainbow* (written concurrently) and anticipates *Women in Love.* Carol Siegel sees the story as a reimagining of GEORGE ELIOT's *The Mill on the Floss* in which Mary's similarities to Maggie challenge Eliot's view of renunciation. Siegel notes connections with KATHERINE MANSFIELD's story "The DAUGHTERS OF THE LATE COLONEL." Janice Hubbard Harris identifies a reversed "Sleeping Beauty" motif: A strong woman awakens a sleeping (or "Oedipally paralyzed") prince. Like Cushman, Mara Kalnins examines the revisions of the story; she argues that the representation of Louisa's sensual awakening constitutes a linguistic breakthrough. In its vocabulary of passion instead of pure social realism and its contextualizing of erotic love within familial dynamics, "The Daughters" exemplifies Lawrence's visionary mode of short fiction.

BIBLIOGRAPHY

Cushman, Keith. *D. H. Lawrence at Work: The Emergence of the Prussian Officer Stories.* Charlottesville: University Press of Virginia, 1978.

Harris, Janice Hubbard. *The Short Fiction of D. H. Lawrence.* New Brunswick, N. J.: Rutgers University Press, 1984.

Kalnins, Mara. "D. H. Lawrence's 'Two Marriages' and 'Daughters of the Vicar.'" *Ariel* 7 (1976): 32–49.

Lawrence, D. H. *The Prussian Officer and Other Stories.* Edited by John Worthen. Cambridge: Cambridge University Press, 1983.

Siegel, Carol. *Lawrence among the Women.* Charlottesville: University Press of Virginia, 1991.

Elizabeth Wilson

DAVIES, RHYS (1901–1978)

Rhys Davies contributed more than 100 stories to English, Welsh, and American periodicals between 1926 and 1978. In addition to his many short stories, he published approximately 20 novels and other writings, including autobiography, biography, drama, and travel books. His long and prolific career naturally engaged a wide range of themes that were compounded by the complexity of his identity. Davies was a gay man and the son of a shopkeeper born into what in his autobiography, *Print of a Hare's Foot,* he described as the "heavily masculine" culture of working-class Wales (59). At a young age, he left his hometown of Blaenclydach to pursue a literary career in London by marketing his Welsh origins. Some of Davies's interest as a writer, therefore, is his negotiation of class, nation, and sexuality. Additionally, as a professional writer who lived entirely by his ability to produce large quantities of fiction, he provides special insights into the culture of the literary market and the short story's position as an unmarketable and therefore more "purely aesthetic" cultural production.

As a professional writer, Davies was a short story writer on off-hours only, for novels were the bread and butter of anyone seeking to make a living by writing. In the preface to his self-edited *Collected Stories of Rhys Davies,* he describes the short story as a "luxury which only those writers who fall in love with them can afford to cultivate" (viii), and he did so, for he believed it to be the more elegant form. Defending the genre in a letter to the *Times Literary Supplement*'s reviewer G. H. Wells, who favored the political realist novel, Davies insists that he "never felt [himself] bowing and prostrate before size and bulk: in fact [he'd] always been suspicious as to the imaginative capability of its producer." The short story, Davies claimed, thrives in lively brevity: "That instinct to dive, swift and agile, into the opening of a story holds, for me, half the technical art; one must not on any account loiter or brood in the first paragraph; be deep in the story's elements in a few seconds" (Davies 1995, viii). In contrast to the novel, "that great public park so often complete with great drafty spaces, noisy brass band and unsightly litter, the enclosed and quiet short story garden is of small importance, and never has been much more" (1955, v). But in this "small importance," Davies later claimed in a letter of 1950, there is a powerful impetus, for in the short story "one can be, so to speak, more human. There is a fire-side, pure tale-telling quality . . . and they can convey with much more success than the novel the ancient or primitive, the intrinsic flavour of a race or people" (letter to Buckin Moon, May 31, 1950, Harry Ranson Humanities Research Center).

Davies's comment on the racial value of the short story belies his more aesthetic claims and reveals his awareness of his marketability as a Welsh writer, for Davies's initial and abiding success in the literary market was as the representative Welshman (and often, consequently, as the authentic voice of the working class). Davies's representations of Welsh communities are often sordid and savage attacks upon a petty and selfish Nonconformist Welsh (i.e., not Anglican). His first three stories, in particular, are recognizably written after the style of Caradoc Evans, whose *My People* (1905) caused a stir in England and elicited the ire of a Wales that felt betrayed by one of its own. But not all of Davies's stories follow this strain of criticism. Many of his stories of Wales are tragic and sympathetic treatments of labor. "On the Tip" (1936), for instance, displays the abiding nobility and humanity of men scraping the most meager living from the dregs of the Depression. Many stories are comic and affectionate, like the rugby-match follies of "Canute" (1949) or the death-mocking revelry of "Mourning for Ianto" (1942). The influence of D. H. Lawrence, with whom Davies became friends before Lawrence's death, is evident in a wide selection of novels and in such stories as "Blodwen" (1931) and "The Skull" (1936). Other stories favor representations of women, especially "Nightgown" (1942), which portrays the demeaning and desperate state of women in a male-dominated society of masculine labor. Davies's frequent sympathy for female characters in working-class Wales also echoes his own feelings of alienation as a gay man. Stories such as "Fear" (1949) and "The Dark World" (1942) reflect the awakening of a mind unsuited to surroundings that entrap their protagonists. More explicitly "queer" stories, such as "The Doctor's Wife" (1931), "The Romantic Policewoman" (1933), and "Wigs, Costumes, Masks" (1949), explore the matrices of power and knowledge in the textual silence surrounding Davies's articulation of gay revelations.

Davies had much to say about nation, class, and sexuality, but he was also concerned with making a living and building a career as a professional writer. He longed for the distinction of highbrow authorship, he dreamed of achieving the success of the best-selling author, but he never succeeded in becoming much more than a moderately well–selling author. Davies's professional anxieties are perhaps best summed up in a review in the *New Age* of a special-edition story, "A Bed of Feathers," published by the Mandrake Press in 1929. The reviewer dismissed Davies as "the highbrow's Elinor Glynn." Davies took this review to heart, referring to it twice in his personal correspondence, and it is an apt description of a writer who longed for success, who resented the market that denied it to him, and who cultivated an aesthetic distance and highbrow indifference to shore up some authorial authenticity. This aesthetic indifference and antipathy to the market is evident in his conception of the short story, but it also appears in several of the stories themselves. For instance, Davies describes a publisher in "Doris of Gomorrah" (1933) who "made spectacular sums of money on tasteless books that the public could respect as safely as the tapioca puddings they resembled." For Davies, the short story had an almost magical quality that could dispel his Grub Street dependence on novel writing. As he lamented to a poet friend, Phillip Henderson, at the outset of his career, "All I can say is get a couple of decently written novels done and you'll soon get enough to buy yourself a couple of sausages for dinner for at least a year" (September 16, 1928,

MS22C03E #31 National Library of Wales). The short story would bring no sausages, but it did feed Davies's aesthetic fantasies.

Aside from being a true craftsman of a large and varied oeuvre of stories, and aside from being a site for complex negotiations of identity, Davies's career also places the short story within the complexities of its circulation in such wide-ranging literary markets as magazines, special editions, anthologies, collections, and collectors' shops. Some very good work has been conducted on Davies's writing, but he is still an understudied figure in the forms and contexts of the short story genre. (See WALES.)

BIBLIOGRAPHY

Davies, Rhys. *Collected Stories of Rhys Davies.* London: Heinemann, 1955.

———. *Print of a Hare's Foot, An Autobiographical Beginning.* 1968. Bridgend, Wales: Seren, 1998.

———. Uncollected papers and letters. Harry Ransom Humanities Research Center, University of Texas, Austin.

———. Uncollected papers and letters. National Library of Wales.

Osborne, Huw Edwin. "Rhys Davies, Professional Writer: Identities in the Marketplace," *North American Journal of Welsh Studies* 3, no. 1 (Winter 2003): 1–32.

S., J. Review of *A Bed of Feathers,* by Rhys Davies. *New Age,* 18 July 1929, p. 143.

Stephens, Meic. *Rhys Davies, Collected Stories.* 3 vols. Llandysul, Wales: Gomer, 1998.

———. *Rhys Davies: Decoding the Hare—Critical Essays to Mark the Centenary of the Writer's Birth.* Cardiff: University of Wales Press, 2001.

Huw Osborne

"DEAD, THE" JAMES JOYCE (1915) JAMES JOYCE began writing "The Dead" in 1907, somewhat later than the other stories in *Dubliners,* the collection in which it was finally published in 1915. It is considerably longer than the other stories, and some commentators regard it not as a short story but as a novella. In addition to the difference in form from the other stories, it also seems to have a different moral perspective or stance toward Ireland. It is generally seen as playing an important transitional role between Joyce's earlier, shorter work and the longer, more technically

involved later work. Like most of Joyce's other narratives, not much seems to be happening in terms of surface action. The story's real resonance comes from the complex narrative and thematic subtleties incorporated into its underlying structure. Like all of Joyce's fiction, it has provoked an enormous amount of critical and interpretive attention. It has been dramatized and was made into a film by John Huston in 1987.

The events themselves are easily summarized: Two elderly unmarried women—Julia and Kate—and their niece Mary Jane are giving their annual epiphany season dinner and dance in their home on Usher's Island in Dublin at the turn of the century. Their nephew, Gabriel Conroy, the main character from whose perspective most of the action is revealed, arrives at the party with his wife, Gretta. They greet and converse with the other guests, with whom they are familiar. Much of this disjointed conversation is reproduced. The self-absorbed Gabriel, a teacher and literary man, is nervous about delivering some after-dinner remarks he has prepared. Memories of the past, associations with various guests, and concerns about how he is regarded flit through his mind. He is also irritated with some of the guests and feels that his talk will be above the heads of his audience. When the time comes to deliver his comments, he praises his two aunts and their niece highly and celebrates the values of the past. After the dinner, he and his wife return in a cab to a hotel room they have rented for the occasion of the dinner. Gabriel feels lustful toward his wife, but these feelings are undercut by Gretta's memories of Michael Furey, an early suitor of hers who died when he was only 17. First Gretta falls asleep, and then, finally, Gabriel.

Underneath these mundane actions lies the story's rich interpretive potential. The title of the story suggests its major theme: the awareness of the claims of the past—the dead—on an individual and his willingness or reluctance to accept those claims. The story incorporates many of these associations with the past through various motifs that run through the story. The first word of the story, for instance, is "Lily," the name of the caretaker's daughter who welcomes the guests to the party. The associations that can be made with *lily* include half a dozen potential connections with death and its counterpart, resurrection. The lily is a common flower at funerals because it also suggests resurrection. In addition, it is the emblem of the archangel Gabriel, who welcomes those who have died into heaven, so it prefigures the appearance of Gabriel Conroy. A lily's whiteness might also suggest snow, a major motif in the story, in its associations with cold—a deathlike quality—but also in its ability to cover, preserve, and finally provide the sustenance for rebirth or revitalization. The setting of the story during the epiphany season—something that is never mentioned explicitly but must be deduced from the text—has suggested to many commentators that in the course of the story Gabriel Conroy moves toward his own epiphany, or sudden insight into the true nature of things.

One of the story's major issues is the degree of Gabriel's commitment to Ireland and things Irish. Intellectually he is inclined to associate himself with the "east," or Europe and England—with new trends. Molly Ivors, his colleague and an Irish nationalist who attends the party, teases him by making fun of these inclinations. Emotionally, he comes to realize in the course of the story, he cannot shake off identifications with Ireland, or the "west." Other motifs in the story suggest these ingrained cultural identifications: the old stories being told, the memories of deceased friends, the associations of specific images linked to Ireland's past. These and other evocative aspects of the story remain implicit, and their meanings remain suggestive rather than clear-cut or definite. The deliberate ambiguity contributes to the story's rich potential of meaning.

Another important pattern is Gabriel's growing self-awareness. What exactly this awareness consists of is, however, open-ended. The story's final scene in the hotel room pulls together many of the issues Gabriel has been grappling with and involves the forging of a new dimension of his identity—a realization, for instance, of a more complex meaning of love and his deeper connections with his heritage. The final paragraph shifts into an even more poetic mode, using the snow outside the window to suggest links with a greater humanity, a kind of universality and universal experience that Gabriel may be now acknowledging or at least be aware of. The language of this scene also contains repetitions of images and symbols employed earlier in the story.

Whether Gabriel will awaken a new man is unclear. One extreme would be to assume the terms of Gabriel's sleep, "The time had come for him to set out on his journey westward," are figurative terms for his death—that nothing has happened. Another view might focus more on the story's hints of resurrection or rebirth and argue that the old Gabriel must die in order that the new individual might be born and that he will awaken with a heightened awareness. A middle view might see his final realization as the semiconscious, dreamlike state between wakefulness and sleep, and perhaps only a passing perception. Some commentators, like Richard Ellmann, whose highly regarded biography of Joyce includes a useful essay on the story, have argued that in "The Dead" Joyce gives a rendering of himself if he had stayed in Ireland and not gone into self-imposed exile in order to dedicate himself to his art.

BIBLIOGRAPHY

Ellman, Richard. *James Joyce.* New York: Oxford University Press, 1982.

Joyce, James. *Dubliners: Text, Criticism, and Notes.* Edited by Robert Scholes and A. Walton Litz. New York: Penguin USA, 1996.

Schwarz, Daniel. *James Joyce's "The Dead": A Case Study of Contemporary Criticism.* New York: St. Martin's, 1994.

Tom Loe

DEBITS AND CREDITS RUDYARD KIPLING (1926)   The publication of this collection marked the end of a long fallow period for RUDYARD KIPLING in which he struggled with depression (following his son, John's death in WORLD WAR I) and a creative block. The collection of 14 stories, 19 poems, and two scenes from an unfinished play received a mixed response, although some did see Kipling as having returned to the form of his earlier works. The collection contains some of Kipling's most famous stories, including "The Janeites," which famously describes the sense of kinship created between men as a result of a shared passion for the works of Jane Austen. "A Madonna of the Trenches" focuses on the aftermath of the war and in particular on a man whose mind has been shattered not only by what he has encountered but also by his family life.

World War I also features in "A Friend of the Family" and "The GARDENER," a story Kipling composed after a visit to the war cemetery at Bois Guillaume near Rouen on March 14, 1925. He was familiar with the bureaucracy of identifying bodies and notifying next of kin from his work with the War Graves commission.

In "The Gardener" Helen Turrell returns from recuperating in France with the infant son of her dead ne'er-do-well brother and an unsuitable woman. She raises Michael with great devotion and allows him to call her "Mummy" at bedtime. Before beginning Oxford, Michael enlists in the army. He is soon listed as missing. Helen is informed that he is buried in a military cemetery in Belgium. On her way to visit the grave, Helen encounters two women. One is distraught because she cannot find her son's grave; the other visits the cemetery ostensibly to take photos for her grieving friends, but the real reason, as she confides to Helen, is to visit the grave of a lover whom she could never acknowledge. Helen encounters a man in the cemetery who "looked at her with infinite compassion." He tells her, "I will show you where your son lies." Leaving the cemetery, she again sees the man, "supposing him to be the gardener."

Understatement and irony throughout the story lead up to this short exchange, the mystery of the story. What is the relationship between Helen and Michael? Is she, as many critics suggest, actually his mother? Has her life been a series of lies to cover up the birth of an illegitimate son? The passage refers to John 20:14–15 in the Bible. Mary Magdalene at the tomb of Jesus turns to a man who asks her why she is weeping; she answers him, "supposing him to be the gardener." Is Christ the gardener providing Helen with heavenly consolation? Does the accompanying poem's reference to Mary Magdalene and the themes of deception and discovery illuminate the ambiguity of the story? Or, as Dillingham has argued, is the story "a study of the excruciating and prolonged pain of bereavement" (68) in which religion brings no consolation? Is a biological connection necessary to explain Helen's profound grief, or does parenthood mean more?

As in other stories in the collection, inconsistencies and incomplete explanations force the reader to question the veracity of the third-person narrative. Conventions and social forms are rigidly upheld by society, and the messy, emotional disturbances of life are covered up and repressed. Kipling's language conveys through casual narrative the pain and grief that lies below the surface. The horror of Helen's loss is underscored by the narrator's calm, ironic revelation that "by means of time-tables made clear, how easy it was and how little it interfered with life's affairs to go and see one's grave." Michael's death, the catastrophe of the story, is contained: "a shell-splinter dropping out of a wet dawn killed him at once. The next shell uprooted and laid down over the body what had been the foundation of a barn wall, so neatly that none but an expert would have guessed that anything unpleasant had happened." Like other stories in the collection this hints at hidden secrets and a private self. Kipling also reveals how repression of pain, love, and grief seem to be necessary for society to maintain order, but the price it ultimately exerts on individuals is shown in exquisite detail.

BIBLIOGRAPHY

Bauer, Helen Pike. *Rudyard Kipling: A Study of the Short Fiction.* New York: Twayne, 1994.

Dillingham, William B. "Rudyard Kipling and Bereavement: 'The Gardener,'" *English Language Notes* 39, no. 4 (2002): 60–71.

Gilbert, Elliot. "Kipling's 'The Gardener': Craft into Art," *Studies in Short Fiction* 7 (1970): 308–319.

Kipling, Rudyard. *Debits and Credits.* 1926. New York: House of Strauss, 2003.

Lewis, Lisa. "Some Links between the Stories in Kipling's *Debits and Credits*," *English Literature in Transition* 25, no. 2 (1982): 74–85.

Shanks, Edward. Review of *Debits and Credits. London Mercury* 14 (1926): 649–651.

Margaret Godbey O'Brien

DECADENCE   A literary movement of the late 19th century that interacted with and resulted from AESTHETICISM. There is little agreement among critics regarding a defining set of features to encompass decadence, especially since the term has been burdened with its origins from the Latin *decadere,* a falling away from or decline, and the French *décadence,* a waning or downfall. Walter Pater's early influence on this movement is found in the conclusion to his *Studies in the History of the Renaissance* (1873), where he encourages artists "to burn always with this hard, gemlike flame, to maintain this ecstasy, is success in life." The 1880s and 1990s associated the idea with the scandalous French "yellow" novelist Joris-Karl Huysmans's *À rebours* (1884) and OSCAR WILDE's *The Picture of Dorian Gray* (1890), texts that read as breviaries of decadent themes and style. Shocking statements of perversity, sensuality, and sexual excess are mixed with a preference for art over nature, a love of artificial effects, an affinity for the city over country, and a preoccupation with exoticism; in addition, decadent literature is filled with the idea of ennui or moral exhaustion and synaesthetic experiences found in music, alcohol (such as absinthe), drugs (such as hashish or opium), sexual perversity, and various forms of art. The movement had a disdain for any traditional, natural, political, or moral ideals; rather, the importance of nonconformist form and subject matter were foregrounded. Authors of the short-lived decadent movement are illustrators, poets, short fiction writers, and novelists, including Charles Baudelaire, ERNEST DOWSON, J. K. Huysmans, Théophile Gautier, Stephane Mallarmé, Paul Verlaine, and Oscar Wilde; recently, scholars have also been interested in the work of female authors such as Rachilde (Margaret Eymery). The short fiction of the decadent movement (e.g., ELLA D'ARCY) was concentrated in the periodical press; in particular, John Lane's controversial *YELLOW BOOK* and later the *Savoy* created by Arthur Symons and Aubrey Beardsley were popular vehicles for decadent work and short story writers.

BIBLIOGRAPHY

Bernheimer, Charles. *Decadent Objects.* Baltimore: John Hopkins University Press, 2002.

Robbins, Ruth. *Pater to Foster, 1873–1924.* London: Palgrave, 2004.

Sarah Maier

DE LA MARE, WALTER (1873–1956) Walter de la Mare was born in Charlton, near Woolwich, London, the sixth child in a family of seven. Sent to the choir school at St. Paul's Cathedral, he left at 17 to begin a career immediately as a statistical clerk with the Anglo-American Oil Company, the newly established London office of J. D. Rockefeller's Standard Oil. This period, lasting from 1890 to 1908, also marked the beginnings of de la Mare's career as a writer. Slowly and patiently educating himself, he experimented with different forms of fiction and poetry on wastepaper sheets after hours and began to publish pseudonymously under the name Walter Ramal. First came a number of serialized short stories, which began to appear in 1895, followed by his first collection of poetry, *Songs of Childhood*, in 1902, and then several novels, including *Henry Brocken* (1904) and *The Return* (1910). De la Mare was to prove an enormously prolific writer, producing over 1,000 poems, roughly 100 stories for children and adults, and several volumes of edited anthologies and collections of critical essays. Official and popular recognition arrived, respectively, with the championship of the establishment writer Henry Newbolt, who obtained for him a royal bounty grant of £200 in 1908, and the publication of *The Listeners* in 1912, de la Mare's first widely read collection of poetry for adults. These landmarks were quickly followed by his best-known collection of poems for children, *Peacock Pie* (1913), and a civil list pension (1915). By the time of his death, he had been awarded the Order of Merit and had been appointed a Companion of Honour by the British monarch. His ashes were buried, appropriately enough, in the crypt of St. Paul's.

As this brief summary suggests, de la Mare's status has largely been defined by his official popularity, his prodigious output (particularly of poetry), and his appeal to several generations of children. Such a view has had a tendency to limit the sense of his critical value in general and has also, perhaps, obscured the appreciation of his short stories in particular. As might be suggested by the broad range of his literary production, these stories are enormously various and were produced for many different occasions and over an extended period of time. Yet even his first published tale, "Kismet" (1895), sets out the underlying tapestry of dark themes and suggestions that are repeatedly woven through his narratives. A seaman hitches a lift on a cart back to his own village, hoping to delight his wife by his unexpected return. He finds a comfortable box on which to sit, but his driver is inexplicably surly so he decides to make the final part of his journey on foot. When he arrives, however, the cart stands outside his door, and the driver is inside, light streaming from the bedroom window. His wife is dead; the man who has brought him there is her undertaker, and the box on which he sat is her coffin. But even before this denouement, both main characters feel a vague presentiment of foreboding that they do not fully understand. In the traveler's case, it is centred on "the pitiless cold stare of the moon upon all and the silence of death." He is afraid but does not know why he fears, and his heart is thus eaten away. Controlling the structure of our experience and the innocence of life, even of childhood, is a dark, unknown well of the fearful, the archaic, or simply the unknown. De la Mare's characters feel it as the sensation of a gaze, a sense that all is not quite right, an actively lurking corruption, or merely a dangerous lack of knowledge.

For both John Atkins, one of de la Mare's earliest critics, and Julia Briggs, the author of perhaps the most perceptive essay on his stories, death is the central and pervasive theme in his work. It expresses itself as both an exploration of the experience of death and, as Atkins puts it, the passage between "the tomb and the waste," the journey from death to what lies beyond, from the known, or apparently known, to what can never be fully comprehended. Unlike Mr. Bloom, the subject of "A Recluse" (1926), who is "interested in edges no longer" because he has moved over death's "borderline," de la Mare's characters are constantly concerned with the dynamics and the rhetoric of the edge, how it is measured and described. Where they never remain is in what the narrator of "A Recluse" calls the "central": "it has been explored; it is safe; you know where you are." As several observers have noted, in negotiating these borderlines effectively, de la Mare takes lessons from the short stories of HENRY JAMES. His prose, particularly in stories like "The Trumpet" (1936) or the sublimely malevolent "Seaton's Aunt" (1922), is nearly as intricately dense and operates a version of James's rhythmic "economy" in linguistically measuring the distance between the mundane and the extraordinary, the known and the unknown. Most often, however, its function is to map the impossibility of deciding between the two. Along with the work of many of his contemporaries, like ARTHUR MACHEN, M. R. JAMES, and

Algernon Blackwood, a significant proportion of de la Mare's tales could be described as ghost stories, but, as with James, we can never be entirely certain in each instance that the cause is supernatural. In any case, de la Mare's stories are most consistently preoccupied with being disconcerted by that which lies beyond the visible, known, or understood.

Set against his modernist contemporaries, figures like VIRGINIA WOOLF and JAMES JOYCE, who worked to redefine the short story, de la Mare's language has come to be seen as conventional and his sentiments complacent. In his quiet, careful negotiation of limits to the human experience, however, and his location of a precise and densely allusive prose answerable to those challenges, his own tales may have the potential to make equal, although different, claims on our attention.

BIBLIOGRAPHY

Alkins, John. *Walter de la Mare: An Exploration,* London: Folcroft, 1973.

Briggs, Julia. *Night Visitors: The Rise and Fall of the English Ghost Story.* London: Faber, 1977.

de la Mare, Walter. *Short Stories, 1895–1926.* edited by Giles de la Mare. London: Giles de la Mare Publishers, 1996.

———. *Short Stories, 1927–1956.* Edited by Giles de la Mare. London: Giles de la Mare Publishers, 2001.

Whistler, Theresa. *Imagination of the Heart: The Life of Walter de la Mare.* London: Duckworth, 1993.

David Towsey

"DEMON LOVER, THE" ELIZABETH BOWEN (1941)

Published first in the *Listener* and reprinted in ELIZABETH BOWEN's collection *The Demon Lover and Other Stories* (1945), the title story is based on a traditional "border ballad" or folksong of the same title, the oldest version of which, "A Warning for Married Women," collected by English diarist Samuel Pepys in 1703, has much in common with Bowen's tale: A married woman is carried away by a vengeful lover who returns from the dead to punish her for breaking a vow. Bowen sets her version in London during the Blitz of WORLD WAR II. Kathleen Drover has come up from the country to gather some belongings from the shut-up family home. The eerie atmosphere of the bombed city and the silent house creates rising tension. Mrs. Drover finds a letter that cannot have been delivered by post: It is from "K," her soldier fiancé who died during WORLD WAR I. The letter reminds her of a promise she made him and announces his arrival later that afternoon. Terrified, she remembers parting from him, his cruelty, and her mother's warnings. She felt overwhelmed by the promise, which is never specified but seems to involve staying true to each other through eternity. She did not grieve much at his death, and in her 30s she married an unremarkable man with whom she lived an ordinary life. She cannot even remember her soldier fiancé's face. Not sure if the part-time caretaker is in the house or not, Mrs. Drover gathers her things and leaves in a waiting taxi, heartened by the presence of the driver. In a shocking ending, the taxi speeds off before Mrs. Drover can give directions, and as she is thrown against the partition between the seats, she sees the driver's face and screams. The last glimpse of her is her hands beating against the windows as the taxi drives into the twilight.

"The Demon Lover" lends itself to multiple interpretations. On one level, it is a modern ghost story, with its sinister revenant. The story has many features of a ghost story, or even of gothic: the atmospheric setting, seemingly supernatural coincidences of timing and place, a woman in peril, and the startling ending. Others have seen it as a more straightforward work of realism; the soldier, who somehow has survived World War I, is a psychopathic stalker who has been triggered by the current war into tracking his former lover. Thus the story leaves open the possibility that the caretaker is actually the fiancé in disguise. Another reading suggests that the soldier is a figment of Kathleen's imagination. There are a number of hints in the story that she is not an emotionally strong woman; there is something almost childlike about her, and she seems uncomfortable with powerful feelings. In this reading, the stress of the war has brought her to a nervous breakdown. Nonetheless, by bringing a character from World War I into the setting of World War II, Bowen is also asking readers to make some connection between the wars, to find similarity in the inescapable dislocation and transformation of the familiar during war. The domestic setting also raises questions about the home and security: War is destroying Mrs. Drover's comfortable, upper-middle-class existence. In the postscript to *The Demon Lover and Other Stories,* Bowen notes that her stories are about wartime rather than warfare. As such, they are about impressions and psychological states rather than concrete war experiences. "The Demon Lover" is typical of her work in this and in its fascination with the darkness beneath the ordinary surface.

BIBLIOGRAPHY

Bowen, Elizabeth. *The Demon Lover and Other Stories.* London: Chatto and Windus, 1945.

Calder, Robert L. "'A More Sinister Troth': Elizabeth Bowen's 'The Demon Lover' as Allegory," *Studies in Short Fiction* 31 (1994): 91–97.

Coates, John. "The Moral Argument of Elizabeth Bowen's Ghost Stories," *Renascence* 52, no. 4 (Summer 2000): 293–309.

Reed, Toni. *Demon-Lovers and Their Victims in British Fiction.* Lexington: University Press of Kentucky, 1988.

Terri Doughty

"DESTRUCTORS, THE" GRAHAM GREENE (1954)

"The Destructors" first appeared serialized in two parts in *Picture Post* on July 24 and 31, 1954, and then was published in the collection *Twenty-one Stories* the same year. GRAHAM GREENE said in the preface to his *Collected Stories,* "I have never written anything better than 'The Destructors,'" yet he adds, "I remain in this field a novelist who has happened to write short stories" (Kelly, 97). The story, as does much of Greene's writing, deals with class differences and violence.

"The Destructors" begins by introducing the reader to a group of children, the Wormsley Common Gang. The story is told in third person, following the gang mentality by not focusing on a particular point of view. The gang's new leader is Trevor, whom they call "T." T.'s father used to be an architect but is now a clerk. T. is able to blend into the group, despite his social class and name, which he announced as a "statement of fact, not as it would have been with the others a statement of shame or defiance" (7). The landscape of Wormsley Common in 1950s London is punctuated by the aftereffects of the Blitz. The gang meet in a carpark, next to a house that survived the Blitz when all those around it were destroyed. Mr. Thomas, or "Old Misery," owns the house, which has fallen badly into decay. T. knows that Christopher Wren designed the house. None of the other children know who Wren is, displaying the class division between T. and the other members.

While Old Misery is away for the August bank holiday, T. proposes that the gang destroy the house, and the leadership changes hands. Blackie, the former leader, goes along with the plan only to gain fame for the gang. The children systematically destroy the house: cutting wires, smashing the bath, collapsing the self-supported spiral staircase. T. finds Old Misery's savings in the mattress and insists on burning the notes one by one. The description of the ash raises images of religious services, as does the unleashing of a flood on the destroyed house. When Blackie asks if T. hates the old man, T. replies, "Of course I don't hate him. . . . There'd be no fun if I hated him" (16).

Old Misery returns early the next day, and T. falters in his leadership. He is called "Trevor," which could crack his authority completely. Blackie supports him, and the gang traps Old Misery in the outdoor lavatory. They toss him food and blanket as a sign that they do not want to hurt him, but they refuse to release him. The gang attaches a rope from a strut supporting the house to a lorry, so the entire house collapses when the lorry driver pulls away in the morning. The story ends as Thomas sobs over the demise of his house while the lorry driver laughs, "There's nothing personal, but you got to admit it's funny" (23).

The house functions as a symbol of old Europe, and the gang members react against the "misery" the previous generations caused them. The decay of the house represents the crumbling social structures of postwar Britain. While Trevor's name sets him apart from the other children, his use of the word "beautiful" to describe the house most strikingly demonstrates how different he is from them. His rage at the house can be seen as a backlash against his own class. As his father created houses, T. destroys them. Greene comments, "Streaks of light came in through the closed shutters where they worked with the seriousness of creators—and destruction after all is a form of creation" (15).

BIBLIOGRAPHY
Greene, Graham. *Twenty-one Stories*. Harmondsworth, England: Penguin, 1981.

Kelly, Richard. *Graham Green: A Study of the Short Fiction*. New York: Twayne, 1992.
Miller, R. H. *Understanding Graham Greene*. Columbia: University of South Carolina Press, 1990.
Watts, Cedric. *A Preface to Greene*. London; New York: Longman, 1997.

Jennifer Young

DETECTIVE FICTION

The history of detective fiction necessarily overlaps with that of other, related fields such as sensation, adventure, thriller, and spy fiction, and, to an extent, its development is dependent on those genres and consequently resistant to definition.

Popular interest in crime had always been evident in the prolific production of the broadsheets, ballads, and anecdotal accounts of criminals' last words that would accompany public trials and executions, but these largely celebrated the heroism of the criminal in his defiance of monarchical authority. With the birth of the police force and institutionalization of the prison system from the early 19th century, the focus of that interest shifted to the protection of society against such criminals and, particularly, to the detective figure in whom that hope of security resided.

The detective story, then, was concerned with the unmasking of a criminal—often a murderer—and bringing him to justice, thus restoring order to society, and the activities of the detective in this pursuit were central to the emerging genre. CHARLES DICKENS made an early contribution with his characterization of Inspector Bucket in *Bleak House* (1852–53), WILKIE COLLINS created Sergeant Cuff in the first full-length detective novel, *The Moonstone* (1868), and ELLEN WOOD had a boy detective in *JOHNNY LUDLOW*. All three authors invoke the authority of the professional police force, but as the genre developed it came to privilege the amateur or private detective.

Edgar Allan Poe had already produced what are widely agreed to be the first detective stories, generating the eccentric figure of the Chevalier Auguste Dupin, whose powers of observation and deduction provided the blueprint from which ARTHUR CONAN DOYLE created Sherlock Holmes. Between Poe's short stories of the 1840s and the creation of Holmes in the 1880s, writers experimented with variations on crime, mystery, and adventure novels, but Doyle in particular took up and renewed interest in the short story form. The circulation of the STRAND MAGAZINE dropped dramatically when Doyle "killed off" Sherlock Holmes in the story "The Final Problem," but the public appetite for more adventures about the popular fictional detective was only whetted by the publication of *The Hound of the Baskervilles* in 1902, a novel set in the years before Holmes's death. Doyle reluctantly resurrected the sleuth and his chronicler, Dr. Watson, in a collection of 13 stories, *The Return of Sherlock Holmes,* in 1905. These much-imitated stories give a good sense of how the detective story might be said to operate at the beginning of the 20th century.

A good example is the story "The ADVENTURE OF CHARLES AUGUSTUS MILVERTON." Milverton is described by Holmes as the "worst man in London . . . the king of all the blackmailers," and it is this form of criminal activity that incurs the greatest revulsion in Holmes and Watson, for the victims are all well-born women. Holmes's usual contempt for the aristocracy is displaced by his concern for the social vulnerability of women, whose indiscretions place their reputations in jeopardy. Yet in avoiding scandal, telling the truth becomes problematic, and Holmes himself has difficulty in ascertaining where the truth lies. His client, Lady Eva, has told him that her letters in Milverton's possession are merely "imprudent," but Milverton asserts that they are, rather, "very sprightly." The nature of the victim's innocence thus comes into question. It also emerges that the law not only is impotent but actually works in favor of the blackmailer. Watson suggests that, in law, Milverton could be apprehended, to which Holmes responds, "Technically, no doubt, but practically not." Armed with a gun, Milverton claims that "the law will support me" should he use it to defend himself from Holmes. Although Holmes has never had qualms about stretching the limits of the law or evading its strictures, he is forced to resort to committing a "morally justifiable" felony to try to retrieve the letters through burglary. Watson's more delicate conscience submits to the "sporting interest" of the crime, by dwelling on the chivalric nature of the motivation behind it. Eventually, justice does not lie in

Holmes's hands but in those of a female victim from the highest ranks of society with whom Holmes has had no business. The victim becomes a criminal avenger, shooting Milverton. That "there are certain crimes which the law cannot touch, and which therefore, to some extent, justify private revenge" is the moral of the story, but where that is the case, the detective's function is compromised and social conventions are distorted.

In another Holmes story, "A SCANDAL IN BOHEMIA" (1891), Doyle develops many of these themes. Watson has married and Holmes now lives alone, and this marginalized lifestyle inheres in his attitude to the legal justice system as it is made clear that he, with Watson's willing cooperation, is ready to break the law "in a good cause." Holmes astounds yet again with his demonstrations of scientific deduction, explaining to Watson, "You see, but you do not observe." His mastery of disguise takes a prominent role in the story. First as a disreputable groom, then as an absent-minded clergyman, Holmes literally impersonates the characters—as Watson says, "his very soul seemed to vary with every fresh part." This acting skill is a transgressive characteristic that raises questions about the stability of Holmes's identity while enabling the detective to infiltrate every level of society in that "good cause."

The plot of "A Scandal in Bohemia" is a simple one. A scandal could ensue if the adventuress Irene Adler sends a compromising photograph of herself with the king of Bohemia to the princess to whom he is now engaged. There appears to be no pecuniary motive for her blackmail but rather the hatred of a woman scorned by her lover. For this reason, her obduracy in holding to her threat cannot be broken by ordinary means, and the King employs Holmes to retrieve the photograph in any way he can. The interest of the tale revolves around the cat-and-mouse game of disguises Holmes plays in order to trick the singer into revealing the whereabouts of the photograph, only to find himself outwitted by her expertise and cunning.

The thematic construction centers around Victorian concerns with gender and class, utilizing polarities to confirm preconceptions that are then undermined in unexpected fashion, thus establishing the detective story as a site of social and cultural debate. In England, the appearance of the NEW WOMAN—the modern, independent woman who challenged the status quo through her incursions into the masculine domain—was causing much public consternation. It was felt that the New Woman sacrificed her essential femininity in pursuing her independence. However, Adler is dissociated from contemporary English girls, in that she is American by birth and has followed an operatic career on the Continent, both details suggesting a far greater freedom from convention and potential for transgression than any English girl could realize. Her unfeminine abilities allow her to disguise herself as "a slim youth," while her description as having "the face of the most beautiful of women, and the mind of the most resolute of men" is regarded as an unseemly combination. Despite these traits, we learn that she was "cruelly wronged" by the king. Although Adler lives at the edge of acceptable social mores, she nevertheless retains her essential femininity through her vulnerability to the masculine hierarchy.

Holmes's admiration for "*the* woman" humanizes the "most perfect reasoning and observing machine that the world has seen," making him a more accessible character, and that admiration is stirred by Adler's resoluteness. Her moral integrity in refusing to give in to the king's demands is sharply contrasted with the king's own selfish class-consciousness, which values position over ethics. The forms of society are questioned from the start when middle-class Watson describes the foreign sovereign's attire as "akin to bad taste." Holmes's cool, admonitory rejoinder to the king that Adler "seems, indeed, to be on a very different level to Your Majesty" and his request for her photograph over any financial reward clearly suggest that the lower-class Bohemian soul is more discerning of moral principle than the Bohemian king.

Despite the vividness of Doyle's representation of Holmes, it is possible to argue that the structure and limits of the short story form encouraged detective fiction writers to focus on the puzzle element of the plot. Characterization and setting were necessarily reduced to a minimum, and interest in the detective and his methods took precedence over questions of social realism. Serial publication also ensured the continued consumption of this form and, in the wake of the spectacular suc-cess of Holmes and Watson, the detective short story was taken up by many writers. G. K. CHESTERTON developed the Father Brown stories, which were nearly as successful as Doyle's, while writers such as ARTHUR MOR-RISON, L. T. MEADE, Ernest Bramah, and R. Austin Freeman all produced their own versions of the eccentric detective. Nor were all detectives male; Catherine Pirkis's "lady detective," Loveday Brooke (1893), and Baroness Orczy's Lady Molly of Scotland Yard (1910) were rare, but not unpopular, female sleuths in what was becoming a formulaic tradition.

That the genre was quickly established was clear from the numbers of parodies, pastiches, and imitators that proliferated after Doyle. The idea of fair play between author and reader came to be expected, and authors generally adhered to "rules" by which intelligent readers could be expected to solve the mystery for themselves, although this also led to debates over the literary value of these throwaway puzzles. E. C. Bentley's *Trent's Last Case* (1913) reworked and expanded the short story into a full-length novel that utilized more psychological methods in solving the mystery and directed authors toward the broader possibilities of the novel form of detective fiction. In the aftermath of WORLD WAR I, detective stories turned to a nostalgic revisioning of English life and to testing the boundaries of fair play. AGATHA CHRISTIE, probably the best-known author to emerge in the golden age of British detective fiction, the interwar years, challenged the rules with her 1926 novel *The Murder of Roger Ackroyd*. Other authors experimented with specialisms such as locked-room mysteries or so-called impossible crimes, but all tended to hark back to prewar social certainties and drew on more extensive characterization, albeit within a restricted social field. Dorothy L. Sayers, Margery Allingham, Ngaio Marsh, Michael Innes, and John Dickson Carr, all of whose detectives owe their construction to variations on eccentric, amateur, or gentlemanly backgrounds, were among some of the most popular authors of this period. Although the detective fiction of this golden age tended to run to novel-length productions, readers were also avid for the many collections and anthologies of short stories published at the time, in which celebrated detectives practised their extraordinary skills in classic, abbreviated style.

At the same time in America, pulp magazine stories by writers such as Dashiell Hammett and, later, Raymond Chandler featured tough, lone private eyes and created a subgenre known as hardboiled detective fiction, which offered a much more realistic response to interwar social conditions and often presented the detective in some form of conflict with law and order. After WORLD WAR II, British authors followed suit and abandoned golden age nostalgia, incorporating more realistic elements and dealing with more plausible criminal acts in line with the prevailing social condition. Detectives became less extraordinary and were less likely to be gentlemanly amateurs but rather policemen whose character flaws and imperfect private lives were also a product of that society. Authors such as P. D. James, Julian Symons, Ruth Rendell, and Colin Dexter developed the complexity of their detective figures through serial publication, while also placing more emphasis on the psychological motivation and circumstantial conditions that underpin the crimes. Apart from her policeman Adam Dalgliesh, James also created a female professional detective, Cordelia Gray, in *An Unsuitable Job for a Woman* (1974), giving a contemporary response to concerns about the feminist movement.

The realistic trend continued, although often utilizing an unusual or self-contained setting, as in Dick Francis's world of horse racing, Ellis Peters's medieval monastery, or W. J. Burley's Cornwall. Other subgeneric developments include the police procedural novel, which concentrates on police teamwork and its methodologies. More recently, the forensic specialist who can pin down criminal identity through scientific evidence and psychological profiling has become the new detective hero, against whom the anonymous urban serial killer has become the ultimate opponent.

BIBLIOGRAPHY

Chandler, Raymond. *The Simple Art of Murder.* Boston: Houghton Mifflin, 1950.
Doyle, Arthur Conan. *The Adventures of Sherlock Holmes.* London: Newnes, 1892.
Haycraft, Howard. *The Art of the Mystery Story: A Collection of Critical Essays.* New York: Carroll & Graf, 1983.
Ousby, Ian. *Bloodhounds of Heaven: The Detective in English Fiction from Godwin to Doyle.* Cambridge, Mass.: Harvard University Press, 1976.
Priestman, Martin. *Crime Fiction from Poe to the Present.* Plymouth, England: Northcote House, 1998.
Symons, Julian. *Bloody Murder: From the Detective Story to the Crime Novel.* London: Penguin, 1985.

Therie Hendry-Seabrook

"DEVASTATING BOYS, THE" ELIZABETH TAYLOR (1966)

Published in *McCall's* magazine in May 1966, ELIZABETH TAYLOR's "The Devastating Boys" is a witty, poignant depiction of the change that occurs in the marriage of Harold, a self-involved Oxford archeology professor, and his wife Laura, when two black children from London come to stay with them one summer. Harold is a dominating husband who has provided a model for an overbearing character in their neighbor Helena Western's novel; Harold himself does not recognize himself in the character simply because the fictional man is a barrister: "[T]hat character, with his vaguely left-wing opinions and opinionated turns of phrase, his quelling manner to his wife . . . could have nothing to do with him, since he had never taken silk. Everyone else had recognized and known, and Laura, among them, knew they had." While Harold's ego does not allow him to imagine past his professorial identity, his self-deprecating wife is aware of others' perceptions of their marriage. The story's first sentence portrays Harold's unreasonable dominion over his wife with admirable economy, while making his extemporizing about his own foibles comical: "Laura was always too early; and this was as bad as being late, her husband, who was always late himself, told her." It has been Harold's idea that they take in two poor urban children: "[H]e read of a scheme to give London children a summer holiday in the country. . . . 'Some of the children will be coloured' caught his eye. . . . He had made a long speech to Laura about children being the great equalizers, and that we should learn from them, that to insinuate the stale prejudices of their elders into their fresh, fair minds was such a sin that he could not think of a worse one." Harold is a theorist, an intellectual who has liberal ideas about life, which he has not bothered to live very intimately or observe very closely. Laura has been in the trenches; with their own children, "any little bothers Laura had hidden from him."

Laura is described as "a woman who had never had any high opinions of herself." She has loved being a mother, but her children are now grown up and gone: "Her children had been her life, and her grandchildren one day would be; but here was an empty space. Life had fallen away from her." Laura is a very private person, not a woman who enjoys socializing with the other professors' wives. Taylor depicts Laura's quandary as that of an intelligent, reclusive woman without any work that feels important to her at present. Laura is a woman who finds a worthwhile identity through mothering but who lives in an era that does not offer her the possibility of using her talent for nurturing in a job as well. Yet though Laura does not think she is good with other people's children, she finds she is a success with the boys from London. The story, like so much of Taylor's fiction, has a feminist impulse both in its championing of the beleaguered Laura, taught that she is insignificant in comparison to her important husband, and in the recognition that Laura's maternal qualities of patience, love, and humor are not so common.

The story opens with Laura waiting at the train station on a beautiful July morning for Septimus Smith and Benny Reece, the poor "coloured" children who are coming from London to the country. She herself is the mother of daughters, the "biddable children," and until the last minute Laura has imagined that she will be sent little girls: "Six-year-old boys, and she had pictured perhaps eight- or ten-year-old girls, whom she could teach to sew and make cakes for tea, and press wild-flowers as she had taught Imogen and Lalage to do."

The flamboyant half-caste Benny ("Laura hoped that this would count in Harold's eyes") and the self-dramatizing West Indian Sep are a far cry from Laura's domestic, literary-named daughters. The boys revel in the domestic appurtenances familiar to the middle classes: brushing their teeth and taking baths, talking on the telephone. They are unintimidated by Laura, her big house, Harold, or other upper-class people like the writer Helena, whom they gleefully imitate. Soon Laura too is imitating Helena: "Aren't they simply *devastating* boys?" Laura feels emboldened by the boys to be witty: She also plays cricket with Sep and Benny and feels proud of their politeness at Helena's, "just as

if they were her own children." When Laura mentions to Harold that Sep might be a great athlete, he replies that Sep has rickets: "One of her children with rickets, she had thought, stricken." Meanwhile, Harold has become more appreciative of Laura, has noticed when she is tired, and has himself played with the boys, told them stories, taken them—albeit reluctantly—to church. Laura recognizes that the boys' vacation has been a success for her, and for Harold. Harold the archaeology professor, who early in the visit is "agonized" by Sep's breaking of one of his sherds, is now focusing more on the living than the relics of the dead. By the story's close, Harold has come to a new awareness of Laura's gifts. On the day the boys leave to go back to London, Harold comes home early, imitates Benny's and Sep's slang ("Shall we make tracks?"), and takes his wife to an intimate lunch in the country. Harold, "who could not believe that he had any particular idiosyncrasies to be copied," at last sees that the drama of life is based on the recognition of individuality. Harold learns from the authenticity and exuberance of the boys to appreciate not only them but himself and his loving wife as well: "'Don't fret,' he said. 'I think we've got them for life now.'"

BIBLIOGRAPHY

Elizabeth Taylor. *The Devastating Boys*. London: Chatto and Windus, 1972.

Deborah Deneholze Morse

"DIARY OF ANNE RODWAY, THE" WILKIE COLLINS (1856)

First published in CHARLES DICKENS's magazine *Household Words* (July 19 and 26, 1856), the story was included in WILKIE COLLINS's short story collection *The Queen of Hearts* (1859) as "Brother Owen's Story of Anne Rodway."

The narrative is composed of a series of excerpts from the diary of Anne Rodway, a "plain needlewoman." In the opening series of entries, Anne recounts her concern over her troubled friend and fellow lodger Mary Mallinson. One evening, Anne is given a dreadful fright when she finds Mary sleeping heavily, her room in total disarray. She discovers a bottle of laudanum and jumps to the conclusion that Mary has given in to her despair and has attempted to end her life. Anne manages to awaken Mary, who reassures her that she is accustomed to taking a few drops of laudanum each night to help her sleep. Mary admits, however, that given her overwhelming debts, her ineptitude for needlework, and her estrangement from her family, her life is hardly worth living. Anne is haunted by Mary's parting words: "I began my life wretchedly, and wretchedly I am sentenced to end it."

A number of days are marked in Anne's diary, but there are no corresponding entries. Finally, Anne returns to her narrative with news of a "dreadful calamity"—one evening, not long after the laudanum incident, two policemen show up at the lodging house carrying the almost lifeless body of Mary. They found her lying in the street having suffered a blow to the temple. The doctor who is called in concludes that Mary is the victim of a freak accident: She likely suffered a fainting fit, fell down on the street, and hit her head on the "kerb-stone." While Anne stays up that evening keeping watch over the unconscious body of her friend, she discovers in one of Mary's tightly clenched hands what appears to be a torn piece of a man's necktie. Anne immediately concludes that Mary has been the victim of foul play, but when the doctor returns the next morning to check on Mary, he dismisses the torn cloth as significant evidence that a crime has been committed. Shortly thereafter, Mary dies. Some time passes, and then, by complete chance, Anne discovers the missing section of the tie in a rag and bottle shop. With this vital clue, she vows to track down the murderer of her friend: "[A] kind of fever got possession of [her]—a vehement yearning to go on from this first discovery and find out more, no matter what the risk might be." The seamstress-turned-detective tracks down the owner of the tie, a "crooked-back dwarf." Through a series of bribes, the dwarf leads her to the murderer, a drunk by the name of Noah Truscott, who coincidentally was also the wicked ruin of Mary's father.

"The Diary of Anne Rodway" is an early example of Collins's experiments with narrative form and perspective. Thematically, the story is provocative not simply because it features the first fictional female detective but because that amateur detective is an uneducated, working-class needlewoman who exposes the incompetence of male authority as represented by the doctor and the police. Anne Rodway sets a pattern for the strong, independent heroines that appear throughout Collins's fiction: women who often dominate and control the action while the men passively stand by. Indeed, through her ingenuity and perseverance, Anne cracks the case single-handedly, but it is her absent fiancé, Robert, who ultimately reaps the rewards of her efforts. Mary's long-lost brother reappears on the scene and expresses his gratitude by securing a job for Robert so that he can marry Anne. This so-called happy resolution of narrative events invites the reader to consider the nature of Anne's success—whether Anne's containment within the domestic sphere is reward or punishment for her transgressive acts.

The story also features the dream as a cryptic and awful foreboding, blurring the boundaries between the natural and supernatural and reflecting Collins's interest in contemporary dream theory. Collins had begun to use the dream as a narrative device in his novel *Basil* (1852), and he would continue to explore in more sophisticated ways the dream as psychic transmission in novels such as *The Woman in White* (1860) and *Armadale* (1866). Finally, the appearance of the "crooked-back dwarf," though his role in the narrative is minimal, introduces another key feature of Collins's fiction: the "freak." Collins does not, however, showcase characters with various physical and psychological abnormalities simply for comic effect; rather, his fictional grotesques are figures whose motivations in the narrative are always ambiguous and discomfiting to characters and readers alike.

BIBLIOGRAPHY
Collins, Wilkie. *Complete Short Fiction*. London: Constable, 1998.

Maria Bachman

DICKENS, CHARLES (1812–1870)

Born on February 7, 1812, in Portsmouth, Charles Dickens was to become the most successful and influential writer of the Victorian period. In his lifetime he produced 14½ novels (*The Mystery of Edwin Drood* was left unfinished at his death), countless sketches, short stories, dramas, articles, novellas, and even travel writing. He ran his own magazines and toured Britain and

America performing spectacular readings from his own works. Dickens's almost pathological industriousness led to an early death at age 58.

Dickens had a difficult early life. His parents, John and Elizabeth, had an unstable existence, Dickens's father always living beyond his means (he was later immortalized in the character of *David Copperfield*'s Mr. Micawber). The Dickens family was never really able to settle and moved a great deal around the south of England. Their situation changed drastically from month to month. John Dickens's profligacy and fiscal mismanagement culminated in his being sent to Marshalsea debtor's prison, where he was joined by his wife; the young Charles was taken out of school at age 12 and sent to work in a blacking factory for six shillings a week. Although the young Dickens was at the factory for only a matter of months, he had no way of knowing at the time that he would not be stuck there forever. Factory life was so terrifying for the young boy that it proved to be a formative experience for the man. He never spoke about Warren's Blacking Factory to his family for the rest of his life. His early fiction, however, repeatedly returned to the dejected boy's early life. All of his work from *Oliver Twist* (1837) to *Little Dorrit* (1857) draws, in different ways, from these experiences. Dickens's pathology of ceaseless work was surely driven by the need to stay out of the debtor's prison and to stay out of the factory.

He began his adult employment in 1828 as a parliamentary reporter. His first literary work, "Mr. Minns and His Cousin," appeared on December 1, 1833, and later was published in SKETCHES BY BOZ (1836–37). In 1836 Dickens was approached by two young publishers, Edward Chapman and William Hall, to write what was to become *The Pickwick Papers;* this was also the beginning of a 23-year relationship with a young illustrator, Hablot Knight Browne ("Phiz"). The young publishers earned £14,000 from *Pickwick,* and Dickens had begun his career as a novelist. His reputation was solidified and established by the works that followed: *Oliver Twist* (1837), *Nicholas Nickleby* (1839), *Barnaby Rudge* (1841), *Martin Chuzzlewit* (1843), *Dombey and Son* (1848), *David Copperfield* (1850), *Bleak House* (1853), *Hard Times* (1854), *Little Dorrit* (1857), *Tale of Two Cities* (1859), *Great Expectations* (1861), *Our*

Mutual Friend (1865), and *The Mystery of Edwin Drood* (1870). Dickens married Catherine Hogarth in 1836, and the first of their 10 children was born in 1837. Although they remained married, Dickens always seemed to have a chaotic love life. The death of his sister-in-law, Mary Hogarth, in May 1837 was a spectacular disturbance to him. He suspended the monthly numbers of *The Pickwick Papers* and *Oliver Twist* and kept her clothing for years afterward. His first love, Maria Beadnell (whom he courted from 1830 to 1833) made a brief return to his life some 10 years later. After their disappointing meeting he used her for the comically overemotional Flora Finching in *Little Dorrit.* He also had a long-lasting affair with an actress, Ellen Ternan, whom he met in August 1857. Dickens left her £1,000 in his will. She married in 1876, and there is no evidence to suggest that she ever mentioned her affair with Dickens to any of her family.

Dickens's novels are widely available and have been much studied. However, he also made considerable contributions to the British short story, most notably, *Sketches by Boz* and his Christmas books. *A CHRISTMAS CAROL* (1843, full title: *A Christmas Carol in Prose, A Ghost Story of Christmas*) is by far the best-known Christmas story in the English language. It is probably the most-adapted story of the 20th century. Within two months of its publication there were eight stage versions, and film versions have steadily appeared since 1935. Dickens achieves an unusual mixture of economic realism and the fairy tale in this story; the resulting specific historicity and atemporality have contributed to the story's longevity. The core economic message of the *Carol* is to beware of capitalism. The *Carol,* like *The Chimes* (1844), *The Haunted Man* (1848), and the other Christmas books, is also interested in the humanizing affects of memory. In all cases the raw edges of character derive from a kind of amnesia; it is a trope that is peculiar to Dickens' Christmas fiction.

Much of Dickens's short fiction was tied up with his involvement in various magazines. He edited three magazines—*Bentley's Miscellany* (1837–39), *Household Words* (1850–59), and *All the Year Round* (1859–70)—all of which featured his own short stories (e.g., "HUNTED DOWN" [1859]), as well as works by WILKIE COLLINS, ELIZABETH GASKELL, and Edward Bulwer

11118

DIXON, ELLA HEPWORTH

Lytton. His short fiction principally focuses on themes of imprisonment, debt, crime, reform, new money, impoverishment, and class mobility (e.g., "The POOR RELATION'S STORY," "The Tuggses at Ramsgate"), suggesting that Dickens's literary success was both the cause and beneficiary of his chaotic and tumultuous personal life. For the Dickens canon, it was a small price to pay.

BIBLIOGRAPHY

Carey, John. *The Violent Effigy: A Study in Dickens' Imagination.* London: Faber, 1973.
Dickens, Charles. *A Christmas Carol.* London: Chapman and Hall, 1843.
———. *The Cricket on the Hearth.* London: Chapman and Hall, 1845.
———. *The Posthumous Papers of the Pickwick Club.* London: Chapman and Hall, 1836–37.
———. *Sketches by Boz.* London: Macrone, 1836–37.
Dyson, A. E. *The Inimitable Dickens.* London: Macmillan, 1970.
Flint, Kate. *Dickens.* Brighton, England: Harvester, 1986.
Glancy, Ruth. *Dickens' Christmas Books, Christmas Sketches and Other Short Fiction: An Annotated Bibliography.* New York: Garland, 1985.
Kaplan, Fred. *Dickens: A Biography.* London: Hodder, 1988.

Vybarr Cregan-Reid

DIXON, ELLA HEPWORTH (C. 1855–1932)

Ella Hepworth Dixon was the seventh of eight children of Marian (Machon) and William Hepworth Dixon. Her family deftly managed to be both artistic and respectable. Dixon's mother held fashionable salons, informal gatherings where conversation is the focus, which attracted an ever-changing mix of literary and visual artists. Her father was well known as the editor of the *Athenaeum,* a leading periodical of the day, and made a point of encouraging women writers by treating them as professionals. Dixon's parents gave her an unusual artistic education for a Victorian girl of the upper middle class. She traveled often to the continent, studying language, philosophy, and piano in Heidelberg and, even more unconventionally, painting in two artists' studios in Paris.

Though Dixon detested the necessity of doing so, she used her recently deceased father's name and his connections in London publishing to launch her career as a journalist and short story writer; she understood that men held the power in the business world and that becoming a successful professional writer was, at best, very difficult for women. Her work appeared in variety of periodicals throughout her career, including the *YELLOW BOOK,* the *Times* (London), the *Illustrated London News,* the *Manchester Guardian,* and the *Westminster Gazette.* She was also a regular contributor of both short stories and articles to *Woman's World* under OSCAR WILDE's editorship, and she edited the *Englishwoman* from 1895 to 1896.

Dixon used her short stories (collected in *One Doubtful Hour,* 1904) to explore how women were economically and spiritually exploited by men in Victorian culture. With her constant attention to the reality of Victorian women's lived experience, Dixon was known then and now as a NEW WOMAN writer (see also ELLA D'ARCY, GEORGE EGERTON, and VERNON LEE). Though very much part of decadent literary circles (see DECADENCE), Dixon was also keenly critical of how male artists' aesthetic appreciation of women allowed them to fix women as art objects without any sort of independent agency. Dixon's first long work, *My Flirtations,* was published under the humorous pseudonym Margaret Wynman in 1892. The series of connected short stories depict Margaret's flirtations with different types of men, who are obvious parodies of well-known fin de siécle figures like Oscar Wilde and Richard Le Gallienne. In the end, however, Margaret agrees to a loveless marriage because her husband will rescue her from a debt incurred in ignorance.

Though also a journalist and short story writer, Ella Hepworth Dixon is best known for her *Story of a Modern Woman* (1894), a short bildungsroman chronicling the life of Mary Erle from idealistic childhood to disillusioned adulthood. Clearly drawn from Dixon's own life experiences, the novel begins with Mary trying to make her way in the London publishing world after the death of her father. In this novel, as well as her other stories and nonfiction work, Dixon is particularly concerned with the lives of "odd women," upper-class women who had few prospects for marriage (due to the lack of marriageable men resulting from casualties sustained by England during the Napoleonic wars) and had few professions open to them for economic survival. Toward the end of the 19th century, these women were called New Women for their departure from conventional Victorian feminine behavior and their political activism around a variety of issues, including women's role in marriage, women's legal status, and education for women.

Significantly, in the novel, Dixon also reveals something of the manner in which female short story writers might establish a career for themselves in the male-dominated world of 1890s London publishing. In the character of Mr. Bosanquet-Barry and his AESTHETIC affectations, Dixon spoofs Oscar Wilde, her own editor at *Woman's World,* and criticizes the decadents for viewing women as aesthetic objects rather than as thinking individuals and the capitalists for concerning themselves only with what will sell. She also criticizes the way he and other bohemian male artists treat women through the nameless editor of *The Fan,* who only gives Mary any attention once he realizes that she is an upper-class lady. The critical moment in Mary's career comes after she has had several pieces published and goes to her editor with an idea for a novel about the life of the modern woman. Her editor refuses to publish her novel on the grounds that the newly literate lower classes will not read it, and he tells her that she must stick to conventional marriage plots with happy endings. Mary's own life has no such happy ending, and the novel ends with her disappearing back into the London suburbs after visiting her father's grave. The novel is striking for the way it merges French-influenced naturalism and social Darwinism to explore the social structures that exploit women in Victorian society and how all women must ultimately bow in some way to these systemic pressures.

BIBLIOGRAPHY

Ardis, Ann L. *New Women, New Novels: Feminism and Early Modernism.* New Brunswick, N.J.: Rutgers University Press, 1990.

Dixon, Ella Hepworth. *My Flirtations.* London: Chatto & Windus, 1892; Philadelphia: Lippincott, 1893.

———. *One Doubtful Hour and Other Side-lights on the Feminine Temperament.* London: Richards, 1904.

———. *The Story of a Modern Woman.* London: Heinemann, 1894; New York: Cassell, 1894.

Stetz, Margaret Diane. "Ella Hepworth Dixon." In *Dictionary of Literary Biography,* Volume 197: *Late-Victorian and Edwardian British Novelists,* Second Series, edited by George M. Johnson, 99–109. Detroit: Gale Research, 1999.

———. "Turning Points: Ella Hepworth Dixon," *Turn-of-the-Century Women* 2 (Winter 1984): 2–11.

Lisa Hager

"DOLL'S HOUSE, THE" KATHERINE MANSFIELD (1923)

Published in *The Dove's Nest,* KATHERINE MANSFIELD's last collection of short stories, "The Doll's House" belongs with "Prelude" (1920) and "At the Bay" (1922) among the Burnell stories, a trilogy based on the re-creation of a New Zealand childhood that threads family life with social satire while exploring issues of identity and belonging. The story, divided into three sections, uses the central metaphor of the doll's house, which also provides the linear and dramatic framework of the narrative. It begins with the arrival of a completely furnished doll's house sent to the Burnell children by "dear old Mrs. Hay," a friend of the family. When Pat, a servant, opens the house, Isabel, Kezia, and Lottie cannot believe their eyes: "It was too marvellous; it was too much for them." But while her sisters admire this imitation of gaudy bourgeois comfort, Kezia, Mansfield's recurring figure of the open-minded girl, is drawn by the perfection of an "exquisite little amber lamp" that looks "real" to her.

In the second and third sections of the story, the doll's house becomes a source of social and psychological conflict as it is turned into an instrument of power by Isabel, the eldest Burnell sister, and the other schoolchildren invited to share her euphoric pride. Cruelly excluding the Kelvey girls from their companionship and from the pleasure of seeing the doll's house because they are the daughters "of a washerwoman and a gaolbird," Isabel and her friends reproduce their parents' prejudiced views and social sense of self-gratification without questioning them. The narrative works up to an epiphanic climax when Kezia, "the potentially free subject," to use Kate Fullbrook's terms (113), breaks with social and family conventions by opening "the big white gates" of her home and her heart to allow Lil and Else Kelvey a hurried glimpse at the doll's house. Over a short moment of symbolical intensity, the three children are drawn together in a shared experience of vision and beauty: "[Else] put out a finger and stroked her sister's quill; she smiled her rare smile. 'I seen the little lamp,' she said."

As are most of Katherine Mansfield's stories, "The Doll's House" is poised dialectically between the external world of social reality and an internalized world of subjective perceptions. Its MODERNISM lies in its refusal to rely on narratorial intrusions (the text is full of ironic insights but is never judgmental) and in its use of point of view and indirect free form to convey inner feelings, of symbol and metaphor as structural elements, and of epiphany as the ephemeral moment when the focal character and the reader might gain access to truths hidden to ordinary perceptions: Not only do Kezia and the Kelvey sisters know that the doll's house is a social symbol of status and discrimination, they also see in its little lamp the metaphorical values of shared knowledge and emotion, while the whole story suggests that artistic creation may be a redeeming act of inclusion and fulfillment.

"The Doll's House" is also typically Mansfieldian in the way the narration oscillates between ironic distance and emotional empathy, using "impersonation" as a form of speech representation that captures the subtle nuances of a character's tone of voice and makes for immediacy but also ambiguity and ironic contrasts. However, the epiphanic accomplishment characterizing this story makes it different from most of the other short fiction by Mansfield: Far from being an experience of self-deception or self-betrayal, the expected revelation is here a "blazing" if evanescent moment of discovery and happiness.

BIBLIOGRAPHY
Fullbrook, Kate. *Katherine Mansfield.* Bloomington: Indiana University Press, 1986.
Kobler, J. F. *Katherine Mansfield: A Study of the Short Fiction.* Boston: Twayne, 1990.
Mansfield, Katherine. *The Dove's Nest and Other Stories.* London: Constable, 1923.

Anne Besnault-Levita

DOWSON, ERNEST (1867–1900) Primarily known as a decadent poet of the late 19th century (see DECADENCE), Ernest Dowson also made several prose contributions to significant periodicals of the period, including the YELLOW BOOK, and published *Dilemmas; Stories and Studies in Sentiment* in 1895. Dowson spent his childhood traveling the Continent with his consumptive parents as they sought various treatments. His parents' ill health, bankruptcy, and eventual suicide were the recurring disturbances in Dowson's life that influenced his decision to leave Oxford after studying classics there for only a few terms. Dowson was a member of the Rhymers' Club and friend of OSCAR WILDE and Aubrey Beardsley. Best known for falling in love with the young daughter of a restaurant owner who married a waiter, Dowson converted to Catholicism before dying of tuberculosis.

Dowson's work reflects his personal and decadent preoccupations. Dowson's attraction to the innocence and purity of adolescent girls informs "Apple Blossom in Brittany," as Benedict Campion struggles with the decision to marry Marie-Ursule or support her desire to join a convent. Campion ultimately argues that to lose her to the convent was "the only way in which he could keep her always" (327) after he realizes that her idealized appeal would be sullied by marriage. "The Dying of Francis Donne" deals with a doctor's sudden realization that he is going to die. The story vividly re-creates the contemplation and anticipation of death and creates an atmosphere of ennui as Donne deteriorates until an equally sudden understanding makes sense of his distorted life at the moment of death. Dowson's interest with death, drugs, and altered states runs throughout his work and is well represented in a number of very short stories that, combined with several poems, became *Decorations* in 1899. In the supremely decadent "Absinthia Taetra," various poetic features are incorporated in the narrative to reproduce the experience and futility of drinking mind-altering absinthe. Dowson's characteristically abrupt but conclusive manner of ending his stories is apparent in "The Visit," as the narrator's supposedly welcome encounter with Death leaves the reader pondering just how eager the narrator was to see Death.

BIBLIOGRAPHY
Ernest Dowson. *Dilemmas; Stories and Studies in Sentiment.* London: John Lane, 1895.
———. *Decorations.* London: John Lane, 1899.

Tony Garland

DOYLE, ARTHUR CONAN (1859–1930)

Born in Edinburgh in 1859, the second of 10 children, Arthur Conan Doyle was brought up in an atmosphere of financial and emotional strain. His father, Charles Altamont Doyle, came from an artistic, Catholic family, being the son of John Doyle, a noted caricaturist whose brother Richard—known as "Dicky"—was famous for his work on *Punch*. Charles pursued his own artistic talents as an architect in the Edinburgh Office of Works and struggled to supplement his salary with artwork and illustrations, but he gradually succumbed to a combination of alcoholism and epilepsy and was eventually institutionalized in an asylum, where he died in 1893. Doyle's mother, Mary, also a Catholic, ran a boardinghouse to bring in much-needed income and was able to pay for her son's education at a Jesuit public school. When Doyle decided to take up a medical career, he had to support himself through his degree at Edinburgh University, taking jobs as a doctor's assistant to cover his expenses, but in his spare time he was already writing—and publishing anonymously—short adventure stories (e.g., "The CAPTAIN OF THE POLE STAR" [1883]). Doyle qualified as a doctor in 1881, eventually setting up a successful practice in the English town of Southsea and going on to specialize in ophthalmology, but intermittent periods of quiet allowed him to return to writing and in 1887 he published *A STUDY IN SCARLET*, the first book to feature Sherlock Holmes, in the *Beeton Christmas Annual* of 1887; it came out in book form the following year with illustrations by his father. The tale was advertized as a "story of thrilling interest."

Although Doyle had no intentions at this stage of working further on his detective creation, *A Study in Scarlet* nevertheless furnished most of the basic ingredients for Holmes's later adventures while also providing inspiration for future authors of detective fiction. The first part of the story, taken from "the reminiscences of John H. Watson, M.D.," is of particular interest for the detailed introduction to Holmes. Watson is the only source of information here, as he will be in subsequent stories, and the reader shares his initial uncertainties about and his developing admiration for the enigmatic Holmes. These uncertainties arise from the fact that he cannot identify who Holmes is or what he does; Holmes cannot be fitted into any conventional social construction. Watson provides what will become the archetypal portrait of the sleuth: He is tall, thin, and hawklike; his interests, as Watson lists them, lean to the sciences; while his personality is by turns indolent and energetic. He is an isolated individual—the visitors whom Watson takes at first for friends are merely clients—and yet his personality reveals a measure of sensitivity. When Watson congratulates him on bringing "detection as near an exact science as it ever will be," Holmes "flushe[s] up with pleasure," but he is also ambitious, declaring: "I know well that I have it in me to make my name famous." The relative haplessness of the Scotland Yard detectives, Gregson and Lestrade, is made clear from the start; Holmes characterizes them as "conventional—shockingly so." Unconventional himself, Holmes prefers to rely on the street Arabs, who can "go everywhere and hear everything." The fast-moving narrative of this section follows "the scarlet thread of murder" in the deaths of two Americans, Enoch Drebber and Joseph Stangerson. The police investigation flounders for lack of interpretable clues, but through Holmes's intervention and independent lines of enquiry, the murderer is swiftly apprehended.

Doyle's literary ambitions, however, revolved around what he would term "better things," and he constantly aspired to acclaim for what he regarded as his more serious work. The success of his historical novel *Micah Clarke* (1889) led to the offer of a commission from the American *Lippincott's Magazine,* for which Doyle agreed to contribute a second novel about Holmes, *The Sign of Four* (1890). At the same time, however, another of his historical novels—*The White Company*—was being serialized in the *Cornhill Magazine*. Doyle's medical practice was losing ground, and as he noted in his autobiography, it now seemed the opportune moment to further his "literary prospects."

The appearance of the new *STRAND MAGAZINE* in 1891 offered Doyle the chance to capitalize on the speedy financial return that could be gained from short story publication, and the 12 *ADVENTURES OF SHERLOCK HOLMES* duly appeared over the following year. The magazine's editor, George Newnes, insisted on high-quality production with an abundance of illustration, and the artist Sidney Paget created the visual image of Sherlock Holmes that has persisted in the public mind ever since. Priced sixpence, the magazine was accessible to a broad audience, and Doyle's contributions were particularly successful. The collected set both played off and increased the stories' popularity. The contemporaneity of the stories, the accurate urban topography and recognizable setting of Baker Street, and the employment of current technologies and scientific advances all provided a thoroughly modern background against which the detailed personal histories of the protagonists unfolded and promoted a sense of continuity.

The term *adventure* captures the flavor of these early cases, as Holmes happens across strange and puzzling, rather than obviously criminal, situations. "The Red-Headed League" stages a bizarre cover-up for a bank robbery, while "The Engineer's Thumb" provides a similarly convoluted scenario for a gang of coiners. Mystery may depend on the concealment of identity, as in "The Copper Beeches" and "A Case of Identity Or the MAN WITH THE TWISTED LIP." The initial impetus for this last tale sends Watson out to track down an opium addict, Isa Whitney, but, having found him, the doctor soon yields his active, professional role to resume his function as chronicler of a very different story. The linchpin of the narrative is the opium den that Watson has entered undisguised, as a respectable visitor, only to find Holmes immersed in the impersonation of an old addict himself—"very thin, very wrinkled, bent with age." Holmes is caught up in unraveling the mysterious disappearance of an upright middle-class family man, Neville St. Clair. The testimony of Mrs. St. Clair, along with evidence of bloodstains in the living quarters above the opium den, leads Holmes to deduce that her husband has been murdered by the lodger, Hugh Boone, a professional beggar. Boone is notable both for his financial success and for his "repulsive" appearance of bright red hair, coupled with a disfiguring facial scar "from eye to chin" that has contracted to twist "one side of the upper lip, so that three teeth were exposed in a perpetual snarl." Characterized as "sinister," Boone is marked as the prime suspect not only through his association with the Lascar and the evils of the opium trade but also because his brutish physiognomy would typically be understood to denote criminality. That this is a

disguise donned by St. Clair so that he can inhabit the illegal but lucrative world of beggary is ironic in that the appearance of extreme disfigurement, which even "a wife's eyes could not pierce," was chosen for its pitifulness and usefulness when begging, rather than for its criminal aptness. St. Clair is predominantly concerned with maintaining the respectable identity he has achieved through his ambitious social mobility, but the integrity of that position is fractured by his leading of a double life. Although Holmes's own "mastery" of appearances assists him in his pursuit of his "natural prey," his very success in this also carries transgressive overtones. The ease with which he can apparently transform his features speaks of the depth of impersonation of which he is capable, a depth that suggests an all-too-familiar knowledge of the criminal underworld. That Holmes can insinuate himself so credibly into such an environment raises questions about his own respectability and yet constitutes one of the intellectual tools with which he can penetrate the mystery surrounding St. Clair. Smoking an ounce of shag tobacco while perched on "a sort of Eastern divan," Holmes creates an atmosphere resonant of the opium den in which he finally detects the truth behind the distraction of appearances. A court case is avoided on the basis of St. Clair's "solemn oaths" to do away with Hugh Boone. Holmes's initial theory about the relationship between the two "characters" is thus inverted, and his detective abilities are seen to depend on the perspective from which he observes the facts of a case, rather than from an impartial desire to uphold the law.

In the same collection, "The Beryl Coronet" and "The Noble Bachelor" showcase the complexity of Holmes's detective methods, while in "A SCANDAL IN BOHEMIA" no real crime is perpetrated. Within the framework of Watson's narration, the myriad criminal characters, their victims, and the supporting characters seem to exist merely to place Holmes in a theatrical spotlight, and the collection familiarized readers with the extent of Holmes's extraordinary powers of penetrating observation and deduction. The disparity between the professional doctor's diagnostic skills and those of the amateur sleuth favoured Holmes as by far the more effective doctor of society's ills. In this society the operations of the police also seem pedestrian by contrast with Holmes's successes, a trope that Doyle developed from the works of Edgar Allan Poe and WILKIE COLLINS. Yet the mysteries that Holmes encounters rarely present the threat of extreme danger, nor is murder the staple crime it would become for later DETECTIVE FICTION. Although murder is committed in "The Speckled Band," the impact of personal grief or trauma is secondary to the intellectual solving of the puzzle. In both "The Blue Carbuncle" and "The Boscombe Valley Mystery," Holmes protects the criminals he has unmasked. Like Poe's Dupin, the great detective straddles the law and criminality, serving justice according to his personal moral code rather than society's, but by the end of the 12 stories in *Adventures,* Holmes is nevertheless clearly established as the guardian of Victorian middle-class values and security.

Although the stories were extremely successful, Doyle quickly tired of his ingenious hero and famously "killed" the sleuth in a climactic confrontation with his enemy, Professor Moriarty, at the Reichenbach Falls in *The Final Problem* (1893). Doyle could now pursue his copious production of novels of action and adventure, as well as taking a post as war correspondent in Egypt and later supporting the British management of the Boer War and overseeing a field hospital in South Africa. This patriotism may have been behind his knighthood in 1902, and it would return in a very public manner during World War I when, as war correspondent again and contemporary historian, he was vocal in promoting the British position, most notably in *The British Campaign in France and Flanders* (1916–20).

Despite his other interests, which included standing—unsuccessfully—for Parliament, the clamor of the reading public for more stories about Holmes induced Doyle to write *The Hound of The Baskervilles* (1902), a short novel that purports to be an adventure from Holmes's earlier career and has since become one of his best-known works, adapted many times for film and television. Holmes is presented at the peak of his capacity as "scientific machine," countering local superstition about the eponymous hound with unrivaled forensic detective skills and the unwitting aid of his chronicler, Dr. Watson. The book's success persuaded Doyle to resurrect Holmes in *The Return of Sherlock Holmes* (1905), and the detective made his final appearance in 1927 in the collection *The Case-Book of Sherlock Holmes.*

World War I marked a turning point in Doyle's literary focus. While attending the Jesuit school, Doyle seems to have abandoned his Catholicism and later took up the study of psychic phenomena. After 1918 he wrote prolifically about spiritualism, an interest that, while touching a public nerve in the aftermath of so many deaths, would eventually involve him in some ridicule for his investigations into the claims of psychic mediums and for his support of the so-called Cottingley Fairies photographs. Meanwhile, Doyle continued to write poetry, pamphlets, short stories, and more adventure novels, creating such vigorous characters as Professor Challenger in *The Lost World* (1912) and BRIGADIER GERARD in his own set of adventures.

Doyle married twice, his first wife Louise dying of tuberculosis in 1906, and his second wife, Jean, surviving him after his death in 1930. Surrounded by women as a child—he had only one younger brother, and Charles was a distant, when not actually absent, father—his attitude toward women has been the subject of much critical attention. Some find a misogynistic streak in his literary treatment; others see it as indicative of the status quo, whereby women were viewed as the weaker sex, Doyle's daughter contended that Doyle took an idealistic and protective view of women. Apart from Irene Adler, who outwits Holmes, incurring his admiration in "A Scandal in Bohemia," female characters certainly tend to be deployed merely as victims and catalysts of the mysteries and, in this sense, the detective stories clearly show an affinity with the patriarchal fictions of empire and adventure that were so popular at the time. Indeed, in the stories produced during and after World War I, Holmes is often involved in solving crimes against the nation rather than crimes against the individual, further reflecting contemporary preoccupations.

Although Doyle's literary output was vast and his public activities diverse, it is for the 56 short stories and four short novels of Sherlock Holmes's exploits that he is nowadays remembered. While this may not tally with Doyle's own assessment of serious literary accomplishment, his work has been key in the development of the short story. Written at a time when the periodical press and the public lending libraries had an increasing impact on the consumption of accessible literature, the Holmes stories, with their serial nature, guaranteed readership loyalty, while the character himself is an embodiment of the concise and unique completeness that is central to the short story form. Arguably formulaic in characterization and plot, the stories nevertheless provided a relevant reworking of Poe's original detective, Dupin, retaining his psychological expertise but utilizing all the modernity of science, technology, and medicine to create a new blueprint for detective fiction that still resonates today.

BIBLIOGRAPHY
Booth, Martin. *The Doctor and the Detective: A Biography of Sir Arthur Conan Doyle.* New York: Thomas Dunne Books and St Martin's Minotaur, 1997.
Doyle, Arthur Conan. *The Adventures of Sherlock Holmes.* London: Newnes, 1892.
———. *A Study in Scarlet.* London: Ward Lock, 1888.
———. *The Captain of the Polestar and Other Tales.* London: Longman, 1890.
———. *The Hound of the Baskervilles.* London: Newnes, 1902.
———. *The Memoirs of Sherlock Holmes.* London: Newnes, 1894.
———. *Memories and Adventures.* London: Hodder & Stoughton, 1924.
———. *The Return of Sherlock Holmes.* London: Newnes, 1905.
———. *The Sign of Four.* London: Blackett, 1890.
Green, Roger Lancelyn, and John Michael Gibson. *A Bibliography of A. Conan Doyle.* Oxford: Clarendon Press, 1983.
Stashower, Daniel. *Teller of Tales: The Life of Arthur Conan Doyle.* London: Penguin, 1999.

Therie Hendry-Seabrook

"DREAM CARGOES" J. G. BALLARD (1991)

Included in the American edition of J. G. BALLARD's *War Fever,* "Dream Cargoes" summarizes some of the staple ingredients of Ballard's writing while also prefiguring the ecological themes of his novel *Rushing to Paradise* (1994). The story focuses on Johnson, a "deck hand on the lowest grade of chemical waste carrier," who unexpectedly achieves his first command. Tricked by Captain Galloway into joining the crew of the *Prospero,* Johnson decides to remain when the others aban-don ship. The drunken, intemperate Galloway has been bribed into transporting unspecified but highly toxic "organic by-products." Prohibited from weighing anchor, the freighter drifts forlornly until entering the path of a hurricane. As the chemicals spill into the sea, the ship fatally holed, Galloway and his men take the remaining lifeboat. Johnson, however, elects to stay behind and become "master of his own fate." This opening description recalls Ballard's debt to JOSEPH CONRAD, in this instance to both "YOUTH: A NARRATIVE" and *The SHADOW-LINE.* However, whereas in "Youth" it is the narrator who leads the crew to safety, Johnson's refusal to leave not only introduces a different narrative trajectory but also resists a more conventional romantic heroism. Instead, the allusions to Prospero and the hurricane indicate that this story is to also become a rewriting of Shakespeare's *The Tempest.*

Running the ship to ground on a forgotten atoll, once used by the U.S. Military as a garbage dump, Johnson sleeps until he is disturbed by Christine, a marine biologist. While Johnson has slept, the leaking chemicals have begun to affect the local environment, changing a spoiled wilderness into a profusion of new, giant, and hybrid plant forms. Christine's hope is to uncover the secret of what has happened before the U.S. Navy "scorch[es] the island with flame-throwers." After four months, the island has been transformed into a "botanical mad-house," Johnson has become immensely strong, and Christine is carrying their child after "one brief act of love, over so quickly that he was scarcely sure it had ever occurred." Whereas Christine, who divides her time between the island and the mainland, remains dedicated to her scientific investigation, Johnson has become oversensitive toward the island and its exotic wildlife.

By the following week, Johnson has begun to hallucinate and to lose all sense of passing time: "He stared at Christine, aware that the colours were separating themselves from her skin and hair. Superimposed images of herself, each divided from the others by a fraction of a second, blurred the air around her, an exotic plumage that sprang from her arms and shoulders. The staid reality that had trapped them all was beginning to dissolve." While recalling the hallucinogenic imagery of his novel *The Crystal World* (1967), the story also recounts one of his major themes: the recovery of nonlinear time from an imposed chronological order. Johnson's behavior, though, proves too much for Christine. While he pictures her as an angelic, Ariel figure, Christine radios a passing U.S. naval cutter, effectively the Caliban to Johnson's Prospero. Christine's commitment to rationality, her treatment of nature as an object of study, means that she cannot align herself with Johnson's almost mystical insight in which he has come to believe "that he was responsible for the transformation." However, as the cutter prepares to take Christine and Johnson back to the mainland, Johnson leaps overboard, hoping that he can "climb the trees and release the birds" in their mutual "escape from time." Whereas the narrator of Conrad's "The SECRET SHARER" has to abandon his double in order to take his place within human society, Ballard's protagonist refuses the profanity of public time and, instead, rejoins the sanctity of his own private vision.

BIBLIOGRAPHY

Ballard, J. G. *The Complete Short Stories.* London: Flamingo, 2001.

Paul March-Russell

"DUALITISTS, THE" BRAM STOKER (1887)

First published in the *Theatre Annual* (1887), "The Dualitists," frequently cited as demonstrating one of BRAM STOKER's favorite themes, male bonding, evokes a world of children's adventure stories. As in much of Stoker's fiction, the driving force grows out of an innate male lust for violence. Two young boys, Harry Merford and Tommy Santon, are each given an identical knife as Christmas presents. Armed with these symbols of manliness, self-possession, and self-ownership, the boys put their weapons to the test by "hacking" them against the other like fencing swordsmen. When the knives become worn out, the boys look for other paired objects that they might use to continue their game—furniture, dolls, pet rabbits—before deciding on two human weapons: a set of identical baby twins belonging to neighbors Ephraim and Sophonisba Bubb. In the climax of the story, the boys smash the twins together in "apotheosis of art." When Mr. Bubb tries to wrest his children from their torturers, he misses and

blows off the heads of his own children with a "double-barrelled gun." The boys wave the torsos of the twins like trophies. When the mutilated bodies are thrown into the air, the parents try to catch them but are killed by the weight of their children's bodies falling on top of them, thus ensuring the extinction of the whole Bubb family. With Harry and Tommy acting as the only witnesses, a coroner's court concludes that the parents ("inhuman monsters, maddened by drink") must have been guilty of infanticide and suicide. Tommy and Harry meanwhile are feted as heroes.

This macabre story depends for its effectiveness partly on the doubling that is so insistent a feature of Stoker's fiction and in gothic writing generally. The infanticide and parricide of the two boys is graphically depicted, and the narrative gains much from our being forced to respond to the suggestion that the mutant violence emerging in the story is latent in everyone—even small children. The events of the narrative are presented in matter-of-fact terms, even humorously; we are not asked to weep for the murdered children and their parents. As elsewhere in Stoker's fiction, the tradition of the gothic horror tale is transformed and domesticated, with the ensuing paradox that the appalling wickedness and gruesome crimes are perpetuated by small children running out of control in commonplace, ordinary modern settings. Related to this is the way the narrator stresses the narcissism of the two spoiled boys. Their heroism surpasses the likes of Napoleon and Nelson (the figures the boys claim as the inspiration for their game); they view themselves not as "unregenerate youths" but as heroes, not as butchers but as musketeers, demonstrating their manhood by mimicking accepted masculine codes, refusing Bubb's mandate to come down off the roof: "'Never!' Exclaimed the heroic two with one impulse, and continued their awful pastime with a zest tenfold" (57).

In a preface to the story, Peter Haining has suggested that Stoker developed the idea for it by watching Henry Irving's performances in the dueling epic *The Corsican Brothers* by Alexandre Dumas père, a story of twin brothers separated at birth but held together by a psychic bond. The domestic setting may also owe something to Edgar Allan Poe's tale of doubling, "William Wilson" (1839). Critics have also detected political overtones, seeing the story as Stoker's allegorization of Anglo-Irish relations during the 1880s, a time when Irish resentment against British rule was prompting an escalation of armed resistance to the British authorities.

BIBLIOGRAPHY

Stoker, Bram. *Bram Stoker's Midnight Tales.* Edited by Peter Haining. London: Peter Owen, 1990.

Hughes, William, and Andrew Smith, eds. *Bram Stoker: History, Psychoanalysis and the Gothic.* London: Macmillan, 1998.

Valente, Joseph, "'Double Born': Bram Stoker and the Metrocolonial Gothic," *Modern Fiction Studies* 46 (2000): 632–645.

Peter Matthias

DUBLINERS James Joyce (1914)   James Joyce wrote most of the short stories in *Dubliners* in Trieste in 1905. Even after finding a publisher, however, concerns about content (in particular, his liberal use of actual people and place-names from Dublin) stalled publication until 1914. One of the more notable characteristics of the collection is that even while the central protagonist changes from one story to the next, the sequence of stories is such that *Dubliners* largely gives the effect of a central character aging, as each successive story focuses on a marginally older protagonist.

Dubliner's was written against the backdrop of British colonial oppression and the repressive religious institutions of the Catholic Church, both of which haunt the many characters in these stories and provide *Dubliners* with a consistent theme and atmosphere. It is often noted, for instance, that the stories are predominantly about the social, economic, and political paralysis that is a consequence of such repression. In "Eveline," the title character's inability to escape her ailing and abusive father is mirrored in her inability to leave Ireland for Argentina with Frank. Even as Little Chandler of "A Little Cloud" is inspired to greater things on the occasion of Ignatius Gallaher's visit from London, where he has become a successful journalist, Dublin is ultimately represented as paralytic to ambition and repressive of literary and creative pursuits. Critics find corroboration for this reading in the fact that Joyce not only wrote *Dubliners* in Trieste

but lived almost exclusively in Europe from 1902 until his death.

Dubliners is perhaps most remarkable aesthetically, however, for Joyce's development and implementation of the epiphany. In the epiphany of "A Little Cloud," when Little Chandler finally becomes cognizant of the paralysis that accompanies marriage and fatherhood, he screams into the face of his infant son; this, in turn, only intensifies his paralysis regarding his relationship with his wife. While not written in the stream-of-consciousness narrative style that Joyce first made famous with *A Portrait of the Artist as a Young Man* and remastered for *Ulysses,* the stories are replete with self-conscious characters who second-guess and reconsider their actions in the face of the paralysis that overwhelms and represses them. James Duffy of "A Painful Case," for instance, "lived at a little distance from his body, regarding his own acts with doubtful sideglances." It is worth noting that this self-consciousness—perhaps best embodied by the narrator of "Araby," who, in his own epiphanic moment as he leaves the fair, having failed in his quest to purchase a gift for Mangan's sister, "saw himself as a creature driven and derided by vanity"—only makes the paralysis of the characters more intense. Eveline's inability to leave her position is intensified by her realization that she has so few options. In "The Boarding House," Mr. Doran's "notion that he was being had" provides him little relief in the face of the owner's machinations to see him paired with her daughter.

In the final analysis, *Dubliners* is populated by characters suffering a peculiar sort of paralysis in which their knowledge about the futility of their position does little to help them understand the appropriate means of escaping it. In addition to being notable for their artistic achievements, the stories are also important to Joyce scholars both because they follow a similar chronological arc to Joyce's *Portrait of the Artist as a Young Man* and *Ulysses* (at the beginning of *Portrait* Stephen Daedelus is very young, and we see him at various distinct ages as the novel progresses; *Ulysses* picks up where *Portrait* leaves off) and because some of the characters that are introduced in *Dubliners* can be found again in the allusion-packed *Ulysses*.

BIBLIOGRAPHY

Beck, J. Warren. *Joyce's Dubliners: Substance, Vision, and Art.* Durham, N.C.: Duke University Press, 1969.

Ellman, Richard. *James Joyce.* New York: Oxford University Press, 1982.

Joyce, James. *Dubliners.* New York: Penguin, 2000.

Torchiana, Donald T. *Backgrounds for Joyce's Dubliners.* Boston: Allen & Unwin, 1986.

Daniel Jernigan

DUEL, THE JOSEPH CONRAD **(1908)** As with many of his shorter pieces, JOSEPH CONRAD interrupted work on a novel—in this case *Chance*—to write the Napoleonic novella *The Duel*. It was originally published serially in Britain as "The Duel—A Military Tale" in *Pall Mall Magazine* in January through May of 1908. That same year, in July through October, it was published in the United States, in *Forum,* as "The Point of Honor." Following the serial publication in Britain, *A Set of Six* was released in August 1908, in which *The Duel* was collected with five shorter works. Both the novella and the book received good reviews on both sides of the Atlantic; critics cited the thrilling pace, directness, and credibility of the narrative, as well as its comic and ironic under- and overtones. Favorable comparisons were made to the work of Turgenev and Meredith, while a French reviewer called the novella "artistically imperfect" though showing "prodigious imagination." *The Duel* is, characteristically for Conrad, an ironic dramatization of apparently actual events: a duel in which the duelists fought again and again throughout most of the Napoleonic period. This particular duel achieved sufficiently legendary status to be retold, or synopsized, in print with every subsequent resurgence of dueling. It is believed—and Conrad suggests as much in his preface to *A Set of Six*—that the source of the novella lies in one of these many retellings, such as that which appears in the September 1858, number of *Harper's New Monthly Magazine* (though it is unlikely Conrad saw this particular one).

In Conrad's version of the tale, two young hussars—light cavalry officers in Napoleon's army—become embroiled in a duel, the cause of which only they (and the reader) know. They face off against each other in several bloody but nonfatal encounters over a period spanning 16 years. Their duel is suspended, however, whenever they are called to duty in support of Napoleon's own long-running and wide-ranging duel against the rest of Europe, or whenever one outranks the other—dueling with inferiors being an even greater crime than dueling itself. The feud—and it does resemble a feud more than a duel—comes to an end when the hubris of one of the combatants gets the better of him, leaving him with two empty pistols and facing a well-armed opponent. Of the two main characters in Conrad's story, Armand D'Hubert is clearly the protagonist. The other, Gabriel Florian Feraud, from the manner in which Conrad characterizes him from the outset, is obviously the antagonist. Feraud is a professional duelist; he is the instigator in every encounter with D'Hubert. He is the one who, when he has all but forgotten about D'Hubert and the duel, is set off yet again by even the slightest mention of his opponent. Feraud (mis)reads every transfer of duty and promotion granted to D'Hubert as personal affronts. D'Hubert, on the other hand, is the unwilling, yet complaisant, victim of Feraud's rage. Today, these two could be classified as codependent, as D'Hubert's willing submittal to his nemesis's every summons enables Feraud to act out his rage against the lot he was dealt in life. D'Hubert cannot and will not disengage from Feraud, who cannot and will not disengage from him. It is a point of honor in both cases for both men, and it must be worked out between them.

Perhaps the most significant irony—and a significant element of Conrad's creative reworking of a well-known story—is that the events following the initial confrontation between D'Hubert and Feraud are, in effect, a duel over dueling. Though the story is told from a third-person, omniscient point of view, readers' knowledge of the circumstances and the characters involved is focalized through D'Hubert. Conrad skillfully uses this narrative technique to build sympathy for his protagonist. The narrative itself is compressed between a beginning and an ending that frame as well as define the story. It begins with a misreading of events and intentions by Feraud. He is to be placed under house arrest for dueling, a violation of his Emperor's rules; his rage at the general who orders him placed under arrest is transferred to the messenger,

D'Hubert. The ending, and the literal end of the duel, occurs when D'Hubert leaves Feraud no room to misread the real meaning of honor. As in Sir Walter Scott's tale, "The TWO DROVERS," it is the act of a relatively minor character—in this case, the general requesting the arrest of Feraud—that serves as the unintentional catalyst, precipitating the events in an otherwise nonreactive yet potentially volatile situation.

BIBLIOGRAPHY

Conrad, Joseph. "The Duel." In *A Set of Six,* 8th ed. London: Methuen & Co. Ltd., 1926.

The Duellists. Dir. Ridley Scott. Perf. Keith Carradine and Harvey Keitel. 1977. DVD. Paramount Pictures, 2002.

Ferguson, J. DeLancey. "The Plot of Conrad's *The Duel,*" *Modern Language Notes* 50, no. 6 (1935): 385–390.

Knowles, Owen, and Gene Moore. *Oxford Reader's Companion to Conrad.* Oxford: Oxford University Press, 2000.

James Fromm

DU MAURIER, DAPHNE (1907–1989)

Novelist, dramatist, short story writer, and biographer, Du Maurier is best known for her 1940 novel *Rebecca,* widely considered to be the 20th century's first major gothic novel. Her grandfather was *Trilby* author George du Maurier. Originally from London, du Maurier spent the bulk of her adulthood in Cornwall, which frequently provided the evocative setting for her suspense fiction. In 1932, Du Maurier married a Grenadier Guards officer, Major Frederick Arthur Browning. The couple had three children. Du Maurier followed her husband to his various postings both within and outside the United Kingdom. During this time, Du Maurier produced many of her best-known works including *Rebecca* and *Jamaica Inn* (1936), both of which evoke the Cornwall home she missed while living abroad. During her early and middle writing career, Du Maurier was extremely popular. However, the works of her later career, other than *The House on the Strand* (1969), were not as well received. Recently her work has been reevaluated, and her literary standing has once again risen.

Du Maurier published her first short story, "And Now to God the Father," in the May 15, 1929, edition of the *Bystander,* a periodical edited by her uncle William Beaumont. On June 26 she published a second story, "A Difference in Temperament," in the same periodical. This led to her first collection, *The Apple Tree and Other Stories,* in 1952. This volume included her best-known short story, "The Birds." She was inspired to write the story after seeing a farmer being attacked by a flock of seagulls as he plowed his field. Expanding on this incident, Du Maurier developed her story of birds becoming progressively more hostile to humans when an especially rough winter has led to food scarcity. Alfred Hitchcock's 1963 film adaptation of the story displeased Du Maurier, largely because he set it in California rather than Cornwall, a setting she considered a vital part of the story.

Du Maurier's second collection of short stories, *The Breaking Point,* was published in 1959. Two notable stories in this collection are "The Alibi," about a man who exchanges his boring life for a more exciting one and ends up being charged with murder, and "Ganymede," about a man who journeys to Venice in an unsuccessful attempt to escape his homosexuality. Her third collection of short stories, *Not after Midnight and Other Stories,* contains the chilling story "Don't Look Now." Du Maurier is at her best when creating atmospheric settings, and the Venice of this story is dark, labyrinthine, and nightmarish. In this story, a married couple is vacationing in Venice to ease their grief over their daughter's death. They meet two elderly English sisters who tell them their daughter's spirit is there and is communicating that they must leave Italy immediately. The wife does leave, but the husband stays and meets a terrifying end. "Don't Look Now" was also made into a film (1973) but was more faithful to the original story than *The Birds.* Perhaps because of the popularity of this story, the collection was republished in 1971 as *Don't Look Now.*

Du Maurier's writing style is easily readable but at times uneven. Nevertheless, her best works are truly masterpieces of gothic suspense. Probably because of its popular appeal, Du Maurier's work has not been the subject of much scholarly criticism. Avril Horner's *Daphne Du Maurier: Writing, Identity, and the Gothic Imagination* (1998) is a notable examination of Du Maurier's gothic work. A recent biography, Margaret Forster's *Daphne Du Maurier: The Secret Life of the Renowned Storyteller* (1993), though authorized by the

Du Maurier family, provides new—and sometimes shocking—insights into Du Maurier's life and work.

BIBLIOGRAPHY

Forster, Margaret. *Daphne Du Maurier: The Secret Life of the Renowned Storyteller.* New York: Doubleday, 1993.

Horner, Avril. *Daphne Du Maurier: Writing, Identity, and the Gothic Imagination.* New York: St. Martin's, 1998.

Du Maurier, Daphne. *The Apple Tree and Other Stories.* London: Gollancz, 1952.

———. *The Breaking Point.* London: Gollancz, 1959.

———. *Classics from the Macabre.* London: Gollancz, 1987.

———. *Echoes from the Macabre.* London: Gollancz, 1976.

———. *Not after Midnight and Other Stories.* London: Gollancz, 1971.

———. *The Rendezvous and Other Stories.* London: Gollancz, 1980.

Leah Larson

DUNMORE, HELEN (1952–)

Born in Yorkshire in 1952, Helen Dunmore has achieved recognition for both her poetry and prose writing in a notably prolific career. After studying English at the University of York, she taught in Finland for two years before returning to England, where she has worked at the University of Bristol and as a reviewer for the *Times* and the *Observer.* Her first book of poetry, *The Apple Fall,* was published in 1983, and her next collection, *The Sea Skater* (1986), won the Alice Hunt Bartlett Award in 1987. Dunmore admits that she was "very intimidated by prose" and did not publish her first novel, *Zennor in Darkness,* until 1993. This won the McKitterick Prize in 1994, and Dunmore's third novel, *A Spell of Winter* (1995), won the inaugural Orange Prize for Fiction in 1996. Since then she has written five more novels; *The Siege* (2001) was short-listed for both the Whitbread Novel Award and the Orange Prize for Fiction. Dunmore has also written several books for children, winning the Signal Poetry Award in 1995 for *Secrets* (1994).

Dunmore's two volumes of short fiction both show the influence of her time in Finland, and the great majority of the stories in her first collection, *Love of Fat Men* (1997), concentrate on Scandinavian characters and settings. The opening story, "Love of Fat Men," introduces Ulli, a frequently recurring character who embodies Dunmore's central themes of fraught family relationships, social alienation, and emotional dislocation. These themes also feature in the non-Ulli stories, such as "Annina" and "North Sea Crossing," but Ulli's repeated appearances in the book allow for a greater development of Dunmore's bleak perspective on human interaction. The Ulli stories run from her childhood to early adulthood, but their lack of chronological order further emphasizes Dunmore's focus on the fragility of the bond between parent and child. The young Ulli's naively hopeful attempts to foster communication in "Family Meetings" are made all the more poignant by the earlier stories "Ullikins," in which an older Ulli has voluntarily estranged herself from her parents and brothers, and "Spring Wedding," in which 16-year-old Ulli secretly worries that she is pregnant. Dunmore's characters consistently lack emotional honesty, reflecting the individual's confusion in postmodern society, where conventional ideas about role and identity are constantly being remade.

Ulli reappears less frequently in Dunmore's second volume of short fiction, *Ice Cream* (2000), but her presence in "The Kiwi Fruit Arbour," which follows directly from "Spring Wedding," further complicates the focus on parent-child relationships. In "The Kiwi Fruit Arbour" there is no doubt that Ulli is pregnant, but the conspicuous absence of a child in her later life provides new insights into the precarious nature of her subsequent relationships, lending new significance to the previous Ulli stories. However, while *Ice Cream* traces the same lines of emotional enquiry as *Love of Fat Men,* it ranges more widely in characterization and setting. The opening story, "My Polish Teacher's Tie," reflects Dunmore's interest in social marginalization but in the more mundane context of a primary school, while "Leonardo, Michaelangelo, Superstork" is an unexpectedly futuristic tale of eugenics that gives an ethical resonance to the familiar theme of parenthood. Dunmore's stories repeatedly question accepted notions about belonging and love by highlighting the limits of our emotional understanding, often producing unsettling meditations on the lawlessness of human emotions.

Dunmore has been most highly praised for the inspired lyricism of her prose, particularly in relation to the sensuousness of her descriptive writing. While these two collections contain precisely observed and often disturbing bleak dissections of human relationships, Dunmore's real strength lies in her ability to evoke physical sensation. She repeatedly uses food, weather, and landscape to generate intensely memorable images that emphasize the indefinably complex and transient nature of the impulse and instincts that inform her fiction.

BIBLIOGRAPHY

Dunmore, Helen. *The Apple Fall.* Newcastle upon Tyne, England: Bloodaxe, 1983.

———. *Ice Cream.* London: Viking, 2000.

———. Interview with Robert McCrum. *Observer* (June 10, 2001). Available online. URL: http//:www.books.guardian.co.uk/departments/generalfiction/story/0,,504308,00.html. Accessed May 11, 2006.

———. *Love of Fat Men.* London: Viking, 1997.

———. *Secrets.* London: Bodley Head, 1994.

———. *The Siege.* London: Viking, 2001.

———. *A Spell of Winter.* London: Viking, 1995.

Rochelle Sibley

DYSON, JEREMY (1966–   )

Born and raised in Leeds, Jeremy Dyson is now better known for being the cocreator of the town of Royston Vasey and the unseen face of *The League of Gentlemen,* the cult television comedy series in which it features. Having studied both philosophy at Leeds University and screenwriting at the Northern School of Film and Television, it is perhaps no surprise that as well as his work on television he was asked to write the foreword for a recent translation of Dostoevsky's *The Double.* He has published one collection of short stories: *Never Trust a Rabbit* (2000). Treading the spectrum from Edgar Allan Poe to Mervyn Peake, his view on the world, while skewed, is still familiar. It is in provoking this sensation of recognition that he is able to unsettle the reader.

"City Deep," a disturbing story, seems remarkably prescient with its main character's stated fear of traveling on the London Underground in case of "[s]ome terrible bomb left by a vengeful terrorist." It then takes this fear further and darker in a way that recalls the gothic tales of the early 20th-century writer H. P. Lovecraft. Another story that stands clear from the rest is "At Last," in which two young Jewish boys, led to fear that the crowd that they can hear gathering in the streets is a mob that has "come for the Jews again," find that it is a gathering of fellow Jews walking the streets in an affirmation of life. While ostensibly positive, this story seems representative of the collection: It discomfits evens as it uplifts, reminding the reader of the terrors of the Holocaust. In the final story, "All in the Telling," Dyson brings the collection to a close with a howl of outrage in which the telling of stories is equated, and then replaced, with purchased sex.

Critics have been largely positive about Dyson's writing, listing a number of writers whom they feel Dyson emulates, but it is his contemporary resonance that makes him interesting. His gothic influences are tempered with modern fear and anger that make the stories his own.

BIBLIOGRAPHY

Dyson, Jeremy. *Never Trust a Rabbit.* London: Duck Editions, 2000.

———. *What Happens Now.* London: Abacus, 2006.

Dyson, Jeremy, et al. *The League of Gentlemen: Scripts and That.* London: BBC Books, 2003.

Calum Kerr

E

EAST WEST SALMAN RUSHDIE (1994) SALMAN RUSHDIE's only collection of short stories, *East West*, is organized into three sections, "East," "West," and "East, West," with three stories in each. In an interview for the *Bookseller* in 1994, Salman Rushdie firmly locates himself in the title of *East, West:* "[T]he most important part of the title was the comma. Because it seems to me that I am that comma—or at least that I live in the comma." All of the stories in this collection deal with representations of home and with people whose homes become uncertain. A longing for home connects the first story in the collection, "Good Advice Is Rarer Than Rubies," to the last, "The Courter." In the first story, a confident woman fails her English immigration interrogation in order to remain in Lahore, Pakistan, as an ayah (or nanny). "The Courter" sees another ayah return to India to repair a heart murmur caused by homesickness. "The Courter" is a classic episode from a bildungsroman, or tale of development, in which a schoolboy portrays a few short years of his life in a clash of language, unrequited lusts, and the raging arguments and efforts of politeness that define family life.

In the "West" section, Rushdie shifts the firm ground from beneath three great Western tales that have acquired mythical status: those of Hamlet, Christopher Columbus, and the Wizard of Oz. "Yorick" begins in Rushdie's characteristic style, with an extended flow of disjointed narration: The first sentence is more than a page in length. "At the Auction of the Ruby Slippers" is a bitter story of loss and gain; the auction house becomes a microcosm of contemporary society, where the rich and powerful are protected from the outcasts, orphans, tramps, and political refugees who inhabit small sections of the overcrowded room.

In "Christopher Columbus and Queen Isabella of Spain Consummate their Relationship (Santa Fe A.D. 1492)," Columbus waits for the royal commission that will permit him to travel west and reach America. The story asks a recurring postcolonial question when it contests the notion that he discovered the Americas. Perhaps the most poignant story in the collection is "The Free Radio," in which overpopulation leads to mass sterilization. The narrator's perspective transforms the social realism into a tale of one man's hope and dependence. The beautiful young man, waiting for the free radio from the government that he believes is part of the sterilization deal, clings desperately to the empty space next to his ear, where he hopes that his recompense, the acknowledgment for his sacrifice, will reside.

BIBLIOGRAPHY
Rushdie, Salman. *East, West.* London: Jonathan Cape, 1994.
Reder, Michael R., ed. *Conversations with Salman Rushdie.*
   Jackson: University Press of Mississippi, 2000.

Jenni Ramone

EBONY TOWER, THE JOHN FOWLES (1974) According to JOHN FOWLES: "The working title of this collection of stories was *Variations*, by which I meant

131

to suggest variations both on certain themes in previous books of mine and in methods of narrative presentation" (119). The four stories in the collection, are "The Ebony Tower," "Poor Koko," "The Enigma," and "The Cloud." A striking feature is the inclusion of a translation of a medieval French tale, "Eliduc," which is preceded by an introduction in which Fowles highlights a personal and a general theory of fiction. Fowles remarks that in reading stories such as "Eliduc," "the writer of fiction . . . is watching his own birth" (120). The stories deal with conflicts in love, sex, and guilt; the reconciliation of opposites, the functions of art and the artist; and the paradoxes of free choice. The implicit devices of the collection are the epigraphs at the beginning of each story and the patterns of intertextuality and allusion, of quest, adventure, disappearance, and nature. However, Fowles himself writes, "Again and again in recent years I have told visiting literary academics that the key to my fiction, for what it is worth, lies in my relationship with nature" (2005, 35).

The title story, "The Ebony Tower," shows the tragedy of authenticity and choice when a young English painter and art critic, David Williams, goes to hunt Henry Breasley, an aging expatriate artist living in Brittany. "Eliduc" presents the medieval theme of romance with its aura of courtly love. "Poor Koko" is an ordeal of a particular night, where the narrator is the subject of his narrative encounter with a burglar. "Koko" is a Japanese word and means correct filial behavior, "the proper attitude of son to father" (186). "The Enigma" falls into a subgenre of DETECTIVE FICTION in which the mystery is not solved and no solutions are hinted at. The narrative of the last story, "The Cloud," circles around two families who spend a day near a forest beside a river. Catherine, a recently widowed artist, is reminiscent of the fairy tale princess who, lost in the woods, disappears under mysterious circumstances.

BIBLIOGRAPHY
Fowles, John. *The Ebony Tower*. London: Cape, 1974.
———. *The Tree*. London: Vintage, 2005.

Krishna Barua

"EBONY TOWER, THE" John Fowles (1974)

In "The Ebony Tower," John Fowles wrote a variation on his novel *The Magus* (1965). Both narratives present a young man who, guided by an older mentor figure, has to make life-determining decisions while being tempted by an artistic young woman. In this short story, the artist and art critic David Williams travels to France to interview fellow painter Henry Breasley, an old man who lives with Diana (the Mouse) and Anne (the Freak), his two beautiful young muses, in an enchanted forest, "the sacred wood of the mythical quest" (Barnum 134). The theme of mystery and romance introduced through the almost magical quality of its location finds reinforcement through the story's intertextual links to Marie de France's medieval *lai* "Eliduc," a translation of which Fowles included with his short stories. Both narratives investigate the trials of romantic love, the conventions of society, and the necessity to stay true to personal feelings. Williams, however, proves to have an immature, or at least conventional, personality, being driven by the rules and regulations of British bourgeois life. Drawn between his unexciting marriage and the temptations that the highly intelligent, artistic, emotional, and sexually uninhibited Mouse represents, he chooses to honor his marital vows and thereby betrays his emotional self. Indeed, Williams's inability to express his innermost thoughts and feelings in a personal, truthful fashion also characterizes his critical writing, in which he succumbs to recent aesthetic fads and squanders his original artistic talent.

Echoes of the kinds of psychoanalytic theories popularized by Carl Jung are omnipresent in the short story. They find their way into the constellation of characters, with Breasley representing a mentor figure and the two characters Diana and Anne representing realizations of womanhood as either spiritual muse or sexual vamp. Williams's conflict also stands for the struggle between his repressed needs and wishes, what Jung called *shadow,* and his outer mask of convention and conformity, the *persona.* His inability to bring these two sides into harmony shows Williams to be a highly flawed and inauthentic character. His excessive reliance on theoretical frameworks appears as his fundamental deficiency.

Where Williams is cerebral, Breasley is physical. While the former sees in art predominantly an intellectual exercise, the latter thinks of his work as an emotional, sexual, and fundamentally intimate activity.

The conflict between mind and body that these two approaches represent comes down heavily in favor of Breasley's physical version of art. Williams's highly abstract views on (often also highly abstract) art Fowles presents as inauthentic, irrelevant, and self-congratulatory. In Barry Olshen's words, Fowles ostracizes "the failures of the age" (95). The story's implicit references to Williams's repressed and futile sexuality further emphasize the masturbatory tendencies of his theoretical discourse.

In "The Ebony Tower," Fowles draws a negative picture of his contemporaries' modes of criticism, condemning them as overly abstract and out of tune with real-world issues.

BIBLIOGRAPHY

Acheson, James. *John Fowles.* London: Macmillan, 1998.
Conradi, Peter. *John Fowles.* London: Methuen, 1982.
Foster, Thomas C. *Understanding John Fowles.* Columbia: University of South Carolina Press, 1994.
Fowles, John. *The Ebony Tower.* 1974. London: Cape, 1984.
Olshen, Barry. *John Fowles.* New York: Ungar, 1978.

Gerd Bayer

ECSTASY Irvine Welsh (1996)   Irvine Welsh's second collection of short fiction was published in 1996, arriving in the midst of the author's greatest moment of popularity. Danny Boyle's film adaptation of *Trainspotting* had been released earlier that year, and its remarkable success had sparked interest in the first novel as well as Welsh's subsequent work. The publication of *Ecstasy* was apparently hastened in order to capitalize on the momentum created by the film. Despite impressive sales, however, the book was poorly received by reviewers, and its lukewarm reception marked the beginning of a critical backlash against an author who had to that point been embraced by both the literary establishment and the popular marketplace.

"Ecstasy" is the more familiar name of MDMA, the pleasure drug of choice of the so-called chemical generation associated with Britain's rave scene of the 1980s and 1990s. Welsh's work began to be embraced by young clubgoers following the 1994 publication of *The Acid House,* whose title alluded to one of their preferred musical styles. The title and packaging of *Ecstasy* indicate a continued attempt on the part of author and publisher alike to appeal to this youth subculture. Ecstasy, along with other concoctions favored by ravers, LSD and Temazapan, figures heavily in these stories. Indeed, some reviewers of *Ecstasy* found Welsh's tone uncomfortably evangelical on the subject, although the pharmaceutical catastrophe underlying the second story, "Fortune's Always Hiding," might be seen as a counterargument to the book's occasional eulogies for chemically-induced altered states of consciousness.

The first novella, "Lorraine Goes to Livingston," centers on the transformation of Rebecca Navarro, a pampered and successful writer of popular romances, whose banal style Welsh parodies in excerpts from Rebecca's work. While recovering from a stroke, Rebecca learns the truth about her husband, Perky, an apparently doting man who is secretly disdainful of her and pursues a sexually adventurous life hitherto unknown to his wife. With the assistance of her young nurse, Rebecca plots her revenge on the unsuspecting Perky. The second story, "Fortune's Always Hiding," is a tale of the bloody revenge wreaked by Samantha, a victim of Tenazadrine, a fictional painkiller that recalls a genuine pharmaceutical disaster of the late 1950s: the introduction of Thalidomide, a drug intended supposed to relieve morning sickness in pregnant women, which resulted in thousands of dead and malformed infants all over the world. The final novella, "The Undefeated," is a surprisingly conventional romance that brings together Lloyd, an aging raver growing uncomfortable with the continuing aimlessness of his life, and Heather, a woman freeing herself from a dull, confining marriage.

Ecstasy's subtitle—"Three Tales of Chemical Romance"—highlights what was for many an ultimately disappointing aspect of this collection: Welsh's unlikely foray into romance. That all three of these novellas might fairly be labeled "romances" at all is open to question, most obviously in the case of "Fortune's Always Hiding," whose "romance" involves the revenge-obsessed Samantha and Dave, an east London thug whom Samantha manipulates into assisting in the mutilation and murder of the man who brought to Britain the deadly drug that left her with no arms.

Clearly, the genre takes on some unaccustomed shapes in Welsh's hands. However, some of the inherited conventions of romance do make their presence felt in *Ecstasy*. There is a new emphasis in these stories on female characters as central figures, and the first and final stories end happily and with scenes of integration—most neatly so in "The Undefeated," with its final note of true love found; Welsh mocks the popular romance in his first story only to embrace its fundamental outline without apparent irony in his last. In hindsight, Welsh himself has acknowledged the weaknesses of *Ecstasy* in comparison with other work. Arguably his least successful book, *Ecstasy* nonetheless demonstrates Welsh's continuing willingness to experiment with a variety of styles and genres.

BIBLIOGRAPHY
Welsh, Irvine. *Ecstasy*. New York: Norton, 1996.

Brian Patton

EDGEWORTH, MARIA (1768–1849)
Born on New Year's Day in 1768, Maria Edgeworth was the eldest daughter of an Irish landowner living in Oxfordshire. Her first publication, *Letters for Literary Ladies* (1795), defended women's right to education. In 1796 she published *The Parent's Assistant,* a collection of short stories for children. The collection was both influential and popular; it eventually ran to seven volumes. In 1800, she published her first short novel, *Castle Rackrent*. Like *The Absentee* (1812), *Castle Rackrent* explores the profligacy and dire irresponsibility of an Irish landowner in the 18th century. In 1823 she visited Walter Scott, who became probably her most enthusiastic reader. *The Absentee* prompted Scott to return to his manuscript of *Waverley* (1814), making Edgeworth partially responsible for the explosion of the historical novel in the 19th century. Her work was wide-ranging; she was interested in notions of nationality, gender, education, colonial politics, and the nature of authorship. For most of the 20th century she was all but ignored, but she has recently begun to be republished and reread, and a number of interesting studies of her work have appeared, most notably, by Marilyn Butler.

BIBLIOGRAPHY
Butler, Marilyn. *Maria Edgeworth: A Literary Biography.* Oxford: Clarendon Press, 1972.
———. *Romantics, Rebels and Reactionaries: English Literature and Its Background 1760–1830.* Oxford: Oxford University Press, 1981.
Edgeworth, Maria. *Castle Rackrent.* Edited by George Watson. Oxford: Oxford University Press, 1964.

Vybarr Cregan-Reid

EGERTON, GEORGE (1859–1945)
George Egerton was the pseudonym of Mary Chavelita Dunne (later Bright), one of the so-called NEW WOMAN writers of the 1890s. Born on December 14, 1859, in Melbourne, Australia, she was the eldest of six children. When she was a young woman, her personal life was fraught with difficulties, including a short, brutal elopement with a bigamist friend of her father's, Henry Higginson. From 1888 until his death in 1889, Egerton lived with Higginson in Norway, where she learned Norwegian and read such writers as the German philosopher Friedrich Nietzsche and the Scandinavian writers Henrik Ibsen, August Strindberg, Olaf Hansson, and the novelist Knut Hamsun (with whom she had an affair). Upon her return to London, she married George Egerton Clairmonte, who had recently returned from Africa, in 1891; he seemed incapable of employment, so Egerton began to write for financial support and divorced him in 1901. After purchasing a penny exercise book, she wrote her short stories in sepia ink and then sent them to T. P. Gill, the literary columnist for the *Weekly Sun,* for his opinion. Although he praised their originality in his column, he clearly found them shocking in their outspoken discussions of sexuality. Ironically, he believed they were the work of a male author and wrote to Egerton, asking her to edit them before publication. Once he learned her true identity, Gill encouraged her to submit them to William Heinemann; ultimately, it was John Lane at the Bodley Head who chose to publish them as KEYNOTES, the inaugural (and eponymous) volume in his series (1893); he had them bound with a frontispiece and cover illustrated by Aubrey Beardsley. Included in the collection was the much-anthologized story "A CROSS LINE." Egerton followed this with the short story collections *Discords*

(1894), *Symphonies* (1897), *Fantasias* (1898), and two later texts, a fictionalized collection of letters in *Rosa Amorosa* (1901) and the autobiographical novel *Wheel of God* (1898).

Her writing created a stir with its frank depiction of the "terra incognita" of woman's psychological complexity and her honest representation of women's sexuality. She was variously praised for her original themes and stylistic advances, which anticipate MODERNISM while showing influence from the naturalist school, and reprimanded for her audacity. In the December 1893 volume of *Review of Reviews,* the critic remarked that the writer of *Keynotes* was a "woman [who] has crystallised her life's drama, has written down her soul on the page," while *Punch* caricatured her text as "She Notes" by "Borgia Smudgiton"; Hugh Stutfield wrote in "Tommyrotics" and "The Psychology of Feminism" that Egerton was neurotic, her themes were inappropriate for a woman, and her texts were morbid depictions of modern life. Her ability to write psychological snapshots of a woman's life at moments of crisis or to discuss alcoholism, suicide, conventional attitudes on respectability, and woman's essential nature prefigures the state of consciousness found in the work of modernists such as JAMES JOYCE and VIRGINIA WOOLF, making her an important although often-neglected figure in the development of the late Victorian short story. In 1901, after various rumored affairs with literary men, Egerton formed a lasting marriage with Reginald Golding Bright, a dramatic agent 15 years her junior. She finished her writing career between 1908 and 1925 with plays (*His Wife's Family, Backsliders,* and *Camilla States Her Case*) that she refused to have listed on her official bibliography; even though they were of interest to prominent actresses, they had no commercial success. She died in Crawley, Sussex, on August 12, 1945. (See also "A NOCTURNE.")

BIBLIOGRAPHY

Egerton, George. *Discords.* London: Virago, 1983.
———. *Keynotes.* London: Virago, 1983.
Stubbs, Patricia. *Women and Fiction: Feminism and the Novel 1880–1920.* Brighton: Harvester, 1979.

Sarah Maier

ELIOT, GEORGE (MARY ANN EVANS) (1818–1880)

George Eliot grew up in the rural country of Warwickshire, near the Midlands town of Coventry, the daughter of an estate manager. Formidably intelligent, she acquired a profound education in languages, philosophy, theology, and science and became the most intellectual British novelist of the 19th century and one of the most highly regarded. A woman of great mental and personal courage, she abandoned traditional religious faith, moved in progressive intellectual and political circles, and lived with a man, George Henry Lewes, with whom she was not married, for 24 years. Famous, above all, for her complex and long novels of social and psychological life—such as *Adam Bede* (1859), *The Mill on the Floss* (1860), *Middlemarch* (1872), and *Daniel Deronda* (1876)—she also wrote short fiction, which plays an important, if secondary, role in her output.

Eliot's first pieces of extended fiction were three long short stories, "The SAD FORTUNES OF THE REVEREND AMOS BARTON," "Mr. Gilfil's Love Story," and "JANET'S REPENTANCE," first published in *Blackwood's Edinburgh Magazine* in 1857 and later published in book form by Blackwood in 1858. The setting of all three stories is typical of Eliot's fiction—the rural English Midlands 30 to 60 years before the texts' time of publication. Also typical are the omniscient, third-person narrators, who intervene to comment on action and character. These realist stories present a wide social range of characters, and the narrator constantly points to the interrelationship of personal development and the social and economic circumstances of characters' environments. The action depicted is melancholy. Amos Barton is a study in misplaced and destructive idealism, Mr. Gilfil's love for Caterina can not save her, and "Janet's Repentance" is a vivid depiction of drunkenness and domestic violence. Wisdom comes only through loss and suffering, although others may learn from the protagonists' examples.

The short novel *Silas Marner: The Weaver of Raveloe* (1861) has a similar place and time setting to that of *Scenes of Clerical Life.* Like all of Eliot's fiction, it is a bitter critique of selfishness and materialism. Silas is a stranger in the village of Raveloe (Eliot frequently writes about outsiders) who, embittered by his relationships with human beings inside and outside the village, becomes a miser, obsessed with the gold he earns and hoards. The melodramatic plot involves the theft of his money and the appearance in his home of a child, Eppie, whom he adopts and whose golden hair replaces the stolen money. Silas learns humanity through the girl and becomes part of the community. The short novel demonstrates Eliot's interest in and high regard for socially lowly life.

Eliot published two further short stories, "The LIFTED VEIL" (1859) and "BROTHER JACOB" (1864), both of which are much less known than her other works. "The Lifted Veil" has marked gothic elements and echoes Edgar Allan Poe's and Nathaniel Hawthorne's fiction. Latimer, the protagonist, discovers that he has the powers of foreseeing events and of seeing into the minds of those who surround him. Neither of these gifts are viewed positively: The visions of the future are sad, and the gift of knowing people's thoughts is a curse. This is ironic, given the stress that Eliot places elsewhere on the moral value of an ability to understand others. Bertha, Latimer's wife, is a version of the beautiful egoistic women that recur throughout Eliot's work, Hetty Sorrel, Rosamond Vincy, and Gwendolen Harleth, but the supernatural and gothic elements are unusual in her fiction. "Brother Jacob" is a comic moral fable, in which the egoist David Faux is made to pay for his crimes by his mentally subnormal brother.

BIBLIOGRAPHY

Eliot, George. *The Lifted Veil and Brother Jacob*. London: Penguin, 2001.
———. *Scenes of Clerical Life*. Oxford: Oxford University Press, 2000.
Levine, George, ed. *Cambridge Companion to George Eliot*. Cambridge: Cambridge University Press, 2001.
McDonagh, Josephine. *George Eliot*. Plymouth, England: Northcote House, 1999.
Nestor, Pauline. *George Eliot*. London: Palgrave, 2002.

David Malcolm

ELPHINSTONE, MARGARET (1948–)

Born in Kent, Margaret Elphinstone spent her first 10 years in Kent, Sussex, and Somerset. She moved to Scotland in 1970 to study at the University of Glasgow. Her first story, "Spinning the Green," published in *Dis-patches from the Frontiers of the Female Mind* (1985), is a pastiche based on a number of traditional fairy tales, particularly *Beauty and the Beast*. The story suggests an environmentalist agenda, as the Beast is a collective name for a group of women who are reminiscent of the Greenham Common women who mounted a long campaign against nuclear weapons in the 1980s, in which Elphinstone took part, and who lived outdoors on the land surrounding an air force base. In the story the women are determined to protect nature from the risks of permanent damage caused by pollution; they keep "spinning the green," an action evocative both of the fairyland atmosphere and the ecological agenda at the core of the story.

In the 1980s and 1990s, Elphinstone's interest in environmental matters inspired two gardening handbooks: *The Holistic Gardener* (1987), coauthored with J. Langley, and *Organic Gardening* (1990). Her early novels, *The Incomer* (1987) and *A Sparrow's Flight* (1989), also belong to this phase. Folk tradition (the use of magic, references to witchcraft, tarot imagery) and science fiction (the environmentalist catastrophe, the future dystopian setting of the stories) merge in these novels. Her collection of stories *An APPLE FROM A TREE* (1991) follows the same path. The stories all disclose environmental concerns, often filtered through an encounter with an otherworldly creature. This happens in the first story, significantly titled "The Green Man" which deals with an art teacher, Sara, and her magical adventure with Lin, a "green man." Similar magical-realist experiences are shared by other human protagonists of Elphinstone's stories, including Alison and her alter-ego Nosila in the title story of the collection. Two related stories, "Conditions of Employment" and especially "The Cold Well"—inspired by a visit to Sellafield nuclear station—reinstate Elphinstone's involvement in the peace movements and in ecological issues.

Since the publication of the collection, Elphinstone has abandoned fantasy mostly in favor of historical fiction, beginning with *Islanders* (1994), set in 12th-century Shetland, which was followed by *The Sea Road* (2000)—winner of the Scottish Arts Council Book Award in 2001—set in 11th-century Greenland and Vinland. Both stories reveal Elphinstone's interest in Scandinavian lore, a field Elphinstone started to explore from 1972 to 1980, during the years she spent working as a librarian and volunteering for an archeological expedition in Shetland. An imaginary island is the setting for *Hy Brasil* (2002), a novel cast in the utopian genre with a hint of mystery.

Elphinstone's next novels marked a return to historical fiction: *Voyageurs* (2003), short-listed for the 2005 Great Lakes Book Award, explores Native American culture through the eyes of a Quaker traveling across the Canadian border during the 1812 war with the United States. *Gato* (2005), a novella written in collaboration with the Highland Adult Literacy Education and set in the Middle Ages, is the story of a child raised in a mill; the plot involves the miller, his wife, a Spanish Friar, and his cat. Her novel *Light* (2006) explores life on a small island off the Isle of Man in the first half of the 19th century.

Margaret Elphinstone is also the author of articles on Scottish women's writing and is professor of writing at Strathclyde University.

BIBLIOGRAPHY

Elphinstone, Margaret. "Spinning the Green." In *Despatches from the Frontiers of the Female Minds,* edited by Jen Green and Sarah Lefanu, 15–26. London: The Women's Press, 1985.

———. *An Apple from a Tree and Other Visions.* London: The Women's Press, 1991.

———. *Gato.* Dingwall: Sandstone Vista Series, 2005.

Gifford, Douglas. "Contemporary Fiction II: Seven Writers in Scotland." In *A History of Scottish Women's Writing,* edited by Douglas Gifford and Dorothy McMillan, 604–629. Edinburgh: Edinburgh University Press, 1997.

McGillivray, Alan. "Interview with Margaret Elphinstone," *Laverock* 1 (1995): 29–38.

Monica Germana

"END OF HER JOURNEY, THE" LUCY CLIFFORD (1887)

"The End of Her Journey," by LUCY CLIFFORD was initially published in two installments in the monthly magazine *Temple Bar* (June–July 1887). The story was topical, appearing at a time when newspapers were hotly debating the "marriage question." It opens by detailing the seemingly uneventful life of Mildred Archerson, wife of an affable and popular barrister, Edward ("Teddy"). Teddy Archerson is a familiar type, the sociable but morally lightweight man whom everybody likes. Neglected by Teddy and barely noticed by their acquaintances, Mildred lives a lonely and monotonous existence in London, longing for her husband to spend time with her. The story is told mostly from Mildred's perspective, although we do get some idea of the sense of boredom she inspires in her husband. To all appearances Mildred is dull and charmless. Yet her silence masks a deep unhappiness; "[D]eaf and dumb the woman's soul lived within its prison, unconsciously beating against its bars, longing to escape, wondering and weeping at its own limits, its own blindness, its own incapacity, having no power at all except to suffer without seeing the reason of it, or knowing any remedy" (197). While technically a free woman, Mildred seems to inhabit a kind of subterranean existence, viewed as irredeemably marginal by everyone around her. As spectacle of imprisonment and frustrated sexuality, Clifford's portrait of a seemingly ordinary woman is both complex and poignant. Partly this is because her heroine cannot voice what she feels.

Generically "The End of Her Journey" can be labeled sensation fiction and invites comparison with the kind of literature made famous by such writers as WILKIE COLLINS, MARY ELIZABETH BRADDON, and ELLEN WOOD in the 1860s and 1870s. The sensation novel was a "novel with a secret," which brought adultery, bigamy, illegitimacy, suicide, and murder into the confines of the respectable middle- or upper-class drawing room. In "The End of Her Journey," Mildred's world is quite literally destroyed when an acquaintance tells her that Teddy has been seen at Clapham Junction railway station with another woman. Soon afterward she spots a list of charitable donations in the newspaper, including one from a "Mrs. Edward Archerson," and this makes her more curious. Exhibiting unexpected determination, she assumes the disguise of a collector for charity and explores the suburban streets of Clapham. Eventually she finds herself in a small house with Teddy's photo in the drawing room, and then she comes face to face with her husband's illegitimate second family—a young woman and a small boy. The true reason behind Teddy's long absences is made blindingly obvious. The discovery is a moment of personal cataclysm for Mildred, reminding her of what she lacks. But it is also apparent that she has undergone an awakening. Silently she goes back home, saying nothing as to her real identity. She does not confront her husband, and when he suggests that she go on a cruise for the sake of her health, Mildred agrees, accepting Teddy's excuses for not accompanying her. She goes alone, committing suicide on the voyage. The conclusion of the story shows Teddy and his new family happy in their pretty new home. Only when his new wife draws a picture of the mysterious woman who visited her and the reason for Mildred's death becomes clear is Teddy forced finally to realize the horror of his own moral decay; he is a man whose selfishness prompted his wife to throw herself overboard so that he might be free.

The ending of this story is like other works by Clifford in that it stresses the power of the past to haunt the present. But throughout, Clifford is also interested in the underside of domesticity, in female lives lived in a male-dominated society and the callousness and victimization this may involve. Mildred is in thrall to old-fashioned ideas, ideas that have in truth left her lonely and unfulfilled. While Clifford does not offer an explicit a feminist critique of her society in the way that, for example, outspoken NEW WOMAN writers of the 1890s such as GEORGE EGERTON or Mona Caird do, there is no doubt about Teddy's weakness as a man and a husband. At the same time, Mildred's discovery prompts a move from passivity to activity; she begins to take matters into her own hands, striving to effect a scheme of what she regards as her personal destiny. Just how we interpret the news of Mildred's suicide is unclear. Is it an act of self-assertion? An act of courage? Or is it a pyrrhic victory? After all, Mildred can get Teddy's attention only by obliterating herself.

BIBLIOGRAPHY

Chisholm, Monty. *Such Silver Currents: The Story of William and Lucy Clifford, 1845–1929.* Cambridge: Lutterworth Press, 2002.

Devine Jump, Harriet, ed. *Nineteenth-Century Short Stories by Women: A Routledge Anthology.* London: Routledge, 1998.

Andrew Maunder

ENGLAND CALLING JULIA BELL AND JACKIE GAY **(2001)**   Since the devolution of power to Scotland and Wales at the end of the 1990s, England has been questioning its own identity and offering a different image from that of the overruling power it projected in the past, presenting instead a local, approachable, and contradictory picture. *England Calling,* a dense and vibrant volume of short stories, is a translation into fiction of that introspective attitude. The editors Julia Bell and Jackie Gay had previously compiled the anthology *Hard Shoulder* (1999), in which 16 writers each produced a story about Birmingham. The success of this venture in regional writing led them to carry out the more ambitious project of *England Calling,* in which the country as a whole could be represented.

As the editors state in the introduction, at the beginning of the 21st century, England is undergoing a process of change, and they simply want to illustrate this mutation: "These writers are not only telling stories of the landscapes of England, but peeling back the layers of Englishness in the process—Englishness as it is now: multicultural, messy, survivalist" (xi). The main idea behind the project, therefore, is fiction as a contribution to self-knowledge or, to paraphrase Patricia Waugh, "reading the age through its imaginative literature" (2).

The 24 contributors to this volume (editors included) come from every corner of England. The book begins with a vigorous representation from the north, followed by stories from different parts of the Midlands, the east coast, London, and the home counties, the south and the southwest. Some of the contributors were already well-established writers at the time of the book's launch, including columnist Julie Burchill, spoken-word performer Joolz Denby, and veteran novelist Jane Rogers, but many were still in the first stages of their literary careers. The University of East Anglia, where Julia Bell teaches creative writing, appears to be the breeding ground of a significant number of the writers in this collection. In fact, the anthology has been criticized for being too strongly influenced by techniques taught in creative writing courses (Blincoe). In any case, what the authors of *England Calling* see in this restless country are scenes of an urban, modern, and highly commercialized society where history is now called heritage tourism. City centers have been redeveloped to erase their dirty past. The same colorless shopping centers replace old markets everywhere. Affluent young professionals line up to get cappuccinos in recently opened Starbucks in the main streets of similar towns: "Carshalton could look exactly the same as Croydon, Sutton, Kingston, Ashford and Woking" (207). The stories in this collection accurately reflect the state of the country at the start of the new millennium; a blunt pragmatism has invaded people's consciences, shopping is the new religion, and old ideals have vanished in the air: "Now, I wonder why we cared so much," says one story's protagonist, who once joined Greenham Common Women's Camp to protest U.S. missiles being based in the country: "Everybody wants an ecstasy lifestyle" (150).

Although there are descriptions of middle-class interiors, suburban comfort, and hidden neuroses, the real energy in the anthology comes from the outcasts, the no-hopers, people living on the dole, confused old hippies, or kids from street gangs. The local pub, usually in the middle of an urban wasteland, or the block of flats in a council estate are therefore frequent settings. The longing for some kind of spirituality, whether religious or other, is another recurrent feature in the collection. Perhaps to compensate for the absence of a sense of community in their lives, the characters search for meaning everywhere: in a bleeding statue, in a newspaper enterprise doomed to failure, or in a game of chess with an old man. Whether this should be interpreted in terms of postmodern nostalgia (and its subsequent paralysis) is another matter.

BIBLIOGRAPHY
Bell, Julia, and Jackie Gay, eds. *Hard Shoulder*. Birmingham: Tindal Street Press, 1999.
———. *England Calling*. 2001. London: Phoenix, 2002.
Blincoe, Nicholas. "Left with the Dregs," *New Statesman* (July 16, 2001). Available online. URL: http://www.newstatesman.com/200107160043. Accessed July 4, 2006.
Waugh, Patricia. *Harvest of the Sixties*. Oxford: Oxford University Press, 1995.

José Francisco Fernández

"ENGLISHMAN'S HOME, AN" EVELYN WAUGH (1938) This story, collected in *Work Suspended and Other Stories* (1943), demonstrates not only Waugh's comic genius but also his penetrating social criticism of English life in the period between World Wars I and II. Mr. Beverley Metcalfe has retired to the village of Much Malcock, where he and his wife have settled into what they expect will be a comfortable existence of gardening, leisure, and civic responsibility among the gentry of the English countryside. A lifelong city dweller, Metcalfe is woefully unfamiliar with the customs of country life. He congratulates himself for having purchased only a small acreage surrounding his new retreat. Metcalfe's new existence is threatened when another outsider arrives in the village and purchases an adjoining plot of land with plans to establish a new scientific-industrial complex that will destroy not just Metcalfe's new lifestyle but the comfort and property values of his neighbors as well. In a series of conversations and meetings with his neighbors, Metcalfe discovers that the recently sold land has traditionally been regarded as belonging to his own estate. Angered at his failure to secure the now-threatened property in the first place, Metcalfe's neighbors refuse to assist him in a joint effort to buy back the property. This modern fable of the city mouse transplanted to the country ends with a delightful reversal that underscores the changing conditions of English country life in the last years before the outbreak of World War II.

As in much of Waugh's fiction, the satirical force of the story is conveyed through the rich characterization of Metcalfe and his neighbors at Much Malcock. Beverley Metcalfe is a former cotton trader from Alexandria, a past president of the British Chamber of Commerce, and by far the wealthiest of the denizens of Much Malcock. However, Metcalfe's wealth and his pride in his own business acumen fail him in his efforts to secure his own lifestyle and the fellowship of his neighbors. Lady Peabury of Much Malcock House is a semireclusive widow who devotes her time to the decadent practice of reading novels before noon and raising terriers. Colonel Hodge, who lives at Much Malcock Manor, is the leading patron of the local Boy Scouts and a vociferous critic of the Bolshevik tendencies of the village parson. Mr. and Mrs. Hornbean, who occupy the lowest social stratum of the village's upper crust, inhabit the Old Mill, where they devote themselves to the bohemian pleasures of pottery, gardening, vegetarianism, and a running critique of rampant modern capitalism. Together, these good citizens of Much Malcock represent the changing landscape of English rural life between the wars. They struggle to maintain the traditional, agricultural, paternalistic culture of an England that is in the midst of modernization.

The source of the threat to their way of life, the outsider who threatens their idylls with his blueprints for an industrial complex in the midst of their pastures and vistas, proves in the end a confidence man whose schemes are motivated by his desperate need to raise funds in order to pay the taxes on his own country estate. After finally purchasing the infamous property in question at several times its value, Metcalfe donates the property to the Boy Scouts for their use as a camp and unveils plans to build them a new lodge for their meetings. Although he proves a poor excuse for a supposedly skilled businessman, Metcalfe finds himself at the story's conclusion as the new chief philanthropist in the village of Much Malcock.

BIBLIOGRAPHY

Stannard, Martin. *Evelyn Waugh: The Early Years, 1903–1939.* New York: Norton, 1986.

Waugh, Evelyn. *The Complete Stories.* Boston: Little, Brown, 1998.

Tony Rafalowski

"ENIGMA, THE" JOHN FOWLES (1974)

"The Enigma" is one of five short stories included in the collection *The EBONY TOWER*. JOHN FOWLES's working title for the collection was *Variations;* although he was convinced by his publisher to discard the original title, the stories constitute variations in more than one sense. They recapitulate and prefigure the themes of Fowles's novels, offer variations on narrative techniques and generic conventions, and playfully subvert customary distinctions between fiction and reality.

All of these aspects can be seen in "The Enigma." The title refers to a quasi detective mystery: the sudden and inexplicable disappearance of John Marcus Fielding, a 57-year old, rich, happily married Tory member of Parliament. After some discreet and futile investigations led by Fielding's wife, the police are approached and a young detective, Michael Jennings, is assigned the case. Jennings questions Fielding's family members, friends, colleagues, and political rivals. All he receives are variations, competing versions of the man's personality, motives, and possible whereabouts. The more he questions, the less he knows. As Fielding has never been a major political figure, and as the investigation into his disappearance yields no results, the police lose interest in the case. The official inquiry gradually dwindles, and the young investigator's professional interest in the (potentially) criminal mystery gives way to his passionate interest in another kind of mystery. He falls in love with Isobel, Fielding's son's girlfriend, and comes to realize that "the tender pragmatisms of flesh have poetries no enigma, human or divine, can diminish or demean" (247).

"The Enigma" anticipates the major themes and narrative strategies of Fowles's later novels: the endorsement of freedom as the highest human good; the view of life as an ultimate mystery that defies all attempts at rational explanation; the refusal of closure, suggesting the impossibility of resolving the mystery of human existence; female characters as existential heroines triggering the male protagonist's awakening; a metafictional element of a story-within-a-story, ironically and playfully undermining the customary distinction between fiction and reality.

The notion of freedom is explored on several levels. In the fictional world, none of the characters (but Isobel) is free. They are all scripted by their social roles. The most conventional figure is Fielding's wife, for whom the fear of scandal overrides the concern for her husband. The omniscient narrator describes her as a woman who believes that "what one did was never so reprehensible as letting it be generally known" (196); the young investigating sergeant comes to see her as "a woman welded to her role in life and her social status" (222). Fielding's son, Peter, is torn between his criticism of his parents' conformism and his enjoyment of its benefits. Fielding, the missing man, seems to be the least free character; this lack of freedom, his total subservience to his public persona, is one of the hypothetical reasons for his absconding and potential suicide.

Freedom is a central notion in existentialist thought, and John Fowles has often been considered an existentialist writer (although he repudiated this classification late in life). In existentialist philosophy, existence precedes essence: Humans do not have an essential, innate nature but create themselves and their fate through their actions, and principally through interactions with other human beings. The only character in the story representing this kind of freedom is Peter's girlfriend, Isobel. As noted by most critics, Isobel is cast in the mold of Fowles's typical female protagonists—independent, free, full of life. In his collection of essays, *Wormholes*, Fowles acknowledges, "The female characters in my books tend to dominate the male ones. I see man as a kind of artifice, and woman as a kind of reality. The one is a cold idea, the other is a warm fact" (23).

From a different (and playfully ironic) perspective, the story celebrates not only the male protagonists' (Fielding, Jennings) liberation from the shackles of duty and convention, but also the fictional characters' emancipation from the tyranny of their author. John Marcus Fielding is a rebel character who walks out on his creator. In the famous chapter 13 of *The French Lieutenant's Woman*, Fowles professes his belief that "it is only when our characters and events begin to disobey us that they begin to live" (81). The fictional characters' freedom to evolve independently of the novelist's plot entails the readers' freedom to supply the ending to this plot. Therefore, the mystery of Fielding's disappearance has no closure; each reader is left to supply his or her own conjectures regarding Fielding's motivation and his fate. "The kind of writing I have always admired," admits Fowles, "makes reading active too—the book reads the reader, as radar reads the unknown" (*Wormholes*, 11).

Mystery is the narrative kernel of the DETECTIVE story, and "The Enigma" is framed as a detective story. Traditional detective fiction is a genre that foregrounds the pursuit of knowledge. It proceeds from a twofold assumption: Truth exists, and it can be discovered by the inquiring mind. But in "The Enigma" the opposite is the case. The more the young sergeant inquires, the less he knows. The impossibility of knowledge is refracted from the characters to the reader, transforming "The Enigma" into a paradigm of the postmodern metaphysical detective story, which, in the words of Patricia Merivale and Susan Elizabeth Sweeney, "ask[s] questions about mysteries of being and knowing [that] transcend the mere machinations of the mystery plot" (2).

"The Enigma" is distinctly postmodern in two other respects, its metafictional concern and the blurring of distinctions between reality and fiction. Both are suggested in the final conversation between Isobel and Jennings. The young girl, who is a writer, offers her own theory of Fielding's disappearance and teases the investigator: "Let's pretend everything to do with the Fieldings, even you and me sitting here now, is in a novel. A detective story. Yes? Somewhere there is someone writing us, we are not real" (236). Isobel's hypothesis offers a playfully ironic instance of metafiction, defined by Patricia Waugh as "fictional writing which . . . draws attention to its status as an artefact, in order to pose questions about the relationship between fiction and reality" (2). These questions, conveying the characters' concern about their ontological status, are refracted from the fictional world to the world of the reader, who begins to wonder whether he also, like Fielding, Jennings, and Isobel, has not been scripted by a master novelist.

BIBLIOGRAPHY

Fowles, John. *The Ebony Tower*. Boston: Little, Brown and Company, 1999.
———. *The French Lieutenant's Woman*. New York; Barnes and Noble, 1998.
———. *Wormholes*. London: Vintage, 1999.
Merivale, Patricia, and Susan Elizabeth Sweeney, eds. *Detecting Texts: The Metaphysical Detective Story from Poe to Postmodernism*. Philadelphia: University of Pennsylvania Press, 1999.
Waugh, Patricia. *Metafiction*. London: Routledge, 2001.

Ilana Shiloh

"ENOCH'S TWO LETTERS" ALAN SILLITOE (1973)

"Enoch's Two Letters," included in the volume of short-stories *Men, Women and Children* (1973), constitutes an excellent first insight into the universe of ALAN SILLITOE. Among the nine stories in the collection, it is perhaps the one that has reached the widest and most enduring popularity.

"Enoch's Two Letters" is an example of the author's affinity with the helpless. It is primarily concerned with the problems of communication. Enoch is an eight-year-old boy. His parents' marriage is in crisis, and both his mother and his father decide to leave the other, coincidentally on the same day. As a consequence, when Enoch returns from school he finds an empty house with not even a note from his parents. Enoch does not seem to understand exactly what has happened, and the remainder of the story focuses on the development of the child's feelings as he slowly becomes conscious of his circumstances. He makes his way to grandmother's house, where two letters arrive, from the mother to the father and vice versa, to confirm Enoch's abandonment.

Sillitoe's straightforward, apparently simple style; the strong interest that he shows in the existential dilemmas of life; and the way he reveals a deeper concern with brutality or apathy when characters face difficulties might be said to bring him close to the works of the existentialists, including authors such as Jean-Paul Sartre and Albert Camus.

Although the collection met with a mixed critical response, most of it criticizing the improbability of the parents' departure, the story has always found favor with readers. *Men, Women and Children* also includes a sequel to the story, "The End of Enoch?," in which Sillitoe reveals the protagonist's eventual fate.

BIBLIOGRAPHY

Sillitoe, Alan. *Men, Women and Children*. London: W. H. Allen, 1973.

Rafael R. Pleguezuelos

"EPISODE, AN" W. Somerset Maugham
(1947) Appearing in *Creatures of Circumstance* (1947), the last collection of short stories to be published in W. Somerset Maugham's lifetime, "An Episode" hinges on a twist. Far from revealing psychological abnormality, however, "An Episode" depicts a painfully human response to a romantic relationship.

Told as a story-within-a-story, "An Episode" is narrated in two voices. In the frame story, the unnamed narrator describes his friend Ned Preston, a bachelor who is unable to hold a job because of his tuberculosis.

He instead volunteers with prisoners in Wormwood Scrubs. At a dinner party, Preston tells the sad story of Fred Manson, a postal worker who fell in love with a young middle-class woman, Grace Carter. Her father, who began as an errand boy, owns a draper's shop and has four assistants working beneath him; Grace's mother is a former servant. The class issues brought to the fore in this story indicate Maugham's awareness of the struggles of the working classes to move up the social ladder and their fears that their offspring will reject their effort. Grace's parents are determined that Grace should marry a gentleman, but she rejects their arguments, remaining faithful to Fred even after he is convicted of postal fraud. That he stole money in order to maintain her middle-class lifestyle is accepted by Grace as proof of his love.

The reader of "An Episode" would expect the climax to stem from the couple's social inequalities. Maugham, however, is only providing a smokescreen for the story's true emotional center. Grace and Fred remain committed to each other during his time in prison until two weeks before Fred's release, when he breaks off their engagement. His reason is that he has thought about Grace so much during his incarceration that he is thoroughly bored with her. The party guests laugh at this conclusion, so Preston refrains from telling them the coda, which only the narrator learns: that Grace, upon learning of Fred's decision, calmly states that there is nothing more to do but put her head in the gas oven. The final sentence of the story is Preston's laconic statement: "And she did."

Maugham makes no major developments as a storyteller with this tale, and unlike other stories in *Creatures of Circumstance,* "An Episode" lacks the exotic setting for which he became so well known. In his introduction to the fourth volume of his *Collected Short Stories,* Maugham states that he writes about people who, through some accident, "have been involved in unusual contingencies." Here, the contingency is something so tragic and yet simultaneously so ludicrous that the deep poignancy of "An Episode" is indeed difficult not to respond to with laughter.

BIBLIOGRAPHY

Archer, Stanley. *W. Somerset Maugham: A Study of the Short Fiction.* New York: Twayne, 1993.

Curtis, Anthony, and John Whitehead, eds. *W. Somerset Maugham: The Critical Heritage.* London and New York: Routledge and Kegan Paul, 1987.

Maugham, W. Somerset. *Collected Short Stories.* Vol. 4. London: Vintage, 2002.

———. *Creatures of Circumstance.* London: William Heinemann, 1947.

Tracey Rosenberg

"ETERNAL MOMENT, THE" E. M. FORSTER (1928)

Appearing in the collection *The Eternal Moment and Other Stories,* "The Eternal Moment" falls into the pattern set by E. M. FORSTER's other "conversion" tales featuring the English aboard. Outwardly the story is a simple one: Miss Raby, a middle-aged novelist, tries to take stock of her life and the decisions she has made in it by returning after 20 years to the Alpine village of Vorta, a place she has immortalized in her most successful novel, "The Eternal Moment." Thanks to the publicity she has given the village through her book, it has become a fashionable and prosperous tourist resort. Horrified by the crass commercialization that has taken place, and blaming herself for what she sees as the spiritual degeneration of the village's inhabitants, Miss Raby seeks sanctuary at rustic inn where she stayed on her first visit. Seeking to make some kind of atonement, she decides to make contact with Feo, a porter who, 20-years earlier, had announced his love for her on the mountainside, causing her to flee panic-stricken and offended. Feo, however, is no longer the handsome, upright man Miss Raby pictures in her mind. Now he is a bloated, cynical slob who revels in the newfound wealth that the tourists bring to the village and makes sure he gets his fill. Miss Raby decides that this loss of native simplicity and natural honor is also her fault. She reminds Feo of their last meeting, but this time it is Feo who panics, thinking he is being trapped. Realizing he is not, he then decides that this middle-aged woman is making a pass at him and winks meaningfully at her. This leering behavior upsets Miss Raby again, but sticking to her desire to make amends she offers to adopt one of Feo's three children, her plan being that if she can remove him from the atmosphere of the village he will be spared the taint of its new vulgarity and he can be educated to share what she con-

siders her own refined spiritual values. Feo refuses the offer, worried that his wife would read too much into the relationship between himself and this unmarried Englishwoman. Miss Raby initially feels insulted, but she comes to believe that her encounters with Feo have expanded her vision of life—a sentiment similar to that propounded in Forster's novels *Where Angels Fear to Tread* (1905) and *A Room with a View* (1908).

Part of the interest of this particular story lies in the fact that it is questionable whether Miss Raby has come to any deeper understanding. She is as blinkered and inward-looking as she ever was; she has no real desire to meet with real life and has no desire to bear a child of her own (seeing this as a job for lower-class women, not educated ones); her moral gesture to Feo is just that—a gesture. Thus the story's title appears powerfully allusive, but it may also be ironic. Miss Raby will remember the moment, but it is doubtful that it will prompt her to change her philosophy of life or that she is any more clear-sighted.

BIBLIOGRAPHY
Forster, E. M. *The Eternal Moment and Other Stories.* London: Sidgwick and Jackson, 1928.

Andrew Maunder

"EVELINE" JAMES JOYCE (1904)

This much-anthologized short story by JAMES JOYCE was first published in *The Irish Homestead* on September 10, 1904, and later became part of his famous collection *Dubliners* (1917). In contrast to the three stories of childhood that precede it, "Eveline" opens with the 19-year-old young woman of the title reminiscing about her childhood. She watches with her face pressed against the window as people pass by outside, and she recalls the field in which she used to play with other children before her father would hunt them down with his blackthorn stick. Even with this image of brutality, Eveline thinks that her father "was not so bad then," when her mother was still alive. Now her siblings have grown up, and their childhood friends have left Ireland or died, and Eveline muses that she will soon leave home as well. The knowledge that she will leave soon causes her to examine her surroundings critically. She notes the yellowed picture of an unknown priest and the familiar objects covered in dust. She wonders if leaving home is wise. At home at least she has food, shelter, and the people she has always known. She wonders what will be said about her when it is discovered that she ran away with a man. She imagines what life will be like in her new home in a distant country when she is married. When she is married, she thinks, people will treat her with respect, not like her mother was treated. She feels threatened by her father's violence, which has given her heart palpitations. Only lately has he begun to threaten her, saying what he would do to her if not for her dead mother's sake, whereas when she was younger he never went after her because she was a girl. Now she is left alone in the house with him, and the weekly struggles to get money from him for the keeping of the house are beginning to wear on her. She keeps his house in addition to working as a nanny for two children, and while recognizing that it is a hard life, she wonders if she should leave it to journey with Frank to Buenos Aires, where she will become his wife. She met Frank as he was standing outside his lodging house, and she finds herself enraptured by his tales of faraway places and adventures on ships. Her father forbade the affair upon learning that Frank was a sailor. Eveline thinks of her father's kindness when she was sick and of her happy times with him when her mother was alive. From outside the window comes the song from a street organ, and it recalls to her the promise she made to her mother to keep the home together. Her mother's pitiful life and death terrify Eveline as she thinks of her mother's last cry, *"Derevaun Seraun! Derevaun Seraun!"* This cry has been read as a Gaelic phrase meaning either "the end of pleasure is pain" or "the end of song is raving madness." Resolving that she must escape and that she has a right to happiness, she decides that she will leave with Frank.

Eveline holds Frank's hand at the station, feeling the crowd about her and catching sight of the great dark mass of the boat. She prays for guidance and wonders if she can back out after all that Frank has done for her. The boat's whistle startles her, and she feels Frank pulling her, urging her to come with him. Silently, Eveline grabs the railing and refuses to let go. Frank is carried along by the crowd, and Eveline, "passive, like a helpless animal," refuses him any sign of recognition or farewell.

As in "A LITTLE CLOUD," the protagonist feels that freedom can be achieved only through exile, a belief also adopted by Joyce's Stephen Dedalus in *A Portrait of the Artist as a Young Man* (1914). Freedom for Eveline appears even more complicated because she is a woman and must choose not whether to be a solitary exile but whether to remain in her father's house or travel abroad with Frank. She is caught between the possible husband and the probable abusive father.

A strong Catholic sensibility and the maternal voice are among the forces that pull Eveline from the waiting ship. The face of the unknown priest that hangs on the wall of her home as well as the deathbed promise to her mother form twin nets with which Joyce himself was all too familiar. Eveline's decision to stay may also be read as a choice for community, however ruptured, over isolation in a strange country. Eveline's home, although certainly not idealized, stands in stark contrast to Frank's lodging house, a temporary abode. Her promise to her mother to hold the home together suggests the hope of unity and stability. Her mother's dying words haunt the text, and Eveline ultimately turns against pleasure and song, which her mother warns lead to pain and madness.

Eveline has traditionally been read as a character who fails to take advantage of her chance to escape. Given the opportunity to leave an abusive father and limited economic potential, Eveline is unable to leave Ireland's shores. Bound by her promise to her mother, she cannot leave even when a sailor has a home waiting for her in Buenos Aires. However, critics such as Hugh Kenner and Katherine Mullin have argued that Eveline is wise to let Frank leave without her. Kenner points out the undercurrent of sexual danger that runs throughout the story and argues that if Eveline left with Frank, she would most likely be seduced and abandoned in England. Mullin points out that 1889 saw a boom in migration to Argentina, but that trend had completely died out by 1904, largely because of Argentina's reputation as a land of betrayal, exploitation, and disappointment. Purity tracts of the 1880s told stories of girls lured from Ireland by the promise of marriage and sold into the white slave trade, and such stories captivated the public imagination. Joyce may have had such stories in mind as he was composing "Eveline," especially since at the same time he was trying to convince Nora to leave Ireland with him. The story underscores the particularly vexed and sexually precarious position of women leaving Ireland.

BIBLIOGRAPHY

Joyce, James. *Dubliners: Text, Criticism, and Notes.* Edited by Robert Scholes and A. Walton Litz. New York: Penguin USA, 1996.

Kenner, Hugh. *Joyce's Voices.* Berkeley: University of California Press, 1979.

Mullin, Katherine. "Don't Cry for Me, Argentina: 'Eveline' and the Seductions of Emigration Propaganda." In *Semicolonial Joyce,* edited and with an introduction by Derek Attridge and Marjorie Howes, 193–208. Cambridge: Cambridge University Press, 2000.

Torchiana, Donald T. *Backgrounds for Joyce's Dubliners.* Boston: Allen & Unwin. 1986.

Julieann Ulin

"EVELINE'S VISITANT" MARY ELIZABETH BRADDON (1867)

"Eveline's Visitant" first appeared in *Belgravia,* the magazine MARY ELIZABETH BRADDON (1835–1915) edited, in January 1867. In a change of direction for Braddon—who usually wrote about sensational happenings in contemporary Britain—the action takes place in early 18th-century France. The two protagonists are cousins, André and Hector de Brissac, who quarrel about a woman. Hector, the "rough . . . ill-mannered boor," strikes André, the "favourite," who is seriously insulted and wants to avenge this "brutal outrage" through a duel. André's last words before death are, "It is my will to haunt you when I am dead." André is buried in the old family vault, and Hector inherits the château and its wealth. After some months, Hector meets Eveline and marries her, but their blissful life is shattered by the recurring presence of a strange man who seems to haunt Eveline. In fact, it is the ghost of André, carrying out his oath by haunting Eveline until she dies.

This short story epitomizes Braddon's skillful writing of chilling sensational stories. Her narrative uses three different time frames: the story time (the duel and its consequences in the past), the telling time (Hector's backward glance cast on his own past life), and the reading time, with several ominous signs scattered in the narrative to confirm to the reader that this is a ghost story. The action opens in a strange atmosphere at dawn; there is a ghost, silent and invisible but with the power to intrude into impenetrable places closed by locked gates and surrounded by a "moat ten feet wide and full of water." In fact, the ghost is "no one" but still haunts the text as a phantom. Ironically, the hunting costume André was wearing the day of the duel becomes a haunting costume for Eveline.

The story also highlights Braddon's treatment of women. They fall into two categories: the wicked ones and the angels. The former ("beautiful vipers"), responsible for the duel between the men, are put in opposition to the angels, embodied by Eveline Duchatel. The latter is submissive and pure; she personifies the ideal woman, the enlightening source of life for Hector. Under her influence, his life, once characterized by loneliness, "grew bright." But this blissful existence does not last since the story quickly turns to Eveline's inexorable physical and mental degradation. It is precisely on this point that Braddon's story is highly ambivalent, a kind of constant ironic undermining of human powerlessness in the face of supernatural usurpation. The physician cannot cure Eveline and shares her husband's utter inability to protect her. The husband's protective role is nullified further when Eveline dies. On her deathbed, "*he* was by her side," "he" standing not for the husband but for the ghost as if he had taken Hector's place in Eveline's heart and mind. Ironically, the angel, Eveline, becomes another wicked woman, who confesses her sin to her husband before dying: She was fascinated by this phantom, her "phantasm." The reader is left with old Hector's ambivalent last question: "Was the fatality that overshadowed us any work of hers?" as if Hector's ghost was not his responsibility but hers. Is not the title of the short story "Eveline's Visitant"? Is she not the one haunted by this "shadowy form"? The unsettled end leaves the reader with a feeling of uneasiness as chilling as the presence of the ghost itself.

BIBLIOGRAPHY

Dalby, Richard, ed. *The Cold Embrace and Other Ghost Stories.* Ashcroft, British Columbia: Ash Tree Press, 2000.

Marion Charret-Del Bove

"EVERMORE" JULIAN BARNES (1995) First published in the *New Yorker* and subsequently collected by JULIAN BARNES in *CROSS CHANNEL*, "Evermore" is the story of Miss Moss, an elderly woman who proofreads dictionaries and who for countless years has made an annual trip through France to visit World War I memorials, including the gravesite of her brother, Samuel M. Moss. The title of the story is derived from a phrase carved into many of the headstones and memorials she encounters during her journey: "Their name liveth for evermore." As Miss Moss travels from one burial site to the next, from Thiepval to Maison Blanche to Sam's resting place at Cabaret Rouge, she explains her understanding of what it means to grieve and shares her concerns for how the memory of the war and the soldiers' sacrifice will be transferred to future generations.

The plot of "Evermore" consists of minimal action, but underneath the subtle, omniscient narration, BARNES constructs a story rich in meaning and purpose. The basic structure of the story follows Miss Moss as she makes what may be her last journey to France, her last opportunity to honor her brother and those who died fighting in the war. As in much of Barnes's works, a heavy use of factual details supports the story. Outlining the route she will take, the cities she will travel through, and the locations she will visit provides insight into Moss's exacting character. As a proofreader, she is naturally drawn to the lists of soldiers' names etched into the memorials, referring to them as "the official graffiti of death," and she takes special interest in learning the numbers of casualties in specific battles. By including such specifics, the story generates a tone of gravity and loss that underscores Moss's journey of grief.

Commemorating her brother's death becomes Moss's defining character trait. She is "a connoisseur of grief" who believes the time spent at his gravesite is "the most vital of her life." She is so consumed by her grief that she describes it as "a caliper, necessary and supporting; she could not imagine walking without it." Over time, her remembrance of Sam changes: "[I]t became work, continuity; instead of anguish and glory, there was fierce unreasonableness, both about his death and her commemoration of it." She is equally concerned with the quality of the memory, and she worries that time will lessen the importance of the soldiers' deaths. Just as the dictionary labels words "obsolete" or outdated, she fears the world will soon label World War I antiquated and trivial.

Such observations expand the scope of the story to include questions of how a nation commemorates its dead and ensures the continuation of a national memory. Miss Moss wonders whether others will continue to remember the soldiers after she has died, whether "there was such a thing as collective memory, something more than the sum of individual memories." She has hope that "those too young to have original knowledge could be given memory, could have it grafted on." But having lived with her grief for many years, she knows too well how unlikely it is that the graves will be untouched and preserved for evermore. "What if memory-grafting did not work, or the memories themselves were deemed shameful?" she questions. "Then the great forgetting could begin, the fading into the landscape." Her poignant lament serves as a cautionary warning of history's slow amnesia and the certainty of death.

BIBLIOGRAPHY

Barnes, Julian. *Cross Channel.* New York: Vintage, 1997.
———. "Evermore," *New Yorker,* 13 November 1995, pp. 104–112.
Cook, Bruce. "Julian Barnes' Short Stories Explore English-French Relations," *Chicago Tribune,* 21 April 1996, p. 3.
Pierce, Peter. "Evermore: Stories of the Great War by Rudyard Kipling and Julian Barnes," *Critical Review* 42 (2002): 65–71.
Roberts, Ryan. Julian Barnes Website. Available online. URL: www.julianbarnes.com. Accessed May 11, 2006.

Ryan Roberts

EXHIBITIONISM TOBY LITT (2002) *Exhibitionism* is TOBY LITT's second collection of short stories, in which he moves away from the consumer culture of *ADVENTURES IN CAPITALISM* and embarks on a deconstruction of sex, the masculine condition, and the minutiae of contemporary life. Litt still retains his fetishization of the body, which he cultivated in *Adventures in Capitalism* and employed so successfully in *Corpsing* (2000) and *deadkidsongs* (2001), but infuses it with a sense of pulp, namely, a delightful fascination with authoritarian figures, eroticism, and violence. Playing on the mordant subtexts of everyday conversation and creating numerous female stereotypes, Toby Litt's second collection is brutal and nasty but an important part of his literary oeuvre.

"Mapmaking among the Middle-Classes" is an excruciating comedy of manners, focusing on the relationship among the self-concerned Josh; his weak, tearful and pregnant wife, Selina; and Ian, the embittered bachelor who is the real father of Josh's prospective child. Ian's recollection of the conception is "clogged in cobwebs of frozen vodka" (57); the act "had been overheard, although no one now admitted to eavesdropping" (65). Litt's knowing use of the middle-class virtues and such titles as "In the Realm of the Sensitive" creates what is essentially a painful parody of polite society's indiscretions.

Story to Be Translated from English into French and Then Translated Back Again (without Reference to the Original) focuses on the sexual extremities of Edith and her lover Antoine. The main narrative involves Antoine's seduction of a young female chemist, ice-blonde, who accuses him of "making pornography" (156), a word that "fascinates" her (156). Each part of the seduction is interspersed with a flashback to Edith, alone and tied up, commenting on her desires for Antoine to indulge in greater extremities: "[S]ince when does a woman have to beg a man for pain?" (157).

"Tourbusting 2" is a meditation on rituals, portraying a burgeoning rock musician, Brian, who feels compelled to return to the library where the dowdy Lindsay Wagner works. Lindsay, his band's first and most loyal fan, recommends Strindberg for him to read and then disappears, leaving Brian to discover that her dilapidated home is a world away from the pseudointellectual image she created.

"Alphabed" echoes IAN MCEWAN's early short stories in its descriptions and exhibits the same sordid dirty realism as McEwan's *FIRST LOVE, LAST RITES* (1975) and *In Between the Sheets* (1978). Each page is headed with a letter of the alphabet from A to Z, and the narratives can be read in any order. After endless scenes of sexual experimentation, the unnamed male, "he," realizes "[t]hat this is the state they are themselves tending towards: deliquescence" (206).

BIBLIOGRAPHY

Litt, Toby. *Exhibitionism*. London: Hamish Hamilton, 2002.

Martin Colebrook

F

"FALL RIVER AXE MURDERS, THE"

ANGELA CARTER (1981) "The Fall River Axe Murders" was first published in the *London Review of Books* in 1981 under the title "Mis-en-scene for Parricide"; it later appeared under its more familiar name in ANGELA CARTER's 1985 short story collection, *BLACK VENUS* (*Saints and Sinners* in the United States). The story revisits the case of Lizzie Borden, whose legend is summed up by the gruesome children's rhyme that serves as the story's epigraph: "Lizzie Borden with an axe / Gave her father forty whacks. / When she saw what she had done / She gave her mother forty-one." On August 4, 1892, in Fall River, Massachusetts, Borden's parents were bludgeoned to death in the family home by an unknown assailant. The 32-year-old Lizzie, the younger of the Bordens' two daughters, was the prime suspect but was acquitted in 1893, and the case was never officially solved. Still, popular memory has clung to Lizzie Borden in the form of the axe-wielding caricature of the familiar rhyme.

Carter's account humanizes the caricature by inviting us to imagine the world of Lizzie Borden in the months and days leading up to the murderous events that the story stops just short of presenting. Carter places a heavy emphasis on the stifling atmosphere of the Borden home at the time of the killings—on the "dementing" summer heat of Fall River; on the heavy, hot and confining clothes deemed proper for women of Borden's class regardless of the intense heat; and on the claustrophobic qualities of the Borden family home

itself, "a house without passages" whose narrow rooms "lead in and out of one another like a maze in a bad dream." This close and confining atmosphere suggests the social and cultural circumstances of Lizzie Borden: a spinster condemned to lifelong residence in the home of her father and stepmother, a gentlewoman cut off from the society of her social equals because of the quirks of her father, who shuns "The Hill," where Fall River's other middle-class families reside. Carter creates a portrait of a woman imprisoned in her own mind-numbing, duty-bound, and joyless life.

Carter employs the techniques of realistic narrative to complicate a story that has been reduced to the crude outlines of folk legend. She situates the Borden family within the carefully delineated social space of Fall River, reminding us of the town's economic base, its class and gender divisions, and the Protestant ethos that informs every part of life there. Her narrator adopts the guise of an invisible intruder in the Borden household, recounting events as they unfold as though before our eyes, even slipping on occasion into the mind of Lizzie herself, but never providing more than a tantalizing glimpse of the mystery's impenetrable center.

However, Carter's aim is not to present yet another in a long line of supposedly authoritative accounts of the Fall River murders. Working against these realistic qualities are the numerous reminders of the tricks and habits of storytellers, who transform events into narratives in part through distortion and omission. The story alludes to several fairy tales, those old, simple, and familiar narratives that exert their shaping influence on new ones. Carter's narrator also reminds us explicitly of the selective nature of historical narratives, introducing and then omitting an often-forgotten figure, John Vinnicum Morse, a visitor in the Borden household whose presence in the story would only diminish its "emblematic effect"—and so he is promptly erased, taking with him any claim of truth that might have been made for Carter's often hyperrealistic narrative.

Like many of Carter's stories, "The Fall River Axe Murders" mingles elements of fiction and critical commentary. Carter's narrator shifts between her narration of events and her direct addresses to the reader; the resulting is a story that is at the same time an analysis of earlier versions of the story and a sceptical interrogation of historical narratives in general.

BIBLIOGRAPHY
Carter, Angela. *Black Venus*. London: Chatto and Windus, 1985.

Brian Patton

"FAMILY SUPPER, A" KAZUO ISHIGURO (1982)

One of Kazuo Ishiguro's best-known short stories, "A Family Supper" was first published in the journal *Firebird* in 1982. It has subsequently reappeared several times in journals and anthologies.

Narrated in Ishiguro's characteristic understated and quietly sophisticated style, the short story begins by describing the fatal outcome of consuming certain parts of the fugu fish. The reader is then told that the narrator's mother died from fugu poisoning. The narrator, a young Japanese man who has apparently lived in California for a while, visits Japan two years after her death and is given details of the circumstances surrounding the death by his father. The story describes the complex tensions attendant on the family supper on the first day of his arrival. While the narrative avoids any obvious attempt to render the setting of the story "exotic," references to ghosts, hara-kiri, and fugu itself impart the feel of a Japanese locale.

The story raises several questions but leaves them unanswered and hints at a number of possibilities that it refrains from resolving—did the mother kill herself?

Does the father too want to commit suicide? Is the fish he has prepared for the supper also poisonous? While it would not be easy to identify the central theme of the "The Family Supper," the relationship among the three characters who appear in the story—the widowed father, his son, and his college-going daughter—draws attention to generational conflict. There are also complex tensions informing the relations between the father, who not only has apparently lived in Japan all his life but is uneasy in a rapidly changing and modernized Japanese society, and his son, who has lived in the United States and who possibly had an American girlfriend. This theme reflects Ishiguro's own position as a British citizen of Japanese origin who described himself in an interview as "neither very English" nor "very Japanese."

BIBLIOGRAPHY
Barry, Lewis. *Kazuo Ishiguro—Contemporary World Writers*. Manchester and New York: Manchester University Press, 2000.
Mason, Gregory. "An Interview with Kazuo Ishiguro," *Contemporary Literature* 30 (1989): 335–346.

Brinda Charry

"FIGURE IN THE CARPET, THE" HENRY JAMES (1895)

The narrator of "The Figure in the Carpet," published in *Cosmopolis* in 1896, spends the tale trying to get a grip on the overarching design in the novels of his idol, Hugh Vereker, who dismisses the narrator's laudatory review for its failure to understand the core of his work. The novelist believes critics have missed the grand design of his art, expressed in every element of his oeuvre, but the critic, seeing, cannot see. Vereker characterizes this design as the source of life, as something vital, but the commentator calls it a figure in a carpet, something static and graspable. Another novelist, Gwendolen Corvick Deane, learns the secret and uses it in her work, to the improvement of her art. She and her first husband die before the narrator can learn the secret.

Both Vereker and the narrator are among HENRY JAMES's characters who see themselves as artist-failures. Some critics regard the tale as an expression of James's own sense that he was misunderstood and was, hence, a failure. In the tale, the narrator cannot fathom the heart of Vereker's work, nor can he appropriate its power, as Gwendolen Corvick Deane does. The relationship between artist/creator and reader/critic is important in the text. The metaphors for the informing principle of Vereker's work suggest fundamental differences between an artist, whose work is shaped from and shapes life, and a critic, whose work defines and mummifies the words of others. The piece also suggests a divide between idol and disciple. James's tale, in its skillful revealing and omitting, raises more questions than it answers and has become a mine for biographical critics, psychoanalytic theorists, and reader-response analysts.

BIBLIOGRAPHY
James, Henry. *The Figure in the Carpet and Other Stories.*
    London: Penguin, 1986.

Karen Keck

FIN DE SIÈCLE   French for the "end of the century," also used by the British during the 1890s, particularly in reference to the literary mood of the time and to the "naughty nineties." This transitional period of endings and beginnings between the Victorians and MODERNISM saw a collision of ideas between convention and the avant garde that some critics have referred to as the "ambivalence of modernity." Initially, the term represented an impetus for positive change and liberality of thought, but it was marred by what is now considered a certain degree of resistance to French aesthetic influences and practices. A period of technological advancement, educational reform, eugenic debates, and psychological theorization, the last decade of the 19th century also saw a clash of ideas on women's rights, sexual politics, gender identity, open marriage, and, where the OSCAR WILDE trials became emblematic of the excessive concern over moral frailty, sexual inversion or homosexuality. As a result, the term became pejorative, much like DECADENCE, in its suggestion of moral ambiguity and a general disappointment in life; it became equated with apocalyptic terms like *fin du globe* and metaphors of illness such as *mal du siècle*. Further, aesthetic advancement in literature and the arts was seen to be infused with an alleged perversity and moral ambivalence, while general concerns over the decline of empire were mixed with theories of degeneration and fantasies of racial decline. One of the most important developments of this period was a revisioning of literary culture in a broad sense, which saw the emergence of both "high" and "low" literary texts. The decline of the three-volume novel allowed for the tremendous increase of popular print culture in the periodical press—including *Blackwood's,* the YELLOW BOOK, the *Savoy*—which saw the intense development of short fiction (see MAGAZINES: LATE VICTORIAN). Literature of the period, particularly short fiction published in such periodicals, engaged with all of these controversial issues and expressed a restlessness and morbidity that made society uncomfortable during the end of the century. (See also NEW WOMAN, GEORGE EGERTON.)

BIBLIOGRAPHY
Ledger, Sally, and Scott McCracken, eds. *Cultural Politics
    and the Fin de Siècle.* Cambridge: Cambridge University
    Press, 1995.
Ledger, Sally, and Roger Luckhurst. *The Fin de Siècle: A
    Reader.* Oxford: Oxford University Press, 2000.

Sarah Maier

FIREWORKS: NINE PROFANE PIECES ANGELA CARTER (1974)   A collection of ANGELA CARTER's short stories written during 1970–1973, her early experiments with short fiction. These stories introduce most of the issues that became Carter's hallmarks in her major novels and short fiction—androgyny, incest, loneliness, rape, sadism, slavery, the blurred margins between imagination and reality, the intrusion of the supernatural in the natural world, and mirrors as the replica and re-creation of reality. In many of her stories in *Fireworks* Carter mingles magic realism, the narrative mode that includes fabulous and bizarre events in its objective, realistic reportage, with surrealism, wherein the subconscious mind is represented in art and literature by juxtaposing fantastic, seemingly contradictory images to create an unreal effect.

"A SOUVENIR OF JAPAN" captures the loneliness of a British woman caught in a monotonous physical affair with a Japanese man and living in Shinjuku, where appearances veneer reality. The story is an attempt by the narrator, who feels like "a female impersonator," to maintain the facade of being in love while she is painfully aware of the general objectification of women as sexual beings in the male-dominated world. In "The Executioner's Beautiful Daughter" time appears to be petrified, and the descriptions of the sordid lives of the inhabitants of the village resonate with the two hideous events in the story—the beheading of the incestuous son and the repetition of the incestuous act by the executioner father. "The Loves of Lady Purple" is a feminist satire on the enigmatic relationship between the creator and the created. The story lashes out at male fantasies and depicts the animated puppet prostitute Lady Purple killing the puppet master, appropriating the role he has assigned her, and looking for a brothel to gratify her insatiable sexual needs.

"The Smile of Winter" poignantly captures the sorrow of the forlorn narrator through strikingly desolate images of the sea beach. The self-reflexive elements draw attention to the whole process of writing a story about the insensitivity of nature to human suffering as a cathartic exercise. "Penetrating to the Heart of the Forest," with its double entendre in the title, provides incestuous undertones to the myth of the Fall of Man. Here a brother and a sister, during their search for the legendary Upas Tree, discover their latent sexuality, which they can explore only with each other. In "Flesh and the Mirror" the mirror reflects the moral aridity of the narrator as she engages in sex with a stranger to overcome her loneliness when her lover has betrayed her expectations.

"Master" portrays the perverted sadistic treatment of a female slave, significantly named Friday by the master, and ends fittingly with poetic justice. "Reflections" contains strong gothic elements with its grotesque characters and events, the mirror playing the pivotal part in the transition of the protagonist from the rational world to the irrational one. "Elegy for a Freelance," using the backdrop of political unrest during wars, presents the cycle of retribution and justice wherein the act of punishing the assassin itself becomes a debatable crime.

BIBLIOGRAPHY

Carter, Angela. *Burning Your Boats: Collected Short Stories.* With an introduction by Salman Rushdie. London: Vintage, 1996.

VanderMeer, Jeff. "Angela Carter." The Modern World. Available Online. URL: http://www.themodernword.com/scriptorium/carter.html. Accessed July 30, 2005.

Preeti Bhatt

"FIRST CONFESSION" FRANK O'CONNOR (1939)

First published in *Harper's Bazar,* "First Confession" is possibly FRANK O'CONNOR's funniest story. It juxtaposes Catholic concepts of innocence and sin, redemption and damnation, with the anxious logic of a boy of about seven encountering them for the first time. The narrator, Jackie, suffers agonies of social and personal mortification when his grandmother, "a real old countrywoman and quite unsuited to the life in town," comes to live with his family in Cork. With the landmark of his first confession looming, he is convinced that he is destined for damnation as long as she drives him to various sins, up to and including elaborate schemes for her murder. O'Connor mocks prevalent modes of religious instruction and a theological approach focused obsessively on sin and hell. Religion and folk superstition become inextricably mingled in lurid tales of the fate of sinners who have made "bad" confessions (i.e., failed to confess fully and therefore to repent and gain divine forgiveness). Such tales both fascinate and terrify the impressionable Jackie, whose bewildered encounter with the physical layout of the confessional turns into pure farce. Salvation comes, however, with the wonderfully humane pragmatism of the parish priest. In marked contrast to Jackie's teacher, he understands the fundamental innocence underlying childhood sins: Forgoing all attempts at moral or theological exordium in favor of far more effective sympathetic warnings about the horrors of hanging, he sends the much-relieved child, a fully redeemed "sinner," on his way with a minor penance. A richly developed cast of characters is brought to life with remarkable economy in this comic masterpiece.

BIBLIOGRAPHY

O'Connor, Frank. *Collected Stories.* New York: Knopf, 1981.

Muireann O'Cinneide

"FIRST LOVE" SAMUEL BECKETT (1946)

"First Love" was a breakthrough for SAMUEL BECKETT. First

written in French as "Premier Amour" in 1946 (originally published in 1970, translated into English by the author in the same year), the story marked Beckett's turn to first-person narration, a stylistic decision that opened up new opportunities and heralded the development of Beckett's mature fiction.

"First Love" is the story of the narrator's first, and possibly only, love affair, with a prostitute named Lulu, or Anna (the narrator changes the name halfway through). After the death of his father, the protagonist is evicted from his home and begins a vagabond lifestyle until he encounters Lulu on a bench beside a canal. Their courtship consists of short bursts of inconsequential dialogue, coupled with the protagonist's irritation at being disturbed. He manages to stay away from the bench for some time, but finds himself inscribing Lulu's name in a cowpat and thinking of her for as much as half an hour a day. He decides to call this behavior "by the dread name of love." To put an end to this "plight," he returns to meet Lulu once again. She mentions she has a room, and their cohabitation begins. The protagonist removes all of the furniture from one room, pushes the sofa against the wall, and buries himself within. He hopes to be left alone, but wakes one morning to Lulu (now Anna) undressed beside him. He sardonically remarks, "it was my night of love." He is horrified by Anna's ensuing pregnancy, in which he takes no further part, and on the night of his child's delivery he leaves her, with her cries pursuing him down the street.

The real pleasure of "First Love" is in its teller. The protagonist narrator—who appears to have once had ambitions as a writer, but who at the time of writing is nearing the end of his somewhat misanthropic life—relates the story with little sense of propriety, for a traditional cause-and-effect narrative (there are many seemingly unnecessary digressions), for the readers (he overtly abuses them), or for his unethical behavior toward Lulu. There is a detached, irritated quality to the narrator's style, which mixes a disarming use of cliché—"I have no bone to pick with graveyards," for instance—with a matter-of-fact tone: "I didn't understand women at that period. I still don't for that matter. Nor men either. Nor animals." This quotation sums up two of the protagonist's main characteristics: He very

often claims incomprehension, even of the apparently simplest things, and he wishes for a life removed from all women, men, and animals in order to find equilibrium or an escape from himself. These characteristics, along with the derelict remains of a classical education, mark the protagonist as one of the first of Beckett's irritable philosopher-cum-bums who came to dominate his work in the 1940s and 1950s and who are most famously epitomized by the tramps Vladimir and Estragon of *Waiting for Godot.* Summarizing the narrator as a misanthropic, irritable, unethical tramp who wants only to escape the horrors of his own existence does not detract from the humor of "First Love." Indeed, it is the sometimes pitch-black humor of the narrator that keeps both the reader and the narrative (and possibly the narrator) engaged. This detached and deathly humor is perhaps best expressed by the narrator's own epitaph, his only piece of writing that still meets with his approval:

> Hereunder lies the above who up below
> So hourly died that he lived on till now.

BIBLIOGRAPHY
Beckett, Samuel. *First Love and Other Novellas.* London: Penguin, 2000.

Paul Stewart

FIRST LOVE, LAST RITES Ian McEwan (1975) Jack Slay, Jr., has described the appearance of Ian McEwan's first collection of stories, *First Love, Last Rites,* as a "shock into literature," owing to the themes and subject matter contained in the collection's eight stories. The shock derives, first and foremost, from the primary themes and subject matter of most of the stories: A 14-year-old boy rapes his 10-year-old sister in the story "Homemade"; in "Butterflies," a man draws a young girl to a secluded location under a canal bridge, sexually molests her, and drops her body—after she knocks herself unconscious trying to escape him—into the muddy canal waters; in "Cocker at the Theatre," two actors rehearsing a scene in a play engage in sexual intercourse on stage, in front of the entire cast. Such incidents usually stand at the center of the story's plot, but they also often appear scattered throughout the stories in less noticeable ways. While the man lures the girl to her fate in "Butterflies," the two of them pass a group of boys who are preparing to roast a live cat over a fire.

The stories shock at a second level by the neutral and nonjudgmental descriptions of the violence. The narrator of "SOLID GEOMETRY," who causes the wife he has come to hate to disappear using a complex mathematical trick, finishes his tale in this way: "Her voice was quite tiny, 'What's happening?' and all that remained was the echo of her question above the deep blue sheets." The narrators or main characters—six of the stories feature a first-person narrator—express no remorse for their actions and no sympathy for their victims, and the stories themselves do not seem to offer any moral or ethical judgments on anyone or anything. Once the story has committed to an act of murder or sexual perversion, McEwan follows it through to its end, leaving no detail unobserved.

Although most—though not all—of the stories feature violence and sexual perversity, a more clear and consistent connection links all of the stories' narrators or main characters: They are all isolated from human society or are alienated from the dominant culture. It is impossible to say whether McEwan expects the reader to see an inevitable link between these kinds of characters and the violence and perversities in which they engage, but he seems to suggest that isolation and alienation lead to a loss of sympathy for and understanding of others that creates the conditions for such acts.

The quintessential exploration of this theme appears in "Conversations with a Cupboard Man," with a narrator who is initially kept isolated from society without his knowledge; given his freedom, however, he chooses to remain in isolation. The cupboard man narrates his story to a social worker who sits outside his cupboard, listening, and to this worker he describes how his mother kept him in a state of suspended childhood, completely separate from the outside world. He never objected to this treatment for an obvious reason: "I didn't know any other life, I didn't think I was different." She keeps him in a crib until he is 17, feeds him baby food, and tries to construct a special high chair for him when he is 14. She loosens her hold on him when she marries another man, and the cupboard man

finds himself out in the world and forced to fend for himself for the first time. He takes a job as a hotel dishwasher, where he is locked in a large oven by a sadistic chef on two occasions. After taking his revenge on the chef, he leaves the hotel and begins stealing for a living, which eventually lands him in jail. He enjoys the isolation of his cell so much that he asks the warden if he can stay in jail indefinitely; his request is denied, and he is forced to leave. He abandons his subsequent factory job for full-time life in his cupboard, where he remains at the conclusion of the story.

The cupboard man's trajectory is a familiar one in McEwan's short fiction: A character's initial state of involuntary isolation from society leads to voluntary behavior that alienates him from that society. In the cupboard man's case, that behavior—with the exception of his treatment of the chef, which is arguably revenge—takes a relatively innocuous form in his desire for isolation in small, enclosed spaces. In other stories the forms are more violent, perverse, or damaging. The 14-year-old narrator of "Homemade" disparages the "thousands who each morning poured out of the terraced houses like our own to labour through the week" and separates himself from them with his drinking, smoking, and stealing and the rape of his 10-year-old sister. The main character of "Disguises," forced into a curious world of gender confusion by his deceased mother's sister, eventually comes to embrace the little girl's costume she makes him wear and to envision his identity merging with that of a girl he has met at school. The narrator of "Butterflies" suffers from the strange physical defect of having no chin, which frightens people: "[I]t breeds distrust. . . . Women do not like my chin, they won't come near me." When he has his orgasm, he cements the connection between his isolation and his crime: "All the time I spent by myself came pumping out, all the hours walking alone and all the thoughts I had had, it all came out into my hand." Unable to establish meaningful human relations with anyone, the narrator ends up expressing himself in his warped relationship with the little girl.

Even the two stories that do not feature overt acts of violence or perversity, "Last Day of Summer" and "First Love, Last Rites," depend on a background of violence or grotesque and repugnant imagery. In "Last

Day of Summer," a teenager lives in a commune with his older brother after the death of his parents in a car crash. The narrator has an obsessive interest in describing the flesh of an overweight girl who comes to live in the commune and who takes on a maternal role in the house. At the end of the story, the girl's weight causes a boating accident that kills her and a young child; the narrator survives, and the story concludes as he drifts alone down the river on the capsized boat. In "First Love, Last Rites," a young couple living in a dirty flat become obsessed with a rat living in their walls. When they finally manage to kill the rat with a poker, a purple bag containing five baby rats slides out of its belly. The story ends in a moment of seeming hope, as they resolve to clean their flat and take a long walk, but the weight of the story's unrelentingly dark imagery makes it difficult to see real hope in its conclusion.

First Love, Last Rites remains a collection of interest for the study of postwar British literature and for the study of Ian McEwan, who has since achieved wide fame with multiple Booker Prize nominations for his later novels and with the Booker Prize–winning novel *Atonement* (2002). He published only one subsequent collection of short stories, *In Between the Sheets* (1978), which focuses on many of the same themes as his first collection. Although his tendency to depict violence and perversity explicitly has become muted in the novels that followed the publication of his two short story collections, his interest in the origins of violence and evil in the human condition has remained. *First Love, Last Rites* clearly reflects an interest in the nature of violence that featured in many works of British literature in the several decades following World War II, from the savage nature poetry of TED HUGHES and the fictions of William Golding and Anthony Burgess to the quietly violent dramas of Harold Pinter.

With very few exceptions, most of the stories in the collection remain firmly within the tradition of a stark, gritty realism. Elements of postmodernism surface occasionally in the stories, especially in "Solid Geometry," but McEwan's short fiction has little in common with the self-referential or academic fiction of more clearly postmodern novelists and short story writers such as JOHN FOWLES or JEANETTE WINTERSON, who were a dominant presence on the British literary landscape of the 1970s and 1980s.

BIBLIOGRAPHY
Malcolm, David. *Understanding Ian McEwan.* Columbia: University of South Carolina Press, 2002.
McEwan, Ian. *First Love, Last Rites.* London: Cape, 1975; New York: Random House, 1975.
Raban, Jonathan. "Exiles: New Fiction," *Encounter* 44 (June 1975): 81.
Ryan, Kiernan. *Ian McEwan.* Plymouth, England: Northcote House, 1994.
Slay, Jack, Jr. *Ian McEwan.* New York: Twayne, 1996; London: Prentice Hall, 1996.

James Lang

"FISHING-BOAT PICTURE, THE" ALAN SILLITOE (1958)

Like the story "UNCLE ERNEST," this early work has been reprinted many times as part of an ALAN SILLITOE anthology titled *The Loneliness of the Long Distance Runner.* The action takes place in Nottingham during the author's boyhood and youth, the 1930s and the ensuing war years. Written in the first person, the narrator looks back over 28 years of his life, during which time he worked as a postman, married, and became a widower. The marriage was not harmonious; it had been punctuated with rows, separations, and reunions. The picture in the title serves as a metaphor for the relationship, as it goes to and fro between the marital home and the pawnshop before being destroyed in the road accident that kills the narrator's wife, thus ending the marriage.

Although the couple married at a young age and had a low income it is not material poverty that destroys the marriage but a basic incompatibility, made worse by the lack of children. Harry, the narrator, spends his spare time reading books borrowed from the public library, a pastime that annoys his wife, Kathy, who looks for excitement in her daily life. The first major row occurs when Kathy burns her husband's book in a fit of jealous rage. Kathy subsequently leaves her husband to live with a housepainter with whom she had been friendly for about a year. After a ten-year absence, and shortly before the outbreak of World War II, Kathy returns to her hometown and visits her estranged husband. After the death of her housepainter she is now, apparently, on her own. The fishing-boat picture, which was once one of three similar paintings, the other two having been destroyed in a quarrel, becomes the focus of attention. Responding to Kathy's apparent affection for the picture, Harry wraps it up and makes a gift of it to her. The picture is of little monetary value but has sentimental significance as it was a wedding present, for which reason Harry is surprised to see it in a pawnbroker's shop a few days after parting with it. He buys it from the pawnbroker, takes it home, and hangs it up in its old place. Throughout the war years Kathy continues to visit Harry, borrowing money and admiring the picture as she did before pawning it. Six years after the first time she took the picture Harry again wraps it up and makes a gift of it to her, only to find it in the pawnshop again. This time it is Kathy who retrieves it, but only to lose it in the road accident that takes her life. At his wife's funeral Harry learns that she had been living with another man. With his marriage finally at an end, Harry replaces neither his wife nor the picture but broods on the meaning of his life. This story is a close study of marital disharmony and deceit and the man's inability to acknowledge or express his deepest feelings.

BIBLIOGRAPHY

Stilitoe, Alan. *The Loneliness of the Long Distance Runner.* New York: Plume, 1992.

Irene Wiltshire

"FLY, THE" KATHERINE MANSFIELD (1922)

One of the most anthologized of KATHERINE MANSFIELD's short stories, along with "The GARDEN-PARTY," "The Fly" was published in the *Nation* in 1922. Conscious of its appeal to perceptive readers, Mansfield avoided the publication of this story in a magazine, unlike others at that time that were intended just for money. She wrote it while she was staying in Paris undergoing Dr. Manhoukin's new treatment for tuberculosis, and it is considered "her own little masterpiece" and "one of her principal achievements" (Alpers 258, 356). Like other Mansfield stories ("The Child-Who-Was-Tired" is the clearest example), "The Fly" has been seen as drawing on Chekhov, particularly on his story "Small Fry," in which an abused clerk, who is writing a letter to his

hated superior, crushes a cockroach and tosses it into the flame of the lamp.

"The Fly" is the story of old Woodifield and his boss, who is never referred to by his name. The former worked for the latter until a heart attack forced him to retire prematurely. Since then, every Tuesday he visits the boss. This Tuesday is different because old Woodifield mentions that his daughters have recently visited the graves of his son and the boss's son, both of whom died in WORLD WAR I. This stirs the superior's sorrow, for he has not overcome the loss of his only child. He feels the urge to be alone and expels Woodifield from his office. Suddenly, a fly falls into the inkpot. After playing with it, the boss finally drowns the fly and is grasped by a profound fear of death, which is the only facet of his life that he cannot control.

This story has aroused endless academic explanations. Some, like Cherry A. Hankin (245–246), find autobiographical connections, in which the boss stands for Mansfield's father (Harold Beauchamp, a bank director) and the dead son for Mansfield's brother Leslie (killed in the war six years previously, as in the story). Others, like Ken Arvidson (217), find in this narrative Mansfield's ultimate perception of the artist as an impersonal entity who kills sentimentalism, like a god who controls everything, but is vulnerable to death. In any case, this story reflects the importance of cyclical time and its connection with senility and the loss of power. Woodifield's premature retirement has involved his seclusion in the house with his wife and daughters, a domestic realm and private sphere, away from the external, masculine space of work, that forces him to live in a cyclical and repetitive time. In turn, the boss, although older than Woodifield, still remains in the public eye almost like a scarecrow; his senility is observed in his circular perception of time, always coming back to the moment when he lost his only son. It is a story of self-deception, narrated from the point of view of the boss.

BIBLIOGRAPHY

Alpers, Antony. *The Life of Katherine Mansfield.* Oxford: Oxford University Press, 1980.
Arvidson, Ken. "Dancing on the Hand of God: Katherine Mansfield's Religious Sensibility." In *The Critical Response*

to *Katherine Mansfield,* edited by Jan Pilditch, 211–218. Connecticut and London: Greenwood Press, 1996.

Hankin, Cherry A. *Katherine Mansfield and Her Confessional Stories.* London and Basingstoke: MacMillan, 1983.

Tate, Trudi. *Men, Women and the Great War: An Anthology.* Manchester: Manchester University Press, 1995.

Gerardo Rodriguez-Salas

FORSTER, E. M. (1879–1970)

Edward Morgan Forster (called Morgan by his family and friends) was born into a middle-class family, and his father died before he was two years old. Raised by his mother and grandmother in rural Hertfordshire, he attended Tonbridge School as a day student and then King's College, Cambridge, where he studied classics and history. During two extended trips abroad between 1901 and 1903, he wrote his first short stories, "The STORY OF A PANIC" in Italy and "The ROAD FROM COLONUS," in Greece (see the introduction to *Collected Tales*). These two stories and "The OTHER SIDE OF THE HEDGE" were his first publications, all printed in the new liberal monthly magazine *Independent Review* during 1904. His travels inspired the theme of rustic simplicity as a liberating agent for the rigidity and intellectual narrowness of middle-class English life that he would later use in his stories and novels.

Nicholas Royle has noted that a good deal is known about Forster's "surface life" (5). In the years prior to World War I, Forster worked energetically on his writing, finding outlets in a variety of popular magazines. Around this time he also participated in the Bloomsbury gatherings of intellectuals and writers, informally led by Virginia Woolf and named for the quarter in London where many of them lived. When Forster returned from Egypt in 1919, where he had been working for the Red Cross, he worked briefly as literary editor of the *Daily Herald* before going to India as secretary to the maharajah of Dewas State. His experience of colonial administration led to the writing and publication of *A Passage to India* in 1924. He was the first president of the National Council for Civil Liberties; was an honorary fellow of King's College, Cambridge, from 1945; and was awarded the prestigious Order of Merit by the queen in 1969.

Although he appeared to be an "establishment" figure, Forster was also, as Nicholas Royle notes, always slightly "anti-authoritarian" (5) and more openly critical of English social conventions and male gender roles than some of his contemporaries. Despite his seeming misogyny (the fact, for example, that many of his women characters are very unsympathetically drawn), critics have made a strong case for a transgressive or "new" Forster, noting the motifs of conversion and the antiestablishment impulses that underlie a good deal of his work (Royle, 6). As a young man Forster knew Edward Carpenter, an early advocate of gay rights, and this association is often said to have helped him come to terms with his own homosexuality, although Forster never felt sure enough of his reputation to make this side of his life public or to allow his novel *Maurice* (1971) to be published in his lifetime. This aspect of Forster is also evident in the short stories. Forrest Reid wrote of the "deeper and more hidden things touched on," by which he meant the homoerotic aspects in many of the stories (quoted in Herz, 250). "ARTHUR SNATCHFOLD" (1928), while conforming to other stories of awakening, is a protest against the criminalization of homosexuality that was in force until 1967. "The Other Boat" (1958) is a story of an interracial affair between a young Indian man, Cocoanut, and the English narrator Lionel, which takes place on a ship. Lionel ends the relationship by murdering his lover.

For much of his life and increasingly since his death in 1970, Forster has been remembered primarily for his novels about Edwardian England, with his literary reputation resting primarily on *Where Angels Fear to Tread* (1907), *A Room with a View* (1908), and *Howard's End* (1910), all of which have been lavishly filmed. However, during a literary career spanning 70 years, Forster was prolific in a variety of genres: In addition to six novels, he wrote as many as 15 plays, over 50 short stories, and a large body of criticism. Forster's short stories were clearly important to him. In 1910 he wrote to the publisher Edward Garnett about *The Celestial Omnibus and Other Stories* (1911), asking, "Do you remember some short stories of mine? I have at last entrapped a publisher into taking them. I am very glad, for I think them better than my long books—the only point of criticism on which I have ever disagreed with you!" (quoted in Herz, 24). Later, he wrote to a friend, Jessica Darling, "Thank you for what you say about my short stories. I would rather people praised them than anything else I wrote" (quoted in Herz, 24). In fact, both *The Celestial Omnibus and Other Stories* (1911) and Forster's second collection, *The Eternal Moment* (1928), received mixed reviews, although the first was overall more highly regarded than the second. A third collection, *The Life to Come,* was published posthumously in 1972.

Forster considered his short stories fantasies; in 1944 he wrote, "I like the idea of fantasy, of muddling up the actual and the impossible until the reader isn't sure which is which" (1972, 226). Some of his short stories make use of supernaturalism. For example, in "The Celestial Omnibus" (1908) a boy travels on a mysterious bus above London and meets literary heroes and authors. Other stories, such as "The Road from Colonus," suggest mystical forces that could transform the circumscribed consciousness of ordinary people, but do not employ explicitly supernatural devices. Still other stories, such as "The Other Side of the Hedge," are fantasy with overtones of allegory. Of fantasy novels, Forster writes, "The power of fantasy penetrates into every corner of the universe, but not into the forces that govern it" (Forster 1954, 110). So it is with Forster's short stories: He takes ordinary protagonists and nonchalantly expands the limits of their perception far beyond the scope of everyday reality in order to dramatically reveal the awful mediocrity and conformity structuring that reality.

BIBLIOGRAPHY

Beauman, Nicola. *Morgan: A Biography of E. M. Forster.* London: Hodder and Stoughton, 1993.
Forster, E. M. *Aspects of the Novel.* 1927. Reprint, New York: Harcourt, Brace and Company, 1954.
———. *The Celestial Omnibus and Other Stories.* London: Sidgwick and Jackson, 1911.
———. *Collected Tales.* New York: Knopf, 1947.
———. *The Eternal Moment and Other Stories.* London: Sidgwick and Jackson, 1928.
———. *Howard's End.* London: Arnold, 1908.
———. *The Life to Come and Other Stories.* London: Arnold, 1972.
———. *Two Cheers for Democracy.* London: Arnold, 1972.
———. *Where Angels Fear to Tread.* Edinburgh: Blackwood, 1905.
Herz, Judith Scherer. *The Short Narratives of E. M. Forster.* London: Macmillan, 1988.
Royle, Nicholas. *E. M. Forster.* Plymouth, England: Northcote House, 1999.

Susan Russo

FOWLES, JOHN (1926–2005)

Born in Essex, Fowles served in the Royal Marines. After his discharge, he attended the University of Edinburgh and completed a B.A. at New College, Oxford University, in 1950. Thereafter he became a teacher in France, Greece, and Britain until 1963, when he began to devote his energies full time to his writing.

Fowles is best known for his novels, which present flawed characters confronting complex existential dilemmas. They include *The Collector* (1963), about a uninteresting clerk with an extensive butterfly collection who buys a remote cottage and imprisons a vibrant, privileged young woman in the basement; *The French Lieutenant's Woman* (1969), a Victorian story with authorial intrusions about a young man's uncertain attempts to understand the emotional crisis haunting a mysterious young woman's existence; and *A Maggot* (1985), an experimental narrative into which extranarrative documents intrude and in which the more conventional elements have been drawn from an elastic synthesis of the mystery/detective and science-fiction genres.

Fowles's only collection of short fiction was *The EBONY TOWER* (1974). The collection contains the title novella as well as four short stories. The basic situation in the title novella is broadly similar to that in his novel *The Magus* (1965): A young, married British writer named David Williams travels to Brittany to interview a reclusive, expatriate artist. He finds the artist living with two young women whom he has nicknamed the Mouse and the Freak to emphasize their respective roles as literary caregiver and pleasure giver. The women complement each other, and the protagonist discovers that although their relationship with each other is, in its essence, the artist's creation, it may be as important to them as their relationships with him. Indeed, the artist's estate has provided them with a welcome refuge but has gradually come to seem a place of confinement. Williams becomes tentatively involved with the Mouse, whose real name is Diana, but ultimately it becomes clear that he does not understand his own needs any better than he understands hers.

The four short stories in *The Ebony Tower* are "Poor Koko," "The ENIGMA," and "The Cloud." "Poor Koko" centers on a biographer who retreats to a country cottage to finish a book on Thomas Love Peacock. He is surprised by a burglar who not only ties him up and abuses him but also destroys both his book manuscript and his typewriter. "The Enigma" concerns a policeman's investigation of a man's mysterious disappearance and exploits the conventions of the mystery/detective genre. Set in southern France, "The Cloud" wryly populates an idyllic picnic in an Edenic location with a cast of unself-consciously superficial, crassly self-indulgent, and boorishly self-important British vacationers.

BIBLIOGRAPHY

Acheson, James. *John Fowles.* New York: St. Martin's, 1998.

Baker, James R., and Dianne Vipond, eds. John Fowles Special Issue. *Twentieth Century Literature* 42, no. 1 (Spring 1996).

Foster, Thomas C. *Understanding John Fowles.* Columbia: University of South Carolina Press, 1994.

Fowles, John. *The Ebony Tower.* London: Jonathan Cape, 1974; Boston: Little, Brown, 1974.

Palmer, William J., ed. John Fowles Special Issue. *Modern Fiction Studies* 31, no. 1 (Spring 1985).

Martin Kich

"FOX, THE" D. H. LAWRENCE (1918 AND 1921) D. H. LAWRENCE wrote the first version of "The Fox" in December 1918. This version of the story was a straightforward tale about two women, whose lesbian partnership is implicit. Jill Banford is diffident and timid, whereas the more physical Ellen March is capable of strenuous farming chores. Struggling for comfort and an effective agricultural existence in an unfamiliar rural residence, the city women are troubled by a fox who deftly robs them of domestic fowl. A young man, Henry Grenfel, enters the women's lives. After killing the fox, he wins March, and Banford, despite her vociferous complaints, loses her lover. To retain any companionship with March, she must assist

her with the wedding, galling as this is. March has taken the easier option, choosing heterosexuality over lesbianism. As homosexuality was not made legal in Britain until 1967, such a move is understandable. The relationship between Banford and March has been courageous and unconventional, but a heteronormative status quo is established by the story's end. There is a triumph for normative sex, but the story is a tragedy because a flourishing, nonnormative relationship has been thwarted.

In 1921, Lawrence revised "The Fox," crafting a longer and more brutal, violent, and successful story. In the new version, Henry deliberately kills Banford by allowing a tree to fall on top of her. This dramatic climax is patently symbolic in its phallocentric imagery. The axe shaft and the tree trunk, both profoundly phallic, are wielded by the masculine Henry. The homosexual female, Banford, has lost her lover, March, to the heterosexual male, Henry. Henry not only has won March through loaded discourse but also has contrived a callous murder. It is not relevant to speculate about whether March suspects the truth behind her former lover's death. What is important is that even before the killing, March meekly accepts Henry's advances instead of valuing and privileging her existing relationship. Banford becomes less sympathetic as the narrative progresses. She whines and nags March about her indulgence toward Henry but fails to articulate any convincing argument about the efficacy of her same-sex partnership with March. Banford's loquacious impotence—Linda Ruth Williams describes the character as a "fretful, manipulative caricature of passive-aggressive femininity" (63)—contrasts the physicality of the confident Henry. Only one warrior is equipped to inspire the loyalty and sexuality of the easily swayed March: The male wins easily.

When he first arrives, Henry is less confident. A low-ranking soldier in World War I, he previously fled to Canada. He grew up in the farmhouse with a now-deceased relative, so he soon claims mastery of the home and its surroundings. He kills the fox, replacing it as the aggressive male threat to the female couple's way of life. Significantly, March had a clear opportunity to shoot the fox but hesitated, gripped by its striking appearance and stealthy character. She is intrigued by the male fox, as she is later intrigued by Henry, who eventually conquers her. Henry wins March, gaining her hand, but he does not necessarily win her heart. Lawrence's major achievement in "The Fox" is to legitimize the homosexual love that Banford feels for March. Henry's triumph is a victory for heterosexual-dominated society, but it is clearly not a triumph for March, who shows little indication of genuine affective desire for her new, male partner. Before Henry wins March, his sexual lust for Banford is expressed through Lawrence's use of free indirect speech; the sexuality that exists between Banford and March is, inevitably, noted more coyly.

A 1967 film version of "The Fox," directed by Mark Rydell, sensationalizes the sexuality essential to the dangerous love triangle and, arguably, dilutes the impact of Lawrence's discreet, moral insistence on the merits of all forms of love.

BIBLIOGRAPHY

Hubbard Harris, Janice. *The Short Fiction of D. H. Lawrence.* New Brunswick, N.J.: Rutgers University Press, 1984.

Kincead-Weekes, Mark. *D. H. Lawrence: Triumph to Exile, 1912–22.* Cambridge: Cambridge University Press, 1996.

Lawrence, D. H. *The Cambridge Edition of the Works of D. H. Lawrence: "The Fox," "The Captain's Doll," "The Ladybird."* Edited by Dieter Mehl. Cambridge: Cambridge University Press, 2002.

Nelson, Jane A. "The Familial Isotopy in 'The Fox.'" In *The Challenge of D. H. Lawrence,* edited by Michael Squires and Keith Cushman, 129–142. Madison: University of Wisconsin Press, 1990.

Tate, Trudi. "Lawrence's Tales." In *The Cambridge Companion to D. H. Lawrence,* edited by Anne Fernihough, 103–118. Cambridge: Cambridge University Press, 2001.

Williams, Linda Ruth, *D. H. Lawrence.* Plymouth, England: Northcote House, 1997.

Kevin De Ornellas

G

"GABRIEL-ERNEST" Saki (H. H. Munro) **(1909)** A slyly rebellious, blackly comic story that unites the Edwardian author's common themes of sexual ambiguity, metamorphosis, and reminiscent of an Oscar Wilde campiness. "Gabriel-Ernest," first published in the *Westminster Gazette* on May 29, 1909, was one of Saki's first published stories as a full-time writer, when he had settled in London after six years as a newspaper correspondent in Europe.

A "wild beast" in Van Cheele's woods turns out to be a boy who cheerfully admits to eating "child-flesh." Van Cheele passes the boy off as a lost, savage waif, but when he is later found lying naked in the bachelor's morning-room, Van Cheele's aunt christens him "Gabriel-Ernest" and enlists his help with her Sunday school children's tea. Van Cheele discovers that the boy turns into a werewolf at dusk, but he is too late to save a child whom Gabriel-Ernest escorts home—the sun sets, the victim screams, and the two vanish. When Gabriel-Ernest's clothes are discovered near a stream, Van Cheele's aunt, thinking the pair drowned, naively mourns "her lost foundling. It was on her initiative that a memorial brass was put up in the parish church to 'Gabriel-Ernest, an unknown boy, who bravely sacrificed his life for another.'"

This daring, sexually transgressive story offers a tantalizing parallel between the "unknown boy" and Hector Hugh Munro, whose private world remains unknown but who, when he transformed into his satirical alter ego Saki, savaged with ink-tipped claws the conventional, bourgeois Edwardian world. Munro would later fight and die in World War I, sacrificing his private life for a brief, manly, patriotic life as a defender of the very society he seemed so disillusioned with as Saki.

Saki's interest in adolescent boys—from his frequent protagonists Reginald and Clovis to the doomed young dandy Comus Bassington in *The Unbearable Bassington* (1911)—is most obviously gilded with homoeroticism in "Gabriel-Ernest." The strange boy's taste for devouring other boys may reflect Munro's possible hidden homosexual interest in younger lovers (explored in A. J. Langguth's 1981 biography). Munro, through Saki, seems to allude coyly to the impossibility of discussing homosexuality in a post-Wilde England when Van Cheele notes that the wolfish lad should not talk about devouring young boys because "Such dreadful things should not be said even in fun." Van Cheele later covers up the naked youth with a copy of the *Morning Post,* the paper for which Munro was a correspondent. Saki's tales often involve a boy gaining temporary triumph over an intolerant guardian—probably based on the strict aunts who raised Munro in Pilton—but here the aunt blindly sees only the good in the lycanthropic Gabriel-Ernest, going so far as to innocently erect a memorial to his murderous behavior. In this cheeky allegory, then, the physical, moral, and sexual deviance of the beastly youth is unwittingly endorsed by the aunt (a typically matrimony-endorsing, heterosexuality-upholding figure in literature), but Gabriel-

Ernest himself survives, untamed by conformist, conservative Edwardian society.

"Gabriel-Ernest," with its "wild, nude animal" antihero reposing regally in a bourgeois dining room, owes much of it campy clash of nature and culture to Oscar Wilde, literary defender of "the love that dare not speak its name." Saki's title is probably an homage to Wilde's *The Importance of Being Earnest,* where "earnest" was a pun on "uranist," a late 19th-century term for a homosexual. The lordly Van Cheele, the artist Cunningham, and Gabriel-Ernest also echo the male characters that form the triangle at the heart of *The Picture of Dorian Gray.*

This metamorphosis story also rewrites Ovid's myths of the lupine Lycaon and the eroticized youth Narcissus (in which a self-absorbed youth is mourned by a woman), while offering a more original, imaginative version of Walter Pater's cannibalism- and pederasty-tinged look at the Greek wine god in "A Study of Dionysus" (*Greek Studies,* 1895).

BIBLIOGRAPHY

Saki. *The Complete Saki.* Harmondsworth, England: Penguin, 1982.

Brian Gibson

GALLOWAY, JANICE (1956–)

Born in Saltcoats, Scotland, in 1956, Galloway studied music at the University of Glasgow and worked as a teacher in Ayrshire for 10 years, before her writing career established her as one of the leading authors in Scotland.

Her debut novel, *The Trick Is to Keep Breathing,* published in 1990, was an immediate success, short-listed for the Whitbread First Novel, Scottish First Book, and Aer Lingus Awards and winning the Mind/Allan Lane Book of the Year. Dealing with a woman's nervous and emotional breakdown following her lover's death, the novel is an exploration of Joy's postbereavement struggle to continue a normal life. Her lonely existence, whose grieving crises are cleverly diluted by the author's ironic wit and tinted with Scottish sarcasm, is driven by a desperate effort to find the "trick," the way out of her posttraumatic depression. The novel's acclaim was accompanied by the popular reception of its stage adaptation, performed in Glasgow

(Tron Theatre), London (Royal Court), and Toronto (Du Maurier Theatre).

Galloway's subsequent works received increasing critical attention and prestigious awards: Galloway's second book, the short story collection BLOOD (1991), was short-listed for the Guardian Fiction Prize, People's Prize, and Saltire Award and was a New York Times Notable Book of the Year. Ordinary situations (moving into and redecorating a new house) and everyday scenarios (a visit to the dentist's), glimpses of real life, are observed with an almost cinematic technique and often presented as fragmented capsules of human existence. The stories are linked by a shared element of traumatic revelation, invariably disclosing the grotesque and surreal aspects within the characters' apparently normal routines.

Galloway's unsentimental stance on human relationships and particularly the dysfunctionality of romantic love is apparent in her second collection of stories, *Where You Find It* (1995). As in her previous works, ordinary rituals of average life stories—from the accurate confection of Valentine's Day heart-shaped sandwiches to women comparing notes on men's kissing attributes—are laid bare, their lack of depth inexorably exposed by Galloway's unforgiving wit.

BIBLIOGRAPHY

Christianson, Aileen, and Alison Lumsden. eds. *Contemporary Scottish Women Writers.* Edinburgh: Edinburgh University Press, 2000.
Galloway, Janice. *Blood.* London: Cape, 1991.
———. *Clara.* London: Cape, 2002.
———. *Where You Find It.* London: Cape, 1995.

Monica Germana

GALSWORTHY, JOHN (1867–1933)

A prolific writer of novels, plays, and short stories, Galsworthy is generally known for the series of novels that make up *The Forsyte Saga*—the first of which, *The Man of Property,* appeared in 1906—which detail the lives of a wealthy London family over several generations. The sequence was televized to great acclaim in 1967 and again in 2002–2003. A lawyer by training with a strong social conscience, Galsworthy launched his career as a writer with a collection of short stories, *From the Four Winds,* published in 1897, followed by the collection *A Man of Devon* (1901). Other collections include *On Forsyte Change* (1930), a collection of short stories focusing on incidents in the lives of his most famous fictional family, and *Five Tales* (1818), which contains his most anthologized tale, "The Apple Tree." In this story an unhappily married man returns to the idyllic farm where he had stayed 25 years before and remembers his romance with an innocent girl whom he proposed to but abandoned. Their meeting under an apple tree is a deliberately symbolic one, evoking the prelapsarian state of Adam and Eve in the Garden of Eden before the Fall. Like much of Galsworthy's work, the story contains a strong element of social commentary, particularly on the operation of the class system. The story was made into a film in 1988. At the end of his career, Galsworthy's reputation led to his being awarded the Nobel Prize for Literature in 1932.

BIBLIOGRAPHY

Galsworthy, John. *The Forsyte Saga.* Oxford: Oxford University Press, 1998.
———. *From the Four Winds.* London: Unwin, 1897.
———. *A Man of Devon.* London: Blackwood, 1901.
Ginden, James. *John Galsworthy's Life and Art.* Ann Arbor: University of Michigan, 1987.
Lanier, Doris. "The Blackbird in John Galsworthy's 'The Japanese Quince,'" *English Language Notes* 30, no. 2 (1992): 57–62.
Sternlicht, Stanford. *John Galsworthy.* Boston: Twayne, 1987.

Andrew Maunder

GAMES AT TWILIGHT AND OTHER STORIES Anita Desai (1978)

This short story collection by the Indian-born writer Anita Desai (b. 1937) addresses social alienation and the isolation of the self. By focusing her work on the domestic sphere and on the self, Desai has established a new trend in Indian writing in English. The characters' inability to come to terms with the clash between inner and outer worlds gives rise to two main reactions: For some, the quest for identity is characterized by a need to prove their worth through outside acknowledgement (an influence of Western culture originating with the British Empire); for others, the response is one of oblivion as regards their own personality (a reflection of a Hindu heritage).

The title story is an account of a conflict experienced by a child protagonist who is anxious to win a game of hide-and-seek at all costs. Ironically, when Ravi finally comes out of his hideous hiding place to claim victory, the other children have forgotten all about him and are playing a different game. The ultimate feeling of disillusionment experienced by the young protagonist triggers his awareness of the meaninglessness of his desire for recognition.

In "Private Tuition by Mr. Bose" and "Sale," the protagonist, a Sanskrit teacher in the former, a painter in the latter, is faced with the insensitivity of his customers, which bruises his sense of self-worth. In "Sale," the artist's representation on the canvas of a beautified reality serves as an escape from his painful and grim personal life. His customers, who seek a comforting representation of life, leave without purchasing any paintings. Both protagonists are caught between antagonistic worlds: the outside world with the helpless pupils and the unappreciative customers and the sweet realm of domestic occupations with wife and child. In both stories the need for creation and material needs come into conflict. The ending of "Sale" shows the character in a pathetic light as he resorts to begging, thereby reducing his art to a mere means of survival.

In "Surface Textures," Harish, a responsible man with a family, is bewitched by the sight of a melon that decisively alters his life: He withdraws from the everyday world and roams the streets, foraging for a texture that will quench his craving for sensuous perception. The final irony lies in the fact that, although he has abandoned his family, Harish is revered like a saint. Another story of obsession, "The Accompanist," examines the life of a character whose sole raison d'être lies in his submission to a famous musician. Bhaiyya's inner world is disrupted when his childhood friends suggest that he perform solo, reminding him of his musical talents as a child. A reconstruction narrative built on reminiscence around the symbol of the tyrannical father's house takes place. The constricting prison of the childhood home has been replaced by concert halls, which have become a refuge from the outer world. To heal a sense of divided self, the character has refashioned his inner world. Leading the life of the Ustad's accompanist symbolizes a new narrative of his sense of self. For both protagonists the significance of their past life has been erased by their newly found meaning in life.

The setting and images of urban India, the pervading atmosphere of India's hot summers, and the evocation of the stifling environment of crowded homes all furnish a vivid picture of Indian life. Desai employs the journey of the inner self as a postcolonial literary trajectory: To generate an alternative construct, her writing relies on the narratives of self and family, time and recollection (with the interrelatedness of past and present), and space. With its exploration of the internal landscape and its exposition of the discrepancy between the inner being and the outside world, Desai's writing, exemplified in this short story collection, constitutes an attempt toward the decolonization of self in Indian literature.

BIBLIOGRAPHY

Desai, Anita. *Games at Twilight and Other Stories.* London: Penguin, 1978.

Florence Libert

GARDAM, JANE (1928–)

Jane Gardam was born in Coatham, North Yorkhire, in 1928. She won a scholarship to the University of London to study English and then developed a career in journalism. Gardam came to literary prominence with *Black Faces, White Faces* (1975), a collection of linked short stories about Jamaica, which won the David Higham Prize for Fiction and the Winifred Holtby Memorial Prize. Gardam also attracted critical acclaim for her first adult novel, *God on the Rocks* (1978), which won the Prix Baudelaire and was short-listed for the Booker Prize. Her other novels include *The Queen of the Tambourine* (1991), which won the Whitbread Novel Award; *Faith Fox* (1996); and *The Flight of the Maidens* (2000).

In *Black Faces, White Faces,* Gardam explores familial interaction and the breakdown of communication that frequently leads to isolation, despair, and mutual misunderstanding. Stories of domestic British frustrations, displaced into a "foreign" environment, are played out against an enigmatic Jamaican backdrop, complete with murderous glens, awakening desires, and the fear of abandonment. Gardam's British characters often display a residually colonialist attitude toward Jamaica and its people. This is particularly evident in "Something to Tell the Girls," in which Miss Dee-Dee and Miss Gongers of Harrogate Hall, two elderly spinster teachers, treat the local Jamaicans naively and patronizingly as they get lost and risk danger away from the tourist trail. The elderly women are discovered teaching English folk songs to local children by a former student, Mrs. Ingham, who features in the earlier story "The Weeping Child." The interaction of the characters from distinctly separate stories concretizes the sense of time and place in this collection and operates as an effective technique to create additional layers of claustrophobia.

Gardam continues her exploration of the fraying remains of the colonialist spirit and the exploitation of its infrastructure in the first and last stories in *The Pangs of Love and Other Stories* (1983), winner of the Katherine Mansfield Award. In "The First Adam," the colonial drive is provided by modern business opportunities in Hong Kong as an English businessman describes his work as his mistress; the wife he barely knows is distant and removed at home in Welwyn. The final story, "The Last Adam," is an example of Gardam's frequent engagement with religious systems, which are often revealed as lacking in any spiritual depth, as Mother Clare oversees the closure of a redundant Catholic mission in India. In contrast, the title story from *The Pangs of Love* is more superficially lighthearted than the other stories in the collection. It is a self-consciously feminist reworking of Hans Christian Anderson's story "The Little Mermaid" in which the younger sister of the self-sacrificing original mermaid determines to be "free of the terrible pangs of love that put women in bondage." The younger, "coarser" sister tracks down the handsome prince who captured her sister's heart and attracts him with her feisty nature and feminist sensibilities. However, he refuses to give up his existing life (and, indeed, to swap his legs for a tail) as requested by his new love. The mermaid is left alone, fighting off bitterness and denying that she is now aggressive. The idea of sacrifice is treated with the recurrence of religious symbolism in the story "The Easter Lilies." Here, the elderly Miss White becomes fixated on saving her financially troubled church money by requesting some lilies from Malta, where she has recently stayed. However, she dies as she is laying out the lilies in church. Having bequeathed her estate to the church, her death saves it. The Easter setting of the story contextualizes her actions in terms of a thoroughly mundane and frugal version of Christian sacrifice.

Gardam's third collection of stories, *Going into a Dark House* (1994), was awarded the PEN/Macmillan Silver Pen Award (1995). In "Zoo-Zoo," two Catholic nuns communicate more of a connection with a wildcat escaped from the zoo than with Sister Alfege, whom they had recently taken to a hospice to die. As do Gardam's other religious characters, the nuns lack any real sense of a fundamental faith. Similarly, rather than overtly displaying religious acts of devotion and inner faith, the Quaker community in "The Meeting House" lives by religious routines. These routines are disrupted by the arrival of a homeless family who squat in the community house and deliberately disrupt ceremonies. The death of this family in a car accident enables the Quakers to retake their meeting place; they are left with the supernatural, ghostly presence of the family, but this is reassuring rather than threatening. This story thereby provides an example of how Gardam represents the supernatural as a means whereby communication and reconciliation can be attained between people previously alienated. This theme is also explored in "Dead Children," wherein a mother grieves for the loss of her children, who have become adults with whom she no longer has any connection. The supernatural meeting among the three of them, when the woman is elderly and the children very young, offers a channel whereby an emotional connection can be made. Miscommunication and lack of connection between familial generations is also central to the last story in *Going into the Dark House,* "Telegony," which is subdivided into three parts. Each part focuses on a different generation of the same family, which is dominated by a lack of understanding and empathy.

Gardam's other short story collections include *Missing the Midnight: Hauntings and Grotesques* (1997), which extends her use of the supernatural into the realm of magical realism, and *The Sidmouth Letters* (1997), which melds past and present, the title story

exploring Jane Austen's love life. In addition to short stories and novels for adults, Gardam is a successful writer of nonfiction and children's fiction. Her nonfiction includes a book about Yorkshire, *The Iron Coast* (1994), and her writing for children includes *Bilgewater* (1977), originally written for children but now reclassified as adult fiction. She won the Whitbread Children's Book Award for *The Hollow Land* (1981); published a collection of short stories set on a farm for children, *A Few Fair Days* (1971); and has written novels for teenagers, *A Long Way from Verona* (1971) and *The Summer after the Funeral* (1973).

BIBLIOGRAPHY

Gardam, Jane. *Black Faces, White Faces.* London: Abacus, 1982.
———. *A Few Fair Days.* London: Hamish Hamilton, 1971.
———. *God on the Rocks.* London: Hamish Hamilton, 1978.
———. *Going into a Dark House.* London: Abacus, 1997.
———. *The Hollow Land.* London: Julia MacRae, 1981.
———. *Missing the Midnight: Hauntings and Grotesques.* London: Sinclair-Stevenson, 1997.
———. *Old Filth.* London: Chatto & Windus, 2004.
———. *The Pangs of Love and Other Stories.* London: Abacus, 1984.
———. *The Sidmouth Letters.* London: Hamish Hamilton, 1978.

Jo Trevenna

"GARDENER, THE" RUDYARD KIPLING (1925)

The critic Edmund Wilson described "The Gardener" as the finest written by RUDYARD KIPLING. Possibly the most celebrated story by Kipling to deal with the legacy of WORLD WAR I, it is also (with the exception of "MARY POSTGATE") the most contentious. Much of this debate centers on the relationship between the protagonist and her "nephew" as well as the ambiguous religious allusion that closes the text.

Kipling establishes a closed community built around discretion and moral conduct in the opening words of the story: "Every one in the village knew that Helen Turrell did her duty by all her world." The tale Helen tells her neighbors is that her brother, reputed to be "a black sheep," died in India shortly before the birth of his illegitimate son. Helen, convalescing in the South of France because of "lung trouble," "most nobly" assumed responsibility, arranging for the child to be brought to her from India and nursing him through an illness before returning to the village "thin and worn but triumphant." Helen christened the child Michael and raised him as her nephew.

Kipling introduces important incidents from Michael's childhood and adolescence. At six years old, Michael asks Helen why he cannot call her "Mummy." Helen allows him to do so, but only at bedtime and between themselves. However, she makes a point of informing her neighbors because "it's always best to tell the truth." Michael is upset when he learns that she has told and threatens to hurt Helen when he is dead. When, as a schoolboy, Michael breaks down Helen's "stammered defences" in order to confirm his illegitimacy, he receives the assurance from her "that nothing on earth or beyond could make any difference between them."

Michael enlists at the start of the war and is killed (in circumstances that closely resemble the death of Kipling's own son). Seeing the war as part of an industrial process, Helen comments, "I'm being manufactured into a bereaved next of kin." The making of mourners is described as another arm of the militarized state. Grief, too, is no more than a routine: "[T]he ease with which she could slip Michael's name into talk and incline her head to the proper angle, at the proper murmur of sympathy." Following the armistice, Michael's body is discovered and identified, and Helen prepares to visit the war cemetery where he has been buried.

For his description of Hagenzeele, Kipling drew on his own experience of Rouen Cemetery. Arriving at the Central Authority in France, Helen encounters a Lancashire woman in search of her son, also illegitimate: "His proper name . . . was Anderson, but, coming of respectable folk, he had of course enlisted under the name of Smith." On the train to Hagenzeele, Helen meets Mrs. Scarsworth, who claims not to have lost anyone but visits the cemeteries on behalf of those who have. Scarsworth initially appears as a ghoulish kind of tourist armed with her Kodak camera: "[W]hen I've got enough commissions for one area to make it worth while, I pop over and execute them." Later in their hotel, though, Scarsworth admits to Helen that there is

"one, d'you see, and—and he was more to me than anything else in the world." Under the cover of her commissions, Scarsworth visits his grave: "He was everything to me that he oughtn't to have been—the one real thing . . . and I've had to pretend he wasn't. I've had to watch every word I said, and think out what lie I'd tell next, for years and years!" Helen responds by reaching out to Mrs. Scarsworth; the latter's reaction ("Is that how you take it?") suggests a bond between the two women.

The following day, Helen visits the cemetery by herself and gets lost among the "merciless sea of black crosses." She meets a gardener who asks her for whom she is looking. Helen replies, "Lieutenant Michael Turrell—my nephew." The gardener responds by saying, "I will show you where your son lies." Enough has been implied in the story to suggest that Michael is, indeed, Helen's son, so that, though moving, the gardeners words are not wholly unexpected. What is surprising, however, is that this mysterious figure should know Michael's true identity. The story's final words ("and she went away, supposing him to be the gardener") are an allusion to John 20:15, in which Christ is compared to a gardener. This conclusion has provoked much debate. Does the gardener have Christlike qualities, is he literally Christ, or is it a case of mistaken identities in which redemption is the most important factor? In terms of the short story form, this ending is quite different from the "twist in the tail" that Kipling often uses in his earlier stories, in which the surprise of the ending is not forecast previously in the text, as it is in "The Gardener." Instead, by breaking with the patterns of his own fiction, Kipling appears to suggest that redemption is possible in an otherwise Godless universe only by breaking with the polite codes that prevent truth. By dismantling the structures of his own writing, Kipling points to the excessive grief and trauma that a hypocritical society merely seeks to repress.

BIBLIOGRAPHY

Kemp, Sandra. Kipling's Hidden Narratives. Oxford: Basil Blackwell, 1988.

Lewis, Lisa, ed. "The Gardener." The New Reader's Guide to the Works of Rudyard Kipling. Available online. URL: http://www.kipling.org.uk/rg_gardener1.htm. Accessed May 12, 2006.

Rutherford, Andrew, ed. *Kipling's Mind and Art.* Edinburgh: Oliver & Boyd, 1964.

Paul March Russell

"GARDEN-PARTY, THE" KATHERINE MANSFIELD (1921)

KATHERINE MANSFIELD incorporated literary MODERNISM into the genre of the short story in *The Garden-Party and Other Stories,* published in 1922. The title story, written in 1921, emphasizes mood, emotion, and relationships of characters rather than plot and reveals the interior world of protagonist Laura, Mansfield's representative, as she confronts class distinctions and considers the meaning of life and death.

Born in New Zealand in 1888, Mansfield moved to England in 1909. A visit from her brother in 1915 a month before he died in World War I stirred memories of her earlier life, and she began to place many of her stories in her homeland. "The Garden-Party," one of the stories set in New Zealand, pictures the cloudless blue sky "veiled with a haze of light gold, as it is sometimes in early summer" (534) and the karaka trees "with their broad, gleaming leaves, and their clusters of yellow fruit" (536).

The first half of the story deals with preparations for the garden party: the placement of the marquee, the positioning of the pots of canna lilies, the preparation of the 15 types of party sandwiches. Mansfield uses her clear, lyrical prose to create the magnificence of the day. The rose bushes "bowed down as though they had been visited by archangels" (534), and Laura sees the karaka trees as "proud, solitary, lifting their leaves and fruits to the sun in a kind of silent splendor" (536).

The attraction Laura feels toward the working class becomes apparent during her encounter with the men who come to put up the marquee. The smile of "a lanky, freckled fellow" is "so easy, so friendly" (535) that it puts her at ease. When he pinches a sprig of lavender and smells it, she reflects, "Why couldn't she have workmen for friends rather than the silly boys she danced with and who came to Sunday night supper?" (536).

Into this "perfect day" (534) intrudes the news of the death of a neighbor who lived in one of the "little cottages just below" (541). Laura decides immediately that the party must be canceled. Her sister Jose rejects the idea as foolish, and her mother seems "amused"

(543) at the suggestion. Back in her room, Laura pictures the body of the dead man being carried into his house, but the scene seems "blurred, unreal" (544), and the party activities soon crowd it out.

As the family nibbles on party food after the guests have left, Mrs. Sheridan decides to send a basket of leftovers to the bereaved family and appoints Laura, who is horrified at what she considers to be her mother's insensitivity, to make the delivery. On her way to the house, the surroundings take on symbolic meaning. She walks down the gleaming white road outside her family's garden gates, crosses a wide road, and enters a "smoky and dark" lane (546). Approaching the house of the grieving family, Laura sees "a dark knot of people" (546). Inside she finds, to her amazement, that the dead man appears "wonderful, beautiful" (548). Later, when her brother asks about her visit, she responds, "'It was simply marvelous'" (548), but she is unable to complete her sentence "'Isn't life—'" (549). She realizes that life and death are too complex to put into words—or to understand, for that matter.

Mansfield wrote "The Garden-Party" while she was dying of tuberculosis. She knew life and death and the joy and grief of both. In the introduction to *The Short Stories of Katherine Mansfield,* J. Middleton Murray, Mansfield's husband and primary publisher, wrote of his wife, "She loved life—with all its beauty and its pain" (xi). In "The Garden-Party" Laura experiences both the beauty and pain of life, but Mansfield, true to what George McLean Harper calls her "penetrating honesty" (232), leaves Laura at the end of the story groping for a satisfactory definition of life.

BIBLIOGRAPHY

Harper, George McLean. *Literary Appreciations.* Freeport, N.Y.: Books for Libraries Press, 1937.
Mansfield, Katherine. *The Short Stories of Katherine Mansfield.* New York: Alfred A. Knopf, 1965.

Charlotte S. Pfeiffer

GASKELL, ELIZABETH (1810–1865)

The title of Arthur Pollard's 1966 study of Elizabeth Gaskell, *Mrs. Gaskell: Novelist and Biographer,* provides valuable insight into how her achievements have traditionally been discussed. Although she published more than 40 short stories and essays during her lifetime,

Gaskell is remembered today almost exclusively for novels such as *Mary Barton* (1848) and *North and South* (1854) and her landmark biography of Charlotte Brontë (1857). Anyone who ignores her short fiction, however, will obtain only a partial understanding of the author, for Gaskell often used her short stories to explore subjects and settings she excluded from the novels that made her famous. For this reason alone, they are worthy of far greater critical attention.

Born on September 29, 1810, Elizabeth Stevenson was raised by her aunt in Knutsford, Cheshire, a town that later became a model for the fictional Cranford. At age 22 she married William Gaskell, a Unitarian minister, and moved to the industrial city of Manchester. Her first published work was the short essay "Clopton Hall," which appeared in William Howitt's *Visits to Remarkable Places* in 1840. The success of her first novel, *Mary Barton,* brought Gaskell to the attention of CHARLES DICKENS. A professional relationship and personal friendship between the two sprang up that, although strained at times, lasted for the rest of his life. Beginning with "LIZZIE LEIGH" in 1849, Dickens published a number of her short stories (e.g., "A MANCHESTER MARRIAGE" [1858], *A DARK NIGHT'S WORK* [1863]), the novel *North and South,* and the novella "MY LADY LUDLOW" (1858) in his periodicals *Household Words* and *All the Year Round.* By the time of her death on November 12, 1865, Gaskell had achieved substantial popularity in Great Britain and ranked among the country's literary elite.

As a novelist, Gaskell operates almost exclusively within the domain of realism. Works such as *North and South* offer sympathetic and detailed portrayals of mid-19th-century working-class and middle-class life that were drawn in large part from her personal experiences working among the poor with her husband in Manchester. In her stories, however, she explores different eras and different settings. "The Grey Woman" (1861), for instance, takes place during the French Revolution, "The Poor Clare" (1856) harkens back to the mid-1700s, and "Six Weeks at Heppenheim" (1862) is set in Germany. Gaskell also frequently incorporates elements of the gothic and supernatural into her short fiction, as in "LOIS THE WITCH" (1859), a fictional account of the Salem witch trials and one of her most striking

and fully realized tales. Other works that follow this pattern include "The OLD NURSE'S STORY" (1852) and "Curious, if True" (1860). Nine of these ghostly stories were recently collected by Penguin in the volume *Gothic Tales.*

BIBLIOGRAPHY

Foster, Shirley. *Elizabeth Gaskell: A Literary Life.* Basingstoke, England: Palgrave Macmillan, 2002.

Gaskell, Elizabeth. *A Dark Night's Work and Other Stories.* Edited by Suzanne Lewis. Oxford: Oxford University Press, 1992.

———. *Gothic Tales.* Edited by Laura Kranzler. New York: Penguin, 2000.

Martin, Carol A. "Gaskell's Ghosts: Truth in Disguise," *Studies in the Novel* 21, no. 1 (Spring 1989): 27–40.

Matsuoka, Mitsuhara. The Gaskell Web Project. Available online. URL: http://lang.nagoya-u.ac.jp/matsuoka/Gaskell.html. Accessed on May 12, 2006.

Pollard, Arthur. *Mrs. Gaskell: Novelist and Biographer.* Cambridge, Mass.: Harvard University Press, 1966.

Stephen E. Severn

"GIOCONDA SMILE, THE" ALDOUS HUXLEY (1921)

Originally published in the April 1921 issue of *The English Review* and later included by ALDOUS HUXLEY in *Mortal Coils* (1922), "The Gioconda Smile" is inspired by the story of Harold Greenwood, a man who had been acquitted of poisoning his wife. The story's title alludes to the enigmatic grin of Leonardo da Vinci's "Mona Lisa del Gioconda." Thanks to Huxley's adaptation of the story for the screen in 1947 (renamed *A Woman's Vengeance* by Universal Studios) and subsequent dramatization for the stage in 1950, "The Gioconda Smile" has become one of the author's most famous works.

Henry Hutton, the philandering middle-aged banker at the center of Huxley's story, having grown weary of caring for his invalid wife, prides himself on his ability attract women. The narrative opens as Hutton pays a surprise visit to his wife's closest friend, Janet Spence. Unabashedly flirting with the 36-year-old spinster despite experiencing a profound sense of boredom in her presence, Hutton invites Janet to have lunch with him and his wife Emily the next afternoon. After kissing Janet's hand, Henry departs, leaving Janet thoroughly charmed by his behavior. Despite Janet's desire to accompany Henry to his automobile, Hutton insists that he go alone, concealing the fact that his young mistress, Doris, is waiting for him.

At the next afternoon's luncheon, the normally sickly Emily Hutton feels surprisingly robust and allows herself to eat stewed currants, the digestion of which doctors had deemed too taxing for her fragile constitution. Despite Henry's half-hearted protests, Janet insists the man allow Emily to indulge her appetite. As the Huttons' maid brings the party their after-dinner coffee, Emily remembers that she must take her medication, and Henry volunteers to retrieve it while the women prepare their coffee.

Not long after Emily takes her medicine and drinks her coffee she begins to feel ill and returns to the house to rest. While in the garden, Janet informs Henry that Emily "is dreadfully ill . . . anything might happen" (101). Despite Janet's ominous comment and under the pretense of having made an appointment with a colleague, Henry leaves to spend the evening with Doris, dismissing Emily's sudden illness as the inevitable result of her unwise decision to eat the stewed currants. Upon Henry's return later in the evening, the family doctor informs him that Emily is dead; her heart, because of chronic vascular disease, could not handle the strain caused by the stewed currants.

After a brief period of mourning, during which Henry appears to have reformed his libertine lifestyle, he marries Doris long before the traditional period of grieving has passed. Spurned by the object of her desire, Janet Spence accuses Henry of having poisoned his wife. After a preliminary investigation reveals traces of arsenic in the Huttons' garden, police exhume Emily's body and arrest Henry for murder. Responding to a doctor's inquiry shortly after Hutton's execution, Janet admits that it was she who had put arsenic in Emily's coffee, presumably with the intent of marrying the newly widowed Henry herself.

The short story demonstrates what Nicholas Murray has called the "morbid interest in human decay and debility . . . evident in much of Huxley's early work" (142). Additionally, Huxley's use of satire in "The Gioconda Smile" criticizes the hedonistic zeitgeist of the Jazz Age, in particular such prevalent social ills as infidelity and egocentrism. Furthermore, by writing with "the coldness of the vivisectionist" (Murray, 142), Huxley presages the hard-boiled attitude and meticulous attention to detail found in the crime fiction of James Cain, Raymond Chandler, Dashiell Hammett, and Horace McCoy that was popular in the 1930s and 1940s.

BIBLIOGRAPHY

Clark, Virginia M. *Aldous Huxley and Film*. London: Scarecrow Press, 1987.
Dunaway, David King. *Huxley in Hollywood*. New York: Harper & Row, 1989.
Huxley, Aldous. *Collected Short Stories*. London: Chatto & Windus, 1957.
Murray, Nicholas. *Aldous Huxley: A Biography*. London: Little, Brown, 2002.

Erik Grayson

"GOOD-BYE, GOOD-BYE" ELIZABETH TAYLOR (1958) ELIZABETH TAYLOR's poignant short story "Good-bye, Good-bye" was first published in the magazine *Woman and Beauty* and then collected in *The Blush and Other Stories* in 1958. The story's title points to its theme of two painful farewells. These leavetakings occur between adulterous lovers, Peter and Catherine, the first recalled by Peter in retrospect, and the second occurring at the end of the story. "Good-bye" is a quintessential Taylor story for a number of reasons: It is informed by a Brontëan tale, the obsessive love of Catherine and Heathcliff in Emily Brontë's *Wuthering Heights*; it is quietly dramatic, portraying a momentous event in the lives of people doing ordinary things; and it demonstrates an uncanny knowledge of children's lives, of their fears and certainties. Only the trenchant wit in much of Taylor's fiction is not much in evidence, as she depicts the quiet despair of an impossible love.

From the story's first words, it is infused with a sense of Peter's urgent recklessness on the night before he leaves a second time for South Africa: "On his last evening in England he broke two promises—one, that he would dine with his brother, and another, older promise made to a woman whom he loved." The second sentence starkly addresses the hopeless quandary of the lovers' thwarted desire for each other: "When he and Catherine had tried, years before, to put an end to this impermissible love for one another the best they could decide was to give it no nourishment and let it wither if it would."

Despite his promises, Peter decides to revisit the scene "where they had sometimes been together," Catherine's summer house by the sea. Here, the pervasive mood of repressed passion and regret is explicitly connected to the romantic Heathcliff and Catherine. Early on, Peter exclaims over Catherine's daughter Sarah's eyes: "'Oh, Catherine's eyes, those eyes!' he thought. 'The miracle, but the enormity, that they should come again; clearer, more beautiful'—he could not think it." Readers of *Wuthering Heights* will remember the scene in which Heathcliff is disarmed by the eyes of the second Cathy and her cousin Hareton, which "are the eyes of Catherine Earnshaw," as the narrating housekeeper Nelly Dean tells us. Peter's love is unchangeable, like Heathcliff's. Such allusions to the Brontës' fiction are common and powerful in Taylor's early fiction, from the gift of the book *Wuthering Heights* in Taylor's first novel, *At Mrs. Lippincote's* (1945), through the reworking of *Jane Eyre*'s governess tale in Taylor's second novel, *Palladian* (1946), to the frustrated, enduring love of Catherine and Vesey in *A Game of Hide-and-Seek* (1954). The Brontës' works are a marker of a shared literary inheritance between Taylor and her readers and between Taylor's characters as well. Although Taylor's fiction is most often compared to Jane Austen's, Taylor in fact is much more likely to evoke the turbulent passions of the Brontës' novels in the repressed subtext of her stories.

A book of selected short stories by Taylor published in 1995 is titled *Dangerous Calm*. This sense of the threat pervading the ordinary informs "Good-bye, Good-bye" as well. All through the introductions to the children and their friends—"Lucy, this is Mr. Lord. He gave you your Fairy-Tale book that you love so much"—there is the secrecy of their illicit past just behind the facade of Peter the avuncular, the memory of a passion that threatened these very children's security. In fact, Peter is not a kindly uncle but the man who—like Heathcliff to Brontë's Catherine—was like a god to the children's mother: "Mr. Lord." The romantic sunset, "explosive, Turneresque brilliance above the sand-hillocks," is backdrop to a tense, discreet inter-

play between the lovers that resonates with memories of their forbidden meetings.

But the evening is experienced differently by Catherine than by Peter, even though she is deeply shaken by the encounter with her lost lover. Her eyes fill with tears when Peter praises her four children; it is her love for them that has divided Peter from her, her inability to make the children's world unstable, much less to forsake them. In particular, Catherine identifies with her 16-year-old daughter Sarah, suffering because the boy she likes does not come to the beach that night: "'It is worse for her now,' Catherine thought, and she felt hostility towards men. 'As it is worse for me.'" Catherine vacillates between thinking that Peter has become judgmental and admitting miserably to herself, as Peter plays affectionately with her little girl Lucy, "A barren evening. Nothing said; nothing felt, but pain. The wheel starting to creak again, starting to revolve in agony." Catherine is unable to tell Peter what she feels because the children are there, and they must not know, must not be hurt: "'I am in love with you still. In love, certainly. And there isn't a way out and never will be now.' Her eyes might say this without Lucy knowing, and she turned to him so that before he went away he could be a witness to her constancy." Taylor's quiet understatement, her fiction of manners, does seem informed in this passage by Austen. There is something of Jane Austen about this straining effort to communicate love despite all constraints, the resonance of Anne Elliot in *Persuasion* trying to tell Wentworth that she loves him without saying the words in a public place.

This love, unlike Anne's and Wentworth's, will not end happily. In the end, the lovers must simply know that theirs is an unchanging passion because they recognize the other's suffering. When Peter asks Catherine for her forgiveness because he has disturbed her life, she responds, "I might have done the same." While they have "no time" to talk alone, Peter knows that Catherine "was waiting for tears to recede, her head high, breath held. If he kissed her, she would fail, would break, weep, betray herself to the children." Peter immediately thinks "To have thought of her so long, imagined, dreamed, called that child 'Catherine' for her sake, started at the sight of her name printed in a book, pretended her voice to myself, called her in my sleep, and now sit close to her and it is almost over." Their sad reunion is punctuated by the children's picnic, by the children's voices and needs, until the end, when Peter's final "good-bye, good-bye" echoes that of the older children's departing guests, as if Peter were leaving Catherine only for an evening instead of a lifetime.

BIBLIOGRAPHY
Taylor, Elizabeth. *The Blush*. London: Peter Davies, 1958.
———. *Dangerous Calm: The Selected Stories of Elizabeth Taylor*. Edited by Lynne Knight. London: Virago, 1995.

Deborah Deneholz Morse

"GOOD LADY DUCAYNE" Mary Elizabeth Braddon (1896)

Although not a vampire story in the strictest sense, Mary Elizabeth Braddon's "Good Lady Ducayne," first published in the Strand Magazine in 1896, is now frequently included in vampire anthologies. In this story, Bella, a young girl, is hired as a companion to a mysterious old woman, Lady Ducayne. The pair, accompanied by Lady Ducayne's physician, travel to Italy. There Bella becomes increasingly weak and complains of nocturnal mosquito bites. A brother and sister she meets at the Italian resort become concerned about her rapidly deteriorating condition. The brother, a physician, investigates and discovers that Lady Ducayne and her doctor have been using a machine to transfuse Bella's blood into the old woman. Lady Ducayne is convinced that a constant supply of young blood will enable her to live forever, and it is revealed that Bella is not the first to be used for this procedure. However, unlike the other victims, Bella survives.

This readable story is important because it is the first to combine traditional vampire superstitions with the Victorian interest in technology, especially in transfusion. This interest would be developed the following year in Bram Stoker's *Dracula*. Braddon's story also contains many of the characteristics of the traditional gothic tale, including an exotic setting and an innocent young heroine who is in the thrall of a more powerful person. As in Samuel Taylor Coleridge's "Christabel" and Sheridan Le Fanu's "Car-milla," the powerful person is another woman. However, in stark contrast to the youth and beauty of the women in these works, Lady Ducayne is grotesquely ugly because of her unnaturally advanced age. Even though the supply of youthful blood keeps her alive, Lady Ducayne cannot stop the aging process. This aspect of the story perhaps makes it especially pertinent to modern readers.

BIBLIOGRAPHY
Stephenson, Glennis, ed. *Nineteenth-Century Stories by Women: An Anthology*. Peterborough, Ont.: Broadview Press, 1993.

Leah Larson

GOOD TIMES, THE James Kelman (1998)

The Good Times is a sequence of 20 first-person stories documenting the inner lives of working-class men and boys in Scotland. James Kelman portrays his characters empathetically in their common struggle to survive poverty, boredom, and failure with their self-respect intact. Each story evokes a distinct "male consciousness," often by setting private, inward experience against the pressures of public situations: We encounter these men and boys in the workplace, in the schoolyard, in shops and pubs, on the subway, and in the family home. Narrated by males ranging from childhood to late middle age, a strong memento mori ("remember, you must die") theme links the stories to larger philosophical issues. The reflections of all the protagonists—disaffected boys and yearning teenagers; a deluded 30-something divorcé; manual toilers, both embittered and cavalier; moody philosophical husbands—have a decided existential flavor, though the tone of the stories ranges from silly humor to devastating grimness. Many build toward an existential climax, involving a moment of authentic decision between resignation and a liberating sense of responsibility for one's own fate. In "It Happened to Me Once," an unemployed man waiting to collect his social security money is annoyed by another man waiting in line, someone he regards as a loser but in whom he recognizes his own desperate condition. The narrator's paranoia lends the tense encounter an unbearable sense of dread and prompts a dismal epiphany.

In contrast, in "Yeh, These Stages," a depressed man whose girlfriend has left him wallows in self-pity before being spurred into life by a mysterious knock at the door, which he opens only to find that there is no one there. The "human absence" is an emblem of the world's indifference to his plight; a man previously in "the kind of despair that makes suicide a positive move" realizes that the world will carry on with or without him, and he finds in this thought an invigorating sense of independence, even hope.

Awareness of one's own mortality and limitations looms large in *The Good Times,* and all Kelman's characters seem to struggle toward accepting, without despair, that "they werent going to play for Rangers, they werent going to play for anybody; and they werent getting the good job, they werent getting this that or anything." (Glasgow Rangers is one of the two dominant teams in Scottish soccer.) This struggle begins early in life. The boy narrator of "Joe Laughed" is so irritated by his friends' senseless and "childish" behavior that he despairs of being part of society at all. In a fit of despair he imagines completely abdicating from the roles—son, friend, teammate, neighbor—that community life imposes on him. This fantasy of total withdrawal into self-absorption shows its comic potential in "Gardens Go on Forever," in which the fanciful imagination of the narrator and the absurd conversations he has with his workmate result in one of Kelman's funniest stories. At the end of a typically anarchic chain of daydreams, the relaxed and flippant protagonist envisages his own funeral. His oppressive job does not move this character (unlike others in the collection) to bitterness but underscores the freedom that comes with absolute existential responsibility. The narrator of "Oh My Darling" agrees: "If people do want to change their lives then it is their responsibility and not mine, nor is it anybody else's, it's theirs, theirs and theirs alone. But they should be happy, content, just to be living instead of not yet entering into the slipstream."

In Kelman's view, the brute truth of the memento mori has carpe diem ("seize the day") as its everyday meaning; life is for living, nothing more. "The Norwest Reaches" warmly evokes the humble comforts of family life, while the intrusion of social class into romantic relationships is brilliantly captured in "Oh My Darling" and "Constellation." "Strength" hauntingly explores the painful closeness of the long-married, when personal, individual memories and the hurt of regret have become shared property. The protagonist's wife has a morbid fascination with a motorcycle accident from her husband's teenage years, in which he and his then girlfriend were nearly killed. Far from feeling troubled or jealous at the thought of her husband's former lover, she dwells uncomfortably on the relationship, wondering what might have been if not for the girlfriend's interfering mother: "I know ye loved that wee lassie, but it doesnay bother me. Even if ye had got killed the gether, the two of ye, it still wouldnay bother me. I just admire ye both, I do." The genuine selflessness of this sentiment is clouded over by the implication that the character would be unmoved had her future husband died before meeting her, which concedes that the married couple's own, subsequent relationship was no kind of romantic destiny but the product of contingent circumstances. Doing without such comfortable myths ("we were made for each other") demands the strength of the story's title: Those myths are a kind of emotional crutch, comparable to the pouffe (footrest) the wife uses for her immediate comfort, but which, over time, the husband fears will leave her spine warped and twisted. The wife's "raking up" of old memories is symbolically connected to her stubborn refusal to sit up straight; "ye'll just suffer for it" is her husband's half-pitying, half-reproving warning. The distorting effect of loneliness on a middle-aged bachelor is the topic of the collection's most shattering story, "The COMFORT"; its deft examination of masculinity, morality, and death might almost be read as *The Good Times* in miniature.

BIBLIOGRAPHY

Kelman, James. *The Good Times.* New York: Anchor Books, 1999.

Scott Hames

GREENE, GRAHAM (1904–1991)

Born into prosperous circumstances in Berkhampstead, Hertfordshire, on October 2, 1904, Graham Greene was the son of the headmaster of Berkhampstead School. Bullied for being the headmaster's son, the young Greene made several suicide attempts; thanks to his psychiatrist, he began to write and made the acquaintance of several well-known authors, including WALTER DE LA MARE. Greene later attended Oxford University, where, neglecting his studies, he developed an interest in politics, joined the Communist Party, and completed his first novel, *Anthony Sant,* which was never published. Greene's first successful job was as a subeditor with the *Nottingham Journal.* While working there he met his wife, Vivien Dayrell-Browning. A devout Catholic, Vivien encouraged Greene to convert to the faith in 1926. Greene began writing full time after the success of his first published novel, *The Man Within* (1929). His works include *Brighton Rock* (1938), *The Heart of the Matter* (1948), and *The Quiet American* (1955). His novels made him successful, and he lived very comfortably in London, Antibes, and Capri, separating from but never divorcing his wife. Toward the end of his life, Greene lived in Vevey, Switzerland, where he died in 1991.

Although Greene is most famous for his novels and journalism, he also wrote many short stories. These have received little attention, and Greene himself seems to have encouraged this neglect. He commented that they were not to be taken seriously. Several, however, have been widely acclaimed, including "The DESTRUCTORS," "A LITTLE PLACE OFF THE EDGWARE ROAD," and "The INVISIBLE JAPANESE GENTLEMAN." Critics have tended to agree that Greene was not a stylistic innovator and tended to be influenced by older masters of the short story form, including HENRY JAMES and SOMERSET MAUGHAM. Also apparent are some of the same preoccupations that appear in Greene's novels, including, as Richard Kelly notes, "clever similes, seedy atmospheres, and recurrent themes such as innocence and betrayal" (84). Kelly is one of a number of critics who also see in Greene's works a kind of therapeutic writing out of a troubled personal life, demonstrated by "a sense of betrayed innocence; an authoritarian and puritanical father; clever school bullies; fear of the dark, birds, and water; fear of and fascination with sexuality; fear of boredom" (84).

BIBLIOGRAPHY

Greene, Graham. *Collected Short Stories.* London: Penguin, 1986.

Kelly, Richard. *Graham Greene: A Study of the Short Fiction.* Boston: Twayne, 1993.

Mudford, Peter. *Graham Greene.* Plymouth, England: Northcote House, 1996.

Andrew Maunder

"GREEN TEA" JOSEPH SHERIDAN LE FANU **(1872)** The first story in SHERIDAN LE FANU's sensation collection *In a Glass Darkly.* This collection of stories forms a unified whole, held together by a frame story that resurfaces at the beginning and end of each consecutive episode.

Written in the wake of the so-called Sensational Sixties, *In a Glass Darkly* forms part of the Victorian sensation genre popularized by WILKIE COLLINS, MARY ELIZABETH BRADDON, and ELLEN WOOD. It transposes the gothic into domestic or urban settings, adding an interest in new medical, specifically psychological, theories. In the frame story, the medical secretary of the fictitious German physician Dr. Hesselius sets out to edit accounts of mysterious, enigmatically supernatural occurrences. Capitalizing on the mid-Victorian fascination with clinical treatments, psychosomatic disorders, and the increasingly problematic mind/body split, the ghost stories that follow are thus presented as medical accounts: "Here and there a case strikes me as of a kind to amuse or horrify a lay reader with an interest quite different from the peculiar one which it may possess for an expert." As in the majority of Victorian sensation stories, horror is shown to be breaking into or, with a twist that is even more calculated to disturb, out of the mundane. This introduction of the gothic into the everyday middle-class home constitutes an important disruption of Victorian ideals of domesticity. As Lillian Nayder argues in a study of Wilkie Collins, it generates a specifically "domestic Gothic."

While the later stories in *In a Glass Darkly* tend to return to the foreign scenes and aristocratic trappings that characterize the 18th-century gothic genre, "Green Tea" admirably exemplifies the popularity of the Victorian domestic gothic in its choice of a suburban setting. Mr. Jennings, the unfortunate victim of supernatural phantasms, is a quiet, scholarly clergyman. His first encounter with the demon is set in an omnibus that takes him from the City, London's commercial district, to a quiet, upmarket Victorian suburbia. The only drugs or stimulants featured in the story are pots of the titular green tea.

Connected to this projection of a disturbingly familiar horror, in which dark suburban streets, empty omnibuses, and insomnia become the signs of a developing phantasmagoria, or nightmare, is the ambiguous function of modern medical research in the story. Dr. Hesselius is the author of essays on "Metaphysical Medicine" and a follower of the 18th-century cosmologist Swedenborg. His interpretations of Jennings's malady are influenced by his belief in metaphysics. Jennings admits that his extensive consumption of green tea has affected his nerves, which might account for his visions of the monkeylike demon that haunts him from the omnibus to his suburban home and ultimately drives him to suicide. However, whether the demon is solely the creation of dyspepsia and affected nerves or a true vision remains tantalizingly unsolved. Jennings's reasoning proves ineffective: "'I've been sitting up too late, and I daresay my digestion is quite wrong, and with God's help, I shall be all right, and this is but a symptom of nervous dyspepsia.' Did I believe all this? Not a word of it." After Jennings's death, Dr. Hesselius concludes that his patient inadvertently opened an "inner eye," and yet his diagnosis of this "sublimated," "precocious," or "interior" vision is strictly couched in clinical terms. Similar ambiguity is central to the following stories in the book, including the influential vampire story "Carmilla."

BIBLIOGRAPHY

Harris, Sally. "Spiritual Warnings: The Ghost Stories of Joseph Sheridan Le Fanu," *Victorians Institute Journal* 31 (2003): 9–39.

Le Fanu, Joseph Sheridan. *In a Glass Darkly*. London: John Lehman, 1947.

McCormack, W. J. *Sheridan Le Fanu*. Stroud, England: Sutton, 1997.

Nayder, Lillian. *Wilkie Collins*. London: Prentice Hall, 1997.

Tamara Wagner

"GREVILLE FANE" HENRY JAMES (1892)

"Greville Fane" is from the group of stories that HENRY JAMES published during the 1890s in which he explored the relationship between the writer and the critic. Yet while the story is a portrait of the artist, it was also conceived as a joke at the expense of parents who vainly prepare their offspring to follow in their own footsteps. This second, comic aspect of the narrative turns the story (as James admitted) into an anecdote. This effect was, probably, James's intention. Whereas his other literary portraits, such as "The FIGURE IN THE CARPET," appeared in highbrow or avant-garde publications, "Greville Fane" featured in the popular, mainstream journal the *Illustrated London News*. Nevertheless, critics have emphasized James's unusually sympathetic portrait of his protagonist, the female novelist.

The story is narrated by a book reviewer who is employed to write an obituary of Mrs. Stormer. Stormer is a romantic author who, while writing under the pseudonym Greville Fane, has managed a household and raised a family. The critic personally likes her ("a dull, kind woman"), although he despairs of her work: "She could invent stories by the yard, but she couldn't write a page of English." Fane is not without skill; what she lacks is a sense of art as struggle: "[G]enius always pays for the gift, feels the debt, and she was placidly unconscious of obligation." Instead, Fane prefers to think of herself as "a common pastry cook, dealing in such tarts and puddings as would bring customers to the shop." Despite her artistic shortcomings, Fane is regarded affectionately by James's narrator. In this respect, she resembles woman-novelists, such as MARY ELIZABETH BRADDON, MARGARET OLIPHANT, and Mrs. Humphrey Ward, whom James admired for their industry in spite of their uneven talent. Fane's matronly qualities contrast her with the sexually provocative NEW WOMAN, such as GEORGE EGERTON, whom James described as writers of "the larger latitude." Though written in a lighter vein, the story shares with "The Private Life" (also published in 1892) the attempt to distinguish the writer from the authorial persona.

Here, this distinction allows James to explore the sadness behind Fane's celebrity: Mrs. Stormer's misguided attempt to train her son, Leolin, to be a great novelist. She shows him the sights of Europe, but Leolin grows up to be lazy and self-indulgent. After his mother's death, Leolin ransacks her unpublished papers to make money. James compounds Mrs. Stormer's misery by portraying her daughter, Ethel, as a snobbish and spoiled girl who disdains her mother's writing while drawing upon her fortune. Though the depiction of Leolin and Ethel is scathing, the satire is at Mrs. Stormer's expense, in particular, her belief that talent can be acquired. Instead, James reaffirms the claim from his essay "The Art of Fiction" (1884) that artistic genius is inherent: "The deepest quality of a work of art will always be the quality of the mind of its producer" (182). Though Mrs. Stormer's foolishness adds to her humanity (in contrast with her children), at the end of the story the focus moves away from her abilities as a writer to her virtues as a mother. Consequently, having begun as a consideration of the woman writer, the story ends as a speculation on motherhood.

BIBLIOGRAPHY

Chapman, Sara S. *Henry James' Portrait of the Writer as Hero.* Basingstoke, England: Macmillan, 1990.

James, Henry. "Greville Fane." In *The Complete Tales of Henry James,* vol. 8, edited by Leon Edel, 433–452. London: Rupert Hart-Davis, 1963.

James, Henry. "The Art of Fiction." *Longmans Magazine* 4 (September 1884): 180–186.

———. "The Art of Fiction." In *The Critical Muse: Selected Literary Criticism,* edited by Roger Gard, 186–204. London: Penguin, 1987.

Paul March Russell

GREYHOUND FOR BREAKFAST JAMES KELMAN (1987)

JAMES KELMAN's second book of stories is his largest and most diverse. Varied in tone, style, length, and intensity, the collection shows a writer experimenting with a range of techniques and subjects and discovering the strength of his talent in a few powerfully realized short works. The extremely short stories include both realistic urban tableaux capturing snapshots of working-class life and enigmatic, highly stylized fragments that show the influence of surrealism and absurdism. A brief sketch of a young married man's temptation by a prostitute, "dear o dear," is a concrete prose poem arranged as a silhouette of the shape of a streetwalker. "A Sunday Evening" provides a morbidly tender window into the intimacy and monotony of settled domestic routine. Here, and throughout the volume, Kelman captures an extraordinarily deep sense of his characters' subjectivity, often at moments of inner drama within outwardly mundane situations. Many stories show men and boys in moments of solitude, attempting, and usually failing, to seize small freedoms from "ordinary" contexts of unfreedom, be it economic, social, or sexual. The narrator of "Getting Outside" wavers between "bloodcurdling screams of horror" and strict control of his emotions, as he escapes a tense situation inside a house only to be faced, outside, with an equally anxious private one. Enduring the situation counts as a tiny victory for this character. The theme of survival hauntingly recurs in "A History," in which an evening stroll by the beach prompts the protagonist's detached, overly tidy meditations on time and fate. This train of thought, but not the coolly ambivalent narrative voice that conveys it, is disturbed by the memory of finding a drowned man along the same stretch of beach. The narrator dwells on the particulars of the body's imagined history but steers clear of sentimentality. Whether the detached tone he adopts is a sign of coldness or of stoical resignation is left ambiguous, as is the nature of the narrator's sympathy as he continues to muse: "He would have been dead in twenty minutes, maybe less. If I had been God I would have allowed him to survive for twenty hours." Is this imaginary postponement supposed to allow the man time enough to save himself or simply to prolong his struggle against an implacable fate? Which does the narrator value more highly: human life or the futile impulse to preserve it? We are left uncertain, and disturbed. In "Greyhound for Breakfast," a grown man also finds solace in loneliness after a doomed attempt, worthy of a schoolboy, to reinvent himself as a dog-racing man. This experimental collection shows the emergence of Kelman's characteristic thematic and formal interests and points toward the disciplined but expansive style of *The GOOD TIMES.*

BIBLIOGRAPHY

Kelman, James. *Greyhound for Breakfast.* London: Secker & Warburg, 1987.

Scott Hames

"GUESTS OF THE NATION" FRANK O'CONNOR (1931)

Published originally in *Atlantic Monthly* and then in a collection of stories also titled

Guests of the Nation (1931), this is the most widely read and commonly anthologized of FRANK O'CONNOR's works.

In this story, set during the Anglo-Irish War (1919–21), the narrator, Bonaparte, and his fellow Irish soldiers, Noble and Donovan, are charged with guarding two English prisoners. The two Englishmen, Belcher and Hawkins, live in relative comfort in the home of an elderly Irishwoman, playing cards with their hosts in the evenings, sharing in household chores, and living more as welcome guests than as prisoners. To his profound distress, Bonaparte learns from Donovan that they must execute their "guests" in reprisal for the English killing of Irish prisoners. Donovan shoots both prisoners, but Hawkins survives and Bonaparte has to kill him with a bullet to the head. The story closes with Bonaparte feeling lost and alone, changed forever by the terrible experience.

Although O'Connor was an ardent Irish patriot, "Guests of the Nation" focuses not on the Irish cause but rather on the inhumanity of war more generally. "Guests" is essentially an initiation story: Early on, the youthful protagonist longs to join a fighting brigade, but when he reaches his painful epiphany at the story's end, Bonaparte is clearly disabused of any youthful romanticism about war. The central theme of the story lies in the conflict between duty and friendship. O'Connor shows that while in other circumstances these Irish and British soldiers might be fast friends, duty to their cause dictates that the Irish soldiers must effectively murder their "guests," who are enemies only in name. O'Connor emphasizes the humanity of the English prisoners through carefully developed characterization that highlights their differences: Belcher is large, reticent, and happily domestic, while Hawkins is small, loquacious, and concerned with international politics and religion. In the end, Bonaparte learns that doing one's duty in war can have life-altering consequences and that the soldier's business in war is essentially murder.

As the story's title suggests, one of its hallmarks is irony. Among the most notable ironies is how thoroughly friendly Bonaparte and Noble become with the English prisoners—the persistent use of the word "chum" by both English and Irish characters becomes intensely ironic as the story progresses. Rather than confront one another as truly hostile opponents, the four men engage in the friendly competition of card games and the sorts of arguments over politics and religion that occur between pals in any corner tavern. Irony is paramount when Hawkins, a self-professed communist, and the Irish Catholic Noble discuss politics and religion in such a civil fashion, since politics and religion were, of course, central to the larger Anglo-Irish conflict. The many rich and pervasive ironies reward rereading, and the grim denouement has a powerful impact: "Guests" stays with the reader long after the initial reading.

BIBLIOGRAPHY

Evans, Robert C., and Richard Harp, eds. *Frank O'Connor: New Perspectives*. West Cornwall, Conn.: Locust Hill, 1998.

McKeon, Jim. *Frank O'Connor: A Life*. Edinburgh: Mainstream, 1998.

Sheehy, Maurice, ed. *Michael/Frank: Studies on Frank O'Connor*. London: Macmillan, 1969.

Chip Rogers

H

"HALF BROTHERS, THE" Elizabeth Gas-
kell **(1859)** Published in the collection *Round the
Sofa and Other Tales* (1859), "The Half Brothers" is, as
its title suggests, about two brothers, and it recalls
those Old Testament brothers divided by enmity: Cain
and Abel, Jacob and Esau, Joseph and his brothers.
However, this story of brothers is one of faithful love, a
tale that embodies Christian self-sacrifice and forgiveness as it portrays one brother as a savior. As in many
of Elizabeth Gaskell's stories, the mother's love is
redemptive, while the father's harshness is fatal, a sin
for which he ultimately repents.

Gaskell's tale is told in the first person by the younger
brother about his half-brother Gregory. The narrator,
who never gives his name, has been the petted child of
his mother's second marriage to a wealthy farmer, William Preston. His older brother Gregory is the son of his
mother's first marriage, when she was only 17, to a
young farmer who died of consumption three years
after the marriage. Gregory is the only surviving child
of this union, born after his father's death and just a
week after his older sister died of scarlet fever. The
mother's grief at the double loss of husband and daughter is so intense that she is "just stunned with this last
blow." She is unable to cry until Gregory is born, when
she weeps "day and night, day and night." Gregory is
then everything to her, and "she seemed after that to
think of nothing but her new little baby."

The story issues from this mother's intense love for
her children, a love that triumphs over the cold harshness of her second husband. William Preston is jealous
of his pretty wife's passionate love for Gregory when
she clearly does not love him, although "a more dutiful
wife, I have heard him himself say, could never have
been." The farmer "wanted her to love him more, and
perhaps that was all well and good; but he wanted her
to love her child less, and that was an evil wish." Eventually, Preston viciously "cursed and swore" at Gregory, and his tirade brings on the early birth of Gregory's
half-brother. After this, the narrator tells us that his
Aunt Fanny declared that her sister "Helen did not
wish to live, and so just let herself die away without
trying to take hold on life." Before Helen dies, she
enjoins Gregory to love his baby brother.

Gregory grows up neglected and scorned. He is
"lumpish and loutish, awkward and ungainly, marring
whatever he meddled in, and many a hard word and
sharp scolding did he get from the people about the
farm. . . . I am ashamed—my heart is sore to think
how I fell into the fashion of the family, and slighted
my poor orphan step-brother." But Gregory, who is
termed "sulky" and "stupid" even by his Aunt Fanny, is
praised by Adam the shepherd, who "said he had never
seen a lad like him." Adam, named for the father of
mankind, is the first good father Gregory has known,
and the boy flourishes as a shepherd under his loving
tutelage.

Adam's faith in Gregory is justified when Gregory rescues his younger brother, who is desperately lost at night
in a snowstorm on the fells. Gregory appears like the

Good Shepherd himself, "wrapped in his maud," and he and his collie Lassie—who has also been abused by Mr. Preston—together save Gregory's young brother. Gregory gives his cloak to his brother, and he himself freezes to death, his last words to his brother a remembrance of their mother's deathbed wish that they love each other.

The narrator's father is utterly transformed by Gregory's sacrifice. He cries for the first time in the story, painful, "unwonted" tears that connect his grieving for Gregory to his wife's mourning for her dead little girl. Gregory's "still, cold face" links him to the narrator's previous description of his dead half-sister's "pretty, pale, dead face," the beloved, imagined faces their narrating brother recalls. Preston's final tribute to the courageous boy he scorned is twofold. His last words are "God forgive me my hardness of heart towards the fatherless child!" and after his death his family finds instructions that he is to be buried at the foot of Gregory's grave. The final act of repentance, though, is the narrator's. His words serve as testament to the power of the Word. In recording Gregory's act of brotherly love, the narrator pays homage both to him and to their mother, whose love engendered such self-sacrifice.

BIBLIOGRAPHY
Elizabeth Gaskell. *Round the Sofa.* London: Sampson, Law, 1859.

Deborah Denenholz Morse

"HAMMER OF GOD, THE" G. K. Chesterton (1910)

A short story by G. K. Chesterton originally published in The *Story-Teller* magazine in 1910, published in America's The *Saturday Evening Post* in 1919 as "A Bolt from the Blue" and collected in *The Innocence of Father Brown* in 1911. This story is the fourth to feature as a detective the unassuming Roman Catholic priest Father Brown, who solves crimes through his knowledge of evil in everyday life.

The plot concerns two brothers, Colonel Bohun, a drunkard and playboy, and Reverend Bohun, curate of an Anglican church. The story commences with the Reverend Bohun meeting Colonel Bohun in the town square as the minister is on his way to church and the military man is making his way to continue an adulterous affair with the blacksmith's wife. The reverend castigates the colonel for his blasphemous ways and continues on to the church to engage in prayer, only to be interrupted by the news that his brother has been struck dead in the square. The body is lying in the center of the square with its skull completely flattened, and a tiny hammer is found next to the body. Father Brown arrives on the scene just as the town's suspicion focuses on the blacksmith, who turns out to have a firm alibi for the time of death. The blacksmith, a staunch Presbyterian, proffers a biblically accented theory that God smote the colonel down in punishment for his sins. Father Brown assures the townspeople that a man has committed the crime but that the joke that the blacksmith threw the hammer from the next town comes closest to the true explanation of it. The priest then escorts the minister to the top of the church steeple, where he confronts him with his knowledge that the minister himself murdered his brother by dropping the small hammer from that great height. He further tells the reverend that he will make no mention of the crime's solution, offering the man a chance to redeem himself. The story ends with the curate confessing his guilt to the police.

Like Chesterton's other Father Brown stories, "The Hammer of God" offers symbolic imagery and metaphysical ruminations along with a murderer who has been established as the least likely suspect. Echoing the biblical story of Cain and Abel, Chesterton portrays Reverend Bohun as confused by the great height of the church into believing he had the authority of God to choose who deserves life and who death. A description of the gothic architecture of the church edifice as offering a "topsy-turvy" view of the world melds with a larger statement about the dizzying heights offered by a religiosity cut off from human compassion. Father Brown offers the curate a paradox: "Humility is the mother of giants. One sees great things from the valley, only small things from the peak." But ultimately, the curate comes across as a fundamentally good man, who repents for his crime by asserting his free will over his false conception of himself as godhead.

BIBLIOGRAPHY
Chesterton, G. K. *The Innocence of Father Brown.* New York: Quiet Vision Press, 2001.

Jennifer A. Halloran

"HAPPY PRINCE, THE" Oscar Wilde **(1888)** Arguably the most popular of Oscar Wilde's fairy tales, "The Happy Prince" is the first story in *The Happy Prince and Other Tales,* which was published in 1888. The narrative, which has been favorably compared to the work of Hans Christian Andersen and Andrew Lang, tells of the transformation of a swallow and a young prince.

The story begins with the swallow's decision to leave his earthbound wife, a reed, to join his fellow birds in Egypt. Having waited in the hope that his wife would accompany him, the bird migrates alone. After a day's flight, he seeks shelter from the elements beneath the bejeweled statue of a young man and falls asleep. Falling water awakens the swallow, who finds that the annoying moisture is not rain but teardrops from the statue's sapphire eyes. The beautiful prince explains that he grew up removed from ordinary concerns in the palace of Sans Souci and knew only human happiness; however, since he was now outside that cultivated environment, he saw the grief of the people he had ruled and wept for their sorrows, despite having a leaden heart.

The swallow becomes, reluctantly, the prince's messenger. The bird takes the rubies that adorn the prince's sword to a seamstress whose son is ill, delivers the prince's sapphire eyes to a poet starving in a garret, and gives the gold leaf that covers the statue to the poor of the city. Eventually, however, the bird dies in the cold, and the statue of the prince grows shabby. The mayor tears down the statue and has it melted for a new monument. As the mayor and the town councillors squabble over which of them deserves the honor, a workman notices that the leaden heart has not melted and discards it. An angel from heaven finds the dead bird and the rejected heart to be the most valuable items in the city, and God grants the bird and the prince eternal life in the garden of paradise.

The fairy tale, whose moralism seems antithetical to Wilde's aesthetic (see AESTHETICISM), is consistent with Wilde's sense of art. The genre, which may seem as simple as the lines of an Oriental drawing, has additionally a self-contained beauty: complete in itself and internally balanced. Paradoxically, the form presents truth without a slavish imitation of real life.

Short narrative, and the fairy story in particular, seem well suited to Wilde's talent as a raconteur: These forms are compact and to the point, and they can blend sheer delight with surprising depth. Some critics, however, see Wilde's success as a teller of fairy tales (whatever their appeal to an adult audience) as a symptom of his emotional immaturity. Another view might be that Wilde was playing with his audience in presenting a serious message for adults in a seemingly frivolous form for children.

Paradox is an important element in "The Happy Prince." Although the statue has a heart of lead, it is purer than the gold leaf that clothes the body of the statue, and the prince's artificial heart is more sympathetic than the human hearts within the presumably democratic leaders of the town. The metal heart is closer to the biblical heart of flesh than the living prince's heart was. The prince has a greater beauty after stripping himself of his outward attractions; the nobility of his soul is greater than that of his blood. The allegedly democratic rulers of the town, the mayor and the council, lack that inherent nobility of action and show less concern for the poor than does the aristocratic prince. Finally, the two most precious items in the city are on a dust heap; they seem to the inhabitants to be useless now that they have been used to improve the lot of the poor. All the good the prince and the swallow have done seems to have been for nothing, but it earns them a great reward.

Christian commentators on the story have seen the prince as a Christ figure who empties himself as a sacrifice for others. These critics also see "The Happy Prince" as a fable of a transformation from selfish interest to agape, the highest form of love. The prince has been aware only of aesthetic beauty; the bird cares only for himself. The sight of the unfortunate brings them to express a generalized love for humanity fully and unselfishly. Like Christ, the prince ultimately dies for his people.

Some have seen in this story a blend of Pater's valuation of ancient Greek ideals with Christian principles. The emphasis on physical beauty comes from Pater's thought, while the later emphasis on spiritual beauty comes from Christianity. Other recent commentators have focused on the elements of the story that seem to express Wilde's sexual preference, and some look at the tale as a coded coming out. The fact that the swallow leaves his wife and keeps the company of a handsome young man has received emphasis and attention, as has the fact that none of the marriages in *The Happy Prince and Other Tales* produce offspring. Queer theorists see childless marriages in literature as a way of masking homosexual union, and other scholars have seen in the friendship between the prince and the swallow a veiled but unmistakable indication of sexual preference. They class this story with other Victorian literature in which strong same-sex friendship is a cover for homosexual love. The emphasis on the aesthetic beauty of the prince's statue and the growing sensitivity of the prince are also seen as peculiarly homosexual concerns. Those who draw on Wilde's biography note that he once remarked that his fairy stories were not just for children but also for a particular kind of adult, one who presumably could break the code.

Wilde himself, however, argued that life imitates art, rather than the reverse, and he saw in this tale a prefiguring of his transformation from the carefree, possibly careless, celebrity to the wiser and more compassionate man who emerged from Reading Gaol.

BIBLIOGRAPHY

Duffy, John-Charles. "Gay-Related Themes in Wilde's Fairy Tales," *Victorian Literature and Culture* 29 (2001): 327–349.

Knight, G. Wilson. "Christ and Wilde." In *Oscar Wilde: A Collection of Critical Essays,* edited by Richard Ellman, 138–149. Englewood Cliffs, N.J.: Prentice Hall, 1969.

Martin, Robert K. "Oscar Wilde and the Fairy Tale: 'The Happy Prince' as Self-Dramatization," *Studies in Short Fiction* 16 (1979): 74–77.

Wilde, Oscar. *Complete Shorter Fiction.* Oxford: Oxford University Press, 1992.

Karen Keck

HARDY, THOMAS (1840–1928)

On June 2, 1840, Thomas Hardy was born to Thomas and Jemima Hand Hardy in Higher Bockhampton, Dorset, and into the old Dorchester family. Encouraged by his mother in his love of reading, the young Hardy read Dryden's *Virgil* at age 10 and attended the village school. Hardy later graduated from the British School at Dorchester, where he had received a strong education grounded in the classics under the direction of Wiliam Barnes, a Dorchester schoolmaster and a poet of some distinction. At age 16 Hardy became the apprentice to an architect who specialized in church restoration. During this period, Hardy made the acquaintance of his great friend, Horace Moule. The Cambridge-educated Moule encouraged Hardy's literary inclinations and promoted his friend's career as an author. While employed as an assistant architect in London, Hardy read furiously at the British Museum in his spare time, and he began his lifelong passion of writing poetry before beginning his attempts at fiction. All of his early attempts to publish his poetry in periodicals failed.

Returning to Dorset because of ill health in 1867, he wrote his first novel, *The Poor Man and the Lady;* aware that the public craved fiction over poetry, he desired to be a successful author, a goal he believed could be achieved only in prose. His first novel being rejected by publishers and consequently lost, Hardy went on to publish anonymously the sensational *Desperate Remedies* (1871), which earned a passionless reception from the reviewers. Despite this inauspicious beginning, Hardy has come to be perhaps the most renowned English man of letters of his time. Having a worldwide reputation, he is regarded as one of the major late 19th-century novelists and an influential force as an early 20th-century poet. In 1870, Hardy met Emma Lavinia Gifford, whom he married September 17, 1874. Their early marriage was happy, but they later grew apart as Hardy's literary, philosophical, and theological interests drew him further into questioning his faith; ultimately, after the the 1876 suicide of Moule, his atheism and sadness at the loss of his friend cast a shadow over Hardy's remaining life and work. By now, Hardy was well known in literary circles, and among his best friends were Edmund Gosse, the country's most influential literary critic, and the author James Barrie. In 1885, after the publication of *The Trumpet Major* (1880) and *Two on a Tower* (1882), Hardy returned to Dorchester and Max Gate, the Victorian mansion he had designed himself. Despondent in his marriage, Hardy was guaranteed fame if not happiness by his tragic novel *The Mayor of Casterbridge* (1886) and the mellower *The Woodlanders* (1887) He continued to write throughout his life, producing a total of 14 novels that were both serialized in leading periodicals of the day and published in traditional two- and three-volume formats and later in one-volume form.

By the early 1890s, Hardy's career was at its peak, but he balked at the respectability imposed on him as a novelist. In *Tess of the D'Urbervilles* (1891), Hardy consciously rebelled against his public and critics. The novel provoked a furious reaction that was only eclipsed by Hardy's final novel, *Jude the Obscure* (1895). In an attempt to enter public debate over the issues of authorship, responsibility, and morality, Hardy participated in various periodical forums on the subject of writing fiction; perhaps the most important of these was an essay he wrote for the *New Review* in January 1890, "Candour in English Fiction," which clearly states his belief that the task of the writer to create an honest portrayal of life. His other important essays include "The Dorsetshire Labourer" (*Longman's Magazine,* 1883), "The Profitable Reading of Fiction" (*Forum,* 1888), and "The Science of Fiction" (*New Review,* 1891).

Aside from his novels, Hardy was a prolific writer of short stories; he wrote 53 short stories, often for the MAGAZINE market, before collecting 37 in four volumes: WESSEX TALES: *Strange, Lively, and Commonplace* (six short stories written between 1879 and 1888 published in one and two volumes in 1888, including the much-anthologized "THE WITHERED ARM"), *A Group of Noble Dames* (10 short stories written between 1878 and 1890 published in 1891), *Life's Little Ironies: A Set of Tales with Some Colloquial Sketches Entitled "A Few Crusted Characters"* (nine short stories written between 1882 and 1893 published in 1894, including "ON THE WESTERN CIRCUIT" and "THE MELANCHOLY HUSSAR OF THE GERMAN LEGION"), and *A Changed Man, The Waiting Supper, and Other Tales* (12 short stories written between 1881 and 1900 published in 1913). These collections of short fiction were both well received and illustrative of the narrative techniques, themes, issues, folklore, and characters found in his novels (see "THE ROMANTIC ADVENTURES OF A MILKMAID"). Other stories, notably "AN INDISCRETION IN THE LIFE OF AN HEIRESS" (1878), were never collected by Hardy into a volume but have also come to be much studied.

Hardy claimed that a "story must be exceptional enough to justify its telling. We tale-tellers are all Ancient Mariners, and none of us is warranted in stopping Wedding Guests . . . unless he has something more unusual to relate than the ordinary experience of every average man and woman" (Brady, 4). Although sometimes uneven in quality—often under the pressure of publishing deadlines for periodicals—the tales are expressions of everyday life and its difficulties in Wessex (Hardy's fictional Dorset) as well as expressive of his all-encompassing beliefs in the importance of law, social justice, the plight of children (especially when illegitimate), the victimizing power of public opinion, and the role of family history in the life of an individual. Hardy's characters—in both his short and his long fiction—are posed at the nexus of a complex web of social intricacies, and his portraits challenge the inconsistencies in Victorian mores and conventions. Editors often viewed them as too outspoken for Victorian audiences. For example, *A Group of Noble Dames* was intended for serialization in the *Graphic* in 1890; upon receipt of the manuscript, the assistant editor, William Locker, wrote to Hardy that the directors of the paper had been offended by the collection because "Many fathers are accustomed to read or have read to their family-circles the stories in the *Graphic;* and I cannot think that they would approve for this purpose a series of tales almost every one of which turns upon questions of childbirth, and those relations between the sexes over which conventionality is accustomed . . . to draw a veil" (Millgate, 72). He then demanded that Hardy make major revisions to "Barbara of the House of Grebe," "The Marchioness of Stonehenge," "Anna, Lady Baxby," and "The Lady Icenway," while the last two stories, "Squire Petrick's Lady" and "Lady Mottisfont," were completely rejected. The humiliation for an author of Hardy's standing was almost unbearable. He believed in an ethics of compassion and strove to drive his readers away from complacent assumptions and conventional, unquestioned reactions to the realities of human existence if only the editors would allow his fictions to stand as he had conceived them rather than bowdlerize them for publication.

Following the extensive compromises he had to make in order to see *A Group of Noble Dames, Tess,* and

Jude published, and after the intensely controversial reception of *Tess* and *Jude,* Hardy turned away from writing fiction for good in order to return to his first love, poetry. After the publication of *The Dynasts* (1903–6), Hardy declined the offer of a knighthood and was, instead, awarded the highest honor that can be bestowed on an author by the Crown, the Order of Merit, in 1910. In 1912, Emma died, and Hardy felt a profound sense of guilt over the last years of their marriage; however, less than two years later, on February 10, 1914, Hardy married Florence Emily Dugdale, who was 37 years his junior.

In addition to scores of letters and notebooks, Hardy left an autobiography in two volumes, *The Early Years of Thomas Hardy 1840–1891* and *The Later Years of Thomas Hardy 1892–1928,* which was published post-humously under the name of Florence Emily Hardy in 1928 and 1930, respectively; they have since been republished and reedited as his own work in one volume, *The Life and Work of Thomas Hardy.*

At his death in 1928, Thomas Hardy's ashes were buried in Westminster Abbey and his heart was buried in his first wife's grave.

BIBLIOGRAPHY

Brady, Kristin. *The Short Stories of Thomas Hardy.* London: Macmillan, 1982.

Hardy, Thomas. *Collected Short Stories.* London: Macmillan, 1888.

———. *A Group of Noble Dames.* London: Osgood, 1891.

———. *Life's Little Ironies.* London: Osgood, 1894.

———. *Wessex Tales.* London: Macmillan, 1888.

Millgate, Michael. *Thomas Hardy.* Oxford: Oxford University Press, 2004.

Ray, Martin. *Thomas Hardy: A Textual Study of the Short Stories.* Aldershot, England: Ashgate, 1997.

Widdowson, Peter. *Thomas Hardy.* Plymouth, England: Northcote House, 1996.

Sara Maier

HARLAND, HENRY (1861–1905)

Although American by birth (brought up in Connecticut and New York) Henry Harland moved to Britain in 1889. There, as editor of the YELLOW BOOK (April 1894–April 1897), Harland shaped the British short story through his selections and his peevish criticism. The *Yellow Book*'s prospectus declared, "It will publish no serials; but its complete stories will sometimes run to a considerable length in themselves." Harland had a personal stake in the *Yellow Book:* He was a writer himself, producing small corpus of dated, stylized work. The mannered stories in *A Latin-Quarter Courtship* (1889), *Grey Roses* (1895), and *Comedies and Errors* (1898) fall into two categories: reminiscences of the Latin Quarter and tales of nonexistent Eastern European royalty. At least one of his own short stories appeared in each of the 13 quarterly volumes of the *Yellow Book,* and he often paid contributors out of his own pocket.

Writers of the 1890s identified Harland with the art of the short story. Richard Le Gallienne, a regular contributor to the *Yellow Book,* recalled Harland "excitedly propounding the *dernier mot* on the build of the short story or the art of prose. . . . The polishing of his prose was for him his being's end and aim, and I have often seen him at that sacred task of a forenoon, in his study-bedroom, still in pajamas and dressing-gown, with a coffee-pot on the hearth, bending over an exquisite piece of handwriting, like a goldsmith at his bench." More distinguished writers shared this view. HENRY JAMES, for instance, called Harland "The Story-teller at Large" in an essay remarking how the short story had "of late become an object of almost extravagant dissertation" (650).

Harland's only signed, published remarks on the art of the short story appeared in the *Academy* for July 1897. This essay, "Concerning the Short Story," distinguishes between the "normal man" and the "artist." The normal man or "manufacturer" of fiction is content to work with "idea" or an "incident," while the artist begins with an "impression." This "is never a simple thing, which can be conveyed in two minutes' conversation. It is never an obvious thing. It is always a complex thing, it is always elusive. It is a thing of shades and niceties and fine distinctions." Moreover, brevity alone does not make a story a short story, distinguished as art: A "story is a short story, no matter how many pages it may cover, in which you have expressed your impression with the greatest possible economy of means. The manufacturer's economy was an economy of matter; the artist's economy must be an economy of means." For such reasons, "the short story will never be popular in England."

One of Harland's most notoriously successful fictions was his own biography. Though born and brought up in Connecticut and New York, he claimed to have been born in St. Petersburg and educated at the University of Paris. So goes the account that persisted in the *Dictionary of National Biography* until its 2004 revision.

BIBLIOGRAPHY

Beckson, Karl. *Henry Harland: His Life and Work.* London: 1890s Society, 1978.

Harland, Henry. *The Cardinal's Snuff Box.* London: John Lane, 1900.

———. "Concerning the Short Story," *Academy* (June 5, 1897): 6–7.

———. *Comedies and Errors.* London: John Lane, 1898.

———. *Grey Roses.* London: John Lane, 1895.

———. *A Latin-Quarter Courtship.* London: Cassell, 1889.

James, Henry. "The Story-Teller at Large," *Fortnightly Review* 69 (April 11, 1898): 650–654.

Mix, Katherine Lyon. *A Study in Yellow: The Yellow Book and Its Contributors.* Lawrence: University of Kansas Press, 1960.

"What the 'Yellow Book' Is to Be—Some Meditations with Its Editors," *Sketch* 5 (April 11, 1894): 557–558.

Winnie Chan

HARTLEY, L. P. (1895–1972)

Born in Whittesley in Cambridgeshire, Leslie Poles Hartley served in the British army from 1916 to 1918 but did not see combat. After his discharge, he completed a B.A. at Balliol College of Oxford University in 1922. Although he tutored at a preparatory school in the early 1920s and lectured at Trinity College of Cambridge University in 1964, for the most part he concentrated on his writing. He inherited a financial interest in a brickworks from his father, and it provided him with a comfortable income that made it unnecessary for him to teach or to seek other work to supplement his earnings from his books.

In addition to being a prolific author of novels chronicling the manners, habits, attitudes, and mores of upper-middle-class British society in the early to mid-20th century—*The Shrimp and the Anemone* (1944), *Eustace and Hilda* (1947), and *The Go-Between* (1953) are the best known—he also published several collections of short stories. There are many connec-

tions between Hartley's novels and stories, but even though his novels often had their beginnings in his stories, he viewed the stories as important works in themselves, and he concentrated a great deal on their structures, pacing, and details. Indeed, although the settings and characters are similar in Hartley's stories and novels, the stories typically explore situations and themes that are considerably more gothic than those treated in the novels. In the manner of his acknowledged influences—Edgar Allan Poe, CHARLOTTE BRONTË, Nathaniel Hawthorne, and HENRY JAMES—Hartley emphasizes psychological issues that are brought to a crisis by preternatural influences. In his most macabre stories, Hartley moves beyond the gothic into the horror genre. Of his gothic stories, "Two for the River," in which the spirit of a house objects to being sold and responds in a violent manner, and "Someone in the Lift," in which a young boy inadvertently kills his father, who is dressed as Santa Claus, are among his most fully realized efforts. Of his horror stories, "The Killing Bottle," "Night Fears," "Please Do Not Touch," and "The Travelling Grave" are among the most chillingly effective.

BIBLIOGRAPHY

Hartley, L. P. *Complete Short Stories of L. P. Hartley.* London: Beaufort Books, 1973.

———. *Collected Macabre Stories.* Leyburn: Tartarus Press, 2001.

———. *The Killing Bottle.* London: Putnam, 1932.

——— *Mrs. Carteret Receives and Other Stories.* London: Hamish Hamilton, 1971.

——— *Night Fears and Other Stories.* London: Putnam, 1924.

——— *The Travelling Grave.* London: Arkham House, 1948.

———. *Two for the River.* London: Hamish Hamilton, 1961.

———. *The White Wand and Other Stories.* London: Hamish Hamilton, 1954.

Jones, E. T. *L. P. Hartley.* Boston: Twayne, 1978.

Wright, Adrian. *Foreign Country: The Life of L. P. Hartley.* London: A. Deutch, 1996.

Martin Kich

"HAUNTED HOUSE, A" VIRGINIA WOOLF (1921)

In 1921 VIRGINIA WOOLF published her first collection of short stories, titled *MONDAY OR TUESDAY,* which included "A Haunted House" as the opening piece. Although she continued to publish short fiction, this proved to be the only collection of such work published in her lifetime. Leonard Woolf, her husband, later chose the story for inclusion in the posthumous *A Haunted House and Other Stories* (1944).

Just 10 paragraphs long, "A Haunted House" depicts an unnamed, ungendered character who perceives (or perhaps dreams) that a loving but long-deceased couple haunts the country house he or she inhabits. Centuries ago, a woman died there, and her lover left for faraway lands, returning only in death. Reunited, the pair now wander around the rooms and the surrounding gardens, reminiscing to each other about the past, searching for "their joy." This search disturbs the contemporary couple currently in residence: As they try to sleep or read, they sense movement—doors opening and shutting, the ghosts walking, the house beating as if it were a human heart.

Formally, the story resembles a prose poem more than a traditional narrative. Several repeated lines ("safe, safe, safe") act as refrains, and repeated phrases ("treasure buried") serve as poetic conceits, or unifying metaphors. The structure also prefigures the stream-of-consciousness style and seamless use of multiple points of view that Woolf perfected in novels like *Mrs. Dalloway* (1925) and *The Waves* (1931). As in these other texts, here she creates a collage of bits of dialogue, forcing the reader to unravel the identity of each speaker or pronoun. Sometimes the ghosts speak to each other; sometimes they speak to the inhabitants of the house. Likewise, sometimes the couple speaks to each other; sometimes they speak to the ghosts; sometimes they speak directly to the reader.

The action, however, occurs not in the plot but in the thematic amalgamation. Concerns more fully explored in later Woolf works, including sensual perceptions of the natural world, the relationships between individuals, and a preoccupation with mortality, gestate in "A Haunted House." Our inability to decide conclusively whether the narrator imagines, dreams, or actually witnesses any supernatural phenomenon echoes *The TURN OF THE SCREW* (1897), a novella by HENRY JAMES in which an interpretation of the story hinges on an evaluation of the protagonist's sanity and trustworthiness. Like James, Woolf reacts against the constricting social mores of Victorian society: In contrast to the repressive atmosphere of late 19th-century England, an exuberant sexuality infuses this story, from its descriptions of light altering the colors of apples, leaves, and roses, traditional symbols of carnal love and knowledge, to the ghosts' recollections of their "kisses without number."

These traces of romantic pleasure may stem from the house's real-life inspiration—Asheham, an estate in Sussex rented by Woolf and her sister in 1911. Virginia and Leonard courted along its grounds, and they spent their first night as a married couple beneath its roof. But Asheham itself iterates Talland House, where Woolf summered happily as a child and to which she imaginatively returns throughout her oeuvre (Lee, 25). However, an unease permeates the story, reminding us that the house is, after all, haunted.

"A Haunted House" concludes with the narrator waking in the night, frantic, crying out. Indeed, Woolf rented Asheham after her doctors advised her to leave London to recuperate from a mental breakdown, and the story might therefore be read as a portrayal of someone suffering from psychological torment. Published just two years after the signing of the Treaty of Versailles, which ended WORLD WAR I, the story also reflects a very real loss: Close to 3 million soldiers suffered casualties, almost 1 million fatally, during the so-called Great War. A whole generation of European men and women lay buried, and their ephemeral sacrifice haunted the country.

BIBLIOGRAPHY
Benzel, Kathryn N., and Ruth Hoberman. *Trespassing Boundaries: Virginia Woolf's Short Fiction.* New York: Palgrave, Macmillan, 2004.
Lee, Hermione. *Virginia Woolf.* London: Vintage, 1999.
Woolf Virginia. "A Haunted House." In *Monday or Tuesday: Eight Stories.* 1921. Reprint, New York: Dover, 1997.

Jessica Allen

HAUNTED MAN AND THE GHOST'S BARGAIN, THE CHARLES DICKENS (1848)

Originally slated to appear in 1847, "The Haunted Man and the Ghost's Bargain," the fifth and last installment of the Christmas book series was delayed because of

CHARLES DICKENS's exhaustion at maintaining the serialization of *Dombey and Son* (1846–48).

In the 1852 preface to his collected *Christmas Books,* Dickens wrote that his purpose for this series was "to awaken some loving and forbearing thoughts, never out of season in a Christian land." By the last two stories in this series, however, critics were losing patience with the didacticism and sentimentality of the Christmas stories, though they sold relatively well. *The Haunted Man* sold about 18,000 copies between December 19 and Christmas, making a profit of almost £800. In comparison with his novels and with the first three Christmas books, *The Haunted Man* is sparsely furnished with the realistic details, the characters, the humor, and the incidents that otherwise fill Dickens's fiction.

According to Harry Stone, Dickens's Christmas book method takes "a protagonist who displays false values" and makes him, "through a series of extraordinary events, see his error" (494). *The Haunted Man* opens with an esteemed professor of chemistry sitting alone indulging in an extended period of despair after the death of his sister and the loss of the woman he had wished to marry. Redlaw's grief is deepened by the fact that his best friend seduced his sister and married his lover. Significantly, in the August before Dickens sat down in October to complete the story, Dickens's own beloved sister, Fanny, had died of tuberculosis.

In the tale, Redlaw is strangely unsurprised when an exact copy of himself appears in spirit form. This phantom doppelgänger haunting Redlaw is not possessed of goodwill toward his material other, like Marley or the three ghosts of *A CHRISTMAS CAROL,* but rather tempts Redlaw to extend his withdrawal from the rest of humanity. Redlaw expresses a desire to be relieved of his sorrow, and the spirit offers him a gift that, at first, very much appeals to Redlaw: the loss of any and all sorrowful memories. Redlaw accepts, and though his own painful memories ebb away, he also finds that he possesses a sort of Midas touch that removes the sorrowful memories from anyone he meets. Furthermore, he realizes that he has lost his ability to express or feel human compassion. In a November 1848 letter, Dickens wrote, "my point is that bad and good are inextricably linked in remembrance, and that you could not

choose the enjoyment of recollecting only the good" (*Letters,* 5:443).

Only the wife of the custodian of the college, Milly, who has experienced the death of her child, and the young animalistic street urchin she has newly adopted are immune to his Midas touch: The child because he has no humanity to lose and Milly because she contains humanity to an extraordinary degree. Redlaw realizes the monster he has become, and Milly helps him and those whom his touch has crippled (including the son born of the marriage between his former love and his former best friend) restore their memories and their full humanity. Rather than social reform, *The Haunted Man* emphasizes "the reformation of the individual heart" (Kaplan, 180). Redlaw, as the great professor, contrasts the wisdom learned from books with the wisdom learned from the emotions.

The story ends with a Christmas banquet underneath the prayerful inscription on a generations-old portrait in the Great Hall of the school: "Lord keep my Memory green." Redlaw finally understands the ambiguity of the inscription and prays that his own recollections—of the good as well as of the painful—shall be kept alive.

BIBLIOGRAPHY

Dickens, Charles. *The Letter of Charles Dickens: The Pilgrim Edition,* vol. 5: 1847–1849. Edited by Graham Story and Kenneth Fielding. New York: Oxford University Press, 1981.

Kaplan, Fred. *Dickens: A Biography.* Baltimore: Johns Hopkins University Press, 1988.

Thomas, Deborah A. *Dickens and the Short Story.* Philadelphia: University of Pennsylvania Press, 1982.

Stone, Harry. "Dickens' Artistry and *The Haunted Man,*" *South Atlantic Quarterly* 61, no. 4 (1962): 492–505.

Chris Barnes

HEART OF DARKNESS JOSEPH CONRAD (1899)

The essay "Geography and Some Explorers" (1924) describes JOSEPH CONRAD as a schoolboy amusing classmates by pointing to Africa on a map and declaring, "When I grow up I shall go there." Eighteen years later, in 1890, Conrad obtained a post as steamboat captain with a trading company in the Belgian Congo (now Democratic Republic of the Congo). He undertook the 1,000-mile journey up the Congo River to Stanley Falls, where a great depression fell on him. His encounter with the grim reality of European exploitation undermined his faith in commerce with developing countries. He returned to England in 1891 and checked into a hospital for malaria and dysentery. Conrad went to sea just once more after returning from Africa, choosing to devote his time instead to writing literature. In 1897, he wrote about the disillusioning experience in Africa for *Blackwood's Magazine,* which serialized *Heart of Darkness* in three parts (February, March, and April) and afterward published a revised version of the story in a separate volume, YOUTH: A NARRATIVE; and Two Other Stories (1902).

Conrad's most famous novella, *Heart of Darkness* (adapted into Francis Ford Coppola's film *Apocalypse Now* in 1979) is a fictional treatment of his experiences in Africa. Charlie Marlow recounts the traumatic Congo expedition to four companions aboard the *Nellie,* a cruising yawl anchored in the Thames estuary. London has also been "one of the dark places of the earth," Marlow begins, thus evoking European imperialistic history at the beginning of his tale about a journey through Africa in search of a white explorer, reminiscent of Henry Stanley's famous discovery of Doctor David Livingstone. At the first company station along the Congo, Marlow finds malnourished native workers dying before the eyes of an immaculately dressed chief accountant. The company agents, ironically described as "pilgrims," turn out to be little more than European colonists intent on exploiting the natives for profit. The corruption Marlow encounters at each stage of the journey—a French ship firing blindly into the continent, the rapacious Eldorado Exploring Expedition—starkly contrasts with the lofty rhetoric about bringing civilization to Africa.

At each stop Marlow hears of a legendary ivory trader named Kurtz, whose "moral ideas" might redeem the colonial enterprise. After long delays at the Central Station, Marlow pilots the steamer upriver amid perilous snags, shallows, and fogs. Just a few miles from Kurtz's outpost, natives attack the steamer with arrows and kill Marlow's helmsman with a long spear before being frightened away by the steamboat whistle. A Russian traveler reveals that the ambush has been ordered by Kurtz, who wishes to remain among the natives. Far from civilizing them, Kurtz has himself "gone native" by attending mysterious rituals, obtaining ivory through tribal warfare, involving himself with a native woman, and surrounding his hut with human heads. Kurtz's eloquent report about educating the natives for the International Society for the Suppression of Savage Customs ends with the contradictory postscript: "Exterminate all the brutes!" Marlow finds devoted native attendants carrying on a stretcher the dying, emaciated Kurtz, whose final words resonantly express a sense of horror. When Kurtz's fiancée in Belgium asks about Kurtz's last words, Marlow lies to protect her innocence and says that her name had been spoken last. The narrative ends with Marlow's audience aboard the *Nellie* reflecting on what they have just heard.

The frame narrative, or what is essentially a story-within-a-story as an unnamed narrator listens to Marlow's tale, distances the audience from the traumatic experience and enables Marlow to describe events only partially understood at the time. Marlow's confusion is registered through a process Ian Watt calls "delayed decoding," or the deferred explanation of sense impressions, as when "sticks" flying through the air turn out to be arrows. Like the figurative journeys in many of Conrad's plots, Marlow's journey is both a literal journey into Africa and a metaphorical journey into the depths of consciousness. Marlow faces a "choice of nightmares" between the inhumane commerce of the company manager and the tortured idealism of Kurtz, who at least struggles with moral convictions. Kurtz is the conflicted representative of European imperialism ("All Europe contributed to the making of Kurtz") in whom Marlow finds a double or alter ego with whose moral struggle he can identify. According to Marlow, Kurtz at least judges himself in the end with the famously ambiguous last words "The horror! The horror!" Conrad's ambivalent attitude toward colonialism—the African novelist Chinua Achebe called Conrad "a thoroughgoing racist" while other critics have considered the novella progressive in its critique of imperialism—has been a major reason for enduring interest in the story.

BIBLIOGRAPHY
Achebe, Chinua. *Hopes and Impediments: Selected Essays 1965–1987.* London: Heinemann, 1988.

Apocalypse Now (1979). Directed by Francis Coppola. Written by John Milius and Francis Coppola. Paramount Pictures, 1992.

Conrad, Joseph. *Heart of Darkness*. Oxford: Oxford University Press, 1990.

———. *Last Essays*. New York: Doubleday & Page, 1926.

Kimbrough, Robert, ed. *Heart of Darkness: Norton Critical Edition*. 3rd ed. New York and London: Norton, 1988.

Said, Edward W. *Culture and Imperialism*. London: Chatto and Windus, 1993.

Watt, Ian. *Conrad in the Nineteenth Century*. Berkeley: University of California Press, 1979.

Matt Rubery

"HIGHLAND WIDOW, THE" WALTER SCOTT (1827)

This story by the celebrated Scottish novelist Sir WALTER SCOTT (1771–1832) first appeared as part of the collection *Chronicles of the Canongate*. Here, Chrystal Croftangry, the narrator of the collection, retells the widow's story from the memorandum of a late friend, Martha Bethune Baliol. She herself hears the story from her Highland tour guide, Donald MacLeish. The narrative begins with Mrs. Bethune Baliol's Highland tour, which climaxes with her encounter with the mysterious "Woman of the Tree," Elspat MacTavish. Elspat's husband, the cateran (warrior) Hamish MacTavish, known as MacTavish Mhor, is feared throughout the Highlands and the Lowlands until the failure of the Jacobite rebellion against King George II in 1745; some time thereafter, he is killed. Elspat escapes and raises their son, Hamish Bean, to emulate his father's life as a cateran. But while she refuses to acknowledge that Scottish ways have forever altered, Hamish realizes that there is no place for a cateran in modern Scottish culture; finally, after much harrying by his mother, he disappears, only to reappear as an enlisted soldier en route to America. For Elspat, this is an unthinkable betrayal: By joining the Black Watch, Hamish has simultaneously accepted the power of the Hanovers and abandoned the old feuds between the MacTavishes and the other Highland clans. But knowing that Hamish fears the scourging that awaits any soldier who deserts, Elspat persuades him to stay with her until his leave is nearly up—then drugs his drink. Too late, Hamish awakens to find that he has, for all intents and purposes, become a deserter; even so, he vows to return and receive his punishment. Once again, Elspat foils him. When Hamish's sergeant, Allen Breack Cameron, comes to arrest him, Elspat successfully encourages Hamish to shoot him—thereby ensuring his own execution. She desperately seeks to save him from his fate, but all for naught. After hearing of his death, Elspat isolates herself in her grief, refusing to have anything further to do with human society. As her own end approaches, she sneaks past the women asked to watch her and disappears.

Scott first heard this tale from Mrs. Anne Murray Keith and started working on his own version in late May 1826. (He was beginning his desperate attempt to write himself out of £121,000 worth of debt, incurred when the Ballantyne Press collapsed in January of that year.) The first of three stories in *The Chronicles of the Canongate: First Series*, "The Highland Widow" addresses many themes familiar from Scott's novels: the intricate cultural clashes of Highland and Lowland Scots, as well as Scots and English; the role of women in creating and maintaining folk traditions; the power of landscape; the psychology of superstition; and, above all, the sad but inevitable collapse of the old ways in the face of modernization. In some ways, the story functions as a sequel to Scott's *Waverley* (1814), insofar as it traces the collapse of Highland culture in the wake of the Jacobite rebellion. Bethune Baliol's Highland tour also partly echoes Waverley's own educational wanderings across the Scottish landscape. Elspat herself is an especially gloomy version of one of Scott's female types, ominous, more or less prophetic, and occasionally insane: Other variations on this theme include Meg Merrilies of *Guy Mannering* (1815), the madwoman Madge Wildfire of *The Heart of Midlothian* (1818), and Alice Grant of *The Bride of Lammermoor* (1819). Elspat's unwillingness or inability to recognize historical change, with tragic results, is yet another of Scott's frequent preoccupations. As is so often the case, Scott represents historical change as simultaneously inevitable and painful; both Caroline McCracken-Flesher and Graham Tulloch have noted Scott's ambivalence about English attitudes to Highlanders, which partly precipitate Hamish's death. If Elspat's wild yearning for the vanished past comes across as an entirely unviable option, it is not clear that Scotland's embrace of English ways—as symbolized by the Black Watch—represents something altogether desirable.

BIBLIOGRAPHY

Cooney, Seamus. "Scott and Progress: The Tragedy of the 'Highland Widow,'" *Studies in Short Fiction* 11 (1974): 11–16.

McCracken-Flesher, Caroline. "Pro Matria Mori: Gendered Nationalism and Cultural Death in Scott's 'The Highland Widow,'" *Scottish Literary Journal* 21 (1994): 69–78.

Scott, Walter. *Chronicles of the Canongate: First Series.* Edinburgh: Cadell and Co.; London: Simpkin and Marshall, 1827.

Tulloch, Graham. "Imagery in 'The Highland Widow,'" *Studies in Scottish Literature* 21 (1986): 147–157.

Miriam Elizabeth Burstein

HILL, SUSAN (1942–   )

Susan Hill was born in Scarborough, Yorkshire, in 1942. She is married to a Shakespeare scholar, Stanley Wells. Hill's semiautobiographical writings include *The Magic Apple Tree* (1982) and *Family* (1989), the latter relating the death of her premature child, Imogen. Hill's novels include *Strange Meeting* (1971), *I'm the King of the Castle* (1970), and a series of crime novels. The recent *The Pure in Heart* (2005) continues Hill's exploration of the crime genre. Hill is best known for her ghost story *The Woman in Black* (1983), the dramatization of which has had a long and successful run in London's West End. *The Woman in Black*'s supernatural narrative, gothic characterization, and claustrophobic sense of isolation locate it firmly within the realm of the modern gothic. Hill's interest in supernatural fiction and her interest in the short story form itself, is demonstrated by her editorship of numerous collections including *The Walker Book of Ghost Stories* (1990).

While the supernatural dominates deathly experience in *The Woman in Black,* Hill's short stories are more frequently dominated by emotionally gritty realism in their representations of death and an internalized sense of isolation and alienation. Death is the main stimulus for change in characters' circumstances, and change itself represents a major source of anxiety for the majority of Hill's protagonists, as in "HOW SOON CAN I LEAVE?" As such, Hill frequently explores the changes faced by children approaching maturity and the elderly facing lonely death.

Hill relies heavily on pathetic fallacy and seaside locations to layer the intensity of anxiety in her prose. In *The Albatross and Other Stories* (1971), which won the John Llewelyn Rhys Memorial Prize, Hill uses a seaside setting to shroud characters with an expectancy of death and to create a sense of claustrophobic entrapment. In her afterword, Hill identifies the inspiration for "The Albatross" as Benjamin Britten's "Sea Interludes" from the opera *Peter Grimes.* As such, the bleak power of the sea dominates the story as the protagonist, Duncan, struggles to find his own identity independent of his mother, whose body is eventually enveloped by the brooding sea.

A seaside setting offers more carnivalesque potential in the title story from *A Bit of Singing and Dancing* (1973), as Esme, a repressed middle-aged woman whose domineering mother has recently died, takes in a lodger—the singing and dancing seaside entertainer, Mr. Curry. Like many of Hill's protagonists, Esme has yet to reach adult independence and emotional maturity despite being middle-aged, as the bonds between parent and child (of whatever age) predominantly constrict and suffocate in Hill's stories. This comic use of the seaside location in "A Bit of Singing and Dancing" is rare in Hill's work, however; "The Badness Within Him" in the same collection returns to the use of the sea as a deathly signifier. Here, the young boy, Col, struggles with an overpowering sense of change that foreshadows and, indeed, predicts the drowning of his father and his epiphanic understanding of his new position as dominant male in the family. In fact, the loss of parents or of sons and daughters is a key Hill theme. In "Elizabeth," from *Listening to the Orchestra* (1996), the death of the young girl's mother creates a vacancy of responsibility that the daughter is trapped into filling, thereby creating parallels with Col's experiences. In "Father, Father," from *The Boy Who Taught the Beekeeper to Read,* the death of the mother and remarriage of the father leave two grown-up daughters distraught and unable to form new independent identities. Hill's exploration of the entrapment caused by familial relationships runs parallel to a sense of individual isolation, which is frequently positioned paradoxically both as the result of familial relationships and as the only alternative to such entrapment.

Hill's collection *The Boy Who Taught the Beekeeper to Read* (2003) returns in the title story to examining the relationship of need between the old and the young. As in "The Custodian" and "Halloran's Child" in *A Bit of Singing and Dancing,* the isolated adult is revealed to be in far more emotional need than the child. Such dependency inevitably leads to an increased sense of isolation following the maturation and departure of the child.

By returning to established themes, Susan Hill has honed her distinctive voice as a short story writer. Moreover, through her work as editor of a range of collections, including *The Random House Book of Ghost Stories* (1991) and *The Penguin Book of Modern Women's Short Stories* (1991), Hill continues to promote and explore the short story form.

BIBLIOGRAPHY

Hill, Susan. *The Albatross and Other Stories.* London: Penguin, 1989.
———. *A Bit of Singing and Dancing.* London: Penguin, 1973.
———. *The Boy Who Taught the Beekeeper to Read.* London: Chatto & Windus, 2003.
———. *Listening to the Orchestra.* Ebrington: Long Barn Books, 1996.
———. *The Magic Apple Tree,* London: Penguin, 1982.
———, ed. *The Penguin Book of Modern Women's Short Stories.* London: Penguin, 1991.

Jo Trevenna

HILL BACHELORS, THE WILLIAM TREVOR

(2000)   Mary Fitzgerald-Holt has noted that *The Hill Bachelors* represents a marked change of style from WILLIAM TREVOR's previous collections. "Gone are the dramatic moments of confrontation, the sometimes strident exposures of painful truths" (174), she writes. Indeed, this collection has a much quieter feel, this conveyed through an economic use of words and a consistent tone of gentle tolerance. Many of the characters are as seedy as those in previous Trevor collections: confidence tricksters, petty thieves, and mendacious hypocrites are as prevalent as before. The difference is that secrets are revealed slowly, without the dramatic sensa-

tionalism that characterizes, for example, the revelations made by the ranting Cynthia in 1981's "Beyond the Pale." In "Three People," two seemingly innocuous persons have transgressed seriously: Vera has escaped punishment for murdering her dependent, handicapped sister, and Sidney has perverted the course of justice by providing a false alibi. These horrendous secrets are not revealed in a destructive flash but are discreetly and quietly presented to us—not to any other character in the text.

Several stories are set in England, but the stories set in Ireland convey the most consistent and memorable theme: the decline of rural Irish customs. The sober pace and tone is appropriate to this theme: Rural Irish families, routines, and traditions are dying not with cataclysmic flashes but with anticlimactic whimpers. "Of the Cloth" focuses on the quiet life of a Church of Ireland clergyman in remote Ennismolach. Underlining the steadfast dignity of the clergyman, Trevor insists that Reverend Grattan Fitzmaurice is as Irish as any Catholic: "[H]e belonged to this landscape." A contrast is made between the sparseness of Fitzmaurice's existence (the rectory has a negligible staff and a minute congregation) with the apparent wealth of a nearby, fresh flower–decorated Catholic church. But we gradually realize that Trevor is not mourning the decline of Irish Protestantism. Instead, the insistence is that the Roman Church is in decline—falling attendances underline the Catholic Church's lessening influence. The confidence of the Catholic priests is a front: Their status will soon be as sorry as that of the already marginalized Fitzmaurice. The Protestant tradition has declined already; the Catholic tradition is undergoing a similar decline.

In "The Virgin's Gift," another sort of rural decline is subtly accounted for: the passing of family-scale agriculture. Michael has willingly undergone many years of hermitage, inspired by instructions apparently sent by the Virgin Mary in his sleep. Called upon again, this time to return to his country-dwelling family, he goes home. His aged parents appreciate this change, but there will not be a perpetuation of their livestock-rearing and crop-sowing subsistence. Michael still seeks only peace. Significantly, he is an only child; he chose a religious life instead of a married life with a young woman, Fódla. Trevor does not tell us whether Michael's following of the Virgin's callings is delusional—Trevor never judges his characters in such a manner—but it is clear that Michael's religious devotion causes the ending of one family's local-scale farming. In the title story, 29-year-old Paul does continue rural traditions: He takes over the family's farm after his father's death. His older brothers have all progressed to married lifestyles in commercial environments distanced from the farm's remoteness. The problem is that Paul cannot find a marriage partner. Women invariably reject Paul—transparently, he seeks a wife only to share farm chores. Trevor articulates the tragedy of this enforced solitariness through an elegiac narrative. Paul accepts that he is destined to be a "hill bachelor," a loner who will never pass the farm down to an heir. He is resigned to the inevitable decline of rural traditions in his area, just as Trevor accepts with melancholy that traditional rural sensibilities in Ireland have generally given way to industrial-scale agriculture and urban-influenced attitudes and mores.

BIBLIOGRAPHY

Fitzgerald-Holt, Mary. *William Trevor: Re-imagining Ireland.* Dublin: The Liffey Press, 2003.

Kiberd, Declan. "Demented Bachelors," review of *The Hill Bachelors. London Review of Books,* 8 March 2001, pp. 30–31.

MacKenna, Dolores. *William Trevor: The Writer and His Work.* Dublin: New Island Books, 1999.

Ormsby-Lennon, Hugh. *Fools of Fiction: Reading the Fiction of William Trevor.* Dublin: Maunsel and Co., 2004.

Trevor, William. *The Hill Bachelors.* London: Viking, 2000.

Kevin De Ornellas

HOMOSEXUALITY   Same-sex desire has been represented in literature as far back as Plato's *Symposium* in Ancient Greece. However, the terms *homosexuality* and, slightly later, *heterosexuality,* were not coined until late 19th-century sexologists such as Havelock Ellis and Richard Krafft-Ebing sought to categorize variations in human sexual behavior. Indeed, many literary historians and queer theorists today agree with Michel Foucault's assertion that although same-sex erotic and sexual behavior has always existed, "the homosexual" did not emerge as an identity category until late-Victorian times. Others, however, citing 18th-century mollyhouses, or gathering places for homoerotically inclined men, argue that identity was in place much earlier. Initially, the term *homosexuality* was intended to garner compassion for those whose emotional and sexual attraction and behavior was oriented toward their own sex, thus shifting homosexuality (then also called sexual inversion) from a crime to a disorder. However, attitudes toward homosexuality as sin, disease, or crime continue to persist alongside beliefs that it is a normal sexual orientation or choice.

Literary references to homosexuality often cite historical trends and events including the following: 18th and 19th-century romantic female friendship, or "Boston marriage"; OSCAR WILDE's 1895 trial for "gross indecency"; the 1928 obscenity trial over Radclyffe Hall's novel *The Well of Loneliness;* Paris lesbian salons and the Berlin queer milieu of the 1930s (see Christopher Isherwood's "SALLY BOWLES"); Nazi persecution of homosexuals; mid-20th-century styles of butch and femme; the 1969 Greenwich Village Stonewall rebellion; the emergence of gay liberation and activism inspired by feminist and racial justice civil rights movements; the American Psychological Association's deletion of homosexuality as a disorder in 1973; and the emergence of HIV/AIDS and Thatcher/Reagan antigay policies in the 1980s. More recent events include the development of sex-change techniques; increasing reference to gay, lesbian, bisexual, and transgendered (LGBT) persons in movies and television; current debates over "gay genes," gay marriage, gay adoptions and gays in the military; and the emergence of LGBT studies and queer theory as academic disciplines. Representations of homosexuality may reflect the autobiographical impulses of gay authors: Examples include E. M. FORSTER, SOMERSET MAUGHAM, and SYLVIA TOWNSEND WARNER and many writers associated with AESTHETICISM and DECADENCE. Alternatively, homosexuality might mark characters as evil, especially in the evocation of lesbianism to pathologize female power and/or sexuality, as in SHERIDAN LE FANU's Carmilla.

Contemporary authors such as A. S. BYATT, WILL SELF, and JEANETTE WINTERSON frequently refer to queerness directly. However, earlier writers are often more oblique, signaling homoeroticism or homosexual acts through metaphor or allusion to figures like Sappho, St. Sebastian, or the Bible's David and Jonathan or Naomi and Ruth. Or they may encode same-sex desire through sensual language, phallic images, or labial and clitoral references to flowers, pearls, seeds, and so forth. Since the sex-gender system of Western society dictates both gendered behavior and sexual object choice according to one's biological sex, gender-bending and cross-dressing characters may be read as a feminist critique of rigid gender roles but may also provide a queer critique of compulsory heterosexuality. The same is true for characters who resist heterosexual relationships or suffer unhappy marriages while enjoying positive same-sex friendships (as in HENRY JAMES, VERNON LEE, and VIRGINIA WOOLF). Additionally, homoerotically inclined authors of either sex sometimes identify with the figure of the adolescent boy, both for his youthful beauty and for his relative freedom from the expectations of heterosexual adulthood (e.g., J. M. Barrie, creator of Peter Pan).

To avoid anachronism, critics discussing authors and texts prior to the 20th century often use alternate terms in lieu of gay, lesbian, bisexual, or homosexual, such as homoerotically inclined, lesbian-like, antiheteronormative, or queer. The latter two terms may also be applied to transgendered and intersexed subject positions. Readers should be aware that native and non-Western perceptions of same-sex desire, behavior, and identity may vary greatly from Western models of homosexuality.

BIBLIOGRAPHY

Abelove, Henry, et al., eds. *The Lesbian and Gay Studies Reader.* New York: Routledge, 1993.

Duberman, Martin, ed. *A Queer World: The Center for Lesbian and Gay Studies Reader.* New York: New York University Press, 1997.

Foucault, Michel. *The History of Sexuality: An Introduction.* Vol. 1, 1978. New York: Vintage, 1990.

Sedgwick, Eve Kosofsky. *Between Men: English Literature and Male Homosocial Desire.* New York: Columbia University Press, 1985.

Jill R. Ehnenn

"HORSE DEALER'S DAUGHTER, THE" D. H. LAWRENCE (1922)   D. H. LAWRENCE tried

unsuccessfully to get the *English Review* to publish "The Horse Dealer's Daughter," written in 1917 and originally titled "The Miracle." However, in 1921 he revised the story, retitled it "The Horse Dealer's Daughter," and included it in his second volume of short stories, *England, My England* (1922). The story was an immediate success and to this day remains one of Lawrence's most anthologized pieces of writing, second only to "The ROCKING-HORSE WINNER" (1926).

"The Horse Dealer's Daughter" begins with the disbanding of the Pervin family: Mabel Pervin and her three brothers, Malcolm, Fred Henry, and Joe, all must leave their home after their father has died and left them in debt. The Pervin brothers state openly what they intend to do with their futures; Mabel, however, is strangely silent about her intentions. Mabel's sole connection to a family member is with her mother, who died when Mabel was just 14. Now, as a 27-year-old woman, Mabel still feels deep and worshiping love for her mother. Lawrence states simply that this intense love for her dead mother makes Mabel feel "her own glorification, approaching her dead mother, who was glorified" (143). Mabel's intent is to follow her mother to the grave.

Little physical notice is taken of Mabel except by Dr. Jack Ferguson, a Pervin family friend, who finds Mabel's "steady, dangerous eyes" emotionally unsettling (141). Present in this story is Lawrence's interest in the development of the individual identity as it pertains to larger questions of community. Both Mabel and Jack Ferguson find themselves alienated in their respective communities; Mabel does not fit into her family, and Jack Ferguson does not feel comfortable in the "alien, ugly little town" of people for whom he cares (144). Mabel's attempted suicide, by drowning, propels these two alienated people together. Dr. Ferguson rescues Mabel from the pond into which she has walked, although he cannot swim, out of duty as a medical man. After dragging her from the cold and murky waters, he resuscitates her, takes her back to her own house, undresses her in the kitchen, and wraps her naked body in warm blankets. When he gives her some brandy she comes into full physical consciousness and asks him the question that will change their lives forever: "Do you love me, then?" (148). The conversation between Mabel and Jack Ferguson, following this question, illustrates one of the recurrent themes in Lawrence's stories, the complicated problem of defining the exact nature of love between men and women. Lawrence shows that love is what draws these two people together. However, in this story love has many meanings. Love is emotional desire, sexual passion, and possession of another person.

Mabel's prolonged nakedness forces Jack to address his burgeoning desire for her. Finally, Mabel's intense need for Jack's love compels him to abandon the pretense of helpful doctor, to embrace his newfound love for her. Although there is final recognition between Mabel and Jack for their love of each other, this is a love story without a happy ending. At the moment that Jack declares definitively that he wants her, that he is even willing to marry her immediately, Mabel is "frightened . . . almost more than her horror lest he should *not* want her" (152). Lawrence was a writer who sought to represent human nature in all its complexities. Thus, in this story, love is imperfectly felt and experienced.

BIBLIOGRAPHY

Delany, Paul. *D. H. Lawrence's Nightmare: The Writer and His Circle in the Years of the Great War.* New York: Basic Books, 1978.

Harris, Janice Hubbard. *The Short Fiction of D. H. Lawrence.* New Brunswick, N. J.: Rutgers University Press, 1984.

Lawrence, D. H. *England, My England and Other Stories.* London: Penguin, 1995.

Worthen, John. *D. H. Lawrence: A Literary Life.* New York: St. Martin's, 1993.

Barbara Tilley

"HOUSE OF THE FAMOUS POET, THE" MURIEL SPARK (1959)

Originally published in the *New Yorker*, "The House of the Famous Poet" is set in 1944 during the shelling of London and follows the narrator as she travels on the night train from Edinburgh to London to resume work at her civil service position. Aboard the train, she meets two other passengers: a soldier returning to his post and a domestic worker named Elise. The soldier's generosity with his cigarettes forms a bond between the two women, and Elise ultimately invites the narrator to stay at the home where she is employed. Enchanted by the conversation, the desire to stay in London, and Elise's aristocratic accent, the narrator accepts the invitation. However, almost immediately she regrets it. Viewed standing and in the light of day, Elise has a bearing of almost oppressive exhaustion, a quality that then permeates everything with which she is associated, including the home in which she works. As a result the narrator becomes increasingly uncomfortable with her promise to spend the night with Elise. This discomfort is heightened when the speaker discovers that the home in which she is to spend the night is, as the title tells us, the house of the famous poet. With new eyes, the narrator examines her surroundings. They no longer speak of Elise's exhaustion but of the mind of the poet. The narrator's discomfort now stems from the feelings of intrusion into the private world of this poet who is both known and unknown to her. As she prepares to leave the home the next day, she again meets the soldier from the train. The story then enters the world of magical realism. Short on funds, he sells her an abstract funeral in return for train fare. While she ponders the funeral and what it must look like, the soldier gets off the train only to reappear moments later as a notion of himself. Though intrigued by the concept of the abstract funeral, the narrator ultimately discards it, finding that it fails to meet her expectations; she desires a real funeral. At the close of the story, the narrator relates that not long after her stay in the house of the famous poet, it was bombed, killing Elise and the famous poet and destroying his house.

As many of her works are, "The House of the Famous Poet" is based on events from MURIEL SPARK's own life. A civil servant during World War II, Spark had stayed with a woman working in the house of Louis MacNeice on her way back to work after a trip to Edinburgh. Though none of the events mentioned in the latter part of the story occurred, Spark points to this experience as the catalyst that inspired her to write. In fact, throughout the story, the narrator discusses her need to record these and other events. Not surprisingly, these particular events are also recounted in other Spark works, including her autobiography, *Curriculum Vitae,* and an essay titled "The Poet's House."

To a large extent, the primary theme of the short story is how perception mediates reality. As a result, reality is flexible and revisable. The overrun nature of the house changes from being indicative of Elise's exhaustion to hinting at the mind of the famous poet. Moreover, this plastic reality allows for some of the postmodern play. The story shows a clear self-consciousness in the construction of the narrative and in the choice of detail. The latter parts of the story, most specifically the description of the house, the recurrence of the notion of the solider, and the poet's death, evoke the gothic and magical realism in their associations with death and the supernatural. Furthermore, although "The House of the Famous Poet" lacks some of the characteristics of Spark's larger oeuvre, especially the prolepsis found in works such as *The Prime of Miss Jean Brodie* and *The Driver's Seat,* the narrator's tone and the focus on descriptive detail hint at Spark's experimentation with the nouveau roman found in her longer works.

BIBLIOGRAPHY

MacLachlan, Christopher. "Muriel Spark and the Gothic." In *Studies in Scottish Fiction: 1945 to the Present,* 125–145. Frankfurt: Peter Lang, 1996.

McQuillan, Martin, ed. *Theorizing Muriel Spark: Gender, Race, and Deconstruction.* New York: Palgrave, 2002.

Rankin, Ian. "The Deliberate Cunning of Muriel Spark." In *The Scottish Novel since the Seventies: New Visions, Old Dreams,* 41–53. Edinburgh, Edinburgh University Press, 1993.

Spark, Muriel. *Complete Short Stories.* London: Penguin, 2001.

Mary M. Husemann

"HOW SOON CAN I LEAVE?" Susan Hill (1973)

Susan Hill's 1973 widely anthologized short story "How Soon Can I Leave?" relates the relationship of Miss Roscommon and Miss Bartlett, two unmarried women living in the coastal town of Mountsea. Hill's simple, straightforward style of writing is evident in this story. Sparse yet realistic details provide the reader with a complete picture of the characters and situations, making the story interesting and absorbing.

Miss Bartlett, a woman in her 40s, comes to Mountsea, though the reader does not learn how or why. After winter storms flood her waterside cottage—perhaps symbolic of life itself—she moves in with Miss Roscommon, an older woman who enjoys domestic pursuits and having someone to benefit from them. Their relationship appears to be mutually beneficial: Miss Roscommon has someone to watch over, and Miss Bartlett has a safe place to pass the winter. One winter turns into seven years, all following a similar pattern, with Miss Bartlett making crafts for sale and Miss Roscommon running the business and domestic sides of their lives. Then, Miss Bartlett's 47th birthday, along with a visit to Miss Roscommon by her young niece and her new husband, bring Miss Bartlett to an emotional crisis of sorts. She decides to move out of Tuscany, Miss Roscommon's house, and settle into her little cottage again. Once there, she will make new plans for her future.

She postpones this decision-making again and again, however. The reader has already learned that this is typical of Miss Bartlett—she makes very few intentional commitments because she believes that committing to one plan or place means permanently ruling out any other path. Hill describes Miss Bartlett's life as drifting, similar to the sections of the pier that break off into the sea during the fierce winter storms that were the initial cause of her living arrangement with Miss Roscommon.

These same winter storms slowly wear at Miss Bartlett's determination to be independent from her former housemate. She wishes there were someone to comfort her during the storms that frighten her. Though she has rebuffed Miss Roscommon's recent efforts to take care of her, one particularly harsh storm changes Miss Bartlett's resolution to live on her own. She returns to Tuscany in the morning to reestablish their friendship, though she envisions herself refusing Miss Roscommon's tendencies to treat her as a child or pet. Yet instead of presenting the cheerful reunion the reader expects, Hill ends the story with a twist: Miss Roscommon has died in the night, during the storm, alone.

A few themes and ideas are constant in the story. Hill makes frequent use of contrast, both obvious and subtle. Miss Roscommon and Miss Bartlett are the most noted example. Miss Roscommon is a no-nonsense sort of woman, while Miss Bartlett is perceived by others as dreamy and artistic. Contrast is shown in other areas of the story as well, such as Miss Bartlett herself. She tells herself that she is an independent adult capable of any adventure or journey she can dream, yet her outward actions seem to demonstrate the exact opposite. Even the weather in the winter and in the summer are contrasted with each other.

In addition, the story explores ideas of childhood and independence. Children who are different and misunderstood by adults are featured in other works by Hill, a subject that stems from her vivid memories of her own childhood. In this story, Miss Bartlett is the child. She recalls scenes from her girlhood that she has allowed to define her adulthood. Although Miss Bartlett's mother is dead at the time of the story, she is in fact a character because her presence is so vivid in Miss Bartlett's life. When her mother is not discussed, Miss Roscommon takes over the role of Miss Bartlett's deceased mother.

BIBLIOGRAPHY
Hill, Susan. "How Soon Can I Leave?" In *Penguin Modern Stories*. London: Penguin, 1971.

Amber Cason Wingfield

HUGHES, TED (1930–1998)

Poet, children's author, dramatist, critic, and essayist, Edward James Hughes was born in Mytholmroyd, Yorkshire. His father returned from the Dardanelles, the only survivor of his regiment. As a child, Hughes frequently accompanied his gamekeeper brother in retrieving the bodies of birds and small animals. These formative experiences of life's frailty and the bleakness of the Yorkshire moors had a profound effect on Hughes's writing. As a young man, Hughes won a scholarship to study English at Cambridge but became bored and transferred to archaeology and anthropology. It was at Cambridge that he met the American poet Sylvia Plath, whom he married in 1956.

Hughes is best known as a poet, having published 14 anthologies of poetry that focuses on the frailty of life and the prevalence of violence in nature and the human psyche (e.g., "The RAIM HORSE"). However, he also published a well-known short story, "The Iron Man" (1968). This was originally a bedtime story Hughes made up to tell his own children, and he said he had "just wrote it out" as he told it. In stark contrast to much of his poetry, Hughes suggests, through the retelling of the George and the Dragon myth, that friendship with the enemy is the key to suppressing terror. Its belated sequel, "The Iron Woman" (1993), has a myth about writing poetry as its central theme. Most of Hughes's stories have been criticized for being of inferior quality to his poetry.

BIBLIOGRAPHY
Feinstein, Elaine. *Ted Hughes*. London: Weidenfeld and Nicolson, 2001.
Hughes, Ted. *The Iron Man*. London: Faber and Faber, 1968.
———. *The Iron Woman*. London: Faber and Faber, 1993.
———. *Wodwo*. London: Faber and Faber, 1967.
Sagar, Keith. "Edward James (Ted) Hughes." In *Oxford Dictionary of National Biography,* edited by H. C. G. Matthew and Brian Harrison. Oxford: Oxford University Press, 2004. Available online. URL: http://www.oxforddnb.com. Accused July 5, 2006.

Radcliff Gregory

"HUNTED DOWN" CHARLES DICKENS (1859)

First published in the *New York Ledger* in three parts in 1859, this story is one of the few by CHARLES DICKENS that is widely regarded as DETECTIVE FICTION. It is narrated by Mr. Sampson, the retired chief manager of an insurance office, who is a believer in physiognomy—reading faces—as a means of interpreting character. He recounts how at work he had a glass partition through which he could see but not hear visitors, and how one day he saw a gentleman for whom he conceived an immediate and intense dislike. The man is well dressed and about 40, and he wears his hair "elaborately brushed and oiled" and "parted straight up the middle." The parting in his hair becomes the focus of Sampson's dislike, for to him it seems to declare, "You must take me, if you please, my friend, just as I show myself. Come straight up here, follow the gravel path, keep off the grass, I allow no trespassing."

Over the course of several encounters, Sampson's instinctive dislike is overcome by Slinkton's apparent politeness and generosity. Sampson writes a life insurance policy for Slinkton's friend, Beckwith, with Slinkton as character reference and beneficiary. But all is not as it seems. Several months later Sampson meets Slinkton and his niece, Miss Niner, at the beach at Scarborough. Miss Niner confides that she is ill and will soon die, just as her sister did not long before, and praises her uncle for his devotion. She also points out an "invalid old gentleman" and his servant on the sands who have been shadowing her. When Slinkton leaves to go swimming, Sampson reveals that she is in danger—not from her "shadow" but from her uncle. The "invalid" and the servant have been waiting to spirit her away to safety.

A couple of months later Sampson is called in to see Slinkton's neighbor and friend, Beckwith. His rooms are dingy and he is apparently an inveterate drunkard whose drinking has been encouraged by Slinkton for the £2,000 in insurance money that his policy will pay. But Slinkton has been drawn into a trap. Beckwith is no drunk; he has been throwing away the brandy his "friend" has been plying him with. He reveals that he is Meltham, the insurance agent who made out the policy for Slinkton's dead niece, and that he has thrown himself in Slinkton's path to hunt him down by finding evidence of a worse crime: the murder of his niece and attempted murder of her sister. Finding Slinkton's journal that recounts dates and doses of poison, he has the evidence he needs for Slinkton to be prosecuted. However, Slinkton poisons himself and dies before he can be turned over to the authorities. Meltham, torn with regret that he could only save the second sister—he was the mysterious "shadow" on the beach—dies a few months later, leaving all he has to Miss Niner.

For a story that revolves around deception, this tale is interesting given the subterfuge of its narrator, the apparently forthright Mr. Sampson. Early in the story he mentions but fails to name a visitor to his home, who was undoubtedly Meltham. He obscures the reason for his trip to Scarborough as a need for "a breath of sea air"—in actuality, the invalid he meets on the beach is Meltham in disguise, at the ready to rescue Miss Niner. Similarly, he explains his appearance at Beckwith/Meltham's rooms at the end of the story as an appointment in "some chambers in the Temple." Of course, within the world of the story, Sampson must hide the truth to protect Miss Niner and to trap Slinkton. But his deceptions in relaying his story to

the reader are of a different order: Their function is to keep the reader in suspense. They enable him to give the impression that he is recounting the events of the story as he experienced them while withholding information crucial to understanding Slinkton and the trap laid for him.

The necessity for a narrator-detective to share information with the reader was later enshrined as one of the "10 commandments" for how detective fiction should work by Ronald Knox, but Sampson is not the detective of the story. His astute perceptions about Slinkton's real character merely ensure that he is more readily persuaded to rescue Miss Niner and aid in Slinkton's exposure by the story's detective: Meltham.

Dickens had a strong interest in crime and police work. He wrote articles about his expeditions into London's underworld with Inspector Field of Scotland Yard (the model, it is widely believed, for Inspector Bucket in his novel *Bleak House*), as well as about infamous criminals of the day, including the "gentleman" poisoners, Thomas Griffiths Wainewright and Dr. William Palmer. These two murderers have been suggested as inspirational in Dickens's portrayal of Slinkton. Palmer's 1856 trial caused a national sensation, for the doctor had poisoned at least 16 people, including his own children, his mother-in-law, and his wife (on whom he had taken out a large insurance policy). In his article "The Demeanour of Murderers" (published in *Household Words* in June 1856), Dickens suggests that such apparent "complete self-possession" as Palmer's during the trial is in fact "always to be looked for and counted on, in the case of a very wicked murderer." Further, he declares, "Nature never writes a bad hand. Her writing, as it may be read in the human countenance, is invariably legible, if we come at all trained to the reading of it."

Like Palmer, Slinkton is a contradiction: He can pass as respectable and so carry out his terrible crimes, yet apparently the physical signs of guilt that indicate his criminality are "written" on his face. This premise was comforting: Through research and education the world could be made predictable. Criminals could be detected and caught, and the world made safe from their predations. Such a perception was crucial to the subsequent rise of criminal anthropology that sought to tie physical characteristics (e.g., a sloping forehead) to criminal behavior. But it was also crucial to the emergence of the classic detective genre that became popular in the final decade of the century and beyond, with its detectives such as ARTHUR CONAN DOYLE's Sherlock Holmes, who could use the science of deduction to unravel even the most complex mysteries.

BIBLIOGRAPHY

Allingham, Philip V. "Dickens's 'Hunted Down' (1859): A First-Person Narrative of Poisoning and Life-Insurance Fraud Influenced by Wilkie Collins." The Victorian Web: Literature, History, and Culture in the Age of Victoria. Available online. URL: http://www.victorianweb.org/authors/dickens/pva/pva19.html. Accessed on Feb 10, 2005.

Dickens, Charles. Hunted Down. London: Peter Owen, 1996.

Gerri Brightwell

HUXLEY, ALDOUS (1894–1963)

Most often associated with *Brave New World*, his 1932 dystopian novel, the poet, playwright, essayist, novelist, and short story writer Aldous Leonard Huxley was born on July 26, 1894, in Surrey, England. As one of the youngest members of an accomplished literary and scientific family, the precocious Aldous benefited tremendously from the intellectual atmosphere surrounding him. Initially intending to pursue a career in medicine, Huxley entered Eton College in 1908, where he remained until 1911, when an eye infection nearly blinded the boy. With the help of braille, Huxley managed to continue his education at home in preparation for the university studies he hoped to undertake upon regaining his vision. In 1916, Huxley earned his bachelor's degree from Balliol College, Oxford.

After resigning from a post at Eton in 1919, Huxley married Maria Nys and began working as a journalist. Although much of his time was spent in writing for the *Athenaeum, House and Garden,* and the *Westminster Gazette,* the young writer managed to publish a third volume of verse and began work on his first novel, *Crome Yellow.* By 1923, Huxley's success as a writer enabled him to work on his craft full time; he produced five short story collections, which helped establish him as one of the dominant literary voices of the interwar generation. For example, the stories in *Mortal Coils*

(1922) attempt to capture something of the post–World War I sense of cynicism, selfishness, and lack of humanity, which seemed to have replaced older values of loyalty, family, and religion. This collection contains Huxley's most frequently anthologized story, "The GIOCONDA SMILE," which was later filmed. Several of the stories in *Little Mexican, and Other Stories* (1924), including the title story, paint a similarly bleak view of human relations in which exploitation of children by parents and of servants by employers is rife. A recurrent theme in Huxley's stories is the discrepancy between how things should be—or how characters dream they will be—and the grim reality. He is also interested in people who are emotionally stunted in some way. These are ideas taken up in Huxley's fourth and fifth collections, *Two or Three Graces and other Stories* (1926) and *Brief Candles* (1930).

With the publication of his 12th book, *Point Counter Point*, in 1928 and *Brave New World* (1932), Huxley established himself as one of the foremost writers of his generation. By this time, he had given up writing short stories, claiming to have lost interest in the act of storytelling. In 1937, hoping that the Californian climate would prove better for his failing eyesight (short-sightedness, or a failure to "see," is a recurring theme in his stories) than the harsher climes of Europe, Aldous Huxley moved to the United States. Huxley's relocation also marked a drastic change in the writer's craft. Though he continued writing fiction throughout his life, Huxley moved away from creative writing to focus on philosophical and moral treatises, believing that the latter forms would better convey his philosophical concerns. In addition to the many essays he produced during the late 1930s and early 1940s, Huxley also wrote a number of Hollywood screenplays, most notably the adaptations of Jane Austin's *Pride and Prejudice* and Charlotte Brontë's *Jane Eyre*.

In California, Huxley developed an interest in Hindu philosophy and alternative religions that would continue throughout the remainder of his life. Seeking to expand his consciousness, Huxley studied meditation, hypnosis, and mind-control techniques under the tutelage of several religious figures, including the Swami Prabhavananda and L. Ron Hubbard. Huxley's growing interest in consciousness expansion also led him to experiment with mescaline, psilocybin, and LSD. Meeting with such drug culture icons as Timothy Leary and Dr. Humphrey Osmond, Huxley developed a favorable impression of these emerging psychedelic substances and agreed to participate in a study of mescaline use with Osmond in 1953. In 1954, after taking the drug on two occasions, Huxley wrote *The Doors of Perception,* an influential study of the drug's mind-expansion capabilities. Although Huxley never became a heavy drug user, his lectures on the "visionary experience" one goes through while under the influence of substances such as mescaline, psilocybin, and LSD contributed largely to the writer's popularity among the 1960s Californian hippie culture.

Huxley spent his final years as a visiting professor at institutions such as the University of California at Berkeley, the Menninger Foundation, and the Massachusetts Institute of Technology. In May 1961, a fire destroyed the Huxley home, obliterating the writer's manuscripts, letters, and journals. Diagnosed with cancer of the tongue in 1960, and despite its spreading to glands in his throat by 1962, Huxley continued writing and lecturing until his death on November 22, 1963, in Los Angeles. Although his doctor initially protested, Huxley was given LSD on his deathbed and passed away under the influence of the drug. Aldous Huxley was 59.

BIBLIOGRAPHY

Bedford, Sybille. *Aldous Huxley.* New York: Knopf, 1974.
Dunaway, David King. *Huxley in Hollywood.* New York: Harper & Row, 1989.
Huxley, Aldous. *Brave New World.* London: Chatto and Windus, 1932.
———. *Brief Candles: Stories.* London: Chatto and Windus, 1930.
———. *Collected Short Stories.* London: Chatto & Windus, 1957.
———. *Letters of Aldous Huxley.* Edited by Grover Smith. London: Chatto & Windus, 1969.
———. *Little Mexican and Other Stories.* London: Chatto and Windus, 1924.
———. *Two or Three Graces and Other Stories.* London: Chatto and Windus, 1926.
Murray, Nicholas. *Aldous Huxley: A Biography.* London: Little, Brown, 2002.

Erik Grayson

I

"IMMORTALS, THE" MARTIN AMIS (1987)
This story by MARTIN AMIS appeared in the 1987 collection *Einstein's Monsters,* comprising five short stories and an introductory essay, "Thinkability," relating the author's observations about the nuclear threat's chilling effects on intellectual and spiritual life. Amis later referred to the anthology as the first of a trilogy of major works dealing with the three major problematic events of the 20th century; the other books were the Holocaust novel *Time's Arrow* (1991) and *Koba the Dread: Laughter and the Twenty Million* (2002), about the Russian dictator Josef Stalin's genocidal acts in the 1930s and 1940s. "The Immortals" and the other pieces in *Einstein's Monsters* reflected Amis's increasing concern, bordering on obsession, with the nuclear bomb during the 1980s, and the collection signaled the growing importance of the themes of worldwide crisis and environmental awareness in his work.

"The Immortals," the final and shortest story in *Einstein's Monsters,* was generally considered inferior to the other stories in the collection, particularly the first two, "Bujak and the Strong Force" and "Insight at Flame Lake," both of which focused on the psychological damage, the anxiety and dread, wrought by the theory of nuclear deterrence. "The Immortals" and its predecessor in the collection, "The Little Puppy That Could," were negatively criticized for their showiness, jokiness, and sentimentality. Reviewer Jack Miles, for example, referred to the former as a glorified "comic routine" reminiscent of Mel Brooks's "The Two-Thou-

sand-Year-Old Man." Others, including reviewer Carolyn See, viewed "The Immortals" as integral to a collection that produced a particular response in readers—equal measures of pleasure and horror. According to James Diedrick, the stories failed to fulfill the rhetorical purpose apparently intended by the author, but they succeeded as examples of unconventional writing: "Ultimately, *Einstein's Monsters* is more successful as a set of experiments in fictional technique and tone than as an attempt to locate postmodern malaise exclusively in the nuclear fire zone" (118).

"The Immortals," set some time after the nuclear "apocalypse" (139) and "death typhoon" (141) of 2045—Tokyo was ground zero—is told from the point of view of a character who claims to have roamed the earth since the beginning of time, before the arrival of the "space-seeded life" (137) of plants, dinosaurs, and humans. The narrator, living among the dying, in the first paragraph refers to the "diseases and delusions" (135) of those surrounding him. As mentioned above, the narrator delivers his monologue like a stand-up comedian, punctuating his fanciful tale about the march of global history with one-liners straight out of Borscht Belt traditions: "I once stayed awake for seven years on end. Not even a nap. Boy, was I bushed" (136). He offers quirky observations on the dinosaurs, the Ice Age, classical antiquity, the Middle Ages, the Renaissance, ancient China, and the London of Shakespeare and Ben Jonson.

In a poignant ironic twist, near the end of the story, the narrator reveals that he is occasionally troubled by a particularly disturbing delusion, one that speaks to the true identity of the narrator, whose own mind is diseased: "Sometimes I have this weird idea that I am just a second-rate New Zealand schoolmaster who never did anything or went anywhere and is now painfully and noisily dying of solar radiation along with everybody else." The narrator's grand delusion functions in part as Amis's commentary on the delusions inherent in the nuclear age, particularly the concepts of deterrence and nuclear survivability, as addressed in "Thinkability": "Nuclear weapons deter a nuclear holocaust by threatening a nuclear holocaust, and if things go wrong then that is what you get: a nuclear holocaust." By the conclusion of "The Immortals," the bad jokes and other defense mechanisms have vanished, and the reader is left with a pitiful character, one facing certain destruction with all of his delusions intact.

BIBLIOGRAPHY

Amis, Martin. *Einstein's Monsters.* New York: Harmony, 1987.

Diedrick, James. *Understanding Martin Amis.* Columbia: University of South Carolina Press, 1995.

Miles, Jack. "The Immortals," *Los Angeles Times,* 28 June 1987, p. 13.

See, Carolyn. "Humanity Is Washed Up—True or False?" *New York Times,* 17 May 1987, p. 501.

Philip Booth

"IMPRESSIONS: THE WRIGHTSMAN MAGDALENE" Angela Carter (1992) "Impressions: The Wrightsman Magdalene" first appeared in *FMR Magazine* in February 1992. It was subsequently published in *American Ghosts and Old World Wonders,* the short story collection that appeared the year after Angela Carter's death in 1992, and again in 1995's *Burning Your Boats: The Complete Short Stories.* It is the tale of St. Mary Magdalene's penitence in a cave in the forest of Sainte-Baume where, it is recounted, she arrived alone after having sailed with Mary, mother of Jesus, and others to the coast near Marseille. In this tale Carter's characteristic magic realist approach is discernible only in her representation of saints and miracles, and Mary Magdalene is depicted in her popular role of repentant harlot.

Carter problematizes any simple opposition between vice and virtue suggested by the juxtaposition of a former prostitute and a virgin mother. Carter's narrator describes Georges de la Tour's painting "The Magdalene with Two Flames" ("The Wrightsman Magdalene" of the title): This picture shows a sensual Magdalene meditating upon a burning candle, the flame of which is also reflected in a mirror. The candle flame is the story's central motif. Its contemplation enables the Magdalene's repentance: "The new person, the saint, is being born out of this intercourse with the candle flame" (146). The story's mysterious, first-person narrator (Carter herself?) has been similarly entranced by a flame. She describes how she imagined a candle during the birth of her son: "When the pains came thick and fast, I fixed all my attention on the blue absence at the heart of the flame, as though it were the secret of the flame and, if I concentrated enough upon it, it would become *my* secret, too" (145). These two women, shadowed by the presence of the impressive, impervious virgin, are united by their separate transformations. Justyna Sempruch reads Carter's "black-browed Palestinian" Magdalene (141) as a "paradoxical creature" who escapes from "the limits of cultural boundaries, from the bonds/bounds maintained by traditional structures, religious as well as racial or national" (74). All cultural stigmas and stereotypes are challenged as the experience of the former prostitute in the cave at Sainte-Baume is portrayed equally alongside that of the narrator's labor.

True to its name, "Impressions" is not so much a narrative as a series of observations, centred around the narrator's reflections on two representations of the Magdalene: the Georges de la Tour painting and Donatello's sculpture kept at the Museo dell'Opera del Duomo in Florence, which depicts a Magdalene "dried up by the suns of the wilderness, battered by wind and rain, anorexic, toothless, a body entirely annihilated by the soul" (143). The poetic or literary description of artistic objects is known as ekphrasis, and in "Impressions" it is used to conjure the disparity between these different portrayals. The conflict that results implies Mary Magdalene's mystery, her unknowability. While Carter's narrator remains at all times entranced by the penitent, the variances between the two artistic works suggest that the society that may condemn the Magda-lene is also the society that may not understand her.

The story concludes by implying that a worldlier, earthier experience—like the Magdalene's—may pro-duce a different sort of birth. The figure in "The Mag-dalene with Two Flames" holds a skull in her lap, "where, if she were a Virgin mother and not a sacred whore, she would rest her baby" (146). The skull is memento mori, a reminder and augury of death. Mary Magdalene has labored to bring her own enlighten-ment into the world. She has arrived at a revelation of the human condition in its inevitable mortality. The possibility of transformation is thus denied to neither the mother nor the nonmother. Carter presents revela-tion in a story that, given the frailty of its plot, is almost a nonstory. Ideals about the exclusivity of traditional or romantic means for attaining enlightenment are thus unsettled and challenged by "Impressions: The Wrightsman Magdalene," be these means childbirth or realist narrative itself.

BIBLIOGRAPHY

Carter, Angela. *American Ghosts and Old World Wonders.* London: Chatto & Windus, 1992.

Sempruch, Justyna. "The Sacred May Not Be the Same as the Religious: Angela Carter's 'Impressions: The Wrights-man Magdalene' and 'Black Venus.'" *Women: A Cultural Review* 16, no. 1 (2005): 73–92.

Michelle Kelly

"INDISCRETION IN THE LIFE OF AN HEIRESS, AN" THOMAS HARDY (1878)

First published in the *New Quarterly Magazine* in July 1878, "An Indiscretion" was never collected by THOMAS HARDY into any of the four volumes of short stories that he produced during his lifetime. Its eventual printing in 1934 caused a public dispute to erupt between Flor-ence Hardy, his widow, and Sydney Cockerell, his lit-erary executor. Much of the story's essential plot was clearly drawn from *The Poor Man and the Lady,* Hardy's first novel, which he wrote in 1867 and 1868 but never published.

"An Indiscretion" details a forbidden relationship between Egbert Mayne, a poor schoolteacher in the town of Tollamore, and Geraldine Allenville, the privi-leged daughter of a member of the local gentry. Egbert's desire for Geraldine is kindled when he saves her from being killed by a mechanical threshing machine. After the incident, Geraldine visits Egbert at his school under the pretense of inspecting it on behalf of her father, Squire Allenville, and a tentative friendship between them begins to take shape. When Egbert's grandfather is in danger of being turned out of his house by the squire, Egbert prevails on Geraldine to intercede, and she does. The two continue to meet clandestinely, and one night he kisses her in the schoolhouse.

Despite a series of missteps, the relationship grows until Egbert, conscious of the dangerous social gap between them, determines to leave Tollamore for Lon-don, where he hopes to build his reputation and for-tune to a level that will allow him to finally marry Geraldine. After five years of steady effort, he achieves a modest amount of social success as a writer and pub-lishes two books. At first, he maintains a correspon-dence with Geraldine, but this soon dwindles when her father learns of their relationship. When he hears that her family is visiting London, he contrives to sit near her at the opera. Quietly sneaking behind her, Mayne grabs her hand, and she declares that she remains "Yours now as then" (87). His hopes are quickly dashed, however, when he soon learns that her father has arranged for her to marry Lord Bretton.

Dejected, Egbert returns to Tollamore, where Geral-dine's wedding is to take place. There, he experiences more emotional upheaval when he hears Geraldine's voice outside his window. Still in love with him and fearful of Bretton, she has run away from her father's house. Determined to save his lover, Egbert arranges for them to be married secretly, and they elope to the seaside town of Melport. After the ensuing scandal, Geraldine returns to the squire's house to attempt a reconciliation. The encounter with her father puts too much strain on her fragile state; she suffers a ruptured blood vessel and collapses. At Geraldine's request, Egbert is eventually admitted to the home, but Mr. Allenville ignores him. Geraldine's health declines and she dies. Egbert sits on the right side of the bed hold-ing her hand "while her father and the rest remained on the left side, never raising their eyes to him and scarcely ever addressing him" (113).

Thematically, "An Indiscretion" establishes the author's (very personal) preoccupation with questions of social standing. But, unlike such later novels as *Tess of the d'Urbervilles* and *Jude the Obscure,* in which Hardy rails against the Victorians' fundamentally snobbish attitudes about class, here he seems much more muted. The difficulties experienced by Egbert and Geraldine in their relationship are not used as the vehicles for scathing social commentary. A useful point of comparison is the conclusion of *Tess.* Each text closes with its heroine dying as a result of circumstances that stem directly or indirectly from her desire to marry outside of her social station. But, whereas the narrator of *Tess* greets her death with the embittered, ironic proclamation that "'Justice' was done, and the President of the Immortals . . . had ended his sport with Tess" (314), the narrator of "An Indiscretion" displays an unmistakable relief that "this strange family alliance was at end for ever" (113). Though a sense of sadness pervades the scene, the indignation that constitutes a hallmark of Hardy's mature writings is noticeably absent.

BIBLIOGRAPHY

Dalziel, Pamela. "Hardy's Unforgotten 'Indiscretion': The Centrality of an Uncollected Work," *Review of English Studies: A Quarterly Journal of English Literature and the English Language* 43, no. 171 (August 1992): 347–366.

Hardy, Thomas. *An Indiscretion in the Life of an Heiress and Other Stories.* Oxford: Oxford University Press, 1994.

Stephen E. Severn

"INDISSOLUBLE MATRIMONY" REBECCA WEST (1914)

Rebecca West (1892–1983) was born Cicely Isabel Fairchild. Following a brief period on the London stage, West took her nom de plume from the outspoken heroine of Henrick Ibsen's *Rosmersholm* when she began her writing career with the suffragette magazine the *Freewoman.* Besides her fiction, literary criticism, journalism, political analysis, and history, West's most notable feminist writings include a piece on the suffragette Emily Davidson, who threw herself in front of the king's horse at the Derby. In 1912 she wrote a taunting critique of H. G. WELLS's *Marriage,* calling him "the Old Maid of novelists." Piqued by West's acerbic wit, the celebrated novelist invited her to tea, a meeting that marked the start of their stormy 10-year affair (the 45-year-old Wells was married). In 1914, West gave birth to their son Anthony.

That same year West published her short story "Indissoluble Matrimony" in the first issue of Wyndham Lewis's *Blast* alongside the work of Ezra Pound and Ford Madox Ford, firmly establishing her place amongst the modernists (see MODERNISM). She was a committed and outspoken suffragette, and her views on female sexuality remain distinctly modern. Like Lewis, West mocks English middle-class respectability and exposes the fear and loathing fueling obsessive propriety. In addition, the young West masterfully demonstrates how discourses of race are inextricably bound to issues of class, gender, and sexuality. While providing a darkly ironic psychological commentary on "the tie that binds," this incisive feminist reveals an all-too-clear understanding of the power struggle that shapes modern marriage.

"Indissoluble Matrimony" is presented from the husband's point of view, thereby providing direct insight into a white middle-class male's fearful view of the emergent New Woman and her rise in social status. To complicate matters, we learn that George Silverton's wife Evadne has "black blood in her," although she looks almost white. In contrast to her repressed, sickly husband, who has "a natural incapacity for excitement," Evadne is bursting with life. Physically strong and athletic, she is repeatedly compared to an animal or described as catlike, emphasizing her sensuous nature. George, who has always been slightly scared of women, is initially seduced by the sound of her voice, her soulful singing, finding her exotic and falling in love with her childlike simplicity: her helplessness, her innocence, and her natural sexuality, so free of complexity in contrast to proper, white middle-class women. However, after 10 years of marriage, the prudish George now finds his wife's "voluptuous presence" intolerable and is consumed by his "sense of outraged decency."

Although the couple had fancied themselves "orthodox Radicals" in the early years of their marriage, Evadne has gone on to embrace socialism, which George finds too extreme—a violation of his deeply entrenched middle-class values. After marrying, moreover, Evadne began studying economics and writing for the socialist press. Learning that the socialist candidate for the town council has asked his wife to speak at a local meeting pushes George over the edge. In the face of Evadne's intellectual superiority and her unflinching determination to make this speech, George becomes enraged. When Evadne storms out of the house, George follows her, imagining she is off on some secret tryst, since his middle-class beliefs dictate that feminine virtue and female sexuality are not compatible.

Evadne, we discover, has gone for a moonlight swim in the lake on the neighboring moor. By the time George catches up to her, he is overcome with murderous rage; they engage in a deadly struggle, during which Evadne disappears into the darkness of the pond, so that George believes he has drowned his wife. Ravaged but alive, he slowly makes his way home, savoring his one night of triumph over a woman. However, when George finally arrives home, he finds Evadne tucked into their warm bed, sleeping soundly. Shivering with cold, George collapses into the bed, surrendering to the primal power of the female body. "Bodies like his," he realizes, "do not kill bodies like hers." Once the irony evaporates, West leaves her readers with Freudian insight into the unconscious forces that render the marriage bond "indissoluble."

Widely regarded as an important feminist writer, West developed similar ideas in her novels. *The Return of the Soldier* (1918), dealing with a soldier who is suffering from shell shock and the women who wait for him, reveals West's grasp of Freudian psychology as well as her socialist sympathies. In her second novel, *The Judge* (1922), she bravely explores the torment of a single mother and the legacy it bestows: "Every mother is a judge who sentences the children for the sins of the father."

BIBLIOGRAPHY

Glendinning, Victoria. *Rebecca West: A Life*. London: Weidenfeld and Nicolson, 1987.

Marcus, Jane. *The Young Rebecca: Writings of Rebecca West, 1911–1917*. New York: Viking Press, 1982.

Norton, Ann V. *Paradoxical Feminism: The Novels of Rebecca West*. Lanham, Md.: International Scholars Publications, 2000.

West, Rebecca. *The Only Poet and Short Stories*. London: Virago, 1992.

Elaine Pigeon

"INTERLOPERS, THE" SAKI (1919)

A story that illustrates SAKI's (H. H. Munro's) lesser-known talent for pathos, "The Interlopers," collected in the posthumous anthology *The Toys of Peace* (1919), is a sort of Balkan gothic romance that moves from thrilling to hopeful to tragic, thanks to Saki's usual twist ending.

On a stormy winter evening, Ulrich von Gradwitz searches his Carpathian forest for his longtime foe, Georg Znaeym. The disputed land has been the cause of a bitter, raging blood feud between the families "for three generations." Ulrich has long dreamed of shooting "down his neighbour in cold blood" and his arch-nemesis desires the same end for him. The two men suddenly come face to face beneath an enormous beech tree. As they hesitate to shoot, the storm brings down the tree, pinning them next to each other. Injured and bloody, the enemies laugh at each other's fate. Ulrich tells Georg that his men will soon be there to deal with him as a poacher, while Georg counters that his men are not far behind him; they will reach him first and then roll the tree onto Ulrich. Georg notes that, with their lives in the balance, there are "no cursed interlopers to come between us"; by the end of the night, one of them will die at the hands of the other and his men. Yet slowly, wracked with pain as they consider their imprisonment, the neighbors begin to realize the folly of their lifelong animosity. They agree to be friends, imagine the surprise of the village at the sight of them riding into the "market-square together," and then call out for their men in a spirit of cooperation and renewed hope. Ulrich sees figures approaching, and Georg asks whose men they are. But they are not men; they are wolves.

Munro was a reporter in the Balkans from 1902 to 1904 for *The Morning Post*, and many of the stories he wrote as Saki use the area as an untamed frontier backdrop for slightly exotic suspense tales of passionate violence or family secrets, from the terrorist attack in "The Easter Egg" to a mystical death in "The Wolves of Cernogratz." In contrast to many of Saki's Balkan stories, however, which tend to show the area as a pseudo-Oriental other on the wild fringes of Europe, "The Interlopers" shows its two protagonists as ultimately just as fate-controlled and pretense-bound as any of Saki's English characters.

In comparing men to beasts—indeed, suggesting that men are lesser creatures, for they refuse to rise above petty blood feuds yet cannot shake off the hypocritical, self-contradictory codes "of a restraining civilization"—and eliciting the reader's sympathy for the men's newfound amity, only to show that their friendship comes too late, Saki champions indifferent nature and implacable fate over the false civility and trivial covetousness of man. Ironies abound in this barbed fable: Hunters become the hunted, property disputers are trapped on the land, and public enemies in life become private friends in death.

BIBLIOGRAPHY

Saki. *The Complete Saki.* Harmondsworth, England: Penguin, 1982.

Brian Gibson

"IN THE CAGE" HENRY JAMES (1898)

"In the Cage," a realist novella, was first published during what is known as HENRY JAMES's 'middle period.' In this phase of his writing, James focused on political and social themes rather than on his more typical explorations of the nature of American consciousness set in Europe.

"In the Cage" is the story of an unnamed young woman who works in a telegraph office in London and is engaged to a successful grocer, Mr. Mudge. Longing for the higher-class position her family once held, she spends her long workdays speculating about the lives and circumstances of her wealthy customers, based on clues she derives from the encoded words of their telegraphs. A dashing young wealthy couple in the telegraph office especially captures her fancy. Surmising that this pair—Lady Bradeen, a married woman, and Captain Everard, a bachelor—are having an illicit relationship, the telegraphist becomes preoccupied with developing a narrative about them based on the numerous frantic telegraphs through which the two orchestrate their meetings. The telegraphist focuses especially on Captain Everard, who, she feels, appreciates her intimate and perceptive understanding of his situation.

Mr. Mudge, undeterred, continues his entreaties for the telegraphist to transfer to an office closer to his grocery store, and she delays this commitment. Captain Everard and Lady Bradeen's affair seems to become more and more precarious, and the telegraphist tracks the case fervently, suffering deeply when weeks go by with few or no visitations from Captain Everard. Finally, just when it seems the relationship will be exposed, the telegraphist is able to help the captain retrieve an incriminating document, using her obsessive memory for the bits of information she has gathered about the couple. After this narrow avoidance of scandal, Lady Bradeen's husband dies, and she and the captain are on their way to a legitimate relationship. Upon hearing this news, the telegraphist resolves abruptly to join Mr. Mudge and the marriage and home he has offered her, and the story ends.

One reason that "In the Cage" is significant in James's oeuvre is that its main character has to work for a living; this novella thus offers evidence for what John Carlos Rowe has called "the other Henry James," the novelist who sympathizes with financial hardship and class oppression. "In the Cage" explores in particular the changing position of women in fin de siècle London and the dangers of exposure inherent in the far more public role the New Woman could play, especially when she was required to work for a living.

"In the Cage" has also been touted as an exploration of the artistic consciousness. Critics such as Leon Edel and L. C. Knights contend that the telegraphist's experiences represent the plight of the artist. In this light, the artist (who may be James himself) is fated to observe the world from behind bars that prevent him or her from acting in the world, but this position allows the artist to concoct representations of it from an alternate perspective.

A final important theme of the novella is the nature of knowledge and information. The story illustrates both a modern, technological form of information dissemination, the telegraph, and the kind of subjective, inductive knowledge gathering of which the telegraphist is exceptionally capable. In this novella, this combination is dangerous, an invitation to scandal. This anxiety prefigures the interest and concern that early 20th-century writers continued to have with the spread of new technologies. "In the Cage" not only presents the issue of knowledge thematically but also conveys it stylistically: James's characteristically ambiguous style of writing—a precursor, many critics claim, to the literary style of MODERNISM—necessitates the same interpretive acuity that the telegraphist has so skillfully honed.

BIBLIOGRAPHY

Edel, Leon. *Henry James: A Life.* Rev. ed. New York: Harper, 1985.

James, Henry. *In the Cage.* London: Hesparus, 2002.

Knights, L. C. "Henry James and the Trapped Spectator." In *Explorations: Essays in Criticism Mainly on the Literature of the Seventeenth Century,* 155–169. London: Chatto, 1946.

Rowe, John Carlos. *The Other Henry James.* Durham, N.C.: Duke University Press, 1998.

Amy Jamgochian

"IN THE GREAT WAR" FAY WELDON **(1985)** FAY WELDON's early collection *Polaris and Other Stories* both reflects and anticipates the concerns that engage her writing in its myriad permutations, before and since. By the time the collection was published, Weldon was a familiar female voice, in no small part because of her prolificacy (she had published nine novels and an earlier short story collection, not to mention the numerous television productions to her credit). The 12 "parables of modern life," as the cover blurb describes the collection, offer a variety of ways in which Weldon's skilled voice—ironic, sharp, unforgiving— narrates the center of human existence: love. The story "In the Great War" can be seen as a microcosm of her themes, characters, and strategies.

"In the Great War" introduces characters that are familiar inhabitants of Weldon landscapes: female protagonists whose husbands or significant others leave them or cheat on them because they, being women, are too independent or too dependent, thus foregrounding the impossibility of pleasing the fickle male; women who have no compunction about poaching other women's spouses; mothers who resent/abandon their children; and children who are initially creatures of incredible selfishness but who mature by the end of the tale, ready, perhaps, to take on their own role as responsible adults and future parents. The male char-

acters, objects of passion and obsession for the female protagonists, are conveyed in a manner to create confusion in the reader as to the source of such attraction, and, as characters, even those portrayed to be living the male ideal are much less interesting and dynamic than the women.

"In the Great War" chronicles the lives and loves of Patty, whose husband Arthur leaves her for a more feminine woman, and her 19-year-old daughter Enid, who makes being feminine her life's goal and succeeds in enticing her formerly married professor to marry her. Patty is a woman "who was what she was" (129) and so is easily defeated by Helene, "the enemy at the gate with her slim legs and bedroom eyes" (129). Enid, Patty's daughter, is irrevocably scarred by her father's abandonment, blaming her mother on the one hand— "Do we have to eat this? No wonder Dad left home!"— but taking up "the armoury her mother never wore" on the other, in order to avenge them both (131). Arthur, Patty's husband, is persuaded "without much difficulty . . . to leave Patty and Enid, give up his job, paint pictures for a living and think the world well lost for love" (130–131). Neither Walter Walther, Enid's 48-year-old professor, nor his wife Roseanne, older than Walter by four years, "stand a chance against Enid" (133), just as her mother before her "didn't stand a chance against Helene" (129). The light mocking voice of the omniscient narrator spares none of the characters, and while ostensibly sympathetic to their behavior, the narrator often critiques it. For example, the narrator tells us that Helene is cross with Enid for doing what she herself had done with Enid's father—"She was an old retired warrior, sitting in a castle she'd won by force of arms, shaking her head at the shockingness of war" (135)— thus exposing the wicked naivete of both women.

The story utilizes Weldon's typical narrative structure: short paragraphs created of brief and pointed sentences, serving to convey information that may often be quite devastating in a disarmingly humourous manner, a legacy from Weldon's successful advertising days. The voice is familiar, even gossipy, in the manner of Victorian address to the "dear reader," often punctuated with exclamation marks. For example, we are informed that Patty is taking estrogen and becoming more like Helene as a result, with a potted geranium on her windowsill: "A geranium! Patty, who could never see the point in potted plants!" (135). The juxtaposition of the geranium as an example of Patty's newfound femininity with the estrogen as its source highlights Weldon's acuity about life's ironies. The implication is, of course, that she has been "improved" and that by becoming more "feminine" she has in fact become less bitter and kinder. Indeed, at Enid's wedding she "actually saw the point of shaking [Arthur's] hand and even laying her cheek against his, in affection and forgiveness" (136).

Accordingly, Enid marries Walter Walther, whose name is an example of Weldon's bestowal of ridiculous names on her male comic heroes (think Bobbo in *The Life and Loves of a She-Devil*) so that even if they cease to behave in a manner worthy of scorn as a narrative progresses, the reader is always reminded of their initial preposterous state. (Walter's name has the added weight of being a weapon, one favoured by James Bond, no less, thus foregrounding his role in the women's hostilities.) Wedded bliss, however, does not last, despite Enid's best efforts: "Her curtains were always fully lined, her armpits smooth and washed, never merely sprayed. Enid never let her weapons get rusty. She would do better, thank you, than Patty, or Helene, or Roseanne" (137). And yet, she does not. The failure of these concrete manifestations of the good wife reflect Weldon's consistent engagement with the ways in which women measure their self-worth on the basis of male-defined criteria of what that worth entails. Thus, Enid's desire to have a baby precipitates Walter's ultimate betrayal. After Roseanne sends their daughters to live with Walter and Enid (another common antimaternal characteristic in Weldon's writings, appearing prominently in another story in the collection, "Christmas Lists"), Walter abandons the pregnant Enid and returns to Roseanne. It seems that Enid is doomed to misery.

However, Weldon does offer a message of limited hope through sisterhood for such misguided women. The war ends when Enid fittingly gives birth to a daughter and rejoices, although the "birth of a girl was . . . cause for commiseration rather than rejoicing." She "abandoned a battle which was really none of her making; she laid down her arms" (142) and embraces her mother, stepmother, and stepdaughters. She lives with her daughter and stepdaughters in a home with no men, returns to college, and succeeds in a new career. In the closing paragraph we are told she has become "something of a propagandist in the new cold war against men . . . walk[ing] around linked arm-in-arm with women" (143). What, after all, could be more natural than women linked? But Weldon does not offer this unity of females as an unambiguous solution to the hostilities and travails of women for and against the gender divide. In the story's last lines she reminds us that however "treacherous" the old "male allies" had been, "[w]ho is to say what will happen next?" (143). Whenever Weldon has chosen to investigate that particular question, be it in *Polaris* or in her writings since, she has done it with an unflinching eye for the truth of the way many women live their lives.

BIBLIOGRAPHY
Weldon, Fay. *Polaris and Other Stories.* London: Hodder and Stoughton, 1985.

Nancy Peled

"IN THE SHADOW OF WAR" BEN OKRI (1983)

First published in the *West Africa* magazine in 1983, "In the Shadow of War" was later included as the first story in the collection *Stars of the New Curfew* (1988). Based largely on BEN OKRI's experience of the Nigerian civil war and written from the perspective of a child, it relies a good deal on economy and intensity of expression for its narrative power. The story is written in a bare, realistic style that vividly captures the shades of a murky war. Okri's method seems to be to allow the description to speak for itself while significant details pile up and suggest the hallucinatory visions the war causes.

The story opens with the arrival of three soldiers in a village close to the express road. The soldiers are observed in their activities by Omovo, the child protagonist, who is glued to the news reports on the radio, much to the annoyance of his father. Down below, the soldiers go on drinking wine and while away their time in playing draughts. The soldiers call to the children playing near them in order to find out more about a veiled woman who has been walking through the village. One of the soldiers tells Omovo that they suspect the woman may be a spy.

Omovo returns to his position beside the window to wait for the woman in the headscarf to appear. As reported, she does not have a shadow and her feet do not touch the ground. She is unfazed by the children's attempts to disturb her. While waiting for the strange woman to appear, Omovo dozes off and wakes up late in the afternoon to realize that the veiled woman has just crossed the village, with the soldiers in pursuit. This time the woman is carrying a red basket on her head. Omovo sees her go into a cave full of women and children. On her way back she is intercepted by the soldiers and killed when she refuses to give them information. Omovo, the sole witness, runs home but faints on the way. He wakes up to find his father drinking with the soldiers, who have carried him back from the forest. Okri's story has been described as an "antiquest" (Thorpe). In a society destroyed by ethnic warfare, the stance of the impartial witness is effectively embodied in the experience of the uninvolved, sensitive child.

BIBLIOGRAPHY

Moh, Felicia Oka. *Ben Okri: An Introduction to His Early Fiction*. Enugu, Nigeria: Fourth Dimension Publishing, 2002.

Okri, Ben. *Stars of the New Curfew*. London: Penguin, 1999.

Thorpe, Michael. Review of *Stars of the New Curfew*. *World Literature Today* (Spring 1990): 349.

R. S. Nanda

INTIMACY HANIF KUREISHI (1998)

Intimacy is the most unapologetic and autobiographical work to date from Hanif Kureishi (b. 1954) and was published in 1998 to a roar of controversy. Critics were appalled by what they saw as the novella's barely veiled depiction of Kureishi's real-life breakup with partner Tracey Scoffield. Like Kureishi, *Intimacy*'s narrator Jay is a successful British-Asian writer who, also like Kureishi, leaves the mother of his two children for a much younger woman who plays in a rock band. Jay is an unrepentant philanderer and self-obsessed misogynist whose callousness to his wife and children is only occasionally mitigated by moments of narcissistic concern for the pain they will feel on losing him. Their loss, by contrast, barely seems to register to him. In

one of the novella's most notorious and frequently cited lines, Jay opines "there are some fucks for which a person would have their partner and children drown in a freezing sea" (96). During a brief moment of guilt about his imminent and unannounced departure, Jay consoles himself by imagining that his partner Susan will eventually find another man and forget her pain. "Not that there will be a queue," he thinks. "Nevertheless, the most grotesque people get laid, and even married" (95). This vicious contempt for a character seemingly based on his own former partner has proved too much for many reviewers to stomach. More generous critics have recognized the book as an ironic critique of the way egotism is justified through the popular bourgeois mantra of fulfilment, self-expression and creativity and as an important contribution to the burgeoning genre of male confessional writing popularized by writers such as Nick Hornby, Blake Morrison, and Andrew O'Hagen.

Like much of Kureishi's recent work, *Intimacy* departs dramatically from the writer's earlier thematic investment in issues of postcolonialism, race, and sexual identity. In its style and psychological purview, the novella seems to have far more in common with the work of the great 19th-century Russian realists whom Kureishi (and Jay) admires so much than it does with the politically charged explorations of ethnicity and gender in the writing of other British-Asian contemporaries such as Monica Ali, Suhayl Saadi, and Meera Syal. There is no "plot" in a conventional sense: The narrative is composed of Jay's internal musings on the night before he is set to leave his family for good. As he spends what this family little suspects is his last few hours with them, he contemplates both telling Susan about his plans and calling them off entirely. Jay is a character too enamored with the contemplation of "the splendours and depths of [my] own mind" (29) to make decisions easily. He rationalizes his numerous infidelities and his recent besottedness with the young "part-woman" (117) Nina on the basis that he still believes in "the possibilities of intimacy. In love" (106). This alleged faith in idealized love seems unconvincing when read against Jay's frequently evinced dread of emotional closeness and committed monogamy. He castigates Susan because she, unlike himself, "lacks detachment" (88), a failing he ascribes to all the women he has been with: "Whenever I was with a woman, I considered leaving her. . . ." Given this psychology, it seems unlikely that Jay, as he himself seems only too aware, will ever find enduring happiness with anyone. The narrative seems to hint that his flight from the domestic home is less of a liberating rejection of middle-class values than the very epitome of them—what, after all, could be more clichéd or depressingly routine than the midlife crisis–induced confusion of novelty with real change and growth? Jay occasionally approaches this realization—"what is the point of leaving if this failure reproduces itself with every woman?" he wonders—but ultimately remains caught in his own illusions, declaring as he walks hand in hand with the nubile and accommodating Nina that "the best of everything had accumulated in this moment. It could only have been love" (123). The draw of *Intimacy* lies in its brutally honest depiction of the often humorous albeit repellent extent of human narcissism and in its ambiguous position between the intimacy of autobiographic confession and the greater detachment of fictional satire.

BIBLIOGRAPHY

Kureishi, Hanif. *Intimacy*. London: Faber, 1998.

Christine Fergus

"INVISIBLE JAPANESE GENTLEMEN, THE" GRAHAM GREENE (1965)

"The Invisible Japanese Gentlemen" first appeared in the *Saturday Evening Post* in November 1965. The piece was later published in the volume of short stories *May We Borrow Your Husband?* in March 1967. The volume is subtitled "And Other Comedies of the Sexual Life," and indeed the collection of stories is significantly lighter in tone than much of GRAHAM GREENE's work. There is a distinct sense of amusement prevalent throughout the volume, and while the authorial focus is still unreservedly on human relationships, the seriousness with which Greene had previously approached such issues is conspicuous by its absence.

"The Invisible Japanese Gentlemen" is set in a fashionable London restaurant and is primarily a studied piece of observation rather than of action. Greene's examination of the processes of recognition and alienation, of the way people interact, observe one another, and coexist, raises a number of fundamental questions regarding the relationship of the individual to the world as a whole.

The plot is simple, taking place within a few brief minutes and confined to three tables in the corner of the restaurant. The characters remain seated, stationary throughout the body of the text, and the only movement in the piece is that of the narrator's gaze as he surveys the room. Communication is virtually nonexistent as, although the girl and her fiancé talk profusely, they rarely connect. Their conversation is broken, a series of unfinished questions and statements, unformulated responses and throwaway, irrelevant comments. Her speech constantly intersects his as she strives to make herself heard, lamenting, "Darling, you don't listen, do you?" They are continually talking at cross-purposes, and it is as if two separate conversations are taking place. Their effort to converse becomes a battle of words in which both speak but neither listen, and the connection is lost irrevocably.

The girl herself is particularly isolated, surrounded by words that mean nothing to her. Even the titles she chooses for her books are rejected and replaced with somebody else's misinterpretations. The softness of the title "The Ever-Rolling Stream" sits in stark contrast to the publisher's choice, "The Chelsea Set." Even her fiancé cannot feel an affinity for her artistic sensibility. His response to "The Azure Blue" reveals their interplay to be more of a process of alienation than a lovers' discourse.

The Japanese gentlemen of the title are indeed invisible to their fellow diners. Their conversation cuts across the various other dialogues, momentarily distracting the narrator from his observations. Physically situated directly between the couple and the narrator, their language, their "incomprehensible tongue," quite literally forces a distance between the main characters. Yet despite their violent intrusion into the dialogue they remain unnoticed, "invisible" to the girl. Absorbed in her own attempts to dominate the speech she is unable to recognize the very existence of others.

Greene's story functions as a cutting critique of the way in which language can isolate rather than connect, and it exposes the tenuous links that bind human to human and individual to individual.

BIBLIOGRAPHY
Greene, Graham. *Collected Stories: 21 Stories.* London: Penguin, 1993.

Alice Smith

IRELAND   Historians of the Irish short story tradition regularly highlight its origins in the Gaelic oral tradition and the short realistic, supernatural tale called an *eachtra* (Averill, 20). These remnants of the oral tradition can be seen in stories written in English by MARIA EDGWORTH, Gerald Griffin, and William Carleton at the beginning of the 19th century and by Daniel Corkery, GEORGE MOORE, and SOMERVILLE AND ROSS toward the end. Like the stories produced in SCOTLAND in the 19th century, Irish stories tended to be proudly national in character, anecdotally describing scenes, memories, customs and modes of life in isolated settings. Their writers also tried to capture local dialect—or a selective version of it—giving voice to the Irish peasantry. The *eachtra*'s emphasis on dramatic stories of fantastic, creepy events was also one of the factors behind the emergence of a parallel Irish tradition of ghost stories and gothic tales most famously represented by SHERIDAN LE FANU, OSCAR WILDE, and BRAM STOKER. Yet all these writers wrote in English for practical reasons. Few of them could speak the language, and they also had to sell their stories to magazines with English audiences.

Although critics recognize the importance of the Irish short story to the country's literary history, there is some difference of opinion about its dominant characteristics. This is because the short story in Ireland has been created out of a number of opposing political and cultural positions: Catholic/Protestant, landowner/peasant, country dweller/city dweller, exile/homebody. Some critics writing about the Irish short story as it developed in the early part of the 20th century have suggested that the genre became a hybrid form, taking elements of the oral tradition but mixing them with the experimental forms used by Russian writers like Ivan Turgenev and MODERNIST writers (see JAMES JOYCE). Other critics take as a starting point Ireland's long-held status as a colonial subject under English rule. H. E. BATES's description in *The Modern Short Story* (1941) is typical: "The Irish short story has been bred of vastly different qualities from the English. Where art and people fight for existence, whether against religious, moral or political tyranny or against plain indifference, and where such art is naturally poetic and such people are naturally and proudly belligerent, the tendency of all expression is bound to be revolutionary" (148–149). Corkery's stories in *The Hounds of Banba* (1920), set at the time of the Easter Rising of 1916 and the Anglo-Irish war fit this pattern. They offer revolutionary adventurers as heroes performing daring, sometimes brutal, deeds in the name of the nationalist struggle and trying to evade capture by the notorious section of the English army dubbed the "Black and Tans."

Another recurrent theme in the Irish short story is the formative influence of the Catholic Church and other official institutions on daily life. According to many critics, it is the individual's ability to look or leap beyond the forces around them—either physically or imaginatively—by which characters are judged. This feeling is particularly strong in Irish writing of the first half of the 20th century. As Deborah Averill writers, "Most Irish writers regarded their society as peculiar, self-defeating, and out-of-step with other western societies" (24). After the establishment of the Irish Free State in 1922, there was a deliberate policy on the part of the new government to encourage an Ireland that stood apart from world affairs. In this oppressive atmosphere divorce was forbidden and sexual transgressions punished; Irish became the official language of the country, and in 1937 the new constitution confirmed the Catholic Church as the country's spiritual leader. The Censorship Act of 1929 resulted in the suppression of writers' works, and several went into exile, including Liam O'Flaherty and SAMUEL BECKETT. This feeling of isolation was fostered by Ireland's decision to remain neutral in World War II. Of the writers who remained in Ireland, many, including FRANK O'CONNOR and SEAN O'FAOLAIN, painted an ambivalent picture of postrevolutionary Ireland and the sense of disillusionment they felt (see O'Connor's "The GUESTS OF THE NATION" and O'Faolain's "The Patriot"). In these stories, which mix romance and realism, the countryside, the Gaelic language, and the peasantry become symbols of old values that have slowly been lost.

One of the claims made by O'Connor, and others in his generation, was that he and his compatriots had had to specialize in the short story because their society was simply too inward-looking, small-minded, and rigid to allow the kind of wide scope needed by the novelist. By the time O'Connor died in 1966, writers who dared to be outspoke—EDNA O'BRIEN and JOHN MCGAHERN, for example—could still expect to face a torrent of criticism. Since then, however, as the Church and State have become less directly influential, the theme of the individual versus the oppressive state no longer preoccupies short story writers quite as much. According to Maurice Harmon, writing in 1982, "The struggle now is not with laws of church and state or with social conformity, but with personal relationship and through individual powers of perception and understanding" (65). Many critics would debate Harmon's assertion about the extent of this shift—the violence in Northern Ireland remained something that many writers felt obliged to confront—but the context for and nature of Irish short stories has widened. For example, as Dermot Bolger points out, it is by no means certain that Irish writers necessarily consider themselves postcolonial subjects needing to work out their own and their country's vexed relationship with England. Since the 1970s Clare Boylan, Neil Jordan, John McCardle, BERNARD MCLAVERTY, and WILLIAM TREVOR are just some of the writers who have benefited from an expanding Irish publishing industry and its increased willingness to publish stories dealing not with the rural scene or revolutionary nationalism but with the details of daily life in modern Ireland, "the drama of human interaction and the nuances of the individual's inner life" (Harmon, 66). (See also JAMES JOYCE and ELIZABETH BOWEN.)

BIBLIOGRAPHY

Averill, Deborah. *The Irish Short Story from George Moore to Frank O'Connor.* New York: University Press of America, 1982.

Bates, H. E. *The Modern Short Story.* Boston: The Writer, 1941.

Bolger, Dermot, ed. *The New Picador Book of Contemporary Irish Fiction.* London: Picador, 2000.

Harmon, Maurice. "First Impressions." In *The Irish Short Story,* edited by Patrick Rafroidi and Terence Brown, 63–78. Lille: Publications de l'universite de lille III, 1982.

Thompson, Richard. *The Appeal of the Modern Irish Short Story.* New York: Whitston, 1989.

Joe Davis

J

JAMES, HENRY (1843–1916) Born on April 15, 1843, in New York City, Henry James was the second of the five children of Henry James (1811–82) and Mary Walsh James (1810–82), and much of his emotional life was shaped by his lifelong rivalry with his older brother, William (1842–1910). Of his three younger siblings, Henry was closest to his only sister Alice (1848–92), the youngest. The family traveled in Europe before settling in Newport, Rhode Island. Although Henry attended Harvard Law School for a term and studied visual art briefly, he was educated among his family. In his youth, he became friends with his cousin, Minny Temple (d. 1870), whose death at 24 had a lasting impact on him and his art. He also met William Dean Howells (1837–1920), who published James's work in *Harper's*; Oliver Wendell Holmes (1841–1935); and Thomas Sergeant Perry, with all of whom he maintained friendships into his adult life. At 17, James suffered an injury that prevented him from serving in the U.S. Civil War; some scholars suggest that the injury was also responsible for James's celibacy, a subject of recent biographical discussion.

James began his writing career anonymously in 1864 with the publication of a short story, "A Tragedy of Error," and a book review in *North American Review.* His first signed work appeared the following year. He serialized his first novel, *Watch and Ward,* in 1871 and published a volume of short stories, *A Passionate Pilgrim and Other Tales,* in 1875. He also published a travel book and a novel, *Roderick Hudson* (1876). He moved to Europe and took rooms on Bolton Street in London. He resided in England for the rest of his life and became a British citizen in 1915. He seems to have enjoyed his participant-observer status in British and French society and among the American expatriates and visitors in Europe.

The success of *DAISY MILLER* (1878) brought both praise and blame. His portrait of a young ingenue is considered a fine re-creation of youth and innocence, but it offended some in the United States who felt that no properly brought-up young woman would behave as Daisy does in going out unescorted to meet a man. The novella establishes James as a master of prose fiction and features a characteristic Jamesian theme of the brash innocence of the New World in contrast with the corrupt, jaded, and sometimes jealous propriety of the Old World. James also has a talent for exemplifying the innocence of Americans through the consciousness of young women. He shows astute psychological observation in his novellas, such as *Washington Square,* and novels, such as *The Portrait of a Lady,* that concern young women coming to maturity.

James met Constance Fenimore Woolson (1840–94) in 1880 and developed a close friendship with her. They seem to have shared living quarters in Bellosguardo near Venice in 1887, and Alice James sent Fenimore a message from her deathbed in 1892, the year that Robert Louis Stevenson (who had named James as his executor) died. Two years later, Fenimore was found dead in Venice; James believed she had committed suicide. Biographical critics see the influence of the friendship most strongly in the short novel *The Aspern Papers* (1888) and in "The Beast in the Jungle" (1902). Three other deaths in this period had an impact on James's life: that of Clover Hooper Adams by her own hand in 1885, that of Elizabeth Boott Duveneck after childbirth in 1888, and that of Fanny Kemble from old age in 1893.

In 1890, James began a five-year attempt to change the direction of his career. He was successful as an author of short stories, novels, travel writing, and miscellaneous essays, but he wanted to write for the stage. He failed notoriously. His adaptation of *The American* (1891) was considered pale and unoriginal in comparison with the novel (1877). Some plays were never staged, and *Guy Domville* opened in 1895 on the same night as Wilde's *The Importance of Being Earnest*. *Domville* was criticized for its melodrama, as were some of James's early novels, and it closed after its first night. Although James did not achieve the reputation as a dramatist that he sought, the experience sharpened his skill with dialogue in his fiction.

He experimented more successfully when he turned to writing ghost stories in 1898. *The Turn of the Screw* (1898) is a fine example of a ghost story with ambiguous supernatural and psychological elements, as is "The Jolly Corner" (1908). He became known as the Master for his extraordinary skill in composing exquisite fiction, both short and long. Among the former are "Brooksmith," "Greville Fane," "The Figure in the Carpet," "The Real Thing," and "The Tree of Knowledge."

After his 50th birthday in 1893, James, all too aware of the passing of his youth, seems to have looked to young men for emotional sustenance. He had a particularly affectionate correspondence with a sculptor, Hendrik Christian Andersen (1872–1940). He also developed friendships with younger writers, including Joseph Conrad (1857–1924), Stephen Crane (1871–1900), and H. G. Wells (1866–1946). He broke with Wells over a satirical chapter in *Boon*, the alleged literary remains of George Boon, in 1915, as he had earlier broken with Thomas Perry over the latter's criticism of James's decision to live abroad. (James encountered Perry in France in 1907 and resumed the friendship.) James formed other important friendships, perhaps more like that with Fenimore, late in life with Edith Wharton (c. 1861–1937) and Lucy Clifford.

In 1899, James bought Lamb House in Rye, where he settled to write in quiet. He published *The Wings of the Dove* (1902), *The Ambassadors* (1903), and *The Golden Bowl* (1904). He lectured in the United States in 1904 and published a book about his travels. His reputation grew, and he published from 1906 to 1909 *The Novels and Tales of Henry James* (the New York Edition). He wrote prefaces that note the origins of his fictions and create his aesthetic for fiction; he rewrote some of his early work in his mature style. The exhaustion from the endeavor seems to have triggered a brief breakdown. Oxford awarded him an honorary degree in 1912. For his 70th birthday, his friends and literary colleagues commissioned a portrait by John Singer Sargent (1856–1925), which a suffragette wielding a meat cleaver attacked in 1914; she protested not the subject or the painter but the plight of women painters. The painting was later repaired. James received the Order of Merit about two months before his death after a series of strokes on February 28, 1916.

BIBLIOGRAPHY

Edel, Leon. *Henry James: A Life.* New York: Harper and Row Publishers, 1985.

James, Henry. *Collected Stories.* 2 vols. London: Everyman, 2000–2001.

———. *Complete Stories 1864–1874.* New York: Library of America, 1999.

———. *Complete Stories 1874–1884.* New York: Library of America, 2000.

———. *Complete Stories 1884–1891.* New York: Library of America, 2000.

———. *The Complete Tales of Henry James.* 12 vols. Edited by Leon Edel. Philadelphia and New York: J. B. Lippincott Co., 1962–1964.

———. *The Portable Henry James.* Edited by John Anchard. New York: Penguin Books, 2004.

Kaplan, Fred. *Henry James: The Imagination of Genius.* New York: William Morrow and Co., 1992.

Novick, Sheldon M. *Henry James: The Young Master.* New York: Random House, 1996.

Karen Keck

JAMES, M. R. (1862–1936)

Montague Rhodes James was born in Goodnestone, Kent, the fourth and youngest child of his family. He was a solitary child and spent more time in libraries reading archaic texts than playing with other children. His zeal for reading led him first to Eton College and then King's College, Cambridge, where he excelled and was quickly promoted to fellow, them dean and tutor. In 1905 he was made provost for King's College, and from 1913 to 1915 he served as vice chancellor for the university. In 1918, he returned to Eton as provost, where he remained until his death in 1936.

Despite his exhaustive career as a scholar, James is remembered instead for his ghost stories, the first of which was published in the 1904 collection *Ghosts of an Antiquary*. The sources for these tales can be traced to his childhood, when he suffered from chronic nightmares, and his Dickensian pastime of telling ghosts stories on Christmas Eve, which began during his time as a student at Eton. The success of his first volume of ghost stories prompted four more collections, including *More Ghost Stories of an Antiquary* (1911), *A Thin Ghost and Others* (1919), *A Warning to the Curious* (1925), and *The Collected Ghost Stories of M. R. James* (1931). The impact of his stories not only on his contemporaries but on present-day writers such as Terry Lamsley and Fritz Leiber has led to his being considered the father of the modern ghost story. The recurring theme in James's works is not only the psychology behind the ghost story but his emphasis that the events told are factual accounts; he thus draws his reader into believing in the supernatural because of recovered documents or trustworthy narrators, as in one of his most famous stories, "Oh, WHISTLE, AND I'LL COME TO YOU, MY LAD." (See also "LOST HEARTS.")

BIBLIOGRAPHY

Cox, Michael. *M. R. James*. Oxford: Oxford University Press, 1993.

James, M. R. *Casting the Runes and Other Ghost Stories*. Oxford: Oxford University Press, 2002.

———. *Collected Ghost Stories*. London: Wordsworth, 1992.

———. *The Haunted Doll's House and Other Ghost Stories*. London: Penguin, 2000.

Amanda Mordavsky

"JANET'S REPENTANCE" GEORGE ELIOT (1858)

"Janet's Repentance" is part of a trio of stories by GEORGE ELIOT that was first serialized as *Scenes of Clerical Life* in *Blackwood's Edinburgh Magazine*. The other two stories in the group are "The SAD FORTUNES OF THE REVEREND AMOS BARTON" and "Mr. Gilfil's Love-Story." This story focuses on Janet Dempster, whose alcoholic husband verbally and physically abuses her. Janet herself turns to alcohol. Though she has friends and a mother, Janet initially refuses their gentle offers of assistance. After Dempster comes home drunk and in so fierce a mood that he throws Janet out in her nightdress, Janet turns to her friend Mrs. Pettifer for help and shelter. After this she accepts the help of an Evangelical minister, Mr. Tryan, whom she had earlier reviled since her religious loyalties were to her pastor, Mr. Crewe.

When Janet's husband has an accident, she takes care of him, but he dies of his injuries. After her husband's death, more friends rally around Janet. Though she is tempted to take up drinking again, Janet manages, with the help of Mr. Tryan, to stay sober. Unfortunately Mr. Tryan is ill with consumption (tuberculosis); Janet does her best to see that he is comfortable and accepts the help of others before he dies of the disease. The end of the narrative speaks of Janet as a living memorial to Tryan.

The help Janet receives from Mr. Tryan is an instance of the working out of Eliot's humanism. Eliot handles even the character of the drunken, violent Robert Dempster with compassion in this story. The events of the story go beyond church factional bickering and exposure of alcoholism to offer insights into the human condition. Eliot's omniscient narrator often takes a compassionate stance and offers broad understanding of everyday struggles and suffering: "Yet surely, surely the only true knowledge of our fellow-man is that which enables us to feel with him—which gives us a fine ear for the heart-pulses that are beating under the mere clothes of circumstance and opinion" (229). The narrator also clearly expresses the idea that people need one another in order to be fully human and alive. One of the ways the reader sees Janet's transformation is through Janet's renewed need to help others and to reestablish friendships she had neglected while she was bound to Dempster. Critics also cite the story as an example of realism, as Thomas Noble points out, however, realism is not a word Eliot used, but she wrote of trying to honestly portray real people and their struggles (viii). Human experience in Eliot's fictional world always involves trials and personal challenges that her main characters learn to meet and work through with the help of others. Her characters often have changes of heart brought about by circumstances that are at least initially beyond their control. Eliot sees that the human soul is "full of unspoken evil and unacted good" (252).

BIBLIOGRAPHY

Demetrakopoulos, Stephanie. "George Eliot's 'Janet's Repentance': The First Literary Portrait of a Woman Addict and Her Recovery," *Midwest Quarterly* 35, no. 1 (1993): 95–108.

Eliot, George. *Scenes of Clerical Life.* Edited by Thomas Noble. Oxford: Oxford University Press, 2000.

Hertz, Neil. *George Eliot's Pulse.* Palo Alto, Calif.: Stanford University Press, 2003.

Susan Bernardo

"JE NE PARLE PAS FRANÇAIS" KATHERINE MANSFIELD (1918)

A pivotal story in KATHERINE MANSFIELD's career, "Je ne parle pas français" is also a key modernist short story (see MODERNISM). The piece was composed over two weeks in the last year of WORLD WAR I, at the time when Mansfield was developing the fatal stages of the tuberculosis that would kill her. She wrote to her husband John Middleton Murry that the story was a "cry against corruption" (1951, 149), and it reveals a more cynical, more cruel view of human personality than her earlier stories. It is also the first story told in a persona not her own. "Je ne parle pas français" was originally published privately by Murry's Heron Press; early reviews noted a similarity to the work of Fyodor Dostoyevsky, particularly to *Notes from Underground.* The story was included in the 1920 collection *BLISS,* published by Constable, but only after Mansfield agreed to cut several passages consisting of explicit sexual material. *Bliss* as a collection received generally positive reviews, and "Je ne parle pas français" garnered quite a bit of attention for its amoral narrator and frank subject matter.

The story is told from the point of view of Raoul Duquette, who describes himself as "twenty-six years old and a Parisian, a true Parisian." Raoul is a writer whose book titles (*False Coins, Wrong Doors, Left Umbrellas*) reveal the emptiness of his being and the deceptiveness of his nature. He claims he has no memories of childhood save one: a sexual encounter with an African laundress (one of the suppressed passages). Raoul traces his own adult sexual deviance—he is promiscuous and irresistible to women, probably bisexual, a sometime prostitute and procurer—to this incident. He maintains that people have no soul: "I don't believe in the human soul. I never have. I believe that people are like portmanteaux—packed with certain things, started going, thrown about, tossed away, dumped down, lost and found, half emptied suddenly, or squeezed fatter than ever, until finally the Ultimate Porter swings them on to the Ultimate Train and away they rattle." These themes of deviance, of emptiness, permeate the whole text. Raoul's reflections on the nature of human experience and personality, especially when he sees the sentence *je ne parle pas français* on some blotting paper in the café, bring Raoul to recollections of his friend, an English writer named Dick Harmon with whom he was infatuated. They spent a great deal of time together when Dick was first in Paris, making a study of French literature. Raoul was insulted when Dick suddenly had to return to England, but agreed to help him find rooms some time later when the Englishman came back to Paris, this time with a beautiful young woman named Mouse. It is Mouse's line "je ne parle pas français" that gives the story its title and haunts Raoul; it is what she says to him upon meeting him and her final words to him the last time he sees her. A few hours after their arrival in Paris, Dick abandons her, ostensibly to return to his mother. Raoul promises to come back again to see Mouse and make sure she is all right, but he never does.

In the creation of the narrator Raoul, Mansfield establishes a character who is entirely artificial, who sees himself as a literary creation and the world around him as text. He is an unreliable narrator, a figure who illustrates Mansfield's ideas about the tenuousness of the self and the impossibility of taking action and representing experience. This was a wholly new direction for her as a writer, resulting in her first truly modernist story. According to her letters, the tension between

Frenchness and Englishness is also crucial, a tension that characterizes modernism as a whole as the text moves between symbolism and a self-conscious irony in regarding those symbols. Everything about Raoul, including his Frenchness, is in some sense a self-reflective creation. Finally, the representation of sex—including Raoul's purported homosexuality—is quite daring, and Mansfield uses it to contribute to the ambiguity that surrounds him and his actions in the story.

Little critical attention was paid to this story for many years, as critics were not entirely certain how it fit into the Mansfield canon; it seemed a radical departure from what earlier critics called her "lyrical," "delicate," or "feminine" style. In recent years, however, the story's engagement with homosexuality and desire, as well as its blurring of boundaries between masculinity and femininity, have made it a much-discussed text.

BIBLIOGRAPHY

Dunbar, Pamela. *Radical Mansfield: Double Discourse in Katherine Mansfield's Short Stories.* New York: St. Martin's, 1997.

Henstra, Sarah. "Looking the Part: Performative Narration in Djuna Barnes's *Nightwood* and Katherine Mansfield's 'Je ne parle pas français,'" *Twentieth-Century Literature* 46, no. 2 (2000): 125–149.

Mansfield, Katherine. *Letters to John Middleton Murry.* New York: Knopf, 1951.

———. *Short Stories of Katherine Mansfield.* 1937. Edited and with an introduction by John Middleton Murry. New York: Knopf, 1967.

Meisel, Perry. "What the Reader Knows; or, The French One." In *Katherine Mansfield: In from the Margin,* edited by Roger Robinson, 112–118. Baton Rouge: Louisiana State University Press, 1994.

Janine Utell

JOHNNY LUDLOW ELLEN (MRS. HENRY) WOOD (1868)

Johnny Ludlow was the title character, orphaned teenage narrator, and pseudonym adopted by ELLEN WOOD for her most popular and highly regarded series of short stories, which appeared irregularly in the *Argosy,* the monthly periodical Wood edited, between January 1868 and June 1891. Wood probably invented the Johnny Ludlow persona to conceal the fact that she was the author of almost half of the contents of her magazine. The stories began as a series of almost naive rural schoolboy sketches but soon deepened in complexity to encompass a wide range of genres and themes, including political agitation, rural deprivation, legal inequality, bigamy, crime, and even social comedy. The tales are mainly rooted in realism, although Wood's predilection for sensation is also evident in many narratives. Although there are more than 90 individually titled stories, only those that have been reprinted in modern anthologies are discussed here.

The first series of 1874, originally simply called *Johnny Ludlow,* was a collection of 26 of the more somber stories Wood had written up to that date. In "Lease the Pointsman" the eponymous railway worker, in a moment of extreme stress, fails to change the points at a busy junction, causing the deaths of a colleague and several passengers. He suffers agonies of conscience because he is aware that his lapse of memory is responsible for the deaths. "Reality or Delusion?" is a ghost story involving a love triangle among two strong-willed women and a vacillating young man, who ultimately proves to be a thief. He commits suicide only to reappear briefly as a ghost to his original lover. "Going through the Tunnel" is an early ingenious crime story set in a railway carriage. A wallet is stolen when a train plunges into a dark tunnel, but the thief is the least likely suspect—a formula that later became a cliché.

The second series (1880) included Wood's name on the title page for the first time. G. K. CHESTERTON reprinted "Abel Crew" in an anthology of early DETECTIVE FICTION. Crew, an herbalist, is indicted for manslaughter when the pills he supplies are believed to have caused the death of twins. However, he is eventually freed when it is discovered that a young woman kept her own similar-looking pills on top of the same cupboard, and the wrong medicine was accidentally administered to the children.

The best story in the third series (1885) is "Jellico's Pack," in which a group of working-class women are fleeced by an unscrupulous draper who tricks them into buying on credit. A near suicide of one of the women is averted by the financial intervention of Johnny.

The fourth series (1890) contains "A Curious Experience," one of the best of all Victorian ghost stories. Four visitors to a spa lodging house each attempt to sleep in a specific room but instead endure the torment of a restless night. It is later discovered that a doctor, a previous tenant, probably poisoned his wife there. The supernatural presence ensures that this woman's story of oppression can never be entirely forgotten.

Dorothy L. Sayers reprinted "The Ebony Box" from the fifth series (1890) as an example of an early crime story. A small box full of gold pieces goes missing, and a young man who is suspected of taking it is ostracized. However, the box was accidentally caught up in some heavy material and is eventually relocated. The young man is triumphantly exonerated. Sayers did Wood a disservice by reprinting this tale, since there are several superior Johnny Ludlow crime stories.

The only tale that has been reprinted from the sixth series (1899) is "The Mystery at Number Seven." A woman servant is found dead at the bottom of some stairs and is believed to have been murdered by a milkman. However, it is later discovered that her closest female friend killed her in a brief moment of jealous insanity because the milkman preferred her.

Toward the end of Wood's career she found the planning and writing of long novels too tiring, but she continued to invent novellas for Johnny Ludlow, her favorite character, and these tales are her most enduring legacy to the short story format.

BIBLIOGRAPHY

Flowers, Michael. "The *Johnny Ludlow* Stories," Available online URL: http://www.mrshenrywood.co.uk/ludlow. html. Accessed on August 21, 2004.

Michael Flowers

"JOURNAL OF MISTRESS JOAN MARTYN, THE" VIRGINIA WOOLF (1906)

This story, first published in 1979, was written in 1906 when VIRGINIA WOOLF was considering becoming a historian. The story reflects on the complex relationship between history and fiction. A female historian lights on an old hall in the countryside and asks to be shown the family archives, among which several manuscripts by the owner's ancestors are to be found. She borrows the diary of Joan Martyn, written in the 15th century. The second part of the story consists of Joan's diary, with its double perspective: the historical, seem-

ingly realistic description of her daily life, her encounters with peasants, the preparations for her impending wedding, and the way her mother runs the estate while the men are in the army versus the imaginative dimension of her life, as she reads aloud to the household and welcomes a poet who tells his tales and shows his illuminated manuscripts.

This early work foreshadows later Woolfian themes: the interplay between fact and fiction, the figure of the anonymous author able to capture "the world without a self," and the voice given back to women who have been silenced by patriarchy. However realistic it may seem, with its focus on the ordinary, the story also questions the very notion of realism: The embedded structure and numerous allusions to illuminated pictures suggest that an objective representation of real life is illusory, that reality may be grasped only through the filters of discourse and imagery, in a word, through cultural legacy. The articulation of the present and the medieval past illustrates that we can never reconstruct an exact image of the Middle Ages but can only create our own conception of it. It has been suggested that Woolf's numerous visits to London museums around the time the story was written made her aware of this. As evidenced in the 1905 *Guide to the Exhibition Galleries of the British Museum,* the Department of Manuscripts showed a "Book of Hours, fifteenth century, with autograph inscriptions of Henry VII, Henry VIII" (122) alongside romantic medievalist manuscripts such as *Childe Harold's Pilgrimage* by Lord Byron, an autograph of *Kenilworth* by Sir Walter Scott, and the epilogue to the *Idylls of the King* by Lord Tennyson (122). These items were a reminder of the links between history and fiction and our constant rereading and reassessment of the past and culture.

BIBLIOGRAPHY

Utz, Richard, and Tom Shippery, eds. *Medievalism in the Modern World. Essays in Honour of Leslie J. Workman.* Turhout, Belgium: Brepols, 1998.
Woolf, Virginia. "The Journal of Mistress Joan Martyn." In *The Complete Shorter Fiction of Virginia Woolf,* edited by Susan Dick, 33–62. New York: Harcourt, 1985.
Workman, Leslie K., ed. *Medievalism in England.* Cambridge: Brewer, 1992.

Caroline Marie

JOYCE, JAMES (1882–1941)

JOYCE, JAMES (1882–1941)   Born in Dublin on February 2, 1882, James Joyce was the oldest of 10 surviving children in a family that moved homes continuously because of its fluctuating financial situation. Coming of age in a family in the midst of a long decline, Joyce knew the whole range of Dublin life. Educated in the Catholic Jesuit tradition, he was a gifted student, especially with languages. Drawn to the intricacies, mystery, and ritual of esoteric Catholicism, Joyce attended the Jesuit Clongowes Wood College until he was withdrawn after his father lost his job. Joyce oscillated between periods of intense religious fervor and turning against Catholicism. Like Ireland, Catholicism, even when Joyce appeared to have rejected it, never ceased to be a major force in his writing. In 1893 he attended Belvedere College, where he completed his secondary education, before attending University College Dublin, where the writings of the Norwegian dramatist Henrik Ibsen profoundly influenced him. While in college, he published reviews and articles, wrote plays and poetry, and graduated with a degree in modern language in 1902. After graduation he went to Paris, where he thought he would attend medical school but where he instead began to formulate his "aesthetic system." In 1903 he returned to Dublin to be with his dying mother, an encounter that haunted him throughout his life and is replayed in *Ulysses.* In June 1904 he met Nora Barnacle, and together they left Ireland and traveled to Paris, Zurich, Trieste, and Pola. In 1909 Joyce returned to Dublin to set up Ireland's first cinema, the Volta. He visited Dublin once again in 1912, after which he never returned.

Joyce began publishing stories in the *Irish Homestead,* and these stories eventually became his collection *Dubliners.* Joyce had enormous difficulty securing a publisher for *Dubliners,* which one printer destroyed for its vulgarity, religious slurs, and sexual innuendoes. *Dubliners* was rejected by 12 publishers for its sexuality, immorality, and anti-Catholicism, and especially strong objections were raised to "The Boarding House" and "An Encounter." Grant Richards eventually published the collection in 1914, the same year Joyce's *A Portrait of the Artist as a Young Man* was appearing serially in the *Egoist. Dubliners* was published in New York in 1916. Joyce's *Ulysses,* arguably the central prose work of modern literature, appeared in 1922, the same year as T. S. Eliot's modern poetic masterpiece, *The Wasteland. Ulysses* was not published in the United States until 1934, after a court ruling that it was not pornographic following a complaint by the Society for the Prevention of Vice. Joyce and Nora married in 1931. Joyce's final work, *Finnegans Wake,* appeared under the title "Work in Progress" in the Paris journal *transition* and was published in 1939. Following the outbreak of World War II, the Joyces returned to unoccupied France, but they were forced to leave in 1940 and travel to Zurich, where Joyce died on January 13, 1941.

Critics have argued that *Dubliners* is a study in the economic and spiritual paralysis of the modern city and that the collection is complicated by Joyce's final story, "The DEAD." The opening story, "The Sisters," contains a musing on the word *paralysis,* the condition that afflicts many of Joyce's characters. Joyce wrote his brother Stanislaus that Dublin was a city "suffering from hemiplegia of the will," and paralysis, whether linguistic, economic, sexual, political, cultural, or emotional, is evident from the opening pages of the collection. Alcoholism, miscommunication, abuse, marital problems, and splintered familial relationships in *Dubliners* appear as a product of this paralysis, which itself is a result of the absence of economic and political power due to colonization. The thematic emphasis on failed escapes from Dublin suggests the power of this paralysis.

In addition to composing *Dubliners* to "betray the soul of that hemiplegia or paralysis which many consider a city," Joyce viewed the stories as a series of *epicleti,* the moment of transubstantiation in mass when the common transforms into the sacred. Joyce referred to the revelation of the truth in his stories as his attempt to "give some kind of intellectual pleasure or spiritual enjoyment by converting the blood of everyday life into something that has a permanent artistic life of its own . . . for their mental, moral, and spiritual uplift" (*Letters* 55). Spiritual or artistic transformation is missing in *Dubliners.* Joyce portrays a people sundered from the land and their tradition, isolated and wandering in a city from which they cannot escape. Joyce wrote the stories in a style of "scrupulous meanness," and he composed "The DEAD" partially as a corrective to this cruel anatomy of a city. In contrast, "The Dead" shows a different perception of Ireland, which Richard Ellmann suggests resulted from Joyce's time in Rome. In Rome, an equally Catholic city, the ghosts of the dead remained in the living city, and this refusal of the dead to remain buried constitutes a major theme in Joyce's oeuvre. In "The Dead," both personal and political ghosts haunt the story, and Gabriel Conroy's recognition of his wife's love for her dead lover mirrors the potency of the past in the colonial city. Ellmann calls "The Dead" Joyce's first song of exile.

While Joyce's Irish predecessors in short story writing include William Carleton and GEORGE MOORE, other influences include Guy de Maupassant and Anton Chekhov. In a letter to his brother, Joyce identified his stories as representing the stages of childhood, adolescence, mature life, and public life. As the characters age, the glimpses of possible freedom that characterize the early stories all but vanish, giving way instead to despair and resignation. Joyce's use of stream of consciousness, the epiphanic moment, and vernacular and slang language forecasts his innovation with these techniques in his later work. While early critiques of *Dubliners* emphasized the structure and questioned the unity of the collection, more recent critical interpretations undertake a detailed analysis of the social and political climate of Joyce's colonial Dublin, seeing the paralysis of Joyce's Dubliners as inseparable from their economic and political subjugation by Britain. The critics Vincent Cheng and Emer Nolan have focused on feminism, socialism, and imperialism in Joyce's works.

Joyce's Dublin is a liminal city, a purgatory from which escape is a necessary precursor to success, as in "A LITTLE CLOUD," but escape from Dublin appears problematic, especially for women, as in "EVELINE." The urban landscape of Dublin functions as a character in its own right in Joyce's stories. Writing to publisher Grant Richards in 1905, Joyce stated, "I do not think that any writer has yet presented Dublin to the world. It has been a capital of Europe for thousands of years, it is supposed to be the second city of the British Empire. . . . I think people might be willing to pay for the special odour of corruption which, I hope, floats over my stories" quoted in Oates, 180). Although English domination is most clear in "Eveline," "After the Race" and "Two Gallants," the ripple effects of colonization appear in a number of Joyce's stories. Sexuality is repressed, perverse, absent, or troubling ("A Painful Case," "The Dead," "An Encounter"). In several stories, sexuality is commodified into prostitution, or marriage is seen as prostitution ("A Boarding House," "A Mother," "Eveline"). Alcohol abuse appears in a number of stories, most notably when the characters achieve some recognition of their economic or political impotence ("Grace," "After the Race," "The Dead"). In "A Little Cloud" and "Eveline," alcohol abuse and child abuse coexist. The loss of public power is played out in private domestic space in interpersonal and, more significantly, in cross-generational scenarios. The power struggles between the colonized and the colonizer replicate themselves in the Dublin home, where the result of a loss of public power is the assertion of violence in the private sphere. The ruptured family appears in the relationship between father and daughter in "Eveline," between father and son and husband and wife in "A Little Cloud," and between mother and daughter in "A Mother."

Joyce's vexed relationship to Ireland, though it was at the core of all of his work, appears in his ironic assessment of his country. The stories in *Dubliners* are set in the time of the Irish literary revival, and stories such as "The Mother" and "The Dead" suggest Joyce's resistance to this effort to reject English models of culture for "authentic" Irish representations of Irish life. Joyce rejected much of the Irish revival rhetoric for being sentimental and nostalgic and for seeking to create a mythologized past. Like his protagonist in *A Portrait of the Artist as a Young Man,* Joyce viewed religion and nationality as nets that held back the true artist.

Joyce's chief writings include the poetry collection *Chamber Music* (1907), *Dubliners* (1914), his play *Exiles* (written 1915, published 1918), *A Portrait of the Artist as a Young Man* (1916), *Ulysses* (1922), and *Finnegans Wake* (1939). *Dubliners* represents a significant departure from his earlier writings, and here the natural detail and symbolic systematizing that he masters in his late works first appear. (See also "ARABY.")

BIBLIOGRAPHY
Baker, James R., and Thomas F. Staley, eds. *James Joyce's Dubliners: A Critical Handbook*. Belmont, Calif.: Wadsworth, 1969.
Ellmann, Richard. *James Joyce*. 1959. University Press, New York: Oxford, 1982.
Gifford, Don. *Joyce Annotated: Notes for Dubliners and A Portrait*. 1967. Berkeley: University of California Press, 1982.
Hart, Clive, ed. *James Joyce's Dubliners: Critical Essays*, New York: Viking, 1969.
Joyce, James. *Chamber Music*. London: Elkin Matthews, 1907.
———. *Dubliners*. London: Grant Richards, 1914.
———. *The Letters of James Joyce*. New York: Viking, 1966.
———. *A Portrait of the Artist as a Young Man*. New York: Heubsch, 1916.
Oates, Joyce Carol. "Jocoserious Joyce." In *Contraries*. New York: Oxford University Press, 1981.
Torchiana, D. T. *Backgrounds for Joyce's Dubliners*. Boston: Allen & Unwin, 1986.

Julieann Ulin

"JUDAS" FRANK O'CONNOR (1948)

In "Judas," by FRANK O'CONNOR, a young man's relationship with his widowed mother is damaged by his infatuation with a local girl and consequent loss of illusions. The story explores a painful collision between imagination and "objective reality," an important theme in much of O'Connor's work and a fruitful source of both comedy and pathos for him. The narrator, Jerry Moynihan, an only child with an only child's responsibilities (another significant theme for O'Connor), tells a silent friend about the night he emotionally betrays his mother. Having become infatuated with a nurse, Kitty, Jerry undergoes torments of embarrassment and frustration, seeing her as both morally and socially above him. The agonies and nerves of a shy, idealistic, sexually inexperienced young man are amusingly but touchingly depicted, as are the comic contortions to which they lead. Convinced that the woman he adores is a pure-minded angel, he is dismayed to discover that she sees their relationship in a far more prosaic light and has more experience than him. "Madame Bovary herself had at least the decency to pretend that she didn't like it," he laments. He wants to tell her about his job prospects; she wants to be kissed. Accepting this new type of relationship, Jerry proceeds

home only to be met by his anxious and jealous mother, whose concerns he cruelly repudiates. At cockcrow, however, he repents and goes to her to be comforted. The story's conclusion centers on a curious role reversal, whereby the son's abrupt introduction to adult reality generates the disillusionment of the mother: She is like a struck child "who suddenly saw the stranger in you." The son's realization of what his new adulthood and individual desires have brought about returns them to the relationship of his early childhood, but this, we suspect, is only a temporary respite from the alienating effects of reality.

BIBLIOGRAPHY
O'Connor, Frank. *Collected Stories*. New York: Knopf, 1981.

Muireann O'Cinneide

"JUDGE'S HOUSE, THE" BRAM STOKER (1891)

A horror story, "The Judge's House" first appeared in the December 5, 1891, issue of the *Illustrated Sporting and Dramatic News*. The story was later published in the posthumous collection *Dracula's Guest and Other Weird Stories* (1914). At the time of his death, BRAM STOKER was in the process of compiling several volumes of his earlier short fiction. This first volume of collected stories, with a preface by Stoker's widow Florence, also features "Dracula's Guest," an episode that Stoker had cut from the novel for reasons of length (Senf 36–37).

"The Judge's House" tells the story of Malcolm, a young Cambridge student of mathematics, who is looking for a quiet and secluded spot for study as he prepares for his examinations. Ignoring the protests of the townspeople, he settles into the abandoned former house of a notoriously cruel judge. After a series of escalating encounters with the rats that are the house's only other inhabitants, Malcolm comes face to face with the malevolent spirit of the judge embodied in a giant rat. The unfortunate student is subsequently found dead, hanged at the end of the house's bell pull, fashioned from the same rope used to hang the old judge's victims.

Despite the predictable ending, the story maintains a memorable dimension of horror, achieving its overall effect through Stoker's deployment of a straightforward style. As Daniel Farson notes, the story reads like an accident report (99). The presence of the rats, commonplace yet sinister animals, unifies the tale and contributes to the macabre tone. Stoker's tale borrows elements from SHERIDAN LE FANU's "MR. JUSTICE HARBOTTLE" (1872), just as his most famous novel *Dracula* owes a debt to Le Fanu's vampire story "Carmilla." David Glover characterizes "The Judge's House," whose title is the same as the first chapter of "Harbottle," as a pastiche of the Le Fanu story (29).

BIBLIOGRAPHY
Farson, Daniel. *The Man Who Wrote Dracula.* London: Michael Joseph, 1975.
Glover, David. *Vampires, Mummies, and Liberals: Bram Stoker and the Politics of Popular Fiction.* Durham, N.C.: Duke University Press, 1996.
Senf, Carol A. *The Critical Response to Bram Stoker.* Westport, Conn.: Greenwood, 1993.
Stoker, Bram. *Dracula's Guest and Other Weird Stories.* London: George Routledge, 1914.

Tony Rafalowski

JUNGLE BOOKS, THE RUDYARD KIPLING (1894, 1895)

The Jungle Books includes two volumes of RUDYARD KIPLING's most famous stories, linked by poems, set mostly in India. The best-known stories in the collections are those of Mowgli, the boy raised by wolves. The first volume of *The Jungle Books* features only three Mowgli stories: "Mowgli's Brothers" (first published in *St. Nicholas Magazine,* 1894), "Kaa's Hunting," and "Tiger! Tiger!" The remaining stories, "The White Seal," "Rikki-Tikki-Tavi" (the famous story of the brave mongoose), "Toomai of the Elephants," and "Her Majesty's Servants" are related to the Mowgli stories only insofar as they portray the complex relationship between animals and humans. The second volume features more Mowgli stories: "How Fear Came," "Letting in the Jungle," "The King's Ankus," "Red Dog," and "Spring Running." The remaining stories, "The Miracle of Purun Bhagat," "The Undertakers," and "Quiquern" (about an Inuit hunter), again deal with themes of animal and human interdependence.

The Mowgli stories, though not in chronological order, do follow a master plot, as Mowgli must eventually grow into a man and leave the wild for civilization. Mowgli seems to epitomize the romantic child, living freely and naturally in the jungle. Nature is not idealized, however. The Law of the Jungle (or in the case of "The White Seal," the Law of the Beach) is harsh, and the animal families and communities reflect human social organization, with similar strengths and weaknesses. Whereas earlier interpretations of the books focus on Mowgli as a child hero or as representing humanity expelled from paradise, more recent studies consider the stories to be addressing the relationship between colonizer and colonized. Mowgli at once represents the humans who encroach on the jungle, and he is himself absorbed and made over by the jungle. There is an interesting ecological message in the books.

BIBLIOGRAPHY
Kipling, Rudyard. *The Jungle Books.* London: Penguin, 2000.
McBratney, John. "Imperial Subjects, Imperial Space in Kipling's *Jungle Books,*" *Victorian Studies* 35, no. 3 (1992): 277–293.
Randall, Don. *Kipling's Imperial Boy: Adolescence and Cultural Hybridity.* Basingstoke, England: Palgrave, 2000.

Terri Doughty

JUST SO STORIES RUDYARD KIPLING (1902)

JUST SO STORIES is a collection of short stories, with poems and illustrations, by RUDYARD KIPLING that plays on the *pourquoi* tale, a myth or creation story that explains the existence of something in nature. The first stories grew out of bedtime tales told to Kipling's daughter Josephine, who demanded that they be told "just so," hence the title. These comical parodies of evolution, "How the Whale Got His Throat," "How the Camel Got His Hump," and "How the Rhinoceros Got His Skin," were first published in *St. Nicholas Magazine* (1897–1898). Eight additional stories were published in the *Ladies' Home Journal* and *Collier's Magazine* between 1900 and 1902: "The Elephant's Child," "The Beginning of the Armadillos," "The Sing-Song of Old Man Kangaroo," "How the Leopard Got His Spots," "How the First Letter Was Written," "The Cat That Walked by Himself," "The Crab That Played with the Sea," and "The Butterfly That Stamped." "How the Alphabet Was Made" was added to make 12 stories in the collection. A 13th story, "The Taboo Tale," was added in a 1903 edition but has subsequently been omitted from most editions.

The stories, which seem initially to convey standard moral lessons, like that of the lazy camel punished with a "humph" on his back, mock Victorian didactic fiction for children and become subversive, especially with the elephant's child, who spanks his elders with his new trunk. The collection has many memorable characters, such as the "satiably curious Elephant's Child," the "Mariner of infinite-resource-and-sagacity," and the "Parsee with his hat of more-than-oriental splendour" in "The Elephant's Child." The stories retain the flavor of oral tales. The narrator addresses the reader famously as "Best Beloved," interjects comments, anticipates the reader's questions, and repeats key phrases. Kipling's love of language play and his sensitivity to the sounds of words create vivid tales.

BIBLIOGRAPHY
Kipling, Rudyard. *Complete Just So Stories.* Boston: Little, Brown, 1993.
Knoepflmacher, U. C. "Kipling's 'Just-So' Partner: The Dead Child as Collaborator and Muse," *Children's Literature* 25 (1997): 24–49.

Terri Doughty

"KARAIN: A MEMORY" JOSEPH CONRAD (1897)
One of JOSEPH CONRAD's early Malay stories, "Karain: A Memory" was first published in the November issue of *Blackwood's Magazine* in 1897 and subsequently appeared in *Tales of Unrest* (1898). A story of betrayal and exile and a twofold frame story, it prefigured Conrad's allegorical novels of the British Empire and imperialism in its choice of theme and form.

With its orientalist representation of "a land without memories, regrets, and hopes" (62), "Karain" masterfully expresses the meeting of commercial expansion and European orientalism. A rich past of piratical ventures contrasts ironically with the downsides of imperialist commercialism. In the frame story, the first-person narrator comes across references to political unrest in the Malayan Archipelago in the newspaper. He remembers his encounters with the Malay chief Karain, and his initial reaction is a feeling of nostalgia. The romanticized delineation of the region is sharply posed against the mundane everyday of Victorian London: "Sunshine gleams between the lines of those short paragraphs—sunshine and the glitter of the sea. A strange name wakes up memories; the printed words scent the smoky atmosphere of today faintly" (61). In a juxtaposition characteristic of Conrad's fiction, the commercial trade that takes the narrator to the Far East breaks into a heavily orientalist exotic. In the embedded story, the nameless narrator recounts how he, together with his shipmates Hollis and Jackson, came to Southeast Asia to smuggle guns. Their commercial ventures are at once different from and involved in the continuation of native warfare, including the ambiguously idealized piratical past: "It was almost impossible to remember who he [Karain] was—only a petty chief of a conveniently isolated corner of Minanao, where we could in comparative safety break the law against the traffic in firearms and ammunition with natives" (64). A muted self-irony runs through the story: "He was treated with a solemn respect accorded in the irreverent West only to the monarchs of the stage" (64). The clash of "the irreverent West" with the enigmas of the Orient ultimately becomes central to the resolution of Karain's dilemma. The orientalism that suffuses the story is complemented by an occidentalism that reassesses the (self-)representation of "the West" through its juxtaposition with the changing conceptions of the Orient.

The unfolding of Karain's story is generated as an orientalized ghost story. Karain always appears accompanied by his old sword bearer. After two years of trading, the sword bearer dies, and for once Karain does not pay his usual visit to the smugglers' schooner. Then one night, he arrives on board ship to narrate his story. This ghost story is thus doubly framed. Karain asserts that he is haunted by the ghost of Pata Matara, once his friend, whom he has murdered. Pata Matara's sister, Karain recounts, has brought shame on her people by going to live with a Dutchman, who "said he came to trade" (83). This connection between imperialist commerce and betrayal, including sexual betrayal, runs through Conrad's stories. The Dutchman stands in for the dark side of imperialist trade, as the story capitalizes on Anglo-Dutch colonial rivalry in Southeast Asia. Conrad's most famous novella, HEART OF DARKNESS, establishes a similar juxtaposition between the narrator and the enigmatic Dutchman Kurtz in its representation of European imperialism in Africa. The commercial rapacity of late imperialism and anxieties of degeneration at the fin de siècle form entwined themes that become pivotal to Conrad's MODERNISM.

"Karain" prefigures this allegory, as Karain and Pata Matara embark on an "obscure Odyssey of revenge" (92) in pursuit of the Dutchman and his mistress. This reference to the *Odyssey*, an Ancient Greek epic attributed to Homer accentuates the allegorical levels of the story by imbuing—not without a hint of irony—Karain's tale with an epic and specifically classical dimension. Plagued by dreams of Pata Matara's sister, Karain ultimately shoots his friend instead of the Dutchman. Shortly afterward, he begins to feel haunted by Pata Matara's ghost. Only the old sword bearer can offer him protection. After the old man's death, Karain flees to consult the three smugglers, who represent "the irreverent West." Their rejection of the magical seems to offer a new refuge. At first puzzled by Karain's request of a Western charm to fend off the ghost, they coin just such a specific talisman by capitalizing on a belief in money in their choice of a Jubilee sixpenny piece, a special coin manufactured for Queen Victoria's Golden Jubilee celebrations in 1887: "The thing itself is of great power—money, you know—and his imagination is struck" (100). In this focus on the magic of money and Western coinage, the ironic treatment of commercial imperialism becomes pivotal.

At the same time, Western conceptualizations of order are juxtaposed with an orientalist imaginary of suspended time. The belief in icons of power is ironically treated through its identification with the ghosts that plague the haunted chief. In the narrator's words, as he concludes both framed stories, "that man loyal to a vision, betrayed by his dream, spurned by his illusion, and coming to us unbelievers for help—against a thought. The silence was profound; but it seemed full of noiseless phantoms, of things sorrowful, shadowy, and mute, in whose invisible presence the firm, pulsating beat of the two ships' chronometers ticking off

steadily the seconds of Greenwich Time seemed to me a protection and a relief," (92). Greenwich Time stands for normality. But the end of the story proves that the orientalist imaginary has irrevocably seeped into the empire. The frame story closes with Jackson's assertion that the memory of Karain is more real to him than the bustle of the great metropolis of London. As the narrator self-ironically comments, "I think that, decidedly, he had been too long away from home" (106).

This loss of cultural identity is further developed in Conrad's subsequent "Malay novels," which include such allegorical masterpieces as *Lord Jim* and *Almayer's Folly*. Set in or near the Malayan Archipelago (now Indonesia), they have recently been reassessed for their insights into 19th-century Southeast Asia. Conrad himself, however, emphasized the region's allegorical importance in his works. In *A Personal Record,* he significantly called it a "particular East of which I had but the mistiest, short glimpse."

BIBLIOGRAPHY
Conrad, Joseph. *The Eastern Stories.* London: Penguin, 2000.
———. *A Personal Record.* London: J. M. Dent, 1919.
Hampson, Robert. *Cross-Cultural Encounters in Joseph Conrad's Malay Fiction.* Basingstoke, England: Palgrave, 2000.
White, Andrea. *Joseph Conrad and the Adventure Tradition: Constructing and Deconstructing the Imperial Subject.* Cambridge: Cambridge University Press, 1993.

Tamara Wagner

KELMAN, JAMES (1946–)

James Kelman was born in Glasgow, and the working-class districts of that city are the backdrop for much of his work. Leaving school at the earliest opportunity, Kelman followed his father into the skilled workforce at age 15, beginning a six-year apprenticeship as a compositor, or typesetter. His father's job as a picture framer and restorer involved him in the privileged world of fine art, but in the subordinate position of a manual worker. This contradictory position undoubtedly shaped Kelman's interest in the relationship between social prejudice and ideas of aesthetic worth, which together shape a community's sense of cultural value. In his 1990 essay "Artists and Value" (reprinted in his 1992 *Some Recent Attacks*), Kelman recalls his experience "as a transporter of pictures for various painters and galleries and exhibitions" and his encounters with the concept of "invisibility" that was his as a manual worker. "They saw themselves as 'artists.' The chap who transports their work was the chap who transports their work. They have an inner spiritual life. But the chap doesn't, the chap is a pleb, a servant, brutalized." Many of Kelman's stories (e.g., "THE COMFORT") strive to counteract this invisibility by attending to the inner lives and imaginations of working-class characters, especially men, who are figured not as victims of savage inequality (i.e., products of larger social forces) but as individual human beings, striving for freedom and survival on their own terms.

Kelman's family briefly and unsuccessfully emigrated to California in 1963. Upon returning to Britain, Kelman worked a variety of jobs, including bus driving in Glasgow, factory work in Manchester, and construction labor in London. The everyday lives of blue-collar men both in and out of work, including lone travelers and itinerants, would form the subject matter of his later stories and novels. He began writing at age 22 while working in London, determined to "remain a member of my own community" rather than write from the vantage point of the educated middle-class. When he returned to Glasgow in 1971, he attended extramural classes in creative writing run by the poet and academic Philip Hobsbaum, where he met Alasdair Gray, Tom Leonard, Liz Lochhead, and Agnes Owens. Working independently, these writers sparked an exciting resurgence in modern Scottish literature in the 1980s and profoundly influenced a later generation of Scots writers including IRVINE WELSH, JANICE GALLOWAY, Alan Warner, and Iain Banks.

It is a mistake, however, to read Kelman's work primarily in terms of its Scottishness, or to dwell on its essential connection to Glasgow. Kelman sees himself in existential and anticolonial literary traditions, and his work clearly shows the influence of European modernists such as Franz Kafka, SAMUEL BECKETT, and JAMES JOYCE. Kelman read English and philosophy at Strathclyde University (Glasgow) beginning in 1975. His debut story collection, *An Old Pub near the Angel,* was published in Maine in 1973; *Short Tales from the Night Shift* appeared in 1978. His first major story collection, NOT NOT WHILE THE GIRO, including the famous title story, was published in Edinburgh in 1983, and was

followed in the next two years by the novels *The Busconductor Hines* and *A Chancer,* as well as the story collection *Lean Tales* (with Agnes Owens and Alasdair Gray). All were well received, but it was not until the late 1980s that Kelman became widely known outside Scotland for his innovative narrative technique, which grants the authority of the conventional, third-party narrator to the immediate thoughts and impressions of first-person protagonists and erases the hierarchical division between the language of narration and the language of dialogue. The story collection GREYHOUND FOR BREAKFAST won the 1987 Cheltenham Prize, and *A Disaffection,* a novel about a Glasgow schoolteacher torn between his socialist principles and the function of education in capitalist society, won the 1989 James Tait Black Memorial Prize. *A Disaffection* was also shortlisted for the Booker Prize, which Kelman controversially won in 1994 for the novel *How Late It Was, How Late,* the story of a Glaswegian petty criminal who is blinded in a fight with police he has deliberately incited. The novel's powerful political content, subtle references to canonical literature, and sophisticated critique of social realism were overshadowed by a trivial but vicious newspaper controversy over the "savage" novel's realistic use of profanity. Kelman, in a defiant acceptance speech, compared class prejudice to racism and insisted that "my culture and my language have the right to exist, and no one has the authority to dismiss that right." The short story collection *The GOOD TIMES* (1998) won the 1999 Stakis Prize for Scottish Writer of the Year, and was followed by *Translated Accounts* in 2001, a grim and difficult antinovel set in an unnamed territory under military rule. *You Have to Be Careful in the Land of the Free,* an amusing and inventive yarn about a Scottish emigrant in America, followed in 2004. American readers will find most of Kelman's best short fiction in the collection *Busted Scotch: Selected Stories* (1997).

All Kelman's writing is shaped by his radicalism, and it is impossible to understand his work without understanding his political commitment. He rejects well-meaning, sympathetic stories about the poor and oppressed that represent working-class reality from the outside, but he equally refuses to eulogize from the inside a bygone age of community spirit and sacrosanct working-class values. His unsentimental realism departs from the romantic heroism of William McIlvanney but is distinct from the antiromanticism of D. H. LAWRENCE, ALAN SILLITOE, and Gordon Williams. In American writing, his closest relations in respect of subject matter would include Raymond Carver and Charles Bukowski; in respect to style, Kelman fits somewhere between Damon Runyon and Ernest Hemingway.

BIBLIOGRAPHY

Kelman, James. *"And The Judges Said . . ."* London: Secker & Warburg, 2002.

———. *The Burn.* London: Secker & Warburg, 1991.

———. *Busted Scotch: Selected Stories.* New York: Norton, 1997.

———. *A Disaffection.* London: Secker & Warburg, 1989.

———. *The Good Times.* London: Secker & Warburg, 1998.

———. *Greyhound for Breakfast.* London: Secker & Warburg, 1987.

———. *How Late It Was, How Late.* London: Secker & Warburg, 1994.

———. *Lean Tales.* London: Jonathan Cape, 1985.

———. *Not Not While the Giro.* Edinburgh: Polygon, 1983.

———. *Some Recent Attacks.* Stirling, Scotland: AK Press, 1992.

Scott Hames

KENNEDY, A. L. (1965–)   A. L. Kennedy was born in Dundee on the east coast of Scotland. She studied English and Drama at Warwick University, where she began writing dramatic monologues and short stories. After university she returned to Scotland and worked in various jobs, most significantly as a community arts worker in Clydebank and as a writer in residence for the Hamilton and East Kilbride Social Work Department. It is no accident that her first novel, *Looking for the Possible Dance* (1993), concerns the life of Margaret Hamilton, a community arts worker in the west of Scotland.

Kennedy's fiction engages with those on the fringes of society. Kennedy's gaze is constantly focused on those whom she considers to be unrepresented by the media. In an age when, as one critic puts it, the media is the "seeming verifier of existence" (Dickson, 138), those excluded from media representation are also deemed not to exist. Kennedy's first collection of short stories, *Night Geometry and the Garscadden Trains*

(1990), can be seen as a thematic manifesto that is still pertinent to her most recent work. In the title story, an unnamed narrator attempts to make uncertain sense of a life pulled apart by her husband's adultery. The narrator is unable to come to terms with the fact that the shock waves of her husband's betrayal, cataclysmic to her own life, cannot be acknowledged in the wider world. In a world where millions of people suffer personal disasters every day, her experience is too small to register. The narrator must accept that the lives of "statesmen, or snooker players, or Oscar nominees," those privileged by the global media, will always be more significant than her own.

Often Kennedy's fiction deals with psychological trauma, and especially the trauma that arises from physically or mentally abusive relationships (see "ORIGINAL BLISS"). Close relationships are always a problem since, in Kennedy's stories, communication between individuals is fraught with danger. Misunderstandings and crossed wires abound in her fiction, leading to violence and isolation. Kennedy's characters speak very rarely, since revealing one's identity enables another to manipulate it. For this reason, many of Kennedy's narrators take the form of omniscient third-party voices, and characters' thoughts and feelings are displayed in the free indirect style. Her narrators characteristically make use of heavy irony to emphasize their characters' impossible situations.

Kennedy views the quotidian world of routine and order—in effect, the machinations of any modern city—as a malevolent force. In many of her short stories, female protagonists attempt to escape from or manipulate routine in order to give their lives a private meaning and excitement. These attempts rarely succeed, however, since the new relationships cultivated in this escape from order often mirror the abusive connections they tried to leave behind. In such cases, characters cultivate isolation and social invisibility as a means of self-protection. The confusion the characters feel in this situation is often shown through narrative interruptions and distortions to linear time. The comparable safety of earlier memories can provide a haven from the tumult of the present.

Kennedy's method is to highlight social injustice on the individual level in an attempt to provide a critique of the wider social sphere. Like ALI SMITH, Kennedy deliberately focuses on mundane behaviors, transfiguring the ordinary until it becomes symbolic of a larger order. Neither Kennedy nor Smith rely on pure realism, including in their short stories elements of magic realism and fantasy, often to allegorize very specific situations in a way that ironically highlights their universality.

To date, A. L. Kennedy has written four novels and four collections of short stories, as well as an extended essay titled *On Bullfighting* (2000). She has also written plays for radio and the screenplay for the BFI/Channel 4 film *Stella Does Tricks,* released in 1998. She has edited numerous anthologies. She has twice appeared on *Granta*'s "Best of Young British Novelists" list and is a fellow of the Royal Society of Arts. Kennedy lives in Glasgow and teaches creative writing at the University of St. Andrews. (See also "BREAKING SUGAR.")

BIBLIOGRAPHY

Dickson, Beth. 'Intimacy, Violence and Identity: The Fiction of A. L. Kennedy,' *Revista canana de estudios ingleses* 41 (2000): 133–144.

Kennedy, A. L. *Indelible Acts*. London: Jonathan Cape, 2002.

Kennedy, A. L. *Indelible Acts*. London: Jonathan Cape, 2002.

———. *Night Geometry and the Garscadden Trains.* London: Polygon, 1990.

———. *Now That You're Back.* London: Jonathan Cape, 1994.

———. *On Bullfighting.* London: Yellow Jersey, 1999.

———. *Original Bliss.* London: Jonathan Cape, 1994.

———. *So I Am Glad.* London: Jonathan Cape, 1995.

———. *Tea and Biscuits.* London: Phoenix, 1996.

David Borthwick

"KEW GARDENS" VIRGINIA WOOLF (1919)

"Kew Gardens" was first published as a stand-alone work on May 12, 1919, by Hogarth Press in an initial run of 150 copies. This was quickly followed in June of the same year by a second edition of 500 copies. Its success, fueled by favorable reviews, also ensured the success of Hogarth Press, owned and operated by VIRGINIA WOOLF and her husband. In 1927, a third and limited edition of 500 copies—with woodcut decorations by Woolf's sister, Vanessa Bell, on every page—was issued. The story was later collected with some of Woolf's other short fiction in *Monday or Tues-day* (1921) and *A Haunted House and Other Short Stories* (1944).

"Kew Gardens" is not a story in the conventional sense of the word. While the story elements of scene and characters and atmosphere are present, there is nothing resembling a plot in the expected sense. There is no apparent structure, no framework supporting the story events, no causal chain linking the pastoral opening to the cacophonic closing. Rather, readers appear to discover, one after another, a series of events happening in and around a garden bed in the famous Kew Gardens (located southwest of London near Richmond) on a sunny July afternoon, much as though they were sitting on a nearby park bench and turning their heads to and fro, merely observing, not engaging. From the text, it seems that the events take place on a Sunday afternoon, the day no fee was charged for admission to the gardens. It was the day a family could wander among the garden beds together, the parents reminiscing about their separate pasts, the children chasing butterflies; the day an eccentric elder could be taken out for fresh air and sunshine, where he could talk with the flowers "about the forests of Uruguay which he had visited hundreds of years ago"; the day two elderly busybodies would come together for gossip over tea; the day lovers met and talked in "words with short wings for their heavy body of meaning, inadequate to carry them far."

These glimpses of the lives observed are interlaced with penetrating glances toward and into the garden bed, where a snail and a "high-stepping angular green insect" move about in the parti-colored shade. The entire tapestry is experienced by readers in much the same light as the garden bed itself is seen by one of the gossips: "as a sleeper waking from a heavy sleep sees a brass candlestick reflecting the light in an unfamiliar way, and closes his eyes and opens them, and seeing the brass candlestick again, finally starts broad awake and stares at the candlestick with all his powers." "Kew Gardens" is one of Woolf's early experiments with forms of narration that were later more fully realized in her novels. Rather than a structure of causal relations, of one thing happening because of or as a consequence of some other, the events appear to occur—as Woolf described the particular form in her diary—as though each opens out from another. There is a loose association among events, much as if one were encountering acquaintances unexpectedly and randomly on the street. A conventional reading of point of view in "Kew Gardens" would be that it is told in the third person by an omniscient narrator. One indicator of this point of view is the apparently unrestricted access the reader has to the thoughts and feelings of the characters. While some critics have read the story as focalized through the snail crawling along the floor of the garden bed—or perhaps as focalized in the garden bed itself— a careful reading makes clear that the narratorial presence moves freely among and within the characters much like the butterflies who "crossed the turf in zigzag flights from bed to bed."

BIBLIOGRAPHY

Bishop, Edward L. "Pursuing 'It' through 'Kew Gardens,'" *Studies in Short Fiction* 19, no. 3 (1982): 269–275.

Oakland, John. "Virginia Woolf's *Kew Gardens*," *English Studies* 68, no. 3 (1987): 264–273.

Woolf, Virginia. "Kew Gardens." In *The Complete Shorter Fiction of Virginia Woolf.* 2nd ed. New York: Harcourt, 1989.

———. *A Writer's Diary.* 1953. Edited by Leonard Woolf. New York: Harcourt, 1982.

James Fromm

KEYNOTES AND DISCORDS GEORGE EGERTON (1893; 1894)

John Lane published GEORGE EGERTON's (Mary Chavelita Dunne's) *Keynotes* in 1893 and *Discords* a year later, heading up what would become his new series, "Keynotes," and bringing Egerton fame and notoriety. Aubrey Beardsley's illustration for Egerton's *Keynotes* collection typified the decadent in turn-of-the-century culture. Among the critical responses, Owen Seaman in *Punch* parodied "The CROSS LINE" as "She Notes" by "Borgia Smudgiton," seizing on elements of style and subject, particularly the way Egerton aims to convey a feminine sensibility and a camaraderie between male and female characters.

These stories are innovative in their literary aesthetics and techniques: The writing is characterized by fantasy, impressionism, and truncated open-ended narratives. The stories focus on a woman's sense of self, with descriptions of psychological states and moods. In conveying a peculiarly feminine sensibility, Egerton's prose centers on intuitions and moments of understanding: A sense of immediacy is conveyed by the use of the present tense. Her attention to the relationship between the self and language, its role in constructing experience rather than just expressing it, resembles the perspectives of AESTHETICISM.

The stories are informed by the subject matter and style of Scandinavian naturalism, including the works of Henrik Ibsen, August Strindberg, Bjørnstjerne Bjørnsen, and Knut Hamsun. Egerton lived in Norway and translated Norwegian literature. Although she denied affiliation with the NEW WOMAN movement, Egerton wrote about the concerns of contemporary feminism in *Keynotes* and *Discords*. Disturbing depictions of domestic and sexual violence ("Wedlock," "Gone Under," "Virgin Soil"), alcoholism ("A Shadow's Slant," "Under Northern Sky"), poverty, and prostitution characterize Egerton's treatment of the conditions of married life, in which both working- and middle-class women are vulnerable to economic, physical, and psychological abuse.

While examining the material conditions of women's lives, Egerton also develops a cosmological viewpoint of women that posits an essential female nature of moral and spiritual superiority, which she saw as repressed by the confines of polite urban society and its Victorian mores. Her vision of the true nature of womanhood departed radically and fundamentally from those of her contemporaries in the social and moral purity movement, such as Sarah Grand. Like them, she criticizes male sexual hypocrisy and asserts women's right to make marital and sexual choices, but she also celebrates women who can take pleasure in sexual feelings and power, and she aestheticized their experience ("A Cross Line," "A Little Grey Glove"). She explores their need for fulfillment, insisting on a unique female imaginary and capacity for erotic fantasy, although this model of sexuality, "the primitive, the generic, that makes her sacred, mystic, to the best men" (Egerton, 197), still corresponds to a heterosexual one.

Part of this depiction of real womanhood was of a proactive, sexual maternity in which the woman chooses a eugenically fit mate, which features in many of the stories ("Gone Under," "The Spell of the White

Elf," "A Cross Line"). In "A Cross Line" the heroine fantasizes about riding wildly on a horse; her sexual power and potency—registered further when she recognizes her pregnant state—is depicted in her performance before an admiring and desirous male crowd, "hundreds of faces" gazing at her dressed in a "cobweb garment of wondrous tissue" (20). Yet those deterministic characteristics of Egerton's vision were balanced within a unique imaginary that conveyed optimism and hope. For example, "The Regeneration of Two" concludes with a successful commune of working single mothers and a loving partnership between a New Woman and a New Man based on interdependence, respect, and equality: One of the very few free-love unions to be portrayed as hopeful of success in women's writing at this time.

BIBLIOGRAPHY

Egerton, George. *Key Notes and Discords* (1893, 1894). Edited by Martha Vicinus. London: Virago Press, 1983.

Heilmann, Ann. *New Woman Fiction: Women Writing First Wave Feminism*. Basingstoke, England: Macmillan, 2000.

Ledger, Sally. Introduction. *George Egerton, Keynotes and Discords* (1893). Birmingham: University of Birmingham, 2003.

Richardson, Angelique. *The Eugenization of Love: Darwin, Galton and Late Nineteenth-Century Fictions of Heredity and Eugenics*. Oxford: Oxford University Press, 2003.

Lyssa Randolph

KIPLING, RUDYARD (1865–1936)   Seen by
many critics as the preeminent writer of short fiction in Britain between the 1880s and the 1930s, Kipling was born in Bombay, India, where his father was head of the department of architectural sculpture at the government-sponsored School of Art. Kipling lived in India for the first six years of his life, speaking (as was common among the children of British officials in India) both English and Hindi/Urdu. Indeed, Kipling claimed that he spoke English only "haltingly" at this stage and "thought and dreamed" in Hindi/Urdu. He frequently returns to this India of his childhood in his fiction.

Between 1871 and 1881, Kipling lived in Britain, at first (1871–1877) very unhappily with an English family in Southsea (Kipling writes of this period in "Baa Baa, Black Sheep"), and later happily at a minor private

boarding school for the children of colonial army officers and civil servants (the inspiration for the *Stalky & Co.* stories). He returned to India in 1881, where he worked as a journalist, gathering material that he turned into stories. He published his first stories in the Lahore *Civil and Military Gazette*. Kipling left India, traveled the world, and by 1890, when he settled in London, had become a literary celebrity. Over the next seven years Kipling traveled widely, married an American (Caroline Balestier), and lived for three years in Vermont (where he wrote the stories for THE JUNGLE BOOKS). In 1902 he and his wife settled in Sussex, which was to provide the settings and the topics for many of his later stories. In 1907 Kipling won the Nobel Prize. Despite his successes, Kipling's life was darkened by many sorrows. His daughter Josephine died in 1899; his son John was killed in 1915, fighting in the British Army in France; Kipling himself suffered from serious ill health from 1915 onward. These events are reflected in texts such as his powerful ghost story "They," his stories of World War I (for example, "The GARDENER"), and tales of illness (such as "The Wish House"). Kipling also found himself out of sympathy with many 20th-century literary and political trends, and his reputation went into a severe decline after World War I, to be truly revived only in the last 20 years of the 20th century. There is much that contemporary readers find distasteful in Kipling's work: nationalism, racism, authoritarianism, a distaste for democracy, a crude celebration of violence, and a defense of colonialism. However, many readers have also appreciated his unprejudiced fascination with India and Indians, the breadth of his imagination (encompassing people, animals, machines, the past, the present, and many parts of the globe), the range of his work in terms of genre, and the complex organization of several of his texts (especially with regard to narration).

Kipling is also of importance in British literary history, as he is one of the very few major authors who have dedicated themselves to the short story. Between 1888 and 1932 he published 20 volumes of short stories. During his career, he published only two novels, and one of these, *Kim* (1901), is episodic and at times reads like a collection of connected short stories.

Kipling's Indian stories, most of them published in *PLAIN TALES FROM THE HILLS* (1888), *Soldiers Three*

(1888), *Wee Willie Winkie* (1888), and *Life's Handicap* (1891), are a central part of his output. These include military stories, many of them involving a trio of private soldiers, Mulvaney, Ortheris, and Learoyd. "On Greenhow Hill" is one of the most complex of these and anticipates Kipling's later narrational experiments. Learoyd narrates (it is noteworthy that Kipling allows his lower-class soldiers to tell their own stories) his sad love story, and all the while Ortheris is preparing to kill a deserter from a native regiment. The story brings together a love story, violent death, and the beauty of nature in a striking way. Kipling also produced stories of the officer class of the British Army in India. In "The Man Who Was" (1891) a former officer, captured 30 years previously by the Russians during the Crimean War, makes his way back to the officers' mess of his regiment on the border between India and Afghanistan. The story glorifies the traditions of the British Army and presents the Russians (there is a Russian officer present in the mess) in a most sinister light. Texts like "William the Conqueror" (1898) are very positive portraits of British civilian administrators in India. However, a much more complex note is struck in "On the City Wall" (1888), in which the British narrator is tricked by an Indian prostitute into smuggling a renegade Indian nationalist out of British custody. Similarly, "Without Benefit of Clergy" (1891) is an interracial love story remarkable for its lack of traditional moralizing and racism. "The Mark of the Beast" (1891) and "The PHANTOM RICKSHAW" (1885) are supernatural stories that also fail to show the British in a positive light, while the famous story "The MAN WHO WOULD BE KING" (1888), rather than simply admiring imperial adventure, shows its ultimate failure.

From an early stage, Kipling wrote about children. "Baa Baa, Black Sheep" (1888) is a bleak autobiographical story of adult cruelty and childhood disorientation, while the stories in *Stalky and Co.* (1899) celebrate insubordinate boyish pranks within an overall framework of adult authority. Animals, too, are favorite protagonists. *The Jungle Books* (1894, 1895) are important, but so also are "The Mother Hive" (1908) and "The Bull That Thought" (1926). Kipling wrote many supernatural stories, such as "AT THE END OF THE PASSAGE"

(1891) and "The Wish House" (1924), and also some early science fiction, such as "As Easy As A.B.C." (1912). However, one of the genres Kipling favored was historical fiction. The stories in *Puck of Pook's Hill* (1906) and *Rewards and Fairies* (1910), in which figures from England's history are conjured up to tell their stories, are remarkable exercises in historical imagination, as is a late story about early Christianity, "The Church That Was at Antioch" (1932).

World War I prompted Kipling to write some major stories, marked by the way in which they do not glorify the conflict. "The Gardener" (1926) is a moving story of a woman whose illegitimate son, whom she can never acknowledge as hers, has been killed in France. In "MARY POSTGATE" (1915), despite its apparent anti-German propaganda, the war is reduced to the cruel actions of an elderly lady toward an injured German airman. Death and loss haunt many of Kipling's stories. "They" (1904) is a clear example of this. But there are also stories of regeneration, such as "An Habitation Enforced" (1909) and "My Son's Wife" (1917). One of the most remarkable features of Kipling's output is his experiment with narration. "MRS. BATHURST" (1904) is a radical example: Characters recount events from an angle and with incomplete knowledge; in the end the reader is not quite sure what has occurred. Here Kipling is close to modernist experimentation similar to that in the work of JOSEPH CONRAD and VIRGINIA WOOLF. (See also TRAFFICS AND DISCOVERIES, JUST SO STORIES, and "The RECORD OF BADALIA HERODSFOOT.")

BIBLIOGRAPHY

Gilmour, David. *The Long Recessional.* London: John Murray, 2002.

Kipling, Rudyard. *Collected Stories.* London: Everyman, 1994.

———. *Just So Stories.* London: Penguin, 2000.

———. *Plain Tales from the Hills.* Oxford: Oxford University Press, 2001.

———. *Rudyard Kipling.* Edited by Daniel Karlin. Oxford Authors. Oxford: Oxford University Press, 1999.

———. *Traffics and Discoveries.* London: Penguin, 1992.

———. *War Stories and Poems.* Oxford: Oxford University Press, 1999.

Lowry, Elizabeth. "The Lights That Failed," *Times Literary Supplement,* 19 February 1999, pp. 3–4.

Mallett, Philip. *Rudyard Kipling, A Literary Life*. London: Palgrave/Macmillan, 2003.

David Malcolm

"KISS, THE" ANGELA CARTER (1985)

Part of ANGELA CARTER's collection *Black Venus,* "The Kiss" is set in the "authentically fabulous city" of Samarkand in Uzbekistan. Much of the appeal of the story resides in the evocative portrayal of the city—the details of the firmly geometric designs of buildings and the appearance, makeup, and clothing of the native women. The story seems to have been prompted by legends surrounding Tamburlaine, the Mongol conqueror (1336–1405), and in particular the construction of the Bibi Hanim mosque in Samarkand.

The narrator recounts how Tamburlaine's wife supervised the construction of a mosque as a surprise for her husband to celebrate a great military victory. She asked the architect to complete the final arch in the mosque before her husband returned, but the architect was bewitched by the empress's beauty and requested one kiss in return. She offered him hardboiled eggs dyed in a dozen different colors, arguing that her kiss was no different from that of any other woman and telling him that he could kiss any of her serving women. In response the architect offered her three identical bowls of water, one of which was laced with vodka. On drinking it, the empress spluttered, a reaction that, according to the architect, demonstrated that kissing the woman one loved made all the difference. Admitting defeat, the empress kissed the architect, after which he completed the arch on the same day. When Tamburlaine returned to Samarkand, his wife turned away from him, and the enraged ruler hit her until she admitted her infidelity. Tamburlaine sent his men to the mosque to execute the architect, but he grew wings and escaped to Persia.

As well as demonstrating the tyranny that men have historically used to subjugate their wives, who have much in common with conquered peoples, Carter employs magic realism, combining the techniques of realism and the fantastic so that magical elements grow organically out of the realistic elements portrayed.

BIBLIOGRAPHY
Carter, Angela. *Burning Your Boats: Collected Short Stories.* Introduction by Salman Rushdie. London: Vintage, 1996.
Carter, Angela. *Black Venus.* London: Chatto and Windus, 1985.

Preeti Bhatt

L

"LADY OF THE HOUSE OF LOVE, THE" Angela Carter (1979)

"The Lady of the House of Love," a short story, was first published in Angela Carter's 1979 collection *The Bloody Chamber*. Although *The Bloody Chamber* is composed mainly of retellings of fairy tales, "The Lady of the House" is a gothic vampire tale that contains some conventions usually found in fairy tales, such as the liberating power of love. The story recounts the unenviable, lonely existence of a Transylvanian vampire countess, the "beautiful queen of vampires" (195), a descendant of Vlad the Impaler, who was in actuality a notorious 15th-century Wallachian (Romanian) tyrant who was, according to some noteworthy scholars, the inspiration for the most famous vampire novel of all, Bram Stoker's *Dracula*.

As a member of such a distinctly vicious bloodline, presumably the countess would take great pleasure in the vampire's violent method of feeding, but instead she is a reluctant vampire; there is no enjoyment in feeding for her, it is only a means of survival. Constantly questioning the hand that fate has dealt her, the countess, dressed in her "antique bridal gown" (195), bides her miserable immortality by shuffling through tarot cards, "constructing hypotheses about a future which is irreversible" (197) and, in a taste of bittersweet irony, eternal. As a child, the countess was able to satisfy her hunger by feeding on small animals, but now that she is a woman, only men can provide enough nourishment to sustain her. To survive, the countess employs a governess to assist her; the governess brings young men to the castle, where the countess, outfitted in a "negligee of bloodstained lace" (198), seductively feeds on them. The countess's desire for a mate who is more than a meal is evidenced by her donning of both a wedding gown and negligee, the hallmarks of married life, or at least of a life shared with another. And one day, as in a fairy tale, fate unexpectedly changes everything. Even though the countess did not foresee the event in her tarot cards, her wish for a mate comes true when the governess brings to the castle a young British soldier who is vastly different from any of the other men with whom the countess has had contact.

The young man possesses all the qualities that would constitute a traditional fairy tale prince or the archetypal knight in shining armor. Since he is a soldier, he is heroic; he is also "rational," as is illustrated by his sensible mode of transportation: a bicycle. These qualities, combined with his innocence, signified by his virginity, make him "like the boy in the fairy tale, who does not know how to shudder" (205). The inability to be afraid, however, is the magic elixir that releases the countess from vampirism. When she cuts her hand on a shard of broken glass, seeing her own blood for the first time, the young soldier gingerly kisses her wound. His act of kindness grants the countess the ability to feel for another, and because the capacity to feel is one of the virtues of being human, the soldier's compassion for the countess equips her with the courage and knowledge to become human in her own right.

The next morning, the young soldier wakes to find the countess gone, but he has plans for her—plans to fix her teeth, her eyes, and her "nervous hysteria." In essence he wants to "cure her of all these nightmares" (208). However, with humanity comes mortality, and as the countess was already quite old, death proves to be her true destiny. Nevertheless, as a gothic story, a genre characterized by the irony and contraries, "The Lady of the House of Love" illustrates that death is an escape from the countess's miserable immortal existence; death frees her from a fate that is, for the countess, worse than death.

BIBLIOGRAPHY
Carter, Angela. *Burning Your Boats: The Collected Short Stories.* New York: Penguin, 1995.

Easton, Alison, ed. *Angela Carter: New Casebooks.* New York: St. Martin's, 2000.

Tucker, Lindsey, ed. *Critical Essays on Angela Carter.* New York: G. K. Hall & Co., 1998.

Trudi Van Dyke

"LADY TAL" Vernon Lee (1892)   "Lady Tal," a novella, is the first of three morality tales in Vernon Lee's (Violet Paget's) collection *Vanitas: Polite Stories.* Though described in the dedicatory preface to the volume as "sketches of frivolous women," the stories are not wholly unsympathetic representations of the society women they depict. As such, the stories emphasize the social and economic forces that constrain the lives of such women. "Lady Tal" portrays the relationship between Lady Atalanta Walkenshaw, a rich young widow with literary aspirations, and Jervase Marion, an American psychological novelist, described as "a kind of Henry James, of a lesser magnitude" (194). Holidaying in Venice after completing a novel, Marion has vowed not to pay social calls, not to study people as characters for future novels, and not to proffer assistance to amateur novelists. All three vows are broken when he encounters the enigmatic Lady Tal. Marion learns that Lady Tal married a wealthy older man who died within a year of their marriage, leaving her his entire fortune on the condition that she not remarry. He learns also that she tended to her chronically ill half brother but showed no emotion upon his death. Based on these stories and on his own observations, Marion

concludes that Lady Tal is a heartless woman, a woman without a soul. Fascinated by what he views as a psychological problem, Marion agrees to help Lady Tal with her novel and begins to study her for the purposes of his art. He is at once drawn to and repulsed by Lady Tal, finding in her hints of greatness but believing ultimately that she is too firmly entrenched in frivolous society life to realize her potential.

Marion's perception of her, however, is repeatedly challenged—by Lady Tal's novel, which has "indications of . . . a very decided and unmistakable soul" and, more important, by Lady Tal herself, who, it becomes clear, has a better psychological understanding both of herself and of Marion than he does (213). The story ends when both characters are about to leave Venice. They discuss Marion's next novel, a novel clearly based on their relationship. In Marion's telling, it concerns an older sculptor who makes a fool of himself helping a young woman sculptor. In what appears to be a proposal of marriage, Lady Tal provides a revised account in which the two marry and offers to collaborate on the novel with him. Before she can finish, however, they are driven indoors by a sudden downpour and the story ends. The novella uses techniques of psychological realism in a compelling example of a Jamesian narrative. At the same time, the story has been widely recognized as a satire of Lee's relationship with her mentor Henry James, who was offended by the story and broke off their relationship. And yet, to read the story strictly as a roman à clef does a disservice to Lee's clever use of ambiguity in the narrative to explore themes of reading and misreading and masks and truth. Ultimately, these ambiguities allow for multiple interpretations, forcing readers to come to their own conclusions about the actions, motivations, and future lives of Marion and Lady Tal.

BIBLIOGRAPHY
Lee, Vernon. "Lady Tal." In *Daughters of Decadence: Women Writers of the Fin de Siècle,* edited by Elaine Showalter, 192–261. New Brunswick, N.J.: Rutgers University Press, 1993.

Zorn, Christa. *Vernon Lee: Aesthetics, History, and the Victorian Female Intellectual.* Athens: Ohio University Press, 2003.

Kristen MacLeod

"LAGOON, THE" Joseph Conrad (1897)

"The Lagoon" was one of the first short stories that Joseph Conrad wrote and was his second to be published. The story is set in the Malay Archipelago, which also features in the novels *Almayer's Folly* (1895) and *An Outcast of the Islands* (1896). This location is also the backdrop for "Karain: A Memory" (also 1897), which develops more fully the enigmatic ending of "The Lagoon." Both stories appeared in Conrad's first anthology, *Tales of Unrest* (1898).

"The Lagoon" represents one of Conrad's earliest experiments in what he later described as the "several ways of telling a tale." Though the story introduces themes that Conrad would pursue in other works, "The Lagoon" lacks the technical and intellectual complexity of his later fiction. As Conrad himself wrote, the text features "the usual forests river-stars-wind sunrise . . . and lots of secondhand Conradese" (*Collected Letters*, 301). Despite Conrad's self-deprecation, the story (along with "Karain") was well received following its publication in the *Cornhill Magazine* (see MAGAZINES). As one contemporary reviewer commented, these stories "brought the East to our very doors."

Though "The Lagoon" has as its narrator an anonymous white traveler to whom a tale of violence and passion is told, it differs from "Karain" by being narrated in the third person and by not having a closing frame. Consequently, there is little interaction between either the listener and the storyteller or the author and the reader. The potential ambiguity of the tale is also diminished: It becomes something more easily read and consumed. (Conrad's intention, in part, was to benefit from the huge financial rewards associated with the magazine market.)

"The Lagoon" begins with a white man sailing upstream. He instructs his native crew to tie up for the night in a clearing near where his old companion, Arsat, lives. Arsat is loathed by the sailors not only "as a stranger" but also because "he is not afraid to live amongst the spirits that haunt the places abandoned by mankind." The crew refuses to leave the boat, so the white man goes alone. When he arrives at the hut, he finds Arsat's lover, Diamelan, mortally ill. Unable to help her, Arsat and his visitor sit in silence until "A plaintive murmur rose in the night; a murmur sadden-

ing and startling, as if the great solitudes of surrounding woods had tried to whisper into his ear the wisdom of their immense and lofty indifference." Arsat is now spurred into recounting how he fell in love with Diamelan, a serving girl, and how he and his brother, sword bearers to a tribal chief, had planned to kidnap her from her mistress. When their attempt was discovered, Arsat abandoned his brother to his fate and fled with Diamelan. Arsat is guilt-ridden and convinced that Diamelan's death is retribution for his cowardice. The story's constant suggestion of a supernatural world also hints that the cause of Diamelan's illness is the avenging spirit of Arsat's brother. Nonetheless, this reading remains only a tantalizing possibility, as does Conrad's closing reference to a metaphysical "world of illusions." Though atmospheric, "The Lagoon" is underdeveloped in its symbolism, and contemporary critics have argued that its unsophisticated use of exotic locations erects a safe boundary between the white reader (for whom it was written) and the non-Western, colonial subject.

BIBLIOGRAPHY

Conrad, Joseph. *Collected Letters*. Vol. 1. Edited by Frederick R. Karl and Laurence Davies. Cambridge: Cambridge University Press, 1983.
———. *Tales of Unrest*. London: Fisher Unwin, 1898.
Erdinast-Vulcan, Daphna. *The Strange Short Fiction of Joseph Conrad: Writing, Culture, and Subjectivity*. Oxford: Oxford University Press, 1999.
Karl, Frederick R., and Laurence Davies, eds. *The Collected Letters of Joseph Conrad*. Vol. 1. Cambridge: Cambridge University Press, 1983.

Paul March Russell

LAWRENCE, D. H. (1885–1930)

Born on September 11, 1885, in the Nottinghamshire village of Eastwood, David Herbert Richards Lawrence has been considered one of the most controversial writers of the 20th century. The fourth child of a collier, Lawrence's roots were humble; by his own admission he was "the son of a coal miner, and very ordinary." He was a sickly youth plagued by debilitating bouts of pneumonia and tuberculosis, a weakness that was to haunt him until his early death in 1930. Having studied at Nottingham University College and worked briefly at the Davidson

Road School in Croydon Lawrence was forced by the return of his ill-health to stop working permanently.

In March 1912 Lawrence met Frieda von Richthofen. By May of the same year the couple had eloped to Metz in Germany, Frieda leaving her husband and two children. The couple returned to England in 1914 and were married at Kensington Register Office in July. The years following the outbreak of war in Europe were wretched ones for the Lawrences. Later he wrote, "The War finished me: It was the spear through the side of all sorrows and hopes" (*Letters,* 2: 268). This period was, however, extremely productive for Lawrence. His outrage at the events in Europe stimulated his study of Thomas Hardy, and he wrote some of his most famous novels, *The Rainbow* (1915) and *Women in Love* (1920).

The 1920s was an itinerant decade for Lawrence. In 1917 he and Frieda were evicted from their Cornwall home on charges of spying, exacerbated by Frieda's German origins. In 1919 the Lawrences left England and embarked on a series of travels through four continents. In 1922 they left for Ceylon and then Australia: This journey inspired *Kangaroo* (1923). In September 1922 the couple settled in Taos, New Mexico, a place that was to have huge significance for Lawrence's writing. They spent the summer of 1923 in Mexico, a trip that prompted the composition of *Quetzalcoatl,* an early version of *The Plumed Serpent* (1926). After this decisive break with England, Lawrence returned only once during his lifetime, for just a month in 1925.

Lawrence died in Vence, France, on Sunday, March 2, 1930, after submitting to a final bout of tuberculosis. He was buried there two days later. In 1935 his wife, Frieda, had his body exhumed, cremated, and transported to Kiowa Ranch in New Mexico.

Lawrence's literary reputation and his position within the established canon has been far less stable than that of many of his contemporaries. While figures such as VIRGINIA WOOLF, T. S. Eliot, and JAMES JOYCE have enjoyed a relatively consistent place within the spheres of academic criticism, Lawrence and his work have shifted in and out of favor with alarming frequency. Notoriety dogged Lawrence throughout his lifetime, and very few of his works have escaped accusations of obscenity or hints of scandal. His first compilation of short stories, *The PRUSSIAN OFFICER* (1914), was omitted from the catalogues of Jesse Boot's famous lending libraries because of the overtly sexual undercurrent that suffuses the volume. Shortly after its publication in September 1915, *The Rainbow* (1915) was suppressed and on November 13 was prosecuted and banned under the Obscene Publications Act. *Women in Love* (1920) remained unpublished for nearly three years, only going into print in 1920. *Lady Chatterley's Lover,* published in 1928, marked the height of Lawrence's controversy as a writer. In 1929 the typescripts of *Pansies* were seized by the police, and a London exhibition of Lawrence's paintings was raided for obscenity.

The 1950s saw a turn in the tide of Lawrencian appreciation. Following the efforts of F. R. Leavis in his influential work of criticism *D. H. Lawrence, Novelist* (1955), Lawrence scholarship experienced something of a revival. The famous "Lady Chatterley trial" of 1960 brought Lawrence's work further into the public domain and, in the words of one critic, set Lawrence himself up as the "patron saint" of the 1960s. The end of the transcontinental ban on the novel heralded a new era for Lawrence's writings. *Lady Chatterley's Lover* represented a new model of sexual behavior in which the liberation of body and mind and a complete reverence for the sexual act combined to give an integrity and honesty to that which had previously been considered with shame and opprobrium.

The publication of Kate Millett's *Sexual Politics* in 1970 brought about another shift in Lawrencian criticism. Far from hailing Lawrence's work as sexually liberating, Millett denounced his portrayal of women as both misogynistic and patriarchal. Millett's attack focused on *Lady Chatterley's Lover* and the overt sadism apparent in the story *The Woman Who Rode Away.* While neither Leavis's deification nor Millett's demonization represent the full truth about either the man or the work, this juxtaposition of perspectives is revealing. The desire to categorise Lawrence limits much of the recent criticism. His writing frequently defies such definition and should rather be considered as a series of stages and resting places in his development as both a man and an author. Throughout the body of his work his agenda mutates and morphs, both ideologically and geographically, in line with his own intellectual and, indeed, physical moves. This progression, though obviously manifest throughout Lawrence's novels, can also be charted in microcosm through the body of his shorter fiction. The stories, tales, and short novels provide the reader with a sharp and focused perspective of Lawrence's complex and contradictory journey as a writer.

Lawrence's abilities as a short story writer launched his literary career. His first published work was a piece titled "A Prelude" printed in the *Nottinghamshire Guardian* in the winter of 1907. The story won the newspaper's prize and brought Lawrence his first income for a piece of writing.

Lawrence's contribution to the field of the short story and the novella, or "novelette" as he preferred, was prolific. During his lifetime he published five volumes of short works. *The Prussian Officer and Other Stories* (1914) belongs to the earliest phase of Lawrence's writing and pivots around moments of sexual epiphany, around the strange and unsettling sensation that accompanies the moment within a relationship when the balance of power shifts and reasserts itself. Elizabeth Bates's psychological transformation in the wake of her husband's death in "ODOUR OF CHRYSANTHEMUMS" is considered one of Lawrence's finest moments as a writer.

The collection titled *England, My England* (1922) is Lawrence's final farewell to his homeland and is a clear product of the disillusionment of the war years. Echoing, with a cutting irony, the refrain from W. E. Henley's poem—"What have I done for you / England my England, / What is there I would not do, / England my own?"—Lawrence's sense of rejection, his bitterness and anger at his own country suffuses the volume, in particular, the title story.

The stories in *The Ladybird, the Fox and the Captain's Doll* (1923) mark a transition between Lawrence's rejection of English and European culture and his experimentation with a new symbolism derived from an older and more vibrant civilization. "The Ladybird" in particular embodies the conflict between the will to power and the essential equality of all men. The appeal of the values of "obedience, submission . . . power" were to remain with Lawrence throughout his life, and this quality within his writing has

attracted most criticism. "The FOX" is considered one of Lawrence's best stories.

St. Mawr (1928) and *The Woman Who Rode Away and Other Stories* (1928) draw heavily on Lawrence's stay in New Mexico and Mexico. The juxtaposition of the modern individual with the timeless culture of the American Indians punctuates these tales, and Lawrence's fascination with the anthropological, the ritual, and the primitive is at the forefront of his imagination. Perhaps the darkest of his short works, the stories in these two volumes mark the final stages of Lawrence's development as a writer.

Three volumes of short stories were also published posthumously: *Love among the Haystacks and Other Pieces* (1930), *The Lovely Lady* (1933), and *A Modern Lover* (1934), collecting much of his juvenilia and previously unpublished work.

(See also *The DAUGHTERS OF THE VICAR,* "The HORSE DEALER'S DAUGHTER," "MONKEY NUTS," "The ROCKING-HORSE WINNER," "SAMSON AND DELILAH," and "TICKETS PLEASE.")

BIBLIOGRAPHY

Cushman, Keith. *D. H. Lawrence at Work: The Emergence of the 'Prussian Officer' Stories.* Sussex, England: Harvester, 1978.

Ellis, David. *D. H. Lawrence: Dying Game, 1922–1930.* Cambridge: Cambridge University Press, 1998.

Fernihough, Anne. *The Cambridge Companion to D. H. Lawrence.* Cambridge: Cambridge University Press, 2001.

Harris, Janice Hubbard. *The Short Fiction of D. H. Lawrence.* New Brunswick, N.J.: Rutgers University Press, 1984.

Lawrence, D. H. *England, My England and Other Stories.* Edited by Bruce Steele. Cambridge: Cambridge University Press, 1990.

———. *The Fox, the Captain's Doll, the Ladybird.* Edited by Dieter Mehl. Cambridge: Cambridge University Press, 1992.

———. *Letters of D. H. Lawrence.* Vol. 2. Edited by George J. Zytaruk and James T. Boulton. Cambridge: Cambridge University Press, 2002.

———. *Love among the Haystacks and Other Stories.* Edited by John Worthen. Cambridge: Cambridge University Press, 1987.

———. *The Princess and Other Stories.* Edited by Keith Sagar. London: Penguin, 1971, 1981.

———. *The Prussian Officer and Other Stories.* Edited by John Worthen. Cambridge: Cambridge University Press, 1983.

———. *St. Mawr and Other Stories*. Edited by Brian Finney. Cambridge: Cambridge University Press, 1983.

———. *The Virgin and the Gypsy*. Edited by Brian Finney. London: Penguin, 1982, 1989.

———. *The Woman Who Rode Away and Other Stories*. Edited by Dieter Mehl and Christa Jansohn. Cambridge: Cambridge University Press, 1995.

Thornton, Weldon. *D. H. Lawrence: A Study of the Short Fiction*. New York: Twayne, 1993.

Widmer, Kingsley. *The Art of Perversity: D. H. Lawrence's Shorter Fictions*. Seattle: University of Washington Press, 1962.

Worthen, John. *D. H. Lawrence: The Early Years, 1885–1912*. Cambridge: Cambridge University Press, 1991.

Alice Smith

"LEARNING TO SWIM" Graham Swift (1978)

The title story in the collection Learning to Swim and Other Stories (1982) was originally published in 1978 and is one of Graham Swift's best-known tales. It is representative of this author's short fiction: The plot focuses on domestic strife, and traditional, realist methods of exposition are combined with nonlinear chronology and symbolism.

The motif of marital unhappiness recurs in the collection as a whole. The husbands in the stories fear intimacy and invite betrayal through their inability to connect: Thus in "Learning to Swim" a lesson in surviving the water given by Mr. Singleton to his six-year-old son exposes a tug-of-war between spouses as well as their inability to restore a troubled relationship. The stories differ only in the degree of antagonism exhibited and the variety of pain-inducing strategies each story describes, since all the couples in Swift's stories appear to stay together in order to "conceal their feelings," as the narrator of "Cliffedge" suggests, rather than seek emotional fulfilment.

A third-person, omniscient narrative, "Learning to Swim" exemplifies the cruelty of domestic wars through the portrait of a nuclear family. In this story the human need for emotional dependence and the resentment that emerges from the acknowledgment of such a need are symbolized through a swimming lesson. During a summer vacation in Cornwall, the Singletons, with Paul, their six-year-old son, are spending a day on the beach. While the wife sunbathes and recalls past holidays and important moments in her youth and married life, her reverie is repeatedly interrupted by shouts of "kick!" as her husband impatiently tries to teach Paul how to swim. Her unwillingness to assist with the lesson and the urgency with which the husband commands the boy, refusing to release him before he has acquired the skill, reveal marital unhappiness and chronic resentment between the spouses. Paul's lesson turns into a battle of wills, and the little boy finds himself caught between his instinct for self-preservation and his desire to satisfy his father while retaining his mother's love.

Mr. Singleton, an engineer and builder of bridges, is more interested in water than land: Only when he swims does he "feel quite by himself, quite sufficient." In his daily life he works with solid material, but in his dreams he becomes a water creature: He moves effortlessly "through vast expanses of water," going "for long distances under water" without having to "bother about breathing." He constantly reads to his son from Charles Kingsley's novel *The Water Babies,* a didactic Victorian fairy tale, believing that it is the one story that might transform Paul into the amphibious child he desires. In his infrequent sexual encounters with his wife, Mr. Singleton desires to "swim through her"; he feels that his wife's physical being gets "in the way" of another world where he can be alone and whole.

Mr. Singleton, as his name suggests, resents the physical and emotional demands of married life and has considered leaving his wife for a life of "Spartan purity." His denial of the body sharply contrasts with the pleasure Mrs. Singleton takes in sensual indulgence. She imagines her body to have been carved out of stone; as she lies on the sand in Cornwall, willing herself to become "part of the beach," she lets "the sun make love" to her. Mrs. Singleton's sensual, solid form keeps her husband from liberating himself into liquidity. Caught in this elemental struggle between water and land, male and female, the six-year-old Paul must choose between his parents' conflicting, and to him terrifying, desires: his father's impotent fight against dependence and his mother's suffocating demand for allegiance. While Mrs. Singleton entices Paul out of the water with promises of ice cream and kisses, Mr. Singleton keeps him in the sea in the hope that his son will choose to be a water baby, not a land child. Ultimately, Paul makes an instinctive decision: He breaks away from his parents' self-torturing routine of injury and remorse, and trusting his body to the sea, he swims toward independence in "this strange new element that seemed all his own."

In all the stories in *Learning to Swim,* paternity is unwanted or denied to husbands. When they become fathers, these tortured and torturing men seek to establish their authority and force their beliefs on their sons. Like the 11-year-old Roger in "Gabor," Paul rejects paternal beliefs by swimming "away from his father, away from the shore." Although children embody a mystical promise of regeneration, after long years of strife between the partners the Singleton marriage has been destroyed beyond repair. The story ends with Paul's moment of triumph; although the reader celebrates the boy's courage and unexpected assertiveness, little doubt is left that his parents' struggle will continue unaffected by their son's lesson in survival.

BIBLIOGRAPHY
Swift, Graham. *Learning to Swim and Other Stories.* 1982. London: Heinemann, 1985.

Anastasia Logotheti

LEARNING TO SWIM AND OTHER STORIES GRAHAM SWIFT (1982) *Learning to Swim and Other Stories* is a collection of 11 pieces of varying length, published in Britain in 1982 and in North America in 1985. To date, it is the only short fiction collection GRAHAM SWIFT, a major contemporary British novelist, has published. The majority of the stories were initially published in magazines such as *Punch* and *London Magazine* in the late 1970s. Nearly all of these psychologically complex narratives are set in London, Swift's permanent home, and focus on the need to come to terms with a past crisis and alleviate guilt; the characters range from a successful middle-class doctor to a near-immortal family of clockmakers. The traumatized characters in Swift's early fiction frequently experience disillusionment, guilt, and frustration as well as the need for escape and absolution. Through richly evoked settings and structurally complex plots, these stories suggest that

ambiguity and paradox are inherent in daily existence. Mixing realist and modernist techniques of narration with elements of gothic, Swift subtly draws the psychological portraits of guilt-ridden husbands and wives, tormented sons and grandsons. The ironies of life are constantly revealed to the reader of Swift's early fiction: Along with the unresolved puzzles and mysteries at the core of the human psyche, this contemporary author is concerned with the limits of human knowledge and the ambiguity of human motives.

With the exception of "LEARNING TO SWIM," which uses a third-person, omniscient point of view, all the stories in this collection are told in the first person by reluctant male narrators. Their systematic attempts at concealment expose the past they seek to hide. In "Hotel" the narrator's disillusionment and subsequent collapse stems from his unspoken guilt over the secret that explains his mother's death. In "Seraglio" the husband's guilt over his infidelity masks his inability to accept his wife's miscarriage. In "The Hypochondriac" the doctor's remorse over the death of a patient exposes his phobias and deep unhappiness. These stories exemplify Swift's concern with the nature of guilt and fear as well as his fascination with enigmatic narrators and open-ended stories.

Whether frightening or pathetic, Swift's narrators create a distance from the events by narrating their stories at the end of a crisis. When the narrators manipulate chronological order and favor an impressionistic representation that emphasizes the artificiality of the narrative act, the restructuring of the past becomes a painful process. Such is the case with "The Watch," at 25 pages the longest of the stories in *Learning to Swim.* Narrated through flashbacks by the dying Adam Krepski, the story is a meditation on the nature of time, borrowing as much from magic realism as from satire. Furthermore, in story after story, Swift's narrators are at pains to promote their own versions of events but seem unable to control the narrative. In "The Son," "Cliffedge," and "Hoffmeier's Antelope," the narrator is an observer who presents himself as peripheral to the plot while undermining narrative reliability and producing unresolved enigmas. At the end of these stories, a younger man has been empowered through his ability to subvert the narrative and has emerged as the protagonist in the place of an older man.

In Swift's early fiction the characters' inability to engage in healthy and fulfilling relationships stems from their unwillingness to comprehend how the past shapes the present and to accept their own place in history. Like the Krepskis, masterful clockmakers in "The Watch" who gain immortality through a magical timepiece of their own creation, most of the protagonists remove themselves from the flow of time by denying communication. As Adam Krepski acknowledges, they fail to "make their pact with history." Instead, they haunt the scenes of past crimes and become haunted, literally or metaphorically, by ghosts as well as visions and dreams. In most of the stories the narrators look back at moments of crisis but are unable or unwilling to shoulder responsibility for the catastrophes that bring them to a heightened awareness of their actions.

In *Learning to Swim* Swift explores how cosmic accident and human choice conspire to produce incidents of such devastating potency—a miscarriage or abortion, suicide or incest, a secret adoption or forced childlessness—that his characters have to spend the rest of their lives trapped in the aftermath of the past. The inescapability of history and the pervasiveness of guilt are constant concerns in Swift's early fiction. Unable to accept mortality and paralyzed by phobias, the characters in Swift's short stories are disturbed by universal paradoxes and ambiguities. Swift's narrators pose questions but fear the answers and find few solutions; the protagonists of the short stories in *Learning to Swim* remain alone and unconsoled, locked in their struggle with memory and remorse.

BIBLIOGRAPHY

Swift, Graham. *Learning to Swim and Other Stories.* 1982. London: Heinemann, 1985.

Anastasia Logotheti

LEE, VERNON (1856–1935) "Vernon Lee" was the pseudonym of Violet Paget. Born October 15, 1865, at Chateau Saint-Leonard to Matilda Paget, a strong, intellectual, and unconventional mother, and her second husband, Polish emigré Henry Ferguson Paget, Vernon Lee was raised with her stepbrother,

Eugene Lee Hamilton, as an expatriate in Italy. Her precocious intellect, as evidenced by her fluency in English, French, and Italian, set her apart as a prodigy from an early age; in 1866 she first met her contemporary John Singer Sargent and went on a journey with him to Rome, where she had her first epiphanic experience of art that infused all of her work. In 1870, Lee published her first essay, and it was as a young woman that her fears of not being taken seriously as a writer, especially in the field of aesthetics, led her to adopt her pseudonym (derived from her brother's name) for both professional and personal use. By all accounts, Lee maintained an absolute focus on her work, often to the detriment of her health, as she suffered several breakdowns throughout her life. Lee wrote more than 40 books and 175 articles in several genres (and languages), including aesthetic theory, philosophy, music appreciation, travel essays, psychological inquiries, literary criticism, novel writing, and short fiction.

Lee's fiction, published in such periodicals as the *Contemporary Review,* the *Fortnightly Review,* the YELLOW BOOK, and the *Bookman* and later collected and added to in *Hauntings: Fantastic Stories* (1890), *Vanitas: Polite Stories* (1892), *Pope Jacynth and Other Fantastic Tales* (1904), and *For Maurice: Five Unlikely Stories* (1927), was written quickly and revised little. A combination of Hoffmannian fantasy, romance, and idealism infuse the stories, which have also been lauded for their psychological acuity. In particular, in her extensive collaborations with Clementina (Kit) Anstruther-Thompson, with whom she lived intimately from 1887 to 1897, she explored the "science of the mind and the mind's relations with Body," as well as physical and mental reactions to art, an idea that surfaces frequently in her short stories. She often attempts to capture the ambience of a place, or what she termed the genius loci (spirit of a place), from the past. In *Hauntings,* the description and settings create a suspenseful atmosphere, for which she was praised.

The imagination and scholarship with which Lee's texts are infused is often personified in narrators who are artists or scholars and plots that center on the narrators' obsessions with their object of study. The variety of points of view in these stories adds greatly to their effect; in particular, women who are unable to break from the constraints of society are seen through male characters who misjudge them. Lee questions the place of women artists in a society that also objectifies and disempowers them. Some stories, such as "LADY TAL," have been considered scandalous for their satire of existing authors or movements (as was her first novel, *Miss Brown* [1884]) or for their perceived "diseased sensibility" verging on decadence, as in "Prince Alberic and the Snake Lady."

Lee had several relationships with other women, including Annie Meyer from 1878 to 1880 and the poet Mary Robinson from 1880 to 1887, but later in life she was alienated from most of society because of her obsessive work habits, her physical distance from the literary London community, and her strong pacifist opposition to the Boer War and to WORLD WAR I. Praised by George Bernard Shaw and well regarded in her lifetime as a writer of high scholarship and imagination, despite her sometimes too subtle and convoluted style, Vernon Lee received an honorary doctorate of letters from the University of Durham in 1924. She died on February 13, 1935, of long-term heart trouble at her Florentine villa.

BIBLIOGRAPHY
Colby, Venetia. *Vernon Lee.* Charlottesville: University Press of Virginia, 2003.
Lee, Vernon. *Hauntings.* London: John Lane, 1906.
———. *Pope Jacynth and Other Fantastic Tales.* London: Grant Richards, 1906.

Sarah Maier

LE FANU, JOSEPH SHERIDAN (1814–1873)

A 19th-century Anglo-Irish journalist, novelist, and author of numerous short stories, Joseph Sheridan Le Fanu is now best remembered for his contributions to the mid-Victorian sensation novel, a genre that reached its heyday in the 1860s, and for a number of historical novels set in Ireland. Le Fanu was born in Dublin on August 28, 1814. The son of a clergyman, he came from a wealthy family of Huguenot origins. His ancestors of literary renown included the playwright Richard Brinsley Sheridan and the 18th-century novelist Frances Sheridan, the playwright's mother. In 1826, Le Fanu moved to Abington, in County Limerick, on which he was to base his depictions of rural Ireland and the Irish peasantry. In 1833 Le Fanu entered Trinity College, Dublin, to read law. He graduated in 1837 and was called to the bar in 1839, but to his family's disappointment he never practiced. In 1838 his first story, "The Ghost and the Bone-Setter," appeared in the *Dublin University Magazine,* which also published many of his subsequent stories. As a journalist, Le Fanu edited and owned several newspapers and magazines, including the *Warden,* the *Protestant Guardian,* the *Evening Packet,* the *Dublin Evening Mail,* and the *Dublin University Magazine.* In 1844 he married Susanna Bennett, with whom he had four children. After his wife's early death in 1858 he became a virtual recluse, dubbed the "Invisible Prince" because of his secluded life. His fictional output became even more prolific during his retirement from public life. He increasingly turned to the genre of the ghost story and the popular Victorian sensation genre in his later fiction.

Influenced by Walter Scott, Le Fanu's first full-scale novel, *The Cock and Anchor* (1845), is a historical novel that chronicles old Dublin. Although his subsequent historical novels are often set in England, it has been suggested that the described landscapes acquire additional meaning when they are transferred to Ireland. Michael Begnal, in his early reassessment of Le Fanu's fiction, "writes that Le Fanu's London is Dublin, and his English mansions are in actuality the Irish 'big houses' which were fast disappearing from the contemporary scene" (14). Le Fanu's now best-known works include the mystery novel *Uncle Silas* (1864) and the sensation stories from *In a Glass Darkly* (1872), specifically "GREEN TEA," a story of suburban gothic, and "Carmilla," a vampire story that influenced BRAM STOKER's *Dracula* and was later made into a film that emphasized its lesbian undertones. Le Fanu died on February 7, 1873, the year that saw the publication of his final novel, which had the disturbingly appropriate title *Willing to Die.* A number of his early poems and short stories were collected by A. P. Graves and published posthumously in 1880 as *The Purcell Papers.*

BIBLIOGRAPHY
Begnal, Michael H. *Joseph Sheridan LeFanu.* Lewisburg: Bucknell University Press, 1971.

Le Fanu, Joseph Sheridan. *Green Tea and Other Ghost Stories.* New York: Dover, 1993.

———. *In a Glass Darkly.* Oxford: Oxford University Press, 1999.

McCormack, W. J. *Sheridan Le Fanu.* Stroud, England: Sutton, 1997.

Tamara Wagner

LESSING, DORIS (1919–)

Born in present-day Iran to British parents, Lessing grew up outside of her parents' native England, spending most of her childhood in Southern Rhodesia (now Zimbabwe), where she moved with her family in 1925. Later she would move to England, but the sense of alienation she felt as a white girl in Africa would continue to plague her in England, giving her a sense of permanent homelessness that world surface in many of her works.

A prolific writer, Lessing has worked in multiple mediums, including short and novel-length fiction, poetry, autobiography, science fiction, fantasy, and drama. Lessing's earliest short fiction uses her African homeland as a setting. Her first volume, *This Was the Old Chief's Country* (1951), and her succeeding collection of five short novellas, appropriately titled *Five* (1953), incorporate the interracial and intercultural conflicts that permeated colonial African society. As a result, reviews of these collections invariably focused on the "color question" endemic to colonized South Africa. Such a unilateral critical position unfortunately left many aspects of these works overlooked, such as Lessing's depiction of the horrific power of nature in "A Sunrise on the Veld" and the bankruptcy of Western culture in Africa captured in "Winter in July."

Lessing escaped the thematic profiling of the critics in her subsequent collection of short fiction, *The Habit of Loving* (1957). Although some of the collection's stories are set in Africa, Lessing places others in the Western societies of England and France. These Western settings allow her to elaborate on the sense of Western cultural bankruptcy already present in some of her African fiction. The collection's title story, in particular, presents a collage of characters floating from one relationship to the next, unable to find a permanent cure for their sense of ennui or a stable center to latch onto.

Six years later, Lessing continued to explore the conditions of existential longing in her next collection, *A Man and Two Women* (1963). Like *The Habit of Loving, A Man and Two Women* considers this theme within relationships and within the individual, chronicling psychological and metaphysical torments in marriages and singleness, in Africa and Europe, in men and women. The later collection also includes one of Lessing's most popular and anthologized stories, "TO ROOM NINETEEN," which describes the mental deterioration of a woman trapped in what seemed to be a "perfect" marriage. She can find comfort only in the solitude of an empty hotel room and eventually finds her ultimate consolation in suicide.

Lessing's next two books of short stories, *The Story of a Non-Marrying Man* (1972) and *London Observed* (1992), provide further variations on some of Lessing's favorite themes: radical politics, broken relationships, and the search for permanent happiness. They also reflect an increased interest in aging and the passing of time. Her older characters in "The Sparrows" (1992) and "An Old Woman and Her Cat" (1972) testify to Lessing's awareness of her own aging; "The Sparrows" in particular ponders what the current generation may or may not do with the knowledge and experience of its predecessors.

Such speculations also surface in her most recent collection of short stories, *The Grandmothers* (2003)—a title that explicitly points to Lessing's concern with aging. The title story, like many of its predecessors, deals with convoluted relationships between lovers; however, these relationships also cross generational borders, using intergenerational sex to question the ultimate compatibility between Lessing's peers and the generation following them. Her fantasy piece "The Reason for It" also addresses this question by couching it in a cultural transition within a fabricated fantasy realm. The question remains the same: Will the traditions and ideas of the older generation survive in the years to come?

This inquiry into cultural succession—along with contemporary political concerns, complex and ultimately dissatisfying relationships, and feelings of meaningless and ennui—forms the thematic core of Lessing's 50-plus years of work in the short story genre.

While the broadness of these themes makes her a difficult author to categorize, her depth of insight into the conditions of modern society and the modern psyche preserves her status as one of the strongest voices in the short fiction of the 20th century. (See also "THE ANTHEAP," "MRS FORTESCUE," "THE OLD CHIEF MSHLANGA," and "OUR FRIEND JUDITH.")

BIBLIOGRAPHY

Fand, Roxanne J. *The Dialogic Self: Reconstructing Subjectivity in Woolf, Lessing, and Atwood.* Selinsgrove, Pa.: Susquehanna University Press, 1999.

Greene, Gayle. *Doris Lessing: The Poetics of Change.* Ann Arbor: University of Michigan Press, 1994.

Klein, Carol. *Doris Lessing: A Biography.* London: Duckworth, 2000.

Lessing, Doris. *African Stories.* London: Michael Joseph, 1964.

———. *Each His Own Wilderness.* Harmondsworth, England: Penguin, 1959.

———. *Five.* London: Michael Joseph, 1953.

———. *Going Home.* London: Michael Joseph, 1957.

———. *The Grandmothers.* London: Flamingo, 2003.

———. *The Grass Is Singing.* London: Michael Joseph, 1950

———. *The Habit of Loving.* London: MacGibbon & Kee, 1957.

———. *London Observed: Stories and Sketches.* London: HarperCollins, 1992.

———. *A Man and Two Women.* London: MacGibbon & Kee, 1963.

Josh Miller.

"LET ME COUNT THE TIMES" MARTIN AMIS (1980)

Masculinity in crisis has been a recurrent topic in MARTIN AMIS's fiction. The character John Self, that notorious example of unredeemed machismo in *Money* (1984) immediately comes to mind, but other characters, like Guy Clinch (*London Fields*, 1989), a prototype of hypercorrectness in his dealings with women, suggests the author's interest in exploring different approaches to the problem. In particular, the short story "Let Me Count the Times" displays a full range of Amis's literary abilities in exposing the contradictions of modern men. The story was first published under the title "Vernon" in *Penthouse* in December 1980, later appearing with its present title in *Granta* in 1981. Finally it was included in *Heavy Water and Other Stories* (1998).

The protagonist, Vernon, is a businessman obsessed with calculating arithmetic means of his sexual practices with his wife. Although he loves her and enjoys making love to her, he occasionally feels the urge to abandon their orthodox sexual behavior. Vernon begins to find an outlet for his erotic desires in the form of masturbatory fantasies. Amis's grotesque and mocking style is at its best when he describes the details of Vernon's "affair" with himself: "Vernon did it everywhere. (. . .) With scandalized laughter he dragged himself out protesting to the garden toolshed and did it there. (. . .) Confusedly and very briefly he considered running away with himself" (80). For a while Vernon attempts to keep up both strands of his sexual life: his orthodox conjugal duty, now freed from feelings of guilt, and his perverse but highly satisfactory onanist practices, now expanded into promiscuous imaginary couplings with famous actresses and female characters from literary works. The experience, however, is too stressful for the protagonist, and he collapses in a breakdown of unpredictable consequences.

In this short story Amis makes a fierce criticism of the idea of sex centered on men's needs. Throughout the narrative sex is always something that men do to women. There is also an element of puerile masculine pride in Vernon's obsession with counting the times, correlating his manliness with the number of sexual acts in which he engages. Vernon's masculinity, however, is doomed to collapse because he is subject to what Ian M. Harris (184) has termed "contradictory male messages." Vernon is not able to reconcile his role as a loving husband with the imagined playboy character he has assigned to himself. The resulting anxiety is the cause of his emotional breakdown.

Similarly, Vernon is not able to overcome the strict division of roles that he projects over his wife. On the one hand, she represents the home and "the safety" (77, 90). On the other hand, she has to be degraded because she reveals man's weakness. It is a classic case of masculine schematization, what Jonathan Rutherford has defined as "a projection of the contradictions within male heterosexuality" (51).

However, if in "Let Me Count The Times" Amis dismantles a typical model of masculinity, he goes no further, leaving things as they are. He makes fun of the ridiculous manifestations of a confused modern man but maintains male order in an hegemonic position. First, Vernon's wife is denied all individuality; we never even know her name. Second, she is described along the lines of the classic housewife: kind, patient, understanding. Finally, she does not exist as an agent: Effaced from the narrative, even linguistically she is merely the passive recipient of Vernon's actions. The incomplete nature of this otherwise brilliant satire is perhaps explained by something Amis said in a well-known interview: "I don't offer alternatives to what I deplore" (Haffenden, 14).

BIBLIOGRAPHY

Amis, Martin. "Let Me Count the Times." In *Heavy Water and Other Stories*, 75–93. London: Jonathan Cape, 1998.

Haffenden, John. *Novelists in Interview*. London: Methuen, 1985.

Harris, Ian M. *Messages Men Hear. Constructing Masculinities*. London: Taylor and Francis, 1995.

Rutherford, Jonathan. "Who's That Man?" In *Male Order: Unwrapping Masculinity,* edited by Rowena Chapman and Jonathan Rutherford, 21–67. 1988. London: Lawrence and Wishart, 1989.

José Francisco Fernández

"LETTER, THE" W. SOMERSET MAUGHAM (1927)

For six months in 1921 and four months in 1925, W. SOMERSET MAUGHAM traveled throughout the British-ruled Malay States, befriending the civil servants, planters, officials, and hostesses of the Malaysian colonies—and gathering abundant material for his fiction. "The Letter," one of Maugham's best-known short stories, is the result of these travels. Set against the exotic, vivid backdrop of the British colony at Singapore, "The Letter" depicts the dishonorable effects of jealous passion and deceit while suggesting a subtle tension between the British colonists and their Eastern subjects.

Leslie Crosbie, the wife of rubber planter Robert Crosbie, has been arrested for shooting Geoffrey Hammond, a fellow planter, and claims self-defense. Mr. Joyce, the Singapore lawyer who has been retained in Leslie's defense, finds his position—and his judicial principles—compromised by Crosbie's naiveté, Leslie's practiced dissimulation, and the machinations of his Chinese clerk, Ong Chi Seng, whose Anglicized appearance belies duplicity. Seng, in possession of a letter from Leslie Crosbie to Geoffrey Hammond revealing her infidelity, positions himself as middleman in a discreet but expensive scheme of blackmail. His friend will sell the letter to Robert Crosbie for $10,000. Joyce, at once fascinated and repelled by his client, is moved by her artfully feigned helplessness to take the "unjustifiable" step of accepting Seng's offer, thus shielding Leslie from public humiliation as well as certain conviction. Once Crosbie has read the letter, however, and grasped its implications, Leslie cannot avoid private humiliation.

"The Letter" is notable not only for its suspenseful plot but for Maugham's skillful portrayal of the unrepentant, manipulative, and self-serving character Leslie Crosbie and for his subtle representation of colonial racial tensions: Leslie Crosbie's murderous rage is prompted by her lover's scorn, but it is intensified because he has scorned her in favor of a Chinese woman. Maugham's depiction of the careful, crafty negotiations between Joyce and Seng further underscores the impression conveyed by "The Letter" of two worlds, the colonial and the Oriental, existing in an uneasy balance.

BIBLIOGRAPHY

Maugham, W. Somerset. *The Collected Short Stories*. London: Penguin, 1977.

Sara Atwood

LEVY, AMY (1861–1889)

Amy Levy was born in London in 1861, one of the seven children of Isabel (Levin) Levy and Lewis Levy, a stockbroker. The family, part of the native-born Anglo-Jewish community, practiced Judaism but were not orthodox. In 1879, after graduating from Brighton High School for Girls, Levy entered Newnham College, becoming only the second Jewish woman at Cambridge. Leaving Newnham after her first book of poems was published, Levy traveled in Europe. Residing mostly with her family in Bloomsbury after 1884, the year *A Minor Poet and Other Verse* appeared, she lived the independent life of a NEW WOMAN, frequenting the British Museum's reading room, a meeting place for intellectual women, and becoming active in various organizations for writers as well as the University Women's Club. Levy's poems, essays, and stories appeared regularly in London magazines, and in 1886 she wrote several articles for the *Jewish Chronicle.* By 1887 many of her poems and essays focused on women and the city.

In 1888 she composed both *Romance of a Shop* (1888), a novel that spoofs Victorian realism by exaggerating its conventions, about four orphaned sisters who, in defiance of societal expectations, live on their own and run a business, and *Reuben Sachs* (1889), about the Anglo-Jewish community. Both the Jewish press and gentile reviewers read the latter as an attack on Jewish life, but a few saw that the novel's experiments—its symbolism, unusual degree of allusiveness, and unreliable narrative voices—create a cacophony of contradictory voices on the theme of what it means to be a British Jew and therefore that its unpleasant generalizations about Jews were countered by positive elements. In 1889, Levy produced a slight third novel, *Miss Meredith.* Her vulnerability to "constitutional melancholy" allowed the controversy over *Reuben Sachs* to be a factor in her final slide into severe depression, but Levy's personal life was also a disappointment, and she was growing deaf. During that last summer she corrected the galleys for *A London Plane-Tree and Other Verse.* When Levy committed suicide, Oscar Wilde said in his obituary, "The world must forgo the full fruition of her power," yet she was largely forgotten until 1993, when an edition of much of Levy's work came out that has sparked a revival of interest in her.

Levy published 20 short works of fiction. Of these, 10 were probably written as potboilers. Six stand out as art, four of these well within the tradition of realism—offering complex, well-developed characters, social satire, and a nondidactic concern for social injustice—though all show her penchant for technical innovation. "Between Two Stools" (1883) takes up the dilemma of the woman who has gone to university and become a stranger to conventional late-Victorian middle-class culture. Epistolary in method, it is comic in its representation of both middle-class and university life: The protagonist's ambivalence creates an ambiguity that is moving and powerful. "Sokratics in the Strand" (1884) is daring in its willingness to portray

despair and suicidal impulses; its heavy reliance on dialogue between characters who disagree with each other and the shift to an unreliable narrator brings out contradictory perspectives. "At Prato" (1888) and "The Recent Telepathic Occurrence in the British Museum" (1888) show Levy playing with the fin de siècle interest in fantasy; the latter especially calls to mind HENRY JAMES in its theme of the unlived life.

Levy's stories from her final two years, most written for the *Woman's World,* tend to be brief and show a desire to move away from the detail and sometimes ponderous prose of Victorian fiction although the language is still rich in irony, parody, and allusion. Her last two pieces, "Cohen of Trinity" (1889) and "WISE IN HER GENERATION" (1890), are her best. "Cohen" is a masterpiece of unreliable narrative technique: Its speaker, a Cambridge don, tells of Cohen, a Jew, the gentile's perceptions of this student coming almost entirely from his storehouse of received ideas about Jewish people.

Three of Levy's unpublished stories, that were written while Levy was at Cambridge—"Leopold Leuniger: a Study," "Lallie: a Cambridge Sketch," and "The Doctor"—cry out to be in print. The manuscripts are available at the Amy Levy Archive.

BIBLIOGRAPHY
Beckman, Linda Hunt. *Amy Levy: Her Life and Letters.* Athens: Ohio University Press, 2000.
———. "Amy Levy and the 'Jewish Novel': Representing Jewish Life in the Victorian Period," *Studies in the Novel* 26 (1994): 235–253.
Levy, Amy. *Complete Novels and Selected Writings of Amy Levy.* Gainesville: University Press of Florida, 1993.
Rochelson, Meri-Jane. "Jews, Gender, and Genre in Late-Victorian England: Amy Levy's *Reuben Sachs,*" *Women's Studies* 29 (1996): 173–192.
Wilde, Oscar. "Amy Levy," *Woman's World* 3 (1890): 52.

Linda Hunt Beckman

LEWIS, (PERCY) WYNDHAM (1882–1957)
Wyndham Lewis was born on a yacht off Amherst, Nova Scotia, to an American father and Irish mother. His parents moved to England when Lewis was six and soon after separated. Lewis was raised by his mother and educated at Rugby and the Slade before spending seven years

living a bohemian lifestyle in Europe. On his return he became involved with the avant-garde circles of the *English Review* and Rebel Art Centre and was one of the founders of VORTICISM. Vorticism's manifesto emerged in 1914, in the magazine *Blast* which Lewis edited, but the movement was soon interrupted by World War I. Lewis enlisted in 1916 and saw action in Belgium before returning to the front as a war artist. Lewis's reputation was immensely damaged by his enthusiastic and sympathetic early account of the rise of Nazism in *Hitler* (1931), views he later recanted in *The Hitler Cult* and *The Jews, Are They Human?* (1939). Lewis spent most of World War II in Canada teaching and after the war returned to England, where he served as the *Listener*'s art critic until he became blind in 1951.

Lewis published his first novel, *Tarr,* in 1918; based on his prewar experiences in Paris, it is considered by many to be an important modernist text. Many of Lewis's fictional works of the 1920s and 1930s are marked by a particular style of satirical detached observation of people that Hugh Kenner has called "puppet-fiction." Lewis himself explained the comedy of the "automaton" as follows: "The root of the comic is to be sought in the sensations resulting from the observations of a *thing* behaving like a person. But from that point of view all men are necessarily comic: for they are all *things,* or physical bodies, behaving as *persons*" (quoted in Kenner, 102). He frequently advocated the "external" method of description against the internal, the psychological or time-based approach of his contemporaries Marcel Proust and JAMES JOYCE. Lewis's fictional work was often a vehicle for his political and artistic ideas. *The Apes of God* (1930) satirizes amateur upper-class art lovers and contains thinly disguised caricatures of many of Lewis's contemporaries, including the Sitwells and the Bloomsbury group. *The Childermass* (1928) similarly develops in fictional form Lewis's political ideas from *The Art of Being Ruled* (1926). In 1937 Lewis published what many regard as his best novel, *The Revenge for Love.*

Before World War I, Lewis wrote several short stories for Ford Maddox Ford's *English Review,* and during the war he also contributed stories to the *Little Review.* Probably the best known of these early stories are "Some Innkeepers and Bestre," "The Soldier of Humour," and "Cantelman's Spring-Mate." "Some Innkeepers and Bestre" and "The Soldier of Humour" are good examples of Lewis's external method, eliciting grotesque comic effect from the detailed description of the external mannerisms of their characters. Early stories such as these are often peopled by characters Lewis had met in inns and boarding houses while traveling through Brittany and Spain before the war. "Cantelman's Spring-Mate" describes the sexual encounters of a young infantry officer and a country girl before he is sent to the front; its obscenity caused the *Little Review* to be censored in America. Many of these stories appear in revised form in the 1927 collection *The Wild Body.* In 1951 Lewis published *Rotting Hill,* a collection of short stories portraying the austerity of postwar London and characterized by satirical attacks on the socialist policies of the Labor government.

BIBLIOGRAPHY

Kenner, Hugh. *Wyndham Lewis.* Norfolk, Conn.: New Directions, 1954.

Lewis, Wyndham. *The Wild Body.* 1927. London: Penguin, 2004.

———. *Rotting Hill.* London: Methuen, 1951.

Meyers, Jeffrey. *The Enemy: A Biography of Wyndham Lewis.* London: Routledge & Kegan Paul, 1980.

O'Keefe, Paul. *Some Sort of Genius: A Life of Wyndham Lewis.* London: Jonathon Cape, 2000.

Ben Roberts

"LIFTED VEIL, THE" GEORGE ELIOT (1859)

This story by GEORGE ELIOT was first published in the July 1859 issue of *Blackwood's Magazine.* Latimer, its protagonist and narrator, begins his tale near the end of his life, when he is suffering from acute angina pectoris—a heart disease that functions as a metaphor for his emotional unhealthiness. Able to "foresee when [he] shall die, and everything that will happen in [his] last moments," Latimer hopes to employ his "last hours of ease and strength in telling the strange story of [his] experience." In childhood he was happy, though he suffered from "a complaint of the eyes that made [him] blind for a little while." This first in a lifelong series of bodily and mental disorders draws our attention not only to Latimer's feeble constitution but also to the importance of vision—both physical and metaphysical—in his life story. After his mother dies, Latimer's distant father has him examined by the phrenologist Mr. Letherall. By pronouncing the boy weak in the faculty of analysis but strong in that of fancy, this gentleman invites us to question Latimer's trustworthiness as a narrator.

When Latimer turns 16 he is sent to finish his schooling in Geneva, where he meets and befriends Charles Meunier, a brilliant but uncouth student of medicine who later becomes a celebrated expert in the field. Latimer's "happier life at Geneva" is ended abruptly by a severe illness. During his convalescence, he experiences his first precognitive vision. Although Latimer has "seen no picture of Prague" and the city is to him "a mere name," he envisions crossing a bridge there in startling detail—and, as he later realizes, with absolute accuracy. He likens the "gradual breaking-in of the vision upon [him]" to "the growing distinctness of the landscape as the sun lifts up the veil of the morning mist," and this image of the lifted veil recurs in the remainder of his narrative. At the same time he sees Prague in the future, Latimer also becomes aware of his father's present activities in another part of the house. At first, the boy is pleased by his gifts of precognition and clairvoyance. Believing that he possesses "the poet's sensibility without his voice," he wonders whether his second sight is "the poet's nature in [him], hitherto only a troubled yearning sensibility, now manifesting itself suddenly as spontaneous creation." Soon, however, Latimer experiences a second vision of the future and begins to fear that his newfound ability might be not a power but a disease. Furthermore, he comes "to taste something of the horror that belongs to the lot of a human being whose nature is not adjusted to simple human conditions." The boy discovers that he has, in addition to his other faculties, the gift of telepathy, so that "the vagrant, frivolous ideas and emotions" of one individual after another "force themselves" upon his mind. While Latimer is merely annoyed by his insights into the minds of acquaintances, he suffers "intense pain and grief" when his vision reveals the egoism, pettiness, and darkness of "the souls of those who [are] in a close relation to [him]."

The only character whose thoughts are closed to Latimer is Bertha Grace, his elder brother Alfred's intended fiancée, and her inaccessibility enthralls him. Eventually, Latimer comes to believe that Bertha will wed not his brother but himself—for he envisions the two of them trapped in an unhappy marriage. After gazing on a painting of the notorious 15th-century femme fatale Lucrezia Borgia until he experiences "a strange poisoned sensation," Latimer feels Bertha touch him. At this instant he succumbs to an "intoxicating numbness," a poisoned feeling "like the continuance or climax of the sensation" brought on by the painting—and he sees Bertha as his wife, "every hateful thought within her present to [him]." This glimpse of the future horrifies him, yet still he feels "a wild hell-braving joy that Bertha [is] to be [his]." Latimer's anticipation of their eventual union is realized after Alfred is killed in a riding accident. Bertha and Latimer wed, and during the first phase of their marriage her mind remains a mystery to him. On the night his father dies, however, "the veil which had shrouded Bertha's soul from [him]" is withdrawn, and "from that evening forth, through the sickening years which followed," he sees "all round the narrow room of this woman's soul." After relations with her husband deteriorate into mutual antipathy, Bertha hires Mrs. Archer as a maid and adopts her as a confidant. Mrs. Archer disturbs Latimer, for he sees "in Bertha's mind towards this woman a mingled feeling of fear and dependence." Mrs. Archer falls ill and dies during a visit by Latimer's childhood friend Charles. Immediately after her death, the doctor performs an experimental transfusion on the maid that revives her long enough that she can confess her role in Bertha's Borgia-like plot to poison her husband.

After this scene, Latimer and his wife live apart. He keeps wandering to avoid becoming familiar with others and seeing into their minds, and in his isolation he is metaphysically linked only "with the one Unknown Presence revealed and yet hidden by the moving curtain of the earth and sky." When disease at last forces Latimer to stop traveling, he comes to know not only the secrets of his servants but also precisely how and why they will leave him alone to die. His last words end the tale where it began: "I know these figures I have just written, as if they were a long familiar inscription. I have seen them on this page in my desk unnumbered times, when the scene of my dying struggle has opened upon me." The story's gothic elements include its potentially unreliable narrator, its paranoid tone, and its interest in the pursuit of forbidden knowledge.

BIBLIOGRAPHY

Eagleton, Terry. "Power and Knowledge in 'The Lifted Veil,'" *Literature and History* 9, no. 1 (1983): 52–61.

Eliot, George. "The Lifted Veil." In *"The Lifted Veil" and "Brother Jacob."* Edited by Helen Small, 1–43. Oxford World's Classics. Oxford: Oxford University Press, 1999.

Wilt, Judith. *Ghosts of the Gothic: Austen, Eliot, and Lawrence.* Princeton, N.J.: Princeton University Press, 1980.

Jamil Mustafa

LITT, TOBY (1968–)

Often hailed as one of the most exciting and ambitious young British writers, Litt takes the short story very seriously. His studies for a master's degree in creative writing at the University of East Anglia led to his first collection, *ADVENTURES IN CAPITALISM* (1996), 18 stories analyzing different aspects of 1990s culture. Celebrity culture is satirized in "IYouHeSheItWeYouThey," and would-be fashionable London is the target in "After Wagamama but Mostly Before," the title coming from a chain of Japanese restaurants. The title of the first story in the collection, "It Could Have Been Me and It Was," is inspired by an advertising slogan for the National Lottery. Stories such as "Moriarty," featuring two schoolgirls, Holmes and Watson, carry myriad intertextual references in true postmodernist fashion. The collection marked Litt as a writer who was daring and anarchic and completely in tune with the spirit of the times, managing to "effortlessly surf the twentysomething zeitgeists," as Chris Mitchell has said. However, the collection also prompted the charge—heard a number of times since—that Litt's work lacks gravitas. Matt Seaton notes that

> At his best, Toby Litt seems to revive the spirit of Monty Python, mate it with a strain of magic realism, and let it roam about 1990s London. At his second-best he looks like an author in search of a subject. There's no doubt that *Adventures in Capitalism* marks the arrival of a fresh satirical voice, full of brio. One just hopes that he'll settle down to something more serious.

In the decade since 1996, Litt has shown himself extraordinary prolific, publishing the novels *Beatniks* (1997), *Corpsing* (2000), *Deadkidsongs* (2002), *Finding Myself* (2003), and *Ghost Story* (2004). He has published short stories online and in influential anthologies. His story "The New Puritans" appeared in *ALL HAIL THE NEW PURITANS*, and his work seems to encapsulate many of the ideals of that loose group. His second collection of short stories, *Exhibitionism,* encouraged his reputation as a writer who relishes the chance to tackle so-called adult themes in an explicit, often brutal way. The link among many of the stories in *Exhibition* is sex. Some of them—"On the Etiquette of Eye Contact during Oral Sex," "Legends of Porn (Polly Morphous) Final Shooting Script," and "Alphabed"—have been taken as testament of Litt's apparent desire to play the naughty child and shock the literary establishment. The decision to sell the book with a cover showing a scantily dressed woman on her knees did little to dispel this idea. However, critics more sympathetic to Litt discerned more subtle forces at play. In "Dreamgirls," the narrator dreams of and then comes face to face with a series of fantasy sexual companions—from a 1920s silent film actress, to a nurse, to his mother and the Virgin Mary. Each one demands his attention, and the story can be read as an examination of what it is to have one's fantasies become reality. In "Story to Be Translated from English into French and Then Translated Back (without reference to the original)," a man and a woman indulge in sadomasochistic sex but inevitably replay the master and servant roles society has traditionally had men and women play. In the same collection, Litt showed that he had not lost his satirist's eye. "Mapmaking among the Middle-Classes" examines a London dinner party with all its tensions and petty rivalries. "Mimi (Both of Her) and Me (Hardly There at All)" is a gothic tale in which the narrator takes time out from his research on Dante Gabriel Rossetti (see PRE-RAPHAELITISM) to visit the grave of Rossetti's wife, Elizabeth Siddall, in London's Highgate Cemetery. Once there, he is drawn into a grisly adventure among the tombs with two young women.

Litt has been criticized by critics for favoring style over substance—a flashy, superficial, unfocused writer for a flashy, superficial age, it has been claimed, happy simply to show off his undoubted skill with words. Others, however, would point to his energy and his commitment to experimenting with language and structure, in particular his ability to adopt different voices for different stories. Litt himself has explained that "a short story usually deals either with a moment of chance or of change. Nothing need happen (it can be a moment of chance of change, failed) but there is always the drama of it not happening. . . . Another answer I sometimes give is that a story should contain a situation and a surprise" (2004). Litt's stories certainly fit this pattern. Litt's interest in the structural and the stylistic elements of storytelling is a trait he shares with HENRY JAMES, a writer about whose work he has written and to whom he has, rather surprisingly, been linked. With the publication of Litt's latest novel, *Ghost Story,* in 2004 and its echoes of James's *TURN OF THE SCREW,* some of Litt's admirers seem ready to take this comparison more seriously than before, and he has been acclaimed for exhibiting a new maturity.

BIBLIOGRAPHY

Litt, Toby. *Adventures in Capitalism.* London: Secker and Warburg, 1996.
———. *Beatniks: An English Road Movie.* London: Secker and Warburg, 1997.
———. *Corpsing.* London: Hamilton, 2000.
———. *Deadkidsongs.* London: Hamilton, 2001.
———. *Exhibitionism.* London: Hamilton, 2002.
———. *Ghost Story.* London: Hamish Hamilton, 2005.
———. "How Short Is Short?" Hi-Arts. October 2004. Available online. URL: http://www.hi-arts.co.uk/oct04_feature_toby_litt.htm. Accessed July 10, 2006.
———. "The New Puritans". In *All Hail the New Puritans,* edited by Nicholas Blincoe and Matt Thorne. London: Fourth Estate, 2000.
———. "A Small Matter for Your Attention." In *New Writing* 9, 344–350. London: Vintage, 2000.
Litt, Toby, and Ali Smith, eds. *New Writing 13.* London: Picador, 2005.
Mitchell, Chris. "Shelf Life" Spike Magazine. 1997. Available online. URL: http://www.spikemagazine.xom/0997litt.php. Accessed July 10, 2006.
Seaton, Matt. "Adventures in Capitalism," *Independent* (23 June 1996).
Toby Litt Official Web Site. Available online. URL: http: www.tobylitt.com. Accessed July 10, 2006.

Joe Davies

"LITTLE CLOUD, A" JAMES JOYCE (1914)

"A Little Cloud" was one of the three late additions to the 15 stories that make up the collection *Dubliners.* JAMES JOYCE submitted the first 12 stories to a London publishing firm as early as 1905. When the printers objected to the perceived indecency of some of the phrases in the stories, however, a long and frustrating set of disputes followed. Delayed by these often aggressive disputes, *Dubliners* was not published until 1914. "A Little Cloud," with "Two Gallants" and "THE DEAD," was written after the 12 original stories; it bears witness to its later date of composition in the deftness and precision with which it consolidates the themes of spiritual and social stasis built up in the earlier stories' representation of petty bourgeois Dublin life.

The story hinges on a reunion between two friends after an eight-year separation. One of these friends, the bluff, worldy Gallaher, has "got on" in the world by leaving Dublin and becoming a journalist in London. Chandler has remained in Dublin, become a law-clerk, married, and had a son. Beside what he imagines to be Gallaher's glittering, licentious adventures in the heady world of Fleet Street, Chandler views his own life as inadequate, his ambitions thwarted, his talents neglected. Chandler provides the focal point of the narration; referred to throughout as "Little Chandler," he is not small in physical stature but gives the impression of smallness, and this diminutiveness ironically extends and echoes the pettiness and feebleness of his ambitions (247). Though Joyce uses a third-person narrator in "The Little Cloud," the reader is offered no guidance as to how to judge Chandler or whether such judgment is legitimate at all. Chandler is a pathetic figure but is at the same time a quasi-tragic one, the dowdiness of his dreams only adding to the shallow depths of his suffering.

The story opens with Chandler in an office, follows him down a street walk to a pub, and then arrives at the enclosed space of his home, where his frustration and resentment finally emerge as he shouts at his infant son. This moment of open anger—pathetically directed at a child crying piteously—does not last: Chandler's wife enters the room, rebukes him, and quiets the child while tears of remorse and shame start in Chandler's eyes. The story ends thus, with Chandler trapped physically within the confines of a home his wife rather than he controls. This moment echoes the opening moment of the story, in which Chandler also sits imprisoned, this time at his office desk, bored by and resentful of the duties he nevertheless punctiliously fulfils.

The narrative structure of the story does not justify the conclusion that Chandler has been done for by domesticity, however, though this is a threat and a jeer contained in the ostentatiously ribald stories told by the bachelor Gallaher. It is when Chandler is alone and outside, walking through the streets of Dublin at sunset, that the paucity of his imagination is revealed. Spurred into feeling a vague hope by the expectation of his meeting with Gallaher, Chandler loosens his timid melancholy so far as to see himself as a prospective poet. It is significant that the moment of hope takes place outside: A mawkish rather than a liberating moment, issuing only in immature feelings of superiority and in imitative daydreams, it reveals the role of imaginative dependency in furthering states of unfreedom. As in the rest of the stories in *Dubliners,* it is not life but a surrender to and internalization of soul-crushing conventions that oppresses and fetters otherwise noble souls (603).

BIBLIOGRAPHY

Joyce, James. *Dubliners: Text, Criticism, and Notes.* Edited by Robert Scholes and A. Walton Litz. New York: Penguin, 1996.

Patricia McManus

"LITTLE PLACE OFF THE EDGWARE ROAD, A" Graham Greene (1935)

This story was first published in Graham Greene's debut volume of short stories, *The Basement Room* (1935). The piece emerged again in 1947 in *Nineteen Stories* and then again in 1954 in *Twenty-One Stories. The Basement Room* received a cool response from the critics, and when the collection was republished Greene was apprehensive. In a modest preface he wrote, "I am only too conscious of the defects of these stories. . . . [It] is an exacting form which I have never properly practised." Yet "A Little Place off the Edgware Road" is a masterly handling of the genre, combining many of Greene's own spiritual and religious concerns with a stylistic quality akin to that of Edgar Allan Poe at his most powerful.

As Craven wanders the streets of London, he stumbles upon an old theatre, now the "Home of the Silent Film." Desiring to be "out of the rain," he buys a ticket and plunges himself into the "dead darkness" of the auditorium. The film does not engage him, and it is the cryptic, somewhat sinister interplay between himself and the bearded man in the seat beside him that forms the crux of Greene's story. As the man whispers gently in Craven's ear, it becomes apparent that he is no ordinary filmgoer. His "sticky hands," his enigmatic references to the "Bayswater Tragedy" and the unpleasant "smear" he leaves on Craven's hand as he dashes from the cinema bring both the protagonist and reader to the disturbing conclusion that Craven has been sitting beside a murderer. With a final, brutal twist Greene brings the piece to a conclusion as Craven makes a panicked call to the police. His world closes in on him as he is informed that the murderer has been apprehended; it is the corpse that the police still seek, and the reader's mind is recalled once again to the banner mentioned in the opening paragraphs of the story bearing the message, "The Body shall rise again."

This story combines many themes recurrent within Greene's work. The cinema, fundamental to Greene, provides the setting. A sense of despair and the continual battle fought on the peripheries of insanity define Craven in much the same way that Scobie in the novel *The Heart of the Matter* (1948) or Raven in *A Gun for Sale* (1935) are characterized. As in many of Greene's works, the narrator is male and disillusioned and is pursued by a bitter hatred of both himself and the world around him. Similarly, the piece resonates with a distinctly Catholic sense of guilt and disgust for the corporal, the body.

The distinction between the physical and the spiritual suffuses Greene's writing. The citation from Flaubert that stands as the epigraph to his autobiography, *Ways of Escape* (1980), makes reference to this pervasive preoccupation within his work: "As my body continues on its journey, my thoughts keep turning back. . . ." For Greene, the body and soul are distinct, separate; throughout the story it is the fear that the physical may finally usurp the spiritual that characterizes what Greene calls "Craven's obsession." References to the body punctuate the text and, through Craven's gaze, the reader is made aware of an overwhelming sense of the physical. The statue of Achilles, supposedly immortal but betrayed by the weakness of a single bodily part, opens the piece. The guardsmen's bestialized bodies torment Craven and force him to a recognition of his own revolting physicality.

Craven's experience in the theatre is, in many ways, a foreshadowing of his own death. The very building is reminiscent of a burial chamber, and it is not the murder that so disturbs Craven but rather the continued life of the dead man. The triumph of the physical and the assurance of the resurrection of the body deliver the last blow to Craven's sanity and finally succeed in overthrowing his mind. He does not fear death but rather shies from a continuance of life, as is suggested by his very name.

"A Little Place off the Edgware Road" is much more than a simple thriller. The piece functions as both a psychological portrait and an exploration of the deeper religious and spiritual concerns that pervade all of Greene's writing.

BIBLIOGRAPHY
Greene, Graham. *Collected Stories: 21 Stories*. London: Penguin, 1993.

Alice Smith

"LIZZIE LEIGH" Elizabeth Gaskell (1850)

"Lizzie Leigh" is a story of a fallen woman that was probably begun in the late 1830s (Uglow, 125) but was published in Charles Dicken's *Household Words* from March 30 to April 13, 1850. The story has received a good deal of critical attention from feminist scholars, including Margaret Homans, Christine Krueger, and Deborah Denenholz Morse, who have emphasized the subversive elements in the story. As Coral Lansbury suggests, this tale of a country girl who is seduced and abandoned in the city, where she is forced into prostitution, can be viewed as a reimagining of the prostitute Esther's narrative in Elizabeth Gaskell's novel *Mary Barton* (1848). In this reinscription of Esther's tale, the prostitute's loving mother and surrogate sister are heroes who identify with the fallen woman and who believe in her redemption from sin despite the father's condemnation and the brother's angry shame.

"Lizzie Leigh" opens with the death of Lizzie's father, James Leigh. He has sent Lizzie to Manchester, where, at age 16, she is seduced, impregnated, and cast out by the owner of the factory where she finds work. Both Lizzie's father and the factory owner, her surrogate father/protector, have cast her off. However, as he is dying on Christmas Day, James Leigh at long last forgives his daughter with his final breath: "I forgive her, Annie! May God forgive me!" His death frees his wife to act independently, prompted by her love for her daughter and the New Testament message of forgiveness for all. On the evening of her husband's death, Christmas night, Anne asks her mild, sweet younger son Tom to read the parable of the Prodigal Son. Her stern older son Will understands the reference to his fallen sister and listens sullenly, as "to him it recalled the family's disgrace." As the story progresses, Will—the son most like his dead father—is enlightened as to the real meaning of Christian love and forgiveness. This new father then gives promise of a transformed masculinity imbued with the love of the Son.

The story might have been called "Anne Leigh," because the story's overt focus is the heroic mother, who moves to Manchester to seek her prodigal daughter. She wanders the streets in a red cloak, a marker with which Gaskell identifies the loving mother with her fallen daughter, the "scarlet woman." Anne does not find Lizzie but instead meets the tolerant, self-sacrificing Susan Palmer, who has taken in Lizzie's child, thrust upon her in the street. This assumption of maternal duties by a young unmarried woman defines Susan's goodness; as Patsy Stoneman states, "the care of children is Elizabeth Gaskell's crucial test of moral values" (49). Gaskell's characteristic narrative strategy crosses the boundaries of Victorian womanhood in identifying the pilgrim-named Susan Palmer—who lives on the symbolic Crown Street—with the fallen woman Lizzie, as well as with the courageous mother Anne and with Lizzie's child, Anne's namesake Nanny.

When the rigid, angry Will Leigh, now in love with Susan Palmer, fears that she will scorn Lizzie, Anne Leigh argues that Susan is a Christian who will love her fallen sister: "She's not one to harden her heart against a mother's sorrow. . . . She's not one to judge and scorn the sinner. She's too deep read in her New Testament for that." The silent wife Anne ultimately becomes the powerfully voiced mother, commanding her son to forgive his sister and her illegitimate child: "I am your mother, and I dare to command you, because I know I am in the right, and that God is on my side." Will quietly submits. As Christine Krueger has argued, Anne's words are a preachment, a legacy from the evangelical tradition, giving Anne a "prophetic role" that "enables [her] to appropriate privileged language on behalf of a fallen woman" (169).

Despite this pact of tolerance and forgiveness, the tale culminates in the death of Lizzie's child Nanny. James Leigh's judgments and the factory owner's callous abandonment of the pregnant young girl are coupled with Susan Palmer's drunken father's irresponsibility, which causes the accident in which little Nanny dies. Through her sacrificial death—symbolically, by falling—all of the women of the tale are united in Susan's house, and they are identified with one another and with the dead child. As Margaret Homans argues, "In this part of the story, there is general but not disturbing uncertainty as to who is daughter, who is mother, and of whom. Three mothers contemplate, in grief, the faces of two daughters, one who is dead, one who is 'like one dead'" (231).

The story's ending is poignant but somewhat contradictory. Gaskell calls for forgiveness for the fallen woman Lizzie but suggests the need for her continual purification and the expiation of her sin through celibacy, sorrow, and good works—but not through death, as with Esther in *Mary Barton* or the saintly heroine of *Ruth.* Lizzie lives with her mother in a secluded cottage near the old Leigh farm, where the now-married Susan and Will are raising a large family. While Lizzie becomes nearly beatified through her service to others—"many hearts bless Lizzie Leigh"—Susan is "the bright one who brings sunshine to all. Children grow around her and call her blessed." Again the pure mother and the prostitute are aligned, both "blessed" by others. They are also identified when Susan's daughter Nanny, named for Lizzie's dead child, becomes Lizzie's surrogate daughter and companion. The final scene of the story shows this second Nanny and Lizzie together in the lonely moorland churchyard where Lizzie's child is buried, and "while the little creature gathers daisies, and makes chains, Lizzie sits by a little grave, and weeps bitterly."

BIBLIOGRAPHY

Gaskell, Elizabeth. "Lizzie Leigh." In *Nineteenth Century Short Stories by Women,* edited by Glennis Stephenson, 249–283. Peterborough: Broadview Press, 1993.

Humans, Margaret. *Bearing the Word.* Chicago: Chicago University Press, 1986.

Krueger, Christine. *The Reader's Repentance.* Chicago: Chicago University Press, 1992.

Stoneman, Patsy. *Elizabeth Gaskell.* Brighton: Harvester, 1987.

Uglow, Jenny. *Elizabeth Gaskell.* London: Faber, 1999.

Deborah Denenholz Morse

"LOIS THE WITCH" Elizabeth Gaskell **(1859)** Elizabeth Gaskell's story "Lois the Witch" was first published in Charles Dickens's magazine *All the Year Round* in October 1859. Set during the Salem, Massachusetts, witch trials of 1692, the story offers a fictionalized chronicle of Lois Barclay, a young English girl accused of witchcraft and eventually condemned to death for her alleged crime. Closely paralleling the historical events that tore the community of Salem asunder, "Lois the Witch" begins when a few young girls accuse others in the community of being witches. To support their accusations, the girls simulate fits, behaving as though they are possessed by evil forces. The panic that the girls help create, turning neighbors and loved ones alike against one another, spreads throughout the village, establishing an atmosphere "not so unlike the overpowering dread of the plague, which made some shrink from their best-beloved with irrepressible fear" (152). With this comparison, the story uses an unflattering chapter of American history to illustrate deftly, in hauntingly realistic detail, the depth of the human capacity for insanity when confronted with delusion and mass hysteria, and the tragic and often bloody consequences of such fanaticism.

In the narrative, Lois is sent to New England to live with her Puritan relatives following the death of her parents. Lois's relations include three cousins, Prudence, Faith, and Manasseh, as well as her Aunt Grace. As an outsider in the community, Lois is perceived as different, even by the members of her own family. In a dose of harsh reality, as the story progresses, it is Lois's family that becomes the most adamant in accusing her of practicing witchcraft. Lois's indictment escalates, as each relative comes forward with alleged evidence to prove that Lois is a witch. Prudence, so unlike her name, is the first to accuse Lois of being a witch. Despite Prudence's reputation for taking an "impish delight in mischief" (147), the accusations are given a considerable amount of credence by the community because Prudence's sister Faith professes to believe that Lois is a witch as well. However, Faith too has ulterior motive: unrequited love. Faith is jealous of Lois, who has won the favor of the man Faith desires.

In addition, Lois's Aunt Grace supports her daughters' allegations because she believes that Lois has placed a spell on her son Manasseh, causing him to fall in love with her. Although mad even before Lois came to live with the family, Manasseh claims that he hears voices informing him that he is destined to marry Lois. Lois, however, sees Manasseh's so-called prophecy for what it is: a figment of his imagination. Lois even informs Manasseh after one "proposal," "I may take a dream to be truth, and hear my own fancies, if I think about them too long" (137). Aunt Grace pleads with Lois to release Manasseh from his alleged enchantment, but Lois maintains her innocence, and Grace too vehemently curses her. Lois, however, protests her innocence to the very end; before her hanging, she makes a heartfelt statement through her tears: "Sirs, I must choose death with a quiet conscience, rather than life to be gained by a lie. I am not a witch" (184). Although some doubt Lois's guilt because they do not believe a witch can cry, the execution is performed and Lois dies.

The story ends with Lois's intended husband, Hugh Lucy, arriving from England to claim his bride. When he finds that Lois is deceased, he lives the remainder of his life as a bachelor in reverence to Lois. Years later, Prudence reveals that there was no truth to the accusations of witchcraft that she leveled at Lois; she seeks repentance for the entire community of Salem, but as Hugh Lucy insists, "No repentance of theirs can bring her back to life" (191). With this story, Gaskell chillingly demonstrates that sometimes human beings can inflict far worse horrors on one another than any supposed supernatural force can.

BIBLIOGRAPHY
Duthie, Enid L. *The Themes of Elizabeth Gaskell.* Totowa, N.J.: Rowman and Littlefield, 1980.
Gaskell, Elizabeth. "Lois the Witch." In *Cousin Phyllis and Other Tales,* 105–193. New York: Oxford University Press, 1981.
Wright, Terence. *Elizabeth Gaskell: "We Are Not Angels": Realism, Gender, Values.* New York: St. Martin's, 1995.

Trudi Van Dyke

LONDON As the paradigmatic site of literary production in the English language, England's capital city can easily claim to be the home of the short story, and the place of London within the short story genre, is one that must always remain incomplete.

The work of George W. M. Reynolds (1814–79) is perhaps indicative of the difficulties that plague London literary history. He was also the author of *The Mysteries of London, Faust, The Mysteries of the Court of London,* and *Reynolds's Miscellany.* Reynolds was one of the foremost literary celebrities of the day. A best-selling author, immensely popular with working-class audiences for his gothic tales of crime and adventure, he issued the first series of his immensely popular *Mysteries of London* in 1844. These "Penny Dreadfuls," as they were nicknamed, outsold all other serialized publications of their time, including those of CHARLES DICKENS. The miscellany is a genre that is intrinsically linked to the short story, and a great deal of Reynolds's prose conforms to the conventions of the short story. Yet Reynolds is now completely lost to the literary tradition. With his disappearance it becomes clear how many paradoxes plague the city's literary history: Are we attempting to write the history of the London short story according to the reception of those works as they were published, or are we concerned with posthumous reputation, with the history of the city's literature as it now stands?

While such questions are difficult to answer, the most obvious place to begin an account of the London short story is with Charles Dickens, whose work straddles the popular and literary traditions. While Dickens is largely recalled as the author of compendious novels, or "loose baggy monsters," as they were infamously labeled, he also penned more than 70 short stories, including the prose sketches and short works that made up *The Pickwick Papers* and SKETCHES BY BOZ. These short stories manage to capture London through a range of techniques, including descriptive prose and the characterization of London cockney archetypes. The majority of Dickens's short stories conform to a narrative style that has as its foundation the oral storytelling tradition. These stories are usually told directly; some, like the Christmas stories, are designed to be read aloud. This feature is one that results in a curious style of storytelling that is often seen as antithetical to the taut, psychological short story of Edgar Allan Poe. Indeed, Dickens's short stories have as their central feature what Deborah Thomas has referred to as "imaginative license," and this emphasis on creativity and its transformative potential is at the heart of Dickens's London short stories.

In opposition to Dickens's stories of whimsy and imagination are those of his American contemporary, Edgar Allan Poe. Often considered the master of the short story genre, Poe's often gothic studies draw the contradictory and relentless experience of the city into the psychological space of the short story. "The Man of the Crowd," one of Poe's best-known stories and possibly the archetypal text of the modern urban short story, is indicative of the way in which London becomes transformed through the short story genre. Here London is the space in which the anonymity and disorienting nature of modernity is to be found. The narrator's mission to find the mysterious man of the crowd becomes a mission to understand how humanity can ever become reconciled to the horror and wonder of modern urban experience.

The late 19th century saw the urban gothic become the dominant paradigm in the London short story as it infused the genre-fiction of such writers as ROBERT LOUIS STEVENSON and ARTHUR CONAN DOYLE. *The ADVENTURES OF SHERLOCK HOLMES* (1892) is undoubtedly one of the most famous volumes of short stories in the English language. In these tales, Conan Doyle plays out the complex relationship between reason and the unknown that was at the heart of late-Victorian culture. London is a site in which Holmes, the master of rationality, sets out to uncover the ineffability at the heart of the city. At the beginning of "A Case of Identity," Holmes makes this desire clear: "If we could fly out of that window, hand in hand, hover over this great city, gently remove the roofs, and peep in at the queer things which go on, the strange coincidences, the plannings, the cross-purposes, the wonderful chains of events, working through generations, and leading to the most *outré* results it would make all fiction with its conventionalities and foreseen conclusions most stale and unprofitable." Doyle here establishes the paradox of attempting to write the city: Its complexity makes any attempt to encapsulate it impossible. The short story is only capable, then, of rendering this impossibility. Reason and the desire to catalog the city must give way to the partiality of impression.

The modernist attempts to record the city are also marked by this sense of fragmentation, the short story being the ideal form for presenting this fracturing of narrative perspective (see MODERNISM). VIRGINIA WOOLF, perhaps the most famous London modernist writer, was responsible for taking the literary impression to its most celebrated form in her celebrated "stream of consciousness" style. For Woolf, London was the site in which the excesses of sensory experience were intertwined with subjective memory and a public gaze, which produced the fragmented, abstract form of her most famous London work, *Mrs. Dalloway*. Yet the novel was predated in July 1923 by the publication of "Mrs. Dalloway in Bond Street" in the magazine the *Dial*. The story encapsulates the tone and subject matter of the later novel, featuring the sensory experience of Big Ben, the austere emptiness of the Admiralty Arch, and the unrelenting traffic of crowds in Bond Street alongside the internal musings of Clarissa. The partiality of this narrative fragmentation was to become one of the hallmarks of modernist aesthetics, rendering the city as fleeting impression rather than as archetypal entity.

The post-1945 period has, to a large degree, seen a decline in the short story as a London genre. While a great deal of short story writing has been produced, many of the city's better-known contemporary scribes, such as Peter Ackroyd, Hanif Kureishi, and Zadie Smith, limit themselves to the far more lucrative production of novels, while others, such as IAIN SINCLAIR, incorporate the short story into their genre-defying literary practice. Yet that is not to say that London is not the site of short story production. Writers such as MARTIN AMIS and WILL SELF continue the tradition of the London short story. With the publication in 2006 of Iain Sinclair's edited volume of short fiction, poetry, and documentary titled *London, City of Disappearances*, perhaps short fiction will return to its place within the London tradition.

BIBLIOGRAPHY
Davies, Andrew. *Literary London*. London: Macmillan, 1988.

McLaughlin, Joseph. *Writing the Urban Jungle: Reading Empire in London from Doyle to Eliot*. Charlottesville: University Press of Virginia, 2000.

Onega, Susan, and John A. Stotesbury, eds. *London in Literature: Visionary Mappings of the Metropolis*. Heidelberg, Germany: C. Winter, 2002.

Poe, Edgar Allan. *The Complete Illustrated Stories and Poems*. London: Chancellor Press, 1994.

Reynolds, G. M. W. *The Mysteries of London*. North Staffordshire, England: Keele University Press, 1996.

Sinclair, Iain, ed. *London, City of Disappearances*. London: Penguin, 2006.

Robinson, Alan. *Imagining London, 1770–1900*. Basingstoke, England: Palgrave Macmillan, 2004.

Thomas, Deborah. *Dickens and the Short Story*. Philadelphia: University of Pennsylvania Press, 1982.

Wolfreys, Julian. *Writing London: The Trace of the Urban Text from Blake to Dickens*. Basingstoke, England: Macmillan, 1988.

Woolf, Virginia, *The Complete Shorter Fiction of Virginia Woolf*. Edited by Susan Dick. London: Hogarth Press, 1989.

Alex Murray

LONELINESS OF THE LONG DISTANCE RUNNER, THE ALAN SILLITOE (1959) This is the bleak title novella in a collection by ALAN SILLITOE. Although Sillitoe dislikes the label, the story is invariably grouped with other works by the so-called Angry Young Men of the period, works "dominated by a mood of bitterness and defiance" (Byars, 585). (See also KINGSLEY AMIS and STAN BARSTOW.) LIke Sillitoe's famous novel *Saturday Night and Sunday Morning* (1958), in this story the author adopts the persona, colloquialisms, and imagined writing style of a young, badly educated working-class man, in this case, Smith. (He is given no other name.) A 17-year old from Nottingham, Smith sees the world as divided between Out-laws and In-laws, whose battles take place in insti-

tutions such as Borstal (a reformatory) in the county of Essex, where he has been sent as punishment for robbery. "Them bastards over us aren't as daft as they most of the time look. . . . They're cunning, and I'm cunning. . . . If only 'them' and 'us' has the same ideas we'd get on like a house on fire, but they don't see eye to eye with us and we don't see eye to eye with them" (7).

In Borstal power is represented by the "governor." When this patronizing middle-class man discovers that Smith has a talent for running, he has the idea of making him the winner of the national long-distance championship being held in Essex. Smith, despite his contempt for the governor's plan, agrees to train for the race because running makes him feel mentally and physically free, as opposed to feeling like "a cut-balled cockerel" (19). However, he also decides to lose the race deliberately in order to strike back at the governor and publicly affirm his own values, despite knowing that he wil be punished for doing so. Organized sport, in this instance, seems to be associated with the establishment; talent gets hijacked by those in charge for their own ends. As Smith explains, "Our doddering bastard of a governor, our half-dead gangrened gaffer, is hollow like an empty petrol drum, and he wants me and my running life to give him glory, to put in him blood and throbbing veins he never had." Smith views himself as a human racehorse, running for "a bit of blue ribbon and a cup for a prize," which will become the possessions of the institution, not himself (8). Although "The Loneliness of the Long-Distance Runner" seems to be a story of defeat, it has also been read as a gesture of self-assertion and refusal on the part of a young everyman to accept the smug, comfortable values of a decaying older generation—represented by the governor (a kind of surrogate father). "I'm a human being and I've got thoughts and secrets and bloody life inside me that he doesn't know is there" (13). One of the messages of the story is that the Borstal system fails to work; men like the governor cannot hope to change Smith.

As more about the journey the protagonist has taken is revealed, readers' responses to him can become confused. Sillitoe himself has noted that "Smith is a . . . complex character. What his trouble is, we don't go into" (quoted in Hanson, 39). Smith regards himself as outside the "normal" boundaries of society; he is isolated and committed to life as an Out-law, which requires craftiness and deceit if he is to remain free. He has no intention of getting an honest living; he is motivated not by need but by pleasure and excitement. He is crude, callous, and self-centered, and he has a potential for violence—as when he imagines what he would do with power: "And if I had the whip-hand I wouldn't even bother to build a place like this to put all the cops, governors, posh whores, penpushers, army officers, Members of Parliament in; no, I'd stick them up against a wall and let them have it" (15). When he leaves Borstal, he avoids National Service because he has developed pleurisy and is pleased by this; at the time he is writing he has just stolen another £628 and is planning to steal more. At the same time, however, the story also invites sympathy for Smith, in part through the first-person narrative; Smith confides in the readers and encourages the feeling that he telling the truth (although it is questionable how truthful or reliable a narrator he actually is). He is self-reliant and determined but cannot imagine success because there will always be someone in authority waiting to stop him. We learn something of his working-class family; his father has died agonizingly from cancer of the throat; his slatternly mother has a "fancy man" and has squandered the insurance money from her husband's death. Except for his friend Mike, he seems to have always been alone. As Smith recalls his father's death during the last stage of the race in a way he never has before, he finds inspiration in his father's refusing medication and hospitalization and ultimately choking in his own blood: "If he had guts for that then I've got guts for this" (51). Claire Hanson reads the mixture of blood, tears, and self-awareness as a form of rebirth. Smith "comes alive through the vision of his father's death, sight, sound, taste and smell, as well as existential nausea come into play to emphasize his newfound awareness" (Hanson, 44). In this reading Smith achieves a tragic and almost heroic status. As Bayer argues, "[r]unning, the dominant, symbolic action in the story, suggests three motifs: the experience of life, the endurance test, and the lonely journey or pilgrimage" (586). Alan Penner further suggests that rather than a sign of "moral decay" Smith's rebellious gesture is the demonstration of a "Christ-like passion for a tragically deluded society suicidally hostile to life" (46). However, readers might also consider how much Smith actually changes. The story ends with the words "That I do know" (54), suggesting that Smith has learned something. He is still, however, a small-time crook; he may always be so.

A film of *The Loneliness of the Long Distance Runner*, directed by Tony Richardson and starring Tom Courtney, Michael Redgrave, and Avis Bunnage, was released in 1962.

BIBLIOGRAPHY
John Bars. "The Initiation of Alan Sillitoe's Long Distance Runner." *Modern Fiction Studies* 22, no. 4 (1976): 584–590.
Hanson, Claire. *Understanding Alan Sillitoe*. Columbia: University of South Carolina Press, 1999.
Penner, Alan. *Alan Sillitoe*. New York: Twayne, 1972.
Sillitoe, Alan. *The Loneliness of the Long-Distance Runner*. London: Flamingo, 1993.

Andrew Maunder

"LORD ARTHUR SAVILE'S CRIME" OSCAR WILDE (1891)

Subtitled "A Study of Duty," "Lord Arthur Savile's Crime" was published in a volume called *Lord Arthur Savile's Crime and Other Stories*. OSCAR WILDE had previously sold it in 1887 to the magazine *Court and Society Review*. Lord Arthur stands at the brink of his wedding to his beloved Sybil Merton when he goes to a party at Lady Windermere's and meets a cheiromantist, or palm reader—her pet entertainer for the time. When Lord Arthur has his palm read privately by Mr. Podgers the cheiromantist, he learns that he is destined to murder a distant relative. To clear the way for his marriage to Sybil, he decides to get the murder over with; however, it turns out that Lord Arthur is an inept murderer. Both of his attempts at the crime—giving his second cousin, Lady Clementina, a poison pill for her next attack of heartburn and sending a dynamite-rigged exploding clock to the Dean of Chichester—fail. Lady Clementina dies but does not take the pill he gave her, and the clock acts an entertaining toy for the Dean's family. Just when Arthur is about to give up, he sees Podgers on a bridge at the Thames and has the inspired notion that action will do the trick. He grabs Podgers by the legs and tips him into the river. The story ends happily as Sybil and Lord Arthur, having been married by the Dean of Chichester, converse with Lady Windermere. Sybil tells her friend that Lord Arthur takes one subject so seriously that he must not be kidded about it—cheiromancy.

The story is a humorous critique of the Victorian notion of duty and the idea of the heroic quest as it juxtaposes Lord Arthur's determination to clear the way for his marriage by committing murder with the reader's knowledge that murder cannot masquerade as duty. This opposition creates irony throughout the story. Wilde also satirizes the idea that the aristocracy can be moral exemplars for society. When Lord Arthur makes the arrangement for the exploding clock to be sent to the dean, for example, he contacts a Russian anarchist and agrees, on his honor, not to give any information to Scotland Yard about him. Lord Arthur also takes Lady Windermere's taste for novelty as a premise for serious action. His killing of Podgers does not mean his denial of belief in chiromancy, but it strikes the reader as a moment of poetic justice as the origin of Savile's murder attempts becomes the fulfillment of his quest. The story's tone, especially in a passage that describes Lord Arthur's despair at not being able to commit a murder, clearly mocks the norms of melodrama: "When he got upstairs, he flung himself on a sofa, and his eyes filled with tears. He had done his best to commit this murder, but on both occasions he had failed, and through no fault of his own" (47). Most of the story's satire focuses on Lord Arthur, but other characters are not spared. Sybil, in her role as unquestioning wife and patient fiancée, is also part of the satire. She is ridiculously loyal to Lord Arthur even when he travels abroad and delays their wedding without giving her or her parents an explanation. Lady Windermere's trendiness comes through again at the end of the story: Her new fad is telepathy. Lady Windermere ironically observes about Arthur's loyalty to cheiromancy, "I never heard such nonsense in all my life" (52).

BIBLIOGRAPHY

Wilde, Oscar. *Complete Shorter Fiction*. Oxford: Oxford University Press, 1992.

Susan Bernardo

"LORD EMSWORTH AND THE GIRL FRIEND" P. G. WODEHOUSE (1935) This is one of a number of Wodehouse's stories to feature the dimwitted aristocrat Clarence Emsworth. This character—a favorite with Wodehouse fans—first appeared in "The Custody of the Pumpkin" in the *Saturday Evening Post* in 1924. Other stories featuring Emsworth—including "Lord Emsworth and the Girl Friend"—appeared intermittently through the 1920s and eventually were collected in *Blandings Castle and Elsewhere* (1935). The title

of the collection refers to the country house in the rural county of Shropshire where Emsworth lives. Bumbling and divorced from the events of the outside world, Lord Emsworth cares little for his immediate family. His younger son, Freddie, is always getting into scrapes, and his sister, Lady Constance Keeble, tries to domineer over him, often in alliance with McAllister, the gardener, a dour Scotsman who bullies him but whom he needs and is afraid to get rid of. Lord Emsworth realizes that "he is no longer captain of his soul; that he is to all intents and purposes ground beneath the number twelve heel of a Glaswegian head-gardener." Emsworth, good-natured but rather blinkered and scared of human society (including women), finds consolation in caring for his prize-winning pig, the Empress of Blandings.

In this story, Blanding's Castle has been commandeered by Constance to play host to a garden fete, "a noisome rash of swings, roundabout, marquees, toy balloons, and paper bags"—much to Emsworth's annoyance. As the crowds ("the peasantry") pour in and strangers are milling around, the lonely Emsworth, who has been dressed up for the occasion, is told "to go and be genial." He meets a young working-class girl from a London slum; this is Gladys—the girlfriend of the title. Thirteen years old, pert and unafraid, with a face of "wizened motherliness," she wins over Emsworth when she tells him how she threw stones at the tyrannical head gardener who chased her as she tried to pick some flowers. In her willingness to challenge McAllister, this young girl is the very opposite of Lord Emsworth. Impressed, Emsworth views Gladys as "a superwoman" and, inspired by her example, begins to stand up to his sister and the gardener, wresting back control—albeit temporarily—of his own garden. The story seems to show how people from different backgrounds can interact and learn from each other.

The struggle for power between Emsworth and his gardener and sister provides much of the story's humor. However, as in other Blandings stories, it is sometimes difficult to ascertain whether Wodehouse is inviting us to condemn or support his aristocratic hero. Wodehouse has been accused of being rather too bewitched by the world he describes, so that what starts out as satire ends up being a nostalgic account of harmless eccentrics and lazy summer days ("so warm, so fair, so magically a thing of sunshine and blue skies and bird-song"). The bond between the childlike Emsworth and Gladys is touching, and she brings out the chivalric instincts in the old man. In this sense the story seems to fit with Evelyn Waugh's comment that Wodehouse's world and characters are "idyllic" and "Edenic in their innocence." "For Mr. Wodehouse there has been no fall of man" (cited in Leader, 49). Wodehouse, Waugh argues, wants to preserve this unspoiled world. Yet the presence of Gladys and the throwing open of Blandings to the outside world—in this case underprivileged schoolchildren—is a reminder that not all of England enjoys the same halcyon existence. Gladys and her hungry brother Ern have been "reared among the tin cans and cabbage stalks of Drury Lane," and the flowers and food at Blandings are a vision of a world that they can only dream about. Emsworth's distaste at the invasion of his home by the working classes can be read as quirky and amusing, and his sister Constance's patronizing attempts to engage in social work can be seen as deserving of mockery. Attempts to make the children take tea irrevocably break down: "All civilized laws had obviously gone by the board and Anarchy reigned in the marquee." Emsworth, who prefers to wear the clothes of a workingman rather than a collar and top hat (which keeps getting knocked off), also wants to rebel against the do-gooders. In this sense, an unusual link is established between him and his working-class guests. However, it is also possible to stress the selfishness of Emsworth: He does not really want to mix with these people and resents their annual appearance in his world; they threaten its orderly existence.

BIBLIOGRAPHY

Leader, Zachery, ed. On Modern British Fiction. Oxford: Oxford University Press, 2002.
Wodehouse, P. G. Blandings Castle and Elsewhere. London: Everyman, 2002.

Andrew Maunder

"LOST HEARTS" M. R. JAMES (1895, 1904)

One of M. R. JAMES's earliest ghost stories, frequently anthologized. James read aloud a version of "Lost Hearts" to his colleagues in the Chitchat Society, Cambridge, in October 1893. The story subsequently appeared in the *Pall Mall Magazine* (December 1895), and James later gathered it into *Ghost Stories of an Antiquary* (1904), his first and most important collection of supernatural tales. The tale opens in 1811, when a young orphan, Stephen Elliott, arrives at Aswarby Hall, the Lincolnshire estate of his elderly cousin Mr. Abney, an aloof yet kindly amateur researcher of classical antiquities. Stephen gradually becomes aware that Mr. Abney's historical pursuits are neither innocent nor benign—indeed, these studies have necessitated the boy's presence as an "inmate" at Aswarby Hall—and the story acquires much of its weird atmosphere from the way James deftly intermingles depictions of childhood innocence with a series of sudden occult awakenings. In one memorable instance, Stephen sleepwalks from his bed and glimpses a visionary horror secreted away within "an old disused bathroom": "A figure inexpressibly thin and pathetic, of a dusty leaden colour, enveloped in a shroud-like garment, the thin lips crooked into a faint and dreadful smile, the hands pressed tightly over the region of the heart."

With its leisurely progression toward a striking denouement, its couching of supernatural incident within an everyday setting, and its smart placement of antiquarian detail, "Lost Hearts" is a prime example of James's methods and preoccupations. Because of its thematic concerns with the return of paganism into a later epoch, the tale should also be read within the fin de siècle context of decadence and occult spiritualism that produced ARTHUR MACHEN's *The Great God Pan* (1894). Several BBC radio and television productions have been made of this story.

BIBLIOGRAPHY

Ackroyd, Peter. Albion: The Origins of the English Imagination. London: Chatto & Windus, 2002.
Briggs, Julia. Night Visitors: The Rise and Fall of the English Ghost Story. London: Faber, 1977.
James, M. R. Ghost Stories of an Antiquary. Edited by E. F. Bleiler. New York: Dover, 1971.
Sullivan, Jack. Elegant Nightmares: The English Ghost Story from Le Fanu to Blackwood. Athens: Ohio University Press, 1978.

Charles L. Sligh

"LOTUS, THE" JEAN RHYS (1967)

"The Lotus" was first published in *Art and Literature* in 1967 and later published in the collection *Tigers Are Better Looking* in 1968. Although according to JEAN RHYS's letters most of the stories in the collection were ready in 1945, their publication was possible only because of Rhys's literary resurrection after the publication of her novel *Wide Sargasso Sea* in 1966. Like many other stories in the collection, "The Lotus" is set in London. The third-person narrative follows the point of view of Ronnie Miles and focuses on his downstairs neighbour, Lotus Heath, a middle-aged woman writer. Ronnie invites Lotus over for a drink, despite the disapproval of his wife, Christine, who believes Lotus to be "a tart." Lotus tells the couple about her work, ignoring Christine's sarcastic comments about her writing and her insinuations that she is drinking too much. When Ronnie accompanies Lotus back to her small basement flat, he sees photographs of her as a young woman. The striking beauty of these photographs evokes the older woman's growing sense of loss. In the intimacy of this small but crowded space, Lotus tells Ronnie about the pain of her loneliness and marginalization in London: "I've had enough. I've had enough, I can tell you. The things they say. The things people say!" Back in his flat, some minutes later, Ronnie notices a strange noise coming from the street: Lotus is running naked up the street until she is, finally, caught by two policemen. One of the policemen tries to find out if the Mileses or any of their neighbors know Lotus, suggesting that her behavior was probably triggered by "something more than drink." Ronnie, however, claims not to know anything about his neighbor. He goes back to his bedroom, where his wife Christine is lying in bed, peaceful and happy as a little child, ignoring "the whole sordid affair." The desire that Christine's uncontaminated happiness provokes in Ronnie further intensifies the isolation and the grotesque marginalization of Lotus Heath.

Early reviewers, writing in 1968, saw *Tigers Are Better Looking* as confirming Rhys's interest in the lives of underdogs and read the bleak ending of "The Lotus" as a critique of the hypocrisy of English manners. Others read the story as autobiographical, highlighting possible links between the two middle-aged women writers, Lotus Heath and Jean Rhys. For many feminist and postcolonial critics it is the "naked" portrait of social discrimination, exclusion, and alienation that makes story so powerful. Even though Lotus's ethnicity is not clearly conveyed in this story, critics have tended to read "The Lotus" alongside other short stories by Rhys whose figures are outsiders, in terms of class, race, or gender. The name Lotus evokes that sense of displacement, evoking the transplant of an exotic flower to the urban London scene. The lotus flower is native to eastern Asia but is widely cultivated outside Asia for its large pink or white flowers. While these colors emphasize the energy, exuberance, and creativity of Rhys's character, they also suggest her potential alienation and marginality. Lotus's naked body as she runs alone in the streets of London is, in this sense, a striking image of dispossession and loss. The erasure of Lotus's identity is prefigured through several references to death, such as Christine's sarcastic comments on Lotus's age: "Most people go on living long after they ought to be dead, don't they?" Similarly, at the end of the story, when Ronnie is talking with the policeman, he impulsively asks, "Is she dying?" The narrative, framed, woven, and constructed through male perspective, also emphasizes the silencing of Lotus. The dislocation of the typically modernist epiphany—the last paragraphs of the story focus not on Lotus but on Christine—confirms again the deletion of Lotus's subjectivity from the white male narrative. This obliteration is particularly poignant because Lotus, the woman exiled from the narrative, is herself a writer.

BIBLIOGRAPHY

Rhys, Jean. *Collected Short Stories.* London: Norton, 1992.

Susana Araujo

"LOVE AMONG THE HAYSTACKS"
D. H. LAWRENCE (1930) Although "Love among the Haystacks" was published posthumously in November 1930, two letters date its composition between July 30, 1908, and November 7, 1911. In the first letter, D. H. LAWRENCE writes at length to Blanche Jennings about his fortnight's work at the hay harvest in Greasley (*Letters,* 21–26). In the second, he describes "a rather ripping long short story" (*Letters,* 85) to Edward Garnett, which has been identified as "Love among the Haystacks." However, the similarities between the story's diction—for example, the description of the "large lime tree," which "teemed with scent that seemed almost like a voice speaking" (*Letters,* 104)—and that of the letter to Jennings, describing the "big lime trees, murmuring and full of the scent of nectar" (*Letters,* 23–24), suggest that the story was written closer to July 1908 than to November 1911.

Like much of Lawrence's writing, the story is based on people and places known by him and is semiautobiographical. The Wookey family are a characterization of the Chambers family, with whom Lawrence was intimately connected through his relationship with Jessie Chambers. Their realistic rather than sentimental presentation is given in the dialectal forms of their dialogue. They are portrayed again as the Saxton family in *The White Peacock* and as the Leivers family in *Sons and Lovers*. Likewise, Greasley, the setting for the story, retains its proper name and landmarks, such as the vicarage mentioned in the letter, whereas in the novels that share its Nottinghamshire setting, real locations are described under allusive names, such as the fictionalization of the Chamberses' Felley Mill Farm as Strelley Mill in *The White Peacock* and Lawrence's birthplace, Eastwood, as Bestwood in *Sons and Lovers*.

Another common factor between "Love among the Haystacks" and these two early novels is their opening paragraphs, in which the narrative moves from a panoramic view of the landscape to characters' perceptions of it. By contrasting different perspectives of the landscape, such as Maurice's immediate, exclusive view of the haystack versus Geoffrey's speculative "large view" (88) of the countryside from it, Lawrence develops a method of characterization that he applies to subsequent novels, notably the opening of *The Rainbow*, in which inward- and outward-looking views of the known world are used to distinguish between the male and female members of the Brangwen family, respectively. Views of the landscape, such as Maurice's perception of the colliery's "elfish" lights, the iron-foundry's "red-flare," and the "dim breathing of town-lights" (106), also reflect Lawrence's anxiety about England's ecological destruction at the hands of its mechanized, urban society.

The plot centers on the sibling rivalry between Maurice and Geoffrey Wookey and their respective sexual initiations the night after the hay harvest. The language of the consummations is handled with the delicate metaphorical suggestion characteristic of Lawrence's early writing. Indeed, the story is drawn upon again in *The Rainbow* as Will and Anna "consummate" their love after making a new "stook" one night during the corn harvest. "Love among the Haystacks" is typical of the early fiction in that for both brothers "the whole feminine sex ha[s] been repre-sented by their mother" (89), and the story tells how such oedipal bonds are broken. In so doing it explores how lovers subvert and are constrained by social taboos, as in Maurice's engagement to Paula, a Polish refugee. Himself a traveler and outsider for most of his life, Lawrence gives sympathetic treatment to characters like Paula and Lydia, who is trapped in a loveless marriage to a gypsy. Such themes continue to be explored in later stories. "Love among the Haystacks" demonstrates Lawrence's imaginative attachment to his experiences in the countryside of his youth and the importance of the short story to him as a document thereof. Moreover, it exemplifies his use of the short story both as an aesthetic form in its own right and as a sketchbook for descriptions and characterizations that appear in his work in other genres.

BIBLIOGRAPHY
Kearney, Martin F. *Major Short Stories of D. H. Lawrence: A Handbook.* New York: Garland, 1998.
Lawrence, D. H. *Letters of D. H. Lawrence.* Vol. 1: *1901–1913.* Edited by James T. Boulton. Cambridge: Cambridge University Press, 1979.
———. *Love among the Haystacks and Other Stories.* Edited by John Worthen. Cambridge: Cambridge University Press, 1987.

Oliver Taylor

"LOVE AND FRIENDSHIP" JANE AUSTEN (1790, 1922)

This parody of sentimental fiction is JANE AUSTEN's best-known juvenile work. It was written in 1790, when she was only 14, but did not appear in print until 1922.

Austen's novella is a mock epistolary romance consisting of 15 letters written by a woman named Laura to the daughter of her friend. In her first letter, Laura uses rhetoric typical of novels of sensibility when she offers to give an account of "the fortitude with which I have suffered the many Afflictions of my past Life" in the hopes that it will provide the girl with "a useful Lesson" (75). Through Laura's narration of her own early adventures, Austen sends up the emotive heroines, stilted diction, and pseudodidacticism of sentimental novels. Austen's witty story can be read as a moral satire to the extent that it exposes the spuriousness of Laura's claims to virtue and, by extension, the dubious morality of much sentimental fiction.

Austen, making fun of the idealized heroines of romance, has Laura begin her narrative by describing how beautiful, accomplished, and virtuous she was at 18. By her own account, her only flaw was a "sensibility too tremblingly alive" (76). The first incident in her story is the arrival of a mysterious young man at her parents' cottage. The noble youth, named Edward, has run away from home because he scorns to marry the woman his father has chosen for him: "Never shall it be said that I obliged my Father" (79). Edward declares his passion for Laura, and they are married at once. This episode ridicules two conventions of sentimental fiction: the portrayal of tyrannical parental authority and the formation of sympathetic bonds between characters. The second of these sentimental tropes is parodied again when Edward and Laura move in with Edward's friend Augustus and his wife Sophia. Laura describes her first meeting with Sophia as follows: "We flew into each others arms and after having exchanged vows of mutual Friendship for the rest of our Lives, instantly unfolded to each other the most inward Secrets of our Hearts—" (83–84).

The household is broken up when Augustus is sent to debtor's prison and Edward disappears. Laura and Sophia travel to Scotland to seek assistance from Sophia's relations. Laura explains in passing that they could not take refuge with her parents, as they had died some time earlier. With this fleeting remark, Austen exposes the hypocrisy of Laura, who, for all her tender sensibility, has little real compassion. The death of Laura's parents also affords Austen the opportunity of mocking the well-worn literary cliché whereby an orphaned heroine is discovered to be of high birth. At an inn, Laura and Sophia meet an elderly gentleman who readily acknowledges both as his long-lost granddaughters. After this providential reunion, the heroines proceed to the home of Sophia's cousin, Macdonald, where they convince his daughter to break her engagement with a suitable young man, because "he had no soul" and his hair was not auburn (91). After they help her elope with a fortune hunter and are caught stealing banknotes, Macdonald sends them away.

As the heroines sit by a stream, they witness a carriage overturning. The passengers, who lie "weltering in their blood," are none other than Edward and Augustus. Laura explains that upon making this discovery, she and Sophia lose their senses: "Sophia faint-

ing every moment and I running Mad as often" (96). The coup de grâce of Austen's parody of the sentimental heroine occurs when Sophia's acute sensitivity proves fatal. As a consequence of having fainted repeatedly "in the open Air as the Dew was falling" (98), Sophia catches a cold, never to recover. On her deathbed, she gives her friend the following advice: "Run mad as often as you chuse; but do not faint—," a lesson that serves as the ironic moral of Laura's tale (99).

"Love and Friendship" introduces themes that Austen developed more fully in novels such as *Sense and Sensibility* (1811) and *Northanger Abbey* (1798, 1818). Stylistically, it offers an excellent early example of Austen's deft use of irony. It is also important for its critique of romance, which set precedents for the realism that came to characterize her approach as a writer.

BIBLIOGRAPHY
Austen, Jane. *Catharine and Other Writings.* Edited by Margaret Anne Doody and Douglas Murray. Oxford: Oxford University Press, 1998.

Natalie Neill

LOWRY, MALCOLM (1907–1957)

Born in Cheshire on July 28, 1907, Malcolm Lowry was the son of a wealthy cotton broker and regarded himself as a composer of popular music before he turned to writing. The established facts of Lowry's early life are that he was educated at Cambridge University from 1929 to 1932, went to sea, and lived in New York from 1934 to 1936, where he was treated for alcoholism in Bellevue Hospital. Lowry's accounts of events, however, have often displayed a tendency to exaggeration and self-martyrdom. When Lowry left England for the six-month voyage that would result in his first published work, *Ultramarine* (1933), it was by no means a self-exile but rather a low-risk adventure, embarked on by a young graduate with less proficiency as a seaman than his later work implies. While Lowry's writing is frequently described as autobiographical, it is the contradictions or parallels among stories that constitute their artistry; the author thereby comments on the fluidity of identity and the instability of memory. In contrast, Lowry can also be considered a travel writer selling his experiences; more than one authorial persona in the later short stories has bemoaned becoming a "literary" writer by accident, an attitude that Lowry's biographer, Douglas Day, has also attributed to Lowry himself. This factor may account for some of the shortcomings several critics have detected in Lowry's work, namely, a poor sense of plot and an almost solipsistic preoccupation with his own life.

Lowry's most important work is *Under the Volcano* (1947), a novel often ranked among the greatest works of the 20th century by a British author since *Ulysses*. Based loosely on Dante Alighieri's *Inferno,* the novel narrates several hallucinatory hours in the life of a dipsomaniac British consul on the Mexican Day of the Dead (Lowry lived in Mexico from 1936 to 1938). *Under the Volcano* has received the lion's share of attention from critics and readers of Lowry alike, but it is relevant here because the complexity of the design recurs within many of his short stories, especially within the collection *Hear Us O Lord from Heaven Thy Dwelling Place* (1962). Intertextualities in Lowry's work are generally either occult and mystical references—allusions to the mythologies of the Old World and the New—or references to episodes from the author's own life, previously recounted from a younger (or a more-or-less inebriated) perspective. The first story in the collection ("The Bravest Boat") is the most artistically satisfying and the most self-contained. The premise is that a balsa-wood boat launched on a New England beach eventually reaches the woman who becomes the protagonist's wife after reading the letter sealed inside. Although hyperbolically sentimental in some passages, the story also displays Lowry's poetic prose at its most visionary. In lines worthy of Herman Melville, Lowry imagines the boat passing glaciers, as "saber-winged birds with iron beaks" pass overhead. In its mindless encounter with figures of the sublime—the full force of the elements—the boat seems more pathetic and more absurd than the *Pequod.*

Later in the collection, Lowry revisits the trope of a chance encounter after many years with an emblem of a past that seems to be a portent of divine mysteries ordaining human lives. In this case, the protagonist discovers the same elephant that (Hannibal-like) he had to transport by sea years before, an experience he had lucratively novelized. "Elephant and Colosseum" [sic] is not, however, as effective as "The Bravest Boat"—the

descriptions of Roman architecture and the lives of artists who have passed through the city are accomplished, but the author neglects to prioritize either the allegorical episodes or the descriptive passages and fails to integrate them convincingly. "Through the Panama" (from the same collection) is in effect the bones of an uncompleted novel, or a plan for the novel-cycle *The Voyage That Never Ends,* interspersed with notes on the modernist precursors whom Lowry admires. Most of Lowry's short fiction may be read for its mastery of language, but not all of it shows the work of a writer who has understood the potential of the form.

A major exception to this tendency is Lowry's reimagining of his time spent in Bellevue, *Lunar Caustic* (1968). His most significant work after *Under the Volcano,* this novella deserves consideration both for the writer's candor in his depiction of alcoholism and for the intensity of the purgatorial vision recounted. Comparisons to Dante are inevitable, but there is no "debt" to speak of. Here, as in such stories as "The Forest Path to the Spring," Lowry demonstrates the use of traditional narratives to locate order and design in the universe, even when living "under the volcano." Whether by deliberate intention or failure of imagination, the story's lack of resolution and the inertia of the main character throughout succeed in conveying the horror of delirium tremens and foreshadow the longer fall into a still-darker spiritual abyss that culminated in Lowry's death in 1957 (widely reported as suicide, though never confirmed).

BIBLIOGRAPHY

Asals, Frederick, and Paul Tiessen. *A Darkness That Murmured: Essays on Malcolm Lowry and the Twentieth Century.* London: Toronto University Press, 2000.

Day, Douglas. *Malcolm Lowry.* London: Oxford University Press, 1974.

Grace, Sherrill. *The Voyage That Never Ends: Malcolm Lowry's Fiction.* Vancouver: University of British Columbia Press, 1982.

Lowry, Malcolm. *Dark as the Grave Wherein My Friend Is Laid.* New York: New American Library, 1968.

———. *Hear Us O Lord from Heaven Thy Dwelling Place.* London: Jonathan Cape, 1962.

———. *Ultramarine.* Philadelphia: Lippincott, 1962.

———. *Under the Volcano.* New York: Reynal and Hitchcock, 1947.

M. A. T. Mellor

MACAULAY, ROSE (1881–1958) Born in Rugby, England, to a family of scholars and clerics, Emilie Rose Macaulay spent much of her childhood in Varezze, a seaside village in Italy, where her father worked as a translator. From her time on the Mediterranean, and from her many and varied travels thereafter, she acquired her love of classical archaeology, of swimming, and of adventure in general. After returning to England to study modern history at Somerville College, Oxford, she moved to London, where she quickly succeeded in the fields of journalism, fiction, and criticism. Working as a nurse and a civil servant for the War Office and the Propaganda Department during World War I, she also immersed herself in London's literary community and befriended many fellow writers: Rupert Brooke, ELIZABETH BOWEN, Rosamond Lehmann, VIRGINIA WOOLF, Christopher Isherwood, W. H. Auden, and E. M. FORSTER, to name a few. Never married, she nevertheless had a decades-long affair with a married writer and former Catholic priest, Gerald O'Donovan, who was her muse, writing critic, and best friend until his death in 1942. A prolific author and renowned wit, she published 35 books during her lifetime and is best remembered for her anguished post–WORLD WAR II novel *The World My Wilderness,* her travel books, and her comic novel *The Towers of Trebizond.* She was named Dame Commander of the British Empire shortly before her death in 1958.

Predominantly a novelist and critic, Macaulay nevertheless wrote one of the most incisive and evocative short stories of World War II London. Predating her neoromantic and similarly haunting *The World My Wilderness* and a precursor in morbid meditation to *Pleasure of Ruins* (1953), "Miss Anstruther's Letters" (published in 1941 by Storm Jameson) tells the disconcerting story of Miss Anstruther, a single, elderly woman with strong autobiographical parallels to Macaulay herself, reacting to the destruction by bombing of her central London house. Like Macaulay when her London flat was bombed, Miss Anstruther loses everything of significance, most importantly her library and the letters from her recently dead lover. The few illegible scraps of love letters she finds among the wreckage become symbols of the Blitz itself, reminders of the profound losses, uprootedness, fragmentation, and anxiety of a city under siege. Indeed, she loses herself in losing her letters: The paper trail of her existence is no longer accessible, and Miss Anstruther, now a mere shade of her former vitality, creeps toward the fate of her lover and his letters by observing life with all of the distance and apathy of one already half-dead. Upon its publication, "Miss Anstruther's Letters" was widely hailed as one of the most touching and accurate depictions of Blitz-era peril. It is valuable for its geographical and historical specificity as well as its biographical parallels to Macaulay's own life, but its use of the imagery reminiscent of the Renaissance poets Dante and Milton and its poignant eloquence render it a free-standing masterwork.

BIBLIOGRAPHY

Boston, Anne, ed. *Wave Me Goodbye: Stories of the Second World War.* London: Penguin, 1988.

LeFanu, Sarah. *Rose Macaulay: A Biography.* London: Virago, 2003.

Macaulay, Rose. *And No Man's Wit.* London: Collins, 1940.

———. *They Were Defeated.* London: Collins, 1932.

———. *The World My Wilderness.* London: Collins, 1950.

Kristin Anderson

MACHEN, ARTHUR (1863–1947) Arthur

Machen was born in Caerleon-on-Usk, Wales, the only child of an Anglican priest and his wife. Born Arthur Llewellyn Jones, Machen adopted his mother's maiden name for his literary career. As a child, he spent his days exploring the Welsh landscape and was preoccupied with the Roman artifacts repeatedly uncovered during his childhood. Although he was an astute learner, his parents could not afford to send Machen to Oxford, where his father had studied, and he instead moved to London in 1881 at age 18 to pursue a career in journalism. This led to the publication of his long poem *Eleusinia* (1881), which proved to be a complete failure. Undeterred, in 1884 Machen published *The Anatomy of Tobacco* and in 1887 *The Chronicle of Clemendy,* both of which met with moderate success. However, his short stories of the 1890s would bring him his greatest success. In 1894 John Lane published Machen's *The Great God Pan* in his Keynote series, which caused Machen to be labeled a decadent (see DECADENCE), despite Machen's insistence that his work was not decadent. John Lane published another Machen success in 1895, *The Three Impostors,* in which Machen used his friend W. B. Yeats as the model for one of his characters. Although he continued to write through the end of the century, he did not publish any other works until after 1900, a lapse some scholars attribute to his link with the decadents and their unpopularity after the OSCAR WILDE trials.

Machen's name returned to print at the beginning of the 20th century with his famous semiautobiographical *The Hill of Dreams* (1907). Much to Machen's dis-

may, the text was considered by a critic to be the most decadent book ever written because of its somewhat occultist themes. After this novel Machen's writing significantly changed. Continuing his career as a journalist for the *Evening News* through WORLD WAR I, Machen wrote a piece of fiction in 1914 that resulted in a national debate. "The BOWMEN" told the story of celestial angels that helped the British avoid defeat during the battle of Mons against Germany. Although Machen insisted that the piece was fictional, people continued to write to the *Evening News* with "proof" that that the event really happened. Machen continued to write fictional pieces about World War I but with little success. Only in the 1920s did Machen regain some of his previous success as a writer when Vincent Starrett led an American revival of his supernatural texts from the 1890s. Unfortunately, Machen had already sold his rights to his works, and he remained poverty stricken throughout the rest of his life.

Although Machen's works do not all belong to one genre, his most successful works are, according to Vincent Williams, examples of both fantastic and supernatural fiction. S. T. Joshi, however, argues that these works belong in the subgenre of weird fiction. In *The Great God Pan* and "The Inmost Light," Machen combines science and the supernatural to create female monsters. Helen Vaughn, from the former text, is a female incarnate of Jack the Ripper who chooses wealthy male victims but exhibits the same frenzy as the 1888 serial killer. Machen's works demonstrate his obsession with the mysteries of the universe but his rejection of the possibility of finding their solutions. Machen's short-lived involvement with the Hermetic Order of the Golden Dawn in 1899 increased his interest in the unexplained and his contempt for scientific materialism. Machen's contrast between science and the fantastic influenced contemporary and present-day authors, including H. P. Lovecraft, Clive Barker, and Ramsay Campbell.

BIBLIOGRAPHY

Joshi, S. T. *The Weird Tale.* Austin: University of Texas Press, 1990.

Machen, Arthur. *Arthur Machen: Selected Letters.* Edited by Roger Dobson, Godfrey Brangham, and R. A. Gilbert. Wellingborough, England: Aquarian Press, 1988.

Machen, Arthur. *The Bowmen and Other Legends of the War.* London: Simpkin, 1915.

———. *The Great God Pan.* London: John Lane, 1894.

———. *Tales of Horror and the Supernatural.* Horams: Tartarus Press, 1997.

Reynolds, Aidan, and William Charlton. *Arthur Machen: A Short Account of His Life and Works.* London: John Baker for Richards Press, 1963.

Williams, Vincent. "Arthur Machen and the Supernatural in English Fiction, 1880–1980." Master's thesis, University of London, 1990.

Amanda Mordavsky

MACLAVERTY, BERNARD (1942–)

Born in Belfast, Bernard MacLaverty lived there until 1975, when he left Northern Ireland for Scotland. He is the author of four volumes of short stories and four novels. Two of the novels, *Lamb* (1980) and *Cal* (1983), were filmed from screenplays by MacLaverty. Many of his short stories have been filmed for television and broadcast as radio plays.

Northern Ireland and its troubled political situation almost always provide the settings and characters for MacLaverty's short fiction. However, in most of MacLaverty's stories Northern Irish violence is in the background, referred to or hinted at but rarely brought to the center of a story. MacLaverty writes predominantly about figures on the margins of society, especially children, the old, and the poor, and often focuses on the experience of women. His fiction frequently hints at problems that underlie everyday life, dialogue or actions subtly revealing depths of suffering. Despite the darkness of his topics, MacLaverty's work is sometimes humorous, although the comedy is overshadowed by a sense of the unhappiness of life.

MacLaverty's first collection of short stories is appropriately entitled *Secrets* (1977). In "The Exercise" a boy does not tell his father that his help with the boy's homework has been useless. In "Secrets" another boy uncovers his great-aunt's romance from the time of World War I. MacLaverty also shows his skill in evoking the secret lives of the lost and the unhappy—a lonely priest in "St. Paul Could Hit the Nail on the Head," a 50-year-old failure in "A Happy Birthday," and a down-and-out in "A Present for Christmas."

The stories in *A Time to Dance* (1982) deal with outsiders similar to those in *Secrets*. In the title story, Nelson is in rebellion against school and his mother, a striptease dancer, whose life he only partly understands. "My Dear Palestrina" involves a working-class boy who is gifted musically. His teacher, the mysterious immigrant Miss Schwartz, opens the world of music to him but is rejected by his community when, unmarried, she becomes pregnant. Many of the characters in the stories in this collection are orphans or are isolated in some way. For example, "The Daily Woman" is a harrowing tale of sexual exploitation and loneliness. Humor is, however, apparent in some stories, as in "Phonefun Limited," although even here there are suggestions of secret unhappiness. "Father and Son" is unusual in that it presents the violence of Northern Ireland directly.

Two stories in *The Great Profundo* (1987) are typical of MacLaverty's work. In "Words the Happy Say" two lonely people cannot overcome their inhibitions to form a relationship. "Some Surrender" presents, largely through dialogue, the complex relationship between a father and his son. The father is an unbending Protestant; the son has left the family to attempt an unsuccessful relationship with a Catholic woman. Although *Walking the Dog* (1994) shows MacLaverty attempting new things, many of the stories explore characters who are familiar from the author's earlier work. Two stories stand out. In "Walking the Dog" the protagonist is picked up by a murder team. He does not know whether they belong to the Irish Republican Army or to a Protestant paramilitary group. They do not know whether he is a Catholic or a Protestant and ask him questions to find out. Because he does not know who his captors are, he does not know how to answer. "A Silent Retreat" presents conversations between a Catholic schoolboy and a young Protestant special policeman in the early 1960s. Their attempts at communication break down and suggest the violent future of Northern Ireland.

BIBLIOGRAPHY

Griffith, Benjamin. "Ireland's Ironies, Grim and Droll: The Fiction of Bernard MacLaverty," *Sewanee Review* 106, no. 2 (Spring 1988): 334–338.

MacLaverty, Bernard. *Cal.* 1983. London: Vintage, 1998.

———. *The Great Profundo.* London: Cape, 1987.

———. *Secrets.* 1977. London: Vintage, 1997.

———. *A Time to Dance.* London: Cape, 1982.

———. *Walking the Dog.* 1994. London: Penguin, 1995.

David Malcolm

MAGAZINES, VICTORIAN (1830–1880)

For many, perhaps most, Victorian readers, fiction was packaged within the pages of a magazine or newspaper rather than between the covers of a book. During the 1830s and 1850s the reduction and eventual abolition of the notorious stamp duty and taxes on advertising and, in 1861, on paper, together with publishers' perception of an expanding market, encouraged the proliferation of magazines.

Although the monthly and weekly magazines are more frequently associated with serialized long fiction—and it is arguable that the heyday of the short story belongs to the end of the century—in fact periodicals encouraged the production of short fiction throughout the Victorian age and helped the development and popularity of subgenres such as ghost stories, sensation fiction, and detective fiction.

In the early decades (the mid-1820s to mid-1850s) the illustrated ANNUALS, designed for the Christmas and gift market, played a part in popularizing short fiction, since by their nature they were unsuitable for serialized novels. MARY RUSSELL MITFORD, whose series of tales "Our Village" had transformed the fortunes of the *Lady's Magazine* in the early 1820s, was a notable contributor, as was MARY SHELLEY, who provided many short stories for such publications as the *Keepsake.* Editors sought celebrity contributors, and among writers of short fiction for *Heath's Book of Beauty* during the Countess of Blessington's editorship were Sir Edward Bulwer Lytton and the Earl of Beaconsfield (former Prime Minister Benjamin Disraeli). Later, the special Christmas numbers of magazines like CHARLES DICKENS's *Household Words,* which had accelerated the demise of the expensive annuals, exploited the attraction of the short story for holiday reading. Meanwhile such lively monthlies as *Bentley's Miscellany* and *Fraser's Magazine* were also publishing fiction. *Oliver Twist* appeared in *Bentley's; Fraser's* carried some of William Makepeace Thackeray's early work. ELLEN WOOD was certainly not alone in launching her career as a novelist through magazine fiction when, during the 1850s, she supplied, for modest remuneration, some 150 short stories to Harrison Ainsworth, then the editor of *Bentley's* and the proprietor of the *New Monthly Magazine.*

Dickens's *Household Words* (1850–59) a cheap (twopenny) and innovative weekly magazine, was aimed at a much broader audience than the purchasers of monthlies. Its professed ambition was to usurp the penny dreadfuls while bringing to its readers a deeper knowledge of their own society and the wider world, but always in a highly imaginative and entertaining way. Dickens's strong editorial control over both it and *All The Year Round,* which he launched in 1859 following his split from Bradbury and Evans, imparted a distinct personality to both magazines. *All The Year Round* is distinguished by its commitment to serialized fiction, but *Household Words* also made a major contribution to the publication of contemporary fiction.

WILKIE COLLINS collaborated with Dickens on stories and wrote original fiction for *All the Year Round,* whose staff he joined in 1865. Eliza Lynn Linton was a regular writer of short stories. Percy Fitzgerald, introduced to Dickens by John Forster, became a prolific contributor to both magazines over a period of 20 years; he said that the "mere connection" with *Household Words* was for an author a passport to other journals.

"LIZZIE LEIGH" by ELIZABETH GASKELL opened *Household Words,* which later published the CRANFORD stories and others, including "The OLD NURSE'S STORY" and various Christmas number offerings. She found the discipline of serial writing, however, uncongenial, complaining that with *North and South* every page was "grudged" her. As a result she preferred not to write for *All The Year Round,* though she found herself committed to allowing her powerful novella "LOIS THE WITCH" to appear there. Afterward she sent what she regarded as her best work to the *Cornhill Magazine. All The Year Round*'s prioritization of serial fiction perhaps inevitably, if somewhat paradoxically in view of Dickens's high-minded opposition to the crude criminal literature that was a staple of the penny dreadfuls, led to an emphasis on sensation and mystery to keep readers hooked. The magazine's early success was built on *A*

Tale of Two Cities, Great Expectations, and *The Woman in White.*

In the more favorable financial climate of the 1860s, new monthly magazines like the *Cornhill* rose to challenge old established ones. *Blackwood's Magazine,* founded as long ago as 1817, was one of the survivors. By 1830 it had established its character and niche in respectable society, offering a mixture of creative literature, reviews, and essays on domestic and foreign affairs, largely eschewing anything controversial. Faced with competition from the newcomers, it made little attempt to emulate their innovations, hanging on to its core, albeit shrinking, readership by sticking to its editorial principles—the tradition of maintaining contributors' anonymity, imposing minimal editorial interference, and developing a loyal group of writers. One of its longest-standing relationships was with (MARGARET) OLIPHANT, who became *Blackwood*'s major literary reviewer in 1854, regularly supplying serials, short stories, and essays almost until her death in 1897. A fierce critic of the sensation novels of the 1860s, she was nevertheless an admirer of Wilkie Collins's artistry, and one of the finest of her own short stories, "The Library Window," has strong gothic overtones.

Elsewhere, popular novelists ran their own magazines. In 1867, the sensation novelist MARY ELIZABETH BRADDON launched the monthly *Belgravia,* whose title she described as "the best bait for the shillings of Brixton and Bow." It became a vehicle for her own sensation fiction, though she also published work by other writers. Only after the magazine's sale to Chatto & Windus in 1876 did novelists of the caliber of Wilkie Collins, Mark Twain, and THOMAS HARDY appear within its covers, but with the loss of Braddon's work its circulation declined rapidly. Another sensation novelist who successfully edited and contributed fiction to her own magazine was Ellen Wood. Her "JOHNNY LUDLOW" series of short stories was one of *Argosy*'s most popular features.

Fiction was a staple, too, of many women's magazines, from the romantic tales in fashion papers like the *Ladies' Cabinet* to the educational stories of Charlotte Tonna, the one genre of fiction considered acceptable in the evangelical *Christian Ladies' Magazine,* which Tonna had formerly edited.

BIBLIOGRAPHY

Law, Graham. *Serializing Fiction in the Victorian Press.* London: Palgrave, 2000.

Wynne, Deborah. *The Sensation Novel and the Victorian Family Magazine.* London: Palgrave, 2001.

Barbara Onslow

MAGAZINES, LATE VICTORIAN/EDWARDIAN (1880–1914)

By the 1890s the short story was ubiquitous in magazines and newspapers, which printed not only countless short stories but also debates over the genre's form and aims. As HENRY JAMES observed in 1898, the short story was "an object of almost extravagant dissertation." Critics continue to trace the short story (as a "tale") back to Edgar Allan Poe, but at the end of the 19th century even the term "short story" was of recent coinage. By the end of the century writers on both sides of the Atlantic were weighing in on the aesthetics and moral purpose of the short story. HENRY HARLAND and Robert Barr, magazine editors who were also prominent short story writers, condemned British readers for not tolerating the subtlety that should define the genre. Between 1884 and 1901 Brander Matthews, a professor of English at Columbia University and a writer of short stories, honed his theory of the short story as an artistically superior genre, first appearing in an anonymous article in the *Saturday Review* and then, after several refinements in other venues, culminating in a short book, *The Philosophy of the Short-story.* Like Frederick Wedmore, who warned that "a short story should never be a 'novel in a nutshell,'" many critics agreed that a short story differed from a novel not just in length but in kind. Neither novels nor poetry nor plays received such tortured attention to their aims and poetics, and the short story's peculiar position in this debate is suggestive. Indeed, the short story was the only major genre to have developed out of this commercial transformation of the literary field.

This "extravagant dissertation" was certainly a response to the even more extravagant efflorescence of short stories in magazines. The rise of both the short story and the periodical belonged to wider-ranging changes in the literary profession. The late 19th century saw the end of the circulating library system and the three-volume novel, but it also ushered in international copyright and the literary agent. While it is now common for a short story to be published for the first time in a collection of short stories, the vast majority of short stories a century ago appeared first—and, more often than not, only—in magazines and newspapers. The expansion of the periodical press began after the 1850s, when the repeal of taxes on paper encouraged the founding of new periodicals. This production accelerated with the implementation of new technologies for reproducing illustrations and for mass printing. By the end of the century, the extent of the periodical press was enormous, and in order to attract their share of a swelling middle-class readership, periodicals competed with one another for fiction. After decades during which Mudie's Circulating Library had provided novels for all middle-class Victorians, fiction had become a necessity for any periodical seeking popularity. By the 1890s this fiction was, more often than not, short fiction. While the most eminent authors could command commissions for serials, the short story involved much less complicated business arrangements than did serials. Distinguished primarily by its length, the short story defined itself commercially in terms of a word count, which came to occupy a predictable place in most periodicals' "Editorial Notes" to aspiring contributors. Inevitably, writers found themselves paid by the word, an arrangement that eloquently illustrates the economic pressures on literary production.

As the century drew to a close, British periodicals of nearly every description were publishing short stories, accustoming readers to a genre that until recently had attracted virtually no serious attention in Britain. A culture of the short story was born. The market was crowded with periodicals devoted to short fiction, including, in 1897, *Short Stories, Stories, Home Stories, Complete Stories, Favourite Stories,* the *London Story Paper, Popular Stories,* and *Striking Stories.* Periodicals that did not advertise their loyalties to the short story in their titles nonetheless featured them prominently. Not surprisingly, periodicals would carve out their niches through their identification with a certain kind of short story. The STRAND was the place to find a detective story, the *Idler* a

humorous one, the YELLOW BOOK an aestheticist or risqué one (see AESTHETICISM), and so on. In most cases, however, a story in one of these periodicals would have been at home in many others. Rare was the magazine without short stories, which readers could count on finding in *Badminton* or the theosophical *Longman's Lucifer.* By the end of the century, a successful magazine required short stories. For example, a note to the second volume of the *Pall Mall Magazine* in 1894 wistfully apologized for not providing such fiction, promising "A choice assortment of short stories, of which it is still sought to make a peculiar and distinctive feature." As H. G. WELLS later recalled of the period,

> No short story of the slightest distinction went for long unrecognized. . . . Short stories broke out everywhere. Kipling was writing short stories; Barrie, Stevenson, Frank Harris; Max Beerbohm wrote at least one perfect one, "The Happy Hypocrite"; Henry James pursued his wonderful and inimitable bent; and among other names that occur to me, like a mixed handful of jewels drawn from a bag, are George Street, Morley Roberts, George Gissing, Ella d'Arcy, Murray Gilchrist, E. Nesbit, Stephen Crane, Joseph Conrad, Edwin Pugh, Jerome K. Jerome, Kenneth Graham [sic], Arthur Morrison, Marriott Watson, George Moore, Grant Allen, George Egerton, Henry Harland, Pett Ridge, W. W. Jacobs (who alone seems inexhaustible). I dare say I could recall as many more names with a little effort. (1–6)

Developing rapidly throughout the 1880s and 1890s in periodicals, the mass media of the day, the short story created many reputations. So many periodicals had erupted in the press that, as Wells recalled, even examples "of the slightest distinction" found a place in print somewhere. The genre saturated the culture and commerce of an era that saw massive shifts in the way literature was acquired, produced, and consumed.

BIBLIOGRAPHY
Altick, Richard. *The English Common Reader.* 1957. London: Ohio University Press, 1995.

"Directory of Magazines, Reviews, and Periodicals: Monthly and Weekly Magazines." In *Mitchell's Newspaper Press Directory*. London: C. Mitchell, 1898.

"Editorial Preface," *Pall Mall Magazine* 2 (March 1894): ii.

Harris, Wendell V. *British Short Fiction in the Nineteenth Century: A Literary and Bibliographic Guide.* Detroit: Wayne State University Press, 1979.

Harte, Bret. "The Rise of the Short Story," *Cornhill* 7 (July 1899): 1–8.

"How to Write a Short Story," *Bookman* 5 (March 1897): 42–46.

Matthews, Brander. *The Philosophy of the Short-story.* New York: Longmans, Green, 1901.

———. "The Philosophy of the Short-story," *Lippincott's* 36 (October 1885): 366–374.

———. "Short Stories," *Saturday Review* 87 (July 5, 1884): 32–34.

"On Magazine Articles." In *Literary Year-Book,* edited by F. G. Aflalo, 153–155. London: George Allen, 1897.

Orel, Harold. *The Victorian Short Story: Development and Triumph of a Genre.* Oxford: Oxford University Press, 1986.

Wedmore, Frederick. "The Short Story," *Nineteenth Century* 43 (March 1898): 407.

Wells, H. G. Introduction to *The Country of the Blind,* 1–6. London: Thomas Nelson and Sons, 1913.

Willing's Press Guide and Advertiser's Directory and Handbook. London: James Willing, 1890–1900.

Winnie Chan

MAGAZINES, EARLY 20TH-CENTURY

(1914–1939) Alvin Sullivan begins his account of magazine publishing in the 20th century by stressing the "destruction" of periodical literature as it had been practiced in the 19th century (xv). The grand quarterly magazines like *Blackwood's* and the *Edinburgh Review* and monthlies like the *Cornhill* lost much of their influence because of changes in circulation and readership. By 1914 the magazines seemed old-fashioned to the new cultural elite, at a time when MODERNISM had began to take shape and "new expressions, new moulds for our thoughts & feelings," in KATHERINE MANSFIELD's words, took over (quoted in Hankin, 204). After WORLD WAR I, writers looked elsewhere to publish their work and still had plenty of choice. The so-called "high culture" magazines, such as the *London Mercury* (1919–39), published work by VIRGINIA WOOLF, Mansfield, WALTER DE LA MARE, ELIZABETH BOWEN, D. H.

LAWRENCE and FRANK O'CONNOR. The "little" magazines, *New Stories* (1934–36) and the *New Adelphi* (1927–55), published the innovative and the experimental. Other magazines, such as the *Bermondsey Book,* published from London's East End (1923–30), had a strong social conscience and printed the work of authors who dealt with working-class subjects, including A. E. COPPARD and Liam O'Flaherty. Then there were the publishers who saw themselves as catering for the suburban train commuter or his wife through the *STRAND, Storyteller, Hutchinson's Magazine, T.P.'s and Casell's Weekly, Good Housekeeping, Woman's Own,* and the *Ladies' Home Journal*—all designed to appeal to middle- and working-class readerships.

What becomes clear in looking at magazines from the interwar years is that the boundaries between "high" and "popular" culture were not always clear cut. A high-culture magazine, aptly named *Coterie* (1919–21, 1925–57), published several new writers now considered classic, notably Virginia Woolf, ALDOUS HUXLEY, and Hilda Doolittle, as did the *Criterion* (1922–39). Woolf, though, also published her stories in U.S. magazines, notably *Harper's* and *Harper's Bazaar,* and wrote for *Vogue.* Also in the 1920s, AGATHA CHRISTIE's stories featuring her most famous detectives—the eccentric Belgian Hercule Poirot and the elderly English spinster Jane Marple—had considerable popular appeal in a host of middlebrow magazines such as the *Sketch, Flynn's Weekly,* the *Story Teller,* and *Cosmopolitan,* as did those of her rival, Dorothy L. Sayers. Science fiction writers could send stories to *Novae Terrae* (New worlds); children's writers might approach *Sunny Stories,* edited (from 1926) by Enid Blyton. North American magazines—the *New Yorker* and William Randolph Hearst's *COSMOPOLITAN*—would also buy serials and short stories from British writers.

BIBLIOGRAPHY

Hankin, Cherry, ed. *Letters between Katherine Mansfield and John Middleton Murray.* London: Virago, 1988.

Sullivan, Alvin, ed. *British Literary Magazines: The Modern Age, 1914–1984.* New York: Greenwood, 1986.

Andrew Maunder

MAGAZINES, LATE 20TH-CENTURY

(1939–2000) It is often claimed that outlets for short fiction declined in the second half of the 20th century after WORLD WAR II. During the war, short story publication in magazines was dominated by two fairly new journals: *Horizon,* edited by Cyril Connelly (1940–50), and *Penguin New Writing,* edited by John Lehmann (1940–50). Connelly referred to his magazine as "a child of war," and both magazines reaped advantages from the fact that older publications like the *Criterion* and the *London Mercury* had been forced to shut down. The writing in these magazines was not, however, dominated by stories about the war. Connolly argued that "the war is the enemy of creative activity and the writers and the painters are wise to ignore it" (quoted in Sullivan, 202). *New Writing,* founded by John Lehmann in 1936, published stories by established names—E. M. FORSTER, V. S. PRITCHETT, and ELIZABETH BOWEN—but tried to mix them with working-class writers, democratically trying to "break down the barrier between these and the other team, to provide a place of cross fertilization of their talents" (quoted in Sullivan, 301). Other magazines included *Orion, Daylight,* and the *Windmill,* as well as the middlebrow *Penguin Parade* (1937–48) and *English Story.*

The decline in outlets for short stories in the postwar years—the genre's supposedly "sad economics and its general neglect by the book-buying public"—is one of the issues discussed in a special issue of the influential *London Magazine* in September 1966. In a polemical essay, V. S. Pritchett wrote that "the periodicals on which the writer can rely have almost all vanished, driven out by expensive printing, by television and the hundred and one diversions of an extravert and leisured society" (6). Another contributor, Francis King, noted how "Every apprentice writer has learned this dismal truth. *London Magazine, Encounter, The Cornhill,* two or three women's glossies, in which the author's name appears in smaller type than the most insignificant of photographers or nondescript of models—these are the only outlets for the short story writer in this country" (11). Romantic fiction in magazines such as *Nomad, Woman's Journal, Secrets,* and *She* was booming. Otherwise, by the 1970s publishers and agents seemed to push their authors away from stories toward the more profitable form of the novel. Although throughout the 1980s magazines like *Stand* and *Granta* (relaunched in 1979) gave considerable space to short stories, it is only since the mid-1990s, which saw the rise of the World Wide Web and the emergence of online magazines and blogs, that British short story writers looking to make their work available to domestic audiences have begun to feel the tide turning.

BIBLIOGRAPHY

Granta. Available online. URL: http://www.granta.com. Accessed January 4, 2006.

King, Francis. "The Short Story," *London Magazine* 6, no. 6 (September 1966): 11–12.

London Magazine. Available online. URL: http://www.thelondonmagazine.net. Accessed January 4, 2006.

Pritchett, V. S. "The Short Story," *London Magazine* 6, no. 6 (September 1966): 6–8.

Ross, Alan. Introduction to *London Magazine* 6, no. 6 (September 1966): 5.

Sullivan, Alvin, ed. *British Literary Magazines: The Modern Age, 1914–1984.* New York: Greenwood, 1986.

Andrew Maunder

MAGRS, PAUL (1969–)

Paul Magrs was born in 1969 in Tyneside, an industrial region of northeast England that encompasses Newcastle and Middlesborough. Magrs (pronounced *maws*) studied for an M.A. in creative writing and completed his Ph. D., focusing on ANGELA CARTER as a "queer" writer, at Lancaster University. His first published creative writing in 1995 was a short story, "Patient Iris," in *New Writing Four,* edited by A. S. BYATT and Allan Hollinghurst, but it was his debut novel, *Marked For Life,* published the same year, that established his literary standing. This first novel establishes key themes and a Carteresque, playful fascination with the boundaries between reality and fantasy, particularly in relation to sexuality and desire, often revisited by Magrs.

In his collection of short stories *Playing Out* (1997), Magrs explores these realms of fantasy and reality and the slippage between them as the protagonists of the stories play out their desires. The Tyneside dialect evident in "Judith's Do Round Hers" firmly locates the story in the world in which Magrs grew up and invites realist assumptions. Indeed, this story rotates around the mundane and the everyday world of domesticity and the protagonist's worldview, dominated by television fantasies and obsessions. The fantasies explored in other stories in the collection are, however, much broader in scope. In "The Furrier the Better," the fantastic is embodied in genetically engineered furry crocodiles bred for the fur trade. These bizarre animals are discovered by a lighthouse keeper whose animal rights activist girlfriend turns out to be the daughter of the woman behind the fur-breeding experiment; ultimately he becomes involved in the killing of the mutant crocodiles. Personal ethics are thereby dismissed in the face of financial gain as these fantastic creatures are commercially exploited.

Several of the stories in the collection are self-consciously preoccupied with the act of reading itself. In "Ariel's Tasty Dog," the struggling mature student Kerry is given an electric drill by the fairy Ariel (from William Shakespeare's play *The Tempest*) and his yellow pit bull terrier to enable her to put up bookshelves for her growing book collection. These books offer intellectual freedom for Kerry but represent a focus of mocking distrust for her husband. The slippage between reality and fantasy facilitated by books is developed in "Seven Disenchantments," in which a book "with empty pages" contains Japanese paper flowers that expand in water and turn into real lovers for the protagonist.

Magrs has contributed stories to wide range of publications including *The Gay Times Book of Short Stories* (2000) and *Crossing the Border: Tales of Erotic Ambiguity* (1998), edited by Lisa Tuttle. In the latter collection, "Nude on the Moon" features Liz, a cross-dresser on a touring holiday with her lover, Cliff. The story focuses on moments in which Liz passes successfully as a woman and those in which she is exposed as a man and the consequences of these moments.

One important subgenre of Magrs's writing includes the novels and short stories based on the cult science fiction series Doctor Who. Magrs's contribution to the *Short Trips* collections of Doctor Who short stories maintains his interests in established themes and the boundaries between reality and fantasy. In "Kept Safe and Sound," Magrs's child protagonist, Jack, is an avid collector of the rare Books of Mayhem series, much to the disapproval of his overprotective mother. These books represent Jack's desire for maturity and independence. During his quest to find the last book in the series in a market, Jack discovers the once-beloved robot dog, K9, one of Doctor Who's most trusted companions. Every time Jack goes back to the marketplace, he sees that more of K9 has been dismantled to form spare parts for other equipment. The relationship between K9 and Jack develops until the climax of the story, when Jack secures the last volume in the Books of Mayhem series and steals the remains of the robot dog to record his time-traveling stories.

A child protagonist is the focus of Magrs most controversial novel, *Strange Boy* (2002). The book attracted much publicity because the 10-year-old child, David, is homosexual and the book is aimed at the teenage market. The "strangeness" experienced by David is displaced into the realm of fantasy through his beliefs in magical powers, which are revealed as real at times. Through its exploration of sexuality, desire, fantasy and magic, *Strange Boy* thereby continues to develop themes central to Magrs's short story and novel writing.

BIBLIOGRAPHY

Magrs, Paul. "Kept Safe and Sound." In *Short Trips: Companions,* edited by Jacqueline Rayner, 73–82. Maidenhead: Big Finish Productions, 2003.

———. *Marked for Life.* London: Vintage, 1995.

———. "Nude on the Moon." In *Crossing the Border: Tales of Erotic Ambiguity,* edited by Lisa Tuttle, 71–98. London: Indigo, 1998.

———. "Patient Iris." In *New Writing Four,* edited by A. S. Byatt and Allan Hollinghurst, 64–72. London: Vintage, 1995.

———. *Playing Out.* London: Vintage, 1997.

Jo Trevenna

"MANCHESTER MARRIAGE, THE" ELIZABETH GASKELL (1858)

This story was first published in the extra Christmas number of *Household Words* (edited by CHARLES DICKENS) and was republished in ELIZABETH GASKELL's collection *Right at Last and Other Tales* (1860). It tells the story of Alice Openshaw, who moves from Manchester to London with her children and second husband, Thomas. Alice is an orphan brought up by relatives; she escaped their house by marrying her cousin, Frank Wilson. When he is lost at sea, she must make a living to support herself and her baby daughter. With her mother-in-law and loyal maid, Norah Kennedy, Alice opens a lodging house. Quiet, undemonstrative Alice attracts the notice of Thomas Openshaw, a well-to-do but gruff lodger. He and Alice marry and, after her mother-in-law's death, move to London.

Openshaw's relatives, the Chadwicks, come to visit. One evening they all go out, leaving the servants to take care of the house and children. A strange man calls and insists on talking to Norah. To her horror, she recognizes him as Frank Wilson: After being held captive by "savages" for many years, he has returned and is desperate to find his wife. Norah must relay the shocking news that she has remarried, but to placate him she lets him see his sleeping daughter. Unfortunately, little Ailsie wakes up and the next day reveals that Norah has had a male visitor. When Mrs. Chadwick's expensive brooch goes missing (it is later found that Mrs. Chadwick has only mislaid it), suspicion falls on Norah and her male visitor. While Thomas Openshaw does not suspect her of theft but of gullibility in letting the man into the house, her refusal to explain the strange man's visit angers him. Distraught, Norah flees to Wilson's hotel room but he is gone: Inconsolable over the loss of his wife and child, he has drowned himself. Eventually Openshaw finds Norah, and she confides the secret of his wife's unwitting bigamy. Mortified that he has unknowingly so hurt another man, Openshaw resolves to give him a proper burial and to keep the truth from Alice.

The dreadful secret of inadvertent bigamy at the heart of this story was soon to become a mainstay of the genre of sensation fiction that burgeoned in the 1860s and focused on "sensational" wrongdoing. It is a crucial part of the plot of such immensely popular works as ELLEN WOOD's *East Lynne* (1861) and MARY ELIZABETH BRADDON's *Lady Audley's Secret* (1862) and *Aurora Floyd* (1862–63). Like so many sensational tales, "The Manchester Marriage" makes the role of the servant prominent and draws attention to tensions between middle-class employers and their lower-class servants at a time when the majority of the middle class employed domestic staff.

Victorian middle-class employers wanted to see themselves as surrounded by servants who worked out of a sense of devotion rather than for money. However, they could not escape the reality that their staff had to be paid and that they tended to change positions frequently. In fiction, servants therefore tended to be portrayed either as sinister, self-serving professionals (for example, Crawford in Gaskell's "Right at Last") or as loyal but inept retainers, like Norah. Unable to explain her behavior without revealing the secret from which she is protecting her employers, Norah brings their suspicions and anger down on herself. But through this twist of irony, she becomes the means by which the middle-class characters are judged: The saintly Alice Openshaw never doubts her character and never discovers the truth about her marriage; Thomas Openshaw suspects Norah not of theft but of breaking domestic rules by having a lover and allowing him into the house. It is he who has to bear the burden of the secret Norah reveals, and it is he who must make amends to Frank Wilson. He must also learn to treat his wife with a new "reverence" and "tenderness"—and is rewarded by making "a large fortune" in business. As for the Chadwicks, their certainty that Norah is dishonest (they even hire a detective to follow her) and their part in provoking the crisis by misplacing the brooch in the first place means that their moral character becomes tainted.

At the end of the story, Norah is rewarded for her loyalty by being welcomed back into the household with her reputation intact and by being allowed to continue serving her employers. Devoted servitude, the story implies, is not just a duty the lower class owes to the middle but is a role the lower class treasures. In a sense, "The Manchester Marriage," like many other stories that feature servants, uses Norah to carry out the "dirty" work of discovering and helping resolve middle- and upper-class secrets. Just as in real life maids were responsible for the dirtiest of housework—for instance, cleaning fireplaces, scrubbing floors, and emptying chamber pots—so in fiction they take on a similar task: They are the ones who come across secrets and expose them. Although this means that wrongs can be righted and it forces the middle and upper class to live up to the moral superiority they use to justify their social status, it is also a way of keeping the lower class in its place. Servants not only clean up the real-life dirt, the dust and refuse, but also deal with the metaphorical dirt of their employers' secrets. In both cases, the dirt servants have to deal with helps explain their low social position: the dirt makes them dirty (even though it is not their own), and therefore they deserve to be the ones who serve rather than the ones who are served. In "The Manchester Marriage," the unfairness of the accusations against Norah points to Gaskell's sympathy for working women, but ultimately, the story is one about middle-class characters—their flaws and their redemption—not about the plight of the many thousands of women who worked as servants.

BIBLIOGRAPHY

Davidoff, Leonore. *Worlds Between: Historical Perspectives on Gender and Class.* New York: Routledge, 1995.

Gaskell, Elizabeth. "The Manchester Marriage." In *Nineteenth Century Short Stories by Women,* edited by Harriet Devine Jump, 93–116. London: Routledge, 1998.

Gerri Brightwell

"MAN OF THE HOUSE, THE" FRANK O'CONNOR (1949)

"The Man of the House" first appeared in the *New Yorker* in 1949 and has been anthologized in the collections *More Short Stories by Frank O'Connor* (1953), *Traveller's Samples* (1951), and *Collected Stories* (1981). This short story was one of more than 40 stories by FRANK O'CONNOR that the *New Yorker* published. O'Connor, whose real name was Michael O'Donovan, wrote over 200 short stories, many centering on children's experiences in Ireland. Some of O'Connor's stories are overlooked because of their simplistic nature and childlike focus. The author was an only child born to a sensitive mother and an alcoholic father in Cork. Many of his short stories and the first part of his autobiography, *An Only Child* (1961), feature remnants of his childhood experiences, including his relationship with his mother and the family's abject poverty. "The Man of the House" provides a glimpse of life from the point of view of a young boy who feels responsible for the care of a sick mother.

At the start of the story Gus, the narrator, admits that he has his shortcomings. His attention span is fairly low, and he has to concentrate in order to be responsible and help his mother. He becomes the man of the house as he gives her the orders she expects from men. The mother, with a cough that could be deadly consumption or a simple cold, takes her son's orders and lies down for the day. Gus quickly takes over as head of the household and, accordingly, becomes the good Christian while other children are heathens. However, a young girl easily convinces Gus to taste his mother's medicine, and it is soon gone. Feeling tricked and guilty, Gus runs home in tears and confronts his mother and her friend Ms. Ryan with the empty medicine bottle. His mother is simply grateful that Gus is home, and she then gets up to take care of him. Ms. Ryan levels her judgment against Gus, naming him a simple child after all. In the end, now sick and feeling defeated, Gus happily falls back into the role of a child who is dearly loved by his mother, heathen or not.

As is true of most of O'Connor's protagonists, Gus does not mind being judged by the likes of Ms. Ryan or others in the community. Above all, he seeks the love of his mother and the comfort of her caretaking. Though he tries to be a good man of the house to help his ailing mother, what he truly prays for and happily receives is the permission to be a child and make mistakes. Ms. Ryan tries to use religion as a way to force Gus into being a good man, but Gus manages to brush off her judgment in the light of his mother's love and acceptance.

It is possible to argue that young Gus mirrors the young Michael O'Donovan/Frank O'Connor. Both face poverty and judgment at a young age because of an absentee father and medieval ideas about children. However, both also find solace in their mother's love. The close relationship between mother and son compensates for the boy's struggle over having to grow up quickly and replace a father who cannot or will not assume his role in the household. The story suggests that a mother's love is strong enough to allow moments when Gus, and perhaps O'Connor in his life, can make the mistakes necessary to learn how to be a proper and successful adult.

BIBLIOGRAPHY

O'Connor, Frank. *Collected Stories.* New York: Knopf, 1981.

Sheehy, Maurice. *Studies on Frank O'Connor.* New York: Knopf, 1969.

Steinman, Michael A. *Frank O'Connor at Work*. Houndmills, England: Macmillan, 1990.

Tomory, William M. *Frank O'Connor*. Boston: Twayne, 1980.

Christine Brown

MANSFIELD, KATHARINE (1888–1923)

Katherine Mansfield is undoubtedly one of the most original and influential British short story writers of the 20th century. VIRGINIA WOOLF famously remarked that Mansfield's was "the only writing that I have ever been jealous of" (Woolf, 2:227). A native New Zealander and the author of five collections of stories, two of which were published posthumously, Mansfield dramatically reimagined the possibilities of the genre by developing a unique, impressionistic style that focuses primarily on capturing internal states, not describing external appearances. Her stories tend to eschew traditional narrative practice, sometimes beginning in midsentence and often concluding without discernible resolution. A biting ironic tone and the frequent employment of subtle but crucial symbolism are further hallmarks of Mansfield's style.

Her personal association with members of the Bloomsbury circle, such as Woolf, T. S. Eliot and D. H. LAWRENCE—coupled with the fact that her stories are formally challenging, focused on internal, psychological experience and explore themes of alienation and despair—has led most literary critics to classify Mansfield as a modernist (see MODERNISM). Although the label fits to a large degree, her writing at times displays a sentimentalism and nostalgia that is absent from that of many of her contemporaries. This is particularly apparent in stories that she based on her childhood experiences in New Zealand, such as "The Prelude" and "At the Bay" and in some of the selections from *The Garden-Party and Other Stories* (1922), the last volume published during her lifetime. Moreover, she generally rejects the use of obscure, erudite allusions in her work, a practice that modernist authors like Eliot, JAMES JOYCE, and Ezra Pound favor heavily.

Mansfield was born Katherine Mansfield Beauchamp in 1888 in Wellington, New Zealand. Her father, Harold Beauchamp, was a prominent local businessman who was later knighted. In 1903, she moved to Britain to attend Queens College but returned to New Zealand in 1906. She was a rebellious child who began writing poetry, stories, and snippets of novels at a young age. In 1908 she left her homeland forever and moved to London. Free from the direct control of her family, she impulsively married a young music teacher named G. C. Bowden only to leave him the same day. Shortly afterward, she became pregnant by a violinist named Garnet Trowell and journeyed to Germany to have the baby, which was eventually stillborn. Her experiences on the continent provided the material for her first volume of short stories, *In a German Pension* (1911).

Upon her return to Britain, she became involved with John Middleton Murry, a publisher who had founded *Rhythm,* a small, avant-garde journal. Murry and Mansfield's relationship would continue in fits and with several interruptions until their marriage in 1918. The death of Mansfield's younger brother Leslie in World War I put a further strain on her already fragile mental state. Like many artists at the time, she was deeply troubled by the war, but this did not deter her from a daring venture near the front lines in France to visit her lover, Francis Carco. A fictional account of the event can be found in "An Indiscreet Journey," and Carco provided the model for the narrator of "JE NE PARLE PAS FRANÇAIS." "The Prelude," perhaps the greatest of Mansfield's New Zealand stories, appeared in 1918. Loosely based on the move of her family home from Wellington to Kaori, it is broken into 12 sections and stands as one of her longest works.

Unfortunately, Mansfield's physical condition was declining, and she was soon diagnosed with tuberculosis. She moved to the French Riviera in the fall of 1920 in search of a healthier climate. There, she composed *BLISS AND OTHER STORIES,* her second volume of short stories, which appeared in December 1920 and contained the short story "PICTURES." Shortly afterward, she moved to Switzerland and began work on the stories that would make up *The Garden Party and Other Stories,* including "The DAUGHTERS OF THE LATE COLONEL," "The GARDEN-PARTY," and "MISS BRILL." Released in February 1922, it cemented Mansfield's literary reputation. In his introduction to the posthumous collection *The Short Stories of Katherine Mansfield,* Murry claims that the volume "finally established her as the most remarkable short-story writer of her generation" (ix).

Sadly, time was running out for his wife. She began four months of intensive irradiation treatment in January 1922 under the direction of a questionable Russian doctor named Manoukhin. Not surprisingly, the treatment took its toll on her. In the last few months of her life she wrote very little new fiction. "The FLY," however, dates from this period. A remarkable portrait of an old businessman's inability to cope with his son's death in the war, it was no doubt based on Mansfield's father's experiences. "The Canary," Mansfield's last complete story, was finished in July 1922. Desperate to find a cure and disenchanted with traditional medicine, she joined the Gurdjieff Institute for the Harmonious Development of Man in Fontainebleau, France, later that year. Not surprisingly, the program there did nothing to stave off her illness, and she died on January 9, 1923.

Over the next few years, Murry oversaw the release of a great deal of Mansfield's work, including her final two volumes of new stories, *The Doves Nest and Other Stories* (1924), featuring "The DOLL'S HOUSE," and *Something Childish* (1924). His editorial choices on *The Journals of Katherine Mansfield* (1927) and *Selected Letters* (1928) worked to paint an incomplete picture of his wife that suppressed the more difficult and conflicted aspects of her character. That misconception remained firmly in place until the eventual publication of her full journals and more complete editions of letters.

Thanks in part to the rise of feminist studies, critical interest in Mansfield has risen steadily over the past several years. A recent book-length study, Angela Smith's *Katherine Mansfield: A Literary Life,* provides an effective starting point for most scholarly study, while Andrew Bennett's "Hating Katherine Mansfield" offers a particularly interesting analysis of the complicated relationship between Mansfield and Virginia Woolf.

BIBLIOGRAPHY

Bennett, Andrew. "Hating Katherine Mansfield," *Angelkai: Journal of the Theoretical Humanities* 7, no. 2 (December 2002): 3–16.

Mansfield, Katherine. *The Katherine Mansfield Notebooks Complete Edition*. Edited and with an introduction by Margaret Scott. Minneapolis: University of Minnesota Press, 2002.

———. *The Short Stories of Katherine Mansfield.* 1937. Edited and with introduction by John Middleton Murry. New York: Knopf, 1967.

Pilditch, John. *The Critical Response to Katherine Mansfield.* Westport, Conn.: Greenwood Press, 1996.

Smith, Angela. *Katherine Mansfield: A Literary Life.* New York: Palgrave, 2000.

———. *Katherine Mansfield and Virginia Woolf: A Public of Two.* Oxford: Clarendon Press, 1999.

Woolf, Virginia. *The Diary of Virginia Woolf.* Vol. 2. Edited by Anne Oliver Bell. New York: Harcourt Brace Jovanovich, 1977–84.

Stephen E. Severn

"MAN WHO COULD WORK MIRACLES, THE" H. G. WELLS (1898)

"The Man Who Could Work Miracles" by H. G. WELLS was published with the subtitle "A Pantoum in Prose" in the *Illustrated London News* in the summer 1898 edition, before being included in *Tales of Space and Time* in 1899. It deals with the complexities of both space and time and the scientific consequences of the actions of George McWhirter Fotheringay, described as "not a very exceptional man" (5), who acquires the miraculous power to realize his smallest whim just by imagining it. Fotheringay is apprehensive about his gift and tentatively practices lighting candles and turning water different colors. His miracles are mundane, and it is only when Fotheringay attends church on Sunday that he discloses his secret to the minister, Mr. Maydig, who sees the larger possibilities of the gift and sets about providing increasingly benevolent miracles for Fotheringay to perform. Fotheringay becomes apprehensive, not that he is performing extraordinary miracles but that he might not be ready for work the next morning. Maydig's suggestion that he perform a biblical miracle and stop the rotation of the Earth results in the destruction of the world, leaving Fotheringay alone. After some careful thinking, he wills his power gone and everything as it was before he acquired his power, effectively erasing the entire story from his mind and returning the story to its beginning.

Wells's story negotiates tensions between imaginative possibilities and scientific certainties in a complex mixture of scientific and logical reasoning that preempts many modern science fiction narratives. The story has been repeatedly used, and the double themes of mind over matter and maintaining the status quo rather than dealing with a phenomenon well beyond the understanding and ability of human beings speak of both human frailty and the cognitive superiority of the individual thinker. The story suggests the potentially disastrous consequences of ignoring and misunderstanding science but also establishes science as an impassionate constant, even against the power to perform miracles. The miracles represent the limitless possibilities of human beings but are set against individuals' limited ability to comprehend the complete consequences of their actions. In addition, the conflict between science and religion finds an interesting and ultimately unfulfilled expression in the story. Inherent in Fotheringay's acquisition of the power to perform miracles but inability to master them is the human inability to comprehend the power of religion. The circumstances of Fotheringay's biblical miracle and its disastrous result suggest, rather than science triumphing over religion, a connection between the two in which humans are ineffectual agents for the implementation of divine intervention. Through careful narrative positioning, Wells achieves a complex web of ideas that Michael Draper describes as a revival of 18th-century "clarity, detachment and narrative freedom." The reader and narrator are afforded a privileged perspective and a secure position from which they alone can view the dangerously volatile nature of existence. The story ends optimistically, as Fotheringay, introduced as an individual "greatly addicted to assertive argument," effectively thinks himself out of a cataclysmic situation to produce an effective, if slightly convenient, resolution.

At the end of the story Fotheringay resolves an uncontrollable situation with a modest understanding of his own limitations. He becomes a hero who saves the world precisely because he is not heroic and is willing to sacrifice his power to reestablish the balance between science and miracles. In "The Man Who Could Work Miracles," Wells successfully navigates distinctions between fantasy and reality to produce exceptional science fiction writing that is at once believable and extraordinary. Wells depicts a world where the individual is powerless to act for the good of mankind, and while the story challenges our faith in an eternal stability of existence, it optimistically prioritizes the individual's role in maintaining the balance of existence, suggesting that nothing is impossible but everything carries significant consequences.

BIBLIOGRAPHY
Draper, Michael. *H. G. Wells*. London: Macmillan, 1987.
Wells, H. G. *Thirty Strange Stories by H. G. Wells*. New York: Carroll and Graf, 1998.

Tony W. Garland

"MAN WHO WOULD BE KING, THE"
RUDYARD KIPLING (1888)   Written when RUDYARD KIPLING was in his early 20s, "The Man Who Would Be King" was first published in India in 1888. It appeared as the last of four stories collected in *The Phantom Rickshaw and Other Eerie Tales*.

The story is an example of a frame narrative; it consists of two stories, nested one within the other. The unnamed narrator is a correspondent for the *Backwoodsman*. He is an active character in the outer, frame narrative and a passive observer and transmitter of the inner story. He tells of meeting two adventurers, Peachey Taliaferro Carnehan and Daniel Dravot, who have decided to leave an India that "isn't big enough for such as us" (161). They have entered into a contract to become Kings of Kafiristan, a forbiddingly remote and at that time largely unexplored area in northeast Afghanistan—unexplored, that is, by European colonizing powers. Two years after they set out, a barely recognizable, barely human Peachey returns alone to tell how, by exploiting religious, Masonic, and military ritual, the two initially succeeded in their scheme: "Kings we were with crowns upon our heads—me and Dravot" (168). But, in a failure to understand the importance of the ruse behind the ritual, Dravot sought to establish a dynasty by exploiting yet one more ritual of power, that of intermarriage with the local population. When Dravot's flesh is ripped by the bite of the woman whom he is intent on marrying, the obscuring veil of power is ripped aside, and the god-kings are exposed as mere men.

The title declaims, and the opening epigraph supports, a theme grounded in the contrasts developed by the story: There are things to be learned and done and not forgotten by the man who really would be king. Ironically, the men who would be kings, Peachey and Danny, are among those least likely to become real kings. They are initially identified by the narrator as loafers and intermediates, referring both to their social and financial status—as when riding in railway coaches—and to their condition of being suspended between the ruled and those who rule them. Yet, the intermediate positions they have occupied, as "[s]oldier, sailor, compositor, photographer, proof-reader, street-preacher, and correspondents of the *Backwoodsman* when we thought the paper wanted one" (161), have provided them with the opportunity and wherewithal to exploit each end of the social and political spectrum to prey upon the other for personal gain.

The tale told by Peachey to the narrator both mirrors and parodies the colonial spirit—the motives, efforts, and goals of the BRITISH EMPIRE in India. When Kipling wrote the story, Britain was actively competing with Russia for influence in central Asia, particularly in Afghanistan. Ostensibly in an effort to protect colonial holdings in India, Britain was, under the guise of geographical survey, making exploratory forays into the Afghan territories. This background intrigue provided knowledgeable contemporaneous readers with a strong sense of presence for the story, which was also given a certain credence by Dravot's fantasy of receiving a knighthood from Queen Victoria for gifting her with his little empire—a northern buffer with which to protect her own. The root *kafir* in *Kafiristan* is an Arabic word loosely translated as unbeliever, or infidel; hence, Kafiristan was, at the time Kipling wrote the story, the land of the unbelievers. In an interesting twist of historical irony, today Kafiristan is called Nuristan; quite literally, it is now the land of the enlightened, having fallen prey to one of the oldest forms of imperialism, religious conversion.

BIBLIOGRAPHY

Bauer, Helen Pike. *Rudyard Kipling: A Study of the Short Fiction.* New York: Twayne, 1994.

Kipling, Rudyard. "The Man Who Would Be King." In *Fictions of Empire,* edited by John Kucich, 56–87. New York: Houghton Mifflin Company, 2003.

The Man Who Would Be King. Dir. John Huston. Perf. Sean Connery, Michael Caine, and Christopher Plummer. 1975. DVD. Warner Home Video, 1997.

Marx, Edward. "How We Lost Kafiristan," *Representations* 67 (1999): 44–66.

James Fromm

"MAN WITH THE TWISTED LIP, THE"

ARTHUR CONAN DOYLE (1891) A detective story first published in *The STRAND MAGAZINE* in December 1891, as the sixth story in ARTHUR CONAN DOYLE's 12-part series *The ADVENTURES OF SHERLOCK HOLMES* (1891–92), and subsequently published as part of that collection.

Holmes and Watson investigate the disappearance of Neville St Clair, a rich man whose wealth has been accumulated from financial interests in the City. On a visit to London from their suburban home, St Clair's wife had seen her husband struggling in the window of a East End Thames-side house, but on forcing her way in (with the help of the police) found the room occupied solely by Hugh Boone, a crippled and facially deformed beggar. St Clair has disappeared, although evidence of him remains—his jacket is found in the Thames, and a box of bricks bought for his son is discovered in the house. Boone is arrested on suspicion of murder. Holmes's conclusion that St Clair is dead is, however, challenged by a letter from St. Clair to his wife, assuring her of his safety. After much consideration and consumption of tobacco, Holmes realizes that Hugh Boone and Neville St Clair are the same person, the gentleman disguised by the beggar's idiosyncratic physiology. Boone is therefore innocent of the murder of St Clair, who has made his fortune in the City by posing as a beggar, an imposture he started as an exercise in investigative journalism. The police agree not to take action if St Clair ends the fraud.

The narrative elegantly combines the techniques of the detective story with concerns of social welfare, as Holmes can solve the mystery of St Clair's disappearance can only by blurring distinctions between social classes. The text has been profitably read by Audrey Jaffe in the context of the urban surveys undertaken by Henry Mayhew in *London Labour and the London Poor* (1861–62, 1864), an exercise in social typology where types such as the "true" and "false" beggar are defined and codified. By presenting a character who is both suburban gentleman and fraudulent city beggar, the story articulates late-Victorian concern about the role of the philanthropic middle class, and the distinction between the deserving and undeserving poor. The geography of the narrative is significant in this context: St Clair moves between the affluent suburbs and the deprived East End of London, and the story is notable (as Franco Moretti points out) as being the only Holmes adventure in which the detective visits the East End.

The story has also been argued to have autobiographical significance. Stephen Knight reads St Clair's financially motivated imposture as a parallel to Doyle's own situation in writing the Holmes stories, which he regarded as purely lucrative work that distracted him from more respectable literary endeavours. (This disillusion may explain a notable lapse in continuity in the story, when Watson's wife calls him "James" rather than "John.") The position of the story supports Knight's analysis: "The Man with the Twisted Lip" was the last of the first batch of Holmes stories Doyle submitted to the *Strand Magazine,* after which the magazine's literary editor, Greenhough Smith, agreed to a substantial rise in Doyle's pay for the subsequent six stories, which would complete the first series of *The Adventures of Sherlock Holmes.*

BIBLIOGRAPHY

Doyle, Arthur Conan. *The Adventures of Sherlock Holmes.* London: Newnes, 1892.

Jaffe, Audrey. "Detecting the Beggar: Arthur Conan Doyle, Henry Mayhew, and 'The Man with the Twisted Lip,'" *Representations* 31 (1990), 96–117.

Knight, Stephen. *Form and Ideology in Detective Fiction.* London: Macmillan, 1980.

Moretti, Franco. *An Atlas of the European Novel 1800–1900.* London: Verso, 1998.

Christopher Pittard

MARS-JONES, ADAM (1954–)   A writer, reviewer, essayist, and lecturer, Adam Mars-Jones is an all-around man of letters. Born in London in 1954, he was educated at Cambridge University before studying and eventually teaching creative writing at the University of Virginia. He regularly contributes both articles and reviews to most of the newspapers, and his name frequently appears in the contents of *Granta.* He has published two collections of short stories, *Lantern Lecture* (1981) and *Monopolies of Loss* (1992), on his own and a further collection, *Darker Proof: Stories from a Crisis* (1987), with Edmund White. He published the novel *The Waters of Thirst* in 1993, and after a long break from published fiction, two more novels, *Box Hill* and *Everything Is Different in Your House,* and a book of two novellas, *Hypo Vanilla,* have been slated for publication late in 2006 and 2007.

Lantern Lecture, his first collection, published in 1981 and winner of the Somerset Maugham Award 1982, contains just three stories that at first glance seem unconnected. On deeper inspection, they all show a rich knowledge of class structures and boundaries. Mars-Jones exploits these with carefully handled satire to create three very different narratives. "Lantern Lecture" charts the life of Phillip Yorke, a typically eccentric aristocrat, and the decline of his family's fortunes. Told in many small sections with no discrimination about order or chronology, it contrives to deliver all the information necessary to encompass a whole life. In the second story, "Hoosh-Mi," Mars-Jones follows what happens when the queen contracts rabies from one of her corgis. The characters include many ancillary staff members as well as the royal family, and the relationships exposed seem to hold the most interest for the author. "Bathpool Park" is a tale of both trial and crime interwoven with a critique of both the judiciary and the police force. Reminiscent of both P. G. WODEHOUSE and Evelyn Waugh, these stories are mostly light in nature but contain carefully barbed attacks on the establishment.

The stories contained in the collaboration with Edmund White, *Darker Proof: Stories from a Crisis,* exhibit the same voice and awareness of society's structure, but they are turned to the more serious subject of the AIDS crisis among the gay community. His five stories, "Slim," "An Executor," "A Small Spade," "The Brake," and "Remission," move comfortably between the painfully serious side of living with the virus and the absurdity that always accompanies chronic illness. Mars-Jones's 1992 collection, *Monopolies of Loss,* continues his exploration into what it is to live in the shadow of HIV.

In 1993 he published his single novel to date, *The Waters of Thirst,* which combines the light, satirical touch of *Lantern Lecture* with the subject matter from his later work, showing the problems of being both affluent and gay in the late 20th century. Since the publication of *The Waters of Thirst,* Adam Mars-Jones has been a constant contributor to publications as an article writer, often but not exclusively on gay issues, and an editor of story collections.

BIBLIOGRAPHY

Mars-Jones, Adam. *Lantern Lecture.* London: Faber and Faber, 1981.
———. *Monopolies of Loss.* London: Faber and Faber, 1992.
———, with Edmund White. *The Darker Proof: Stories from a Crisis.* London: Faber and Faber, 1987.
———. *The Waters of Thirst.* London: Faber and Faber, 1993.
———, ed. *Mae West Is Dead: Recent Lesbian and Gay Fiction.* London: Faber and Faber, 1983.

Calum Kerr

"MARY POSTGATE" RUDYARD KIPLING (1915)

Possibly the most anthologized of RUDYARD KIPLING's short stories, "Mary Postgate" was published in 1915, soon after the start of German air raids on English towns in the middle of WORLD WAR I. John Kipling, the writer's son, was reported missing in November 1915. This short story has been seen as Kipling's personal response to the effects of the war back home. It later appeared in *A DIVERSITY OF CREATURES.*

Miss Mary Postgate is a put-upon lady's companion, middle-aged and drab. She is devoted to her employer's nephew Wynn, who, when war breaks out, joins the flying corps and is killed in a plane crash. Mary, who views herself as his surrogate mother, is full of anger with the German enemy. While buying paraffin to burn Wynn's clothes, she witnesses the violent death of a child, Edna Gerrit. Back in the garden with the fire ablaze, she comes across a German pilot seriously hurt by his fall through the trees. She tends the fire and ignores his dying cries for help. Then, hot and excited, she goes indoors to have tea.

The extent of Mary's callousness toward the airman has shocked readers. Some have suggested that the heroine's attitudes are Kipling's own. Others have read "Mary Postgate" as a piece of propaganda intended to inspire English readers to behave in a similar way if the occasion demanded it. The English gentleman, Wynn, becomes a sacrificial figure, but his very name hints at victory. The German airman falls into an Edenic garden where he pleads for mercy with an Englishwoman, but instead of giving way the virgin spinster gives him death. This Englishwoman is inspired by war and does her duty.

Others have suggested, however, that it is more plausible to see the story as a disturbing psychological study of what the horrors of war do to seemingly civilized people. Mary's desire for revenge is governed by hatred of the havoc wrought by air raids, though she overlooks the fact that Wynn dies while in training to carry out similar raids. The story also contains various hints that invite the reader to question Mary's reliability. Mary mourns Wynn but forgets his cruel treatment of her. She is convinced that a bomb has fallen and killed the child, Edna, but no one else believes this. It is partly this belief that prompts Mary to let the young German pilot die, although he speaks French and may not be German at all. It is also clear that having this man at her mercy gives the resentful spinster a sense of release and of power after years of being patronized and imposed on. It has been suggested that the apparent pleasure Mary takes in a man's dying agony may even carry sadistic sexual overtones. According to this reading, Kipling does not support his protagonist's actions but merely records her response to the situation, leaving his readers to make up their own minds.

BIBLIOGRAPHY

Gilbert, Elliot. *The Good Kipling.* Athens: Ohio University Press, 1971.
Kipling, Rudyard. *War Stories and Poems.* Oxford: Oxford University Press, 1999.
Parry, Ann. "'The Years Between': Rudyard Kipling and the Great War," *Kipling Journal* 62, no. 245 (1988): 42–61.
Pierce, Peter. "Evermore: Stories of the Great War by Rudyard Kipling and Julian Barnes," *Critical Review* 42 (2002): 65–71.

Andrew Maunder

MATISSE STORIES, THE A. S. BYATT (1993)

The Matisse Stories, a collection of three tales informed by specific Matisse line drawings included within the text itself, was published to enthusiastic reviews following A. S. BYATT's celebrity as the Booker Prize–winning author of *Possession* (1990). Most reviewers focused on the visual character of Byatt's prose, emphasizing its relationship to the painterly character of Matisse's work. Geoff Dyer suggests that Byatt's style, which "contrives to be both exquisite *and* bland," is "almost a mirror image of Matisse's art." Other commentators have looked beyond the sensuous surface, examining instead the stories' characters and themes. For Sheryl Halpern, "they're about less-than-serene Matisse-lovers: middle-aged academics and artistic also-rans who see themselves and their desires in the master's nudes, interiors and still lifes," while Michele Roberts has viewed the collection as a feminist triptych focusing on the female body as a vehicle for themes of "cruelty, destruction, selfishness, dishonesty and self-annihilation."

The first story, "Medusa's Ankles," is introduced by Matisse's line drawing of a woman's head, her coils of abundant hair flowing sensuously downward, and takes place in a beauty salon, where postmodern narcissi preen and primp in front of sleek mirrors. Susannah, a successful classics scholar, is burdened with increasing anxiety regarding her aging appearance. She encounters Lucian, an ironic artist-hairdresser whose melodramatic posturings offer a telling contrast to the potent formal dignity emanating from Matisse's "Rose Nude," a print that hangs above the doorway. Gradually, Susannah taps into this hidden power of the femme fatale, and when she finally sees her own elaborately coiffed image in the mirror, themes of vanity, illusion, identity, and mortality coalesce into a shocking realization—"*I look like a middle-aged woman with a hair-do*" (23)—an epiphany that results in the rage-fueled destruction of the entire salon by this contemporary Medusa.

"Art Work" features the Dennisons—Debbie, a former art student who now writes commercial articles for *A Woman's Place,* and Robin, a painter of brilliant color who presides over the family from his third-story studio—and explores issues of art, creativity, sacrifice, and exploitation surrounding the couple's Guyanese housekeeper, Mrs. Sheba Brown. When the formally trained Robin fails to secure a show in the Florimel Gallery, Mrs. Brown succeeds as a feminist collagist,

her "soft sculptures," sewn together from discarded clothes and other common domestic materials, serving as a sartorial protest on women's subjugation. Thus, Mrs. Brown is seen as "a recycler of culture, reversing the flow of western appropriation of the Third World" (Kelly, 58) and as offering alternative strategies of image making to a moribund art world. After her success, both Debbie and Robin reinvigorate their art, Debbie becoming a successful wood engraver, and Robin achieving a "loosed, slightly savage energy" (90) in his increasingly abstract paintings.

"The Chinese Lobster" repositions these feminist concerns in a new context, an off-campus meeting in a Chinese restaurant between the dean of women's studies, Gerta Himmelblau, and a visiting art professor, Peregrine Diss. Diss has been accused of sexual harassment by a suicidal art student, Peggi Nollet, whose dissertation, "The Female Body and Matisse," is supported by her smearing of Matisse reproductions with either blood or feces, a talentless strategy that enrages the authoritative professor. Surprisingly, Gerta sides with Diss, not the disturbed young woman, as Byatt explores issues of identity politics, appropriation, domination, and aesthetics by showing the two aging academics bonding over a highly stylized, visually sensual gastronomic experience that mirrors Matisse's "silent bliss. *Luxe, calme et volupte*" (121). Byatt's art is highly visual, and *The Matisse Stories* exhibits her understanding of the modernist master's accomplishments. Her own vivid visual sense conceives of "any projected piece of writing or work as a geometric structure [of] various colors and patterns" (Kellaway, 45), a strategy commensurate with Matisse's brilliant work from which this collection takes its name.

BIBLIOGRAPHY

Byatt, A. S. *The Matisse Stories.* London: Chatto & Windus, 1993.

Dyer, Geoff. "Precious in the Pink," *Guardian,* 11 January 1994, p. G8.

Franken, Cristien. *A. S. Byatt: Art, Authorship, Creativity.* New York: Palgrave, 2001.

Halpern, Sheryl. "Just a Bit of Byatt; Thin but Satisfying Read," *Montreal Gazette,* 26 March 1994, p. 13.

Kellaway, Kate. "Self-Portrait of a Victorian Polymath," *Observer,* 16 September 1990, p. 45.

Kelly, Kathleen Coyne. *A. S. Byatt.* Twayne's Author Series. New York: Twayne, 1998.

Roberts, Michele. "Matisse: All the Nudes That's Fit to Print," *Independent,* 9 January 1994, Reviews, p. 31.

Randall S. Wilhelm

"MATTER OF SENTIMENT, A" SAKI (H. H. MUNRO) (1911)

The general plot of SAKI's "A Matter of Sentiment" is quite similar to that of a number of his previous short stories: A group of familiar characters gathers under the auspices of a particularly stuffy English hostess and undertakes a decidedly aristocratic activity. But at the core of the story rests a decided phobia toward the rising Prussian empire and German people, as well as a pronounced anxiety about the international dynamic of the time and England's own position within it, themes that would predominate in Saki's later stories. "A Matter of Sentiment" marks a particular shift in Saki's perception from a respect for, to an outright concern over, England's lack of preparation for the eventual military conflict with the Germans that Saki felt to be lurking on the horizon.

The story opens with the various members of Lady Susan's house party furtively discussing a horse race, an activity Lady Susan strongly disapproves of, just as she seems to disapprove of almost every other activity. Nevertheless, the members of the house party are able to telegraph in their bets after receiving advice about which horses to bet on through a butler who has a relative working at a nearby racing establishment. The bitter disappointment over losing leads one member of the party to blurt out the name of the winning horse, Sadowa, in front of Lady Susan. To the surprise of everyone gathered, Lady Susan reveals that she herself had placed a wager on Sadowa, despite her purported objection to horse racing. She explains that she placed the bet because she was intrigued by the horse's name. Lady Susan reveals that Sadowa was named after a battle during the Franco-Prussian War, which began on her wedding day and ended on the day her first child was born. Her placement of the bet, which, as she admits, goes entirely against her inclinations and beliefs, is merely a matter of sentiment. The story concludes with a chorus of frustrated groans from the members of the house party.

"A Matter of Sentiment" is very much a story of its time. The horse race mirrors the international situation from the English perspective throughout the 1910s. Furthermore, none of Lady Susan's guests are quite sure which horse to support and place their money on, just as England, at the time, was undecided regarding whom it should support in the increasingly volatile and tense European arena. The sense of doubt surrounding the race can be seen as indicative of England's own hesitation and anxieties about the nature of international alliances. Sadowa was not, in fact, a battle in the Franco-Prussia War, as Lady Susan claims it was, but rather a battle in the earlier Prussian War with Austria. Lady Susan's apparent confusion about Sadowa might be Saki's mockery of what he considered the intellectual and historical ignorance of the English upper-classes. Also, Sadowa, an early victory for the Prussians, might have been a source of the evolving English fear of the Germans, who had developed into a significant threat since the Prussian-Austrian war. In that respect, Lady Susan's interest in that particular historical event can be said to mirror the general mentality of the English people at the time, in Saki's view. The fact that her bet was placed simply as "a matter of sentiment" strongly suggests Saki's concern that any rumor or notion about the Prussian empire was capable of shifting, without reason or logic, the popular opinion and sentiment of the English people.

BIBLIOGRAPHY

Birden, Lorene M. "Saki's 'A Matter of Sentiment.'" *Explicator* 56, no. 4 (1998): 201–204.
Langguth, A. J. *Saki.* New York: Simon and Schuster, 1981.
Saki. *The Complete Saki.* New York: Penguin Classics, 1998.

James R. Fleming

MAUGHAM, W. SOMERSET (1874–1965)

William Somerset Maugham was born January 25, 1874, in Paris, where his father was a solicitor in the British Embassy. Ironically, though Maugham would ultimately become one of 20th-century Britain's best-known writers, the future author of 20 novels, 31 plays, nine volumes of short stories, and numerous volumes of prose nonfiction spoke fluent French as a child and learned English only as a second language.

Maugham's mother died in 1882, when he was eight years old, and his father died two years later. The orphaned Maugham, whose three older brothers were away at school in England, was sent to live with his uncle, the Reverend Henry McDonald Maugham, in Whitstable, Kent. The reverend and his wife were childless, and their home proved an awkward place for a young boy. Maugham suffered from a stammer as a boy, which added to his sensitivity and loneliness. In 1887, Maugham was sent to the King's School in nearby Canterbury, which he attended until he was nearly 18. At King's he suffered under the torment of his classmates, who mocked his stammer, and the ignorance of his rough, ill-educated masters. Upon leaving school he abandoned plans, more his uncle's than his own, to enter the church, deciding instead to spend a year abroad. In Heidelberg he attended lectures at the university and began to study and appreciate art, literature, and the new religious ideas. During his year abroad, he traveled to other parts of Germany, as well as to Switzerland and Italy, thus fostering what would become a lifelong wanderlust.

When he returned to England in the spring of 1892, Maugham found himself faced with the necessity of choosing a career. Uninterested in the professions—the law, the army, the navy, the church—he ended up becoming an articled clerk in a chartered accountant's office, a position secured for him by his uncle. Maugham detested the work and quit after only six weeks, thereby losing most of the money paid for his articles. He turned instead to medicine and in 1892 entered the medical school at St. Thomas Hospital, London, where he qualified as a physician and surgeon in 1897. Maugham never practiced as a doctor, but his observations as an intern working among the poor of London provided excellent training for a writer. He learned a great deal about human nature during this time and poured his experience into his first novel, *Liza of Lambeth,* written when he was 23 and still a medical student. Indeed, Maugham's tendency to write about his fellows offended many people throughout his career, including the inhabitants of Whitstable, who found themselves unflatteringly reflected in the pages of *Cakes and Ale* (1930).

Unlike many writers, Maugham did not begin writing short stories as an apprenticeship to writing novels. Finding that novel writing did not bring him the financial independence he desired, he turned next to playwriting, publishing his first play, *Marriages Are Made in Heaven,* in 1902. During the period 1905–15 he wrote many successful comedies, becoming the most popular dramatist of the day and gaining entrée into fashionable London society, experiences that would influence his later novel *Theatre* (1937). In 1915, at the height of his success as a playwright, Maugham wrote the autobiographical novel *Of Human Bondage* in an attempt to exorcise the demons of an unhappy childhood. The novel remains his best-known work and was made into a film (as were several of Maugham's novels and plays) in 1934. Traveling in Samoa and Tahiti in 1916–17, Maugham began researching the life of Paul Gauguin. In 1919 he published *The Moon and Sixpence,* a novel suggested by the artist's life. Around this time he began working seriously on short stories. His travels provided the inspiration for the collection *The Trembling of a Leaf: Little Stories of the South Sea Islands* (1921) and for his most famous (and much-filmed) story "Rain," about the relationship between the prostitute Sadie Thompson and a bigoted clergyman, Reverend Davidson. Like many of Maugham's stories, this is told in the first person and builds toward a strong, shocking climax.

During the World War I, Maugham served in a Red Cross ambulance unit and was later invited to join the British secret service, MI6. His wartime travels took him to Belgium, Russia (where he was involved in trying to prevent the Russian Revolution), America, and the Far East. His experiences were the inspiration for ASHENDEN (1928), a series of stories about a secret service agent, as well as for several novels and tales, such as *The Painted Veil* (1925) and "The LETTER" (1927), set in the Far East and based on a real-life murder case of 1911. These stories, in their colonial settings and interrogation of imperial attitudes, are reminiscent of the works of JOSEPH CONRAD and RUDYARD KIPLING. They have also been accused of being inherently misogynistic.

After World War I, Maugham, now a celebrated playwright, novelist, and short story writer, purchased the Villa Mauresque in the south of France. In autumn

1940, having successfully sought treatment for his stammer with a London doctor, Maugham spent time in the United States, traveling among various cities and giving speeches and readings to an admiring American public. Maugham wrote his last play, *Sheppey*, in 1933, and his last novel, *Catalina*, in 1948; thereafter, he wrote only essays, including his final publication, the book of reminiscences *Purely for My Pleasure* (1962). Maugham celebrated his 80th birthday at the famous Garrick Club in London, joining CHARLES DICKENS, William Makepeace Thackeray, and ANTHONY TROLLOPE as the few literary men to be so honored. W. Somerset Maugham died in the south of France in 1965, aged 91.

Maugham's stories are concerned with representing the truth of human experience, depicting the petty foibles and flaws, as well as the strengths, of humanity (e.g., "A STRING OF BEADS" and "An EPISODE"). He did not shrink from modeling fiction on life, often closely enough to offend the living models. In *The Summing Up* (1938), a memoir and meditation on his craft, Maugham declares that the greatest benefit of his medical education, and the most valuable training for his career as a writer, was the opportunity to experience "life in the raw" (42). His fiction reveals this fascination with the "discrepancies of human nature" (44).

BIBLIOGRAPHY

Calder, Robert. *Willie: The Life of W. Somserset Maugham*. London: William Heinemann, 1989.

Archer, Stanley. *W. Somerset Maugham: A Study of the Short Fiction*. New York: Twayne, 1993.

Maugham, W. Somerset. *The Collected Short Stories*. London: Penguin, 1977.

———. *The Summing Up*. New York: Signet, 1964.

Whitehead, John. *Maugham: A Reappraisal*. Totowa, N.J.: Barnes and Noble, 1987.

Sara Atwood

"MAURICE, OR THE FISHER'S COT" MARY SHELLEY (1820)

"Maurice, or The Fisher's Cot" was originally written by MARY SHELLEY (1797–1851) as a gift for Laurette Tighe, the daughter of Mrs. Mason (Lady Mountcashell), one of the Shelleys' acquaintances in Pisa in 1820, and the former pupil of Shelley's mother Mary Wollstonecraft. Denied publication by Shelley's father, William Godwin, for his Juvenile Library, the story remained unpublished until it was discovered in 1997 by descendants of Laurette Tighe.

Written in three "volumes" in imitation of the popular novels of the day, and employing a modified version of the frame narrative Shelley had used in her well-known novel *Frankenstein*, "Maurice, or the Fisher's Cot" tells the story of its title character, who at the beginning of the story is participating in the funeral of Barnet, an old fisherman. A traveler who witnesses the funeral learns about young Maurice and is then introduced to him, and Maurice explains his decision to leave his parents because of the cruel mistreatment by his supposed father, Daddy Smithson. Changing his name from Henry to avoid detection, Maurice decides to make his own way and not return until he can support himself. His travels have taken him to the recently widowed Barnet, who agrees to let Maurice live with him in exchange for some minor chores and, more important, companionship. Maurice quickly becomes a favorite of the village, assuming in some ways the late Dame Barnet's position in the community by reading from the Bible and teaching other children how to read. After Maurice completes his story, the traveler tells him about the kidnapping, some 11 years earlier, of his own son, for whom he spends two months each year looking near the area of his disappearance. After Maurice's status as the traveler's son is confirmed, aided by the remorseful confession of Dame Smithson to Henry's kidnapping, father and son return to Windsor, though Henry's father purchases Barnet's cottage and the two continue to visit the village for two months every year. After an extended absence, a grown Henry returns one day to discover that the cottage has collapsed. He builds a new house near the old location and offers it to another poor fisherman's family in remembrance of kind old Barnet.

The most commonly identified characteristics of Shelley's novella are the recurring themes of loss, suffering, and alienation. In this context, biographical parallels are particularly significant, especially in terms of the loss of a child. By the time she began to compose the novel, Shelley had already endured the deaths of three children. Mrs. Mason had to surrender her claims to her seven children by her first husband when she left him for George Tighe. For both women, therefore, the painful separation from one's offspring would have been a very meaningful subject. Throughout Maurice's history, however, his experiences of mistreatment and uncertainty fail to diminish his innate goodness, diligence, and compassion. In this regard, the novella can also be seen to contribute to the nature/nurture debate. In contrast to the creature in Shelley's *Frankenstein,* for example, who is portrayed as good until society's abuse causes him to become violent, Maurice never loses his original fine qualities, despite the suffering he endures. As in the novel, Shelley also incorporates into "Maurice" a discussion of the therapeutic values of nature, a theme widely treated in the literature of the romantic period, as both Henry and his father appreciate the wonders of nature. It is this appreciation, ironically, that originally leads to Henry's kidnapping, which occurs after his father and mother take a walk along a river, leaving their son in the hands of a nurse who promptly falls asleep, giving Dame Smithson her opportunity.

BIBLIOGRAPHY

Markley, A. A. "Lost and Found," *Romanticism on the Net* 15 (August 1999). Available online. URL: http://www.erudit. org/revue/ron/1999/v/n15/005868ar.html. Accessed May 23, 2006.

Mekler, L. Adam. "Placing *Maurice* within the Shelley-Godwin Circle," *CEA-MAGazine* 14 (2001): 23–33.

Shelley, Mary. *Maurice, or the Fisher's Cot.* Edited by Claire Tomalin. New York: Knopf, 1998.

Adam Mekler

MCEWAN, IAN (1948–)

Ian McEwan was born on June 21, 1948, in the military garrison town of Aldershot, England, to David and Rose Lilian McEwan. His mother's first husband died during World War II; she subsequently married David, then a sergeant major in the British military. McEwan's childhood was spent in empire outposts such as Singapore and Libya, until he was sent to a boarding school in Suffolk.

He enrolled at the University of Sussex in Brighton in 1967 and graduated with a degree in English in 1970. From there he enrolled in an M.A. program in English at the University of East Anglia, where he was allowed to submit some of his short fiction as a part of the requirements for his degree. Under the guidance of British novelist Malcolm Bradbury, McEwan wrote more than two dozen short stories and earned his degree in 1971. Several of the stories written during that period were published in British and American periodicals, as well as in McEwan's first two books, both short story collections: *FIRST LOVE, LAST RITES* (1975), winner of the Somerset Maugham Award, and *In between the Sheets* (1978). The shocking nature and the literary quality of these stories earned McEwan enough critical and popular attention to enable him to pursue writing as a full-time career, an occupation to which he has devoted himself ever since.

McEwan's two collections of short stories, both written in the earliest years of his career as a professional writer, explore the multiple forms of depraved and socially unacceptable behavior—sadism, rape, bestiality, pedophilia, castration, murder—of which seemingly normal human beings are capable. Most of the characters who commit these acts are alienated from the dominant culture in which they live, and they all narrate their tales in neutral and rational tones, with the sort of attention to detail that one expects of sympathetic fictional narrators. McEwan's short fiction puts the reader in the difficult position of determining whether these characters are simply aberrations, monsters created by their heredity or their environment, or whether they represent the worst aspects of human nature. His stories are by turns shocking, prurient, innovative, and repulsive, but given the level of critical attention they have continued to receive throughout McEwan's long career, they undoubtedly constitute an important contribution to the genre of short fiction in the latter half of the 20th century.

First Love, Last Rites opens with a teenager recounting a dreamy memory of washing a bedspread with his younger sister sitting nearby; by the end of the story we discover that this memory comes at the conclusion of a horrifying incident in which the young man has raped the 10-year-old girl. Sexual molestation of a young girl appears again in the story "Butterflies," in which a facially deformed man leads a girl to a secluded spot along a city canal, entices her into a sexual encounter, and then pushes her body into the canal when she falls and is knocked unconscious while trying to escape from him. Death, violence, and sexuality—especially deviant forms of sexuality (incest, rape, transvestism, voyeurism)—dominate the collection. Most of the stories are narrated in the first person, and most of these narrators—and the main characters in the other two stories—are loners, isolated from the world around them by temperament or by other characters in the story (as in "Last Day of Summer," in which an orphaned boy lives in a commune with his older brother and his friends). The characters offer few explicit motivations for their actions; the are primarily observers, and neutral ones at that. They rarely make judgments about their own actions or about the actions of others.

The more violently shocking elements of McEwan's short fiction are somewhat muted in his second collection, *In between the Sheets*. The emphasis in these stories falls more upon the abnormal and the delusional. No doubt there is violence in these stories. For example, the main character in "PORNOGRAPHY," a pornographic bookseller who has passed along his venereal disease to two nurses, winds up on a makeshift operating table at the end of the story, about to undergo castration at their hands. But there is in this collection far more abnormality than violence: In "Dead as They Come" a rich man falls in love with a store mannequin and brings her home to live with him as his mistress; in "Reflections of a Kept Ape" the title character (an actual ape), who lives with a female novelist, reflects longingly on the eight days he spent as her lover; an Englishman in Los Angeles, in the midst of his narrative of exile, "PSYCHOPOLIS," tells the story of a man whose lover asks him to urinate on himself in the middle of a restaurant, and after he has done so she introduces him to her just-arrived parents.

The settings for the stories in both collections are urban, often London, and McEwan's depicts the city as dull, dark, and decaying. The stories all seem to take place under the "uniformly grey skies" mentioned by the narrator of "First Love, Last Rites." Clear connecting lines run between these settings, the themes of isolation and alienation, and the behavior of the characters. The stories depict contemporary urban existence as monotonous and conformist, from which setting any

individuals who do not fit into the common molds are outcast and exiled. These exiles, in turn, assert their individuality in any way that becomes available to them; murder or sexual perversity serves here as a form of self-expression, as a rejection of the values of contemporary society. In that sense, these characters and their stories stand easily within the 20th-century literary tradition of alienation and rebellion.

McEwan continued to explore the same themes in his first published novel, *The Cement Garden* (1978), in which the backyard cement slab of the title serves as a metaphor for McEwan's perception of modern urban life. The appearance of this novel essentially marked the end of McEwan's career as a publishing writer of adult short fiction. He has written in a variety of genres since then—including novels, plays, an oratorio, and motion picture and television scripts—but has published less than a handful of adult short fiction since then. Critical acclaim for McEwan's novels has built steadily throughout his career, evident from the four nominations for Britain's prestigious Booker Prize he has received for *The Comfort of Strangers* (1981), *Black Dogs* (1992), *Amsterdam* (1998), and *Atonement* (2002). *Amsterdam* won the prize in 1998. (See also "SOLID GEOMETRY.")

In the mid 1980s, McEwan's fiction moved into new territories. While traces of his interest in violence and abnormal psychological states remain, these subsequent works express much greater interest in broader questions of politics and history. With each subsequent novel, too, McEwan's narrators become more readily understandable and sympathetic; they are often artists or writers, they have relationships with spouses and children, and they pay attention to world history and politics in ways that are completely absent in the short story collections.

McEwan did return to the short story in 1994 with the publication of his collection of stories for children, titled *The Daydreamer*. The title character in this collection is Peter Fortune, a 10-year-old English boy with a vivid imagination and a tendency to let his mind wander into elaborate daydreams.

Although McEwan has published little short fiction since the late 1970s (he has published excerpts from his novels in popular and literary magazines), the nature and quality of his two adult short fiction collections, as well as the literary fame McEwan has subsequently achieved, ensure his stories a place in the literary canon of postwar British literature.

BIBLIOGRAPHY

Malcolm, David. *Understanding Ian McEwan*. Columbia: University of South Carolina Press, 2002.

McEwan, Ian. *Atonement*. London: Jonathan Cape, 2001.

———. *The Daydreamer*. London: Jonathan Cape, 1994.

———. *First Love, Last Rites*. London: Cape, 1975.

———. *In between the Sheets*. London: Cape, 1978.

———. *Saturday*. London: Jonathan Cape, 2005.

Roberts, Ryan. IanMcEwan.com. Available online. URL: http://www.ianmcewan.com. Accessed May 23, 2006.

Ryan, Kiernan. *Ian McEwan*. Plymouth, England: Northcote House in association with the British Council, 1994.

Slay, Jack, Jr. *Ian McEwan*. New York: Twayne; London: Prentice Hall, 1996.

James Fromm

MCGAHERN, JOHN (1934–)

One of the most highly regarded contemporary Irish novelists and short story writers, McGahern grew up in rural western Ireland, a setting he returns to throughout his fiction. He is the author of six novels (*The Barracks* [1963] and *Amongst Women* [1990] are the most famous), a play, and three collections of short stories. His *Collected Stories* was published in 1992. His short fiction shows the influence of Irish writers such as GEORGE MOORE and JAMES JOYCE and of Continental European writers such as Anton Chekhov. His stories are described as realistic but also as possessing features of poetry. Although now widely celebrated, McGahern has been a controversial figure. His second novel, *The Dark* (1965), was banned in Ireland, and McGahern was forced to go into exile in Britain and America for several years.

McGahern's first collection of short stories, *Nightlines* (1970), presents childhood, adolescent, and adult experience, mostly in rural Ireland. The time setting is the 1950s and 1960s in some stories, but in others it is left indefinite. This ambiguity and the interweaving of texts concerning characters of different ages suggest that the collection is offering a generalized view of human life. Conflicts between father and son (so much

a part of McGahern's fiction as a whole) are central to stories such as "Wheels" and "Korea." "Coming into His Kingdom" and "Lavin" are accounts of sexual initiation, while adult sexuality is the focus of "My Love, My Umbrella." All of these stories suggest a dark vision of human life, often marked by emotional and social paralysis and disappointment. "Strandhill, the Sea" and "The Recruiting Officer" exemplify this. Stories set outside Ireland, "Hearts of Oak, Bellies of Brass" (set among London building workers) and "Peaches" (a story of sexual and political tensions in Franco's Spain), offer no relief from the pessimistic vision of the world. "Korea" is typical of this vision: A young man believes that his father wants him to emigrate to the United States so that he can be conscripted to fight in the Korean War and thus earn money for his father, especially if he is killed.

Getting Through, McGahern's second collection of short stories, was published in 1978. All the stories are about failure, and the title suggests that the best a person can do in life is endure. "The Beginning of an Idea" is unusual in McGahern's work in that it has a female protagonist; she has to survive the stupidity and brutality of men. The elderly, the middle-aged, and the young all face similar disappointments and difficulties. In "All Sorts of Impossible Things" the protagonist reflects that it is best to put aside dreams and desires. "Swallows" shows two musicians who have chosen not to realize their gifts. "The Wine Breath" depicts an elderly priest who sees his life as empty and unfulfilled. A more positive note is struck in the picture of the strengths of a traditional rural community in "Faith, Hope, and Charity."

High Ground (1985) shows a deepening and development of McGahern's short fiction. All of these stories deal with outsiders who seek a place in some community. Particularly striking are "Oldfashioned," "Eddie Mac," and "The Conversion of William Kirkwood," which center on the experience of Protestants in a post-1922 independent Ireland and are marked by historical breadth and complexity. Other texts return to familiar territory of sexual failure and family tensions. "Bank Holiday," however, ends optimistically. *Collected Stories* contains one major new story, "The Country Funeral," a complex text about the strengths and evils of modern rural and urban Ireland that reflects McGahern's concerns in his later novels.

BIBLIOGRAPHY

McGahern, John. *Amongst Women.* London: Faber, 2000.
———. *The Barracks.* London: Faber, 1963.
———. *Collected Stories.* London: Faber, 1992.
———. *The Dark.* London: Faber, 1965.
———. *The Leavetaking.* London: Faber, 1984.
———. *Nightlines.* London: Faber, 1970.
———. *That They May Face the Rising Sun.* London: Faber, 2002.

David Malcolm

MEADE, L. T. L. T. Meade was the pen name of Elizabeth Thomasina Toulmin-Smith (1854–1914). Meade was born in Ireland, the daughter of an Anglican clergyman, and her ambition to write scandalized her respectable family. Until recently Meade was best known for penning more than 250 novels for children and teenage girls, such as *Girls of Merton College,* and editing the girls' magazine *Atalanta.*

Meade, with her physician collaborators Robert Eustace (Dr. Eustace Robert Barton, 1854–1943) and Clifford Halifax (Dr. Edgar Beaumont, 1860–1921), wrote several series of DETECTIVE FICTION, usually involving a medical theme. With Halifax, Meade wrote a number of mysteries collected as *Stories from the Diary of a Doctor* (1894), and with Eustace Meade she wrote "The Secret of Emu Plain" (1898) and a series of mysteries featuring the female detective Florence Cusack, including the often-anthologized "Mr. Bovey's Unexpected Will" (1899) and "The Outside Ledge" (1900). For these stories, Halifax and Eustace typically supplied medical details that Meade developed into a means of either committing or solving a crime.

The most famous of Meade's detective stories, written with Robert Eustace, were published in the STRAND from October 1902 to March 1903 and were later collected in a volume titled *The Sorceress of the Strand* (1903). Of the tales' oddities, the most striking was the central character Madame Sara, a female and foreign manifestation of the arch-villain, so diabolically clever that, as the writing duo known as Ellery Queen stated, she "made [traditional] rogues like Colonel Clay and Raffles look like sissies" (Russell, x). Meade's stories

establish that Madame Sara's femininity and foreignness—she is half Indian and half Italian—enable her to baffle the detectives completely and to circumvent the ideals of justice upheld by contemporary Holmesian heroes of popular detective fiction.

BIBLIOGRAPHY

Adrian, Jack, comp. *Strange Tales from "The Strand."* Oxford: Oxford University Press, 1995.
Cox, Michael, ed. *Victorian Detective Stories.* Oxford: Oxford University Press, 2003.
Marcus, Laura, ed. *Twelve Women Detectives.* Oxford: Oxford University Press, 1997.
Meade, L. T. *The Sorceress of the Strand.* London: Ward Lock & Co., 1903.
———. *Stories from the Diary of a Doctor.* London: Newnes, 1894.
Russell, Alan. "Introduction." In *Rivals of Sherlock Holmes: Forty Stories of Crime and Detection from the Original Magazines,* i–xv. Secaucus, N.J.: Castle Books, 1978.

Jennifer Halloran

"MELANCHOLY HUSSAR OF THE GERMAN LEGION, THE" THOMAS HARDY **(1890)** THOMAS HARDY first published this story as "The Melancholy Hussar" in the *Bristol Times and Mirror* in 1890 and revised and reprinted it several times, notably in *Life's Little Ironies* (1894) and in the Wessex Edition of his *Wessex Tales* (1912). He had begun working on the story some time before July 1888 but then laid it aside for more than a year before offering it for publication in October 1889. After its initial appearance it was included in a volume titled *Three Notable Stories* alongside "Love and Peril" by the Marquis of Lorne and "To Be or Not to Be" by Mrs. Alexander.

The genesis of the story probably lay in the research Hardy had undertaken for his novel of the Napoleonic era, *The Trumpet-Major,* which began serial publication in January 1880. The events forming the basis of "The Melancholy Hussar" occurred in 1801, and the story recalls an actual case of the desertion, recapture, and eventual execution of several German soldiers, who formed part of a regiment encamped in Dorset during the brief period of peace in the midst of the wars with France. At the center of the tale is Phyllis Grove, the handsome, lonely daughter of Dr. Grove, a retired professional man of intensely reclusive habits. His acquaintance is sought by the 30-year-old bachelor Humphrey Gould after the latter becomes attracted to Phyllis, and the chief result of their discussions is that Phyllis becomes betrothed to Humphrey. Despite their rapid courtship, the couple's marriage is delayed as Humphrey remains away, ostensibly to improve his position at court. In the meantime, Phyllis finds herself drawn to a corporal of the Hussars named Matthäus Tina. Matthäus is deeply dissatisfied with the state he finds himself in, being eager either to return to his native Germany or to engage his enemies on the battlefield. As his feelings for Phyllis intensify, Matthäus determines to desert his regiment and flee to Germany, taking Phyllis with him. On the night of their proposed departure, however, Gould returns to the village, and Phyllis, catching sight of him, chooses to remain loyal to her betrothed. Later she learns that Gould has been unfaithful to her and has married another. Matthäus is subsequently captured and executed as a deserter. Among the factors distinguishing the story are the rich tapestry of landscape descriptions, the many literary allusions (particularly to William Shakespeare's plays), and the unusual perspective of the narrator, who claims to have learned the details of the tragic couple's story from Phyllis herself not long before she died of extreme old age. A film adaptation titled *The Scarlet Tunic* was produced in 1996.

BIBLIOGRAPHY
Hardy, Thomas. *Wessex Tales.* Oxford: Oxford University Press, 1998.
Orel, Harold. *The Victorian Short Story: Development and Triumph of a Literary Genre.* Cambridge: Cambridge University Press, 1986.
Ray, Martin. *Thomas Hardy: A Textual Study of the Short Stories.* Aldershot, England: Ashgate, 1997.

John Ballam

"MERE INTERLUDE, A" Thomas Hardy (1885)

A fine example of Thomas Hardy's skillful use of irony, this story alerts readers to the danger of making hasty decisions. The heroine, Baptista Trewthen, attempts to create a better life for herself through marriage, but she encounters unusual obstacles to her plans. She hates her new job as a schoolteacher and decides to marry David Heddegan, an older man whose wealth will guarantee her a more comfortable lifestyle. However, on her way home to be married in the island village of Giant's Town, Baptista is delayed in the port city of Pen-zephyr, where she meets an old school friend, Charles Stow. Also a teacher, Charles is dismayed at Baptista's decision to marry a much older man and claims that he would have asked for her hand himself had she waited. Charles then convinces Baptista to marry him immediately. While waiting for a connecting steamer in Pen-zephyr, Charles decides to swim in the sea. The current carries him away, and although Baptista seeks help from the local villagers, Charles drowns. Baptista, now a widow, continues her journey. She has kept the marriage secret for propriety's sake and cannot delay her arrival without inciting concern. Once at home, she cannot find an opportunity to announce her marriage to Charles, and she quietly marries Mr. Heddegan the next day. Baptista settles into a quiet existence with Heddegan until a glazier, who was a witness to her first marriage, chances upon her one day. When the witness realizes that Baptista has kept Charles a secret, he blackmails her, but Baptista soon confesses the truth to Heddegan. Far from being angry, Heddegan promptly confesses that he too has been widowed. He had married a woman from Pen-zephyr just before her death and was now responsible for her four daughters. He admits that he married Baptista so that he could bring the girls home for her to teach since they are too old to attend school. Baptista is angry at having been deluded, but she doggedly undertakes the task of educating the girls. Eventually, she learns to love them and develops a friendship, if not a love, for Heddegan.

Hardy published "A Mere Interlude" in the *Bolton Weekly Journal* and later collected it as part of *A Changed Man and Other Tales* (1913). It was widely reprinted and pirated in Britain and in the United States, although Hardy himself did not consider the tale especially good. The story's title establishes the irony that pervades the plot, since the interlude of Baptista's first marriage is far from trivial. Moreover, Baptista's fate may be a warning to Hardy's readers to avoid making quick, unreasoned decisions that ignore potentially negative consequences. Like many of Hardy's other tales, "A Mere Interlude" engages the Woman Question, an interest in gender relations that emerged from Victorian England and that encouraged the exploration of women's roles. Baptista's limited choice—marriage or teaching—can be interpreted as Hardy's sympathetic gesture toward women and the state of dependence in which they often found themselves. When Charles coerces Baptista into marriage and Mr. Heddegan conceals his true motives, Baptista slips easily into the role of victim. Her passivity embodies the submission expected of the traditional English housewife, but her fate may suggest the inadequacy of such an obedient role. Although she rouses herself to admirable activity to thwart the glazier's blackmail plan, she lapses quickly into her usual passivity and must learn to live with her fate.

BIBLIOGRAPHY

Hardy, Thomas. *A Changed Man and Other Tales.* 1913. Gloucester, England: Alan Sutton, 1984.

Larkin, Peter. "Irony and Fulfilment in Hardy's 'A Mere Interlude,'" *Journal of the Eighteen Nineties Society* 9 (1978): 16–22.

Rogerson, Ian. "The Illustrations in 'A Mere Interlude,'" *Thomas Hardy Journal* 16, no. 3 (2000): 63–64.

Turner, Paul. *The Life of Thomas Hardy: A Critical Biography.* Oxford: Blackwell, 1998.

Ben P. Robertson

MEW, CHARLOTTE (1869–1928)

Charlotte Mew was born and lived the rest of her life in the famous Bloomsbury district of London. Her father, Fred, worked as an architect for his father-in-law's firm, and provided for his wife, Anna Maria, and four surviving children a middle-class standard of living during his life. After his death in 1898, however, the family was forced to accept reduced economic circumstances, renting out part of their house and living in its basement. By this time the family consisted of Charlotte's mother and two sisters. In the late 1880s, her brother Henry had been sent to Peckham House Lunatic Asylum after showing signs of mental illness, most likely schizophrenia; her sister, Freda, also showed indications of mental breakdown and was confined to the Isle of Wight County Mental Hospital in the early 1890s. As a result of their siblings' schizophrenia,

Charlotte and her sister Anne agreed never to marry and have children. Insanity and the fear of insanity appear as themes in many of Mew's pieces, most explicitly in the poems "Ken" (1916) and "On the Asylum Road" (1916). At particular points in her life Mew exhibited erratic, irrational behavior, and she committed suicide in 1928 by drinking disinfectant, probably because she recognized the telltale signs of mental degeneration and preferred death to commitment and madness.

Mew's earlier writings consist of short stories and articles published in periodicals, but she began writing poetry almost exclusively after 1915. Her career began somewhat sensationally. Her story "Passed" was published in the second number of the *YELLOW BOOK* in 1894, the literary and art journal that folded because of the scandal created by the 1895 Oscar Wilde trial in which he was charged with homosexuality. Despite Mew's own probable homosexuality, she maintained a strong aversion to any hint of scandal. As a result, she never published in the *Yellow Book* again and disassociated herself from its community of contributors. It would be five years before Mew published anything else, and she did so then out of financial necessity after the death of her father. Fortunately, Mew found the journal *Temple Bar* amenable to her work. She placed her short story "The China Bowl" there in 1899 and continued to publish most of her work in the journal until it quietly folded in 1905.

Besides mental illness, themes of guilt, renunciation, religious doubt, and death figure prominently in Mew's poetry and prose. Her short story "A WHITE NIGHT" (1903) describes the live burial of a Spanish nun by monks from the point of view of an Englishman who witnesses the incident unnoticed. The narrator, Cameron, perceives the scene as a spectacle and views the nun's passivity as a conscious renunciation of her life. In her poem "Madeleine in Church" (1916), Mew traces the thoughts of a woman in the threws of religious doubt. The poem exemplifies literary modernism in its use of fragmented or disjointed language to reflect the realistic workings of an individual mind.

Mew's poetry attracted notice and gained respect after "The Farmer's Bride" (1912) appeared in the *Nation*. Her admirers included THOMAS HARDY, VIRGINIA

WOOLF, Ezra Pound, D. H. LAWRENCE, and May Sinclair. In 1916, Harold Monro of the Poetry Bookshop collected and published a volume of Mew's poems under the title *The Farmer's Bride*. *The Farmer's Bride* was republished in 1921 with additional poems. (See also "SOME WAYS OF LOVE.")

BIBLIOGRAPHY
Fitzgerald, Penelope. *Charlotte Mew and Her Friends*. London: Collins, 1984.
Mew, Charlotte. *Collected Prose and Poems*. London: Fyfield Books, 2003.

Melissa McLeod

"MISS BRILL" KATHERINE MANSFIELD (1920)

Written in 1920 and included in KATHERINE MANSFIELD's short story collection *The Garden-Party and Other Stories*, "Miss Brill" narrates a day in the life of an aging spinster, Miss Brill, who perceives life as a play and is aware of her role as an actress, playwright, and director in the metaphorical representation. Alone and with no friends, she spends her Sundays visiting the local park, listening to the band, and observing people's lives around her. Since it is the first Sunday of a new season, she decides to celebrate by wearing a shabby fox-fur collar that has been long stored in an old box. This scene is part of her own play, in which she is one of the protagonists, until she is awakened from her idyllic dream by the comment of a couple, who laugh at her decrepit state, making her conscious of her age and terrible loneliness. Feeling utterly miserable, she returns home, locks herself in her bedroom, and throws the fur into the box, from which she hears a little cry of anguish.

This story was originally published in the *Athenaeum* (November 26, 1920) and, despite the opinion of some critics, like Richard F. Peterson, who sees it as a story "better suited for melodrama than the delicate art of the modern short story" (385), its general public acclaim was unprecedented, as Mansfield herself acknowledged (*Letters,* 130, 136). As opposed to other stories that she might have written just for money, like "Mr. and Mrs. Dove" or "See-Saw," the quality of this piece of fiction derives from the author's almost obsessive reworking on it:

I chose not only the length of every sentence, but even the sound of every sentence—I chose the rise and fall of every paragraph to fit [Miss Brill] on that day at that very moment. After I'd written it I read it aloud—number of times—just as one would *play over* a musical composition, try to get it nearer and nearer to the expression of Miss Brill—until it fitted her. (*Letters,* 165)

Pamela Dunbar (66) notes that the stylistic flourishes in the story (such as frequent repetitions, omissions, and exclamations) capture Miss Brill's personality (her lack of confidence, tenderness, and defiant, gushy gaiety). Indeed, together with "Poison" and "The Lady's Maid," "Miss Brill" is considered by some to be one of Mansfield's best stories written at that time (321).

"Miss Brill" reflects two of Mansfield's central preoccupations in her narrative: the use of metafiction and the figure of the old, lonely spinster. With the former, Mansfield intends to dismantle the artificiality of language, which creates illusions of identity and a false sense of belonging, to show finally that we are puppets manipulated by society. Miss Brill is conscious that she is "composing" a play and that we are reading her work of art. Everything is artificial: the "great spots of light," her old job as an actress, the landscape as if it were a backdrop, the people as "members of the company," "a little 'theatre' dog," and the couple who ridicule her as a "hero and heroine." As Miss Brill thinks, "They were all on the stage. They weren't only the audience, not only looking on; they were acting. Even she had a part and came every Sunday. No doubt somebody would have noticed if she hadn't been there; she was part of the performance, after all" (334). She feels overjoyed, godlike, until the young couple's comment brings her back to reality: She is "an old mug," like the fur she is wearing (shabby, with a need to belong and shine with a little glamor); she is, after all, an illusion of identity in the fictional play of life, in which she ultimately does not have a role.

This evanescent identity connects with the topic of the aging spinster, and Miss Brill is its perfect epitome. Mansfield's taste for symbolism can be observed in the character's name: It is a kind of *flat*fish, living isolated in the bottom of the sea, where it blends in with the sand because of its color. Therefore, this old lady is presented as a social outcast, an insignificant and invisible animal who adopts a superficial identity to survive in a system of appearances, condemned to live in a vicious cycle, like the "fried whiting" that bites its own tail, with which she is compared in the end. Mansfield herself considers Miss Brill as "my insect *magnificat* now & always" (*Letters,* 109), and her social criticism is conspicuous in the story: She parodies the isolated figure of the old expatriate woman who never matures, does not have access to the emblematic institution of marriage, and wastes her time leading other people's lives. The old spinster, including such figures as Miss Brill, Ada Moss in "PICTURES," the protagonist in "The Canary," and Miss Bray in "Second Violin," is the most pathetic of all Mansfield's heroines. The box into which she throws the fox fur could represent the most tragic of deaths: the coffin where she is buried alive.

BIBLIOGRAPHY
Alpers, Antony. *The Life of Katherine Mansfield.* Oxford: Oxford University Press, 1980.
Mansfield, Katherine. *Collected Stories.* London: Penguin, 1981.
———. *The Collected Letters of Katherine Mansfield.* Oxford: Clarendon Press, 1996.
Peterson, Richard F. "The Circle of Truth: The Stories of Katherine Mansfield and Mary Lavin," *Modern Fiction Studies* 24, no. 3 (1978): 383–394.

Gerardo Rodriguez Salas

"MISS OGILVY FINDS HERSELF" RADCLYFFE HALL (1934)

A story exploring sexual inversion first published in 1934 in a collection with the same title. Radclyffe Hall (the pen name of Maguerite Radclyffe Hall [1883–1943]) wrote "Miss Ogilvy Finds Herself" in 1926 before beginning work on *The Well of Loneliness* (1928), a novel notorious in its day for its open treatment of lesbianism. The short story fits within the tradition of psychological fiction represented by such authors as May Sinclair, Dorothy Richardson, and Rebecca West.

The story opens with the disbanding of Miss Ogilvy's ambulance unit at the end of World War I. This opening sequence is marked by a sense of regret rather than victory. The reason for this initial dark atmo-

sphere becomes clear in the next sequence, in which Miss Ogilvy, now on a train back to England, remembers "all that had gone to the marring of her from the days of her earliest childhood." Through these memories, the reader glimpses Miss Ogilvy's unhappy childhood. Shy and awkward, Miss Ogilvy grows up plagued by the fact that she does not fit the usual stereotypes about young women. She prefers sports and physical activities instead of dolls and dresses; she prefers the company of men to women and fears and loathes her few male suitors. When her father dies, Miss Ogilvy is looked on as the natural heir to his position as head of the family. She is happy with this new role until the outbreak of the war. Desperately desiring to be active in the war effort, she fights to be placed in an ambulance unit in France. Her years on the front are Miss Ogilvy's happiest, for she is accepted and rewarded for her courage and capability. However, at the end of the war, the illusion that the world has been transformed and now accepts people like Miss Ogilvy is destroyed. Back at home with her sisters, Miss Ogilvy finds that she is again expected to try to fit herself to the old gender stereotypes. Disheartened, Miss Ogilvy decides to take a trip to a small island off the south coast of Devon. She seems strangely linked to the island, even remembering details about it despite having never visited it before. Here the story slips into the fantastic, for suddenly Miss Ogilvy closes her eyes and in a sort of trance sees the island as it would have appeared in the Bronze Age. She also sees herself as a young warrior walking with a young woman. The narration slowly elides the presence of Miss Ogilvy and focuses on this couple as they make their way to a cave on the island to make love. The story ends the next morning, when Miss Ogilvy is found dead sitting at the mouth of the same cave.

"Miss Ogilvy Finds Herself" was not well received on its publication in 1934, perhaps partly because the acclaim that Hall had won for her previous novels had been compromised by the publication of *The Well of Loneliness* and the obscenity trials that followed. Even today, "Miss Ogilvy" continues to be overshadowed by *The Well of Loneliness*. Hall, however, viewed this short story as a necessary experiment that would help her write *The Well of Loneliness*. She connects Miss Ogilvy to this other study of congenital inversion in an author's note, in which she writes:

> Although Miss Ogilvy is a very different person from Stephen Gordon, yet those who have read *The Well of Loneliness* will find in the earlier part of this story the nucleus of those sections of my novel which deal with Stephen Gordon's childhood and girlhood, and with the noble and selfless work done by the hundreds of sexual inverted women during the Great War: 1914–1918. (Cline, 171)

Perhaps because it is not a full-length study of sexual inversion, "Miss Ogilvy" seems to lend itself to a more general reading than *The Well of Loneliness,* which is often discussed purely in terms of its position in a genealogy of lesbian literature. Sally Cline notes in her biography of Radclyffe Hall, "Looking at the body of her work, it is clear that what interested her were the emotions and position of the stranger in society" (4). Miss Ogilvy is portrayed as a sexual invert. However, what drives the story is not her sexual inversion but rather her outsider status and her frustrated attempts to feel at peace in a society that rejects those who do not conform to its expectations. Though "Miss Ogilvy Finds Herself" belongs within the genealogy of lesbian literature alongside Hall's *The Well of Loneliness,* it is also noteworthy as an illuminating and sympathetic portrayal of a person living outside the norms set by society.

BIBLIOGRAPHY

Cline, Sally. *Radclyffe Hall: A Woman Called John.* London: John Murray, 1998.

Franks, Claudia Stillman. *Beyond the Well of Loneliness: The Fiction of Radclyffe Hall.* Avebury: Avebury Publishing, 1982.

Newton, Esther. "The Mythic Mannish Lesbian: Radclyffe Hall and the New Woman," *Signs* 9 (Summer 1984): 555–575.

Tate, Trudi, ed. *Women, Men, and the Great War: An Anthology of Stories.* Manchester, England: Manchester University Press, 1995.

Heather Edwards

"MISS PULKINHORN" WILLIAM GOLDING (1960)

Written in 1951 but not published until 1960, when it appeared in the magazine *Encounter,* "Miss Pulkinhorn," by Nobel Prize–winning author William Golding (1911–93), was published in book form only after a dramatized version was broadcast on BBC radio in 1960. The Miss Pulkinhorn of the title is a witchlike spinster with fanatically strong but conventional Anglican beliefs who devotes her time to cleaning and guarding Salisbury Cathedral. Bigoted and uncharitable, with a strong sense of her own righteousness, Miss Pulkinhorn is endured but not popular with anyone, including the narrator, Sir Edward, who studies Miss Pulkinhorn from the vantage point of the organ loft. As he explains caustically, "She was a great one for the cathedral and I don't suppose she ever missed a service, but sat out the lot, simmering with disapproval" (100). Miss Pulkinhorn regards herself as the cathedral's guardian, exorcising anyone she regards as undesirable or morally suspect. The result is not pleasant. "[B]elieve me," announces the narrator, "when so much bigotry and ignorance gets mixed up with jealousy on however high a plane, it curdles into a poison that can turn a woman into a witch." (101).

Miss Pulkinhorn's dislikes extend to the showiness of High Church practices, notably the Reservation of the Sacrament in the chapel of St. Augustine. In Holy Communion, the sacrament is the consecrated bread (the body of Christ), some of which may be kept after the service in a designated place in order that those who did not attend can commune with it later. The narrator explains that whenever the sacrament is reserved in the chapel, a light is lit; when it is not, the light is put out.

Miss Pulkinhorn's special hatred is directed toward a bedraggled old man who comes to worship the sacrament every day. It is not clear whether the old man is mad or a mystic. He prays devotedly in front of a stained-glass window that depicts the Biblical father and son Abraham and Isaac in spectacular colors, and in doing so he imitates Abraham's gesture of revelation: "God appearing from a great burst of colour, smiling in a friendly, fatherly way, and Abraham below in the right-hand light, smiling up with face and hands lifted" (102). These extravagant displays infuriate Miss Pulkinhorn. "She came to hang all her feelings on his alleged superstition; and I think she was jealous—jealous of his simplicity and fervour; jealous of his devo-

MITFORD, MARY RUSSELL 289

tion with all the dreadful energy of childless and ignorant women" (102). Matters come to a head one night when the narrator, filled with foreboding, returns to the cathedral. As the caretaker makes his rounds, the two men find the old man praying as usual. However, although the light is on, the cupboard that holds the sacrament and to which he has been praying is empty. The old man, feeling that his gestures have been revealed to be meaningless, collapses and later dies. The narrator thinks he can see Miss Pulkinhorn in the darkness of the cathedral and suspects that she has managed to break into the cupboard using the pin of her brooch and remove the sacrament in order to teach the old man a lesson, destroy his illusions, and end his joyfulness. Miss Pulkinhorn cannot cope with the fact that the narrator knows her secret and dies soon after, telling Sir Edward that her conscience is clear.

On one level, the story is about fanaticism and the desire for control. Miss Pulkinhorn, as Joasiane Paccaud-Huguet notes, is "ghoulish figure possessed by the desire for mastery over the worldliness of life that escapes her grasp[;] she perversely uses the tramp to confirm her own authority. . . . By lighting the candle in the absence of the Sacrament she diverts the symbolic meaning of the light, traps her victim into a parody of revelation which leaves him scandalously exposed—the effect being not humility but humiliation and death" (66). But also in evidence is the narrator's own mastery over Miss Pulkinhorn. By knowing her secret, he gains a godlike power over her. The story is also about the loss of innocence—the narrator's misogynistic jibes at Miss Pulkinhorn's unmarried state, together with the descriptions of the tramp's ecstatic poses, suggest that as in the Bible there is a link between knowledge and sexual innocence. There is also the gap between image, reality, and the value placed in the life of the church on symbols, whether the communion bread or Abraham's gesture. Critics have suggested that the work taps into other common ideas within Golding's work as a whole. According to Steven Metcalf, these include "the unreliability of our understanding of our own motives, the vulnerability of the more innocent, and the totality of self-deception in the less innocent." Golding told an interviewer, "I am

treated as a philosopher, as a theologian as a historian, as a psychologist, if not a psychiatrist, but, in fact, what I am at bottom is a storyteller and . . . what I am really interested in is what gives power to a story" (quoted in Regard, 18).

Bradbury, Malcolm, ed. *Penguin Book of Modern Short Stories.* London: Penguin, 1988.
Metcalf, Steven. "Island Skies," *Times Literary Supplement,* 2 September 2005.
Paccaud-Huguet, Josianne. "Rites of Perversion in Miss Pulkinhorn." In *Fingering Netsukes,* edited by Frederic Regard, 63–81. London: Faber, 1995.
Regard, Frederic. *Fingering Netsukes.* London: Faber, 1995.

Joe Barker

MITFORD, MARY RUSSELL (1787–1855)

Poet, novelist, and dramatist, Mary Russell Mitford was born at Alresford, Hampshire, in 1787, the only child of George Mitford and his wife, Mary Russell, an heiress. Initially the family was wealthy, but the extravagance of George Mitford, a compulsive gambler, reduced them to poverty. The task of supporting them fell on their daughter, and she pursued it with great success. Her first published work, *Miscellaneous Poems* appeared in 1810. It was followed by the equally popular *Poems on the Female Character* in 1813. Her tragedy *Julian* was performed at Covent Garden in 1823, followed by *Foscari* in 1826 and *Rienzi* in 1828. Mitford gained a much wider reputation, however, with a series of country sketches, drawn from her observations of her own village, Three Mile Cross. The series *Our Village* was initially published starting in 1819 in the *Lady's Magazine,* boosting the magazine's sales considerably. The sketches were much admired for their rambling charm, and their detailed, realist descriptions of village life and customs. They were often seen as comparable in spirit with the countryside writings of George Crabbe. Mitford was also credited with preserving for posterity a way of life that was fast dying out in the wake of the Industrial Revolution, which was causing rural communities to break up. The sketches were published in five volumes (1824–32). Typical of the gentle, seductive tone is "Cousin Mary" (1824), an uplifting tale of a penniless girl who leaves the countryside to become a governess in a polluted industrial town. Her goodness is eventually recognized by her employer, who marries her. Mitford published other works, including a novel, *Belford Regis, or Sketches of a Country Town* in 1835, but she never recaptured the success of the sketches. She never married but by the time of her death in 1855 was a literary celebrity, much feted by a large circle of famous admirers, including Elizabeth Barrett Browning and Alfred Tennyson.

BIBLIOGRAPHY

Edwards, P. D. *Idyllic Realism from Mary Russell Mitford to Hardy.* London: Macmillan, 1989.

Mitford, Mary Russell. *Our Village: Sketches of Rural Life, Characters and Scenery.* London: 1824–32.

Raymond, Meredith, and Mary Sullivan, eds. *Women of Letters: Selected Letters of Elizabeth Barrett Browning and Mary Russell Mitford.* Boston: Twayne, 1988.

Andrew Maunder

MODERNISM The term *modernism* is used to define a loose literary movement of the early 20th century; its dates are subject to question, but some critics situate it between about 1890 and the outbreak of World War II. It can also be used to denote a style of literature rather than a particular cohesive movement. As a term describing both a movement and a mode it has several defining characteristics, including experimentation with narrative technique, structure, style, the use of time and space, and individual subjectivity and consciousness. In addition, it has come to be associated with the exploration of certain themes, such as alienation and isolation, gender and sexuality, and the darker side of human psychology. These elements may all be seen in the short fiction of the period; indeed, many critics claim that the modernist period was a time that saw a great flourishing of the genre.

The 19th century was a high point for the British novel, yet the short story remained, for much of the century, undefined and amorphous. Editors, readers, and critics did not reach a consensus on what constituted the short story, also referred to as a sketch, tale, or miscellany. Authors famed for their novels, such as CHARLES DICKENS and ANTHONY TROLLOPE, expressed ambivalence about the short story as a form. There existed no real audience for the short story; fiction

writers relied primarily on readers of novels for their income and audience, so they devoted their time to writing triple-decker novels. Rather than expend their energy on short fiction, they would serialize their novels, guaranteeing an audience for themselves and profits for their editors and publishers. The Victorian period witnessed a dramatic rise in literacy as well as in the publishing of periodicals, contributing to the growth of an audience for fiction. Serials such as *Bentley's Miscellany, London Magazine,* and *Athenaeum* specialized in and encouraged the publication of fiction (see MAGAZINES). At the same time, however, short stories were often relegated to the status of filler material, and it was conventional wisdom in the publishing world that collecting an author's short fiction in book form for sale was bad business: There was simply no market for it.

Several intersecting factors in the 1880s and 1890s contributed to the solidification and flourishing of the short story as a genre. First, there emerged a large number of new periodicals devoted to fiction: The STRAND MAGAZINE and *Blackwood's,* as well as shorter-lived but nonetheless important serials like The YELLOW BOOK and the *Savoy.* At the same time, the triple-decker novel and its serialization fell in popularity. Later there would be a number of crucial "little magazines," such as the *Egoist,* the *Little Review,* and the *New Age,* dedicated to the publishing of serious modernist fiction. Second, practitioners of the genre found the short story conducive to the kinds of aesthetic, philosophical, and psychological explorations they wished to make. Whereas earlier the amorphous quality of the short story made it difficult to define, publish, and market, writers in the late 19th and early 20th century discovered that such a flexible genre lent itself to technical, stylistic, and thematic experiments. The movement toward psychological realism, as well as symbolism and the AESTHETICISM of the fin-de-siècle could be accommodated in the short story as practiced by precursors of modernism, such as OSCAR WILDE, THOMAS HARDY, and JOSEPH CONRAD; by true modernist short story writers, such as KATHERINE MANSFIELD; and by novelists who wrote and published short stories, such as JAMES JOYCE, VIRGINIA WOOLF, and D. H. LAWRENCE. Collections such as Hardy's *Life's Little Ironies* (1894),

Joyce's DUBLINERS (1914), Mansfield's BLISS (1920), Woolf's MONDAY OR TUESDAY (1921), and Lawrence's *England, My England* (1922) showed the growing interest in short story collections as valid and valuable contributions to the literary marketplace and exemplified the transformation of narrative through modernist concerns, both technical and thematic. Often, these concerns intersect, particularly in the interest in and representation of individual subjectivity.

Important precursors to the modernist short story include the works of Wilde, Hardy, and Conrad. These authors exemplify a number of crucial developments in the genre at the turn of the century. Wilde was a key figure in fin-de-siècle England, parlaying aestheticism into fiction that seems on the surface merely witty and sophisticated but that, on closer examination, has something significant to say about the relationship between reality and art and about the artifice of human psychology and behavior. Wilde's story "LORD ARTHUR SAVILE'S CRIME" (1891) is the tale of a wealthy and delicate young man on the eve of his wedding who learns through a palm reader that he will murder someone. Horrified, he postpones his wedding and decides to preempt the inevitable by killing one of his relatives. What seems at first to be a grim tale of murder and corruption becomes instead a witty reflection on performance, on blurring the boundaries between truth and fiction, as Wilde satirizes the attitude that anything can be rendered into an aesthetic experience, including duty and murder.

The relationship between truth and fiction is a primary concern in modernist literature. A grimmer reflection on the relationship between truth and fiction and on the ways art can function as a trap is Hardy's story "ON THE WESTERN CIRCUIT" (1891). Here, an illiterate servant girl becomes pregnant by a young law clerk moving from London through the countryside on one of his periodic rounds to hear cases. They begin a correspondence, but unbeknownst to him the girl's sensitive and beautiful letters are composed and written by her employer, who herself falls desperately in love with the man. When the deception is revealed on the day he marries the servant girl, he realizes that through the letters he has fallen in love with the mistress and trapped himself in a marriage that can only ruin him. The story is an excellent example of Hardy's preoccupation with inexorable forces like lust and fate that trap individuals. In its frank treatment of sexuality, as well as its interest in the nature of texts and interpretation and the seductive quality of language, Hardy's story shows much affinity with later modernist stories.

Conrad shares Wilde's and Hardy's concentration on psychology; his texts also exemplify a 20th-century concern with the consequences of empire and postcolonial modes of inquiry. His novella HEART OF DARKNESS works through this concentration on psychology and subjectivity by employing a variety of experimental narrative techniques, namely, an unreliable narrator and an impressionistic representation of events. Conrad rejects a stable perspective and a linear narrative to tell the story of Marlow and his trip into the Congo to find Kurtz, an ivory trader rumored to have gone insane in the jungle. The story, told from Marlow's point of view, is always unstable; one is never sure where one is or what one knows, just as Marlow is unsure. The reader is forced to piece information together from impressions, from clues, mirroring Marlow's knowledge gathering as he travels into the unknown.

The emphasis on the processes of subjectivity and the narrative techniques that arise from this preoccupation in modernist short fiction are exemplified in the work of Joyce, Mansfield, and Woolf. Joyce's stories in *Dubliners* are famous for their use of the epiphany, a moment of being or feeling in which the character comes to a realization. These stories are also notable for their lack of resolution, for the seeming failure of the plot to resolve itself. For instance, "ARABY" and "EVELINE" both focus on a moment of realization on the part of the main character, only to show that such a realization does ends not in clarity or resolution but in further paralysis. Joyce's use of stylistic experimentation is notable as well, as stories are told not only from the point of view of the boy or of Eveline but also in the individual voice, a striking use of free indirect discourse. Mansfield, too, in such stories as "JE NE PARLE PAS FRANÇAIS" and "Bliss," refuses to offer resolution to the inner conflicts of the characters. Furthermore, she focalizes her narratives through the perspectives of her characters only to show how little they know and understand not only others but also themselves. For Mansfield's characters, their own subjectivity remains a mystery.

Mansfield's stories also share with those of other modernist writers, like Lawrence, a concern with the representation of sexuality and desire and their relationship to alienation and isolation. For these authors, and for many modernist writers, desire does not bring two people together but rather provides a moment to show how there can be no true connection. Mansfield's story "Bliss" and Lawrence's story "The HORSE DEALER'S DAUGHTER" illustrate the modernist impulse to address sexuality, gender, and desire while also showing how it contributes to isolation and how it forms a most unknowable part of the human psyche.

Further exploration into the processes of subjectivity and their relationship to time and space can be seen in Woolf's fiction. Her story "KEW GARDENS" begins with an image of the flowers in the gardens, their shifting colors serving as a symbol for the shifting perspectives of the people walking along the paths. The story is told from several points of view, different people thinking their own thoughts or having their own conversations as they walk. The moments are meant to be seen as occurring simultaneously, a moment in time when an experience is focalized through many subjectivities. The story ends with a return to the symbol of the flower, a moment of movement and of stasis. The short fiction of the period relies heavily on symbols such as this one; in "Bliss" Mansfield uses a pear tree to signify the female protagonist's burgeoning sexuality, and Lawrence uses animal symbolism extensively to similar purpose in his work, including stories such as "The Horse Dealer's Daughter."

This intersection between symbolism and psychological realism, the importance of narrative experimentation, and the shared themes discussed are key characteristics of modernist short fiction. The modernist period, by all accounts, was a moment of great artistry in the genre.

BIBLIOGRAPHY

Childs, Peter. *Modernism.* New York: Routledge, 2000.

Flora, Joseph, ed. *The English Short Story, 1880–1945: A Critical History.* Boston: Twayne, 1985.

Hanson, Clare. *Short Stories and Short Fictions, 1880–1980.* New York: St. Martin's, 1985.

Head, Dominic. *The Modernist Short Story: A Study in Theory and Practice.* New York: Cambridge University Press, 1992.

Morrisson, Mark. *The Public Face of Modernism: Little Magazines, Audiences, and Reception, 1905–1920.* Madison: University of Wisconsin Press, 2001.

Orel, Harold. *The Victorian Short Story: Development and Triumph of a Literary Genre.* New York: Oxford University Press, 1986.

Janine Utell

MONDAY OR TUESDAY VIRGINIA WOOLF (1921)

One of the first books produced by Leonard and VIRGINIA WOOLF's Hogarth Press, *Monday or Tuesday,* a collection of short stories, is representative of Woolf's style, relying on her ranging interior narrative voice, the stream-of-consciousness technique for which she and other modernist writers have become famous (see MODERNISM). There are eight stories in the collection: "A HAUNTED HOUSE," "A Society," "Monday or Tuesday," "AN UNWRITTEN NOVEL," "A String Quartet," "Blue and Green," "KEW GARDENS," and "The Mark on the Wall." Some of the stories reveal Woolf's interest in gender. "A Society" is about a group of women who meet every week to debate issues of the day. The story also raises questions about female creativity. This is also the theme of the important story "An Unwritten Novel," which Woolf claimed marked a breakthrough in her invention of a modern style. She described the lightning-speed composition of "An Unwritten Novel" as a "great discovery [that] showed me how I could embody all my deposit of experience in a shape that fitted it" (letter to Ethel Smyth, October 18, 1930).

"An Unfinished Novel" is the story of one woman trying, on a train ride, to imagine a how a stranger lives. The narrator stares over her newspaper and creates a name and story for the passenger sitting across from her, calling her "Minnie Marsh" and deciding that she is going to visit her brother John, sister-in-law Hilda, and their children Bob and Barbara in Eastborne. Working as a novelist does, she imagines what Minnie's private sins might be and forms an antagonist for the story, James Moggridge. Here Woolf essentially compares any attempt at communication with the creative act of writing a novel: A good novel, like a good relationship, builds the hidden personality that Woolf calls the "figure behind the ferns" in "An Unwritten Novel" (16). The narrator's observation of "Minnie" over the top of the *Times,* in which she's reading a story about the Peace Conference, echoes Woolf's own later, famous claim in "Mr. Bennett and Mrs. Brown" that "in or about December, 1910, human character changed." The wartime switch from Victorian to modernist style meant a switch from structuring a truth from reportage and physical details to reconstructing the truth of inner lives. The story ends when the narrator watches "Minnie" step off the train to meet her actual son. The reality does not match what the narrator predicted, and she feels her distance from this other human being, coupled with an ongoing need to imagine what others feel. "It's you, unknown figures, you I adore," Woolf writes (21).

"An Unwritten Novel" also rehearses some lines that find development in later novels such as *Mrs. Dalloway,* including the narrator's musing that Minnie "committed some crime!" (12) and that there was "a parting, was it, twenty years ago" (12) and her image of Minnie's shopping in a store alone, fingering rose print. Some of Woolf's other prominent themes also appear, including the importance of the body (in Minnie's uncontrollable twitch), the metaphor of knitting socks as creation inside the passing of time, and the empathetic gap between social classes (Minnie's lower social standing keeps her unknowable for the narrator).

Monday or Tuesday was generally positively received. Harold Child wrote in the *Times Literary Supplement* (April 7, 1921) that Woolf constructed a map of realistic psychological detail in which "all [is] so trivial, all so significant." In *New Statesman* (April 9, 1921), Desmond MacCarthy credited Woolf with framing the inner life as "incomparably . . . more vivid and real" than mere physical details. An unsigned review in *Dial* (February 1922) critiqued some of the stories for lack of form. The reviews did, however, acknowledge what Woolf was trying to do with the short story. These stories can also be read as Woolf's own answers to the problems she poses in "Modern Novels" (*Times Literary Supplement,* 1919; later revised and printed as "Modern Fiction," 1925) and later in "Mr. Bennett and Mrs. Brown" (*New York Evening Post,* 1923). In both of those essays, Woolf calls for a fiction that deemphasizes physical details in favor of greater psychological acuity. She blames popular genre expectations for disconnecting fiction from the sloppier experience of real mental life.

BIBLIOGRAPHY
Virginia Woolf. *Letter of Virginia Woolf.* Vol. 4. Edited by Joanne Trautman. New York: Harcourt 1981.
———. *Monday or Tuesday.* New York: Dover, 1995.

Ilana R. Simons

"MONKEY NUTS" D. H. LAWRENCE (1922)
"Monkey Nuts" was first published in the *Sovereign,* in August 1922, and was included by D. H. LAWRENCE in *England, My England and Other Stories* published in October the same year. It has appeared in a number of anthologies since that time. The action takes place at the end of WORLD WAR I in a rural situation somewhere in England. There are three main characters: Albert, an army corporal; Joe, a younger and more junior soldier; and Miss Stokes, a land army girl.

The story opens with the two men working in the goods yard of the village railway station. They work well together as they load goods onto railway wagons. The goods, which consist of coal, timber, or hay, are usually brought to the yard by male workers, but one day an assignment of hay is brought from a local farm by Miss Stokes. The girl is attracted to Joe, and before long he receives a telegram inviting him to meet her one Saturday evening. Joe does not respond to the invitation, but on another occasion he and Albert meet the girl on the way home from a visit to the circus. Miss Stokes makes physical overtures to Joe, and he begins to meet her outside working hours on a regular basis. The relationship between the two men then starts to deteriorate. They continue to work together, to share the same lodgings and even the same bed, but an edginess creeps into their conversation. When Joe admits to Albert that he does not want the girl, the older man stands in for him at their next date, but the girl tearfully rejects him. The following day Miss Stokes arrives at the goods yard as usual, but for the last time.

Neither of the men see her again. Joe's response is one of relief, though details of his relationship with the girl are not revealed.

The story is a study of male bonding unsuccessfully challenged by a predatory woman. The close male relationship has been forged during wartime conditions, and these same conditions have promoted, in the girl, feelings of independence and a desire to take control of her life. There is a certain amount of physical contact between the two men and between the girl and Joe, and the suggestion is that Joe prefers Albert's embrace to that of Miss Stokes—lending to a queer reading of the story. Suspense is maintained throughout the story, and the conclusion is open-ended. Because of this lack of closure, the reader is left to wonder about the girl's circumstances and the likely future of the two men.

BIBLIOGRAPHY

Lawrence, D. H. *The Tales of D. H. Lawrence.* London: Martin Secker, 1934.

Sagar, Keith. *A D. H. Lawrence Handbook.* Manchester, England: Manchester University Press, 1982.

Thornton, Weldon. *D. H. Lawrence: A Study of the Short Fiction.* New York: Twayne Publishing, 1993.

Irene Wiltshire

MOORCOCK, MICHAEL (1939–)

Born in London on December 18, 1939, Michael Moorcock is surely the most prolific of all contemporary British writers. Beginning as an editor in the 1950s, Moorcock has published close to 100 novels in a range of genres, from fantasy to science fiction, the espionage thriller, and London myth. While Peter Ackroyd may claim the title of contemporary Dickens, it is Moorcock, in his prolific and fantastical output, who can lay claim to being truly Dickensian.

Moorcock's literary career began in 1956, when he was 16 and became editor of *The Tarzan Chronicles* before going on to edit the *Sexton Blake Library.* But it was as the editor of the *New Worlds* magazine from 1964 to 1971 and again from 1976 to 1996 that he moved to the forefront of an alternative British literature. Under his direction this SCIENCE FICTION journal became one of the most important outlets for British countercultural writing of the 1960s.

Yet Moorcock is best known as the author of numerous science fiction and fantasy series. Among these the *Elric* novels are some of the most famous. Along with this series are the more than 15 novels in the *Eternal Champion* cycle, in which the figure of the eternal champion recurs throughout time and in many different incarnations, making up the Multiverse. Among Moorcock's most well-regarded works is the Jerry Cornelius saga, a scathing satire of the modern age, including events such as the Vietnam War. Moorcock has also written a range of books outside the genres of fantasy and science fiction, including the erotic *Brothel in Rosentrasse* and a series of novels that investigate the events that led to the Holocaust, including *Byzantium Endure* and *The Laughter of Carthage.*

While Moorcock is best known as a novelist, he has also written a large number of short stories, notably the collections *London Bone* and *The Stealer of Souls and Other Stories.* Published as a collection in 2001, *London Bone* is composed of eight stories that were published between 1990 and 2000. Most of the works are set in London and are written in first- or third-person narratives, focusing on typically eccentric characters. "The Clapham Antichrist" is the humorous story of Edwin Begg, a onetime vicar turned proselytizer whose history is recounted by a narrator, a Moorcock, thinly veiled, who generously endorses Begg's antagonistic indictment of postwar Britain. The story, tracing the decay of London, enacts a model of social critique similar to Moorcock's London novels, *Mother London* and *King of the City,* blending social history and autobiography. The title story of the collection, while continuing the theme of critique set in London, is focused around the fantastic. "London Bone," indicative of Moorcock's uncanny use of dystopic realism, may be one of the most inventive and idiosyncratic London short stories. The tale is narrated by Raymond Gold, a traditional cockney entrepreneur, who describes himself as "an art representative, a professional mentor, a tour-guide, a spiritual bridge-builder . . . a cultural speculator." This colorful scalper becomes embroiled in a scandal whereby the city becomes obsessed with grave robbing, the trade in London's dead becoming the dominant cultural expression of the zeitgeist. The trade reaches the point at which the government is actively selling off London bone under the slogan of "let the dead pay for the living for a change." The story is a wildly imaginative critique of the contemporary British heritage economy, in which the seemingly inexorable commodification of the past is leading to the destruction of the city and the nation's psyche.

The Stealer of Souls and Other Stories, published in 1963, is more indicative of Moorcock's prolific and influential career as a writer of fantasy. The collection of stories is set in the empire of Melnibone, which flourished on Earth either 10,000 years before or after history had been recorded. The stories follow events in the life of Elris, the hero of Moorcock's cycle. The stories are narrated in a conventional narrative style, yet they utilize the defamiliarizing effects of fantasy, such as unusual names, mythic gods of the elements, and nonexistent historical events to render the narrative uncanny. The cumulative effect, as in a great deal of Moorcock's fantasy, is something akin to reading a contemporary action novel written by the early 19th-century poet William Blake. The individual stories take the form of the fantastic and otherworldly popular short story, one that has both a long history and massive popularity.

BIBLIOGRAPHY

Greenland, Colin. *Michael Moorcock: Death Is No Obstacle.* Manchester, England: Savoy, 1992.
Moorcock, Michael. *King of the City.* London: Scribner, 2000.
———. *London Bone.* London: Scribner, 2001.
———. *Mother London.* London: Scribner, 1999.
———. *The Retreat from Liberty: The Erosion of Democracy in Today's Britain.* London: Zomba, 1983.
———. *The Stealer of Souls and Other Stories.* London: Granada, 1968.

Alex Murray

MOORE, GEORGE (1852–1933) George

Moore's career lasted from 1882 to 1933, straddling the Victorian and the modernist periods (see MODERNISM). As such, Moore proves an intriguing transition figure particularly because of his influence on the emergence of the modern short story and such modernist authors as JAMES JOYCE. Ever changing in his tastes and enthusiasms, Moore is not an author who can be easily labeled, and any list of his publications reveals that he revised and republished his works constantly. Instead of concentrating on one genre, he experimented with plays, novels, reviews, memoirs, and short stories. His career also shows experimentation with realism, naturalism, and even symbolism. But despite his fluctuating allegiances to genres and styles, there remain common threads that connect his varied works. He repeatedly turned his attention to the plight of women and the experience of the single woman at the turn of the century. In addition he was interested in contemporary ideas about hysteria and sexual repression, themes that arise in the representation of unstable subjects in the collection of stories *Celibates* (1895).

George Moore was born at Moore Hall, County Mayo, in 1852 to Mary Blake Moore and George Henry Moore, an Irish Catholic landowner and member of Parliament. As the eldest son, George Moore inherited his family's large estate when his father died in 1870. Although prodded by his family to pursue a military career, Moore chose to pursue a career in painting. When he turned 21 in 1873, the new master of Moore Hall left for Paris. After formal studio training, Moore chose to pursue a different kind of education in the cafés of Paris. Here he became acquainted with some of the major artists and authors of the period, including Édouard Manet and Émile Zola. Moore eventually abandoned painting for writing, but his contact with the French impressionists and French naturalism would continue to influence his writings even after he left Paris behind in 1880 because of reduced rent receipts from his estate in Ireland. He began publishing short stories, articles, and reviews for various periodicals. His first novel, *A Modern Lover,* was published in 1883. However, it was the publication of *Esther Waters* in 1894 that established his career because of the wide acclaim it received. It remains the work for which Moore is most often remembered.

In 1899, Moore's career took a new turn when Edward Martyn and W. B. Yeats invited him to take part in the creation of the Irish National Theatre. Moore moved to Ireland in 1901; however, he soon split from the venture because of artistic and personal differences with Yeats and Martyn. Moore remained in Ireland for a decade and devoted himself to expanding literary possibilities there. One result of this project was his collection of short stories exploring Irish themes, *The Untilled Field* (1903). Echoes of *The Untilled Field,* particularly its exploration of the themes of exile and stagnation, are found in James Joyce's DUBLINERS as well as the work of SEAN O'FAOLAIN and FRANK O'CONNOR. As a result, Moore is often viewed as the father of the modern Irish short story. In addition, *The Lake* (1906), a novella that grew out of a story initially intended for *The Untilled Field,* is echoed in the work of modernists because of its experimentation with narration and style.

Moore's final break with the Irish literary scene occurred with the publication of his three-volume memoir *Hail and Farewell* (1911–14), which included satirical accounts of the major participants of the Irish Literary Revival. He returned to London in 1911 and continued to write and publish almost continuously until he died in 1933.

BIBLIOGRAPHY

Frazier, Adrian. *George Moore: 1852–1933.* New Haven, Conn.: Yale University Press, 2000.

Moore, George. *Collected Short Stories.* London: Pickering and Chatto, 2006.

———. *The Untilled Field.* Gerards Cross, England: Colin Smyth, 2000.

Owens, Graham, ed. *George Moore's Mind and Art.* Edinburgh: Olive & Boyd, 1968.

Heather Edwards

"MORPHO EUGENIA" A. S. BYATT (1992)

"Morpho Eugenia" is the first of two novellas published together as ANGELS AND INSECTS in 1992 (the other being "The Conjugal Angel"). Both novellas reflect and develop A. S. BYATT's enduring interest in the Victorian period: Her previous novel, the Booker Prize–winning *Possession: A Romance* (1990) cut between the present day and the mid-Victorian period and has been a huge international success. The two novellas, however, remove the frame of the present-day detective story (as in *Possession*) and are set wholly in the 1860s and 1870s.

Eugenia is the youngest daughter of the affluent and philanthropic Reverend Harald Alabaster. Alabaster invites the impoverished, recently shipwrecked William Adamson to stay at their house. The young naturalist is recently returned from entomological research in South America. At the Alabasters' home he meets and instantly falls in love with Eugenia. Their engagement is hasty and they quickly marry. Their marriage does nothing to quell Eugenia's brother Edgar's hatred for William, but this animosity is not the only reason for William's feelings of unease. Even within the marriage, things are not straightforward. Eugenia's enigmatic behavior is puzzling to him; while remaining socially distant, she is sexually enthusiastic, producing five children in quick succession. William finds a confidante in another outsider, Matty, a penniless and resident relative of the Alabaster family. Retreating from his marriage, he spends increasing amounts of time either with Matty or investigating local insect colonies. Through Matty, William discovers the terrible truth of the corruption at the heart of the well-to-do family. The passages in which Eugenia reveals her incestuous relationship with her brother are quiet, alarming, and unsettling. Adamson returns to the Amazon to continue his entomological studies with Matty Crompton.

A. S. Byatt's sensational story touches on many of the key themes of the Victorian period and the late 20th century: sex and sexuality, the disjunction between religion and science, and the anxieties of class and sexual difference. The title of the novella also reflects one of the key themes of the text: the 19th century's seeming inability to conceptualize womanhood. Eugenia is created and imprisoned by William's incapacity to see beyond the categories of angel and insect.

The novella also attempts to articulate the seismic epistemological and ontological shift caused by Charles Darwin's theory of evolution, espoused in *On the Origin of Species* (1859). But why should such a moment in the 19th century be of interest to a late 20th-century audience? Sally Shuttleworth accounts for it as kind of cultural and psychological shift. She suggests that "[f]or the Victorians, there was a decisive crisis of faith, a sense that the world was shaking under them, an ecstatic agony of indecision. For the postmodern era, no such form of crisis seems possible, for there are no fixed boundaries of belief. It is an age of 'ontological doubt' without any fixed points of faith against which it may define itself." (155).

Angels and Insects was adapted for the cinema in 1995 starring Kristen Scott Thomas, Mark Rylance, and Patsy Kensit.

BIBLIOGRAPHY
Byatt, A. S. *Angels and Insects.* London: Vintage, 1992.
Shuttleworth, Sally. "Writing Natural History: 'Morpho Eugenia'." In *Essays on the the Fiction of A. S. Byatt: Imagining the Real,* edited by Alexa Alfer and Michael J. Noble, 147–160. Westport, Conn.: Greenwood, 2001.
Todd, Richard. *A. S. Byatt.* Plymouth, England: Northcote, 1997.

Vybarr Cregan-Reid

MORRISON, ARTHUR (1863–1945)   Arthur

Morrison grew up in Poplar, part of London's East End; his father was an engine fitter. Before devoting himself to a writing career, Morrison worked as a clerk for Walter Besant's People's Palace, a charity set up to help improve conditions in the slums. He later helped edit the organization's magazine, the *Palace Journal.* His stories of East End poverty appeared in *Macmillan's Magazine,* the *National Observer,* and the *New Review.*

Morrison's stories were collected as *Tales of the Mean Streets* (including "A Street" and "Lizerunt") and were designed to show readers something of the brutality and hopelessness of life in the dark side of the British Empire's capital. Morrison insisted that while he was presenting life in the East End as it really was, he did not see himself as belonging to any particular school, neither realism nor naturalism.

His first novel, *A Child of the Jago* (1894), incorporated many of the same ideas, in particular the impact of such conditions on children's lives. The book prompted considerable controversy. Morrison turned increasingly toward detective fiction, though he returned to the East End in *To London Town* (1899), *The Hole in the Wall* (1902), and another collection of short stories, *Divers Vanities* (1905). Morrison's startling evocations of the London slums have come to be viewed as influential in raising awareness of the "other" side of the city and recognized for their impact not only on other writers but on social reformers.

BIBLIOGRAPHY
Krzak, Michel "Arthur Morrison's East End of London." In *Victorian Writers and the City,* edited by Jean-Paul Hulin and Pierre Coustillas. Lille, France: L'Université de Lille III, 1979.
Morrison, Arthur. *A Child of the Jago.* 1896. Chicago: Academy Chicago Publishers, 1995.
———. *Martin Hewitt, Investigator.* 1894. London: Lightning Source, 2004.
———. *Tales of the Mean Streets* 1894. Chicago: Academy Chicago Publishers, 1997.
Swafford, Kevin R. "Translating the Slums: The Coding of Criminality and the Grotesque in Arthur Morrison's *A Child of the Jago," Journal of the Midwest Modern Language Association* 35, no. 2 (2002): 50–64

Andrew Maunder

"MORTAL IMMORTAL, THE" MARY SHELLEY (1833)   This gothic short story by Mary Shelley

(1797–1851), the author of *Frankenstein: Or The Modern Prometheus* (1818), explores the implications of immortality. In the story, alchemy, or artifice, overrides natural law and makes the impossible dream of immortality possible. The story contains many of the motifs found in Shelley's famous novel, including a protagonist who impulsively and thoughtlessly moves forward with a scientific experiment, the effects of which he is ill-prepared to face. The story is narrated by the 323-year-old Winzy, who, as an aspiring scientist of 20, apprenticed himself to Cornelius Agrippa, a figure whose influence makes itself felt in *Frankenstein* as well. Tormented by the thought that his beloved Bertha holds him in contempt because of his poverty, Winzy imbibes a potion that Agrippa has described as "a philter to cure love." Winzy does not realize that this is an "elixir of immortality" that will cure not only love but "all things" through the distanced perspective of immorality.

Immediately after he drinks most of the elixir, a heated disagreement between Bertha and her wealthy (but tyrannical) protectress convinces Winzy that Bertha is in fact devoted to him. Bertha leaves her patron's home, rejecting the wealthier match her patron has championed. Winzy and Bertha marry, and they are happy until it becomes clear to both the couple and the townspeople that while Bertha is aging naturally, Winzy is not. The couple is ostracized, and on Agrippa's deathbed, the truth comes out. Winzy, horrified, realizes that he may never die. He recounts the painful later years of his marriage, condemning his wife for her self-conscious affectations of youth, while recognizing that, although his deception is not as obvious as Bertha's, he, too, lives a lie. He is by all appearances a young man of 23, even though he is well past 50. When an aged Bertha dies, severing Winzy's final connection to humanity, he becomes a "sailor without rudder or compass—tossed on a stormy sea" for centuries. The story closes with Winzy's proposed exploration of the Arctic, to find either death or glory.

With its emphasis on the natural supernatural, Shelley's story is in the gothic mode, but it strays from gothic conventions by setting the narrative in the present. Shelley also explores the typically feminine motif of being trapped in and defined by one's body and, in her tormented narrator, reveals the psychological damage that can accompany this condition. (See also "MAURICE, OR THE FISHER'S COT.")

BIBLIOGRAPHY
Shelley, Mary. "The Mortal Immortal." In *Nineteenth Century Short Stories by Women,* edited by Harriet Devine Jump, 73–83. London: Routledge. 1998.

Anita Rose

"MR. JUSTICE HARBOTTLE" Sheridan Le Fanu (1872)

This story is reprinted in Joseph Sheridan Le Fanu's collection of weird tales, *In a Glass Darkly* (1872), which purports to consist of nonfictional case studies first collected by Dr. Martin Hesselius and then edited and published by his literary executor. As the story's editor notes at its outset, its provenance is complex. "Mr. Justice Harbottle" is the second and less technical of two narratives about the judge acquired by Dr. Hesselius, the first written by a Mrs. Trimmer and the second by Anthony Harman, Esquire. Unable to find the first account, among Dr. Hesselius's papers the editor discovers in the doctor's "escritoire a note to the effect that he had lent the Report of Judge Harbottle's case written by Mrs. Trimmer, to Doctor F. Heyne." Requesting this manuscript from Dr. Heyne, the editor is informed that the doctor returned the document to Dr. Hesselius. As proof, Dr. Heyne sends "a line written long since by Doctor Hesselius" that "acknowledged the safe return of the papers." The editor feels secure in reproducing Mr.

Harman's account, as the "late Dr. Hesselius, in another passage of the note" avers that regarding "the facts (non-medical) of the case, the narrative of Mr. Harman exactly tallies with that furnished by Mrs. Trimmer." After these involved explanations, yet another narrative frame is introduced. Writing 30 years after his conversation with an elderly man who lived in Judge Harbottle's house, Mr. Harman relates this gentleman's tale of an encounter there with the ghosts of the judge and a man whom he had convicted of forgery and executed, Lewis Pyneweck. Mr. Harman writes to a friend some years his senior for more information about the house and its most infamous inhabitant. Writing back to Mr. Harman, this friend recounts the events of the narrative proper, which take place during his father's lifetime, in 1746. At the story's outset, Judge Harbottle speaks with a mysterious old man, Hugh Peters, who warns him that a cabal is forming to judge England's judges. It plans to begin with Judge Harbottle, who has come to its attention by manipulating a jury into convicting of forgery Lewis Pyneweck, whose wife the judge has seduced and brought into his own home as a housekeeper. Though disturbed, the judge is suspicious and canny enough to order Peters followed. When the man is revealed to be a fraud and the plot merely a trick to frighten him, Judge Harbottle is relieved; however, he soon realizes that the disguised Mr. Peters bore a strange resemblance to the jailed Pyneweck. After making inquiries "whether any one was personating Pyneweck in prison, and whether he had thus or otherwise made his escape," the judge is reassured that the prisoner is safe and there is "no question as to his identity." Judge Harbottle later sentences Pyneweck to death, only to see him appear again in court some time after his hanging. Shortly after this strange visitation, the judge receives a letter informing him that on the 10th of the month he is to be tried for the wrongful execution of Pyneweck. He dismisses this letter as another hoax, but later he dreams that he is sentenced to death on the 10th of the following month by "a dilated effigy of himself." When this date arrives, Pyneweck's ghost appears to several members of Judge Harbottle's household, and the judge himself is found hanged. "Mr. Justice Harbottle" is noteworthy for its many gothic features, including its intricate narrative structure, its doppelgangers, and its exploration of the uncertain boundary between madness and the supernatural.

BIBLIOGRAPHY
Le Fanu, Sheridan. *In a Glass Darkly*. Oxford: Oxford University Press, 1999.

Jamil Mustafa

"MRS. BATHURST" RUDYARD KIPLING (1904)

"Mrs. Bathurst" is one of the most ingeniously crafted and enigmatic stories by RUDYARD KIPLING. Originally published in the *Windsor Magazine* as the fourth of a set of six stories, each featuring the character Petty-Officer Pyecroft, the story is far more complex than its predecessors. Instead of the garrulous Pyecroft acting as the main narrator, the tale of doomed love is told by three men, Pyecroft, Pritchard, and Hooper, each complementing the others by narrating only as much of the story as he honestly knows. Consequently, there is no one definitive version of the story: The reader is dependent on each narrator supplying his contribution. At the same time, the reader is kept at a distance by the inclusion of a fourth, anonymous narrator, whose first-person narration frames those of his companions. By distancing the reader from the narrative, the reader is encouraged to question both the meaning and the making of the text.

The success of Kipling's conceit, though, also depends on his effective use of time, place, and atmosphere. These elements are established in the story's opening: "I found myself stranded, lunchless, on the sea-front with no hope of return to Cape Town before 5 p.m." By chance, the narrator meets his friend Hooper, a railway inspector. Hooper has a "souvenir" from up-country for the narrator but is interrupted by Pyecroft and his shipmate, Pritchard. Brought to South Africa on imperial duty, Kipling's protagonists are themselves adrift, temporarily suspended while waiting either for the next train or for ship repairs to be made. In the meantime, there is little to do but talk. They swap stories about other migrant figures, such as Boy Niven, who, on the promise of land, "lured seven or eight able-bodied seamen and marines into the woods of British Columbia." The characters they describe, snatches of lives spent (or misspent) in the service of empire, are both shadowy and mysterious. While these stories are being exchanged, the reader is uncertain when the tale of Mrs. Bathurst will itself begin, if she is related to any of these characters, or if there will be a principal narrator.

The talk turns to Warrant-Officer Vickery who, four months previously, deserted by going up-country. Hooper presses them for identifying marks, and Pyecroft describes Vickery's mechanical false teeth. The desertion is doubly strange since Vickery was close to receiving his pension. Pyecroft speculates that the cause may have been the owner of "a little hotel at Hauraki—near Auckland": a woman named Mrs. Bathurst. Pritchard is shocked at the suggestion, not only because Vickery was married with a child but because of the sublime goodness of Mrs. Bathurst. Vickery seems to have met her in New Zealand, but Pyecroft acknowledges that his information is second-hand: "I used to think seein' and hearin' was the only regulation aids to ascertainin' facts, but as we get older we get more accommodatin'."

The decisive event, Pyecroft recalls, occurred during a cinema show: "We saw London Bridge an' so forth an' so on, an' it was most interestin' . . . the pictures were the real thing—alive an' movin'." Then, suddenly, Pyecroft and his companions recognize Mrs. Bathurst: "She came forward—right forward—she looked out straight at us with that blindish look which Pritch alluded to. She walked on and on till she melted out of the picture." The effect of this on Vickery is dramatic: He returns compulsively to the cinema show, his false teeth clicking "like a Marconi ticker," convinced that Mrs. Bathurst is looking for him. Vickery's increasingly erratic behavior climaxes in his desertion.

This passage has provoked much debate. The film seems to have been shot during the South African War; Pyecroft and Vickery apparently see it just before Christmas 1902. Whether Vickery left England before or after Mrs. Bathurst's arrival is unclear. Equally unclear is why Mrs. Bathurst is in England: Has she discovered Vickery's adultery? Vickery refers to his wife as "my lawful wife," implying that Mrs. Bathurst is his unlawful bride and that his crime is bigamy. However, Vickery also refers to murder. It has been suggested that Mrs. Bathurst is dead (whether or not the victim of murder) and that Vickery has been possessed by her ghost. It could equally be that the innocent sight of Mrs. Bathurst reminds Vickery of a lapse into temptation—there is no evidence that he betrayed his wife—and that, fearing the loss of his moral code, he disappears from the story. As Hooper comments, a man either "goes crazy—or just saves himself."

Kipling leaves his coup de grâce, though, to the very end. Hooper returns to the subjects of the false teeth and of up-country. He tells the others that two tramps had been discovered in a forest, petrified after being struck by lightning, "One of 'em was standin' up by the dead-end of the siding an' the other was squattin' down lookin' up at him." The only identifying mark that remained from the standing man was a set of false teeth. At this point, Hooper removes his hand from his waist pocket, apparently containing the souvenir for the frame narrator, to reveal—nothing. The irresolution of Kipling's text places the burden of interpretation on the reader. The ending, though, complements the beginning of the story. The reactions of Pritchard and Pyecroft suggest that they have been convinced, despite the lack of evidence, that the standing body is Vickery. At the same time, the absence of a coherent meaning diverts the reader away from a central focus to the peripheries of the narrative—how the story is told rather than what is told, when and where the story is set (especially the outposts of Empire), and who is telling the story. Kipling's perennial insistence on the lives and language of working men is here counterpointed by the stray characters within empire: the Greek merchants, the "dirty little Malay boys," and the "heaps of tramps."

BIBLIOGRAPHY

Bayley, John. *The Short Story: Henry James to Elizabeth Bowen.* Brighton: Harvester Press, 1987.

Bodelson, C. A. *Aspects of Kipling's Art.* Manchester, England: Manchester University Press, 1964.

Everett, Barbara. "Kipling's Lightning-Flash," *London Review of Books,* 10 January 1991, pp. 12–15.

Kipling, Rudyard. *Mrs. Bathurst and Other Stories.* Oxford: Oxford University Press, 1991.

Lodge, David. *After Bakhtin: Essays on Fiction and Criticism.* London: Routledge, 1990.

Paul March-Russell

"MRS. FORTESCUE" Doris Lessing (1964)

Doris Lessing (b. 1919) once called her sequence of novels *Children of Violence* "a study of the individual conscience in its relation with the collective" (quoted in Whittaker, 37). More often than not, it is female figures that she depicts in closely observed detail, showing women's struggles to gain personal and sexual freedom. However, in the short narrative "Mrs. Fortescue," first published in *Winter's Tales* in 1964, the protagonist is an adolescent male, a 16-year-old boy passing from childhood innocence to a sexually driven awakening, a "new state of mind" (507) that plunges him into uncertainty.

Fred Danderlea is the loutish schoolboy son of parents who run a liquor shop in London, on the floor above which the family—parents, son and 17-year-old daughter—lives in cramped and squalid quarters that are never free from the pervasive odor of whiskey and stale beer wafting up from below. As is so often true in Lessing's work, the topographical layout embodies the family constellation: The children have to pass through the parents' bedroom to get to their own room, a single room shared during their childhood and only recently divided into two by a make-shift partition, which gives "at least the illusion of privacy" (508). Whereas Fred is still subject to the disciplined round of school, his sister Jane has left school and dolls up every evening for a night on the town; she is transformed by her newfound independence, being no longer the childhood companion of innocent summer holidays, but now a "cool, flip girl" (510) who despises her younger brother. On the upper floor lives Mrs. Fortescue, no longer young, who departs the house every evening attired in a fur coat and heavily made up—an "old tart" going about her business, as Fred is informed by a friend. His curiosity aroused, Fred follows her, confirming his suspicions that she is a prostitute, and is then enlightened by his parents, whose matter-of-fact account of their lodger's doings fills him with a sense of shame and degradation at his parents' deception of him. They have for years concealed this "horror, years-old, and right over their heads, part of their lives" (513). Nonetheless, he is drawn inexorably into this mixture of fascination and horror, and one evening, after providing himself with a half-full bottle of whiskey from his father's supplies, he waits for Mrs. Fortescue to return home, lures the already somewhat intoxicated woman into her quarters, and after plying her further with whiskey pulls off her clothes and in a violent sexual union achieves "the goal of his hot imaginings of these ugly autumn nights in one shattering spasm" (519) that nevertheless fills him with "no less hatred." After this act of violence, he humiliates her even more by turning the light on, so he can see her old, ugly body, and calling her a "filthy old whore" (520). Mrs. Fortescue's parting comment, "That wasn't very nice, was it?" (520), applies to both parties and, though understated, returns them to the quasi adult-child relationship that existed before.

That same day, after following his sister into town and observing her staring at an advertisement of a man wearing a revolver in his belt and then an assortment of lipsticks "in all the pink-orange-scarlet-crimson shades" (514), he places on her bed an old inoperative revolver of his father's, together with an array of lipsticks instead of bullets. After his "victory" over Mrs. Fortescue he confronts his sister, and in a gesture of scarcely restrained violence he points the gun at "that woman his sister in her terrifying intimacy of warm pink" (521). The "pink pink pink everywhere" takes him back to Mrs. Fortescue's room. Both women wear similar pink gowns, and the "fleshly" colors pink and red serve as a leitmotif for Fred's (incestuous) sexual desire. Through his aggression the boy has changed and triumphed: He thinks he has "regained his sister" and "come level with her again" (521). Freudian critics would argue that fragmentation of his adolescent identity, symbolized by the room plan, is overcome, as the divided compartments of his mind—ego, superego, and id—are reunited through his violent sexual initiation. Fred's postlapsarian identity and sexual awakening is on the one hand a liberating experience that gives him a feeling of superiority over his sister and parents; on the other hand, "this ferment of his craziness" (514) does leads not into new maturity but into a crude form of violent masculinity. The story is a kind of Bildungsroman (story of development) that demonstrates the hollowness of its achieved goal.

BIBLIOGRAPHY
Lessing, Doris L. *Stories*. New York: Vintage Books, 1980.
Whittaker, Ruth, *Doris Lessing*. Basingstoke, England: Macmillan, 1988.

Heike Grundmann

"MY LADY LUDLOW" Elizabeth Gaskell **(1858)**   First published in Charles Dickens's magazine *Household Words* from June 19 until September 25, 1858 and reprinted in Round the Sofa in 1859, "My Lady Ludlow" is presented as one of a "chain" of stories connected by a prologue. As Jenny Uglow argues, "My Lady Ludlow" has been the "least regarded" of Elizabeth Gaskell's longer stories and deserves more critical attention (468). The novella, or long story, is one of Gaskell's historical fictions; a tale within its main story is set during the French Revolution—as in "My French Master"—a time that influences all of the history that is related thereafter. "My Lady Ludlow" focuses in part on the bygone era of its aged aristocratic heroine, who is indelibly influenced by the terrors of the French Revolution, which occurred in her middle age. In many senses, however, the story centers more on the inevitability of change, on the transformations of the present moment—reforms in English culture that perhaps have staved off the revolutions that ignited France both in 1789 and in 1848. As Terence Wright has argued, "For Mrs. Gaskell a far more fundamental characteristic of the natural in history than attachment to the past . . . is the tendency to change" (74).

The theme of social change inheres not only in the story of Lady Ludlow herself but in that of the story's narrator. "My Lady Ludlow" is narrated by an old woman, Margaret Dawson, a distant kinswoman who was taken on as a kind of ward to Lady Ludlow at age 16, when Margaret's clergyman father dies. Margaret is crippled during the course of the story, and her resultant intimacy with kindly Lady Ludlow is intensified because of Margaret's infirmity. (In *Round the Sofa*, Margaret Dawson is the infirm old woman on the sofa, and "My Lady Ludlow" is her contribution to the stories the group round the sofa tells.) Like Gaskell's other physically disabled characters, Margaret is treated sympathetically, and her crooked body—like the Reverend Thurston Benson's in *Ruth*—is allied to quick perception and memory. The tone of the narrative is in part elegiac, as Margaret tells the story long after her own departure from Hanbury Court and Lady Ludlow's subsequent death. Margaret is recalling not only a past historical period and a figure who represents that past—her beloved Lady Ludlow—but also Margaret's own hopeful youth, her own personal history, now rendered idyllic with the passage of time and life in more ordinary circumstances: "Like a piece of seawreck, I have drifted away from those days: quiet, happy, eventless days, very happy to remember!"

Margaret tells the story of the aristocratic, well-meaning Lady Ludlow's losing battles against the insurgence of the lower and middle classes and her acquisition thereby of a fuller Christian outlook of true goodwill toward all. Margaret details the kindly but reactionary countess's slowly altering views on issues ranging from the education of the lower classes to the social acceptance of an illegitimate girl who becomes a respected schoolteacher. Occasionally, Margaret's tone is darker, more critical of the status quo, as when she deeply resents the formalities of mourning offered for the unknown Lord Ludlow when he dies far away in Vienna, while her own hardworking, poor clergyman father was not so honored by the parishioners among whom he labored:

> It might arise from my being so far from well at the time, which produced a diseased mind in a diseased body; but I was absolutely jealous for my father's memory, when I saw how many signs of grief there were for my lord's death. . . . My father had spent the best years of his manhood in labouring hard, body and soul, for the people amongst whom he lived. . . . And yet when he died . . . the sounds of every-day life still went on, close pressing around us. (161)

"My Lady Ludlow" focuses on central Gaskellian themes: the nurturance of children, female bonds of friendship, the knowledge of character over time, and the democratizing influence of education and Christianity. In particular, it is concerned with honoring those who nurture others' inherently good qualities with no regard to class origin. While Lady Ludlow's generosity in taking in orphaned gentlewomen is admired, there are others in the story who raise up those who are marginalized by society. Mr. Horner, Lady Ludlow's solicitor, takes on the poacher's son, Harry Gregson, as his protégé and heir when Horner sees that the boy is bright and devoted. His mentorship is all the more significant because the countess is deeply opposed to teaching the lower classes to read, since she has witnessed what she thinks of as the results of educating the masses in the bloodletting of the French Revolution. Eventually, Lady Ludlow does see Harry's promise, and she is instrumental in getting Mr. Horner's inheritance to the boy, so that he can go on to university with "Mr. Horner's money—or my lady's money, or Harry Gregson's money, call it which you will" (207). Mr. Gray, the intensely devout, consumptive young minister, encourages Harry's father Job Gregson, the hapless poacher, who ultimately becomes Lady Ludlow's gamekeeper. The idiosyncratic spinster Miss Galindo, who as a young girl was befriended by Lady Ludlow, many years later takes in Bessy, the orphaned illegitimate daughter of her girlhood lover.

The end of the story takes the measure of Lady Ludlow's social and moral progress and of the reformist tendencies in English culture that have prevented the countess's feared revolution. In a letter from Miss Galindo to Margaret Dawson, who has been away from Hanbury Court for a year, we learn that Lady Ludlow has a party to which she invites those she would not formerly have allowed within her doors as guests: Mrs. Brooke, the rich grocer's wife, and the illegitimate Miss Bessy—whose name was unmentionable when she first arrived in Hanbury, but who is now engaged to Mr. Gray, the evangelical, reformist vicar. Mr. Gray himself is invited, despite his former dispute with Lady Ludlow over building a school for the poor, which the noblewoman now supports. At the party Lady Ludlow looks "like a splendid fairy queen of mature age, in black velvet, and the old lace, which I have never seen her wear before since my lord's death" (208). Lady Ludlow graciously rescues Mrs. Brooke from a social faux pas: "What does my lady do? Ay! There's my own dear Lady Ludlow, God bless her! She takes out her own pocket-handkerchief, all snowy cambric, and lays it softly down on her velvet lap, for all the world as if she did it every day of her life, just like Mrs. Brooke, the baker's wife" (210).

Lady Ludlow's kind gesture takes on a sacred resonance, as she saves Mrs. Brooke from ridicule. She is a "fairy queen" who experiences a resurrection into the true significance of Christian good works, and as she performs her social ritual with the "snowy cambric," she quietly enacts a reformation of consciousness in her audience. Those who have mocked Mrs. Brooke's social ineptness are silenced, while the purest Christian soul in the room, Mr. Gray, is "made so happy by this pretty action of my lady's, that he talked away all the rest of the evening, and was the life of the company."

The story closes with the sad news of the deaths of Lady Ludlow and Mr. Gray. But the reformist and Christian work they have accomplished in their different spheres is indicated by the final line of the narrative: "As I dare say you know, the Reverend Henry Gregson is now vicar of Hanbury, and his wife is the daughter of Mr. Gray and Miss Bessy."

BIBLIOGRAPHY
Gaskell, Elizabeth. *My Lady Ludlow and Other Stories.* Oxford: Oxford University Press, 1989.
Uglow, Jenny. *Elizabeth Gaskell: A Habit of Stories.* London: Faber, 1999.
Wright, Terence. *Elizabeth Gaskell: "We Are Not Angels:" Realism, Gender, Values.* London: Macmillan, 1995.

Deborah Denenholz Morse

"MY OEDIPUS COMPLEX" FRANK O'CONNOR (1963)

In this story by FRANK O'CONNOR, the narrator, young Larry Delany, is to some extent an alter ego of O'Connor's, and his growth into adulthood is charted in several other stories. The comic discrepancy between the title's lofty psychological analysis and Larry's disgruntled, colloquial narrative voice sets the tone for O'Connor's astute depiction of a child's perception of adult relationships and sexuality. This Freudian reference is appropriate: The boy lives happily alone with his mother until his father's return from World War I. Father and son resent each other's claim to the mother's attention, but they eventually reconcile and bond with each other. Larry's bemused exasperation at adult unreasonableness, his curious mixture of perceptiveness and naivete regarding

the world around him, and his inability to comprehend the mysterious appeal his father possesses for his mother are all vividly rendered. The reconciliation of father and son brought about through mutual resentment at their joint exclusion from the mother's bed and attention in favor of a new baby is both entertaining and touching. Later stories focus on Larry's gradual loss of innocence, an important theme for O'Connor; here, childhood innocence remains intact, but Larry's jealousy and hostility keeps it far from sentimentalized. Moreover, well-meaning adult attempts to keep children in ignorance only complicate matters: Larry's mother's claim that a new baby will cost 17 and sixpence lead Larry to suspect that she is being "too exclusive," since the poor family up the road can clearly afford a "cheap baby." We glimpse initial hints of the father's alcoholism and the mother's anxieties, which other Delany stories turn to tragicomic effect. The story also gives a strong sense of life in early 20th-century Cork, with its daily economies, sense of community, and subtle class divisions.

BIBLIOGRAPHY
O'Connor, Frank. *My Oedipus Complex and Other Stories.* New York: Penguin, 1963.

Muireann O'Cinneide

"MYSTERIOUS KÔR" ELIZABETH BOWEN (1944)

"Mysterious Kôr" was first published in the 1944 volume of John Lehmann's *Penguin New Writing.* The next year ELIZABETH BOWEN placed the story last in her collection of wartime stories *The Demon Lover,* which was published in 1946 in the United States as *Ivy Gripped the Steps and Other Stories.* In the prefaces to these collections, Bowen accentuated the placement of "Mysterious Kôr" by noting "the rising tide of hallucination" in the order of the stories. Set in London during the Blitz, the story explores the psychological impact of WORLD WAR II on a soldier on leave, his lover, and her chaste flatmate. The lovers, Arthur and Pepita, begin the story near Regent's Park searching for a secluded place for lovemaking. They grow frustrated, discuss the lost city Kôr, and end their tryst unconsummated at her flat, where her roommate Callie naively welcomes them. Callie, a "brotherless virgin," at once makes their lovemaking impossible, becomes an object of Arthur's desire, and displaces her own romantic fantasies onto the couple. Harold Bloom suggests that the story is "almost a novella, complete in its radical incompleteness as an action, as a complex sexual encounter that does not take place" since "[n]othing happens, yet everything takes place that can occur, psychologically and metaphysically" (6).

The hallucinatory effects of the story conflate time and place. Chief among these effects are the processes of psychological displacement and the "[f]ull moonlight" pervading the night landscape. This opening image of "Mysterious Kôr" makes "the futility of the black-out . . . laughable," since the moonlight exposes the city and creates easy targets for bombers. However, the Londoners do not fear the Germans; they fear "something more immaterial." Such ambiguous, suggestive descriptions create the air of mystery in the story. Eudora Welty considers "Mysterious Kôr" Bowen's "most extraordinary story" in which the "deserted other city of Kôr occupies the same territory as bombed out London through the agency of the full moon at its extreme intensity." In this vein, Clare Hanson finds the story to be surrealist in that it expresses "desire through the kind of dislocated images which occur in dreams" (86).

Often anthologized, "Mysterious Kôr" draws its name from Rider Haggard's fantasy adventure novel *She* (1887). Bowen had read the novel when she was 12, and in a 1947 broadcast she explained the persistent intoxication and allure of the novel and its exotic locale in the lost African city Kôr. Despite the preoccupations of working as an air-raid warden during the Blitz, Bowen remembered the escapism and power of words proffered by Haggard's novel, and she drew on what she found to be the moral of the novel to create her story.

In the first spoken words of the story, Pepita tells Arthur that London is Kôr. Pepita feels that "here's there" and "now's then." She confides in him that she thinks of the city "all the time," and recites some lines from an Andrew Lang sonnet, also inspired by *She,* which suggests that the theme of lost love makes the power of *She* transferable to "whatever spot." At the same time, Pepita is aware of the divergent historical contexts between the late 19th century and the 1940s.

In a comment reminiscent of Joseph Conrad's *Heart of Darkness,* she explains that then "they thought they had got everything taped . . . even the middle of Africa." Now she realizes how even imaginary places such as Kôr keep endless the possibilities of exploration and enchantment.

Bowen's wartime stories occupy nearly a singular spot in documenting the effect of World War II on Britain. Along with the work of Henry Green, "Mysterious Kôr" and her other wartime stories convey the persistence of British culture in the twilight of the BRITISH EMPIRE. London survives the war, but the empire has gradually dissolved. At one point in Haggard's novel, Ayesha, the "She" of the title, says that her "empire is of the imagination." In this sense, Bowen's story is a significant transitional text in the field of postcolonial literature. The Kôr of British colonial adventure becomes a London whose reach in less expansive but whose people hold promise for the future. At the end of the story, Callie puts her loss of "love for love" into the relative perspective of the "war's total of unlived lives," and Pepita dreams of entering Kôr with Arthur as "the password, but not the answer."

BIBLIOGRAPHY

Bloom, Harold. Introducing to *Modern Critical Views: Elizabeth Bowen,* 1–11. New York: Chelsea, 1987.

Bowen, Elizabeth. *The Demon Lover.* London: Cape, 1945.

———. *Ivy Gripped the Steps and Other Stories.* New York: Knopf, 1946.

———. "Rider Haggard: She." In *The Mulberry Tree,* 246–250. London: Virago, 1986.

Haggard, Rider. *She.* 1887. New York: Modern Library, 2002.

Hanson, Clare. *Short Stories and Short Fictions, 1880–1980.* London: Macmillan, 1985.

Lang, Andrew. *The Grass of Parnassus.* 1888. London: Longmans, 1892.

Lassner, Phyllis. *Elizabeth Bowen: A Study of the Short Fiction.* New York: Macmillan, 1992.

Welty, Eudora. "Seventy-Nine Stories to Read Again," review of *The Collected Stories of Elizabeth Bowen, New York Times Book Review,* 8 February 1981, p. 22.

Damon Franke

N

NAIPAUL, V. S. (1932–) Vidiadhar Suraj-prasad Naipaul's life story is told in some variation in many of his fictional narratives: the migration of his grandparents from northern India to the Caribbean as indentured laborers; his birth in Chaguanas, Trinidad, on August 17, 1932 and his upbringing in a large Brahmin family among a diverse community of Africans, Caribbeans, Chinese, Indians, and Europeans; his father Seepersad's career as a journalist and author; his education at a racially mixed colonial school; his scholarship to Oxford and subsequent residence in England, where he still lives. Naipaul's biography is especially important since his writing is a mixture of fiction and autobiography commonly referred to as semiautobiographical. The anonymous narrators of his stories often resemble Naipaul himself in their imaginative attempts to impose order on traumatic histories. All share his sense of exile as an Indian who never lived in India, a West Indian never at home in the West Indies, and a resident of England separated from the English heritage of which he is now inescapably a part. He has never lost the feeling of living "in the other man's country."

After Oxford, Naipaul worked as an editor for the BBC series *Caribbean Voices*. Naipaul's story collection *Miguel Street* (1959), his first complete work though the third to be published, is a series of sketches of eccentric local characters drawn from the streets of Trinidad. These stories are brief and concise and are narrated from a child's viewpoint with an adult's retrospective judgment. The opening story, "Bogart," portrays an uncommunicative man, named after the American film actor, who impresses his friends with a hard-boiled attitude. Like many of the book's characters, absurd poses cover an underlying despair. What is at first amusing expresses the poverty of life in a decolonized nation with little opportunity. The title character of the story "Man-man" is a local eccentric of dubious sanity who runs in every election, barks like a dog, and announces himself as a new messiah until the crowd, at his bidding, ties him to a cross and throws stones at him. Man-man's performance leads the narrator to question whether he is mad at all and to implicate the community for going along with such destructive fantasies. The broken Trinidadian English spoken by the characters implies a transitional society without England's stability or its own autonomy. The comic tone is characteristic of Naipaul's early fictions, which are often farcical accounts of formerly colonized citizens adjusting to independence. Only later in his career would Naipaul recognize his comic style, in which anxiety lies just beneath the surface of the jokes, as a way of coping with a harsh world.

Naipaul's early novels examine the residual effects of the British Empire on Caribbean life and are considered by many to be his finest. *The Mystic Masseur* (1957; made into a film by Merchant and Ivory in 2002) established Naipaul's reputation in Britain seven years after his arrival, but *A House for Mr. Biswas* (1961) is the novel that would make him famous. This novel is Naipaul's effort to adapt the forms of European fiction to non-European communities without a stable sense of history or tradition. Mohun Biswas's efforts to obtain a home and, more important, a secure place in the world are the subject of this novel. He dies without having paid off the mortgage. It is the last of Naipaul's comic works, often described as Dickensian in its blend of caricature and social realism. Many consider this novel to be Naipaul's best work for its balance of unique colonial life with universal human suffering.

Later novels like *A Bend in the River* (1979) and *Guerillas* (the novel that established his reputation in the United States in 1975) move away from West Indian settings to explore various forms of exile and colonial heritage. *The Mimic Men* (1967) uses flashbacks rather than chronological narrative to explore the colonial past of displaced Trinidadian Ralph Kripal Singh, who moves between London and the fictional island Isabella. Naipaul later described the novel as a concrete way of writing about "colonial schizophrenia" in which men imitate or mimic the former imperial power because they have grown to distrust everything about themselves. The best-seller *The Enigma of Arrival* (1987) is heavily autobiographical in its hauntingly beautiful account of the author's attempt to settle in the rural village of Wiltshire, where England's imperial past is imprinted on the landscape. Seemingly benign aspects of the English estate, like the creeping ivy, in fact show the effects of imperialism. Whereas the early works rely heavily on slapstick comedy, a pervasive sense of sadness and loss pervade this elegiac novel.

In a Free State, the sequence of three stories awarded the Booker Prize in 1971, explores the experience of homelessness that features in nearly all of Naipaul's work. Paul Theroux describes the book as the "fiction of rootlessness." These stories speak for the homeless and the exiled: an Indian in the United States, a West Indian in Britain, and an Englishman in Africa. Freedom is an insecure state that often ends in violence and humiliation in these stories. The prologue takes place aboard a ship bound for Egypt on which an English traveler, who considers himself "a citizen of the world" with little use for nationality, consequently finds himself unprotected from the cruel harassment of the other nationalistic passengers. The first story, "One out of Many," tells of Santosh, an illegal immigrant from India, who discovers the high cost of freedom once he is no longer able to rely on Hindu traditions. This lesson is painfully clear when he accidentally calls his employer *sahib* ("master") in a servile, undignified way that exposes the close relation between slavery and the migrant's servility. "In a Free State," the third story, portrays Bobby and Linda, ineffectual English civil servants in the midst of a civil war in a recently independent African state. This story links political and sexual disorder before ending, like many of Naipaul's fictions, in a humiliating act of violence that turns upside down the power roles.

Naipaul is a prolific—and controversial—travel writer who has written extensively on the West Indies, India, Africa, Asia, and the American South. These pieces express Naipaul's vivid descriptive ability, sense of detachment, and dissatisfaction with former colonies (including a notorious remark in *The Middle Passage* that "nothing was created in the West Indies"). Many of the travelogues criticize postcolonial countries for a lack of economic stability, authentic culture, and progressive vision. His travel writings are among his most controversial, leading to charges of Eurocentrism, racism, and nostalgia, especially in his negative conclusions about Islamic nations. He has been accused of speaking from a privileged position that discounts the extent to which formerly colonized people share his experience of displacement, hybridity, and shame. Like the story collections, these travelogues often comprise self-contained episodes thematically linked together, as in *A Way in the World* (1994), which presents semiautobiographical stories about historical figures like Sir Walter Raleigh who have visited the West Indies, or in the travel book *Beyond Belief: Islamic Excursions among the Converted People* (1998), which Naipaul describes as "a book of stories."

Naipaul's reputation as "the world's writer" comes from the ever-broadening geography of his writing as well as his claim that he does not to speak for any country. We are left with two Naipauls not easily reconcilable: the controversial personality famous for irascible and provocative commentary and the measured prose stylist who writes with a graceful touch comparable to the finest modernist authors. While we may squirm at the crude remarks he makes in interviews, the fiction itself often manages to escape such reductive vision in its remarkable philosophical and aesthetic breadth for which Naipaul was awarded the Nobel Prize in 2001. The title of his Nobel lecture, "Two Worlds," expresses his sense of never feeling at home in the world, which has inspired his best writing. It is these moments of insight into the psychological effects of the colonial past, the unseen wounds inflicted on a society, for which he will be remembered and celebrated.

BIBLIOGRAPHY

Bhabha, Homi. "Naipaul's Vernacular Cosmopolitans," *The Chronicle of Higher Education,* 26 October 2001, p. B13.

Jussawalla, Feroza, ed. *Conversations with V. S. Naipaul.* Oxford: University Press of Mississippi, 1997.

Schiff, Stephen. "The Ultimate Exile," *New Yorker,* 23 May 1994, pp. 60–71.

Gorra, Michael Edward. *After Empire: Scott, Naipaul, Rushdie.* Chicago: University of Chicago Press, 1997.

Naipaul, V. S. *The Guardian of Gurudera and Other Stories.* London: Deutsch, 1976.

———. *A House for Mr. Biswas.* London: Deutsch, 1971.

———. *In a Free State.* London: Deutsch, 1971.

———. *Literary Occasions.* London: Picador, 2003.

———. *A Man of Mystery and Other Stories.* London: Penguin, 1998.

———. *Miguel Street.* London: Deutsch, 1959.

———. *Reading and Writing: A Personal Account.* New York: New York Review of Books, 2000.

———. "Two Worlds." Nobel lecture. December 7, 2001. Available online. URL: http://www.nobel.se/literature/laureates/2001/naipaul-lecture.html. Accessed June 2, 2006.

Matthew Rubery

"NAPOLEON AND THE SPECTRE"

CHARLOTTE BRONTË (1833, 1925) CHARLOTTE BRONTË wrote "Napoleon and the Spectre" in 1833, when she was 17. The story is taken from the manuscript of her novella *The Green Dwarf.* In its original context, the tale is overheard being told by "a little dapper man" to a group of Frenchmen at an inn (1996, 127). When it is finished, Napoleon himself enters the inn and arrests the little man for having recounted such a "scandalous anecdote" (1996, 130). Although extracts from the story appeared in a literary journal in 1897, it was not published in its entirety until 1919, when Clement Shorter printed a limited edition for private circulation.

It was published for a wide audience for the first time in *The Twelve Adventurers and Other Stories* (1925) and has since appeared in editions of Brontë's juvenilia and in various short story anthologies.

Brontë's amusing ghost story is a gothic parody and a satire of patriarchal authority. Her irreverent portrayal of Napoleon, or "Nap," may owe, in part, to a friendly rivalry with her brother Branwell, who was her early writing partner. Branwell chose Napoleon to be the hero of his earliest stories, while Charlotte preferred the Duke of Wellington (Alexander, 27). Her spoof begins abruptly with the line, "Well, as I was saying, the Emperor got into bed." The unnamed storyteller proceeds to relate that Napoleon's repose is disturbed by strange noises. A groan emanating from a closet causes him to leap out of bed and threaten to shoot whomever is inside. The only response is a "short, sharp laugh" (1996, 139), which may suggest to the reader that the mysterious occupant is already dead. When Napoleon opens the closet door he hears a rustling noise. But he soon realizes that the sound was caused by a cloak that had fallen from its peg, so he returns to bed, "[h]alf-ashamed" of his superstitious fears (1996, 140). This unsatisfactory explanation, which fails to account for the groan or the laughter, parodies a gothic device popularized by the novelist Ann Radcliffe, whereby seemingly supernatural events are depicted, only to be explained later in rational terms. Through her humorous invocation of the "explained supernatural," Brontë foreshadows the bathetic ending of the story.

Just as Napoleon is about to close his eyes again, a specter appears before him. Although its identity is as yet unknown, Brontë's comic-grotesque description provides the initiated reader with several clues. It wears "a black cravat very tightly round its neck, and confined by two little sticks behind each ear. The countenance was livid; the tongue protruded from between the teeth, and the eyes all glazed and bloodshot started with frightful prominence from their sockets." (1996, 140). An example of the story's pervasive irony occurs when this dreadful figure addresses Napoleon gravely as the "lifter of the Eagle Standard!" (1996, 140), an impressive title incongruous with the image of the emperor huddled in bed "[s]weating with terror" (1996, 140).

The wall of the bedchamber opens, and the ghost leads Napoleon through a passage and out onto the streets of Paris. They arrive at a grand house and enter a large hall, where Napoleon sees a row of masked women and hears a wild strain of eerie music. The mystery is elucidated when Napoleon comes to his senses and finds himself in the midst of a ball that Marie Louise (his second wife) is throwing. He has been sleepwalking and now stands before his wife and her guests in his nightgown. When he asks dazedly for "Piche," the identity of the specter is revealed: General Charles Pichegru was arrested for his involvement in a plot to overthrow Napoleon and was found strangled to death in his cell while awaiting trial. Although it was sometimes thought he had committed suicide, this story suggests that the narrator (and perhaps Brontë herself) believed Napoleon to be guilty of his murder (1996, 138). Brontë's satire ends with a comic flourish. When the humiliated emperor realizes it has all been a dream, he is seized with a "fit of catalepsy" that lasts for two days (1996, 143).

In juvenile works such as "Napoleon and the Spectre," Brontë practiced her technique as a writer and explored themes she would develop in her mature novels. For example, the trope of the explained supernatural is used for comic effect in this early story but is treated more seriously in *Jane Eyre* (1847), in which mysterious noises and occurrences at Thornfield Hall are ultimately attributed to Rochester's mad wife. In both instances, Brontë depicts the apparently supernatural in order to create an atmosphere of suspense and explore the theme of imagination itself.

BIBLIOGRAPHY

Alexander, Christine. *The Early Writings of Charlotte Brontë.* New York: Prometheus, 1983.

Brontë, Charlotte. *Charlotte Brontë: Juvenilia, 1829–1835.* Edited and with an introduction by Juliet Barker. London: Penguin, 1996.

———. "Napoleon and the Spectre." In *The Twelve Adventures and Other Stories,* 137–43. London: Hodder, 1925.

Natalie Neill

"NEEDLECASE, THE" ELIZABETH BOWEN (1941)

This short story was published in ELIZABETH BOWEN's 1941 collection *Look at All Those Roses.* "The Needlecase" recounts the arrival of Miss Fox, a young seamstress, at the home of the Forresters, a formerly aristocratic family that no longer has the means to keep up the family home or the manner of living expected of them. They have hired Miss Fox to give their home and their clothes a semblance of wealth in order to help woo the heiress to whom the currently absent eldest son Arthur has become attached: "Everyone knew, Arthur knew, that Arthur must marry money." This, it is made clear, is but the latest in a series of eligible young women that Arthur has hoped to marry, and his absence throughout the narrative is portrayed as typical of the young man, whose duty is essentially to be agreeable to others in the hope that this will one day make him his fortune.

The Forresters are able to afford the seamstress's services only because she, too, has fallen into desperate circumstances: She has an illegitimate child she is working to support. The family is both fascinated by the newcomer and her story and eager for her services; one of the daughters, Toddy, rushes to the attic where Miss Fox has been installed, bringing her dresses in need of repair. As Miss Fox looks over the work at hand, Toddy inspects the seamstress's belongings, most notably the needlecase of the title. "'As large as a family Bible,' said Toddy, pleased. And like a family Bible, it had a photo stuck inside." The photograph is of the woman's illegitimate son, and the seamstress soon snatches the needlecase away. The family continues to discuss the two matters at hand: the scandalous story of their current visitor, and their current misery while waiting for the money that will be the result of Arthur's potential marriage. When the second daughter, Angela, comes to speak to the mysterious Miss Fox, she is told a story: Miss Fox has met the absent Arthur at another house where she was employed. He asked her for one of her sewing dummies to use in a game, and despite her best judgment ("I should have known better; I ought to have known my place."), she lent it to him. The dummy fell and was damaged, and though Arthur was sorry, he never made amends, and Miss Fox's reputation suffered. While telling this tale, the seamstress offers her needlecase to Angela, who is repairing a stocking, and the photograph inside takes on new significance: The boy in the picture is the very image of Arthur himself.

The device of using a family that has lost its wealth and the ancestral home that is slowly bankrupting them is a recurrent theme in Bowen's work, and though it is never explicitly stated, this theme undoubtedly alludes to the decaying situation of the Anglo-Irish (portrayed in such Bowen novels as *The Last September, A World of Love, The House in Paris,* and *The Heat of the Day* as well as in short stories such as "The Back Drawing-Room," "Her Table Spread," "Sunday Afternoon," and "A Day in the Dark"). Analyses of "The Needlecase" often focus on the strong implications of class hierarchy: The name of the main character, after all, alludes to the fox hunt, one of the aristocracy's favorite ways of amusing themselves. However, as the conclusion of the short story makes clear, the character is associated not only with animals but also with objects: She substitutes herself for the dummy in her story, a comparison reinforced by the narrator's description of the character as "sculpted" and "carven." Indeed, the other principal character in the story is wholly object: The family home is both the setting of the narrative and the motivation and justification for the action. The description of it as "a disheartened edition of Mansfield Park" obviously refers to the Austen novel of the same name and further emphasizes the importance of class distinctions in the story. Like Mr. Bertram, absent while attending to his plantations, Arthur resorts to questionable means to keep the family home in existence; like Fanny Price, Miss Fox is both accepted and kept apart from the aristocratic family with whom she has a close bond. (Acknowledged or not, her son represents the next generation of Forresters.) The difference in the fortunes of the Austen and Bowen heroines suggests that in Ireland, the breach between the Protestant ascendancy and their Irish neighbors cannot be easily "patched up," even by the talented seamstress.

BIBLIOGRAPHY
Bowen, Elizabeth. *Collected Stories of Elizabeth Bowen.* London: Vintage, 1999.

Shannon Wells-Lassagne

"NEWS OF THE ENGAGEMENT" ARNOLD BENNETT (1907) A lighthearted story published in Arnold Bennett's *The Grim Smile of the Five Towns.* The story is narrated by a young man, Philip, who travels from London to his childhood home in Bursely, one of the five towns indicated in the title of the collection. In the story, Philip returns home to visit his widowed mother for Christmas and also to inform her of his engagement to a young woman named Agnes. Although Philip regularly writes to his mother, he feels it impossible to explain his feelings for Agnes and their recent engagement in a letter. Upon greeting his mother, Philip notices that she is more excited and nervous than usual, and he guesses that she has somehow discovered his engagement. His suspicions are further raised when he sees that the dining table has been set for three. Instead of Agnes, however, an old family friend, Mr. Nixon, arrives for dinner. Philip admits that he is slightly dismayed since he desires to disclose his news to his mother in private. Unable to stop thinking of his engagement, Philip leaves dinner momentarily to dispatch a letter to Agnes informing her of his safe arrival. When he returns home he is met by a solitary Mr. Nixon, who tells Philip that he has become engaged to his mother. Mr. Nixon explains that they had gradually fallen in love, but that Philip's mother did not feel comfortable disclosing the news in a letter. Philip laughs at the irony of the situation and decides not to reveal his own good news that evening. At the conclusion of the story, Philip admits that he had never thought of his mother as a woman with a future; he had never before realized that she was desirable.

While Bennett (1867–1931) is perhaps best known for his realist provincial novels, such as *The Old Wives' Tale* (1908) and *Clayhanger* (1910), he was also a prolific short story writer. In fact, he first received critical attention in 1895 with the publication of his short story "The Letter Home" in the *YELLOW BOOK*. Throughout his lifetime, Bennett published seven volumes of short stories.

Bennett was born in Hanley, Staffordshire, one of the five pottery towns that served as the setting for much of his fiction. In "News of the Engagement," Philip returns home to the potteries from London and assumes that nothing has changed in his sleepy childhood town. He is surprised to learn, though, that life has changed for his mother. Philip's surprise that a man might desire his mother and that "her lonely existence in that house was not all that she had the right to demand from life" reveals his naïveté and his youthful self-absorption (244). His realization also highlights the fact that women's sexual existence did not end in youth or middle age. Bennett felt impelled to represent this in his fiction. He once claimed, "I had always revolted against the absurd youthfulness, the unfading youthfulness of the average heroine" (preface to *The Old Wives' Tale*), and his novel *Leonora* (1903), in which the heroine is 40 years old, is an early manifestation of this revolt. The desire to depict realistic lives of older women would later influence his writing of *The Old Wives' Tale,* which traces the lives of its two heroines, Constance and Sophia, from youth to old age.

BIBLIOGRAPHY

Bennett, Arnold. "News of the Engagement," In *The Tales of the Five Towns*. London: Chatto & Windus, 1964.

———. *The Old Wives' Tale*. 1908. New York: The Modern Library, 1999.

Broomfield, Olga. *Arnold Bennett*. Boston: Twayne, 1984.

Lucas, John. *Arnold Bennett: A Study of His Fiction*. London: Methuen, 1974.

Tara MacDonald

NEW WOMAN A term coined by British feminist Sarah Grand in an 1894 essay to describe an independent woman who seeks achievement and self-fulfillment beyond the realm of marriage and family. According to Grand, the New Woman "proclaimed for herself what was wrong with Home-is-the-Woman's-Sphere, and proscribed the remedy" (142). In a historical moment when women were beginning to attend university, enter the professions, and campaign for political representation, Grand's coinage of this term struck a chord, providing a label for a new style of femininity that had already emerged in Anglo-American culture. Soon, the "New Woman" became a trans-Atlantic stereotype; she was an educated young woman of "advanced," feminist views who lived an independent, Bohemian lifestyle. The stereotypical New Woman was associated with various ideographic "props." Bicycles and latchkeys symbolized her freedom to move about public space; cigarettes, books, spectacles, and golf clubs symbolized her adoption of

masculine pursuits and activities. The New Woman was mostly a middle- and upper-class figure; wealth and class position facilitated her choice to forgo the economic security of marriage and provided her with social privileges like a university education. While often the target of social derision in the popular press, the New Woman was also a mode of articulating real shifts in the relative freedom and occupational choice available to young women from the 1880s. As an image of modern femininity, she was a source of alarm to cultural conservatives, who considered her an emblem of degeneracy.

On the heels of the New Woman phenomenon, a new literary genre emerged called New Woman fiction. Most New Woman novels and short stories are realist or naturalist in genre, but they attempt a more candid account of women's experiences and psychology than previous writers had done. As GEORGE EGERTON put it, in literature, "there was only one small plot left for [woman] to tell: the terra incognita of herself, as she knew herself to be, not as man liked to imagine her—in a word, to give herself away as man had given himself away in his writings" (quoted in Nelson, 3). Egerton, like many New Woman writers, treated women's sexuality with a frankness that shocked many of her contemporaries. In 1893, she published a series of short stories in the *YELLOW BOOK,* an avant-garde British magazine associated with the Aesthetic movement (see AESTHETICISM); the series, titled *Keynotes,* was a cultural sensation, as was her second series of short stories, *Discords* (1894). The *Yellow Book* was a key forum for British New Woman short fiction, also publishing Netta Syrett's "Thy Heart's Desire" (1894), Victoria Cross's "THEODORA: A FRAGMENT" (1895), and Ada Radford's "Lot 99" (1896). Other British New Woman writers included Sarah Grand, ELLA D'ARCY, Olive Schreiner, and Mabel Wotton.

Although "New Woman fiction" was a predominantly British term, it is now commonly applied to turn-of-the-century U.S. writing as well. New Woman short fiction in the United States includes work by Charlotte Perkins Gilman (such as "The Yellow Wallpaper" [1892]), Kate Chopin (such as the novella *The Awakening* [1899]), and Edith Wharton. African-American women writers of the period, including Pauline

Hopkins and Jessie Redmon Fauset, applied New Woman themes to the unique social conditions of African-American women. New Women writers on both sides of the Atlantic were heavily influenced by Henrik Ibsen, a Norwegian dramatist whose plays often focused on women's experience. Other male writers of the period who wrote about New Women include George Gissing, THOMAS HARDY, HENRY JAMES, and George Bernard Shaw. The term "New Woman" is particularly associated with the years 1880–1920, but its meaning has become somewhat adaptable, and it is continuously reinvented to describe new developments in feminism.

BIBLIOGRAPHY

Egerton, George. *Keynotes and Discords.* Edited and with an introduction by Martha Vicinus. London: Virago, 1983.

Grand, Sarah. "The New Aspect of the Woman Question," *North American Review* 158 (March 1894): 270–276. Reprinted in Nelson, 141–146.

Ledger, Sally. *The New Woman: Fiction and Feminism at the fin de siècle.* Manchester, England: Manchester University Press, 1997.

Nelson, Carolyn Christensen, ed. *A New Woman Reader: Fiction, Articles, Drama of the 1890s.* Peterborough, Ontario: Broadview, 2001.

Richardson, Angelique. *Women Who Did: Short Stories by Men and Women.* London: Penguin, 2002.

Elizabeth Carolyn Miller

NIGHTS H.D. (HILDA DOOLITTLE) (1935) Hilda Doolittle (1886–1961), an American-born author who worked under the penname H. D., did much of her writing while living in London, England. She was initially best known for her poetry despite an abundant corpus of plays and fiction and nonfiction prose. It was thought for many years that Ezra Pound (the modernist poet to whom she was engaged briefly; see MODERNISM) was largely responsible for developing H. D.'s early "imagistic" style. However, recent criticism suggests that H. D.'s idiom originated with her and in fact influenced Pound. Her later marriage to poet Richard Aldington led to her involvement with the magazine the *Egoist,* which she edited for a short time. More than two decades after her death in 1961, H. D. gained significant critical attention due in large part to the work of feminist critics Susan

Stanford Friedman and Rachel Blau DuPlessis, who read H. D.'s prose and poetry with a critical eye toward feminine, lesbian, and bisexual discourses. Texts such as Friedman's *Penelope's Web: Gender, Modernity, H. D.'s Fiction* (1990) helped bring H. D.'s prose into the critical fold. Referring to H. D.'s maternal, life-giving poetics as the "gynopoetic," Friedman is one of many critics who view the author's work as a precursor to that of French feminists, including Julia Kristeva and Helen Cixous (11). Miranda Hickman's *The Geometry of Modernism* (2006) calls yet more attention to H. D.'s important prose work, taking into account the past three decades of H. D. criticism. By focusing primarily on *Nights,* which previously had been underrepresented in H. D. criticism, Hickman does important work toward challenging some of the assumptions about H. D.'s oeuvre that have reigned since the 1980s. "With its presentation," writes Hickman, "of an idealized geometric body, *Nights* not only offers an alternative to the childbearing body but in fact indicates a profound discomfort with that body, resisting its dominion and even critiquing its entailments for women" (331).

Written under the pseudonym John Helforth, *Nights* is one of H. D.'s several romans à clef, including *HERmione* and *Bid Me to Live.* Based on her own life, these narratives helped the author work through challenges related to her writing, mental health, and bisexuality. One of five novellas in a series, *Nights* was published first in a tiny edition for H. D.'s friends in 1935 and republished for larger distribution in 1986, with an introduction by the author's daughter, Perdita Schaffner. Schaffner was adopted during H. D.'s lifetime by her female partner, Winifred (Bryher) Ellerman, and Bryher's husband of convenience, Kenneth Macpherson, who had also been H. D.'s lover. Bryher and Macpherson are recast as the characters Renne and Neil, respectively, in *Nights.*

Nights begins with a prologue in Part I by the fictional John Helforth, seen by many as "H. D.'s alter ego" (Doolittle, ix). As John Helforth explains, his mission is to read the journal entries and try to understand the protagonist's suicide. Part II consists of the journal entries by the protagonist of the story proper, Natalia, who, in turn, is a thinly veiled representation of H. D. herself. By writing a version of herself in Natalia and rewriting another version in John Helforth (both of whom are written over the living, breathing author, H. D.), the author creates a text in which she is at once male and female, dead and living, writer and critic, recalling the palimpsest structure often attributed to H. D.'s work. Literally, a "palimpsest" is a manuscript in which later writing has been superimposed on earlier (effaced) writing; this was initially practiced as a means of conserving paper. For H. D. the palimpsest structure enabled her to rewrite classical myths with a female voice, express bisexuality in artistic form, and replicate aspects of the human psyche with which H. D. and her analysts (including Sigmund Freud) were concerned. In *Nights,* this structure also contributes to the mysterious atmosphere surrounding Natalia's apparent suicide and the critical reading John Helforth must perform to uncover the mystery.

John Helforth serves as a narrative device for critical distance from Natalia's journal entries. H. D. therefore was able to write Natalia's intensely emotional, "high flown," "cryptic" journal entries while preserving a critical distance resembling that of the detective or the psychoanalyst (ix). DETECTIVE FICTION was popularized during the 19th and 20th centuries by authors such as WILKIE COLLINS, ARTHUR CONAN DOYLE, AGATHA CHRISTIE, and Edgar Allan Poe. John Helforth in *Nights,* however, bears a stronger resemblance to later versions of the disorganized and often psychologically disturbed detectives of the 20th century in fictions by authors such as Raymond Chandler and Dashiell Hammett. The gothic and mystical elements of the earlier detective fictions can be traced in *Nights,* while the psychoanalytic elements of the later detective fictions are particularly relevant: The suicide itself, after all, suggests that the most troubling mystery is that of the human mind.

Having faced excessive trauma, including the birth of a stillborn child and the loss of her brother in the war, H. D. sought distance from her immediate environment—as a psychoanalyst maintains distance from her analysand—and left London. Like H. D., Natalia has been living abroad for many years, prompting her friends to question: "O, she's always abroad, why doesn't she stay in England?" This "living abroad" is itself redoubled in H. D.'s case, for she is already an American abroad in England who then imagines herself "abroad" when out of England. Therefore, H. D. represents in the figure of Natalia her own otherness, or "alterity," relative to national English society, as well as to conventional sexual norms within that society. Moreover, *Nights* gestures toward the postwar desire among Londoners to travel abroad in an effort to escape the tragic events they had faced.

Natalia's journal entries tell the story of her life leading up to the suicide. In an attempt to heal the pain she has sustained as a result of her desertion by her husband, Neil, in his pursuit of an openly gay lifestyle, Natalia has sex with a young man named David Leavenworth. The relationship that develops between Natalia and David primarily constitutes the action of the journal entries, but the most crucial elements of the text involve the mental, spiritual, bodily, and linguistic challenges she must face as a result of Neil's abandonment, her bisexuality, and the writing itself. Contrasting the organic fluidity of the stream of consciousness with the "psycho-surgical" invasiveness of psychoanalytic thought, Natalia's prose reveals H. D.'s struggles in a rich, highly stylized, but accessible narrative. Natalia's journal entries effectively probe the unsolvable problems of H. D.'s life, and they appropriately leave open the many questions they pose.

BIBLIOGRAPHY
Doolittle, Hilda (H. D.). *Nights.* New York: New Directions, 1986.
DuPlessis, Rachel Blau. *H. D.: The Career of That Struggle.* Brighton and Sussex: Harvester Press, 1986.
Friedman, Susan Stanford. *Penelope's Web: Gender, Modernity, H. D.'s Fiction.* Cambridge and New York: Cambridge University Press, 1990.
Guest, Barbara. *Herself Defined: The Poet H. D. and Her World.* Garden City, N.Y.: Doubleday, 1984.
Hickman, Miranda. *The Geometry of Modernism: The Vorticist Idiom in Lewis, Pound, H. D. and Yeats.* Austin: University of Texas Press, 2006.

Lindsay Holmgren

"NOCTURNE, A" GEORGE EGERTON (1897)

This story by the NEW WOMAN writer GEORGE EGERTON (Mary Chavelita Dunne) (1859–45) first appeared in the collection *Symphonies* published by John Lane.

While surveying the "human flotsam and jetsam" (187) of the Thames embankment one night from his room, the narrator, a young bachelor, sees a woman in distress, reeling at the river's edge. Fearing she may be suicidal (and believing her to be genteel), he leads her back to his flat to recover, where she stays the night and leaves the following morning. This unconventional meeting of the lives of a struggling, modern young woman and a sympathetic New Man allows Egerton to challenge social and sexual mores, using a realism that hints at the emotional and material crisis of the young woman at its center.

This New Woman figure mixes typically feminine modesty and sensitivity with qualities of frankness and openness that the narrator finds compelling. While the discretion of the incident is established, as is the woman's "purity" and shabby genteel respectability, there is clearly a sexual and romantic tension experienced by the narrator. The woman undresses from her wet costume in an adjoining room, recalling Sue Bridehead the heroine in THOMAS HARDY's novel *Jude the Obscure* (1895), but the sense of scandal does not have a tragic note. An ideal of equitable companionship between the sexes is conveyed: They enjoy a cigarette together, and she shakes his hand in "an honest grip, like a nice lad might have done" (192). He recognizes "the kin feeling of race" (192): Like many of Egerton's characters, they are both of Irish descent—a reference to the author's own parentage. The next morning the woman recounts her story to him: Orphaned, bereaved, and fallen on hard times, she is struggling to make a living, latterly as a writer, and is in ill health. Eager to assist her, he writes an introduction to recommend her to a woman editor he knows. A second, brief, encounter follows that evening, ending the story on a positive note for her future—she has got work—if a wistful one for his: "It was jolly to have a woman—a woman of that kind, you know—taking an interest in one's first editions" (196).

BIBLIOGRAPHY

Egerton, George. "'A Nocturne,' *Symphonies.*" London and New York: John Lane, 1897. Reprinted in *Women Who Did: Stories by Men and Women, 1890–1914,* Edited by Angelique Richardson, London: Penguin, 2002.

Lyssa Randolph

"NOT NOT WHILE THE GIRO" JAMES KELMAN (1983)

"Not not while the giro" is the title story of JAMES KELMAN's breakthrough collection. Waiting for his giro (unemployment allowance) the hero of this freewheeling black comedy epitomizes the qualities of Kelman's writing that led one early reviewer to proclaim him "both angrier and funnier than [Samuel] Beckett." The dark humor and mock-heroic digressiveness of SAMUEL BECKETT are clear influences on Kelman's style, and the famous lines that close Beckett's *Molloy* ("I can't go on, I'll go on") might serve as a précis of this story's plot. It begins with a Beckettian "bellyful of lamentations": A penniless bachelor in a rooming house relates the circumstances of his penury and the seeming impossibility of improving his lot. Yet by the end of the story, our hero's account of his pitiful, going-nowhere existence has evolved into a richly ironic fantasy of independent nomadism, a life of never-ending escape from stagnation. This character has nothing to live for, save his giro (i.e., his means of "going on," of pointlessly surviving), so he escapes into a fantasy of another sort of "giro": a circuitous walking trip around the coastal roads of Scotland, or, possibly, an endless hike shuttling between the northern- and southernmost points of Great Britain. Along the way, we are treated to James Kelman's first truly exceptional performance as a prose stylist and his arrival as a humorous writer.

The story begins and ends in media res, highlighting the unbroken routine of the hero's life as well as his inability to pin down his roving imagination. He begins with an inventory of his present state of deprivation: He is nearly out of the "one essential luxury" of tobacco, but he does possess a curious asset: his coat. "My coat is in the fashion of yesteryear but I am wearing it. . . . This shrewd man I occasionally have dealings with refused said coat on the grounds of said lapels rendering the coat an undesired object by those who frequent said man's premises. Yet I would have reckoned most purchasers of 2nd hand clothing to be wholly unaware of fashions current or olden." The irony of this overly formal diction stems from the vast discrepancy between the hero's gallant, decorous language and his economic circumstances: the "shrewd man [he] occasionally has dealings with" is not a business associate but a pawnbroker.

Kelman exploits this talent for mimicry to satirize the pomposity and politics of the 1980s British establishment. His character's mock-ceremonious speech, with its evocations of tradition and authority, embodies a romantic fantasy about British culture and society. Kelman lampoons the aristocratic fiction that sees the British working class either as plucky self-starters "playing the game"—full of cheerful self-reliance and dogged resolution to better their lot—or as dissipated, insolent parasites. By this mythology, poverty is always the fault of the lazy poor. The system of values this mythology depends on never questions the virtues of free-market capitalism; it is a worldview that excludes the reality of the protagonist's position as an unemployed bachelor struggling to survive.

Though narrated in the first person, this story forecasts Kelman's later experiments in rendering a first-person experience of reality in more objective, third-person form. The comic tension of its speeches often derives from its convincing mimicry of a richly descriptive, inflated style of upper-class speech. The polished narrative voice found in the novels of Sir WALTER SCOTT, for example, which speaks in a language of gentle authority and sensitive discernment, richly embroidering the less sumptuous reality perceived by lower-class characters, is put into the mocking mouth of a ne'er-do-well. In other circumstances, presumably, the learning and wit displayed by this character could be put to more productive use; as the protagonist muses, "one's mental capacities would be bound to make more use of their potential without problems at the fundamental level"—that is, the economic level. The essentially political point of the story is to remind us that an expensive education is not a prerequisite for formidable powers of linguistic invention, and that the economic conditions of this man's existence prevent him from reaching his potential.

The giro of the title can also refer to a circuit or tour, which is what the protagonist imagines a carefree life to consist of. He imagines the delicious freedom of itinerant begging, not having to depend on government assistance to survive: "The minimum money required. Neither broo nor social security. The self sufficiency of the sweetly self employed." A giro-free life of independent subsistence is, thus, a life of never-ending "giro," giro without end. The story's warmly sardonic climax imagines the carefree existence of the Scottish Coast Road walker. It is the wonderfully inventive, anarchic imagination of the protagonist that makes his life worth living, even in the most brutal conditions.

BIBLIOGRAPHY

Kelman, James. *Not not while the giro.* Edinburgh: Polygon, 1983.

Scott Hames

NOT THE END OF THE WORLD KATE ATKINSON (2002)

KATE ATKINSON entered the ranks of critically acclaimed contemporary writers with her debut novel, *Behind the Scenes at the Museum* (1995). Awarding that novel the prestigious Whitbread prize for Overall Book of the Year in 1995 (see AWARDS AND PRIZES), the judges commended Atkinson for both her ambitious historical scope and her command of narrative models. The attention to the everyday material details of a historical period, combined with the stylistic range, nonchalantly including realism, parody, fantasy and tragedy, which distinguished *Behind the Scenes at the Museum*, also features in Atkinson's three later novels.

Although her novels have generated much critical attention, Atkinson first published short stories; she cites the work of two American short story writers, Robert Coover and Donald Barthelme, as having propelled her into becoming a writer herself. All the stories collected in *Not the End of the World* (2002) reflect Atkinson's overriding interest in the dense and inescapable significances of personal relations in women's lives. The stories are crowded with families, friendships, births, marriages, estrangements, and deaths. But while private life and the suffering it inflicts provide the framework for these texts, and while family life in particular generates their emotional depth, Atkinson is nothing if not a historically sensitive writer who weaves social and political events and anxieties into the context and textures of her characters' lives.

"Charlene and Trudi Go Shopping," a story commissioned for the Ilkley Literary Festival in 2001, begins with two friends shopping for a birthday present. They wander through an elegant and expensive department store uninspired by the mountains of goods on display but compensating for the banality or inaccessibility of the merchandise by undertaking imagined voyages of exotic, indulgent consumption. The narrative is impersonal and elliptic: The narrator reveals only slowly, but then unambiguously, that the city the two friends move around in is a battleground. Bombs explode softy in the distance, electricity and water supplies are turned off, and citizens sleep with guns under their pillows in a story that comments obliquely but effectively on the atmosphere of fear and anxious stoicism that emerged in the Western world after September 11, 2001.

This is the pattern for the stories in the collection: All celebrate the richness and strangeness of the imaginative lives of individuals while revealing the painful, often violent, disconnections between the world as it is and as it could be (550). Atkinson creates exuberant, sometimes frenetic stories out of the materials of her characters' personal lives.

BIBLIOGRAPHY

Kate Atkinson. *Not the End of the World.* London: Doubleday, 2002.

Charlotte Moore. "Not the End of the World," *Spectator* 23 November 2002.

Patricia McManus

O

O'BRIEN, EDNA (1936–) Born in Tuam-graney, County Clare, Ireland, Edna O'Brien attended the Pharmaceutical College of Ireland. She left school to marry the Czech novelist Ernest Gebler, and by the time they divorced a dozen years later she had established herself as a writer. Although her literary reputation rests primarily on her novels and short fiction, she has written at least nine stage plays, eight screenplays, and seven teleplays. She has also taught at the City College in New York.

Of O'Brien's 15 novels, her best-known may be those comprising the Country Girls trilogy: *The Country Girls* (1960), *The Lonely Girl* (1962), and *Girls in Their Married Bliss* (1964). In these novels, she treats the coming-of-age of two young women who struggle with the constraints of the very parochial social and moral expectations for Irish women. Because of its frank treatment of female sexuality, the trilogy (as well as some of O'Brien's subsequent novels) was banned in Ireland. From the start, her depiction of Irish society has seemed a revealing and affirmative testimony to her Irish admirers and a betrayal to her Irish detractors. In the 1990s, O'Brien produced another trilogy: *House of Splendid Isolation* (1994), *Down by the River* (1997), and *Wild Decembers* (2001). In these novels, she depicts the political factionalism, the religious fervor, the disturbed family relations, and the intensely personal feuds that together define a kind of rural Irish life far removed from the postcard pictures of idyllic villages among rolling emerald-green pastures.

The best stories from O'Brien's first four short story collections have been collected in *A Fanatic Heart* (1984). For the most part, these stories are set in the Ireland of O'Brien's youth and told in retrospect from a female point of view. The stories exhibit a consistent awareness of how the passage of time brings memories of joys and sorrows, accomplishments and disappointments, yearnings and resentments, with much the same underlying sense of loss as in her novels. The distance between event and memory and the immediacy that the memory provides create a great ambivalence in the recollection. It is like looking through a long tube at a brightly lit scene.

In his review in the *Washington Post,* Jonathan Yardley compares O'Brien's stories to those of Flannery O'Connor. Although both authors often enter into difficult territories with little armor but an ironic sense of the grotesque, O'Brien's stories are distinguished in that their tellers have a more direct stake in their telling. In "My Mother's Mother," the narrator describes how her grandmother reacted to her grandfather's dying suddenly and frightfully while saying a rosary. In "A Rose in the Heart of New York," O'Brien chronicles the lifelong tension between an Irish woman and her daughter and thereby explores maternal love as a necessary and fundamentally good impulse that inevitably has destructive repercussions in the lives of both mother and daughter.

The title story in O'Brien's most recent collection, *Lantern Slides* (1990), is a retelling of JAMES JOYCE'S "The

DEAD." Using the poignant ironies of Joyce's story as a counterpoint, O'Brien provides a barbed satire on the social and cultural pretensions of young Dubliners who are on the make professionally and sexually. Beyond the obvious influence that Joyce has had on subsequent generations of Irish writers, O'Brien has also expressed her special feeling for his work in her widely reviewed book on him for the Penguin Lives series, *James Joyce* (1999). (See also "SISTER IMELDA," "WHAT A SKY.")

BIBLIOGRAPHY

Lynch, Rachel Jane. "'A Land of Strange, Throttled, Sacrificial Women': Domestic Violence in the Short Fiction of Edna O'Brien," *Canadian Journal of Irish Studies* 22 (1996): 37–48.

O'Brien, Edna. *A Fanatic Heart: Selected Stories of Edna O'Brien.* New York: Farrar, Straus, 1984.

———. *Lantern Slides: Stories.* New York: Farrar, Straus, 1990.

———. *The Love Object.* London: Jonathan Cape, 1968.

———. *Mrs. Reinhardt and Other Stories.* London: Weidenfeld and Nicolson, 1978. Republished as *A Rose in the Heart.* Garden City, N.Y.: Doubleday, 1979.

———. *Returning.* London: Weidenfeld and Nicolson, 1982.

———. *A Scandalous Woman and Other Stories.* New York: Harcourt, 1974.

O'Hara, Kiera. "Love Objects: Love and Obsession in the Stories of Edna O'Brien," *Studies in Short Fiction* 30 (Summer 1993): 317–325.

Pearce, Sandra Manoogian. "Edna O'Brien's 'Lantern Slides' and Joyce's 'The Dead': Shadows of a Bygone Era," *Studies in Short Fiction* 32 (1995): 437–444.

Martin Kich

O'CONNOR, FRANK (1903–1966)

Born Michael Francis O'Donovan in Cork, Ireland, Frank O'Connor grew up in a poverty made worse by his father's heavy drinking. O'Connor's formal education was minimal, consisting of a brief enrollment in a school run by the Christian Brothers. Although only in his mid-teens, he fought in the Irish Republican Army (IRA) in the rebellion against British rule. Indeed, even after Irish independence had been secured, he continued to fight with the IRA against the continuing British and Protestant domination of Northern Ireland. Because of these activities, he was forced to live a tran-

sient existence, and he ultimately served a short prison term. During this period he adopted the name Frank O'Connor, a nom de guerre that would shortly become his nom de plume. By the time he was released from prison, he had educated himself thoroughly enough to secure a series of positions as a librarian in Sligo, Cork, and Dublin.

In the early 1930s, O'Connor began contributing stories to George Russell's *Irish Statesman,* and for the first time his work received widespread attention. From 1935 to 1939, he served on the board of directors of the Abbey Theater, where four of his plays were produced. He subsequently served as the poetry editor of *Bell,* a literary journal published in Dublin. Between 1931 and 1952, O'Connor published six collections of short stories (including the volume *Selected Stories* in 1947), one collection of poems, one novel, a biography of the Irish Republican leader Michael Collins, and three volumes of travel writing. Ironically, because of his persistent difficulties with Irish censors, his stories about Irish nationalism were published for the most part in the United Kingdom.

As if to signal his willingness to emigrate to the United States, in the 1940s O'Connor began to publish his books, sometimes initially, in the United States. On the basis of his prodigious output and his growing literary stature, which was reinforced by the publication of *The Stories of Frank O'Connor* in 1952 and *More Stories by Frank O'Connor* in 1954, he secured a series of teaching positions at such prestigious American universities as Harvard, Northwestern, and Stanford. Although he regularly contributed stories to periodicals such as *Atlantic, Esquire, Harper's,* and the *New Yorker,* his productivity over the last 15 years of his life to slowed considerably; he published only two new collections of short stories and a memoir over that period.

A great deal of O'Connor's work has, however, been published posthumously. Ten new thematic collections of his stories have appeared, including some previously unpublished work, as well as another memoir and a collection of his correspondence. But the three volumes that have been most integral to sustaining his critical reputation have been his *Collected Stories* (1981), *The Frank O'Connor Reader* (1994), and a highly regarded collection of his critical writing, *The Lonely Voice: A Study of the Short Story* (1985).

In his best short stories, O'Connor deftly integrates a colloquial narrative voice with carefully conceived narrative structures. His stories bridge the folk traditions of Irish lore and the conventions of modernist fiction. What might seem merely local color in other contexts is culturally resonant in his stories. Within this framework, O'Connor is able to shift naturally between humor and pathos, sentiment and irony. The stories are typically set in rural Irish communities, with characters drawn from the whole spectrum of Irish society. Often treating political or religious themes, the stories typically explore conflicts that arise between the sensibility and the needs of the individual and the customs and expectations of the community.

O'Connor's most widely anthologized story has been "GUESTS OF THE NATION," the title story of his first collection. Set during the Irish rebellion, it concerns the fate of British prisoners who must be executed in reprisal if the British follow through on their threat to execute captured Irish volunteers for sedition. Of course, the Irish have no formal facilities for holding prisoners and no formal protocols for carrying out executions. Instead, in the domestic environment of their own communities, they come to know their prisoners as individuals and, when they are called upon to execute them, naturally feel much more emotionally conflicted than the guards at a prison might feel.

Other notable stories include: "FIRST CONFESSION," which depicts the first religious rite in a boy's coming of age; "The Drunkard," which explores the relationship between a man's chronic drunkenness and his wife's responses to it; "In the Train," which delineates the ironies of "country justice"; and "The Long Road to Ummera," in which a lifetime of conflicts between a mother and son come to a head over her burial wishes. (See also "THE MAN OF THE HOUSE," "MY OEDIPUS COMPLEX," "JUDAS.")

BIBLIOGRAPHY

Alexander, James D. "Frank O'Connor in the *New Yorker,* 1945–1967," *Eire-Ireland* 30 (Spring 1995): 130–144.

Bordewyk, Gordon. "Quest for Meaning: The Stories of Frank O'Connor," *Illinois Quarterly* 41, no. 2 (1978): 37–47.

Matthews, James H. *Frank O'Connor.* Lewisburg: Bucknell University Press, 1976.

O'Connor, Frank. *Collected Stories.* New York: Knopf, 1981.

———. *For a Two-Hundredth Birthday.* Edinburgh: Tragara, 1986.

———. *A Frank O'Connor Reader.* Syracuse, N.Y.: Syracuse University Press, 1994.

———. *Guests of the Nation.* London: Macmillan, 1931.

———. *Masculine Protest and Other Stories.* London: Pan, 1969.

———. *More Stories by Frank O'Connor.* New York: Knopf, 1954.

———. *My Oedipus Complex and Other Stories.* New York: Penguin, 1963.

———. *A Set of Variations.* New York: Knopf, 1969.

———. *The Stories of Frank O'Connor.* New York: Knopf, 1952.

Tomory, William M. *Frank O'Connor.* Twayne's English Author Series, no. 297. Boston: Twayne, 1980.

Wohlgelernter, Maurice. *Frank O'Connor: An Introduction.* New York: Columbia University Press, 1977.

Martin Kich

"ODOUR OF CHRYSANTHEMUMS"

D. H. LAWRENCE (1911, 1914) A short story published in the *English Review* in 1911, shortly after D. H. LAWRENCE's first novel, *The White Peacock,* and subsequently republished in revised form in Lawrence's first, and perhaps most important, collection of short stories, *The PRUSSIAN OFFICER AND OTHER STORIES,* in 1914. While the collection is now seen as an important landmark in Lawrence's development as a storyteller, "Odour of Chrysanthemums" attracted the attention of author and editor Ford Maddox Ford, who later stated that it convinced him that Lawrence was a major writer in the making. The story now exists in the two published versions mentioned above and in two unpublished proof versions.

The story is set in the vicinity of Eastwood, in a coal-mining town in Nottinghamshire. The opening image of "small locomotive engine, Number 4," which comes "clanking, stumbling" down the line, is among Lawrence's best drawn. A woman, Elizabeth Bates, watches the train going by. She then returns home to get tea ready and, along with her two children, John and Annie, awaits the return of her husband, Walter Bates, from his day at the pit. Elizabeth, struggling to raise her family and careworn, but still feeling slightly superior to her husband and her dreary surroundings, provides the focus of the story. She becomes increasingly angry and restless as the wait gets longer and she suspects that Walter is at the pub getting drunk. Eventually her anger is tinged with anxiety and fear for his safety, and she sets out to look for him. Her husband's workmate Jack Rigley informs her that he left Walter working in the mines and offers to make further inquiries. Elizabeth returns home, and soon afterward her mother-in-law, the elder Mrs. Bates, comes in to inform her that Walter has had an accident at the pit. News then arrives that he has been killed. His body is brought back home, where it is laid out and washed by his wife. The story ends with an exploration of Elizabeth's inner feelings about and response to this event.

"Odour of Chrysanthemums" is among Lawrence's most popular works today, but early reactions to this and other stories in the collection as a whole were mixed. Reviewers expressed admiration for the young writer's technique but also felt that the author was dark and morbid in his style, inclined toward a "hideous form of naturalism" (*Standard,* 4 December 1914), and was "pitiless in his cruelty, relentless in his realism" (*Saturday Review,* 9 January 1915). The intense, dramatic quality of this story is in many ways characteristic of Lawrence's early writing. With its focus on character rather than plot and its interest in the "inner life," the story is a deliberate departure from the brand of realism characteristic of the writing of Lawrence's Edwardian predecessors, though the symbolic function of the recurring chrysanthemum motif draws on some of the conventions of late 19th-century realism. The chrysanthemums that are referred to repeatedly in the story tie the plot together and are associated with the cycle of life, marriage, and death. The setting, along with the carefully etched details, indicates the author's personal knowledge and experience of a landscape and way of life characteristic of a mining town in the early twentieth century. The poverty of the family, the degenerate lifestyle of the husband, the relationship between the husband and wife, and finally the accidental death of the young miner itself (themes Lawrence was to return to in his novel *Sons and Lovers* and

again in his play *The Widowing of Mrs. Holryd,* which is in many ways a rewriting of "Odour of Chrysanthemums") are clearly drawn from Lawrence's own life. Lawrence realizes the most important theme of the story, the ultimate estrangement and alienation of human beings from one another and the fundamental solitariness of the human state, by locating the action in a specific sociocultural context and by drawing attention to the complexities of the relations and conditions characteristic of that particular context.

BIBLIOGRAPHY

Lawrence, D. H. *The Prussian Officer and Other Stories.* Cambridge: Cambridge University Press, 1983.

Schulz, Volker. "D. H. Lawrence's Early Masterpiece of Short Fiction: 'Odour of Chrysanthemums,'" *Studies in Short Fiction* 28 (Summer 1991): 363–396.

Stovel, Nora Foster. "D. H. Lawrence and 'The Dignity of Death': Tragic Recognition in 'Odour of Chrysanthemums,' *The Widowing of Mrs. Holroyd,* and *Sons and Lovers,*" *D. H. Lawrence Review* 16 (1983): 59–82.

Brinda Charry

O'FAOLAIN, SEAN (1900–1991)

The novelist, critic, and editor Sean O'Faolain, born in Cork on February 22, 1900, as John Francis Whelan, is best known for his short stories about Ireland's lower and middle classes. His major concerns were individuals' struggle to achieve dignity as human beings within a society that tends to be excessively paternalistic and restrictive, Ireland's conflicts in reconciling past history with present reality, the decline of the nationalist ideals, and the failings of Irish Roman Catholicism.

O'Faolain was the youngest son of a family of three boys to parents who both had come from the country. As a child he experienced a dull and restrictive life that resulted from his parents' ambitions and excessive emphasis on frugality, prayer, hard work, and respectability. O'Faolain began his education at the Lancastrian National School; in 1914 he went to the Presentation Brothers Secondary School. Visits to the Cork Opera House across the street from his house and annual vacations to the country in Rathkale brought release from his confined existence. His father, a police constable in the Royal Irish Constabulary, was devotedly loyal to the British Empire, an attitude young

O'Faolain shared until the martyrdom of the leaders of the Easter Rising in 1916, when he began to rebel against the restrictions and false loyalties of his family. O'Faolain began to identify in a romantic way with the poor and repressed as well as with the cultural past of Ireland; by 1917 he spoke Gaelic fluently and changed his name to O'Faolain. In 1918 he attended a summer school where he met Eileen Gould, whom he married 10 years later.

When he entered University College Cork in 1918, his nationalist passion became even more intense. He was a revolutionary for six years, first in the Volunteers and then during the Irish civil war (1922–23) in the Irish Republican Army (IRA), doing scouting, carrying dispatches, and doing police work. In the civil war he was successively a bomb maker, a guerilla, a director of propaganda of the First Southern Division of the IRA, and finally, in Dublin, director of publicity for the whole Republican movement. He protested against the Republican defeat and could not accept the reality of the treaty with England. He became disillusioned, however, when he realized that the Republicans lacked a worthwhile social and political program. He went back to the university and took an M.A. in Irish literature; he taught at a school and then took an M.A. in English literature to improve his job qualifications. His successful application for a Commonwealth Fellowship gave him the time he needed to recover from his bitterness and to put his life in perspective. He left for America in September 1926 and stayed for three years at Harvard University, studying philology. Eileen Gould joined him in 1928 and they married in Boston, later went to London, and then in June 1933 returned to Ireland, where O'Faolain hoped to live by his pen. Eileen and Sean O'Faolain had two children, Julia (b. 1933) and Stephen (b. 1938).

His first book of short stories, *Midsummer Night Madness,* which shows the influence of JAMES JOYCE and GEORGE MOORE, was published in 1932 and immediately was banned. It is an attempt to come to terms with his own experiences during the Anglo-Irish War and the civil war—the guerrilla fighting, executions, reprisals, bombmaking, and violence. The central figure of all his stories is a romantic young rebel who has come to question the purpose of his life. "Fugue" and "The Patriot" serve as terminal points in the rebel's progress from identification with romantic nationalism to his rejection of abstract political causes and his detachment from violence in favor of human relationships and domestic peace. O'Faolain's biographies of Irish national figures, *King of the Beggars, A Life of Daniel O'Connell* (1938) and *The Great O'Neill* (1972), show a similar development from identification with heroes as the epitome of Irish pride, passion, and hope to a more sober view of the inconsistencies and contradictions in these heroes' characters and in Irish character in general. His first biography of De Valera in 1933 was openly propagandist, but he later revised his view of De Valera's policy and criticized him for his cultural parochialism and isolationist economic policy, which kept Ireland from a deeper contact with the outside world.

For O'Faolain Ireland after 1923, was introverted, narrow-minded, and frustrating in its emphasis on materialist middle-class values and its lack of artistic and intellectual interests, exacerbated by censorship and the increasing influence of the Catholic Church on political decisions. The novels O'Faolain published between 1932 and 1942 are concerned with the fate of the individual caught up in an inhibiting environment. In his first novel, *A Nest of Simple Folk* (1934), the escape to personal freedom is inextricably bound with the cause of national liberty. *Bird Alone* (1936) and *Come Back to Erin* (1940) share the sociological and moral approach to Irish issues, emphasizing the way men are affected by their surroundings. Fighting for the rights of the individual became the centerpiece of his editorials in the *Bell* magazine, which he founded and edited from 1940 to 1946. Here O'Faolain advocated a realistic literature of the everyday. Writers such as Frank O'Connor, Liam O'Flaherty, and O'Faolain himself produced short stories with this emphasis, but the magazine failed nevertheless.

His second collection of stories, *A Purse of Coppers* (1937), shows the emergence of a distinctive pessimistic point of view and a greater technical ability. It raises the issue of individual freedom from the frustrations of a stagnant postrevolutionary society. In the prologue story, "A Broken World," O'Faolain shows the inability of progressive forces within society (the priest who wants to reform the land) to arouse a lethargic, almost vegetative peasantry to activity and the improvement of the whole society. Unlike the priest, who is corroded by the knowledge of failure, the narrator sees Ireland ready for a dawn, as indicated by the final word of the story, which ends on a wave of romantic hope. A restrictive society maiming its members is also shown in the stories "A Born Genius," "The Old Master," "Sinners," and "Discord," which demonstrate the shortcomings of Catholic priests in a modern world.

In *The Short Story* (1948) O'Faolain formulates some of the theories of the short story evident in his writings: the avoidance of elaborate introductions, his method of informing by suggestion while avoiding excessive detail, deployment of mood of place, the implication of a general moral or idea, and his indebtedness to Chekhov. In his next collections, *Teresa* (1947), *The Man Who Invented Sin* (1948), and *The Finest Stories of Sean O'Faolain* (1957), the bitterness and frustration give way to a concentration on the variable nature of man and an attentiveness to the complexity of human nature. The narrator is no longer haunted by frustration and loss but stands both detached from and sympathetic to his characters. His collection *I Remember! I Remember!* (1961) shows a greater refinement of feeling and technique in the development of a mature omniscient voice as he meditates on the universal themes of growth and change. "Lovers of the Lake" shows his amused interest in the religious and emotional confusion, the clash of rationalism and sentimentality, of a middle-aged pair of adulterous lovers, a topic of close interest to O'Faolain, who despite many adulterous affairs (with ELIZABETH BOWEN, Honor Tracy, and Alene Erlanger, among others) could not shed his religious heritage entirely.

The warm reception of O'Faolain's work allowed him to give lecture tours at Princeton University (1953) and to teach at Boston College in 1964 and at Wesleyan University in 1966. He was director of the Arts Council of Ireland between 1957 and 1959. His cosmopolitanism was further enhanced by his travel writing, especially about Italy, when he worked for *Holiday*. Many of his later short stories were first published in the *Playboy* magazine. His wife Eileen died in 1988, and Sean O'Faolain died at his home in Dublin on April 20, 1991.

BIBLIOGRAPHY

Arndt, Marie. *A Critical Study of Sean O'Faolain's Life and Work.* Lewiston, N.Y.: Edwin Mellen Press, 2001.

Butler, Pierce. *Sean O'Faolain: A Study of the Short Fiction.* New York: Twayne, 1993.

Harmon, Maurice. *Sean O'Faolain: A Life.* London: Constable, 1994.

O'Faolain, Sean. *Bird Alone.* Jonathan Cape, 1936.

———. *The Collected Stories of Sean O'Faolain.* 3 vols. London: Constable, 1980–82.

———. *Constance Markievicz.* London: Jonathan Cape, 1934.

———. *The Finest Stories of Sean O'Faolain.* Boston: Little, Brown, 1957.

———. *The Heat of the Sun, Stories and Tales.* London and New York: Penguin, 1966.

———. *I Remember! I Remember!* Boston: Little, Brown, 1961.

———. *Midsummer Night Madness and Other Stories.* London: Jonathan Cape, 1932.

———. *A Nest of Simple Folk.* London: Jonathan Cape, 1933.

———. *A Purse of Coppers: Short Stories.* London: Jonathan Cape, 1937.

———. *The Short Story.* London: Collins, 1948.

———. *Teresa and Other Stories.* London: Jonathan Cape, 1947.

Rippier, Joseph S. *The Short Stories of Sean O'Faolain: A Study in Descriptive Techniques.* Gerrards Cross, England: Colin Smythe, 1976.

Heike Grundmann

OKRI, BEN (1959–)

Ben Okri was born on March 15, 1959, in Minna, a small town in central western Nigeria, a year and a half before Nigerian independence. His father, a member of the Urhobo ethnic group, worked in the railways but left soon after his son's birth for England to study law. Okri was taken as an infant to London, where he grew up. The Okri family returned to Nigeria in 1965 to find it moving into a bitter and murderous period of civil war, later known as the Biafran War (1967–70), which would wreck the Nigerian hope of a strong and united republic, creating a violent legacy of communal conflict and military takeovers. Okri completed his secondary education at Urhobo College, Warri, and moved to Lagos, where his father had set up his practice as a lawyer in difficult circumstances. Okri worked in a paint company but also tried his hand at writing stories and articles for newspapers. These early efforts dealt exclusively with

Nigerian themes, particularly the corruption and violence that gripped the country in the 1970s. Okri tried in vain to study science in a Nigerian university, but he did manage to secure a government scholarship for liberal arts study in England and in 1978 began to study comparative literature at the University of Essex. Although he was unable to complete the course, the experience at Essex shaped him as a writer and paved the way for his literary success later.

Okri's first two novels, *Flowers and Shadows* (1980) and *The Landscapes Within* (1981), showed his preoccupation with the plight of Nigerians in a strife-torn society and captured something of the turbulence of his childhood and youth (see "IN THE SHADOW OF WAR"). Okri then honed his skills as a storyteller in a series of short stories set mostly in Lagos. These were subsequently collected in *Incidents at the Shrine* (1986) and *Stars of the New Curfew* (1988). By this time Okri was living in England and, among other odd jobs, served as the poetry editor of *West Africa* magazine. He also did a two-year stint with the BBC World Service as broadcaster for their Network Africa program. Most of his stories from this period convey an oppressive sense of helplessness in the Nigerian society in the face of the depredation of a corrupt elite, rendered from the sensitive perspective of a child or an artist figure. Okri pooled his knowledge of both the African and the European traditions to produce accounts of the human spirit overtaken by brutal circumstances and sought to blend the ingredients of Western realism with the mystical and mythical nature of West African reality. This happy combination led to the Booker Prize–winning *The Famished Road* (1991), the first novel in a trilogy narrating the melancholy but magical saga of postindependence Nigeria. Using the figure of the spirit-child *abiku* from Yoruba mythology, Okri traverses the forbidden space separating the human world from the world of the spirits, enriching the narrative with multiple layers of meaning. The quest of the child protagonist Azaro is continued in the sequels—*Songs of Enchantment* (1993) and *Infinite Riches* (1998). Okri has published two volumes of poems.

A recipient of many literary awards, Okri was honored with an OBE in 2001. Often bracketed with SALMAN RUSHDIE and Gabriel García Márquez as a writer whose works embody elements of magical realism and postmodernism, Okri's best work should also be understood in the context of the daily, difficult struggles of the Nigerians after independence.

BIBLIOGRAPHY

Cooper, Brenda. *Magic Realism in West African Fiction.* London: Routledge, 1998.
Fraser, Robert. *Ben Okri.* Plymouth, England: Northcote House, 2002.
Hattersley, Roy. "Ben Okri: A Man in Two Minds." *Guardian Saturday Review* (August 21, 1999). Available online. URL: http://www.guardian.co.uk/saturday_review/story/0,3605,268270,00.html. Accessed June 1, 2006.
Okri, Ben. *The Famished Road.* London: Vintage, 1992.
———. *In Arcadia.* London: Weidenfeld and Nicolson, 2002.
———. *Incidents at the Shrine: Short Stories.* London: Heinemann, 1986.
———. *Infinite Riches.* London: Phoenix, 1998.
———. *Songs of Enchantment.* London: Jonathan Cape, 1993.
———. *Stars of the New Curfew.* London: Penguin, 1999.

R. S. Nanda

"OLD CHIEF MSHLANGA, THE" DORIS LESSING (1964)

One of DORIS LESSING's many stories concerning relations between white settlers in Southern Africa and the black communities they have displaced, "The Old Chief Mshlanga" was first published in 1964 in *African Stories*. The story recounts the awakening of a historical and political consciousness in a young white woman who has been inculcated to regard the South African landscape as her own and to regard the Africans who live in it as "an amorphous black mass . . . who existed merely to serve" (12). As a child, the narrator fails to see the African landscape as it really is, instead projecting a world she has taken from fairy tales and stories about England. She, along with the other white children, have been taught to view Africans through a "consciousness of danger" (12), a fear against which the children defend themselves by mocking and humiliating the black people they encounter. This part of the narrative, in which the young child walks through the veld accompanied by dogs and a gun for her protection, is narrated in the third person, perhaps to generalize her experience as an attitude held by many white children but perhaps also as if the narrator cannot quite bear to recognize her early attitudes as her own.

In a shift to the first-person, we learn of the adolescent girl's encounter one day with the elderly Chief Mshlanga. The old chief's quiet dignity and his courtesy as he speaks with the girl eventually lead to a change in her attitude. Now she sees that it is African soil she walks on and that the African people have an existence independent of her. Suddenly the discomfort she has felt in previous exchanges disappears: "it seemed it was only necessary to let free that respect I felt when I was talking with old Chief Mshlanga, to let both black and white people meet gently, with tolerance for each other's differences: it seemed quite easy" (15). The narrator's curiosity about the chief and his kraal (village) is intensified when she learns that the cook in her family's home is the chief's son. Setting out one day to find the kraal, she experiences an unprecedented "terror of isolation" (17) in the vastness of the veld. She arrives at the kraal only to have an awkward encounter with the chief: Divisions between African and white settler make genuine social interaction impossible, and she realizes she is an intruder in their village and on what was once their land. Her earlier experience of defamiliarization in the veld has been a prelude to her intellectual and emotional realization that the earth is not really owned by the white settlers at all.

The subtlety of Lessing's depiction of her narrator's evolution is that it shows her later position of "tolerance" to be a false solution to real problems. As is made clear by an incident related at the end, in which her father confiscates the chief's goats and finally has his kraal removed from what is now the government's land, the land that the white settlers consider their own has been taken from the Africans, who have no right of appeal to the legal system, which represents the interests of the whites: "'Go to the police, then,' said my father, and looked triumphant. There was, of course, no more to be said" (20). In the face of such historical and material injustice, the narrator's previous belief in the "easiness" of relations between blacks and whites is revealed to be a complacent delusion that suppresses recent history and the stark inequalities it has produced. She has learned that "if one cannot call a country to heel like a dog, neither can one dismiss the past with a smile in an easy gush of feeling, saying: I could not help it, I am also a victim" (19).

BIBLIOGRAPHY
Lessing, Doris, *This Was the Old Chief's Country: Collected African Stories.* Vol. 1. 1964. London: Michael Joseph, 1973.

Victoria Margree

"OLD NURSE'S STORY, THE" ELIZABETH GASKELL (1852)   This story first appeared in CHARLES DICKENS's magazine *Household Words*. It begins with the old nurse of the title, Hester, describing her years in service with the Furnivall family over three generations. Having begun in her adolescence as a nurse for the young Miss Furnivall, Hester then cares for this lady's daughter, Miss Rosamond. When the story starts, Hester is telling a tale to the adult Miss Rosamond's children about their mother's childhood experiences with the supernatural at Furnivall Manor. After the young Rosamond is orphaned, she and Hester come to live at the manor with the elderly Miss Grace Furnivall and her longtime maid and companion, Mrs. Stark. The only other inhabitants of the household are the servants James, Dorothy, and Agnes. As winter approaches, Hester sometimes hears music coming from the great organ in the manor's hall—an instrument that, she discovers to her horror, is "all broken and destroyed inside," though its surface appears "brave and fine." This massive, booming organ was the property of the late Lord Furnivall, a music lover who played it in life and continues to do so after death. A key symbol in the book for patriarchal power, it also functions as a metaphor for the Furnivall family itself, whose impressive lineage belies a hidden corruption. This manifests itself when Rosamond disappears during a snowstorm and nearly dies of exposure, claiming to have followed a spectral child into the elements.

The crisis rouses Hester into demanding the family history from Dorothy, who reluctantly recounts the story of Grace and her elder sister, Maude. Both women were great beauties in their youth, and they were bitter rivals for the affection of a foreign musician who came to the house at the behest of their father, Lord Furnivall. Maude married the man in secret and bore a daughter, whom she kept hidden from her family in a nearby farmhouse. Her husband returned briefly from abroad to toy with her own and her sister's affections, but soon he departed forever and deserted them both. Maude shocked Grace by telling her that "all the time the dark foreigner had been mocking her with pretended love— he was her own husband." The embittered Grace then began to spy on her sister, eventually learning of the daughter's existence and betraying her sister to Lord Furnivall. During a winter storm the old lord confronted Maude and her child, striking the latter with his crutch before turning mother and daughter out of the house and into the winter storm to die. During this scene, Grace stood beside her father and against her sister.

After hearing this tale, Hester wishes "Miss Rosamond and [herself] well out of that dreadful house for ever," but she cannot leave her charge and dares not take her away. Her adventures at the manor climax during a terrible storm, when the ghosts of Lord Furnivall, Maude, and the girl appear to Rosamond, Hester, Grace, and Mrs. Stark. The specters act out the tragic scene from their past, and when Lord Furnivall raises his crutch to strike his granddaughter, Grace begs him to "spare the little innocent child!" At this moment an apparition of the young Grace materializes to stand beside her father, and "the terrible phantoms [move] on, regardless of old Miss Furnivall's wild entreaty." Struck with palsy, Grace collapses to the floor. On her deathbed she repeats the story's moral: "What is done in youth can never be undone in age!" ELIZABETH GASKELL's ghost story is gothic by virtue of its specters, its framed narratives, and its investigation of tragic family histories and provides an example of the sensational stories of secrecy and family skeletons later popularized by WILKIE COLLINS, MARY ELIZABETH BRADDON, and ELLEN WOOD.

BIBLIOGRAPHY

Gaskell, Elizabeth. "The Old Nurse's Story." In *Nineteenth Century Short Stories by Women,* edited by Harriet Devine Jump, 93–116. London: Routledge, 1998.

Jamil Mustafa

OLIPHANT, MARGARET (1828–1897) Margaret Oliphant, the youngest of three surviving children, was born near Edinburgh, where her father was a minor customs official. She does not seem to have had any formal education. Her childhood was fairly nomadic as her father took up different posts in Glasgow and Liverpool. He was a weak, vacillating man, in marked contrast to her mother, who was energetic and inspirational. Ineffectual men were to recur in most of Oliphant's narratives, especially her short fiction. In 1852 she married Francis Oliphant, a cousin and a stained-glass artist. Seven years later her husband was dead, leaving her with three children (another two died in infancy) and debts, which had to be paid. To raise money she wrote two short stories, "The Rector" and "The Doctor's Family," published in one volume, which were the first narratives in *The Chronicles of Carlingford,* the series that made her reputation. The remaining works in this series are long novels similar to ANTHONY TROLLOPE's Barsetshire novels, in that they are set in a small provincial town, focus on the doings of clergymen and their families, and are striking for their portrayals of strong, independent women. Despite her success, Oliphant never received what she perceived as adequate repayment for her labors. Oliphant's continual need for money was exacerbated in 1866 when she took on the additional responsibility of providing for her widowed brother and his three children.

Oliphant's prolixity meant that she was probably most suited to the writing of novels, although she occasionally returned to the short story, especially in her ghost stories and supernatural fiction, which she titled *Stories of the Seen and Unseen.* These tales, written mainly in the final two decades of her life, have often been reprinted, both in modern collections and individually in various anthologies, and these are her most lasting legacy to the short story format. Elizabeth Jay has said that Oliphant, in her ghostly narratives, "discovered a place to ponder further upon irresolvable paradoxes and gender-related confusions."

Oliphant took unusual pains with "A BELEAGUERED CITY" (1879), and carefully revised the narrative. In this novella a series of narrators relate their version of what occurred when a French town was possessed by spirits, which could be sensed by only one male inhabitant but by all the female citizens. The city's dead ancestors return as a punishment for the secularism of the modern age, while the current inhabitants are forced into exile. The mayor and the priest are eventually allowed back into the town, where they celebrate a mass that exorcises the phantoms. The remaining citizens can now return, and Oliphant ends her novella on an ironic note as the men once more take up their positions of authority.

"The Open Door" (1882) is one of the most frequently anthologized Victorian ghost stories. A young boy hears a ghostly cry emanating from a ruined building on the estate his father is renting, and his health deteriorates as he worries about the ghost's torment. The sounds are eventually tracked to the sill of an open door in the ruins. The local minister realizes that the ghostly voice is a prodigal son who needs to be reunited with his mother in the "Unseen." The minister exorcises the ghost largely through his empathy with the ghost's plight, and with the exorcism the ailing boy is restored to good health.

Oliphant's late story "The Library Window" (1896) is the most widely praised. An adolescent girl visits a Scottish aunt and each day sees more clearly a figure of a man writing at a desk in the library window opposite to her room. She becomes obsessed with this man, who seems to recognize her, but a visit to the library reveals that there is no window, and she falls into a fever. Many years later she has been married, has had children, and is now widowed, but what she saw in the library window remains the most vivid experience of her life.

Other supernatural tales written by Oliphant include "The Secret Chamber" (1876), "Earthbound" (1880), "The Lady's Walk" (1883), "Old Lady Mary" (1884), "The Portrait" (1885), "The Land of Darkness" (1887), and "The Story of a Wedding Tour" (1894).

BIBLIOGRAPHY

Clute, John. "Mrs. Oliphant." In *Supernatural Fiction Writers,* vol. 1: *Fantasy and Horror,* edited by E. F. Bleiler, 261–268. New York: Scribners, 1985.

Jay, Elizabeth. *Mrs. Oliphant: "A Fiction to Herself."* Oxford: Clarendon Press, 1995.

Oliphant, Margaret. *The Autobiography of Margaret Oliphant.* Peterborough, Ontario: Broadview, 2001.

———. *A Beleaguered City and Other Tales of the Seen and Unseen.* Edited by Jenni Calder. Edinburgh: Canongate, 2000.

———. *The Widow's Tale and Other Stories.* Edinburgh: Blackwood, 1898.

Michael Flowers

"ON THE EDGE OF THE CLIFF" V. S. PRITCHETT (1979)

"On the Edge of the Cliff" first appeared in the *New Yorker* in 1978 and was the title story for a collection of nine short stories published in 1979, in the latter part of V. S. PRITCHETT's writing career; "On the Edge of the Cliff" explores the tension between two sets of romantic partners with remarkable age differences. The story follows Harry, a widower and retired professor in his 70s, and Rowena, an artist in her 20s, through the early stage of their romantic relationship. However, the story questions Harry's relationships with women and their attitude toward him—his wife Violet, who committed suicide; Daisy, who nearly broke up his marriage; and now Rowena, his young girlfriend by whom he wants to be loved yet to whom he never quite reveals himself. V. S. Pritchett, sometimes called the English Chekov, does not pass judgment on these characters but rather gives the reader the opportunity to understand these relationships.

Throughout "On the Edge of the Cliff" there is an ease between Harry and Rowena yet also an ever-present awareness of the difference in their ages. Pritchett does not fall into typical readerly expectations of a romantic relationship between younger woman and older man—the relationship is not primarily sexual. Rowena is sensitive to and cautious of bringing attention to Harry's age. The narrator portrays Rowena as very childlike. She reads Harry's facial expressions like a child would a parent's: "she saw by his leaden look that the subject was closed." She sees Harry without his dentures and responds "with a horror she tried to wipe from her mind." Harry thinks of the relationship: "There are rules. . . . It has to be played as a game." He performs certain tones of voice and censors some of his own emotions. As he stands on the cliff, Rowena asks him what he is thinking. His honest reply would be, "these days I think only of death," though he says to her "You." Harry thinks she carries an "arrogance" of youth: "Like all girls she wanted to leave her mark on places. . . . Ownership! Power!" However, Harry seeks some form of conquest over her; he thinks to himself, "How marvelous. She is jealous, after all. She loves me." The difference in their age is magnified during this day, the day of their first sexual encounter. Harry takes Rowena to the fair and then to Withy Hole and the cliffs. Before he jumps into the water, he breaks a "rule" and allows her to see him naked in the daylight—something he never does, as it foregrounds all of the evidence of his old age. That night, Rowena enters his bed for the first time, and she says, "I've come to see the Ancient Mariner."

The story juxtaposes this relationship with that of Daisy Pyke, a middle-aged woman, and Stephen, her younger lover. The couples encounter each other at the fair. Harry and Rowena presume Stephen to be Daisy's son. A few weeks later, Daisy unexpectedly visits Harry at home one afternoon. The reader learns that she nearly caused Harry's marriage to end. As Daisy speaks "in her old hard taunting style," Harry momentarily recalls her allure—past and present. Harry reveals himself to Daisy; the thoughts of death he censors from Rowena, he confides to Daisy: "I only think of death now."

The contrast between Daisy and Stephen brings into focus the difference between Harry and Rowena. The two never speak of their ages, and it is only at the end of the story that the difference is noted verbally. With surprise, Harry tells Rowena that Stephen is Daisy's lover. Her response is, "'You can't mean that.'. . . putting on a very proper air. 'She's old enough—'." At the end of the story, the reader has the sense that Harry and Rowena's relationship will move into a new phase, further defining Harry as inextricable from his past loves. As Harry wants to tell Rowena, but keeps to himself, "Girls were like flowers with voices and he had spent a lot of his life collecting both. When young girls turned into women they lost his interest: he had always lived for reverie."

BIBLIOGRAPHY

Pritchett, V. S. *The Cab at the Door and Midnight Oil.* New York: Modern Library, 1994.

———. *The Complete Collected Stories.* New York: Random House, 1990.

———. *The Pritchett Century.* Edited by Oliver Pritchett. New York: Modern Library, 1999.

Stinson, John J. *V. S. Pritchett: A Study of the Short Fiction.* New York: Twayne, 1992.

Treglown, Jeremy. *V. S. Pritchett: A Working Life.* New York: Random House, 2004.

Alissa Appel

"ON THE WESTERN CIRCUIT" THOMAS HARDY (1891)

"On the Western Circuit" addresses many of the same questions of sexuality, propriety, and class structure that dominate much of THOMAS HARDY's longer fiction, but it does so from a fundamentally different perspective. Like such novels as *Tess of the D'Urbervilles* and *Far from the Madding Crowd,* the story is set in the author's mythical Wessex. But whereas those texts focus on the rustic life of the countryside, "On the Western Circuit" is very much a tale of the city. It details the growth and eventual collapse of an unusual love triangle among Charles Bradford Raye, a London attorney; Mrs. Edith Harmon, the wife of a wine merchant in the town of Melcaster; and Anna, a pretty but poor and uneducated country girl whom Mrs. Harmon has brought to town to train as her domestic servant.

As the story opens, Raye is watching Anna ride a merry-go-round at a fair in the town square. He engages her in conversation, and she quickly becomes enamored of him. When Anna is late returning home, Mrs. Harmon goes to look for her, and she too finds herself drawn to Raye's charms. The trio are pressed so tightly together by the crowd that Raye mistakenly grabs Mrs. Harmon's hand instead of Anna's, but because he is "so gentlemanly, so fascinating, had such beautiful eyes" (99–100), she does not object to the contact. After this initial encounter, Raye extends his stay in Melcaster to continue his dalliance with Anna. They meet repeatedly over several days. He views the affair as merely a "passing desire," while she becomes his in "body and soul" (100). When Raye eventually leaves to go "on the Western Circuit" and try cases throughout Wessex, he leaves an address for Anna to write him in London. When no letter is comes, he sends a quick note imploring her to correspond with him. The response that arrives catches him completely off guard: "He had received letters from women who were fairly called ladies, but never so sensible, so human a letter as this" (104). The cause of Raye's surprise is quickly revealed. Anna, who is illiterate, has had Mrs. Harmon help her craft the response. Raye is intrigued, and the correspondence between the lovers increases, though Anna plays an increasingly marginal role in composing the letters that supposedly come from her. Mrs. Harmon, overcome by her own attraction to Raye, uses the notes as an outlet for her own fantasies, and they come to represent her desires, not Anna's. For her part, Anna works diligently to improve her penmanship and reading skills but makes little progress.

Problems arise when Anna becomes pregnant by Raye and Mr. Harmon turns her out of his house. Mrs. Harmon now writes to Raye without any consultation from her former charge. Raye, unaware of the deception, believes that Anna, despite being a poor rural girl, possesses dramatic "powers of development" and with "a little private training in the social forms of London" will make "as good a professional man's wife as could be desired" (111). He determines to marry her, and a wedding in London is planned. The ceremony is attended by Mr. and Mrs. Harmon and a friend of Raye's. Afterward, when Raye asks Anna to draft a note to his sister, her illiteracy can no longer be concealed. When Mrs. Harmon confesses the entire affair in private to Raye, he declares, "in soul and spirit I have married you" (117), and the two share a long, passionate kiss. Although she recognizes that he has been "ruined" socially, she asks for his forgiveness. He bestows it, noting, "It serves me right," and they part (117). In the story's conclusion, Raye peruses Mrs. Harmon's letters with "dreary resignation" as he and Anna ride the train to their honeymoon.

Thus, as is typical in Hardy's writing, "On the Western Circuit" closes on a note of despair. At the same time, a sense of poetic justice—something frequently missing from Hardy—pervades the scene as well. Although Raye has certainly been deceived by Mrs. Harmon and now must live with an "unlettered peasant chained to his side" (117), his situation ultimately stems from his willingness to exploit Anna's naiveté for a romantic dalliance that is meaningless to him but threatens to destroy her social respectability. The conclusion saves Anna from the disgrace of having a child out of wedlock even as it punishes Raye for have trifled with her in the first place. To his credit, the young lawyer does feel despair but not bitterness. He forgives Mrs. Harmon and acknowledges that he has earned his fate.

From a textual perspective, "On the Western Circuit" presents a challenge for critics. It was first published serially in the *English Illustrated Magazine* and *Harper's Weekly* in 1891 and then included in the volume *Life's Little Ironies* in 1894. For the serial version, Hardy altered language to deemphasize Anna's physical relationship with Rayes and her pregnancy and made several material changes to the structure of the story itself, such as transforming Mrs. Harmon into a widow. Unfortunately, the typescript Hardy used to make these revisions was sold at auction in 1988 and is no longer available for study.

Like much of Hardy's short fiction, "On the Western Circuit" has received relatively little critical attention. Kristin Brady's *The Short Stories of Thomas Hardy,* however, serves as a useful starting point for further analysis. Those Alan Manford's editorial notes to Oxford's 1996 edition of *Life's Little Ironies* provides a convenient introduction to the story's textual issues, while Martin Ray's *Thomas Hardy: A Textual Study of the Short Stories* explores them in much greater depth.

BIBLIOGRAPHY
Brady, Kristin. *The Short Stories of Thomas Hardy.* New York: St. Martin's, 1982.
Hardy, Thomas. "On the Western Circuit." In *Life's Little Ironies.* 1894. Edited by Alan Manford. Oxford: University Press, 1996.
Plotz, John. "Motion Sickness: Spectacle and Circulation in Thomas Hardy's 'On the Western Circuit,'" *Studies in Short Fiction* 33, no. 3 (Summer 1996): 369–386.
Ray, Martin. *Thomas Hardy: A Textual Study of the Short Stories.* Aldershot, England: Ashgate, 1997.

Stephen E. Severn

"ORIGINAL BLISS" A. L. KENNEDY (1997)

"Original Bliss" takes as its theme a situation prevalent in many of A. L. KENNEDY's short stories: A frustrated female character, hemmed in by the mundane routines of her life, must enter a period of struggle in order to maintain her identity in a world that would deny her the opportunity to be anything other than the sum of her domestic roles. Kennedy's portrayal of these struggles relies on a detailed depiction of psychological turmoil. Many of her stories end at a liminal moment, a moment at which a leap of faith must be made. Kennedy's stories are generally open-ended, abandoning her protagonists at the crucial juncture where they must either choose to take responsibility for themselves or regress to their earlier state of hopelessness.

This novella is the title story of Kennedy's 1997 collection. The novella focuses on Margery Brindle, significantly referred to for much of the story simply as Mrs. Brindle. Margery Brindle's life is controlled by her husband, a masculine archetype, who requires that she fulfill certain prescribed roles that almost wholly involve serving his needs and whims. Mrs. Brindle is able to cope with these restrictions thanks to her particular conception of God, a hybrid figure who performs the functions of lover and confidant, as well as being a moral guardian and vengeful disciplinarian.

The story follows the repercussions of Mrs. Brindle's loss, not of a strictly orthodox religious faith but of this specific conception of God. Kennedy shows that Mrs. Brindle's mind is beginning to rebel against its own self-imposed shackles, which have been constructed from the limited ideological material she has had access to in her circumscribed life. Mrs. Brindle's life, however, is bearable only because of her apparent adherence to guidelines set down by this higher power. Without any sense that her God, purveyor of part moral guidance and part mortal fear, provides an overarching set of moral and spiritual guidelines, Margery Brindle's life becomes an existentially oppressive void of monotonous routine tasks.

The novella begins as Mrs. Brindle, unable to sleep, attempts to evade the dark hours by watching television. The program she happens to see introduces her to Professor Edward E. Gluck, a leading academic in the field of cybernetics and the author and practitioner of a self-help regime he refers to simply as "The Process." Margery is attracted by the fact that Gluck appears to understand perfectly the conditions of his own existence and their link to his constant psychic and spiritual contentment. Gluck becomes an omni-present figure, appearing on Margery's radio and in the magazines she reads. Encouraged by his claim that she too can be "the miracle that makes itself," she lies to her husband about a visit to a sick relative before traveling to a conference in Germany at which Gluck is the keynote speaker.

Margery's uncharacteristic flight begins her journey away from her old life and into a moral maze. She and Gluck become friends, though the erotic tension between them causes the return of Mrs. Brindle's personal God, which at first, she relishes. Gluck's Process, too, proves to be fallible: Despite his ability to help others, he is unable to cure himself of his addiction to hard-core pornography. After they return to their previous lives, a growing need develops between Margery and Gluck as both of them become increasingly unable to deal with the conditions of their own existence. After Margery is subjected to Mr. Brindle's domestic violence, she again takes flight from Glasgow and arrives at Gluck's home in London. Once there, Margery is not required to act as a servant, while her presence prevents Gluck from using pornography. It is here, though, that Margery makes the discovery that sex can be a form of need rather than a duty or requirement. Gluck's tentative moves toward a consummation of their relationship, however, involve elements of his deviant sexuality. In a symbolic scene, he attempts to shape and possess Margery in a way that reduces her identity and is thus comparable to her subjection beneath Mr. Brindle's will. Faithful to her marriage vows, and as her God reasserts himself, Margery again flees Gluck's presence and returns to her old life.

In "Mr. Brindle's House," Margery awaits guidance or punishment from her personal God. After a torturous wait, Margery decides to initiate the inevitable violence herself. She is severely injured by her husband, who then takes an overdose of painkillers and dies. Gluck and Margery are reunited in the hospital, and she is discharged into his care. The novella ends as Margery and Edward consummate their relationship under the watchful eye of a "Jealous, Patient Love"—a God of their own mutual creation and the culmination of their Process.

"Original Bliss" shows Margery Brindle's move toward catharsis through a series of incidents that can almost be described as purgatorial. She and Gluck must learn to live both with and without one another in order to test their love and, crucially, their faith. The novella essentially charts the relationship between two badly damaged individuals who, despite their vast differences in life and lifestyle, are able to use their juxtaposition to achieve a kind of spiritual equilibrium. The ending of the novella, however, remains ambiguous. Margery and Edward have, to this point, enjoyed a relationship based on its illicit nature: Both have used the relationship as an escape from a particular conception of reality. It remains to be seen whether they are capable of forging a relationship now that its function as emotional outlet has been exhausted. It is characteristic of Kennedy's style that the removal of the impediment to the relationship, Mr. Brindle, does not amount to resolution. Kennedy's characters live in a complicated world, and there can be no final escape from its demands.

BIBLIOGRAPHY
Kennedy, A. L. *Original Bliss.* London: Jonathan Cape, 1994.

David Borthwick

"OSTLER, THE" WILKIE COLLINS (1855)

"The Ostler" was originally published in the special Christmas issue of *Household Words* in 1855, and WILKIE COLLINS later expanded this supernatural story for inclusion in *The Queen of Hearts* (1859) as "Brother Morgan's Story of the Dream Woman." Collins then significantly lengthened the story as a public reading text for his American lecture tour of 1873–74 and printed yet another revised version, titled "The Dream Woman," in *The Frozen Deep and Other Stories* (1874).

"Unlucky" Isaac Scatchard is an honest and humble ostler who has never had the good fortune to marry or secure stable employment. On his 40th birthday, Isaac journeys from the small cottage that he shares with his widowed mother to seek a position on the distant estate of a gentleman. Upon his arrival however, Isaac is informed that another man has been hired as the stable helper. Unable to make the return journey until the next morning, Isaac seeks lodgings for the night in an isolated road side inn. After he shares a modest meal and amiable conversation with the proprietor, the

household retires to bed. Later, Isaac is abruptly roused from his slumber by a "strange shivering" that courses through his body and by "a dreadful sinking pain at the heart." His eyes are drawn to the foot of his bed, where he is confronted with the vision of a fair, flaxen-haired woman staring intently at him with a knife clasped in her hand. She approaches him and repeatedly attempts to stab him, but he is able to dodge her blows. As the flame on his candle flickers out, so too does the apparition of the woman. The next morning, Isaac is left wondering whether the fair woman with the knife was "the creature of a dream, or that other creature from the unknown world called among men by the name of ghost?"

Upon his return home the next day, Isaac recounts his dream to his mother, who insists on recording every detail, including the date and time of the vision, which happens to be the exact date and time of his birth. Seven years later, Isaac encounters a woman of "lost character," Rebecca Murdoch, to whom he is strangely drawn. She soon "takes possession, not of his passions only, but of his faculties as well." When Isaac brings her home as his wife-to-be, with great alarm his mother immediately points out Rebecca's uncanny resemblance to the dream woman. Against his mother's violent protestations, Isaac gives in to his "fatal passion" and marries Rebecca. After a few months of quiet marital bliss, however, she becomes strangely altered in character and temperament and takes to drinking. As she lies on her deathbed, Isaac's mother beseeches her son to separate from the woman who means him harm. It is advice that he once again does not heed. On Isaac's birthday, Rebecca fulfils the dream prophecy by attacking him in his bed with a knife. She disappears, but Isaac is left in a state of perpetual anxiety that the dream woman will one day return to complete her fatal purpose.

Not only does "The Ostler" represent one of Collins's earliest contributions to the ghost story, but the narrative's engagement of the supernatural, particularly in the form of visions, dreams, and fate, to generate sensation and suspense, beckons to what would become one of the hallmarks of Collins's fiction. Isaac's prophetic vision anticipates some of the more complex dream sequences in works such as *The Woman in White* (1859–60) and *Armadale* (1866).

The dream woman is also one of Collins's early characters who confounds and disrupts the prevailing stereotypes of women in fiction. While she is described as "fair" with "flaxen hair"—the Victorian embodiment of innocence and virtue—the dangerous and desirable dream woman is, in fact, what nightmares are made of. She is likely the prototype for the "dangerous experiment" that Collins suggested in an essay the year after "The Ostler" was published. In "A Petition to the Novel-Writers," written for *Household Words* in 1856, Collins challenged other writers "to overthrow the established order of things" and introduce "a jovial dark sister and a dismal light [one]" in their fiction.

Finally, the dream woman's so-called bewitching of Isaac—a phrase that appears repeatedly in revised versions of the story—hints at the ostler's unstable state of mind, a state in which passion and reason commingle and confound. This image of madness is a fictive strategy that Collins repeatedly returns to and develops throughout his fiction as a means to generate fear and suspense as well as to engage in contemporary debates and theories on the nature of insanity.

BIBLIOGRAPHY

Collins, Wilkie. *Complete Short Fiction*. London: Constable, 1998.

Maria Bachman

"OTHER KINGDOM, THE" E. M. FORSTER (1911)

Throughout his fiction, E. M. FORSTER exposes the artificiality of cultural boundaries, blurring the distinctions between self and other. Many of the stories contain doubles and reflected selves and posit conflict between body and soul. His fictional world often has elements of classical mythology and Greek tragedy, although this is one area that some readers have been quick to criticize as unconvincing and forced. VIRGINIA WOOLF referred to Forster as "an uneasy truant in fairyland" and to the world of his collection *The Celestial Omnibus* as a "freakish land where boys leap into the arms of Pan and girls become trees" (quoted in Herz, 161). Woolf was referring in particular to "The Story of a Panic" and a companion piece of fantasy, "The Other Kingdom," an Edwardian reworking of the Daphne-Apollo myth, in which a young girl,

Daphne, escapes the ministrations of her tutor, Mr. Inskip, who is trying educate her in Pygmalion fashion into a fitting wife for her fiancé Harcourt Waters. The nearby beech wood (the "other kingdom") is the only place where Daphne feels free, and it is here that she finds her true identity in nature while she dances around the trees in a green dress. Her fiancé disapproves of the hold that the wood has over her and fences it in so that it is accessible only via a little bridge. This attempt to control and possess Daphne's spirit is the final straw: "Oh fence me out, if you like! Fence me out as much as you like. But never in." Faced with the prospect of lifelong imprisonment as Harcourt's wife, Daphne flees to back to the natural world of the wood and, like Daphne in the Greek myth, metamorphosizes into a tree. The story seems intended to highlight how modern man has lost respect for and appreciation of a natural system of values and beliefs, uncontaminated by commerce and money.

BIBLIOGRAPHY

Forster, E. M. *The Celestial Omnibus and Other Stories*. London: Sidgwick and Jackson, 1911.
Herz, Judith Scherer. *The Short Narratives of E. M. Forster*. London: Macmillan, 1988.

Andrew Maunder

"OTHER SIDE OF THE HEDGE, THE" E. M. FORSTER (1904)

This short story was first published in the liberal monthly *Independent Review* in 1904. Later it was reprinted in E. M. FORSTER's first short story collection, *The Celestial Omnibus and Other Stories* (1911), and in *The Collected Tales of E. M. Forster* (1947). In his introduction to the latter volume, Forster calls all of the included pieces fantasies. "The Other Side of the Hedge" is narrated by an unnamed 25-year-old protagonist who identifies himself with the group "we of the road." Walking along a dusty road bordered by tall, dry hedges, he becomes exhausted but is revived by a "puff of air" coming through the hedge (*Tales,* 40). Enticed, he wedges himself through the hedge and falls into a moat on the other side. A middle-aged man rescues him, and the narrator sees that the sparsely populated landscape is open and lush compared with the narrow, dry road.

1 of one word

The older man explains that this place leads nowhere. Believing that the place is a prison, the narrator becomes increasingly agitated, especially when his attempts to compete with the older man and to measure his own progress are frustrated. A solitary runner and a woman singing by herself puzzle him. When he wonders aloud what it all means, the older man tells him several times that "It means nothing but itself" (*Tales*, 44). The narrator wishes to leave, but the older man insists on showing him a white gate in the hedge that opens onto the road. He explains that humanity went out the gate long ago, but the road doubles back and runs close to the hedge. The narrator stubbornly insists that the road moves forward to an unknown goal. Attempting to leave again, he is held in check by the older man. After the narrator refuses milk, fruit, and flowers offered by the inhabitants of the land, the older man brings him to another, semitransparent gate that opens in from the road. When the narrator sees the road again he loses self-control, gulps beer stolen from a man passing by, and succumbs to exhaustion. The older man shuts the gate and tells him that humanity will return by this gate. Before the narrator falls asleep he hears nightingales, smells hay, and sees the stars coming out. In the final moment, he recognizes the man whose beer he stole as his brother, whom he had left behind on the road a year ago.

In this story, Forster draws his imagery from English country roads, which are often bordered by tall hedges, in order to contrast English notions of progress and "race" (in the double sense of competition and English civilization) with the unregimented, pastoral beauty of landscapes modeled on the Greek and Italian countryside. A recurrent image in his novels and other short stories, rustic landscapes reveal to Forster's characters the possibility of humanistic liberation from stultifying, socially inculcated routines and sharply limited individuality. In this story, the people on the other side of the hedge are kind and unworried, and they pursue activities for their own sake (and thus resemble the Eloi, meek people who also live on fruit and gather flowers in H. G. WELLS's science fiction novel *The Time Machine* [1895]). But the narrator, who is "of the road," is so mentally and physically confined to a narrow life of mandatory "advancement," symbolized by the dusty road boxed in by "brown crackling hedges" and a "strip" of sky, that he cannot see the point of any other way of life (*Tales*, 41, 48). This story can also be read as an allegory, in which the other side of the hedge is Arcadia and the narrator's brother represents death (he carries a scythe and causes the narrator to lose consciousness).

BIBLIOGRAPHY
Forster, E. M. *The Collected Tales of E. M. Forster.* New York: Knopf, 1947. Reprinted 1979.

Sarah Russo

"OUR FRIEND JUDITH" DORIS LESSING (1960)

A short story originally published in *Partisan Review* (1960) and later collected in DORIS LESSING's volume of short stories *A Man and Two Women* (1963). Written more than a decade before the mainstream feminist movement and two years before her influential novel *"The Golden Notebook"* (1962), "Our Friend Judith" portrays an independent, intelligent, and self-sufficient woman who is a source of bewilderment and rumor to those around her.

Judith Castlewell, the protagonist, is a woman whom others find impossible to categorize. At the story's beginning, the unnamed first-person narrator says that Judith has been called a "typical English spinster," but that this label is clearly insufficient. The narrator laments that Judith is so misunderstood but is frustrated by her own inability to understand her friend. The story is structured around a series of anecdotes about Judith, each of which is a source of gossip between the narrator and her close friend Betty. Whenever Betty or the narrator sees Judith, they call the other to "report" on her, as though Judith is a source of excitement in their own more mundane lives. The story is typically realist in that the narrator probes Judith's motives, psychology, and inner life by analyzing the outer "facts" of her existence, but it is also critical of psychological realism as a genre, since Judith remains an enigma no matter how many "facts" the narrator uncovers. Judith has lived alone for 20 years, in a small, shabby London flat. She is beautiful yet dresses to appear plain; she attracts men but prefers to live alone and maintain casual sexual relationships with married men. She is a poet, but her poems focus on "scientific, mechanical, and chemical imagery" rather than personal expression. She likes cats but cannot inhibit their freedom by keeping them as pets.

In the second half of the story, Judith takes a long trip to Italy to get away from her lover, who has annoyed her by offering to divorce his wife and marry Judith. Betty decides to visit Judith and writes a long letter to the narrator describing Judith's life in Italy: She has adopted a cat and begun a romance with an Italian barber named Luigi Rineiri. Judith's behavior in Italy upsets Betty because it is uncharacteristic of the cool and aloof person she imagines Judith to be. Intrigued, the narrator decides to go to Italy herself. By the time she arrives, however, Judith has unexpectedly left. The traumatic death of a cat, it seems, has led Judith to believe there is a "complete gulf of understanding" between herself and the Rineiri family. Back in London, the narrator asks Judith to explain her actions. Judith is offended by the narrator's snooping and ironically proclaims in the last lines that Betty and the narrator are strange and incomprehensible women.

Like much of *A Man and Two Women,* this story focuses on a relationship among three people: Betty, Judith, and the narrator. Betty and the narrator are very much alike; they are both conventional, middle-aged, married housewives. As the title "Our Friend Judith" suggests, the two women have nearly identical views and imagine that this consensus gives them moral authority: They are "normal"; Judith is "abnormal." Nonetheless, Lessing suggests that Judith's independent femininity is both incomprehensible and secretly tantalizing to them. Like much of Lessing's fiction, the story opposes traditional and modern women and reveals women's growing discontent with limited social roles. The story is also characteristic of Lessing's postmodernism in that it challenges the traditional enlightenment conception of self. The narrator and Betty struggle to locate Judith's "real" or "authentic" self, but the story suggests that no such self exists. Judith is a fragmented, unpredictable character rather than a unified and knowable one. And at the end of the story, when Judith calls the narrator and Betty "strange," Lessing reminds readers how little they know of the story's anonymous narrator. She, it seems, is just as enigmatic as Judith.

BIBLIOGRAPHY

Gardiner, Judith Kegan. "Gender, Values, and Lessing's Cats," *Tulsa Studies in Women's Literature* 3, no. 1–2 (1984): 111–124.

Michael, Magali Cornier. *Feminism and the Postmodern Impulse: Post–World War II Fiction.* Albany: State University of New York Press, 1996.

Sprague, Clair. *Rereading Doris Lessing: Narrative Patterns of Doubling and Repetition.* Chapel Hill: University of North Carolina Press, 1987.

Waugh, Patricia. *Feminine Fictions: Revisiting the Postmodern.* London: Routledge, 1989.

Elizabeth Carolyn Miller

P

PAIN, BARRY (1864–1928)

The son of a Cambridge linen draper, Pain studied classics at the local university, where he attracted a reputation for his witty stories in a university magazine, *Granta.* Subsequently, his long career included contributions to the *Cornhill,* the STRAND, *Black and White, Punch,* the *Idler,* and many other periodicals (see MAGAZINES). Thanks to his popular "Eliza" stories, which satirize social-climbing suburbanites, Pain is often characterized as a humorist, but his varied output ranges from social commentary to the supernatural. His short fiction is far superior to his rambling novels, and some of his most interesting stories use light humor to critique literary fashions, including the short story itself. Published in *Black and White* in 1894, "The Autobiography of an Idea" is narrated by an idea for a short story, which observes that "it is an exceedingly rare thing for a single short story to attract any attention at all." But the short story resulting from the idea is so original that it captivates a readership that transcends classes and tastes, from the posh country house to the plebeian public house.

Pain's later critical writings reveal his optimism about the British reading public as an improving influence on literature. An important index to this influence is the taste for short stories and especially readers' impatience with formulaic iterations of the genre popularized by the magazines. In the early years of the 20th century, Pain wrote not only in but also about the genre, first a textbook for the London Correspondence College (1906) and then a defense of the British short story (1912). Like many commentaries of the time, the latter volume acknowledges that "Artistic work is rarely popular. . . . If the most artistic work is that which makes the greatest demand on whom it is submitted, then no kind of literary work is more artistic than the short story." Unlike his contemporaries, who blame a newly educated mass readership for slowing the development of the short story, Pain champions the British reader as discriminating and capable of elevating the genre's "most artistic work." His book is as much a defense of the British reader as it is a defense of the short story. Acknowledging the poor quality of most magazine stories, he points out that readers "are growing weary of the magazine story made like a flabby pudding from an aged recipe. They are watching with less interest the monthly parade of stock characters through plots of worthless ingenuity. The time will come when such readers will want more—will they get it?" Far from condemning readers, Pain exhorts writers to abandon the cynical reconfiguration of characters and excitements: The short story is the locus of literary change.

BIBLIOGRAPHY

Pain, Barry. *Collected Tales.* London: Mark Secker, 1916.
———. *Eliza.* London: Cassell, 1908.
———. *The Eliza Stories.* London: Pavillion, 1984.
———. *The Short Story.* New York: George H. Doran, 1912.

Winnie Chan

"PARSON'S DAUGHTER OF OXNEY COLNE, THE" ANTHONY TROLLOPE (1861)

Patience Woolsworthy, the parson's daughter, is beautiful, talented, and witty, but she does not bother to list these qualities in her estimation of herself. Instead, the strong-willed "Patty" strives to be sensible and free from the tendencies of romantic heroines. When Captain John Broughton comes to visit from London, his aunt, who is also Patience's neighbor and confidant, suggests that he might fall in love with Patty. And indeed, he does. But Patience, though she returns his love passionately, refuses to show it. She tells the captain to go away to consider his affections and return only when they are certain. For four months, Patience keeps her secret and goes about her ordinary life uninterrupted. When Broughton returns and presses her for a vow of love, she takes it as proof of his certainty and finally confesses her full heart to him. The engagement is promptly announced, but that very evening the captain begins to doubt his decision. He worries that Patience is ill-suited for London society and resolves to instruct her. The resulting tensions lead Patty to dissolve the engagement, contending that the gift of her heart should not be weighed against the gift of his fortune or status. The captain eventually marries an heiress, while Patty remains "an old maid."

Typical of ANTHONY TROLLOPE's realism, this story deromanticizes the lovers and the love affair for the reader. Trollope undermines traditional marriage plots not only by canceling the marriage but also by withholding the details of courtship until after the engagement occurs. Furthermore, romantic sentiments appear entirely untrustworthy here. Patty's initial reluctance to confess her love is justified by Broughton's abruptly cooled ardor after the engagement. And ultimately, their break is precipitated by Patty's romantic ideal that Broughton should value her love apart from realistic concerns for wealth and status.

BIBLIOGRAPHY

Trollope, Anthony. *Complete Short Stories.* Forth Worth: Texas Christian University Press, 1979–83.

Katherine Malon

"PENANCE, THE" SAKI (1870–1916)

One of SAKI's [H. H. Munro's] tragicomic explorations of the gap between imaginative children and conventional adults, "The Penance" first appeared in the *Westminster Gazette* on September 24, 1910.

Octavian Ruttle has recently killed the neighboring children's tabby cat, which he thought had been killing his chickens. The children, unfortunately, witnessed the death over the wall between the houses, and they utter one word in unison to the feline-slayer: "Beast!" Ruttle's peace offerings to the children are spurned, and he soon realizes that, in fact, rats have been eating his poultry. One afternoon, desperate to placate his little foes, he brings out his two-year-old daughter Olivia to charm them and picks some flowers from his garden for the three siblings. But while his back is turned, the children take Olivia to Octavian's piggeries, where they hoist her onto a sty roof, threatening to throw her to the swine. As the parties negotiate terms, Olivia falls into the muck. Octavian tries to reach his slowly sinking daughter but cannot move in the quagmire of mud. Panic-stricken, he agrees to the children's demands—for half-an-hour, he will stand in a white sheet by the cat's grave, holding a candle and saying, "I'm a miserable Beast"—and the trio pass a short ladder down to him so he can crawl slowly across it and extricate his daughter from the mire. That evening, Octavian serves his penance, and "the next morning his eyes were gladdened by a sheet of copy-book paper lying beside the blank wall, on which was written the message 'Un-Beast.'"

Saki is an expert illustrator of the difference between adults' and children's worlds, exemplified here by the "high blank wall" between Octavian and his unnamed juvenile opponents, a barrier that "would not be more impervious to his explanations than the bunch of human hostility that peered over its coping." As in the better-known "Sredni Vashtar" (published just four months earlier) or "The Lumber-Room" (1913), children's private, devoutly animist rituals and beliefs eclipse their public ties to family, friends, or neighbors. The children morally equate humans and beasts by suggesting that Olivia's death is compensation for their cat's and telling Octavian that he is a "Beast." In an echo of "The SCHARTZ-METTERKLUME METHOD," they use their basic knowledge of bloody events in adult history against adults. The "standing puzzle" of this intelligent, moral child-force reveals the blandness, immorality, and hypocrisy of an unfeeling, hidebound Edwardian society.

Many critics have pointed out that Ethel Munro's biography of her brother suggests that Munro's harsh upbringing in the household of two aunts in Pilton—as outlined in his sister's 1924 memoir—is reflected in Saki's stories of children wreaking revenge on adult guardians. "The Penance," with its children growing up in England while their parents are "in India," certainly seems inspired by the animal-loving Munro's children's time together in 1870s Devon while their father was in Burma, when, as Ethel writes in her 1924 memoir, "there were the three of us, and we lived a life of our own, in which the grown-ups had no part."

BIBLIOGRAPHY

Saki. *The Complete Saki.* Harmondsworth, England: Penguin, 1982.

Brian Gibson

"PHANTOM RICKSHAW, THE" RUDYARD KIPLING (1885)   Written when RUDYARD KIPLING was 19, this story first appeared in the 1885 *Quartette,* the Christmas annual of the *Gazette.* An ironic and haunting ghost story, "The Phantom Rickshaw" has a message: Using people, specifically women, as mere sex objects will bring suffering and death. Jack Pansay, the only one who sees the ghost of Mrs. Agnes Keith-Wessington, cannot understand why he is being haunted, even though everyone around him, including his fiancée, Kitty Mannering, and his doctor, Heatherlegh, regard him as a "blackguard." Returning to India after vacationing in England, Jack, a civil servant of the British Empire, has a casual shipboard fling with Agnes but then abruptly and cruelly severs the relationship. When Jack announces to Agnes his engagement, she dies of grief. The apparition that haunts Jack is this scene of his announcement: Agnes seated in a yellow-banded rickshaw, looking frail and sorrowful, her golden head leaning out, a handkerchief pressed to her face. During subsequent encounters Jack demands an

explanation for the haunting, and Agnes's ghost replies: "Jack! Jack darling! Its some hideous mistake. . . . *Please* forgive me and lets be friends" (122). Kitty, disgusted by Jack's bizarre behavior and conversations with invisible people but more so by his treatment of Agnes, breaks off their engagement. Haunted and abandoned, Jack dies, creating much speculation about the cause of his death.

The ghost story has two parts: The brief first part told by an unnamed narrator and the longer second part. The first part constructs a plausible scenario for the willing suspense of disbelief necessary for fantasy tales. However, Heatherlegh's first explanation, that Jack died of overwork, is ironic, for Jack frequently vacations in both England and India. Heatherlegh's second explanation, that Jack is crazy and has a devilish attitude, is more plausible given his cruelty toward Agnes.

The second part is the ghost story narrated by Jack. When medical cures fail, Heatherlegh suggests that Jack write his hauntings down to cure him of his delusions, but the therapy fails, making Jack an object of ridicule and providing fodder for more storytelling. Although neither Jack nor the reader discovers what the ghost's words mean, they are prophetic: Jack roams the streets of Simla with the ghost of Agnes as his only friend.

Although Kipling has generally been faulted for his sympathy with Britain's imperialism, "The Phantom Rickshaw" suggests the colonial subject's insight into the inevitable failure of imperialism. The story's unusual opening, "One of the few advantages that India has over England is a great knowability" (113), is followed by a description of India's excessive hospitality. The "knowability" reflects, perhaps, India's knowledge that Britain, flattered by its glory and power, had failed to clothe its own naked greed and was unaware of its nakedness. Britain had become so accustomed to fleecing its colonies, the first narrator says, that "every Englishman in the Empire . . . may travel anywhere and everywhere without paying hotel-bills" and that "globe trotters who expect entertainment as a right, have . . . blunted this open-heartedness" (113). Heatherlegh concocts stories that have the appearance of rational explanations and disseminates these stories to spare Jack further humiliation, just as the British Raj had methodically disseminated narratives of its own altruism in bringing enlightenment to the so-called uncivilized natives of India. But just as Jack's arrogance and greed for sexual adventure bring about loss and death, the unchecked greed and glory of the British Empire brought loss and death to British citizens, reflecting the Indian philosophy that people who did wrong eventually paid the price for their wrongdoing. Nonetheless, "The Phantom Rickshaw" is first and foremost a haunting ghost story, comparable to Poe's "The Tell-Tale Heart" and "The Black Cat," that launched Kipling's career in the genre of the supernatural.

BIBLIOGRAPHY
Kipling, Rudyard. *Phantoms and Fantasies.* New York: Doubleday, 1965.
————. *Something about Myself.* London: Macmillan, 1937.
Ricketts, Harry. *The Unforgiving Minute: A Life of Rudyard Kipling.* London: Chatto & Windus, 1999.

Sukanya Senapati

"PICTURES" KATHERINE MANSFIELD (1919) Though this story was originally published in 1917 for the *New Age* as "The Common Round," KATHERINE MANSFIELD changed its original dialogue form and set it out as a narrative under the title "Pictures." This new version appeared in the autumn issue of *Arts and Letters* in 1919 (later to be included in Mansfield's collection *Bliss and Other Stories,* 1921) and was enthusiastically acclaimed by readers. Like "MISS BRILL," this is the story of an aging spinster, Miss Ada Moss, a desperate penniless actress who calls herself "old girl." Although she studied in the College of Music, has a good contralto voice, and used to sing in concerts in the West End, there is no place for her in a world that only values physical appearance and youth. The story has a bipolar structure: On the one hand is Miss Moss's idealism in her dream to become a successful actress; on the other hand is the dominant reality, sordid and asphyxiating, that gradually suffocates this woman's expectations. Her final acquiescence to reality happens at the end of the story, when she is invited to have a drink with and is picked up by a lecherous and threatening man. This dichotomy can be synthesized by the image of the mirror, ubiquitous in the story, which represents Miss Moss's two sides: The idealist one is the flesh-and-bone

lady who has internalized the romantic values traditionally required of women, while the realist one is the mirror image that mocks her. Mansfield parodies not only the harmful effect of sentimentalism in young girls but also its lifelong determinism in women's lives, so that even mature women like Miss Moss live in a false dream that condemns them to failure and frustration. This story draws on Mansfield's earlier experience, from 1913 to 1916, occasionally acting as an extra in films.

BIBLIOGRAPHY
Mansfield, Katherine. *Bliss and Other Stories.* London: Bloomsbury, 1994.

Gerardo Rodriguez Salas

"PING" SAMUEL BECKETT (1966) "Ping" was first written in French (titled "Bing") in 1966 and was translated by the author in 1967. It came at a time when SAMUEL BECKETT was pushing the boundaries of what was possible in both prose and drama and creating radically challenging texts. As such, "Ping" is undoubtedly a difficult story to read and interpret, yet experiencing the text can be thrilling and even strangely moving.

Beckett's extreme minimalist style creates a text of 1,030 words with an entire vocabulary of just 120 words, of which just 7 words appear only once. The density of repetition is the first thing the reader encounters. Key words or word groups, such as "all known," "bare white body fixed," or "legs joined like sewn," are repeated again and again, often with slight variations or subtly different orders. The effect can often be that the words swim before the eyes, or that certain rare words—such as "unover" or "haught"—suddenly grab the attention. This repetition is further heightened by Beckett removing many of the nuts, bolts, and punctuation marks of grammar, as in the first sentence: "All known all white bare white body fixed one yard legs joined like sewn." However, while the language seems impenetrable, a syntactical rhythm begins to emerge that limits the relationships among words while maintaining the possibility of other relationships that, in turn, can create other possible interpretations.

Beckett has reduced elements such as setting, character, and plot to an absolute minimum. The setting is a white box, one yard square and two high. In the box is a white body, apparently fixed, its legs and heels together "like sewn" with the palms of the hands hanging forward; the only sign of color is "the eyes only just light blue almost white," which are the only things still "unover."

The third element is that of the title: "ping." Many commentators have seen the "ping" as an external noise, part of a mechanism that rings slight changes in the box, as in the following sentence, in which the "ping" seems to alter the apparently fixed body: "Light heat white planes shining white bare white body fixed ping fixed elsewhere." Quite where or how the body might be fixed elsewhere is not said. This interpretation gains credibility from the association of "ping" with "murmur," which also seems to be an external sound and might offer the hope of a world beyond the box: "Ping murmur only just almost never one second perhaps a way out . . . Ping murmur perhaps a nature" If the "ping" is a sound external to the box, then it at least admits of some hope; there is something "out there," if only the remains of a mechanism. The second possibility is that "ping" is allied to the consciousness of the figure in the box. In this reading, the "ping" rings mental changes, such as the intrusion of images and memories, however brief, into the otherwise narrow field of the consciousness's perspective, which is primarily concerned with stating the "all known" of the situation in the box.

Given the difficulties of arriving at a stable interpretation, the following description of what might be said to occur in the story must be taken as extremely tentative. A figure is trapped within a white box. This figure, through an impersonal narration, attempts to state the "all known" of the situation in the box. The obsessive repetition of these elements suggests that the figure cannot finally state all that is known and thus bring the attempts at statement to an end. The desire to state "all known," all that is here and now, is frustrated by the intrusion, heralded by the "ping," of an elsewhere that is "known not." This elsewhere is at first imagined spatially as if there were "a nature" beyond the box. Yet the murmurs and images increasingly become a question of memory rather than place. The dominant recurring memory, no more than a trace, is of "blue and white in the wind." These traces "of old" are "unover,"

as if they have to be suppressed in order for the figure to live within the "all known" of the box. Memory ultimately focuses on a second pair of imploring black and white eyes. The figure manages to quash the memory of the blue and white in the wind and resolves that "that much memory henceforth never" before, in the final sentence, quashing the memory of the black eyes, thus allowing the figure's consciousness to be no longer elsewhere but here and now within the known. Only then, finally fixed, can the obsessive voice come to a close and all come to an end: "Head haught eyes white fixed front old ping last murmur one second perhaps not alone eye unlustrous black and white half closed long lashes imploring ping silence ping over."

Multiple different readings are possible: that the figure is struggling to recall rather than to suppress memory, that the final black eyes are those of some interrogator, that the word *ping* comes to mean or even name the figure itself, that references to the palms and torn flesh create associations with Christ. This list is by no means exhaustive. These equally plausible interpretations point to one of the story's major achievements. The reader is tantalized by images or traces that seem to offer hope of a coherent interpretation. On second glance, these traces are replaced by others that offer a different and no less coherent interpretation. In this way, the reader is placed in a situation similar to that of the figure in the box, desperately trying to make the "not known" into the "known," to make the words that slide into one another on the page come together and finally settle into a stable meaning. The result is that we do not read about something but rather that something happens to us as we read.

BIBLIOGRAPHY
Beckett, Samuel. *Six Residua*. London: J. Calder, 1978.
Lodge, David. "Some 'Ping' Understood," *Encounter* 30, no. 2 (1968): 85–89.

Paul Stewart

PLAIN TALES FROM THE HILLS RUDYARD KIPLING (1888)

The first edition of *Plain Tales from the Hills* contains 40 stories written by RUDYARD KIPLING between 1884 and 1887. Most of the stories were first published in the *Civil and Military Gazette,* of which

Kipling was assistant editor, in Lahore, India, between 1884 and 1887.

The stories are short and were designed to fit a column and a half of the *Gazette*. The majority concern Anglo-Indian life, usually, though not always, contemporary. The subjects are personal and professional rivalries, love affairs and flirtations, dances, sporting occasions, government policies, job searches in the British administration, and the work of British officials and businesspeople. In addition, some stories focus exclusively on military life. Four of these deal with a trio of private soldiers, one of whom, the Irishman Mulvaney, is the principal narrator of three of them. *Plain Tales from the Hills* also contains stories with Indians as their central characters. Even in these, however, there is mostly an interaction (usually unfortunate) between European and Indian characters at the center of the text.

The collection's title is ambiguous. These are tales not just of the Indian plains but also of life in mountainous northern India (for example, in Simla, the summer capital of British India). They are "plain" not in the sense of being simple but rather in the sense of being outspoken. Many are scarcely "tales" in any developed sense but have plots without much complexity and seem much closer to gossip and anecdote than to short stories by Kipling's contemporaries de Maupassant or Chekhov.

The principal narrator of the stories is anonymous but presents himself as a knowledgeable observer of Anglo-Indian and Indian life who is able to move from the world of powerful imperial administrators through the various ranks of European and Indian society to the world of some of the lowest of British India. Indeed, the theme of knowledge recurs in the narrator's comments on life and in characters like the policeman Strickland or the drunkard McIntosh Jellaludin, who has adopted an Indian way of life. The narrator often addresses the reader directly, frequently mentioning stories that he will not tell at the moment. As a whole, the stories are marked by a negative view of British India. Bureaucratic infighting and incompetence, a struggle for easy and lucrative postings, and cruelty and callousness in personal relationships fill the stories. The racism and violence

of Kipling's narrator and characters are hard for modern readers to accept, and they are not part of his cynicism toward the world he depicts. However, approval is given to some characters: the enterprising (and naked) British soldiers who take a town in Burma; the imperial administrator who is wise enough to listen to a child; the resourceful Mrs. Hauksbee, who often does good; and Eurasian Michele D'Cruze, who maintains British imperial authority in the face of a riot.

It is noteworthy that many of the stories in *Plain Tales from the Hills* involve the crossing of borders, usually racial ones. In this respect, "Beyond the Pale" stands as a complex examination of Kipling's fascination with the Indian world but his insistence on the terrible consequences of passing too far into that world. The concluding story of the collection, "To Be Filed for Reference," presents a similarly ambiguous version of the topic.

BIBLIOGRAPHY

Kerr, Douglas. "Plain Tales from the Hills (1888)." Literary Encyclopedia. Available online. URL: http://www.LitEncyc.com. Accessed June 5, 2006.

McGivering, John, ed. Notes on stories in *Plain Tales from the Hills*. The Kipling Society: Readers' Guide. Available online. URL: http://www.kipling.org.uk/booKmart_collects.htm#plain. Accessed June 5, 2006.

David Malcolm

"PLAYING SARDINES" MICHÈLE ROBERTS (2001)

Playing Sardines (2001), the collection in which the short story of the same name appears, is MICHÈLE ROBERTS's second independently authored collection of short stories. Chronologically and thematically it may be considered alongside Roberts's most recent novels, including *The Looking Glass* (2000), *The Mistressclass* (2003), and *Reader, I Married Him* (2005). These texts are distinguished by their sensuous language, particularly with regard to food, and although Roberts's use of religious themes is still apparent, it is much less prominent than in her earlier works. According to Sarah Sceats, Roberts "evokes food almost as a constituent of female sensuousness and contingency, suggesting a knowledge and understanding more visceral than cerebral" (127). In many of Roberts's texts food preparation and enjoyment serve as a vehicle through which women explore their identities. In particular, her stories often link food to the construction of national identity and expose the difficulties inherent in navigating two cultural backgrounds. Roberts herself is half English and half French, and from this personal experience she is able to construct characters who must straddle two cultures with opposing expectations. This struggle ultimately strengthens the character's sense of identity.

"Playing Sardines" describes a young Englishwoman's experiences in Italy as the wife of an architectural historian. It is written in the style of a love story, but the amorous exchange occurs not between the husband and wife but rather between the woman and the Italian culinary arts. As she patrols the markets for food and *art brut,* her husband pursues his latest female conquest. The narrator lacks the sophistication he desires in a wife: She wears the wrong clothes and does not possess the mannerisms of a proper *signora.* She, in turn, feels that there is an impersonal distance between her husband and his food that represents his lack of understanding of its true beauty. She is more comfortable in the kitchen with the village women and the livery boy, where the connection to the food is more visceral and therefore more real. Ultimately she returns to England as a single woman but with a greater understanding of herself.

In this story, Roberts draws an explicit connection between food and the human body. "Playing sardines" refers both to the tedious process of opening a tin of sardines and a child's game in which bodies pile on top of one another in the dark. Within the language of the text, there is a strong contrast between the narrator's meticulous observation of details and her husband's sweeping generalizations about Palladian architecture. She transgresses Italian custom at the level of the dinner guest but finds a more visceral connection with Italian food in the kitchen. It is this connection that she retains as part of her identity when she returns to England.

BIBLIOGRAPHY
Roberts, Michèle. *Food, Sex, and God: On Inspiration and Writing.* London: Virago, 1998.
———. *Playing Sardines.* London: Virago, 2001.

Sceats, Sarah. *Food, Consumption and the Body in Contemporary Women's Fiction.* Cambridge: Cambridge University Press, 2000.

Sherah Wells

"PLEASURE-PILGRIM, THE" ELLA D'ARCY (1895)
When ELLA D'ARCY's collection of short stories *Monochromes,* which includes "The Pleasure-Pilgrim," was published in 1895, she was a fixture of the 1890s London literary scene. She was an editor of the provocative journal *The YELLOW BOOK* and was compared favorably to writers such as Ethel Coburn Mayne, JOSEPH CONRAD, and HENRY JAMES. "The Pleasure-Pilgrim" takes up the theme of the American girl abroad, which had been popularized by James in *DAISY MILLER,* thus prompting a reviewer in the *Chicago Tribune* to accuse D'Arcy of knowing nothing about American girls.

In "The Pleasure-Pilgrim," Campbell, an Englishman vacationing at Schloss Altenau (a German castle converted into a boardinghouse for tourists), meets Lulie Thayer, an American traveling with her female companion. Campbell is immediately drawn to Lulie, despite his misgivings about her frankness and apparent freedom. His friend Mayne, who is also staying at the Schloss, notices Campbell's attraction to Lulie and informs him that Lulie is an egregious flirt and is considered an adventuress. He tells Campbell that he himself had once engaged in a flirtation with Lulie and that Lulie had sent her companion, Miss Dodge, to proposition him on Lulie's behalf. To further his point, Mayne shows Campbell a beribboned stick—on the ribbon, he claims, are the names and dates of Lulie's conquests.

Campbell becomes disillusioned with Lulie as a result of his conversation with Mayne. The next morning Miss Dodge assures Campbell that Lulie was speaking to him in earnest and that she is so upset by his coldness that she has taken ill. When Campbell relays this information to Mayne, Mayne cynically tells Campbell that Lulie is a consummate actress and is merely playing the part of a love-struck woman. Later Lulie, having recovered, asks Campbell whether he will at least accept her love even if he cannot return it and becomes vexed when Campbell tells her that he does not believe her feelings for him are genuine. Campbell admits that, in his view, genuine love is by nature passive; he moreover reveals to her his anxiety about her relationships with other men. Lulie tries to assure him that this is the first time she has ever been in love. Agitated, Lulie declares that she would rather die than suffer any more of Campbell's rejections.

One rainy day, Lulie asks Campbell if he would like to shoot with her. She brings him her pistols and tells him that a crackshot rancher from Montana taught her how to use a gun. Campbell immediately becomes jealous, despite Lulie's assurances that the rancher was not one of her romances. Lulie tries to explain to Campbell that her childhood, a gadabout existence without a stable home, is what has made her so unconventional. Campbell, however, keeps insisting that she is defiling the nature of love by her actions. He claims that if Lulie truly loved him as she says she does, she would be so disgusted by her past experiences with men that she would shoot herself. Lulie asks him if that gesture would finally convince him of her love and Campbell quickly says that it would. Lulie suddenly takes the pistol and fatally shoots herself. After the suicide, Miss Dodge tells Campbell that Lulie killed herself because she did not want to live without his love, while Mayne maintains that Lulie, the consummate actress, was simply ending her performance as the tragic lover.

"The Pleasure-Pilgrim" is an excellent example of both NEW WOMAN fiction and the transition to MODERNISM. Lulie is punished by both Campbell and Mayne for her supposed promiscuity, specifically by their conviction that a promiscuous woman cannot love genuinely. Lulie's actions, moreover, are left deliberately ambiguous. We are never sure whether Mayne's or Miss Dodge's interpretation of Lulie's suicide is correct. Is she a practiced adventuress, merely seeing Campbell as her latest conquest? Or is she a woman who loves Campbell so passionately that she cannot foresee living without him? D'Arcy raises many questions in this story concerning women's sexuality and the disjuncture between the act of romance and the feelings that underscore it. This story is a criticism of Victorian men's fears of sexual, independent women; also implicit, however, is a criticism of the New Woman's inability to love in a way that will lead to a happy resolution.

BIBLIOGRAPHY

D'Arcy, Ella. *Monochromes.* London: John Lane, 1895.

Maier, Sarah E. "Subverting the Ideal: The New Woman and the Battle of the Sexes in the Short Fiction of Ella D'Arcy," *Victorian Review* 20 (1994): 35–48.

Windholz, Anne M. "The Woman Who Would Be Editor: Ella D'Arcy and the *Yellow Book,*" *Victorian Periodicals Review* 29 (1996): 116–130.

Heather Marcovitch

"POOR RELATION'S STORY, THE"

CHARLES DICKENS (1852) One of two short stories by CHARLES DICKENS that appeared in the Christmas number of *Household Words* in 1852, *A Round of Stories by the Christmas Fire.* The story was later published by Chapman and Hall in *Christmas Stories* (1859), a volume that included all the Christmas numbers of *Household Words* from 1850 to 1859.

After a brief introduction, the story is handed over to the "poor relation," who begins the first round of stories to be told around the Christmas fire. He opens with a confession that he is not what the family supposes him to be, recounting what everyone believes is true: that he is "nobody's enemy but my own," ruined by being too friendly in business, too trustful in love. Sixty years old, he lives on a small allowance in a lodging and spends most of his days wandering through the City of London, visiting offices and countinghouses until he returns, alone, to his room. While he spends most of his time alone, his happiest days are those spent with his cousin's child, Little Frank. The child is like the poor relation, easily ignored and quiet, and the old man likes to walk with him and see the sights since they "understand each other." He awaits the sad time when Little Frank will go to school and when he himself will die, leaving behind for his small friend only a little miniature of himself.

After recounting this "general impression" of his life, the poor relation goes on to reveal that "this is all wrong" and that, in fact, he lives in a castle. The balance of the story skillfully interweaves what everyone believes has happened to the poor relation with what he now claims to be true. When he was disinherited by his uncle for choosing to marry a poor girl, he was not, as his relatives believe, rejected by this woman for a wealthier man; instead, he insists, he married her and raised a family and that his first grandson "is so like Little Frank, that I hardly know which is which." Instead of being swindled by a business partner he trusted too much, he maintains, they had a "prosperous and happy partnership" that resulted in the marriage of their two eldest children. He ends the story by declaring that he does not know what loneliness is and that he always has some child or grandchild visiting to keep him company. As the story closes, one of the group listening begins to ask about the poor relation's "castle," and the man reveals to all that his castle "is in the Air."

The structure of this story follows the framework of Dickens's early Christmas stories, in which each tale is told by one person sitting around the fire. This structure suggests "Dickens's continuing obsession with the narrator-story relationship," as the stories revealed their narrator's characters while also "gaining effect from their particular teller" (Glancy, 60). The substance of the story demonstrates Dickens's belief that the Christmas season could be used for moral purposes and his almost obsessive insistence on childhood innocence and morality. Little Frank's relationship with the old man idealizes a bond that nurtures the child and accepts him for who he is. The poor relation models the power of the human spirit to overcome adversity and still remain hopeful, all the while dreaming of a world where humans are compassionate and where capitalism coexists with benevolence.

BIBLIOGRAPHY

Dickens, Charles. *Christmas Books, Tales and Sketches.* Garden City, N.Y.: Nelson Doubleday, Inc., 1956.

Glancy, Ruth F. "Dickens and Christmas: His Framed-Tale Themes," *Nineteenth-Century Fiction* 35 (June 1980): 53–72.

Jordan, John O., ed. *The Cambridge Companion to Charles Dickens.* Cambridge: Cambridge University Press, 2001.

Beth Callaghan

"PORNOGRAPHY" IAN MCEWAN (1978) The short story "Pornography" opens IAN MCEWAN's second collection of short stories, *In between the Sheets* (1978). The story returns to the familiar themes of McEwan's earlier collection of stories, *FIRST LOVE, LAST RITES* (1972), with its focus on the relationship between sexuality and violence.

The main character, O'Byrne, works in his brother Harold's pornography shop in London. O'Byrne resents his older brother and works listlessly for him as his brother updates his shop to focus on selling American pornography, more lucrative than its British equivalents. O'Byrne spends his free time drinking with his brother's friends and visiting the flats of two nurses, both of whom work at the same hospital but in different wards. Pauline, in the children's ward, is passive and quiet; Lucy, from the other side of the hospital, leads O'Byrne into increasingly unusual sexual games and activities, including an episode in which she urinates on him as he achieves orgasm. O'Byrne, despite his initial distaste for such activities, eventually submits and begins to enjoy them. Infected with a venereal disease at the opening of the story, O'Byrne knowingly spreads it to both nurses. He suspends both relationships during the two weeks he receives medical treatments, which sap his sexual desire. When he returns to Lucy's flat for a prearranged assignation, she plies him with food, wine, conversation, and sexual titillation. She ties him up on the bed, and O'Byrne prepares for a new game of domination and submission. Instead, Pauline arrives at the flat, and the two nurses begin sterilizing surgical equipment, preparing to castrate O'Byrne. He struggles desperately against his bonds, though he seems perversely excited at the prospect of his own castration, and manages to free one hand in the story's final paragraph. The story's concluding lines, however, suggest that his sexual excitement will not allow him to escape, and the final line of dialogue from Lucy indicates that the operation has begun.

Narrated in spare, unemotional prose, the story depicts a set of characters who use other human beings as they use their sexuality: as means to pleasurable ends, with little consideration for the effects of their actions on others. Harold uses his customers for their money, which buys him expensive clothing, O'Byrne uses Pauline and Lucy for his sexual pleasure, and they do the same to him. No character in the story has any redeeming qualities; at the warehouse O'Byrne visits to purchase pornography for the shop, the workers, whose evident distaste for their own product might render them morally sympathetic, are presented as physically repulsive creatures.

Like much of McEwan's early work, including his two collections of short stories and his first several novels, "Pornography" contains some elements of postmodernism in its unflinching and uncritical depiction of seemingly horrific subject matter. But the story contains none of the self-conscious or playful narrative style usually associated with postmodernism, and in that respect it may be aligned more closely to a stark, gritty form of realism. The focus on violence and sexuality in stories such as this one invites comparison to the short fictions of MARTIN AMIS published around this same time.

BIBLIOGRAPHY

McEwan, Ian. *In Between the Sheets, and Other Stories.* London: Cape; New York: Simon & Schuster, 1978.

Ryan, Kiernan. *Ian McEwan.* Plymouth, England: Northcote House in association with the British Council, 1994.

Slay, Jack, Jr. *Ian McEwan.* New York: Twayne; London: Prentice Hall, 1996.

James Lang

PORTRAIT OF THE ARTIST AS A YOUNG DOG DYLAN THOMAS (1940)

The 10 stories in this collection were written in Laugharne during 1938 and 1939 (though not in the order in which they appear in the volume), and the collection signaled the emergence of Welsh writer Dylan Marlais Thomas (1914–53) as a master of autobiographical prose as well as poetry. In contrast to his early stories, which were introspective, obscure, and surreal, Thomas now turned to the world about him, drawing extensively on his experiences as a journalist and releasing a spring of comedy and nostalgia. The stories give a coherent picture of the growth of a poet's mind, each dealing with a state of his childhood, youth, or early manhood as well as giving a faithful depiction of Swansea during the Depression—its poverty and unemployment and the destruction and decadence of Welsh culture. Thomas denied the influence of JAMES JOYCE's *Portrait of the Artist as a Young Man,* saying, "I made a bit of doggish fun of the *painting*-title and . . . intended no possible reference to Joyce." He added, however, that "the shaping of some of my *Portrait* stories might owe something to Joyce's stories into the volume *Dubliners*"

(quoted in Ackerman, 185). As Joyce's DUBLINERS encapsulates a people, time, and place, so does Dylan Thomas's *Portrait,* and despite the gently satiric tone, the narrator shows compassion for the suffering of his characters and delights in their humanity.

In the opening story, "The Peaches," Thomas explores his family origins by depicting his mother's relations' life on their small, impoverished farm in Dyfed. The story opens with a journey from town to country in spring, at night, which becomes a rite of passage for the boy. While waiting for his Uncle Jim, who stops for a drink and leaves him alone in the darkness, the boy experiences a nightmarish and surreal enlargement of his imagination. The story depicts the rural world as empathizing with nature ("I felt all my young body like an excited animal surrounding me" [14]) but hopelessly decayed at the same time, and thus symptomatic of the economic plight of Welsh rural areas during the 1930s. Uncle Jim is a drunkard who sells his farm stock for alcohol, Auntie Annie is kind but ineffectual; the son Gwilym is supposed to be training for the ministry yet is a sexual fantasizer and masturbator who terrorizes young Dylan and his friend Jack with his preaching. The title-giving peaches are not the luscious fresh fruit but a tinned version, which becomes a symbol of a helpless gesture of Welsh hospitality. As a luxury for the poor Welsh peasants, Auntie Annie offers the peaches to wealthy Mrs. Williams, mother of Jack, who cruelly rejects them out of snobbishness. The final humiliation is reached when Jack flees home, leaving the "ruin of Gorsehill" (18) behind. Pathos and comedy are well balanced throughout, and the story gives an idea of the young boy's sensitivity.

In "A Visit to Grandpa's" the world of his father's family is depicted as an equally strange mixture of the everyday and the surreal, the hilarious and the serious. His grandfather rides horses in his dreams, and while awake he tries to walk in his best waistcoat to nearby Llangadock to be buried there, because "the ground is comfy" (24). When the neighbors find grandpa, he refuses to return home, standing "like a prophet who has not doubt" (24). The precision of topographical detail and deep knowledge of Welsh traditions that emphasize a person's place of burial make this a memorable story of the Carmarthenshire district of Thomas's youth.

The following eight stories, all but three of which are written in the first person, explore aspects of the protagonist's life from childhood to late adolescence. In "Patricia, Edith and Arnold," a story written in the third person, the child glimpses an adult world of chaotic sexual relations and unhappiness. Young Dylan observes how two women who have found out that they have received similar tokens of love and love letters from the same man try to settle their dispute. Forced to decide between the two women, the narcissistic suitor turns both of them against him, as female solidarity finally overcomes sexual jealousy. Similar in theme is "Just Like Little Dogs," in which the protagonist, now older, again observes the tragicomic arbitrariness of sexual relations and the pain that is yet involved in them.

For Thomas, the most important relationships are masculine friendships, and women merely feature as mothers or as objects of desire, usually superior to the protagonist. "The Fight" details the odd development of a childhood friendship that begins with a fight between two boys and results in the decision that they will edit a magazine together. Similarly, in "Where Tawe Flows" the poet, now somewhat older, attends a meeting of men who plan to collaborate in the writing of "a Novel of Provincial Life" that centers again around sexuality and death. Friendship and the creative process are closely linked, and each aids the development of the other.

Several of the stories explore the developing sexuality of the adolescent poet. "Extraordinary Little Cough" is a story of pubescent love, a nostalgic account of a camping outing to Rhossili and its beach. Other stories, such as "Who Do You Wish Was with Us" and "Old Garbo," deal with the theme of death. The title figure of "Old Garbo" is Mrs. Prothero ("We call her Old Garbo because she isn't like her, see" [95]), an old working-class woman who believes that her daughter and new grandchild have died in childbirth. After a collection is made for her, the daughter is found to be alive, and the mother, drunk and unable to face her friends, throws herself into the river. The story depicts Swansea as a city of two halves—a respectable part and a disreputable dock area—in which the narrator, who works as a journalist for a Swansea newspaper, shifts between the two areas. This is in contrast to his boss, Mr. Farr, who tries to shut his eyes against the poverty, unemployment, and misery.

The concluding story, "One Warm Saturday," Thomas's favorite, exudes an atmosphere of missed opportunity. The poet is wandering by himself about Swansea on an August bank holiday and contrasts himself in his isolation with the happy families on the sands. Thomas gives a humorous and self-mocking portrait of the artist here: "He thought: Poets live and walk with their poems; a man with vision needs no other company. . . . But he was not a poet living and walking, he was a young man in a sea town on a warm bank holiday, with two pounds to spend; he had no vision, only two pounds and a small body with its feet on the littered sand; serenity was for old men" (102). Characteristically, the protagonist falls in love with a beautiful girl and fantasizes about sexual fulfillment, but he loses track of her in the nightmarish world of a labyrinthine house full of stairs and doors; Alfred Tennyson's dramatic poem spoken by a madman, "Come into the garden Maud" (1855), provides heightened ironic effects. In these stories love is a frustrating and unsatisfying experience of isolation and loss.

The collection is unified not only through the protagonist and the Swansea setting but also by the theme of increasing alienation. As young Thomas encounters various worlds, his desire to belong intensifies while his ability to belong decreases (Davies, 180). The growth of the young man into a poet is a process of distancing himself from his hometown environment. (See also WALES.)

BIBLIOGRAPHY

Ackerman, John. *A Dylan Thomas Companion: Life, Poetry and Prose.* Basingstoke, England: Macmillan, 1991.

Davies, James A. *A Reference Companion to Dylan Thomas.* Westport, Conn.: Greenwood Press, 1998.

Thomas, Dylan. *Portrait of the Artist as a Young Dog.* Introduction by Aeronwy Thomas. London: Phoenix, 2001.

Heike Grundmann

POTTER (HEELIS), BEATRIX (1866–1943)

Helen Beatrix Potter was born in South Kensington, London. Although she had a younger brother, Beatrix grew up alone, tutored by governesses, while her brother was sent away to school at a young age. The family's comfortable income provided for trips to the country throughout Beatrix's youth, which became more frequent during her teen years after her father inherited a fortune.

From 1881 to 1897 Beatrix made regular entries in a coded journal. With its memories of her childhood and its record of her forays into painting and authorship as well as a variety of natural sciences, this journal has offered a detailed glimpse of the developing writer. Potter would first appear as an author not of children's books, but of a paper, "On the Germination of the Spores of *Agarincineae,*" read before the Linnean Society in 1897. The first of her children's tales, *The Tale of Peter Rabbit,* was published privately in two small editions (1901, 1902) before being published with new color illustrations by Frederick Warne & Co. Over the next two decades, Warne would publish the remainder of Potter's "little books" featuring animal characters, many based on Potter's own pets, culminating in the collected TALES OF BEATRIX POTTER.

After her marriage to William Heelis in 1913, Potter slowly moved from life as a children's author to life as a prominent farmer and landowner. In keeping with her love of nature, Mrs. Heelis used the profits from her successful books to buy property throughout the Lake District, often with the help of the National Trust, in order to save it from development.

Today, while Potter's books remain popular children's classics worldwide, attention has shifted to include her interest in scientific and environmental issues, through both her tales and her work in and around the countryside. Potter is remembered not only as an author whose subtly rhythmic prose and beautiful illustrations have charmed generations of children but also as an artist of the English landscape, an accomplished amateur scientist, and a careful farmer and preserver of the English countryside.

BIBLIOGRAPHY

Grinstein, Alexander. *The Remarkable Beatrix Potter.* Madison, Conn.: International Universities Press, 1995.

Potter, Beatrix. *The Complete Tales of Beatrix Potter.* London: Frederick Warne, 2002.

———. *The Journal of Beatrix Potter from 1881 to 1897.* Transcribed by Leslie Linder. London: Frederick Warne & Co., 1966.

Taylor, Judy. *Beatrix Potter: Artist, Storyteller and Countrywoman.* London: Frederick Warne & Co., 1987.

Andrea Cabus

PRE-RAPHAELITISM The Pre-Raphaelites were a group of authors in the later 1840s through the close of the 1890s who espoused a distinctive artistic philosophy. In form, Pre-Raphaelite short stories exhibit a highly finished style that reflects and embodies the aesthetic programs of their authors. Such works characteristically make use of themes and imagery drawn from ghost stories, fairy tales, medieval romances, and the lives of saints and painters.

The foundation of the Pre-Raphaelite movement came in 1848, when a band of young British artists chose the title "Pre-Raphaelite Brotherhood," thus signaling their break from what they regarded as the artificiality of painting styles that prevailed in the studios of London's Royal Academy of Art. At the head of the group stood Dante Gabriel Rossetti (1828–82), a painter-poet who, inspired by the examples of Dante Alighieri (1265–1321), William Blake (1757–1827), and John Keats (1795–1821), strove to realize a strikingly original inner vision in a variety of visual media and writing genres. Throughout the breadth of his work, Rossetti shows himself to be concerned primarily with dramatizing the artist's struggle to achieve an intermingling of spiritual ideal with material form. His prose fiction—largely untouched by criticism, unlike his paintings—evidences several of his most important explorations of this theme. Indeed, Rossetti's tales "Hand and Soul" (1849) and "St. Agnes of Intercession" (1850) may be read as aesthetic allegories in which the artist works to discover the limits of his art. "Hand and Soul" first appeared in the short-lived Pre-Raphaelite magazine, the *Germ* (1850). The story uses its pseudohistorical trappings to relate the life-legend of an apocryphal 13th-century painter, Chiaro dell'Erma. Chiaro undertakes a hard pilgrimage toward artistic and spiritual enlightenment, passing from an art based on a kind of naive naturalism to devotional works increasingly abstract and moral in their presentation. The climactic moment in the tale comes during a great religious festival in Pisa. Warring factions among the Pisan families come to blows beneath Chiaro's newly hung artwork in the Church of San Petronio: "the whole archway was dazzling with the light of confused swords . . . and there was so much blood cast up the walls on a sudden, that it ran in long streams down Chiaro's paintings." Witnessing this incident, the painter despairs at the ineffectiveness of his art and falls into a feverish swoon. The image of his own soul then appears to him, taking the shape of a beautiful woman who instructs him to "Set thine hand and thy soul to serve man with God." Rossetti's "St. Agnes of Intercession" owes something to the weird tales of Edgar Allan Poe (1809–49). This unfinished story tells how an artist working in 19th-century London discovers uncanny doubles for himself and his fiancée in portraits painted by a 15th-century Florentine artist.

Rossetti's taste for the supernatural, his love of things medieval and mystic, and his highly wrought prose style greatly influenced the short fiction written by the second generation of Pre-Raphaelites, a stellar group of younger artists and writers that included the poet Algernon Charles Swinburne (1837–1909); the designer, poet, and social critic William Morris (1834–96); and the painter Edward Burne-Jones (1833–98). Swinburne's short stories merit special attention because of the sheer variety of their forms. His *Triameron* (1861) is a series of interlocked prose tales modeled on the works of Boccaccio; tales such as "Dead Love," "The Portrait," and "The Chronicle of Tebaldeo Tebaldei" demonstrate his confidence in employing a pastiche of earlier styles and conventions. Swinburne's parodic reviews are literary hoaxes in which imaginary reviewers critique imaginary publications, and these faux reviews should be read as consummate works of short fiction. Morris's early Pre-Raphaelite prose tales—such as "The Story of the Unknown Church" (1856), "The Hollow Land" (1856), and "Golden Wings" (1856)—take up the aesthetic concerns first announced by Rossetti, granting especial attention to the problematic relationship of past and present. Morris's later prose romances, such as *The Wood beyond the World* (1894) and *The Sundering Flood* (1898), draw heavily on his studies of Icelandic sagas and medieval romance. Swinburne, Morris, and

Burne-Jones all published their early short fiction in the pages of the *Oxford and Cambridge Magazine* (1856). This important avant-garde periodical helped pass on the influence of the Pre-Raphaelite prose tale to writers of the aesthetic movement, such as Walter Pater (1839–94), OSCAR WILDE, William Sharp ("Fiona Macleod"; 1855–1905), and VERNON LEE (See AESTHETICISM.)

BIBLIOGRAPHY

Lang, Cecil Y. *The Pre-Raphaelites and Their Circle.* Boston: Houghton Mifflin, 1968.

Morris, William. *News from Nowhere: and Other Writings.* Edited by Clive Wilmer. London: Penguin, 1993.

Rossetti, Dante Gabriel. *Collected Poetry and Prose.* Edited by Jerome McGann. New Haven, Conn.: Yale University Press, 2003.

Swinburne, Algernon Charles. *Major Poems and Selected Prose.* Edited by Jerome McGann and Charles L. Sligh. New Haven, Conn.: Yale University Press, 2004.

Weeks, John. *The Dream-Weavers: Short Stories.* Santa Barbara, Calif.: Woodbridge, 1980.

Charles L. Sligh

PRITCHETT, V(ICTOR) S(AWDON) (1900–1997)

Long since recognized as one of the great masters of the British short story form, the man who became V. S. Pritchett was born in Ipswich, Suffolk, the son of a salesman. After leaving school at age 16 he worked in the leather industry before moving to Paris in 1920. He began writing and had his first short story, "Rain in the Sierra," published in the *New Statesman* in 1926. After that he became a prolific writer of stories, novels, and articles, producing work well into his 90s. During his long career, Pritchett often tried to define what made a good short story. For example, in the second installment of his autobiography, *Midnight Oil,* he argued that the form "concentrates an impulse that is essentially poetic." In the introduction to the *Oxford Book of Short Stories* (1981), he championed brevity and the "discipline of form" of the poet. He also argued that the writer has to "suggest" rather than show and that it is up to the reader to play an active part in making meaning. Critics have noted that because of his longevity, Pritchett's stories, while centered on universal themes, provide a snapshot of 20th-century social change. The story "The Saint" focuses on a teenager's loss of Christian faith; "The Camberwell Beauty" is a moving study of the customers and staff of a London antique shop; "The Accompanist" is about a woman who plays the piano for a living, but as the story progresses readers comes to realize that she is also an accompanist in life as well as in music.

BIBLIOGRAPHY

Allen, Walter. *The Short Story in English.* New York: Oxford University Press, 1981.

Baldwin, Dean. *V. S. Pritchett.* Boston: Twayne, 1981.

Pritchett, V. S. *Collected Stories.* New York: Random, 1983.

———. *Complete Essays.* New York: Random, 1992.

Stinson, John. *V. S. Pritchett: A Study of the Short Fiction.* New York: Twayne, 1992.

Joe Davis

"PROPHET'S HAIR, THE" SALMAN RUSHDIE (1981)

Extensively anthologized, SALMAN RUSHDIE's "The Prophet's Hair" was initially published in the *London Review of Books* and the *Atlantic.* The story was later included in a limited, privately printed edition in 1989, along with a companion piece, "The Free Radio," in the wake of the controversy generated by *Satanic Verses* and the proclamation of the fatwa against Rushdie. A revised version of the story appears in Rushdie's short story collection of 1994, EAST WEST.

As its title indicates, the story is about a sacred object, a strand of the prophet Mohammed's hair, an object of worship for devout Muslims. Rushdie tackles the issue of religious belief in a modern secular context. The story has its origin in an actual theft of the relic from its location at the Hazratbal mosque in Kashmir in the early 1960s. The relic was subsequently recovered and restored to the shrine after authentication by the Muslim priests. The story presents Rushdie at the peak of his storytelling power. It not only grips the reader's attention through its simple narration—what Goonetilleke calls "whatnextism"—but also demonstrates the wit and flippancy for which the author is so famous.

The story spans a week in the family life of Hashim, a rich and comfortable Kashmiri moneylender. It narrates a series of disasters that befall ill-fated Hashim's placid household once he fortuitously comes into the possession of the prophet's hair. The reader gets a taste of things to come in the first paragraph. It contains two long sentences, neatly divided into well-executed clauses—one setting the time and the landscape and the other disclosing the fatal injuries of Atta, the son and heir, incurred while in search of a professional thief to steal the ominous relic from the accidental possession of his ungovernable father.

From the beginning Rushdie maintains a fast pace, inserting flashback scenes and self-reflexive remarks. There is an engaging account of the sudden appearance of the relic in Hashim's life and his transformation into a devout and bullying father and husband, swearing by the Holy Book all the time. There is a repeat journey made by his daughter, Huma, in the footsteps of her unsuccessful brother, to contact the redoubtable Sheikh Sein to draw up a secret plan to dispossess her obdurate father of his fatal obsession. The events converge in the cross-purposes of the fateful night when the master burglar arrives in the moneylender's place to carry out the prearranged plan. It all goes awry, leaving a trail of devastation that all but wipes out the moneylender's clan, consigning the lone surviving member, the wife, to the lunatic asylum.

Although the story is full of blood and carnage, its shifting tone and emphasis on the role of chance in the unfolding of events, often produce a comic effect. Neither the passionate belief in a transcendent order of things nor the secular reason of the rationalist deciphering the causality of events is allowed to have the last word in the story. The reader's sense of bracing confusion is heightened in the last two paragraphs, in which the narrator announces an unequal reversal of fortunes in the dead burglar's wife and sons. The meaning of the relic as a symbol or icon remains unresolved.

BIBLIOGRAPHY

Goonetilleke, D. C. R. A. *Salman Rushdie.* London: Macmillan, 1998.

Richards, Fiona. "The Desecrated Shrine: Movable Icons and Literary Irreverence in Salman Rushdie's 'The Prophet's Hair,'" *SOAS Literary Review* 2 (2000). Available online. URL: http://www.soas.ac.uk/soaslit/issue2/RICHARDS. PDF. Accessed June 5, 2006.

R. S. Nanda

PRUSSIAN OFFICER AND OTHER STO-RIES, THE D. H. LAWRENCE (1914) The publi-
cation by Duckworth of D. H. LAWRENCE's first volume of short stories on November 26, 1914, collected writing from as early as 1907. Except for the unpublished DAUGHTERS OF THE VICAR, the book was compiled from work that had previously appeared in journals such as KATHERINE MANSFIELD's Blue Review, Austin Harrison's English Review, and Ezra Pound's Smart Set. "A Fragment of Stained Glass" (formerly titled "Ruby Glass") and "The White Stocking" represent revised versions of two of the stories Lawrence submitted under pseudonyms to the Nottinghamshire Guardian's 1907 Christmas competition. "A Prelude," the third story and the winning entry in the Guardian's "Most Enjoyable Christmas" category, was published under the name of Jessie Chambers (Lawrence's then lover) but, like stories such as "LOVE AMONG THE HAYSTACKS," was omitted from The Prussian Officer. Indeed, Lawrence extensively revised all of the included stories before their collection. As he wrote to Edward Marsh in July 1914, "Lord, how I've worked again at those stories—most of them—forging them up" (Letters, 287).

However, Lawrence's hand was not the only one to shape the collection. Duckworth's editor, Edward Garnett, was responsible for its title and for rearranging the stories into an order different from that given by Lawrence. In July, Lawrence had suggested that the projected title of the volume change from The Goose Fair to The Thorn in the Flesh, and in October 1914 he proposed The Fighting Line as a title to Garnett: "After all" he wrote, "this is the real fighting line, not where soldiers pull triggers" (Letters, 292). In reply, Garnett told Lawrence that it would be titled The Prussian Officer, an amendment that caused Lawrence to write in a letter to his literary agent, J. B. Pinker, that "Garnett was a devil to call my book of stories The Prussian Officer," (Letters, 296).

A letter to Garnett dates the composition of the volume's title story in early June 1913. Lawrence considered "The Prussian Officer," originally titled "Honour and Arms," "the best short story I have ever done" (Letters, 209). Like "The Thorn in the Flesh," the story tells of a German soldier, Bachmann, who deserts the army during WORLD WAR I in order to escape the violence

exacted on him by his superiors. Other characters in the collection, such as Elsie Whiston in her affair with Sam Adams in "The White Stocking" or Louisa Lindley in her engagement to Alfred Durant despite the protestations of her family in Daughters of the Vicar, escape social conventions in order to live. The influence of Lawrence's Study of Thomas Hardy (begun in the summer of 1914) can be detected. Like THOMAS HARDY's characters, Lawrence's characters' tragedy is that despite their escape they die either from their "own lack of strength to bear the isolation and the exposure, or by direct revenge from the community, or from both" (Phoenix, 411): The orderly dies, Bachmann is arrested, Elsie's husband strangles her to make her give up Sam, and Louisa and Alfred are obliged to emigrate to Canada. Be it battlefield violence or domestic violence, the emotional and physical damage is plain. In "The Shadow in the Rose Garden" the title character is the former lover of a woman who discovers him as a lunatic; the war has made him a shadow of his former self. Although critics responded to these stories as "morbid," "brutal," and "depressing," scenes such as Bachmann and Emilie's lovemaking the night before he is recaptured show human beings alive and living in such a way as they ask. As Lawrence argued in Study of Thomas Hardy, "What does money, power, or public approval matter? All that matters is that each human being shall be in his own fullness" (Phoenix, 406).

Money matters were, however, influential in the creation of the volume itself. Since Lawrence was impelled to write professionally—as he wrote in a letter, "I've got to earn my living by prose" (Letters, 231)—placing short stories in magazines rather than writing novels, whose publication process was lengthier, offered a more stable income. "A Sick Collier," which appeared in The Prussian Officer, is one of four "journalistic" pieces engaging with the miner's strike at the end of February 1912. The strike began at Alfreton pit, not far from Lawrence's birthplace, Eastwood, when the miners demanded a minimum wage. Both the location and the cause were dear to Lawrence. Indeed, possible methods of political change and social reconstruction are proposed throughout his work. "The Christening" and "ODOUR OF CHRYSANTHEMUMS" are also based on mining families. The latter was printed in the English

Review in June 1911 but dates in composition from 1909. Its description of the miner Rigley's scar, "caused by a wound got in the pit, a wound in which the coal-dust remained blue like tattooing" (189), is copied almost verbatim in the description of Walter Morel's "blue scars, like tattoo marks, where the coal-dust remained under the skin" (235) in *Sons and Lovers,* and it illustrates one of *The Prussian Officer*'s many intertextual relationships.

In January 1914, Lawrence wrote to Edward Garnett telling him that he was "going through a transition phase" (*Letters,* 263). *The Prussian Officer* stories are documents of Lawrence's earliest writing, and their revision and collection are testimony to his development and transition as a writer. Their themes are perennial in his oeuvre and are often reworked in his later writing; in particular, the love triangle among a gamekeeper, his betrothed, and her former lover in "Shades of Spring" became the central conflict in *Lady Chatterley's Lover.*

BIBLIOGRAPHY

Cushman, Keith. *D. H. Lawrence at Work: The Emergence of the Prussian Officer Stories.* Hassocks: Harvester, 1978.

Kearney, Martin F. *Major Short Stories of D. H. Lawrence: A Handbook.* London: Garland, 1998.

Lawrence, D. H. *Phoenix: The Posthumous Papers of D. H. Lawrence.* Edited by Edward D. McDonald. London: Heinemann, 1936.

———. *The Collected Letters of D. H. Lawrence.* Edited and with an introduction by Harry T. Moore. 2 vols. London: Heinemann, 1962.

———. *The Prussian Officer and Other Stories.* Edited by John Worthen. Cambridge: Cambridge University Press, 1983.

Oliver Taylor

"PSYCHOPOLIS" Ian McEwan (1987) The

final story in Ian McEwan's collection *In between the Sheets* (1978), "Psychopolis" was originally published in *American Review* and anthologized in the influential *The Penguin Book of Modern Short Stories* (1987), edited by Malcolm Bradbury, McEwan's former tutor at the University of East Anglia. The story concerns an Englishman and his relationships with three Americans and with music but ultimately with America and the psychopolis, the city of the mind. It opens with the protagonist chaining the feminist Mary to his bed for the weekend, on her request. The act becomes one of commitment to a promise, and despite Mary's begging to be freed, he refuses. The narrator attempts to resist the banality of Los Angeles by playing his flute. When he finally releases Mary, he tells her that in just one week the city has completely changed him. The rhythm of the story is the transitions between intense moments, public revelations of inner angst and heated exchanges, juxtaposed with the narrator's contemplation of nothingness.

The story moves on to describe the development of the Englishman's friendships with George Malone, who owns the store beneath his apartment, and with Terence Latterly, a man nothing like the stereotypical American but who rather resembles a Renaissance prince and who is researching a thesis on George Orwell. Listening to Terence's stories, the narrator becomes depressed and comes to believe that there is no escape from the kind of superficial lifestyle represented by Los Angeles. He tries to lift his mood with his music but soon lapses into a deep depression.

George appreciates his music and takes him to bars where people make public their personal grief on stage. The final section brings all the characters together for a showdown. The Englishman is leaving for New York, and George invites them all to a farewell party at his house, telling the visitor to bring his flute. As Terence and Mary meet for the first time, the conversation turns to Los Angeles; both of them praise the city, but Terence's falsity becomes all too obvious. McEwan comments on the social mores of the English and the Americans, as the narrator tells Mary that in England strangers would not immediately talk about being physically abused by their parents. Mary replies that the English tell each other nothing. He retorts that between telling nothing and telling everything there is very little to choose.

George introduces his guests to his two children, whom he is bringing up as Christians, and then the party turns nasty. The guests' conversation moves from how Christians have ruined the world to gun ownership. When George pulls out his gun, Terence takes it and aims the gun at his host with the words, "death to gun owners." Suddenly etiquette reasserts itself: The

guests eat and their conversation moves onto safe subjects; American politeness and hospitality takes over.
The narrator plays his Bach sonata, and while he does
so, images of his time in America flow through him,
thoughts of the city without a center, without citizens,
existing only in the mind, the psychopolis. He stops
abruptly but his fellow guests do not notice. Then,
however, there is a true moment of warmth as they
clap and the musician is overwhelmed by nostalgia for
this version of America.

BIBLIOGRAPHY
McEwan, Ian. *In between the Sheets.* London: Cape, 1978.

Jason Lee

"PUMPKIN PIE" FAY WELDON (1991)   FAY
WELDON's story "Pumpkin Pie," published in the 1991
collection *Moon over Minneapolis: Or Why She Couldn't
Stay,* uses a shifting style of narration and integrated
symbolism to comment on class and gender issues.
The story follows Antoinette, a maid to the rich and
absurd Honey Marvin, as Antoinette prepares the
Marvin household for Thanksgiving. While the narrative voice and tone fluctuate throughout the story,
ultimately the plot serves as a warning against class
domination.

"Pumpkin Pie" demonstrates the concern with class
and gender relationships that is evident in much of
Weldon's fiction. As Lana Faulks writes of Weldon's
later work, "Domestic and romantic scenarios parallel
the political line, with children and women grouped
among the powerless who, especially those of the lower
classes, remain victims of the powerful" (57). In
"Pumpkin Pie" Antoinette must acquiesce to the ludicrous whims of her employer. Honey, whose name
reflects an outer façade that is wryly dismissed throughout the story, throws out a refrigerator and destroys a
$500 centerpiece with no sense of consequence. Antoi-
nette wishes for such a refrigerator, even if it would
only fit sideways in her kitchen or in a backyard, but
she would not dream of asking for it. When Antoinette
takes discarded paper home from work for her children to build collages with, Honey notes that no items,
even "apparently discarded" ones may "be removed
from the dwelling" (85).

Beyond material concerns, the work Antoinette
endures is also demeaning. Although she has her own
family, including a new grandchild and a daughter in
crisis, she is expected to serve the Marvin family on
Thanksgiving Day or risk losing her job. She polishes
silverware that was carefully polished and wrapped
away the season before and bakes pumpkin pie while a
vicious dog lacking proper housetraining creates
messes afoot. The dog becomes a symbol for the larger
power system, as Antoinette tolerates its cruelties, pla-
cates its anger, gives in to its whims, and cleans up its
messes.

Faulks notes that "Weldon relishes the mundane,
exaggerating human circumstances and nuances, crys-
tallizing our most intimate interactions so that we may
look more closely at the daily act of living, in particular
our relations with others. Out of these particulars, she
proposes a large social vision: the powerful lack compassion and victims will do anything to be empowered" (3). It is difficult not to sympathize with
Antoinette. Even Honey's ill husband becomes a burden to Antoinette with his need for special cholesterol-
free food, and we are left with the feeling that he too is
a pawn in Honey's drive to control others.

The narrator asks us what we feel, who we identify
with: "A bit of all of them? I hope so. That way progress lies. If it hurts, it heals" (85). Nonetheless, the narration primarily follows Antoinette as she prepares for
Thanksgiving dinner, and it is the power dynamic
between Antoinette and Honey that creates tension as
Honey's frivolous requests show her absurdity (and,
implicitly, the absurdity of much of the behavior of
those in power).

While Honey may hold the overt power, Antoinette
exercises cunning of her own as she sneaks out of Honey's kitchen to visit her own family, realizes Honey's
pie will be burnt, and so returns to Honey's with her
own family's egg-laden (and cholesterol-containing)
pumpkin pie. She feeds the burnt cholesterol-free pie
to the dog and covers up the switch. When Honey
asks, "You didn't put egg yolk in it, did you? Because,
as you know, egg yolk can kill my husband," and
Antoinette replies, "Why, ma'am here's the proof no
egg yolk went into that pumpkin pie" (87) while showing a previously obtained bowl of egg yolks, we can see

Antoinette's strategic power and sneaky meanderings. Ultimately the story is a warning that the oppressed will create their own kind of power, and it will be to the detriment of those who thoughtlessly wield control. The pumpkin pie represents the commodities of time, enjoyment, and family holiday taken from Antoinette and granted to Honey through Antoinette's labor. Weldon writes that the poor "begin to know that the pumpkin pies of the poor taste as good if not better than the pumpkin pies of the rich; so if you can't make your own, do without, and let the hired help stay home for a change. Or you'll find cholesterol in your pie and a knife in your back, and a good thing too" (88).

The beginning and ending narrator is didactic, preaching about the proper treatment of others. Perhaps it is the voice of the author who ends the story, "See the drop of blood on the page? That's mine. That's just the beginning" (88). Because the ending is left ambiguous, we can speculate whose blood is on the page. Did the narrator bleed, or cause another to bleed? Her words are also on the page, intense like blood, and embracing both condemnation and culpability—as, we are meant to infer, must we all.

BIBLIOGRAPHY

Faulks, Lana. *Fay Weldon*. New York: Twayne, 1998.

Weldon, Fay. *Moon over Minneapolis: Or Why She Couldn't Stay*. New York: Penguin, 1992.

Rachel Liberatore

"PUSS-IN-BOOTS" ANGELA CARTER (1979)

This story is the most ebullient of the reimagined fairy tales in ANGELA CARTER's 1979 collection *The BLOODY CHAMBER*. The volume's title suggests the more characteristic tone of these tales of sex, violence, and the struggles for power within male-female relationships in a patriarchal world. While thematically linked to its companions, "Puss-in-Boots" strikes a much lighter, comic note.

Versions of this animal-helper tale had been published by Straparola and Basile before the 1697 appearance of Perrault's "The Master Cat, or Puss in Boots"; however, the Perrault tale—the first literary version to feature a male Puss and to introduce the unusual footwear—has become most familiar. In this version, the titular cat, the meager inheritance of the third son of a miller, promises to improve his master's fortunes in exchange for a bag and a pair of boots. Using the bag to trap a variety of game, the cat makes a series of gifts to the king on behalf of his master, eventually persuading the king that his poor master is a man of great property, worthy of the hand of the princess, whom the young man eventually marries.

The moral of Perrault's tale is a dubious one—success through deception. Carter's version enthusiastically dismisses any question of such somber containment, revelling instead in the triumph of the roguish Puss and his allies over the story's hypocritical guardians of morality. Carter's Puss plays matchmaker for his love-struck master, whose beloved is the beautiful young wife of an elderly miser, a woman locked away and jealously guarded by a crone of a governess. Puss's scheming allows his master first to see and eventually to have two sexual encounters with the young woman before the conspirators manage to dispatch the husband and governess and live happily—and carnally—ever after. Like earlier versions of the tale, Carter's story is about the gulling of the wealthy and powerful by their supposed inferiors, but it seems to take particular delight in this upsetting of the order of things.

Much of the story's exuberance derives from the distinctive voice of its narrator, Puss himself, whose earthy and unapologetic vitality anticipates that of Fevvers, the winged wonder who narrates Carter's carnivalesque novel *Nights at the Circus* (1984). Puss is playful, irreverent, and entirely at home in his own body, as he demonstrates throughout in the attention he gives to the cleaning of his "sparkling dicky" between amorous encounters with the young wife's female tabby. Puss's earthy humour and behavior provide an ironic counterpoint to the actions of his human companions, particularly his master. Where Puss greets the tabby with "the customary tribute of a few firm thrusts of my striped loins," the lovelorn young man turns to high-flown romantic complaints—"A princess in a tower. Remote and shining as Aldebaran. Chained to a dolt and dragon-guarded"—prompting his animal companion to pause momentarily in the cleaning of his genitals and fix the man "with my most satiric smile." The lover's later attempts at poetry are greeted with equal contempt; to Puss's mind, this is all "sentimental havering," a tiresome prelude to the sexual pleasure the two lovers eventually enjoy, much to the delight of their feline go-between.

A recurrent theme in *The Bloody Chamber* is the embracing of an animalistic carnality as a means of refusing the division of masculine and feminine passions into the separate realms of Beauty and the Beast. Both "The Tiger's Bride" and "The COMPANY OF WOLVES" conclude with potential female victims of bestial lovers becoming instead equally carnal partners. In the lighter "Puss-in-Boots," this theme is played out again, but in the high-spirited, comic mode that would become the hallmark of Carter's last novels, *Nights at the Circus* (1984) and *Wise Children* (1991).

BIBLIOGRAPHY
Carter, Angela. *The Bloody Chamber* (1979). London: Vintage, 1995.

Brian Patton

R

"RAIN HORSE, THE" Ted Hughes (1967)

Only two characters appear in Ted Hughes's best-known short story: an unnamed man and a black horse. The man, returning to a rural landscape after a 12-year absence, is attacked inexplicably by the horse but escapes muddy and unharmed. Compared with Hughes's opaque, enigmatic poems "The Horses" (*The Hawk and the Rain,* 1957) and "A Dream of Horses" (*Lupercal,* 1960) the equine references seem straightforward, even simplistic. According to Hughes's biographer and critic, Keith Sagar, the story was influenced by an incident in Hughes's childhood at the Don in Old Denady, South Yorkshire. However, Sagar notes that the story is also clearly influenced by characters' encounters with horses in D. H. Lawrence's works, particularly *The Rainbow* and "A Modern Lover." As the appropriation of Lawrentian antecedents indicates, the horse is figured not just as a protagonist in a naturalistic story but as a symbol in a psychological crux for the unnamed male.

No reason is given for the man's return to the place he left more than a decade previously. He has no affection for the countryside and is naively dressed in a business suit. He feels only anger and boredom. In other words, there is a void in the man's interaction with the rugged, rural environment. He is here because he has to be, not because he wants to be. Leonard M. Scigaj has argued that the horse's attack begins only when the man consciously ignores its unusual behavior. The horse is a symbol of lack. For Scigaj, that lack is sexual:

"The horse symbolizes the repressed libidinal energies of the man's own psyche" (62). Indeed, no mention of a sexual partner is forthcoming at any point, so Scigaj's insistence that the horse represents an unrealized carnality that rears its head despite the man's attempts to repress it is convincing. But the horse may be seen as a more generalized symbol of the man's disenfranchisement from the countryside, as an iconic, zoomorphized signifier of the antagonism between the man and an almost personified countryside.

The horse's acts of violence—which are thwarted only by the man's forceful throwing of large stones—may also be seen as representative of the essential violence of the agricultural industry to which the man returns so unenthusiastically. The man remembers a display of foxes' cadavers, recalling their bloody teeth. Men not only carry out violence against animals but exhibit the carcasses that result. References are made to gates and fences, stressing that the farmlands constitute property, territory marked out by acquisitive human hunters. Indeed, the narrator notes that "A loop of the river bordered all this farmland"—humans have exploited nature's borders to mark out their territory, making the farm seem almost castlelike with its surrounding moat. Farmers use nature only in order to fight it.

The farm's shed is packed with tractors, a plough, binders, and an oil drum; the heavy odors are not bucolic but are caused by paraffin, creosote, and fertilizer. Little is natural about farming on this scale.

Unusual though the horse's violence appears, it is linked to the quotidian, nonnatural violence that farmers wreak perpetually on the fauna and flora in their fields. The narrator asserts that the landscape "looked lifeless and desolate." Previously, the sky has repeatedly been described as "grey"—the color of a corpse. Despite the presence of fecund rabbits (that are considered only as a nuisance) and the lonely horse, this is an almost dead landscape, one rendered unrecognizable through farming. The story suggests that Hughes had prescient fears about the impact of intensive agriculture on the countryside, because pastoral biodiversity is as absent in this story as the man's sexual satisfaction and spiritual contentment.

BIBLIOGRAPHY

Hughes, Ted. "The Rain Horse." In *Wodwo*. London: Faber and Faber, 1967.

Sagar, Keith. *The Art of Ted Hughes*. Cambridge: Cambridge University Press, 1980.

———. *Ted Hughes*. Windsor: Profile, 1981.

Scigaj, Leonard. *Ted Hughes*. Boston: Twayne, 1981.

Kevin De Ornellas

"REAL THING, THE" HENRY JAMES (1892)

"The Real Thing" was published in 1892 in *Black and White* (see MAGAZINES) and is considered among HENRY JAMES's finest short stories. The tale explores the complicated interplay of life and art, of object and imagination. The unnamed narrator is an illustrator and portrait painter whose encounter with an impoverished but indisputably upper-class couple, the Monarchs, changes his art for the worse. When they first appear, he expects a commission for a double portrait, but they want to earn money as models, since other jobs are closed to them as members of the upper class. Although he assesses their photographic realism as perfect for advertising, he agrees to use them as figures in his work. He cannot, however, transmute their impervious facticity: They are as they are, and illustration requires that the artist remake or complete the subject. Miss Churm and Mr. Oronte, the models he usually employs, seem unmistakably lower class but can be transformed into the characters needed for an illustration. The narrator wishes to help the Monarchs but seems flummoxed when confronted

with their stolidity and with his inability to remake them, even as artistic representations of the upper class. In the end, however sympathetic he is to their poverty, he cannot endure the change in his style or the thought of employing them as his servants. He pays them to go away but lives with the memory and its unspoken lesson.

The story is one of reversals: The Monarchs have had a reversal of their fortunes and expectations in life. The artist pays his sitters, who would ordinarily pay him. Mrs. Monarch is, on the surface, more of a servant when asked to prepare tea for the artist and Mr. Oronte than the lower-class Miss Churm is in similar circumstances. The lower-class models better represent the noble class in art than do the upper-class models. Finally, the narrative reverses the reader's expectation that a momentous life experience will have a positive effect on an artist's work.

Critical attention, however, has focused on the teller of the tale. The narrator may belong to the class of Jamesian artist-failures; some have called this story a parable of mastery as it seeks to define the artist's control over his subject in the conversion of the potential of reality into the realization of art. Others have seen in this tale a moral fable in which one man learns compassion as he negotiates the tensions among social class, artistic sensibility, and ethical rectitude. Some critics say the artist renounces his talent for the good of the Monarchs, while others suggest the artist reaches the limit of his talents as he finds he cannot remake them. Biographical critics believe that the story, with its origins in an anecdote told by George DuMaurier, expresses James's fear that the material from which he made his fiction was beyond his control, that life might master him before he could master it through art. Others have proposed that James, in spite of saying that art shapes life, sees factual life as more solid and more important than the felt life of the imagination. The implications of the story, however, remain as mysterious as the title itself: Readers do not know if the Monarchs are, as the narrator states, the "real thing" or if the art made from imaginative incompleteness is the real thing. The ending, furthermore, remains as mysterious as that of James's novel *What Maisie Knew*: The worth of the experience is never told.

BIBLIOGRAPHY
James, Henry. *Complete Stories*. New York: Library of America, 1996.
Lackey, Kris. "Art and Class in 'The Real Thing.'" *Studies in Short Fiction* 26 (1989): 190–192.
Sonstegard, Adam. "'Singularly like a bad illustration:' The Appearance of Henry James' 'The Real Thing' in the Pot-Boiler Press," *Texas Studies in Language and Literature* 45 (2003): 173–200.
Wagenknecht, Edward. *The Tales of Henry James*. New York: Frederick Ungar Publishing Co., 1984.
Whitsitt, Sam. "A Lesson in Reading: Henry James's 'The Real Thing,'" *Henry James Review* 16 (1993): 304–314.

Karen Keck

"RECORD OF BADALIA HERODS-FOOT, THE" RUDYARD KIPLING (1890)

First published in November 1890 in the *Detroit Free Press* (British edition) Christmas number, later reprinted in RUDYARD KIPLING's collection *Many Inventions* (1893). Kipling's only London slum story, "The Record of Badalia Herodsfoot," based on his observations of the poor living near his London lodgings, is connected to a broader movement of fictional and nonfiction studies of the London poor in the 1880s and 1890s, with characters such as Lascar Loo, a dying prostitute whose name evokes Asian sailors and opium dens. Kipling's Badalia is a typical resident of Gunnison Street until her abusive husband, Tom, leaves her for another woman. Then Badalia finds her calling as an assistant to Christian charitable workers: Unlike the Reverend Eustace Hanna or the innocent Sister Eva, Badalia knows what help her neighbors really need. Here, Kipling criticizes middle-class relief workers who claim to know what is good for the poor without ever really understanding their lives. Badalia is successful because she understands the social Darwinian creed of Gunnison Street: the survival of the fittest. Badalia uses her strength to defend the weak from those, like Lascar Loo's mother, who would prey on them.

Badalia falls in love with Reverend Hanna but recognizes that he could never imagine loving a woman of her class and that he is in love with Sister Eva. Tom Herodsfoot, who has moved a few blocks away with Jenny, soon begins to fight with his new "wife." When Jenny calls in the police and Tom feels humiliated, he returns to Badalia to reassert his masculine authority. Encouraged by Lascar Loo's mother, Tom beats Badalia, trying to make her give up the money she holds in trust. Jenny arrives on the scene, and she and the injured Badalia agree to protect Tom from the law. On her deathbed, Badalia notes the futility of her love and tells Reverend Hanna he should marry Eva. In the end, Lascar Loo's mother is again stealing Loo's comforts: Nothing has changed on Gunnison Street. The story's irony is highlighted by the epigraph from Victorian poet Robert Browning's "Pippa Passes": "God's in his heaven / All's right with the world!" What is normal in Badalia's world seems emphatically wrong. Despite the grim humor of the narrator's cynical observations and the depressing inability of the women to transcend the laws of Gunnison Street, the narrative treats Badalia's circumstances with sympathy: The story should encourage readers to rethink Kipling's reputation for misogyny.

BIBLIOGRAPHY
Bauer, Helen Pike. *Rudyard Kipling: A Study of the Short Fiction*. New York: Twayne, 1994.
Johnson, Patricia E. *Hidden Hands: Working-Class Women and Victorian Social-Problem Fiction*. Athens: Ohio University Press, 2001.
Kipling, Rudyard. *Many Inventions*. Available at: http:// whitewolf.newcastle.edu.au/words/authors/K/ KiplingRudyard/prose/ManyInventions/inde x.html. Accessed June 5, 2006.

Terri Doughty

RELIGION

Short stories, because of their length, have the potential to present religious ideas with vivid brevity. This explains their presence in scriptures and sermons. Consequently, parables have migrated from faith to faith, as, for instance, tales from the Buddhist Jatakas were adapted into Christian hagiography and allegory in the medieval anthology *Barlaam and Josaphat*. In this case, the short stories were disguised as entirely Christian, but whether concealed or not, a combination of imagery from more than one faith is a fairly common occurrence in narratives.

As illustrative of medieval short stories in verse, consider one of the most famous groupings, Geoffrey Chaucer's *The Canterbury Tales* (c. 1380s). It concludes with "The Parson's Tale," in which loving a "wyf" (i.e., wife) or any other being more than God is deemed one's "mahmet" (a word oddly conflating "Mohamed" with pagan idolatry).

Idolatry from many sources serves as a unifying theme of the collection, as in "The Merchant's Tale," in which Proserpina, whose very name alludes to a Greek goddess, nonetheless denounces "false gods." "The Second Nun's Tale" extols St. Cecilia, who died rather than sacrifice to an idol. Designed as an apologue against idolizing wealth, "The Pardoner's Tale" is a Christianized story of Buddhist origin. Despite being set in a pre-Christian past in which all its main characters are pagans, "The Knight's Tale" implicitly brings in Christian condemnation of them. Palamon's idolatry in mistakenly worshiping Emelye as Venus gives Arcite pretext for saying that he himself was the first to love her as a human being—the origin of their fatal quarrel. "The Prioress's Tale" portrays Judaism as involving idolatrous human sacrifices—a charge complicated by the unreliability of its narrator, who openly violates the rules of her order. Indeed, *The Canterbury Tales* are famous for exposing hypocrisy, perhaps because Chaucer shared a patron with the precursor of Protestantism, John Wyclif, whose version of the Bible may have influenced Chaucer's language. In addition to seasoning his narratives with the dynamic conflicts of Christianity versus Islam, paganism, and Judaism, Chaucer may thus be giving an early form of Protestant/Catholic controversy.

Typical of medieval fiction, multireligious allusions in *The Canterbury Tales* are all reconciled to a Christianity that bickered among its factions but had not yet experienced the Protestant-Catholic wars. In reaction against these, 18th-century fiction often expressed deism, which tried to limit religion to the abstract common ground between all theistic faiths. Such sentiments appear particularly in the mouths of Near Eastern characters in the many imitations of the *Arabian Nights* after its 1706–08 translation into English. Near the end of that century, however, the influence of Voltaire's oriental tales brought an anti-Christian tinge to deism in some British short stories, notably William Beckford's.

Although deism per se passed out of fashion, 19th-century authors continued to treat religion in a vague, abstract, or indirect manner, as in CHARLES DICKENS's Christmas stories, which promote a nonsectarian charity and piety. RUDYARD KIPLING had been forced as a child to memorize passages from the Bible as punishments, so that he gained an almost encyclopedic knowledge of that book and a tendency to allude to it, while simultaneously resenting it. In his collection of short stories *The JUNGLE BOOKS,* he thus parodies the fundamentalist assumption that God's law is eternal truth: Baloo, the teacher of the Indian Jungle Law, describes it as timeless, while the narrator counters that in fact it evolved. As a Mason, Kipling looked for partial truth in all religions; that Masonic orientation surfaces frequently, as when the jungle animals who keep the law can gain each other's help by pronouncing the "Master-Word," comparable to a Masonic recognition sign. By the end of the century, the so-called DECADENCE movement fascinated many readers with stories of foreign faiths, which helped them break free from Christian strictures.

With the rise of 20th-century MODERNISM and thereafter, the number of religious points of view have proliferated in short stories. Practically any conceivable belief has been advocated or even preached; D. H. LAWRENCE's and E. M. FORSTER's have turned their sexual attitudes into mysticisms associated with various non-Christian faiths and contrasted with Christianity. JAMES JOYCE took the Christian concept of epiphany and made it a structural principle of *DUBLINERS,* stories used as weapons in his attack on Catholic culture, particularly the doctrine of priestly celibacy.

Today, the rainbow of multiculturalism in British short fiction means that, unlike in Chaucer's time, authors can no longer take for granted an audience's deep familiarity with any single tradition. Religions, ranging from orthodox faiths to what used to be called heresies, nonetheless continue to contribute imagery to short stories. SCIENCE FICTION and fantasy (major genres since the 1960s) usually involve such religious themes as apocalypse, golem, shaman, paradise, damnation, salvation, enlightenment, reincarnation, and messiah. Despite religion's importance to the British short stories, it has received relatively little study. Not only are there no books focusing on that topic, but general works such as *A Dictionary of Biblical Tradition* in *English Literature* devote only a little attention to short fiction in contrast to the tome's encyclopedic coverage of other genres. At present, scholarship on religion in short fiction consists primarily of works on major authors rather than on the genre itself.

BIBLIOGRAPHY

Besserman, Lawrence L. *Chaucer and the Bible: An Introduction, Critical Review of Research, Indexes, and Bibliography.* New York: Garland, 1988.

Ellis, Roger. *Patterns of Religious Narrative in The Canterbury Tales.* Totowa, N.J.: Barnes & Noble, 1986.

Glancy, Ruth. *Dickens' Christmas Books, Christmas Stories, and Other Short Fiction: An Annotated Bibliography.* Garland Dickens Bibliographies. New York: Garland, 1985.

Griffin, Ernest G. *Bibliography of Literature and Religion.* Edmonton: University of Alberta, 1967.

Jeffrey, David Lyle, ed. *A Dictionary of Biblical Tradition in English Literature.* Grand Rapids, Mich.: William B. Eerdmans, 1992.

Korte, Barara, Nicholas Poussin, and Claudia Sternberg. *Multicultural British Short Stories.* Stuttgart, Germany: Recala, 1997.

Walter, Dennis. *Dickens and Religion.* London: Allen and Unwin, 1981.

Wright, T. R. *D. H. Lawrence and the Bible.* London: Cambridge University Press, 2000.

Jim Whitlark

RHYS, JEAN (1890–1979)

Now considered a major 20th-century British author, Jean Rhys finally achieved acclaim almost 40 years after her first publication, with the *Wide Sargasso Sea* (1966), her retelling of *Jane Eyre* from the perspective of Mr. Rochester's mad Creole first wife. With her consistently sleek modernist style, Rhys creates two worlds, equally complex and dark: the Caribbean world of her childhood and the demimonde of London and Paris between the world wars.

Rhys was born Ella Gwendolen Rees Williams on Dominica on August 24, 1890, to a Welsh doctor and a Creole descendant of plantation owners. Though she left Dominica in her teens, her Caribbean childhood heavily influenced her fiction. Left destitute after her father's death, she survived by holding a variety of jobs including chorus girl and model. In 1919 she married Jean Lenglet, a self-styled journalist who was actually a French spy involved in various criminal activities. The couple moved to Paris, living in poverty except when Lenglet earned money through dubious means. They had two children: One died in infancy, and the other spent long periods separated from Rhys. Rhys tried to ease their poverty through translation work, meeting a Mrs. Adams who was impressed with Rhys's style and asked to see original works, which she forwarded to writer and publisher Ford Madox Ford. In 1923, Ford suggested she adopt a pen name and began to mentor her. The same year Lenglet was arrested, tried, and imprisoned. Once again left in poverty, Rhys developed a closer relationship with Ford. He helped shape her style and wrote the introduction for her first collection of stories, *The Left Bank, and Other Stories* (1927). Here, Rhys draws from her experiences of living on the edges of and observing society in Paris, Vienna, and southern France. The collection includes works as short as the one-page sketch "In the Luxenbourg Gardens" and as long as the novella "Vienne," a fictionalized account of her first marriage. The collection introduces Rhys's sleek, modernist style and the outsiders and outcast observers peopling her works.

In 1928 Rhys returned to England, placing herself under the protection of Leslie Tilden Smith, her literary agent and second husband. Her period with Tilden Smith, 1928–40, was her most productive. During this time she published her first four novels: *Postures* (1928; republished as *Quartet* in 1929 by Simon and Schuster), *After Leaving Mr. Mackenzie* (1931), *Voyage in the Dark* (1934), and *Good Morning Midnight* (1939). During this period she also began work on her future masterpiece, *Wide Sargasso Sea.*

Tilden Smith went to war in 1940, and with his death in 1945 Rhys lost her steadying force, sinking into alcoholism. She took up with Smith's cousin, Max Hamer, marrying him in 1947. Their marriage lasted until Hamer's death in 1966, but it was a troubled one. Like Lenglet, Hamer was imprisoned for illegal activities. Rhys disappeared totally from the literary scene. When actress Selma Vas Dias wanted to dramatize *Good Morning Midnight,* she was surprised to find Rhys still alive and encouraged her literary comeback. Although unpublished since 1939, Rhys had been working on what would become her posthumously published autobiography, *Smile Please* (1979), and her second collection of short fiction, *Tigers Are Better Looking* (1988).

In 1966 *Wide Sargasso Sea* brought Rhys immediate critical and financial success. She next published *Tigers Are Better Looking, with a Selection from the Left Bank* (1968). Of the 17 stories in the collection, nine were originally published in *The Left Bank and Other Stories.* Although the new stories mostly were written during Rhys's productive period with Tilden Smith, two stories were written between 1945 and 1968: "The Day They Burned the Books" and "Let Them Call It Jazz." In this volume, Rhys continues her focus on the outsider and the outcast. In "The Day They Burned the Books," Rhys expands her examination of society to include an indictment of racism in her native Dominica.

Her final short story collection, *Sleep It Off, Lady* (1976), is a retrospective of Rhys's life and writing. The stories fall into three sections: youth, adulthood, and old age. The first are all set in the West Indies, and Rhys returns to her earlier themes centering on the conflicts among black and white native islanders and recent British immigrants. In these four stories, either the narrators or the main characters are children. The second group centers on young adult women. All but one of these stories return to the territory of Rhys's earliest works: the music hall, the theater, the brothel, the bleak and shallow lives of those who inhabit this territory. Although the situations are similar to those of her earlier works, here Rhys approaches the subject matter from the perspective of one who has lived through this hard life instead of being in the midst of it. In the final story of this section, "The Insect World," Rhys creates a Kafkaesque nightmare in which a young woman's descent into insanity is juxtaposed with London during the blitz. Although the female characters in the final four stories in the collection bear striking similarity to those in the rest of the collection, they are now elderly. In "Rapunzel, Rapunzel," an elderly woman still looks young and beautiful because of her long, thick, but now white, hair. A barber promises to trim her hair but cuts it all off. Without her hair, the woman is old and ugly and quickly succumbs to illness. In the final story in the collection, "I Used to Live Here Once," Rhys returns to the West Indies. In this short gothic gem, the narrator

returns to her childhood home. The children she calls out to do not answer her calls, seem to look right through her, and complain of a sudden chill. It is only then that the narrator realizes that she is dead.

Recently, Postcolonial theorists have been very interested in Rhys's works, especially *Wide Sargasso Sea.* She has also been studied in the context of her modernist contemporaries, with a focus on her novels. Although many of her shorter works represent the finest of her writing, they have not received much scholarly attention. (See also "THE LOTUS.")

BIBLIOGRAPHY

Angier, Carole. *Jean Rhys: Life and Work.* New York: Little, Brown, 1990.

Malcolm, Cheryl Alexander, and David Malcolm. *Jean Rhys: A Study of the Short Fiction.* New York: Prentice Hall, 1996.

Maurel, Sylvie. *Jean Rhys.* New York: St. Martin's, 1995.

Rhys, Jane. *The Left Bank, and Other Stories.* London: Cape, 1927.

———. *Tigers Are Better Looking, with a Selection from the Left Bank.* London: André Deutsch, 1968.

Sternlicht, Stanford V. *Jean Rhys.* New York: Twayne, 1997.

Leah Larson

"ROAD FROM COLONUS, THE" E. M. FORSTER (1903)

"The Road from Colonus" was written by E. M. FORSTER in 1903, shortly after he had visited Olympia in Greece. He had gone there as part of a cruise group made up largely of classical scholars against the enthusiasm and knowledge of whom Forster felt dull and irritable.

For a public school– and Cambridge-educated young man of Forster's time, Greece came too well mediated, too known in advance, and could inspire in the sensitive young artist only the disappointments of rehearsed responses. This fear of being unable to respond adequately to the essential vitality of the external world is a fear that was to haunt Forster's early work. Philip Herriton in *Where Angels Fear to Tread* (1905) is frozen into the painful position of a spectator, unable to engage wholly or fully with anything around him that does not comply with the straight and civilized lines of the actions and etiquette he knows. Likewise, Rickie Elliot in *The Longest Journey* (1907) fears that too much culture and self-consciousness has undone his capacity to respond to life with the abandon life sometimes urgently demands.

Unlike Herriton or Elliot, Mr. Lucas, the central character of "The Road from Colonus," sees life not from the intense and anxious perspective of early manhood but from the weariness and greediness of old age. His age indeed forms the story's matrix as that which all the characters, Lucas himself included, struggle to give meaning to. Lucas is holidaying in Greece with a party that includes his daughter Ethel, a woman destined by her authoritarian father to serve as the helpmeet and comfort of his old age; Mr. Graham, a young man of impeccably imperialist manners; and Mrs. Forman, one of those well-meaning but cruelly complacent older women who punctuate Forster's fiction.

Lucas has dreamed of a trip to Greece for 40 years. Long a Hellenist, his desire to immerse himself in the Greece he has dreamed of has only been sharpened by the social and physical symptoms of the onset of old age. The attention and consideration he is constantly the object of threaten his independence, making that independence both more valuable and more difficult. Greece disappoints him: He can but look at it through the eyes of an old man, and to those jaded eyes, Greece itself appears as an old man. It is the ambiguity with which Forster presents this terrible loss of hope that gives this otherwise slight story its narrative interest and emotional depth. Lucas is an unlikably patrician figure, arrogant and irritable. Why should the external world conform to his desires? But why should it be unbearably sad when, as he does by the story's end, he gives up on the hope that it would or even could?

The story opens on the threshold of a moment that is to challenge Lucas's surrender to the inevitability of time. A discontent that had been growing in him blossoms on a trip to Olympia, issuing in a momentary rebellion against the authority of the young over the old, and against the tyranny of common sense and habit over beauty, peace, and solitude. His rebellion is defeated. He is physically lifted from the place he desires to stay in and led impassively away, back to his now despised, empty life and away from that which had promised him happiness and beauty. The scene in which Lucas is overcome is a triumph of precision and

conciseness and provides a moment of sadness that gives the story as a whole its affective power.

Read with Forster's "The STORY OF A PANIC," a story in which a rebellion succeeds as the boy Eustace seizes himself out of the grip of domesticity and polite power, "The Road from Colonus" shows Forster again tackling the terrors of direct experience. The well-mannered but no less cutting conflicts that thread this story pit the visible world against the invisible and convention against desire in a sharp analysis of cruelty's resting place in duty and self-deception.

BIBLIOGRAPHY
Forster, E. M. *The Celestial Omnibus and Other Stories.* London: Sidgwick and Jackson, 1911.

Patricia McManus

ROBERTS, MICHÈLE (1949–)

Emerging from a group of women writers influenced by the 1970s feminist movement, Michèle Roberts has won a place on the literary stage with her 11 novels, two collections of short stories, and poetry, the most significant of which is collected in *All the Selves I Was* (1995). Obsessed with food, sex, and God, also the title of her 1998 collection of essays, Roberts's sensuous prose nevertheless insists on a feminist politics of location and the specificity of women's lives: "If you write specifically, admitting where you are coming from—female, French, Catholic—then you have to take the risk that some people won't always be comfortable" (White, 126).

Born in 1949 to a French mother and English father, Roberts grew up mainly in England but spent summers in Normandy. Many of her texts, particularly her earliest novels, *A Piece of the Night* (1978) and *The Visitation* (1983), display autobiographical elements, and Roberts's experience of two languages and two cultures informs and enriches much of her writing. *Daughters of the House* (1992) presents this sense of dual culture in the cousins Léonie and Thérèse, who are engaged in a battle over their shared English and French past. This novel won Roberts a Booker Prize nomination, the WH Smith prize, and general acclaim, something that had largely eluded her in the publication of her previous five books.

Brought up a Catholic and educated in a convent school, Roberts rejected the Catholic Church in favor of feminism during her days studying English at Oxford. Nevertheless, the shades of the faith have not left her work, peopled as it is by nuns, guilty daughters, and saints. This obsession with exorcising the ghosts of Catholicism led her to write *The Wild Girl* (1984), an alternative, feminine gospel story. Inevitably controversial, this is a brave novel but ultimately conservative and uneven. Other works, such as *The Book of Mrs. Noah* (1987) and *Impossible Saints* (1997), use religious figures and imagery to more creative ends, producing fantastic and even grotesque novels, many of which explore and subvert malign aspects of Catholic heritage.

Roberts's two collections of short stories, *During Mother's Absence* (1993) and *Playing Sardines* (2001), demonstrate her ability to produce rich and often poetic short fiction. This is no surprise since her longer works often blur the boundaries between the novel and the short story; *Flesh and Blood* (1994), *The Book of Mrs. Noah,* and *Impossible Saints* consist of numerous stories held together in complex ways. The short story collections explore many of the issues central to Roberts's novels and poetry, manifesting strong feminist impulses, and they also demonstrate her interest in formal experimentation, including stories as diverse as the glossary of French terms that evoke childhood in "Une Glossaire" (in *During Mother's Absence*) and a diary made up of lists ("Lists" in *Playing Sardines*), in which mundane reminders to visit the supermarket and clean the church metamorphose into details of a murder.

From dead nuns on biers in *A Piece of the Night,* to dead lovers for dinner in "The Cookery Lesson" (*Playing Sardines*), Roberts's fiction continues to entertain and unsettle. She is willing to take the risk that people will find her work uncomfortable. (See also "The BISHOP'S LUNCH.")

BIBLIOGRAPHY
Brown, Georgina. "From Hand to Mouth," *Independent,* 12 March 1993, p. 21.
Hanson, Clare. "During Mother's Absence: The Fiction of Michèle Roberts." In *British Women Writing Fiction,* edited by Abby H. P. Werlock, 229–247. Tuscaloosa: University of Alabama Press, 2000.
Roberts, Michèle. *All the Selves I Was.* 1995. London: Virago, 2000.
———. *Daughters of the House.* 1992. London: Virago, 1993.
———. *During Mother's Absence.* 1993. London: Virago, 1994.
———. *Food, Sex and God: On Inspiration and Writing.* London: Virago, 1998.
———. *The Looking Glass.* London: Little, Brown, 2000.
White, Rosemary. "Michèle Roberts: An Interview," *Bête Noire* 14/15 (1994): 125–140.

Sarah J. Falcus

"ROCK, THE" E. M. FORSTER (1947) Described by E. M. FORSTER, in his introduction to *The Collected Short Stories of E. M. Forster* (1947), as "a complete flop," "The Rock" was rejected by editors in Forster's lifetime and was eventually published only in the posthumous *The Life to Come and Other Stories* (1972). The story's neglect, by Forster and others, may be attributed to neither its brevity (it is not four pages long) nor its theme (how to measure worth) but to the disjunction between them.

The rock of the title is a rock treacherously placed in the water off the North Coast of Cornwall. A man—we do not learn his name—holidaying in Cornwall sails one day too close to the rock; his boat capsizes, and he is left stranded on the rock but is then rescued by three village men. The rescued man discovers or rediscovers (there is no suggestion that he was unhappy before his holiday) his love of life; his love for his wife and hers for him is equally transfigured. So great is his gratitude, however, that he cannot decide how to fulfill his obligation to his rescuers. This is the dilemma the story turns on: The question is not merely how to measure the worth of a life saved but how to recognize and respect the different measures of worth borne out of different needs (229).

BIBLIOGRAPHY
Forster, E. M. *The Life to Come and Other Stories.* London: Penguin, 1975.

Patricia McManus

"ROCKING-HORSE WINNER, THE" D. H. LAWRENCE (1926) David Ellis, in his account of D. H. LAWRENCE's late years, explains that the author was paid 15 pounds for allowing the publication of "The Rocking-Horse Winner" in Cynthia Asquith's 1926 anthology, *The Ghost Book*. This, states Ellis, was a bargain, because "The Rocking-Horse Winner" became one of the most acclaimed, anthologized, and translated stories of the century. The story first appeared in the July 1926 issue of *Harper's Bazaar* before surfacing in Asquith's collection. It was grouped, posthumously, with other Lawrence works in the 1933 collection *The Lovely Lady*.

The story's plot is simple. A young boy, Paul, is harassed by two complementary pressures: ghostly and maternal. His mother, Hester, is tortured by a sense of fiscal limitation: Socially pretentious, she cannot accept the family's level of income. Paul hears his mother insist that "There *must* be more money!"—and ghostly voices endlessly repeat this phrase, haunting and taunting him. Paul, encouraged by an opportunistic gardener, learns that he has an uncanny ability to predict the outcome of major horse races. He does this by galloping on a rocking-horse, discovering answers from some indefinable source. His motivation is to rectify his family's supposed impoverishment. After one supreme, successful effort to predict a Derby winner, Paul falls into a coma and dies, leaving the family rich but without a male heir.

Critical reaction to the story can be as complex as the story is straightforward. Many see the story as a tongue-in-cheek morality tale: The urge for financial gain outweighs familial affection, and money is more important than children's welfare. Janice Hubbard Harris points to a deeper Lawrentian trait in the story. The sexually frustrated Hester turns her son into a "desirable opposite" of her disappointing husband: Paul's accumulation of wealth is as spectacular as his father's is average. Other critics, notably W. D. Snodgrass, have concentrated on the onanistic elements of Paul's retreat into a world that only he is privy to: Satisfaction is achievable only behind the closed doors of an uneasy, intimacy-bereft home. Perhaps Lawrence also mocks the (mainly) masculine desire to control the external by such feats as prophesying races. Being able to predict the outcomes of sporting events is a fantasy that appeals to all acquisitive persons. "The Rocking-Horse Winner" continues to hold attention. It has

been filmed three times, notably by Anthony Pelisser (1950). Its disturbing focus on a boy's relationship with a rocking-horse, together with Lawrence's novella about the eponymous stallion St. Mawr, influenced Peter Schaffer's equally disturbing play about a youth's breakdown, *Equus*.

BIBLIOGRAPHY
Ellis, David. *D. H. Lawrence: Dying Game, 1922–30*. Cambridge and New York: Cambridge University Press, 1998.

Harris, Janice Hubbard. *The Short Fiction of D. H. Lawrence*, 224–227. New Brunswick, N.J.: Rutgers University Press, 1984.

Lawrence, D. H. "The Rocking-Horse Winner." In *The Lovely Lady*. London: Martin Secker, 1932.

Snodgrass, W. D. "A Rocking Horse: The Symbol, the Pattern, the Way to Live," *Hudson Review* 11 (1958): 191–200.

Kevin De Ornellas

"ROMANTIC ADVENTURES OF A MILKMAID, THE" THOMAS HARDY (1883)

In this much-anthologized story, THOMAS HARDY combines realism and imagination to create a romance that illustrates the danger of allowing sexual desire to influence one's marriage choice. Set in the village of Silverthorn in Hardy's Lower Wessex, "The Romantic Adventures of a Milkmaid" focuses on Margery Tucker, a young milkmaid whose rustic life is unsettled by the Baron von Xanten. Margery unwittingly prevents the baron's suicide when they first meet, and when von Xanten offers a reward in gratitude, Margery asks him to take her to a ball. The experience sours Margery's relationship with her fiancé, the local lime burner Jim Hayward. She has fallen in love with the luxury of the baron's world and desires the baron for herself. When she misses her own wedding to meet with the baron, the nobleman finally realizes the damage he has done. He helps Jim impress Margery with expensive furniture and other household items, but she still resists Jim's advances. Finally, the baron, apparently on his deathbed, arranges a surprise marriage ceremony for Margery, and she marries Jim on the condition that their bond is kept secret. They live apart for several months until Jim settles on two new schemes to attract Margery's attention. He joins the yeomanry regiment to impress her, and he courts a local widow, Mrs. Peach, to incite Margery's jealousy. The schemes succeed until the baron, now in better health, returns and whisks Margery away toward the coast where his yacht is moored. Von Xanten asks Margery to join him abroad, but when she refuses, he returns her to Silverthorn, where she finally reunites with Jim. Years later, Margery and Jim learn that the baron has killed himself, and Margery admits that she would have accompanied von Xanten had he pressed her to do so.

Hardy published this tale concurrently in the *Graphic* in Britain and, serially, in *Harper's Weekly* in the United States. Contemporary reviewers criticized the improbabilities in the text, and subsequent critics have dismissed it as a mere potboiler not worthy of critical attention. Indeed, Hardy's biographer Michael Millgate notes that although Hardy included the story in the collection *A Changed Man and Other Tales* in 1913, even he had a "low opinion" of the entire volume. However, "The Romantic Adventures," often reprinted and pirated, was popular with the public, and it deserves serious scrutiny. Margery's experience with von Xanten and Jim provides a fine example of female subjection in the 1840s society in which the tale takes place. Beyond its examination of women's roles, the tale also provides cautionary advice to readers who might aspire to higher social standing. The true genius of Hardy's story lies in its attention to psychological nuance as the relationship between Margery and the baron unfolds and complicates Margery's marriage decision. By the end of the story, the innocent relationship of the carefree country girl with the dark, brooding, Byronic foreigner transforms into a complex of unstated sexual desire. Hardy develops the characters well enough for readers to speculate about their motivations and to sympathize with their anxieties. Simultaneously, he introduces enough ambiguity to give the characters vitality and mystery. The baron, for example, could be interpreted symbolically as a satanic figure whose purpose is to tempt the inhabitants of Silverthorn and disrupt their idyllic pastoral existence. Given the length of the tale, critics are unable to agree on whether it is a short story, a novella, or a short novel. Regardless, it effectively displays Hardy's characteristic style and poetic fascination with detail.

BIBLIOGRAPHY
Allingham, Philip V. "The Initial Publications of Thomas Hardy's Novella 'The Romantic Adventures of a Milkmaid' in the *Graphic* and *Harper's* (Summer, 1883)," *Thomas Hardy Journal* 16, no. 3 (2000): 45–62.
Benazon, Michael. "'The Romantic Adventures of a Milkmaid': Hardy's Modern Romance," *English Studies in Canada* 5, no. 1 (1979): 56–65.
Hardy, Thomas. *Collected Stories.* Edited by F. B. Pinion. London: Macmillan, 1998.
Millgate, Michael. *Thomas Hardy: His Career as a Novelist.* New York: Random House, 1971.

Ben P. Robertson

ROUND THE SOFA ELIZABETH GASKELL (1859)

Round the Sofa, a two-volume collection of stories, short novels, and essays by ELIZABETH GASKELL, was made up of earlier works published previously in magazines, notably CHARLES DICKENS's *Household Words* (see MAGAZINES) and, in America, in *Harper's New Monthly Magazine.* The disparate stories are held together by a framing device of a narrator who claims to be writing down other people's stories. The storytelling begins when Miss Greatorix visits her friend Mrs. Dawson and asks to tell the first story, the novella "MY LADY LUDLOW." When she has finished, Mr. Dawson then offers to tell another story, "An Accursed Race," which he has prepared for his local philosophical society. Miss Greatorix politely agrees and finds that "I found it, on the whole, more interesting than I anticipated" (II, 2). He is followed by Miss Duncan, a governess who, "in a high-pitched, ill-assured voice," reads "The Doom of the Griffiths." Like many of the stories in the collection, this is about the history of a family, in this case about the extinction of an ancient line. In "The Poor Clare" a woman mistakenly curses her granddaughter.

The most striking of these family stories is "The HALF-BROTHERS," which focuses on a Cumberland farmer, William Preston, and the familial divisiveness he brings about by favoring his own son over his despised stepson, Gregory. Gaskell underpins the narrative with a succinct and unsentimental exposition of the social and economic pressures on women during the 19th century, of which the two boys' mother's second marriage, which she undertakes out of dutiful necessity, is the direct and inevitable result.

Through the first-person narration of the younger half brother, Gaskell creates complex temporal and emotional links between past causes and present effects that have their mimesis in the setting and the language. While the bleak and pitiless northern landscape is deployed to reflect Preston's hardness of heart, that same environment nevertheless nurtures Gregory as a simple but loving shepherd, trained by "old Adam" and accompanied by faithful Lassie. Gregory embodies the Christlike qualities of humility and self-sacrifice—the "good parts" that he has inherited from his mother—through which he is able to rescue his seemingly privileged brother from a "desolate, helpless death" and redeem Preston from his role as "wicked step-parent." Preston's burial at the foot of the grave shared by Helen and Gregory may be interpreted as evidence of the humility he has finally achieved in accepting the dominion of spiritual over passionate love.

BIBLIOGRAPHY

Elizabeth Gaskell. *Round the Sofa.* London: Sampson Low, 1859.
Watson, J. R. "*Round the Sofa:* Elizabeth Gaskell Tells Stories." *Yearbook of English Studies* 26 (1996): 89–95.

Therie Hendry-Seabrook

RUSHDIE, SALMAN (1947–)

Salman Rushdie was born in Bombay just two months before Indian independence (August 15, 1947), the moment in history that inspired *Midnight's Children,* winner of the Booker Prize in 1981 and of the Booker of Bookers, for the best work awarded the prize in its first 25 years. This period of extreme cultural flux is portrayed through a generation of children born with magical gifts when colonial rule ended. Rushdie is a prominent postcolonial writer, a magic realist, and a political satirist, and he is studied alongside contemporary South Asian, South Asian Diaspora, and British writers. He is frequently compared to JAMES JOYCE, Gabriel García Márquez, Milan Kundera, and Günter Grass, whose novel *The Tin Drum* is sometimes regarded as an intertext for *Midnight's Children.* Rushdie's recurring themes include the home, exile,

belief, fame, commerce and corruption, the figure of the storyteller, and mutation. His stories are invariably told through unreliable narration, intrusive external narrators, or a disruption of the order of narrative.

As well as eight novels, including *Shame,* which won the Prix du Meilleur Livre Etranger, and *The Satanic Verses,* which was awarded the Whitbread Prize for Best Novel, Rushdie published a collection of short stories, EAST WEST, in 1994. Mythmaking and the origin of myths dominates the collection. Although themes range from Christopher Columbus to contemporary immigration procedures and from the power of religious relics to severe mental illness, the stories consistently express a longing for home, or for a definition of home.

Rushdie's 1997 short story "The Firebird's Nest" was included in the 2004 anthology *Telling Tales,* edited by Nadine Gordimer. In this evocative and tense story, an American woman marries an older, Indian man whose hometown, where women die by spontaneous combustion, is destroyed by drought and economic hardship. "The Firebird's Nest" revises the Bluebeard fairy tale in which a new bride discovers the murdered bodies of previous wives. ANGELA CARTER, who was also an obvious influence on Rushdie's writing, also based her acclaimed short story "The BLOODY CHAMBER" on the Bluebeard tale.

While studying history at Cambridge University, Salman Rushdie was a member of the Cambridge Footlights theater, which may have encouraged his preoccupation with the stage, actors, and cinematic imagery. Before becoming a full-time writer, Rushdie worked in advertising, and the language of advertising pervades his work, with its fast-paced, innovative style.

In 2004, Rushdie became president of the American division of the international writers' organization for freedom of expression, PEN. Rushdie is known outside the world of literature for the political significance of his 1988 novel *The Satanic Verses* and the subsequent fatwa, or death sentence, pronounced by the Ayatollah Khomeini of Iran without any legal process, which forced Rushdie into hiding for more than 10 years. A good example of the vast critical commentary relating to this period of his career is Sara Maitland and Lisa Appignanesi's *The Rushdie File* (1989), a comprehensive collection of contemporary journalism and critical writing.

Rushdie has published two collections of nonfiction, *Imaginary Homelands* in 1991 and *Step across This Line* in 2002. *The Jaguar Smile,* a piece of extended narrative journalism documenting Nicaragua and the Sandinista political movement, was published in 1987. His short story "At the Auction of the Ruby Slippers" in *East West* refers to *The Wizard of Oz,* a film that he considers a seminal work and a formative influence on his career; he describes the film as his "very first literary influence" in *Step across This Line,* and he discusses it in a 1992 work of film criticism.

BIBLIOGRAPHY

Appignanesi, Lisa, and Sara Maitland, eds. *The Rushdie File.* London: Fourth Estate, 1989.

Cundy, Catherine. *Salman Rushdie.* Manchester, England: Manchester University Press, 1996.

Reder, Michael R., ed. *Conversations with Salman Rushdie.* Jackson: University Press of Mississippi, 2000.

Rushdie, Salman. "At the Auction of the Ruby Slippers." In *East West.* London: Jonathan Cape, 1994.

———. "The Firebird's Nest." In *Telling Tales,* edited by Nadine Gordimer, 45–64. London: Bloomsbury, 2004.

———. *The Ground Beneath Her Feet.* London: Vintage, 1999.

———. *The Jaguar Smile.* London: Vintage, 1987.

———. *The Moor's Last Sigh.* London: Vintage: 1995.

———. *Shame.* London: Vintage, 1983.

———. *Step across This Line: Collected Nonfiction 1992–2002.* London: Vintage, 2002.

Jenni Ramone

S

"SAD FORTUNES OF THE REV. AMOS BARTON, THE" GEORGE ELIOT (1857)

Encouraged by George Henry Lewes, Mary Ann (Marian) Evans purposed to write publishable fiction and began with a title that came to her in the middle of one night, "The Sad Fortunes of the Rev. Amos Barton." She conceived a story that would be the first in a series of sketches called *Scenes from Clerical Life*. Once completed, the story was accepted by *Blackwood's Edinburgh Magazine* to run anonymously in two installments, January and February 1857. Only after John Blackwood pressed for the author's identity (after *Adam Bede*) did she put forth her now familiar pseudonym, GEORGE ELIOT: "George" in honor of her partner's Christian name, and "Eliot" as a "good mouth-filling, easily pronounced word" (Cross, I:310). Most readers were sure that the stories had been penned by an actual clergyman, so realistic were their portrayals of clerical life.

Eliot believed that literature should depict truth, especially the reality of everyday life, with all of its ordinariness, flaws, and obtuseness. Therefore, Amos Barton is an unglamorous, mediocre man; he is "in no respect an ideal of exceptional character . . . far from remarkable,—a man whose virtues were not heroic . . . but [he] was palpably and unmistakably commonplace." His deficiencies as a minister include a pompous oratorical style, and many of his ideas have no relevance or lucidity for his parishioners. Worse, he is a grammatical buffoon. Barton incomprehensibly "preached Low-Church doctrine—as evangelical as anything to be heard in the Independent Chapel," that is, a belief in the infallibility of the Bible and an emphasis on the personal experience between parishioner and God. But he is also High Church, meaning that he performs rituals such as treating communion as an instrument of grace that imparts salvation to its partakers. He also insists on ecclesiastical authority, which most Low Church followers reject. For these reasons he is ineffectual as a pastor; he is duplicitous and lacks a single conviction of his own. This character reflects the way Eliot perceived Christianity in her day.

In contrast, Eliot describes Barton's angelic wife, Milly, as a gift to him and all humanity: "Happy the man, you would have thought, whose eye will rest on her in the pauses of his fireside reading—whose hot aching forehead will be soothed by the contact of her cool soft hand—who will recover himself from dejection at his mistakes and failures in the loving light of her unreproaching eyes." Milly is Eliot's notion of a true Christian, one who practices charity with sympathy and humility. Inexplicably, Amos allows a countess to stay with them, when they can barely feed and clothe their own brood of six children. Milly literally works herself to death in caring for all of them. Eliot, in subscribing to the theories of positivism that discounted the possibility of spiritual intervention, creates a good woman who does good deeds but, without spiritual wherewithal beyond herself, becomes depleted and dies. Milly is buried like a Madonna figure, with her dead baby in her arms. At this point the readers, like the parishioners of Shepperton, sympathize with the reverend's suffering and are motivated to treat others with compassion. Milly's sacrificial death brings out the best in Barton's neighbors: "Amos failed to touch the spring of goodness by his sermons, but he touched it effectually by his sorrows." The neighbors reach out to comfort and help with his children, but not before they instigate the loss of his job. His reduction to sheer humanity establishes him as one of them. This, to Eliot, is the best that humans can do: learn to sympathize with others, realize and accept our own frailties, and make better choices prompted by feeling-based ethics.

"The greatest benefit we owe to the artist," Eliot wrote, "is the extension of our sympathies" (*Essays,* 270). By being initiated into literary realism, readers may be moved to do what is ethical in their own lives. This was Eliot's "religion of humanity" that impelled the production of her first short story. She had finished translating two philosophical discourses with premises that, in effect, raided Christianity of the power of the cross. The first was David Strauss's *Life of Jesus* (1846), which considered the Gospels to be no more than myths that contained some kernels of truth. Strauss discounted all that was supernatural in the Bible, seeing it merely as the product of an unsophisticated, ignorant culture. This assertion undermined one of the foundational truths shared by the Evangelical sect—of which Eliot was once a follower—the absolute authority of a literal interpretation of the Bible. At the center of Evangelicalism is Jesus, the only begotten son of God, who gave his life on the cross for the remission of human sin and then arose from the dead. Removing the spiritual from Christianity, for Eliot and many Victorians like her, left a quandary as to what, if anything, to retain from faith. For her, the answer came from her study and translation of Ludwig Feuerbach's *The Essence of Christianity* (1854), which identified benevolence, humanity, and ethics as the enduring, useful values of Christianity. To believe this is to completely deny the centrality of the Cross to any of those virtues and leads the question, What is Christianity without Christ?

Eliot was also a determinist, perceiving a universe that is absolutely rational and believing that everything happens because of what has gone before, that no one makes moral choices or exercises free will. However, Eliot believed that studying the past can help people learn from mistakes and thereby positively influence the future. This is why she sets "Amos Burton" in the past, so that readers can learn from the reverend's mistakes and make informed decisions accordingly. The reverend is a pathetic representative of Christianity, as impecunious in his faith as he is in his emotional and financial provision for his family. He is spiritually detached from humanity. In his own suffering, he never prays, never asks God to provide for the material needs of his family, never trusts God for anything. Indeed, neither does Milly, nor do any of the people of Shepperton. In her own life, Eliot herself no longer looked for the divine but found divinity in all humanity. The purpose of literature, as Eliot explained in a letter was a moral one, to encourage uplifting feelings that would lead people to do what is socially right. This is what she set out to do in writing fiction.

After "Amos Barton," Eliot wrote "Mr. Gilfil's Love-Story" and "JANET'S REPENTANCE," which were bound in a book in 1858.

BIBLIOGRAPHY
Cross, John. *George Eliot's Life as Reflected in Her Letters and Journals.* 4 vols. Edinburgh: Blackwood, 1884.

Gribble, Jennifer. Introduction. *Scenes of Clerical Life,* by George Eliot, ix–xxxvii. London: Penguin, 1999.

Eliot, George. *Essays of George Eliot.* Edited by Thomas Pinney. New York: Columbia University Press, 1963.

———. *Scenes of Clerical Life.* 1858. Edited and with an and introduction by David Lodge. London: Penguin, 1973.

Haight, Gordon S. *George Eliot: A Biography.* Oxford University Press, 1968.

———, ed. *The George Eliot Letters.* 9 vols. New Haven: Yale University Press, 1954.

McCormick, Kathryn. "George Eliot's First Fiction, Targeting *Blackwood's,*" *Bibliotheck* 21 (1996): 69–80.

Brenda Ayres

SAKI (HECTOR HUGH MUNRO) (1870–1914)

The man who became known as Saki was born in Akyab, in northwest Burma, on December 18, 1870, to a family with strong military connections on both sides. On the death of his mother, he and his older brother and sister were sent to live with their grandmother and aunts in Devon. The figure of the domineering, repressive woman who bullies and browbeats or simply fails to love a young boy appears in many Saki stories and may reflect the unhappiness of the years between the children's return to England when Saki was two years old and their father's retirement and return when Saki was 17. A delicate child, Munro was not sent to school until he was 12. Two years at Pencarwick school at Exmouth was followed by two at Bedford. His father's return released him from formal education and the aunts alike, though informal studies continued during extended trips to Europe.

Munro followed his father and brother into service in the Burmese Police Force, where he spent most of his time investigating, and adopting, the flora and fauna of his district. After several bouts of malaria, he was invalided home and spent the next three years writing a history of the Russian Empire. An introduction from a family friend led to his producing a series of political satires illustrated by Francis Carruthers Gould, a well-known political cartoonist, later collected as *Alice in Westminster,* and he also began to publish short stories. He became a foreign correspondent of the Tory *Morning Post,* based in the Balkans, which provided him further opportunities for enjoying the wild landscapes he loved; Russia, where he witnessed the St. Petersburg Massacre in 1905; and finally Paris. After the death of his father, Munro returned to England and took rooms in Mortimer Street and a cottage in Surrey where he installed his sister, whom he visited frequently. He was now able to earn a living from his fiction. His short stories appeared in a number of periodicals, but chiefly the *Westminster Gazette.* He was a popular guest and host, known for his impeccable manners and impeccable tailoring. He enjoyed the theater and ballet, but he kept a fairly low profile and did not move in the circle of duchesses and wealthy hostesses depicted in his stories. In 1914, though past the age of military service, he enlisted as a trooper, but he soon transferred to the 22nd Royal Fusiliers and was sent to the front. A dedicated soldier, he refused a commission on a number of occasions but eventually accepted promotion to lance-sergeant.

Munro was killed at Beaumont-Hamel on the Somme in November 1916. He was one of a group of infantrymen resting on the lip of a crater between bombardments. His last words were, "Put that bloody cigarette out," and then he was shot through the head by a sniper presumably aiming for the glowing tip of the cigarette.

The pseudonym *Saki* is thought to be taken from *The Rubáiyát of Omar Khayyám,* in which Saki is a cup-bearer. Saki's writing is elegant, economical, and witty. The tone of the short stories is worldly, flippant irreverence delivered in astringent exchanges and neat epigrams, such as "To have reached thirty . . . is to have failed in life" ("Reginald on the Academy") and "brevity is the soul of widowhood" ("The Match-Maker"). The protagonist is often a young man; fastidious, fashionable, witty, hedonistic, vain, self-centered, and materialistic. His charm lies chiefly in his youth, and he is determined to hang on to it. There are hints at decadence, though the youth's crimes are usually no worse than mischief.

The other major strand of Saki's writing is the supernatural. In a number of stories a supernatural creature or being becomes an agent of revenge for the crimes of the overbearing woman against the boy or man in her power. The tone in these stories is completely ruthless; the women, it is suggested, have deserved their respective gruesome fates, and neither the narrative voice nor the characters waste a moment's pity on them. In "Sredni Vashtar" a ferret is magically transformed into a gigantic ur-ferret that kills the guardian who has made Conradin's life a misery. Conradin watches. Finally, "out through the doorway came a long, yellow-and-brown beast, with eyes a-blink at the waning daylight, and dark wet stains around the fur of jaws and throat." Unwilling to break the news to the bereaved boy, the servants hesitate outside the door behind which Conradin calmly consumes buttered toast. This audacious heartlessness also provides much of the humor of the stories. When a hyena devours a gypsy child, a character asks, "'Do you think the poor little thing suffered much?' 'The indications were all that way,' I said; 'on the other hand, of course, it may have been crying from sheer temper. Children sometimes do'" ("Esmé"). (See also "GABRIEL-ERNEST," "The

INTERLOPERS," "The PENANCE," "The SCHARTZ-METTER-KLUME METHOD.")

BIBLIOGRAPHY

Langguth, A. J. *Saki: A Life of Hector Hugh Munro: With Six Short Stories Never Before Collected.* New York: Simon and Schuster, 1981.

Saki. *The Complete Saki.* Harmondsworth, England: Penguin, 1982.

Spears, George James. *The Satire of Saki: A Study of the Satiric Art of Hector Munro.* New York: Exposition Press, 1963.

Sandie Byrne

"SALLY BOWLES" CHRISTOPHER ISHERWOOD (1937)
In 1929, after the publication of his first novel *All the Conspirators,* Christopher Isherwood (William Bradshaw, 1904–1987) moved to Berlin, where he intermittently spent the next four years. Isherwood intended to write a novel about his experiences with the residents of the Berlin underworld and began writing one in 1932, which he titled *The Lost.* He never completed that novel; instead, he wrote a series of short stories, some of which, like "Sally Bowles" (1937), were published in magazines throughout the 1930s. In 1939, his stories about his Berlin years were published in the story collection *Goodbye to Berlin.*

The story "Sally Bowles," with its eponymous heroine, is perhaps the best known of Isherwood's works because of its various theater and film adaptations. John Van Druten adapted the story for the stage in 1955 as *I Am a Camera,* with Julie Harris as Sally Bowles. Harold Prince directed *Cabaret,* the musical adaptation of Van Druten's play, with music and lyrics by John Kander and Fred Ebb, in 1966. In 1971, Bob Fosse directed the acclaimed film *Cabaret,* with Liza Minnelli as Sally Bowles. The musical version of Isherwood's story has been revived successfully several times since then.

Isherwood's story spans about a year, from autumn 1930 to 1931, and is loosely based on his friendship with Jean Ross who, like Sally, was an English expatriate working as a second-rate cabaret singer and actress in Berlin in the early 1930s. "Sally Bowles" is less a traditional story than a series of vignettes in which Isherwood's alter-ego strikes up a friendship with the free-spirited Sally and accompanies her on a series of misadventures. Sally's story is structured around her affairs with three men: Klaus, her accompanist, who leaves for London to pursue a career as a musician for film scores; Clive, a rich American who pampers both Sally and Christopher; and George, a 16-year-old con artist from Poland. Christopher is a witness to the first affair, a participant in the second, and the instigator of the third.

The vignettes follow this order: Christopher meets Sally at the home of Fritz Wendel, a businessman and playboy, and later goes to hear her act at the Lady Windermere, a seedy cabaret. He then helps Sally through a brief affair with Klaus and gets involved in her affair with Clive, who showers them both with gifts. Christopher, Sally, and Clive make plans to leave Berlin for an extended world tour, but Clive disappears abruptly, leaving Sally and Christopher a brief message and three hundred-mark notes. Shortly thereafter, Sally discovers she is pregnant and arranges to have an abortion. Despite her efforts to act nonchalantly, the abortion puts a strain on her friendship with Christopher, and he leaves Berlin for a time. Upon his return, he renews his relationship with Sally, which sours when she asks him to ghostwrite an article for her and dismisses his effort. In revenge, Christopher sets Sally up with a con artist, who sleeps with Sally and then steals her money. Sally manages to charm the local police into helping her by insisting that she was engaged to the young man.

Sally's friendship with Christopher gives these scattered episodes coherence, and her affairs chart the developments in their relationship. Sally, untalented and naive, holds enough fascination for Christopher to cause him to fall in love with her deeply, albeit platonically. Along with some of the other characters in *Goodbye to Berlin,* Sally is often seen as representing the spirit of post–World War I Germany during the so-called Weimar Republic, an unbridled hedonism that lacks the capacity for reflection on one's actions. The rise of Hitler and the Nazis is apparent in the story but is kept in the background, largely because Sally finds them irrelevant. (At one point, she expresses ignorance over a bank collapse that has the rest of the characters panicking.)

Sally's manner of living, along with that of characters such as Fritz Wendel, Klaus, and Clive, show not only a complete disregard for the encroaching Nazi presence but also a lack of forethought that causes them to resort to drastic measures in a crisis. Both Klaus and Clive disappear when their relationships with Sally intensify, and Sally herself has an abortion and promptly quarrels with Christopher. Anti-Semitism is also an undercurrent, especially in Fraulein Mayr's warning to Sally against Jewish abortionists. A determinedly anti-Fascist writer, Isherwood's decision to keep these events in the background in "Sally Bowles" is deliberate, his point being that the transition from the Weimar era to a Nazi culture was helped by people's refusal to give these disturbing elements proper attention.

BIBLIOGRAPHY
Isherwood, Christopher. *The Berlin Stories*. New York: New Directions, 1988.
———. *Christopher and His Kind*. New York: Farrar, Straus & Giroux, 1976.
Page, Norman. *Auden and Isherwood: The Berlin Years*. London: Macmillan, 1998.
Piazza, Paul. *Christopher Isherwood: Myth and Anti-myth*. New York: Columbia University Press, 1978.

Heather Marcovitch

"SAMSON AND DELILAH" D. H. LAWRENCE (1917)

This story was first published by D. H. LAWRENCE in March 1917 in the *English Review* and appeared in the *Lantern* in June the same year. It was included in *England, My England and Other Stories*, published in October 1922, and has since appeared in a number of anthologies. The action takes place during the first year of World War I, in an isolated tin-mining village in West Cornwall. The two principal characters are an estranged man and wife, Willie and Alice Nankervis. Secondary characters include their teenage daughter Maryann, a group of miners, and a group of soldiers.

The story opens as a solitary man arrives at the village on a cold winter evening. He enters the village inn, where he finds the landlady, Alice, playing cards with a group of miners. After he has ordered a drink, the remaining characters make their entrance: the soldiers, shortly followed by Maryann. The men order food, and after they have finished their meal, most of the soldiers retire to bed. When the miners leave the premises, the landlady is left in the company of the stranger and the sergeant. Although she declares it is closing time, the stranger remains seated and states his intention to spend the night at the inn. A heated conversation follows in which the stranger insists he is the landlady's husband, returning home after an absence of nearly 16 years. The landlady tries to evict the stranger with the help of the soldiers, and the sergeant, who has witnessed the stranger's declaration, advises him to leave the inn for the night and to seek a reconciliation on another occasion. When the man refuses to leave, the soldiers, at the landlady's behest, tie him up with a grass rope and leave him outside the inn, though the knots are left loose. In due course the man works the rope free and returns to the inn. He finds a solitary light still on, in the kitchen, and the back door open. He enters and finds his wife sitting by the kitchen fire. Alice does not express surprise at seeing her husband again so soon after he was turned out of the inn, but she does express anger about his long absence, suggesting that she needs her husband but is reluctant to admit it. Willie makes physical advances to her and reminds her that she is still his wife.

The action is rooted in a specific geographic place, but the relationships transcend this specificity. The Cornish mining industry and the proximity of the Atlantic Ocean tie in with the husband's occupation and with his absence in America. On a wider front the story may be read as a study of complex feelings between a man and his wife. It is a study of face-saving behavior, as exemplified by Alice's initial rejection of her husband, juxtaposed with deeper human needs, as signified by the open back door and the warm kitchen fire. The story has no real closure, and the reader is left to wonder how such a dichotomy between surface appearance and pride on the one hand and suppressed desire on the other might be resolved.

BIBLIOGRAPHY
Lawrence, D. H. *The Tales of D. H. Lawrence*. London: Martin Secker, 1934.
Sagar, Keith. *A D. H. Lawrence Handbook*. Manchester, England: Manchester University Press, 1982.
Thornton, Weldon. *D. H. Lawrence: A Study of the Short Fiction*. New York: Twayne, 1993.

Irene Wiltshire

"SCANDAL IN BOHEMIA, A" ARTHUR CONAN DOYLE (1891)

Coming after two novellas featuring Sherlock Holmes (A STUDY IN SCARLET and The Sign of Four), "A Scandal in Bohemia," a short DETECTIVE story, first appeared in the STRAND magazine in July 1891. It recounts the case of the king of Bohemia, who asks the famous consulting detective for help in retrieving a photograph that could doom his impending marriage to the daughter of the king of Scandinavia. He has been involved in an affair with Irene Adler, an American-born actress, famous beauty, and "well-known adventuress," and has unwisely left her in possession of irrefutable proof of their relationship: a photograph of the two of them together. She threatens to make the picture public should he announce his engagement. Since she will not give up the photograph, the king has tried to steal it, but all his attempts to recover it have failed.

Holmes pursues the case by disguising himself as an unemployed groom. He gains information about Adler's household and unintentionally becomes a witness to her secret marriage to a lawyer. In the guise of a clergyman he returns to her house and, with Dr. Watson's help, tricks her into revealing the whereabouts of the photograph. They plan to return the next day with the king to seize it, but Adler outwits them: She has guessed the identity of the "clergyman" and follows them back to Baker Street disguised as a young man. Having confirmed her suspicions that the formidable Holmes has discovered her secret, she flees with her husband. When the detective and his party arrive the next morning, they find only a letter to Holmes and another photograph: a portrait of Adler. Now that she is married to another man, she no longer wants revenge against the king for abandoning her—though she keeps the incriminating photograph to protect herself against "any steps which he might take in the future." Despite being bested by a woman, Holmes's mission has been accomplished: The king's secret will remain safe, and the political turmoil its revelation would have caused has been avoided.

"Scandal" is notable not only because it is one of the few stories in which Holmes is outwitted but also because to him Adler becomes "the woman." Watson explains that Holmes did not feel "any emotion akin to love" for her since such a feeling would have been "abhorrent to his cold, precise but admirably balanced mind." However, Holmes himself describes her as "the daintiest thing under a bonnet on this planet" and as having "a face that a man might die for." Scholars have speculated on whether Holmes's admiration is purely for Adler's intellect or whether he is sexually attracted to her. Either way, the story does not fundamentally undermine the stereotypes of its day that defined women as intellectually inferior to men, despite Watson's comment at the end of the story that Holmes "used to make merry over the cleverness of women, but I have not heard him do it of late." Adler has, as the king tells Holmes, "the face of the most beautiful of women," but she also has "the mind of the most resolute of men." Given that she also disguises herself as a man to follow Holmes and Watson, the story suggests that her intellect is more a male trait incongruously found in a woman rather than evidence of female intelligence. Further, since Adler is an actress and adventuress (in other words, morally suspect), her combination of female beauty and male intellect becomes tinged with immorality: It is not what is expected of a respectable woman. By the story's end, though, she is married to a lawyer and has left the country, doubly ensuring that she will not pose a threat to the status quo.

ARTHUR CONAN DOYLE's success with the 60 Holmes stories he wrote between 1887 and 1927 made the detective genre very popular at the end of the 19th century and the beginning of the 20th. However, he was not the first to create a detective in the classic tradition. "Scandal" shows many similarities to American Edgar Allan Poe's detective story "The Purloined Letter" (1845), in which a member of the French royal family wants to avoid scandal by retrieving an incriminating letter. In both stories the detectives use ratiocination (a system of deduction) as the basis for their crime solving and show an almost uncanny ability to interpret evidence. As Holmes does in many other stories, early in "Scandal" he demonstrates this skill to Watson before taking on the case at the center of the story: On first seeing Watson he recounts to him some of the circumstances of his home life, startling the doctor with his eerily accurate account.

As a classic detective, Holmes is preoccupied with restoring a social harmony disturbed by crime. On occasion, though, his investigations put him on the wrong side of the law: In "Scandal" he deceives Adler into letting him into her house, engages Watson's help in throwing a smoke bomb through her window, and would steal her photograph given the opportunity. However, such lawbreaking is portrayed as legitimate because, as Holmes says, "the cause is excellent!" He does not merely enforce legal codes by catching criminals. Instead, he is often called on to fulfill functions the police are unable to, operating outside the law to enforce a higher moral standard or—as in "A Scandal in Bohemia"—to avert political disaster. Although the king of Bohemia is at fault for abandoning Adler, this wrongdoing is overshadowed by the story's insistence on the need to save his upcoming marriage: It is a matter that, as the king puts it, is "of such weight it may have an influence on European history."

The Bohemian king, however, does not escape from the story unscathed: He is described as being dressed "with a richness which would, in England, be looked upon as akin to bad taste" and, with his heavy coat and fur boots, gives "the impression of barbaric opulence which was suggested by his whole appearance." When he laments that the clever Irene Adler is not "on [his] level" and so could never have been his wife, Holmes responds, "From what I have seen of the lady she seems indeed to be on a very different level to your Majesty." In the world of the story, royalty—especially foreign royalty—does not occupy the top rungs of a hierarchy where intellect is what counts.

BIBLIOGRAPHY

Doyle, Arthur Conan. *The New Annotated Sherlock Holmes.* New York: Norton, 2005.

Krumm, Pascale. "'A Scandal in Bohemia' and Sherlock Holmes's Ultimate Mystery Solved," *English Literature in Transition* 39, no. 2 (1996): 193–203.

Roth, Marty. *Foul and Fair Play: Reading Genre in Classic Detective Fiction.* Athens: University of Georgia Press, 1995.

Gerri Brightwell

"SCHARTZ-METTERKLUME METHOD, THE" SAKI (H. H. MUNRO) (1911)   "The Schartz-Metterklume Method" is one of Edwardian writer SAKI's mordantly humorous stories of rebellion against rigid, stodgy adulthood, but this time the attack is launched by another adult rather than a child. The story, which first appeared in the *Westminster Gazette* on October 14, 1911, offers one of Saki's favorite conceits—an elaborate hoax that rattles bourgeois Edwardians' pretense and certitude—wrapped in Saki's exact prose and sparkling wit, the lightness of tone masking dark farce and disturbing undercurrents.

Lady Carlotta, taking a brief stroll at a small country station while she waits for her train to resume its journey, notices a horse burdened by a carter's heavy load and tries to intervene. The train then leaves without her, and Lady Carlotta is suddenly confronted with an "imposingly attired lady" who confuses her for her children's new governess, just arrived. Lady Carlotta pretends she is the "Miss Hope" that Mrs. Quabarl was expecting and drives with the mother of four to her new home. After suggesting better automobiles and, at dinner, recommending wines superior to the vintage on offer, "Miss Hope" reassures her employers, who wish their children to be immersed in the stories of historical figures, that she will be teaching history according to the "Schartz-Metterklume method." The next day, Mrs. Quabarl finds her immobile daughter Irene personifying Rome, while sister Viola, clad in a wolf skin, is Romulus and Remus, and brothers Claude and Wilfrid have left, in Irene's words, "to fetch the shabby women." Mrs. Quabarl rushes to the lawn and finds her two sons dragging off the lodge keeper's daughters while Lady Carlotta, wielding a cricket bat, looks on impassively. Appalled by her governess's method of teaching history to her children by having them reenact it, Mrs. Quabarl dismisses her, and Lady Carlotta tells her to hold onto her luggage until she telegraphs them her address. Her luggage, she adds, consists merely of "a couple of trunks and some golf-clubs and a leopard cub"; with that, "Lady Carlotta strode out of the Quabarl horizon."

Saki, often considered a misogynist writer because of his attacks on female guardians and satires of suffragettism in some of his stories, reveals a much more conflicted attitude toward women in this story, which champions the single female over the married mother within a tale of infighting between two bourgeois ladies. Lady Carlotta is a strong-willed, single NEW WOMAN, ("You may be very clever and modern, Miss Hope," her employer tells her), yet her fierce independence is brought out by Mrs. Quabarl, a typically Sakian battle-axe wife. Mrs. Quabarl's imperious, condescending attitude irritates Lady Carlotta, who cattily pursues an elaborate hoax—with children as the secondary victims—in order to undermine the self-satisfied mother who, along with her husband, is easily cowed by anyone who seems more cultured or lofty than she.

Lady Carlotta is no more petty than, and just as witty as, Saki's dandy protagonists Clovis or Reginald when she flippantly concocts and then justifies Canon Teep's assault on his wife with a "soda-water syphon" because "Mrs. Teep is quite the most irritating bridge-player that I have ever sat down with." This comment, typical of Saki's religion-mocking antiheroes, also suggests Saki had as much common with his devious female antihero Lady Carlotta as he did with his male pranksters, for he was an avid bridge-player. As a child Munro also, according to his sister Ethel, relished acting out historical battles, tormented governesses, and was once scolded by an aunt for using the word "debauchery" after a Roman history lesson.

Saki, who often uses wild beasts or vengeful children to mischievously undermine prosaic adults who wish to stifle creativity and ignore the power of fantasy, not only uses a woman here as the maverick trickster and victimizes children—who are shockingly taught about rape by Lady Carlotta—but reveals the contradictions of his class views. Lady Carlotta, as Miss Hope, is a problem for Mrs. Quabarl because she does not know her place and thus presages the class confusion and disintegration that would envelop England after the war: "When the new governess failed to express wondering admiration of the large newly purchased and expensive car, and lightly alluded to the superior advantages of one or two makes which had just been put on the market, the discomfiture of her patroness was almost abject." Yet in Saki's canon, the lower classes are rarely represented in a complex way, and here they are dismissed as the brief butts of Lady Carlotta's elaborate pedagogical prank. Lady Carlotta, resentful at her employer's condescending treatment of her supposed governess, has her young charges abduct the lodge keeper's children, pretending they are the soon-to-be-raped Sabine women.

As disturbing as Lady Carlotta's "Schartz-Metterklume method" (the name may be a shot at the militancy of pre-WORLD WAR I Germany) is, however, Saki's argument seems to be that history is often a series of messy, bloody events, from war and conquest to repression and rape. The use of supposedly innocent women and children to illustrate such a lesson only makes Saki's point more disturbingly powerful. In "The Toys of Peace," too, Saki mocks the attempt of pacifist educators to have children play with peaceful toys by having the children quickly resort to acting out gory battles with the playthings instead; often in Saki's stories, children and animals conquer the adult world because they are closer to the wild, natural order of things than the bland, supposedly civilized world of Edwardian England.

Many critics have noted Saki's clever reworking of his own plots in other stories. This tale resembles Clovis's tricking of a sheltered rural couple in "The Unrest-Cure," while the use of children in the reenactment of a classical myth with sexual undertones recalls Reginald's bacchanalian expedition with a church youth group in "Reginald's Choir Treat." In its conceit of reenacting history, "The Schartz-Metterklume Method" echoes the overly realistic charades in "A Matter of Sentiment." Indeed, an early scene detailing Lady Carlotta's refusal to leave her painting and extricate an annoying neighbor from the attentions of a boar-pig may have sowed the seeds of inspiration for Saki's later stories "The Stalled Ox" and "The Boar-Pig."

BIBLIOGRAPHY
Saki. *The Complete Saki*. Harmondsworth, England: Penguin, 1982.

Brian Gibson

SCHREINER, OLIVE (1855–1920)

Olive Emilie Albertina Schreiner was born in South Africa March 24, 1855, to missionary parents Rebecca and Gottlob Schreiner. Because of her family's financial difficulties, she worked as a governess for a number of years. In 1881 she returned to England with hopes of becoming a medical doctor, which she quickly abandoned. She arrived in England with *The Story of an African Farm* in hand and saw it published to great success in 1883. In 1889 she returned to Africa and three years later married Samuel Cronwright. Schreiner gave birth to a daughter in 1895 who did not survive. Throughout much of her life she campaigned for women's rights and worked against the imperialist policies of the South African government.

Schreiner is perhaps best known for her novel *The Story of an African Farm,* originally published under the pseudonym Ralph Iron, and the feminist classic *Women and Labour* (1911), which addresses female parasitism and argues that women's marginalization should be a concern for all of society, not just women. *The Story of an African Farm* focuses on the lives of two girls—the passionate, independent Lyndall and her more traditional and domestic cousin, Em—and Waldo, the son of a farm worker who, like Lyndall, desires something more from life. Because of her feminist views, Schreiner is often included among NEW WOMAN writers (late 19th-century women authors who advocated new possibilities for women in regard to marriage, motherhood, and the workplace).

In addition to these better-known works, however, Schreiner also wrote a number of short stories. These stories, often allegorical, frequently deal with relationships between men and women and contain female characters who must choose between love and freedom. In "Three Dreams in a Desert," for example, the narrator has three dreams about the plight of women. In the first, she sees a woman struggling, heavy with burdens, and is told that the woman *"must help herself"* (311). In the next, we meet another woman seeking "the Land of Freedom" (314). This woman learns that it will be a difficult journey, but that her sacrifices and struggles will make it easier for future women who seek the same path. The woman is also told that she cannot bring men with her to the Land of Freedom— men must find their own way, and humankind will be stronger for it. The final dream brings an optimistic view of the future in which women and men walk hand in hand and look into each other's eyes without fear. Similar themes are found in the short fable "Life's Gifts," another story of a sleeping woman, in which a woman dreams she is given the choice between freedom and love. The woman chooses freedom, and although she gives up love, the narrator hears her

"laugh in her sleep" (317). The struggles of the enlightened woman are found again in "The Buddhist Priest's Wife" (Schreiner's favorite of her own short stories), which portrays a male intellectual who desires a traditional, passive wife instead of a female intellectual for his companion.

BIBLIOGRAPHY

Burdett, Carolyn. *Olive Schreiner and the Progress of Feminism: Evolution, Gender, Empire.* New York: Palgrave, 2001.

First, Ruth. *Olive Schreiner.* New York: Schocken, 1980.

Heilman, Ann. *New Woman Strategies: Sarah Grand, Olive Schreiner and Mona Caird.* Manchester, England: Manchester University Press, 2004.

Monsman, Gerald Cornelius. *Olive Schreiner's Fiction: Landscape and Power.* New Brunswick, N.J.: Rutgers University Press, 1991.

Elaine Showalter, ed. *Daughters of Decadence: Women Writers of the Fin-de-Siècle.* New Brunswick, N.J.: Rutgers University Press, 1993.

Melissa Purdue

SCIENCE FICTION   The term *science fiction* was first used by Hugo Gernsback, founder of the magazine *Amazing Stories,* in 1929. It now refers to virtually any fiction that involves some element of futuristic technology, alien encounter, or supernatural phenomenon. Some critics prefer to define science fiction by its overall aesthetic rather than specific plot elements; Farah Mendlesohn argues that a "sense of wonder" is the unifying characteristic (1).

Because the topics that can be covered within science fiction are so wide-ranging, there is a risk of expanding the category so much that it collapses. Subgenres have therefore developed over the past century—including scientific romance, utopias and negative utopias, alternative history, time travel, and cyberpunk—which offer more closely defined boundaries. One of the inherent hazards of writing science fiction stems from this broad range: A work of science fiction must establish its contexts immediately, so that the reader is clear whether the story addresses the moral implications of destructive power (Fredric Brown's "The Weapon," 1951) or is an alternative history in which the Nazis were victorious (William L.

Shirer's "If Hitler Had Won World War II," 1961). This issue is particularly a problem for short stories, which must establish time, place, and environment with a rapidity that longer works do not require. Skilled writers are able to incorporate the necessary exposition in the forward movement of the story without resorting to long paragraphs of explanation.

The roots of British science fiction can be traced back several centuries, incorporating speculative works such as Thomas More's *Utopia* (1516), Jonathan Swift's *Gulliver's Travels* (1726), and Mary Shelley's *Frankenstein* (1818). The Victorian period provided the beginning of modern science fiction short stories, including what-if alternative histories such as George T. Chesney's "The Battle of Dorking" (1871). The most influential writer of this period to be identified with science fiction is H. G. WELLS, a trained biologist who melded speculations about science with cautions about the morality of abusing it and the alienation that it could cause to members of the general public. Stories such as "The Stolen Bacillus" and "The Argonauts of the Air" were forward-thinking in regard to the social and ethical dangers of modern technology.

Speculative fiction was not popular among magazine readers of the late 19th and early 20th centuries, and the brutal realities of World War I made it even less so. The Wells-influenced period of British science fiction ended in the mid-1930s, followed by a period in which American science fiction gained supremacy. The periodical *New Worlds* played a major role in the reestablishment of British science fiction following World War II, publishing a wide range of stories, including Arthur C. Clarke's "The Sentinel" (1951), which later became the basis for the movie *2001.* When MICHAEL MOORCOCK took over the editorship in 1964, he did so with the intention of giving science fiction the opportunity to equal, if not surpass, mainstream realistic writing. The best-known writer to come out of his editorship is J. G. BALLARD; whose story "Billenium" (1961) offers a nightmare vision of the dangers of unchecked population growth on the urban environment. Another influential source of short fiction was the 1968 anthology *England Swings SF.* This period, in which the clichés of science fiction were being rejected by younger writers in favor of avant-garde influences,

is known as the New Wave. Many authors were unhappy with this label, however, feeling that it was used to describe a commercial product.

The 1970s became a dead zone. *New Worlds* folded in 1976, and British science fiction writers soon had nowhere to publish stories in their own country. In 1982, the magazine *Interzone* began filling the void, becoming a crucible for new writers such as Nicola Griffith, Charles Stross, and Ian R. MacLeod. Three volumes of an anthology titled *Other Edens,* edited by Christopher Evans and Robert Holdstock, showcased British short fiction in the late 1980s, and other magazines and anthologies began opening the field again. Modern science fiction is a more international field than it has ever been, but British magazines and anthologies (such as the series *Infinities: The Very Best of British SF Today*) continue to play a major role in the field.

BIBLIOGRAPHY

Aldiss, Brian, with David Wingrove. *Trillion Year Spree: The History of Science Fiction.* Thirsk, England: House of Stratus, 2001.

James, Edward. *Science Fiction in the 20th Century.* Oxford and New York: Oxford University Press, 1994.

James, Edward, and Farah Mendlesohn, eds. *The Cambridge Companion to Science Fiction.* Cambridge and New York: Cambridge University Press, 2003.

Mendlesohn, Farah. "Introduction." In *The Cambridge Companion to Science Fiction,* 1–15. Cambridge and New York: Cambridge University Press, 2003.

Ruddick, Nicholas. *Ultimate Island: On the Nature of British Science Fiction.* Westport, Conn.: Greenwood, 1993.

Shippey, Tom, ed. *The Oxford Book of Science Fiction Stories.* Oxford: Oxford University Press, 2003.

Tracey Rosenberg

SCOTLAND It is often noted that during the last 20 years the Scottish short story has flourished. The international success of IRVINE WELSH's *Trainspotting* (1993) led to a tour of the United States and Australia by Welsh, accompanied by JAMES KELMAN and Duncan MacLean, on which the trio performed readings from their latest works. Kelman is one of a number of prize-winning Scottish writers. His novel *How Late It Was, How Late* won the Booker Prize in 1994, and the short story collection *The GOOD TIMES* (1998) won the 1999

Stakis Prize for Scottish Writer of the Year. Duncan MacLean won a national award for his collection *Bucket of Tongues* (1992); A. L. KENNEDY and JANICE GALLOWAY have also won prizes. According to Jurgen Neubauer, "Scottish fiction has become a popular event within the British literary scene and seems to address readers far beyond Scotland with a directness rarely achieved by other British authors of the last two decades" (9).

A popular—if simplistic—way of reading Scottish fiction since the 1980s is to connect recent success with political developments, in particular, the campaign for independence from England. In 1979, there was a good deal of disappointment and anger when the Devolution Bill, which was intended to give Scotland its own parliament, was defeated (Neubauer, 9). In the following decades fiction began to thrive, "as though," Cairns Craig suggests, "the energy that had failed to be harnessed by the politicians flowed into other channels" (quoted in Neubauer, 9). As in discussions of the Irish short story (see IRELAND), it has become commonplace to argue that when a country struggles politically to establish its sovereignty, literature works to safeguard national identity. Ian Bell, editor of a collection of writings about national literatures, *Peripheral Visions,* sees in Scottish writing of the past twenty years "a radical literature of [political] resistance and reclamation" (219). Certainly in the contemporary Scottish short story there is some interest in what it means to live in Scotland. Unlike previous internationally famous Scottish writers such as ARTHUR CONAN DOYLE and MURIEL SPARK—both of whom made indirect use of their Scottish backgrounds—Kelman, Galloway, Welsh, and Banks set their stories in Scottish cities in the present. Considerable use is made of local dialect, something that, in discussions of Scottish literary history, has been seen as anticolonial resistance to linguistic colonialism and the encroachment of Standard English. (Older examples include the work of WALTER SCOTT, John Galt, and ROBERT LOUIS STEVENSON).

Although it is questionable whether the population of any country can have a completely unified sense of national identity that its literature both expresses and preserves, this has proved a popular way of thinking about Scottish stories and their genesis. For example, it is generally accepted that the origins of the Scottish short story lie amongst the Gaelic and Scots oral storytelling traditions of folktales and ballads. In the 16th and 17th centuries songs such as "Otterburn," "The Bonnie Earl o'Moray," and "The Wife of Usher's Well" existed alongside a mass of fireside stories passed down from generation to generation. In his introduction to *Classic Scottish Short Stories,* J. M. Reid suggests that it was these traditions that Scottish writers of the early 1800s, such as John Galt, Walter Scott, and James Hogg tried to capture. In doing so, they helped set in motion the development of different strands of Scottish short story writing. According to Tim Killick,

> Short fiction . . . played its part in imagining (or re-imagining) Scottish history, and in particular oral history. Scotland's tradition of oral transmission encompassed the ballads and songs mentioned above, but it also included the multifarious branches of folklore, fairy tales, curious anecdotes, ghost stories, shaggy-dog stories, and the many other modes of storytelling and narrative ephemera that can be incorporated into the loose designation of 'tales' and which formed much of the country's short fiction output. (49)

Scott's "Wandering Willie's Tale," which appears in his novel *Red Gauntlet* is a much-anthologized example of a folk legend redone for an expanding audience of readers. Also important are Hogg's reworking of old legends in the collections *Winter Evening Tales* (1820) and *The Shepherd's Calendar* (1829), Galt's *Annals of the Parrish* (1821), and Allan Cunningham's *Traditional Tales of the English and Scottish Peasantry* (1822). As Killick notes, many of these tales were published initially in magazines with a wide circulation, including *Blackwood's Edinburgh Magazine* and the *London Magazine,* whose readers enjoyed the "rich and poetic preprint oral history" these stories seemed to capture, allowing the readers to engage with a picturesque culture and style different from their own (50).

The stories also created a powerful image of the Scots. Although some authors did not shy away from pointing out the hardship and the sordid reality faced by their subjects, the "kailyard" or community story, with its tendency toward allegory and parable, helped create a stereotyped and sentimentalized idea of Scotland, one that often bore little relation to what life—whether in the Gaelic highlands and isles or in the city—was actually like. J. M. Barrie's stories from the early 1900s, in particular, are often cited as evidence of the refusal to acknowledge that by the mid-19th century, Scotland was an industrial nation.

In the 20th century, there was much greater readiness to confront industrialization and to make use of local color. Notable examples in the 1930s and 1940s include the stories of George Mackay Brown, set mostly in the Orkneys, and those of George Friel, Edward Gaitens, and Margaret Hamilton, many of which are set among the industrial shipbuilding communities on the River Clyde in Glasgow and are characterized by their attempt to portray realistically the privations of working-class people. This pattern and the interest in working-class life have been continued by contemporary short story writers. The urban settings of writers like Kelman and Welsh force the reader to confront contemporary youth culture as it is plagued by violence, unemployment, crime, and AIDS.

Also important to the Scottish story tradition is the ghost story. In the 19th century *Blackwood's Magazine* (see MAGAZINES) became well known for its supernatural stories, and the Scottish writers who published in the magazine often drew on early legends and tales. Scott's story "The TWO DROVERS" appeared in 1827, "My Aunt Margaret's Mirror" and "The Tapestried Chamber" in 1828. Early 19th-century Scottish writers were often influenced by the supernatural works of German writers—E. T. A. Hoffman and the brothers Grimm—and stories became increasingly sophisticated. In the decades of religious debate and uncertainty of the 1880s and 1890s, many later writers—for example, JOHN BUCHAN and Robert Louis Stevenson (as in "THRAWN JANET")—saw the ghost story as offering a useful framework to explore what one critic has called a "peculiarly Scottish sense of evil" but also to tackle questions of death, psychology, morality, and religion, particularly Calvinism (Warner, 337). Others like MARGARET OLIPHANT (as in "A BELEAGUERED CITY" (1878), "The Open Door" (1879), and "The Library Window") believed in spirits and tied to encourage sympathy for the creatures who had crossed back into the world of the living. But Oliphant exploited, as many Victorian writers of ghost stories did, the form's potential for exposing the underside of culture, in particular, its ability to represent lost, marginalized, and voiceless subjects.

A number of recognizable characteristics emerge in these 19th-century stories that still appear today: cultural antagonisms between Highland and Lowland Scots, the blurred distinction between fact and fiction, decline of folk traditions and the encroachment of modernity on the lives of the poor, the power of superstition and the dangers of evil spirits, the uneasy relationship with England and the recurrent issues of "Scottishness," national identity and oppression. What is also true, however, is that many contemporary short story writers resist these traditional routes. A. L. KENNEDY, for example, has written that "my whole understanding of my writing and my method of making it does not stem from literary or national forms and traditions." Instead, Kennedy emphasizes the international context of her work (100). James Kelman rejects the idea of "some 'mystical' national culture," preferring to focus on the local Glaswegian context rather than the national one (Neubauer, 24). As Neubauer observes, these and other modern Scottish writers—Carl MacDougall, Agnes Owens, Alisdair Gray, Jeff Torrington—"do not necessarily embrace nationalist politics: they work from socialist, feminist or sub-cultural positions that are both specifically local and at the same time cut across national borders" (25) In the 21st century, the modern Scottish short story should be read as part of a complex literary evolution.

BIBLIOGRAPHY

Bell, Ian. "Imagine Living There: Form and Ideology in Contemporary Scottish Fiction," In *Studies in Scottish Fiction 1945 to the Present,* edited by Susanne Hagemann, Scottish Studies 19, 217–234. Frankfurt: M. Lang, 1996.

Burgess, Moira. "The Glasgow Short Story," *Laverock* 2 (1996). Available online. URL: http://www.arts.gla. ac.uk/ScotLit/ASLS?Laverock_Glasgow_ShortStory.html. Accessed July 10, 2006.

Kelman, James. *Some Recent Attacks: Essays Cultural and Political.* Edinburgh, Scotland: AK Press, 1992.

Kennedy, A. L. "Not Changing the World." In *Visions of Nationhood in Contemporary British Fictions,* 100–102. Cardiff: University of Wales Press, 1995.

Killick, Tim. "Truth, Imagination and Tradition: Allan Cunningham and Scottish Short Fiction," *Scottish Studies Review* 6, no. 2 (2005): 49–59.

Letley, Emma. *From Galt to Douglas Brown; Nineteenth Century Fiction and Scots Language.* Edinburgh, Scotland: Academic Press, 1988.

Neubauer, Jurgen. *Literature as Intervention: Struggles over Identity in Contemporary Scottish Fiction.* Marburg: Tectum Verlag, 1999.

Peripheral Visions: Visions of Nationhood in Contemporary British Fictions. Cardiff: University of Wales Press, 1995.

Reid, J. M., ed. *Classic Scottish Short Stories.* Oxford: Oxford University Press, 1989.

Urquhart, Fred, and Giles Gordon, eds. *Modern Scottish Short Stories.* London: Faber, 1978.

Warner, Fred B. "Stevenson's First Scottish Story," *Nineteenth Century Fiction* 24, no. 3 (December 1969): 334–44.

Andrew Maunder

SCOTT, SIR WALTER (1771–1832)

Born in Edinburgh on August 15, 1771, Sir Walter Scott was the son of Walter Scott, a lawyer and strict Presbyterian, and Ann Rutherford Scott. Despite a series of lingering childhood illnesses, Scott enjoyed a pastoral childhood in Sandyknowe, listening to tales of Jacobean martyrs and outlaws and learning to recall local ballads from memory. He began attending the high school and the University of Edinburgh at age eight, though he later remarked that he was a lackluster and largely self-taught student. Nevertheless, he developed into an omnivorous reader while in school, with a particular taste for romances and adventure stories, and took part in a number of literary circles and groups while in college.

Scott's literary career began with his translation of Goethe's *Goetz von Berlichingen* into English in 1799 and his poetic contributions to Monk Lewis's *Tales of Wonder.* Scott's first important publication was *Minstrelsy of the Scottish Border,* in 1802 though his 1805 ballad *The Lay of the Last Minstrel* marked the beginning of his popular literary career. From that point Scott lived the life of a Scottish man of letters, gaining further fame and acclaim for such highly popular poetic works as *Marmion: A Tale of Flodden Field* (1808) and *The Lay of the Lake* (1810). Scott turned from poetry to novel writing in 1814 with *Waverly* and continued writing novels until the end of his life, producing such now canonical works as *Rob Roy* (1818) and *Ivanhoe* (1819) at the rate of over one a year. Scott died after a prolonged illness on September 21, 1832, as one of the most famous men of English letters. Though his reputation declined shortly after his death, Scott is now considered to be among the most potent literary forces of the romantic age, and the strength of his many contributions to Western literature cannot be denied.

Scott has often been praised for his short stories despite having written only a handful of them, and a number of critics position Scott as the founder of the modern English short story. Among his most accomplished and widely read stories are "The Surgeon's Daughter," "The HIGHLAND WIDOW," and "The TWO DROVERS." The latter two stories were originally published in 1827, in the initial volume of the first series of Scott's *Chronicles of the Canongate* collection. This volume also included such supernatural stories as "My Aunt Margaret's Mirror" and "The Tapestried Chamber," as well as the anecdotal sketch "The Death of the Laird's Jock."

The primary difference between Scott's short stories and his novels lies in the type of figures he chooses as his protagonists. Unlike his novels, which tend to be set against grand historical backdrops and feature heroic characters, such short stories as "The Two Drovers" and "The Highland Widow" do not involve grand historical happenings, and their protagonists are not the sort of characters that tend to make history. In Scott's short stories, history can occur even among the most basic people in the most common locales and circumstances. Both "The Two Drovers" and "The Highland Widow" explore the implications of historical happenings and drastic social changes and upheavals on common people. Throughout his short stories. Scott presents a vision of history as the end result of economic and cultural tension. W. J. Overton has speculated that the inherent structural limitations of the short story provided Scott with both the freedom and the discipline that his novels lacked, allowing him to represent brief, character-centered experiences of historical happenings and changes.

Scott's abandonment of the short story genre owed, at least in part, to his concern that his readers would find the literary form of the short story to be something of a low literary form, and therefore he would not be able to command the high rates he required, at the time, to avoid bankruptcy. Also, the publishing conditions of the time were best suited for fiction that could be published over the course of two or three volumes, a demand that better suited novels than short stories.

BIBLIOGRAPHY

Scott, Walter. *The Two Drovers and Other Stories.* London: Oxford University Press, 1987.

W. J. Overton. "Scott, the Short Story, and History: 'The Two Drovers,'" *Studies in Scottish Literature* 21 (1986): 210–225.

James R. Fleming

"SECRET GARDEN, THE" G. K. CHESTERTON (1910)

A detective story first published in the monthly magazine *The Storyteller* in October 1910, and subsequently in the collection *The Innocence of Father Brown* (1911).

Father Brown attends a dinner party held by the chief of the Paris police, Aristide Valentin. The party is interrupted by the discovery in the garden of an unidentified corpse that is dressed for dinner but whose head is completely severed from its body. Besides entries from the house, the garden is bounded by three high walls offering no access to the outside. It is quickly established that the murder weapon is a saber forming part of the dress of one of the guests that is found outside the house. Suspicion falls on Valentin's guest of honour, Julius Brayne, an American millionaire and financial supporter of religious institutions. Brayne's sudden, suspicious disappearance and the discovery of dollars on the body support this theory. The next morning, a second head is recovered from a Parisian river, although its body is missing. The body in Valentin's garden is identified as Arnold Becker, the twin of a recently guillotined German criminal. Various questions remain: What was Brayne's motive? Why was such an ostentatious method of murder used? and How did Becker manage to enter the sealed garden without being seen? Father Brown realizes that the second head belongs to Brayne and that the body and head in the garden do not match. It was Brayne who

was murdered in the garden; his head and the saber were then thrown over the garden wall and Becker's head substituted. Furthermore, Brown explains that the second head is not that of Arnold Becker but that of his twin brother, executed the previous day. The murderer must be somebody with access to the guillotine—Valentin himself, who, while demonstrating to Brayne his ability with the saber in the garden, beheaded him from behind. Valentin's motive is ideological; as an atheist determined to do anything to break "the superstition of the cross," he wished to prevent Brayne making a substantial donation to the Church of France. The story ends with Valentin's suicide by drug overdose.

"The Secret Garden" was the second story (after "The Blue Cross") to feature the amateur detective Father Brown, a character based on a friend of Chesterton's, Father John O' Connor. The story belongs to the subgenre of the "locked room mystery," in which a crime appears to have taken place in impossible circumstances (the genre takes its name from the frequently employed mystery of a murder victim found alone in a room locked from the inside); here, the locked room is the sealed garden. Critics of detective fiction have noted that the locked room genre makes particular use of paradox, and the form is particularly suited to Chesterton's approach to detective fiction, which uses the devices of the genre to illustrate a moral insight. "The Secret Garden" reinforces a central argument of the Father Brown stories, that as a Catholic, Brown is more sensitive to the nature of evil than non-believers, an argument represented by the explicitly stated theological contrast between the two detective figures of the story, the Catholic Brown and the atheist Valentin, whose rationalism paradoxically makes "mercy even colder than justice." The seemingly impossible crime also encapsulates the wider concern of the Brown stories with the nature of miracles. The solution to the mystery is seen not as a materialist explanation for this miracle but rather as a process of demystification. This underlies the ideological stance of much of Chesterton's detective fiction—that spiritual truth is characterized by simplicity and the clarity of faith, as opposed to the complexity and obfuscation of bad religion and superstition.

BIBLIOGRAPHY

Chesterton, G. K. *The Innocence of Father Brown.* Oxford: Oxford University Press, 1987.

Finch, Michael. *G. K. Chesterton: A Biography.* London: Weidenfeld and Nicholson, 1986.

Kayman, Martin A. "The Short Story from Poe to Chesterton." In *The Cambridge Companion to Crime Fiction,* edited by Martin Priestman, 41–58. Cambridge: Cambridge University Press, 2003.

Sweeney, S. E. "Locked Rooms: Detective Fiction, Narrative Theory, and Self-Reflexivity." In *The Cunning Craft: Original Essays on Detective Fiction and Contemporary Literary Theory,* edited by Ronald G. Walker and June M. Frazer, 1–14. Macomb: Western Illinois University, 1990.

Christopher Pittard

"SECRET OF THE GROWING GOLD, THE" BRAM STOKER (1892)

Like several of the stories collected by BRAM STOKER's widow, Florence, in the posthumous collection *Dracula's Guest* (1914), "The Secret of the Growing Gold," revolves around issues of gender relations and repressed desire. It was first published in the illustrated magazine *Black and White* (1892). The beautiful Margaret Delandre scandalizes her community by running off with a neighbor, Geoffrey Brent. They live together as man and wife. Several years later, rumors circulate that Margaret has been drowned. In fact she has been murdered—strangled by Geoffrey Brent in order to smooth the way for his marriage to a rich heiress. Geoffrey hastily buries Margaret under the hearthstones in the hall of his ancestral home, unable to move her body without being discovered. In the meantime Margaret rises from the dead, armed with the power to terrify Brent and his new wife literally to death; they watch in terror as her still-growing hair forces its way through cracks in the broken stones to invade the supposedly impregnable domestic space.

As a ghost story and tale of decay and imprisonment, "The Secret of the Growing Gold" is haunted, like many of Stoker's texts, by the traces of influential male writers—Washington Irving, Edgar Allan Poe, and SHERIDAN LE FANU. Prior victimization or neglect of women by men or by society more generally also provides the explanation for numerous ghost stories by Victorian women writers, and Stoker uses the generic conventions of the ghost story to expose female powerlessness and exclusion. Stoker also draws on well-established gothic conventions and symbolism, including the familiar motifs of confinement, repression, regression, and entrapment—the captive woman under threat and the brutish, sexually threatening aristocratic man. The subterranean aspects of the story remind us that Stoker's social landscape is based on the premise of traditional male/female hierarchies, it is the figure of the repressed and excluded sexual woman who becomes empowered. Stoker also uses images of darkness and death to show how women's hair is linked in the masculine imagination with a fear of women's sexuality. Stoker's biographer, Barbara Belford, has suggested that the story may have been inspired by a real-life event: the exhumation, seven years after her death, of Elizabeth Siddall by her husband, the pre-Raphaelite poet and painter, Dante Gabriel Rossetti in 1869 (see PRE-RAPHAELITISM). Rossetti wanted to retrieve a notebook containing copies of his unpublished poems. When the coffin was opened, the poems were retrieved from the strands of Siddall's still-growing blond hair.

BIBLIOGRAPHY

Belford, Barbara. *Bram Stoker.* New York: Da Capo, 2002.

Claire Stewart, "'Weird Fascination': The Response to Victorian Women's Ghost Stories." In *Feminist Readings of Victorian Popular Texts,* edited by Emma Liggins and Daniel Duffy, 108–125. Aldershot: Ashgate, 2001.

Moody, Nickianne, "Visible Margins: Women Writers and the Ghost Story." In *Image and Power: Women in Fiction in the Twentieth Century,* edited by Sarah Seats and Gail Cunningham, 77–90. London: Longman, 1996.

Stoker, Bram. *Bram Stoker's Midnight Tales.* Edited by Peter Haining. London: Peter Owen, 1990.

Andrew Maunder

"SECRET SHARER, THE" JOSEPH CONRAD (1910)

In late 1909, JOSEPH CONRAD broke off working on his political novel about Russia, *Under Western Eyes,* to write the short story "The Secret-Sharer: An Episode from the Sea." First issued in two parts in 1910, in the August and September issues of *Harper's Monthly Magazine,* it was later published, in October 1912, as the second of three stories in the collection

'Twixt Land and Sea: Tales. The story is generally accepted as Conrad's rewriting of a killing, subsequent escape, and apparent suicide, all of which events took place on the tea clipper *Cutty Sark* in 1880, combined with his personal experience of first command on *Otago* in 1888.

In the story, a ship's captain, the unnamed narrator of the story, reflects from some point late in life on an unusual experience he had during the initial weeks of his first command of a sailing vessel. While waiting for sufficient wind to take his ship out of the Gulf of Siam (now the Gulf of Thailand), the untried and inexperienced captain takes aboard his ship an escapee who has swum from another ship in the gulf. The swimmer, named Leggatt, was first mate of *Sephora,* the other ship, and was being held for eventual trial for having killed a ship's hand. Leggatt tells his version of the circumstances leading to his present condition, admitting the killing but refusing to stand trial: "you don't see me coming back to explain such things to an old fellow in a wig and twelve respectable tradesmen, do you? What can they know whether I am guilty or not—or of *what* I am guilty, either?" (536). Convinced, for a variety of reasons, that Leggatt's act was justified, the captain-narrator recounts how he hid Leggatt in his stateroom for several days before facilitating a complete escape. An undercurrent of tension drives the story, as the captain-narrator obsesses over the inadvertent discovery of Leggatt by his crew. This tension reaches an initial peak with the arrival of Archbold, captain of *Sephora.* As representative of the law and arbiter of justice aboard his ship, he is seeking to recover the escapee. The final peak occurs as the captain-narrator unwillingly accedes to Leggatt's desire to be marooned on one of the many islands in the gulf. He tells of putting his ship and crew through a difficult and dangerous maneuver at night—presented to the crew as an effort to catch off-shore breezes. Close to a shoreline that threatens the integrity of the ship and the safety of the crew, Leggatt and the captain-narrator part ways, each now apparently in control of his own destiny.

From the opening lines—and as a natural consequence of the narrator's first-person point of view—readers are placed in a position sympathetic to the inexperienced captain: seeing with his eyes, feeling his

reactions to the sensory impressions he is experiencing. This sympathy is transferred, against the grain of social conscience, through the narrator to Leggatt by the forceful associations of shared background, education, and class, as well as through continuous references to Leggatt as "my double," "my other self," and "my secret self."

Conrad had variously considered naming the story "The Second Self" or "The Other Self" or "The Secret Self" before settling, with his publisher's assistance, on the title by which readers now know the story. Much critical capital has been generated and spent on readings of the story through close readings of that title. As a function of shifting the emphasis placed on the crucial terms *secret* and *sharer,* for example, the title can point to a reading as the narrator's finally sharing a secret out of his past with some unidentified interlocutor. It could also suggest a variety of readings constructed around the idea of an illicit sharer of one's clothing, food, fears, bed, and beliefs who is secreted, kept hidden, from the prying eyes of others on board the ship. Critical notions spun from secrets and sharing are supported by the sometimes overwhelming recurring motif in the story, that of the double or doubling. Aside from the many explicit textual references on the part of the narrator connecting Leggatt to him, their apparently close resemblance is reinforced by the almost too obvious visual sign of paired bunches of bananas tied and hanging from the central ceiling beam in the ship's saloon. The doubling of selected consonants in Leggatt's name is highlighted by the singular L, which is later doubled by the L-shape of the captain-narrator's stateroom where Leggatt is hidden. While the ship repeatedly doubles back and forth, tacking across the windless gulf toward the open sea, life aboard becomes interminably tedious, heightening the physical and psychic tensions of the young captain. The narrator recounts experiencing a sense of psychic schism, a sort of doubling of his self, brought on in part as a consequence of the ethical dilemma he faced: Leggatt violated the law, both of the land and of the sea, yet the captain-narrator understands the extenuating circumstances under which the event occurred and sympathizes with Leggatt. In the end, as the ship approaches the rocky shoals surrounding the island of Koh-ring, where Leggatt completes his escape, the now tightly focused but terrified captain reenacts with important variations Leggatt's apparently murderous act.

The early uncertainty of the captain as to his readiness to command is mirrored in the later uncertainty of the mature and apparently successful narrator; for example, regarding the name of the captain of *Sephora,* he says, "it was something like Archbold—but at this distance of years I hardly am sure" (530). This lack of surety, though, is counterbalanced by the certainty with which the captain-narrator, as participant and teller, adheres to Leggatt's version of the events on *Sephora.* So certain is he of that truth that he declines to relate Archbold's version in favor of painting a picture of a petit tyrant, unfit to command a ship. Uncertainty is manifest both as reflecting and as amplifying the situation aboard ship; in his duplicitous dealings with his crew and when facing down Archbold, where he feigns deafness, the captain-narrator's behavior raises the question of reliability. Close attention by the reader to this behavior and to evidence provided by the narrator's own admission of a faulty memory reveals an ambivalent and ironic cast to what on a first reading appears to be a happy ending to the story.

BIBLIOGRAPHY
Conrad, Joseph. "The Secret Sharer." Edited by Daniel R. Schwarz. New York: Bedford/St. Martin's, 1997.
———. "The Secret-Sharer: An Episode from the Sea," *Harper's Monthly Magazine* 121 (1910): 349–359, 530–541.
Schwartz, Daniel. *Rereading Conrad.* Columbia: University of Missouri Press, 2001.
Watt, Ian. *Essays on Conrad.* Cambridge: Cambridge University Press, 2000.

James Fromm

"SEFTON CHURCH" Laetitia E. Landon (1834)

This short story by Laetitia Landon (1802–1838), one of the most popular writers of the early 19th century, takes the form of a humorous monologue, most likely spoken by an older, opinionated, and unmarried woman. Landon spoofs, subverts, and exposes the foolishly sentimental ideals and assumptions so popular among women writers of the time—

sentimentality that would later in the century prompt GEORGE ELIOT (Mary Anne Evans) to rail against "silly novels by lady novelists." A disastrous wedding at Sefton Church has occasioned the monologue, and in it, the narrator is amusingly cynical about a number of respected institutions, including marriage.

The narrator begins with a wry observation on the "series of mistakes" that pass for human life. It is a mistake, she decrees, to be born, to live, to die, and to marry. Of these, only the decision whether to marry is our own. Inspired by this cheerful thought, she meditates whether she has known any happy couples and at last thinks of one. The wife lives "at Amsterdam and he in Demerara," and the narrator declares that they write one another the most affectionate letters.

However, the marriage at hand is not nearly so promising. The reader learns that the bridegroom has abandoned his bride (and wedding guests, much to the annoyance of the narrator) at the altar. When the misfortune is announced, a young naval lieutenant steps forward and volunteers to marry the young woman, who replies, "Well . . . it is a pity to be drest for nothing" and accepts his proposal: They (foolishly) marry on the spot.

In the course of her witty observations about love, courtship, and marriage, the narrator waxes subversive about the social duties of middle-class women, hero worship, and sentimental hyperbole. She notes that for many women, change of scene seems to equal change of self, hence the "modern" mania for social calls. While waiting for the groom to appear, she notices a plaque vowing to "long preserve" the memory of a fallen war hero, and she slyly notes that, since the country appears to neither remember nor care, the plaque is a lie. In short, conventions surrounding love, marriage, female friendship, and honor are all exposed as the provinces of fools. "Sefton Church" is a character study of a genteel old spinster who is surprisingly frank in her criticisms of social mores and delightfully wicked in her pronouncements on sentimentality and love.

BIBLIOGRAPHY
Landon, Laetitia E. "Sefton Church." In *Nineteenth Century Short Stories by Women,* edited by Harriet Devine Jump, 87–89. London: Routledge, 1998.

Anita Rose

SELF, WILL (1961–) After graduating from Oxford University and working as a cartoonist for the *New Statesman* and *City Limits*. Self has written collections of short stories: *The Quantity Theory of Insanity* (winner of the 1992 Geoffrey Faber Memorial Prize), *Grey Area* (1994), *Tough, Tough Toys for Tough, Tough Boys* (1998), and *Dr. Mukti and Other Tales of Woe* (2004), the title story of the last being a novella. An anthology of Self's short stories is due for publication in 2005.

Self began to establish himself as a major British writer with *The Quantity Theory of Insanity* (1991) and *COCK AND BULL* (1992), an intriguing dual novella. In *Cock* a submissive woman grows a penis and rapes her husband. In *Bull* an amateur front-row prop rugby player called Bull grows a vagina on the back of his knee and becomes pregnant. Such savage commentaries on the social construction of reality through the exploration of paranoid satirical worlds that sit within the apparently real world, combined with the quotable asides of wry wit and philosophical insight, make comparisons to Jonathan Swift (1667–1745) and OSCAR WILDE apposite. As Jules Smith has noted, Self's other predecessors and influences include Philip Roth (black humor and linguistic invention), J. G. BALLARD (black humor and inner space), MARTIN AMIS (tough deadpan voice), and even ROALD DAHL. Through his appearance on numerous television shows, regular newspaper columns, and well-publicized consumption of illegal drugs, Will Self has become a version of a fictional character himself. Self is now the preeminently visible male writer-celebrity, intellectual, and wit of his generation in British culture. His work as a writer, critic, and social commentator encapsulates a 21st century desire to move beyond the hypocrisy and meaninglessness of consumption, hedonism, and nihilism that epitomized so much of the 1980s and 1990s.

If it were possible to nail down Self's body of work to two words, these might be *transgressive* and *comic*. The precision of the prose expertly conveys postmodern angst. As in *Cock and Bull,* gender issues, especially the role of men, are continually important elements of the fiction. With the photographer David Gamble, Self produced *Perfidious Man* (2000), a textual-visual commentary on the state of masculinity. Some of his other key subjects are death, suicide, drugs, psychosis, and, in particular, psychology and psychiatry. Underlying these is an investigation of spirituality and religion and the way humans manufacture meaning. In Kafkaesque fashion, the stories frequently probe the absurdities of the mental health system, questioning accepted notions of reality and sanity. The egomaniac psychiatrist Dr. Zack Busner appears as an antagonist in many of the short stories and in the longer fictions *Dr. Mukti* and *Great Apes*. Through this interweaving of the long and short fiction, Self has created a highly original fictional world in which aberrant psychology dominates and accepted versions of normality are challenged. The stories, long and short, delve deep into the contemporary mind, unnervingly unearthing the repressed, animal, and coacal that drive the frequently unconscious human animal.

BIBLIOGRAPHY

Self, Will. *Cock and Bull*. London: Bloomsbury, 1992.
———. *Dr. Mukti and Other Tales of Woe*. London: Bloomsbury, 2004.
———. *Feeding Frenzy*. London: Viking, 2001.
———. *Grey Area*. London: Bloomsbury, 1994.
———. *How the Dead Live*. London: Bloomsbury, 2000.
———. *Perfidious Man*. London: Viking, 2000.
———. *Short Stories*. London: Viking, 2005.
———. *Sore Sites*. London: Ellipsis, 2000.
———. *Tough, Tough Toys for Tough, Tough Boys*. London: Bloomsbury, 1998.
Smith, Jules. "Will Self." The Film and Literature Department of the British Council. Available online. URL: http://www.contemporarywriters.com/authors/?p=auth88. Accessed June 6, 2006.

Jason Lee

"SELFISH GIANT, THE" OSCAR WILDE **(1888)** This fairy tale by OSCAR WILDE was published in 1888 in a volume called *The Happy Prince and Other Tales*. After being away on a trip, a giant returns to his home only to find that children are playing in his yard and garden. He drives them from the garden and posts notices warning trespassers that they will be prosecuted. The absence of the children causes the garden to fall into a wintry state while the rest of the world experiences all the seasons in their normal order. The seasons refuse to come to the giant's garden because he is too selfish. Eventually the children make their way back to the garden, spring returns, and the giant enjoys the children's company. He has a special friendship with the smallest boy and helps him into the bough of a tree since the boy cannot reach it alone. One day the small boy stops coming to the garden. The giant grows old and has not seen the boy for years, so he is surprised one day in winter when he sees the boy outside. The boy has nail prints in his hands and feet, which prompts the giant to offer to kill the person who hurt the boy, but the boy tells the giant that "these are the wounds of love" and says he will take the giant with him to his garden called Paradise. Later the Giant is found dead lying under the tree, "all covered with white blossoms" (114).

The story shows the nature of real love and compassion first through the softening of the heart of the giant and later through the appearance of the boy as a Christlike figure. The link between nature following its seasonal course and the children's happiness indicates that it is more natural to be happy and congenial than isolated and selfish. Critics of the story have also pointed out that the relationship between the giant and the small boy gestures toward the possibility of so-called homosocial bonds between men. In the story the boy is so touched by the giant's conversion to generosity that he hugs and kisses him. The boy's gesture is catalyst for the return of the other children, who do not believe in the giant's change of heart until they see the giant helping the smallest boy into the tree and the boy embracing him. This embrace is proof that the giant is no longer wicked. The relationship with the boy remains important for the giant even after years pass and he grows too old to play with the children. The boy as savior of the adult at the end of the story illustrates the role a youth can play in the mind and heart of a man. Beauty, youth, and sincere affection attract and ultimately save the giant in both the Christian sense and a personal sense. The story offers readers a sad but beautiful ending as the giant dies but also will join the boy in heaven. The white blossoms that cover the giant's body at the end link him both with the tree the boy sat in and with the boy's purity.

BIBLIOGRAPHY

Kingston, Angela. "Homoeroticism and the Child in Wilde's Fairy Tales," *Wildean: The Journal of the Oscar Wilde Society* 19 (July 2001): 43–53.
Wilde, Oscar. *Complete Shorter Fiction.* Oxford: Oxford University Press, 1992.
Zipes, Jack. *Fairy Tales and the Art of Subversion: The Classical Genre for Children and the Process of Civilization.* New York: Routledge, 1983.

Susan Bernardo

SHADOW-LINE, THE Joseph Conrad (1917)

This late novella, originally written in 1915, reworks themes from Joseph Conrad's earlier writing, while also acting as an ambiguous response to World War I. (Conrad's son, Borys, enlisted and became a second lieutenant while Conrad worked on the text.) Nevertheless, the genesis for the story dates as far back as 1899, when Conrad had in mind a story titled "First Command," a possible follow-up to "Youth: A Narrative" (1898). *The Shadow-Line* shares with its predecessor the theme of innocence versus wisdom but differs from Conrad's earlier work through the conspicuous presence of evil and death. Unlike of Heart of Darkness (1899), with its mysteries, *The Shadow-Line* is altogether more explicit, a directness that some critics have taken for a lack of sophistication.

In retrospect, this criticism appears to be overly harsh. The text is not simply a rehashing of old ideas; instead, its exploration of masculinity accords with the sexual interest of Conrad's later novels, such as *Victory* (1915) and *The Rescue* (1920). Furthermore, while the story draws on Conrad's own experiences as commander of the *Otago* in 1888, the text not only edits this material but also transforms it through repeated allusion to Samuel Taylor Coleridge's poem "The Rime of the Ancient Mariner." Conrad was not averse to this form of intertextuality: The journey described in *Heart of Darkness* plays self-consciously on Dante's descent into the Inferno.

The intertextual design of *The Shadow-Line* has three effects. First, Conrad avoids a straightforward, autobiographical account. Instead, by drawing on Coleridge's epic poem, Conrad heightens his own material. The readers' attention is drawn to the way the story is narrated and, in being made aware of Conrad's literary conceit, readers are also invited to question what they are being told. In this respect, the text shares the same degree of rational skepticism as the narratives of "YOUTH," "KARAIN: A MEMORY," and "The SECRET SHARER." This additional effect transforms what might have been a seafaring yarn into a quest for knowledge.

Conrad's third achievement is to reinforce the theme of possession. While the metaphor of the shadow-line refers, in one sense, to the separation of youth from maturity, in another sense it refers to the proximity of life to death. The young sea captain is haunted by various kinds of specter. On the one hand, he is inspired by the fatherly Captain Giles ("a man should stand up to his bad luck, to his mistakes, to his conscience, and all that sort of thing") while fearing his own failure ("And here is proof positive, I am shirking it, I am no good"). On the other hand, the narrator is curious about his predecessor, who died at sea, but not before he went insane. The narrator's curiosity is stoked by his first mate, Mr. Burns, who is convinced that the dead captain has cursed the ship. Burns, an intermittently comical and sinister figure, is another kind of phantom, teasing the narrator with suggestions of devilry and enchantments. His role is balanced, though, by the steward, Ransome, on whom the narrator comes to rely. Just as the narrator is shadowed by these different figures, each representing an aspect of his psyche (his fears and desires, hope and despair), so Conrad's narrative is itself haunted by Coleridge's poem. Not only are the events broadly similar to those the Ancient Mariner experiences (the curse, the becalmed sea, the sick and dying crew), but the injunction upon tale-telling is also reminiscent. Whereas Coleridge's sailor is compelled to recite his story, so Conrad's text is subtitled "A Confession." Whether Conrad's narrator has truly crossed "the other side of a shadow" into a state of self-fulfillment or whether he remains trapped within the "great mirror of my despair" (the opening epigram from the poet Charles Baudelaire) is left unresolved.

BIBLIOGRAPHY

Erdinast-Vulcan, Daphna. *Joseph Conrad and the Modern Temper*. Oxford: Clarendon Press, 1991.

Lothe, Jakob. *Conrad's Narrative Method*. Oxford: Clarendon Press, 1989.

Schwarz, Daniel R. *Conrad: The Later Fiction*. London: Macmillan, 1982.

Paul March Russell

SHELLEY, MARY (1797–1851)

English romantic novelist, biographer, writer of short stories, and editor, Mary Wollstonecraft Shelley was, until the late 20th century, famous for only one book: *Frankenstein, or, The Modern Prometheus* (1818). She was born Mary Godwin on August 30, 1797, in London as the daughter of the writer and feminist Mary Wollstonecraft (1759–1797) and the revolutionary and philosopher William Godwin (1756–1836). Her mother died 11 days after her birth from puerperal fever, and Mary Shelley had to bear the double burden of the notoriety of her dead mother and the absence of a nurturing parent. In November 1812 she met the married poet Percy Bysshe Shelley (1792–1822), and they fell in love, eloping on July 28, 1814.

They traveled through France, Switzerland, Germany, and Holland, returning to England on September 14, a trip that served as the basis for the first part of Mary Shelley's *History of a Six Weeks' Tour,* published anonymously in 1817. In 1816, while staying in Geneva, Shelley wrote first the story and then the novel *Frankenstein, or, The Modern Prometheus,* a probing analysis of the psychology of modern scientific man, of the dangers inherent in scientific research, and of the technological exploitation of nature. Apart from creating the myth of a manmade monster, the novel also founded a new genre, science fiction, and would become a favorite of the film industry. The manuscript was revised by her husband, who undercut her unsympathetic depiction of the ambitious male protagonist; in 1831 she revised her novel herself. Apart from its criticism of science, the novel can also be read for its depiction of the traumas of birth, death, and the rejection of a child by a parent, as well as its scathing feminist critique of the destruction of family values by male hubris.

Biographical readings of Shelley's work are commonplace. For example, Shelley's anger and depression following the deaths of her children—Clara Everina (b. 1817) in September 1818 in Venice and William in Rome in 1819—partly as a result of her husband's carelessness, found an outlet in the writing of *Mathilda*. This novella was begun on her husband's birthday, August 4, 1819. Shelley projected much of her hostility toward her abandonment by both father and husband into it. *Mathilda* is a father-daughter incest fantasy. Mathilda, who is raised by her aunt after her mother's death in childbirth, is reunited with her father when she is 16 and she lives with him happily until he reveals to her that he loves her in an illicit way. Rejected by his virtuous daughter, the father commits suicide; she is later rejected by the young poet Woodville, a character resembling Mary Shelley's husband, as he also puts his poetic vocation above family and love. Shelley's ideology of the family always creates close analogues between fathers and husbands, betraying a life long obsession with her own father.

The birth of her only surviving child, Percy Florence, in 1819 alleviated Mary Shelley's acute depression and partially reconciled her to her husband. But Percy Shelley's sudden death by drowning on July 8, 1822, deprived her not only of financial security but also of support and intellectual partnership. In 1824 she began her apocalyptic novel *The Last Man,* an attempt to come to terms with her loss as well as her anger at the husband who had left her alone. It is a roman à clef, depicting both her husband and Lord Byron as freedom fighters but also as egotistical ideologues. War, disease, and the plague destroy all but three of the human race, two of whom drown on a superfluous trip to Greece. While the all-extinguishing plague could be read as a metaphor for the French Revolution, the novel also clearly criticizes male exploitation and irresponsibility.

Mary Shelley had to borrow money to return to London with her son Percy Florence in 1823, where she supported herself economically by writing novels, stories, encyclopedia articles, and reviews. Her novels *Ladore* (1835) and *Falkner* (1837) both depict an idyllic relationship between loving fathers or father substitutes and devoted adolescent daughters, a relationship uninhibited by other family members (as mothers are absent). These daughters receive a strongly gendered education: They become sweet and pliable, obedient angels in the house who cannot image a life without their fathers. Read against the grain, these novels betray a painful recognition of the damage done to women by a family ideology that insists that women (not men) have to sacrifice their personal ambitions and desires to the welfare of the family (i.e., husband and father). They show Shelley's growing awareness of the destructiveness of the sexual and emotional exploitation of women who find their self-definition and self-fulfillment only through love for their fathers and their husbands.

Shelley's short stories have long been ignored as mere commercial writing, but they can be read as an exploration of female identity through plot devices of cross-dressing, disguise, and identity switches. In "A Tale of the Passions," published in 1823 in the *Liberal,* she develops the topic of female-to-male cross-dressing. While the heroine Despina's male attire enables her to serve her male leader, thereby being a means of her female servitude, she also succeeds, albeit through her death, in disempowering the evil Lostendardo. "Transformation," published in *The Keepsake for 1831* (see ANNUALS), deals with the psychological metamorphosis of the narrator Guido, who undergoes the transformation of his own body into that of a mysterious dwarf. Through this enforced renegotiation of his identity, his treatment of and orientation toward women is altered. In "The Sisters of Albano" and "Ferdinando Eboli," published in *The Keepsake for 1829,* issues of gender and class are dealt with. Both stories involve siblings who experiment with exchanging identities by exchanging clothes. While the sisters of Albano sacrifice their lives for each other, the two brothers in "Fernando Eboli" are poised as enemies, and the evil brother uses the clothes of the other to improve his social status and gain his lover. Again, the woman, Adalina, escapes her imprisonment by disguising herself as a page to rescue her lover. The same motif is repeated in "The False Rhyme," published in *The Keepsake for 1830,* in which a wife takes her husband's place in prison to enable him to go on fighting in the service of his king (who had wrongfully convicted him). Here the woman is the ultimate example of a perfect wife who sacrifices her health and liberty for the masculine values of a male, military state. In "The Brother and the Sister: An Italian Story," published in *The Keepsake for 1833,* another young woman worships her older brother, who is a father and guardian figure; she cross-dresses to follow him and reunite the male opponents through her love. While cross-dressing cannot be read as a destabilization of the status quo, Shelley's stories at least draw attention to the arbitrary nature of gender categories. The women who transgress gender boundaries in her stories are similar to Shakespeare's cross-dressing heroines, and like Shakespeare, Shelley also has to affirm the patriarchal convention in the end, even if only to satisfy her audience.

Shelley was determined to give her son Percy Florence the education of a gentleman and to reconcile him with his grandfather, Sir Timothy Shelley, who finally granted her a small allowance of £200 per annum. To achieve this she sacrificed her London life and spent three years in a flat in Harrow so that Percy could be a day scholar at that school. Her son was devoted to her and took her, with his friends, on his travels in Italy. In 1848, after the long-expected death of Sir Timothy, Percy gained accession to the baronetcy and married Jane St. John, who admired her mother-in-law. Having long suffered from psychosomatic illnesses, headaches, nervous irritability, and depression, Mary Wollstonecraft Shelley finally succumbed to a paralysis and died in February 1851, at the age of 53. (See also "MAURICE OR THE FISHER'S COT.")

BIBLIOGRAPHY

Bennett, Betty T., ed. *Mary Shelley in Her Times.* Baltimore, Md.: Johns Hopkins University Press, 2000.

Fisch, Audrey A., ed. *The Other Mary Shelley: Beyond Frankenstein.* New York: Oxford University Press, 1993.

Schor, Esther H., ed. *The Cambridge Companion to Mary Shelley.* Cambridge: Cambridge University Press, 2003.

Shelley, Mary. *Frankenstein; or, The Modern Prometheus.* Revised ed. 3 vols. London: Henry Colburn & Richard Bentley; Edinburgh: Bell & Bradfute; Dublin: Cumming, 1831.

———. *Mary Shelley: Collected Tales and Stories, with Original Engravings.* Edited by Charles E. Robinson. Baltimore: Johns Hopkins University Press, 1976.

———. *Mounseer Nongtongpaw; or The Discoveries of John Bull in a Trip to Paris.* London: Proprietors of the Juvenile Library [M. J. Godwin & Co.], 1808.

Williams, John. *Mary Shelley: A Literary Life.* Basingstoke, England: Macmillan, 2000.

Heike Grundmann

"SIGNALMAN, THE" CHARLES DICKENS (1866)

A much-anthologized story that first appeared in *Mugby Junction,* the extra Christmas number for CHARLES DICKENS's magazine *All the Year Round* in 1866. It later appeared in a one-volume edition of all the Christmas numbers from *All the Year Round* (1859–1867) published by Chapman and Hall in 1868.

The story is told by a commonsensical narrator "who had been shut up within narrow limits all his life" and now wants to learn more about the railroad. In pursuit of this quest, he approaches the signalman with questions about his post. Over the course of several visits, the narrator learns not only about the signalman's job but about the strange specter the man has seen while working. The signalman explains that several times he has seen an apparition that has tried to warn him of some danger; after the first visitation, "the memorable accident on this Line" occurred, and after the second, a train on which a "beautiful young lady had died instantaneously" passes. The specter has now returned a third time, this time without incident, and the signalman explains that he torments himself in trying to discover its meaning, expecting another disaster anytime. The narrator himself struggles with this story, judging the man to be disturbed and fearing that the worker's unstable mind will affect his ability to perform his job. Finally, the narrator decides to leave the signalman for the night, but he agrees to return to accompany the man to "the wisest medical practitioner" the next day. As the narrator approaches the signalman's post the next night, he sees what the man had described as the apparition—but this time, the ghost is a real man, and the narrator soon discovers that the signalman has been killed. The specter-made-real is the train conductor, and he reenacts for the narrator the gestures he performed in order to warn the signalman to get out of the way of the oncoming train. The story ends with the eerie revelation that the words the narrator conjured in his own mind as he watched the signalman's demonstration of the specter's warning gestures are the very words that the train conductor uttered in trying to warn the signalman of impending danger.

"The Signalman" is the last of many ghost stories Dickens wrote, particularly in his Christmas numbers, the most famous of which is *A CHRISTMAS CAROL* (1843).

He commented to ELIZABETH GASKELL in 1851 that ghost stories are good for "illustrating particular states of mind and processes of the imagination" (quoted in Thomas, 15–16). The narrative of "The Signalman" achieves this goal effectively, demonstrating the trauma and agony of the railroad worker, who is warned of impending danger yet cannot discover the precise meaning of these warnings and is therefore powerless to avert disaster. The substance of this story might be connected to Dickens's real-life trauma in a train crash in 1865, when he narrowly escaped death as the train he was on jumped the tracks, but symbolically the tale is "a powerful and suggestive image of man's alienation by technological progress" (Mengel, 274). The railroad worker's post lies in a sort of technological hell, within a "deep trench" made "through a clammy stone" that the narrator remarks is "as solitary and dismal a place as ever I saw."

The intensity of this story lies in its ambiguity, as Dickens leaves many questions open to interpretation. It is never clear whether the signalman has really seen a spirit, and Dickens even suggests that either the signalman or the narrator might themselves be ghostly visitors. By leaving these issues unresolved, Dickens suggests that rational and scientific explanations of the world may not be sufficient to explain the scope of human experience.

BIBLIOGRAPHY
Dickens, Charles. *Christmas Books, Tales and Sketches.* Garden City, N.Y.: Nelson Doubleday, 1956.
Mengel, Ewald. "The Structure and Meaning of Dickens's 'The Signalman,'" *Studies in Short Fiction* 20 (Fall 1983): 271–280.
Thomas, Deborah A. "Introduction." In *Charles Dickens: Selected Short Fiction.* Baltimore: Penguin, 1976.

Beth Callaghan

SILLITOE, ALAN (1928–)

Sillitoe grew up in the Midlands city of Nottingham during the period between the two world wars. A laborer's son and one of a large family, he left school at 14. His subsequent education was derived mainly from his own wide reading and travel. His working-class Nottingham background invites a comparison with D. H. LAWRENCE, and his birth two years before Lawrence's death suggests that he might have been Lawrence's literary heir. While there are parallels, however, there are also divergences. Lawrence's mother had been a schoolteacher, but neither of Sillitoe's parents had the benefit of further education. Both writers left school early, but while Lawrence trained as a pupil-teacher, Sillitoe became a factory worker. Both writers developed tuberculosis when they were young, but only for Sillitoe was this a catalyst for change. Since Sillitoe's illness was diagnosed while he was still serving in the Royal Air Force, he left the service with a modest pension that enabled him to live in France and Spain while he persevered with his writing. Sillitoe's first full-length novel, *Saturday Night and Sunday Morning* (1958), focuses on the hedonistic lifestyle of Arthur Seaton, a young factory worker who rejects all forms of authority. The novella "The LONELINESS OF THE LONG DISTANCE RUNNER" (1959) takes as its hero, or antihero, a juvenile delinquent who is serving time in a young offenders' institution. Both of these works became successful films in the 1960s and typified the social realism associated with that decade, though Sillitoe rejected labels such as "working-class" and "angry young man." Like Lawrence, Sillitoe has worked in more than one genre: poetry, drama, the novel, the novella, the short story, and travel writing. Sillitoe was aware of Lawrence's position in the literary canon but saw him as representing the end of a line, while his own ambition was to break new ground.

Many of Sillitoe's short stories, especially the early ones such as "UNCLE ERNEST," have characters who are on the margins of society, have been abandoned ("ENOCH'S TWO LETTERS"), or are stuck in situations where they are unable to move on, as in "The FISHING-BOAT PICTURE." Sillitoe's strengths include an ability to create a self-contained environment with minimal reference to extraneous values, and to delineate the mundane quality of lives that are circumscribed by limited education and repetitive work.

Sillitoe belongs to a generation of writers born in the 1920s in the Midlands or the north of England (STAN BARSTOW, John Braine, John Wain, and Keith Waterhouse), all of whom began their writing careers during the postwar years and who made a major contribution to the development of 20th-century provincial writing.

Sillitoe's work has not yet been fully appraised, but he stands apart from his contemporaries for his fidelity to the experience of lower-class life. He is regarded by many reviewers as a master of the short story. His most recent collection, *Alligator Playground,* appeared in 1997.

BIBLIOGRAPHY
Atherton, S. S. *Alan Sillitoe: A Critical Assessment.* London: Allen, 1979.
Sillitoe, Alan. *Alligator Playground.* London: Flamingo, 1997.
———. *Life without Armour.* London: Harper Collins, 1995.
———. *The Loneliness of the Long Distance Runner.* London: Pan, 1959.
———. *Raw Material.* London: Allen, 1972.

Irene Wiltshire

SIMPSON, HELEN (1957–) Helen Simpson was born in Bristol and raised in London. She studied English literature at Oxford University, where she wrote her masters thesis on restoration farce. After leaving Oxford with an M.Litt degree, Simpson won the *Vogue* Talent Contest and worked for the next five years as a staff writer for the British edition of *Vogue.* After leaving *Vogue* and becoming a freelance writer, Simpson contributed articles and short stories to a variety of publications and published two cookbooks. Simpson has won a variety of literary awards for her short stories, including the Somerset Maugham Award and the Sunday Times Young Writer of the Year Award (both for *Four Bare Legs in a Bed and Other Stories* [1990]), the Hawthornden Prize (for *Hey Yeah Right Get a Life* [2000]), and the 2002 E. M. Forster Award. Though Simpson's only full-length work was an early suspense novel, *Flesh and Grass* (1990), *Granta* magazine picked her as one of the 20 Best Young British Novelists in 1993. Simpson's short stories have been critically praised on both sides of the Atlantic for their depth and subtlety as well as their realism, wit, and emotional intimacy.

Each collection of Simpson's stories tends, at least roughly, to chart the emotional and intellectual progression of various women at remarkably similar positions in their lives. Newlywed women were the primary focus of *Four Bare Legs in a Bed.* In the title story, a bored young woman dreams every night of being romantically involved with a variety of different partners, including her husband's friend. In "An Interesting Condition," Simpson writes of an prenatal class full of perplexed and frightened mothers-to-be, one of whom suggests to the other mothers that they wear a Venetian carnival mask to avoid the embarrassment of being recognized during delivery. Throughout the stories in this collection, Simpson refuses to limit herself to the confines of contemporary reality; she transports her readers across both time and space, setting her stories in not only late 20th-century London but also Renaissance country villages and fascist future states. Imminent motherhood and the anxieties surrounding the question whether to have children were the primary themes of Simpson's 1995 collection, *Dear George.* In "When in Rome," a young girl feels a sense of triumph and relief when she realizes that she is not pregnant. In "Heavy Weather," a woman suffers the acute loneliness, exhaustion, and exclusion of her roles as a mother and wife. "To Her Unruly Boyfriend" is a modern-day reworking of Marvell's "To His Coy Mistress," as a desperate young woman tries to convince her wayward lover to have a child with her.

In the collection *Hey Yeah Right Get a Life,* Simpson examines how motherhood can destroy relationships between both lovers and friends. In "Café Society," Simpson keenly demonstrates the difficulty of holding a conversation when a young child is present. In "Wurstigkeit," Simpson tells a virtual fairy tale involving two businesswomen eluding their families by visiting a clandestine women's clothing shop that requires a secret password in order to gain entrance. Despite the misery and desperation a number of the mothers in her stories feel, Simpson's outlook on motherhood remains ultimately optimistic. She tends to center her later stories on the moments of epiphany that can occur between mothers and children that make the sacrifice of motherhood ultimately worthwhile. Throughout her 2005 collection *Constitutional,* Simpson explores the trials and tribulations of women as they enter into middle age and begin to contemplate the imminence of age and death. In the title story (see "CONSTITUTIONAL"), a pregnant middle-aged woman takes a long walk after a funeral, during which she darkly reflects on death, birth, and the circularity of human existence. In "Every Third Thought," a cancer panic sweeps across a group of women, all of whom promptly begin to weigh the odds of their own demise from the disease.

Like her literary idols Anton Chekhov and KATHERINE MANSFIELD, Simpson demonstrates a particular gift for the conveyance of unadulterated human emotion throughout her fiction. She is able to philosophize over the particularities of every day life in a remarkably genuine and realistic manner, without slipping into heavy-handed pathos or cliché. As dark, cynical, and downright grotesque as her stories can often be, Simpson maintains a sharp sense of humor and strong sense of irony no matter the nature of her subject matter. Throughout her short stories, Simpson walks the fine line between stark realism and satire with both wit and grace.

BIBLIOGRAPHY

Simpson, Helen. *Constitutional*. London: Jonathan Cape, 2005.
———. *Dear George and Other Stories*. London: Heinemann, 1995.
Four Bare Legs in a Bed and Other Stories. London: Heinemann, 1990.
———. *Hey Yeah Right Get a Life*. London: Jonathan Cape, 2000.
Taylor, D. J. "The Grim Reaper of Hampstead," *Independent on Sunday*, 1 January 2006.

James R. Fleming

SINCLAIR, IAIN (1943–)

Born in Wales on June 11, 1943, the son of a doctor, Iain Sinclair is, perhaps more than any other contemporary writer, recognized as the scribe of LONDON. Sinclair was educated at the London School of Film Technique and Trinity College, Dublin, where his study focussed on theatre, literature, and filmmaking. Unlike other contemporary writers, such as MARTIN AMIS or Peter Ackroyd, who began their literary careers as journalists, Sinclair's literary development was anything but orthodox. In the 1970s he established his own publishing house, Albion Press, while supporting himself financially by working in a brewery, a mail-sorting center, and a cigar-packing factory and as a gardener and a secondhand book dealer.

It was was with the publication in 1975 of *Lud Heat* that Sinclair began to develop his London mythography for which he is now renowned. *Lud Heat* is an eclectic combination of free-verse poetry, diary entries, and literary and cultural history that attempts to plot "lines of influence" that have had an influence over the city's history. Throughout the rest of the 1970s and the early 1980s Sinclair continued to publish poetry and mythography with little critical success. It was not until the publication of *White Chappell, Scarlet Tracings* in 1987 that Sinclair began to be recognized as an important voice in contemporary British fiction. This novel was an investigation into the Jack the Ripper murders of 1888. This was followed in 1991 by *Downriver,* for which Sinclair won the James Tait Black Memorial Prize, and *Lights Out for the Territory*. This collection of documentary prose, uncovering the "secret history" of London, was universally praised as an original investigation of the city, both past and present. Its success was followed by that of *London Orbital* (2002), a prose collection that documented a series of walks around the M25, the freeway that circles London. Since then Sinclair has continued to publish prolifically, including his 2004 novel *Dining on Stones,* and in 2005, *The Edge of Orison,* a documentary of a series of walks based on John Clare's journey from an insane asylum to his home village.

Sinclair's oeuvre is, if nothing else, resistant to any genre classification. Yet several of his works can be classified as short stories, in particular the 1997 collection *Slow Chocolate Autopsy.* The collection features a range of prose pieces centered on the character "Norton, prisoner of London." Norton is confined to the geographical limits of the city yet is free to move through time, acting as witness to a range of historical events. "The Fifth Man in the Garden" is representative of Sinclair's stylistic and thematic preoccupations, as well as his approach to the short story. Here Norton is present at the murder of Christopher Marlowe in Deptford on May 30, 1953. The story largely consists of Norton's musings over the event, his desire to intervene so as to write his own name into literary history. Yet wracked by apathy and indecision, Norton walks away—into the familiar contemporary landscape of redevelopment and pollution. Here, as so often, Sinclair combines literary history with social critique, the past with the present, attempting to undermine the stable categories of time and canonical literary history that have had such a profound effect on our understanding of literary London. While this is the only recognizable collection of short stories, all of Sinclair's narratives, both fictional and documentary, are episodic and fragmental, and all blur the boundary between fiction, nonfiction, and autobiography; passages of the novel *White Chappell, Scarlet Tracings,* the 12 "vessels" of *Downriver,* and the essay collection *Liquid City* all could be classified in the short story genre as well as the dedicated short story collection *Slow Chocolate Autopsy.*

BIBLIOGRAPHY

Bavidge, Jenny, and Robert Bond, eds. *City Visions: The Work of Iain Sinclair.* Cambridge: Cambridge Scholars Press, 2006.

Bond, Robert. *Iain Sinclair.* Cambridge: Salt, 2005.

Sinclair, Iain. *Dining on Stones.* London: Penguin, 2004.

———. *Liquid City.* London: Reaktion Books, 1999.

———. *London Orbital.* London: Granta, 2002.

———. *Lud Heat and Suicide Bridge.* London: Vintage, 1995.

Sinclair, Iain, with David McKean. *Slow Chocolate Autopsy.* London: Phoenix, 1997.

Wolfreys, Julian. *Writing London.* Vol. 2: *Materiality, Spectrality, Memory.* Basingstoke, England: Palgrave Macmillan, 2004.

Alex Murray

"SIR EDMUND ORME" HENRY JAMES (1892)

"Sir Edmund Orme" is one of HENRY JAMES's many tales that revolve around strange apparitions. A fascination with occult (magical, theosophical, mysterious, or even spiritual) phenomena is evident in many of James's tales and short stories. Like his contemporaries GEORGE ELIOT (Mary Ann Evans) and MARGARET OLIPHANT, James wrote a number of texts that feature communication between the dead and the living, clairvoyance, and similar phenomena. Other members of James's family shared his interest. His father, Henry James, Sr., for example, was a well-known theologian interested in mysticism; his brother, William James, a professor at Harvard University, became involved in experimental psychology such as that led by the Society for Psychical Research (SPR) in England. In fact, one year after the society's instantiation in England,

William founded the American Society for Psychical Research and conducted scientific experiments on the survival of the human spirit after death, communication with the dead, and telepathy. Critics such as F. O. Matthiessen helped bring the family into fame, while Leon Edel and other major literary critics collected and critiqued Henry James's work, helping establish him as a leading literary figure.

"Sir Edmund Orme" is an example of James's many narratives that employ ideas about the occult and spirit worlds. First printed in the Christmas 1891 edition of the populist periodical *Black and White,* "Orme" was probably designed to entertain a popular audience interested in such ghost stories as CHARLES DICKENS's famous *A CHRISTMAS CAROL* (1843) and George MacDonald's "Uncle Cornelius His Story" (1871). Moreover, like virtually all of James's narratives, "Orme" addresses the challenges posed by Victorian codes of decorum and control that placed often unbearable pressures on members of society: As they are presented by James, these pressures could lead to disaster or even death.

"Orme" is framed by an unnamed, first-person narrator who possesses papers that apparently belonged to the also unnamed first-person narrator of the story proper. This recalls the structure of one of James's most famous stories, *The Turn of the Screw* (1898), in which an unnamed first-person narrator frames the story. The story, in turn, is related to an audience by Douglas, the owner of the sheets on which the story was written by an unnamed governess. One of the more important differences between *The Turn of the Screw* and "Sir Edmund Orme" concerns the existence of the ghosts around which the stories revolve. The likelihood of the ghosts' existence differs in the two stories largely as a result of the narrator's reliability (or unreliability). While the existence of the ghosts in *The Turn of the Screw* is consistently in doubt because of the narrating governess's psychological instability and questionable objectivity, the ghost of Sir Edmund Orme is presented as a matter of fact, for the narrator's mental wellness, objectivity, and sincerity are not in question. Moreover, the narrator in *The Turn of the Screw* cannot secure a witness to corroborate her sightings, whereas the narrator in "Sir Edmund Orme" is himself the witness, for he perceives the ghost of Orme, which has been haunting another character, Mrs. Marden, for some time.

In the story, Mrs. Marden is shaken on several occasions by the sight of a gentleman whom no other character besides the narrator is able to see. Once certain that the narrator can, in fact, see him, Mrs. Marden reveals that the gentleman is the ghost of her deceased lover whom she abandoned in her youth to marry Captain Marden, inciting Orme to commit suicide. According to Mrs. Marden, she is being punished for so mistreating her lover, and she fears that the same fate awaits her daughter. Mrs. Marden's beautiful, coquettish daughter, Charlotte, has stolen the unnamed narrator's heart along with, apparently, those of a number of other suitors. Fearing that her daughter will abandon the narrator as she herself abandoned Orme, Mrs. Marden tries to prevent the disaster by encouraging the relationship. Charlotte, however, is not interested in marrying the narrator. Mrs. Marden eventually reveals that her own mother and sister had placed a similar pressure on her: Although she did not love Orme, they had promoted her relationship with him. At the end of the tale, Orme appears to Mrs. Marden as she lies ill in bed, Charlotte and the narrator at her side. To accommodate her mother, Charlotte implies that she will, indeed, devote herself to the narrator. Mrs. Marden dies, her punishment executed with a final, ambiguous gasp from an unknowable source.

The story can be read in a number of ways. In one sense, the dead Orme and the living narrator could be said to fight over possession of Charlotte. In another sense, "Orme" can be read as a tale of irony in which Mrs. Marden commits the same error as did her mother before her by virtually forcing Charlotte to love the narrator with no regard for her daughter's true feelings, thus leading to her ultimate punishment in death. Still another interpretation is the narrator's own: It is a case of retributive justice in which the spell has been broken by his and Charlotte's commitment to each other. Yet more readings are possible, and this equivocation, characteristic of Henry James's fiction, is due to his particularity of language and skillful use of narrative devices that appeal "to wonder and terror and curiosity and pity and to the delight . . . of the mystified state" (*Art*, 253).

BIBLIOGRAPHY

James, Henry. *The Art of the Novel: Critical Prefaces.* New York: Scribner, 1937.

———. *The Turn of the Screw and Other Stories.* Oxford: Oxford University Press, 1992.

Matthiessen, F. O. *The James Family, Including Selections from the Writings of Henry James, Senior, William, Henry and Alice James.* New York: Knopf, 1947.

Lindsay Holmgren

"SISTER IMELDA" EDNA O'BRIEN (1981)

Though it recycles characters and situations from her justly famous *Country Girls* trilogy, EDNA O'BRIEN's "Sister Imelda" is satisfying on its own and is a condensed introduction to some of the things O'Brien does very well. Ostensibly a story of the convent school days of a teenage Irish girl and her charged relationship with the titular nun-teacher, what goes on between the lines makes the story compelling and wonderful. O'Brien's story develops the peculiar relationship between two women in the service of articulating a larger thematic point about the nature of lesbian relationships.

The relationship between the unnamed narrator and her young and worldly teacher, Sister Imelda, routinely crosses the line between platonic and sub-rosa sexuality. This relationship is hardly novel, even if one overlooks treatments of similar material in the O'Brien's corpus. But what it striking is the skill and knowing humor with which O'Brien presents the material; in a seduction sequence that plays out in a home economics classroom and nods equally to the jam-puff sequence in GEORGE ELIOT's *Mill on the Floss* and Christina Rossetti's "Goblin Market," O'Brien turns up the heat when her narrator remembers "testing orange cakes . . . and letting me lick the line of half-baked dough down the length of the needle" (130). Elsewhere, O'Brien deploys religious imagery with a wink when she writes that it "was not difficult to imagine Sister Imelda, face downward, arms outstretched, prostrate on the tile floor" (131). On its own, either of these phrases could be the product of a hormonally excited teen girl, but taken together with similar phrases throughout the story, they create an overall hothouse atmosphere that is almost stifling.

The story makes repeated reference to secret languages and other signs between women. Lesbianism in

"Sister Imelda" is coterminous with a religious vocation, since both call for renunciation. Imelda instructs the narrator in how to understand sapphic love by giving the narrator a chrysanthemum to smell, which "had no smell . . . only something faint that suggested autumn" (127), and a picture of the Virgin and Child that is "so pale that it was almost gray" (128). This lack of color and the fragility of lesbian relationships is contrasted in the story's final sequence, in which the narrator notes how, in heterosexual relationships, "our skins were smothered beneath layers" of makeup (142) the artificial plumage required to attract a man. The narrator also finds childbearing viscerally repulsive: "mating could only lead to one's being a mother and hawking obstreperous children out to the seaside" (142). The story is the narrator's apologia, a brief and incomplete explanation of why she has not entered the sisterhood or searched for love with other women.

O'Brien writing style might be described as a free direct discourse: A straightforward description will suddenly curve into more personal, enlivened territory. It is not only through her narrative voice, though, that O'Brien demonstrates her knowledge of JAMES JOYCE: A reference to the nuns' shapes echoes the description of Mangan's sister in "ARABY," and the extended reverie that narrator and her friend Baba share about Sister Imelda's experience with men is indebted to Gretta's final encounter with Michael Furey in "THE DEAD." However, here that story is considered childish fantasy, not the invitation to melodramatic solipsism that it is in Joyce's hands. O'Brien explodes naive conceptions throughout her story, giving in their place a layered presentation of the relationship between two women and the way that relationship, even having failed, lingers for one of them.

BIBLIOGRAPHY
O'Brien, Edna. *A Fanatic Heart: Selected Stories of Edna O'Brien.* New York: Farrar, Straus & Giroux, 1984.

Matthew Dube

SKETCHES BY BOZ CHARLES DICKENS (1834–1836)

Sketches by "Boz" Illustrative of Every-day Life and Every-day People is a collection of CHARLES DICKENS's first-published works. He had begun his literary publishing career proper on December 1, 1833 (at age 21), when "A Dinner at Poplar Walk" (later titled "Mr. Minns and His Cousin") appeared in the *Monthly Magazine.* The pseudonym *Boz* derived from Dickens's younger brother's pronunciation of Dickens's nickname, Moses. Other tales of "every-day life" appeared in the *Morning Chronicle,* the *Evening Chronicle,* and *Bell's Life in London.* The publisher John Macrone first approached Dickens regarding a collection in October 1834, offering Dickens £100 for the copyright (later in his career, Dickens bought it back for more than £1,000). Macrone also managed to interest the most successful illustrator of his day, George Cruikshank, who was to contribute 40 illustrations to the edition. The collection was first published in 1836, the day after Dickens's 24th birthday. This first series of sketches was successful enough for Dickens and Cruikshank to begin work on a second volume almost immediately. The second series coincided with Dickens's frenetic writing of installments for *The Pickwick Papers.* As early as this was in his career, Dickens had already begun a feverish and eclectic working routine that almost certainly contributed to his relatively early death.

There are 56 sketches in all; structurally and stylistically they have more in common with the modern short story than they do with the Victorian one. They draw on the novelistic device of depicting the everyday in often obscure, odd, and fantastical ways by defamiliarizing it, but not so much that the sketches lose their focus. The sketches are almost exclusively comical. "Greenwich Fair" has one of the funniest opening paragraphs that Dickens would ever write. "The Tuggs's at Ramsgate" is a hilarious satire of new money and its associated new pretensions to aristocracy. The tale is an articulate representation of the need to perform one's identity through external commodities rather than actions; it comically portrays the disjunction between interior life and exterior lie—the new disease of modernity. Such a notion of the necessity of performance, imitation, and impersonation in everyday life is also explored in the sketch "Astley's," which recounts a visit to Astley's Circus undertaken by the narrator, who then reflects nostalgically on the wonder of the circus in days supposedly long gone by.

The timbre of Dickens's narration suggests that nostalgia as a historical epoch never existed at all. Dickens also found plenty of space to include some social criticism, most notably in "Gin-Shops," "Criminal Courts," "A Visit to Newgate," "The Black Veil," and the moral lessons of "The Drunkard's Death." Of all the sketches, these tend to be the weakest, striking a slightly melodramatic, monotonous note. In short, *Sketches by Boz* foretells many of Dickens's qualities as a novelist: funny and serious, subtle and melodramatic, tiresome and mesmerizing.

BIBLIOGRAPHY

Dickens, Charles. *Sketches by "Boz" and Other Early Papers.* Edited by Michael Slater. Columbus: Ohio State University Press, 1994.
Flint, Kate. *Dickens.* Brighton, England: Harvester, 1986.

Vybarr Cregan-Reid

SMITH, STEVIE (1902–1971)   Stevie Smith

(Florence Margaret Smith) was born in Hull, one of two sisters. When her father left the family for the navy, Stevie and her sister were taken by their mother to an aunt's home in Palmers Green, a north London suburb. Themes of abandonment and female independence characterize Smith's fiction as well as her poetry. A product of one of the first schools in England founded for girls, she never attended university or married but worked instead as a secretary in a publishing firm, where she wrote fiction on office time in the 1930s and 1940s.

After her suicide attempt in 1953, Stevie Smith retired and devoted the rest of her life to writing and caring for "the noble aunt who so long tended us" ("A House of Mercy"). Although Smith is best known for her eight books of poetry, for which she won the Chalmondeley Award and the Queen's Gold Medal in 1969, she also wrote three novels and 10 short stories. Like the poetry, her fiction features naughty children, quarrelsome men, and women who are ambivalent about it all.

Although separated by a century, Stevie Smith and GEORGE ELIOT treat the idea of gender roles in a strikingly similar manner; moreover, Smith shares an affinity for feminism with VIRGINIA WOOLF. Smith's fiction is contemporaneous with that of ELIZABETH BOWEN, Kay Dick, and Naomi Mitchison but is less thematically traditional in terms of family and work. Today, Margaret Drabble, Anita Brookner, and Margaret Atwood directly descend from her line.

More conventional in style than her novels, Smith's short stories frequently feature Helen, a writer who is a thinly disguised version of Smith herself. In "The Story of a Story" (1946), Helen's friend's husband files a libel suit that prevents the publication of her story about the couple; Smith contrasts the wife's intelligence with the husband's legalism. Helen/Smith confronts her friend's ambivalence as the married woman proclaims both her independence and her need for companionship. Although the husband wins the lawsuit, he loses his wife, who had come to regard herself as his slave. Helen appears again in "Beside the Seaside" (1949), ironically subtitled "A Holiday with Children." The unmarried writer Helen vacations with a married friend and her children. The boy's frequent pranks and tantrums upset Helen so much that she eventually hits him with a rolled magazine and orders him to shut up. Adult and child collide in the story, paralleling the clash of competing impulses in women's lives.

In "Getting Rid of Sadie" (1955), a brother and sister devise a plan to murder a cruel governess, aptly named Sadie. Ten years later, the now-grown siblings reflect on their failed attempt and Sadie's authoritative behavior, admitting the seriousness of their scheme. This story, as well as "The Story of a Story" and "Beside the Seaside," points to another theme typical of Stevie Smith: Her work subverts the assumption of the innocence of children; indeed, it examines the very nature of assumptions themselves.

Besides contributing to feminist fiction, Smith also contextualizes her work in pre- and postwar England. Having served as a fire watcher in the West End of London, she depicts characters who walk to work amid fragments of broken glass, suffer through rations and shortages, and take geopolitical stands on the issues of the day. One of Helen's chief complaints in "Beside the Seaside" targets not only her friend's inability to stand up to her own children but also her ignorance of the cataclysmic potential of the atom bomb. It is Stevie Smith's janus-faced ability to look inward and outward simultaneously that distinguishes her short fiction from that of her female contemporaries.

BIBLIOGRAPHY

Civello, Catherine A. *Patterns of Ambivalence: The Fiction and Poetry of Stevie Smith.* Camden House: Columbia, S.C., 1997.

Smith, Stevie. *The Collected Poems of Stevie Smith.* New York: Oxford, 1976.

———. *Me Again: Uncollected Writings.* Edited by Jack Barbera and William McBrien. London: Virago, 1981.

Spalding, Frances. *Stevie Smith: A Critical Biography.* London: Faber and Faber, 1988.

Cathy Civello

"SOLID GEOMETRY" IAN MCEWAN (1975)

IAN MCEWAN departs somewhat from his typical style and subject matter in the story "Solid Geometry," published in his first collection of stories, FIRST LOVE, LAST RITES. As in the rest of the stories in the collection, the main character of the story has little regard for other human beings and seems inclined toward violence and unusual sexual desires; unlike the other stories in the collection, though, this one combines elements of history, the supernatural, and metafiction in ways that anticipate many of McEwan's later novels.

The story begins with the unnamed narrator's description of a penis that his great-grandfather purchased at an auction and preserved in formaldehyde. The narrator has this heirloom on his desk, and he reflects on it frequently as he spends his days reading and editing his great-grandfather's copious diaries. The story alerts the reader in the opening pages to a potentially sinister ending when the narrator notes that he used to fantasize about leaving his wife when he had finished the editing project, "but now there is no need at all."

Like many of the main characters and narrators in McEwan's short stories, this first-person narrator has little human connection with or sympathy for the people in his life—in this case, his wife Maisie. When she describes her nightmares to him and begs him to stay awake with her, he responds "through a yawn" that he has to get up early and falls immediately back to sleep. In another episode, the narrator locks himself in the bathroom one evening to write in his own diary and prevents his wife from entering despite her urgent pleas for access. When he finally comes out of the bathroom, she hits him on the head with a shoe and locks herself in; when she, in turn, opens the door of the bathroom, he has been lying in wait with the shoe and returns the favor. As the narrator's obsession with the diary becomes more intense throughout the story, his relationship with his wife becomes increasingly cold. The depiction of this relationship echoes a major theme that dominates the stories in *First Love, Last Rites:* the potential for violence lying beneath the surface of everyday sexual and social interactions.

As the narrator delves more deeply into his great-grandfather's diary, he ponders the disappearance of his great-grandfather's friend, named only "M" in the diary. Eventually the narrator discovers that the disappearance of M coincides with a section of the diary he has previously neglected, since it consists mostly of discussions of geometrical principles. He decides to read these sections more carefully, and here McEwan inserts a long passage from the diary, written in his grandfather's 19th-century diction. The passage describes his great-grandfather's account of an international conference of mathematicians in which a Scottish mathematician claimed to have proved the existence of "plane without a surface." After demonstrating the existence of this plane by folding a piece of paper in such a way that it disappears, this mathematician then contorts his body in the same proportions and directions and slowly causes his body to disappear entirely. The narrator gathers, from the following pages of the diary, that his great-grandfather accomplished this same astonishing feat by rediscovering the plane without a surface and causing his friend M to disappear.

These excerpts from the diary appear in two long sections, separated by an interlude in which Maisie, stung by the narrator's lack of interest in her sexually, smashes the jar containing the formaldehyde penis. Upon finishing the section of the diary devoted to this geometrical miracle, the narrator uses his great-grandfather's precise directions to reproduce the trick of the disappearing paper. Maisie enters his study as he completes the exercise, and the narrator immediately forms his plan to cause the disappearance of another "M." He plies her with food and wine, and—in the final scene, which Maisie initially interprets as foreplay—begins to bend her into position. He describes the event with the admiring eyes of a mathematician contemplating a formula: "the positioning of her limbs expressed the breathtaking beauty, the nobility of the human form, and, as in the paper flower, there was a fascinating power in its symmetry." He completes his trick, and at the end of the story his wife has become the final plane without a surface.

In a handful of its elements, the story echoes themes that dominate the collection in which it appears: the narrator's indifference to the fate of those around him and his complete focus on his own self-interest and pleasure, the sudden outbursts of violence in otherwise seemingly benign people and situations, and the interest in the most grotesque and unusual forms of human sexuality and desire (such as the preserved penis, which becomes an object of horror when it has been removed from the formaldehyde: "grey, limp, and menacing, transformed from a treasured curiosity into a horrible obscenity").

The story's turn to the past, though, has parallels in no other story in this collection, which otherwise depicts people and situations in 1970s England. The use of history in this story, to be sure, seems purely functional: It removes the discovery of this fantastic disappearing process into the distant past, which discourages the reader from demanding much detail about the scientific nature of the plane without a surface. McEwan's venture into the past in the story signals an interest in history that becomes dominant in his later fiction but remains undeveloped here. The same can be said for his use of the supernatural in the story. This theme plays a central role in later novels such as *Black Dogs*, but here it seems to offer an unusual variation on a typical plotline in his short fiction: the gradual deterioration of sexual desire and sexual relationships into violence. The narrator offers no speculation on where Maisie might disappear to, no reflections on the cosmological or theological implications of such an action. His interest in the disappearing trick is purely self-interested; once Maisie has disappeared, he has no further use for it.

In its depiction of the supernatural, and in the narrator's search through the diaries of his great-grandfather for the secret of the plane without a surface, "Solid Geometry" contains elements of gothic fiction, with a modern twist. One final element of the story, though, aligns it more closely with the late 20th-century movement postmodernism. Many postmodern works contain metafictional elements, in which characters or the narrator call attention to the work of art as a work of art. This happens midway through the story, when Maisie accuses the narrator of talking as if they were in a fiction seminar: "Perhaps we *are* in a fiction seminar," the narrator replies. The obvious connection between a fiction seminar and a work of fiction constitutes a warning to the reader not to swallow the reader's supernatural elements too easily.

The story's title helps illustrate its theme: The narrator views his world and the people in it as mathematics problems. From his perspective, the search for the fate of M in the diaries is no different from the trick of making his wife disappear: Both involve solving puzzles—and puzzles must be solved, regardless of the outcome for those around him. This narrator, like most narrators and main characters in McEwan's fiction, lives to satisfy his own pleasure; the distinctive element of this story is that the narrator's pleasure lies in the abstract pleasure of solving mysteries, rather than in the pleasures of violence or deviant sexuality.

BIBLIOGRAPHY
McEwan, Ian. *First Love, Last Rites.* London: Cape; New York: Random House, 1975.

Malcolm, David. *Understanding Ian McEwan.* Columbia: University of South Carolina Press, 2002.

Raban, Jonathan. "Exiles: New Fiction," *Encounter* 44 (June 1975): 81.

Slay, Jack, Jr. *Ian McEwan.* New York: Twayne; London: Prentice Hall, 1996.

James Lang

SOMERVILLE, E., AND MARTIN ROSS (EDITH ANNA OENONE SOMERVILLE [1858–1949] AND VIOLET MARTIN [1862–1915])

Although they wrote a number of novels, essays, reminiscences, and travel books together, including what has been called the finest Irish novel of the 19th century, *The Real Charlotte* (1894), the literary partnership of Somerville and Ross is best remembered for the popular series of stories featuring the "Irish R.M." ("Resident Magistrate"). Edith Somerville spent most of her life at Drishane, the family home, in Castletownshend, Ireland; the hilly landscape of the coast of West Cork provided the setting for the stories. Like her second cousin, Violet Martin, she devoted much of her time and energy to maintaining the family estate in the face of economic pressures and political changes in Ireland. Martin, also the daughter of an Anglo-Irish Protestant landowning family, lived at their estate, Ross, in County Galway until her mother's death in 1909; thereafter she resided with Somerville at Drishane. The two women met in 1886 and soon began a remarkably successful and long-lasting collaboration. The first of the "Irish R.M." stories appeared in the *Badminton Magazine* in 1898, and the humourous depiction of the clash of English orderliness and Irish subversion proved immediately popular. There were eventually three collections: *Some Experiences of an Irish R.M.* (1899), *Further Experiences of an Irish R.M.* (1908), and *In Mr. Knox's Country* (1915), as well as a volume containing all 34 stories, *The Irish R.M. and His Experiences* (1928; later retitled *The Irish R.M. Complete*). The stories were accompanied by Somerville's whimsical illustrations (she had a secondary career as a painter).

The hero and narrator of these stories is Major Sinclair Yeates, an Englishman in his 30s who has recently left the British army and obtained a position as resident magistrate in Skebawn. Unfamiliar with the people and their ways, his predilection for organization, routine, and a certain amount of comfort is constantly frustrated by the very un-British attitudes and conditions to be found in this remote corner of the United Kingdom (Ireland at this time being part of the British Empire). Among the vivid characters he encounters are his rascally landlord, Flurry Knox ("who looked like a stableboy among gentlemen, and a gentleman among stableboys"), and his aunt, the fearsomely eccentric Mrs. Knox (who dresses "as if she had robbed a scarecrow"). Yeates is often bemused by his neighbors but never loses his fundamental openness and good humor. Though a representative of the Crown, he often finds himself manipulated into undermining the standards he has been sent to uphold, and he comes to learn that being a magistrate in West Cork

involves a good deal of winking at the letter of the law: "I realized for the hundredth time the magnificent superiority of the Irish mind to the trammels of officialdom, and the inveterate supremacy in Ireland of the Personal Element" ("Poisson d'Avril"). Much of the humor of the stories comes from Yeates's dry narration of the chaos and near disasters all around him, as when a pleasure boat runs aground: "We were not, so far, at the bottom of the sea, but during the next ten minutes the chances seemed in favour of our getting there" ("The House of Fahy").

The authors were enthusiastic sportswomen, and their knowledge of fox hunting informs about one-third of the Irish R.M. stories (which are sometimes mistakenly remembered as hunting tales merely, like the works of R. S. Surtees). Given that Somerville and Ross took scrupulous care in reproducing the speech of County Cork (for which FRANK O'CONNOR praised them), it is ironic that the stories have generally been more popular in Britain and in the rest of the English-speaking world than in Ireland, where the authors have frequently been seen as condescending members of the gentry. Somerville and Ross regarded themselves as inheritors of the Irish comic tradition begun by MARIA EDGEWORTH. In addition to O'Connor, the Irish R.M. has found admirers in ELIZABETH BOWEN and WILLIAM TREVOR. The stories were successfully adapted for a television series in the 1980s and have often been anthologized.

BIBLIOGRAPHY

Robinson, Hillary. *Somerville and Ross: A Critical Appreciation.* Dublin: Gill & Macmillan, 1980.
Somerville, Edith Oenone, and Martin Ross [Violet Florence Martin]. *The Irish R.M. Complete.* London: Faber and Faber, 1962.
Tillinghast, Richard. "The Uneasy World of Somerville and Ross," *New Criterion* 13, no. 8 (April 1995): 23–30.

Andrew J. Garavel

"SOME WAYS OF LOVE" CHARLOTTE MEW (1901)

CHARLOTTE MEW published "Some Ways of Love" in the *Pall Mall Magazine*. Opening with an epigraph from the French writer Anatole France's novel *At the Sign of the Queen Pédauque* (1893) that talks of the impenetrability of the soul and the cruel birth of love,

Mew addresses here themes that recur in her fiction and poetry: the inability of individuals to truly know one another and the failure or renunciation of love. "Some Ways of Love" is structured in four parallel parts, showing Captain Allan Henley alternately with two women he loves: Lady Ella Hopedene and Mildred Playfair. Initially, the boyish Allan woos the more experienced Ella, who, although loving him, refuses to answer his proposal until he comes back from serving in the Boer War, believing that she is nobly offering him a way out if he changes as he matures. He is too callow to understand her real emotions. Next, we see him some time later, on a ship returning to England, out of love with Ella and wooing Mildred. Honorable to a fault, he tells Mildred that he has made a prior commitment to Ella and must be released by her before he can wed Mildred. Hopeful, he tells Mildred that Ella is incapable of deep feeling. When he returns to Ella, she reveals her love in the shock of seeing him. Additionally, she reveals that she is dying, with only a year to live. Ever the gentleman, Allan pretends that he has always loved her and says they will be married. Finally, he returns to Mildred, who cannot understand the emotional nuances and refuses to wait for him. Both recognize that he has betrayed Ella.

The dialogue and descriptions are typical of popular magazine fiction of the day. Yet despite the clichés and contrivedness of the plot, "Some Ways of Love" is still interesting for its implied criticism of modern notions of honor and gentlemanliness. Although Allan initially blames Ella for not giving him a clear answer the first time, it is his choices and behavior that are condemned in the story as well as the codes and mores by which he lives. This questioning of heterosexual courtship rituals links "Some Ways of Love" to NEW WOMAN fiction of the period, in which writers like GEORGE EGERTON and Netta Syrett challenged traditional relations between men and women. The story also illustrates well Mew's characteristic style. At the beginning of the third section, the worldly Ella is reading *Ramuntcho* (1897), a novel of manners by another French writer, Pierre Loti, noted for his intimate style and evocation of sensory impressions. Ella comments that his work can be "enervating," but Mew's own style, focusing on deep emotions that usually must be repressed and organized around moments of intense, almost painful, perception, can be equally intense. In a biographical link, Penelope Fitzgerald suggests that Ella might be named after the writer ELLA D'ARCY, with whom Mew eagerly and rather too fervently pursued a friendship during the period she wrote this story. As did most of Mew's attempts at forming relationships, this one failed, life imitating art or vice versa.

BIBLIOGRAPHY

Fitzgerald, Penelope. *Charlotte Mew and Her Friends*. London: Collins, 1984.
Mew, Charlotte. *Charlotte Mew: Collected Poems and Prose.* Edited with an introduction by Val Warner. Manchester, England: Carcanet Press; London: Virago, 1981.

Terri Doughty

"SOUVENIR OF JAPAN, A" ANGELA CARTER (1974)

One of the short stories from *Fireworks: Nine Profane Pieces,* "A Souvenir of Japan" reflects the influence of ANGELA CARTER's residence in Japan (1970–72) on her writing. Written soon after her divorce from her first husband, this short story set in Shinjuku delineates the complex relationship between a British woman and her Japanese lover through descriptive snapshots. Critics have examined the story as an "evocation of culture clash—between men and women even more than between Japan and England" and have drawn particular attention to its autobiographical resonances as the narrative of a woman coping with personal loss (VanderMeer) and to the realistic setting of the story (Lurie).

The story captures the disillusionment experienced by the female narrator-protagonist and her lover, who are trapped in a static relationship based purely on physical attraction. In an alien country, the narrator is continually conscious of her otherness, not least because of her involvement with a younger man, Taro. She is also acutely aware of the status of women as objects of men's passion in the obtrusively patriarchal setup of the Japanese society and candidly assents to this kind of inferior treatment of women rather "than never . . . be valued at all." (31). Taro is obsessed with the idea of being in love but paradoxically experiences a feeling of extreme boredom as a consequence of "an affair which is so isolated from the real world" (33).

The story is marked by a tone of sadness and resignation at the transience of all objects of beauty and the human inability to delve beneath the surface appearance of things.

Throughout the story Carter tries to capture something of the culture and the customs of Japan. The name *Taro* originates from the Kabuki tale of Momotaro, the boy who was born from a peach, a story of unnatural birth. The narrator draws a parallel between the living man and the mythical character; both share "an inhuman sweetness of a child born from something other than a mother" (30). The Japanese fireworks, *hannabi,* form an ironical backdrop to the narrative. Carter's fascination with mirrors is also apparent, as the city is described as a cold hall of mirrors that replicates reality as a series of perplexing yet intangible images.

Like many of Carter's stories, "A Souvenir of Japan" appears feminist in its sympathies, largely because of its candid acknowledgement of the unequal treatment of women in a world that privileges men. The story draws on the conventions of postmodernism in the way it calls attention to the fictionality of the characters and the story. The narrator explicitly points out that Taro might be an invention of her mind and his name merely an exercise of her choice. Similar to the houses in this Japanese city of appearances, which are insubstantial and disappear overnight, the edifice of Carter's story is also an illusionary construct.

BIBLIOGRAPHY

Carter, Angela. *Burning Your Boats: Collected Short Stories.* Introduction by Salman Rushdie. London: Vintage, 1996.

Lurie, Alison. "Winter's Tales." New York Times on the Web. (May 19, 1996). Available online. URL: http://www.nytimes.com/books/98/12/27/specials/carter-boats.html. Accessed June 7, 2006.

VanderMeer, Jeff. "Angela Carter." The Modern World. Available online. URL: http://www.themodernword.com/scriptorium/carter.html. Accessed June 7, 2006.

Preeti Bhatt

SPARK, MURIEL (1918–2006)

Muriel Spark was a Scottish novelist, short story writer, critic, poet, and playwright who won international acclaim primarily for her fiction, which reveals her sensitive observation of the human propensity to evil, her narrative skills, and her dexterous techniques for conveying epistemological truths.

Spark was born in Edinburgh of a Jewish father and a Christian mother. Her mixed religious parentage influenced her deeply, as is revealed in her story "The Gentile Jewess" and in the novel *The Mandelbaum Gate* (1965). Spark left for Rhodesia when she was 19 and was married there. Many of her stories are set in Africa against the backdrop of British colonial rule. Spark returned to England in 1944, her marriage having broken up. She held a variety of writing jobs during World War II, working in a branch of the Intelligence Service, at the press offices of other organizations, and as editor of the *Poetry Review* for a year.

In 1951, Spark entered a short story competition organized by the *Observer* and won the first prize for the story "The Seraph and the Zambesi," which, as the title indicates, was a combination of realistic, fantastic, and supernatural strands. In 1954 Spark was received into the Roman Catholic Church. In her autobiography, *Curriculum Vitae* (1992), Spark acknowledged that her conversion decidedly influenced her creativity and literary talent. Her first novel, *The Comforters,* was published in 1957, and the appreciative response it received established Spark's reputation as a novelist in the literary world. Spark wrote 22 novels, most famously, *The Pride of Miss Jean Brodie,* and published several editions of her short stories.

The form of the short story is suited to Spark's writing style thanks to her economy of expression and her use of irony and contingency as the pivot of her plots. The fantastic often occurs in Spark's stories, a mode of fiction in which the possible and the impossible coexist, baffling the characters, the reader, and at times the narrator. Sinister coincidences recur in Spark's stories, and supernatural undercurrents lurk beneath the surface. Spark subverts the traditional narrative form by using of time shifts, giving away suspense, and blurring the margins between fantasy and reality. Her fiction has also been seen as significant for its engagement with the social, cultural, and intellectual issues of the post-1945 period, which at times shape the entire narrative.

Spark's story "Bang-Bang You're Dead" alternates descriptions of an old film reel as it is being watched with traditional third-person narration relating events in the life of a young girl, Sybil, living in an African colony and her look-alike, Désirée. Here a childhood mock-shooting game is eerily replicated in the later life of the girls, causing gruesome consequences. "The Portobello Road" is a tale of deceit, malice, and murder narrated in the first person by a ghost; it mingles realism with the paranormal. "The Black Madonna" uses irony as a tool to denounce the human inclination to question Divine Will and to represent racial prejudice. "The Go-Away Bird" contrasts a British African colony with Britain and satirizes the exploitative nature of sophisticated societies as well as the limited awareness of human beings. (See also "You Should Have Seen the Mess," "The house of the Famous Poet.")

BIBLIOGRAPHY

Cheyette, Bryan. *Muriel Spark.* Writers and Their Work. Devon, England: Northcote, 2000.

Mengham, Rod. "1973 The End of History: Cultural Change According to Muriel Spark." In *An Introduction to Contemporary Fiction,* 123–134. Cambridge: Polity, 1999.

Spark, Muriel. *All the Stories of Muriel Spark.* New York: Norton, 2001.

———. *The Complete Short Stories.* London: Penguin, 2001.

———. *Open to the Public: New and Collected Short Stories.* New York: New Directions, 1997.

———. *The Young Man Who Discovered the Secret of Life and Other Stories.* London: Travelman, 1999.

Preeti Bhatt

SPEAKING WITH THE ANGEL Nick Hornby (2000)

Speaking with the Angel is the result of editor Nick Hornby's request to a group of writer friends to help in a charity with which he was personally involved. Hornby is the father of an autistic boy, and part of the profits from the anthology went to a London school for autistic children. This collection, therefore, was inspired by extraliterary concerns. But *Speaking with the Angel* is atypical in other senses as well. There is no common factor linking the stories of the collection: The pieces do not follow a previously designed set of rules, as in the anthology *All Hail the New Puritans* (2000); nor do they revolve around the same subject matter, as in *Disco Biscuits* (1999); nor is there any similarity in the geographical origin of the contributors, as in *England Calling* (2001).

The volume edited by Hornby is even more exceptional as not all the contributors are habitual writers of short fiction. Of the 12 authors involved in the project (Hornby included), only five of them can claim short story writing among their creative interests: Melissa Bank, Zadie Smith, Nick Hornby, Dave Eggers, and Irvine Welsh. Roddy Doyle has occasionally produced a story for a collective volume, but he is above all a novelist. Robert Harris, Helen Fielding, and John O'Farrell are also novelists. The list of contributors also includes a sports columnist, Giles Smith; a scriptwriter, Patrick Marber; and an actor, Colin Firth. As a result of this heterogeneous group of authors, the stories in the collection stand out for their great disparity of styles and attitudes: Robert Harris's piece is a political satire, a *divertimento.* Zadie Smith's story could have fit into any anthology by young authors of the same period. It fulfills, for instance, the requirements of the New Puritans' manifesto. Helen Fielding's contribution deals with the weapons of seduction used by women and could easily have been published in a woman's magazine. These are but three examples of the different directions in which the collection points, but they show that, from a literary point of view, it is an irregular volume.

Despite the outstanding variety of the stories, if there is something close to a predominant tone in the anthology it is that of controlled transgression. Frank O'Connor (4) argued that the territory of the short story belonged to a submerged population group, but a significant number of the protagonists of the stories in *Speaking with the Angel* are comfortably ensconced in the middle classes. Many of the characters in these stories have a glimpse of a wild life outside their well-established routines: A prime minister escapes temporarily from his security service; two teenagers lose their virginity; a middle-aged man finds a breach in his solid existence in the form of a rat. But things usually return to normal. Only two of the authors in the volume transgress the limits of normalcy and in so doing connect their stories with one of the touchstones of the genre itself, what Claire Larriere has defined as "a voice of rebellion" (196) that characterizes the short story. Eggers writes a brilliant, weird, and fantastic story about a dog who considers his life from eternity. The brio and energy of his discourse manages to transmit a full range of purely physical emotions. On the other side of the spectrum, Welsh produces a grotesque and sardonic story of a young man who is punished after his death for his homophobic attitudes. The Scottish author's contribution may be thought by some to surpass the limits of political correctness and good taste, but it also dares to play with conventions relating to time and space. The stories by Eggers and Welsh, in short, add spice to a reasonably well-seasoned collection.

BIBLIOGRAPHY

Bell, Julia, and Jackie Gay, eds. *England Calling.* 2001. London: Phoenix, 2002.

Blincoe, Nicholas, and Matt Thorne, eds. *All Hail the New Puritans.* London: Fourth Estate, 2000.

Champion, Sarah, ed. *Disco Biscuits.* London: Sceptre, 1999.

Hornby, Nick, ed. *Speaking with the Angel.* London: Penguin, 2000.

Larriere, Claire. "The Future of the Short Story: A Tentative Approach." In *The Tales We Tell: Perspectives on the Short Story,* edited by Barbara Lounsberry, Susan Lohafer, Mary Rohrberger, Stephen Pett, and R. C. Feddersen, 195–199. Westport, Conn., and London: Greenwood Press, 1998.

O'Connor, Frank. *The Lonely Voice: A Study of the Short Story.* 1962. Cork, Ireland: Cork City Council, 2003.

José Francisco Fernández

"SQUAW, THE" BRAM STOKER (1893)

An unseasonable short story that BRAM STOKER wrote in 1893 for *Holly Leaves* (the Christmas number of the *Illustrated Sporting and Dramatic News*), "The Squaw" is set in Nuremberg, a city that Stoker had visited in 1885. A self-regarding, unnamed Englishman who is touring the region with his new bride, Amelia, narrates it. Also among the party is a boastful, uncouth man from Bleeding Gulch, Nebraska, Elias P. Hutcheson, who regales his companions with stories of his adventures in the American West and his cruel treatment of Native Americans. While visiting the city's medieval castle, the three tourists climb up to the battlements. Looking down they see a mother cat on the ground playing with her kitten. Hutcheson drops a pebble down to help the play but misjudges his aim, and the stone crushes the kitten's skull. The mother cat glares at Hutcheson, licks the kitten's wound, and, realizing that it is dead, tries to climb up the wall looking "the perfect incarnation of hate." The angry cat prompts Hutcheson to remember his encounters with the Native Indian Apaches and Comanches and, in particular, an Indian squaw who had lingered over the torture of a "half-breed" who had killed her papoose. The cat stalks Hutcheson, following him and his English companions into the notorious torture tower. Among the gruesome items on display is the infamous Iron Virgin, a "rudely shaped figure of a woman . . . Mrs. Noah in the children's Ark." The tourists learn that in earlier, less civilized times, the prisoner used to be put inside the heavy iron sarcophagus, whose door in front was operated by a rope attached to a pulley system. The queasy twist to the tale comes when Hutcheson insists on climbing into the contraption. As the attendant slowly feeds the rope, the vengeful mother cat appears. She springs at the attendant, who lets go of the rope. Inside, Hutcheson far from enjoying his deadly coupling, is impaled and castrated and his skull is crushed. The narrator retrieves the bloody corpse, and immediately the mother cat sits on it licking the blood that "trickled through the gashed socket of his eyes." Furious at another man's being unmanned at the hands of the unholy alliance of the iron woman and the cat, the narrator seizes an old executioner's sword and cuts the cat in two. "No one will call me cruel for doing so," he assures us.

As Lillian Nayder has noted, crucial to this gruesome story is the obvious anxiety about powerful women. According to Nayder, Hutcheson represents the colonist-as-rapist, who takes virgin territory and is subsequently punished. The story's fears about women's sexuality (figured in the Iron Virgin) invite Freudian readings. They are also intertwined with a wider anxiety about the figure of the murderous mother, Amelia, who stands at the center of middle-class ideology as the touchstone of moral and familial virtue. This story is also disturbing because it invites us to identify totally with the narrator's point of view and embrace his system of values. The thrust of his ideology seems plain—women's capacity for monstrosity and the need to keep a vigilant watch on them.

BIBLIOGRAPHY

Hughes, William, and Andrew Smith, eds. *Bram Stoker: History, Psychoanalysis and the Gothic*. London: Macmillan, 1998.

Nayder, Lilian. "Virgin Territory and the Iron Virgin: Engendering the Empire in Bram Stoker's *The Squaw*." In *Maternal Instincts: Versions of Motherhood and Sexuality in Britain 1875–1925,* edited by Claudia Nelson and Ann Sumner Holmes, 75–97. New York: St. Martin's, 1995.

Stoker, Bram. *Dracula's Guest and Other Weird Stories*. London: George Routledge, 1914.

Andrew Maunder

STATE OF THE ART, THE Iain M. Banks (1991)   *The State of the Art* was Iain M. Banks's fourth publication and is his only collection of short stories to date. The collection is divided into one novella, *The State of the Art,* and seven other short stories, ranging from gothic horror to SCIENCE FICTION to political polemic, which further advance the already substantial corpus of writing about The Culture, Banks's vision of a Utopian society.

"Road of Skulls" is the first story in this collection and portrays two drunken peasants, Mc9 and his anonymous companion, riding in a beast-drawn cart toward an unnamed city that is moving away from them as swiftly as they approach it. The Road of Skulls of the title is constructed out of people who have opposed the empire and have consequently been vanquished. This is a brief but dark satire exploring Banks's fascination with the gothic, which recurs in his more conventional fiction, including such novels as *Song of Stone* (1997) and *The Wasp Factory* (1984).

"A Gift from the Culture" is a morality tale that adds further to Banks's analysis of the contradictions which occur in the utopian society of The Culture. Wrobik, a former woman, former Culture citizen who has changed into a homosexual living in the Free City of Vreccis, "where nothing is free"(13), is being blackmailed into carrying out an assassination attempt by attacking a starship carrying the city's returning admiral. It transpires that the starship will also be carrying an esteemed member of The Culture, therefore forcing Wrobik to decide whether to pay off his debt, leave his lover, and destroy the ship

or to escape from the city and remain loyal to his former Culture life. In the end the ship is destroyed, and Banks's customary political commentary informs the subtext of the final lines: "I could still see the line of light that had briefly joined me to the starship; bright path indeed. . . . A bright path in the soft darkness of the mind. I raced down to join all the other poor folk on the run" (28).

The novella *The State of the Art* is another example of Banks's strong socialist perspective. He portrays Earth in the political upheaval of 1977, told by the drone Dziet Sma, who finds that an ally has "gone native." To rescue this ally, Dziet must endure the hypocrisy, empty rhetoric, and strange "humanish" activities of the humans. At one point the Earth is referred to as "more dross than anything else," and this novella seems to have provided the starting point for such later work as *The Player of Games* (1992) or *Against a Dark Background* (1995).

BIBLIOGRAPHY

Banks, Iain M. *The State of the Art*. London: Orbit, 1991.

Martin Colebrook

STEVENSON, ROBERT LOUIS (1850–1894)   Stevenson wrote travel tales, letters, fables, essays, and poetry but remains best known for his fiction, most of which appeared in short story and short novel form. He was born in Edinburgh on November 13, 1850, into a well-to-do and strongly religious family of lighthouse and harbor engineers. When he was a child, frequent ill-health enforced prolonged periods of physical inactivity but stimulated his imagination in stories of fantasy and adventure. Later he studied first engineering and then law at Edinburgh University and also began to follow his inclination to be a writer, publishing articles and essays in journals. In 1873, following a major dispute with his father over his increasing agnosticism, he left Edinburgh and headed eventually to France, where he fell in love with a married American woman, Fanny Osbourne. His travels in Europe led to his first notable literary successes, the travel books *An Inland Voyage* (1878) and *Travels with a Donkey* (1879). *Edinburgh: Picturesque Notes* also appeared in 1878. In 1879 he married the now-

divorced Fanny in America and returned to Britain, where he was reconciled with his father. In 1881, a collection of his essays, *Virginibus Puersique,* was published; he also began his celebrated pirate yarn *Treasure Island* (published in 1883). The following year saw the publication of *New Arabian Nights,* in which he consciously imitated the romance formula of the famous Oriental tales to describe a series of colorful adventures in contemporary London. In the summer of the same year he wrote "THRAWN JANET," one of his best-known works. Rendered superbly for the most part in Scots dialect, it is the story of a small Scottish parish in bygone days where a woman is believed to be in league with the devil. It was published in the 1887 collection *The Merry Men and Other Tales and Fables,* which includes two other tales of supernatural interest: "Markheim," about a murderer confronted by a strange visitor, and "Olalla," a kind of vampire tale (though it lacks the lurid sense of the later *Dracula*) about a decaying aristocratic Spanish family, one of whom, at least, displays a predilection for sucking human blood.

In 1886, two texts appeared that cemented Stevenson's reputation as one of the leading writers of the day: the Scottish historical romance *Kidnapped* and *The STRANGE CASE OF DR. JEKYLL AND MR. HYDE,* the perennially popular tale of a doctor, who by means of a drug, periodically changes into and is ultimately consumed by his bestial alter-ego. The text demonstrates Stevenson's abiding interest in the nature of evil, which probably arose from his Calvinist upbringing; it is also notable for the way it interrogates Victorian ideals of respectability and propriety. Other themes that emerge include the troubled father-and-son relationship, a recurrent theme in Stevenson's fiction, perhaps understandably in view of his own experiences; here Jekyll is father and Hyde is rebellious son. Not the least interesting aspect of the story is its setting: Nominally London, it has, as many critics have noticed, a distinct Edinburgh feel. Stevenson also used an Edinburgh setting for his grisliest tale, "The Body Snatcher," based on the exploits of the infamous grave-robbing pair Burke and Hare. The story appeared in the posthumous 1905 collection *Tales and Fantasies* and often features in gothic and ghost story anthologies.

Stevenson also continued writing essays, many of which engaged current literary issues, most notably the vigorous debate between realism and romance. One of the most important is "A Humble Remonstrance," written in 1884 in response to HENRY JAMES's "The Art of Fiction" and later collected in *Memories and Portraits* (1887). It argues cogently that literature is, in essence, artifice and cannot be like life, as James would have it. Out of this a correspondence and friendship began between the two writers.

In 1887 Stevenson went to America and the South Seas, settling at last in Samoa, where he found the climate exceptionally genial for his continuing poor health. This period saw him return to preoccupations with his native land in the historical novels *The Master of Ballantrae* (1889); *Catriona* (1893), a sequel to *Kidnapped;* and the unfinished *St Ives* and *Weir of Hermiston.* But he also produced important factual accounts of the Pacific, *A Footnote to History* (1892) and *In the South Seas* (1896), and two pieces of fiction that are now counted among his most significant works, "The BEACH OF FALESÁ" (1892) and *The Ebb Tide* (1894). Both provide damning pictures of the colonial enterprise in the Pacific. The former proved especially controversial for its time, as it uncovers the colonial corruption and miscegenation that was rife in the area. It appeared in the 1893 collection *Island Nights' Entertainments,* alongside "The Bottle Imp" and "The Isle of Voices," two stories that draw on Polynesian traditions.

Stevenson died suddenly at his Samoan estate, Vailima, on December 3, 1894, of a brain haemorrhage. A rash of glowing biographies and recollections of his life followed, which built up a picture of a romantically restless and roving figure and prompted an inevitable critical backlash in due course. His storytelling gifts—the economical yet elegant prose style, skillful delineation of character, and compelling plots—have never been in much doubt. However, largely because of his preferred choice of material, he has often been regarded as being no more than a romancer and entertainer. That said, scholars are now taking note of more modern aspects of his work—his critique of imperialism in his South Sea writings, for one. Moreover, he has attracted greater attention as a literary theorist; although he did not really experiment with the form of the short story or novel, he had a keen awareness of the mechanics of storytelling, as several of his essays witness.

BIBLIOGRAPHY

Gray, William. *Robert Louis Stevenson: A Literary Life.* Basingstoke, England: Palgrave, 2004.

Maixner, Paul, ed. *Robert Louis Stevenson: The Critical Heritage.* London: Routledge and Kegan Paul, 1981.

Orel, Harold. *The Victorian Short Story.* Cambridge and New York: Cambridge University Press, 1986, 115–137.

Sandison, Alan. *Robert Louis Stevenson and the Appearance of Modernism: A Future Feeling.* Basingstoke, England: MacMillan, 1996.

Stevenson, Robert Louis. *The Ebb-Tide.* London: Heinemann, 1894.

———. *Island Nights Entertainments.* London: Cassell, 1893.

———. *Memories and Portraits.* London: Chatto and Windus, 1887.

———. *The Merry Men and other Tales and Fables.* London: Chatto and Windus, 1887.

———. *The Story of a Lie.* London: Cassell, 1883.

———. *The Strange Case of Dr. Jekyll and Mr. Hyde.* London: Longmans, Green, 1886.

———. *Treasure Island.* London: Cassell, 1883.

———. *Weir of Hermiston: An Unfinished Romance.* London: Chatto and Windus, 1896.

Gurdip Panesar

STOKER, BRAM (1847–1912)

Born into an Irish-Protestant family at Clontarf near Dublin, Abraham ("Bram") Stoker grew up in modest circumstances, as the third child of Abraham Stoker, a civil service clerk, and his wife Charlotte Blake Thornley. He was a sickly child but by 1864, however, he seems to have recovered sufficiently to enter Trinity College, Dublin, where he became a prize-winning athlete and cultivated the image of a hearty, masculine sportsman, attributes that he would also bestow on the heroes of his novels. When, in 1870, Stoker graduated with an M.A. in mathematics, he dutifully followed his father into the civil service. He also took on the role of (unpaid) drama critic of the *Dublin Evening Mail* and began contributing stories to magazines. He formed a passionate attachment to Walt Whitman, and in 1876 he had an emotional first meeting with the actor Henry Irving. Two years later Stoker eagerly accepted the invitation to become business manager for Irving's new company at London's Lyceum Theatre. He left his job and hurriedly married his fiancée, Florence Balcombe (who counted OSCAR WILDE among her former suitors).

Stoker worked devotedly for Irving for 28 years, but he also found time for active literary career, writing more than 30 short stories and 12 novels. His first novella, *The Primrose Path,* a violent antialcohol story about Irish immigrants in London, was serialized in the Dublin-based *Shamrock* magazine in 1875. The second story written for the *Shamrock,* "Buried Treasures," was published in 1875 and was the first of Stoker's adventure stories. Stoker's commitments to Irving prevented him from writing for most of the 1880s, but in the 1890s and 1900s he began writing again. *The Snake's Pass* was published in 1890, followed by *The Watter's Mou* (1894), *The Shoulder of Shasta* (1895), *Dracula* (1897), *Miss Betty* (1898), *The Mystery of the Sea* (1902), *The Jewel of the Seven Stars* (1903), *The Man* (1905), *Lady Athlyne* (1908), *The Lady of the Shroud,* and his swan song, *The Lair of the White Worm* (1911). The quality of these works varies enormously, but their diversity is a reminder that Stoker is a figure who cannot be conveniently classified with a single label. He was a very adaptable writer who could move between different genres—adventure stories, historical romances, NEW WOMAN fiction. Stoker's most famous (and much-filmed) novel *Dracula* has been analyzed as a piece of gothic fiction but also as a symbolic text whose vampires and monsters express some of the wider fears coming to the surface in the Britain of 1897.

Stoker's diverse output also included short stories written expressly for the expanding MAGAZINE market. Eventually he had enough to publish three collections of short stories. *Under the Sunset* (1882) is a series of dark allegorical tales for children set in a mythic land that is bordered by a dark wilderness ruled over by the King of Death. In *Snowbound: Records of a Theatrical Touring Party* (1908), a group of actors and backstage crew take turns relating weird stories from their past, which encompass murder and adultery. *Dracula's Guest* (1914) was published posthumously and includes the title story, which originated as part of *Dracula* but did not make it into the final version. The stories cover a remarkably wide range of subjects: murder, adultery, degeneration, love, adventure, betrayal, and weird or supernatural events—haunting, the return of the dead, second sight, and doubles. Like the novels, they interweave ideas taken from different sources—racial theory, international politics, sexology, and psychology. They all have very different settings: "The SECRET OF THE GROWING GOLD" has an aristocratic setting; "The SQUAW" (1893) is a horrifying account of the death of an American tourist in Nuremberg; "The Coming of Abel Behenna" (1914) is a story about a man's return from the dead and is set in small fishing community in rural Cornwall. Some critics have given biographical readings of Stoker, suggesting that Stoker's use of the family as an organizing theme in many of these stories and his dramatization of the darker side of male-female relations were prompted by his own experiences as son, husband, and employee or were even a kind of private therapy—a way of tackling his own personal ghosts and sexual hang-ups. Certainly these stories tend to present a very bleak vision of family life: The domestic realm is a space of safety but also of danger, whose boundaries are shifting and unstable. They focus in uncomfortable ways on the problematics of sexual passion and marriage and on homes in which violence, or the possibility of violence, is always lurking. A key presence is the figure of the female monster. In the much-anthologized story "The Squaw," the "savage" malevolent mother of the title is the starting point for interrogating the symbolic function of the mother, and the female rebellion that follows is not only political but also biological. Stoker's short stories are often overlooked, but they are interesting in their own right as texts that test some of the themes, situations, characters, and techniques that recur in his full-length novels.

BIBLIOGRAPHY

Hughes, William, and Andrew Smith. *Bram Stoker: History, Pyschoanalysis and the Gothic.* London: Macmillan, 1998.

Glover, David. *Vampires, Mummies and Liberals: Bram Stoker and the Politics of Popular Fiction.* Durham, N.C.: Duke University Press, 1996.

Hughes, William. *Beyond Dracula.* London: Macmillan, 2000.

Stoker, Bram. *Dracula.* London: A. Constable & Co., 1897.

———. *Dracula's Guest and Other Weird Stories.* London: George Routledge, 1914.

———. *Snowbound. The Record of a Theatrical Touring Party.* London: Collier, 1908.

———. *Under the Sunset.* London: Sampson Low, 1882.

Andrew Maunder

"STOLEN LETTER, THE" WILKIE COLLINS (1854)

"The Stolen Letter" was originally published as "The Fourth Poor Traveller" in *The Seven Poor Travellers,* the extra Christmas number of CHARLES DICKENS's *Household Words* (December 1854). At this time, WILKIE COLLINS was a protégé of Dickens. The story was subsequently reprinted in *After Dark* (1856) as "The Lawyer's Story of a Stolen Letter."

While sitting for his portrait, an attorney, Mr. Boxsious, recounts the time he helped out his young friend, Mr. Frank Galtiffe. In his story, Frank, the son of a rich country squire, falls in love with his younger sister's governess and is intent on marrying her. This alliance, however, does not meet the approval of his father, who takes it upon himself to send the governess, Miss Smith, away with first-rate references and a generous monetary compensation. Mr. Frank is not one to give up so easily; he follows the governess and threatens to take his own life if he is prevented from marrying his beloved. The old squire finally concedes to the engagement when he finds out that the poor young governess's deceased father had come from a "good" family and had served in the army before becoming a wine merchant.

Preparations are made for the wedding day, including an announcement in the county paper that highlights the superior pedigree of the governess's father, though omitting the part about his subsequent career path. In the meantime, however, Mr. Frank receives a disturbing note. The sender claims to have a letter in his possession that implicates the governess's father in an attempted forgery. This letter, he threatens, will be turned over to the local newspaper unless he receives payment of £500.

The lawyer comes to Mr. Frank's aid and offers to retrieve the letter from the blackmailer. If he succeeds, Mr. Frank will pay the lawyer the £500; if he does not obtain the incriminating document, his professional services are free. With the aid of two servants, the lawyer executes an elaborate search-and-surveillance plan to gain access to the blackmailer's rooms and steal back the letter. Using the only clue he has at hand, a puzzling numerical inscription, Boxsious demonstrates his remarkable powers of deduction in recovering the original letter. At first he meticulously searches, "on the usual plan," every possible inch of the room: designs on the wallpaper, the placement and construction of the furniture, the window counterpane, even the fringes on the bed, all to no avail. Then he chastises himself for almost overlooking the obvious, the place where he was standing—the carpet. By applying the numerical inscription "5 alone" and "4 across" to the pattern in the carpet, he discovers the hiding place of the original letter. Ultimately, he turns the tables on the blackmailer—"a nice irritating little plan"—by replacing the letter from beneath the carpet with a piece of paper on which he has inscribed, "change for a five hundred pound note." The marriage of Mr. Frank to the governess can thus take place without the threat of scandal, while the duped blackmailer quietly slips out of town, presumably never to be seen or heard from again.

Though clearly influenced by Edgar Allan Poe's "The Purloined Letter" (1845), "A Stolen Letter" is an early example of Collins's numerous and varied contributions to the genre of detection fiction. While the detective work of "A Stolen Letter" is performed expertly by a respectable and professional male, the lawyer Mr. Boxsious, in much of Collins's subsequent fiction (his short stories and his novels) acts of ratiocination are performed by a motley (and often transgressive) cast of amateur detectives, who in various ways outwit their social and intellectual superiors in the course of their investigations. The stolen letter, of course, serves as a motif that runs throughout Collins's fiction as well: the buried writing or "dead secret" that will not remain hidden.

BIBLIOGRAPHY

Collins, Wilkie. *Complete Short Fiction*. London: Constable. 1998.

Maria Bachman

"STORY OF A NON-MARRYING MAN, THE" Doris Lessing (1973)

Published in 1973 in *The Sun between Their Feet,* the second volume of Doris Lessing's *Collected African Stories,* "The Story of a Non-marrying Man" is paradoxically titled since it concerns a man who has in fact married bigamously many times. The story opens with an adult narrator recounting a time from her childhood on a South African farm when an aging vagrant, Johnny Blakeworthy, called on her parent's hospitality and stayed with them for a night. This being an unremarkable occurrence in the 1930s Depression, the experience is remembered by the narrator only because of the letter sent by Johnny a few days later, thanking the family for their hospitality. It was a "bread and butter letter" (31), as the narrator calls it, a sign of Johnny's now long-distant upbringing as a polite English boy. Years later, now a young woman, the narrator hears a story of a friend's aunt who had been happily married for a number of years to man called Johnny, only to have him walk out on her without explanation, leaving only a letter thanking her for a nice time, "like a letter after a party or something" (32). The man, it turned out, was already married. Eventually the narrator uncovers the story of Johnny Blakeworthy through a short story in a local newspaper: Johnny has left a trail of "wives" across Southern Africa, and the pattern is always the same: The women have considered Johnny a good husband and then have been shocked by his sudden departure followed only by his "thank you" letter which despite its good intentions, has wounded them with its implication that he was only ever a guest in their lives.

In Lessing's novels marriage is frequently portrayed as an enclosure for women (Budhos, viii). Here, the same is true for the man. A predominant theme in the story is that of "going native." The aging Johnny whom the narrator meets "at the end of his life" and "at the beginning of mine" (28) has discarded the paraphernalia of life in white society and appears to live a nomadic existence, living on maize-meal porridge as the Africans do. Later we learn that he lives in an African settlement, living "in kindness" (40) with an African woman whom the community elders have chosen for him. One of the most interesting allusions in Lessing's economic but richly suggestive prose comes when the narrator refers to white society's attitude toward going native. Alongside the anger—the white man gone native perhaps fails to uphold the distinctions that racist ideology demands—is a "bitter envy" (29), as if they too have yearned for the lifting of the restrictions of life in colonial society.

The word "marrying" takes on a larger significance in the story than the uniting of husband and wife and should perhaps be read instead as any act of joining or fixing together that might be considered constraining. Johnny is a drifter who has refused to be married to any place, occupation, or relationship in a white town life that he finds "suffocating" (40). As a figure in the text, he also resists being married to any one narrative. Johnny is an elusive character who is only partially captured through the multiple narratives that structure the text. His story is told in fragments by the anonymous narrator, by the narrating "I" of the newspaper fiction, by the "true-life" account of its author, and in the reported stories of Johnny's fictional and real wives. Johnny is the only person not to tell his story, writing only his "thank you" letters to the women he possibly loved but could not stay with. "The Story of a Non-marrying man" is in some ways a narrative about a man who eludes narrative, leaving only traces to be interpreted by those who are established in the white society, for which the figure that rejects its values exerts a powerful fascination.

BIBLIOGRAPHY

Budhos, Shirley. *The Theme of Enclosure in Selected Works of Doris Lessing.* New York: Whitson, 1987.

Lessing, Doris. *The Sun between Their Feet: Collected African Stories.* Vol. 2. London: Michael Joseph, 1973.

Victoria Margree

"STORY OF A PANIC, THE" E. M. FORSTER (1904)

When, at age 22, E. M. FORSTER graduated from Cambridge University, a legacy from his aunt gave him the freedom to indulge his passion for European travel, particularly to Italy, something that makes itself felt in much of his work. Returning to England in 1903, Forster began writing in earnest, and in 1904 the *Independent Review* accepted "The Story of a Panic" for publication. This early story contains many of the ideas that resurface in later works: A blinkered middle-class Englishman (or woman) is shaken out of his (or her) complacency by an encounter with a member of a different social group or, if the setting is another country, with a foreigner. During a holiday in Italy, Eustace, the young hero, is liberated by an encounter with the half-man/half-goat god Pan. Eustace then astounds his companions by flinging his arms around a young Italian waiter, Gennaro. The story ends in tragedy when Gennaro is killed after trying to rescue Eustace, who has been locked in his room by his worried traveling companions. The narrowness of the English is harshly exposed, and their bigoted and stiff codes of behavior compare unfavorably with the relaxed attitudes of the Italians. Other stories in the collection in which this story later appeared, *The Celestial Omnibus and other Stories* (1911), explore this theme, notably "The OTHER SIDE OF THE HEDGE" and "The ROAD FROM COLONUS." In "The Story of a Panic," Forster also employs, for the first time, one of his favorite devices: characters as uncomprehending narrators, "treacherously involved in the story's events, but . . . unwittingly instrumental in the triumphant conclusion" (Herz, 30).

BIBLIOGRAPHY

Forster, E. M. *The Celestial Omnibus and Other Stories.* London: Sidgwick and Jackson, 1911.

Herz, Judith Scherer. *The Short Narratives of E. M. Forster.* London: Macmillan, 1988.

Andrew Maunder

"STORY OF THE ELDEST PRINCESS, THE" A. S. BYATT (1994)

"The Story of the Eldest Princess" is one of the five stories that appeared in A. S. BYATT's collection *The Djinn in the Nightingale's Eye* (1994). It is an ostensible fairy tale that in fact subverts the assumptions of the genre in sometimes explicit, sometimes subtle ways. One of the consequences of this subversion is self-reflexivity; another is a feminist rewriting of the conventions of the genre. Two other stories in the same collection, "Gode's Story" and "The Glass Coffin," first appeared in Byatt's Booker Prize–winning novel, *Possession* (1990). With "Dragons' Breath" and "The Djinn in the Nightingale's Eye," this collection takes a post-Victorian and occasionally postmodern look at the fairy tale.

"The Story of the Eldest Princess" begins with the quintessential fairy-tale opening sentence: "Once upon a time, in a kingdom between the sea and the mountains, between the forest and the desert, there lived a King and a Queen with three daughters" (41). Divested of specifics like time, place, and individual personalities, this incipit is the formula for a typical fairy tale. The plot revolves around a quest, usual in fairy tales. The reason for the quest is self-evidently trivial: The sky has begun to change color. It is no longer blue but green, and the people hold the king and the queen responsible.

The eldest princess, as is the wont in fairy tales, is the first to set off on the quest to bring back the single silver bird that will turn the sky blue. At this point the narrative informs us that the princess is a reader of books and is thus aware of the pattern of fairy-tale narratives. In these tales the eldest princess and the second invariably fail in fulfilling the terms of the quest and are punished for their transgressions, while the third princess succeeds in the quest as well as in redeeming her sisters. The eldest princess wants to reject this predestined role and choose her own destiny. The rest of the story is about the ways in which the eldest princess makes decisions, each time ruling against precedents and sometimes even against counsel, thereby asserting her independence. In the process she strays from the road and into the forest, rescuing a wounded scorpion, a toad, and a cockroach before reaching the haven of the old woman, where they are all healed.

A notable anti-fairy-tale move the princess makes is to reject a potential lover and husband, whom she could perhaps have elevated to the rank of prince. But after his innate cruelty is revealed by the creatures she rescues, the princess rejects marriage, another patriarchal destiny that the conventional fairy tale has determined for its princesses. In the encounter with the toad in another instance, the toad tells the princess that she must not suppose that he will transform into a handsome prince "or any such nonsense" (55). This is a direct allusion to many fairy tales in which the princess kisses the toad and he changes into a charming prince.

Needless to state, the princess accepts his terms while helping him.

"The Story of the Eldest Princess" ends with the protagonist finding her destiny in the cottage of the old woman, who applauds the eldest princess's intelligence in recognizing that she was trapped in a story that she could choose to leave, and who also tells stories to explain the eventual fate of the other two princesses. The quest is fulfilled by the second princess, but its fulfillment is token rather than real: Soon enough people begin to grumble against the blue sky, as they miss the green one that they had become familiar with.

One of the most obvious ways in which "The Story of the Eldest Princess" challenges the genre of the fairy tale is by liberating the central character from her fixed role and by letting her get ahead of the plot. When she thinks, "I am in a pattern I know" (48), the Princess's knowledge becomes power, and her empowerment is manifested in the way she gives a new life to an old story. "The Story of the Eldest Princess," especially in its ending, is an affirmation of the idea that stories lead to stories and new stories come out of the old.

BIBLIOGRAPHY:

Byatt, A. S. *The Djinn in the Nightingale's Eye: Five Fairy Stories.* London: Chatto & Windus, 1994, 41–72.

———. *Possession: A Romance.* 1990. London: Vintage, 1991.

Sudha Shastri

"STRAIGHT FICTION" Martin Amis (1995)

"Straight Fiction" is not the first story in which Martin Amis depicts an upside-down world in a short story. In "The Time Disease," published in *Einstein's Monsters* (1987), Amis imagines a postnuclear society where to be ill is a sign of health, of being in tune with a sick world where those who suffer from "time" (rosy cheeks, appetite, fits of energy) are condemned to a certain death. In "Career Move" (1992) poets live in luxury, courted by multinational companies, whereas scriptwriters have to wait long years to see their material published in obscure magazines.

In "Straight Fiction," first published in *Esquire* in 1995 and later included in *Heavy Water and Other Stories* (1998), most of the population is gay while heterosexuals are a beleaguered minority who begin to stand up for their rights. Cleve, the protagonist of the story, is scandalized when a famous actor comes out in a magazine as being "totally het" (195). Although the main character prides himself as being a liberal homosexual, he observes with dismay that straight people increasingly show affection in public places; bookshops display sections on straight studies, and on television heterosexual demonstrations are receiving important news coverage: "Here was a big item about Straight Freedom Day, as celebrated in San Francisco, 'the straight capital of the world'" (204).

Not everyone is as tolerant as Cleve, of course. "They sick, men" (205), says Kico, one of the promiscuous acquaintances of Cleve's partner, who believes that heterosexuals should be killed or sent to Madagascar. Things get worse for the straights as a new disease spreads among this layer of the population. "A spokesman for the Anti-Family Church Coalition predictably announced that the straight subculture had brought this scourge on itself" (214).

In "Straight Fiction" and the other stories in which Amis uses such drastic changes of perspective, the author forces the reader to consider his or her everyday assumptions from a fresh approach. Situations normally taken for granted are questioned, prejudices are revealed, and the possibility is raised that some of our interpretations of reality are ideologically biased and therefore subject to change. From a different point of view, "Straight Fiction" is an excellent showcase for Amis's stylistic creativity. Practically every feature that has made him a literary innovator can be found in this narrative. This story is an example of prose in which Amis feels "the need to stamp each sentence with his literary personality," a technique that, according to ADAM MARS-JONES (457), "defeats his ambitions as a literary artist." In any case, verbal excess is Amis's trademark, as he told Christopher Bigsby in an interview: "I don't like this clear-as-a-mountain-creek kind of writing, this vow-of-poverty prose" (179) and in "Straight Fiction" the stylistic explosion takes place in the form of neologisms, puns, tongue twisters, impossible word formations, surprising sound patterns, typographic experiments, etc., apart from his usual recourse to irony, conceit or hyperbole. The reading of this story is an experience that overwhelms the reader.

As usually happens in Amis's work when he exposes a problem in fictional terms, it is not free of controversial aspects. Gay people, who have traditionally been marginalized, here occupy a position of hegemony, but the only female character is the one who worries about domestic chores: "The cooker, the clothes dryer, the conversion of the box room – should she paint it blue or pink?" (214). Furthermore, the author's tendency to sort things out at the end, to put everything back in a "natural" order, casts some doubts on Amis's commitment to a real critique of preconceived ideas.

BIBLIOGRAPHY
Amis, Martin. *Einstein's Monsters.* 1987. London: Penguin, 1988.
———. "Martin Amis Interviewed by Christopher Bigsby." In *New Writing,* edited by Malcolm Bradbury and Judy Cooke, 169–184. London: Minerva and The British Council, 1992.
———. "Straight Fiction." In *Heavy Water and Other Stories,* 195–221. London: Jonathan Cape, 1998.
Mars-Jones, Adam. "Fireworks at the Funeral," *Times Literary Supplement,* 1 May 1987, p. 457.

José Francisco Fernández

STRAND MAGAZINE, THE (JANUARY 1891–MARCH 1950)

When, on December 13, 1949, the *Strand* announced that it would cease publication the following March, a columnist in the *Times* called the monthly "a popular influence of great importance in that lively period of English story-telling . . . which reached its height in the 'nineties.'" From the magazine's inception in January 1891, few could deny either its popular influence or its great importance. Offering what its publisher called "a shilling's worth of reading at half the price," the first issue sold more than 200,000 copies; subsequently, circulation would often reach half a million copies monthly.

Before the *Strand,* the serial novel dominated magazine fiction in Britain. While many British magazines published short fiction, none did so exclusively, and they paid little attention to either the form or its poetics. Publisher George Newnes (1851–1910) had already made a fortune with *Tit-Bits,* a weekly digest of excerpts designed to entertain a newly educated mass market. The *Strand* was supposed to be a more sophisticated production, but Newnes restricted its fiction to short stories in order to appease fickle readers unlikely to keep up with every issue, as well as impatient ones unwilling to wait for the next installment of a serial. By first publishing translated stories from the Continent, the *Strand* popularized conventions of the genre from traditions with established poetics for composition and idioms for critique.

Still, the magazine did not achieve its legendary status until June 1891, when ARTHUR CONAN DOYLE's "A SCANDAL IN BOHEMIA" became the first Sherlock Holmes short story to be published in it. Though issued within the past five years, *The Sign of Four* and *A Study in Scarlet,* book-length works that had featured the detective, had attracted little notice. As a set of related but not serial stories, the Holmes adventures forged a community of readers without necessitating a cohesive, loyal readership—which, paradoxically, the *Strand* attracted anyhow. Doyle later recalled inventing the short story series, featuring "a character which carried through, and yet installments which were each complete in themselves, so that the purchaser was always sure that he could relish the whole contents of the magazine. I believe that I was the first to realize this and "'The Strand Magazine' the first to put it into practice." Through the short story series, the *Strand* redefined the short story as a distinctively British genre and drew to it a readership arguably more loyal than any of the more conventional serial novels had ever enjoyed. In its six decades in print, the magazine included stories by RUDYARD KIPLING, H. G. WELLS, W. SOMERSET MAUGHAM, P. G. WODEHOUSE, Dorothy Sayers, and numerous others.

As the dominant publisher of short stories at a crucial time when the genre's poetics were being defined, the *Strand* attracted many imitators that multiplied its influence in shaping the modern British short story. A revival of the *Strand* launched in Birmingham, Michigan, in 1997 quite appropriately specializes in "short stories," defined as "tales of mystery and suspense."

BIBLIOGRAPHY

Beare, Geraldine. *Index to The Strand Magazine, 1891–1950.* Westport, Conn.: Greenwood, 1982.

Doyle, Arthur Conan. *Memories and Adventures.* Boston: Little, Brown, 1924.

Jackson, Kate. *George Newnes and the New Journalism in Britain, 1880–1910: Culture and Profit.* Aldershot, England: Ashgate, 2001.

Pound, Reginald. *Mirror of the Century: The Strand Magazine 1891–1950.* New York: A. S. Barnes and Co., 1961.

Winnie Chan

STRANGE CASE OF DR. JEKYLL AND MR. HYDE, THE ROBERT LOUIS STEVENSON (1886)

Longman, Green, and Company published ROBERT LOUIS STEVENSON's *The Strange Case of Dr. Jekyll and Mr. Hyde* in 1886 as a "shilling shocker." Stevenson reputedly developed the storyline from a dream he had about a man forced into a cabinet after ingesting a potion that would convert him into a brutal monster. The composition of *Dr. Jekyll and Mr. Hyde* began in September 1885, and the final draft was submitted for publication later that same year. Unlike most 19th-century literary works, Stevenson's manuscript was released in book form instead of being serialized in a popular magazine. The publishers withheld its release until January 1886 because booksellers had already placed their Christmas stock. Within six months, Stevenson's novella sold more than 40,000 copies in England and America.

Dr. Jekyll and Mr. Hyde debates the conflict between good and evil and the correlation among bourgeois values, urban violence, and class structure. Dr. Jekyll is a seemingly placid character whose often-debated scientific research has nonetheless gained him respect amid his peers. The potion that Jekyll develops causes an unexplainable transformation into the violent Mr. Hyde. The Mr. Hyde alter-ego may represent an uncontrollable subconscious desire driven by anger and frustration toward an oppressive English class structure. Hyde's numerous rampages include trampling a young girl and murdering the prominent English politician Sir Danvers. Although Jekyll prefers living the life of "the elderly and discontent doctor" (84), he cannot control his urge for "the liberty, the comparative youth, the light steps, leaping impulses, and secret pleasures" that the Hyde persona offers him. Dr. Jekyll's desired liberty is perhaps caused by the restricted lifestyle that bourgeois cultural codes imposed on English society. Several Victorian social critics maintained that inner-city

London dwellers were a debased life form living in junglelike conditions analogous to those in Africa. In 1890, William Booth, the founder of the Salvation Army, claimed that England needed rescuing from its continually degenerating condition since its citizens were gradually turning into "[a] population trodden with drink, steeped in vice, [and] eaten up by every social and physical malady" (quoted in Stevenson, 183). Stevenson's text describes how hidden desires have always existed in a seemingly perverted civilization.

Literary critics have stressed that Stevenson's success in the "shilling shocker" market both helped and hindered his career. The rapid success of *Dr. Jekyll and Mr. Hyde* led Henry James to remark that Stevenson's novella was at first too popular a work to be comfortably called a masterpiece. Henry James was not questioning Stevenson's talent as a writer but rather was noting that the book's quick popularity defined it as a story that was easily accessible to the mass public.

Playwright Richard Mansfield produced a stage version of *Dr. Jekyll and Mr. Hyde* in 1888. Shortly after Mansfield's play opened, several East End London prostitutes were murdered by a serial killer nicknamed Jack the Ripper. English newspapers initially termed the slayer the "Whitechapel murderer" and "Leather Apron" before settling on "Jack the Ripper." Reporters based their stories on the possible correlation between the killings and Mansfield's theatrical representation of violence. Mansfield's play was eventually closed because such parallels made it seem as though Jack the Ripper was mimicking the violence depicted in Mansfield's play, marking the first time that the concept of Mr. Hyde was used in reference to sequential crime sprees. Reports from the *Daily Telegraph* further damaged the profits for Mansfield's play by stating that "there is no taste for horror" (17) on the London stage. *Dr. Jekyll and Mr. Hyde* remains a significant canonical text that uses its patchwork narrative to explore the conflation of reality and fictional representation that most postmodern writers still examine.

BIBLIOGRAPHY

Caler, Jenni. *The Robert Louis Stevenson Companion.* Edinburgh: P. Harris, 1980.

James, Henry. "Robert Louis Stevenson." Reprinted in *The Strange Case of Dr. Jekyll and Mr. Hyde,* edited by Martin A. Danahay, 140–141. Orchard Park, N.Y.: Broadview Literary Texts, 1999.

Rose, Brian A. *Jekyll and Hyde Adapted: Dramatizations of Cultural Anxiety.* Westport, Conn.: Greenwood, 1996.

Saposnik, Irving S. "The Anatomy of Dr. Jekyll and Mr. Hyde." In *The Definitive Dr. Jekyll and Mr. Hyde Companion,* edited by Harry M. Geduld, 108–117. New York: Garland Publishing, 1983.

Stevenson, Robert Louis. *The Strange Case of Dr. Jekyll and Mr. Hyde.* Edited by Martin A. Danahay, 29–91. Orchard Park, N.Y.: Broadview Literary Texts, 1999.

Wedgewood, Julia. "Appendix F: Contemporary Review April 1886, xlix, 594–5." Reprinted in *The Strange Case of Dr. Jekyll and Mr. Hyde,* edited by Martin A. Danahay, 139–140. Orchard Park, N.Y.: Broadview Literary Texts, 1999.

Gerardo Del Guercio

"STRING OF BEADS, A" W. Somerset Maugham (1943)

A story within a story, "A String of Beads" draws much of its thematic complexity from the counterpoints it provides between the two levels of its narrative. The broader narrative is told in the first person by a male speaker who has been invited to a dinner and has been seated next to a woman named Laura. Almost immediately, she indicates her eagerness to share with him a story that evolved out of an incident at another dinner party. Presumably because he is a writer to whom others are perpetually offering stories, he expresses his hope that she will find something else to talk about.

Despite his obvious reluctance to hear it, she persists with her story. She attended a dinner party at the Livingstones, who, because they had been a guest short, had invited their governess, Miss Robinson, to join the party. Another guest was Count Borselli, a world-renowned expert on gemstones. After confirming that Mrs. Lyngate's pearls were indeed worth the £8,000 she paid for them, he suggested that Miss Robinson's seemingly much more modest string of pearls was actually worth some £50,000. Miss Robinson stated, however, that she paid just 15 shillings for the pearls. As she did so, two men arrived wishing to question her. The assumption that the men were policemen generated speculation among the guests about Miss Robinson's possible criminal activities and criminal acquaintances. But when Miss Robinson shortly returned to the dinner party, she revealed that the two men were actually the jewelers from whom she had bought her inexpensive necklace, which, as Borselli immediately noticed, she was now wearing. When she had taken it back to them to have its clasp repaired, they had mistakenly given her the much more expensive necklace. After she had readily agreed to exchange the necklaces, they had, however, presented her with a reward of £300.

Extending beyond the events of the dinner party, Laura's story hinges on what Miss Robinson eventually did with the £300. When it came time for her vacation, she informed Mrs. Livingstone that she meant to spend the entire sum living in luxury for at least a month at a seaside resort. Before that month was quite up, she informed Mrs. Livingstone that she would not be returning to her position as governess because she had entered another profession. In the meantime, Laura has discovered that Miss Robinson has become a courtesan, living first with a wealthy Argentinian and then leaving him for an even wealthier Greek.

Although the narrator suggests that Laura's story is of little use to him because he has already written several well-known stories featuring necklaces, he does actually use it, recognizing that its point of interest has nothing to do with the string of pearls. Indeed, when Laura goes on to tell him that, for the story to be satisfying, Miss Robinson should not become a wealthy courtesan but should, instead, marry a disabled war veteran who scrapes by on the salary he earns at a bank, he interjects that such a resolution might be rather "dull," and she responds that it would nonetheless be "moral." In the narrator's view, the story is an exposé of Laura's class consciousness and her rigid belief that to act morally is to accept one's place in the hierarchical social structure in which she and the Livingstones conveniently hold a privileged place.

BIBLIOGRAPHY

Maugham, W. Somerset. *The Collected Short Stories.* London: Penguin, 1977.

Martin Kich

STUDY IN SCARLET, A ARTHUR CONAN DOYLE (1887)   A detective fiction novella first pub-

lished by ARTHUR CONAN DOYLE in *Beeton's Christmas Annual,* and published subsequently as a separate edition by Ward, Lock and Company in 1888, *A Study in Scarlet* marks the first appearance of Sherlock Holmes.

The story begins with the narration of Dr. John Watson, an army doctor who, following the battle of Maiwand, has chosen to settle in London. He is introduced to Sherlock Holmes, a man of unusual habits. It becomes clear that Holmes is a consulting detective when he is called upon by the police to investigate the murder of Enoch Drebber in an empty house near Brixton. The police misread the word "Rache" written in blood at the crime scene as "Rachel"; Holmes reads the clue correctly as German for "revenge." Drebber's secretary, Joseph Stangerson, is accused of the murder but is later found murdered. Through the reading of fine details and other investigations, Holmes concludes that the killer is a cab driver, Jefferson Hope. Hope's arrest leads to the second half of the novella, a third-person narrative concerning the foundation of the Mormon community in Utah. Because the father of Hope's fiancée has broken with Mormon tradition, they have murdered him and kidnapped Hope's fiancée. Hope swears revenge against the two prominent conspirators, Drebber and Stangerson, and follows them from America to London. He poisons Drebber, leaving his message written in blood from a nosebleed caused by an aneurism. Hope finds Stangerson and stabs the secretary in self-defence when Stangerson attacks him. The final chapters, again narrated by Watson, describe Holmes's deductions in solving the mystery and relate how Hope dies before facing trial.

Although marking the first appearance of what was to become one of English literature's most famous characters, *A Study in Scarlet* was relatively unsuccessful on first appearance; the popularity usually associated with Holmes did not arise until the *Strand Magazine's* publication of the first series of short stories in 1891 as *The Adventures of Sherlock Holmes.* Doyle had completed the novella in 1886 and had been rejected by three publishers (including the *Cornhill Magazine*) before being accepted by the London firm Ward, Lock and Company, which paid £25 for the copyright on condition that its publication wait until

1887, as (in their words) "the market is flooded at present with cheap fiction."

The story contains many of the elements that would become a feature of the Holmes stories: Holmes's deductive (or more accurately, abductive) method that draws inferences from tiny clues, Watson's narration, and the incompetence of the police, among others. Doyle would use these in his second Holmes novella, *The Sign of Four* (1890), a text with a similar narrative structure to that of *A Study in Scarlet,* in which Watson's narration describing the investigation contains another narrative that describes the actions of the criminal. These narrations correspond to the formalist categories of *szujet* and *fabula,* respectively, as outlined by Tzvetan Todorov in his influential discussion of detective fiction. Significantly for a genre concerned with policing social and national boundaries, the embedded narrations of both stories describe how criminality in London originates from overseas (in *The Sign of Four,* a murderous conspiracy begins in colonial India, in a plot that bears comparison with Wilkie Collins's *The Moonstone* [1868]), and the threat of the criminal foreigner is reiterated throughout the Holmes stories, as it is through much late-Victorian detective fiction. In *A Study in Scarlet,* the idea finds expression through Watson's description of London as "that great cesspool into which all the loungers and idlers of the Empire are irresistibly drained." The novella thus suggests a link between criminality and empire, which would be explored in Doyle's subsequent stories.

BIBLIOGRAPHY

Doyle, Arthur Conan. *A Study in Scarlet.* London: Ward Lock, 1887.

Eco, Umberto, and Thomas A. Sebeok, eds. *The Sign of Three: Dupin, Holmes, Peirce.* Bloomington: Indiana University Press, 1983.

Stashower, Daniel. *Teller of Tales: The Life of Arthur Conan Doyle.* London: Allen Lane, 2000.

Thompson, Jon. *Fiction, Crime and Empire: Clues to Modernism and Postmodernism.* Urbana: Illinois University Press, 1993.

Todorov, Tzvetan. *The Poetics of Prose.* Translated by Richard Howard. New York: Cornell University Press, 1977.

Christopher Pittard

SUFFRAGETTE FICTION   The struggle for women to gain the right to vote was fought not only in the political arena but in literature. Although the suffrage movement can be dated to the mid-19th century, its literature as a distinct category is generally located between 1900 and 1919. Fiction concerned with the suffrage movement should be seen as a part of a wider discourse on the social and political role of women and as a manifestation of the belief that because polite requests for the vote had failed, demands were now in order. The literary importance to the campaign can be seen from the existence of the Women Writers' Suffrage League, founded in 1908 by playwright and novelist Cecily Hamilton. Members were required to have earned payment for their writing, which ensured that they were seen as professional working women who could provide an active voice for the movement.

Suffragette was a term invented in 1906 to describe militant prosuffrage activists, and many suffragette stories focus on women who are storming Parliament or who have been to prison for similarly disruptive offences. Evelyn Sharp's "The Black Spot of the Constituency" involves public speakers who create a bond with their impoverished listeners in part because they, too, have been to Holloway Prison. In many cases, suffragette literature was used as a vehicle for social change in which the message was of primary importance. These works were intended to be accessible to working-class women, so the requirements of telling a clear story surpassed the literary experimentation demanded by modernism.

Some participants in the suffrage movement felt that the restrictions on women as a gender were more important than class barriers, and the fiction demonstrates how women of the middle classes were made aware of the wrongs done not only to them but to working-class women who were unprotected when they worked outside the home. W. L. Courtney, in the title story of his collection *The Soul of a Suffragette,* offers his middle-class heroine a vision of "a great sisterhood, united in aims, fervent and unwearied in well-doing, always ready for sacrifice . . . towards a distant and shining goal." These stories also show a breakdown of barriers between the sexes; both "The Soul of a Suffragette" and Sharp's "The Women at the

Gate" demonstrate how easy it becomes for suffragettes to converse with unknown men when they are thrown together, even as spectators, for the cause.

Suffragette stories were also used as an attempt to dispel the stereotypes of suffragettes as ridiculous, mannish women attempting to encroach on male privilege rather than use their influence within the home. Gertrude Colmore's "Pluck" deliberately mocks the alleged differences between "true" women and unsexed suffragettes, establishing her protagonist as dainty, genteel, and stylish before a man in the room identifies her as a notorious suffragette. The Women Writers' Suffrage League was particularly concerned that suffragette characters should be seen as positive role models, using such portrayals to change social attitudes toward the suffrage cause.

BIBLIOGRAPHY

Courtney, W. L. *The Soul of a Suffregette and Other Stories*. London: Chapman and Hall, 1913.

Joannou, Maroula, and June Purvis, eds. *The Women's Suffrage Movement: New Feminist Perspectives*. Manchester and New York: Manchester University Press, 1998.

Nelson, Carolyn Christensen, ed. *Literature of the Women's Suffrage Campaign in England*. Peterborough, Ontario, and Orchard Park, New York: Broadview Press, 2004.

Norquay, Glenda. *Voices and Votes: A Literary Anthology of the Women's Suffrage Campaign*. Manchester and New York: Manchester University Press, 1995.

Claire Eustace, Joan Ryan, and Laura Ugolini, eds. *A Suffrage Reader: Charting Directions in British Suffrage History*. London and New York: Leicester University Press, 2000.

Tracey Rosenberg

SWIFT, GRAHAM (1949–)

Graham Swift is a major contemporary British author whose reputation has been firmly established by the seven novels he has published to date. Swift is less known for his short fiction since he has published fewer than 20 stories, and all represent his early work. Swift began his apprenticeship as a writer through short fiction at a time when he claims to have had "no conception of how to write a novel" (Hartung-Brückner, 469). In 1982, 11 of Swift's short pieces, almost all previously published in well-established British periodicals and anthologies of new writing, were collected in LEARNING TO SWIM AND OTHER STORIES. These stories are of undeniable merit. In *The Penguin Book of Modern British Short Stories* (1987), a collection of 34 pieces, Malcolm Bradbury includes one of Swift's stories, "Seraglio," as representative of the work of an "outstanding young literary generation."

Swift's short stories challenge the norms and conventions of the genre. The traditional short story, as A. S. BYATT defines it in *The Oxford Book of English Short Stories* (1998), requires "unity of form . . . that only one thing should happen, that an episode or incident should be developed, or an emotion caught, with no space for digression, or change of direction or tone" (xvi). Swift's stories do not follow this norm. Instead, his stories seem to belong to a category that Byatt terms "the great English story" which is "shocking" and "hard to categorise" and that breaks "all the rules of unity of tone and narrative" (xvi).

Born in South London in 1949, Swift belongs, along with MARTIN AMIS, JULIAN BARNES, Kazuo Ishiguro, SALMAN RUSHDIE, and IAN MCEWAN, to a postwar generation of male novelists and short fiction writers who began their literary careers in the 1970s, achieved acclaim in the 1980s, and, since the 1990s, have been considered mainstream. Like most of his fellow writers, Swift has received formal training in literature: Having completed his early schooling at a prestigious public school, Swift went on to study English at the Universities of Cambridge and York for a period of almost 10 years. A thorough education in English literature has provided Swift with what he defines as "a very strong sense of tradition" (Bernard, 223). While departures from realism through metafictional irony and self-conscious paradox are obvious in the confessions of Swift's frequently unreliable narrators, who teeter on the verge of a mental breakdown, his narratives remain as morally committed as any tale by CHARLES DICKENS. The coexistence of opposites in Swift's fiction—the fragmentation, nihilism, and alienation characteristic of modernism along with the humanism and engaging storytelling of realism—appears in the works of his contemporaries, such as Ishiguro and Barnes, as well. Yet Swift is a less prolific, quieter representative of his literary group; he focuses on writing novels. Unlike Barnes or Amis, he has forgone writing short stories, the genre that helped him launch his career, believing that a writer should "concentrate," not "dissipate," his talent (Rosenberg).

Graham Swift's career began in April 1976 with the publication of "The Recreation Ground," a 20-page story in *London Magazine,* which is not included in the collection *Learning to Swim.* Narrated in the first person, this bleak tale illustrates Swift's preoccupation with tormenting father figures within an urban landscape that symbolically reflects the narrator's angst. The unnamed adolescent protagonist strives to liberate himself from an overbearing, violent, sadistic father and a manipulative, neurotic, masochistic mother. Like all of Swift's protagonists in the stories, he seeks escape but remains in awe of "Dad" and imprisoned in the present; his tormented struggle for survival in an alien environment becomes a motif in Swift's early fiction.

In 1982 the critical reception of *Learning to Swim* in Britain was favorable. In the *Times Literary Supplement* Alan Hollinghurst praised the author's "meticulous" manner of analysis, comparing Swift's techniques to those of HENRY JAMES. The *Times* reviewer called the stories "admirable" and "impressive." However, when *Learning to Swim* appeared in the U.S. market in 1985, American reviewers in the *Washington Post* and the *New York Times* gave the stories more mixed reviews.

For a perceptive reader such as fellow author Hilary Mantel, the stories in *Learning to Swim* "reach out beyond their own confines, as if they were trying to become novels." Indeed, these vignettes of existential crisis often deal with events that are barely contained or analyzed in the text. The stories in *Learning to Swim* reveal Swift's preoccupations with the function and modes of narrative, the relationship between the individual and history, and familial oppression and self-induced guilt.

Despite having published 16 stories between 1976 and 1982, Swift has not built a body of short fiction, dedicating himself to writing novels. In a 1994 interview Swift admits that not having written any short stories "for a long time . . . occasionally troubles" him (Hartung-Brückner, 471). Still, the publication of an eight-page piece entitled "Our Nicky's Heart" in the magazine *Granta* in 2000 suggests that Swift may produce more stories in future. In this story the narrator,

Mark Randall, a 38-year-old veterinarian, assumes the observer position, like Derek in "Hoffmeier's Antelope," one of the stories in *Learning to Swim,* while Mark's mother and her other son's "heart" dominate a plot concerned with the aftermath of his adolescent brother's accidental death. The barely disguised sibling rivalry that Mark exhibits is reminiscent of the narrator of "Cliffedge," another of the stories collected in *Learning to Swim.*

Nicky buys a motorcycle but soon afterward has a fatal accident at age 17. At the doctors' request, his mother decides to donate his heart but finds her intense grief at her son's loss suspended by the knowledge that part of Nicky lives on. When the narrator discovers that his brother's heart was transplanted into a female patient of their mother's age, he withholds the truth to spare her from identifying with that patient and wanting to place "Nicky's heart . . . safely inside her." Mark manipulates the facts, becoming a guardian of secrets, aware that this is "the biggest lie of [his] life." Like the narrators of "Cliffedge" and "Hotel," Mark reveals his repression through his serene tone and controlled expression. Concerned with sibling rivalry and using a reluctant narrator, "Our Nicky's Heart" is a typical Swiftian tale on a par with the best of the stories in *Learning to Swim.*

All of Graham Swift's short stories examine human weaknesses in the context of contested family relations. Despite the variety of plots and settings, Swift's protagonists are all tormented: They feel abandoned, insecure, and undeserving. Through intricately structured vignettes from everyday life, most frequently told through first-person narratives, Swift has established himself as an explorer of universal binaries: mortality and posterity, ignorance and knowledge, suffering and guilt. His masterful command of the short story genre ensures he has a place among the more prolific practitioners of his generation.

BIBLIOGRAPHY

Bernard, Catherine. "An Interview with Graham Swift," *Contemporary Literature* 38, no. 2 (1997): 217–231.

Bradbury, Malcolm. "Introduction." *The Penguin Book of Modern British Short Stories,* 11–14. London: Penguin, 1987.

Byatt, A. S. "Introduction." *The Oxford Book of English Short Stories.* Oxford: Oxford University Press, 1998.

Evans, Stuart. "Very Ordinary People," Review of *Learning to Swim*. *Times,* 26 August 1982, p. 6.

Gorra, Michael. "When Life Closes In," Review of *The Sweet-Shop Owner* and *Learning to Swim*. *New York Times Book Review,* 23 June 1985, pp. 11–12.

Hartung-Brückner, Heike. "The Question of History and Writing: An Interview with Graham Swift," *Germanisch-Romanische Monatsschrift* 46 (1996): 469–471.

Hollinghurst, Alan. "Falling Short," Review of *Learning to Swim*. *Times Literary Supplement,* 27 August 1982, p. 920.

Mantel, Hilary. "Blood Ties," Review of *Ever After*. *New York Review of Books,* 11 June 1992, pp. 23–25.

O'Mahony, John. "Triumph of the Common Man." *Guardian* March 1, 2003. Available online. URL: http://books.guardian.co.uk/departments/generalfiction/story/0,,904963,00.html. Accessed June 7, 2006.

Rosenberg, Scott. "Glowing in the Ashes." Interview with Graham Swift. *Salon* 14 (May 6, 1996). Available online. URL: http://archive.salon.com/weekly/swift960506.html. Accessed June 7, 2006.

Swift, Graham. *Last Orders*. London: Picador, 1996.

———. *Learning to Swim and Other Stories*. 1982. London: Heinemann, 1985.

———. *The Light of Day*. London: Hamish Hamilton, 2003.

———. *Out of This World*. London: Penguin, 1980.

———. *The Sweet-Shop Owner*. London: Allen Lane, 1980.

Untitled review of *Learning to Swim*. *Times Literary supplement,* 16 April 1993, p. 22.

Wheeler, Wendy. "Swift, Graham." *The Literary Encyclopedia*. Available online. URL: http://www.LitEncyc.com. Accessed June 7, 2006.

Anastasia Logotheti

T

"TALE, THE" Joseph Conrad **(1917)** In his Preface to *The Nigger of the Narcissus* (1897), Joseph Conrad had coined very early his now famous literary manifesto: "My task which I am trying to achieve is, by the power of the written word to make you hear, to make you feel—it is, before all, to make you *see*. That—and no more, and it is everything." Twenty years later, and after Conrad's most celebrated texts had been published, "The Tale" reads like a rather unclassifiable shorter text that returns to and questions Conrad's essential preoccupation with seeing, vision, and truth.

"The Tale," written in 1917, during World War I, was published posthumously in Conrad's last collection of short stories, *Tales of Hearsay,* in 1925, and is an uncompromising modernist rejection of the notion of truth, stigmatized as a pathological illusion. In *Lord Jim* (1900), Conrad had already attempted to defuse the naturalist craving for truth through Marlow's oxymoronic definitions: "I was made to look at the convention that lurks in all truth and on the essential sincerity of falsehood" (59), or "He felt confusedly but powerfully, the demand of some such truth or some such illusion—I don't care how you call it, there is so little difference, and the difference means so little" (135). In "The Tale" Conrad sets out to represent the morbidity of what he calls "the passion for truth," and this short story, ostensibly set in a dense fog, where characters powerlessly "try to see—what they could see," ends on a crisis of knowledge with the commanding officer's final words, "I shall never know."

The structure of the story relies on three embedded narrations: It starts with an anonymous, third-person narrator, who gives a vague frame for the story. Two unnamed people, probably lovers, are alone at twilight in an undetermined "long room," during an unspecified war. The woman asks the man for a tale, like those he used to tell her "in the days before the war." He first objects that "now, you see, the war is going on," thus sharing in the modernist conviction that the war made it impossible to resort to old words. He nevertheless agrees to embark on the tale, and the second level of narration begins. He tells the story, of a commanding officer of a British warship and a Northman, the owner of a neutral boat. After passing by an unidentified floating object, which the community officer assumes could be a barrel left there by a "false" neutral ship after it was used to refuel an enemy submarine, the ship is forced to retreat in a cove because of a dense fog. There the ship comes across the Northman's neutral boat, and the commanding officer suspects that the Northman could very well be involved in such treachery. He thus boards his boat to listen to the Northman's tale, the third story-within-a-story. Although the commanding officer is unable to find any loophole in the Northman's version, confirmed by his log-book, that he is utterly lost and does not know his position in the fog, the officer's suspicion turns into certainty, his "passion for truth" tells "another tale." He therefore orders the Northman's ship out of the cove, purposefully giving the crew false directions that lead them to shipwreck

415

without any survivors. After a few slips of the tongue that gave him in, a few rash irruptions of the first-person pronoun in his tale, the commanding officer confesses that this was indeed his own story, emphasizing the character's and the reader's sense of alienation.

"The Tale" is a thus a modernist story in that it dissolves the central concepts of vision, truth, and knowledge: Conjuring up several blurring elements—twilight, the sea as an opaque surface, the fog (a "blind white stillness [that] took possession of the world")—Conrad makes it clear that seeing should not amount to the illusion of seeing through, that truth is a morbid fantasy, and that any type of literature that craves knowledge is an illusion. The opacity of the world cannot be solved, and language should therefore try to inscribe such opacity, replacing knowledge with doubt, assertion with wondering: "His lips outlined themselves firmly under his yellow moustache. But they twitched. Did they twitch?"

BIBLIOGRAPHY

Conrad, Joseph. *Tales of Hearsay.* New York: Fisher Unwin, 1925.

Erdinast-Vulcan, Daphna. *The Strange Short Fiction of Joseph Conrad.* Oxford: Oxford University Press, 1999.

Hawthorn, Jeremy. *Joseph Conrad: Narrative Technique and Ideological Commitment.* London: Edward Arnold, 1990.

Lothe, Jakob. *Conrad's Narrative Method.* Oxford: Clarendon Press, 1989.

Nathalie Jaëck

TALES OF BEATRIX POTTER, THE

BEATRIX POTTER (1903–1913)   The tales written by BEATRIX POTTER are undoubtedly some of the most enduring works for children ever published. Arising from Potter's fascination with animals and their world, the books' attention to historical detail and her precise use of language made them classics in their own time.

Originally written as a letter to the son of her former governess, "The Tale of Peter Rabbit" was published privately in 1901. Warne's, a publisher that had previously rejected the work, later brought out a commercial edition that sold its entire run before publication day and sold 50,000 copies by the end of 1903. This ensured that further books would be well received.

The exact number of the tales depends on definition; there were 23 books, but two of them ("The Tale of Mr. Toad" and "The Tale of Pigling Bland") were longer than the others and were issued as part of a separate series. Three works—"The Story of a Fierce Bad Rabbit," "The Story of Miss Moppet," and "The Sly Old Cat"—were originally issued in a foldout panoramic format, and only two were reissued as regular books. Between 1901 and 1913, Potter wrote and published 20 books with Warne. Her marriage in 1913 provided her with different priorities, and although she wrote 11 further books between 1917 and 1956, some of them based on her home at Hill Top Farm, her earlier oeuvre is by far the strongest.

Although Potter's books are not preachily didactic, several of her animal characters find that disobeying orders can lead to near-tragic consequences. It is not a coincidence that Potter was influenced by the fables of Aesop, which also use animals as a means of demonstrating moral behavior. Moreover, although the stories have happy endings, they do not deny the cruelties of nature or the dangers in which the characters often find themselves. Potter modeled some of her work on fairy tales ("The Tailor of Gloucester" pays homage to the Grimm brothers' fairy-tale "The Elves and the Shoemaker") and folktales ("The Tale of Squirrel Nutkin" explains why squirrels chatter and sometimes have short tails), but the true basis of her stories stems from her exceptionally keen observations of animal and human behavior.

Although Potter claimed that her isolated childhood was not an unhappy one, her parents were very strict. By making pets of wild animals collected on vacations—even when she noticed how captivity did not suit them—she may have been creating a space in which she was not powerless and thus attempting to exert authority over her life. Not until she was in her 40s did Potter truly escape the restraints placed on her by her parents, who resisted both of her attempts at marriage. Even her will dictated how her personal items were to be maintained at Hill Top Farm, which is now a National Trust property. Potter denied that her stories offered psychoanalytic interpretations of her own life, but her subject matter and attention to detail allow for a reading of the tales in which the author is not merely observing the animal world but establishing it within confines she controls.

BIBLIOGRAPHY

MacDonald, Ruth K. *Beatrix Potter.* Twayne's English Authors Series. Boston: Twayne, 1986.

Potter, Beatrix. *The Complete Tales of Beatrix Potter.* London: Frederick Warne, 2002.

Stevenson, Laura C. "'A Vogue for Small Books': The Tale of Peter Rabbit and Its Contemporary Competitors." In *Where Next, Peter Rabbit?: Beatrix Potter Studies X,* edited by Libby Joy and Judy Taylor, 11–27. n.p.: Beatrix Potter Society, 2003.

Tracey Rosenberg

TALES OF THE UNEXPECTED ROALD DAHL (1979)

An anthology of 24 short stories originally published between 1948 and 1979, *Tales of the Unexpected* was released as a tie-in to the eponymous television series hosted by the ROALD DAHL himself. Culled from such successful collections as *Someone Like You* (1953), *Kiss, Kiss* (1960), and *The Wonderful Story of Henry Sugar and Six More* (1977), and spanning three decades of Dahl's literary career, the stories collected in *Tales of the Unexpected* introduce the reader to many of the motifs most frequently found in the author's writing. Dahl's love of painting, fine furniture, wine, and friendly wagers provides Dahl's fiction with the realistic thematic ground from which his strange stories spring. Yet, although the *Tales of the Unexpected* frequently contain elements of horror, science fiction, fantasy, and mystery, Dahl's fiction tends to resist classification as predominantly fashioned in any single genre. Instead, Dahl's stories share the author's singular knack for working humorously macabre plot twists into seemingly mundane narratives.

Originally published in the August 1951 issue of the *New Yorker,* "TASTE" provides as suitable an introduction to Dahl's characteristic style as any story in *Tales of the Unexpected.* Written in the polite, refined language of the British upper classes, "Taste" depicts the genesis and development of a strangely unsettling wager. Mike Schofield, a stockbroker who is uncomfortable with the lack of culture inherent in his profession, challenges the famous gourmet Richard Pratt to guess the breed and vintage of an obscure German claret.

Although the two men have frequently made such wagers in the past, Pratt initiates a bizarre turn of events when he insists that Schofield stake his daughter's hand in marriage against the connoisseur's country estate. With tension building at every moment, Pratt spends an exorbitant amount of time deliberating before finally identifying the wine correctly. As an awed silence envelops the diners, the Schofields' maid, a sort of deus ex machina, reveals that Pratt has cheated: She found his spectacles on the same table where the wine had been stored.

In "Lamb to the Slaughter," made famous by Alfred Hitchcock's dramatization of the tale, Mary Maloney's husband announces that he will be leaving her. Utterly heartbroken by the dissolution of her seemingly happy marriage, Mary clubs her husband over the head with a frozen lamb's leg. With disturbing calm, Mrs. Maloney prepares the couple's dinner as if nothing had happened, leaving the house to purchase some potatoes. Upon her return, Mary reports her husband's murder, using her trip to the grocer's as an alibi. When the police—Mr. Maloney's coworkers—arrive, Mrs. Maloney insists that the men eat the meal she has prepared, thereby destroying all evidence of her crime.

Returning to the wager motif he manipulated so deftly in "Taste," Dahl builds "Man from the South" around a similarly tense, equally strange bet. Here, a young American sailor agrees to wager his pinky against an eerie man's Cadillac to prove that his cigarette lighter will successfully ignite 10 times in succession. As the sailor prepares to make a ninth flick of the wheel, the man's wife enters, sees that the eerie man has raised a meat cleaver over the sailor's head, and pulls it away. Apparently, the man does not have the Cadillac he claims to own, since his wife has won his fortune from him. As the couple leaves the hotel room, the narrator notices that the woman's hand "had only one finger on it, and a thumb" (47).

In "Royal Jelly" a monomaniacal beekeeper weans his baby daughter on the secretion used to nourish queen bees until she resembles the insect. In "Skin" a sadistic art collector arranges for the procurement of a newly discovered painting by Soutine although the painting is tattooed on an elderly man's back. A woman allows her husband to die in a stuck elevator while she visits family in Europe. A neurotic inventor believes he invents a machine that can detect pain in plant life. Kindly old women poison unwitting men.

Although his stories have been compared to those of O. Henry, SAKI, John Collier, and Ernest Hemingway, Roald Dahl holds a unique place among 20th-century short story writers. His style is as inimitable as any of these masters of the form. "Dahl's finest achievement" and ultimate legacy, as Alan Warren observes, "is his near-perfect juxtaposition of humor with horror[,] . . . a slightly tongue-in-cheek quality that actually heightens the tension" of the author's fiction (8).

BIBLIOGRAPHY

Dahl, Roald. *Tales of the Unexpected.* New York: Vintage, 1979.
RoaldDahl.com. "Roald Dahl Biography." The Official Roald Dahl Website. Available online. URL: http://www.roalddahl.com. Accessed June 8, 2006.
Treglown, Jeremy. *Roald Dahl: A Biography.* New York: Farrar, Straus & Giroux, 1994.
Warren, Alan. *Roald Dahl.* San Bernadino, Calif.: Borgo Press, 1988.

Erik Grayson

TALES OF UNREST JOSEPH CONRAD (1898)

The five stories included in the collection *Tales of Unrest* (1898) represent some of JOSEPH CONRAD's earliest published writings: They were composed after his first two novels, *Almayer's Folly* (1895) and *An Outcast of the Islands* (1896), and most were published in periodicals in 1896–97. Set in various locales and written in a range of styles, these stories nonetheless, as the collection's title suggests, share certain thematic concerns. The stories are also largely derivative, in particular of French models; the distinct impressionistic style that was to characterize such works as HEART OF DARKNESS (1899), *Lord Jim* (1900), *Nostromo* (1904), *The Secret Agent* (1907) emerges only fitfully in the pages of *Tales of Unrest*.

The collection is framed by two stories set, like Conrad's first two novels, in the Malay Archipelago (modern Indonesia), "KARAIN: A MEMORY" and "The LAGOON." Besides sharing their setting, both pieces are centered on the tales of Malayan men, told at night to more or less anonymous Western auditors—a narrative device that Conrad was to develop more fully in *Heart of Darkness*. "Karain" and "The Lagoon" also share several themes—"betrayal, escape, neglect of important duty"— by which, according to biographer Zdzisław Najder, Conrad was "haunted . . . from the very beginning of his literary life" (257). There are significant differences between the two stories, however. "Karain" is by far the more substantial of the two: Unlike the straightforward, brief "Lagoon," it is divided into six parts, the first three of which serve as a preface to Karain's tale, establishing a contrast between the warlord's theatrical rule and the "reality" of the encroaching darkness outside. The tale itself develops this contrast in a manner that, while comic in its resolution, directly anticipates *Heart of Darkness*. "Karain" also reflects, though in some measure ironically, prevailing racialist attitudes about "Orientals."

Of the other three stories in the collection, "An Outpost of Progress" is the most accomplished. Set in the Congo, it relates the adventures of two bumbling ivory traders who eventually become complicit in the moral squalor of the business and then engage in a squabble that ends in murder and suicide. Because of its setting, "An Outpost of Progress" warrants obvious comparison with *Heart of Darkness;* indeed, Conrad attacks the pretense of a "civilizing mission" in the Congo even more sharply in this story. "Outpost" is also informed by the same racist views of Africans. Conrad himself was fond of the story: The working title of *Tales of Unrest* had been *Outpost of Progress and Other Stories,* and he was later to identify "Outpost" as his best story. Ian Watt observes that while the story owes an obvious debt to Maupassant and Flaubert's *Bouvard et Pécuchet* in its concise, ironic style, it "was easily the most powerful and professional thing Conrad had yet done" (75).

The two stories set closest to home are also the most derivative and least successful. "The Idiots," written while Conrad was on his honeymoon in Brittany and based on his observations of a family from the area, remains, according to one critic, "a creditable imitation" of Maupassant until the end, when it "turns into a pretentious and implausible melodrama." (Graver, 7–8) The collection's other piece, "The Return," the only story not to be published in a periodical first, remains, in Najder's words, "Conrad's least favorite piece of writing" (208). About a woman's return to her husband after an aborted attempt to leave him and his own subsequent departure, the story was, in Conrad's own estimation, "a left-handed production . . . worth while . . . only to see of what excesses I was capable" (*Tales,* 157). Given its subject and its three-part structure, "The Return" nevertheless holds some interest as a contemporary response to Henrik Ibsen's *A Doll's House.*

BIBLIOGRAPHY

Conrad, Joseph. *Joseph Conrad: The Short Fiction.* Edited by Daphna Erdinast-Vulcan, Allan H. Simmons, and J. H. Stape. Amsterdam, Netherlands: Rodopi, 2004.

———. *Tales of Unrest.* Edited by Anthony Fothergill. London: J. M. Dent; Rutland, Vt.: Charles E. Tuttle, 2000.

Graver, Lawrence. *Conrad's Short Fiction.* Berkeley and Los Angeles: University of California Press, 1969.

Najder, Zdzisław. *Joseph Conrad: A Chronicle.* New Brunswick, N.J.: Rutgers University Press, 1983.

Watt, Ian. *Conrad in the Nineteenth Century.* Berkeley and Los Angeles: University of California Press, 1979.

Stan Walker

"TASTE" ROALD DAHL (1945)

"Taste" was first published in *Ladies Home Journal* in 1945. It was reprinted in the *New Yorker* (December 8, 1951), in *Playboy* (April 1956), and in ROALD DAHL's second collection of short stories, *Someone Like You* (1953). Since then, it has been included in numerous anthologies of short stories as a superb model of the genre.

As implied by the title, the narrative's dramatic climax is a ritual of wine tasting. The story takes place during a dinner held at the London home of Mike Scofield, a wealthy and pretentious stockbroker, seeking to make a name for himself as a man of culture. The guest of honor is Richard Pratt, a well-known gourmet, who prides himself on his unfailing taste in food and wine. As on two previous occasions, the host challenges Pratt to identify, by taste, a bottle of exquisite and little-known French claret. In the past, Scofield and Pratt used to bet on a case of the wine itself, but this time, Pratt offers to change the terms of the wager. If he wins, he wants the hand of Scofield's daughter in marriage. If he loses, he is willing to yield his London home and his country house.

The 18-year-old Louise, whom Pratt has been ogling lasciviously all through the meal, is appalled at the offer; so is her mother. But Mike is tempted. Snobbish, self-confident, and greedy, he is certain he cannot lose. The story builds up to the unbearable suspense of the wine tasting, for which the stakes are so high. Pratt seems to be relishing the moment; he also seems to be winning. Just as he triumphantly identifies the year and the vineyard, the Scofields' loyal maid approaches him with a pair of reading glasses. Pratt has left them near that same bottle of wine, which he saw earlier on a shelf in Mike's study, where Pratt had suggested the year before that Mike place the bottle. Livid with rage at being so thoroughly manipulated, Mike is about to assault his guest at the story's end.

"Taste" exhibits most of the features characterizing Dahl's fiction: impeccable narrative structure resolved in a stunning twist, a disturbing blend of realistic and fantastic elements, an undercurrent of evil and cruelty, and social criticism, specifically directed at the power and hypocrisy of adults. Dahl admitted that he spent about six months on each story (viii); the result is lean, perfectly crafted tales, in which no detail is extraneous and each element meaningfully contributes to the whole. In the same way that a gun shown in a film's opening scene must eventually be fired, so the elderly maid hovering in the background finally emerges to the forefront, producing the startling denouement. Similarly, Scofield's account of how Pratt helped him find the optimal place for storing the wine sets the stage for the final revelation.

As critics have noted, Dahl's formula is to take absolutely ordinary characters and plunge them in a deeply disturbing fantasy. This is the basic pattern of "Taste." The opening paragraph sets the realistic tone, reinforced by the presence of a first-person narrator, who functions mainly to lend credibility to the story, as if suggesting, "I was there, I witnessed that." Similarly, the protagonists' outrageous behavior can be accounted for in psychological terms. Mike Scofield is a social climber, motivated by his desire to impress Pratt at all costs and gain the aura of sophistication and culture. He believes himself to be cunning but is no match for the scheming mind of Pratt. Pratt is a man who objectifies human beings (he places a bet on Louise, treating her like an object) and personifies objects (referring to wine as "feminine," "gracious," or "naughty,"). This perspicuous characterization by Dahl makes Pratt's preposterous figure psychologically plausible.

But the carefully constructed realistic narrative has a mythological subtext, consisting of elements traditionally found in fairy tales and folklore. Thus we can find the magical numbers seven and three: There are seven characters (six people at the table and the maid), the maid appears three times, the setting is the third dinner of its kind, and Pratt correctly names the wine after giving two wrong guesses. Another fairy-tale element is the figure of the loyal maid coming to the rescue of the helpless young girl—a function traditionally assigned to the good fairy. The father-daughter relationship in the story echoes the problematic pattern established in classic children's tales, in which real or foster parents neglect or abuse their young ones ("Cinderella," "Hansel and Gretel"), and daughters altruistically sacrifice themselves for their fathers ("Beauty and the Beast"). The principal character, Pratt, metaphorically depicted as all mouth, evokes the traditional figure of the devil. Finally, the central plot element, the fatal bet, belongs with the metaphysical motif found in tales such as Dr. Faustus or Daniel Webster: man's wager with the devil over the human soul.

The realistic and the fantastic perspectives converge to produce mordant social criticism. The world portrayed in "Taste" is one in which the old sacrifice the young on the altar of snobbery, greed, or lust. Despite the happy ending, the story's final effect is profoundly disturbing. We are not inclined to believe that the Scofields will live happily ever after.

BIBLIOGRAPHY
Dahl, Roald. *The Best of Roald Dahl.* New York: Vintage Books, 1978.
Tatar, Maria, ed. *The Classic Fairy Tales.* New York: Norton, 1999.

Ilana Shiloh

TAYLOR, ELIZABETH (1912–1975) Elizabeth Taylor was born Elizabeth Coles in 1912 in Reading, Berkshire, where she attended the Abbey School. She worked as a governess and librarian until in 1936 she married a manufacturer, John William Kendall Taylor, with whom she had a son and a daughter. Taylor settled in the village of Penn, Buckinghamshire, where she wrote her 12 novels, four volumes of short stories, and one children's book between 1945 and 1975, the year she died of cancer. One novel, *Blaming,* was published posthumously in 1976. Taylor's elegant, witty fiction portrays the lives of the well-to-do in England's Midlands, although in her short stories in particular, she ventures at times into the lives of the lower classes. Her work was acclaimed by her literary contemporaries ELIZABETH BOWEN, Rosamund Lehmann, and Ivy Compton-Burnett in England and by Eudora Welty in the United States. Americans contemporary with Taylor knew her work chiefly from her much-admired short stories, published in the *New Yorker,* the *Saturday Evening Post,* and *Harper's Bazaar,* among other magazines. Reviewers have compared her not only to Bowen and Compton-Burnett but also to Jane Austen, VIRGINIA WOOLF, and the Russian master of the short story form, Anton Chekhov. More recently, Taylor has received critical and popular accolades in England: *Angel* was selected in 1984 as one of the British Book Marketing Council's "Best Novels of Our Time," *The Sleeping Beauty* was made into a BBC TV film titled *The Last Visitor,* and her story "A Dedicated Man" was performed on the BBC's Masterpiece Theater. In 2003 Taylor's powerful narrative *Mrs. Palfrey at the Claremont,* "a haunting, understated study of old age," was listed by the *Observer* as one of the 100 best novels of all time.

Taylor's sharply observed, witty portrayals of the provincial lives of the middle and upper-middle classes immediately place her in Jane Austen's lineage in the domestic fiction of manners. As does the work of the great 19th-century novelists in this tradition—Austen, GEORGE ELIOT, ANTHONY TROLLOPE, HENRY JAMES—Taylor's stories depict sympathetic characters as those who are capable of imaginative empathy, while the darker figures are those impervious to others' needs and desires or actively antagonistic to those around them. Taylor's narratives embody the moral conflict between the destructive egoists and the regenerative, imaginative characters. One of Taylor's most sympathetic characters, the middle-aged publican's wife Phyl in the short story "Flesh," responds to the overbearing owner of her shabby hotel with this insight: "The more monstrous the egoist, she had observed from long practice, the more normal people hope to uphold the fabrication—either for ease, or from a terror of any kind of collapse." The "monstrous egoist" is a familiar figure in the novel of manners tradition.

Taylor's 20th-century redirection of the fiction of manners tradition issues from her connection to a British tradition of between-the-wars women's fiction. The experimental MODERNISM and feminist consciousness of Virginia Woolf influenced Taylor, who named her novel *A Wreath of Roses* after a passage in Woolf's *The Waves* and adopted its focus on the artistic imagination. But Taylor is also close literary kin to Elizabeth Bowen, Rosamond Lehmann, and, in her ironic comedy, Nancy Mitford. In *The Feminine Middle-Brow Novel 1920's–1950's,* Nicola Humble includes Taylor in a group of between-the-wars and post–World War II women writers of both highbrow and popular fiction: Compton-Burnett, E. M. Delafield, Diana Tutton, Margaret Kennedy, E. Arnot Robertson, and Angela Thirkell, among others. In all of her fiction, Taylor connects back not only to Austen's comic consciousness but also to Woolf's feminist project in her concern with the integrity of the inviolate self and with its enemy, the masculine egoists of the world.

Taylor examines the damage wrought by the "monstrous egoist" in nearly every fiction she writes, including her short stories. She expands her consideration of the egoist to include all those, regardless of sex, who disregard other selves. The egoist often has the formal identity of nurturer: mother, father, guardian, tutor. In her earliest volume of stories, *Hester Lilly* (1954), the title story includes an extreme instance of the annihilating power of the egoist in the figure of Muriel, who drives her husband's orphaned cousin from the house in which she is supposed to be sheltered. Three stories from the next volume, *The Blush* (1958), are concerned with the subtle evil wrought by the egoist. In "Poor Girl"—a Jamesian exploration of the psychology of sexual repression in conjunction with the supernatural reminiscent of *The Turn of the Screw*—the philandering father, Mr. Wilson, compromises his son's young governess, while tainting his precocious son's moral nature with evil. Mr. Ransome in "The Primitive" poses naked,

creating himself as objet d'art, while his reluctantly obliging sons paint him; the duke, the duchess, and the tutor, Mr. Gilliat, in "Hare Park," pursue their own concerns at the expense of the family's little boy, the sacrificial Arthur Blanchflower, whose name links him to Taylor's earlier innocent victim, Hester Lilly. In the next collection, *A Dedicated Man and Other Stories* (1965), the title story again tells of the devastating lack of humanity in the snobbish maître d'hôtel, Silcox, who disowns his son and tries to usurp the identity of Edith, the woman he asks to pose as his wife.

Three stories from Taylor's final collection, *The Devastating Boys* (1972), show a progression in Taylor's vision of the egoist, whose self-absorption becomes crueler, more death-dealing. In one of Taylor's stories, the lengthy "Excursion to the Source," the middle-aged widow Gwenda is implicated in the accidental death of her ward, Polly. In "Miss A. and Miss M." the snobbish schoolmistress Miss Alliot betrays her lesbian lover, the kindly Miss Martin, who then commits suicide. In "The Flypaper" an 11-year-old orphan, Sylvia, is left under her grandmother's smothering but ineffectual custody; she is kidnapped by a motherly woman who pretends to protect her.

Despite the ubiquity of deception and betrayal in Taylor's fictional world, there is the possibility of enlightened sympathy and even of moral redemption through imaginative empathy. Again Taylor connects with a central impulse of the novel of manners tradition when she creates sensitive characters with intense moral imaginations, like Henry James's Ralph Touchett (and, of course, Isabel herself) in *A Portrait of a Lady* or Philip Wakem in George Eliot's *The Mill on the Floss*. Taylor's good characters, like those of the other masters in this tradition, are those with imaginations that can take them outside themselves and into other minds, other lives. Their creative vision is opposed to the destruction wrought by the monstrous egoists of Taylor's stories. Taylor believes, like Camilla in *A Wreath of Roses,* that imagination can be cultivated "more than any other quality, perhaps. . . . I value it very highly."

Taylor enlarges the scope of the fiction of manners tradition in her narratives of lower-class characters with compassionate imaginations, which are more common in her later short stories. About the writing of "Tall Boy" Taylor commented, "I always like to stretch my imagination. I once wrote a short story about a West Indian and that was difficult. Trying to imagine his bedsit, his background. It's much more interesting than writing about things you really know more about." In this story, the poor West Indian man, Jasper Jones, creates a sense of community from the photograph of his beloved sisters at home, a birthday card he sends to himself, and the delight of buying cakes for his mates at work:

> They liked the cakes, he kept on thinking. The cakes he'd bought for tea. . . . He ate the beans out of the pan, spooning them up contentedly as he sat on the bed, staring at Opal and Crystal and Sapphyra, who grinned cheekily back at him, sitting in a neat row, their bare feet stuck out in front of them, out of focus, and sharp black shadows falling on their white dresses.

Another central figure in that same collection is the married barmaid Phyl in "Flesh," the sympathetic character who has the insight about the monstrous egoist. Phyl, having an affair while on vacation, is perceived by her lover as "a marvellous Tommy in the trenches" who can say to him, when their liaison is not consummated because of his gout attack, "To me, it was lovely. To me, it was just as good as if we had." Ordinary, unpretentious characters like Jasper and Phyl are, perhaps, unlikely embodiments of beauty, goodness, and imagination, but they are intensely moving.

Taylor's marvelous sense of humor pervades her stories, and she uses her quietly ironic wit both to deflate the self-important and to give power to the insignificant. In the title story of the collection, "The DEVASTATING BOYS," one of Taylor's best-known stories, the self-absorbed anthropology professor Harold is wrenched out of himself by the temporary presence of two poor black children from London whom he has invited, on principle, to his country home. The outrageous Septimus and Benny mock the upper classes' language, in particular, the self-important Helena's slang—"you shake me rigid"—and they elicit witty repartee from Harold's beleaguered, shy wife, Laura, that surprises both partners in the marriage. Through the originality and energy of the London children, Harold learns that Laura, has depths of humor and wisdom that he never suspected: "Harold looked at her as if for the first time in years. She so seldom tried to be amusing." He also discovers that Laura has suffered because of his selfishness. On the day the boys go back to London, he comes home early from work, takes Laura to lunch, imitates the slang of the Black children ("Shall we make tracks?"), and then says simply, "Don't fret. . . . I think we've got them for life." Taylor's art depicts the moments of understanding on which the moral life depends.

There are, as might be expected, several artist figures in Taylor's fiction who possess imaginations vivid enough to bridge the gap between self and other. Catherine, the grieving painter in the story "The Ambush," feels a kinship with her dead lover's brother, the homosexual Esme, because they have both loved passionately. Even in the midst of her own deep pain—"her heart began to ache again and her throat almost shut"—Catherine has the capacity to imagine Esme's peaceful happiness in having his feckless lover Freddie under the same roof as she recalls how she felt about her beloved Noel: "Then the house itself became haunted, enchanted, spellbound with love." Another artist figure who possesses an empathetic imagination is Morland Beddoes, the film director in *A Wreath of Roses.* Morland is introduced into the narrative, significantly, with these words: "Morland Beddoes . . . loved himself only as much as self-respect required, and the reason why he *saw* himself so clearly was that he looked not often, but suddenly, so catching himself unawares." In *Mrs. Palfrey at the Claremont* (1971), the impoverished young novelist, Ludo, begins by exploiting the elderly Mrs. Palfrey in the name of art and ultimately loves her like the faithful grandson she pretends he is—and on her deathbed both imagines and knows him to be. At its most profound, Taylor tells us, art can portray the moral lives to which, at our best, our imaginations can aspire. (See "The BLUSH," "GOOD-BYE, GOOD-BYE.")

BIBLIOGRAPHY

Brown Gillette, Jane. "'Oh, What a Something Web We Weave': The Novels of Elizabeth Taylor," *Twentieth Century Literature* 35, No. 1 (Spring 1989): 94–112.

Grove Robin. "From the Island: Elizabeth Taylor's Novels," *Studies in the Literary Imagination* 11, no. 2 (1978): 79–95.

Humble, Nicola. *The Feminine Middle-Brow Novel 1920's–1950's.* Oxford: Oxford University Press, 2001.

Kingham, Joanna. Introduction. *A Dedicated Man and Other Stories.* London: Virago 1993.

Leclercq, Florence. *Elizabeth Taylor.* Boston: Twayne, 1985.

McCrum, Rob. "The One Hundred Best Novels of All Time," *Observer,* 12 October 2003.

Pritchard, William. *Playing It by Ear: Literary Essays and Reviews.* Amherst: University of Massachusetts Press, 1994.

Taylor, Elizabeth. *The Blush.* London: Peter Davies, 1958.

———. *A Dedicated Man.* London: Chatto and Windus, 1965.

———. *The Devastating Boys.* London: Chatto and Windus, 1972.

———. *Mrs. Palfrey at the Claremont.* London: Chatto and Windus, 1971.

———. *A Wreath of Roses.* London: Peter Davies, 1949.

Deborah Denenholz Morse

"TELEGRAPH GIRL, THE" ANTHONY TROLLOPE (1877)

Unusual both for its time and for ANTHONY TROLLOPE, "The Telegraph Girl" is a sympathetic presentation of a working woman. First published in *Good Cheer,* the Christmas edition of *Good Words* for 1877, the story concerns Lucy Graham, forced to support herself after her brother dies. A kind and respectable widower asks Lucy to marry him, but she refuses because she does not love him. She instead joins the Civil Service—which had been opened to women in 1870, seven years before the story appeared—as a telegraph operator. While Trollope is on record as being against employment for women, his position in this story is less clear-cut: In the end, Lucy marries and is able to quit her job, but her previous employment is not thereby invalidated. It is justified by Lucy's moral stance in refusing to marry for money and security and by the value of work itself—something the workaholic Trollope always respected. In fact, the story came on the heels of an article Trollope wrote for *Good Words,* "The Young Women at the Telegraph Office," and the story as well as the article is full of helpful details on the realities of employment for women—the conditions under which they worked, their salary, the nature of the work itself (including recent technological innovations), and the exact location of the office. Trollope could hardly have provided young women with more encouragement.

Once she has procured a post, Lucy takes lodgings in London with Sophy Wilson, a fellow telegraph girl. Sophy is frankly looking for a husband—a fact that irritates Lucy—and rather forcibly creates a friendship with one of the male-lodgers, Abraham Hart. When Sophy falls ill, Lucy sends her to the seaside at the doctor's recommendation and her own expense; she also, of course, must now pay full rent, and as a result she eats very little. Abraham notices Lucy's increasing thinness and, knowing the reason, offers to help Sophy with the occasional sovereign, thereby freeing some of Lucy's money for food. Lucy, however, refuses to accept the money on her friend's behalf, insisting that it is not proper for men to give money to single women and feeling as strongly that she should not benefit from Abraham's money. Abraham takes a strict ethical position and insists that there is nothing to "confine kindness to this or the other sex." Lucy, however, is attuned to context in a way that Abraham is not. The story's ending, in which Lucy marries Abraham in new clothes bought with his money, seems to support Abraham's way of thinking, but other subtleties of context appear often enough in the story that Lucy's position is also validated. Sophy, for example, while clearly a self-centered flibbertigibbet, is not judged harshly—the standards of moral conduct do not apply to her behavior in the same way they do to Lucy's, for example, because Sophy's nature is weaker.

Though a short story in length, "The Telegraph Girl" is divided into chapters like a novel—a move, perhaps, in the direction of the novella. The story itself is an interesting combination of realism with a more mythical structure; while such works as CHARLES DICKENS's *A CHRISTMAS CAROL* combine the realistic with the fantastic or unlikely by moving back and forth between ordinary and extraordinary events, "The Telegraph Girl" is a work of pure realism throughout but is simultaneously structured like a fairy-tale. Like many a fairy-tale heroine, Lucy falls suddenly upon hard times, undergoes various trials, and is carried away by a lover. This fall-and-redemption pattern exists side-by-side with some of Trollope's most subtle extended psychological examinations of character, to which his shorter works are usually lent.

BIBLIOGRAPHY

Trollope, Anthony. *Complete Short Stories*. Forth Worth: Texas Christian University Press, 1979–83.

———. "The Young Women at the Telegraph Office." Available online. URL: http://www.jimandellen.org/trollope/nonfiction.TelegraphGirls.html. Accessed June 8, 2006.

Anna Peak

"TERRIBLY STRANGE BED, A" WILKIE COLLINS (1852)

"A Terribly Strange Bed" was WILKIE COLLINS's first contribution to CHARLES DICKENS's *Household Words* (April 24, 1852); the story was subsequently included in *After Dark* (1852) as "The Traveller's Story of a Terribly Strange Bed."

The narrator, an Englishman, recounts his visit as a young man to a low gambling house in Paris where he has a remarkable run of luck and breaks the bank playing *rouge et noir*. An old French soldier contributes to the gambler's already intoxicated state by ordering champagne, ostensibly to celebrate the Englishman's remarkable success at the gaming table. After quaffing a second bottle, however, the Englishman comments on the strange side effects that he experiences. The old soldier, who has been watching him closely throughout the evening, orders a pot of coffee to sober him up; the coffee, however, only seems to intoxicate and discombobulate the Englishman further. The old soldier persuades him to sleep off the ill effects of his drinking in a room at the gambling house so that he will avoid being robbed on his way home through the dark city streets.

The Englishman concedes the wisdom of this advice and agrees to meet the old soldier the next morning for breakfast. He retires to his shabby apartment, where, after securing the door and windows and hiding his money under his pillow, he finds himself highly agitated and unable to sleep in a huge four-poster, canopied bed. He attempts to pass the time by taking inventory of the room's furnishings, lingering particularly on a gloomy painting of a swarthy figure wearing a tall, plumed hat. As he stares intently at the painting, he loses himself in reverie of "past scenes and past amusements." In an instant, however, he is jolted back to the present time when he realizes that hat has disappeared from the head of the sinister figure in the painting—the picture seems to be changing right before his eyes. After a moment he deduces that the picture has not in fact changed, but rather the bed's canopy is slowly descending upon him. Paralyzed with fear, the Englishman manages to roll himself out of the bed only moments before he is to be suffocated by the "machine for secret murder."

As he regains his senses, he realizes that he has narrowly escaped a "murderous conspiracy": His coffee has been drugged, and the old soldier and his charlatans have attempted to rob and kill him. He stealthily withdraws from the house and returns later with two police agents, who discover within a "deep raftered cavity" between the floor of one room and the ceiling of his room the machinery of a heavy press designed to smother unsuspecting victims in their sleep. This solves the mystery of the dozens of men who were believed to have committed suicide in the Seine because they had lost everything at the gaming table. They suffered the fate from which the Englishmen only narrowly escaped.

The narrator's frantic questions, "Was I mad? drunk? Dreaming?" invite the reader to consider the uncertainties of perception that are a hallmark of Collins's fiction. The sinister portrait is also symbolic of those psychological ambiguities, particularly the effects of drugs on one's mental state, while in very broad strokes the painting also suggests a theme that Collins returns to again and again: Things are never as they appear. When the narrator goes to the police, for example, he is mistakenly identified as "a drunken Englishman who had robbed somebody."

Finally, the site of the attempted theft and murder by suffocation in a "terribly strange [English] bed" in Paris points to certain sociopolitical anxieties, namely homosexual panic and fears of foreign invasion. The version of the story that appears in *After Dark* is no longer narrated by the victim but rather by the middle-class male artist who is painting his portrait. Some critics have suggested that this shift in perspective and narrative control reveals the tenuous nature of Victorian masculinity, particularly the complex negotiation involved in asserting and maintaining male dominance and control.

BIBLIOGRAPHY

Collins, Wilkie. *Complete Short Fiction.* London: Constable. 1998.

Maria Bachman

"THEODORA: A FRAGMENT" VICTORIA CROSS(E) (1895)

This story by Victoria Cross(e) (Annie Sophie Cory) (1868–1952) first appeared in the avant-garde magazine the *YELLOW BOOK* edited by HENRY HARLAND. Cross's conception of the heiress, Theodora Dudley, presented by the male narrator, Cecil Ray, is of a woman who challenges gender conventions, and the narrative—a number of encounters between the two characters—takes an ambivalent stance on sexual morality. Theodora stands to lose her sizable inheritance if she marries, and this position puts her in the way of being a sexual decadent.

Theodora arouses Ray's social, sexual, and emotional curiosity by "a dash of virility, a hint at dissipation, a suggestion of a certain decorous looseness of morals and fastness of manners" (12). His atypical sexual predilections are hinted at in his remarks to his friend Digby: It is her boyish figure as well as manner, the "full chin" with a trace of a moustache, "that curious masculine shade upon the upper lip" (26) that intrigue him. In a scene of masquerade evoking an Egyptian bazaar, these crossings of racial and gender identities are emphasized further, when Theodora dresses up for Ray and his friend Digby in an Eastern fez hat and tight, silk zouave jacket and smokes a cigarette. Unlike the usual Victorian heroine, Theodora's androgynous figure has "little suggestion of the duties or powers of Nature" (24); she bespeaks "a poor if possible mother, and a still poorer nurse" (21). Desire for the beautiful Theodora is configured as an extension of the doctrine of art for art's sake to pleasure for pleasure's sake, in which sexuality is divorced—even liberated—from nature and its use-value, maternity.

The fragmentary form of the narrative condones the sexually assertive behavior of its androgynous protagonist Theodora, since the story has an open ending, abruptly finishing on a passionate kiss between the two acquaintances without authorial recrimination or resolution. This short story forms the ground of Cross's full-length novel, *Six Chapters of a Man's Life* (1903).

BIBLIOGRAPHY

Cross, Victoria (Annie Sophie Cory). "Theodora: A Fragment." In *Daughters of Decadence: Women Writers of the Fin de Siècle,* edited by Elaine Showalter, 6–37. London: Virago, 1993.

Lyssa Randolph

"THRAWN JANET" ROBERT LOUIS STEVENSON (1881)

ROBERT LOUIS STEVENSON's first Scots-language story, "Thrawn Janet" is a dark tribute to the language and gloomy Calvinism of the writer's native land deserves a prominent place in the canon of Scottish gothic writing. Published in the *Cornhill Magazine* in October 1881 (see MAGAZINES), the story draws on folklore, Calvinist theology, and occult lore to explore what one critic has called a "peculiarly Scottish sense of evil" (Warner, 337). It may be described as a bildungsroman in miniature that charts the conversion of protagonist Reverend Murdoch Soulis from young free-thinking clergyman to fanatical zealot who terrifies the local children with tales of the omnipresence of Satan.

The brief opening section of the story—incidentally, the only part of the narrative written in standard English—describes Soulis in his latter incarnation as devil-obsessed preacher. The rest of the story describes the supernatural circumstances that led to his transformation. Soulis, as the tale's third-person narrator relates, descended on the small rural parish of Balweary some 50 years earlier, then a fresh-faced recent graduate of theology school. He initially puts his parishioners' persistent belief in the existence of witches down to superstition and ignorance, but his convictions begin to change when he takes Janet M'Clour, an "auld limmer" into his house as a servant. In the eyes of the villagers, Janet is an abomination, a loose and corrupt old woman whose illegitimate child, failure to attend church, and delight in walking alone and muttering to herself at twilight is proof that she has sold her soul to the devil. Incensed by the news of her employment, the villagers attempt to dunk her in the river. They are prevented by an outraged Soulis, who accuses them of a lack of Christian charity and escorts Janet safely to his house. On the following morning, she emerges from her room unable to speak and looking as if she has been "thrawn" (thrown) and has broken her neck. Soulis assumes she has suffered a paralytic stroke, but the villagers believe that she is a reanimated corpse. Their interpretation is borne out by events that occur later that summer. A black man (a common incarnation of the devil in Scottish folklore) appears in an abandoned local graveyard and disappears into Soulis's house; later that night, the minister discovers Janet hanging from "a single wursted thread" in her room. It is only when Janet's corpse descends from its suspended position and pursues him through the house that Soulis is forced to abandon his studied rationalism once and for all. Drawing on his remaining strength, he calls on God to consign the revenant to hell. Janet's corpse immediately disintegrates, and Soulis is left a deeply scarred and paranoid man, forever haunted by the material proof of the metaphysical malice whose existence he had once dismissed.

This story provides an early example of the thematic obsession with the pervasiveness of evil that came to dominate so much of Stevenson's later work, most notably in *The STRANGE CASE OF DR. JEKYLL AND MR. HYDE*. Critics have also focused on the narrative's psychoanalytic dimensions—interpreting Janet as an unruly vessel of feminine orality (Fielding)—and on its use of Scots as a strategy of anticolonial resistance to linguistic colonialism (Letley; McCracken-Flesher). This latter reading places "Thrawn Janet" in a tradition whose more recent examples include the work of IRVINE WELSH, JAMES KELMAN, and Laura Hird—one that combines a use of nonstandard English with an almost prurient interest in the darker aspects of human interaction in an attempt to map out a discrete Scottish identity.

BIBLIOGRAPHY

Fielding, Penny. *Writing and Orality: Nationality, Culture, and Nineteenth-Century Scottish Fiction.* Oxford: Clarendon, 1996.

Letley, Emma. *From Galt to Douglas Brown: Nineteenth-Century Fiction and Scots Language.* Edinburgh: Scottish Academic Press, 1988.

McCracken-Flesher, C. "Thinking Nationally/Writing Colonially? Scott, Stevenson, and England," *Novel* 24, no. 3 (Spring 1991): 296–318.

Stevenson, Robert Louis. "Thrawn Janet." In *The Merry Men and Other Tales and Fables.* New York: Scribner, 1909.

Warner, Fred B. "Stevenson's First Scottish Story," *Nineteenth Century Fiction* 24, no. 3 (December 1969): 334–344.

Christine Fergus

"TICKETS PLEASE" D. H. LAWRENCE (1919)

First published in 1919 as "The Eleventh Commandment," this story is set in the Midlands during WORLD WAR I. It depicts a battle of the sexes on the tramways staffed by attractive female conductors, "rash" drivers, and young male inspectors. The name of the male protagonist, John Thomas Raynor, nicknamed "Coddy," emphasizes his sexual appeal. The heroine Annie Stone's last name connects her with the working mother in "The ROCKING-HORSE WINNER," whose heart is stone. Meeting John Thomas at a fair, Annie, a "tartar," lets her guard down. Balking at a "possessive female," John Thomas flirts with others, prompting Annie's jealousy. In retaliation, she rallies the conductors against him. Their surnames suggest he has dallied with them all: Baggaley, Houselay, Sharp, Birkin, and Purdy.

John Thomas withstands their teasing until pressed to choose one of them. When he refuses, Annie leads a frightening attack that transforms the women into Maenads who rip his uniform, almost strangle him, and trample him until he lies bloodied and bruised. After she threatens to break his neck if he plays "tricks," Coddy chooses Annie. When she rejects him, something breaks in her, echoing the "broken manhood" in *Sons and Lovers*. Both have their tickets "stamped."

Kingsley Widmer calls the tone of this story "comic-grotesque . . . from sympathetic bemusement to ideological satire," following love's "rhythm": "attraction to excitement to intimacy to possession to resentment." Others have seen the story as protofeminist in its depiction of women joining forces to overcome the promiscuous male. Janice Hubbard Harris links the story's ritual drama, "a struggle between freedom and responsibility," to Ursula's annihilation of Skrebensky in *The Rainbow* and to the couple in "Wintry Peacock."

BIBLIOGRAPHY

Harris, Janice Hubbard. *The Short Fiction of D. H. Lawrence.* New Brunswick, N.J.: Rutgers University Press, 1984.

Lawrence, D. H. *England, My England and Other Stories.* Edited by Bruce Steele. Cambridge: Cambridge University Press, 1990.

Ramadier, Bernard-Jean. "Dubious Progress in D. H. Lawrence's 'Tickets, Please,'" *Journal of the Short Story in English/Les Cahiers de la Nouvelle* [University de'Angers] 35 (2000): 43–54.

Widmer, Kingsley. *The Art of Perversity: D. H. Lawrence's Shorter Fictions.* Seattle: University of Washington Press, 1962.

Elizabeth Fox

"TO ROOM NINETEEN" DORIS LESSING (1963)

"To Room Nineteen" first appeared in the short story collection *A Man and Two Women* in 1963. Like many of DORIS LESSING's stories, "To Room Nineteen" explores the relationships between genders in the state of marriage.

Susan and Matthew Rawlings marry based on "intelligence": They are well suited to each other, both have careers they enjoy, and they are the centers of their social circle. Susan quits work when she becomes pregnant, and they move to a large house to have four children. When the youngest children begin school, Susan finds herself discomfited, not knowing how to fill the empty time and fearing the "demons" of discontent that wait for her. She resents her ties to the household and family, feeling that the "essential Susan was in abeyance, as if she were in cold storage" (274). Susan begins to go into London to a seedy hotel. In room 19, she searches for solitude and her identity. After Matthew sends a private detective to track her, the hotel room loses the sense of peace, becoming as difficult as her house in Richmond. When Matthew questions her, she invents a lover. Rather than continue to fake her life, Susan goes once more to room 19, where she enjoys her last solitude before turning on the gas and waiting to die.

The story is told in the third person, although a first-person narrator opens the story. This narrator does not appear in the story as a character, instead offering ironic commentary on the state of the marriage and Susan's mental state. "To Room Nineteen" falls into a naturalistic genre, although Susan's visions of the devil in the garden lean toward magic realism. Susan, in her rational way, immediately sees that what she perceived as a devil tormenting a snake was in fact a shadow of a branch.

The physical settings of the short story inform Susan's mental state. Repeatedly, Susan Rawlings finds herself physically trapped: in the garden, in the house, and eventually in room 19. Susan tries to create a room for herself in her home, but it becomes a family room. Her twins, after disturbing her peace, wrap her in a "human cage of loving limbs" (282). Her physical entrapment echoes her mental and emotional entrapment in the roles of mother, wife, and mistress of her house.

Lessing addresses the difficulties of aging women in the story. Two servants bracket Susan's household: Mrs Parkes, who is older than Susan, performs manual household duties: Sophie is hired as an au pair and, at 20, performs the role of mother and mistress of the house while Susan escapes to London. Mrs Parkes and Sophie have no difficulty focusing on and performing their functions. The roles for working women over and under 40 are prescribed, following a Marxist view in which they are overworked and underpaid. The roles available to Susan at 40 are not sufficient to keep an educated yet dependent woman fulfilled.

Susan's descent into madness can be placed in the tradition of Charlotte Perkins Gilman's "The Yellow Wallpaper." Lessing also raises an important issue regarding the balance of emotion and intellect. The Rawlings base their marriage and family on intellectual, rational decisions. Early on, Matthew and Susan laugh at "supporting such an edifice on their intelligent love" (273). When Susan faces emotional upheaval, she does not have the language to discuss it with Matthew. The lack of balance in their lives ultimately destroys Susan.

BIBLIOGRAPHY

Budhos, Shirley. *The Theme of Enclosure in Selected Works of Doris Lessing.* Troy, N.Y.: Whitson Publishing Company, 1987.

Gardiner, Judith Kegan. *Rhys, Stead, Lessing, and the Politics of Empathy.* Bloomington: Indiana University Press, 1989.

Lessing, Doris. *A Man and Two Women.* London: MacGibbon and Kee, 1963.

Schlueter, Paul, ed. *Doris Lessing: A Small Personal Voice.*
London: Flamingo, 1994.

Jennifer Young

TRAFFICS AND DISCOVERIES RUDYARD
KIPLING (1909) This collection from the middle
phase of Kipling's career has been seen to embody the
interests of an author who was increasingly concerned
about the British Empire but who also wanted to shock
a lethargic British public. The waning of Victorianism,
the continuing impact of urbanization, and the recruiting campaigns for the Boer War in South Africa, which
revealed that 60 percent of men were physically unfit
for military service, all meant that it was easy to regard
Britain and the empire as being in a state of transition
and decay, particularly when faced with rivalry from
the United States and Germany.

Not surprisingly, given Kipling's concern for Britain's international standing, several of the stories in
Traffic and Discoveries address questions of imperial fitness and responsibility. Geographically, they range
widely. In "A Captive" the responsible British attitude
is contrasted with that of a thoughtless American profi-
teer, who tries to sell a gun he has invented to the
Boers. Another story, "The Army of a Dream," imagines
an army made up of patriotic volunteers on whom the
Empire can depend, where "every man's capacity for
command must be tested to the utmost" (226). As
Hermione Lee points out, what is in evidence in stories
such as "The Comprehension of Private Copper" and
"A Sahib's War" is that "Kipling's idea of empire . . .
takes the form of 'the day's work' well done," together
with "a belief in the unique British talent for government, efficiency and discipline" (11).

The collection is not all about the administration of
empire. "They" is a ghost story commonly believed to
have been inspired by the death of Kipling's daughter
Josephine in 1892. The most famous story in the collection is "MRS. BATHURST." This is one of Kipling's most
enigmatic and complex stories, looking forward to the
narrative forms of MODERNISM, which would be developed by a younger generation of writers, and demonstrating Kipling's remarkable ear for dialect and
dialogue, as well as his technical control of nuance,
subtly, and ambiguity. Multiple narrators supply inter-

weaving accounts of a mystery that is never fully solved
and continues to fascinate, prompting one reviewer, H.
W. Boynton, to comment on Kipling's growing "habit
of mystification."

The starting points for the character Mrs. Bathurst
are various. In his biography Kipling recalls that he
bought a beer from a remarkable woman in Auckland,
and 10 years later he overheard a petty officer describe
a woman who "never scrupled to help a lame duck or
put her foot on a scorpion." As it appeared in *Traffics
and Discoveries,* it was preceded by "From Lyden's 'Ire-
nius,'" a passage from an unfinished play that refers to
a woman unknowingly responsible for her lover's
death. (Fragments of the play have been published
under the title "Gow's Watch.") Stranded after missing
his boat, the unnamed narrator meets his friend Hooper
at the side of a railway engine in need of repair. On
their way to buy a drink, they run into two sailors,
Pyecroft and Pritchard. The men, questioned by
Hooper, recollect their adventures of the sea: stories of
confusion, desertion, mistaken identity, and technology that either breaks down or results in human suffering and pain. The dialogue is fast-paced and full of
interruptions, realistically capturing the cadence and
slang of sailors. Pritchard recounts the story of Vickery. Each man contributes what he knows of Vickery
and of the attractive widow Mrs. Bathurst, a woman
who ran a hotel and bar in Auckland and affected all
who met her: "'Tisn't beauty, so to speak, nor good talk
necessarily. It's just It. Some women'll stay in a man's
memory if they once walk down a street." Pritchard
and Pyecroft energetically defend Mrs. Bathurst against
any possible role in Vickery's desertion 18 months shy
of his pension. Pyecroft recounts that he has just spent
five nights with Vickery in Cape Town drinking and
going to the cinematograph in order to view 45 seconds of Mrs. Bathurst disembarking from a train in
Paddington Station. The story ends as Hooper reveals
that two tramps were found burnt to death along one
of the railway lines, one of whom bore certain marks
that identify him as the missing Vickery. Hooper does
not reveal that he holds Vickery's false teeth in his
pocket, desiring to spare the comrades further pain.

Deliberately suggesting more than revealing, the
story questions the nature of truth and the ability to

know with any certainty. Any relationship, if there ever was one, between Vickery and Mrs. Bathurst remains ambiguous. Did she return his love? Had she gone to London to seek Vickery only to discover he was married? Critics suggest that Vickery was consumed by guilt, a bigamist who has deserted his wife, the army, and Mrs. Bathurst, and they note his fear of being suspected of murder: "remember, that I am not a murderer, because my lawful wife died in childbed six weeks after I came out. That much at least I am clear of." Kipling's subtle technical skill is revealed with each reading of the story: the atmospheric reality of the dialogue; Vickery's use of Hamlet's last words, "The rest is silence"; the mesmerizing effect of the cinematograph; the identity of the second tramp. Kipling's deliberate ambiguity suggests that love may be a dangerous mystery, one that can drive a man to forsake his duties, but that the true reasons can never be known.

BIBLIOGRAPHY

Bauer, Helen Pike. *Rudyard Kipling: A Study of the Short Fiction.* New York: Twayne, 1994.

Boynton, Henry Walcott. "Rudyard Kipling," *New York Times Review of Books,* 8 October 1904, p. 665.

Kipling, Rudyard. *Traffics and Discoveries.* Edited by Hermione Lee. London: Penguin, 1987.

Lee, Hermione. Introduction. *Traffics and Discoveries.* London: Penguin, 1987.

Lycett, Andrew. *Rudyard Kipling.* Phoenix: Orion Books, 1999.

Mason, Phillip "More Thoughts on Mrs. Bathurst." *Kipling Journal* 66 (1992): 11–20.

Margaret Godbey O'Brien

TRANSATLANTIC AUTHORS

In the late 19th and early 20th centuries, a number of American-born authors established their careers as writers while living in England. Their work fostered a number of shifts in literary styles and devices used in poetry and prose, including short fiction. Texts such as Radclyffe Hall's unpublished "American Authors in England" attest to the relevance of transatlantic authorship as it was understood in the first half of the 20th century. The turn in the second half of the century toward studies of "alterity" or "otherness" has only heightened the critical importance of texts written in England by authors from abroad. In *Culture and Imperialism* (written 15 years after his groundbreaking *Orientalism*), Edward Said explores the problem of otherness in terms of its relationship to Western imperialism. Literary texts, he suggests, are used to uphold the power structures set by dominant societies. As individuals on the margins of society, American authors in England would always be somewhat outside, and their sensitivities to how that alterity is experienced informs their work and enhances our understanding of otherness in ways not merely restricted to nationality.

A few of the best-known authors whose influential work was produced largely during their residence in England are Djuna Barnes (1892–1982), Hilda Doolittle (H. D.) (1886–1961) and HENRY JAMES (1843–1916). Others who visited England in the course of developing their prose include such writers as Samuel Langhorne Clemens (Mark Twain) (1835–1910), Edith Wharton (1862–1937), Gertrude Stein (1874–1946), and Ernest Hemingway (1899–1961). All of these authors wrote in their short fiction about the experience of being an American in England, about England itself, about British participation in the world wars, or about the experience of alterity more generally. It is worthy of note that the highly influential work of the poets T. S. Eliot (1888–1865) and Ezra Pound (1885–1972) was developed during their residence in England. Perhaps the most influential of these writers in terms of the American's experience in England are Henry James and his good friend Edith Wharton, who spent the second half of her life living primarily in Paris. A number of these authors wrote from the margins in other senses as well. For example, they did not necessarily conform to conventional sexual practices, and they frequently problematized conventional conceptions of gender. The female authors were also writing as outsiders in a patriarchal literary history and, in the case of H. D., for example, wrote against the dominant discourses enforced by their male mentors. These writers and the motifs in their prose have helped critics understand writings from the margin. Postcolonial consciousness now governs many refreshed readings of canonical British texts such as those by Jane Austen; a refreshed perspective on British texts written by foreign authors has gained renewed potency in Western society.

Significantly, not only authors but also major ideas and influences moved rapidly across the Atlantic in the 19th and early 20th centuries. The frequent movement of bodies between North America and England was accompanied by advancements in industrial and communication technologies (telegraphs, telephones, airplanes) that fostered the almost instantaneous sharing of ideas. For example, ideas about psychoanalysis and the work of the Society for Psychical Research moved from England to the United States, while the practice of "mediumship" (in which a living individual communicates with one no longer living) moved from the United States to England. Traces of these concepts are notable in the short fiction produced by the authors named above. The short fiction produced by transatlantic authors of this period therefore reflects two important characteristics of late 19th- and early 20th-century British literature. First, the fiction calls attention to questions of alterity both because the authors themselves were outsiders and because the stories they wrote address issues of otherness. Second, the texts produced by these authors contribute to an early corpus of work that reflects the newly established ease with which ideas flowed back and forth between America and England.

BIBLIOGRAPHY

Hall, Radclyffe. "American Authors in England." Radclyffe Hall, 1880–1943 and Una Vincenzo, Lady Troubridge, 1887–1963 Papers, ca. 1900–1962. Harry Ransom Center. University of Texas at Austin.

Said, Edward. *Culture and Imperialism.* New York: Knopf, 1993.

———. *Orientalism.* New York: Vintage, 1979.

Lindsay Holmgren

"TRANSFORMATION" MARY SHELLEY (1830)

Appearing in the popular annual the *Keepsake* for 1831 (see ANNUALS), "Transformation" continues the exploration of romantic conventions and themes of social inequities MARY SHELLEY addressed in earlier works. Though Shelley was known primarily for her literary family and her first novel, *Frankenstein* (1818), her contributions to English romanticism included poetry, travel narratives, mythological dramas, and short stories, which she admitted writing from time to time to make ends meet. For years critics devalued Shelley's short stories for this reason and in doing so overlooked Shelley's experimenta-

tion in her short fiction with traditional elements to create what A. A. Markley calls a "New Gothic."

The central incident in "Transformation" was suggested by Byron's unfinished drama "The Deformed Transformed" (1824). The narrative follows proud and handsome Guido as he journeys to Paris, wastes his inheritance, and indulges in "sleepless, riotous nights." The loss of his fortune sends Guido home to Genoa, where he learns that the Marchese Torella, the wealthy father of Guido's betrothed Juliet, has dissolved the marriage arrangement. But Torella proposes a new agreement: Guido may marry Juliet and inherit her fortune, but only if he agrees to strict spending limits. Offended by the notion, Guido gives in to his "roused pride" and plans to abduct Juliet, but each time his attempts are foiled. While wandering near the seaside, he encounters a misshapen dwarf, "with squinting eyes, distorted features, and body deformed," a creature who "became a horror to behold." The dwarf promises to give Guido a chest full of gold, silver, and jewels if they exchange bodies for three days.

Hoping the fortune can fund his revenge, Guido agrees to the transformation. The dwarf takes advantage of his new form and woos Juliet for himself. Putting aside his pride, Guido wrestles with the doppelganger and, risking eternal entrapment in the dwarf's form, kills him. But Guido wakes to find that both his body and his relationship to Torella and Juliet are restored, and while bearing the pain and regret of his previous ways, Guido becomes "a fonder and more faithful husband."

The story is constructed in a framework familiar to its intended audience (mostly women purchased annuals). While it conforms to typical romantic conventions (natural imagery, the glorification of the commonplace, elements of the supernatural, and the Byronic sinnerhero), "Transformation" also incorporates popular Christian allusions: the prodigal son, the fall of Lucifer, and the Faust myth. Guido takes his inheritance and wastes it on lascivious living, only to return home "the prodigal son of scripture: the fatted calf was killed for him." Guido's subsequent fall into pride is clearly reminiscent of the fall of Lucifer from Heaven, portrayed in Milton's *Paradise Lost.* (The work was a lifelong inspiration for Shelley, challenging her to think in terms of her own mythic scope.)

Similarly, Shelley's knowledge of German literature made the Faust legend a promising and manageable myth for "Transformation." Here the fiendish dwarf assumes the role of Mephistopheles, bargaining with Guido for his soul. The dwarf also reinforces one of Shelley's more popular gothic conventions: the diabolical double, the projection of a split personality; the most obvious use of this convention appears in *Frankenstein,* where the double takes the form of the scientist and his creature. (See also "MAURICE, OR THE FISHER'S COT.")

BIBLIOGRAPHY
Markley, A. A. "Mary Shelley's 'New Gothic': Character Doubling and Social Critique in the Short Fiction," *Gothic Studies* 3, no. 1 (2002): 15–23.
Shelley, Mary. *Collected Tales.* London: Johns Hopkins University Press, 1976.

Greg Stone

"TREE OF KNOWLEDGE, THE" HENRY JAMES (1910)

First published in the collection *The Soft Side,* this HENRY JAMES story revolves around the interlocking relationships of three Londoners with a sculptor, Morgan Mallow, who curiously remains offstage throughout this tightly compressed narrative. Peter Brench, the story's protagonist, carefully conceals both his disregard of the talents of his best friend Mallow and his romantic longings for the sculptor's wife. When Lancelot Mallow, the sculptor's son and godson to Peter Brench, decides to pursue his own artistic ambitions in Paris, Brench is at first strongly opposed to the young man's plans and then takes great pains to ensure that the young artist's education does not lead him to break the closely maintained silence about his father's mediocrity. When Lancelot's efforts fail to meet with success, he returns to London, where he confers with his family's old friend Brench. Having realized the purpose of Brench's opposition to his pursuit of art as well as his godfather's secret desire for his mother, Lance reveals that his mother, too, has always been aware of her husband's lack of artistic ability. The story ends with Brench's realization that his careful actions, designed to protect Mrs. Mallow's sensitivities, have been all in vain.

In a notebook entry dated October 5, 1899, James describes his idea for this story as "practicable on the rigid Maupassant (at extremest brevity) system" (*Notebooks,* 184). The story's almost excessive conciseness marks out this tale as a perfect example of James's characteristic narrative technique of "restricted consciousness." The central character of the story, Peter Brench, from whose perspective this ostensibly simple tale of a love triangle and family dynamics is told, remains throughout the most unknowing of the minidrama's participants. In the preface written for the publication of the collection *The Soft Side,* James characterizes the effects of the technique displayed here as producing "novels intensely compressed" in the guise of short stories (Wagenknecht, 125). Although it is easy to conceive how the materials of a story like "The Tree of Knowledge" could yield a compelling novel, the story itself failed to find a publisher on its own merits and thus appeared first alongside other pieces in an anthology.

BIBLIOGRAPHY
James, Henry. *The Complete Notebooks.* Edited by Leon Edel and Lyall H. Powers. New York: Oxford University Press, 1987.
———. "The Tree of Knowledge." In *Complete Stories, 1898–1910,* edited by Denis Donoghue, 220–234. New York: Library of America, 1996.
Wagenknecht, Edward. *The Tales of Henry James.* New York: Frederick Ungar, 1984.

Tony Rafalowski

TREMAIN, ROSE (1943–)

The daughter of the writer Keith Nicholas Home, Rose Tremain was born in London. For several years, she taught elementary school in London, and for two years, she worked as an editor with the British Printing Corporation. Since 1972, she has concentrated on her writing, though she held an adjunct professorship at the University of East Anglia from 1988 to 1995.

Known primarily as a novelist, Tremain has written 10 novels. In 1983, she was included in a list of the 20 best young British novelists. For *The Swimming Pool Season* (1985), she received the Angel Literary Award. For *Restoration: A Novel of Seventeenth-Century England* (1989), she received a Booker Prize nomination, and for *Music and Silence* (1999), she received the Whitbread

Prize. However, she has also worked extensively as a writer of short stories, and these have been published in three standard collections: *The Colonel's Daughter* (1984), *The Garden of the Villa Mollini and Other Stories* (1987), and *Evangelista's Fan* (1995). In 1996 her *Collected Short Stories* appeared. Tremain's stories are characterized by their careful construction, shrewd pacing, clever turns, elegant and efficient expression, and sophisticated irony and wit.

The stories typically focus on characters whose studied restraint barely contains their great psychological strain. Thus the title story of Tremain's first collection, "The Colonel's Daughter," presents a character study of a woman whose troubled adult life seems to have been preordained by the poems she wrote as a girl, all of which in one way or another concerned death. Trying to redefine herself through radical politics that she only superficially understands, she steals the silver from her parents' mansion, causes the death of a devoted family servant, and ends up being abused by her proletarian lover for her misguided efforts. Another story in the collection, "Dinner for One," brings together a gay chef whose lover has left him for a younger man and a couple ostensibly celebrating their 50th wedding anniversary.

The title story of Tremain's second collection, "The Garden of the Villa Mollini," is a baroque, rather gothic tale about a series of tragic and ironic deaths that mark the construction of an elaborate garden on the estate of a famous and sinisterly self-involved opera singer of the 1880s.

In "Evangelista's Fan," the title story of Tremain's third collection, Salvatore Cavalli, a clockmaker in the Piedmont, Italy, becomes Evangelista Fantino, a barometer maker in London. In "correcting" the calendar, the king of Piedmont has officially eliminated most of Cavalli's life from the historical record. (This circumstance is akin to someone's being born in a leap year on February 29 and technically having a birthday only every fourth year.) In the story, Tremain works around the irony that while erasing one's past may create new possibilities for one's future, it may also eliminate other possibilities that depend on one's past associations. Paradoxically, the story demonstrates how gratification is often heightened by its juxtaposition with regret. In "Two of Them," a teenage boy spends a summer at a seaside resort where his mother is hoping that his father will recover more fully and quickly from a mental breakdown. As the boy tries to come to terms with the immediate reality of his father's delusional episodes and with the broader implications for his family's future, he meets two young women who idyllically initiate him sexually. In "Bubble and Star," a widow enters into a strange relationship with a much younger tough. In trying to redefine herself after her husband's death, she discovers not so much that she is someone very different from who she thought she was but that she is someone very different from who her husband wanted her to be. In the story's climax, as an ultimate gesture of self-assertion, she leaps into Niagara Falls.

BIBLIOGRAPHY

Blom, J. M., and L. R. Leavis. "New Writing: Novels and Short Stories," *English Studies* (October 1988): 410–420.

Blundell, Janet Boyarin. "*The Colonel's Daughter and Other Stories.*" *Library Journal,* 15 May 1984, p. 997.

Field, Michele, and Sybil Steinberg. "Interview: Rose Tremain," *Publishers Weekly,* 5 April 1993, pp. 50–51.

Greenlaw, Lavinia. "Fables of the Fateful," *Times Literary Supplement,* 8 July 1994, p. 19.

Scott, Mary. "The Logic of Surprise," *New Statesman and Society,* 25 November 1994, pp. 41–42.

Tremain, Rose. *Collected Short Stories.* London: Sinclair-Stevenson, 1996.

———. *The Colonel's Daughter.* New York: Summit, 1984.

———. *Evangelista's Fan.* Thorndike, Me.: Thorndike Press, 1995.

———. *The Garden of the Villa Mollini and Other Stories.* London: Hamish Hamilton, 1987.

Martin Kich

TREVOR, WILLIAM (1928–)

Although William Trevor has written 20 novels and 10 produced plays and although his work in those genres has been highly regarded, his short story contributions have made him one of the preeminent figures in that genre in the second half of the 20th century. Trevor's fictions have typically focused on ordinary characters whose complacency is undermined by the intrusion of events from beyond their present place or time. In some instances, incidents or decisions from the characters' own pasts resurface to disrupt the accommodations that they have made to define and sustain their narrow stations in the world. In other instances, social changes or political issues from the broader world are interjected into the equally parochial territories that Trevor has most frequently explored, the rural community and the urban neighborhood, and thereby force the character to confront the equally disturbing consequences of choosing to act or failing to act.

Trevor's style is affectingly suited to his subjects. Relying on direct statement and careful detailing, Trevor manages to convey the quiet ambiguities at the center of his characters' largely unremarkable existence. Readers acquire a poignant sense of the pathos in such circumscribed lives without entering into a false sense of identification with characters' circumstances. The universal implications of the stories' themes are suggested through an intimacy stripped of the excesses of empathy.

An illustrative story may be the title story of one of Trevor's more recent collections, The HILL BACHELORS (2000). The main character is a young man named Paulie who has moved from the rural Irish countryside to the city, where he seems on the verge of realizing the sort of satisfying professional and personal life that he has long imagined for himself. But before he achieves that satisfaction, his father dies, and Paulie feels compelled on many levels to return to the family farm in order to maintain it and care for his now widowed mother. His mother does not fully appreciate what he has sacrificed, but there is no sustained tension between them. In fact, having made his decision, Paulie learns to live with its consequences, and his awareness of those consequences provides a quiet counterpoint, rather than a continuing, corrosive tension, between his comprehension of what his life has become and his intimations of what it might have become. His pointedly undramatic adjustments to his changed circumstances are at the center of the story's understated telling and its themes.

Born William Trevor Cox in Mitchelstown, County Cork, Ireland, Trevor attended St. Columba's College in Dublin from 1941 to 1946 and completed his B.A. at Trinity College in Dublin in 1950. Throughout most of the 1950s, Trevor taught art at secondary schools in County Armagh, Northern Ireland, and at Rugby and Somerset in England. A sculptor of some note, he was especially known for the figures he created for churches, and his work was featured in one-man shows in Dublin and Bath. Trevor's first novel, A Standard of Behavior, was published in 1958, and from 1960 to 1965 he worked as an advertising copywriter with Notley's in London. Three more novels—The Old Boys (1964), The Boarding-House (1965), and The Love Department (1966)—would be published before his first collection of short stories, The Day We Got Drunk on Cake, and Other Stories, appeared in 1967. After the publication of The Boarding-House, Trevor devoted his energies full time to his own writing.

In addition to The Hill Bachelors, his collections of short stories have included The Ballroom of Romance, and Other Stories (1972), Angels at the Ritz, and Other Stories (1975), Lovers of Their Time, and Other Stories (1978), The Distant Past, and Other Stories (1979), Beyond the Pale, and Other Stories (1981), The Stories of William Trevor (1983), The News from Ireland, and Other Stories (1986), Family Sins and Other Stories (1989), Cocktails at Doney's, and Other Stories (1996), Nights at the Alexandra (2001), and A BIT ON THE SIDE (2004). Moreover, his achievement in the genre has been reflected in the publication of the aggregate volumes William Trevor: Collected Stories (1992), Outside Ireland: Selected Stories (1995), and Ireland: Selected Stories (1998).

Trevor has received the Benson Medal from the Royal Society of Literature for Angels at the Ritz, and Other Stories and the Macmillan Silver Pen Award and the Irish Times Literary Award for Fiction for The Hill Bachelors. His stories have appeared in the most prestigious periodicals in Ireland, the United Kingdom, and the United States, as well as in many anthologies. In the last two decades, his stories and novels have frequently and successfully been adapted to television and film. Trevor himself has written the teleplays based on his stories "The Grass Widows," "The Mark-2 Wife," and "O Fat White Woman" (from The Ballroom of Romance, and Other Stories), "Matilda's England" (from Lovers of Their Time, and Other Stories), "The Penthouse Apartment" (from The Stories of William Trevor), and "Events at Drimaghleen" (from Family Sins, and Other Stories).

BIBLIOGRAPHY

Archibald, Douglas, ed. Special Issue Devoted to the Work of William Trevor. *Colby Quarterly* 38, no. 3 (September 2002).

Morrison, Kristin. *William Trevor.* Twayne's English Authors Series, no. 501. New York: Twayne, 1993.

Mortimer, Mark. "The Short Stories of William Trevor." *Etudes Irlandaises: revue Francaise d'histoire, civilisation et litterature de l'Irelande* 9 (December 1984): 161–173.

Tillinghast, Richard. "'They Were as Good as We Were': The Stories of William Trevor," *New Criterion* 11 (February 1993): 10–17.

Trevor, William. *Collected Stories.* London: Penguin, 1993.

Martin Kich

TROLLOPE, ANTHONY (1815–1882)

Anthony Trollope was born in London, the fourth son of Thomas Anthony Trollope, a lawyer and farmer, and Frances Milton. In his *Autobiography* (published posthumously in 1883), the author notes that the family's subsequent poverty made him feel humiliated and miserable in the rigid public social hierarchies at Harrow School and later Winchester, and he was bullied remorselessly. This sense of exclusion was reinforced when Frances Trollope took her three youngest children to America to set up a department store in the city of New Harmony, Tennessee, near Memphis, leaving Anthony behind. In 1832, having returned to England, she published the notorious *Domestic Manners of the Americans,* which brought her fame and marked the start of a highly successful writing career through which she was able to support her impecunious family. Trollope identified with his industrious mother and was scared of his depressive father; nonetheless, much of his work deals sympathetically with individuals who find themselves on the edges of society, unable to exist harmoniously within it. The story "The Spotted Dog," in which the central character plunges from middle-class respectability into the dark abyss of poverty, has been seen as an attempt to write down something of the fear that stayed with Trollope into adulthood. Trollope finally began to achieve a sense of belonging when, aged 19, he joined the London post office as a clerk. Life as a civil servant suited Trollope, and many of his works, notably *The Three Clerks* (1858) and *The Small House at Allington* (1863),

extol the professional opportunities it offered diligent young men.

Trollope is best known for his tremendously popular novels, the most famous of which are set in Barsetshire, a fictional southern county, and deal with the uneasy relationship among ecclesiastical factions in the cathedral town Barchester, the clash between the conservative landowners and the new-monied, modernizers, and the vexed relationships between men and women. Most of Trollope's novels are set in his present day, and he was often praised for the accuracy with which he described modern life. *The Way We Live Now* (1875) is a devastating attack on the corruption of an effete aristocracy and the sexual double-standards of the day. Trollope played out his interest in politics through the so-called Palliser novels, in which his characters navigate their way through the political and marital intrigues of London's parliamentary world. For most of his career, many critics viewed Trollope almost as a protofeminist because of his recurrent interest in the limitations imposed on women by societal conventions and the struggles of women to find personal fulfillment both inside and outside marriage. By the end of her career, however, the works of more daring NEW WOMAN writers such as ELLA D'ARCY and GEORGE EGERTON were beginning to supersede Trollope's polite young ladies, and the literary public began to regard him as rather staid and the old-fashioned spokesman for an unchanging, idyllic rural England of cozy domesticity. Trollope wrote 47 novels at breakneck speed, and at the time of his death had several lined up for publication, including *Mr. Scarborough's Family* (1883), *An Old Man's Love* (1884), and the unfinished, *The Landleaguers* (1883).

Ultimately, Trollope made a deliberate decision to focus on the novel rather than the short story because the expanse of the Victorian novel allowed him to follow his interest in character and its development over a period of several years. But he did publish more than 40 short stories in various magazines, the majority of which were collected into several collections. Some, like *Tales of All Countries* (1861; 1863), *Lotta Schmidt and Other Stories* (1897), and *Why Frau Frohman Raised Her Prices* (1882), were inspired by his foreign travels to Europe and North America. *An Editor's Tales* (1870) drew on Trollope's experiences of the publishing industry. Most of these stories were written for money during a period when Trollope could command high fees but did not have the emotional energy for a longer work.

Trollope established a reputation for himself as a writer of social comedy and an exponent of contemporary realism. The short stories embody many of the same themes that appear in the novels. For instance, great use is made of courtship and romance plots in which a younger character (usually a woman) demonstrates her firm principles by overcoming parental opposition. "The PARSON'S DAUGHTER OF OXNEY COLNE" (1861) portrays the relationship between the title heroine and a young man from outside the community. It shows how the rigid social conventions of the time nearly destroy the blossoming relationship. As in his longer works, like *Rachel Ray* (1863), Trollope is keen to demonstrate the defenselessness of women when left to their own devices; the heroine and her family live a sheltered life in genteel poverty. *La Mère Bauche* (1859) reworks the favorite Trollopian device of the romantic triangle; a struggle between a father and son over the heroine, in this case, has a tragic ending. Unusual among Trollope's stories is "The TELEGRAPH GIRL" (1877), which focuses on the struggles of a young woman who has to work for a living.

The short stories often focus on struggles within families. In "The TWO GENERALS," written during the American Civil War (1863), two Southern brothers, rivals for the same woman, fight on opposing sides. The two brothers vow to kill each other should they meet on the battlefield. The climax comes when the brothers meet; the Southern brother has the opportunity to shoot the Northern but turns away and is himself shot by another Northerner. Trollope was vehemently anti-slavery, but this story also offers insights into his interest in obsessive behavior. Although Trollope's reputation does not depend on these stories, many are good examples of the way in which his works hang on particular moral or ethical dilemmas to which his characters have to find solutions if they are to live their lives successfully. "Why Frau Frohmann Raised Her Prices" describes the slow awakening of a good-hearted but reactionary old shopkeeper to the changes taking place around her.

Believing that love, loyalty, and duty are the most powerful determinants of human behavior, she comes to realize that it is often money that governs what people do, a message that Trollope was never slow to point out.

BIBLIOGRAPHY
Hall, N. John. *Trollope.* Oxford: Oxford University Press, 1991.
MacDonald, Susan Peck. *Anthony Trollope.* Boston: Twayne, 1987.
Smalley, Donald. *Anthony Trollope: The Critical Heritage.* London: Routledge, 1969.
Trollope, Anthony. *Early Short Stories.* Oxford: Oxford University Press, 1994.
———. *Later Short Stories.* Oxford: Oxford University Press, 1995.
Turner, Mark. *Trollope and the Magazines.* London: Macmillan, 2000.

Andrew Maunder

TURN OF THE SCREW, THE HENRY JAMES (1898)

Readers cannot agree on what HENRY JAMES's *The Turn of the Screw* is about. On its publication in 1898 it was received as a ghost story about the haunting of two children. But since the 1920s an alternative interpretation has emerged in which the ghosts are merely the hallucinations of the narrating character's disturbed mind.

The novella opens with a framing narrative in which an anonymous first-person narrator introduces us to Douglas, who promises to present his small circle of friends with a ghost story that is unequalled in its "dreadfulness" (1). The story that follows is related as the first-person account of a young and unnamed woman who is hired by a handsome London bachelor to become governess to his orphaned niece and nephew at his country estate, Bly. On arriving at Bly the governess finds the two children to be beautiful and charming, and she strikes up a friendly relationship with the housekeeper, Mrs. Grose, the only other person in the house. But the governess's joy at this apparently idyllic situation is quickly marred. The young boy, Miles, has been expelled from his boarding school for reasons that are unknown, and she learns of the scandalous events that have preceded her arrival at the house: The previous governess, Miss Jessel, took her own life following the death of her lover, the sinister valet Peter Quint. The governess sees the ghostly apparitions of both Quint and Jessel around the grounds and in the house, but still worse, she comes to believe that the children, too, see the ghosts, that they are in fact being haunted by the dead lovers, who seek to possess the children's souls. A strict condition of her employment being that she never contact the uncle in London, the governess has only Mrs. Grose to confide her fears to, but the latter is a prosaical woman who has seen no sign of the ghosts herself and appears unsure about the governess's claim. Believing that only she can save the children and that this must be done by forcing them to confess the presence of their ghostly companions, the governess confronts first Flora, then Miles. The young girl falls into a dangerous fever and is taken by Mrs. Grose to her uncle in London. Now left alone with Miles, and seeing Quint's "white face of damnation" (84) in the window even as she pleads with boy to give up his name and save his own soul, she presses Miles to her. The boy pulls away, looks frantically around the room, and then falls into the governesses arms, his heart stopped.

Critical reception on first publication was mixed, some reviewers praising it as a "masterpiece" (*New York Tribune,* 23 October 1898; reprinted in James, 150) of storytelling, others reviling it as "the most hopelessly evil story that we have ever read" (*Independent,* 5 January 1899; reprinted in James, 156). But no reviewers doubted that it was a story about the supernatural, in which a young woman battles heroically to save the souls of her two haunted charges. Not until a 1924 article by Edna Kenton was it suggested that the ghosts might not be real since they are attested to by only a single character: "As a tiny matter of literal fact, no reader has more to go on than the young governess's word" (170). The crucial issue became whether the governess was a reliable or unreliable narrator, and in the latter case, it is only she who poses a danger to the children. In 1934 Edmund Wilson published the first Freudian analysis of the story, in which he claimed that the ghosts were the hysterical hallucinations of the sexually repressed governess, who "cannot admit to herself her sexual impulses" (172). Many versions of

this view have since been articulated. The text strongly suggests, for example, that the young governess had fallen in love with the uncle in London, and the sexual couple of the first governess and Quint (who appears in the uncle's clothes) therefore seems like a sort of dream-logic inversion of this first desired coupling. Indeed, the novel became a crucial site of contestation over what is involved in psychoanalytic criticism of a literary text. Shoshana Felman's 1977 intervention criticized Wilson for what she saw as a reductive reading of both the novella and of Freud. Wilson, according to Felman, tries to reduce the text's multiple meanings to a single, literal meaning, that of sex. Stressing that for Freud, sexuality "essentially consists of ambiguity" (210), Felman argues that sexuality is not the text's meaning but rather that through which it "fails to mean" any one final thing (211).

Felman's reading suggests that there is not one correct interpretation of the story, that the text demands a reader who will be attentive to its ability to signify more than one thing at once. As she suggests, it is as if James has included the narrator Douglas's warning "The story *won't* tell . . . not in any literal vulgar way" (3) as an anticipatory rebuke to any reader who will try to reduce the text's indeterminacy by forcing a single meaning on it. As Wilson himself suggests, the novella reveals James to be a master of ambiguity: Almost every event and every utterance is "open to a double interpretation" (171), down to the dying boy's "you devil!" (85), which may be refer to the ghost of Quint that he is finally acknowledging or to the insane governess who is terrorizing him to death.

The novella's ambiguity makes establishing its genre particularly difficult. As a story that involves possibly supernatural happenings centered around a young woman in an isolated great house, it has elements of the gothic. But interpreted as a tale about madness, it seems more like a psychological study. Tzvetan Todorov considered the story a remarkable example of what he called the Fantastic, a fiction that is uncertainly positioned between the supernatural and the natural and that refuses to resolve this indecision at any point (194). With its employment of first-person and possibly unreliable narrators and its ambiguity, the novella may also be considered to display features of MODERN-

ISM. That *The Turn of the Screw* has been such a touchstone for so many critical debates for the last 100 years is testimony to its own uncanny power to haunt.

BIBLIOGRAPHY

Felman, Shoshana. "Henry James: Madness and the Risks of Practice (Turning the Screw of Interpretation)." 1977. In *The Turn of the Screw*. Norton Critical Edition. 196–227. New York and London: Norton, 1999.

The Innocents. Dir. Jack Clayton. Film. 1961.

James, Henry. *The Turn of the Screw*. Norton Critical Edition. New York and London: Norton, 1999.

Kenton, Edna. "Henry James to the Ruminant Reader." 1924. In *The Turn of the Screw*. Norton Critical Edition. 169–170. New York and London: Norton, 1999.

Todorov, Tzvetan. "The Fantastic." 1973. In *The Turn of the Screw*. Norton Critical Edition. 193. New York and London: Norton, 1999.

Wilson, Edmund. "The Ambiguity of Henry James." 1934. In *The Turn of the Screw*. Norton Critical Edition. 170–172. New York and London: Norton, 1999.

Victoria Margree

"TWO DROVERS, THE" WALTER SCOTT (1827)

Although the Edinburgh-born WALTER SCOTT officially published "The Two Drovers" as one among three short tales folded into a framing narrative called *Chronicles of the Canongate,* released for sale November 1, 1827, the story appeared separately a little more than a week earlier, in the October 20 issue of the *London Weekly Review.*

When the story was published Scott was concerned—apparently not without reason—about how readers would respond to it. Certainly, the short format and spare style was not what the author of the celebrated historical novel *Waverley* (1815) was associated with in the minds of his readers. However, since then the story has come to be considered one of the first modern short stories in English. As told by the narrator, the story is divided into two distinct parts. The first part could easily stand alone as a complete story. The ground on which the events play themselves out is well developed, consisting primarily of descriptions of the two protagonists, their relationship to each other, and their individual cultural conditioning. The protagonists, two young men of different and, at the time,

antagonistic backgrounds, have become cross-border friends through mutual trust and respect while engaged in a shared occupation. They are hired drovers who move Scottish cattle from grazing in the Highlands to markets in the north of England. The narrator quickly secures the sympathy of readers for the Scot, Robin Oig McCombich, through a preponderance of detail concerning him, his character, and the culture within which he developed. This sympathy sharpens the tragic consequences of the story's events. While not so fully developed as a character, the other protagonist, Harry Wakefield, also vies for readers' sentiments. The narrative further develops their relationship in describing their amicable and sometimes humorous interactions while on a cattle drive south into England.

Tensions between the two develop when, caught in a disagreement between an English landowner and his unscrupulous bailiff, Harry turns on Robin, even to the extent of rudely rejecting friendly offers of conciliation. Tensions continue to rise along with the pace of narration, building toward a tragic and climactic ending. Goaded on by a drunken herd of his own countrymen that he cannot control, the English drover forsakes his "tolerably accurate sense of law and justice" to defend his wounded pride in the only way he knows. An amateur boxer, he knocks Robin down twice. Robin, for the sake of clan and personal honor, retrieves his long dagger from another drover, returns to the inn where he was assaulted, and kills Harry with a single thrust to the chest, straight through the heart, assuaging his wounded pride and restoring his lost sense of self. The debt of honor is fully paid when Robin is later executed for the murder.

The second part of the tale is an extended, didactic denouement, in which the narrator re-presents and interprets the events of the story through the rhetoric of the English legal system—something with which Scott was familiar. Through the discourse of the judge presiding at the trial of Robin, it is explained that the case against Robin swings on the linchpin of time, a narrative element keenly manipulated by Scott in the story. As the judge reads the circumstances of the case, Robin had adequate time when he went to retrieve his dagger to come to his senses and decide against seeking vengeance. The judge, despite his juridical acuity, fails to understand that Robin had no self to recall, at least not until his honor was restored to him. This is the same honor that demanded that he surrender to his fate. While such a historical event may have occurred—though not in this specific form—and may have been used as a seed from which to grow the tale, it is just as likely that Scott was writing a tragedy in the Aristotelian sense of the word, grounded in his own borderlands experience of the unification of Scotland with England. The story has pronounced connections with classical Greek tragedy, including the foreshadowing of future events through a seer, the role of fate in determining the course of events, the crucial moment when the fortune of a protagonist changes, and the cathartic effect on readers of the tragic sequence taken as a whole. As described by Aristotle in *Poetics,* all of these dramatic elements figure in the development of and response to the events that inexorably unfold between Robin and Harry from beginning to end. (See also "The HIGHLAND WIDOW.")

BIBLIOGRAPHY
Johnson, Christopher. "Anti-Pugilism: Violence and Justice in Scott's 'The Two Drovers,'" *Scottish Literary Journal* 22, no. 1 (1995): 46–60.
Overton, W. J. "Scott, the Short Story, and History: 'The Two Drovers,'" *Studies in Scottish Literature* 21 (1986): 210–225.
Scott, Walter. "The Two Drovers." In *Chronicles of the Canongate.* 1827. Edited by Claire Lamont. Penguin Books: London, 2000.
Wilson, J. "A Review of *Chronicles of the Canongate,*" *Blackwood's Edinburgh Magazine* 22 (1827): 556–570.

James From

"TWO GENERALS, THE" ANTHONY TROLLOPE (1863)

"The Two Generals" first appeared in the Christmas 1863 issue of *Good Words,* the popular monthly magazine launched by Scottish publisher Alexander Strahan in 1860 and edited by the Reverend Norman Macleod. ANTHONY TROLLOPE's involvement with *Good Words* had begun in 1862, with the publication of "The Widow's Mite," and continued into 1864, when he published "Malachi's Cove" in the December 1864 issue. "The Two Generals" has its genesis in Trollope's six-month tour of North America in 1861–62, the same trip that inspired his better-known travel book *North America* (1862). "The Two Generals" is a tale of the American Civil War, in which the personal conflict between the brothers Tom and Frank Reckenthorpe mirrors the civil conflict raging between North and South.

Tom and Frank Reckenthorpe, the sons of Major Reckenthorpe, a former United States senator who is well known and respected in his home state of Kentucky, are political opposites. Tom, the eldest, is a slave-owning Southern gentleman, loyal to the South and its ways. Frank, a West Point–educated army officer, declares himself loyal to the United States government. Though the brothers oppose each other in war, however, they are unfortunately in agreement about loving Ada Forster, an orphaned Northern cousin who lives with the Reckenthorpes. Ada, however, against all her Northern convictions and despite Frank's efforts to dissuade her, loves Tom and has promised to become his wife, intensifying the hostility between the brothers. The war progresses, and Tom and Frank, having risen through the ranks, inevitably meet on the battlefield, where Frank, jealous and hardened, is forced to choose between personal and national loyalty and to admit that love is stronger than politics.

"The Two Generals" demonstrates Trollope's fascination with the human conscience, duty, and moral dilemma, themes Trollope explored at length in novels such as *The Warden* (1855), *He Knew He Was Right* (1867), *Dr. Wortle's School* (1880), and many others. The story is also an example of Trollope's distinct authorial voice, evident here in his commentary on both the American war and the behavior of his characters.

BIBLIOGRAPHY
Trollope, Anthony. *Complete Short Stories.* Forth Worth: Texas Christian University Press, 1979–83.

Sara Atwood

U

"UNCLE ERNEST" ALAN SILLITOE **(1958)**
First published in 1958, "Uncle Ernest" has been
reprinted many times as part of a ALAN SILLITOE's
anthology *The Loneliness of the Long Distance Runner*.
The story is set in a social milieu favored by Sillitoe: a
working-class environment in an English Midlands
town. Ernest acquires the title of uncle when he
befriends two young girls, but he has no natural ties
since his wife has left him and his brothers have left the
district. A survivor of two world wars, he lives alone in
lodgings and makes a living as an upholsterer. Because
of his loneliness, Ernest seeks solace in public houses,
where he can drink beer undisturbed, and in a local
café where he takes most of his meals. One day when
he is eating breakfast in the café, two young girls join
him at his table. When he has overcome his shyness,
Ernest engages in conversation with the children, of
whom the oldest is 12, and learns something of their
circumstances. Their father is dead, their mother is at
work all day, and, as growing children, they are often
hungry. Ernest befriends the children and arranges to
meet them in the café on a regular basis so that he can
buy them food. The relationship that develops between
Ernest and the children eases his loneliness and keeps
him away from the public house and the beer. The
regularity of the meetings and the apparent generosity
of an unkempt middle-aged man toward two young
girls attract the attention of other people, who become
suspicious of his motives. One day when Ernest is buying food for the girls, he is approached by two plain-
clothes police officers who escort him out of the
building. He is not charged with any offence, but he is
cautioned and advised to keep away from the girls.
From then on, the only solace in Ernest's life is the
public house and beer. Officialdom has put a stop to
an innocent occupation and driven him to one that is
potentially more harmful.

This story is characterized by its stark realism,
achieved by closely observed detail. The reader recognizes Ernest's social isolation by the fact that the lavatory attendant is the only person he can rely on to look
after his tools. His low self-esteem is indicated by his
dirty raincoat, unshaven face, and general lack of
cleanliness. His upholstery skills are recognizable in
the particular way he uses his knife to cut the corner of
his bread. The general seediness of the café is evident
through the description of the brown teapot and
cracked cup. The tea leaves left at the bottom of the
cup place the story firmly in an age that predates the
invention of the teabag. All the action takes place
within the confines of the café or immediately outside
it, giving the effect of an enclosed world, as in a stage
play. To the casual observer, a dirty, unkempt, middle-
aged man frequents a café, befriends two children,
and, after a conversation with two police officers, is
seen no more. But Sillitoe has portrayed the inner loneliness of a man, his attempt to assuage his loneliness by
caring for other people, and his final surrender when
his motives are misjudged. The story, therefore, contains psychological realism as well as social realism.

BIBLIOGRAPHY
Sillitoe, Alan. *The Loneliness of the Long Distance Runner.*
  London: Pan, 1959.

Irene Wiltshire

"UNDER THE KNIFE" H. G. WELLS (1896)

Originally published in *New Review* in January 1896, "Under the Knife" was later collected in *The Plattner Story and Others* and was classified as a scientific romance by H. G. WELLS. The story's first-person narrator, who diagnoses himself as suffering a "grey depression" that has resulted in a "deadness of my emotional nature," recounts the anticipation leading up to an operation and the unusual experience of the operation itself. The morbid but surprisingly detached thoughts of dying under anesthesia with which the narrator begins the story anticipate the emergency that arises during the operation. He describes his contemplations of death as "purely personal" because he feels himself "strangely isolated—isolated without regret—from the life and existence about me." The expectation of death provides the narrator with a unique perspective that ultimately contributes to his out-of-body experience. Once the narrator is anesthetized, he discovers he is able to perceive the thoughts and emotions of the surgeons as if they were "bubbles through a stream of frothing meditation." When his vein is accidentally cut, the narrator finds himself permanently disconnected from his body. In his intangible state, the narrator becomes stationary and can only watch as his body, the room, the Earth, and finally all existence move on without him. After an initial reaction of contentment at the peaceful solitude, the narrator becomes terrified by his potentially eternal isolation until he is comforted by a godlike voice reassuring him that "There will be no more pain" and is transported back to his physical form, at which point "the dull melancholy of half a year was lifted from my mind."

"Under the Knife" is an example of science fiction writing that leaves the definition of reality purposefully vague. Whether the narrator actually leaves his body or creates the reality in his own imagination is unclear, but it is also irrelevant. Wells successfully depicts an unreal situation through the plausibly indefinite description of an out-of-body experience combined with the logical application of science to the principles of a disembodied spirit. The narrator's realization that with no physical form he suffers no pain and is no longer subject to the laws of physics is a rational revelation that accentuates the importance of his spiritual and mental suffering and helps the narrator distinguish the source of his depression. It is only by watching the tangible reality of his existence recede beyond his reach that the narrator can understand his own need for it. Tensions between chaos and certainty bring the narrator to an epiphany about the importance of social interaction. After he feels the terrors of isolation, the reassuring but curiously disembodied hand emerging out of a cloud of light and disembodied voice fill the narrator with wonder at the limitless possibilities of the universe.

That the narrator suffers a near-death experience seems certain, as does the fact that such an event might trigger an out-of-body experience. While the narrator's scientific revelations support the logical conditions of his experience, whether he actually leaves his body is as uncertain as it is irrelevant to the outcome of the experience. The narrator's faith in his experience and the sincerity with which he narrates it support his spiritual and emotional transformation. The experience is purposefully mysterious. No explanation is provided, and the idea that humans are social animals whose existence is essentially connected to their physical form is inherent in the conditions of the narrator's departure and return to his body. The final abruptness of the narrator's return to his body and the mundane actions of the surgeons on his return imply that his premonitions of death were not connected to the operation but to his emotional distance and social isolation, both of which are remedied by his out-of-body experience.

BIBLIOGRAPHY
Wells, H. G. *Short Stories of H. G. Wells.* Edited by Ursula le
  Guin. New York: Modern Library, 2004.

Tony W. Garland

"UNWRITTEN NOVEL, AN" VIRGINIA WOOLF (1920)

VIRGINIA WOOLF first published "An Unwritten Novel" in the *London Mercury* (1920) and then in *MONDAY OR TUESDAY* (1921) and the collection *A Haunted House and Other Stories* (1944). Unlike conventional short stories, it does not follow any clear-cut story line. In the framing story, an anonymous narrator gazes at a woman sitting opposite her in a train compartment and imagines her life. The embedded story offers a disrupted syntax and a disconnected series of slices of life: Minnie Marsh at luncheon, Minnie praying or darning, Minnie's boredom or hatred. A leitmotif—the spot on the windowpane Minnie tries to rub away, the itching spot between her shoulders—provides the leading thread; the spot is turned into a metaphor of a sin of which Minnie may be guilty. The story, somewhat following the pattern of a detective story, is presented as a quest for that sin. The spot recalls Nathaniel Hawthorne's allegorical tales, yet here the Christian allegory is subverted, God being derided as "a brutal old bully." If allegory is retained, it is an allegory of artistic creation.

Indeed the story reads as a metaphor of writing, as the narrator who sits watching Minnie, soon identifying with her through the same itching sensation, appears to be the very image of the writer creating a character. Writing is thus indirectly presented as an introspective process based on imagination and inner life—an implicit way of discarding the conventions of realist or mimetic writing that tries to give an illusion of reality by turning toward outer life. In the story-within-the-story the narrator lets the reader see the creative process by laying bare its mechanisms. The characters are presented as being chosen among many: Minnie will be developed while the Moggridges will remain in the dark. Moreover, it is not so much facts that are of interest as the characters' multifaceted selves. The self is elusive and difficult to capture: Like the fragments of eggshell on Minnie's lap, it is a puzzle to be pieced together; like Minnie's glove, it needs mending—a welcome challenge to the writer. As Woolf wrote in her famous essays "Modern Fiction" (1919) and "Mr. Bennett and Mrs. Brown" (1924), her kind of writing is a far cry from what she called "materialist" writing, based on verisimilitude, plot, and facts. Writing here is presented as a moment of being or vision. The imaginative process begins when the two characters are left alone in the train compartment and ends when Minnie gets off the train. The train journey, the isolation of the characters in a closed space, is conducive to a moment of vision, the time of creation; the end of the journey is a moment of crisis when the imaginative process is cut short by the return to reality. But the inexhaustible nature of creation is asserted at the very end, when a new flight of the mind is evoked and the "mysterious figures" take precedence over dull reality.

Similar devices can be found in other Woolf stories—"The Mark on the Wall," "The Lady in the Looking-Glass," or "The Shooting Party." Metaphoric writing is typical of Woolf and of MODERNISM more generally. Under the guise of telling a story, this short story tells the story of writing, adding a metafictional dimension to the narrative impulse; the theoretical principles Woolf expounded in her essays are woven into her story, blurring the dividing line between short story and essay.

BIBLIOGRAPHY

Baldwin, Dean R. *Virginia Woolf: A Study of the Short Fiction.* Boston: Twayne, 1989.

Hanson, Clare, ed. *Re-reading the Short Story.* London: Macmillan, 1989.

Reynier, Christine. "The Short Story according to Woolf," *Journal of the Short Story in English* 41 (Autumn 2003): 55–68.

Woolf, Virginia. *A Haunted House and Other Stories.* New York: Harcourt Brace, 1944.

Christine Reynier

V

VIRAGO BOOK OF FAIRY TALES, THE
ANGELA CARTER (1990) One of the many collections of fairy tales edited by ANGELA CARTER, this is an entertaining and at times ferociously politically incorrect overview, for good and bad, of the female condition, accompanied by Carter's explicit proviso that the notion of a universal sisterhood is just another myth to be wary of. The success of this volume was such as to prompt the publication of a second collection, also edited by Carter: *The Second Virago Book of Fairy Tales* came out posthumously in 1992, with an introduction by Marina Warner.

Carter's main criterion in selecting the fairy tales to be included in these volumes is that the stories should center on a female protagonist. This is the same guiding principle that had informed *Wayward Girls and Wicked Women* (1986), Carter's collection of short stories by 20th-century women writers, significantly subtitled *An Anthology of Subversive Stories* in the 1989 Penguin edition.

The Virago Book of Fairy Tales combines Carter's long-standing fascination with the genre (witnessed also by her work as a translator and editor of *The Fairy Tales of Charles Perrault* [1977] and *Sleeping Beauty and Other Favourite Fairy Tales* [1982]) with the feminist agenda already evident in *Wayward Girls and Wicked Women* as well as in Carter's own work, most notably, perhaps, in her own subversive rewriting of traditional fairy tales in *The BLOODY CHAMBER and Other Stories* (1979).

In the introduction to *The Virago Book of Fairy Tales,* Carter immediately issues a warning to the readers: "you will find very few actual fairies within the following pages." This statement allows Carter to raise a number of crucial questions on both the structure and the themes of her chosen material: Carter points out how the term *fairy tale* refers widely to a corpus of traditional, oral stories, passed on from one generation to the next and being constantly changed and remade in the process. At the same time, Carter also warns the reader that the selected stories will not automatically conform to the customary happy ending, nor will the female protagonists be necessarily represented as lovable, sympathetic heroines. In fact, while fairies are thin on the ground, a whole section of the book is devoted to witches.

Most important, though, through her direct appeal to the readers, Carter effectively takes on the role of storyteller and initiates a dialogue with her audience, thus mirroring the oral, immanent quality to be found in the act of spinning a yarn. Fairy tales lack an original author: What they have is an editor, when they are finally written down, or a performer, when they are still in their fluid, spoken form. Carter's emphasis on this point dismantles the notions of the individuality and originality of the work of art and foregrounds the importance of the context to the reception—and ultimately the interpretation—of a certain narrative.

Even so, according to Carter, the primary aim of the collection is to give pleasure to the readers. After all, fairy tales are "[t]he perennially refreshed entertainment of the poor," an elemental source of fun and diversion, available to everybody and appealing to everybody because they are anonymous and genderless.

To the contemporary reader, fairy tales also have an archival value, insofar as they provide a testimony from a past devoid of technology, when oral storytelling was still a crucial form of communication. As narratives of witness, compared with other literary genres and to recorded historical documents, fairy tales have the advantage of tapping directly into everyday concerns and informal sources, so as to offer an unofficial, alternative version of the past and an equally uncensored vision of the world and of human psychology. *The Virago Book of Fairy Tales* is therefore a self-declared celebration of both the ordinariness and the eccentricities of womanhood, not only through what the characters reveal about the human predicament but also through the extolment of the (female) storyteller's creativity and psychological and social perceptiveness.

Through her introduction, Carter herself comes to embody the figure of Mother Goose, the archetypical narrator of fairy tales. A similarly larger-than-life figure is the eponymous protagonist of the first story in the book: No other character in the collection is perhaps as striking as Sermessuaq, who is so uncontainable as to defy categorization, considering that her story does not belong to any of the seven sections into which the ensuing fairy tales are arranged. Sermessuaq is endowed with an amazing physical strength and charisma: Her power is mentioned in relation to her sexual prowess and her awe-inspiring fertility, as well as to her penchant for exhibitionism. With her swagger, Sermessuaq presides over the rest of the collection and sets its tone: playful and desecrating, occasionally grotesque, and always in-your-face.

Unsurprisingly, the traditional female desire for marriage and/or a family is among the recurrent themes in the collection, which also charts women's anxiety about their own fertility and the trials and tribulations that characters are willing to go through in order to fulfill their maternal instincts (e.g., "Kakuarkshuk," "The Juniper Tree"). Less conventionally, perhaps, the book contains stories focusing explicitly on the need for sexual gratification (e.g., "Blubber Boy," "The Pupil"), as well as traditionally bawdy tales of unfaithful and impudent wives (e.g., "The Resourceful Wife," whose title character cuckolds her husband and then boasts about it to her female friends; "The Hare"; "The Furburger"). There is also a wide selection of tales about wily women and their cunning stratagems to get what they want, often at the (comical) expense of male opposition (e.g., "Aunt Kate's Goomer-Dust," "Clever Gretel").

While love is usually at the top of the characters' wish-list, marriage is often seen as a threat (e.g., the Bluebeard-like Mr. Fox, the equally predatory husband in "Keep Your Secrets," the less gory "The Rich Farmer's Wife"), and family is not always the safe haven it ought to be. The collection contains a veritable host of wicked stepmothers (e.g., the self-explanatory "The Wicked Stepmother," "The Baba Yaga," "The Market of the Dead," "The Little Red Fish and the Clog of Gold," "Beauty and Pock Face") or closer relatives, such as mothers (e.g., "The Mother Who Married Her Son's Wife," "The Good Girl and the Ornery Girl," "Nourie Hadig"), jealous aunts (e.g., "The Girl Who Banished Seven Youths"), or ill-advised fathers (e.g., "The Princess in the Suit of Leather," with the father's threat of incest).

Carter's own favorite tale is "The Wise Little Girl," whose protagonist's intelligence restores justice to her wronged father and wins the czar's love, so that the ensuing happy ending extends to all the main characters. This story makes a good contrast to another Russian tale about a battle of wits: In "Vasilisa the Priest's Daughter" the cross-dressing Vasilisa manages to avoid discovery and protect her true identity from the king's persistent inquisitiveness. Rather than marriage to the most powerful man in the country, Vasilisa's reward for her acumen is the ability to retain her androgynous character and her freedom and to keep on roaming the world unfettered like the fairy tale that bears her name.

BIBLIOGRAPHY
Carter, Angela. *The Virago Book of Fairy Tales*. London: Virago, 1990.
Day, Aidan. *Angela Carter: The Rational Glass*. Manchester, England: Manchester University Press, 1998.
Easton, Alison, ed. *Angela Carter*. London: Macmillan, 2000.

Roemer, Danielle M., and Cristina Bacchilega, eds. *Angela Carter and the Fairy Tale.* Special Issue, *Marvels and Tales* 12, no. 1 (1998).

Stephania Ciocia

VORTICISM   Vorticism was launched onto the British art scene in 1913 by WYNDHAM LEWIS and Kate Lechmere. As a self-conscious avant-garde movement, vorticism drew from and contributed to the heady welter of aesthetic theories, models, and manifestoes that gave European MODERNISM its revolutionary dynamism in the years before World War I (1914–1918).

The establishment of the Rebel Art Centre in London in March 1914, which comprised of artists' studios and lecture and exhibition spaces, modeled on Roger Fry's Omega Workshops but absolutely and publicly opposed to Fry's Bloomsbury postimpressionism, gave the vorticist artists a collective social presence within the metropolitan art world. Artists who adhered to vorticist principles included Jessica Dismorr, Henri Gaudier-Brzeska, Helen Saunders, Edward Wadsworth, Frederick Etchells, Cuthbert Hamilton, Jacob Epstein, and William Roberts.

With the foundation of the quarterly, *Blast: the Review of the Great English Vortex* in June 1914, vorticism gained a public platform from which to both issue manifestoes and demonstrate its aesthetic principles in action. As a polemicist and philosopher of art, as a painter and as a writer, Lewis in particular attacked the turn to interiority and the subjectivism he saw as definitive of Anglo-American modernism (see especially his 1930 satire on the coterie art worlds of interwar London, *The Apes of God*). His vorticist principles and the belief in a necessary and disciplined order that underlay those principles, coupled with his deep and unashamed misogyny, enabled him to produce a writing that, rejecting impressionism as feminine and feminizing, externalizes relentlessly, turning human beings into objects buffeted by innumerable forces. His style is consistently almost oppressively ironic as he parodies the pathetic attempts of would-be-individuals to conceal the brute being of their bodies behind the veils of manufactured personalities and civilizations (Dasenbrock, 227).

The term *vortex,* first used by Ezra Pound, a champion of Lewis and of vorticism, was thus intended to signify a hard, intense, and concentrated energy at the still heart of which stood the vorticist artist. The vortex is the place of essential movement and activity; it draws in whatever rushes toward it and subjects it to its own laws of disorder. At the center of the vortex is a point of still space occupied by the artistic intelligence, by that which gives disciplined form and structure to the expressions of the vortex. This stress on distance, discipline, and order differentiated vorticism from the subjectivist aesthetics of impressionism and postimpressionism, while the aggressive, declamatory boldness of *Blast* defiantly distanced the vorticists from the cultivated amateurism of postimpressionism's English sponsors, the Bloomsbury group, as represented by VIRGINIA WOOLF and KATHERINE MANSFIELD.

BIBLIOGRAPHY
Arts Council of Great Britain, *Vorticism and Its Allies* (Arts Council, 1974; this is the illustrated catalogue to the Hayward Gallery Exhibition of the same year)
Dasenbrock, Reed Way. *The Literary Vorticism of Ezra Pound and Wyndham Lewis.* Baltimore: John Hopkins University Press, 1985.
Edwards, Paul, ed. *Blast: Vorticism 1914–1918.* Aldershot: Ashgate, 2000.

Patricia McManus

W

WALES There is a critical consensus that Wales has achieved its highest artistic potential in poetry. Nonetheless, since the beginning of the 20th century, the short story has proved a distinctive part of Welsh cultural heritage. Although the heyday of the Welsh short story is the 20th century, stories from the 19th century have been recovered as well. For instance, the anthology *A View Across the Valley: Short Stories by Women from Wales, c. 1850–1950* (2002), edited by Jane Aaron, is a collection of stories by Welsh women writing in English. What emerges in this collection remains true for most of the short fiction written in Wales during the period: The settings are mostly rural, set in farmlands, remote villages, and rugged hillsides and valleys. The characters, as Tony Brown has argued, are frequently lonely and detached, as befits a genre seen by critics as peculiarly destined to be a vehicle to portray the lives of the marginalized and the dispossessed.

The writers of Welsh short fiction can be divided into two categories: those writing in Welsh and those writing in English (Anglo-Welsh). Of those writing in Welsh, the most popular are Kate Roberts, R. Hughes Williams, and D. J. Williams, all writing in the early to mid-20th century. All three published stories in Welsh literary journals such as *Y Llenor* (1922–1955), which were established to preserve the culture and language of Wales. Roberts was noted for writing about the ordinary people of Wales, those who worked in the quarries and the iron foundries and who worked the poor soil of Wales. D. J. Williams's first collection, *Storïau'r Tir Glas*

(1936), is loyal to its author's community as well, portraying his "square mile" gently and often humorously. R. Hughes Williams wrote in Welsh and English, frequently focusing on the lives of quarrymen.

The poet Harri Webb describes the Anglo-Welsh as being neither British writing in the British literary tradition nor Welshmen writing in the ancient language of their own homeland. Many Anglo-Welsh writers do not know Welsh or do not know it well enough to create literature in that language. In *Across the Valley: Short Stories by Women from Wales,* many of the stories exhibit the author's feelings of being outsiders. The narrators tell their stories as visitors rather than as members of the community. The stories do not necessarily reflect the reality of Wales but are more an articulation of longing for a homeland seemingly denied them.

The short story came into its own in Wales with the publication of works by Caradoc Evans. His collection, *My People* (1915), written in English, projected an image of Welsh life as narrowly bound up in the often hypocritical Nonconformist religiosity of the chapel-centered communities. His stories helped Welsh writers break away from the moralizing literature of the late 19th century that was often published in magazines for women, such as *Y Gymraes* (1850) and *Y Frythones* (1879–1891), which included didactic stories.

Like many of his contemporaries in the early decades of the 20th century, Glyn Jones, another Anglo-Welsh writer, was raised in a Welsh-speaking family but received an English education. In Jones's stories the tension between individual and community is often felt. Some of his more famous stories ("Price-Parry" and "The Water Music") show the characters overcoming the rift of status or inclination that divides than from the larger community. The alienation Jones felt in his own childhood (described in *The Dragon Has Two Tongues*) becomes a deeply ingrained feature of his stories. He claims that he has never produced any writings that do not have Wales and its people as their subject. His Christian worldview and his painterly talents helped him create deeply loving, detailed pictures of the Wales he loved. Dividing the Welsh short story along gender lines might suggest that the men who wrote short fiction in the 20th century also focused on the natural world of Wales, but unlike the beautiful idealism in the women's stories, their Wales is rugged and violent. Thus, in volumes like Jones's 1998 *Collected Stories,* stories more frequently reflect the natural world than the industrial one that replaced much of Welsh rural life. The characters cope with a harsh land whose natural beauty has been blighted by mining and other industrial damage, and they do so alone. Gwyn Jones's characters are often solitary individuals, not men drawn to rural community life.

One of the most prolific Welsh authors writing in English was RHYS DAVIES, who published more than 100 short stories. His writing was influenced by French and Russian authors, especially Chekhov, and by fellow countryman Caradoc Evans. As a homosexual in a time and place that ruthlessly weeded out all those who deviated from highly prescribed gender roles, Davies moved to London. Often feeling as isolated in England as he had in Wales, Davies continued to write about Wales, the land and its people, constructing a mythical place where the people shrugged off the yoke of the Nonconformist chapel and lived more in touch with nature. Davies's *Collected Stories,* in three volumes, was published posthumously in 1998 and shows the wide range of his talents.

English-language Welsh writers still look to the short story to convey their political and social views. Several anthologies have been published since the 1990s—one, a large volume titled *Momma's Baby (Papa's Maybe)* (2000), includes 55 stories.

BIBLIOGRAPHY

Aaron, Jane. *A View Across the Valley: Short Stories by Women from Wales, 1850–1950.* Aberystwyth: Honno, 2002.

Brown, Tony. "The Ex-centric Voice: The English-Language Short Story in Wales," *North American Journal of Welsh Studies* 1, no. 1 (Winter 2001): 25–41.

Jones, Glyn. *The Dragon Has Two Tongues: Essays on Anglo-Welsh Writers and Writing by Glyn Jones.* Edited by Tony Brown. Cardiff: University of Wales Press, 2001.

Stephens, Meic, ed. *The New Companion to the Literature of Wales.* Cardiff: University of Wales Press, 1998.

Patricia Kennedy Bostian

WARNER, SYLVIA TOWNSEND (1893–1978)

Born on December 5, 1893, at Harrow School, where her father was a master, Sylvia Townsend Warner was precocious and solitary as a child. Gawky, bespectacled, and plain, she would eventually earn the label "the best boy at Harrow," a title curiously presaging her lesbianism in later life (Harman, 30).

In 1923, an interest in witchcraft and the esoteric led Warner to write her first and most famous novel, *Lolly Willowes* (1926). Now upheld by feminists as a polemic against the miseries of spinsterhood and the restorative effects of a rural life for women, for many years it was viewed as no more than an enjoyable and harmless fantasy about witchcraft in the shires. The book became a best seller in both Britain and America and was nominated for the Prix Femina. Her second novel, *Mr Fortune's Maggot* (1927), recounts the tale of a missionary in the South Seas who not only fails to convert any natives but ends up losing his own faith as well. Again, the oddity of the subject matter combined with the cleverness and lyrical quality of the prose ensured its success on both sides of the Atlantic. For many critics, this quality of "credible extra-ordinariness" would become a hallmark of all Warner's best work.

In October 1930 Warner set up home with the female poet Valentine Ackland, to whom she would remain devoted until her death. Tall, short haired, and favoring a mannish trouser-and-tie dress code, Ackland proved to be a complex and at times difficult partner; a closet alcoholic during most of their relationship, she also openly had affairs with other women, causing

Warner considerable anguish. Always politically active, in 1935 the couple became members of the Communist Party and were, for a brief spell in 1936, medical auxiliaries in the Spanish Civil War. In the same year Warner published the story "My Mother Won the War" in the *New Yorker* magazine, the first of more than 150 stories that she placed there over the next 40 years.

Her most fecund period of short story writing took place during the years after World War II. *A Stranger with a Bag* (1966) contains the story "A Love Match," which won the Katherine Mansfield Menton prize in 1968. The story centers on the incestuous relationship between a brother and a sister in the aftermath of Word War I and has been viewed both as an exploration of sexual freedom and as a diatribe against normative heterosexual relationships. The nonfiction work she produced during this period included a translation of Proust's *Contre Sainte-Beuve* (1958) and an acclaimed biography, *T. H. White* (1967).

Devastated by Ackland's death in 1969, Warner resigned herself to her "widowhood," and short stories now became her main creative output. She was made an honorary member of the American Academy of Arts and Letters in 1971. Her long-standing interest in the supernatural being rekindled by Ackland's death, she commenced a period of writing fantasy stories set in an elfin world that were collected into *Kingdoms of Elfin* (1977), the last work published before her death on May 1, 1978.

Indifference to Warner's work appears to have become the default for the majority of literary critics. Inexplicably, given the enormous body and breadth of her work, with its thematic and tonal range, and notwithstanding literary prizes and recognition abroad, she did not merit even the briefest of entries in any edition of the *Oxford Companion to English Literature* published during her lifetime. It is only since the republication of some of her works by the feminist imprint Virago that interest in her novels and stories has been rekindled. (See also "A WIDOW'S QUILT.")

BIBLIOGRAPHY

Davies, Gill, ed. *Critical Essays on Sylvia Townsend Warner.* New York: Edwin Mellen Press, 2006.
Harman, Claire. *Sylvia Townsend Warner.* London: Chatto & Windus, 1989.
Mulford, Wendy. *This Narrow Place.* London: Pandora, 1988.
Warner, Sylvia Townsend. *The Diaries of Sylvia Townsend Warner.* London: Chatto & Windus, 1994.
———. *The Innocent and the Guilty: Stories.* London: Chatto & Windus, 1971.
———. *More Joy in Heaven and Other Stories.* London: Cresset Press, 1935.
———. *The Music at Long Verney.* New York: Counterpoint, 2001.
———. *One Thing Leading to Another and Other Stories.* London: Chatto & Windus, 1984.
———. *The Salutation.* London: Chatto & Windus, 1932.
———. *Scenes of Childhood and Other Stories.* London: Chatto & Windus, 1981.
———. *Selected Stories.* London: Chatto & Windus, 1988.

Gerri Kimber

"WEEKEND" FAY WELDON (1978)

By the 1970s the feminist perspective had become a prominent feature of contemporary culture on both sides of the Atlantic, and it was characterized in part by an insistence on both a national and personal individuality. FAY WELDON's story "Weekend," originally published in the quasi-feminist magazine *COSMOPOLITAN,* is a scathing and poignant exploration of the expectations and assumptions that this powerful social movement engendered. Assembled as a series of separate but linked brief episodes describing the events of a long weekend that an upscale, professional family spends at their "leisure," it presents a devastating account of the demands that the family makes on Martha, the capable, competent modern woman supposedly in charge of everything.

Weldon establishes an aura of brisk authority as Martha organizes and arranges the myriad details required for a successful venture from London "down to their cottage" two hours from the city. Like a litany of necessity, Weldon depicts Martha taking "the country bedding from the airing basket, plus the books and the games, plus the weekend food . . . plus her own folder of work from the office," a list covering every possible need, since leaving anything in the cottage would be, as her husband Martin notes, in the first of a series of typically snide asides, "An open invitation to burglars." The alternation of the endless obligations that Martha accepts with a goodwill that is gradually eroding with an increasingly mordant array of ironic countercomments is the basis for the effective meld of satire and compassion that Weldon brings to the narrative.

Although both Martha and Martin are employed, she is also responsible for the children's needs, organizing meals, operating the household, and driving. When, because of a rare overindulgence on her birthday, she has a minor accident and her license is suspended, Martin must drive, and "every rattle and clank and bump in the engine" reminds her that it is, like everything the hypercritical family points out, "somehow her fault." Martin's address to Martha's practical car, "Come along, you old banger," expresses this casually demeaning attitude, while there is a constant insinuation that she is "all things to all people. . . . It can be done: yes, it can: superwoman." These interjections establish the ethos of Martha's world, a place where, if she asks for any assistance, she hears, "('Don't fuss, darling. You always make such a fuss,')" a parenthetical insertion whose incremental repetition with small variants would wear anyone down.

As the weekend progresses, Martha and Martin entertain Colin and Katie. Katie, "languid, beautiful, elegant," is Colin's "new young wife," replacing Janet, Martha's friend. Katie talks to the men and sneers at the thought of doing any household tasks. Trying to be attractive, attending to the needs of the children, reworking plans as Katie uses up resources supposed to last through the weekend, Martha becomes increasingly frazzled and insecure. Since she loves her work—her "wages were creeping up, almost to the level of Martin's? One day they would overtake. Then what?"—the wear and stress of the weekend are like a burden that Martha accepts because of all the "advantages" of her life. But this time, all of the slights and demands ("Martha dreamt she was eating coal, by handfuls, and liking it") are cast in a different light when her daughter Jenny "started her first period." At this crucial transitional moment, Katie tells Martha to "just sit *down*, . . . you make us all feel bad," and Martin glares at her. This is a moment of revelation for Martha, who sees an unbreakable cycle continuing. "Her daughter," she realizes at the close of the story, "is condemned to repeat the same exhausting pattern, "wife, mother, friend."

BIBLIOGRAPHY
Fay Weldon, "Weekend." In *The Penguin Book of Modern British Short Stories,* edited by Malcolm Bradbury, 309–325. London: Penguin, 1990.

Leon Lewis

WELDON, FAY (1931–)　Born in England, Franklin "Fay" Birkinshaw was taken to New Zealand at five weeks to join her physician father and her older sister. Her mother wrote commercial fiction under the pen name Pearl Bellairs, and her father wrote crime stories. Her parents divorced when she was five, and Weldon lived with only women. She later claimed to have grown up thinking that females dominated the world, but to have learned differently as a student at St. Andrews studying economics. Weldon's first marriage failed, and she was left the single mother of a young son. Starting her writing career as an advertising copywriter, she successfully supported her family.

In her early 30s Weldon discovered psychotherapy, which helped her gain the courage to write fiction full time. The rest of her life would be given to writing about passionate female characters facing not only a male-dominated world but also their own poor self-images. Her female characters struggle to find internal reserves of strength to beat the negative stereotypes that women face in their everyday lives. Along this vein, she has written plays, novels, newspaper and magazine articles, and collections of short stories. In 1996 she won the PEN/Macmillan Silver Pen Award for *Wicked Women.* In October 2002 the Savoy Hotel named Weldon its first writer-in-residence. Because of her overwhelming characterization of troubled women and her commentary on society's ailments, Weldon has been labeled a cultural critic.

The prolific writer's collection *Watching Me, Watching You* (1981) includes a reprint of her first novel, *The Fat Woman's Joke* (1967), as well as short stories. *Polaris and Other Stories* (1985), containing the story "IN THE GREAT WAR," is her second collection, and four others were published in the 1990s: *Moon over Minneapolis or Why She Couldn't Stay* (1991), which contains the story "PUMPKIN PIE"; *Angel, All Innocence and Other Stories* (1995); *Wicked Women* (1997); and *A Hard Time to Be a Father* (1998). *Nothing to Wear* and *Nowhere to Hide* appeared in 2002. The stories in her anthologies are often thematically quite different, but they all show her wry use of humor and irony. Though mostly feminist in nature, her stories take chances with the female characters, creating realistic portrayals that are rough around the edges and not perfect or masculine but simply human. An overall feminine sense of courage and strength helps avoid a masculine outlook; sisterhood solidifies the stories and the characters. Men and masculinity tend to be the antagonists in her stories, manufacturing unstable situations that require women to overcome what is culturally expected of them, as in "WEEKEND." However, Weldon and her stories are not always what some readers and critics expect, and some of her works can seem antifeminist or at least ironic. Critics find Weldon difficult to pin down, assigning her seemingly contradictory labels at the same time—optimistic and negative, progressive and regressive. However, such contradictions characterize life for many women, and Weldon cleverly scripts situations and outcomes for her characters that are as bizarre, untidy, and unlimited as in real life.

Perhaps Weldon's greatest achievement is that she is able not only to expose the limitations put on women but also to force questions about what is considered egalitarian practice by modern society and feminists. Her stories force a self-discovery that is always timely, though it may prove uncomfortable for some.

BIBLIOGRAPHY

Kohn, Rachael. "No Sacred Cows: A Café Talk with Fay Weldon." *The Spirit of Things.* Radio National. Available online. URL: http://www.abc.net.au/rn/relig/spirit/stories/s111756.htm. Posted on March 3, 2000. Downloaded on July 2, 2005.

Mason, Deborah. "Divine Justice," *New York Times,* 29 June 1997.

Pearlman, Mickey, ed. *Listen to Their Voices: Twenty Interviews with Women Who Write.* New York: Norton, 1993.

Stein, Thomas Michael. "Strategies of Subversion in Fay Weldon's Miss Jacobs Stories." In *Engendering Realism and Postmodernism: Contemporary Writers in Britain,* edited by Beate Neumeier, 159–170. Amsterdam, Netherlands: Rodopi, 2001.

Weldon, Fay. *Angel, All Innocence and Other Stories.* London: Bloomsbury, 1995.

———. *A Hard Time to Be a Father.* London: Flamingo/HarperCollins, 1998.

———. *Nothing to Wear and Nowhere to Hide.* London: Flamingo/HarperCollins, 2002.

———. *Polaris and Other Stories.* London: Hodder and Stoughton, 1985.

———. *Watching Me, Watching You.* London: Summit Books, 1981.

———. *Wicked Women.* London: Atlantic Monthly Press, 1997.

Zylinska, Joanna. "Nature, Science and Witchcraft: An Interview with Fay Weldon," *Critical Survey* 12, no. 3 (2000): 108–122.

Christine Brown

WELLS, H. G. (1866–1946)

Herbert George Wells was born in Bromley, Kent, the youngest of three boys in a lower-middle-class family. His mother Sarah was an occasional housekeeper; his father Joseph was a shopkeeper and semiprofessional cricketer but was extremely unsuccessful at the former. At age 17, Wells became a pupil-teacher at the Midhurst Grammar School, the following year winning a scholarship to study science at the Normal School of Science. This was a turning point for Wells; in his first year he studied under T. H. Huxley and excelled in his courses, sparking an interest in science that he would retain for the rest of his life; in fact, Wells would become one of the first professional writers to have a formal scientific education. However, his success did not last, and although he finished three years of study, he did not take a degree. He managed to secure a teaching position in London and, feeling as though he had the financial security to take a wife, he married his cousin Isabel in 1891. The marriage only lasted a few years; by 1894, Wells had divorced Isabel; had eloped with a student named Amy Catherine Robbins, whom Wells called Jane; and was supporting both women, along with Jane's mother. Following in his father's steps financially, Wells was desperate for money, which led him to rework an old story called "The Chronicle Argonauts" for the *National Observer.* The serialized story was a success, and in 1895 it was printed in book form, titled *The Time Machine.* Wells's story explores the extremes of time travel, as well as the sociological structure of civilizations in the future. Wells's first published novel was an antiutopia in that human civilization had degenerated to an animalistic society. The novel version was an even greater success than the serialized story, and it launched Wells's literary career, which thrived during the next 10 years. By 1905, Wells had written 24 more novels, the majority of which are the texts that he is still remembered for today and earned him the recognition as father of science fiction. Wells had great hope that science would foster the progress of society, but he also feared that human nature could destroy civilization with technological knowledge. His works thus explore both the adverse effects of technology on a population, as in *The Time Machine,* and its potential adverse effects on an individual, as in *The Invisible Man.*

In *War of the Worlds* the threat comes from invaders, although the Martians who attack Earth are loosely disguised figures of the European colonists. Having depleted their own natural resources, the Martians come to Earth to use ours, and any resistance seems futile. By the end of the novel, however, human germs are too much for the Martians' immune system, and they capitulate. Although Wells's novel was popular in its own right, it was raised to legendary status when Orson Welles produced a live radio adaptation of the story in America on October 31, 1938. Many listeners tuned in after Welles announced that the story was fiction, and when they heard of the alien invasion, panic struck.

Wells is customarily identified with his science fiction novels, though his short fiction was equally important in his career (see "UNDER THE KNIFE" and "The MAN WHO COULD WORK MIRACLES"). In June 1894, he published a short story called "The Stolen Bacillus" in the *Pall Mall Budget.* The story involves an anarchist scientist who tries to destroy London with a deadly virus. When the plan goes awry, he swallows the potion himself, attempting to continue his plan, only to be stopped when the potion proves nothing more than a practical joke that turns him blue. Although Wells ends the story as a joke, his early preoccupation with the irresponsible scientist is clear. Another of Wells's well-known short stories, "The Country of the Blind," was published in 1910 and is often linked with *The Invisible Man.* It is a tale of a South American village where everyone is blind except one man. In his attempt to rule the blind villagers, he learns that their other senses are more acute and he is in fact not superior to them but an outsider in the village. Wells's story, when read with *The Invisible Man,* underlies the theme that special gifts do not warrant special treatment, and such gifts are only relative to the context in which they are housed.

BIBLIOGRAPHY

Batchelor, John. *H. G. Wells.* Cambridge: Cambridge University Press, 1985.

Parrinder, Patrick. *Shadows of the Future: H. G. Wells, Science Fiction and Prophecy.* Liverpool, England: Liverpool University Press, 1995.

Wells, H. G. *Complete Short Stories.* London: Dent, 1998.

———. *The Door in the Wall and Other Stories.* London: Kennerley, 1911.

———. *Twelve Stories and a Dream.* London: Macmillan, 1903.

West, Anthony. *H. G. Wells: Aspects of a Life.* London: Hutchinson, 1984.

Amanda Mordavsky

WELSH, IRVINE (?1957–)

Irvine Welsh is Scotland's best-known and most controversial contemporary author. Since the publication of his landmark novel *Trainspotting* (1993), made into a film by Danny Boyle in 1996 and translated into more than 33 languages, Welsh has won adulation and excoriation for his hilarious, raw, and often scatological vernacular accounts of Scotland's most impoverished and violent urban communities, such as Leith and Muirhouse. Welsh was publicly denounced in 2004 by fellow Scottish writer Alexander McCall-Smith as "a travesty for Scotland" and a purveyor of "Scottish miserabilism." McCall-Smith's comments represent the sentiments of many critics who have been appalled by Welsh's departure from the quaint loch-and-bagpipes accounts of bonnie Scotland favored by the tourist board and by his use of profane and nonstandard English. Like fellow Scot JAMES KELMAN, whose 1994 receipt of the Booker Prize for *How Late It Was, How Late* caused an uproar among the conservative literary establishment, Welsh frequently writes in the phonetically transcribed idiom of the Scottish working classes, a style that has sometimes proved impenetrable to those who do not understand it and highly offensive to those who do. Welsh has often claimed that his liberal use of swear words aims not simply to shock but to provide a realistic portrait of the speech of Scotland's most neglected inner cities. As such, Welsh can be seen as the inheritor of a realist linguistic literary tradition whose more renowned exponents include William Wordsworth and George Eliot. Indeed, Welsh is arguably a more faithful practitioner of verbal mimeticism than any of his distinguished predecessors. While Wordsworth may have praised the literary use of "language really used by men" in his *Preface to Lyrical Ballads* (1802), he nonetheless composed his poetry in an expurgated medium that excluded the vulgar, profane, or impenetrably regional in order to cater to a wide reading public. Welsh has always been defiantly untroubled by the difficulty that non-Scottish audiences might have in understanding the speech of his Leith characters. Instead of sanitizing the idiom of his native environs, he presents it in all its boisterous glory, refusing to be complicit in the silencing of social have-nots through a rejection and condemnation of their language. Welsh's attitude to the international critics who have challenged his deviation from Standard English seems to be summed up in the response of his character Franco Begbie to the Canadian tourists who cannot understand his heavily accented and profane speech: "These foreign cunts've goat trouble wi the Queen's fuckin English, ken. Ye huv tae speak louder, slower, n likesay more posh, fir the cunts tae understand ye" (115).

Welsh's Scotland is not the romantic, heathery home to colorfully kilted and brave-hearted warriors popularized by Sir Walter Scott and Mel Gibson; it is a rat-infested urban slum, populated by AIDS-infected junkies, football hooligans, sexual deviants, soft-hearted perennial victims, incestuous families, alcoholically fuelled sectarians, and violent psychopaths on both sides of the law. The bleakness of the environment about which he writes is alleviated by the irrepressible and typically scabrous humor of his characters. In *Porno* (2002), for example, the perpetual junkie Spud discusses in group therapy his ambition to become the next drug czar, "cause ay the quality ay the gear these days is pure crap" (72). When told a drug czar is supposed to stop the population from taking drugs rather than increase the quality of their stash, he replies, "What a thankless task for the poor boy. Ah dinnae see but, how they huv tae gie that joab tae a Russian boy when there's plenty punters in Scotland could dae it" (73).

Much of Welsh's writing seems clearly drawn from his own experiences, whether as a child growing up near Muirhouse (one of Scotland's roughest public housing estates, or "schemes"), as a devoted fan of Edinburgh's Hibernian football club, or as a former heroin user and unrepentant imbiber of "Class A's"—hard drugs such as ecstasy and cocaine. Throughout his career, he has cultivated an image of himself as a working-class hustler made rich, if not necessarily good, a self-presentation that may or may not have basis in autobiographical fact.

While known primarily as a novel writer, his output includes works of short fiction including *The Acid House* (1994) and *Ecstasy: Three Tales of Chemical Romance* (1997). Welsh's style in these collections is more picaresque and less character driven than in his longer fiction; he uses the shorter form to experiment with genre, dialect form, and textual form rather than to develop the detailed psychological portraits evident in his longer works. *The Acid House* demonstrates the author's obsessions with drugs, class, thug culture, and the physical and psychological effects of violence. Published in 1994 and made into a film in 1998, the collection is notable for its dark humor, irreverence, and refusal to participate in either the sentimental nationalism or mawkish romanticism often evident in depictions of the Scottish "common folk." In "Eurotrash," for example, a recovering Scottish junkie in Amsterdam responds with curious sangfroid when taken to task by a local barman for the sins of the British Empire. "I was tempted to go into a spiel about how I was Scottish, not British, and that the Scots were the last oppressed colony of the British Empire," he reflects, "I don't really believe it though; the Scots oppress themselves by their obsession with the English which breeds the negatives of hatred, fear, servility, contempt, and dependency" (71). For Welsh, idealization—of one's country or one's class—is an easy lure that is to be avoided at all costs.

Welsh's short story collection *Ecstasy* is a vertiginous and often grotesque exploration of Britain's drug culture, comprising three novellas that borrow from different generic conventions: the historical romance, the gothic tale, and the love story. In "Lorraine Goes to Livingstone," a Scottish nurse helps her ailing romance novelist patient Rebecca Navarro retaliate against her philandering husband Perky. In "Fortune's Always Hiding," a grown-up victim of the birth defect–causing painkiller Tenazadrine uses her sexuality to gain gruesome revenge on the drug's manufacturers: In "The Undefeated," bored middle-class wife Heather finds love and liberation through an ecstasy-fueled romance with Lloyd, from a lower-class area of Edinburgh. All three stories combine Welsh's trademark humor with a fixation on deviant behavior and a critique of the Left's failure to redress or resist the damage done to Britain by Thatcherism. Disgustedly pondering the simple-minded politics of her New Labour husband, Heather muses, "The politics of the last twenty years in Britain are liar's politics. The problem is we are ruled by the weak and the small-minded, who are too stupid to know they are weak and small-minded" (256). Heather's solution to social and personal malaise, like that of so many of Welsh's characters, is psychotropic rather than political: She leaves her husband, becomes a fixture on the Edinburgh rave scene, and takes up with a warm-hearted waster for whom drugs, as Lloyd eloquently puts it, are "a fuckin essential" (213). Such literary scenarios have earned Welsh an unfair reputation as a naive and even dangerous apologist for drug use; yet if drugs sometimes act as catalysts for character liberation in his fiction, they also feature prominently as agents of misery and degradation. Welsh's persistent refusal to engage in any simple-minded valorization—of Scotland over England, of inner-city residents over the suburban middle class, of drugs over sobriety—mark his fitness to document the complexities of 21st-century British urban life.

BIBLIOGRAPHY

Miller, Phil. "Author Describes Irvine Welsh as a 'Travesty for Scotland,'" *The Herald* [Glasgow], 10 January 2004, p. 1.

Morace, R. *Irvine Welsh's Trainspotting.* New York: Continuum, 2002.

Vincent, Sally. "Everybody's Doing It," *Guardian Weekend,* 10 August 2002, pp. 32+.

Welsh, Irvine. *The Acid House.* London: Jonathan Cape, 1994.

———. *Filth.* London: Jonathan Cape, 1998.

———. *Glue.* London: Jonathan Cape, 2001.

———. *Past Tense.* Edinburgh: Clocktower, 1992.

———. *Porno.* London: Jonathan Cape, 2002.

Christine Ferguson

WESSEX TALES THOMAS HARDY (1888, REVISED 1912) The first edition of *Wessex Tales* was published in May 1888 with the subtitle, "Strange, Lively and Commonplace." The volume included five previously published stories: "The Distracted Preacher" (1878–79), "Fellow-townsmen" (1880), "The Three Strangers" (1883), "Interlopers at the Knap" (1884), and "The WITHERED ARM" (1887). A sixth story, "An Imaginative Woman" (1894), was added to the 1896 edition, but this was withdrawn for the 1912 Wessex Edition and replaced with "A Tradition of Eighteen Hundred and Four" (1882) and "The MELANCHOLY HUSSAR OF THE GERMAN LEGION" (dated 1889 but published 1890). Like most of THOMAS HARDY's fiction, all of these stories had first been published in English or American magazines. Almost all are set in eras previous to Hardy's birth in 1840, but in differing ways all embody the economic, social, and cultural nexus of life in his own rural Dorset. As a preparation for writing the stories, Hardy spent considerable time researching details in parish records, in old local newspapers, and even in discussions with elderly inhabitants of the places he describes. Yet for all of his attention to historical accuracy and the meticulous recasting of authentic materials in fictional form, the resulting tales are something more than simply an account of village existence prior to the Industrial Revolution. As Hardy himself says in his preface to the Wessex Edition of the tales (dated May 1912), "the stories are but dreams, and not records" (Hardy, 5). For Hardy himself, each reformulates his own relationship to his rural upbringing, especially as most of the stories were written at a time when he was frequently alternating his place of residence between London and the West Country.

While broadly similar in outlook, the tales themselves vary considerably in length and style, the shortest being "A Tradition of Eighteen Hundred and Four," while the longest, "The Distracted Preacher," is more than five times longer and is divided into seven chapters. Besides the success of *Wessex Tales* as a collection, several of these stories have achieved considerable individual fame and have been reprinted and anthologized many times. One of the most popular is "The Withered Arm," in which Rhoda Brook dreams that she places a curse upon Gertrude Lodge. When the two women finally meet, Rhoda discovers that Gertrude's arm has suddenly and mysteriously withered. Gertrude visits Conjuror Trendle seeking a cure, and he tells her that it was Rhoda who cursed her. Several years later, believing that her husband no longer loves her, Gertrude again visits Trendle, who suggests touching the neck of a recently hanged man as a cure. When Gertrude does so, she immediately sees her husband and Rhoda as they come to collect the body of the hanged man, who is their illegitimate son. Enraged at seeing Gertrude, Rhoda throws her against a wall, fatally injuring her.

BIBLIOGRAPHY
Kramer, Dale. *The Cambridge Companion to Thomas Hardy.* Cambridge: Cambridge University Press, 1999.
Thomas Hardy. *Wessex Tales.* Oxford: Oxford World's Classics, 1998.
Wright, Sarah Bird. *Thomas Hardy A–Z: The Essential Reference to His Life and Work.* New York: Facts On File, 2002.

John Ballam

"WHAT A SKY" Edna O'Brien (1990)

Included in *Lantern Slides,* Irish writer Edna O'Brien's 1990 *Los Angeles Times* Award–winning collection, "What a Sky" narrates a woman's reluctant visit to her elderly father in a nursing home in rural Ireland. The unnamed woman and her father spend an hour talking together. The father dominates the conversation with tales of his difficult youth as an orphan on a horse farm and with recollections of Sister Declan, a nun he had befriended. He glorifies Sister Declan for "her good humour, her buoyant spirit, her generosity, and her innate sense of sacrifice," noting that she preferred to discuss hurley games with her father than gallivant with boys (78). He seems to believe that the qualities he appreciates in Sister Declan are lacking in his own daughter. As the story unfolds it becomes clear to the reader that the father has been estranged from his daughter and would welcome a chance to be reconciled. The daughter comes to the nursing home with the intention of taking her father out to a fine hotel for lunch, but she does not follow through on her plan. Unable to bear an intimate afternoon with her father, the daughter wonders whether she should reveal her own painful past to him or simply maintain the emotional distance. She recalls her childhood struggles and her unsuccessful attempts to earn her father's praise and attention. The daughter lies to her father, telling him that her hired car can only wait an hour and that she needs to return to her hotel.

In the almost unanimous praise allocated to *Lantern Slides,* reviewers applauded O'Brien's use of imagery to convey the emotions of her characters. The title "What a Sky" refers to the story's celestial imagery and is a metaphor for the relationship between father and daughter. At the start of the story, a rainstorm sweeps across the landscape, and a tiny hole opens amid the clouds as the daughter enters the nursing home. This image of an opening in the sky reflects the daughter's consideration of rekindling a relationship with her father. When she leaves the nursing home, both the storm and the opening have passed, signifying another missed opportunity for the father and daughter.

Much of O'Brien's work centers on female identity, particularly Irish women's relationship to Catholicism, family, and country. The stories in *Lantern Slides,* particularly "What a Sky," locate these issues in terms of tragedy. In an interview with Susha Gupta, six years before the publication of *Lantern Slides,* O'Brien identified loss as the most prevalent theme in her work.

Although her sixth collection of short stories has been widely well received, relatively little has been written on *Lantern Slides.* Some critics recognize the presence of the Irish gothic in her stories. Critics have been quick to point out the similarities between the title story of *Lantern Slides* and James Joyce's story "The Dead."

BIBLIOGRAPHY
Fuller, Jack. "Wryly Irish," *Chicago Tribune-Books,* 27 May
    1990, pp. 1, 3.
Leavitt, David. "Small Tragedies and Ordinary Passions,"
    New York Times Book Review, 24 June 1990, p. 9.
O'Brien, Edna. *Lantern Slides: Stories.* New York: Farrar,
    Straus, 1990.
————. Interview with Susha Gupta, *Paris Review* 26, no.
    92 (Summer 1984): pp. 22–50.

Gina Liotta

"WHISTLE, AND I'LL COME TO YOU, MY LAD, OH" M. R. JAMES (1904)

"Oh, Whistle and I'll Come to You, My Lad," is one of the best known and most widely anthologized ghost stories in the English language. It shows M. R. JAMES at the peak of his powers and demonstrates his trademark technique of creating horror by refusing to let its source ever come too clearly into the reader's view. The malevolent specter in "Oh, Whistle" is only briefly and vaguely seen by the story's terrified protagonist Parkins, and its presence is never fully explained. James had an intuitive understanding of the maxim that what you do not see is always much more terrifying than what you do. Despite the enduring favor for his works, James has received relatively little critical attention, perhaps because of enduring academic prejudice against genre fiction or in deference to his own frequent protestations that his stories had no other purpose than to entertain. In addition to its clear entertainment value, "Oh, Whistle" has also been recognized for its implicit critique of modernity (Michalski), its censure of reckless academic curiosity, and its veiled replication of Edwardian social fears about homosexuality (Fielding).

At the story's opening, Parkins, a young professor of ontography (the description of reality, essence, or being) plans a sea-side holiday to the quaint village of Burnstow. He has been forced to take a room with two beds in it, one of which his colleague Rogers teasingly threatens to come down and occupy, saying, "I should do so nicely to keep the ghosts off." Parkins, a convinced rationalist with no time for supernatural mumbo-jumbo, rejects these insinuations but does agree to investigate some old Templar ruins for his friend. While doing so after a day of playing golf, Parkins discovers a curious whistle of some age bearing the Latin inscription "Qui Est Iste Qui Venit" (Who is this who is coming?). He takes the whistle back to his hotel, followed by a shadowy personage who, while apparently running, never seems to catch up with him. Unfazed, Parkins blows the whistle several times in his room, thus summoning huge gusts of wind that he assumes to be coincidental. After a tumultuous night full of nightmares and shuffling noises, he wakes in the morning to discover that both beds look like they have been occupied. Suspecting no more than mundane causes to be at work, he confides the incident to his fellow guest, a retired colonel who takes a different view of things and advises throwing the whistle into the sea. Parkins ignores this advice and is that night awakened by a horrible rustling noise; looking over to the second bed, he sees someone (or something) sit up in it. The thing stands up and, apparently blind, reaches out to feel for the horrified Parkins, who has jumped out of bed. As his eyes adjust to the scene, he realizes that he is looking not at anything human but rather at some type of menacing, immaterial spirit that has swathed itself in the adjoining bed's sheets. As it turns to face him, he sees "an intensely horrible face of *crumpled linen.*" He shrieks and thus gives away his location; the thing moves forward and is about to touch him when the colonel bursts in response to his neighbor's cries. The figure collapses, Parkins is slowly brought back to his senses, and the whistle and the bed linen are duly disposed of. The experience forever changes the badly shaken Parkins, whose "views on certain points are less clear cut than they used to be." Parkins's hubris, like that of so many of James's characters, has been his rash tampering with a past best left alone and his arrogant privileging of rationality over the ever-present and irrepressible order of the supernatural.

BIBLIOGRAPHY
Fielding, Penny. "Reading Rooms: M. R. James and the
    Library of Modernity," *Modern Fiction Studies* 46, no. 3
    (2000): 749–771.
James, Montague Rhodes. *The Penguin Complete Ghost Stories
    of M. R. James.* London: Penguin, 1984.

Michalski, Robert. "The Malice of Inanimate Objects: Exchange in M. R. James's Ghost Stories," *Extrapolation* 37, no. 1 (Spring 1996): 46–62.

Christine Fergus

"WHITE NIGHT, A" CHARLOTTE MEW (1903)

One of several short stories CHARLOTTE MEW published in *Temple Bar* magazine between 1899 and 1905. Mew's poetry is often judged superior to her fiction; however, "A White Night" is a good example of the horror stories popular in the late 19th and early 20th centuries. The setting is somewhat exotic for predominantly Anglican English readers, a remote part of Andalusia, in Catholic Spain. Typical for this type of tale, the narrator establishes realism by claiming to have been told the story by someone who was present at the incident and by giving specific dates and locations initially. Cameron, who is on mining business in Spain, meets his sister, Ella, and her new husband while they are honeymooning. They visit isolated sites and stop in an unspecified one to view a church and convent. Accidentally locked in the church all night, they are horrified witnesses to a bizarre ceremony in which a group of monks bury alive a young woman dressed in white. Cameron justifies his and his brother-in-law's lack of action by claiming that not only were there too many monks for them to overcome but also the unresisting woman did not appear to want to be saved. After the monks leave, Cameron tries to find the flagstone under which the woman is buried, but he cannot distinguish it in the dark and there is no sound to help him find the woman. In the morning, the travelers are let out by a caretaker and leave, at Ella's insistence, to report their experience to a British Consul, who tells them that there is nothing to be done and they should leave Spain immediately. Ella resents her brother and husband for not helping the woman, but Cameron insists that she welcomed her death and that indeed her death was somehow grand, as she had clearly forced the monks into acknowledging her, rather than being discounted as something insignificant.

Mew leaves the reader with a number of unanswered questions. Did the incident really occur, or was it a vision? The story is highly atmospheric, and the darkness of the old stone church is relieved only by the monks' candles, the whiteness of the woman's robes, and the sensory impact of incense and chanting. The Consul seems to believe them, but he also adds the story to his collection of strange local tales. Was the woman a willing sacrifice, or was she a victim of a barbaric punishment? If a punishment, why was she punished? The convent nearby suggests that she was perhaps a nun who had betrayed her vows. There is a certain irony in the woman in white's death, set as it is against the Catholic Church's veneration of the Virgin Mary, highlighted by the prayers of peasant women earlier in the story. Though the monks honor the mother of Christ, their treatment of women on Earth is harsh. Mew emphasizes the alienness of the setting by her description of the un-English landscape and the "oriental" qualities of the architecture. This very foreignness creates distance and perhaps an explanation for Cameron's helplessness. Even so, how are readers to take Cameron's response? Could a woman really welcome such an end? Mew often includes a moral dilemma in her stories. Cameron's repeated insistence that the woman would not have welcomed being rescued suggests that he is trying to convince himself that he acted appropriately. The discomfort generated by "A White Night" derives not so much from the details of the incident itself as from the protagonist's willing detachment from the horror of what he has seen.

BIBLIOGRAPHY
Charlotte Mew. *Collected Poems and Prose.* Manchester: Carcanet Press; London: Virago, 1981.

Terri Doughty

"WHO KILLED ZEBEDEE?" WILKIE COLLINS (1881)

A detective story first published in the *Seaside Library* in January 1881 and reprinted as "Mr. Policeman and the Cook" in WILKIE COLLINS's collection *Little Novels,* (1887).

The story is narrated by an unnamed police detective from his deathbed and is described as a confession to the Catholic priest attending him. The detective recounts how, at an early point in his career, he assisted in the investigation of the death of a Mr. John Zebedee, fatally stabbed in a lodging house where Zebedee and his new wife were staying before emigrating to Australia. Mrs. Zebedee describes how she woke in the night to find her husband dead beside her, stabbed with a knife with the inscription, "To John Zebedee, from —." The investigators question the various inhabitants of the house but center on the provenance of the knife and its unfinished inscription, distributing photographs of the weapon to all police forces and cutlers. Mrs. Zebedee is cleared of suspicion, but the case remains unsolved and is officially closed. The young detective, with the help of the lodging house cook Priscilla Thurlby, carries on an unofficial investigation, during the course of which the two become engaged. On the way to visit Thurlby's parents, the detective makes an unplanned visit to a small town, where he discovers an old cutler's shop that was not included in the original investigation. He finds that the murder weapon was bought and inscribed at this shop; the cutler's records show that the knife was bought by Priscilla Thurlby. Thurlby confesses that she had once been engaged to Zebedee and had bought him the knife as a gift, but before their marriage he abandoned her. Discovering his betrayal, she snatched the knife back (while it was being engraved) and, tracking him to London, used it to kill him. The detective, however, remains too much in love with Thurlby to have her arrested, and they part company. The confession is thus the account of how a detective allowed a criminal to escape.

Although Collins employed the techniques of DETECTIVE FICTION in *The Moonstone* (1868), "Who Killed Zebedee?" represents Collins's attempt to write a more conventional detective narrative featuring a murder mystery and police investigation, but without the complex conspiracy plots that characterized many of Collins's crime-based sensation novels. The role of the official detective force in the story is itself unusual in that later Victorian detective fiction (in the stories of Grant Allen, ARTHUR CONAN DOYLE, ARTHUR MORRISON, and C. L. Pirkis, among others) was dominated by the figure of the amateur or private detective. The story's revelation that the police detective is complicit in the crime by allowing the murderer to escape is more characteristic of late-Victorian crime fiction, which often criticized the official detective force, and is an early example of more self-referential detective stories in which the detective is revealed to be the criminal.

Another Victorian example is Allen's ingenious "The Great Ruby Robbery" (1892), although Collins's work has a greater tendency to draw attention to itself as a narrative: "Who Killed Zebedee?" uses the format of a transcribed confession to foreground its own textuality. Both stories anticipate the development of detective fiction in the 20th century by writers such as AGATHA CHRISTIE and the unwritten rule that the culprit should be the least likely person. Collins's story, in its description of the investigation and particularly in details such as the photographing of the murder weapon, can also be seen as an early form of the police procedural subgenre of 20th-century crime fiction, in which the narrative focus is the work of the investigating officers.

BIBLIOGRAPHY

Collins, Wilkie. *Who Killed Zebedee?* London: Hesperus, 2002.
Cox, Michael. Introduction. *The Oxford Book of Victorian Detective Stories.* Oxford: Oxford University Press. 1993.
Symons, Julian. *Bloody Murder: From the Detective Story to the Crime Novel.* Harmondsworth, England: Penguin, 1985.

Christopher Pittard

"WIDOW'S QUILT, A" SYLVIA TOWNSEND WARNER (1977)

"A Widow's Quilt" was first published in the *New Yorker* magazine on June 6, 1977, just under a year before Warner's death in May 1978. It was subsequently republished in a posthumous collection of her stories, *One Thing Leading to Another* (1984).

In making her selections for *The Oxford Book of English Short Stories* (1998), editor A. S. Byatt claimed that her sole criterion for inclusion was that the stories selected "should be startling and satisfying and if possible make the hairs on the neck prickle with excitement, aesthetic or narrative" (xv–xvi). "A Widow's Quilt" is one such story.

Warner's personal situation at the time of writing is reflected in the story's title. She herself was a "widow," having lost her partner of 40 years, Valentine Ackland, in 1969. However, society accorded her no official title since hers was a lesbian relationship, though the last 10 years of her life were transfused with her sense of bereavement, which touched every aspect of her personal and social life. Claire Harman, the editor of Warner's diaries, talks of the "extraordinary other-life of her bereavement" (ix), and indeed the diary after 1969 contains little that does not refer directly or indirectly to Ackland. The word *marriage* is constantly repeated. In this frame of mind, and knowing how much Ackland would have appreciated the story's irony and magical quality, Warner crafted this unexpectedly menacing tale, whose heroine, according to Byatt, is "precisely and ornamentally stitching a pattern of death" (xxiii).

The initial setting—the American Museum near Bath—acknowledges Warner's large American readership. The widow's quilt of the title still hangs in the museum and is named in its catalog as the "Darts of Death" quilt. The story delineates a childless and loveless marriage between Everard, a hypochondriacal London stamp dealer, and Charlotte, his insular and resentful wife. Charlotte visits the museum with her sister on a day trip and is captivated by the startling black-and-white quilt. On her way back to London she sits on the train "in a dreamlike frenzy" (133), planning her own version. As a gift for Everard from the museum shop, she has chosen some candies flavored with horehound, an ancient Navaho Indian remedy for women in childbirth.

A story that appears to be black and white, a simple narrative of a woman stitching a "widow's" patchwork quilt for pleasure, now transmutes into a macabre tale. Charlotte's crafting of the quilt becomes obsessive, and, as she stitches, Warner reveals the stultifying pattern of this doomed marriage. Secrecy surrounding the quilt becomes "an essential ingredient in her pleasure" (135). Symbolically, on Christmas Eve, Charlotte reveals its existence to Everard, renaming it a "magpie" quilt, thus obscuring its true purpose. As with the horehound, Warner again makes a covert reference to childbirth and pregnancy, since the word *magpie* originates from the Latin word "pica," today used in medical terminology to denote a condition in which a pregnant woman craves and consumes nonfood substances. Though not pregnant, Charlotte's craving for the quilt is all-consuming, and indeed metaphorically she is giving birth—to an entity that becomes larger and more animate by the day: "It had a rationality now, a character" (136). In renaming the

quilt, she seals her own fate; there are fewer more powerful natural symbols of bad luck and malevolence than the magpie. Warner now brings to the fore Charlotte's true purpose—"She was stitching away at Everard's demise" (137). As her true motivation is revealed, the quilt perversely begins to work against her, becoming a worry, a burden, a "drudgery": "She began to make mistakes. . . . Her heart thumped, her fingers swelled" (137), common symptoms of pregnancy. When the quilt is almost complete, Charlotte runs out of thread. Returning from her shopping trip, she climbs the stairs back to her flat, suffers a heart attack, and dies. The quilt has taken approximately nine months to gestate.

With its subject matter of relationships, marriage, death, and widowhood, this outwardly morbid tale can conversely be read as Warner's mourning song, a tribute to her partner and to her love. Toward the end of her life, she wrote in her diary, "Only two things are real to me: my love and my death. In between them, I merely exist as a scatter of senses" (355).

BIBLIOGRAPHY
Byatt, A. S., ed. *The Oxford Book of English Short Stories.* Oxford: Oxford University Press, 1998.
Warner, Sylvia Townsend. *Selected Stories.* London: Chatto & Windus, 1988.
———. *The Diaries of Sylvia Townsend Warner.* Edited by Claire Harman. London: Chatto & Windus, 1994.

Gerri Kimber

WILDE, OSCAR (1854–1900)

Oscar Fingal O'Flahertie Wills Wilde was born on October 16, 1854, in Dublin. The second child of intelligent and eccentric parents, Oscar did his best to continue family traditions: His mother, Jane Elgee (Speranza) Wilde (1826–96) wrote poetry, and his father, Dr. William Wilde (1815–76), was involved in a public sex scandal. Both were Nationalists, and some scholars see Wilde's green carnations (usually taken as the symbol of his AESTHETICISM) and green coats (interpreted by Freud as signals of homosexuality) as expressions of his Irishness and nationalism. Oscar Wilde was educated at Portora School (Enniskellen), Trinity College (Dublin), and Magdalen College (Oxford); he earned a degree in classics at Oxford and won the Newdigate

Prize for the best undergraduate poem. He gained, while still an undergraduate, a reputation as a spokesman for aestheticism, and in the early years of his career he was a celebrity because of his personality rather than his achievements.

His first book, *Poems* (1881), was not successful. The poetry was technically fine but seemed to lack passion. The library of the Oxford Union refused the donation of a signed copy. In part as advertising for the D'Oyly Carte production of Gilbert and Sullivan's operetta *Patience,* which satirizes the aesthete poet, Wilde went on lecture tours. His 1882 tour of the United States was well covered by the press on both sides of the Atlantic. A later lecture tour in Scotland drew less attention.

Following his 1884 marriage to Constance Lloyd (1858–98), Wilde found that he required a larger and steadier income than his lecturing and his wife's marriage settlement brought in. He began to contribute short stories and essays to periodicals and to edit *Woman's World* (originally *The Lady's World*). "The CANTERVILLE GHOST" and "LORD ARTHUR SAVILE'S CRIME" date from this period and are considered among the best of Wilde's short fiction, which shares with his drama witty dialogue and clever plotting.

Wilde's short fiction has affinities besides verbal play with the postmodern: It challenges the reader's expectations in plot and characters. Wilde's writings on aesthetics stress the surface of literature and of life, and that idea fits well with the sense of constructedness that postmodernists prize. Structuralists explore the ways that Wilde's fairy tales fit the standard models, and queer theorists seek expressions of his sexual orientation in all of Wilde's works.

The births of Wilde's sons, Cyril and Vyvyan, in 1885 and 1886 seem to have curtailed Wilde's enjoyment of the role of husband. He began to seek the company of young men and had his first homosexual encounter with Robert Ross (1869–1918). At Cambridge, he told an audience of adoring fans the story that later became "The Happy Prince," one of the most popular of Wilde's fairy stories. The tale became the title story of his first successful book, *The HAPPY PRINCE AND OTHER TALES* (1888).

Some believe he chose to write fairy tales to capitalize on the fame of Hans Christian Andersen (1805–75) and Andrew Lang (1844–1912); Wilde told friends he was fulfilling his duty to his sons in offering moral and aesthetic instruction to them (and to the reading public). *A House of Pomegranates* (1891), a second collection of fairy tales, has also remained popular with readers. Although many critics prefer *The Picture of Dorian Gray* (1891), some scholars rank the volumes of fairy stories among the best of Wilde's nondramatic prose.

With the staging of *Lady Windermere's Fan* (1892), followed by *A Woman of No Importance* (1893), *An Ideal Husband* (1895), and *The Importance of Being Earnest* (1895), Wilde became a successful dramatist whose witty dialogue enchanted audiences as the craft of "The Happy Prince" had delighted the undergraduates of Cambridge. His flamboyant literary style and lifestyle again attracted great comment, praise, and censure. Recent studies of Wilde's short fiction have looked at textual similarities between witty, telling dialogues in his fiction and dialogue in his plays.

In 1892, Wilde became involved with Lord Alfred Douglas (1870–1945), and in 1895, at Douglas's urging, he sued the marquis of Queensbury, Douglas's father, for libel after receiving a card from the nobleman suggesting that he posed as a sodomite. Wilde lost and was prosecuted for the crime of sodomy. Thus began the unraveling of his career. Sentenced to two years of hard labor, Wilde served his time at Pentonville, Wandsworth, and Reading prisons. His wife and children changed their name to Holland and moved to Italy. Wilde was often in poor health during his prison years. He was released in 1897 and moved to France, where he lived in poverty. He also changed his name to Sebastian Melmoth. "The Ballad of Reading Gaol" (1898) is considered the best of his post-prison work. He died on November 30, 1900.

BIBLIOGRAPHY

Ellmann, Richard. *Oscar Wilde.* New York: Knopf, 1988.

Holland, Vyvyan. *Oscar Wilde and His World.* New York: Scribners, 1960.

Pearson, Hesketh. *The Life of Oscar Wilde.* 1954. London: Methuen and Co., 1966.

———. *The Complete Shorter Fiction of Oscar Wilde*. Edited by Isobel Murray. Oxford: Oxford University Press, 1979.

———. *The Importance of Being Earnest and Other Plays*. Oxford: Oxford University Press, 1995.

Karen Keck

WINTERSON, JEANETTE (1959–) Jeanette Winterson was born in 1959 and was adopted by Pentecostal parents. She was raised in a working-class household in Accrington, near Manchester (England), and left home at 16. She supported herself with various jobs, such as driving an ice cream van, while studying for her A levels. She went on to study English at Oxford University. To date, she has published nine novels, one short story collection (*The World and Other Places* in 1998), a children's book (*The King of Capri*, 2003), and a collection of essays, *Art Objects: Essays on Ecstasy and Effrontery* (1995). Furthermore, Winterson has adapted her work for the stage and television and writes regularly for newspapers.

An overview of Winterson's fiction reveals the influence of both MODERNISM and postmodernism in her writing. She expresses an admiration for modernists VIRGINIA WOOLF and T. S. Eliot in *Art Objects,* and their influence permeates all of her writing. Her latest novel, *Lighthousekeeping* (2004), expresses a connection to Woolf in its title, and the style of her sixth novel, *Art and Lies* (1994), has been compared to Woolf's *The Waves* by some critics. The use of postmodern techniques is evident particularly in novels such as *Written on the Body* (1992), in which the narrator's gender is never revealed, and in the self-reflexive use of metafiction throughout her work.

Feminist thinking has also helped shape Winterson's ideas. Sexuality is often a key issue, and gender roles are not taken for granted. The demand for the freedom to love another, regardless of the beloved's gender, is always a recurring feature. Parallels have been drawn between Winterson and the 20th-century writer ANGELA CARTER because of their implementation of magic realism and their specialized use of political ideas (such as feminism). *The WORLD AND OTHER PLACES* (1998) is an imaginative collection of 17 short stories that examine a variety of landscapes and relationships.

BIBLIOGRAPHY

Bengston, Helene, Marianne Børch, and Cindie Maagaard, eds. *Sponsored by Demons: The Art of Jeanette Winterson*. Denmark: Scholars' Press, 1999.

Grice, Helena, and Tim Woods, eds. *"I'm Telling You Stories": Jeanette Winterson and the Politics of Reading*. Amsterdam: Rodopi, 1998.

Jeanette Winterson. Available online. URL: http://jeanettewinterson.com. Accessed June 9, 2006.

Winterson, Jeanette. *Art and Lies*. London: Jonathan Cape, 1994.

———. *Art Objects: Essays on Ecstasy and Effrontery*. London: Jonathan Cape, 1994.

———. *Boating for Beginners*. London: Methuen, 1985.

———. *Gut Symmetries*. London: Granta, 1997.

———. *The King of Capri*. London: Bloomsbury, 2003.

———. *The Passion*. London: Bloomsbury, 1988.

———. *The Powerbook*. London: Jonathan Cape, 2000.

———. *Written on the Body*. London: Jonathan Cape, 1992.

———. *The World and Other Places*. London: Jonathan Cape, 1998.

Julie Ellam

"WISE IN HER GENERATION" AMY LEVY (1890) In "Wise in Her Generation," published posthumously in the *Woman's World* in January 1890, AMY LEVY uses a first-person narrator, Virginia, who has a distinctly tough and cynical voice. Virginia tells how, the previous year, her first social season, she fell in love with a witty and flirtatious lawyer, Philip, who left her to marry a wealthy woman who could further his career. Philip and Virginia meet again at a ball, where she also meets Sir Guy, an aristocrat with £30,000 a year and "a socialist of an advanced type." Still responsive to the personal magnetism of Philip and not able to fall in love with Sir Guy, Virginia is determined to treat men as she has been treated; she sees the courtship ritual as a cruel sport and has "no intention of playing a losing game" again. Admitting that "life can have no such moments in store" for her as those she experienced during her courtship by Philip, she nonetheless informs him, in a conversation that takes place only in her mind, that she no longer loves him. Virginia is determined to abjure self-pity and reproach and to be resilient.

When Sir Guy proposes marriage in a letter, she thinks, "I had won my game," but then she sees her reflection in a mirror: "I was a hundred years old and wrinkled!" The image of herself grown old and corrupt leads Virginia to realize that she must turn her suitor down despite his wealth and prestige: "I will take no undue credit to myself; had no choice in the matter; I simply could not do it." And yet she wonders whether, by the next social season, she will be "capable not only of stalking but also of killing my game" (various meanings of the word *game* are played on throughout). The plot of Levy's final story in part reprises that of her controversial Jewish novel *Reuben Sachs* (1889), in which the male protagonist's betrayal of the woman he loves for self-advancement was usually understood in its own time (and often even in ours) as Levy's attack on Jewish materialism and ambition. That "Wise in her Generation" (like so much of Victorian literature) shows the same values holding sway among gentiles shows that Levy's attack is not on Jews but on the unrestrained individualism and savage competitiveness of her era. She uses the language of social Darwinism to challenge the Victorian doctrine that there was a boundary that protected the private sphere of life from the brutality of market relations. Levy's story ends with the protagonist looking out the window at the London night sky: "Black, black in its heart is the City; the blackness of man's heart is in its huge, hideous struggle for existence. . . . Better be unfit and perish than survive at such a cost."

Formally, what is innovative about the story is that most of what happens occurs inside Virginia's mind. Memory and reflection dominate throughout, and the second part (of six) is an extended meditation on the psychological and moral toll of the values and mores of this predatory world on innocent girls when they go from the protection of home into the fashionable fray. Levy concludes this section with a return to the exterior level of the action, as the protagonist and her former suitor have an exchange that makes explicit the particular bind in which women in this society find themselves, since men are free to be openly ruthless while women are supposed to have a kinder sensibility. Responding to Virginia's observation that "For thorough-going untiring support of one's own interests, there is, after all, no one like yourself," Philip is shocked: "Don't! . . . don't! It doesn't do for a woman to talk like that!"

BIBLIOGRAPHY
Levy, Amy. *Complete Novels and Selected Writings of Amy Levy*. Gainesville: University Press of Florida, 1993.

Linda Hunt Beckman

"WITHERED ARM, THE" THOMAS HARDY (1888)

"The Withered Arm" by THOMAS HARDY depicts the author's fatalistic view of the world. The story, published in *Blackwood Magazine* in 1888 and in the collection *Wessex Tales* the same year, presents the characters as victims of a malevolent power that propels them toward their doom.

The events take place in Wessex, the southwestern area of England where Hardy grew up. The setting establishes the gloomy, brooding tone of the work. Rhoda Brook, a "thin worn milkmaid" (737), and her 12-year-old son inhabit a cottage located on "a lonely spot high above the water-meads . . . not far from the border of Egdon Heath, whose dark countenance was visible in the distance" (738). The wind howls "dismally over the slopes of the heath" (746) as Rhoda and Gertrude Lodge make their way through thick clouds to the house of Conjuror Trendle.

The plot of the story centers on the disfigurement of Gertrude's arm: its cause, cure, and disastrous consequences. Soon after Farmer Lodge brings Gertrude, his young bride, to the community, Rhoda, the mother of Farmer Lodge's son, has a dream in which a ghostly vision of Gertrude pays her a visit, sits on her chest, and flaunts her wedding ring. Rhoda grabs the arm of the specter and throws her to the floor. After the two women meet in person, an affection develops between them, and Gertrude tells Rhoda of the difficulty she is having with her left arm. The problem, Rhoda learns, began at the same time as Rhoda's dream. When the condition of the arm grows worse, Gertrude requests Rhoda's help in locating Conjuror Trendle, who tells Gertrude that the disfigurement is "the work of an enemy" (746). Rhoda, believing that Gertrude now knows that she is the culprit, disappears with her son from the village.

Six years later Gertrude seeks the conjuror again and learns from him that her only hope of a cure is to place the disfigured arm on the neck of a newly hanged victim. Hearing of an execution, she travels to the site of the hanging and arranges with the executioner to touch the dead body before the blood turns cold. Gertrude, feeling her blood turn—as "predicted by the conjuror" (754)—lets out a cry. When a second cry rings out, she turns and sees the parents of the executed young man: her husband and Rhoda Brook.

Fate appears to govern the lives of the characters, whom Hardy treats with sympathy but without emotion. When Rhoda learns that Gertrude's ailment began at the time she wrestled with the specter, she wonders, "O, can it be . . . that I exercise a malignant power over people against my own will?" (743). Conjuror Trendle practices his art against his wishes, and Gertrude carries out his steps for a cure in a desperate attempt to regain the love of her husband. The condemned lad is the victim of chance; the executioner says of him, "If ever a young fellow deserved to be let off, this one does" (753). When the callous and indifferent Lodge changes into "a chastened and thoughtful man" (755), leaving his estate to a reformatory for boys and a small annuity to Rhoda, the reader wonders if his earlier cruelty had been the work of an evil force beyond his control.

Typical of Hardy's writing, the story ends on a dark note. Gertrude dies from physical and mental stress three days after the execution, Lodge lives "in solitary lodgings till his death" (755), and Rhoda's form becomes "bent" (755) and her "once abundant dark hair" becomes "white and worn away at the forehead" (755). "The Withered Arm" depicts the characters moving unwittingly toward an inevitable defeat and reflects the author's belief in the tragic nature of the human condition.

BIBLIOGRAPHY

Hardy, Thomas. *The Thomas Hardy Omnibus.* New York: St. Martin's, 1979.

Charlotte S. Pfeiffer

WODEHOUSE, P. G. (1881–1975) Pelham Grenville Wodehouse was born in Guildford, Surrey, the third in a family of four boys. His father was a magistrate in Hong Kong, and as a result the boys grew up in various schools and spent holidays with various aunts. According to Wodehouse, his childhood was "as ordinary as rice pudding" and com-

pletely happy; nonetheless, aunts are frequent Wodehousian villains. At his prep school, Dulwich College, Wodehouse was a star in various sports and editor of the literary magazine. His father could not afford to send Wodehouse to university, however, and Wodehouse instead began working at the Hong Kong and Shanghai Bank in London, a post he held until 1902, when, at age 20, he left the bank to become a full-time writer. His first book, *The Pothunters,* was published nine days later, and his pace never slackened. From 1902 to 1975 Wodehouse published nearly 100 novels and short story collections, as well as 15 plays and 44 screenplays. He also was a long-time collaborator (as lyricist) with Jerome Kern and Guy Bolton on a number of successful musical comedies; in 1917, the trio had five top shows running simultaneously, a record that still stands.

Wodehouse relocated to the United States in the 1910s, eventually becoming an American citizen. During World War I, he attempted to enlist first with British and then with American forces but was rejected as physically unfit. In 1939, Oxford granted him an honorary doctorate; the following year, while in France, Wodehouse and his wife Ethel were captured by invading German forces and interned for two years. Upon release, the Germans had him make several radio broadcasts, in which Wodehouse made light of his internment. The broadcasts caused a furor, and many considered Wodehouse a traitor; he was the subject of an MI5 investigation, whose results (not released till after Wodehouse's death) were that Wodehouse was wholly innocent of any collaboration with Nazis. The furor eventually died down, and in 1975 Wodehouse was knighted and given a waxwork in Madame Tussaud's. He had no ambitions left, he told the BBC, and died a few weeks later.

His short stories continue to be read and reprinted in many languages the world over. While at the beginning of his career Wodehouse specialized in public school stories and romances, he quickly turned to light comedies with convoluted plots, most of which take place within a Wodehousian universe peopled with hundreds of eccentric characters. During his most creative period (the 1920s through 1950s), Wodehouse established the most important characters and places in this upper-class universe: Blandings, the castle that "has imposters the way some places have mice"; Lord Emsworth of Blandings; his prize pig, Empress of Blandings; his brother Galahad, a soi-disant spreader of "sweetness and light"; Ukridge, an inveterate get-rich-quick schemer; and Mr. Mulliner, a teller of tall tales, all featuring members of an increasingly large Mulliner family. His two most famous creations, however, were Bertie Wooster, an amiable if unintelligent young man-about-town, and his impeccable valet, Jeeves. Wodehouse also wrote a series of golf stories that was reputed to have done much to increase golf's popularity.

Wodehouse's use of language is exceptionally creative; he is one of the second most frequently cited author in the *Oxford English Dictionary,* significantly outpaced only by Shakespeare. His plots, too, while seemingly only, as he described them, "musical comedies without music," manage to be both lighthearted and satirical. The conventions and writing style of the sentimental novel are frequent targets, as are fascist politics and snobbish class attitudes. However, the satire is not reactionary. While servants in Wodehouse's fiction are usually better educated and more intelligent than their masters, they are not necessarily better people. Kindness is the ultimate value in Wodehouse's work, and the most complicated and layered of plots magically resolve for characters who care about others. (See also "LORD EMSWORTH AND THE GIRLFRIEND.")

BIBLIOGRAPHY

Jasen, David. *P. G. Wodehouse: A Portrait of a Master.* New York: Mason and Lipscomb, 1974.

Phelps, Barry. *P. G. Wodehouse: Man and Myth.* London: Constable, 1992.

Wodehouse, P. G. *The Golf Omnibus.* New York: Gramercy, 1996.

———. *Life at Blandings.* New York: Penguin, 1988.

———. *Life with Jeeves.* New York: Penguin, 1983.

———. *Lord Emsworth and Others.* New York: Overlook Press, 2002.

———. *The Most of P. G. Wodehouse.* New York: Touchstone Books, 2000.

———. *The World of Mr. Mulliner.* New York: Avon, 1979.

Anna Peak

WOOD, ELLEN ("MRS. HENRY WOOD," "JOHNNY LUDLOW," "TOM PEPPER") (1814–1887)

The author known as Mrs. Henry Wood was born Ellen Price in the Sidbury area of Worcester, the eldest surviving in a family of 12 children. Unlike her six brothers, who were educated at the nearby prestigious King's School in Worcester, she was educated at home. She seems to have been mainly self-taught, and she read voraciously from her father's extensive library. In early adolescence it was noticed that she was suffering from curvature of the spine. Corrective methods were attempted, but she seems to have remained something of an invalid for the remainder of her life. In 1836 she married Henry Wood, a banker, wine merchant, and former diplomat, and went to live with him in the Gap area in the south of France for the next 20 years. Despite Wood's precarious health, she gave birth to at least five children, one of whom, a daughter, died from scarlet fever.

Wood is best known for her 30 sensation novels, especially *East Lynne* (1861), but she wrote more than 160 anonymous monthly pieces of shorter fiction during the decade before the publication of this novel and more than 100 after. Wood's first traced story, "Seven Years in the Wedded Life of a Roman Catholic," appeared in the February 1851 issue of Harrison Ainsworth's conservative *New Monthly Magazine.* This was followed by several more pieces of anti-Catholic propaganda, but she soon broadened her range to write in many genres, including crime, romance, fictionalized war reports, and sensation. In late 1854 Ainsworth bought *Bentley's Miscellany* and shortly afterward Wood began to contribute concurrently to both periodicals.

Many of Wood's early stories were of novella length, and she later adapted them to form the basis of novels such as *Mildred Arkell* (1865) and *St. Martin's Eve* (1866). The shorter anonymous tales were later reprinted in a more genteel form in her own magazine, the *Argosy.* Wood's purchase of the *Argosy* in late 1867 was a turning point—most of her new novels were serialized in the periodical before they appeared in three volumes, but virtually all her new short fiction written after 1868 appeared there under the pseudonym Johnny Ludlow.

Told in the Twilight (1875), Wood's first non–Johnny Ludlow collection of early short narratives, had disappointing sales figures in comparison with her novels, and some of these tales were reprinted under the less disquieting title *Parkwater* the following year. Apart from three Johnny Ludlow anthologies, these were the only short stories she collected in her lifetime. Wood's son Charles, her literary executor, oversaw the publication of a further three Johnny Ludlow anthologies (two in 1890, and the last in 1899) and four other collections of short fiction: *Lady Grace* (1887), *Adam Grainger* (1890), *The Unholy Wish* (1890), and *Ashley* (1897).

Only one extensive essay has examined Wood's short fiction, but it focuses on her supernatural fiction and is not very well known. Similarly, only one non–Johnny Ludlow tale, "A Mysterious Visitor" (1857), has appeared in a modern anthology. This is a ghost story set at the time of the Indian Mutiny, but the original incarnation in *Bentley's Miscellany* was considerably more violent than the bowdlerized version that appeared in Wood's *Argosy* (1875) and the posthumous collection *Adam Grainger* (1890). Wood's rewriting of her early anonymous work has not previously been remarked on but would repay a scholar's close attention. For instance, "The Parson's Oath" (1855), as it appeared in the *Argosy* and *The Unholy Wish* collection, features the murder of a young girl for no discernible motive. However, in the original anonymous version she was raped, and when she refused to marry her attacker she was shot and buried in his garden. Wood was a more subversive writer, especially before her name became known, than has ever been acknowledged.

BIBLIOGRAPHY

James L. Campbell. "Mrs. Henry Wood." In *Supernatural Fiction Writers.* Vol. 1: *Fantasy and Horror,* edited by E. F. Bleiler, 279–286. New York: Scribners, 1985.

Flowers, Michael. "Ellen Wood's Short Story Collections." Available online. URL: http://www.mrshenrywood.co.uk/short.html. Accessed on August 18, 2004.

Maunder, Andrew. "Ellen Wood Was a Writer: Rediscovering Collins's Rival," *Wilkie Collins Society Journal* 2 (2000): 17–31.

Wood, Ellen. *East Lynne.* 1861. Peterborough, Ontario: Broadview Press, 2000.

———. *St. Martin's Eve.* 1866. London: Pickering and Chatto, 2004.

Michael Flowers

WOOLF, VIRGINIA (1882–1941)

Born Adeline Virginia Stephen on January 25, 1882, Virginia Woolf has become the most celebrated of the modernist writers (see MODERNISM), achieving iconographic status. She was the third child and second daughter of Sir Leslie Stephen (1832–1904) and his second wife, Julia Jackson Duckworth Stephen (1846–95), and she grew up in Hyde Park Gate, London. Her father had been an alpinist in his youth, was a scholar who wrote both history and literary appreciations, and edited *The Dictionary of National Biography.* Virginia was educated at home, where she had free access to her father's library. Her mother died when Virginia was 13, and that event seems to have precipitated the first of several breakdowns that disrupted Virginia's life.

She and her older sister, Vanessa Bell (1879–1961), belonged to a group of artists and thinkers who have come to be known as the Bloomsbury group; they socialized to discuss ideas and had complicated intellectual and sexual relationships with each other. Several of the members, including Clive Bell (1881–1964), Lytton Strachey (1880–1932), and John Maynard Keynes (1883–1946), became, as Woolf did, influences on 20th-century thinking. Woolf was also acquainted with writers including KATHERINE MANSFIELD (1888–1923), ELIZABETH BOWEN (1899–1973), and E. M. FORSTER (1879–1970).

Woolf wrote short fiction like "The JOURNAL OF MISTRESS JOAN MARTYN" for private circulation after she had begun, in 1904, publishing reviews and essays professionally. Some of her early short works show the influence of Jane Austen's style. She married Leonard Woolf (1880–1969), a friend of her older brother Thoby (1880–1906) in 1912 and finished her first novel, *The Voyage Out,* the year after her marriage. It was not published until 1915, however, because of her health. It conveys, as do many of Woolf's stories, such as "An UNWRITTEN NOVEL," her concerns about the roles and positions of women in society. She put forth these views more explicitly in *A Room of One's Own* (1929) and *Three Guineas* (1938).

Woolf's first publisher was her half-brother Gerald Duckworth (1870–1937), who had molested her when both were children. Feminist scholars have focused attention on this trauma and the repeated abuse (psychological and/or sexual) by her half brother George Duckworth (1868–1934) as additional sources of Woolf's mental illness.

In 1917, Leonard and Virginia Woolf founded the Hogarth Press, which published T. S. Eliot's *The Waste Land* as well as Woolf's fiction and translations from Russian and German. They published most of Vita Sackville-West's fiction. Virginia and Vita (1892–1962) had a close friendship between approximately 1925 and 1929 that may or may not have included sexual relations. Early biographers leave the question open, but recent biographers assert that the two had a lesbian affair. Vita is the main character in *Orlando* (1928), Woolf's novel of an Elizabethan man with extraordinary longevity who becomes a woman in the course of that life. The book purports to be a biography, as does Woolf's shorter work, *Flush* (1933), an account of the life of Elizabeth Barrett Browning's spaniel—both play with biographical conventions and expectations. The clear style of *Orlando* skillfully tells a complex plot, and the book was a best seller at the time of its publication.

Leonard was also a writer and worked as an editor to allow Virginia the financial means to write as she pleased. Some of her fiction, both long and short, is conventional in narrative and style, and some of it is innovative in its narrative structure and/or style. Woolf has a distinctive voice, personal and confident, that comes through in all her work, and she is as skilled as a poet in her economy of evocation and in the way that each word of her fiction is right and necessary. The stories contained in the collection MONDAY OR TUESDAY (1921), which include "KEW GARDENS" and "The Mark on the Wall," interlace setting and plot and are typical of Woolf's use of the stream-of-consciousness technique. In total, Woolf published 18 short stories in her lifetime. She was, despite her health, a prolific writer, and her husband attributed that productivity to her habit of writing consistently when she was well. *Mrs. Dalloway* (1925), *To the Lighthouse* (1927), and *The Waves* (1931) are much studied for their unique style and loosely parallel narratives.

Woolf, fearing the onset of another breakdown, committed suicide in 1941 by drowning herself in the river Ouse, near the Woolfs' home in Rodmell, Sussex.

BIBLIOGRAPHY

Bell, Quentin. *Virginia Woolf: A Biography.* 1972. New York: Harcourt, Brace, Janovich, 1974.

Dick, Susan, ed. *The Complete Shorter Fiction of Virginia Woolf.* 2nd ed. San Diego, New York, and London: Harcourt, 1989.

Dunn, Jane. *A Very Close Conspiracy: Vanessa Bell and Virginia Woolf.* Boston: Little, Brown, 1990.

Holtby, Winifred. *Virginia Woolf: A Critical Memoir.* 1932. Chicago: Academy Press, 1978.

Lee, Hermione. *Virginia Woolf.* New York: Knopf, 1997.

Woolf, Virginia. *Between the Acts.* London: Hogarth Press, 1941.

———. *The Common Reader.* London: Hogarth Press, 1925.

———. *Flush.* London: Hogarth Press, 1935.

———. *A Haunted House and Other Short Stories.* London: Hogarth Press, 1944.

———. *Monday or Tuesday.* London: Hogarth Press, 1921.

———. *Mrs. Dalloway.* London: Hogarth Press, 1925.

———. *Night and Day.* London: Duckworth, 1919.

———. *Orlando.* London: Hogarth Press, 1928.

———. *A Room of One's Own.* London: Hogarth Press, 1929.

Joanne Pierce

WORLD AND OTHER PLACES, THE JEANETTE WINTERSON (1998)

The World and Other Places is, to date, JEANETTE WINTERSON's only short story collection. In the afterword of the 1998 edition, Winterson explains how she wrote these 17 stories gradually over 12 years, after the publication of her first novel, *Oranges Are Not the Only Fruit* (1985). There is a pathos invested in many of these stories, but there is also a glimpse of the humor of *Oranges*. This is particularly true of the last story, "Psalms," in which the child narrator and her evangelical mother are replicas of the characters in the novel. Psalms is the unfortunate pet tortoise (who is named, on the mother's insistence, after a book of the Bible) who drowns while the family is on holiday in Blackpool. Both the first and last stories are concerned with loving a pet and therefore explicitly frame the collection. Typically for Winterson, love in the first is frightening and risky and introduces the reader to one of Winterson's dominating concerns: that loving is about taking a chance.

This whole collection is characteristic for its close relationship with Winterson's novels. In "The Three Friends," for example, appearing in *Gut Symmetries* (1997), the three title characters find death after journeying for "that which cannot be found" (49). The story is akin to a quest narrative, or rather a moral fable, and is a reminder of how Winterson adapts different forms for her own use. "Orion" also appears in *Sexing the Cherry* (1989) as Fortunata's story, and the names of the two main characters in "The Poetics of Sex," Sappho and Picasso, are also used in *Art and Lies* (1994). In addition, "Atlantic Crossing" is a condensed version of Winterson's script *Great Moments in Aviation* (1994).

As well as these overt connections, the style of writing also marks these tales as Winterson's work. There are sentences here that are repeated in her novels, such as "What you risk reveals what you value." This appears not only in "Adventure of a Lifetime" and "Orion" but also in *The Passion* (1987) and other novels. Such recycling is open to criticism, but the repetition has the effect of layering Winterson's works with similar meanings. The sentence itself ("what you risk reveals what you value") also indicates that Winterson is inciting the reader to gamble with emotions. Her characters often turn to adultery as a means of escape from the normative effects of institutionalized love. The risk, more often than not, is described as worth it when love has become false or stale.

These stories also have political aspects, especially when late 20th-century consumerism is interrogated. This occurs in "Holy Matrimony," "A Green Square," and, to a lesser extent, "The Green Man," in which the modern world is decried as superficial and meaningless. "Holy Matrimony" maintains Winterson's commitment to a higher faith and criticizes the faithless exchange of vows; marriage is depicted as having become another commodity. "A Green Square" follows immediately after and continues this tone of despair. "The Green Man" conveys a similar sense of despair and questions the life of a married couple once the excitement has begun to pall. These three tales value

love when it is genuine, and they critique conformity and the commodification of desire.

More political reactions can be found in "Orion" and "The Poetics of Sex." In these two stories the influence of feminism is tangible. In "Orion" Winterson rewrites the myth in which Artemis kills Orion with a scorpion as a punishment for raping her, and "The Poetics of Sex" is structured by ignorant homophobic questions asked of lesbians, such as "Don't You Feel There's Something Missing?" and the repeated "Why Do You Sleep With Girls?" This story challenges the marginalizing effects of the dominant heterosexual culture and uses lesbian sexuality to undermine this hegemony.

Recurring Winterson themes are also apparent in the title story. The narrator is a young boy whose family is depicted as so poor that they have to imagine the world and the journeys they could make. This reverence for the imagined journey, the city of the interior, is also evident in *Sexing the Cherry,* in which Jordan's imagination takes the reader to fairy-tale cities.

These journeys in the novel and short story expose an interest in the quest motif and the influence of romanticism and MODERNISM on Winterson's writing. The "other places" extend beyond physical geography and offer travels to richer, imagined landscapes that are escapes from realism. Several of these stories barely have a plot, allowing for a reflection on other concerns, such as the power of language. The use of metafiction, by which the fictionality of the story is self-consciously highlighted, is often touched on in this collection and is a trademark of Winterson's later novels.

The departure from plot has confounded critics of Winterson's work in the 1990s and has contributed to negative criticism of her novels. Because this collection was written over a 12-year period, it is possible to trace a trajectory in the writing that moves increasingly away from the comparatively more grounded *Oranges Are Not the Only Fruit.* In the afterword of *The World and Other Places,* Winterson writes that the nature of time, love, the quest, and the outsider are the compass points of her life and her writing. Furthermore, this collection, alongside her novels, demonstrates that the art of storytelling is another dominant concern for Winterson.

BIBLIOGRAPHY

Cumming, Laura. "Books: Reader, Are You Up to It?" *Guardian*. 27 June 1998, p. 10.

Jeanette Winterson. Available online. URL: http://jeanettewinterson.com. Accessed June 9, 2006.

Winterson, Jeanette. *The World and Other Places*. London: Jonathan Cape, 1998.

Julie Ellam

WORLD WAR I   Long considered the catalyst for World War I, the assassination in Sarajevo of the Austro-Hungarian archduke Franz Ferdinand and his wife by a young Bosnian Serb was merely the final movement in a symphony of events that had been played throughout Europe since the mid19th century: Germany, led by Kaiser Wilhelm II, desired a larger presence on the world's stage and thus began strengthening its naval power. Great Britain, aware that its place in international affairs depended on its ability to defend itself on the water, enlarged its naval capabilities, which led to a German-British arms race. Austria-Hungary annexed Bosnia and Herzegovina in 1908, much to the dismay of Russia, whose foreign policy included a belief in pan-Slavism, or a brotherhood among all peoples of eastern Europe. Populous and increasingly industrialized, Russia also sought an outlet to the Black Sea through the Balkans. The series of so-called Balkan Crises that erupted between 1879 and 1908 further destabilized a region already fractured by nationalist sentiment. Finally, the balance of power created after Napoleon's defeat in 1815 had eroded into two belligerent blocks through the signing of secret treaties: the Triple Entente (Britain, France, and Russia) and the Triple Alliance (Austria-Hungary, Germany, and Italy).

Although Europe was thus prepared to hear the noise of battle, World War I sounded—as well as looked and felt—like no other war before or since. As a result of the assassination, Austria-Hungary, with the help of Germany, decided to invade Serbia; Russia and France reacted angrily. On August 1, 1914, Germany declared war on Russia. Three days later, after the German advance into Belgium, Britain declared war on Germany. All sides believed the war would be over by Christmas. Instead, the war lasted for four years, until the signing of the armistice on November 11, 1918, at a cost of between 9 and 10 million lives and some 20 million serious injuries.

In the years immediately preceding the war, a general sense of decay pervaded English society. The spread of urban areas—and the suburbs, machines, suffragists, and other symbols of modernity contained within cities—threatened the Edenic villages, with their peaceful, quiet optimism, that constituted the very quality of Englishness. Similarly a chasm between the upper and lower classes widened during the Edwardian Period, 1901–1914: Approximately 20 percent of the population lived in luxury, largely as the result of the successful British Empire, while the remaining 80 percent lived in poverty. Writers like H. G. WELLS, E. M. FORSTER, HENRY JAMES, and Ford Madox Ford explored this decadent atmosphere in their prewar work. World War I, however, united the classes under the cause of British patriotism—at least outwardly—and was thus welcomed by assorted members of the literati as a way of healing social fissures.

Capitalizing on this sentiment, the British government created the War Propaganda Bureau (WPB) in fall 1914 to enlist the assistance of writers in maintaining the pervasive good feelings about the war. All told, the WPB produced nearly 1,200 pamphlets by war's end, including "The New Army" by RUDYARD KIPLING and others by ARTHUR CONAN DOYLE, J. M. Barrie, Wells, and Ford, who changed his last name from Hueffer in order to distance himself from his German heritage. The government also carefully controlled the war's portrayal in the media using the 1914 Defense of the Realm Act, which censored news and letters from the fronts and criminalized the publication of works that criticized the government. Succumbing to pressure from other countries, Britain eventually allowed five journalists to cover the war on location.

Not content with simply writing for the WPB, some writers enlisted: Doyle (at age 57) worked as a volunteer, and Ford served as an infantry officer. A prowar tone flowed through many short stories produced between 1914 and 1918, and there is often a celebration of group bravery as in Arthur MACHEN's "THE BOWMEN." "Red Tape" (1914), by May Sinclair, praises the war for its ability to unite. Yet as the war progressed, some writers became more prepared to question its effects, in particular the psychological damage it wrought on individuals. In "MARY POSTGATE" (1915), Kipling's spinster protagonist watches gleefully as a German soldier dies in her rural English hamlet. D. H. LAWRENCE, once suspected of spying for Germany because his wife was German, condemned the war in his 1915 novel *The Rainbow* and portrayed its damaging psychological effects in his 1919 story "TICKETS, PLEASE." KATHERINE MANSFIELD's "Prelude" (1917), with its experimental lack of cause and effect, might be read as an oblique commentary on the confusing tangle of events that preceded the 1914 declarations of war, just as "The FLY" looks at the war's aftermath.

In "His Last Bow" (1917), Sherlock Holmes and Watson meet in the summer of 1914 for their final escapade—to prevent a German spy from leaving England with important state secrets during "the most terrible August in the history of the world" (Doyle, 442). At the close of the story, in an oft-quoted passage, Holmes turns to Watson and says, "There's an east wind coming . . . such a wind as never blew on England yet. It will be cold and bitter, Watson, and a good many of us may wither before its blast. But it's God's own wind . . . and a cleaner, better, stronger land will lie in the sunshine when the storm has cleared" (Doyle, 457). By war's end, the grim calculus had destroyed such vestiges of certainty: During the first four weeks of war, France lost 260,000 troops. On one day in July 1916, 60,000 British soldiers died, mowed down by the recently invented machine gun. Almost 82 percent of all Australians fighting in the war were killed or wounded. Philosopher Walter Benjamin wrote that men returned home from the trenches "silent" (84), and, indeed, several years passed before retellings of the war appeared in poems, novels, and memoirs by such writers as T. S. Eliot, Siegfried Sassoon, and Robert Graves. It took time for writers, especially writers who had not directly participated, to discover a way of chronicling this war—a war that was ostensibly fought to prevent the spread of a perceived barbarianism but was, in its deadlocked trench combat, itself utterly barbaric.

Even as memorials to the war dead sprung up around Europe, doubts about the war's purpose became obvious. Despite the mandates, including Palestine, it received from the League of Nations in 1919, Britain's position as an imperial power was weakened by the war: After fighting alongside British soldiers and for British values, including liberal humanism and enlightenment, colonial subjects from India to Ireland began clamoring for home rule, and Britain ended the war deeply in financial debt to the United States. MODERNISM, an artistic movement that rejected the idea of a single, objective truth; privileged a multiplicity of perspectives; and interrogated uses of form, grew out of such disillusionment. The emphasis on language within literary modernism seemed especially suited to the scrutiny of war that emerged in the 1920s and 1930s in fiction by VIRGINIA WOOLF, JAMES JOYCE, WYNDHAM LEWIS, JOSEPH CONRAD (whose one story about the war, "The Tale" [1925], shrouds the narrative in layers of fog, both real and metaphoric), and Richard Aldington, who explored the newly diagnosed disease shell shock in "The Case of Lieutenant Hall" (1930). These and other writers struggled to find a vocabulary capable of expressing the horrors of modern warfare, and they attempted to break free of a Western literary tradition that tended to portray war as gloriously heroic.

More than 90 years after the first blasts, scholars continue to reflect on World War I: What cultural, social, and economic factors caused such patriotic loyalty in the legions of troops who served? Was the war the result of mad, sadistic statesmen vying for power, or of a global breakdown of concepts of civilization? At what point does fidelity to abstract ideals—democracy, progress, the triumph of good over evil—begin to overshadow the concrete experience of death, devastation, and destruction? Was the war necessary? When, if ever, is war necessary? That writers in the early 20th century also tried to answer these questions speaks not to some literary deficiency or failure but to the queries' significance and to the difficult, dense reality known as the Great War.

BIBLIOGRAPHY

Audoin-Rouzeau, Stéphane, and Annette Becker. *14–18: Understanding the Great War.* Translated by Catherine Temerson. New York: Hill & Wang, 2004.

Benjamin, Walter. "The Storyteller." In *Illuminations,* edited by Hannah Arendt, 83–109. New York: Schocken Books, 1968.

Doyle, Arthur Conan. *Sherlock Holmes: The Complete Novels and Stories.* Vol. II. New York: Bantam, 1986.

Fussell, Paul. *The Great War and Modern Memory.* 1975. Reprint, New York: Oxford University Press, 2000.

Higonnet, Margaret R., ed. *Lines of Fire: Women Writers of World War I.* New York: Penguin, 1999.

Robb, George. *British Culture and the First World War.* New York: Palgrave, 2002.

Tate, Trudi. *Men, Women and the Great War: An Anthology.* Manchester, England: Manchester University Press, 1995.

———. *Modernism, History, and the First World War.* Manchester, England: Manchester University Press, 1998.

Jessica Allen

WORLD WAR II (1939–1945)

World War II officially began when the British Prime Minister, Neville Chamberlain, announced it over the radio on September 3, 1939. As in World War I, Germany was the enemy, along with Fascist Italy and Imperial Japan. Although the catalyst was the German invasion of Poland, the six-year conflict that followed was a very different war from the previous one: It was global, involving several seemingly different wars, on land, at sea, and in the air. From a British perspective, what is most striking about the war is that after the fall of France, Belgium, and Holland, and until the Japanese attack on Pearl Harbor on December 7, 1941, brought the United States into the war, Britain and her colonial troops faced Germany alone and on several fronts. Large areas of the BRITISH EMPIRE were the setting for the fighting; Hong Kong fell to the Japanese in 1941, and Singapore in 1942. At home, the population faced food shortages and rationing. There was an evacuation of troops from Dunkirk in May and June 1940. During the Blitz (from the German word for "lightening"), London and other cities faced sustained bombing for much of 1940–41. Britain waited for Hitler to invade, which seemed highly likely until he diverted some of his attention eastward toward Russia. When Winston Churchill succeeded Chamberlain as Prime Minister in May 1940, he adopted a more bullish tone, promising victory at any cost. Slogans like "Your courage, your cheerfulness, your resolution will bring us victory" were used by the Ministry of Information to bolster morale and helped create a sense that if the "common folk," to use J. B. Priestly's phrase, stood firm, then the enemy would be overcome (Klein, 45).

Historians such as A. J. P. Taylor agree that one of the striking things about World War II is the way it could be presented to the world, at least from Britain's point of view, as "that very rare thing—a just war," (quoted in Klein, 2), a crusade involving the defeat of an evil Nazi state. Unlike World War I, it was not—and has not been—painted as a pointless, tragic conflict (Klein, 2). Widely viewed in this way, and viewed as the war to end all wars, it thus presented a particular challenge to writers. In an important early anthology, *Components of the Scene* (1965), Ronald Blythe describes World War II as "a highly literary war." "Writers," he notes,

> generally believed that they were witnessing dissolution of the old civilized scene and that they had a duty to preserve the great basic values which had created this scene. They also felt that they must resist the new facelessness forced upon Europe by fascist politics and military expediency; that salvation and hope began with the discovery of one's own identity and its maintenance against all the pressures of the emergency. (13)

T. S. Eliot believed that one of the writer's tasks at this time was to preserve the purity of language and not to be sucked into the official language of the bureaucrat and propagandists. Eliot told a fellow poet, Steven Spender, that "it is very important that as many writers as possible should remain detached and not have any official position" (Blythe, 14). The sense of writers scribbling away "above" the war, rather than getting dragged into writing in support of it, as had happened in World War I, was important for many because it suggested the writer's role in maintaining some semblance of civilized values the midst of carnage.

During 1939–45, the short story was seen by some observers as a particularly important genre. Notably, H. E. BATES suggested that the Britain of World War II and "its inevitable aftermath of still more distrustful dislocation" would discover the short story to be the "essential medium for whatever it has to say" because "if no other good comes out of wars, stories will" (quoted in Rogers, xiv). Others, however, expressed themselves unhappy with what emerged, attacking what they saw as the absence of powerful short story writing, arguing that the British stories were too pallid, too concerned with form, and unoriginal. The critic Cyril Connelly, writing in *Horizon* magazine in 1944, observed that "War-writers are disappointing, either because they submit too bare a reportage or derivative *pastiches* by Hemingway." Connelly also warned that the magazine did not want the mundane or the ordinary. *"Horizon,"* he announced, "will always publish stories of pure realism, but we take the line that experiences connected with the blitz, the shopping queues, the home front, deserted wives, deceived husbands, broken homes, dull jobs, bad schools, group squabbles, are so much a picture of our ordinary lives that unless the workmanship is outstanding we are against them" (quoted in Davin, x). Connelly's distaste was shared by Vernon Mallinson, who noted in 1946 that "Nothing written in England since 1939 gives me the slightest indication that this World War, however cataclysmic, has produced or is likely to produce anything immediately significant" (quoted in Klein, 1). It is this kind of response that for many years helped encourage the idea among literary historians that, in contrast to World War I, World War II did not prompt much literary work of great value. Whereas World War I prompted what Vernon Scannell terms a "fixed imaginative landscape," World War II apparently did not have the same resonance. Scannell notes that "the Great War [World War I] has become a powerful myth while the Second World War, to a succeeding generation, has never been other than a historical event." (quoted in Klein, 2).

Although in 1944 critics like Connelly derided the short story, short story writing during the war years played a much greater part in the nation's cultural life than has often been assumed. "Short stories," Anne Boston notes in the introduction to her anthology *Wave Me Goodbye* (1988), "enjoyed an unexpected burst of popularity in wartime, when ordinary life was subject to constant interruption and time was at a premium" (12). This was especially true in the early years of the war when theaters and cinemas were closed and the blackout made it difficult to go out at night. The very shortness of the short story—its ability to capture a single brief incident or "fragment" of life—was seen as one of its advantages. Magazines like *Horizon* (from January 1940) and the long-running *Strand* and *Women's Journal,* along with series such as *Penguin New Writing* (from 1936) and *Bugle Blast,* for the armed forces, gave opportunities to many writers we now regard as important practitioners of the form. These include V. S. PRITCHETT, Julian Maclaren-Ross, ELIZABETH BOWEN, GRAHAM GREENE, "Flying Officer X" (pen name of H. E. BATES), Rosamund Lehmann, and STEVIE SMITH, as well as many others whose work has fallen into neglect: Barbara Pym, Diana Gardner, Joycelyn Brooke, and Alun Lewis.

The themes of these stories are various: foreign travel, combat, death, sexual relations, illness, bereavement, and comradeship all feature. Much of the short fiction of the war is, as Connelly complained, broadly realist. This is perhaps understandable. It is a style that, as Anne Boston notes, "was often the most appropriate medium; it suited the urgency of the time" (12). This is apparent in Boston's anthology—a collection of stories by women writers, in which the focus is largely personal and often domestic, portraying women's lives on home front during and just after the war. In making her selection, Boston makes use of Elizabeth Bowen's important distinction between war stories and wartime ones, which "are more, studies of climate, war-climate, and of the strange growths it raised" (Boston, 15). Notable here are ROSE MACAULAY's "Miss Anstruther's Letters," Diana Gardner's "The Land Girl," Elizabeth Bowen's "MYSTERIOUS KOR," and ELIZABETH TAYLOR's "Gravement Endommagé." SYLVIA TOWNSEND WARNER captures the disruption to family life cause by the war in "Sweethearts and Wives." Another story, "Poor Mary," is about role reversal between a husband who stays behind and works the land and his wife who joins the armed forces. Readers interested in war stories (to use Bowen's terminology) should consult Dan Davin's *Stories from the Second World War* (1982). Like Boston, Davin counsels against viewing the war "only in the comedy and caricature . . . or by films and flashbacks to the Blitz, Churchill, Dunkirk, Colditz and so on which present a heroic myth, perhaps necessary to the nation's sense of itself but nonetheless a myth for all that" (ix). For the most part, Davin's anthology focuses on the armed forces, particularly the privation and dangers of the battlefield. There is little sense of glorification of war in these stories; instead, the focus is on the mental and physical scars that war brings. Although Davin is wary of mythologizing the war, many of the texts present a likable image of the British soldier and conjure up ideas of perseverance and resilience and a shared sense of decency and loyalty.

BIBLIOGRAPHY

Ronald Blythe, ed. *Components of the Scene: Stories, Poems, and Essays of the Second World War.* London: Penguin, 1965.

Boston, Anne, ed. *Wave Me Goodbye: Stories of the Second World War.* London: Penguin, 1988.

Davin, Dan, ed. *Short Stories from the Second World War.* Oxford: Oxford University Press, 1982.

Klein, Holger, ed. *The Second World War in Fiction.* London: Macmillan, 1984.

Rogers, John H. *British Short Fiction Writers 1915–1945. Dictionary of Literary Biography,* vol. 162. Detroit: Gale, 1996.

Scannell, Vernon. *Not without Glory: Poets of the Second World War.* London: Woburn Press, 1976.

Andrew Maunder

Y

YELLOW BOOK, THE   The best known late-Victorian periodical, which ran from its opening volume on April 16, 1894, until its demise in 1897. Run by its editor, HENRY HARLAND, and a subeditor, ELLA D'ARCY, the quarterly was published in London by Elkin Matthews and John Lane of the Bodley Head until October 1894; Lane took over full responsibility when they dissolved their partnership after the second number. In total, 13 volumes of the quarterly were published; for the first four, Aubrey Beardsley was the art director and chief illustrator. It was a nonconformist journal aimed at the literary intelligentsia and was emblematic of the "Yellow Nineties," which aimed to confront conventional attitudes, explore cosmopolitan themes, and provoke discussion on advanced topics. The periodical was unusual in format and content: Each volume was book length (approximately three hundred pages), cost five shillings, and was beautiful in its illustrated, yellow hardcover presentation. Although the first volume was popular enough to run to three printings, it sustained intense criticism for the aesthetic and decadent short stories and poetry that appeared in its pages (see AESTHETICISM and DECADENCE); the appropriateness and quality of Beardsley's artwork were also vehemently attacked. In addition, several parodies of the *Yellow Book* appeared in *Punch*. In spite of its place as the main vehicle for dissemination of ideas such as art for art's sake, the quarterly was unable to sustain viability after OSCAR WILDE was arrested with a yellow book under his arm, although it is believed that the book was not a volume of the *Yellow Book* but rather a French novel in a yellow cover. Indeed, Wilde was never published in the journal, although other important authors of the 1880s and 1890s—such as D'Arcy, GEORGE EGERTON, George Gissing, HENRY JAMES, Richard Le Gallienne, CHARLOTTE MEW, and Victorian Cross—were. A lack of coherent intention became evident as the journal declined, unable to find a balance between original work and critical essays, or between translations of French texts and children's fiction. Eventually, John Lane came to rely on his own authors, and the *Yellow Book* became less the expression of a movement than a publisher's magazine.

BIBLIOGRAPHY

Mix, Katherine Lyon. *A Study in Yellow: The Yellow Book and Its Contributors*. Lawrence: University Press of Kansas, 1960.

Sarah Maier

"YELLOW FACE, THE" ARTHUR CONAN DOYLE (1893)   A detective story first published in the *STRAND MAGAZINE* in February 1893 and subsequently in the collection *The Memoirs of Sherlock Holmes* (1894).

Holmes is consulted by Mr. Grant Munro, on the subject of his wife's mysterious behavior. Munro met his wife, Effie, after the death of her first husband and her child from yellow fever in America. The Munros live at a villa near the South London suburb of Norbury, where one of the few nearby buildings is a cottage. One night, Munro wakes to find his wife leaving the villa and discovers that she has visited the cottage on a number of occasions. When questioned about her secretive visits, Effie pleads with Munro to drop the subject, as the truth will threaten their marriage. During an investigation of the cottage, Munro sees a person in the upstairs window, an "unnatural and inhuman" figure with a yellow face. Holmes surmises that Effie is being blackmailed with a bigamous secret by her first husband, who did not die of fever but has been confined to the cottage with leprosy. Holmes, Watson, and Munro travel to Norbury and force their way into the cottage. They discover that the face at the window was that of a black child wearing a yellow mask in order not to raise suspicion of a black face in rural England. The child is Effie's, and her late husband is revealed to have been African-American. Munro, contrary to his wife's expectations, is happy to adopt the child. Holmes and Watson leave, Holmes fully aware that his detection has been a failure.

The story is notable for two reasons: its emphasis on Holmes's failure to solve the case and its treatment of race. Part of the story's mystery is located in the refusal of the three investigators (all white) to consider that Effie Munro's first husband might be black. This interracial marriage (or, in Victorian terms, *metissage*) combines with the placement of black characters in a white society to produce the narrative's mystery. The child is disguised with a yellow mask so that "those who might see her at the window might should not gossip about there being a black child in the neighbourhood," although this raises the question why such an "unnatural" yellow disguise was chosen and suggests that any skin tone other than black would be acceptable. Similarly, Watson describes a portrait of Effie's first husband as being of "a man, strikingly handsome and intelligent, *but* bearing unmistakable signs upon his features of his African descent" (emphasis added). The story thus illustrates a frequent trope of late Victorian detective fiction, in which mystery is created by the incursion of foreign elements into England (see *A STUDY IN SCARLET*). Such anxieties are developed in the story by references to disease and degeneration: the death of Effie's husband from yellow fever and Holmes's incorrect surmise that her husband may have contracted leprosy. The thematic link between interracial marriage and disease addresses contemporary concern that such marriages would lead to a kind of hereditary impurity, and the use of yellow in the story is also significant in the context of an 1890s association of the color with decadence and moral degeneration (in, for instance, the controversial periodical *The Yellow Book*), allusions that would have been lost had Doyle kept the story's original title, "The Livid Face." Such references are complicated, however, by the ending, in which Holmes's degenerationist theories are discredited and the foreign becomes accepted; Munro adopts his stepchild with the admonition that "I am not a very good man, Effie, but I think that I am a better one than you have given me credit for being." The final image provided by Sidney Paget for the story's publication in the *Strand* illustrates this scene, showing Munro holding his stepdaughter while Holmes looks on approvingly.

BIBLIOGRAPHY
Carr, John Dickson. *The Life of Sir Arthur Conan Doyle*. London: John Murray, 1949.
Doyle, Arthur Conan. *The Memoirs of Sherlock Holmes*. London: Newnes, 1894.
McClintock, Anne. *Imperial Leather: Race, Gender and Sexuality in the Colonial Context*. London: Routledge, 1995.
Thomas, Ronald D. *Detective Fiction and the Rise of Forensic Science*. Cambridge: Cambridge University Press, 1999.

Christopher Pittard

"YOU SHOULD HAVE SEEN THE MESS" MURIEL SPARK (1958)

"You Should Have Seen the Mess" is included in the 1958 collection *The Go-Away Bird with Other Stories* by distinguished Edinburgh-born writer MURIEL SPARK. Since its initial publication, it has become one of Spark's most anthologized stories, probably because of its faultless blend of irony and pathos, its subtle depiction of character through the use of the unreliable narrator, its linguistic and stylistic mastery, and its scathing criticism of English working-class values and the Protestant ethos.

The title aptly conveys the story's central theme and irony. The indignant exclamation "You should have seen the mess" evokes the only criterion by which the main character judges—and misjudges—everything that happens to her. The protagonist-narrator Lorna

Merrifield (note the ironic symbolism of the name) is a 17-year-old working-class girl who continually congratulates herself on avoiding improper behavior, messy situations, and untidy people. She chooses the secondary modern school over the scholastically superior grammar school because the modern school is more "hygienic"; she quits her first typing job in a well-established law firm because the teacups are cracked and the facilities are not spotless; she condemns her well-meaning and educated new friends for their improper language and disorderly habits; and finally she drops her suitor, a rich, loving, and generous artist, because he is not properly tidy.

Lorna is an unreliable narrator. She consistently misinterprets the events and situations she witnesses and experiences. The gap between what the heroine fails to perceive and what the reader readily recognizes is the central source of irony in the story. Thus, when she visits old Mrs. Darby's manor house, she mistakes its antique splendor for decrepit poverty and asks the elderly aristocrat when she is going to be rehoused by the Council. This is a comic instance of Lorna's naïveté, but Lorna's principal character flaw is her blind espousal of her parents' values. These values are subsumed in one term, which Lorna keeps using as her moral yardstick: hygiene.

Spark's stylistic mastery can be seen in the way she repeats a term until it acquires the inverse of its original meaning. Like Shakespeare's rhetorical device in *Julius Caesar,* when Mark Anthony insists that "Brutus is an honorable man" in order to suggest the opposite to his audience, Lorna's absurd reliance on the notion of cleanliness makes the reader realize that *hygiene* can be a dirty word. Throughout the story, cleanliness is associated with hypocrisy, pretentiousness, and plain stupidity. The Merrifields dress their children in their best clothes before sending them to play outdoors, they cleanse their speech of all reference to bodily functions or to death, and they consistently give their daughter irrelevant and damaging advice.

In the autobiographic *Curriculum Vitae,* Spark described the Edinburgh neighborhood of her childhood as "the . . . district where cleanliness and godliness shook hands with each other, honesty was the best policy, all was not gold that glistered and necessity was the mother of invention" (79). This could also serve as an apt description of the Merrifield household, where the sterility of the physical surroundings is extended to language, which becomes fossilized and restricted to a reassuring set of meaningless clichés. A comical instance of this formulaic use of language, symptomatic of the failure to grasp the situation at hand, can be seen in Lorna's assessment of the elegant flat in Curzon Street as "a nice place," which, however, lacked a "Welfare Center . . . where people could go for social intercourse, advice and guidance."

Lorna eventually emerges as a touching figure, both comic and pathetic. If her social inexperience and simple-mindedness are genuinely funny, her unwitting renunciations have tragic implications, for she gradually gives up her chances for friendship, love, and happiness. Art is messy, and so is sex, as the image of the paint oozing out of Willy's tubes seems to suggest. By rejecting all aspects of messiness, Lorna seems to have messed up her life.

BIBLIOGRAPHY
Spark, Muriel. *Curriculum Vitae: Autobiography.* Boston: Houghton Mifflin Company, 1993.
———. *The Go-Away Bird with Other Stories.* London: Macmillan, 1958.

Ilana Shiloh

"YOUTH: A NARRATIVE" JOSEPH CONRAD **(1898)** "Youth: A Narrative" marks an important development in the literary career of JOSEPH CONRAD. It is the first story in which Conrad draws on his own experience and the first to feature Marlow, the narrator also of HEART OF DARKNESS (1899) and the novels *Lord Jim* (1900) and *Chance* (1913). Marlow serves two functions in the story. First, he acts as a persona that allows Conrad to distance himself from the autobiographical element of the text and to give it a shape and a design. Second, Marlow's conversational tone permits Conrad the flexibility to move from the intimacy of a personal account to the intensity of lyric poetry. "Youth" therefore builds on Conrad's success in "KARAIN: A MEMORY" (1897) to relate metaphysical insights ("the romance of illusions," as the frame narrator refers to them here) to the actuality of physical experience.

In his story, Marlow recounts his first voyage to the East, a perilous sea crossing in which he unexpectedly assumes his first command. His listeners (and drinking companions) include a businessman, an accountant, a lawyer, and the anonymous frame narrator, all of whom had begun "life in the merchant service." Marlow recalls how he joined the crew of the *Judea,* bound for Bangkok, under the first-time captaincy of the aging Beard and the first mate, Mahon. Disaster dogs them from the start. Tossed by a gale, they take more than a fortnight to get from London to the Tyne, only to be damaged by a more severe gale and forced into dry dock at Falmouth. Beard refuses to be deterred, and the patched vessel sets sail once more. Near the coast of Western Australia, they discover that the cargo has caught fire. Plowing on, the sailors fight the fire, but the ship explodes. Manning the lifeboats and salvaging as much of the ship they can, the crew head for the coast of Java. Marlow seizes the opportunity not only to command one of the boats but also to lead the others to their destination.

Marlow's tale fictionalizes Conrad's own adventures as second mate of the merchant navy ship the *Palestine,* which left Newcastle for Bangkok in November 1881. Following terrible misfortune, the ship finally arrived the following March at the port of Muntok on Bangka Island off the coast of Java. Though the *Judea* closely resembles the *Palestine,* Conrad makes one major change. Instead of the *Palestine*'s international crew, the *Judea*'s is all British. This alteration may have been made to accommodate the patriotic values of *Blackwood's Magazine,* in which "Youth" was first published. Alternatively, it can be read as an ironic commentary on Britain itself, the *Judea* acting as both a microcosm of British society and an allegory of impending imperial decline.

As do the teasing titles of other short stories by Conrad, the subtitle "A Narrative" also affects the ways the story can be read. First, the subtitle draws the reader's attention to the fact of its narration. In one sense, "Youth" is about storytelling, including the disparity between the acts of telling stories and how they come to be written down (the frame narrator is not even sure how Marlow's name should be spelled). In another sense, by highlighting the story's narration, Conrad raises doubts about the reliability of storytelling and especially Marlow's role. The story successfully sustains the dual perspective of the younger Marlow's boundless enthusiasm and the older Marlow's greater skepticism by ensuring the reader's recognition of both their characters. Nonetheless, while Marlow affectionately mocks his younger self and registers his greater maturity through his insights into the brevity and illusion of youth, the reader is also invited to question the maturity of his older self. The ending in particular, when Marlow invokes his "regret" of youth's passing, suggests that he is still drawn to the glamor of romance. This questioning of Marlow's self-presentation is also aided by the use of the frame narrator, who introduces and closes the story and creates a distance between Marlow and the reader.

In this second sense, in which the reader practically overhears Marlow's conversation with his listeners, the notion of narrative is relevant to an understanding of the story. By recounting his misadventures on board the *Judea,* Marlow can be said to be turning his youth into a narrative—lending it a shape and a significance that it otherwise lacks. Marlow is repeatedly concerned about the mindless destructiveness of time's passing: "youth, strength, genius, thoughts, achievements, simple hearts—all dies. . . . No matter." Instead, he seeks to extract from his youth an event "that seem[s] ordered for the illustration of life, that might stand for a symbol of existence." In other words, he seeks a moment that is not solely the empty and meaningless passage of time, but one through which a purpose may be revealed and an order and a structure may be lent to Marlow's life story. The reader's gradual awareness that Marlow is not only retelling an occasion from his youth but also judging and evaluating its content so that it can be molded into a narrative invites a further questioning of his reliability. A last and most unsettling reading of the story's full title is that youth is itself a narrative, a fiction without any meaning beyond the sea stories that Marlow has read as a boy, the romantic appeal of Byron's poetry (that Marlow buys with his first three-months' pay), or the experiences of the soldier-protagonist in Thomas Carlyle's *Sartor Resartus* (which Marlow reads while the captain's wife mends his clothes). Such a reading would, in effect, support the older Marlow's insight into the futile human struggle for meaning "surrounded by an impenetrable night."

BIBLIOGRAPHY

Bonney, William W. *Thorns and Arabesques: Contexts for Conrad's Fiction.* Baltimore: John Hopkins University Press, 1980.

Carabine, Keith, ed. *Joseph Conrad: Critical Assessments,* Vol. 2. Robertsbridge, England: Helm Information, 1992.

Conrad, Joseph. *Heart of Darkness and Other Stories.* London: Wordsworth, 1995.

Greaney, Michael. *Conrad, Language, and Narrative.* Cambridge: Cambridge University Press, 2002.

Najder, Zdzislaw. *Joseph Conrad: A Chronicle.* Cambridge: Cambridge University Press, 1983.

White, Andrea. *Joseph Conrad and the Adventure Tradition.* Cambridge: Cambridge University Press, 1993.

Paul March Russell

Z

ZANGWILL, ISRAEL (1864–1926)

Israel Zangwill was born in London in 1864 of a Russian Jewish father and a Polish Jewish mother. He first studied at the Jews' Free School of London and then went to London University, where he graduated before becoming a teacher. Zangwill is now largely remembered for his activities within the Zionist movement that he led with Theodore Herzl, and he became one of the founders of the modern state of Israel. His numerous short stories often mirror his activities in the Zionist movement as well as his paradoxical position in English society—a Jew belonging to a second generation of immigrants attempting to build for himself and others a new identity.

Three volumes of short stories constitute Zangwill's work. The collection *Children of the Ghetto* was first published in 1892. These stories follow a family, the Ansells, in the London "ghetto" and the dilemmas the characters have to face as they choose between keeping the old religion and living as Britons. "The Hope Extinct" portrays the effects of an English education on Benjamin, who slowly forgets his Yiddish and remembers an old song his mother used to sing to him in Yiddish only on his deathbed. In "The Hymses' Honeymoon," Esther embodies the link between the time and place of the ancient ghetto and the new era in modern Britain. In both stories the dream is not a dream of integration but a dream of re-creation: the re-creation of an ideal Jerusalem, of a promised land that belongs more to the realm of dreams and literature than to reality. When old Mr. Hyams finds himself alone after his wife's death, he sells his belongings and leaves for Israel, "which had been the dream of his life." But Zangwill shows the illusoriness of this paradise as Hyams finds that the promised land is itself a dream: "somehow it was not *his* Jerusalem, scarce more than his London Ghetto transplanted, only grown filthier, and narrower, and more ragged with cripples for beggars and lepers in lieu of hawkers."

In *Ghetto Tragedies,* published in 1899, Zangwill depicts new people and new adventures. The Jews are no longer the "dreamers of the Ghetto" described in *Children of the Ghetto*. Instead, they emigrate to America where they can live as Jews and Americans, and they build a new life outside the ghetto. This is both a physical journey and a psychic one—a leaving behind of the artificial walls of language and religion.

In *Ghetto Comedies*, released in 1907, Zangwill continued to highlight the choices the Jews had to make at the turn of the century. They could remain eternal dreamers of the ghetto, or they could try to make themselves part of the British nation—by working on Saturdays, enrolling in the army, participating in the political life of the country, or intermarrying. The Jewish sculptor Barstein tells the Jewish Sir Asher, M.P., in the story "The Jewish Trinity" that Asher himself is a trinity: "the Briton, the Jew, and the anti-Semite—three in one and one in three." By calling Sir Asher an anti-

Semite, Barstein refers to the Jews who dreaded the arrival of fresh Jewish immigrants who might tarnish the hard-won image of the Jews in Britain. As critics have noted, it is this kind of engagement with contemporary ideals and anxieties that makes Zangwill's stories valuable examples of the Jewish imagination at the beginning of the 20th century.

BIBLIOGRAPHY

Adams, Elsie. *Israel Zangwill.* New York: Twayne, 1971.

———. "Israel Zangwill: An Annotated Bibliography of Writings about Him," *English Literature in Transition* 13, no. 3 (1970): 209–244.

Leftwich, Joseph. *Israel Zangwill.* London: Clarke, 1957.

Zangwill, Israel. *The Bachelor's Club.* London: Heineman, 1901.

———. *Children of the Ghetto.* London: Heinemann, 1903.

———. *Ghetto Tragedies.* London: McClure, 1893.

———. *The Old Maid's Club.* London: Heinemann, 1902.

Danièle Paycha

APPENDICES

GLOSSARY

This section is intended to provide readers with information about some of the key terms they will encounter in discussions of the short story or novella. Where possible, examples have been given from texts and authors covered in the main section of the volume.

biographical criticism Biographical criticism remains one of the most contentious approaches to the study of literature. For many critics the author's life and the circumstances in which the text was written have little to do with the actual meaning of that text. They argue that every work is an autonomous invention, with its own structure and logic, and therefore should be interpreted independently of biographical details (see formalist criticism). The literary work should not be read as a kind of autobiography or a series of clues to the writer's psyche.

Other literary critics and readers, however, accept the biographical approach as a valuable tool, arguing that knowledge of a writer's life can only deepen their understanding of the text. A reasonable use of biographic details might, for example, help them recognize what might seem to be an arbitrary choice of imagery or allusion. Some of the questions that a reader might ask when using the biographical approach are; To what extent do events in the life of the writer overlap with the events depicted in the literary work? What changes (if any) has the author made to those events

and characters? What are the effects of the changes (or the lack of such changes) for the interpretation of the text? Which sources of influence (people, education, experiences, etc.) are relevant to an understanding of the text? The life of JAMES JOYCE, for example, would inform the reader about the obvious strained relationship between the writer and his family, his complex attitude to the Catholic religion, and his emotional link to his homeland, Ireland. OSCAR WILDE's use of the trope of the mask or the secret life has prompted critics to draw parallels between motifs of secrecy and deception played out in the stories and Wilde's own need to hide his sexuality in 1890s London. Using a biographical approach, it is argued, the reader can gain an insight into the influences and anxieties that helped shape a writer's themes and style.

BIBLIOGRAPHY
Bennett, Andrew. *The Author.* London: Routledge, 2005.

Artemis Rossitsa Terzieva

feminist literary criticism Feminist literary criticism has its origins in the intellectual and political feminist movement. It advocates a critique of male-dominated language and performs "resistant" readings of literary texts or histories. Based on the premise that social systems are patriarchal—organized to privilege men—it seeks to trace how such power relations in society are reflected, supported, or questioned by literary texts and expression.

One of the founders of this kind of approach was VIRGINIA WOOLF, who showed in her 1929 essay *A Room of One's Own* how women's material and intellectual deprivation were obstacles to authorship. Woolf illustrated her case with the abortive artistic aspirations of Shakespeare's fictitious sister Judith. In another essay, "Professions for Women," Woolf also announced the necessity for women writers to kill the "angel in the house," taking her cue from Coventry Patmore's mid-Victorian poem of the same name that glorified a domestic (or domesticated) femininity devoid of any critical spirit.

Another important source of inspiration has been Simone de Beauvoir's 1949 *The Second Sex*. Here de Beauvoir wrote that "one is not born a woman, one becomes one." De Beauvoir's point behind her much-quoted comment was that "'woman' is a cultural construction, rather than a biological one." As Ruth Robbins notes, this remark is important because it highlights the fact that "the ideas about male and female roles which any given society may have come to regard as natural are not really so and that given that they are not natural they may even be changed" (118). All three texts provided ammunition for the women's liberation movement of the 1960s and 1970s and are useful starting points for discussions of short stories that take women and the feminine as central concerns.

The ensuing critical response may best be described as bifurcating into an Anglo-American and a French strand. The former was defined by the greater importance British feminists such as Sheila Rowbotham, Germaine Greer, and Michèle Barrett attached to class. Literary critics working in this school were interested in representations of women in literary texts, an approach most famously encapsulated in Kate Millett's *Sexual Politics* (1970)—probably the world's best-selling doctoral thesis. Groundbreaking as the book turned out to be in reading canonized authors (e.g., CHARLES DICKENS, D. H. LAWRENCE) against the grain and in drawing attention to their suffocating (and often misogynist) representations of women, it was also criticized for its insistence on a male conspiracy. There were objections that its readings were too often based on the assumption that literature simply mirrors reality.

Subsequent critics sought to redress the gaps in Millet's book by setting out to discover and reevaluate neglected female writing. Among those mapping this dark continent (in Sigmund Freud's trope) was Ellen Moers, whose *Literary Women* (1976) is often seen as pioneering in its attempts to focus on noncanonical women writers such as Mary Shelley. The book has since been criticized on account of its unqualified appraisal of "heroism," an appraisal that leaves the concept of the "great writer"—a central category of male literary historiography—intact. One of the terms used by Elaine Showalter in *A Literature of Their Own* (1977) is "gynocriticism," a term intended to indicate her concern with the history of women as authors. In *A Literature of Their Own* Showalter posited the idea of a "feminine" period of literary history (1840–80) in which the experiences of women such as the Brontës, ELIZABETH GASKELL, MARY ELIZABETH BRADDON, and GEORGE ELIOT—notably their use of male pseudonyms and imitation of male standards—demonstrate the obstacles women writers have tended to face. Showalter then described a second phase (1880–1920) that comprised so-called NEW WOMAN writers (e.g., VERNON LEE, GEORGE EGERTON, ELLA D'ARCY) dedicated to protest and minority rights. After 1920, this feminist stage was transcended by a female phase whose major representatives, KATHERINE MANSFIELD and VIRGINIA WOOLF, are said to move beyond mimicry or opposition by asserting feminine identities, no matter how fragile or provisional these might be. Their narratives explore allegedly minor yet personally significant, even epiphanic moments and experiment with gender roles including androgyny and HOMOSEXUALITY. Literary texts of this period can also be said to anticipate postmodernist views of gender in their emphasis on the cultural interpretation of the body as distinguished from the physical characteristics that make people male or female.

Further landmarks in the field of feminist research were provided by Sandra Gilbert and Susan Gubar's *The Madwoman in the Attic: The Woman Writer and the Nineteenth-Century Imagination* (1979) and *The Norton Anthology of Literature by Women* (1985). *The Madwoman,* runner-up for a Pulitzer Prize in 1980, attributed an "anxiety of authorship" to writers such as Jane Austen, the Brontës, and George Eliot. It also posited the widespread imagery of guilt or rage in texts by 19th-century women writers as part of a specifically female aesthetic—an aesthetic whose distinctness from male writers was emphasized in the canon of women's literature as established by the 1985 *Norton Anthology*. Gilbert and Gubar have remained extremely influential, although some critics have questioned the clear-cut separatism of their canon (male versus female) on the grounds that it unconsciously validates the implicit patriarchal ideology.

French feminism shifted the focus onto language. Its proponents drew on Freudian models of infant development that the French psychoanalyst Jacques Lacan had connected with processes of language acquisition and the construction of sexual difference. Lacan's disciples Julia Kristeva, Hélène Cixous, and Luce Irigaray started from the premise that a child's entry into language coincides with the disruption of its dyadic relationship with the mother. Language then reflects a binary logic that works through oppositions such as male/female, nature/culture. This pattern connecting oppression and language tends to group positive qualities with the masculine side. Woman, it is argued, is therefore alienated from linguistic structures and is liable to turn to a different discourse, derived from a preoedipal, "semiotic" period of fusion of mother and child. As so-called *écriture feminine,* this form of writing disturbs the organizing principles of "symbolic" masculinized language. It dissolves generic boundaries, causal plot, stable perspectives, and meaning in favor of rhythmic and highly allusive writing. Such transgression, though, is not gender-specific but can be performed by anyone—indeed, JAMES JOYCE is cited as the major representative of "writing one's body" on the margins of dominant culture.

Both the French celebration of disruptive textual pleasure and the Anglo-American analysis of textual content have come under attack for their underlying assumption that all women—African slave and European housewife—share the same oppression. Postcolonial feminism, as advanced by Alice Walker, bell hooks, Gayatri Spivak, and Chandra Talpade Mohanty, took issue with the reductive ways of representing nonwhite women as sexually constrained, uneducated,

and in need of being spoken for. They also objected to feminism's insistence that women needed to reinforce their homogeneity as a sex, because they felt that this thinking demonstrated an ignorance of plurality and in fact perpetuated the very hierarchies on which patriarchy and Western imperialism had thrived.

From today's perspective, so much has been done to improve female presence that some commentators have suggested that we live in an age of postfeminism. However, there are many who would argue that even in a postfeminist age much needs to be done to highlight the importance of interrogating seemingly natural signs of male/female difference. Recently, critics following Judith Butler have begun to entertain the idea that the very assumption of an innate biological sex might itself be a cultural strategy to justify gender attributes. Whether one accepts this position or not, seeing identities as the embodiments of cultural practices may prompt change. This, in turn, might pave the way for a correspondingly flexible critical approach to identities as things that are entwined with other categories: ethnicity, sexual orientation, social status, health, age, or belief. In this sense, the prefix *post-* should not be read as meaning after feminism or as suggesting a rejection of feminism; rather, it should suggest a more self-reflexive working on the blind spots of former readings. (See also **gender**.)

BIBLIOGRAPHY

Butler, Judith. *Gender Trouble. Feminism and the Subversion of Identity.* 2nd ed. London: Routledge, 1999.

Eagleton, Mary. *Working with Feminist Criticism.* Oxford: Blackwell, 1996.

Gamble, Sarah, ed. *The Routledge Companion to Feminism and Postfeminism.* London: Routledge, 2001.

Hanson, Clare, ed. *Re-reading the Short Story.* New York: St. Martin's, 1989.

Moi, Toril. *Sexual/Textual Politics. Feminist Literary Theory.* London: Methuen, 1985.

Ruth Robbins, "Feminist Approaches." in *Literary Theories,* edited by Julian Wolfreys and William Baker, 103–126. London: Macmillan, 1998.

Showalter, Elaine. *A Literature of Their Own.* Princeton: Princeton University Press, 1977.

Sandra Gottfreund

first-person narration   First-person narrators are characters speaking from their own perspective. As Jonathan Culler states, they may be main characters, minor characters, or even mere observers "whose function is not to act but to describe things to us" (86). With first-person narration a restriction is placed on what can be narrated in that the narrator-character can only relay to events that he or she has seen or been told about.

Unlike omniscient narrators, first-person narrators do not have access to the interiority of other people in the story, to their unexpressed thoughts and ideas. Nor do they have knowledge of all events and circumstances pertaining to the story being related. These restrictions mean that the reader's knowledge is confined to the limits of the narrator's knowledge. However, this apparent constraint can be an asset for the text since it enables the generation of enigmas through what is hidden from the narrator's point of view.

First-person narration can be employed alongside third-person narration. Robert Louis Stevenson's novella *The Strange Case of Dr. Jekyll and Mr. Hyde* (1886, 1998) opens with a third-person narrator describing the lawyer Mr. Utterson: "Mr. Utterson the lawyer was a man of rugged countenance, that was never lighted by a smile" (7). Much of the story—concerned with Utterson's quest to discover the nature of the mystery surrounding his friend Jekyll—is narrated in this mode until the secret is finally revealed in two first-person narratives, letters from Dr. Lanyon and from Jekyll himself. It is not uncommon for fictions related by multiple first-person narrators to take the place of omniscient narration in the late 19th and 20th centuries, perhaps reflecting a cultural sense that a changed world cannot be grasped in a single vision.

A shift from omniscient to first-person narration is also characteristic of the shift from realism to MODERN-ISM that took place at around the beginning of the 20th century. First-person narration is frequently employed in modernist fiction and reflects its concern with subjectivity over objectivity; that is, with the way that an individual mind actively shapes its experience of the world. First-person narration implies that what is relayed is being colored by the character's consciousness, by his or her habits of perception and of creating meaning. An author can allow the reader to realize that a first-person narrator is not entirely reliable, that his or her depiction of events or interpretation of their significance actually distorts the true nature of things. Such first-person narrator is simultaneously an unreliable narrator.

BIBLIOGRAPHY
Abbott, H. Porter. *The Cambridge Introduction to Narrative.* Cambridge: Cambridge University Press, 2002.
Culler, Jonathan. *Literary Theory: A Very Short Introduction.* Oxford: Oxford University Press, 1997.
Stevenson, Robert Louis. *The Strange Case of Dr. Jekyll and Mr. Hyde* [1886] (published with *Weir of Hermiston*). Oxford: Oxford University Press, 1998.

Victoria Margree

formalism   Formalist literary criticism has two defining characteristics. First, it is concerned not with what a literary text means or why it was written but with how it works, that is, how it produces its literary effects, its formal techniques. Second, formalist literary criticism is interested in "literariness," or what makes literary texts different from other types of writing.

There are two main movements associated with formalist criticism in the 20th century: Russian formalism and American New Criticism. The Russian formalists were a loose grouping of Russian literary critics, the main exponents being Victor Shklovsky, Yury Tynyanov, Boris Eikhenbaum, Osip Brik, Grigory Vinokur, and Roman Jakobsen (who was later one of the founders of the Prague School, a key influence on structuralism). These formalist critics were active in Russia from approximately 1914 to 1930, when they came under pressure from a Soviet state hostile to their ideas. The central aim of the Russian formalists was to put the study of literature onto a firm scientific footing and establish it as an independent discipline by clarifying the nature of the literary object. In particular, they aimed to show how literary or poetic language was different from ordinary language. A keystone of their thinking was Victor Shklovsky's concept of defamiliarization (*ostranenie*) or "making strange." For Shklovsky, in our ordinary practical life we use words automatically without really thinking about what they mean; poetry, on the other hand, defamiliarizes and draws attention to language through a variety of formal devices (rhyme, rhythm, unusual combinations of words, and so on). In the case of prose, the formalists made a distinction between *fabula* ("story") and *syuzhet* ("plot"). For literary narrative what is important is not the chronological order of events (the *fabula*) but the way these events are presented by the narrative (the *syuzhet*). The various devices that a prose narrative may use (temporal displacements and condensations, for example) defamiliarize the *fabula* in a similar manner to the way in which poetry defamiliarizes the words of ordinary language. One example of such a literary device in recent British fiction is MARTIN AMIS's short novel *Time's Arrow,* in which a simple reversal of the flow of time defamiliarizes the events of the Holocaust as seen through the eyes of a Nazi doctor.

Although many scholars locate the origins of American New Criticism in the literary criticism of T. S. Eliot and I. A. Richards, the term is most closely associated with critics active in America from the 1930s until the 1960s, particularly John Crowe Ransom, Cleanth Brooks, W. K. Wimsatt, and Allen Tate. The New Critics shared many of the assumptions of the Russian formalists, although the two movements were not connected. In particular, they believed in a close reading of the text itself rather than an interrogation of the intentions of its author (which Wimsatt called the "intentional fallacy"). They were also interested in the formal qualities of the literary text, or what made it irreducible to a simple verbal expression and impossible to paraphrase; for this reason, they were particularly, though not exclusively, interested in poetry.

BIBLIOGRAPHY

Bann, Stephen, and John E. Bowlt, eds. *Russian Formalism: A Collection of Articles and Texts in Translation.* Edinburgh: Scottish Academic Press, 1973.

Bennett, Tony. *Formalism and Marxism.* London: Methuen, 1979.

Jameson, Frederic. *The Prison-House of Language: A Critical Account of Structuralism and Russian Formalism.* Princeton: Princeton University Press, 1972.

Jefferson, Ann, and David Robey, eds. *Modern Literary Theory: A Comparative Introduction.* London: B. T. Batsford, 1986.

Ben Roberts

gender   Although the notion of gender as a variable and unstable construct became an analytical category in the second part of the 20th century, the awareness of the role of history, culture, and language in the establishment of what it means to be a man or a woman dates back to a much earlier period. Since the 17th century, some women and a few men have written in protest of the injustices of a male-dominated society and explored the cultural meanings of femininity and masculinity while suggesting that identity is an experience conditioned by ideology and culture as much as by biology.

As it appears in novels and stories this awareness has been the subject of a good deal of feminist criticism. With seminal works like VIRGINIA WOOLF's "Women and Fiction," Elaine Showalter's *A Literature of Their Own,* and Josephine Donovan's *Women and the Rise of the Novel,* fiction has proved to be a crucial site for the exploration of gender, its construction, and its representations. In many critical works concerned with gender, the question raised is thus not simply, How does literature explore gender construction and differences? but rather, How is literature complicit in maintaining these differences?

In the case of the short story, this type of interrogation has only just begun and remains marginal. The short story is arguably a younger art than the novel, drama, or poetry, but a feminist critic would certainly risk suggesting that the form has suffered less from its being a child of the 19th and 20th centuries than from its position in the hierarchy of genres, as it is often seen to be less important than other forms of literature. As Mary Eagleton suggests in an essay published in 1989, the connections between the short story as a genre and gender is a fruitful territory, yet one that has rarely been explored systematically and theoretically. Of course, there are critical studies of individual authors that focus on gender representation and construction in their corpus. Kate Fullbrook's work on KATHERINE MANSFIELD, published in 1986, is one of those; Earl G. Ingersoll's more recent Lacanian and feminist reading of *Dubliners* is another. Important work has also been done on the literary canon through the rediscovery of women writers who have long been considered second-rate material. In *Women and the Rise of the Novel,*

Josephine Donovan shows how "the framed-novelle, a collection of stories encased in a narrative frame" came to be the dominant genre in the tradition of prose fiction by women from the 15th to the 18th century. Reviving the names and works of Margaret Cavendish (1623–73), Delarivier Manley (1663–1724), Mary Davys (1674–1732), and Jane Baker (1652–1732), she shows how "these women authors recognized the dialogic potential of the genre, and used the frame for feminist comment on and/or ironic treatment of the inset materials, . . . interrogat[ing] misogynist realities, rules and norms about women" (x).

Following a similar path of analysis, Elaine Showalter edited a collection of short stories by fin-de-siècle NEW WOMEN in 1993. Titled *Daughters of Decadence,* the collection included GEORGE EGERTON (1859–1945), Sarah Grand (1854–1943), and Mabel Emily Wotton (1863–1927). In her preface, Showalter begins by stating that "although women were a major presence in the new literary world of the 1880s and 1890s," their work, published in avant-garde MAGAZINES like the *Savoy* and the *YELLOW BOOK,* has long been overlooked or overshadowed by the fiction of their male contemporaries. Here the question of the aesthetic and ideological assumptions behind canonicity is also central. Showalter also underlines the specificity of those short fictions by fin-de-siècle women writers who were often called "literary degenerates" because of their overt feminism and subversive exploration of feminine psychology (Showalter 1993, ix). But above all, Showalter's preface addresses the question of the possible yet problematic link between genre and gender, between women's need for a new artistic mode of expression and their need to find a voice of their own. It is thus commonly acknowledged that at the turn of the century, the end of the dominance of the three-decker Victorian novel, advances in the mass production of magazines, the establishment of new periodicals creating a market for short fiction, and the evolving profitability of the short story genre offered new opportunities for women writers who no longer had to refer to a long tradition of male great masters. For a few decades, FRANK O'CONNOR's theory that the short story "remains by its very nature remote from the community—romantic, individualistic, and intransigent" and that, as such, it attracts "submerged population groups" (88) has offered a reflection on the genre, nonhegemonic and marginal, that might explain women writers' interest in this form, although O'Connor never mentions this point in his analysis. However, the interesting questions raised by the etymological proximity between the words genre and gender are uneasy ones. To what extent can we say that a genre is gendered? Is there a correspondence between the so-called malleability of the short story and its subversive potential, and does this therefore explain women's attraction to it? Can this attraction be proved outside of a given social and ideological context? Last but not least, is there such a thing as a "woman's short story"? In their prefaces to collections of short stories by women, SUSAN HILL and Hermione Lee both tackle the subject cautiously, trying to avoid the traps of essentialism. Hill mentions the "intimacy" of the form, the recurring themes of childhood and women's solitude, and suggests that although the short stories in her collection might be enjoyed by both sexes, they "perhaps do speak, at a certain level, very particularly to other women" (xii). In her introduction to *The Secret Self,* Hermione Lee rejects "a separatist aesthetic theory of the 20th century woman's short story" while suggesting that "some distinctive angles of vision and ways of expression are apparent" in her selection (ix). But as Mary Eagleton rightly concludes, Lee's problem is to find a "concept of gender that she can relate to the short story" (68). It might be argued that unless it is historicized and contextualized, the subtle question of the links between gender and the short story will not receive the theoretical answers it deserves. (See also **feminist literary criticism**, HOMOSEXUALITY.)

BIBLIOGRAPHY

Baldwin, Dean. "The Tardy Evolution of the British Short Story," *Studies in Short Fiction* 30 (1993): 1–10.

Donovan, Josephine. *Women and the Rise of the Novel, 1405–1726.* New York: St. Martin's, 1998.

Eagleton, Mary. "Genre and Gender." In *Re-Reading the Short-Story,* edited by Clare Hanson, 56–68. Basingstoke, England: Macmillan, 1989.

Fullbrook, Kate. *Katherine Mansfield.* Brighton, England: Harvester, 1986.

Hill, Susan, ed. *The Penguin Book of Modern Women's Short Stories.* Harmondsworth, England: Penguin Books, 1991.

Ingersoll, Earl G. *Engendered Trope in Joyce's Dubliners.* Carbondale: Southern Illinois University Press, 1996.

Lee, Hermione. *The Secret Self: Short Stories by Women.* London: Dent, 1985.

Showalter, Elaine, ed. *Daughters of Decadence: Women Writers of the Fin-de-Siècle.* London: Virago Press, 1993.

———. *A Literature of Their Own.* 1977. Princeton, N.J.: Princeton University Press, 1999.

Woolf, Virginia. "Women and Fiction." 1929. In *Virginia Woolf on Women and Writing.* Edited by Michèle Barrett. Reading: Cox and Wyman, 1979.

Anne Besnault-Levita

historicism The basis of historicist criticism is the interpretation of texts with reference to the era in which they were written. It is important, such critics claim, to analyze not only the individual text as an independent entity but the wider sociohistorical context in which it was created and disseminated. Since literature is not an isolated material but a product of its society, literary criticism cannot be properly understood without reference to the time and place it was written or to the people who shaped the literary tastes. Historicist critics believe that readers and critics are equally influenced and informed by the cultural context of their times. A historical approach, then, will blend what is traditionally considered history (i.e., the interpretation of factual documents and events) and literary criticism.

The two main ways in which historicists approach literature are first by providing background information about the historical period in which the text was written and second by analyzing how the literary work reflects the ideas and traditions that shaped the writer, who, it is assumed, was a product of his or her time and place. On a different level, a historical critic may study examples of various critical responses to the work in order to analyze the intellectual currents and readership status at the time.

A more contemporary development, New Historicism, emerged in the 1980s from earlier historical approaches. The New Historicist approach is characterized by a significant difference: an emphasis on a rigorous analysis of historical documents that are contemporaneous with the literary work. One common strategy is the in-depth scrutiny of the differences or similarities between the language of such documents and the language of the literary text. New historicist analysis usually leads to disclosure of cultural attitudes and biases or of affinity between the creative text and the factual documents. For some historicists, literary criticism is a negotiation between past and present texts since the critical act involves both the cultural context in which the text was written and the present cultural context in which the critic works.

Another important characteristic of New Historicist criticism is a preoccupation with the underlying or hidden power structures that simultaneously shape history and culture. Thus, New Historicists study the text in relation to the historical and cultural contexts of the period in which it was created and evaluated to disclose dominant attitudes and power structures at work. These might include attitudes about the role of women or the lower classes. The common understanding that history is not composed of purely objective facts but is interpreted and reinterpreted depending on the power structure of a society is applied to literary texts as well. For the New Historicist it is important to reveal the potentially subversive or conflicting perspectives a literary text carries. Mikhail Bakhtin claims that any social discourse contains many conflicting voices. This is true of the literary text, which is seldom a unified product of social discourse. On the contrary, the text is an excellent example of a collection of diverse, competitive voices—in other words, of social polyphony.

"Ivy Day in the Committee Room" from JAMES JOYCE's collection *Dubliners* may serve as a case study of a historicist approach. Without background information the many allusions, or references to names, would be hardly understandable for the contemporary reader or for the reader outside of Ireland. What, for example, is the Ivy Day from the title of the short story? The obvious historical and political reference in the story is to Charles Stewart Parnell, a political hero of the 19th-century Irish nationalists. Undoubtedly a charismatic leader, Parnell soon lost influence because of an extramarital affair, after which the Catholic church leaders condemned him, and consequently he lost the support of many Irish Catholics. Parnell attempted to continue his work for the cause, but soon afterward he died. Parnell was a symbol of the cause of Irish independence from the British Empire, and his name appears prominently in Joyce's own childhood memories and especially in his novel *A Portrait of the Artist as a Young Man.*

Historicist critics might also think about title of the story. This refers to Ivy Day, which commemorates Parnell's death. He died on October 6, 1891, and the story also takes place on October 6. In the story Joyce does not simply juxtapose nationalists and conservatives but masterfully depicts the real enemy of the cause—the apathy reigning among men. The main issue in the story is the lack of inspiring politicians to lead and motivate people for political action in the elections. Two characters, Jack and Mr. O'Connor, are working for money and the promise of free beer rather than because of real political convictions or because they admire the personality of the candidate, Mr. Tierney. Another character, Mr. Henchy, is constantly worried that Mr. Tierney has forgotten about the promised drinks. The unspoken problem is that the candidates on both sides, now that Parnell is gone, seem to have little political charisma or clear political plans. The conservatives might feel comfortable voting for Mr. Tierney, but his political platform is mediocre, far from the inspirational vision of Parnell. Political recruits, the canvassers, try to lure voters by insincerely praising candidates they personally do not believe in. The poem that Mr. Hynes recites at the end of the story is earnest but has little effect. The insincere or dubious responses of the men in the committee room symbolically stand for the divided Ireland of the early 1900s, and other contemporary sources (newspapers, diaries, poetry, visual imagery) might be consulted to consider how Joyce's story expresses—or does not express—common sentiments of his day. Is this a daring, subversive story? Or were Joyce's views shared by many other people? The overall effect of the story is rather humorous, but the politically sensitive subject may have contributed to the difficulties Joyce faced in publishing the collection *Dubliners.*

BIBLIOGRAPHY
Hamilton, Paul. *Historicism.* London: Routledge, 1996.

Wolfreys, Julian, and William Baker, eds. *Literary Theories.* London: Macmillan, 1998.

Artemis Rossitsa Terzieva

imagery   Imagery can be understood as a form of imitation or mimesis in which "a word or phrase . . . creates a picture in the reader's mind or stimulates a sensory response" (Dietrich and Sundell, 224). While *The Penguin Dictionary of Literary Terms and Literary Theory* identifies three types of imagery—literal, perceptual, and conceptual (413)—most critics distinguish between two types: literal and figurative. In its strictest sense, literal imagery involves a verbal representation of sensory experience. For example, each of the following excerpts from D. H. LAWRENCE's "The Prussian Officer" appeals to one of the five senses: "There was a farm, too, pale blue in shadow, and the timber black" (visual), "Then came the faint clang of the closing of the pot-lid" (auditory), "There was the perfume of clover, like pure honey and bees" (olfactory), "that hard jaw already slightly rough with beard" (tactile). Closely related to tactile and often other types of imagery, kinaesthetic imagery conveys a sense of bodily movement, as in the following sentence: "Struggling to his feet, he lurched away." Though there are references to coffee, wine, and beer in "The Prussian Officer," there is no real use of gustatory imagery, and its absence underscores the orderly's growing dehydration.

Figurative imagery couples concrete images with various figures of speech such as simile, metaphor, metonymy, and personification, to name a few. A good example can be found in JAMES JOYCE's story "ARABY." When the narrator remarks, "my body was like a harp and her words and gestures were like fingers running upon the wires," he is using similes with a combination of visual, auditory, tactile, and kinaesthetic imagery to communicate the exhilaration he feels when he imagines another character, Mangan's sister, whom he has turned into a figure of quasi-religious adoration. Here also, as in other stories in *Dubliners,* Joyce invests the image of the harp with symbolic significance. In "Two Gallants" the main characters Lenehan and Corley pass a harpist, whose instrument, "heedless that her coverings had fallen about her knees, seemed weary alike of the eyes of strangers and of her master's hands." Here, the personified and feminized harp—a traditionally Irish instrument—symbolizes the shabbiness of turn-of-the-century Dublin and also, given its context, yokes the politics of nationalism with prostitution.

As the authors of *The Bedford Glossary of Critical and Literary Terms* point out, often "the key to unlocking the meaning of a work lies in identifying its image patterns and understanding how they work together to suggest or symbolize larger meanings or themes" (Martin and Ray, 211). Whether they have a symbolic function or not, images often lend a story structure through repetition and pattern. In the short stories of both Lawrence and Joyce, for instance, images of light and darkness recur. The color black becomes an important motif for Lawrence and is often associated with masculine rage. In *Dubliners* Joyce makes frequent use of darkness and shadows, and often his characters' moments of epiphany take place, as Little Chandler's does in "A LITTLE CLOUD," when they are "out of the lamplight." In short fiction, as in longer prose narratives and poetry, an accumulation of or variation in imagery can aid in the establishment of setting and atmosphere, as well as contribute to a story's characterization. In the "The Prussian Officer" thermal imagery helps establish both setting and character while contributing to the story's thematic development.

BIBLIOGRAPHY

Cuddon, J. A., ed. *The Penguin Dictionary of Literary Terms and Literary Theory*. Rev. ed. London: Penguin, 1999.
Dietrich, R. F., and Roger H. Sundell. *The Art of Fiction*. 4th ed. New York: Holt, Rinehart and Winston, 1983.
Joyce, James. *Dubliners*. 1914. New York: Dover, 1991.
Lawrence, D. H. *Selected Stories*. New York: Dover, 1993.
Murfin, Ross, and Supryia M. Ray. *The Bedford Glossary of Critical and Literary Terms*. 2nd ed. Boston: Bedford/St. Martin's, 2003.

Jason David Hall

irony The origins of irony—if origins can be traced for so pervasive an aspect of human discourse—are generally attributed to the theater of ancient Greece, where the Eiron (εἴρων) was a comic character who was, literally, a dissembler; that is, he presented himself to others as something other than he really was. This notion of dissimulation is at the root of the conventionally accepted definitions of irony (see, for example, the *Oxford English Dictionary*) as a rhetorical device, utterance, trope, or figure of speech, spoken or textual, that says one thing while meaning—not always clearly so, and never obviously so—something altogether different.

These definitions that have been cobbled together are, however, merely starting points for complicating and problematizing a concept that is often better grasped by example than constrained in a descriptive phrase. As Robert Scholes puts it, irony is "not a mechanical trick but a quality that modulates and complicates the directness of statements" (2001, 46). Consider the indirect point JOSEPH CONRAD successfully makes through his mouthpiece, Charlie Marlow, in "YOUTH" with respect to late 19th-century conventionally romantic associations with "the East." The story of the trials and tribulations of Marlow's journey from England to the East on *Judea* builds to a climactic—and ironic—moment when, anticipating finally hearing the East speak to him, the first "eastern" voice Marlow hears is that of a Westerner berating him violently in English, having mistaken him, possibly, for a local. This is an example of situational irony, an extension of the dramatic irony associated with the stories, incidents, and characters in such plays as Sophocles' *Oedipus Rex* and Shakespeare's *Hamlet* and *Macbeth*.

Irony as both a rhetorical/verbal and a dramatic/situational device is inextricably bound up with point of view in its sense as perspective. Among the participants in a narrative—the characters, the narrator(s), the audience or readers, and the author—there are a variety of perspectives or viewpoints with respect to the story's events as they unfold. Disparities among these viewpoints, disparities in the knowledge of the participants by virtue of their perspectives, limited or omniscient or anywhere between, establish a fertile ground for irony. Readers' awareness of—or even anticipation of—information or conditions provided by the narrator in the telling of, but not available to the characters within, the story can give an ironic (to the reader) cast to characters' actions and interactions. This sense of irony can be initiated by foreshadowing, or prolepsis, similar to that which occurs at the opening of WALTER SCOTT's story "The Two Drovers." With a character not unlike the blind seer Tiresias in *Oedipus Rex,* Scott as author charges the celebratory atmosphere of the start of a Scottish cattle drive with dire warnings of fell deeds; yet the narrator painstakingly develops the uncharacteristically patient and friendly nature of the protagonist, a Scotsman who later forsakes the patience he has learned and commits the very act foreseen, despite having taken actions to avoid it. Sometimes, such ironies are transparent to the reader during a first reading of a story; second and third readings, on the other hand, at some remove from the first uncover ironies not noticed the first time, thus lending credence to the notion that irony is as much in the reader as in the words and situation presented.

BIBLIOGRAPHY

Abrams, M. K., and Geoffrey Galt Harpham. *A Glossary of Literary Terms.* 8th ed. Boston: Thomson Wadsworth, 2005.

Cuddon, J. A. *The Penguin Dictionary of Literary Terms and Literary Theory.* 4th ed. London: Penguin Books, 1999.

Edgar, Andrew, and Peter Sedgwick. *Key Concepts in Cultural Theory.* London: Routledge, 1999.

Scholes, Robert. *The Crafty Reader.* New Haven: Yale University Press, 2001.

———. *Semiotics and Interpretation.* New Haven: Yale University Press, 1982.

Scholes, Robert, and Robert Kellogg. *The Nature of Narrative.* Oxford: Oxford University Press, 1966.

James Fromm

metafiction   Though the term *metalanguage*—a language that describes or analyzes another language—was in use well before the 1960s, it was around this time that theorists including Roman Jakobson (*Linguistics and Poetics* [1960]) and Roland Barthes (*Mythologies* [1957] and *Elements of Semiology* [1967]), whose formalist/structuralist analyses of language and literature would have a significant impact on the direction of literary criticism and theory, were developing theories in which the concept of metalanguage played a central role. In *Mythologies,* for example, Barthes defines his concept of myth in terms of metalanguage: "myth itself, which I shall call *metalanguage,* because it is a second language, *in which* one speaks about

the first" (115). More recently poststructuralist and postmodernist theorists have adopted and adapted the concept of metalanguage to discuss a variety of literary and cultural texts and phenomena. One derivative is metafiction, a term used to describe fictional works (typically but not exclusively prose fiction) that are self-consciously aware of their own fictionality and are given over largely to examinations of the elements of fiction itself. As the authors of *The Bedford Glossary of Critical and Literary Terms* concisely put it, "metafiction means something like 'fiction about fiction'" (259).

Since it was first used by American novelist William H. Gass in 1970, the term *metafiction* has been defined and theorized by a number of literary critics, including Robert Scholes, Robert Alter, Raymond Federman, Linda Hutcheon, Larry McCaffery, Patricia Waugh, and Mark Currie. Of the scholarship available, Waugh's *Metafiction: The Theory and Practice of Self-Conscious Fiction* (1984) is one of the more accessible and useful texts. Waugh provides a concise answer to the question, What is metafiction?: "*Metafiction* is a term given to fictional writing which self-consciously and systematically draws attention to its status as an artefact in order to pose questions about the relationship between fiction and reality" (2). Waugh also analyzes how metafictional writing challenges our understanding of "the world outside the literary fictional text" by provoking questions about representation and identity (2): "If our knowledge of this world is now seen to be mediated through language, then literary fiction (worlds constructed entirely out of language) becomes a useful model for learning about the constructions of 'reality' itself" (3). Clearly, as Waugh suggests, metafiction problematizes more than just the realist text.

While the term *metafiction* may belong to the vocabulary of poststructuralist literary theory, examples of metafiction predate the mid- to late- 20th century. As Waugh points out, nearly all fiction has metafictional properties, but some texts are more self-conscious than others. For example, Laurence Sterne's *Tristram Shandy* (1760–67) offers a riotous send-up of the burgeoning novelistic genre, calling attention to its fictionality at every available opportunity, while Charlotte Brontë's more conventionally realist narrative *Jane Eyre* (1847) has moments when the novel's fictional world is interrupted by Jane's narrating voice—as in the frequently cited line, "Reader, I married him." By unveiling the mechanisms of fictional narrative, Brontë encourages readers to focus on the medium, however briefly. More recently—particularly since the 1950s—self-referentiality in fiction has become more and more common, often to the point that a text's metafictionality is taken as an sign of its postmodernism. For those who find definition by example helpful, the work of writers like Vladimir Nabokov, Donald Barthelme, B. S. Johnson, Thomas Pynchon, and David Lodge, to name just a few, provides some points of reference along what Waugh calls a "spectrum" of metafiction.

Short stories, like novels, can be metafictional, foregrounding themselves as fictional artefacts—*as stories*. Some noteworthy examples include VIRGINIA WOOLF's "An UNWRITTEN NOVEL" (1920); Jorge Luis Borges's collection *Ficciones* (1944), which features his frequently anthologized "Pierre Menard, Author of the *Quixote*"; Robert Coover's "The Babysitter" (1969); B. S. Johnson's "A Few Selected Sentences" (1973); and David Lodge's "Hotel des Boobs" (1986). In contrast to these stories, whose metafictional elements are quite pronounced, JOSEPH CONRAD's *HEART OF DARKNESS* (1902), with its self-conscious nesting of narratives, makes for an interesting debate about the politics of representation—especially in light of Chinua Achebe's 1975 critique and its legacy.

BIBLIOGRAPHY

Barthes, Roland. *Mythologies*. 1957. Translated by Annette Lavers. London: Vintage, 1993.

Murfin, Ross, and Supryia M. Ray. *The Bedford Glossary of Critical and Literary Terms*. 2nd ed. Boston: Bedford/St. Martin's, 2003.

Waugh, Patricia. *Metafiction: The Theory and Practice of Self-Conscious Fiction*. London: Methuen, 1984.

Jason David Hall

myth   Across myriad cultures and epochs, the term *myth* has come to encompass a wide variety of meanings, yet its original definition greatly explains its contemporary usage. Derived from the Greek *mythos,* meaning an authoritative speech, a myth is one central story or plot contained within a greater mythology. A mythology, itself, is any series of stories, narratives, or culturally bound tales meant to perform a particular anthropological function in a particular time period. For example, within classical Greek mythology, myths were often utilized as narratives of explanation by a people who had, as yet, no other method to explain certain phenomena. Hesiod, the first Greek who attempted to explain the creation of the world and life on it, told his narrative through a myth detailing a succession of the births of primal forces: Gaea and Ouranos (Mother Earth and Father Heaven, respectively) were born of the concepts of Love and Light; they begot the "monstrous creatures" who would later inhabit the Earth (Hamilton, 66–67). These creatures became the most remote ancestors of animal life on the planet.

These types of myths focused on the interaction of humans with phenomena outside their sphere of comprehension, such as nature, protoreligious deities, and the general unknown. But over the passage of time and geography, these myths evolved through constant echoing and reinterpretation to reflect other cultural concerns in Western literature, such as the French *pourquoi* (or "why?") tales, the anthropomorphic struggles of good versus evil populating Norse mythology, and even the rise of epic heroes in medieval Europe. In Great Britain, as these tales spread, they became mixed with other cultural ephemera to create a new breed of mythology based on historical precedent, religion, and genre specifications, such as the early romance. Sir Thomas Malory's construction of the contestably historic Arthur of the late 5th to early 6th century in *Le Morte d'Arthur,* for example, blends a variety of cultural materials to tell the tales of the agonism among King Arthur, Lancelot, and Guinevere, thus creating a mythology bound specifically to the Great Britain of the 1500s. As time progressed, Malory's work became imbricated with further stories, poems, and myths of Arthurian legend to create a larger collage of stories surrounding the central core of the myth and thereby create a larger mythos. In turn, critics such as Northrop Frye have stated that "typical forms of myth become the conventions and genres of [modern] literature" (50). To wit, by the 20th century, Malory's version of the myth of Arthur was reenvisioned through T. H.

White's series of stories *The Once and Future King*. This perpetual cycle of the telling and retelling of similar stories is consistent with mythology's power of constant invention and reinvention as espoused by theorists such as Joseph Campbell, whose work, *The Hero with a Thousand Faces,* expands greatly on the topic. (See, for example, Saki's "Gabriel Ernest" and Rudyard Kipling's, *Just So Stories.*)

BIBLIOGRAPHY

Campbell, Joseph. *The Hero with a Thousand Faces.* 2nd ed. Princeton: Princeton University Press, 1968.

Frasier, James George. *The Golden Bough.* New York: Touchstone, 1996.

Frye, Northrop. *Anatomy of Criticism.* Princeton: Princeton University Press, 1973.

Hamilton, Edith. *Mythology.* New York: Warner Books, 1999.

White, T. H. *The Once and Future King.* New York: Putnam, 1958.

Joseph Michael Sommers

narratology   Narratology is, literally, the study of narrative as a broad field of written, spoken, and visual discourse, as opposed to the more narrowly focused and specific fields of the study of fiction, the novel, or the short story. With roots in formalism and structuralism, narratology interrogates and describes, at a variety of levels, the relations among a text, the author, the reader (in a broad sense, taken to include listeners and viewers), the story that is told, the narrator of the story (as an entity distinct from the author), and the narratee (as distinct from the reader). Among the seminal texts contributing to the development of narrative theories are Vladimir Propp's *Morphology of the Folktale* (1928, though not available in English until 1958), Claude Levi-Strauss's *Structural Anthropology* (1958, published in English translation in 1963), and Roland Barthes's essay "Introduction to the Structural Analysis of Narratives" (1977). These works sought—through the application of scientific methods—to develop explications of individual stories as a function of the general structures of, and in, the narratives by which they are told.

There are two general trends in narratology, and most narratologists position themselves somewhere along the continuum between them. In the first and perhaps original instance there is a focus exclusively on the poetics of narrative that is, identification, definition, and elaboration of the terms, relations, and structures necessary to describe narratives of all forms. In the other, there is a purely rhetorical approach, that of describing how and why narratives work on or through readers. These two positions are analogous to the opposite faces of a sheet of paper: Each can be examined in isolation from but cannot exist without the other. One cannot talk about how a particular narrative works without using rules of structure and a taxonomy that are held common among those examining that narrative; nor can the bases of the definitions of the terms and structure come into being without considering how they function in and on a narrative and the reader of that narrative. Some relatively recent narrative studies have extended the theorizing grounded in literary texts toward specific practical applications, influencing such apparently diverse fields as jurisprudence, medicine, and psychology.

As an example of the project of narratology, consider one particular crux among narratologists, the definition of a narrative. The proposed definitions generally agree that narrative consists of the entire act of someone telling (narrating) about some set of events, to some audience, for some purpose. This paraphrase of James Phelan's rhetorically based definition of narrative bounds the narrative act by all of its necessary and sufficient elements: narrator(s), the act of narrating, story, reader(s), and purpose. These elements are necessary in that each is required for narrative to occur (imagine a story without a reader—is it a narrative?); they are sufficient because taken together they constitute the minimum requirements for narrative. Arguably, purpose could be excluded, but the question of motivation for narration is an unavoidable one. Is the purpose of a particular narrative to maintain the memory of a set of events? Is it to promote learning? Or to provide entertainment? Stories are not told for no reason. Going a bit farther along the taxonomic chain, the provided definition of narrative warrants elaboration of at least one further crucial point, the distinction between *story* and *plot* (the related narratological terms borrowed from Russian formalism are *fabula* and *sjužet,* respectively). An origin of this distinction can be traced to E. M. FORSTER's *Aspects of the Novel* (1927), in which Forster clarifies the difference through his now famous formula: "'The king died and then the queen died' is a story. 'The king died, and then the queen died of grief' is a plot" (86). The point is that plot involves a cause/effect and not simply a temporal relation of the events described.

BIBLIOGRAPHY

Abbott, H. Porter. *The Cambridge Introduction to Narrative.* Cambridge: Cambridge University Press, 2002.

Forster, E. M. *Aspects of the Novel.* New York: Harcourt, Brace & World, 1955.

Martin, Wallace. *Recent Theories of Narrative.* Ithaca, N.Y.: Cornell University Press, 1986.

Prince, Gerald. *A Dictionary of Narratology.* Rev. ed. Lincoln: University of Nebraska Press, 2003.

Rimmon-Kenan, Schlomith. *Narrative Fiction.* 2nd ed. London: Routledge, 2002.

Scholes, Robert, and Robert Kellogg *The Nature of Narrative.* Oxford: Oxford University Press, 1966.

James Fromm

naturalism A product of the late 19th century and sometimes seen as an extension of or successor to REALISM, naturalism was a literary movement based on the writings of the scientist Charles Darwin, author of *Origin of Species* (1859). More specifically, naturalist authors were largely interested in maintaining Darwin's suppositions that human beings were soulless creatures, "merely higher-order animals," bereft of free will, whose mannerisms and behavior resulted primarily from their heredity and the influences of a capricious environment (Abrams, 261). Under this framework, a story's character operates by compulsion and drive but cannot control his own destiny. Naturalist authors also relied on journalistic techniques. They focused on an accurate, almost clinical, record of a character struggling to survive some form of displacement from his or her surroundings. There are detailed accounts of environment, and the city is a favorite setting. However, this is not to say that naturalist authors entirely ignored the internal motives of their characters. On the contrary, naturalist characterization depended on fierce internal emotions and drives that most often manifested themselves in rapacious greed and lust.

Although literary naturalism is often seen to have begun with the work of French author Émile Zola (and his 1880 *Le Roman Expérimental*), it also emerged in America, espoused by such authors as Theodore Dreiser, Frank Norris, and Jack London. Literary naturalism is common in British literature as well. Prominent authors such as Arnold Bennett, ARTHUR MORRISON, GEORGE MOORE, and George Gissing all contributed to a larger collection of fiction operating within naturalist mode. In particular, Gissing's works of short fiction, such as *The House of Cobwebs* (1906) and *The Sins of the Fathers and Other Tales* (1924), feature sketches and short narratives replete with naturalist tropes. Several deal with class and money, notably "The Capitalist," a story of "the money-spending, and probably . . . the money-getting, world." More often than not, characters who operate outside the dominant social conventions created in the story find a reader's empathy and interest, especially since they have little control over their eventual fate.

BIBLIOGRAPHY

Abrams, M. H. *A Glossary of Literary Terms.* Orlando, Fla.: Harcourt Brace, 1999.

Joseph Michael Sommers

novella The term *novella* is an Italian word for the realistic tales of the medieval period and is the term from which *novel* is derived. *Novella* has been used interchangeably with *short novel* and *novelette* in the past but lately has come to be regarded as the preferred term for a work of prose fiction between approximately 15,000 and 50,000 words. Aside from this designation of length, which places it somewhere between the short story and the novel, there are no hard-and-fast agreements about its precise definition. To some extent, the difficulty in publishing midlength narratives—usually too long for magazines but too short for stand-alone book publication—has contributed to its being a less popular form. Still, there have been midlength fictional prose works in existence for many centuries, and like the short story and novel, exactly what constitutes the novella's particular shape, aesthetics, and thematic concerns has generated a fair amount of theoretical and critical debate.

On the one hand, it could be argued—with many supporting examples—that the novella has no unique features besides that of length that distinguish it as a narrative. On the other hand, supporters of the idea that the novella is a distinct genre or type of narrative could argue that its middle length and thematic tendency invest it with different qualities from those of the typical short story or novel, especially since the end of the 19th century. This conjecture implies that modern narrative concerns differently affect midlength narratives than shorter or longer types of fiction. This idea presupposes, in other words, that if a writer is working within constraints on length and with certain cultural or philosophical concerns in mind, distinctive patterns within the narrative will result. Perhaps those wishing to express such concerns would also find the conventions of the novella and its intermediate length an ideal form. Usually, then, the notion that novellas are different from other types of narrative is a result of a focus on novellas written in the modern and, to some extent, postmodern eras.

In general, the modernist and postmodernist novellas important to defining the genre have an emphasis on theme and the ways that thematic concerns can be expressed through the developments in and experiments with 20th-century realism. Several histories of the novella as a genre observe the links the novella has with the realism of the Italian novella and the Renaissance stories of Boccaccio. The ties of the novella to satire, apologue, allegory, fable, and parable have also been emphasized. The connection with these types of narrative, which tend to provide a complex moral commentary or polemic, has also been noted, especially in more modern or contemporary novellas that question rather than confirm certitudes of the past. The prototype of such novellas is JOSEPH CONRAD's *HEART OF DARKNESS*.

Most of the great examples of the novella demonstrate that it is truly an international type, at least in its manifestations in Britain, Europe, and the Americas. More than one critic has called the novella a genre of masterpieces. Early such works would include novellas as seemingly disparate as the Irish JAMES JOYCE's "The DEAD," the Austro-Hungarian Franz Kafka's "The Meta-

morphosis," the American Katherine Anne Porter's "Pale Horse, Pale Rider," and the English ELIZABETH GASKELL's "MY LADY LUDLOW" and D. H. LAWRENCE's "THE FOX." An example of a more contemporary novella that shares many traits with these earlier ones is JOHN FOWLES's "THE EBONY TOWER." A useful way of demarcating some of the major differences between short stories and novellas is to compare the two forms in a writer such as Joseph Conrad, who writes both. Another useful comparison can be drawn between the relative directness of the short stories in James Joyce's *DUBLINERS* and the moral complexity and ambiguity of his novella "The Dead" in that same collection.

The definition of the novella that emerges contains a reasonably consistent set of shared features. The tendency of the novella in the modernist period and after, for instance, is to raise questions of an abstract or philosophical nature, especially questions dealing with identity or self-definition. One common feature of the novella that results is a curious individual intensity combined with a sense of distance. This result may be due to the attempt to generate a heightened sense of unique individuality, so highly valued in the 20th century, together with the abstracted and distanced sense of providing an exemplum or parable-like lesson. The emphasis, though, is clearly on character and not on plot or action. There are several narrative tactics for revealing the story that create such an effect. One is related to point of view or focalization. Even though readers may be concerned with one central character, the point of view may shift, may be multiple or mixed, or may be complicated through the use of different narrative "frames." An example is Joyce's "The Dead," which moves from a broadly omniscient perspective to one that is closely tied to the thoughts of Gabriel Conroy and then, in the final scene, back again through metaphor and poetic language to Gabriel's epiphany, an identification with a broader humanity. Another example is the first-person frames that contain Marlow's narrative in Conrad's *Heart of Darkness*. Marlow tells his own story in the first person, but it is an older Marlow relating the story of a younger Marlow, and the older Marlow's story is itself related by an unidentified listener. HENRY JAMES's novellas *DAISY MILLER* and "The *TURN OF THE SCREW*" also have compounded narrative perspectives for creating ironies or multiple levels of meaning that demonstrate the genre's concern with identity. Often novellas develop only one character in depth but balance the realism of that character with other characters or forces that are more stylized and that reveal through suggestive symbol or metaphor hidden aspects of the major character. ROBERT LOUIS STEVENSON's *The STRANGE CASE OF DR. JEKYLL AND MR. HYDE,* for instance, does this even more dramatically than does *Heart of Darkness,* with its Marlow/Kurtz dichotomy.

Commentators have observed that many novellas have triadic arrangements in which characters are juxtaposed to natural forces in the setting that take on the qualities of a character, like the jungle in *Heart of Darkness.* Sequential plot is also deemphasized. Their forms lack clear cause and effect. They often employ a complex structure, utilizing repetition of imagery, motifs, or symbolism that is more important than any sense of plot. A tendency to use language in a way usually associated with poetry makes these novellas' structures resemble the archetypal patterns of classical myth. Such structures may be a way of emphasizing the irrational and may express a disillusionment with established ways to explain thinking. They are generally more associative than linear and, consequently, often disjointed and hard to follow. Sometimes the use of a merely chronological structure in a novella—as in a story structured in terms of a journey, especially a circular journey, a common novella form—undercuts any belief in the primacy of reason. Finally, novellas often conclude with a reflective, epilogue-like commentary that raises questions about earlier presuppositions of order or relationships.

Ultimately, it is important to remember that not all novellas necessarily share these characteristics, and many of the tactics, foci, and styles described above are found in other narrative types. At the same time, they are distinct tendencies and they do set novellas apart from short stories and novels for reasons other than mere length.

BIBLIOGRAPHY
Good, Graham. "Notes on the Novella," *Novel* 10 (1977): 197–221.
Leibowitz, Judith. *Narrative Purpose in the Novella.* The Hague: Mouton, 1974.
Loe, Thomas. "'The Dead' as Novella," *James Joyce Quarterly* 28, no. 2 (1991): 485–497.
May, Charles E. "The Novella." In *Critical Survey of Long Fiction,* English Language Series, vol. 8, edited by Frank N. Magill, 213–352. Englewood Cliffs, N.J.: Salem Press, 1983.
Nemerov, Howard. "Composition and Fate in the Short Novel." Rpt. in *Poetry and Fiction: Essays.* New Brunswick, N.J.: Rutgers University Press, 1963.
Springer, Mary Doyle. *Forms of the Modern Novella.* Chicago: University of Chicago Press, 1975.

Tom Loe

omniscient narrator Omniscience is the quality of the narrator whose knowledge is boundless. The omniscient narrator is not one of the characters within the story (whose knowledge of people and events is limited to what they see or are told of) but rather an all-seeing witness who holds an ideal vantage point above the action. Such narrators are sometimes referred to as telepathic since their knowledge frequently extends beyond all external observable phenomena, actions and speech, to the unexpressed internal worlds of characters—their thoughts, feelings, and beliefs. An omniscient narrator may even know and be able to tell the reader things about characters that the characters do not know themselves—for example, that a character is self-deceiving. DORIS LESSING's "The ANTHEAP" (1953, 1973) uses an omniscient narrator to recount the turbulent process of a young boy's awakening consciousness of the nature of friendship: "Slowly the little boy, sitting alone on his antheap came to an understanding which is proper to middle-aged people, that resignation in knowledge which is called irony" (320). The omniscient narration here is able to relate the boy's innermost and unspoken thoughts, but it also tells us something that the boy at this point cannot know: that his new understanding is one that is normally found in much older people. As such, omniscient narration gives access to a character's perspective, but it may also relate this perspective to a much larger context that the character himself or herself cannot be aware of.

Omniscient narrators may be intrusive, intervening in their own relaying of the narrative to address the reader directly, perhaps commenting on the action so far and offering judgments or even drawing moral lessons. The narrators of many of GEORGE ELIOT's and ANTHONY TROLLOPE's stories are examples of this. While omniscient narrators are typically third person because they are not participants in the narrative events (e.g., "she felt," "they saw"), it is possible for intrusive narrators to refer to themselves in the first person (e.g., "I believe that"). Intrusive narrators tend to foreground the fact of narration: In other words, through their intrusion and address to the reader, they make it clear that a story is a story for someone and told by someone. In contrast, Gustave Flaubert's comment that "the author, in his work, must be like God in the universe, present everywhere but visible nowhere" (quoted in Starkie, 341–342) perfectly captures the position of the nonintrusive narrator: Events are related in the third-person without the presence of a narrating voice or consciousness ever being made obvious.

Omniscience is the dominant narrative mode of 19th-century fiction, and especially of realism. But in 20th- and even in late 19th-century fiction it becomes less popular, frequently being replaced by a number of limited, first-person perspectives or even by unreliable narrators. It is likely that the decline of the omniscient narrator in the late 19th and 20th centuries corresponds to a decline in confidence that the world can be grasped in a single, totalizing vision. (See MODERNISM and postmodernism.)

BIBLIOGRAPHY

Abbott, H. Porter. *The Cambridge Introduction to Narrative.* Cambridge: Cambridge University Press, 2002.

Lessing, Doris, *This Was the Old Chief's Country: Collected African Stories.* 1953. Vol. 1. London: Michael Joseph, 1973.

Starkie, Enid. *Flaubert: The Making of the Master.* London: Weidenfeld and Nicolson, 1967.

Victoria Margree

plot   Plot can be thought of as the imposition of some kind of order on narrations. The events of ordinary life itself can be regarded as having a chronology or time-ordered sequence of events, but a work of fiction selects, orders, and links events or actions besides just providing a chronology and a sequence. This ordering makes up the plot, as distinguished from the simpler chronological ordering, which might be regarded as the story. E. M. FORSTER saw plot as superior to chronology because plot created as well as suppressed connections for tension, suspense, and surprise. His distinction between plot and story (simple chronology) is famous: "'The king died, and then the queen died' is a story. 'The king died, and then the queen died of grief' is a plot." Stories that emphasize causal or cause-and-effect relationships between events are sometimes defined in types or genres that describe those relationships, such as detective stories, mystery stories, sports stories, or adventure stories. They lend themselves to being described in terms of a pyramid, with rising action, a climax, and falling action. We often read such fiction primarily to discover what happens. Causality, for instance, is a major ingredient in the plots of ARTHUR CONAN DOYLE's Sherlock Holmes stories, such as "The ADVENTURE OF THE SPECKLED BAND." Causal relationships are frequently tied to specific discernable episodes or actions of the characters that are distinguishable from one another but still linked in some way. In short fiction, these are usually specific events or actions that might be compared to chapters in longer narratives. They are often action or conflict oriented.

One important kind of order that fictional plot provides is, of course, chronology or sense of time. Whatever else links events, they do have some kind of chronological relationship to one another. The deviation of a story from a straightforward rendering of its chronological sequence is usually thought of as affecting the story's "order," which is a part of plot. Such deviations are common and include such things as flashbacks and flashforwards. Many stories start the action at a particularly dramatic moment, for instance, and then fill in relevant previous events before resuming the action. Time as it relates to plot is also affected by gaps or omissions, which temporarily leave out events that are crucial to the understanding of the story. Gaps are prevalent in the condensed form of short fiction, with the result that much short fiction has a good deal of exposition, or nondramatized explanation. Many stories are told retrospectively—after the events are over—with more mature or more informed narrators who deliberately select events and the order in which they are revealed to promote tension, suspense, or surprise. For this reason, point of view, especially first-person narration, is especially relevant to plot and the relationships of plot and time. The duration of events—over how long a time period a story takes place—in relation to the plot is also important. Some stories cover no more time—or even less—than they take to read; others may cover a lifetime. Nonetheless, most short stories can be read in one sitting, and they all have in one way or another the beginning, middle, and end described by Aristotle. Creating the unity of action and effect characteristic of short fiction requires a careful balance of time in relation to characters, points of view, and plot. Many longer stories have multiple plots or subplots; short fiction, less so.

Stories that deemphasize causality and find other ways of linking their episodes are sometimes regarded as being more literary. Such stories may emphasize as the major structuring element character, setting or sense of place, or tone instead of more traditional plot. Plot and character are especially interdependent, and plots frequently depend on the conflict generated by the main character, the protagonist, and his or her opposite, the antagonist. Still, much modern and contemporary fiction avoids plots based on action or conflict—on cause-and-effect relationships—considering them a distortion of the way life really is. VIRGINIA WOOLF, for instance, argues against plot in the sense of traditionally ordered arrangements that lead directly to some kind of distinct closure. Instead, such writers utilize a more fluid structure, involving patterns that include plot but also subtle or more elaborate, often thematically oriented, features. Stories that are strongly plot oriented and have traditionally defined plots are often described as belonging to the tradition of romance. In contrast, stories that utilize structures organized through features of setting, theme, imagery, and character or that depend on representation of social, psychological, or cultural patterns are allied with realism in its broad sense.

BIBLIOGRAPHY

Brooks, Peter. *Reading for the Plot: Design and Intention in Narrative*. New York: Knopf, 1984.

Forster, E. M. *Aspects of the Novel*. London: Penguin, 1927.

Phelan, James. *Reading People, Reading Plots: Character, Progression, and the Interpretation of Narrative*. Chicago: Chicago University Press, 1989.

Scholes, Robert, and Robert Kellogg. *The Nature of Narrative*, New York: Oxford University Press, 1966.

Thomas Loe

postmodernism   The term *postmodernism* is usually applied to literature written after 1945 and the end of WORLD WAR II, as the West tried to comprehend the devastating events that marked the first half of the 20th century. WORLD WAR I had helped crystallize the tenets of high MODERNISM, and postmodernism was in part a reaction to the carnage of World War II, particularly the unimaginable horrors of the Holocaust and the new threat of atomic annihilation. Any faith in social order had been undermined, and the subsequent paranoia of the Cold War further exacerbated this collective sense of insecurity. Because of the extremity of these events, people found it almost impossible to accept them, and postmodernism evolved as a way of expressing these feelings of shock and dislocation. Postmodernism is essentially concerned with the meaninglessness at the heart of civilization and attempts to undermine accepted ways of thinking by challenging convention.

While some critics view postmodernism as an extension of modernism, others see it as a complete break from the modernist obsession with form and high culture. Certainly, postmodernism disregards rules and conventional concepts of order, suggesting that there is no reality, only interpretation. There are no absolutes in postmodernism, everything is subjective, and individuals shape their own reality through their perceptions. This approach makes postmodernism notoriously difficult to define, but there are some recurring features that can be identified.

Postmodern texts often revel in uncertainty since there is no one "right" way of looking at the events that are being narrated. They may make use of multiple narratives to reinforce an awareness of subjectivity, or they may simply be left open to several interpretations, as is BEN OKRI'S "IN THE SHADOW OF WAR." This story addresses the complex issue of morality in wartime by presenting the reader with a multitude of possible realities. This absence of objectivity emphasizes the role of the reader in postmodern literature—the text waits to be interpreted. SAMUEL BECKETT's "PING" is a more extreme incarnation of this idea. The story is precisely structured around 120 words, repeated in 100 different phrases, and Beckett uses these repetitions to reveal the absurdity of language. The reader is left to piece the text together, while the nameless narrator and high level of abstraction also create a disturbing sense of defamiliarization, questioning the desire for meaning.

Another feature of postmodern literature is the use of popular culture, such as cartoons, films, and pop music, as a field of reference, rather than relying on the "high" art and canonical literature that informed the modernist movement. This reliance on popular culture is often extended to brand names and logos, used in many postmodern texts to illustrate how society communicates through symbols (see, for example, MARTIN AMIS). Some postmodern literature, such as ANGELA CARTER's rewriting of fairy tales in her short fiction, reworks the narratives of popular culture. "The COURTSHIP OF MR LYON" and "The COMPANY OF WOLVES" manipulate well-known stories to create a sense of dislocation but also to comment on the originals and challenge their accepted meanings.

This use of existing narratives or narrative forms is another recognizable feature of postmodern literature, which often blends several genres in a single text. This is clearly seen in SALMAN RUSHDIE's "The PROPHET'S HAIR," which combines the fantastical events of myth with the matter-of-fact narration of more realist literature. This dissolution of absolute definitions further emphasizes the subjectivity of all narration and refutes the possibility of universal order, instead marking the limitations of language and our understanding of reality. These concerns form much of the underpinning of postmodernism: The subversion of accepted forms and the rejection of conventional boundaries allow for greater literary experimentation but still reflect the innate unease that informs contemporary society.

BIBLIOGRAPHY

Appignanesi, Richard, and Chris Garratt. *Introducing Postmodernism*. Cambridge: Icon, 1999.

Sim, Stuart. *The Routledge Companion to Postmodernism*. London: Routledge, 2005.

Rochelle Sibley

psychoanalytic criticism   This term refers to the field of literary criticism that is based on the psychological theories developed most prominently by Sigmund Freud at the turn of the 20th century. Central to Freud's theories was the concept of the Oedipus complex, which Freud derived from his own close reading of a classic literary text, Sophocles' *Oedipus Rex*. Using this play as a dramatic example of universal human impulses, Freud posited that it is the male child's unconscious or unrecognized desire to possess his mother sexually, a desire that is thwarted by the father. The son's jealousy of the father's possession of the mother soon is replaced by the fear of castration by the father, which causes the son to repress his oedipal feelings, isolating himself from his mother and sublimating or redirecting his desire into more socially valued and less threatening goals. During this process, the child experiences a loss of what he has perceived as an ideal relationship with the mother and instead identifies with the father and resolves to have a wife and children of his own.

Jacques Lacan, a later psychoanalytic theorist, proposed that this resolution of the Oedipal conflict occurs in conjunction with the child's acquisition of language, a process Lacan refers to as the entrance into the symbolic order. The unconscious process of substitution of other objects of desire for the mother, Lacan explains, occurs within a metaphorical framework. For the son, the mother remains the original signifier or symbol of his sexual desire. Any objects with which he attempts to replace the original signifier will ultimately be ungratifying, as his desire for his mother will still remain in his unconscious mind. Lacan's recasting of Freud's ideas in linguistic terms highlights his belief that the unconscious mind is in fact structured like a language, where symbols substitute for original concepts or thoughts.

Because of this reformulation, Lacan's theories have lent themselves successfully to literary criticism of various types. In addition to Marxist theorists, feminist critics have used both Lacan's and Freud's ideas in the development of their own systems. Foremost among such critics is Julia Kristeva, who, like other feminist thinkers, has criticized Freud's sexist conceptions of childhood development and their focus on the male. Kristeva dwells on the stage of childhood preceding the Oedipal conflict, labeling as semiotic the period during which the distinction between the child and mother is more fluid. The semiotic, therefore, is opposed to the symbolic and its fixed signs of power that tend to exclude the feminine.

When analyzing a literary text from a psychoanalytic perspective, critics generally focus in greatest detail on one of three subjects: the author, the character(s) in the text, and the reader(s) of the text. BRAM STOKER has proved a favorite subject for psychoanalytic approaches, as have CHARLES DICKENS, HENRY JAMES, and the Brontës. In each instance, readers must take caution not to read too much into a work, especially when focusing on either the author or the characters created by that author, as they generally cannot respond directly to the types of inquiries generated by the critic. What scholars often examine, building on Freud's discussion in his work *The Interpretation of Dreams* (1900), is the relationship between the manifest or most evident content of the work and the latent or hidden meaning beneath the surface. In this way, "symptomatic" places in the text—where things are left unsaid by the characters, where certain kinds of representation recur obsessively, or where pivotal moments in the plot do not receive full description—are examined in order to identify potential desires or conflicts operating in the text. Lacanian or Kristevan readings might include a closer examination of the access to and employment of language by different characters in the text or by the writer him- or herself.

BIBLIOGRAPHY

Eagleton, Terry. "Psychoanalysis." In *Literary Theory: An Introduction.* 2nd ed. Minneapolis: University of Minnesota Press, 1996.

Felman, Shoshana, ed. *Literature and Psychoanalysis: The Question of Reading: Otherwise.* Baltimore: Johns Hopkins University Press, 1990.

Hall, Donald. "Psychoanalytic Analysis." In *Literary and Cultural Theory: From Basic Principles to Advanced Applications.* New York: Houghton Mifflin, 2001.

Adam Mekler

realism Critics admit that one of the most important conditions for appreciating and comprehending British fiction since the mid-19th century is understanding the nature of realism. At the same time, *realism,* a much-used term in the 19th century and in criticism since then, has had such varied meanings, and the history of realist fiction is so diverse and complex, that the term often creates barriers to understanding. Nonetheless there are particular writers about whom this term is always used. For example, ANTHONY TROLLOPE AND GEORGE ELIOT have always been considered securely within this tradition. Nathaniel Hawthorne, in his now famous assessment of Trollope's novels, described them as being "just as real as if some giant had hewn a great lump out of the earth and put it under a glass case, with all its inhabitants going about their daily business, and not suspecting that they were being made a show of" (quoted in Trollope, 145). In his *Autobiography,* Trollope wrote that these comments summed up "with wonderful accuracy the purport that I have ever had in view in my writing." "I have always," he added, "desired to 'hew out some lump of the earth,' and to make men and women walk upon it just as they do walk here among us" (145).

What did it mean for Trollope and others to be judged as exponents of literary realism? The premise of realism seems, of course, straightforward. Ostensibly, *realism* denotes the idea of a narrative reflecting accurately the world around the writer and the lives of the people in that world—a reality taken to be self-evident and available through looking and listening and then recording the world as it is. The assumption here is that there is an unproblematically given reality that literature can imitate in language. However, and as large numbers of critics have pointed out, the idea of such simplicity is misleading. George Levine, for example, has defined realism as "a self-conscious effort," made "in the name of some moral enterprise of truth telling and extending the limits of human sympathy, to make literature appear to be describing directly not some other language but reality itself (whatever that may be taken to be)" (8). In this sense, realism in fiction can be understood as a matter of narrative strategies—a portrayal of society filtered through the eyes of the author and represented through such features as the plot, the voice of the narrator, description, dialogue, and meticulous attention to detail.

Some critics have suggested that realism as a favored literary technique arose in the mid-19th century as a response to particular historical circumstances. According to Lilian Furst, realism was the "product and expression of the dominant mood of the time shaped by the impact of political and social changes" (1–3). Furst points out that technological advances such as the advent of photography have also been seen as influences. In England, the terms *realism* and *realist* began to be used in criticism of the novel in the 1850s. George Henry Lewes seems to have been among the first to apply systematically an aesthetics of realism, as, for example, in his famous essay "Realism in Art: Recent German Fiction" (1858), where he made the announcement that "Art always aims at the representation of Reality. Realism is thus the basis of all Art." For the *Dublin University Magazine,* too, "the novelist's business is to delineate the manners of his own day, and to draw portraits of the people among whom he lives or whom he has opportunities of observing" (Smalley, 361).

The assigning of labels like *real,* and *realistic* is problematic, partly because there was never any manifesto of realism, even though realism, as a matter of style or subject matter or attitude, was at the center of 19th-century critical discussions about fiction. However, as the comments above suggest, it is possible to discern certain shared characteristics. For example, one basic theoretical premise was that art should abandon what, in 1843, a writer for *Fraser's Magazine* (one of the early bastions of realism) called its "wild and whirling . . . rhapsodies[,] . . . the phantoms delirium paints upon darkness" and instead portray things as they really were, in the sense of portraying objectively and concretely the observable details of actual life. As a later reviewer for the same magazine suggested, it was the "novel of daily life . . . of which we are least apt to weary." It was partly for this reason, too, as Trollope argued, that aspiring novel writers should take William Makepeace Thackeray as their model and not the more melodramatic CHARLES DICKENS. This was also why, in turn, novels by Trollope, George Eliot, and ELIZABETH GASKELL were seen to be popular.

"They are what they profess to be," announced *The Times* in 1857, "stories of modern life, told without any attempt at fine writing, without any striving after climaxes and points. . . . They take English life as they find it" (13 August 1857, p. 13).

Although it was generally expected that realism would concern itself with ordinary people, this did not deny the possibility of its being spiritually uplifting. Many believed that realism could (and should) be characterized by the expounding of a moral position or a moral endeavor. Notable in this respect was Theodore Martin, writing in the *Westminster Review* in 1853. Martin argued that the task of the writer should be

> to place before us the men and women who compose the sum of life in the midst of which we are moving, to show them to us in such situations as we might see them in any day of our lives,—to probe the principles upon which the framework of society in the 19th century is based,—to bring his characters to the test of trial and temptation, such as all may experience,—to force us to recognize goodness and worth, however unattractive the guise in which they may appear,—in a word, to paint life as it is . . . to teach wholesome truths for every-day necessities. (374)

In this respect, because readers could recognize themselves or people they might know in the story, the story was a more effective way of encouraging moral lessons.

One further element of realist writing is the use of detail—people's appearances, gestures, furniture, and clothes, together with details about incomes, settings, and family histories. The inclusion of this information can be understood as part of the so-called reality-effect. *Reality effect* is a modern critical term, coined by the French critic Roland Barthes in a famous essay on the function of seemingly arbitrary descriptive detail in realistic narrative. In "The Reality Effect," Barthes, who takes as his example the description by the 19th-century French novelist Gustave Flaubert of Madame Aubain's room in the novel *A Simple Heart,* explains how some kinds of descriptive details appear "useless."

Flaubert's description of a barometer, for example, is "neither incongruous nor significant, and therefore not participating, at first glance, in the order of the notable" (141–142). Yet as Barthes argues, and despite appearances to the contrary, there is a significance to the barometer that stems not from its role in the story but from its status as a "referential illusion." Even when used in stories today, what appears to be a purely superfluous piece of descriptive detail becomes a way of convincing the reader that what is being described really exists, that it is real and that this reality extends to the characters and events of the story. (See also **naturalism**.)

BIBLIOGRAPHY
Anonymous. "British Novelists," *Fraser's Magazine* 61 (1860): 20–35.
Anonymous. "The Novels of Mr. Anthony Trollope," *Dublin University Magazine* 71 (1872). Reprinted in *Trollope: The Critical Heritage,* edited by Donald Smalley. London: Routledge, 1969.
Barthes, Roland. *The Rustle of Language.* New York: Hill and Wang, 1986.
Furst, Lillian, ed. *Realism.* London: Longman, 1992.
Levine, George. *The Realistic Imagination.* Chicago: University of Chicago Press, 1991.
Lewes, G. H. "French Romances." *Fraser's Magazine* 27 (February 1843): 184–194.
———. "Realism in Art: Recent German Fiction," *Westminster Review* 14 (1858): 448–518.
Martin, Theodore. "Thackeray's Works," *Westminster Review* 3 (April 1853): 367–380.
Smalley, Donald. *Trollope: The Critical Heritage.* London: Routledge, 1969.
Trollope, Anthony. *An Autobiography.* Oxford: Oxford University Press, 1980.
Wheeler, Michael. *English Fiction of the Victorian Period.* London: Longman, 1985.

Andrew Maunder

romance   Romance was the preeminent literary genre during the 14th and 15th centuries. The term refers not to a love story, as we might use it today, but to a recognizable story centering on a series of trials or a journey to be undertaken by the hero. The genre sometimes features a supernatural or magical element, as well as some philosophical speculation on the nature of love, chivalry, and honor. Romances tend not to be interested in the interiority of their characters; nonetheless, they can be extremely sophisticated and complex narratives (the English verse romance *Sir Gawain and the Green Knight* is one such example). Although romance became more popular as a prose form during their decline in the 15th century, they were often written in verse. The term *romance* derives from the languages in which romances were originally recited and written, the romance languages being the European vernacular languages derived from Latin. Although the form was eventually succeeded by the novel in the 18th and 19th centuries, it still exists in verse and prose narratives. The emergence of the so-called imperial romance in the 1880s and 1890s involving exciting deeds of derring-do carried out by muscular Englishmen in exotic locations is one way in which the genre lived on. More recently novelists such as A. S. BYATT have returned to the genre in order to refract and subvert the conventions of the novel.

BIBLIOGRAPHY
Fuchs, Barbara. *Romance.* London: Routledge, 2004.
Lewis, C. S. *The Allegory of Love: A Study in Medieval Tradition.* London: Oxford University Press, 1936.

Vybarr Cregan-Reid

setting   *Setting* refers to temporal and spatial conditions, the here-and-now of the story, placing characters and so enabling plot. Setting has since ancient times been theorized as a key aspect of fictional genres of writing. The neoclassical form of Aristotle's dramatic unities—of action, place, and time—typically applies more rigorously the shorter the fiction. While setting in fiction most obviously entails the place and the time of the story, in contemporary theory a complex range of theoretical constructs accounts for the conditions in which the action of a plot occurs. Mikhail Bakhtin's *chronotope* (a site in text for the interaction of time and space) foregrounds elements of setting as essential to dialogic and novelistic writing. Chronotope is for Bakhtin the place where voices meet and where the knots of the narrative are tied together. The term *mise en scène* from film study is relevant because of filmic influences on the 20th century story. *Mise en scène* corresponds to the aspect of theater Aristotle associated with spectacle and refers to everything that is to appear before the camera.

Setting is vital in establishing the mood or emotional tone of a story; In particular, the physical environment of a story allows continuities or discordances to be developed between the inner world of characters and the outer world they inhabit. As such the rhetorical investments of setting are predominantly associated with the tropes metonymy (the relation of contiguity) and synecdoche (the part/whole relationship). Setting may provide a backdrop (or background) for the action of a story, but it may conversely draw the reader's attention and so be foregrounded. In either case, setting may be seen as enabling or limiting the scope of a story's action. Setting may also be closely related to and vital in establishing point of view. This is the case in the opening of JOSEPH CONRAD's (1899) novella *HEART OF DARKNESS,* in which the motion of a ship metonymically establishes the idea of a journey's beginning and so brings the eye of the reader to focus on the imperial center away from which the text will move:

> The Nellie, a cruising yawl, swung to her anchor without a flutter of the sails, and was at rest. The flood had made, the wind was nearly calm, and being bound down the river, the only thing for it was to come to and wait for the turn of the tide.
>
> The sea-reach of the Thames stretched before us like the beginning of an interminable waterway. In the offing the sea and the sky were welded together without a joint, and in the luminous space the tanned sails of the barges drifting up with the tide seemed to stand still in red clusters of canvas sharply peaked, with gleams of varnished sprits. A haze rested on the low shores that ran out to sea in vanishing flatness. The air was dark above Gravesend, and farther back still seemed condensed into a mournful gloom, brooding motionless over the biggest, and the greatest, town on earth.

The conditions of a story (however objective or fanciful) entailed in its setting are closely related to genre and a key determinant of it. In OSCAR WILDE's (1888) children's

story "The SELFISH GIANT," time is cyclical and so eternal in the fairy-tale sense. The story begins in "a large lovely garden, with soft green grass. Here and there over the grass stood beautiful flowers like stars. . . . The birds sat on the trees and sang so sweetly that the children used to stop their games in order to listen to them. 'How happy we are here!' they cried to each other." The landscape of the garden is alive with detail so that the story takes place in an environment that is almost sentient.

Motion between the generality and specificity of setting is a feature of the opening of JAMES JOYCE's story "ARABY" in *DUBLINERS:*

> North Richmond Street, being blind, was a quiet street except at the hour when the Christian Brothers' School set the boys free. An uninhabited house of two storeys stood at the blind end, detached from its neighbours in a square ground. The other houses of the street, conscious of decent lives within them, gazed at one another with brown imperturbable faces.

A claustrophobic sense of surveillance is evoked through extended anthropomorphism (houses *gazed*); the blindness of the street implies the complacency of its inhabitants. From this apparent third-person perspective, the scene setting now moves from the street to the interior of a particular house. An agentless vision of a cold outside world gives way to a first-person narrator's view of what he can hold in his hands:

> Air, musty from having been long enclosed, hung in all the rooms, and the waste room behind the kitchen was littered with old useless papers. Among these I found a few paper-covered books, the pages of which were curled and damp: *The Abbot,* by Walter Scott, *The Devout Communicant,* and *The Memoirs of Vidocq.* I liked the last best because its leaves were yellow.

Joyce's scene setting emphasizes the close relation between the where-things-happen of a story and the manner in which action is made visible to the reader. Independent of and outside the plot of the story is its context: the setting of its composition.

BIBLIOGRAPHY

Bakhtin, Mikhail. *The Dialogic Imagination.* Austin: University of Texas Press, 1981.

Conrad, Joseph. *Heart of Darkness.* Oxford: Oxford University Press, 1990.

Joyce, James. *Dubliners: Text, Criticism, and Notes.* Edited by Robert Scholes and A. Walton Litz. New York: Penguin, 1996.

Wilde, Oscar. *Complete Shorter Fiction.* Oxford: Oxford University Press, 1992.

Christopher Kelen

stream of consciousness   The coining of this term has generally been credited to the American psychologist William James, older brother of novelist HENRY JAMES. It was originally used by psychologists in the late 19th and early 20th centuries to describe the personal awareness of one's mental processes. In a chapter of *The Principles of Psychology* titled "The Stream of Thought," James provides a phenomenological description of this sensing of consciousness:

> Consciousness, then, does not appear to itself chopped up in bits. Such words as "chain" or "train" do not describe it fitly as it presents itself in the first instance. It is nothing jointed; it flows. A "river" or a "stream" are the metaphors by which it is most naturally described. *In talking of it hereafter let us call it the stream of thought, of consciousness, or of subjective life.* (239; italics in the original).

It is helpful at the outset to distinguish stream of consciousness from free association. Stream of consciousness, from a psychological perspective, describes metaphorically the phenomena—that continuous and contiguous flow of sensations, impressions, images, memories, and thoughts—experienced by each person, at all levels of consciousness, that are generally associated with each person's subjectivity, or sense of self. Free association, in contrast, is a process in which apparently random data collected from a subject allow connections to be made from the unconscious, subconscious, and preconscious to the conscious mind of that subject. Translated and mapped to the space of narrative literatures, free association can be one element in the means used to signify the stream of consciousness.

As a literary term, *stream of consciousness* appears in the early 20th century at the intersection of three apparently disparate projects: the developing science of psychology (e.g., investigations of the forms and manifestations of consciousness, as elaborated by Sigmund Freud, Carl Jung, James, and others), the continuing speculations of Western philosophy as to the nature of being (e.g., investigations of consciousness in time by Henri Bergson), and reactionary forces in the arts that were turning away from realism in the late 19th century in favor of exploring a personal, self-conscious subjectivity. The psychological term was appropriated to describe a particular style of novel or technique of characterization that was prevalent in some fictional works, which relied on the mimetic representation of the mind of a character and which dramatized the full range of the character's consciousness by direct and apparently unmediated quotation of such mental processes as memories, thoughts, impressions, and sensations. Stream of consciousness, constituting as it did the ground of self-awareness, was consequently extended to describe narratives and narrative strategies in which the overt presence of the author/narrator was suppressed in favor of presenting the story exclusively through the thought of one or more of the characters in the story. Examples of stream of consciousness techniques can arguably be found in narratives written during the last several centuries, including works by RHODA BROUGHTON and LUCY CLIFFORD in the 19th century. Generally speaking, however, the British writers who are most often cited as exemplars of the stream of consciousness technique are associated with the high modern period of the early 20th century: VIRGINIA WOOLF, JAMES JOYCE, May Sinclair, and Dorothy Richardson.

Bearing in mind the origin of the term, it is easy to see why some Anglo-American literary critics and theorists have subsumed all textual manifestations of the mental activity of characters in a narrative under the overarching term *stream of consciousness.* While convenient, this tendency belies the rich range and depth of narrative methods for representing a character's consciousness, often best described by the terms originally naming them. Consider, for example, the *interior monologue,* in which, a running monologue—similar to those we all experience inside our own minds but that we cannot experience in the minds of others except in fictional narrative—is textually rendered as the unmediated but articulated, logical thoughts of a fictional character. That this monologue is unmediated, presented to the reader without either authorial or narratorial intervention or the common textual signs associated with narrative speech (e.g., quotation marks or attributive verbs), is crucial to establishing in the reader the sense of access to the consciousness of the character. That it is logical and respects grammatical form and syntax, as opposed to appearing as a random collection of disconnected thoughts and images, distinguishes it from another textual rendering of the stream of consciousness, that of sensory impression.

Sensory impression, as a mode of representing the stream of consciousness, occurs as simple lists of a character's sensations or impressions, sometimes with ellipses separating them. These unconscious or preconscious *sensory impressions* represent the inarticulable thoughts, the imaginings of a character that are not experienced as words. To prevent the free associations that stem from such sensory impressions from running away with and destroying the flow and integrity of the narrative, a story must somehow be anchored within the stream of consciousness. One method is a recurring motif or theme. The motif appears on the surface of a character's thoughts and then disappears among the flow of memories, sensations, and impressions it initiates only to resurface some time later, perhaps in a different form, to pull the story back up into the consciousness of both the character and the reader. Consider the example of Virginia Woolf's short story "The Mark on the Wall." The story begins as a meditation, which could easily be read as a spoken monologue, on a series of recollected events but quickly turns, through the motif of a mark seen by the narrator over a mantlepiece on the wall, to a nearly random stream of loosely connected memories and impressions. As the story progresses, the mark and speculations as to its nature and origin appear and disappear as a thread running in and out, binding the loose folds of the narrator's recollections to one another. The narrator's stream of consciousness ranges widely over time and space, whereas the narrator quite clearly remains bound to a particular place and time, anchored—seemingly—by the mark on the wall.

While not generally considered a textual manifestation of stream of consciousness in the conventional sense—in part because it is associated with third-person rather than first-person narration—another method of representing the consciousness of characters is free indirect discourse, or reported or experienced speech. Consider the following, from the ending paragraphs of Joyce's short story "The DEAD":

> He wondered at his riot of emotions an hour before. From what had it proceeded? From his aunt's supper, from his own foolish speech, from the wine and dancing, the merry-making when saying good-night in the hall, the pleasure of the walk along the river in the snow. Poor Aunt Julia! She, too, would soon be a shade with the shade of Patrick Morkan and his horse. (222)

The first sentence is clearly the narrator telling what the character, Gabriel, is thinking; but with the second sentence comes a transition in the form of a series of sensory impressions that moves the reader to Gabriel's own conscious thoughts. In the end, it is not the narrator who thinks, "Poor Aunt Julia!"

BIBLIOGRAPHY

Cohn, Dorrit. *Transparent Minds: Narrative Modes for Presenting Consciousness in Fiction.* Princeton, N.J.: Princeton University Press, 1978.

Bowling, Lawrence Edward. "What Is the Stream of Consciousness Technique?" *PMLA* 65, no. 4 (1950): 333–345.

James, William. *The Principles of Psychology.* 1890. New York: Dover Publications, 1950.

Joyce, James. *Dubliners.* 1916. New York: The Viking Press, 1967.

Woolf, Virginia. *The Complete Shorter Fiction of Virginia Woolf.* 2nd ed. New York: Harcourt, 1989.

James Fromm

structuralism   In general, structure usually refers to the organization of a text—the division of literary units (chapters, stanzas, sections, etc.), the plot and its elements, the patterns of repetition, contrast, imagery, sounds. However, in structuralism, a type of critical approach, the concept of structure is used differently. Through its history in linguistics and anthropology dating back to the 1960s and the 1970s, the term stands for a system of signs that carry meaning. Language is a prime example of such a structure, for it is built of signs whose purpose is to carry meaning. Literary texts are systems heavily dependent on the workings of the language structure.

As understood by the structuralists, a sign is characterized by two important features: arbitrariness and difference. Arbitrariness is the non-preset choice of the sign, while difference is the opposition between signs that is conductive of meaning. The implications for literary criticism are important because these two features lead the reader to weigh the sign of the writer's choice and search for the inner logic behind it. At the same time, the reader can understand how a term is opposed to and different from another term and so produces meaning. One of the frequently used techniques in the analysis of texts is the analysis of binary oppositions, in which contrasting elements are examined as to their relevance to the meaning of the work. Even if the differences between the opposing elements in a text are implicit, a thorough analysis could lead to series of interesting interpretations.

Some of the issues that structuralism considers are the systems of relations (oppositions and differences) between the elements of a text: for example, the apparent opposition between images or the opposition between characters (i.e., as protagonist and antagonist), the circular structure of a text in which the story ends where it has started, or the ways in which setting purposefully limits the action. For the structuralists, then, the internal tensions between the elements of a text create meaning and add to the overall interpretation.

In the short story "Counterparts," JAMES JOYCE uses several structural oppositions to depict the despondent life of his main character, Farrington. On the level of setting, for example, the story leads us through the suffocating offices of the bank where Farrington works, through the gloomy streets of Dublin, to the smoky, raucous pubs and his dreary little house. More interesting, however, is the symbolic opposition between the characters: In the opening scene, Farrington, a tall, bulky man, is furiously scolded by his boss, Mr. Alleyne, a powerful but funny-looking, bald-headed little man. Far from undeserved, the humiliation Farrington has to bear infuriates him and brings out the drinking habit that is one of the reasons for his downfall. There is no opposition on the surface between Farrington and his drinking mates. The appearance of a new man, Weathers, and the subsequent "feats of strength" (arm-wrestling) once again humiliate Farrington because of his defeat by the younger man. The third opposition is between Farrington and his little son, Tom. The obvious physical contrast between the child and the threatening bulk of the father sets the scene for a heartbreaking and meaningless scene of violence. The only available outlet for Farrington's anger is an assault on little Tom, whose miserable cry, "Don't beat me, pa! And I'll . . . I'll say a *Hail Mary* for you," echoes in the empty, somehow godforsaken room. Thus, Joyce skillfully conveys yet another opposition of biblical proportions: the opposition between spiritual innocence and aggressive physicality. This time, again, innocence suffers, while God remains strangely distant.

BIBLIOGRAPHY
Barry, Peter. *Beginning Theory.* Manchester, England: Manchester University Press, 1996.
Wolfreys, Julian, and William Baker, eds. *Literary Theories.* London: Macmillan, 1998.

Artemis Rossitsa Terzieva

structure Structure is generally regarded as consisting of the unifying patterns in a narrative including those related to but also distinct from those of plot. The two concepts are closely related. Many writers associated with realism tried to avoid fiction that was only based on action or conflict and had obvious plots. They made efforts to come up with various writing tactics that could give their work a cohesiveness and at the same time be as close as possible to representing the actuality of experience. These efforts continue today because every era has its own ideas of what makes up actuality. In some ways the term *structure* is analogous to a narrative's overall form or arrangement, especially in its theme-related aspects. The structure of a narrative depends on its repetitions and patterns, whether in its handling of character, setting, imagery, tone, or some other aspect. What sort of unity appears through recurring actions, images, allusions, or descriptions? Are there pervasive metaphors like that of a journey that provide a unifying subtext? These patterns are frequently not immediately obvious and become clear only after a close reading or several careful rereadings. Yet discovering the unifying repetitions is the key to discovering a story's full meaning.

JAMES JOYCE, for instance, unified his short stories primarily around character and the effect of epiphany and the various motifs or clusters of imagery associated with the insights reached by his characters about the nature of the real world. "ARABY" has image patterns of decay, of eyes, and of a journey or quest that help unify the story around its young protagonist's final insights. KATHERINE MANSFIELD's "Bliss" has very different patterns of images but is similar in having a structure that revolves around a series of related images. Not much happens in terms of surface action in these stories. Their impact largely stems from their symbols and the effects on the minds and feelings of their characters. The endings of such stories often lack clear-cut or decisive closure, and the issues they have raised may seem unresolved. Others, like JOSEPH CONRAD's "The SECRET SHARER" and HEART OF DARKNESS, use more traditional adventure plots—stories involving voyages to exotic places—as well as structures depending on motifs. The first has many types of doubling imagery that suggest its theme; the other has patterns of light and dark as well as images connected with rivers and journeys. Both have strong suggestions of myth, which emphasize their themes related to external issues of civilization and the internal voyage of self-discovery. The external journey structurally corresponds with the internal. The complicated point of view, particularly the "tale within a tale," or framed narrative, of *Heart of Darkness,* also provides several possible layers of meaning, or thematic irony, which help shape the story overall and tie its various aspects together. The impressionism characteristic of Conrad's style, especially his use of visual imagery, unifies his stories.

All authors unify their fiction according to their own concerns and interests, which makes every story unique in some way. Structuralists—critics who are primarily interested in a work's all-encompassing arrangements—look particularly at linguistic structures, the creation of meaning from language, and the conceptual and communicative frames of a narrative. Identifying structure can also involve discovering unifying strategies in juxtapositions and correspondences in titles and naming, beginnings and endings, pacing, foreshadowing, and the overall integrity or coherence of style and meaning. A work that attempts to communicate the immediacy of human feeling will have a structural scope very different from a work that is concerned with depicting larger issues, such as exposing the hypocrisy of social conventions. The briefness of short fiction allows for the possibility of a poetic intensity in the way language may be used that would be difficult to sustain in works of greater length.

Thomas Loe

symbolism Symbolism is the expression of one object (an emotion, feeling, or intuition) in terms of another (a color, a landscape, a person) that suggests an analogy between the two. Symbols are a commonplace within many cultures. A fox, for example, may suggest cunning; heroism can be described in terms of a lion. The religious symbolism associated with a cross is instantly understood in many regions. This immediate recognition of symbolic meaning has long been known by storytellers. Religious texts and traditional folktales derive much of their power from their use of symbols: the crown of thorns, for example, in *The New Testament,* or the recurring motifs of color, woods, and physical characteristics in the fairy tales of Charles Perrault and the Brothers Grimm. Symbols were particularly important for the communication of tales. The emotional associations afforded by symbols meant that tales could be effectively conveyed from a speaker to a listener. Subsequent writers, though, have also realized the value of reworking overly familiar symbols in unusual forms. For example, William Blake's poem "The Sick Rose" recasts the traditional symbol for love in ways that suggest physical, moral, or sexual corruption. Blake's use of his chosen symbol evokes multiple and potentially contradictory meanings. This type of intertextuality plays on the reader's almost unconscious attribution of significance to particular symbols.

Symbolism has also played a significant role in the development of prose fiction. Insofar as the novel can be described as a means for understanding the world, symbols introduce an additional layer of meaning and association, but one that is closer to metaphor and fancy than to an empirical comprehension of reality. CHARLES DICKENS, for example, adds a symbolic texture that counterpoints the social realism of his fiction in the references to confinement that persist throughout *Little Dorrit* (1857). In the work of later novelists, such as JOSEPH CONRAD, symbols recur from one text to another, creating a continuous impression throughout his fiction.

Nevertheless, it was the writers of the romantic movement (such as Blake, Samuel Taylor Coleridge, and William Wordsworth) who most of all understood the worth of symbolism. Instead of just mere decoration, the literary use of symbols offers a way of understanding the inner workings of the mind and, in particular, of consciousness. The so-called symbolist movement in France developed this insight further during the second half of the 19th century. Poets such as Charles-Pierre Baudelaire, Jules Laforgue, and Arthur Rimbaud abandoned sequential arguments in favor of fleeting impressions, juxtaposed ideas, and ironic detachment. Symbolism became a method of not only organizing otherwise random material but also observing the poet's own social and psychological life. This rigorous use of symbolism dovetailed with the increasing emphasis on impressionism in the visual arts and, slightly later, with the function performed by symbols in Sigmund Freud's understanding of the unconscious. Symbolism also played a central role in the otherwise open-ended stories of the Russian writers Anton Chekhov and Ivan Turgenev.

While British poets such as W. B. Yeats and T. S. Eliot and the American poet Ezra Pound responded to these developments, the Edwardian novel remained largely tied to conventional notions of plot and chronology until the innovations of MODERNISM. By contrast, the systematic use of symbolism could be applied more effectively to the short story's emphasis on symmetrical or elliptical narratives, characterization, and single effects. Writers such as D. H. LAWRENCE and KATHERINE MANSFIELD feature intricate networks of symbolism in their short stories that alter the reader's experience of the text. The concentration on plot and event is replaced by suggestion and minute detail that need to be pieced together by the reader. Instead of the text as a product that can be consumed, the reader encounters the symbolist story as a process that requires decoding. Consequently, symbolism has strong affinities with the use of epiphany as it was developed by JAMES JOYCE. For modernist writers attempting to create a unified impression from the otherwise random events of psychological and historical reality, symbolism was a powerful tool, especially within the short story.

Paul March Russell

unreliable narrator An unreliable narrator is a first-person narrator whose narration the reader comes to mistrust. The narrator may seem to have limited knowledge, to be mistaken in his or her understanding of people and events, or even to be deliberately misleading the reader. As H. Porter Abbott suggests, the reader begins to sense that the narrator is not the author, that the narrator's perceptions and judgment differ from those of the author figure that we construct in the act of reading, the "implied author" (69). It is possible, though unusual, for unreliable narration to take place through a third-person narrator. Here, the third-person narrator narrates through the consciousness of a character in the story, and that character's limited perspective therefore limits the reliability of the narration.

An author can create an unreliable narrator through a number of techniques: the narration could contain internal contradictions or inconsistencies, the narrator could construct interpretations that seem disproportionate to the evidence, or other characters could offer judgements about the narrating character that call his or her reliability into question. Arguably, all of these techniques are employed in HENRY JAMES's *The Turn of the Screw* (1898, 1999). The critical controversy that has raged over this novella pivots on the question whether the character of the governess is a reliable or unreliable narrator—whether she is correct that the children are being haunted or whether the ghosts are figments of her imagination, created through the force of her unconscious desires. The example of *The Turn of the Screw* illustrates that unreliable narrators are useful for creating ambiguity, for making readers unsure what has happened or how they ought to interpret events.

Unreliable narrators make visible the fact of narration. Where fiction employs omniscient narrators, readers tend not to think so much about the narrator's mediating role between them and the events depicted, concentrating on what is being depicted rather than how it is being depicted. Unreliable narration however, brings narration to the fore to suggest that the activity of telling stories is by no means simple or straightforward, that the way something is told shapes what is being told. Unreliable narration makes readers wonder about who is telling a story and to what purposes and according to what values he or she is telling it. It can suggest that any narrative is necessarily limited or partial in some ways, and as such it implies a critique of the omniscient narrator. Unreliable narration is particularly associated with modernist and postmodernist fiction, perhaps reflecting the questioning of absolute truth characteristic of such works.

BIBLIOGRAPHY

Abbott, H. Porter. *The Cambridge Introduction to Narrative.* Cambridge: Cambridge University Press, 2002.

Booth, Wayne. *The Rhetoric of Fiction.* Chicago: University of Chicago Press, 1961.

James, Henry. *The Turn of the Screw.* 1898. Norton Critical Edition. New York and London: Norton, 1999.

Victoria Margree

BIBLIOGRAPHY

A limited number of studies are devoted exclusively to the British short story. The list that follows comprises the most influential and the most frequently quoted. Readers might also wish to consult the sources recommended at the end of each essay in the present volume, as well as articles on individual stories and authors that appear in the journal *Studies in Short Fiction* (Twayne). Modern reprints of stories by individual authors—Rudyard Kipling, Virginia Woolf, Henry James, Thomas Hardy, Katherine Mansfield—published by Oxford University Press or Penguin invariably carry useful introductory essays setting the author and their works in context.

Baldeshwiler, Eileen. "The Lyric Short Story: The Sketch of a History," *Studies in Short Fiction* 6 (1969): 443–453.

Baldwin, Dean. "The Tardy Evolution of the British Short Story," *Studies in Short Fiction* 30, no. 1 (1993): 1–10.

Bates, H. E. *The Modern Short Story*. London: Michael Joseph, 1972.

Bayley, John. *The Short Story: Henry James to Elizabeth Bowen*. Brighton, England: The Harvester Press, 1987.

Beachcroft, T. O. *The Modest Art: A Survey of the Short Story in English*. London: Oxford University Press, 1968.

Bonheim, Helmut. *The Narrative Modes: Techniques of the Short Story*. Cambridge: D. S. Brewer, 1982.

Boston, Anne, ed. *Wave Me Goodbye: Stories of the Second World War*. London: Penguin, 1988.

Bowen, Elizabeth. "The Short Story in England," *Britain To-Day* 109 (May 1949): 13–17.

Boyce, Benjamin. "English Short Fiction in the Eighteenth Century: A Preliminary View," *Studies in Short Fiction* 5 (1968): 90–102.

Bradbury, Malcolm, ed. *Modern British Short Stories*. London: Penguin, 1988.

Brown, Julie, ed. *American Women Short Story Writers*. New York: Garland, 1995.

Byatt, A. S., ed. *Oxford Book of English Short Stories*. Oxford: Oxford University Press, 1998.

Coldstream, John, ed. *The Daily Telegraph Book of Contemporary Short Stories*. London: Headline, 1995.

Current-Garcia, Eugene. *The American Short Story before 1850: A Critical History*. Boston: Twayne, 1985.

Denisoff, Dennis, ed. *The Broadview Anthology of Victorian Short Stories*. Peterborough, Ontario: Broadview, 2004.

Dunn, Maggie, and Ann Morris. *The Composite Novel: The Short Story Cycle in Transition*. New York: Twayne, 1995.

Ferguson, Suzanne. "Defining the Short Story: Impressionism and Form," *Modern Fiction Studies* 28, no. 1 (Spring 1982): 13–24.

Flora, Joseph, ed. *The English Short Story 1945–1980*. Boston: Twayne, 1985.

Fowler, Alistair. *A History of English Literature*. Oxford: Blackwell, 1987.

Gifford, Douglas, and Dorothy McMillan, eds. *A History of Scottish Women's Writing*. Edinburgh: Edinburgh University Press, 1997.

Gordon, Giles, ed. *The Twentieth Century Short Story in English*. London: British Council, 1989.

Gross, John. *The Rise and Fall of the Man of Letters*. New York: Macmillan, 1969.

Gullason, Thomas. "The Short Story: An Underrated Art," *Studies in Short Fiction* 1 (1964): 13–31.

———. "The Short Story: Revision and Renewal," *Studies in Short Fiction* 19 (1982): 221–230.

Hanson, Clare. *Re-reading the Short Story*. London: Macmillan, 1989.

———. *Short Stories and Short Fictions, 1880–1980*. New York: St. Martin's, 1985.

Harris, Wendall V. "Beginnings of the True Short Story in England," *English Literature in Transition* 15 (1972): 269–276.

———. *British Short Fiction in the Nineteenth Century: A Literary and Bibliographic Guide*. Detroit: Wayne State University Press, 1979.

———. "Vision and Form: The English Novel and the Emergence of the Short Story," *Victorian Newsletter* 47 (1975): 10–13.

Harte, Bret. "The Rise of the Short Story," *Cornhill* 7 (July 1899): 1–8.

Head, Dominic. *The Modernist Short Story: A Study in Theory and Practice*. Cambridge: Cambridge University Press, 1992.

Hill, Susan. *Contemporary Women's Short Stories: An Anthology*. London: Penguin, 1995.

Iftekharrudin, Farhat, Joseph Boyden, and Mary Rohrberger, eds. *Postmodern Approaches to the Short Story*. Westport, Conn.: Praeger, 2003.

Iftekharrudin, Farhat, Mary Rohrberger, and M. Lee, eds. *Speaking of the Short Story*. Jackson: University of Press of Mississippi, 1997.

Ingram, Forrest L. *Representative Short Story Cycles of the Twentieth Century: Studies in a Literary Genre*. The Hague: Mouton, 1971.

Jump, Harriet Devine, ed. *Nineteenth-Century Short Stories by Women: A Routledge Anthology.* New York: Routledge, 1998.

Leader, Zachary, ed. *On Modern British Fiction.* Oxford: Oxford University Press, 2002.

Lee, A. Robert. Introduction. *The Nineteenth Century American Short Story.* Totowa, N.J.: Barnes and Noble, 1985.

Lohafer, Susan. *Coming to Terms with the Short Story.* Baton Rouge: Louisiana State University Press, 1983.

MacDonald, Peter. *British Culture and Publishing Practice 1880–1914.* Cambridge: Cambridge University Press, 1997.

Markham, E. A., ed. *The Penguin Book of Caribbean Short Stories.* London: Penguin, 1996.

May, Charles. *The Short Story: The Reality of Artifice.* New York: Twayne, 1995.

Morrisson, Mar. *The Public Face of Modernism: Little Magazines, Audiences, and Reception, 1905–1920.* Madison: University of Wisconsin Press, 2000.

Myszor, Frank. *The Modern Short Story.* Cambridge: Cambridge University Press, 2001.

Nagel, James. *The Contemporary American Short-Story Cycle: The Ethnic Resonance of Genre.* Baton Rouge: Louisiana State University Press, 2001.

O'Connor, Frank. *The Lonely Voice: A Study of the Short Story.* Cleveland: World Publishing, 1963.

O'Faolain, Sean. *The Short Story.* New York: Devin-Adair, 1951.

Orel, Harold. *The Victorian Short Story: Development and Triumph of a Genre.* Oxford: Oxford University Press, 1986.

Pascoe, Alan. "On Defining Short Stories," *New Literary History* 22, no. 2 (Spring 1991): 407–422.

Perry, Bliss. "The Short Story." *Atlantic Monthly* 90 (1902), 250.

Pilcher, Edward. "On the Conventions of Eighteenth Century British Short Fiction," *Studies in Short Fiction* 12 (1975): 199–203.

Reed, John. "From Aestheticism to Decadence: Evidence from the Short Story," *Victorians Institute Journal* 11 (1982–83): 1–12.

Reid, Ian. *The Short Story.* London: Methuen, 1977.

Rennison, Nick Rennison. *Fifty Contemporary British Novelists.* London: Routledge, 2002.

Richardson, Angelique, ed. *Women Who Did: Stories by Men and Women 1890–1914.* London: Penguin, 2002.

Schroder, Gottfried. "Recent British Short Stories." *Anglistick & Englischunterricht* 50 (1993): 7–31.

Shaw, Valerie. *The Short Story: A Critical Introduction.* London: Longman, 1983.

Showalter, Elaine. "Smoking Room." *Times Literary Supplement* (16 June 1995), 12.

Stephenson, Glennis, ed. *Nineteenth-Century Stories by Women: An Anthology.* Peterborough: Broadview Press, 1993.

Stevenson, Lionel. "The Short Story in Embryo." *English Literature in Transition* 15 (1972), 261–68.

Tate, Trudi, ed. *Women, Men and the Great War. An Anthology of Stories.* Manchester: Manchester University Press, 1995.

Vannatta, Dennis, ed. *The English Short Story 1945–1980.* New York: Twayne, 1985.

Ward, Alfred C. *Aspects of the Modern Short Story: English and American.* London: University of London Press, 1924.

LIST OF CONTRIBUTORS

Maude Adjarian, University of Arizona

Jessica Allen

Kristen Anderson

Alissa Appel, University of Rochester

Susan Araujo

Sara Atwood

Vana Avegerinou, University of London

Brenda Ayres, University of Georgia

Maria Bachman, Coastal Carolina University

John Ballam, Open University

Chris Barnes

Krishna Barua, Gauhati University (India)

Preeti Bhatt, Saint Jayacharya College

Gerd Bayer, University of Wisconsin

Linda Hunt Beckman, Ohio University

Matthew Beedham, Malaspina University College

Anne Besnault-Levita, University of Rouen

Susan Bernardo, Wagner College

Phlip Booth, University of South Florida

David Borthwick, University of Glasgow

Patricia Kennedy Bostian, Central Piedmont Community College

Geraldine Brightwell, University of Alaska, Fairbanks

Angie Brown, Bath Spa College

Christine Brown

Robin Seaton Brown, University of North Carolina, Chapel Hill

Mary Burke, University of Connecticut

Miriam Burnstein, State University of New York

Sandie Byrne, University of Lincoln

Andrea Cabus, Temple University

Beth Callaghan

Elvira Casal, Tennessee State University

Winnie Chan, Rhodes College

Marian Charret Del Bove

Brinda Charry, Keene State College

Muireann O'Cinneide, Oxford University

Stefania Ciocia, University of Kent

Catherine Civello, Dedman College

Wendy Creed, University of Greenwich

Martin Colebrook, University of Hull

Ailsa Cox, Edge Hill University

Lana Dalley, University of Cambridge

Kevin De Ornellas, University of Wales, Bangor

Peter Dempsey, University of Sunderland

Joanna Devereux, University of Western Ontario

Helen Doss, Malcolm X College, City Colleges of Chicago

Terri Doughty, Malaspina University-College

Matthew Dube, William Woods University

Sara Dustin, Florida State University

Heather Edwards

Jill Ehnenn, Appalachian State University

Juan F. Elices, University of la Rioja

Julie Ellam, University of Hull

Sarah J. Falcus, Liverpool John Moores University

Kate Falvey, City Tech, City University of New York

Christine Fergus

Jose Francisco Fernández, University of Almería (Spain)

Michael Flavin, University of York

James R. Fleming, University of Florida

Michael Flowers

Elizabeth Fox, State University of New York

Rosalyn Reso Foy, University of New Orleans

Damon Franke, University of Southern Mississippi

James Fromm, University of Arizona

Andrew Garavel, Santa Cruz University

Tony Garland, University of Leicester

Monica Germana, Derby University

Beth Gibson

Brian Gibson, University of Alberta

Paul Gleason, Cardinal Stritch University

Sandra Gottfreund, Gutenberg University

Erik Grayson, Binghamton University

Radcliff Gregory, Longborough University

Heike Grundmann, University of Heidelberg (Germany)

Gerardo del Guercio, University of Montreal

Lucy de Guilcher

Louisa Hadley, University of Edinburgh

Lisa Hager, University of Florida

Jason David Hall, University of Exeter

Jennifer Halloran, Duke University

Scott Hames, University of Stirling

Ellen Burton Harrington, University of South Alabama

Bridget Hatch, Brandeis University

Therie Hendrey-Seabrook, University of Sussex

Lindsay Holmgren, McGill University

Gail Houston, University of New Mexico

Jonathan Hunt, Santa Clara University

Mary Husemann, University of South Carolina

Nathalie Jäeck, University of Toulouse

Amy Jamgochian, University of California at Berkeley

Daniel Jernigan, Nanyang Technological University (Singapore)

Jason Jones, Central Connecticut State University

Sandro Jung, University of Heidelberg

Matt Kavanagh, McGill University

Karen Keck, Texas State University

Christopher Kelen, University of Macau

Michelle Kelly, University of Sydney

Gary Kerley, Brenau Academy

Calum Kerr, Manchester Metropolitan University

Martin Kich, Wright State University

Gerri Kimber, Queen Mary College, University of London

Tomoko Kuribayashi, University of Wisconsin

James Lang, Assumption College

Leah Larson, Our of Lady of the Lake University

Lucy Le Guilcher, Bath Spa University

Jason Lee, University of Hertfordshire

Marc Leverette, Rutgers University

Leon Lewis, Appalachian State University

Florence Libert

Rachel Liberatore, University of New Mexico

Gina Liotta, Syracuse University

Thomas Loe, State University of New York at Oswego

Anastasia Logotheti, Deree College, The American College of Greece

Tara MacDonald, McGill University (Canada)

Kirsten Macleod, University of Alberta

Sara Maier, University of New Brunswick

David Malcolm, University of Gdańsk (Poland)

Katherine Malon

Paul March-Russell, University of Kent

Heather Marcovitch, Mount Allison University

Victoria Margree, University of Sussex

Caroline Marie

Peter Matthias

Andrew Maunder, University of Hertfordshire

Melissa McLeod, Georgia State University

Jennifer McClinton-Temple, Kings College, Pennsylvania

Patricia McManus, University of Sussex

Adam Mekler, Morgan State University

Michael Mellor, Harvard University

Josh Miller, University of Florida

Elizabeth Carolyn Miller, University of Wisconsin

Amanda Mordavsky, University of Sheffield

Deborah Denenholz Morse, William and Mary College

Neil Murphy, Nanyang University

Alex Murray, Monash University

Jamil Mustafa, Lewis University

R. S. Nanda, Sambalpur University

William Naufftus, Winthrop University

Natalie Neill, York University

Erin Obermueller, St. Louis University

Margaret Godbey O'Brien, Temple University

Barbara Onslow, University of Reading

Huw Osborne, University of Wales

Gurdip Panesar

Brian Patton, King's College

Danielle Paycha, Cergy-Pointoise University

Anna Peak, Temple University

Nancy Peled, University of Haifa (Israel)

Robert Peterson

Charlotte S. L. Pfeiffer

Joanne Pierce

Elaine Pigeon, Université de Montréal (Canada)

Christopher Pittard, University of Exeter

Rafael Pleguezuelos

Matt Potolsky, University of Utah

Melissa Purdue, University of Kentucky

Tony Rafalowski, University of Missouri, Columbia

Jenni Ramone, University of Loughborough

Lyssa Randolph, University of Worcester

Vybarr Cregan Reid, University of Kent, Canterbury

Virginie Renard, Catholic University of Louvain (Belgium)

Christine Reynier, University of Montpellier

Roopika Risam, Georgetown University

Ryan Roberts, Lincoln Land Community College

Sherah Roberts

Ben Roberts

Ben P. Robertson, Troy University
Gerardo Rodríguez-Salas, University of Granada (Spain)
Chip Rogers, Rogers State University
Anita Rose, Converse College
Tracy Rosenberg, University of Edinburgh
Rod Rosenquist, Newbold College
Artemis Rosita Terzieva
Matthew Rubery, University of Leeds
Lauren Rule, Emory University
Paul March-Russell, University of Kent
Sarah Russo, Syracuse University
José Francisco Fernández Sánchez
Juliet Schafer
Sue Ann Schatz, Lock Haven University of Pennsylvania
Robin Seaton, University of North Carolina
John Selvidge, Emory University
Sukanya Senapati, Abraham Baldwin University
Stephen E. Severn, Texas A&M University
Lisa Shahriari, University of Essex
Sudha Shastri, Indian Institute of Technology (India)
Ann Shillinglaw
Ilana Shiloh, Tel Aviv University
Rochelle Sibley, University of Warwick
Illana R. Simons, The New School
Charles Sligh, University of Virginia
Alice Smith, University of Oxford
Alisa Smith-Riel, St. Bonaventure University

Joseph Michael Sommers, University of Kansas
Paul Stewart, Intercollege, Cyprus
Greg Stone, University of Louisiana
Rosemary Sykes
G. G. Taneja, University of Delhi
Oliver Taylor, University of Durham
Barbara Tilley, University of South Florida, Tampa
Tomoko Kuribayashi, University of Wisconsin
Benjamine Toussaint-Thiret
David Towsey, Sussex University
Jo Trevenna, Lord Grey School
Julieann Ulinn, University of Notre Dame
Janine Utell, Widener University
Trudi Van Dyke, William Paterson University
Tamara Wagner, University of Singapore
Stan Walker, Queens College
Lisa Weihman, West Virginia University
Sherah Wells, Warwick University
Shannon Wells-Lassagne, University of South Brittany
Jim Whitlark, Texas Tech University
Elizabeth Wilson
Irene Wiltshire, Salford University
Randall Wilhelm, University of Tennessee
Amber Cason Wingfield, University of South Alabama
Jennifer Young, University of Hertfordshire
Michael Young
Aaron Zacks, University of Texas
Hariclea Zegos

INDEX